C000065427

# Ducati
# 748, 916 & 996
# Service and Repair Manual

by Mark Coombs

**Models covered**

(3756-288-6AG2)

Ducati 748 Biposto, S, SP and SPS models. 1995-on
Ducati 916 Strada, Biposto, Senna, SP and SPS models. 1994 to 1998
Ducati 996 Biposto, S and SPS models. 1999-on

*Note: Does not cover the 748R or 996R*



A book in the **Haynes Service and Repair Manual Series**



ISBN **978 0 85733 957 7**

**British Library Cataloguing in Publication Data**
A catalogue record for this book is available from the British Library.

**Library of Congress Catalog Card Number** 2001131395

**Haynes Group Limited**
**Haynes North America, Inc**

**www.haynes.com**

## Disclaimer

There are risks associated with automotive repairs. The ability to make repairs depends on the individual's skill, experience and proper tools. Individuals should act with due care and acknowledge and assume the risk of performing automotive repairs.

The purpose of this manual is to provide comprehensive, useful and accessible automotive repair information, to help you get the best value from your vehicle. However, this manual is not a substitute for a professional certified technician or mechanic.

This repair manual is produced by a third party and is not associated with an individual vehicle manufacturer. If there is any doubt or discrepancy between this manual and the owner's manual or the factory service manual, please refer to the factory service manual or seek assistance from a professional certified technician or mechanic.

Even though we have prepared this manual with extreme care and every attempt is made to ensure that the information in this manual is correct, neither the publisher nor the author can accept responsibility for loss, damage or injury caused by any errors in, or omissions from, the information given.

# LIVING WITH YOUR DUCATI

## Introduction



## Daily (pre-ride) checks



# MAINTENANCE

## Routine maintenance and servicing

# REPAIRS AND OVERHAUL

## Engine, transmission and associated systems



## Chassis components





# REFERENCE

# Doctor T & The Desmos

by Julian Ryder

More than any other factory, with the possible exception of Norton, the history of Ducati is the history of its racing. From the early days with the lightweight singles in 125 cc Grand Prix racing to the bevel-drive V-twins winning the Imola 200, Mike Hailwood's legendary return to the Isle of Man, a hatful of World TT Formula 2 titles with the Pantah, Daytona Battle of the Twins success with Marco Lucchinelli, the triumphant entry to Superbike racing with the high-tech 888 and then the mighty 916, racing has shown the way. Every one of these victories is engraved on the minds – and hearts – of racing enthusiasts all over the world, there is a romance about Ducati that only an Italian factory could generate. This is underlined by the personal nature of these achievements.

The early success and the credit for laying down the ground rules for every Ducati design since the early '50s is universally acknowledged to belong to the late Fabio Taglioni, an engineer who was as well-known and revered as his designs. Although the man himself was not over-fond of the limelight, he was elevated to the status of demigod by the Ducati faithful. When Taglioni, the man who made desmodromic valve operation work on racing and production motorcycles, stepped down, Massimo Bordi took over and produced a motorcycle that more than matched the best that the giant Japanese corporations could produce. Yet the new 851 Superbike was still recognisably a Ducati. It was a V-twin and it had desmodromic valve operation but it also had fuel injection, water-cooling and four-valve heads. More surprisingly, it eschewed the fashion for aluminium beam frames and stuck with the tubular steel ladder frame that came in with the Pantah in 1980. The 851 and its descendants, the 888, the 916, and the 996 went on to World Superbike glory and in true Ducati tradition created unprecedented demand for its street bikes.

Despite the dominance of the Italian Ducati factory in Superbike racing in the UK, Europe, Australia and the USA, as well as at World Championship level, the company is relatively new. Ducati didn't start making motorcycles until 1950 with a then typically Italian range of small, lightweight bikes. The marque's first giant leap forward came with the arrival of one of the two men who would come to embody Ducati's inimitable Italian flair: Fabio Taglioni.

Taglioni joined Ducati as boss of the technical, planning and experimental department after four years at the small Mondial company where he had worked on their DOHC single-cylinder Grand Prix racers. His job was the complex one of kick-starting the racing programme which had to also fulfil the function of development testbed for the production models.

In under a year from Taglioni's arrival the 98 cc Grand Sport was launched into the highly-competitive 100 cc racing class. This engine was a unit-construction OHC motor with nothing in common with Ducati's earlier pushrod motors or the two-stroke competition. Looking at one of those early GSs you can easily spot the genes of what was to follow, for the overhead camshaft was driven by a bevel-gear-drive via a near vertical shaft enclosed in polished tube that ran up the right-hand side of the barrel. This was the layout that would be followed not just in the 125 cc, DOHC Grand Prix single that was Taglioni's next creation, but in every Ducati built up to 1980. But Taglioni's stroke of genius did not hit the tracks until 1956. The racing world was shaken by the instant success of the new Ducati, basically a standard GS racer with Desmodromic valve gear. In the 125 cc Swedish Grand Prix factory rider Degli Antoni lapped the entire field and set new race and lap records on his way to victory. It was the new bike's first race.

The principle of Desmodromic valve operation is simple: the valves are both opened and closed positively. Instead of being closed by a compressed valve spring extending they are closed by a rocker operated by a third camshaft sighted centrally between and geared to the inlet and exhaust camshafts. Desmodromic valve operation wasn't new, James Norton had roughed out plans for such a system before 1910 and the fabulous pre-War Mercedes W196 Grand Prix

**The 250 cc Desmo single**

**The 900 Darmah**

The M900 Monster

The 900SS Supersport

car had it. The advantages are self-evident, higher rev limits thanks to the prevention of valve 'float' at high revs. That first desmo 125 GP bike revved to 12,500 and was regularly taken to 15,000 rpm by factory testers. Here was a way of allowing four-strokes to rev on without self-destructing. If the principle is simple, the precision needed to make it work in practice most certainly isn't and desmodromics remained in the realms of race-track exotica until 1968 when a 250 and 350 single were launched after being unveiled at the Cologne Show the previous year.

The desmo singles, especially the last yellow, disc-braked versions of the early '70s, introduced a whole generation of enthusiasts to the joys of Ducati ownership. This was, however, not usually an unalloyed joy. Taglioni was above all an engine man and the factory personnel's somewhat, er, Mediterranean attitude to quality control showed through in the experience of ownership. The stories of peeling chrome and self-destructing electrics were by no means apocryphal. These singles were the first Ducatis to be exported in numbers and seemed to addict riders for life or put them off anything Italian for life in equal numbers.

## Changes at the Factory

Unfortunately, while the Ducati company was a world leader in innovation, it was noticeably inept at making a profit. In 1971 it was taken into government 'controlled administration', equivalent to the USA's Chapter 11 bankruptcy, to give it temporary respite from its creditors. Not that this prevented the factory from pulling off one of the most astonishing victories in racing at the Imola 200 in 1972.

Taglioni had designed a V4 in the mid-1960s with the aim of cracking the American market, but the project never got beyond the prototype stage. Instead, it was announced in 1970 that Ducati would build a V-twin based on half the V4. That doesn't seem strange today, but back then the V-twin layout was regarded as an antiquated curiosity. The first V-twins (Taglioni preferred L-twin as the front cylinder was near horizontal) used conventional valve springs, the first Desmo V-twin appeared in 1972 for the prestigious Imola 200. Paul Smart was signed up at short notice to ride the bike alongside factory tester Bruno Spaggiari. They finished first and second, beating factory Triumphs, Nortons and Hondas plus the seemingly almighty combination of Giacomo Agostini and the factory MV Agusta as well as an impressive array of private and semi-works Kawasakis, etc. Just like with the 125 GP racer, this was the desmo twin's first race.

This was the race that founded what is now regarded as the classic family of Ducatis, the bevel-drive desmo V-twins. The first production bikes were a batch of 25 Imola replicas, known as the 750SS, just enough to homologate the model for the new F750 world championship. As with later Ducatis, demand far outstripped supply and led to the development of a whole range of bikes. As we'd come to expect, the motor was a gem but the bits wrapped round it were not for the nervous. American magazine Cycle found a

The 900 Mike Hailwood Replica

The 600SL Pantah

famous of which, a fly trapped for ever in the glass-fibre moulding of the petrol tank, has passed into legend.

The bevel-drive V-twins would go on into the '80s in a variety of guises, the most desirable of which is probably the 900SS, a bigger version of the original Imola replicas. The less-sporty and slightly more civilised versions, like the Darmah, GTS and the S2 simply didn't embody what Ducati was about in the way the Super Sports models did. There was, though, one more bevel-drive 900, and this one wasn't just the result of one of racing's greatest moments but of some quick thinking in the marketing department as well. The event that led to the creation of the 900SS MHR (Mike Hailwood Replica) was the return of Mike Hailwood to the Isle of Man TT. The man regarded as the finest rider ever to grace a racing motorcycle retired from F1 car racing after a bad accident at the Nurburgring in 1974; he chose a Ducati for his comeback to the world stage after a couple of low-profile races in Australia. The 1978 F1 TT was Mike's first Island ride in 11 years and he was 38 years old, yet he won and won convincingly.

While the world of motorcycling went collectively mad, Ducati took advantage of this unexpected success. Mike's bike had of course been a factory special, but the fully-faired version of the 900SS with its red, white and green paintwork went from being a 500-unit limited edition to the factory's best seller for several years. In fact the last ever bevel-drive V-twins were Mille MHRs. Incidentally, the Isle of Man victory gave Hailwood and Ducati a world title, for the F1 TT was effectively a one-race world championship. The V-twin had Ducati's first world title, something the old 125 never had the reliability to do, especially after the great Degli Antoni was killed.

Racing success or not, the road-going bevel-drive Dukes still had many of the problems of the old singles. The antidote to

twins was launched in 1980: the Pantah. The resemblance to the bevel-drive bikes was obvious, although the tunnel housing the shaft drive to the cams was gone, replaced by a polished plate over the toothed belts that would operate the desmodromic valve gear of every new Ducati from now on. The same rocker covers were used, making the engine look a lot more like the old lump than it actually was. The frame was new, too. The old double cradle was gone and in its place was a double ladder frame made of short, straight steel tubes. Like the belt-driven cams, this design set the pattern for every future Duke.

The new belt-driven V-twins couldn't compete with the multi-cylinder opposition in F1 competition, but the 600 cc Pantah was a natural for F2 competition. The British importer entered veteran Tony Rutter on a Pantah-engined bike in the 1981 TT, which he duly won. He also won the world title that year and for the following three years. The last Ducati to be built and sold to the public while Ducati was still being run by the Italian government agency was the F1, a 750 cc belt-drive motor in a chassis that bore a very strong resemblance to the works F2 bikes – despite the seeming conflict in the designations.

Now the F2 championship and even the Battle of the Twins class that the F1 did so well in were all very well, but they were very small beer compared to the F1 title of '78 and the new Superbike class that was starting to take hold in the USA. It looked as if Ducati were set to fade away completely under the dead hand of Italian bureaucracy, or at best become one of those small, enthusiasts-only marques.

## Cagiva Take-over

In 1985 Ducati was bought by the Castiglioni brothers, owners of the Cagiva Group which already owned the old Aermacchi/Harley-Davidson set-up, who were looking to expand

motorcycle manufacturer with which to take on the Japanese. Ducati turned out to be the obvious choice, and they gained an instant North American dealer network by buying the Swedish Husqvarna concern as well.

There was no way the ageing Ducati line-up was going to be able to compete with the Japanese, so the new chief engineer, Massimo Bordi was given the funds to develop a new-generation desmo Ducati. The result was the 851, a completely new motorcycle that nevertheless was very much in the tradition of Taglioni's work, which first saw the light of day at the 1986 Bol d'Or. The motor was a 90° V-twin but to endow it with performance on a par with the four-cylinder Japanese opposition it featured fuel injection and water-cooling plus four valves per cylinder operated, of course, desmodromically. The frame was a steel trellis very much along the lines of the Pantah's.

This is the bike that was developed into the first Superbike racer, the 888, which appeared for the first ever World Superbike Championship race at Donington Park in 1988. Marco Lucchinelli took the new bike to an overall win on its debut. The 888 and its descendants, the 916 and 996, have gone on to win all but three of the World Superbike Championships so far run. This success in what is an increasingly high-profile class, both at the world and domestic level, increased demand for Ducatis drastically, helped by the fact that the depressed value of the Italian Lire on international markets kept prices well below the Japanese competition.

A completely new line was unveiled in 1993, the Monster. Here was a bike as far removed from Ducati tradition as you could imagine, a boulevard cruiser using the old air-cooled motors and built for show, not go. Amazingly, it became a best seller. Further diversification came with the ST sports tourers, which met with critical acclaim but not such impressive sales figures.

The 1995 916 Biposto

The 916 Senna

**The 916 SPS (Sport Production Special)**

**The 2001 996 base model**

Unfortunately, this was not necessarily a recipe for commercial success. The Castiglioni brothers, like many other Italian industrialists, were caught up in the incredibly tangled political situation. The rise in interest rates after the fall of the Socialist government saw them unable to service their loans and on the lookout for cash. Customers noted a difficulty in getting motorbikes, suppliers noted a difficulty in getting paid. That resulted in a new company, Ducati Motor SpA, which came into being in September 1996 as a joint venture between the Castigionis and the Texas Pacific Group, an American investment fund. By 1998, Texas Pacific owned the whole company. The result was a massive increase in personnel, investment in new machinery, a redesign of the corporate logo, and a happier time for customers in general. And while Ducati continues to win races, there are sure to be plenty of them.

## Ducati 916

It is impossible to overstate the impact of the 916, it is simply one of the most important motorcycles ever made. Right from its unveiling at the 1993 Milan Show it was obvious that here was a motorcycle that was absolutely critical to Ducati's future – on and off the track. The looks of the thing, very much in the mould of the sublime Supermono, were enough to set the senses of anyone who has ever felt the slightest desire for any motorcycle aflame. Fortunately, when the bike got into the hands of the magazine roadtesters it was found to go as well as it looked and went straight to the top of the sportsbike tree.

The first 916 in the showrooms was the 1994 Strada followed at the end of the year by the two-seater Biposto. These first bikes were very closely based on the 888 motor (and therefore the Pantah) but with the motor stroked by 2 mm from 64 to 66 mm and using the 94 mm bore from the 888SP. If the motor was very similar, the chassis and styling were on a whole new level. It looked like the big brother of the sublime Supermono, i.e. totally covetable. But it wasn't just pretty, it was also clever. All the ancillary components and systems were tucked into any available space and the result was a shorter wheelbase by 20 mm compared to the 888, yet the motor could still be dropped out of the frame as a unit. The clever bit about the motor was that it was ready to be taken out to a full 1000 cc when the needs of Superbike racing demanded. The designers had looked at the aluminium beam frame as universally used by Japan and, significantly, by the Cagiva 500 cc GP bike, but decided to stick with Ducati's hallmark twin-ladder frame in steel tubing.

About the same time as the Biposto was announced, the SP (or Sports Production)

**The 1998 748 Biposto . . .**

**. . . and 748 SPS (Sport Production Special)**

for the '95 season appeared. But in '95 King Carl Fogarty was racing a 955 cc 916 thanks to a 2 mm overbore as he retained the crown he'd won first time out on the 916. This was the signal for Ducati sales to take off. The 888 had been all well and good, but with it Ducati were still in a niche market. The 916 was thousands of pounds cheaper than the road-going version of Honda's RC45 Superbike, and suddenly what had previously been unobtainable exotica was within the reach of most bikers. It was as if a Ferrari supercar suddenly appeared with the same price tag as a hot-hatch GTi.

There was a school of thought that said the 916 was, well, too much of a good thing on the road. As if in answer to that prayer, in 1995 the 748 appeared. The smaller bike was identical in almost every way to the 916 apart from a reduction of both bore and stroke and just happened to qualify for Supersport racing which pitched 600 cc four-cylinder machines against 750 cc twins. The smaller bike arrived in both Biposto and SP versions, although there was precious little between the performance of the two models.

There was also the Senna, a limited-edition version of the 916 Biposto released shortly after the death of the F1 legend. In fact, far from being limited, two runs were made and the specification wasn't different enough from standard to make it desirable.

The first appearance of the 996 cc capacity came in the factory races for 1997 and then on the SPS (which replaced the SP model) in 1998. The big engine had new crankcases, 98 mm bore and two fuel injectors in each inlet tract. Confusingly, the bike was still called the 916 SPS. This was the last year of the 916 Biposto.

**Foggy in action on the 916 in 1994**

The pressures of World Superbike, where Ducati had suffered since Foggy left and were now suffering even more with him back, led to another limited-edition model in '98, the Fogarty Replica 916SPS. It was a way of getting a frame modification homologated for racing and only 202 were built; one for King Carl himself, one for the Ducati museum and 200 for sale on the UK market. They went at a premium price and helped to pay Carl's wages that year.

The model name was finally changed from 916 to 996 in 1999 with Biposto and SPS versions available. In 2000 the 748 did away with the old Biposto and SPS designations and customers could now buy a plain 748 or 748S. As usual there were also very limited runs of full-race factory bike for the likes of Neil Hodgson, Ben Bostrom and Troy Corser in Superbike and Paolo Casoli, Vitto Guareschi and Fabriziano Pirovano in Supersport. The great thing about the 916 or 748 you can buy is that it takes an expert eye to tell the difference between yours and theirs.


# Acknowledgements

Our thanks are due to Bridge Motorcycles of Exeter who supplied the machines featured in the illustrations throughout this manual. We would also like to thank NGK Spark Plugs (UK) Ltd for supplying the colour spark plug condition photographs, the Avon Rubber Company for supplying information on tyre fitting and Draper Tools Ltd for some of the workshop tools shown.

Thanks are also due to Ducati UK Ltd who provided technical assistance and supplied model photographs. Also to Julian Ryder who wrote the introduction 'Docter T & The Desmos' and to Kel Edge who supplied the colour transparency on the rear cover of Carl Fogarty riding the 916. We are grateful to Ian Falloon, author of the Haynes books *Ducati 916* and *The Ducati Story* for permission to reproduce photographs from these titles.


# About this Manual

The aim of this manual is to help you get the best value from your motorcycle. It can do so in several ways. It can help you decide what work must be done, even if you choose to have it done by a dealer; it provides information and procedures for routine maintenance and servicing; and it offers diagnostic and repair procedures to follow when trouble occurs.

We hope you use the manual to tackle the work yourself. For many simpler jobs, doing it yourself may be quicker than arranging an appointment to get the motorcycle into a dealer and making the trips to leave it and pick it up. More importantly, a lot of money can be saved by avoiding the expense the shop must pass on to you to cover its labour and overhead costs. An added benefit is the sense of satisfaction and accomplishment that you feel after doing the job yourself.

References to the left or right side of the motorcycle assume you are sitting on the seat, facing forward.

**We take great pride in the accuracy of information given in this manual, but motorcycle manufacturers make alterations and design changes during the production run of a particular motorcycle of which they do not inform us. No liability can be accepted by the authors or publishers for loss, damage or injury caused by any errors in, or omissions from, the information given.**

## Performance Data

Maximum power*

| | |
|---|---|
| 748 Biposto | 98 bhp (73 kW) @ 11,000 rpm |
| 748 SPS | 100.3 bhp (75 kW) @ 11,350 rpm |
| 916 Strada/Biposto | 97 bhp (72 kW) @ 9000 rpm |
| 916 SPS | 124 bhp (92 kW) @ 9785 rpm |
| 996 Biposto | 113 bhp (84 kW) @ 8500 rpm |
| 996 SPS | 123 bhp (91 kW) @ 9500 rpm |

Maximum torque

| | |
|---|---|
| 748 Biposto | not available |
| 748 SPS | 52.8 lbf ft (72 Nm) @ 8900 rpm |
| 916 Strada/Biposto | 57.8 lbf ft (78 Nm) @ 6800 rpm |
| 916 SPS | 71 lbf ft (96 Nm) @ 8800 rpm |
| 996 Biposto | 68.7 lbf ft (93 Nm) @ 8000 rpm |
| 996 SPS | 73 lbf ft @ (99 Nm) |

Top speed

| | |
|---|---|
| 748 Biposto | 152 mph (245 kmh) |
| 748 SPS | 162 mph (261 kmh) |
| 916 Strada/Biposto | 162 mph (261 kmh) |
| 916 SPS | 174 mph (280 kmh) |
| 996 Biposto | 164 mph (264 kmh) |
| 996 SPS | 175 mph (282 kmh) |

Acceleration

Time taken to cover a 1/4 mile from a standing start and terminal speed

| | |
|---|---|
| 748 Biposto | 11.8 sec, 115 mph (185 kmh) |
| 748 SPS | 11.08 sec, 126 mph (203 kmh) |
| 916 Strada/Biposto | 11.2 sec, 121.3 mph (195 kmh) |
| 916 SPS | 11.0 sec, 124.5 mph (200 kmh) |
| 996 Biposto | 10.4 sec, 124.5 mph (200 kmh) |
| 996 SPS | not available |

Average fuel consumption

Miles per Imp gal, miles per litre, litres per 100 km

| | |
|---|---|
| 748 Biposto | 45 mpg, 9.8 mpl, 6.3 l/100 km |
| 748 SPS | 45 mpg, 9.8 mpl, 6.3 l/100 km |
| 916 Strada/Biposto | 42 mpg, 9.2 mpl, 6.7 l/100 km |
| 916 SPS | 38.5 mpg, 8.4 mpl, 7.3 l/100 km |
| 996 Biposto | 38 mpg, 8.3 mpl, 7.4 l/100 km |
| 996 SPS | not available |

Fuel tank capacity ........ 17 litres (3.7 Imp gal)

Fuel tank range

| | |
|---|---|
| 748 Biposto | 150 miles (241 km) |
| 748 SPS | 165 miles (265 km) |
| 916 Strada/Biposto | 142 miles (228 km) |
| 916 SPS | 154 miles (248 km) |
| 996 Biposto | 154 miles (248 km) |
| 996 SPS | not available |

*see also manufacturer's power output ratings in Chapter 2 Specifications*

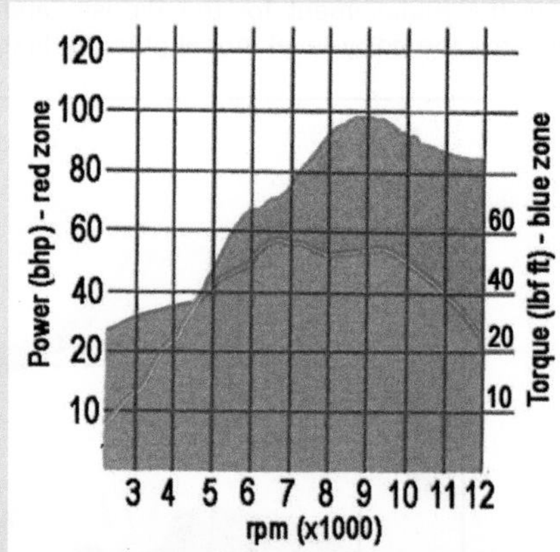


**Power/torque curves for the 916 Strada and Biposto**



# Model development

## 1994 model year

- 916 Strada introduced in February 1994.
- 916 Biposto introduced in December 1994 – The Biposto (dual seat) model was introduced to replace the Strada (single seat) model. Changes included slight revisions to the engine (lighter connecting rods and a different engine management system) and a strengthened rear subframe to cope with the weight of a passenger.
- 916 SP (Sport Production) introduced in November 1994 – The SP was an uprated version of the Strada. Changes to the engine included a different cylinder head with bigger valves, a raised compression ratio, titanium connecting rods, an uprated clutch assembly and a two injector per cylinder engine management system (resulting in a claimed 22 bhp increase in power output). Chassis changes included the fitting of an Ohlins rear suspension unit, cast iron front brake discs and carbon fibre body panels and silencers.

## 1995 model year

- 748 Biposto and SP (Sport Production) introduced – The 748 models are smaller capacity versions of the 916 models with a reduce bore diameter and shorter stroke engine. Although the SP chassis was the same as its 916 counterpart, the engine was very similar to the Biposto model and boasted only a small (6 bhp) increase in power.
- 916 Senna introduced – A limited edition silver coloured model with identification number plaque attached to the top yoke and an identification certificate. The Senna had the uprated chassis components of the SP model, but the standard Biposto engine.

## 1996 model year

- No major changes.

## 1997 model year

- The 916 SPS (Sport Production Special) replaced the SP model. Its engine was uprated to 996 cc by increasing bore diameter by 4 mm.

## 1998 model year

- The 748 SPS (Sport Production Special) replaced the SP model.
- Limited edition (200 units for the UK market) Carl Fogarty 916 SPS replica model. Same as the regular SPS model, but with black five-spoke Marchesini wheels, a titanium exhaust system and carbon-fibre seat unit, graphics from Foggy's bike and his signature on the tank.

## 1999 model year

- 916 Biposto discontinued.
- 996 introduced – Larger capacity version of the 916 introduced in Biposto and SPS (Sport Production Special) versions. The 996 models are similar to the 916 model, but fitted with a two injector per cylinder engine management system.

## 2000 model year

- 748 Biposto and SPS discontinued.
- 748 and 748S introduced – The 748 model was the replacement for the Biposto and became the entry-level model (it is the first head). The 748S replaced the SPS model and was available in single or dual seat versions. Differences to the base model included new five-spoke Marchesini alloy wheels and titanium nitride coated front forks.
- 748R (not covered in this manual) introduced – The 748R was fitted with the new revised 748 cc engine and was only available in limited numbers. Designed purely to homologate the new engine to allow it to be used in Supersport racing.
- 996 model modifications included the fitting of titanium nitride coated front forks (SPS models fitted with new Ohlins forks, Biposto spoke alloy wheels.

## 2001 model year

- 996 SPS discontinued.
- 996S introduced – The 996S retained the SPS engine but had a similar chassis to the Biposto model to keep costs down.
- 996R (not covered in this manual) introduced – The 996R was fitted with the new revised 998 cc engine and was only available in limited numbers. Designed purely to homologate the new engine to allow it to be used in Superbike racing.

### Weights and dimensions

| | |
|---|---|
| Wheelbase | 1410 mm (55.5 in) |
| Overall length | 2030 mm (80.0 in) |
| Overall height | 1080 mm (42.5 in) |
| Overall width (including mirrors) | 780 mm (30.7 in) |
| Seat height | 790 mm (31.1 in) |
| Ground clearance | 150 mm (5.9 in) |
| Dry weight | |
| 748 models | |
| Biposto | 204 kg (450 lb) |
| 748 SP | 192 kg (423 lb) |
| 748 SPS | 194 kg (428 lb) |
| 748 and 748 S | 196 kg (432 lb) |
| 916 models | |
| Biposto | 204 kg (450 lb) |
| Strada and Senna | 198 kg (437 lb) |
| SP | 192 kg (423 lb) |
| SPS | 190 kg (419 lb) |
| 996 models | |
| Biposto | 198 kg (437 lb) |
| S | 195 kg (430 lb) |
| SPS | 190 kg (419 lb) |

Type .....................Liquid-cooled, 90° DOHC vee-twin cylinder with 4-valves per head

Capacity
- 748 models ....................................748 cc
- 916 models
  - SPS ..........................................996 cc
  - All other models ...............................916 cc
- 996 models ......................................996 cc

Bore
- 748 model .......................................88 mm
- 916 model
  - SPS models ....................................98 mm
  - All other models ...............................94 mm
- 996 model .......................................98 mm

Stroke
- 748 model .......................................61.5 mm
- 916 and 996 models ..............................66.0 mm

Compression ratio
- 748 models
  - SP and SPS model ...............................11.6:1
  - All other models ...............................11.5:1
- 916 models
  - SPS models ....................................11.5:1
  - All other models ...............................11.0:1
- 996 models .......................................11.5:1

Engine management (fuel injection/ignition) system
- 916 Strada model .......................Marelli IAW P8 engine management system with one injector per cylinder
- 916 SP and SPS, 996 SPS models .........Marelli IAW P8 engine management system with two injectors per cylinder
- All 748 models, 916 Biposto and Senna models .......Marelli IAW 1.6M engine management system with one injector per cylinder
- 996 Biposto and S models .............Marelli IAW 1.6M engine management system with two injectors per cylinder

Clutch ..................Dry multi-plate, hydraulically-operated

Transmission ........................Six-speed constant mesh

Final drive
- Chain
  - 748 models ............................520 VL4 (94 links)
  - 916 and 996 models .....................525 HV (94 links)
- Ratio (sprocket sizes)
  - 748 models
    - SP and SPS models .....2.64:1 (14 tooth front, 37 tooth rear)
    - All other models .........2.71:1 (14 tooth front, 38 tooth rear)
  - 916 models
    - SP models .............2.57:1 (14 tooth front, 36 tooth rear)
    - All other models .........2.40:1 (15 tooth front, 36 tooth rear)
  - 996 models ..............2.40:1 (15 tooth front, 36 tooth rear)

Type ....................Trellis frame made from steel tubing

Steering head angle
- Models with an adjustable steering head
  - 'Road' position ................................24° 30'
  - 'Race' position .................................23° 30'
- Models with a fixed steering head .....................24° 30'

Trail
- Models with an adjustable steering head
  - 'Road' position .................................97 mm
  - 'Race' position .................................91 mm
- Models with a fixed steering head .....................97 mm

Front suspension
- Type ........................43 mm diameter upside-down hydraulic forks. Later 996 SPS model has Ohlins forks all other models have Showa forks
- Travel ..........................................127 mm
- Adjustments .....................Spring preload, compression damping and rebound damping

Rear suspension
- Type .............Monoshock with fully adjustable suspension linkage. S, SP and SPS models have Ohlins shock absorber all other models have Showa unit
- Travel
  - Shock absorber stroke ...........................71 mm
  - Rear wheel travel ...............................130 mm
- Adjustments .....................Spring preload, compression damping and rebound damping

Tyre sizes
- 748 models
  - Front .....................................120/60 ZR17
  - Rear ......................................180/55 ZR17
- 916 models
  - Front .....................................120/70 ZR17
  - Rear .........................180/55 ZR 17 or 190/50 ZR17
- 996 models
  - Front .....................................120/70 ZR17
  - Rear ......................................190/50 ZR17

Brakes
- Front .......2 x 320 mm discs with Brembo four-piston calipers. SP and SPS models have cast iron discs all other models have steel discs
- Rear ............220 mm disc with Brembo two-piston caliper

working procedures. However enthusiastic you may be about getting on with the job at hand, take the time to ensure that your safety is not put at risk. A moment's lack of attention can result in an accident, as can failure to observe simple precautions.

There will always be new ways of having accidents, and the following is not a comprehensive list of all dangers; it is intended rather to make you aware of the risks and to encourage a safe approach to all work you carry out on your bike.

## Asbestos

● Certain friction, insulating, sealing and other products - such as brake pads, clutch linings, gaskets, etc. - contain asbestos. Extreme care must be taken to avoid inhalation of dust from such products since it is hazardous to health. If in doubt, assume that they do contain asbestos.

## Fire

● Remember at all times that petrol is highly flammable. Never smoke or have any kind of naked flame around, when working on the vehicle. But the risk does not end there - a spark caused by an electrical short-circuit, by two metal surfaces contacting each other, by careless use of tools, or even by static electricity built up in your body under certain conditions, can ignite petrol vapour, which in a confined space is highly explosive. Never use petrol as a cleaning solvent. Use an approved safety solvent.

● Always disconnect the battery earth terminal before working on any part of the fuel or electrical system, and never risk spilling fuel on to a hot engine or exhaust.

● It is recommended that a fire extinguisher of a type suitable for fuel and electrical fires is kept handy in the garage or workplace at all times. Never try to extinguish a fuel or electrical fire with water.

## Fumes

● Certain fumes are highly toxic and can quickly cause unconsciousness and even death if inhaled to any extent. Petrol vapour comes into this category, as do the vapours from certain solvents such as trichloro-ethylene. Any draining or pouring of such volatile fluids should be done in a well ventilated area.

● When using cleaning fluids and solvents, read the instructions carefully. Never use materials from unmarked containers - they may give off poisonous vapours.

● Never run the engine of a motor vehicle in an enclosed space such as a garage. Exhaust fumes contain carbon monoxide which is extremely poisonous; if you need to run the engine, always do so in the open air or at least have the rear of the vehicle outside the workplace.

## The battery

● Never cause a spark, or allow a naked light near the vehicle's battery. It will normally be giving off a certain amount of hydrogen gas, which is highly explosive.

● Always disconnect the battery ground (earth) terminal before working on the fuel or electrical systems (except where noted).

● If possible, loosen the filler plugs or cover when charging the battery from an external source. Do not charge at an excessive rate or the battery may burst.

● Take care when topping up, cleaning or carrying the battery. The acid electrolyte, evenwhen diluted, is very corrosive and should not be allowed to contact the eyes or skin. Always wear rubber gloves and goggles or a face shield. If you ever need to prepare electrolyte yourself, always add the acid slowly to the water; never add the water to the acid.

## Electricity

● When using an electric power tool, inspection light etc., always ensure that the appliance is correctly connected to its plug and that, where necessary, it is properly grounded (earthed). Do not use such appliances in damp conditions and, again, beware of creating a spark or applying excessive heat in the vicinity of fuel or fuel vapour. Also ensure that the appliances meet national safety standards.

● A severe electric shock can result from touching certain parts of the electrical system, such as the spark plug wires (HT leads), when the engine is running or being cranked, particularly if components are damp or the insulation is defective. Where an electronic ignition system is used, the secondary (HT) voltage is much higher and could prove fatal.

## Remember...

✗ **Don't** start the engine without first ascertaining that the transmission is in neutral.

✗ **Don't** suddenly remove the pressure cap from a hot cooling system - cover it with a cloth and release the pressure gradually first, or you may get scalded by escaping coolant.

✗ **Don't** attempt to drain oil until you are sure it has cooled sufficiently to avoid scalding you.

✗ **Don't** grasp any part of the engine or exhaust system without first ascertaining that it is cool enough not to burn you.

✗ **Don't** allow brake fluid or antifreeze to contact the machine's paintwork or plastic components.

✗ **Don't** siphon toxic liquids such as fuel, hydraulic fluid or antifreeze by mouth, or allow them to remain on your skin.

✗ **Don't** inhale dust - it may be injurious to health (see Asbestos heading).

✗ **Don't** allow any spilled oil or grease to remain on the floor - wipe it up right away, before someone slips on it.

✗ **Don't** use ill-fitting spanners or other tools which may slip and cause injury.

✗ **Don't** lift a heavy component which may be beyond your capability - get assistance.

✗ **Don't** rush to finish a job or take unverified short cuts.

✗ **Don't** allow children or animals in or around an unattended vehicle.

✗ **Don't** inflate a tyre above the recommended pressure. Apart from overstressing the carcass, in extreme cases the tyre may blow off forcibly.

✓ **Do** ensure that the machine is supported securely at all times. This is especially important when the machine is blocked up to aid wheel or fork removal.

✓ **Do** take care when attempting to loosen a stubborn nut or bolt. It is generally better to pull on a spanner, rather than push, so that if you slip, you fall away from the machine rather than onto it.

✓ **Do** wear eye protection when using power tools such as drill, sander, bench grinder etc.

✓ **Do** use a barrier cream on your hands prior to undertaking dirty jobs - it will protect your skin from infection as well as making the dirt easier to remove afterwards; but make sure your hands aren't left slippery. Note that long-term contact with used engine oil can be a health hazard.

✓ **Do** keep loose clothing (cuffs, ties etc. and long hair) well out of the way of moving mechanical parts.

✓ **Do** remove rings, wristwatch etc., before working on the vehicle - especially the electrical system.

✓ **Do** keep your work area tidy - it is only too easy to fall over articles left lying around.

✓ **Do** exercise caution when compressing springs for removal or installation. Ensure that the tension is applied and released in a controlled manner, using suitable tools which preclude the possibility of the spring escaping violently.

✓ **Do** ensure that any lifting tackle used has a safe working load rating adequate for the job.

✓ **Do** get someone to check periodically that all is well, when working alone on the vehicle.

✓ **Do** carry out work in a logical sequence and check that everything is correctly assembled and tightened afterwards.

✓ **Do** remember that your vehicle's safety affects that of yourself and others. If in doubt on any point, get professional advice.

● If in spite of following these precautions, you are unfortunate enough to injure yourself, seek medical attention as soon as possible.

The frame serial number is stamped into the right-hand side of the steering head **(see illustration)**. The engine number is stamped onto the bottom of the crankcase, directly in front of the sidestand mounting bracket, and is visible once the left-hand lower fairing panel is removed (see Chapter 8) **(see illustration)**. Both of these numbers should be recorded and kept in a safe place so they can be given to law enforcement officials in the event of a theft.

The frame serial number and engine serial number should also be kept in a handy place (such as with your driver's licence) so they are always available when purchasing or ordering parts for your machine. The numbers contain model specific identification information about the bike.

Once you have found the identification numbers, record them for reference when buying parts. Since the manufacturers change specifications, parts and vendors (companies that manufacture various components on the machine), providing the engine and frame numbers is the only way to be reasonably sure that you are buying the correct parts.

Whenever possible, take the worn part to the dealer so direct comparison with the new component can be made. Along the trail from the manufacturer to the parts shelf, there are numerous places that the part can end up with the wrong number or be listed incorrectly.

The two places to purchase new parts for your motorcycle – the accessory shop and the dealer – differ in the type of parts they carry. While dealers can obtain virtually every part for your motorcycle, the accessory shop is usually limited to normal high wear items such as shock absorbers, tune-up parts, various engine gaskets, cables, chains, brake parts, etc. Rarely will an accessory outlet have major suspension components, cylinders, transmission gears, or cases.

Used parts can be obtained for considerably less than new ones, but you can't always be sure of what you're getting. Once again, take your worn part to the breaker for direct comparison.

Whether buying new, used or rebuilt parts, the best course is to deal directly with someone who specialises in parts for your particular make.

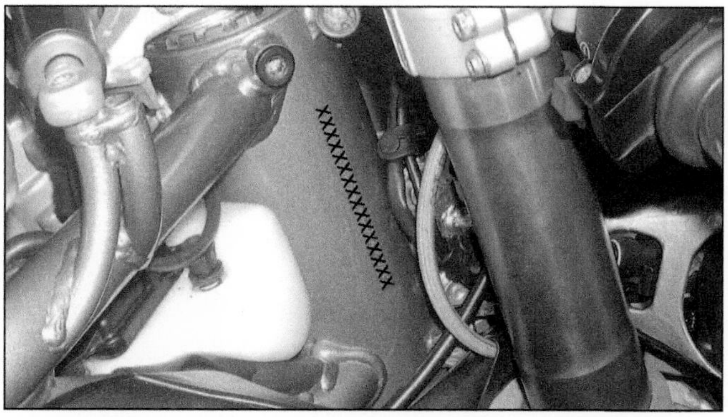

**The frame number is stamped in the right-hand side of the steering head**

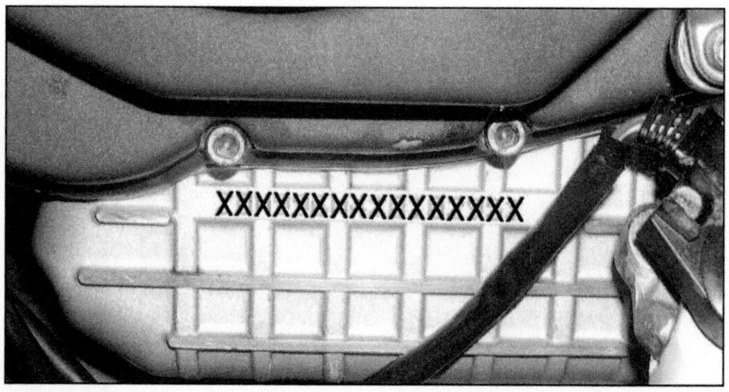

**The engine number is stamped in the bottom of the crankcase on the left-hand side of the engine and is visible once the fairing lower panel is removed**

# Engine/transmission oil level check

## Before you start:

✔ Start the engine and allow it to reach normal operating temperature.

***Caution: Do not run the engine in an enclosed space such as a garage or workshop.***

✔ Stop the engine and support the motorcycle on its sidestand. Allow it to stand undisturbed for a few minutes to allow the oil level to stabilise. Make sure the motorcycle is on level ground.

✔ The oil level is viewed through the window in the right-hand crankcase cover, visible through the aperture in the lower fairing panel. Wipe the glass clean before inspection to make the check easier.

## Bike care:

● If you have to add oil frequently, you should check whether you have any oil leaks. If there is no sign of oil leakage from the joints and gaskets the engine could be burning oil (see *Fault Finding*).

## The correct oil

● Modern, high-revving engines place great demands on their oil. It is very important that the correct oil for your bike is used.

● Always top up with a good quality oil of the specified type and viscosity and do not overfill the engine.

| | |
|---|---|
| **Oil type** | API grade SE, SF or SG |
| **Oil viscosity** | SAE 10W40, 10W50, 20W40 or 20W50 |

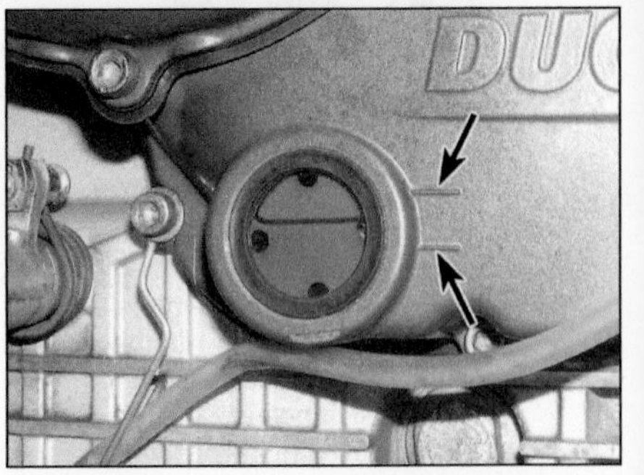

1 With the motorcycle held vertical, check the oil level in the inspection window at the bottom of the crankcase cover. The level should lie between the MAX (upper) and MIN (lower) level marks (arrowed).

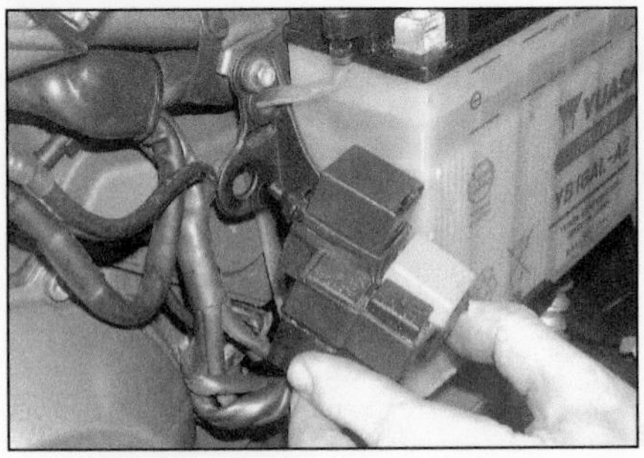

2 If topping-up is necessary, remove the right-hand lower fairing panel (see Chapter 8). Free the relay mounting rubber from the rear of the battery mounting tray to gain access to the oil filler cap.

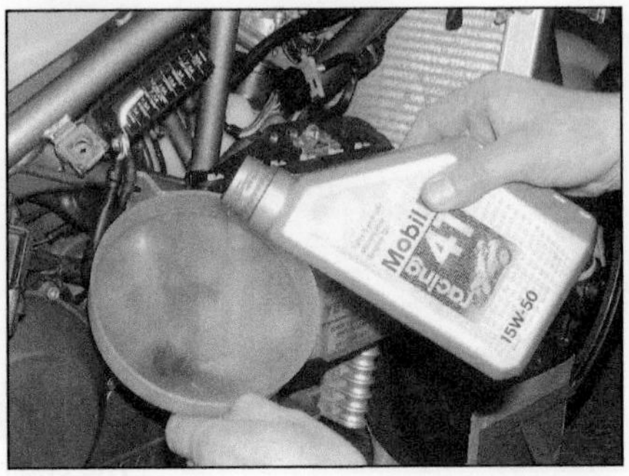


3 Unscrew the cap and add the specified oil to bring the oil level to the upper level mark on the inspection window, but do not overfill.

4 Once the level is correct, securely refit the filler cap ensuring its O-ring is in place. Refit the relay mounting rubber to the battery tray then install the fairing panel.

# Tyre checks

## The correct pressures:

● The tyres must be checked when **cold**, not immediately after riding. Note that low tyre pressures may cause the tyre to slip on the rim or come off. High tyre pressures will cause abnormal tread wear and unsafe handling.

● Use an accurate pressure gauge. Many garage forecourt gauges are wildly inaccurate. If you buy your own, spend as much as you can justify on a quality gauge.

● Correct air pressure will increase tyre life and provide maximum stability, handling capability and ride comfort.

## Tyre care:

● Check the tyres carefully for cuts, tears, embedded nails or other sharp objects and excessive wear. Operation of the motorcycle with excessively worn tyres is extremely hazardous, as traction and handling are directly affected.

● Check the condition of the tyre valve and ensure the dust cap is in place.

● Pick out any stones or nails which may have become embedded in the tyre tread. If left, they will eventually penetrate through the casing and cause a puncture.

● If tyre damage is apparent, or unexplained loss of pressure is experienced, seek the advice of a tyre fitting specialist without delay.

## Tyre tread depth:

● At the time of writing UK law requires that tread depth must be at least 1 mm over the entire tread breadth all the way around the tyre, with no bald patches. Many riders, however, consider 2 mm tread depth minimum to be a safer limit. Ducati recommend a minimum of 2 mm.

● Many tyres now incorporate wear indicators in the tread. Identify the triangular pointer or TWI mark on the tyre sidewall to locate the indicator bar and renew the tyre if the tread has worn down to the bar.

| Load | Front | Rear |
|---|---|---|
| Rider only | 32 psi (2.2 bar) | 35 psi (2.4 bar) |
| Rider and passenger | 36 psi (2.4 bar) | 40 psi (2.8 bar) |

1 Check the tyre pressures when the tyres are **cold** and keep them properly inflated.

2 Measure tread depth at the centre of the tyre using a tread depth gauge.

3 Tyre tread wear indicator bar and its location marking (usually either an arrow, a triangle or the letters TWI.

# Coolant level check

> **Warning:** ***DO NOT leave open containers of coolant about, as it is poisonous.***

## Before you start:

✔ Make sure you have a supply of coolant available (a mixture of 50% distilled water and 50% corrosion inhibited ethylene glycol anti-freeze is needed).

✔ Always check the coolant level when the engine is cold.

***Caution: Do not run the engine in an enclosed space such as a garage or workshop.***

✔ Ensure the motorcycle is held vertical whilst checking the coolant level. Make sure the motorcycle is on level ground.

## Bike care:

● Use only the specified coolant mixture. It is important that anti-freeze is used in the system all year round, and not just in the winter. Do not top the system up using only water, as the system will become too diluted.

● Do not overfill the reservoir tank. If the coolant is significantly above the upper (MAX) level line at any time, the surplus should be siphoned or drained off to prevent the possibility of it being expelled out of the overflow hose.

● If the coolant level falls steadily, check the system for leaks (see Chapter 1). If no leaks are found and the level continues to fall, it is recommended that the machine is taken to a Ducati dealer for a pressure test.

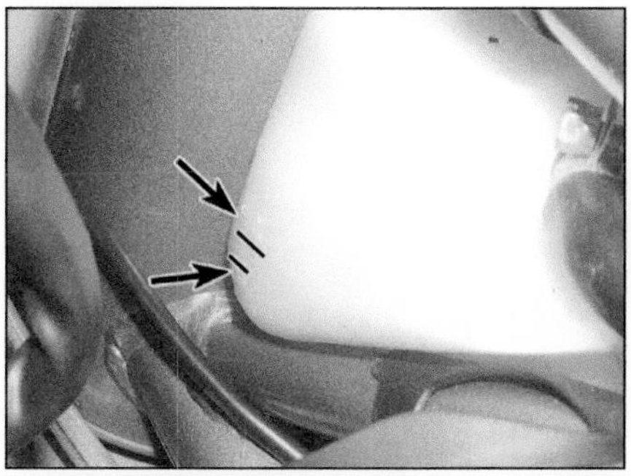

1 The expansion tank is located underneath the front of the fuel tank. The coolant MAX (upper) and MIN (lower) level lines are visible on the side of the tank and the coolant level is visible through the tank.

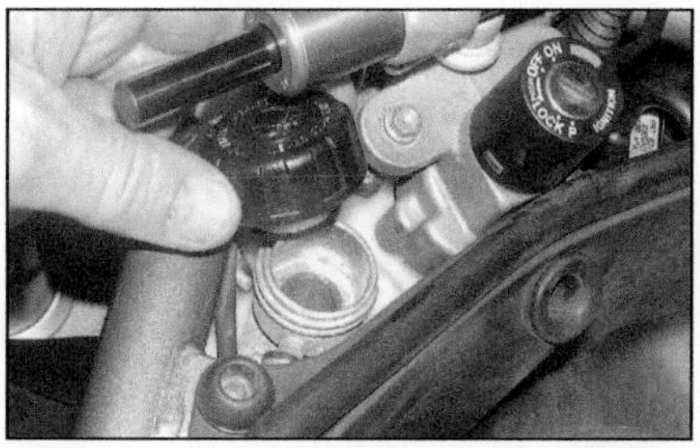

2 If the coolant level does not lie between the MAX and MIN markings, remove the fuel tank to access the expansion tank cap. Note that there is no need to remove the fuel tank completely, access can be gained by unbolting the tank and raising and supporting it, with the hoses and wiring still connected (see Chapter 4). Unscrew the expansion tank cap.

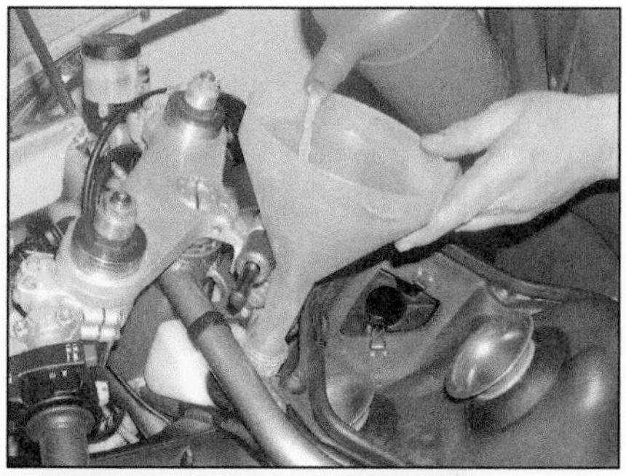

3 Top the coolant level up with the recommended coolant mixture. Once the level is correct, securely fit the cap to the expansion tank then refit the fuel tank (see Chapter 4).

# Suspension, steering and final drive checks

## Suspension and Steering:

● Check that the front and rear suspension operate smoothly without binding.

● Check that the suspension is adjusted as required.

● Check that the steering moves smoothly from lock-to-lock.

## Final drive:

● Check that the drive chain slack isn't excessive, and adjust if necessary (see Chapter 1).

● If the chain looks dry, lubricate it (see Chapter 1).

# Brake and clutch fluid level checks

> **Warning:** ***Hydraulic fluid can harm your eyes and damage painted surfaces, so use extreme caution when handling and pouring it and cover surrounding surfaces with rag. Do not use fluid that has been standing open for some time, as it absorbs moisture from the air which can cause a dangerous loss of braking effectiveness.***

## Before you start:

✔ Ensure the motorcycle is held vertical whilst checking the levels. Make sure the motorcycle is on level ground.

✔ Make sure you have the correct hydraulic fluid. DOT 4 is recommended.

✔ Wrap a rag around the reservoir being worked on to ensure that any spillage does not come into contact with painted surfaces.

## Bike care:

● The fluid in the front and rear brake master cylinder reservoirs will drop slightly as the brake pads wear down.

● If any fluid reservoir requires repeated topping-up this is an indication of an hydraulic leak somewhere in the system, which should be investigated immediately.

● Check for signs of fluid leakage from the hydraulic hoses and components – if found, rectify immediately.

● Check the operation of both brakes before taking the machine on the road; if there is evidence of air in the system (spongy feel to lever or pedal), it must be bled as described in Chapter 7.

1 Ensure the fluid reservoir is as level as possible, then check that the fluid level is between the MAX and MIN level lines on the side of the reservoir.

2 If the front brake fluid level is below the MIN level line, undo the two retaining screws and remove the reservoir cover then lift out the rubber diaphragm and plate.

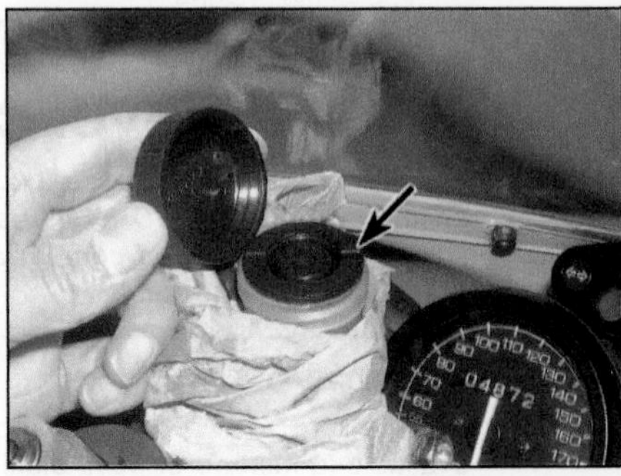

3 If the rear brake or clutch fluid level is below the MIN level line, unscrew the reservoir cover and lift out the rubber diaphragm and plate (arrowed).

4 Top up with new DOT 4 hydraulic fluid, until the level is just below the MAX level mark; do not overfill the reservoir, and take care to avoid spills (see **Warning** above).

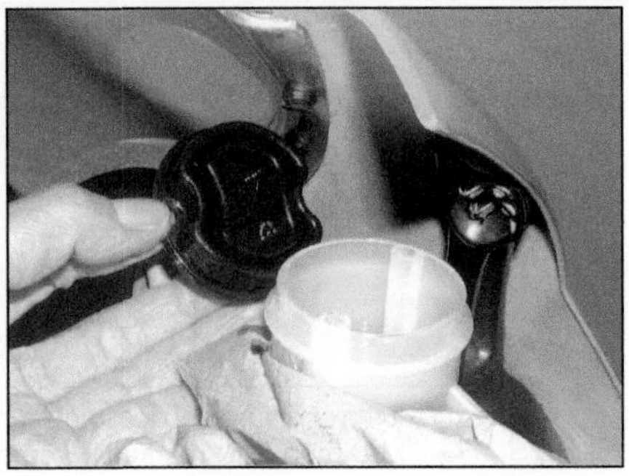

5 When the fluid level is correct, clean and dry the diaphragm, fold it into its compressed state and install it along with the plate. Ensure that the diaphragm is correctly seated before securely installing the reservoir cover. Wipe off any spilt fluid.

6 The rear brake fluid reservoir is located on the right-hand side, between the engine casing and frame tubing.

# Legal and safety checks

## Lighting and signalling:

● Take a minute to check that the headlight, tail light, brake light, instrument lights and turn signals all work correctly.

● Check that the horn sounds when the switch is operated.

● A working speedometer graduated in mph is a statutory requirement in the UK.

## Safety:

● Check that the throttle grip rotates smoothly and snaps shut when released, in all steering positions. Also check for the correct amount of freeplay (see Chapter 1).

● Check that the engine shuts off when the kill switch is operated.

● Check that sidestand return spring holds the stand securely up when retracted.

## Fuel:

● This may seem obvious, but check that you have enough fuel to complete your journey. If you notice signs of fuel leakage – rectify the cause immediately.

● Ensure you use the correct grade unleaded fuel – see Chapter 4 Specifications.

# Chapter 1
# Routine maintenance and servicing

## Contents



## Degrees of difficulty

| | | | | |
|---|---|---|---|---|
| **Easy,** suitable for novice with little experience | **Fairly easy,** suitable for beginner with some experience | **Fairly difficult,** suitable for competent DIY mechanic | **Difficult,** suitable for experienced DIY mechanic | **Very difficult,** suitable for expert DIY or professional |

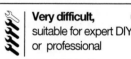

## Specifications

### Recommended lubricants and fluids

| | |
|---|---|
| Engine/transmission oil type | API grade SE, SF or SG motor oil |
| Engine/transmission oil viscosity | SAE 10W40, 10W50, 20W40 or 20W50 |
| Engine/transmission oil capacity (approximate) | |
| 748 models | |
| SPS model | 4.0 litres |
| All other models | 3.5 litres |
| 916 and 996 models | 4.0 litres |
| Coolant type | 50% distilled water, 50% corrosion inhibited ethylene glycol anti-freeze |
| Coolant capacity | 3.5 litres |
| Front fork oil | see Chapter 6 |
| Brake fluid | DOT 4 |
| Clutch fluid | DOT 4 |
| Drive chain | Aerosol chain lubricant for O-ring chains |
| Steering head bearings | Multi-purpose grease |
| Wheel bearings (unsealed) | Multi-purpose grease |
| Swingarm pivot bearings | Molybdenum disulphide grease |
| Suspension linkage bearings | Molybdenum disulphide grease |
| Oil/dust seal lips | Multi-purpose grease |
| Lever/pedal pivots | Multi-purpose grease or dry film lubricant |
| Cables | Cable lubricant or 10W40 motor oil |
| Sidestand pivots | Engine oil |
| Throttle grip | Multi-purpose grease or dry film lubricant |

| | |
|---|---|
| Cylinder identification | Horizontal (front cylinder) No.2. Vertical (rear cylinder) No.1 |
| Engine idle speed | 1000 to 1100 rpm |
| Spark plugs | |
| Type – SPS models | Champion A55V |
| Type – all other models | Champion RA59GC |
| Electrode gap | 0.5 to 0.6 mm |
| Valve clearances (COLD engine)* | |
| Checking clearances | |
| Intake | |
| Opening rocker clearance | 0.05 to 0.18 mm |
| Closing rocker clearance | 0.16 to 0.25 mm |
| Exhaust | |
| Opening rocker clearance | 0.05 to 0.23 mm |
| Closing rocker clearance | 0.11 to 0.20 mm |
| Adjusting clearances | |
| Intake | |
| Opening rocker clearance | 0.16 to 0.18 mm |
| Closing rocker clearance | 0.16 to 0.18 mm |
| Exhaust | |
| Opening rocker clearance | 0.21 to 0.23 mm |
| Closing rocker clearance | 0.11 to 0.13 mm |

**Ducati specify two different sets of valve clearances. The adjusting clearances are for use during reassembly of the valve components (e.g. after cylinder head overhaul or a shim change) and the checking clearances are for use on an engine which has been run.*

| | |
|---|---|
| Cylinder compression | |
| 748 models | |
| Standard | 128 to 156 psi (9 to 11 bar) |
| Minimum | 113 psi (8 bar) |
| 916 and 996 models | |
| SPS models | |
| Standard | 142 to 170 psi (10 to 12 bar) |
| Minimum | 128 psi (9 bar) |
| All non-SPS 916 and 996 models | |
| Standard | 128 to 156 psi (9 to 11 bar) |
| Minimum | 113 psi (8 bar) |
| Maximum difference between cylinders – all models | 28 psi (2 bar) |
| Oil pressure | |
| At 1100 to 1300 rpm | |
| Cold engine | At least 36 psi (2.5 bar) |
| Hot engine | At least 15 psi (1.1 bar) |
| At 3500 to 4000 rpm | 57 to 86 psi (4 to 6 bar) |

## Cycle parts

| | |
|---|---|
| Drive chain freeplay (standard) | 25 mm |
| Drive chain length over 16 links | Less than 256.6 mm |
| Brake pad friction material minimum thickness | 1 mm |
| Brake pedal height | see text |
| Throttle cable freeplay | 1.5 to 2.0 mm |
| Tyre pressures and tyre tread depth | see *Daily (pre-ride) checks* |

## Torque wrench settings

| | |
|---|---|
| Engine oil and filter change | |
| Oil drain plug | 42 Nm |
| Oil filter | 17 Nm |
| Oil pick-up filter bolt | 42 Nm |
| Front sprocket retaining plate bolts | 6 Nm |
| Rear wheel bearing holder clamp bolts | 30 Nm |
| Spark plugs | 20 Nm |
| Steering stem nut | |
| Stage 1 | Tighten to 20 Nm |
| Stage 2 | Slacken by 30° |
| Steering stem nut clamp bolt | 20 to 24 Nm |
| Timing belt tensioner pulley retaining nut | 26 Nm |
| Top yoke clamp bolt | 23 Nm |
| Valve clearance adjustment | |
| Camshaft end cap bolts | 10 Nm |
| Cylinder head oil hose banjo bolt | 12 Nm |
| Cylinder head side cover bolts | 10 Nm |
| Cylinder head valve cover bolts | 10 Nm |
| Brake caliper bleed valves | 12 Nm |

*pre-ride inspection at every maintenance interval (in addition to the procedures listed). The intervals listed below are the intervals recommended by the manufacturer for each particular operation during the model years covered in this manual. Your owner's manual may have slightly different intervals for some items.*

## Daily (pre-ride)

- ☐ See *'Daily (pre-ride) checks'* at the beginning of this manual.

## After the initial 600 miles (1000 km)

**Note:** *This check is usually performed by a dealer after the first 600 miles (1000 km) from new. Thereafter, maintenance should be carried out according to the following intervals.*

- ☐ Check the battery electrolyte level (Section 1).
- ☐ Change the engine oil and filter and clean the oil pick-up gauze filter (Section 8).
- ☐ Clean the air filter elements (Section 10).
- ☐ Check the spark plugs (Section 11).
- ☐ Check the tightness of the cylinder head nuts (Section 12).
- ☐ Check the timing belts (Section 15).
- ☐ Check throttle cable operation and freeplay (Section 5).
- ☐ Check the throttle body synchronisation, engine idle speed and mixture setting (Section 18).
- ☐ Check the cylinder compression (Section 19).
- ☐ Check the engine oil pressure (Section 20).
- ☐ Check the operation of the electric cooling fan (Section 21).
- ☐ Check the operation of the braking system and brake light switch (Section 22).
- ☐ Check the brake pads for wear (Section 2).
- ☐ Check the front sprocket retaining plate (Section 3).
- ☐ Check, adjust and lubricate the drive chain (Section 4).
- ☐ Check and lubricate the stands, lever pivots and cables (Section 6).
- ☐ Check the steering head bearings (Section 24).
- ☐ Check the tightness of all nuts, bolts and fasteners (Section 27).

## Every 600 miles (1000 km)

- ☐ Check the battery electrolyte level (Section 1).
- ☐ Check the brake pads for wear (Section 2).
- ☐ Check the condition of the front sprocket retaining plate (Section 3).
- ☐ Check, adjust and lubricate the drive chain (Section 4).
- ☐ Check throttle cable operation and freeplay (Section 5).
- ☐ Check and lubricate the stand, lever pivots and cables (Section 6).
- ☐ Check the wheel and tyre condition, and the tyre tread depth (Section 7).

## Every 6000 miles (10,000 km)

- ☐ Change the engine oil and filter and clean the oil pick-up gauze filter* (Section 8).

**Ducati specify that the oil pick-up gauze filter only requires cleaning once every two oil and filter changes but we recommend it is cleaned every time the oil and filter are changed.*

- ☐ Renew the fuel filter (Section 9).
- ☐ Renew the air filter elements (Section 10).
- ☐ Renew the spark plugs (Section 11).
- ☐ Check the tightness of the cylinder head nuts (Section 12).
- ☐ Check the tightness flywheel/alternator rotor nut – early (pre 1999 model year) models (Section 13).
- ☐ Check the valve clearances (Section 14).
- ☐ Check the timing belts (Section 15).
- ☐ Check the cooling system (Section 16).
- ☐ Check the fuel hoses and system components (Section 17).
- ☐ Check the throttle body synchronisation, engine idle speed and mixture setting (Section 18).
- ☐ Check the cylinder compression (Section 19).
- ☐ Check the engine oil pressure (Section 20).
- ☐ Check the operation of the electric cooling fan (Section 21).
- ☐ Check the operation of the braking system and brake light switch (Section 22).
- ☐ Check the rear sprocket cush drive rubber bushes for wear (Section 23).
- ☐ Check the steering head bearings (Section 24).
- ☐ Check the wheel bearings (Section 25).
- ☐ Check the front and rear suspension (Section 26).
- ☐ Check the tightness of all nuts, bolts and fasteners (Section 27).

## Every 12,000 miles (20,000 km) or every 2 years

- ☐ Renew the timing belts (Section 28).
- ☐ Change the brake fluid (Section 29).
- ☐ Change the clutch fluid (Section 30).
- ☐ Change the coolant (Section 31).
- ☐ Change the front fork oil (Section 32).

## Non-scheduled maintenance

- ☐ Check for drive chain wear and stretch and sprocket wear (Section 33).
- ☐ Re-grease the suspension linkage bearings (Section 34).
- ☐ Re-grease the steering head bearings (Section 35).
- ☐ Renew the brake hoses and brake master cylinder and caliper seals (Section 36).
- ☐ Renew the clutch hose and master cylinder and slave cylinder seals (Section 37).
- ☐ Check the headlight aim (Section 38).

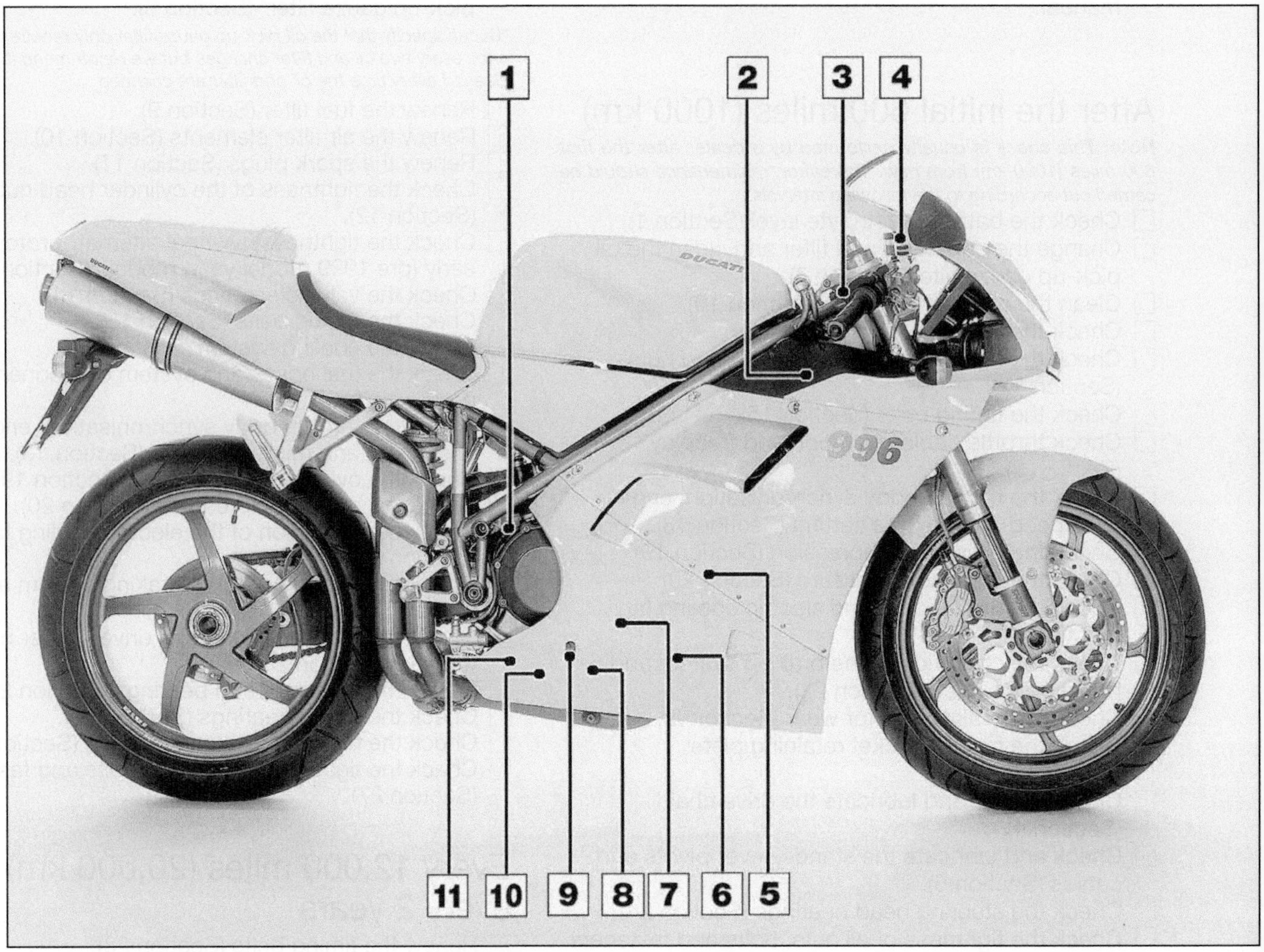


**Component locations – right-hand side**

1 *Rear brake fluid reservoir*
2 *Air filter*
3 *Steering head bearing adjuster*
4 *Front brake fluid reservoir*
5 *Battery*
6 *Oil filter*
7 *Oil filler cap*
8 *Oil pick-up filter*
9 *Oil level inspection window*
10 *Oil drain plug*
11 *Rear brake pedal height adjuster*

**Component locations – left-hand side**

1 *Clutch fluid reservoir*
2 *Coolant expansion tank*
3 *Air filter*
4 *Fuel filter*
5 *Drive chain adjuster*
6 *Rear sprocket cush drive bushes*
7 *Front sprocket retaining plate*
8 *Coolant drain plug*
9 *Front fork dust seal*
10 *Headlight adjuster*

mechanic maintain his/her motorcycle for safety, economy, long life and peak performance.

**2** Deciding where to start or plug into the routine maintenance schedule depends on several factors. If the warranty period on your motorcycle has just expired, and if it has been maintained according to the warranty standards, you may want to pick up routine maintenance as it coincides with the next mileage or calendar interval. If you have owned the machine for some time but have you may want to start at the nearest interval and include some additional procedures to ensure that nothing important is overlooked. If you have just had a major engine overhaul, then you may want to start the maintenance routine from the beginning. If you have a used machine and have no knowledge of its history or maintenance record, you may desire to combine all the checks into one large service initially and then settle into the maintenance schedule prescribed.

**3** Before beginning any maintenance or thoroughly, especially around the oil filter, spark plugs, seat cowling, etc. Cleaning will help ensure that dirt does not contaminate the engine and will allow you to detect wear and damage that could otherwise easily go unnoticed.

**4** Certain maintenance information is sometimes printed on decals attached to the motorcycle. If the information on the decals differs from that included here, use the information on the decal.

# Every 600 miles (1000 km)

## 1 Battery – check

**1** Remove the right-hand lower fairing panel (see Chapter 8) to gain access to the battery.

### Sealed (maintenance-free) battery

**Note:** *On sealed batteries (fitted as standard from 2001 model year), do not attempt to remove the battery cell caps/cover to check the electrolyte level or battery specific gravity. Removal will damage the caps, resulting in electrolyte leakage and battery damage.*

**2** The only check necessary is to ensure the battery terminals are clean and tight and that the casing is not damaged or leaking. See Chapter 9 for further details.

**3** If the machine is not in regular use, disconnect the battery and give it a refresher charge every month to six weeks (see *Fault Finding Equipment* in the Reference section).

**4** On completion, install the fairing panel (see Chapter 8).

### Standard battery

**5** Compare the electrolyte level in each cell to the UPPER and LOWER lines on the battery **(see illustration)**. If the level in any cell does not lie between these marks, remove the cell caps and top up to the upper level mark using only distilled water.

**6** Check the battery for any signs of pale grey sediment at the bottom of the casing. This is caused by sulphation of the plates due to recharging at too high a rate or as a result of the battery being left discharged for long periods. A good battery should have little or no sediment visible and its plates should be straight and pale grey or brown in colour. If sediment deposits are deep enough to reach the bottom of the plates, or if the plates are buckled and have whitish deposits on them, the battery is faulty and must be renewed. Remember that a poor battery will give rise to a large number of minor electrical faults.

**7** Ensure the breather pipe is securely attached to the battery and is correctly routed, without any signs of kinks. Renew the pipe if it is damaged.

**8** Ensure the battery terminals are clean and tight and that the casing is not damaged or leaking **(see illustration)**.

**9** If the machine is not in regular use, disconnect the battery and give it a refresher charge every month to six weeks (see *Fault Finding Equipment* in the Reference section).

**10** On completion, install the fairing panel (see Chapter 8).

**HAYNES HiNT** ***Battery terminal corrosion can be minimised by applying a layer of petroleum jelly to the terminals after the leads have been connected.***

## 2 Brake pads – wear check

**1** A quick check of the brake pads can be made without removing them from the caliper.

**2** The amount of front brake pad wear can be judged by looking at the pads from the rear of the calipers. The groove in the pad friction material, visible through the caliper/pad spring aperture indicates the wear limit **(see illustration)**. Some after-market pads may use different indicators to those on the original equipment as shown; if no wear indicator is visible check the pad friction material is not less than the specified minimum thickness (see Specifications). If either pad has worn down to, or beyond, the cutout/groove in the friction material, or the friction material thickness is less than the specified minimum, all the front brake pads

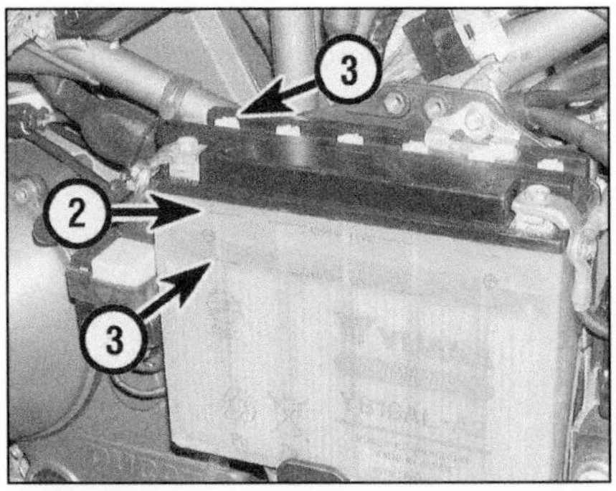


**1.5 Ensure the electrolyte level is between the LOWER (1) and UPPER (2) level marks. If topping-up is necessary, remove the cell caps (3) and add distilled water**

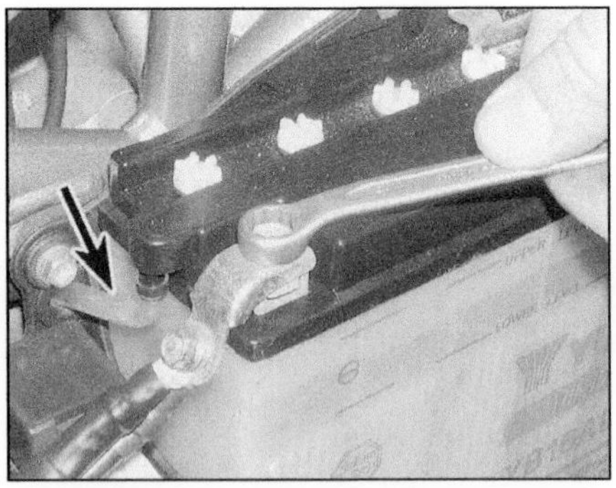

**1.8 Ensure the battery terminal bolts are tight and the breather pipe (arrowed) is in good condition**

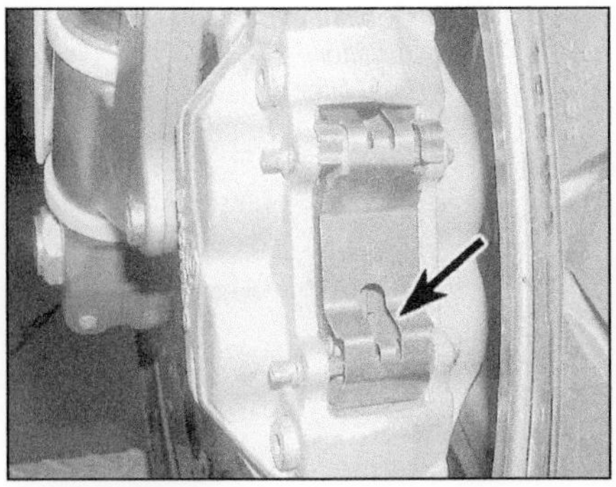

**2.2 Front brake pad friction material is visible through the pad spring aperture (arrowed)**

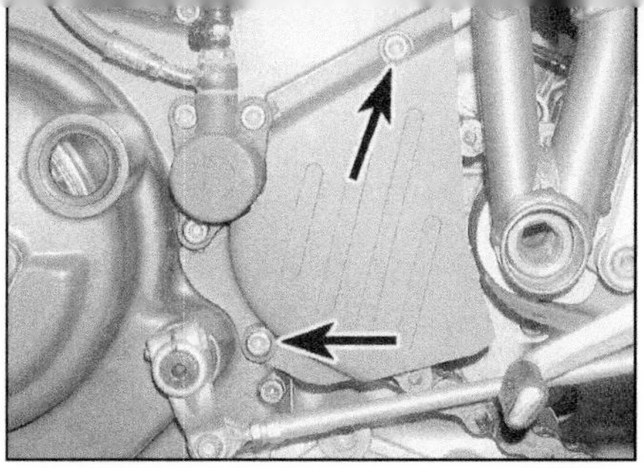

3.2 Undo the bolts (arrowed) and remove the sprocket cover from the engine

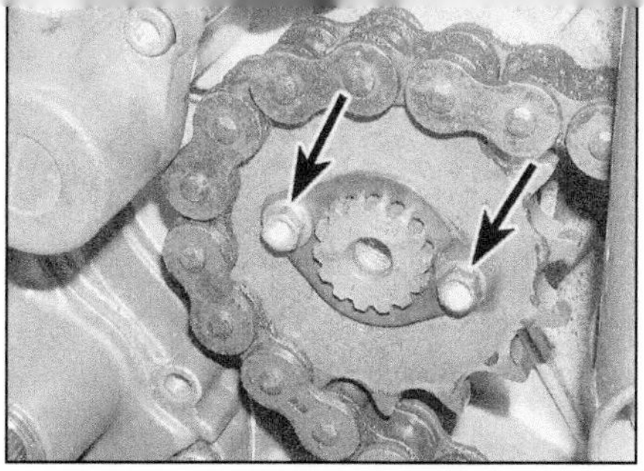

3.3 Ensure the sprocket retaining plate is undamaged and its retaining bolts (arrowed) are tight

must be renewed as a set, i.e. both pads in each caliper.

**3** The amount of rear brake pad wear can be judged by inspecting the pads from the underside of the rear caliper. The friction material of each pad is visible via the caliper aperture. If the friction material of either pad has worn down to, or beyond, the specified minimum thickness, both pads must be renewed as a set.

**4** If the brake pads are dirty, or if you are in doubt as to the amount of friction material remaining, remove them for inspection. Refer to Chapter 7 for details of pad renewal.

## 3 Front sprocket retaining plate – check

**1** Remove the left-hand lower fairing panel (see Chapter 8).

**2** Unscrew the two bolts and remove the sprocket cover from the engine **(see illustration)**.

**3** Clean the area around the front sprocket retaining plate. Check that the retaining plate is securely fitted and that it holds the sprocket securely on the end of the output shaft **(see illustration)**. If the plate shows signs of wear or damage, or no longer retains the sprocket securely, it must be renewed as follows.

**4** Place the transmission in gear then slacken the sprocket retaining plate bolts. Unscrew both bolts then rotate the retaining plate and slide it off the end of the output shaft.

**5** Slide on the new retaining plate, align it with the output shaft groove, then rotate it to line it up with the sprocket holes. Remove all original locking compound and apply a drop of fresh locking compound to each retaining plate bolt then refit the bolts, tightening them to the specified torque.

**6** Ensure the sprocket is securely retained by the plate then refit the sprocket cover, tighten its retaining bolts securely.

**7** Install the lower fairing panel (see Chapter 8).

## 4 Drive chain – check, adjustment and lubrication

### Check

**1** A neglected drive chain won't last long and can quickly damage the sprockets. Routine chain adjustment and lubrication isn't difficult and will ensure maximum chain and sprocket life.

**2** To check the chain, shift the transmission is OFF. Rotate the rear wheel until the chain is positioned with the tightest point at the centre of its bottom run, then place the machine on its sidestand.

**3** Measure the amount of freeplay on the chain's bottom run at a point midway between the two sprockets. Compare your measurement to the value listed in this Chapter's Specifications **(see illustration)**. Since the chain will rarely wear evenly, rotate the rear wheel so that another section of chain can be checked; do this several times to check the entire length of chain. In some cases where lubrication has been neglected, corrosion and galling may cause the links to bind and kink, which effectively shortens the chain's length. If the chain is tight between the sprockets, rusty or kinked, or if any of the pins are loose or the rollers damaged, it's time to renew it. If you find a tight area, mark it with felt pen or paint, and repeat the measurement after the bike has been ridden. If the chain is still tight in the same area, it may be damaged or worn and must be renewed.

***Caution: If the machine is ridden with excessive slack in the drive chain, the chain could contact the frame and swingarm, causing severe damage. Never overtighten the chain as this will place excess strain on the transmission output shaft bearing which could lead to it failing.***

### Adjustment

**4** Rotate the rear wheel until the chain is positioned with the tightest point at the centre of its bottom run, then place the machine on its sidestand.

**5** Slacken and remove the bearing holder clamp bolts from the swingarm **(see illustration)**. Lubricate the threads and underside of the head of each bolt with a smear of molybdenum disulphide grease then refit the bolts loosely to the swingarm.

**6** Using a suitable C-spanner, such as the one supplied in the bike's tool kit, rotate the bearing holder clockwise to slacken the chain or anti-clockwise to tighten it (directions given

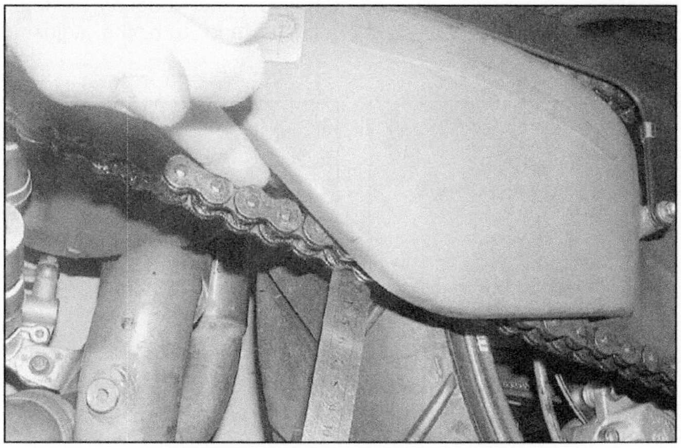

4.3 Measuring drive chain freeplay

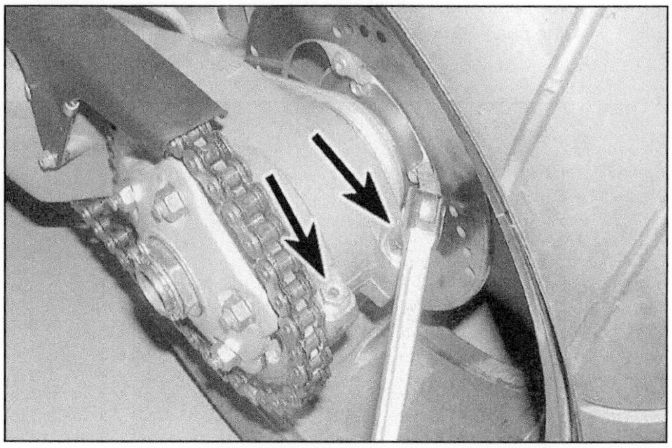

4.5 Slacken and remove the bearing holder clamp bolts (arrowed) from the swingarm

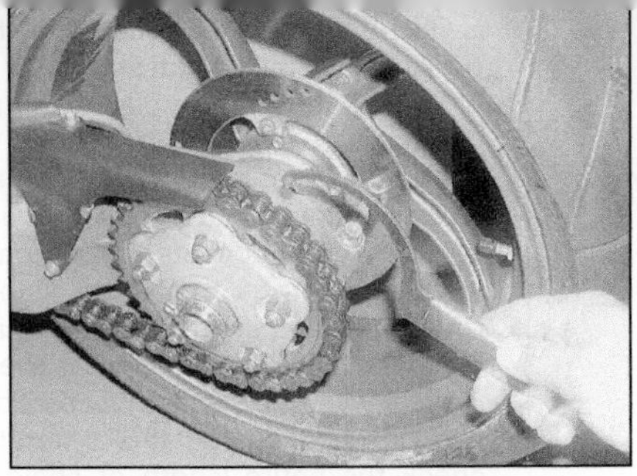

4.6a **Use the C-spanner supplied in the bike's tool kit to rotate the bearing holder**

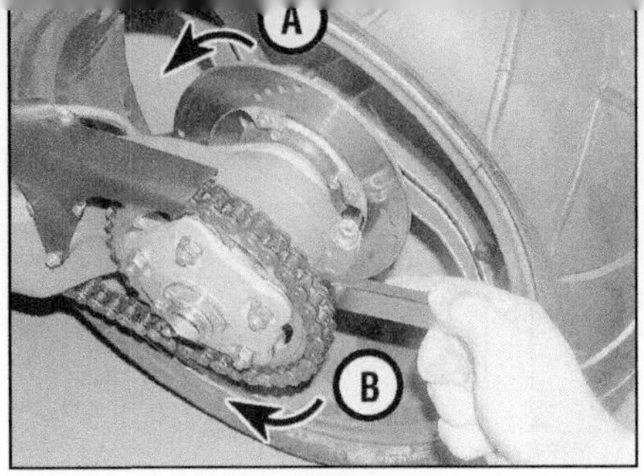


4.6b **Turn it anti-clockwise (A) to tighten the chain and clockwise (B) to slacken it . . .**

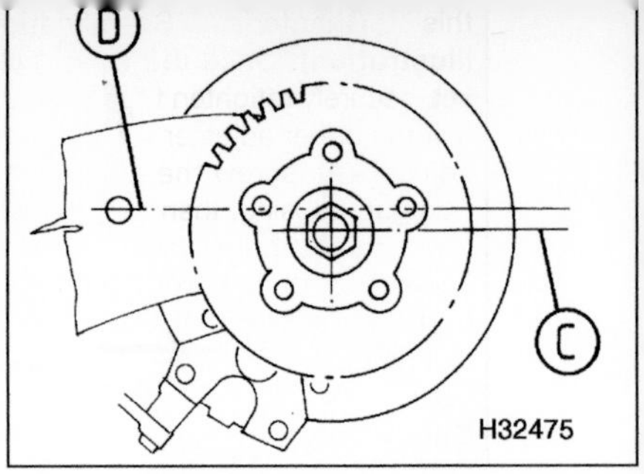


4.6c **. . . to ensure the rear wheel stub axle axis (C) remains below the centre point of the bearing holder (D)**

as viewed from the left-hand side of the bike) until the correct chain tension is obtained **(see illustrations)**. If it is not possible to adjust the chain correctly it is excessively worn and the chain and both sprockets should be renewed as a set (see Chapter 6).

***Caution: Ensure the bearing holder is rotated in the correct direction so that the rear wheel stub axle axis remains below the centre point of the bearing holder* (see illustration)*. If the bearing holder is rotated in the opposite direction, the wheel axis will be above the centre point of the bearing holder. This will result in insufficient clearance between the lower run of the chain and the swingarm and the rear ride height of the bike will be incorrect, adversely affecting the handling.***

**7** When the chain has the correct amount of slack, tighten the bearing holder left-hand clamp bolt to the specified torque then tighten the right-hand clamp bolt to the specified torque. Once both bolts have been tightened, recheck that the left-hand clamp bolt is correctly torqued then recheck the right-hand bolt **(see illustration)**.

## Lubrication

**8** Support the machine on an auxiliary stand so that the rear wheel is off the ground. Rotate the rear wheel whilst cleaning and lubricating the chain to access all the links.

***Caution: Take care not to trap your fingers between the drive chain and rear sprockets as the wheel is rotated.***

**9** Wash the chain in paraffin (kerosene), then wipe it off and allow it to dry, using compressed air if available. If the chain is excessively dirty, it should be removed from the machine and allowed to soak in the paraffin (see Chapter 6).

***Caution: Don't use petrol, solvent or other cleaning fluids which might damage the internal sealing properties of the chain. Don't use high-pressure water. The entire process shouldn't take longer than ten minutes – if it does, the O-rings in the chain rollers could be damaged.***

**10** The best time to lubricate the chain is after the motorcycle has been ridden. When the chain is warm, the lubricant will penetrate the joints between the side plates better than when cold **(see illustration)**. **Note:** *Ducati specifies the use of an aerosol chain lube which is suitable for O-ring chains.*

HAYNES HiNT ***Apply lubricant to the top of the lower chain run – centrifugal force will work it into the chain when the bike is moving.***

## 5 Throttle cable – check and adjustment

**1** Make sure the throttle twistgrip rotates easily from fully closed to fully open with the front wheel turned at various angles. The grip should return automatically from fully open to fully closed when released.

**2** If the throttle sticks, this is probably due to a cable fault. Remove the cable (see Chapter 4) and lubricate it (see Section 6). Install the cable, making sure it is correctly routed. If this fails to improve the operation of the throttle, the cable must be renewed. Note that, in very rare cases, the fault could lie in the throttle body assembly rather than the cable, necessitating the removal of the throttle body assembly and inspection of the throttle linkage (see Chapter 4).

**3** With the throttle operating smoothly, check for a small amount of freeplay in the cable, measured in terms of the amount of twistgrip rotation before the throttle opens, and compare the amount to that listed in this Chapter's Specifications **(see illustration)**. If it's incorrect, adjust the cable to correct it.

**4** Freeplay adjustments can be made at the upper adjuster. Loosen the locknut on the adjuster and turn the adjuster until the

4.7 **Tighten the clamp bolts to the specified torque**

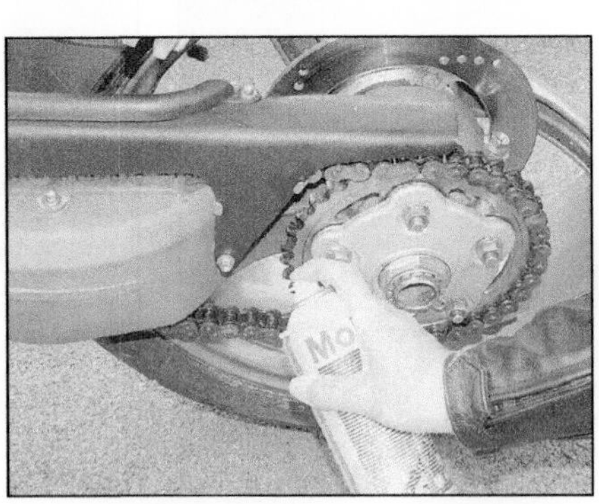

4.10 **Using an aerosol chain lubricant to lubricate the final drive chain**

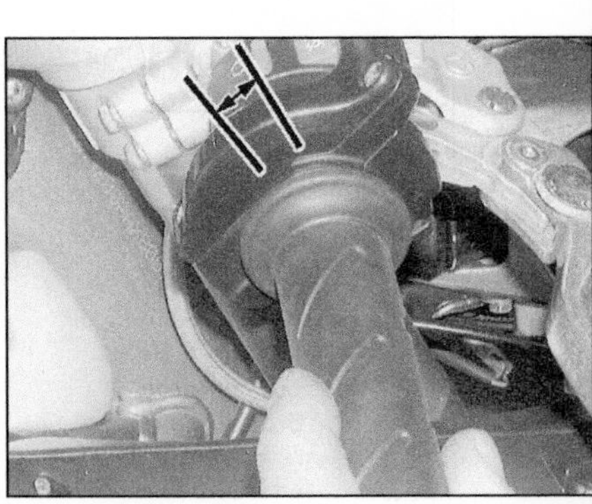

5.3 **Throttle cable freeplay is measured in terms of twistgrip rotation**

this Chapter's Specifications) **(see illustration)**. Once the freeplay is correctly set, securely retighten the locknut.

**5** If the upper adjuster has reached its limit of adjustment, screw the adjuster fully into the twistgrip housing, then remove the right-hand lower fairing panel (see Chapter 8) to gain access to the lower adjuster at the throttle body end of the cable. Slacken the adjuster locknut, then rotate the adjuster to correctly set the twistgrip freeplay **(see illustration)**. Once the freeplay is correctly set, securely tighten the adjuster locknut. Future adjustments can now be made at the upper adjuster. If the cable cannot be adjusted as specified, renew it (see Chapter 4). Once adjustment is correct, install the fairing panel (see Chapter 8).

⚠ ***Warning: Turn the handlebars all the way through their travel with the engine idling. Idle speed should not change. If it does, the cable may be routed incorrectly. Correct this condition before riding the bike.***

**6** Check that the throttle twistgrip operates smoothly and snaps shut quickly when released.

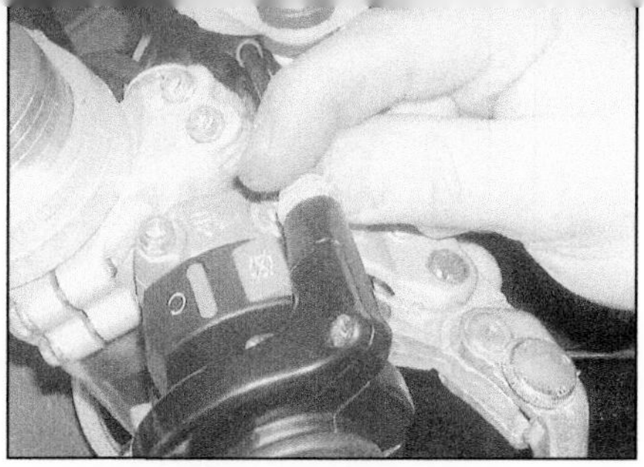

**5.4 Slacken the locknut and adjust the cable freeplay using the upper adjuster on the twistgrip housing**

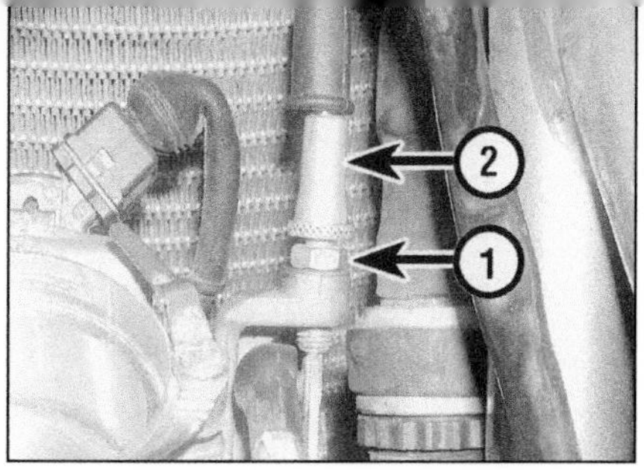


**5.5 Throttle cable lower adjuster on the throttle body (viewed with airbox removed). Slacken the locknut (1) and rotate the adjuster (2) to alter the freeplay**

## 6 Stand, pivots and cables – lubrication

### Pivot points

**1** Since the controls, cables and various other components of a motorcycle are exposed to the elements, they should be lubricated periodically to ensure safe and trouble-free operation.

**2** The footrests, clutch and brake levers, brake pedal, and sidestand pivots should be lubricated frequently. In order for the lubricant to be applied where it will do the most good, the component should be disassembled. However, if chain and cable lubricant is being used, it can be applied to the pivot joint gaps and will usually work its way into the areas where friction occurs. If motor oil or light grease is being used, apply it sparingly as it may attract dirt (which could cause the controls to bind or wear at an accelerated rate). **Note:** *One of the best lubricants for the control lever pivots is a dry-film lubricant (available from many sources by different names).*

### Cables

**3** To lubricate a cable, disconnect the cable at its upper end, then lubricate the cable with a cable oiler clamp, or if one is not available, using the set-up shown **(see illustration)**. See Chapter 4 for the throttle cable removal procedure. The seat cowling lock cable can be unhooked once the seat cowling has been raised.

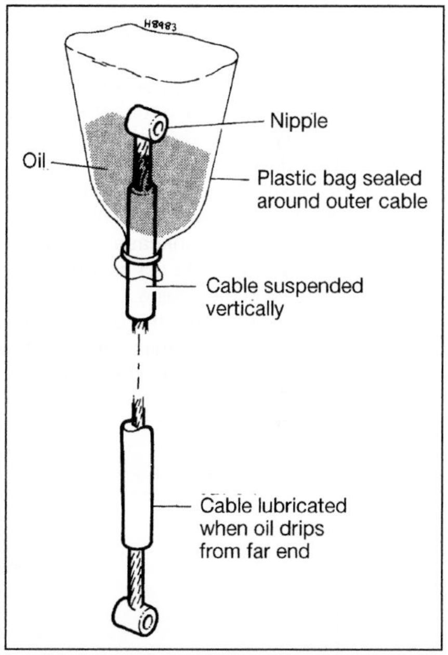


**6.3 Lubricating a cable with a makeshift funnel and motor oil**

## 7 Wheels and tyres – general check

### Tyres

**1** Check the tyre condition and tread depth thoroughly – see *Daily (pre-ride) checks*.

### Wheels

**2** Cast wheels are virtually maintenance free, but they should be kept clean and checked periodically for cracks and other damage. Also check the wheel runout and alignment (see Chapter 7). Never attempt to repair damaged cast wheels; they must be renewed if damaged. Check the valve rubber for signs of damage or deterioration and have it renewed if necessary. Also, make sure the valve stem cap is in place and tight.

# Every 6000 miles (10,000 km)

## 8 Engine – oil and filter change and pick-up filter cleaning

⚠ ***Warning: Be careful when draining the oil, as the exhaust pipes, the engine, and the oil itself can cause severe burns.***

**Note:** *The following procedure includes cleaning the oil pick-up filter. Ducati specify that the oil pick-up filter only requires cleaning once every two oil and filter changes but we recommend it is cleaned every time the oil and filter are changed.*

**1** Consistent routine oil and filter changes are the single most important maintenance procedure you can perform on a motorcycle. The oil not only lubricates the internal parts of the engine and transmission, but also acts as coolant, cleaner, sealant, and protectant. Because of these demands, the oil takes a terrific amount of abuse and should be renewed often with new oil of the recommended grade and type (see Specifications at the beginning of this Chapter).

> **HAYNES HiNT** ***Saving a little money on the difference between good and cheap oils won't pay off if the engine is damaged as a result.***

**2** Before changing the oil, warm up the engine so the oil will drain easily.

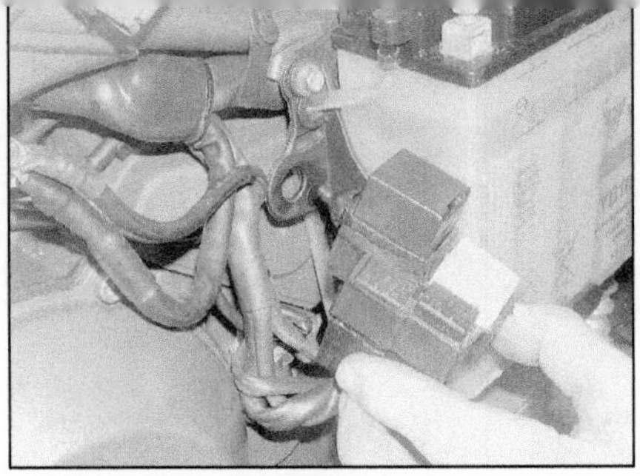

8.3 Free the relay mounting rubber from the battery tray to gain access to the oil filler cap

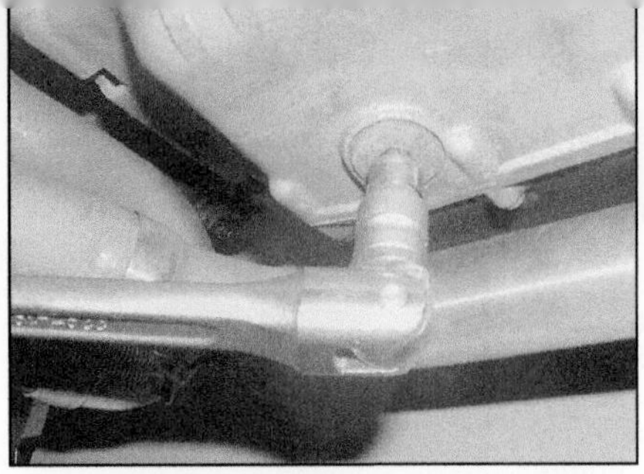

8.5a Unscrew the drain plug from the bottom of the crankcase . . .

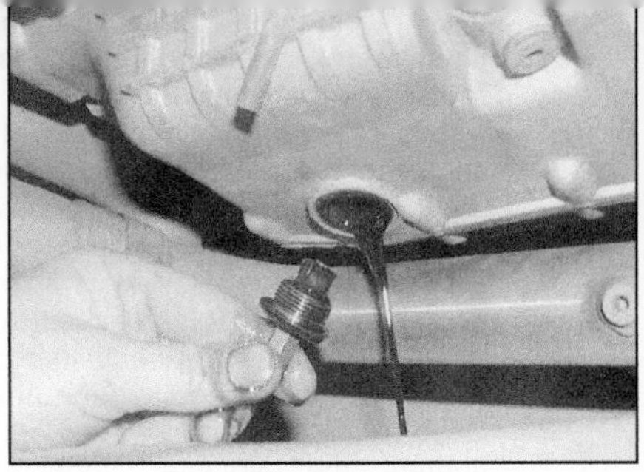

8.5b . . . and allow the oil to drain into a suitable container

**3** Support the motorcycle upright using an auxiliary stand then remove the right-hand side lower fairing panel (see Chapter 8). Free the relay mounting rubber from the rear of the battery tray to gain access to the oil filler cap **(see illustration)**.

**4** Position a clean drain tray below the engine. Unscrew the oil filler cap on the right-hand side crankcase cover to vent the crankcase and to act as a reminder that there is no oil in the engine.

**5** Next, unscrew the oil drain plug from the bottom of the crankcase and allow the oil to flow into the drain tray **(see illustrations)**.

> **HAYNES HiNT** ***To help determine whether any abnormal or excessive engine wear is occurring, place a strainer between the engine and the drain tray so that any debris in the oil is filtered out and can be examined. The drain plug is also fitted with a magnet to attract any stray metal. Small particles of metal are just signs of normal engine wear, but sizeable flakes or chips of metal in the oil or on the drain plug are a sign of internal engine damage.***

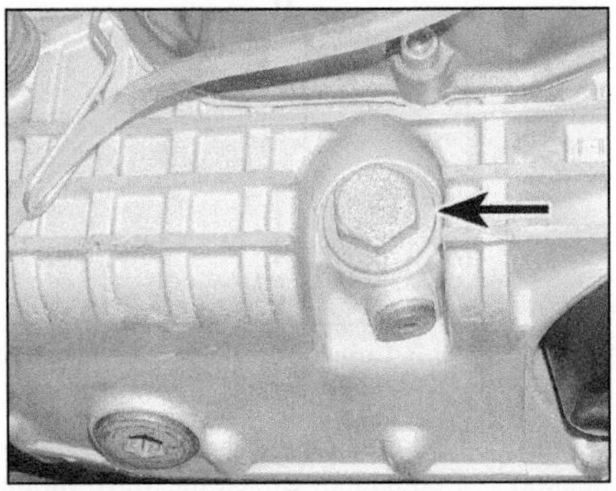

8.6 Unscrew the oil pick-up filter (arrowed) from the right-hand side of the crankcase

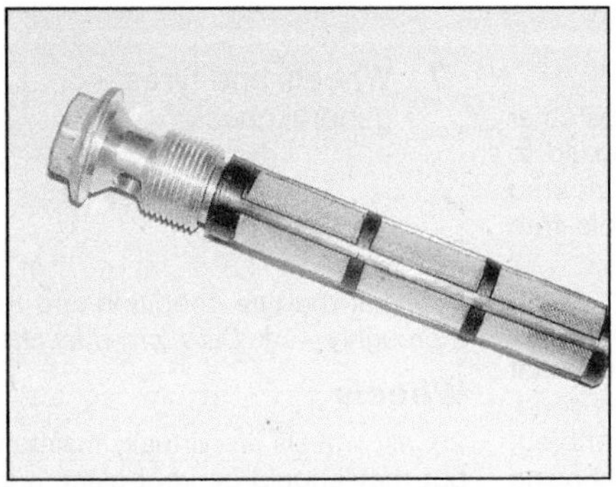

8.7 Ensure the pick-up filter is clean and undamaged

Recover the drain plug sealing washer and discard it; obtain a new one for use on installation.

**6** Unscrew the oil pick-up filter and remove it from the right-hand side of the crankcase **(see illustration)**. Recover the filter sealing washer and discard it; obtain a new one for use on installation.

**7** Clean the pick-up filter in a high-flash point solvent and check it for signs of damage. If the filter gauze shows signs of damage, such as clogging or splitting, it must be renewed **(see illustration)**.

**8** Once all oil has drained from the engine, remove all traces of metallic filings from the drain plug magnet and fit the new sealing washer. Refit the drain plug to the crankcase and tighten it to the specified torque **(see illustration)**.

**9** Ensure the pick-up filter is clean and dry then fit the new sealing washer to it. Screw the filter back into the crankcase and tighten it to the specified torque **(see illustration)**.

**10** Place the drain tray below the oil filter. Unscrew the oil filter using a filter wrench or a strap wrench and tip any residual oil into the drain tray **(see illustration)**. Wipe clean the oil filter mating surface on the crankcase.

**11** Smear clean engine oil onto the rubber seal on the new filter, then manoeuvre the

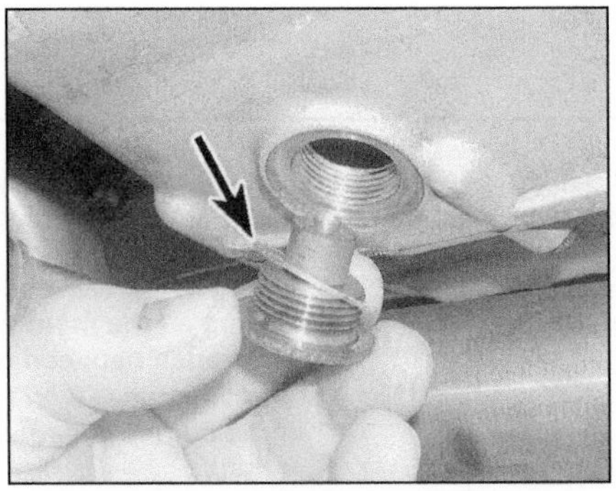

8.8 Fit a new sealing washer (arrowed) then refit the drain plug to the crankcase and tighten to the specified torque

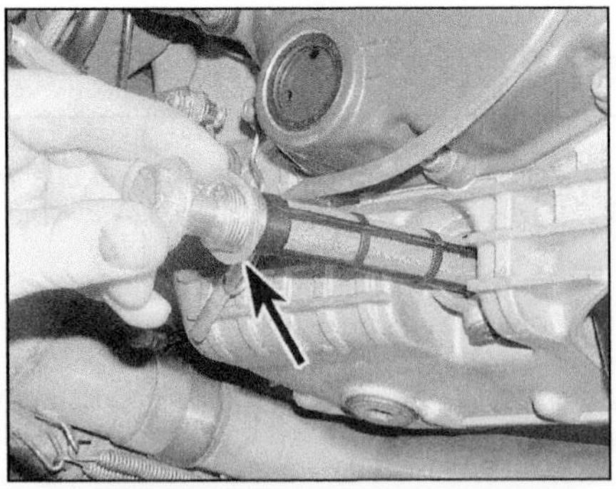

8.9 Fit a new sealing washer (arrowed) to the pick-up filter then refit the filter, tightening it to the specified torque

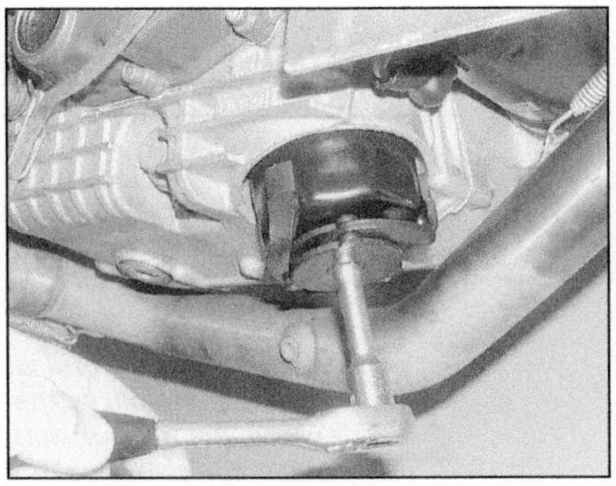

8.10 Slacken the oil filter with a filter wrench and unscrew it from the engine

8.11a Lubricate the rubber seal of the new filter with clean engine oil . . .

8.11b . . . then screw on the filter

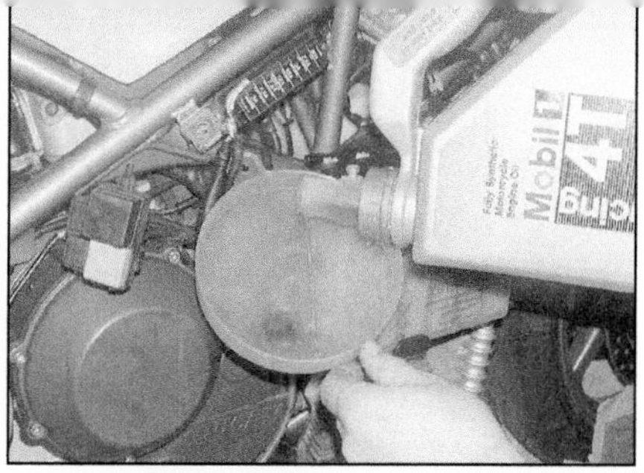

8.12 Refill the engine with the specified type and amount of oil

filter into position **(see illustrations)**. Screw on the filter and tighten it to the specified torque. If a filter wrench is not being used, tighten the filter as tight as possible by hand.

**12** Refill the crankcase to the proper level using the recommended type and amount of oil (see Specifications) **(see illustration)**. With the motorcycle on its wheels and held vertical, the oil level should lie between the upper and lower level lines on the inspection window in the right-hand crankcase cover (see *Daily (pre-ride) checks)*. Install the filler cap. Start the engine and let it run for two or three minutes (make sure that the oil pressure light extinguishes after a few seconds). Shut it off, wait a few minutes, then check the oil level. If necessary, add more oil to bring the level up to the high level line on the inspection window. Check around the drain plug and filters for leaks.

**13** Refit the relay mounting rubber to the battery tray then install the lower fairing panel (see Chapter 8).

**14** The old oil drained from the engine and filter cannot be re-used and should be disposed of properly. Check with your local refuse disposal company, disposal facility or environmental agency to see whether they will accept the used oil for recycling. Don't pour used oil into drains or onto the ground. Note that the old filter should be taken to the oil disposal facility rather than disposed of with the household rubbish.

OIL CARE
FOLLOW THE CODE
OIL BANK LINE
0800 66 33 66
www.oilbankline.org.uk

***Note: It is antisocial and illegal to dump oil down the drain. To find the location of your local oil recycling bank in the UK, call this number free.***

## 9 Fuel filter – renewal

**1** The filter is part of the fuel pump assembly which is housed inside the fuel tank. Refer to Chapter 4 for fuel pump and filter removal and installation details.

## 10 Air filter elements – renewal

***Caution: If the machine is continually ridden in dusty conditions, this task should be carried out more frequently.***

**1** Remove both lower fairing panels and the upper fairing (see Chapter 8). There are two air filter elements; one in the left-hand filter housing and one in the right-hand air filter housing. Each filter element can be renewed as follows.

**2** Trace the wiring back from the turn signal and disconnect the turn signal wiring connectors **(see illustration)**.

**3** Undo the retaining screws and remove the outer cover from the filter housing **(see illustrations)**.

**4** Remove the filter element from the housing, noting which way around it is fitted **(see**

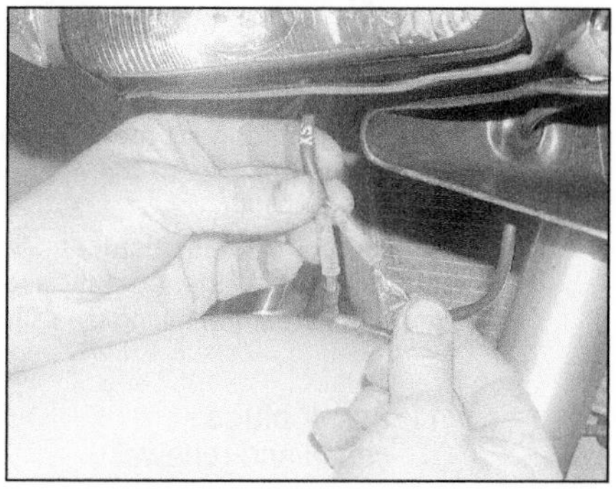

10.2 Disconnect the turn signal wiring connectors so the light can be removed with the air filter housing cover

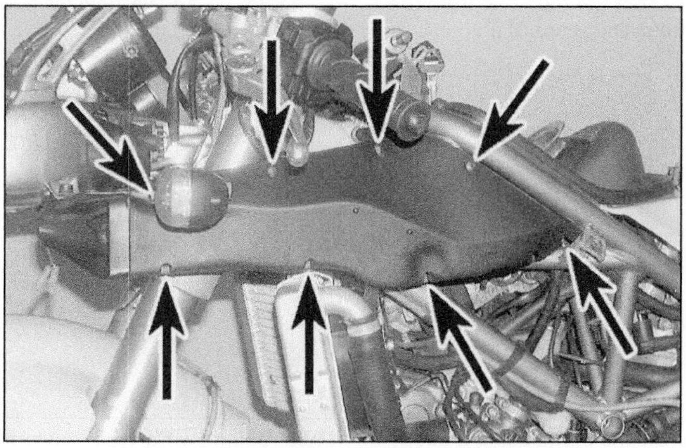

10.3a Undo the retaining screws (arrowed) . . .

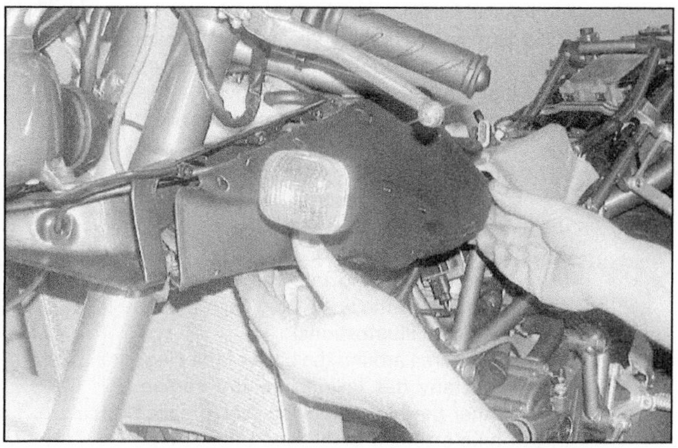

10.3b . . . then remove the outer cover from the filter housing

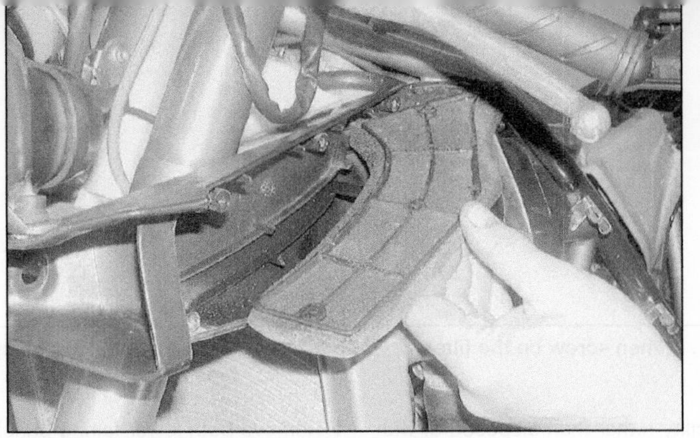
10.4 Remove the air filter element noting which way around it is fitted

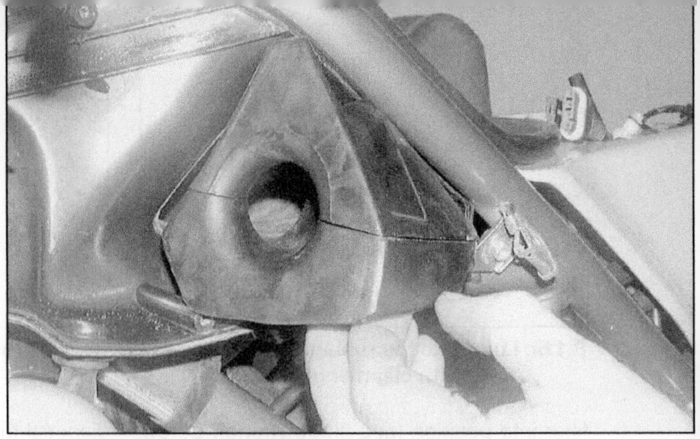
10.5 On 996 models ensure the rubber intake block is correctly seated in the housing

**illustration)**. On 996 models take care not to lose the rubber intake block from the housing.

**5** Wipe clean the interior of the filter housing and cover. On 996 models ensure the rubber intake block is correctly fitted **(see illustration)**.

**6** Install the new air filter element ensuring it is correctly located in the housing slot.

**7** Engage the outer cover correctly with the filter element then seat the cover on the housing, ensuring the turn signal wiring is correctly routed through the hole in the housing. Refit the cover retaining screws and tighten them securely.

**8** Securely reconnect the turn signal wiring connectors then repeat the operation on the other filter housing.

**9** Once both filter elements have been renewed, check the operation of the turn signals then refit the fairing (see Chapter 8).

## 11 Spark plugs – check and renewal

**1** To gain access to the horizontal cylinder spark plug, remove the fairing lower panel and inner panel as described in Chapter 8.

**2** To gain access to the vertical cylinder spark plug, remove the fuel tank (see Chapter 4). Note that there is no need to remove the fuel tank completely, limited access can be gained by unbolting the tank and raising and supporting it, with the hoses and wiring still connected (obviously access will be severely restricted if this method is used).

**3** Clean the area around the plug caps to prevent any dirt falling into the spark plug channels then pull the spark plug cap off each spark plug **(see illustrations)**.

**4** Clean the area around the base of the plugs to prevent any dirt falling into the engine. Using either the plug removing tool supplied in the bike's toolkit or a deep socket type wrench, unscrew the plugs from the cylinder head **(see illustration)**. Lay each plug out in relation to its cylinder; if any plug shows up a problem it will then be easy to identify the troublesome cylinder.

**5** Before discarding the plugs inspect the electrodes for wear. Both the centre and side electrodes should have square edges and the side electrodes should be of uniform thickness. Look for excessive deposits and evidence of a cracked or chipped insulator around the centre electrode. Compare your spark plugs to the colour spark plug reading chart at the end of this manual. Check the threads, the washer and the ceramic insulator body for cracks and other damage.

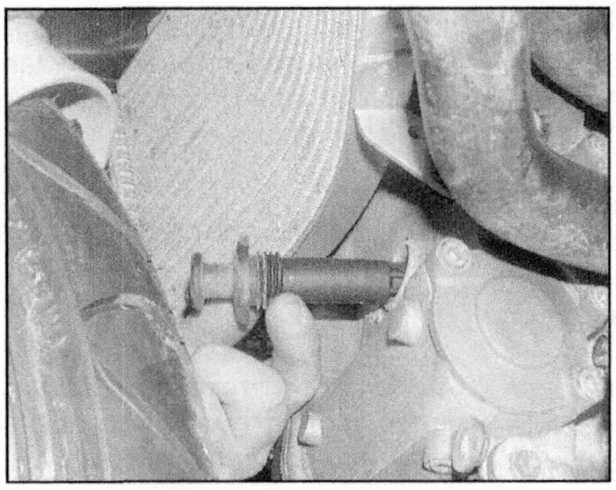
11.3a Disconnect the plug cap from the horizontal cylinder spark plug . . .

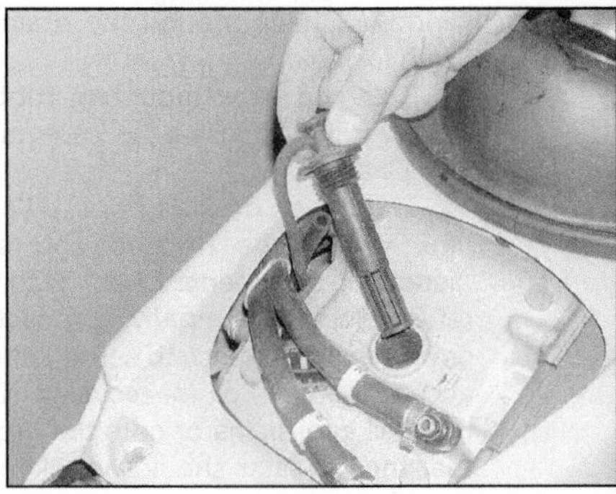
11.3b . . . and vertical cylinder plug

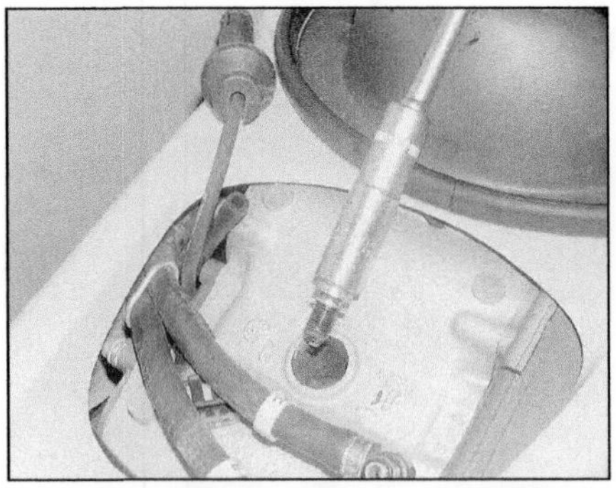
11.4 Unscrew the plugs using a deep socket or the tool supplied in the bike's toolkit

> HAYNES HiNT
>
> ***Stripped plug threads in the cylinder head can be repaired with a thread insert – see 'Tools and Workshop Tips' in the Reference section.***

**6** Before installing the new plugs, make sure they are the correct type and heat range and check the gap between the electrodes **(see illustrations)**. Compare the gap to that specified and adjust as necessary. If the gap must be adjusted, bend the side electrode only

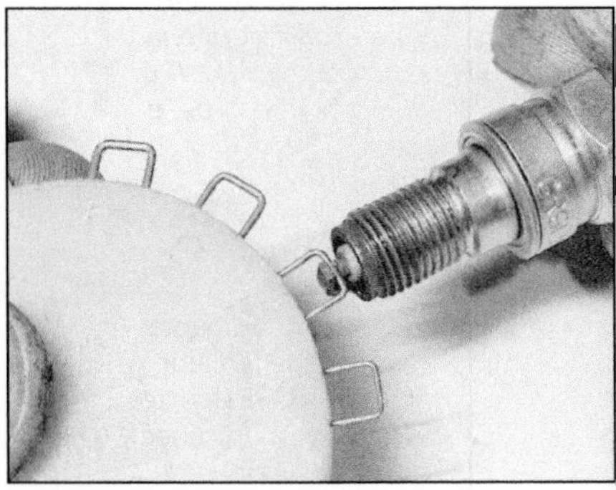
11.6a Using a wire-type gauge to measure the spark plug electrode gap

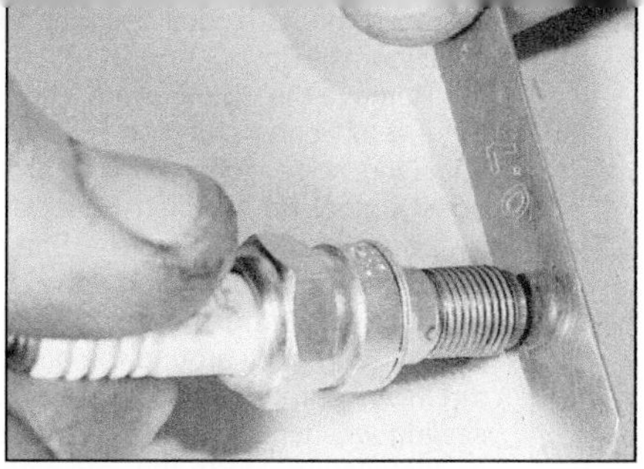

**11.6b Using a feeler gauge to measure the spark plug electrode gap**

and be very careful not to chip or crack the insulator nose **(see illustration)**. Make sure the washer is in place before installing each plug.

**7** Since the cylinder head is made of aluminium, which is soft and easily damaged, thread the plugs into the heads turning the tool by hand. Once the plugs are finger-tight, the job can be finished with a spanner on the tool supplied or a socket drive. Tighten the plugs an additional 1/4 to 1/2 turn or as directed on the plug manufacturer's packaging. If a torque wrench can be fitted to the socket/wrench, tighten the plugs to the specified torque.

> **HAYNES HiNT** ***As the plugs are recessed in the heads, slip a short length of hose over the end of the plug to use as a tool to thread it into place. The hose will grip the plug well enough to turn it, but will start to slip if the plug begins to cross-thread in the hole – this will prevent damaged threads.***

**8** Reconnect both spark plug caps making sure both caps are pushed fully onto the plugs.

**9** On completion, refit the fuel tank and install the fairing panels (see Chapters 4 and 8).

## 12 Cylinder head nuts – tightness check

**Note:** *The Ducati service tool (88713.1139) will be required to enable the cylinder head nuts to be checked. If the tool is not available this check must be entrusted to a Ducati dealer.*

***Caution: The engine must be completely cool before beginning this procedure.***

**1** Remove the airbox (see Chapter 4).

**2** Remove the lower fairing panels and the inner panel (see Chapter 8).

**3** Remove the radiator (see Chapter 3).

**4** Using the service tool (88713.1139) and a torque wrench, check that each cylinder head nut is tightened to the final Stage 3 torque setting (see Chapter 2 Specifications).

**5** Once all nuts have been checked, install the radiator and airbox (see Chapter 3 and 4).

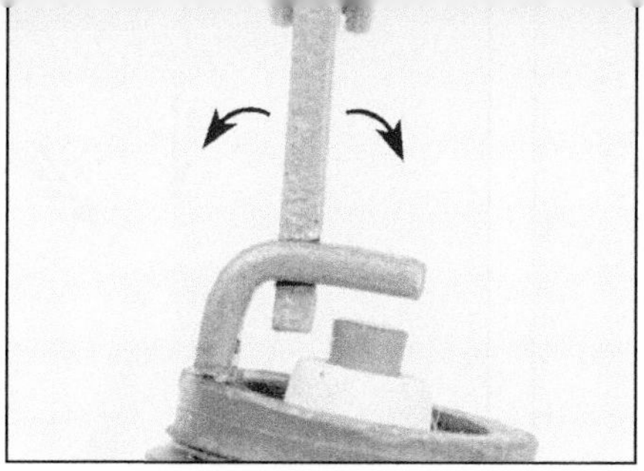

**11.6c Adjust the electrode gap by bending the side electrode only**

**6** Refill the cooling system (see Section 31) then refit the fairing panels (see Chapter 8).

## 13 Flywheel/alternator rotor nut tightness check – early models

**Note:** *This check is only necessary on pre 1999 model year models fitted with the early alternator/flywheel set-up (see Chapter 2, Section 17). Later models with the three-phase alternator do not require checking.*

**1** Remove the left-hand side crankcase cover and check that the flywheel/alternator rotor nut is correctly tightened by applying the specified torque to it (see Chapter 2, Sections 16 and 17 and Specifications).

**2** If the nut is loose or moves when the torque is applied, remove the alternator rotor, flywheel and starter clutch assembly then correctly reinstall the components as described in Section 17 of Chapter 2.

***Caution: If the nut is loose, do not be tempted to remove the nut, apply fresh locking compound to it then fit it and tighten to the specified torque. The washer may have slipped off the rear of the bush and become trapped between the bush and gear. This would cause the flywheel not to seat properly on the crankshaft and will result in serious engine damage.***

**3** If the nut is tight and does not move when the torque is applied, no further action is required.

**4** On completion, refit the left crankcase cover (see Chapter 2, Section 16).

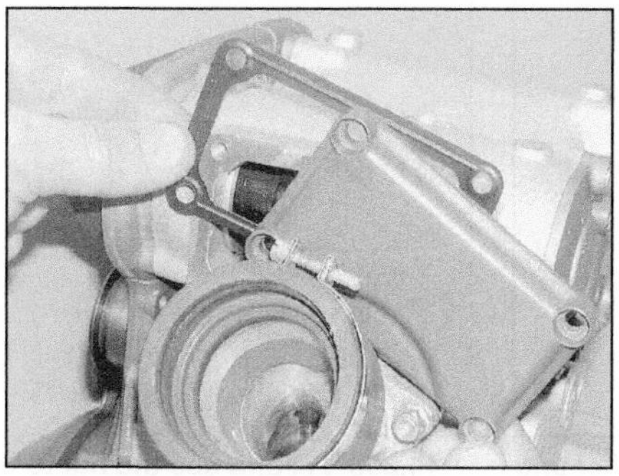

**14.3 Undo the bolts and remove the valve covers and gaskets**

## 14 Valve clearances – check and adjustment

**Note:** *Checking and adjustment of the valve clearances should only be carried out by owners who are familiar with the principles of Desmodromic valve operation. If you are unsure about how it works, entrust the task to a Ducati dealer.*

### *Check*

**1** The engine must be completely cool for this maintenance procedure, so let the machine sit overnight before beginning.

**2** Remove the fuel tank, airbox, throttle body assembly as described in Chapter 4. To further improve access also remove the intake manifolds.

**3** Remove all traces of dirt from around the cylinder head valve covers. Undo the retaining bolts and remove the intake and exhaust valve covers from both cylinder heads **(see illustration)**. Discard the gaskets (where fitted – not all engines have them); new ones will be needed on installation.

**4** Make a chart or sketch of all valve positions so that a note of each opening and closing clearance can be made against the relevant valve.

**5** Referring to Section 6 of Chapter 2, align the engine timing marks to position the horizontal piston at TDC on its compression stroke. With the engine in this position the clearances of all four horizontal cylinder head valves can be checked as follows.

**6** The valve opening clearance is measured between the base of the opening rocker arm and the opening shim which is fitted to the top of the valve stem. To ensure an accurate measurement, using a screwdriver, gently lever up on the closing rocker arm whilst measuring the clearance; this will ensure the valve is firmly seated in the cylinder head. Use feeler gauges to obtain the exact clearance (the gauge should be a light, sliding fit between the arm and shim) and record the measured clearance on the chart **(see illustration)**.

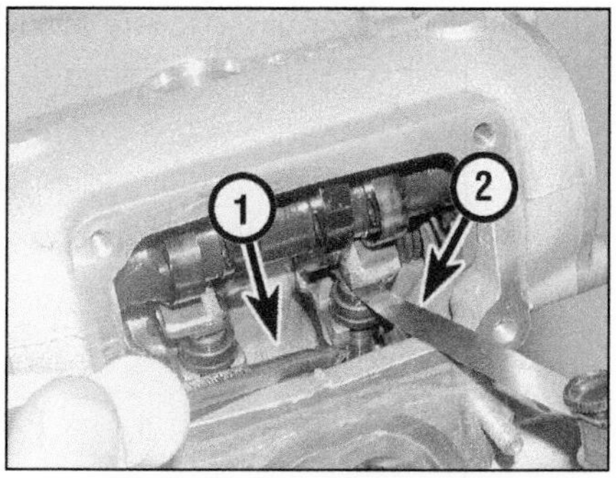


**14.6 Checking a valve opening clearance. Lever the closing rocker arm up with a screwdriver (1) and insert the feeler gauges (2) between then opening rocker arm and shim**

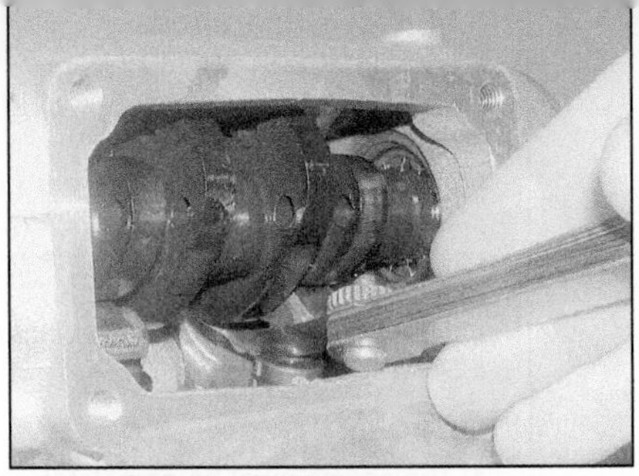

**14.7 Checking a valve closing clearance. Insert the feeler gauges between the rocker arm and camshaft lobe**

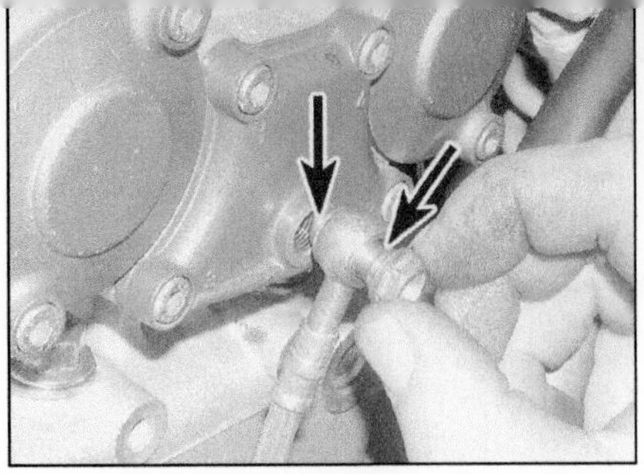

**14.17 Unscrew the oil hose banjo bolt and recover the sealing washers (arrowed)**

**7** The valve closing clearance is far more awkward to check; the clearance is measured between the closing rocker arm and the cam lobe and the rocker arm acts on the rear of camshaft lobe. Use feeler gauges to obtain the exact clearance, sliding the feeler gauges into position from underneath the camshaft **(see illustration)**. **Note:** *Measurement of the closing clearances will be made easier if a set of angled feeler gauges is available.*

**8** Obtain the opening and closing clearances of each of the four horizontal cylinder head valves (a total of eight measurements).

**9** Referring to Section 6 of Chapter 2, rotate the crankshaft through a further 3/4 turn (270°) anti-clockwise to bring the vertical cylinder piston to TDC on its compression stroke.

**10** With the engine in this position the clearances of all four vertical cylinder head valves can be checked as described in Steps 6 and 7. Obtain the opening and closing clearances of each of the four vertical cylinder head valves (a total of eight measurements).

**11** When all clearances have been measured and charted, compare the measurements obtained with the specified checking clearances given in the Specifications. If any clearance is not within the specified limits it must be adjusted as described below.

**12** Once all the valve clearances are known to be correct, ensure the cylinder head and valve cover mating surfaces are clean and dry. Where gaskets were fitted, fit a new gasket to each cover then install the intake and exhaust valve covers on the cylinder head. Where no gaskets were fitted, apply a smear of sealant to the cover mating surfaces then fit the covers. Tighten the cover retaining bolts to the specified torque.

**13** Install the intake manifolds, throttle body assembly, airbox and fuel tank (see Chapter 4).

## Adjustment

**14** Each of the rocker arms has its own shaft which can be withdrawn once the relevant side cover has been removed from the cylinder head. Adjustment of an opening clearance involves partially withdrawing the rocker arm shaft, moving the rocker arm to the side of the valve and removing the shim from the top of the valve stem. This procedure can be carried without disconnecting the timing belts. Adjustment of a closing clearance is far more involved and requires the removal of the timing belt and camshaft. If only the opening clearances require adjustment, follow the opening clearance adjustment procedure. If the closing clearances or both the opening and closing clearances require adjustment, follow the closing clearance adjustment procedure.

### Opening clearance adjustment

**15** Referring to Section 6 of Chapter 2, align the engine timing marks to position the horizontal piston at TDC on its compression valves in the horizontal cylinder head can be adjusted as follows.

**16** Remove the valve covers (see Step 3).

**17** If a left-hand side valve clearance needs adjusting, wipe clean the area around the oil hose union on the left-hand side of the cylinder head. Unscrew the banjo bolt and separate the hose from the head **(see illustration)**. Plug the hose end or wrap a plastic bag tightly around the hose to prevent dirt from entering the system. Discard the sealing washers, as new ones must be used on installation. Undo the retaining bolts and remove the left-hand side cover from the cylinder head to gain access to the rocker arm shafts. Discard the cover gasket; a new one will be needed on installation. **Note:** *On the horizontal head, note the correct fitted location of the radiator locating peg when removing the cover.*

**18** If a right-hand side valve clearance is being adjusted, undo the retaining bolts and remove the right-hand side cover from the cylinder head to gain access to the rocker arm shafts. Discard the cover gasket; a new one will be needed on installation. Cover the timing belt to prevent possible oil contamination.

**19** Each rocker arm shaft is equipped with an M5 thread. The thread is provided to enable a service tool to be screwed into the shaft to draw the shaft out from the head. In the absence of the Ducati service tool (88713.0862), obtain an M5 bolt, nut, washer and a socket to use as a drawbolt. Screw the nut onto the bolt and fit the washer.

**20** Fit the socket to the head of the M5 bolt, then screw the bolt securely into the end of the relevant opening (upper) rocker arm shaft **(see illustrations)**. Partially draw the rocker arm shaft out from the cylinder head, by tightening the nut against the washer and socket, until it is possible to move the opening rocker arm to the side of the valve. Position the rocker arm clear of the valve and remove the opening shim from the top of the valve, using a magnet or a pair of pliers **(see illustration)**.

**21** Using a micrometer, accurately measure the thickness of the shim **(see illus-**

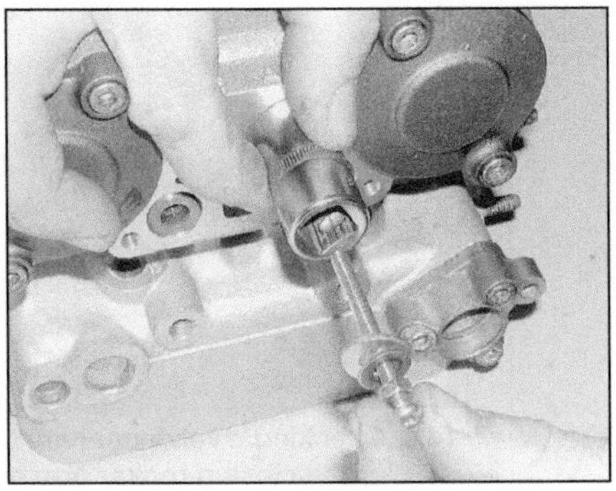

**14.20a Fit the socket, M5 bolt, washer and nut arrangement to the opening rocker arm shaft . . .**

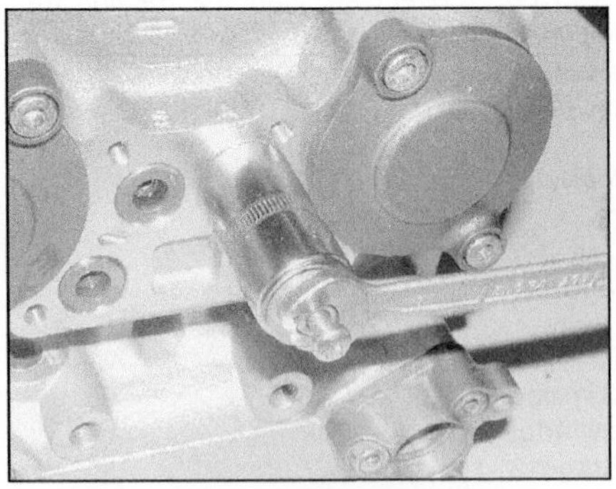

**14.20b . . . and use the nut to draw the shaft out of position . . .**

**14.20c . . . until it is possible to move the opening rocker arm (arrowed) to the side and remove the opening shim from the valve**

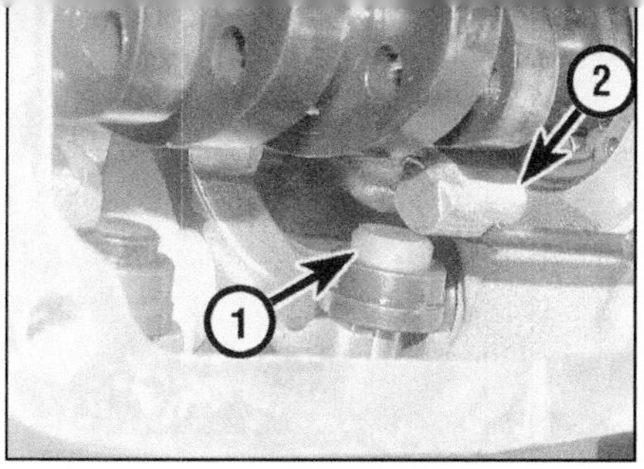


**14.23 Ensure the opening shim (1) is correctly seated then slide the rocker arm (2) back into position**

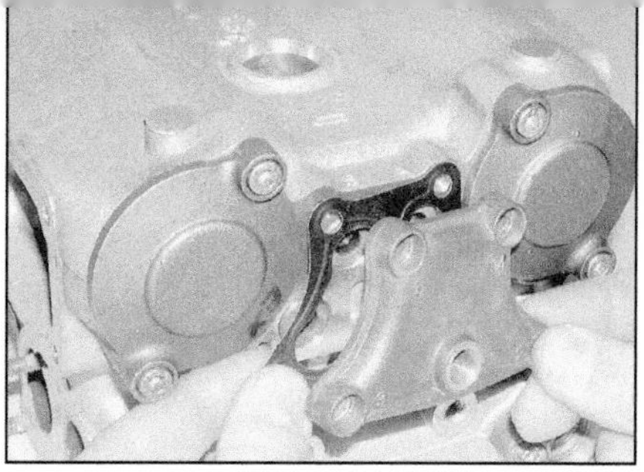

**14.28a Fit the side covers to the head using new gaskets**

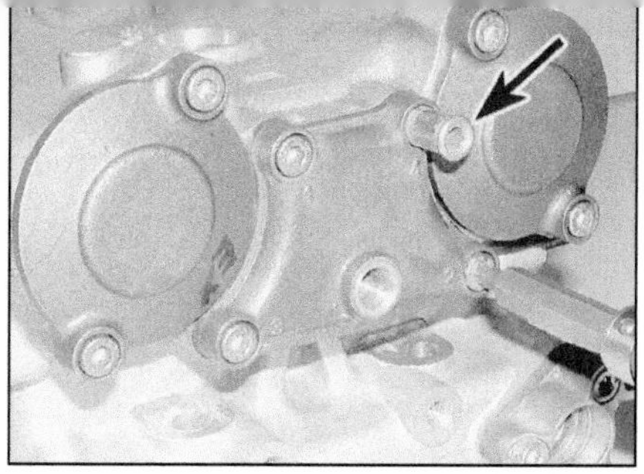

**14.28b On the horizontal cylinder head ensure the radiator locating peg (arrowed) is correctly positioned when fitting the left-hand cover**

**tration 14.44)**. Opening shims are available in 0.05 mm increments from 1.8 mm to 3.45 mm. The new shim thickness required can be calculated using the thickness of the original shim and the measured clearance. If the valve clearance was less than specified, subtract the measured clearance from the specified adjusting clearance then deduct the result from the original shim thickness to obtain the correct thickness of shim required. If the valve clearance was greater than specified, subtract the specified clearance from the measured clearance, and add the result to the thickness of the original shim to obtain the correct thickness of shim required.

**22** Obtain the correct thickness opening shim and fit it securely to the top of the valve stem.

**23** Slide the opening rocker arm back into position between the shim and lobe then press the rocker arm shaft fully into position **(see illustration)**.

**24** Repeat the adjustment procedure, as necessary, on the other valves.

**25** Once all the horizontal cylinder valves are correctly adjusted, rotate the crankshaft through a further 3/4 turn (270°) anti-clockwise to bring the vertical cylinder piston to TDC on its compression stroke (see Section 6 of Chapter 2). Repeat the adjustment procedure on the vertical cylinder valves.

**26** Once all the valves have been adjusted, rotate the crankshaft a few times to settle all shims in position then recheck all valve clearances (see Steps 4 to 10).

**27** On completion of adjustment, ensure the mating surfaces of the cylinder head and covers are clean and dry.

**28** Fit a new gasket to each cover then install the left- and right-hand side covers on the cylinder heads, tightening their retaining bolts to the specified torque **(see illustration)**. On the horizontal cylinder head, ensure the radiator locating peg is correctly positioned on installation **(see illustration)**.

**29** If the left-hand side cover was removed, position a new sealing washer on each side of the oil hose union and screw in the banjo bolt. Ensure the end fitting is correctly positioned in relation to the cylinder head then tighten the banjo bolt to the specified torque.

**30** Ensure the cylinder head and valve cover mating surfaces are clean and dry. Where gaskets were fitted, fit a new gasket to each cover then install the intake and exhaust valve covers on the cylinder head. Where no gaskets were fitted, apply a smear of sealant to the cover mating surfaces then fit the covers. Tighten the cover retaining bolts to the specified torque.

**31** Install the timing belt lower cover and securely tighten its retaining bolts. Install both upper covers, tightening their retaining bolts securely.

**32** Slacken the nut and remove the bolt, spacer, washer and nut used to rotate the crankshaft **(see illustration)**.

**33** Fit a new sealing ring then fit the centre cap to the left-hand crankcase cover **(see illustration)**. Apply a drop of locking compound to the retaining screws threads then fit the screws, tightening them securely.

**34** Install the battery mounting tray and battery (see Chapter 9).

**35** Install the throttle body assembly, airbox and fuel tank (see Chapter 4) then install the lower fairing panels (see Chapter 8).

## Closing clearance adjustment

**Note:** *Adjustment of the closing clearances is an involved and awkward procedure. If several of the clearances require adjustment it may be worth considering removing and overhauling the cylinder head (see Chapter 2). The valve clearances can then be set on the bench before the cylinder head is installed. New half-rings will be required for each shim which is being changed; these must be renewed whenever they are removed.*

**Note:** *The following procedure assumes the clearances of both cylinder heads require adjustment. If only the horizontal cylinder head clearances require adjustment, there is no need to disturb the vertical cylinder timing belt. If only the vertical cylinder head clearances require adjustment, it is possible to release the timing belt tension and disengage the belt from the camshaft pulleys without disturbing the horizontal cylinder timing belt although obviously it will not be possible to remove the belt from the engine.*

**36** Remove the timing belts (see Chapter 2).

**37** Remove the valve covers and the cylinder head side covers (see Steps 3, 17 and 18).

**38** Starting on the horizontal cylinder head, treat each camshaft and its pair of valves as a separate assembly and adjust as follows.

**39** Starting on the first camshaft, remove the opening shims from both valves as described in Steps 19 and 20.

**40** Undo the retaining bolts then ease the camshaft left-hand side cap out of position and remove it from the cylinder head **(see**

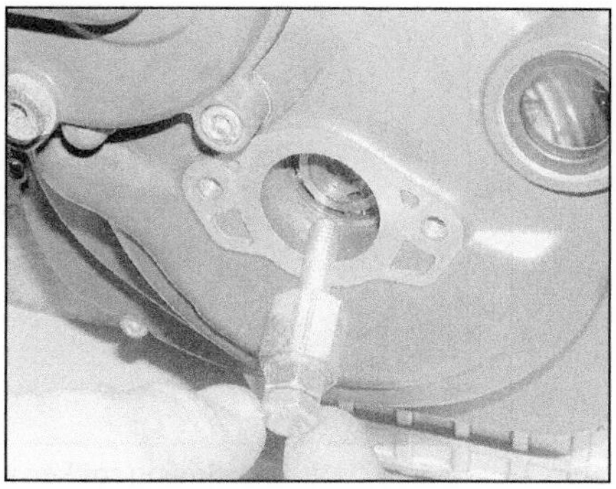

**14.32 Slacken the nut and remove the arrangement used to rotate the crankshaft**

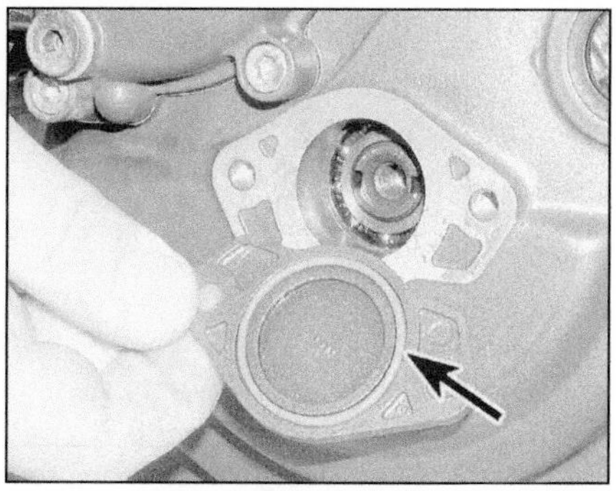

**14.33 Fit a new sealing ring (arrowed) then refit the centre cap to the left crankcase cover**

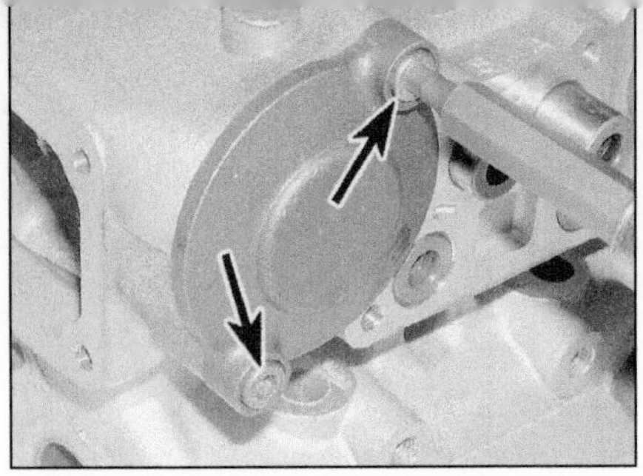

**14.40 Undo the bolts and remove the camshaft left-hand end cap from the head**

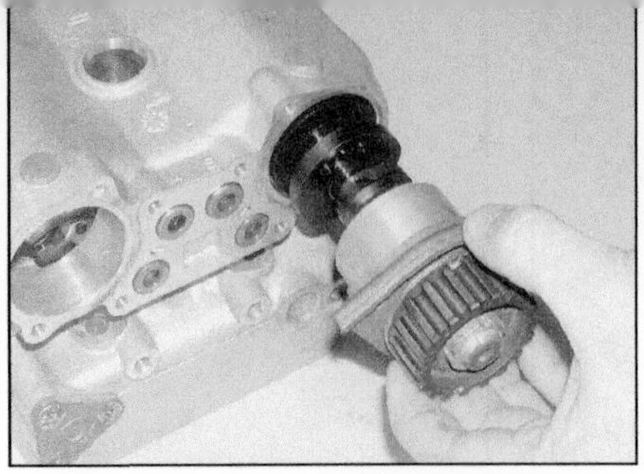

**14.41 Unscrew the right-hand end cap bolts and remove the cap and camshaft assembly**

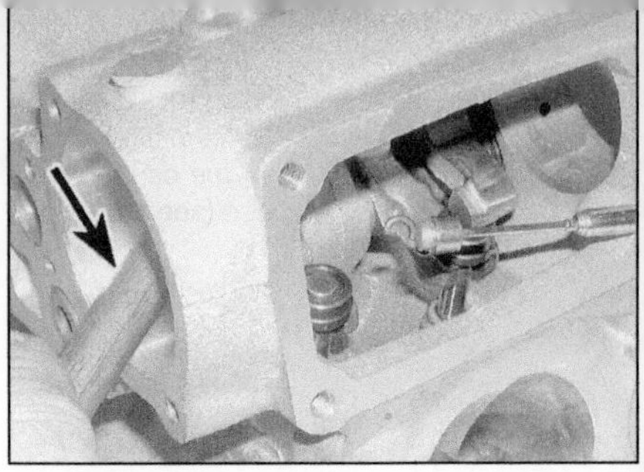

**14.43a Lever the closing rocker arm down using a screwdriver/dowel (1) and remove the half-rings (2) . . .**

**illustration)**. Discard the cap sealing ring; a new one should be used on installation.

**41** Slacken and remove the bolts securing the camshaft right-hand side end cap to the cylinder head. Manoeuvre the end cap and camshaft assembly out of position and remove it from the cylinder head **(see illustration)**. Discard the cap sealing ring; a new one should be used on installation. Note that all the camshafts are different and are not interchangeable (see Section 11 of Chapter 2).

**42** To retain the valve and prevent it falling down into the cylinder (the piston is at TDC and will stop it falling out completely), fit a cable tie to the valve stem. Slide the cable tie down until it abuts the valve guide oil seal then securely tighten it around the valve stem.

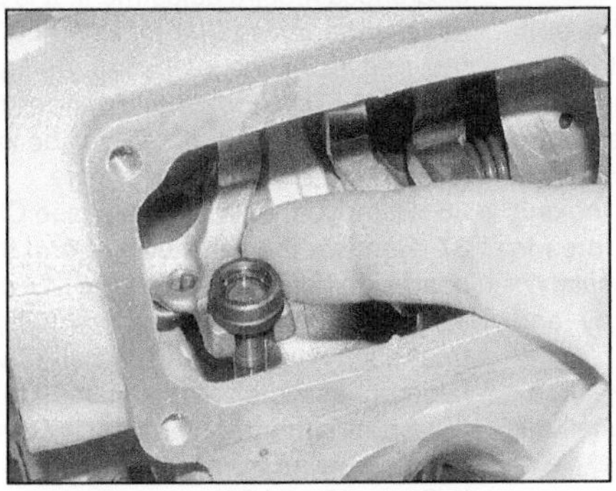

**14.43b . . . then release the rocker arm and slide off the closing shim, noting which way up it is fitted**

**43** With the valve securely retained, insert a screwdriver or wooden dowel in through the camshaft end cap aperture and carefully lever the closing (lower) rocker arm down to relieve the spring pressure from the closing shim. Slide the closing shim down the valve stem and remove the shim retaining half-rings **(see illustration)**. With both half-rings removed, slowly release the rocker arm and slide the closing shim from the end of the valve **(see illustration)**. Discard the shim retaining half-rings; new ones must be used on installation.

***Caution: Take care not to allow the half-rings to drop down into the oil return holes located in the corners of the cylinder head. If any half-ring is dropped it must be recovered before the engine is started***

**44** Using a micrometer, accurately measure the thickness of the shim **(see illustration)**. Closing shims are available in 0.05 mm increments from 2.7 to 3.7 mm. The new shim thickness required can be calculated using the thickness of the original shim and the measured clearance. If the valve clearance was less than specified, subtract the measured clearance from the specified adjusting clearance then deduct the result from the original shim thickness to obtain the correct thickness of shim required. If the valve clearance was greater than specified, subtract the specified clearance from the measured clearance, and add the result to the thickness of the original shim to obtain the correct thickness of shim required.

**45** Obtain the correct thickness closing shim and new half-rings. Apply a smear of grease to the new half-rings to help hold them in position.

**46** Insert a screwdriver or wooden dowel in through the camshaft end cap aperture and lever the closing rocker arm down, ensuring its fork engages correctly with the valve stem. Hold the rocker arm down then slide the new closing shim onto the valve stem, ensuring its flange is facing downwards. Locate the new half-rings correctly in the groove on the valve then slowly release the rocker arm **(see illustration)**.

**47** Ensure that the half-rings are correctly located in both the valve groove and closing shim then forcibly raise the shim to seat the half-rings in the shim recess. Do this either by pushing on the rear of the rocker arm or by lifting the shim with a forked metal tool **(see illustration)**. Ensure the half-rings are in firm contact with the shoulder on the base of the shim before proceeding.

***Caution: It is essential that the half-rings are correctly seated in the closing shim recess. Failure to ensure the half-rings are in firm contact with the base of the shim will make the valve clearance measurements inaccurate, resulting in serious engine damage.***

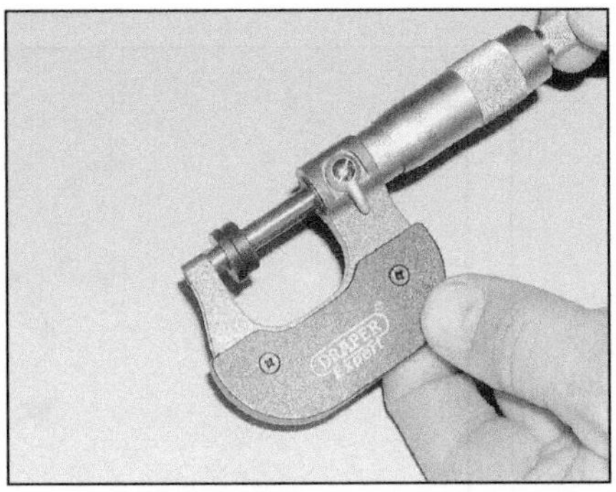

**14.44 Using a micrometer to measure closing shim thickness**

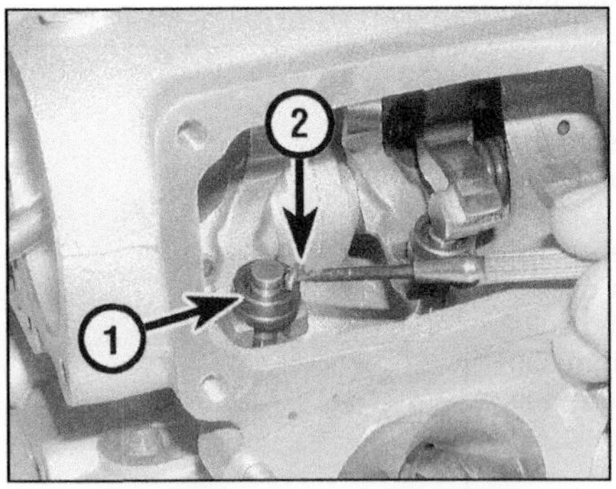


**14.46 Hold the closing rocker arm down then slide on the shim (1 – flange downwards) and locate the new half-rings (2) in the valve groove**

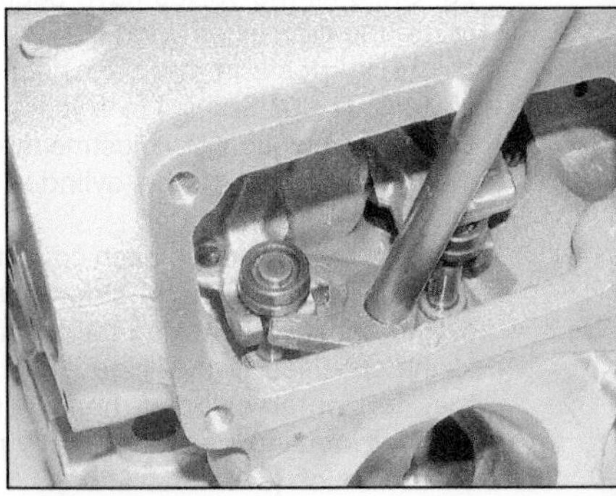

**14.47 Ensure both half-rings are correctly seated then pull up on the shim using a forked tool to seat them correctly in the shim recess**

other valve (where necessary – see Steps 42 to 47).

**49** Once the closing rocker arm clearances are both correctly adjusted, fit the new sealing rings to the grooves on the camshaft left- and right-hand side end caps **(see illustration)**. Lubricate the sealing rings with clean engine oil.

**50** Lubricate the camshaft lobes and bearing surfaces with clean engine oil then install the camshaft and end cap assembly into position, manoeuvring it past the rocker arms, and locate it correctly in the cylinder head. Fit the end cap retaining bolts and tighten them to the specified torque.

**51** Ensure the left-hand side end cap is positioned so that its oilway is facing towards the rocker arms then fit the cap to the head, tightening its retaining bolts to the specified torque **(see illustration)**.

**52** Adjust the opening clearances (where necessary) and install the opening shims and rocker arms as described in Steps 22 and 23.

**53** If necessary, repeat the adjustment procedure on the other camshaft of the horizontal cylinder head.

**54** Align the horizontal cylinder head camshaft pulley timing marks with the O marks on the cylinder head so all the valves are closed.

**55** Position the vertical cylinder camshafts so the valves are all closed then rotate the crankshaft 90° in a clockwise direction to bring the vertical piston to TDC and align its flywheel timing mark with the pointer in the inspection window.

**56** Repeat the adjustment procedure (Steps 39 to 53) on each vertical cylinder head camshaft assembly (as applicable). Once all valves are correctly adjusted, rotate the crankshaft anti-clockwise 90° to bring the horizontal cylinder back to TDC and realign all the timing marks (see Chapter 2, Section 6).

**57** On completion of adjustments, ensure the mating surfaces of the cylinder head and covers are clean and dry.

**58** Fit a new gasket to each cover then install the left- and right-hand side covers on the cylinder heads, tightening their retaining bolts to the specified torque. On the horizontal cylinder head, ensure the radiator locating peg is correctly positioned on installation.

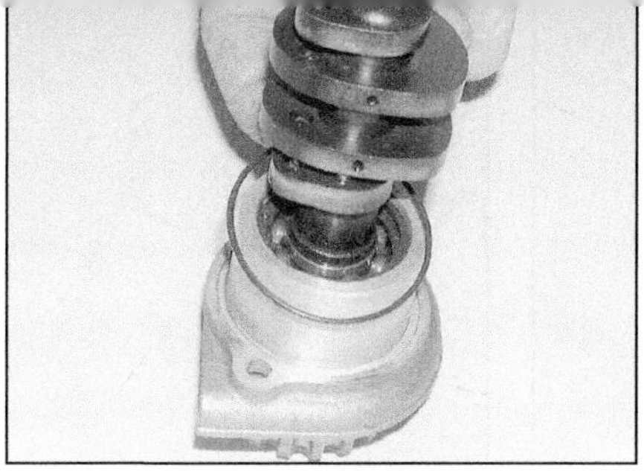

**14.49 Fit new sealing rings to the camshaft end caps prior to installation**

**59** Position a new sealing washer on each side of the oil hose union and screw in the banjo bolt. Ensure the end fitting is correctly positioned in relation to the cylinder head then tighten the banjo bolt to the specified torque.

**60** Fit the timing belts (see Chapter 2). Prior to installing the timing belt covers and valve covers, rotate the crankshaft a few times to settle all shims in position then recheck all valve clearances (see Steps 4 to 10).

## 15 Timing belts – check and tensioning

**Note:** *Access to the Ducati measuring gauge (88765.0999 or 051.2.001.1A), or a suitable aftermarket equivalent gauge, will be needed to accurately check the timing belt tension* **(see illustrations)**. *If a gauge is not available it is recommend that the timing belt check be entrusted to a Ducati dealer.*

### Check

**1** Remove the fairing lower panels (see Chapter 8).

**2** Remove the fuel tank and airbox (see Chapter 4).

**3** Remove the battery and its mounting tray (see Chapter 9).

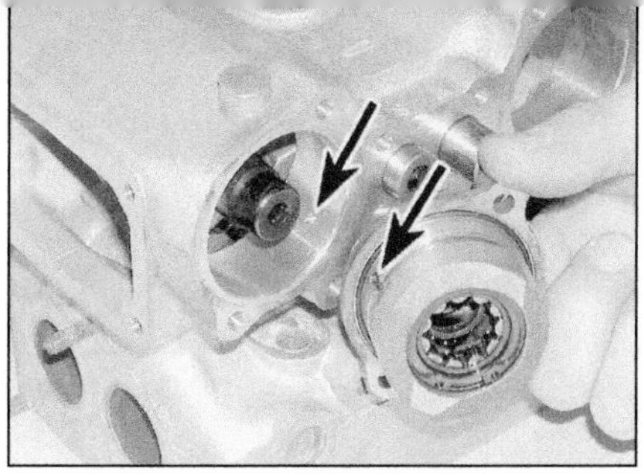

**14.51 Fit the left-hand end cap to the cylinder head ensuring its oilway is correctly aligned with the cylinder head oilway**

**4** Undo the three retaining screws and remove the timing belt upper covers from the right-hand side of both cylinder heads.

**5** Undo the retaining screws and remove the timing belt lower cover from the engine.

**6** Inspect each belt along its backing (flat side) and edges and check that it is not worn or damaged in any way. Check the working face of the belt for damaged teeth, cracking between the teeth and wear of the belt material – a shiny surface indicates extreme wear. If either belt shows signs of wear or damage, renew both belts as a pair (see Chapter 2).

**7** If the belts appear to be in good condition, it is necessary to check the belt tension as follows.

### Tension check using the Ducati measuring gauge

**Note:** *If an aftermarket gauge is being used, follow the instructions supplied by the gauge manufacturer (the belt tension is measured in Lowener units).*

**8** Align the engine timing marks (see Chapter 2, Section 6) to position the horizontal cylinder at TDC on its compression stoke (timing belt tension is always adjusted with the cylinder at TDC on its compression stroke).

**9** Starting on the horizontal cylinder, fit the measuring gauge to the 'top run' of the timing belt, midway between the camshaft pulleys **(see illustration)**.

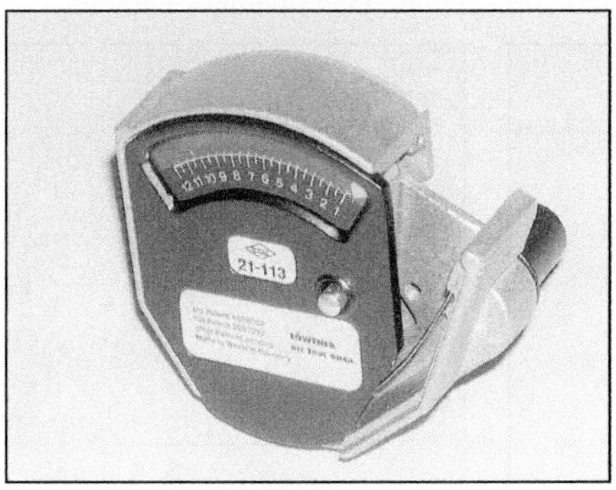


**15.0a Ducati gauge for measuring timing belt tension**

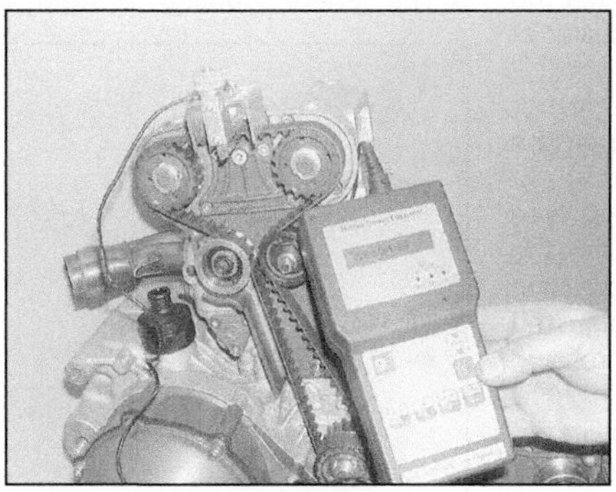

**15.0b An aftermarket timing belt tension gauge**

**15.9 Fit the measuring gauge to the centre of the belt 'top run' so that it is positioned midway between the camshaft pulleys**

**15.11 Adjust the timing belt tension as described in text (shown with engine removed for clarity)**

**10** Slacken the tensioner pulley retaining nut and release the timing belt tension.

**11** Using a 22 mm spanner, rotate the pulley hub anti-clockwise to tension the timing belt whilst observing the measuring gauge pointer **(see illustration)**. Tension the belt until the pointer reaches the end of its measuring scale then gradually release the tension until the needle returns to the 2.5 position on its scale. Hold the pulley hub stationary then tighten the retaining nut to the specified torque. Ensure the gauge reading is still 2.5 then remove the gauge from the timing belt.

**12** Once the horizontal cylinder timing belt is correctly tensioned, rotate the crankshaft 270° anti-clockwise to bring the vertical cylinder to TDC on its compression stroke (see Chapter 2, Section 6). Tension the vertical cylinder timing belt as described in Steps 9 to 11.

**13** Once both belts are correctly tensioned, install the belt lower cover and securely tighten its retaining bolts. Install both upper covers, tightening their retaining bolts securely.

**14** Install the airbox and fuel tank (see Chapter 4).

**15** Install the battery mounting tray and battery (see Chapter 9).

**16** Install the fairing lower panels (see Chapter 8).

### *Tension check without the Ducati measuring gauge*

***Note:*** *If this method is used, ensure that the belt tension is checked by a Ducati dealer at the earliest possible opportunity.*

**17** If the special measuring gauge is not available, an approximate setting may be achieved as follows.

**18** Align the engine timing marks (see Chapter 2, Section 6) to position the horizontal cylinder at TDC on its compression stoke (timing belt tension is always adjusted with the cylinder at TDC on its compression stroke).

**19** Starting with the horizontal cylinder, slacken the tensioner pulley hub retaining nut and release the timing belt tension. Using a 22 mm spanner, rotate the pulley hub anti-clockwise until it is just possible to twist the

**15.19 If a measuring gauge is not available, check the belt tension as described in text**

timing belt through 45° by finger and thumb, midway between the driveshaft and tensioner pulleys **(see illustration)**. The deflection of the belt at the mid-point between the pulleys should be approximately 5.0 mm. Hold the pulley hub stationary then tighten the retaining nut to the specified torque.

**20** Once the horizontal cylinder timing belt is correctly tensioned, rotate the crankshaft 270° anti-clockwise to bring the vertical cylinder to TDC on its compression stroke (see Chapter 2, Section 6). Tension the vertical cylinder timing belt as described in Step 19.

**21** Once both belts are correctly tensioned, install all components removed for access (see Steps 13 to 16).

## 16 Cooling system – check

***Warning: The engine must be cool before beginning this procedure.***

**1** Remove the fairing lower panels (see Chapter 8).

**2** To gain access to the expansion tank cap, remove the fuel tank (see Chapter 4). Note that there is no need to remove the fuel tank completely, access can be gained by unbolting the tank and raising and supporting it, with the hoses and wiring still connected.

**3** The entire cooling system should be each rubber coolant hose along its entire length. Look for cracks, abrasions and other damage. Squeeze each hose at various points. They should feel firm, yet pliable, and return to their original shape when released. If they are dried out or hard, renew them.

**4** Check for evidence of leaks at each cooling system joint. Tighten the hose clips carefully to prevent future leaks **(see illustration)**.

**5** Check the radiator for leaks and other damage. Leaks in the radiator leave tell-tale scale deposits or coolant stains on the outside of the core below the leak. If leaks are noted, remove the radiator (see Chapter 3) and have it repaired at a radiator shop or replace it with a new one.

***Caution: Do not use a liquid leak-stopping compound to try to repair leaks.***

**6** Check the radiator fins for mud, dirt and insects, which may impede the flow of air through the radiator. If the fins are dirty, force water or low pressure compressed air through the fins from the rear of the radiator. If the fins are bent or distorted, straighten them carefully with a screwdriver.

**7** Slowly unscrew and remove the expansion tank cap **(see illustration)**. If you hear a hissing sound (indicating that there is still pressure in the system), wait until it stops before continuing to remove the cap. Check the condition of the coolant in the system. If it is rust-coloured or if accumulations of scale are visible, drain, flush and refill the system with new coolant (See Section 31). Check the cap seal for cracks and other damage. If in doubt about the expansion tank cap's condition, have it tested by a Ducati dealer or renew it. Install the cap and tighten it securely.

**8** Check the antifreeze content of the coolant with an antifreeze hydrometer. Sometimes coolant looks like it's in good condition, but might be too weak to offer adequate protection. If the hydrometer indicates a weak mixture, drain, flush and refill the system (see Section 31).

**9** If the coolant level is consistently low, and no evidence of leaks can be found, have the entire system pressure checked by a Ducati dealer service department or motorcycle shop.

**10** Ensure the pressure cap is correctly installed, then fit the fuel tank and fairing panels (see Chapters 4 and 8).

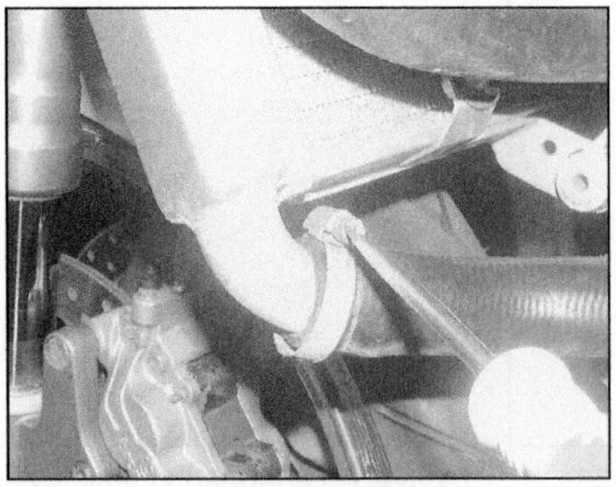

**16.4 Check all coolant hose retaining clips are securely tightened**

**16.7 Coolant expansion tank cap**

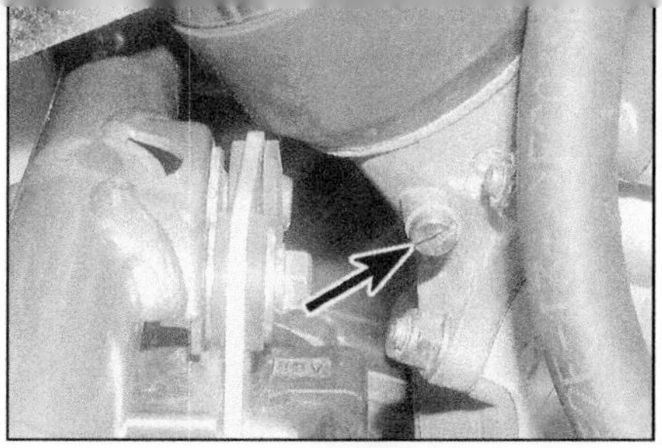

18.6 Remove the blanking screw and washer (arrowed) from the side of each intake manifold and fit the adaptors

## 17 Fuel system - check

***Warning: Petrol (gasoline) is extremely flammable, so take extra precautions when you work on any part of the fuel system. Don't smoke or allow open flames or bare light bulbs near the work area, and don't work in a garage where a natural gas-type appliance is present. If you spill any fuel on your skin, rinse it off immediately with soap and water. When you perform any kind of work on the fuel system, wear safety glasses and have a fire extinguisher suitable for a Class B type fire (flammable liquids) on hand.***

**1** Remove the fuel tank (see Chapter 4).

**2** Check the tank, the fuel pump mounting plate, and the fuel hoses and unions for signs of leakage, deterioration or damage; in particular check that there is no leakage from the fuel hoses. Renew any hoses which are cracked or deteriorated.

**3** Also check for signs of fuel leakage around the fuel injectors. If leakage is present, remove the injectors and renew the injector seals (see Chapter 4).

**4** On completion, install the fuel tank.

## 18 Throttle body - synchronisation, idle speed and mixture setting

**Note:** *Ducati recommend that the throttle position sensor should be checked and adjusted before the throttle body adjustment procedure is carried out. However, adjustment of the sensor requires the use of the Ducati special electronic (Mathesis) diagnostic tester (see Chapter 4). In practice, if the engine has been running well it is unlikely that the throttle position sensor will require adjusting and thus the following procedure assumes adjustment is not necessary. If the throttle position sensor is thought to be in need of adjustment, the bike should be taken to a Ducati dealer who is equipped with the necessary diagnostic tester.*

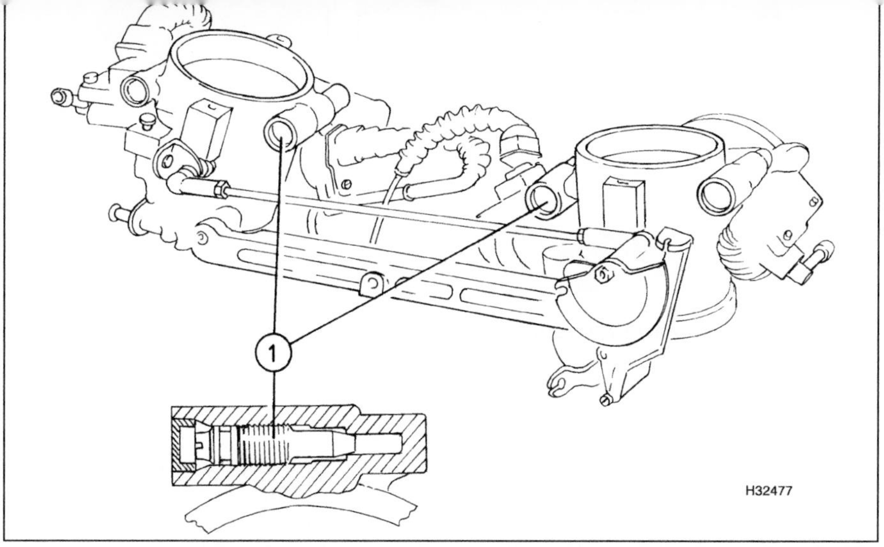


18.9 Throttle body air bypass screw locations (1)

**1** The adjustment procedure is split into two parts; synchronisation and idle speed adjustment are performed first and then the mixture setting is adjusted. Warm the engine up to normal operating temperature before carrying out any adjustments.

### Throttle body synchronisation and idle speed adjustment

***Warning: Petrol (gasoline) is extremely flammable, so take extra precautions when you work on any part of the fuel system. Don't smoke or allow open flames or bare light bulbs near the work area, and don't work in a garage where a natural gas-type appliance is present. If you spill any fuel on your skin, rinse it off immediately with soap and water. When you perform any kind of work on the fuel system, wear safety glasses and have a fire extinguisher suitable for a Class B type fire (flammable liquids) on hand.***

***Warning: Take great care not to burn your hand on the hot engine unit when accessing the gauge take-off points on the cylinder head. Do not allow exhaust gases to build up in the work area; either perform the check outside or use an exhaust gas extraction system.***

**2** Synchronisation is simply the process of adjusting the throttle bodies so that they pass the same amount of fuel/air mixture to each cylinder. This is done by measuring the vacuum produced in each intake manifold. If the throttle valves are not synchronised, the engine will not run smoothly which will result in increased fuel consumption, increased engine temperature, less than ideal throttle response and higher vibration levels. Before synchronising the throttle body assembly, make sure the valve clearances are properly set and the spark plugs are in good condition (see Sections 14 and 11).

**3** To synchronise the throttle body assembly, you will need a set of two vacuum gauges or calibrated tubes (manometer) to indicate engine vacuum, and two adapters to attach the gauges to the engine. **Note:** *Because of the nature of the synchronisation procedure and the need for special instruments, most owners leave the task to a Ducati dealer.*

**4** Start the engine and let it run until it reaches normal operating temperature, then shut it off.

**5** Remove the fuel tank and airbox (see Chapter 4).

**6** The take-off points for each cylinder are located on the side of the intake manifold. Unscrew the blanking screw and sealing washer from each manifold then screw the adapters securely into the threaded holes **(see illustration)**.

**7** Connect the gauge hoses to the adapters. Make sure there are no air leaks, as false readings will result.

**8** Reconnect the fuel hoses and wiring connector to the tank and position the tank so access can still be gained to the throttle body assembly. Take care not to scratch any paintwork, and making sure that the tank is safely and securely supported.

**9** Remove the tamperproof plug from the right-hand side of each throttle body to gain access to the air bypass screws. Screw the bypass screws fully into position until they seat lightly **(see illustration)**. DO NOT force the screws against their seats.

**10** Start the engine and use the throttle twistgrip fast idle button to run the engine at a fast idle. If the gauges are fitted with damping adjustment, set this so that needle flutter is just eliminated but so that they can still respond to small changes in pressure.

**11** The vacuum readings for both cylinders should be the same. If the vacuum readings

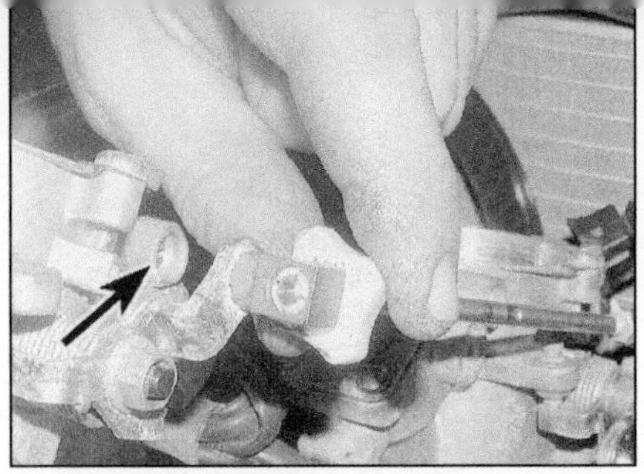

**18.11a Rotate the throttle linkage adjuster knob to synchronise the throttle valves (air bypass screw location arrowed) . . .**

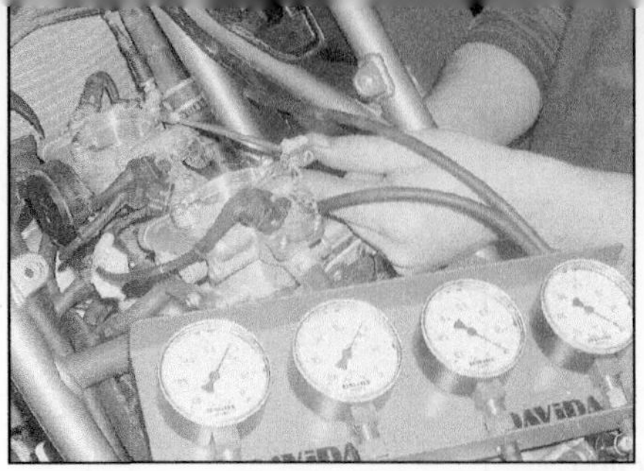

**18.11b . . . so the vacuum gauge readings are the same**

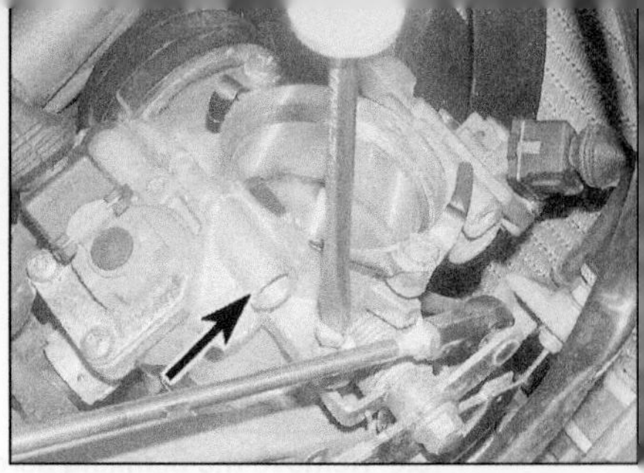

**18.12 If idle speed adjustment proves tricky, use the throttle valve master screw to adjust it (air bypass screw location arrowed)**

vary, use the adjuster knob on the throttle valve linkage to balance the throttle valves **(see illustrations)**.

**12** With both throttle valves correctly synchronised, release the fast idle button then equally unscrew the air bypass screws until the engine is idling smoothly at the specified speed (see Specifications) with the throttle twistgrip released. The objective is to achieve smooth idling with balanced vacuum readings in both cylinders, although this may be difficult if the throttle valves are worn. If it proves impossible to set the idle speed with the air bypass screws, use the screws to balance the vacuum readings then set the idle speed by adjusting the position of the throttle valve master screw **(see illustration)**.

**13** If a CO meter is available, check and adjust the idle mixture as described below.

**14** When all adjustments are correctly set, open and close the throttle quickly to settle the linkage, and recheck the gauge readings, readjusting if necessary.

**15** When adjustment is complete, fit the tamperproof plugs to the air bypass screws. Remove the fuel tank again and disconnect the gauges and adapters. Fit a new sealing washer to each blanking screw and securely fit the screws to the intake manifold threaded holes.

**16** Install the airbox and fuel tank (see Chapter 4).

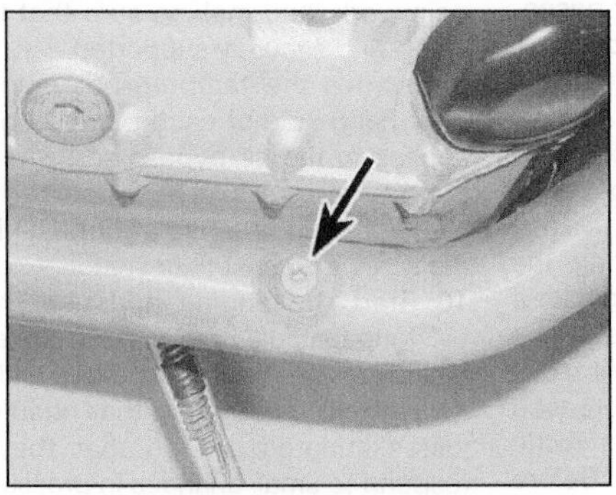

**18.19 Front downpipe exhaust gas take-off plug (arrowed)**

## *Idle mixture (exhaust gas CO level)*

**Note:** *An exhaust gas analyser (CO meter) will be required to accurate set the exhaust gas CO content.*

⚠ ***Warning: Take great care not to burn your hand on the hot exhaust when removing the take-off plugs. Do not allow exhaust gases to build up in the work area; either perform the check outside or use an exhaust gas extraction system.***

**17** The idle mixture (exhaust gas CO level) adjustment is set using the potentiometer on the engine management electronic control unit (ECU). Adjustment will require the use of a good quality exhaust gas analyser. If an analyser is not available, entrust the check to a Ducati dealer. Take-off points are provided on the exhaust front and rear downpipes for exhaust gas CO measurement. Although the horizontal and vertical cylinder settings can be checked separately, they cannot be individually adjusted. Adjustment effects both cylinders equally.

**18** Start the engine and let it run until it reaches normal operating temperature, then shut it off.

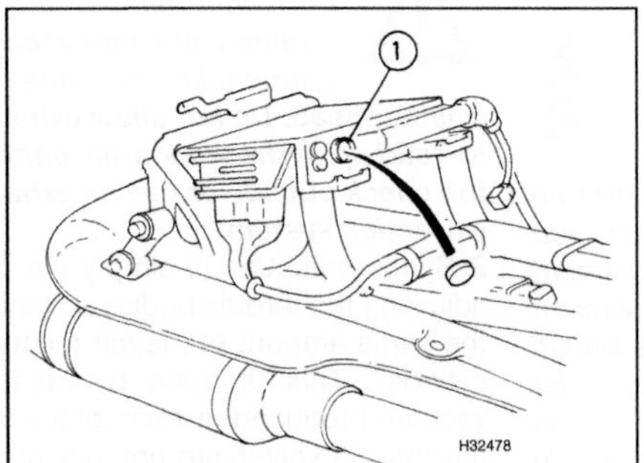


**18.23 On models with a P8 engine management system remove the tamperproof plug from the ECU to gain access to the mixture adjustment potentiometer (1)**

**19** Remove the lower fairing panels (see Chapter 8) to gain access to the exhaust downpipe take-off points. Unscrew the plugs and (where fitted) sealing washers from the front and rear downpipes and insert the exhaust gas analyser probe into the front downpipe **(see illustration)**.

***Caution: Take care not to burn your hands on the hot exhaust!***

**20** Start the engine and run it at a fast idle for a few minutes to clear any excess fuel. Allow the engine to idle and note the reading obtained. Depending on relevant exhaust emission legislation (where applicable), this should be between 1.5 and 6%. If legislation permits, the optimum setting for performance is between 4 and 6%. Repeat the check on the rear downpipe then switch the engine off.

**21** Although a slight difference between the horizontal and vertical cylinder readings is allowable (0.5% difference is permissible), both readings should be similar. If the difference exceeds 1%, then it will be necessary to compensate for this by adjusting the position of the air bypass screws (see Steps 9 to 12). Remove the tamperproof plugs and screw in the air bypass screw of the cylinder which is running the leanest (has the lowest CO reading – this will richen the mixture) and unscrew the bypass screw of the cylinder which is running the richest (has the highest CO reading – this will weaken the mixture). This will affect the vacuum readings between the cylinders but Ducati state that it is preferable to have the mixture settings evenly balanced at the expense of perfect airflow.

**22** Once both cylinders are equal (or within 0.5%), refit the tamperproof plugs to the throttle bodies. The mixture setting of both cylinders can be adjusted as follows.

### Models with a P8 engine management system

**23** The mixture adjustment potentiometer is located on the front of the electronic control unit (ECU). Remove the tamperproof plug to gain access to the adjustment screw **(see illustration)**.

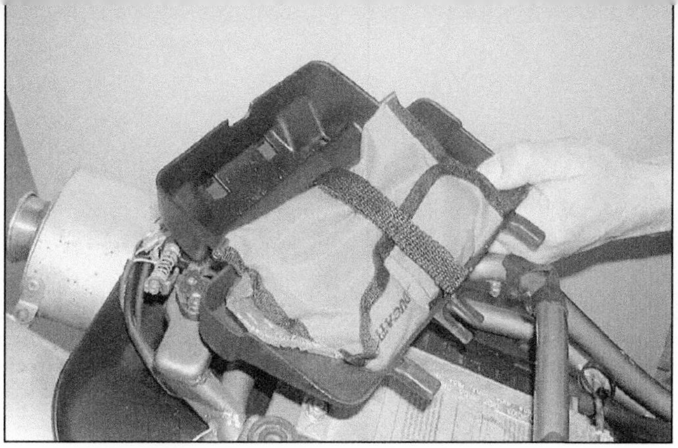

**18.27 On models with a 1.6M engine management system, unclip the toolkit holder to gain access to the ECU . . .**

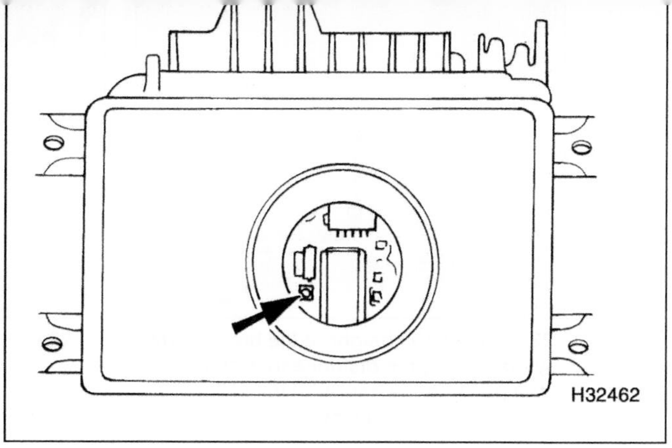


**18.28 . . . then remove the ECU sticker and rubber plug to gain access to the mixture potentiometer (arrowed)**

**24** With the engine at normal operating temperature, start the engine and run it at a fast idle for a few minutes to clear any excess fuel. Allow the engine to idle and note the reading obtained. Adjust the CO level by rotating the screw on the ECU. The screw has an effective adjustment range of approximately 4 turns. Although the screw will continue to rotate beyond this, the movement of the screw will have no effect on mixture adjustment.

**25** Once the mixture setting is correctly set, switch off the engine and refit the tamperproof plug to the ECU.

**26** Remove the exhaust gas analyser and refit the take-off plugs and sealing washers (where fitted) to the downpipes, tightening them securely. Install the fairing panels (see Chapter 8).

### Models with a 1.6M engine management system

**27** Free the toolkit holder from its mounting rubbers and remove it from the bike to gain access to electronic control unit (ECU) **(see illustration)**. Peel the sticker off the top of the ECU then remove the rubber plug to gain access to the mixture adjustment potentiometer. Discard the sticker and obtain a new one.

**28** With the engine at normal operating temperature, start the engine and run it at a fast idle for a few minutes to clear any excess fuel. Allow the engine to idle and note the reading obtained. Adjust the CO level by rotating the potentiometer screw on the ECU printed circuit board **(see illustration)**. The screw has an effective adjustment range of only 270° and must not be forced beyond this. Adjust the CO level by rotating the screw.

***Caution: Never force the mixture adjustment potentiometer screw beyond its stops.***

**29** Once the mixture setting is correctly set, switch off the engine. Securely fit the rubber plug to the ECU casing then fit the new sticker. Install the toolkit holder.

**30** Remove the exhaust gas analyser and refit the take-off plugs and sealing washers (where fitted) to the downpipes, tightening them securely. Install the fairing panels (see Chapter 8).

## 19 Cylinder compression – check

**1** Amongst other things, poor engine performance may be caused by leaking valves, incorrect valve clearances, a leaking head gasket, or worn pistons, rings and/or cylinder walls. A cylinder compression check will help pinpoint these conditions and can also indicate the presence of excessive carbon deposits in the cylinder heads.

**2** The only tools required are a compression gauge and a spark plug wrench. A compression gauge with a threaded adapter for the spark plug hole is preferable to the type which requires hand pressure to maintain a tight seal. Depending on the outcome of the initial test, a squirt-type oil can may also be needed.

**3** Ensure the valve clearances are correctly set (see Section 14), then check the compression pressures using the information given in *Fault Finding Equipment* in the *Reference* section.

## 20 Engine oil pressure – check

**1** The oil pressure warning light should come on when the ignition switch is turned ON and extinguish soon after the engine is started – this serves as a check that the warning light bulb is sound. If the oil pressure light comes on whilst the engine is running, low oil pressure is indicated – stop the engine immediately and carry out an oil level check *(see Daily (pre-ride) checks)*.

**2** An oil pressure check must be carried out if the warning light comes on when the engine is running yet the oil level is good (Step 1). It can also provide useful information about the condition of the engine's lubrication system.

**3** To check the oil pressure, a suitable gauge and adapter will be needed. Ducati dealers use a pressure gauge and adapter which screws into the oil pressure switch aperture in the right-hand crankcase cover (the switch has an M10 x 1 thread).

**4** Remove the oil pressure switch (see Chapter 9) and swiftly screw the adapter and pressure gauge securely into the crankcase cover threads.

**5** Check the engine oil level *(see Daily (pre-ride) checks)* and top up to the upper level mark.

**6** Start the engine and warm it up to normal operating temperature, ensuring that there is no oil leakage from the pressure gauge and adapter.

**7** Once the engine is at operating temperature, increase the engine speed briefly to 4000 rpm whilst watching the gauge reading. The oil pressure should be similar to that given in the Specifications at the start of this Chapter. Once the pressure reading has been obtained, stop the engine and allow it to cool.

**8** If the pressure is significantly lower than the standard, either the pressure relief valve is stuck open, the oil pump is faulty, the oil pick-up gauze filter or main filter are blocked, or there is other engine damage. Begin diagnosis by checking the oil filter, pick-up gauze filter, relief valve, bypass valve, then the oil pump (see Section 8 and Chapter 2). If those items are not faulty, it is possible that the bearing oil clearances are excessive and the engine needs to be overhauled.

**9** If the pressure is too high, either an oil passage is clogged, the relief valve is stuck closed or the wrong grade of oil is being used.

**10** Remove the pressure gauge and adapter from the engine and install the oil pressure switch (see Chapter 9).

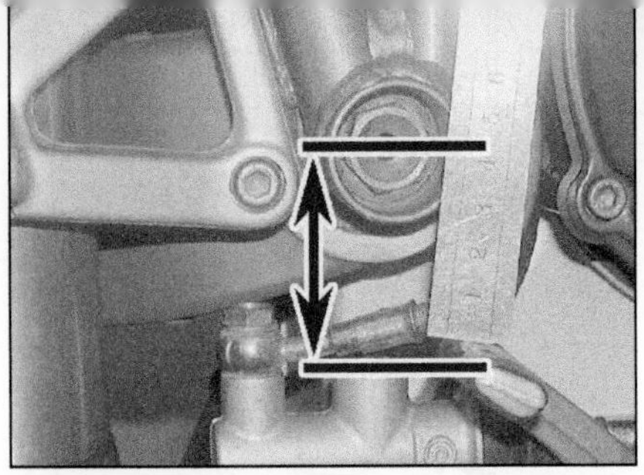

**22.5 Check the height of the brake pedal by measuring the distance from the top of the pedal to the centre of the swingarm pivot**

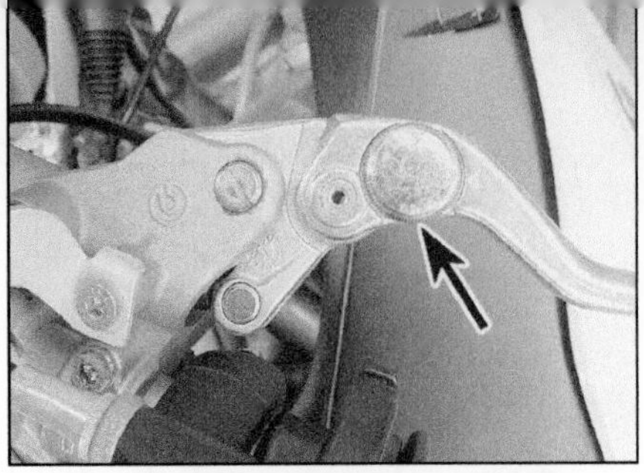

**22.6 Front brake lever span adjuster (arrowed)**

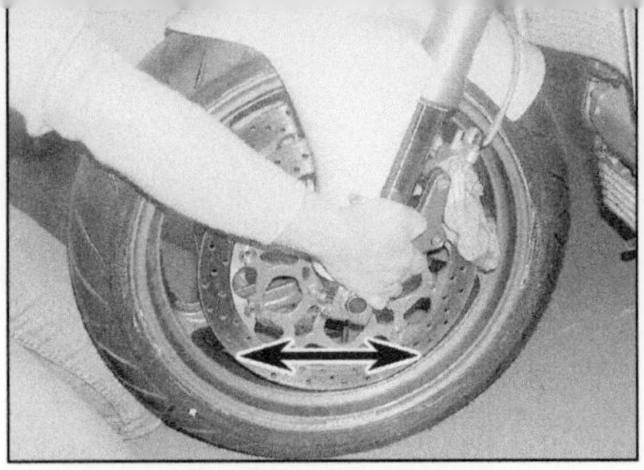

**24.4 Grasp the forks and try to move them backwards and forwards to check the steering bearings for wear**

**11** Check the engine oil level *(see Daily (pre-ride) checks)* and top-up to the upper level mark. On completion, start the engine and check for leaks.

## 21 Electric cooling fan – check

**1** Start the engine and warm it up to normal operating temperature. Allow the engine to idle and check that the electric cooling fan operates correctly.
**2** If the cooling fan fails to operate, inspect the cooling fan circuit as described in Chapter 3.

## 22 Braking system – check

**1** A routine general check of the braking system will ensure that any problems are discovered and remedied before the rider's safety is jeopardised.
**2** Check the brake lever and pedal for loose connections, improper or rough action, excessive play, bends, and other damage. Renew any damaged parts with new ones (see Chapter 7).
**3** Make sure all brake fasteners are tight. Check the brake pads for wear (see Section 2) and make sure that the fluid level in the reservoirs is correct (see *Daily (pre-ride) checks*). Look for leaks at the hose connections and check for cracks in the hoses. If the lever or pedal is spongy, bleed the brakes (see Chapter 7).
**4** Make sure the brake light operates when the front brake lever and rear brake pedals are depressed. The brake light switches are not adjustable. If either fails to operate properly, check it (see Chapter 9).
**5** Check the position of the brake pedal. Ducati recommend that the distance between the top of the brake pedal and the centre of the swingarm pivot bolt should be 46.6 mm **(see illustration)**. However, the pedal height can be altered to suit individual tastes. To alter the pedal height, slacken the locknut and alter the position of the pedal stop bolt. Once the desired pedal height is obtained, hold the stop bolt and securely tighten the locknut. After adjustment ensure that there is approximately 1.5 to 2.0 mm of pedal freeplay before the pushrod contacts master cylinder piston. If not, slacken the pushrod locknut and screw the pushrod in to or out of (as applicable) its clevis. Once the pushrod length is correct, securely tighten the locknut.
**6** On most models the front brake lever has a span adjuster which alters the distance of the lever from the handlebar **(see illustration)**. Pull the lever away from the handlebar and turn the adjuster dial until the setting which best suits the rider is obtained. There are four positions; align the number for the setting required with the triangular mark on the lever bracket.

## 23 Rear sprocket cush drive bushes – check

**1** Support the bike on an auxiliary stand so the rear wheel is raised off the ground.
**2** Firmly grasp the rear wheel and sprocket and check for signs of freeplay between the sprocket and coupling flange. If any sign of freeplay is found, remove the rear sprocket coupling and check the cush drive rubber bushes for signs of wear (see Chapter 6). Renew the bushes as a set if wear is found.

## 24 Steering head bearings – check and adjustment

**1** The steering head bearings can become dented, rough or loose during normal use of the machine. In extreme cases, worn or loose steering head bearings can cause steering wobble – a condition that is potentially dangerous.

### *Check*

**2** Place the motorcycle on an auxiliary stand. Raise the front wheel off the ground either by having an assistant push down on the rear, or by removing the fairing lower panels (see Chapter 8) and placing a support under the engine.
**3** Point the front wheel straight ahead and slowly move the handlebars from side to side. Any dents or roughness in the bearing races will be felt and the bars will not move smoothly and freely. With the wheel pointing straight ahead, tap the end of each bar in turn. The handlebars should move to the full-lock position under the force of gravity alone. If not, and it is not due to interference from wiring or cables, the bearings are too tight.
**4** Next, grasp the fork sliders and try to move them forward and backward **(see illustration)**. Any looseness in the steering head bearings will be felt as front-to-rear movement of the forks. If play is felt in the bearings, adjust the steering head as follows. **Note:** *Freeplay in the fork due to worn fork bushes can be misinterpreted for steering head bearing play – do not confuse the two.*

### *Adjustment*

***Caution: Take care not to damage the paintwork of the fuel tank during the following procedure.***

**TOOL TiP**

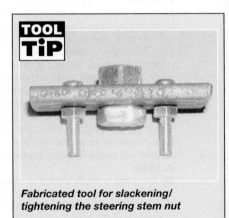

***Fabricated tool for slackening/ tightening the steering stem nut***

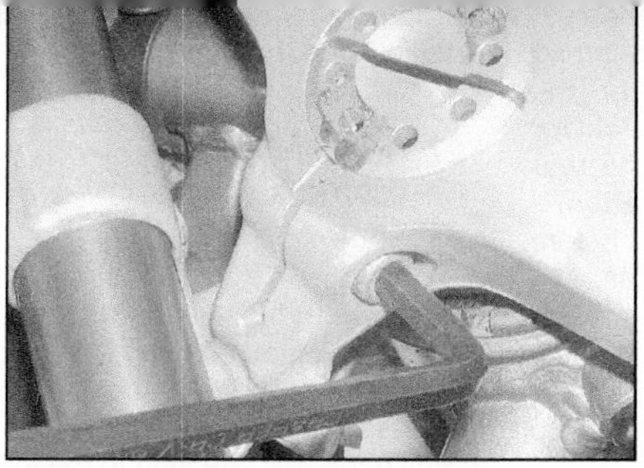

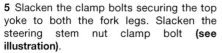

24.5 **Slacken the clamp bolts securing the top yoke to the forks and steering stem nut**

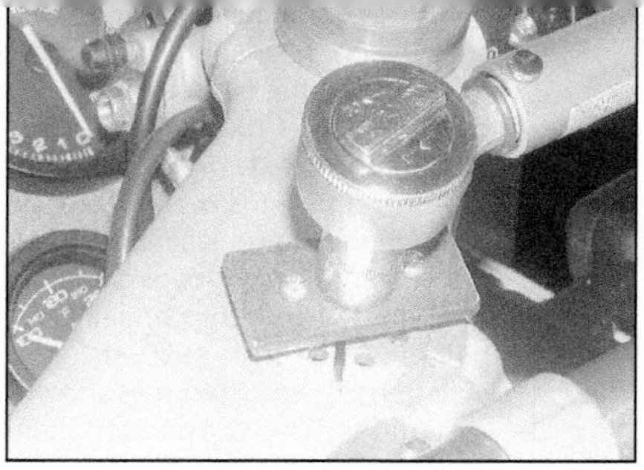

24.6a **Tighten the steering stem nut to the specified torque . . .**

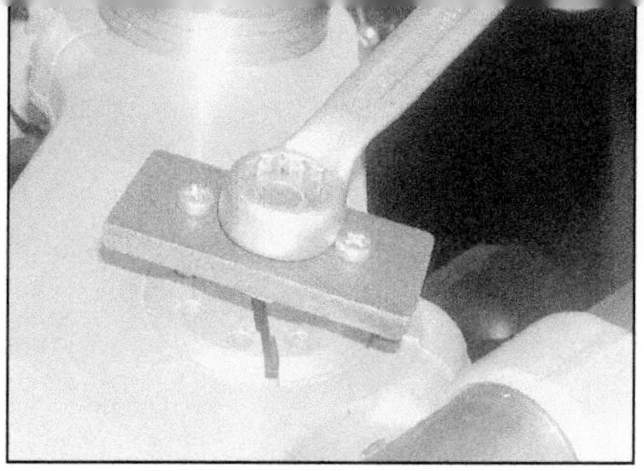

24.6b **. . . then slacken it by the specified angle to correctly set the bearing adjustment**

**5** Slacken the clamp bolts securing the top yoke to both the fork legs. Slacken the steering stem nut clamp bolt **(see illustration)**.

**6** Slacken the steering stem nut, then tighten it to the specified torque to preload the bearings (stage 1). Turn the steering stem from lock-to-lock approximately 5 times to settle the bearings and races in position then slacken the steering stem nut by the specified angle (stage 2) **(see illustrations)**. **Note:** *It is important to check the feel of the steering afterwards as described below; if it is too tight re-adjust the bearings as described below.*

**7** If it is not possible to tighten the nut to the specified torque, slacken the steering stem nut, then tighten or slacken it a little at a time as required until all freeplay in the forks is removed, yet the steering is able to move freely from side to side. Do not turn the nut more than 1/8 turn at a time. The object is to set the steering stem nut so that the bearings are under a very light loading, just enough to remove any freeplay.

***Caution: Take great care not to apply excessive pressure because this will cause premature failure of the bearings.***

**8** If the bearings cannot be set up properly, or if there is any binding, roughness or notchiness, they will have to be removed for inspection or renewal (see Chapter 6).

**9** With the bearings correctly adjusted, press down on the top yoke to ensure it is in firm contact with the steering stem nut shoulder, then tighten the nut clamp bolt to the specified torque.

**10** Tighten the top yoke fork clamp bolts to the specified torque then re-check the bearing adjustment as described above and re-adjust if necessary.

## 25 Wheel bearings - check

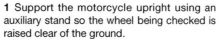

**1** Support the motorcycle upright using an auxiliary stand so the wheel being checked is raised clear of the ground.

**2** Check for any play in the bearings by pushing and pulling the wheel against the hub **(see illustration)**. Also rotate the wheel and check that it rotates smoothly. If any play is detectable in the hub, or if the wheel does not rotate smoothly (and this is not due to brake or transmission drag), the wheel bearings must be inspected for wear or damage (see Chapter 7).

## 26 Suspension - check

**1** The suspension components must be maintained in top operating condition to ensure rider safety. Loose, worn or damaged suspension parts decrease the motorcycle's stability and control.

### *Front suspension*

**2** While standing alongside the motorcycle, apply the front brake and push on the handlebars to compress the forks several times. See if they move up and down smoothly without binding. If binding is felt, the forks should be disassembled and inspected (see Chapter 6).

**3** Inspect the front forks around the dust seal for signs of oil leakage **(see illustration)**. If leakage is evident, the fork seals must be renewed (see Chapter 6).

**4** Check the tightness of all suspension nuts and bolts to be sure none have worked loose.

### *Rear suspension*

**5** Inspect the rear shock for fluid leakage and tightness of its mountings. If leakage is found,

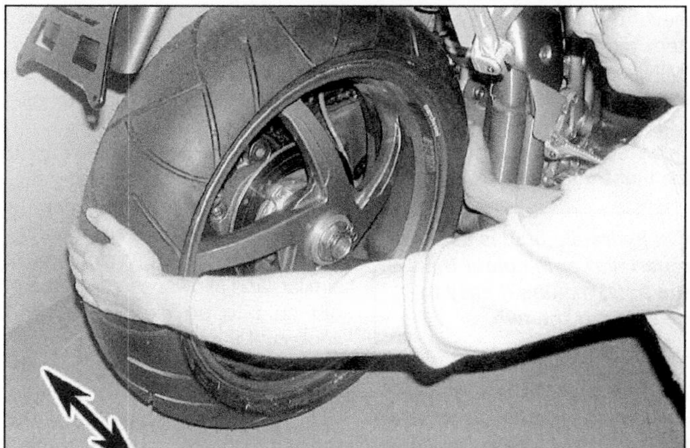

25.2 **Checking for wear in the rear wheel bearings by attempting to move the wheel from side-to-side**

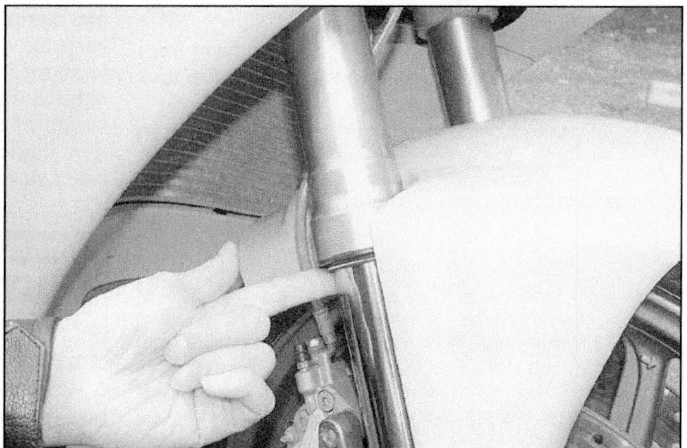

26.3 **Inspect the area around the fork dust seal for signs of oil leakage**

**26.7 Checking for wear in the rear suspension linkage by attempting to move the rear wheel up-and-down**

the shock should be renewed (see Chapter 6).
**6** With the aid of an assistant to support the bike, compress the rear suspension several times. It should move up and down freely without binding. If any binding is felt, the worn or faulty component must be identified and renewed. The problem could be due to the shock absorber, the suspension linkage components or the swingarm components.
**7** Support the motorcycle on an auxiliary stand so that the rear wheel is off the ground. Grab the swingarm and attempt to rock it from side to side – there should be no discernible movement at the rear. If there is a heard, inspect the tightness of all the rear suspension mounting bolts and nuts, referring to the torque settings specified at the beginning of Chapter 6, and re-check for movement. Next, grasp the top of the rear wheel and pull it upwards **(see illustration)** – there should be no discernible freeplay before the shock absorber begins to compress. Any freeplay felt in either check indicates worn bearings in the suspension linkage or swingarm, or worn shock absorber mountings. The worn components must be renewed (see Chapter 6).
**8** To make an accurate assessment of the swingarm bearings, remove the rear wheel (see Chapter 7) and the bolt securing the shock absorber and tie-rod to the swingarm (see Chapter 6). Grasp the rear of the swingarm with one hand and place your other hand at the junction of the swingarm and the frame. Try to move the rear of the swingarm from side to side. Any wear (play) in the bearings should be felt as movement between the swingarm and the frame at the front. If there is any play the swingarm will be felt to move forward and backward at the front (not from side to side). Next, move the swingarm up and down through its full travel. It should move freely, without any binding or rough spots. If any play in the swingarm is noted or if bearings must be removed for inspection or renewal (see Chapter 6).

## 27 Nuts and bolts – tightness check

**1** Since vibration of the machine tends to loosen fasteners, all nuts, bolts, screws, etc. should be periodically checked for proper tightness.
**2** Pay particular attention to the following:
*Footrest and stand bolts*
*Engine mounting bolts*
*Shock absorber and suspension linkage bolts and swingarm pivot bolts*
*Handlebar clamp bolts*
*Front axle bolt and axle clamp bolts*
*Front fork clamp bolts (top and bottom yoke)*
*Rear wheel nut*
*Brake caliper mounting bolts*
*Brake hose banjo bolts and caliper bleed valves*
*Brake disc bolts and rear sprocket nuts*
*Exhaust system bolts/nuts*
**3** If a torque wrench is available, use it along with the torque specifications at the beginning of this and other Chapters.

# Every 12,000 miles (20,000 km) or every 2 years

## 28 Timing belts – renewal

**1** Renew both timing belts as described in Chapter 2.

## 29 Brakes – fluid change

**Note:** *To prevent damage to the paint from spilled brake fluid, always cover the fuel tank when working on the front brake master cylinder, and the surrounding components when working on the rear brake fluid reservoir.*

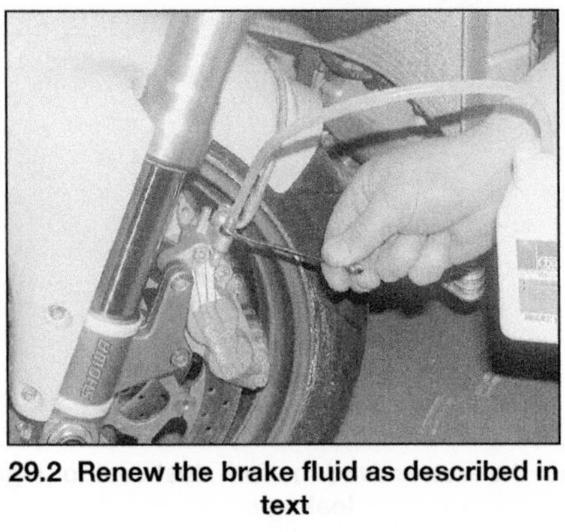

**29.2 Renew the brake fluid as described in text**

**1** The procedure is similar to that for the bleeding of each brake as described in Chapter 7, except that the fluid reservoir should be emptied by siphoning before starting, using a clean poultry baster or similar, and allowance should be made for the old fluid to be expelled when bleeding a section of the circuit.
**2** Working as described, open the bleed valve and pump the lever/pedal gently. Be careful to keep the master cylinder reservoir topped up to above the 'MIN' level at all times or air may enter the system and greatly increase the length of the task. Continue pumping until new fluid can be seen emerging from the bleed valve **(see illustration)**.

> **HAYNES HiNT** ***Old hydraulic fluid is usually much darker in colour than the new, making it easy to distinguish the two.***

**3** When the new fluid is seen to be emerging, hold the lever/pedal and tighten the bleed valve to the specified torque (see Specifications). Where necessary, repeat the operation on the other bleed valve(s) until all old hydraulic fluid has been renewed.
**4** When the operation is complete, wash off all traces of spilt fluid, then top-up the reservoir fluid level (*see Daily (pre-ride) checks*).
**5** Check the operation of the brakes before riding the motorcycle.

## 30 Clutch – fluid change

**Note:** *To prevent damage to the paint from spilled brake fluid, always cover the fuel tank when working on the clutch master cylinder.*
**1** The procedure is similar to that for the bleeding of the clutch hydraulic system as described in Chapter 2, except that the fluid reservoir should be emptied by siphoning before starting, using a clean poultry baster or similar, and allowance should be made for the old fluid to be expelled when bleeding a section of the circuit.
**2** Working as described, open the bleed valve and pump the lever gently. Be careful to keep the master cylinder reservoir topped up to above the 'MIN' level at all times, or air may enter the system and greatly increase the length of the task. Continue pumping until new fluid can be seen

**30.2 Renew the clutch fluid as described in text**

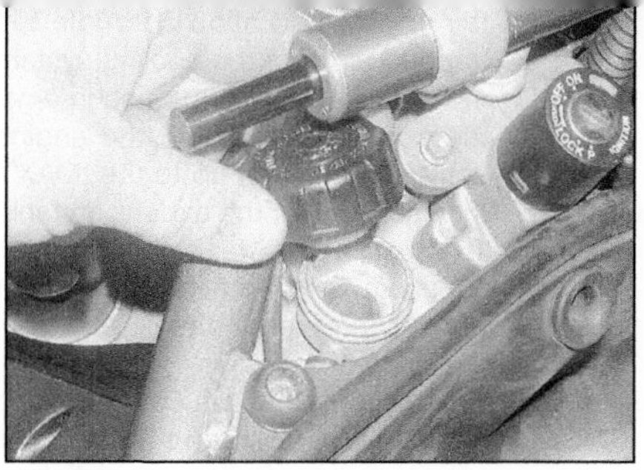

**31.3 Unscrew the cap from the coolant expansion tank**

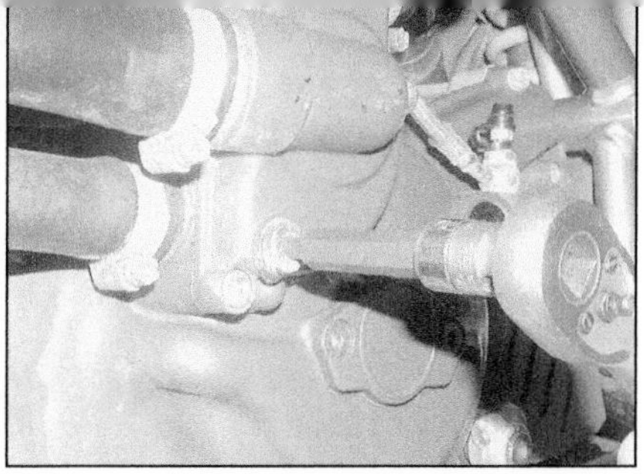

**31.4a Unscrew the drain plug from the water pump cover . . .**

emerging from the bleed valve **(see illustration)**.

HAYNES HiNT *Old hydraulic fluid is usually much darker in colour than the new, making it easy to distinguish the two.*

**3** When the new fluid is seen to be emerging, hold the lever and tighten the bleed valve.

**4** When the operation is complete, wash off all traces of spilt fluid then top-up the reservoir fluid level (see *Daily (pre-ride) checks*).

**5** Check the operation of the clutch before riding the motorcycle.

## 31 Cooling system – draining, flushing and refilling

***Warning: Allow the engine to cool completely before performing this maintenance operation. Also, don't allow antifreeze to come into contact with your skin or the painted surfaces of the motorcycle. Rinse off spills immediately with plenty of water. Antifreeze is highly toxic if ingested. Never leave antifreeze lying around in an open container or in puddles on the floor; children and pets are attracted by its sweet smell and may drink it. Check with your local authority about antifreeze disposal facilities in your area.***

### Draining

**1** Remove the fairing left-hand lower panel (see Chapter 8) to gain access to the drain screws.

**2** To gain access to the expansion tank cap, remove the fuel tank (see Chapter 4). Note that there is no need to remove the fuel tank completely, access can be gained by unbolting the tank and raising and supporting it, with the hoses and wiring still connected.

**3** Slowly unscrew and remove the expansion tank cap **(see illustration)**. If you hear a hissing sound (indicating that there is still pressure in the system), wait until it stops before continuing to remove the cap.

**4** Position a suitable container beneath the water pump on the left-hand side of the engine. Remove the coolant drain plug and its sealing washer and allow the coolant to drain from the system **(see illustrations)**.

**5** To drain the system completely, also unscrew the drain screw and sealing washer from the base of the coolant outlet on the side of the horizontal cylinder barrel and allow the coolant to drain completely from the cylinder barrel **(see illustration)**.

### Flushing

**6** Flush the system with clean tap water by inserting a garden hose into the expansion tank. Allow the water to run through the system until it is clear and flows cleanly out of the drain holes. If the radiator is extremely corroded, remove it (see Chapter 3) and have it cleaned at a radiator shop. Also rinse out the coolant reservoir.

**7** Clean the drain holes, then install the drain plugs using the old sealing washers.

**8** Fill the cooling system with clean water mixed with a flushing compound. Make sure the flushing compound is compatible with aluminium components, and follow the manufacturer's instructions carefully.

**9** Start the engine and allow it to reach normal operating temperature. Let it run for about ten minutes.

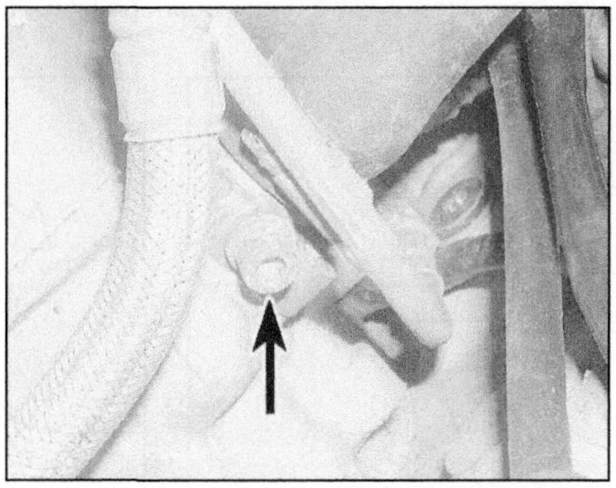

**31.5 Unscrew the drain plug (arrowed) from the base of the coolant outlet union on the left-hand side of the horizontal cylinder**

**31.4b . . . and drain the coolant into a suitable container**

**10** Stop the engine. Let it cool for a while, then cover the expansion tank cap with a heavy rag and unscrew it slightly, releasing any pressure that may be present in the system. Once the hissing stops, remove the cap completely.

**11** Drain the system once again.

**12** Fill the system with clean water and repeat the procedure in Steps 8 to 11.

### Refilling

**13** Fit a new sealing washer to each drain plug, then fit the drain plugs to the water pump cover and coolant outlet, tightening them securely **(see illustration)**.

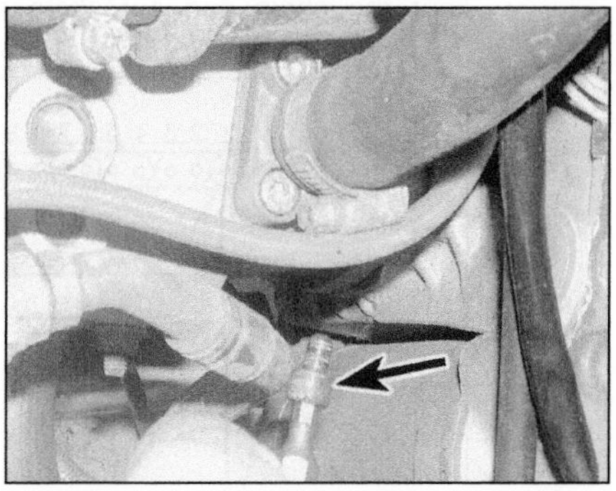

**31.13 Fit a new sealing washer to each drain plug then refit the drain plugs to the pump cover and cylinder outlet and tighten securely**

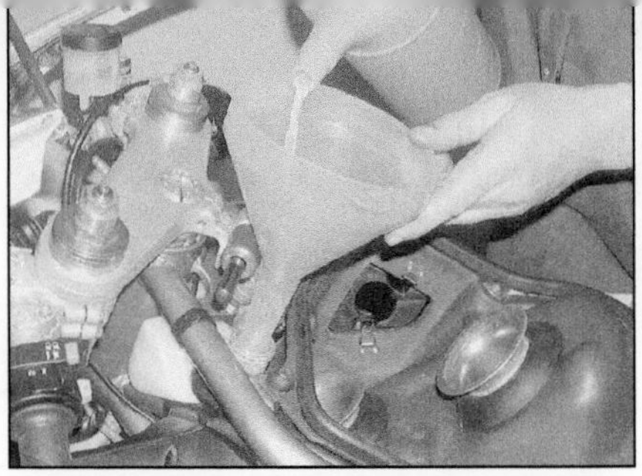

**31.14 Refill the cooling system with the specified type and amount of coolant**

**14** Fill the system with the proper coolant mixture (see this Chapter's Specifications) **(see illustration)**. **Note:** *Pour the coolant in slowly to minimise the amount of air entering the system.*

**15** When the system is topped up to the the engine and allow it to idle to bleed any trapped air from the cooling system. Once no more air bubbles can be seen emerging from the coolant, switch off the engine. Top the coolant level back up to the 'MAX' level mark then securely fit the expansion tank cap.

**16** Seat the fuel tank on the frame then start the engine and warm it up to normal operating temperature and check that there are no coolant leaks.

**17** Let the engine cool, then check the coolant level in the reservoir and top up if necessary (see *Daily (pre-ride) checks)*.

**18** Install the fuel tank and fit the fairing panel (see Chapters 4 and 8).

**19** Do not dispose of the old coolant by pouring it down the drain. Instead pour it into a heavy plastic container, cap it tightly and take it into an authorised disposal site or service station – see **Warning** at the beginning of this Section.

## 32 Front forks – oil change

**Note:** *At the time of writing information was only available for Showa forks. For information on the Ohlins front forks fitted to later SPS models, refer to your Ducati dealer or an Ohlins suspension specialist.*

**1** Fork oil degrades over a period of time and loses its damping qualities and should therefore be regularly changed.

**2** With both forks removed, drain all the oil from the first fork as described in Steps 3 to 11 of Section 7 of Chapter 6 (it is not necessary to dismantle the fork completely), then fill it with fresh oil as described in Steps 36 to 46. Repeat the operation on the other fork, then fit both forks to the motorcycle (see Chapter 6).

# Non-scheduled maintenance

## 33 Drive chain and sprockets – wear check

**1** Support the bike on an auxiliary stand so the rear wheel is raised off the ground.

**2** Check the entire length of the chain for damaged rollers, cracked sideplates, loose links and pins, and renew the chain if damage is found. If the chain has reached the end of its adjustment, it must be renewed.

**3** The amount of chain stretch can be measured and compared to the service limit specified at the beginning of the Chapter. Pull the chain taut and measure along the bottom run the length of 16 pins (from the centre of the 1st pin to the centre of the 16th pin) and compare the result with the service limit specified at the beginning of the Chapter **(see illustration)**. Rotate the rear wheel so that several sections of the chain are measured. If any of the measurements exceeds the service limit the chain and sprockets should be renewed as a set. **Note:** *Never install a new chain on old sprockets, and never use the old chain if you install new sprockets – renew the chain and sprockets as a set*

**4** Undo the two screws and remove the sprocket cover from the engine. Check the teeth on the front sprocket and the rear wheel sprocket for wear **(see illustration)**.

**5** Inspect the drive chain slider on the swingarm for excessive wear and renew it if necessary (see Chapter 6).

## 34 Suspension linkage bearings - re-greasing

**1** Over a period of time, the grease will harden or dirt will penetrate the bearings due to failed dust seals.

**2** The suspension linkage pivots are not equipped with grease nipples and therefore the linkage must be removed and dismantled for greasing of the bearings (see Chapter 6).

**3** Ideally the swingarm bearings should also be re-greased although this is a major operation requiring the removal of the engine from the frame (see Chapter 6).

## 35 Steering head bearings – re-greasing

**1** Over a period of time the grease will harden or may be washed out of the bearings by incorrect use of jet washes.

**2** Disassemble the steering head for re-greasing of the bearings. Refer to Chapter 6 for details.

## 36 Brake hoses, master cylinder and caliper seals – renewal

**1** Brake seals will deteriorate over a period of time and lose their effectiveness, leading to

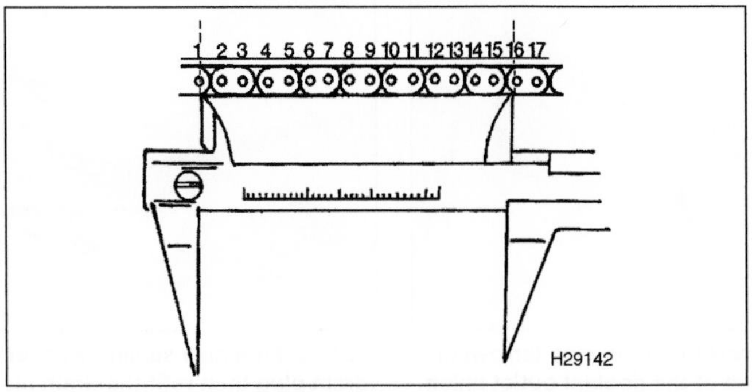


**33.3 Check the condition of the drive chain by measuring the length of a 16 pin section**

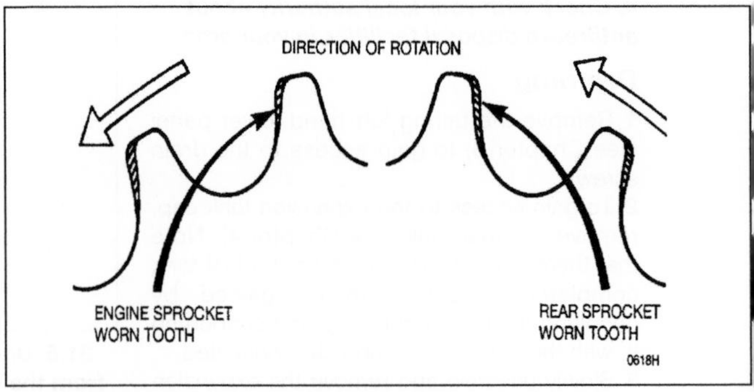


**33.4 Check the teeth on both sprockets to determine whether they are excessively worn**

ingress of air and dirt. Remove the master cylinders and calipers and renew all seals as described in Chapter 7. **Note:** *Check the availability of seals before dismantling the braking system components. It maybe that it is not possible to overhaul the calipers and/or master cylinders (see Chapter 7).*

**2** The brake hoses will in time deteriorate with age and should be renewed regardless of their apparent condition. Refer to Chapter 7 and disconnect the brake hoses from the master cylinders and calipers. Always replace the banjo union sealing washers with new ones.

## 37 Clutch hose, master cylinder and slave cylinder seals – renewal

**1** Clutch master and slave cylinder seals will deteriorate over a period of time and lose their effectiveness, leading to sticking operation or fluid loss, or allowing the ingress of air and dirt. Remove the master cylinder and slave cylinder and renew all seals as described in Chapter 2. **Note:** *Check the availability of seals before dismantling the braking system components. It maybe that it is not possible to overhaul the assembly (see Chapter 2).*

**2** The hydraulic hose will in time deteriorate with age and should be renewed regardless of its apparent condition. Refer to Chapter 2 and disconnect the hose from the master cylinder and slave cylinder. Always replace the banjo union sealing washers with new ones.

## 38 Headlight aim – check and adjustment

**Note:** *An improperly adjusted headlight may cause problems for oncoming traffic or provide poor, unsafe illumination of the road ahead. Before adjusting the headlight aim, be sure to consult with local traffic laws and regulations. Machines in use in the UK should refer to MOT Test Checks in the Reference section.*

**1** The headlight beam can only be adjusted vertically. Before making any adjustment, check that the tyre pressures are correct and the suspension is adjusted as required. Make any adjustments to the headlight aim with the machine on level ground, with the fuel tank half full and with an assistant sitting on the seat. If the bike is usually ridden with a passenger on the back, have a second assistant to do this.

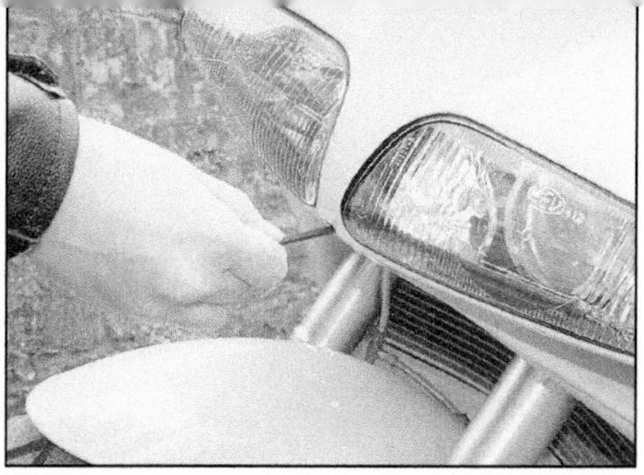

**38.2 Adjusting the headlight beam aim**

**2** Adjustment is made by turning the adjuster located between the main and dipped beam headlights. Remove the cap from the upper fairing and rotate the adjuster with an Allen key **(see illustration)**. Once adjustment is correct, securely fit the cap to the fairing.

# Chapter 2
# Engine, clutch and transmission

## Contents



## Degrees of difficulty

| | | | | |
|---|---|---|---|---|
| **Easy,** suitable for novice with little experience | **Fairly easy,** suitable for beginner with some experience | **Fairly difficult,** suitable for competent DIY mechanic | **Difficult,** suitable for experienced DIY mechanic | **Very difficult,** suitable for expert DIY or professional |

# Specifications

## General

| | |
|---|---|
| Capacity | |
| 748 model | 748 cc |
| 916 model | |
| SPS models | 996 cc |
| All other models | 916 cc |
| 996 model | 996 cc |
| Bore | |
| 748 model | 88 mm |
| 916 model | |
| SPS models | 98 mm |
| All other models | 94 mm |
| 996 model | 98 mm |
| Stroke | |
| 748 model | 61.5 mm |
| 916 and 996 models | 66.0 mm |
| Compression ratio | |
| 748 models | |
| SP and SPS model | 11.6:1 |
| All other models | 11.5:1 |
| 916 models | |
| SPS models | 11.5:1 |
| All other models | 11.0:1 |
| 996 models | 11.5:1 |
| Cylinder identification | Horizontal (front cylinder) No. 2, Vertical (rear cylinder) No. 1 |
| Maximum power (manufacturer's specification) | |
| 748 models | |
| SP and SPS model | 104 bhp @ 11,000 rpm |
| All other models | 98 bhp @ 11,000 rpm |
| 916 models | |
| SP model | 131 bhp @ 10,500 rpm |
| SPS models | 123 bhp @ 9500 rpm |
| All other models | 109 bhp @ 9000 rpm |
| 996 models | |
| S and SPS models | 123 bhp @ 9500 rpm |
| All other models | 112 bhp @ 8500 rpm |

## Cylinder head and valves

| | |
|---|---|
| Valve stem runout | |
| Standard | Not available |
| Service limit | 0.053 mm |
| Valve head runout | |
| Standard | Less than 0.010 mm |
| Service limit | 0.030 mm |
| Valve stem-to-guide clearance | |
| Standard | 0.030 to 0.045 mm |
| Service limit | 0.080 mm |
| Valve seat width | 1.4 to 1.6 mm |
| Valve clearances (COLD engine) | see Chapter 1 |

## Camshafts and rocker arms

| | |
|---|---|
| Camshaft runout | |
| Standard | Not available |
| Service limit | 0.1 mm |
| Rocker arm-to-shaft clearance | |
| Standard | 0.03 to 0.06 mm |
| Service limit | 0.08 mm |

## Cylinder barrels, pistons and piston rings

| | |
|---|---|
| Piston-to-bore clearance | |
| Standard | 0.04 to 0.06 mm |
| Service limit | 0.12 mm |

| | |
|---|---|
| Bore ovality | |
| Standard | Not available |
| Service limit | 0.03 mm |
| Bore taper | |
| Standard | Not available |
| Service limit | 0.03 mm |
| Piston-to-piston pin clearance | |
| Standard | 0.002 to 0.008 mm |
| Service limit | 0.035 mm |
| Piston ring-to-groove clearance | |
| Top compression ring | |
| Standard | 0.025 to 0.070 mm |
| Service limit | 0.150 mm |
| Second compression ring and oil control ring | |
| Standard | 0.020 to 0.055 mm |
| Service limit | 0.100 mm |
| Piston ring end gap | |
| Top and second compression rings | |
| Standard | 0.2 to 0.4 mm |
| Service limit | 0.8 mm |
| Oil control ring | |
| Standard | 0.3 to 0.6 mm |
| Service limit | 1.0 mm |

## Clutch

| | |
|---|---|
| Friction plate thickness | |
| 916 SP and SPS, 996 S and SPS models | |
| Standard | 2.5 mm |
| Service limit | 2.3 mm |
| All other models | |
| Standard | 3.0 mm |
| Service limit | 2.8 mm |
| Friction plate-to-clutch drum clearance | Less than 0.6 mm |
| Clutch plate warpage | Less than 0.2 mm |
| Pushrod runout | Less than 0.3 mm |
| Spring minimum free length | 36.5 mm |

## Crankshaft and connecting rods

| | |
|---|---|
| Crankshaft endfloat | Nil |
| Connecting rod big-end sideplay | 0.15 to 0.35 mm |
| Crankshaft runout | Less than 0.01 mm |
| Main bearing journal out-of-round | Less than 0.01 mm |
| Crankshaft big-end journal (crankpin) diameter | |
| Size group A | 42.006 to 42.014 mm |
| Size group B | 41.998 to 42.006 mm |
| Connecting rod big-end bore | |
| Titanium connecting rods | 45.017 to 45.025 mm |
| Standard connecting rods | |
| Size group A | 45.019 to 45.025 mm |
| Size group B | 45.013 to 45.019 mm |
| Connecting rod big-end bearing running clearance | 0.025 to 0.059 mm |
| Connecting rod small-end-to-piston pin clearance | |
| Standard | 0.015 to 0.034 mm |
| Service limit | 0.065 mm |

## Oil pump

| | |
|---|---|
| Gear teeth clearance | Less than 0.10 mm |
| Gear-to-housing clearance | Less than 0.10 mm |
| Gear-to-pump cover clearance | Less than 0.07 mm |

## Timing belt driveshaft

| | |
|---|---|
| Endfloat | Less than 0.2 mm |

| | |
|---|---|
| **Gear ratios** | |
| 748 models | |
| 1st gear | 2.467:1 (37/15T) |
| 2nd gear | 1.765:1 (30/17T) |
| 3rd gear | 1.400:1 (28/20T) |
| 4th gear | 1.300:1 (26/22T) |
| 5th gear | 1.043:1 (24/23T) |
| 6th gear | 0.958:1 (23/24T) |
| 916 and 996 models | |
| 1st gear | 2.467:1 (37/15T) |
| 2nd gear | 1.765:1 (30/17T) |
| 3rd gear | 1.350:1 (27/20T) |
| 4th gear | 1.091:1 (24/22T) |
| 5th gear | 0.958:1 (23/24T) |
| 6th gear | 0.857:1 (24/28T) |
| Primary drive gear ratio | |
| 748 and 916 models (excluding 916 SPS) | 2.000:1 (62/31T) |
| 916 SPS and all 996 models | 1.843:1 (59/32T) |
| Transmission shaft endfloat | 0.05 to 0.15 mm |
| Selector drum endfloat | 0.10 to 0.40 mm |
| Selector drum groove width | |
| Standard | 8.00 to 8.09 mm |
| Service limit | 8.19 mm |
| Selector fork pin diameter | |
| Standard | 7.66 to 7.74 mm |
| Service limit | 7.50 mm |
| Selector drum groove-to-fork pin clearance | |
| Standard | 0.26 to 0.43 mm |
| Service limit | 0.60 mm |
| Selector fork end thickness (standard) | 3.90 to 4.00 mm |
| Gear selector fork groove width (standard) | 4.07 to 4.19 mm |
| Selector fork end-to-gear groove clearance | |
| Standard | 0.07 to 0.29 mm |
| Service limit | 0.40 mm |

## Torque settings

| | |
|---|---|
| Camshaft end cap bolts | 10 Nm |
| Clutch centre nut | 186 Nm |
| Clutch cover screws | 9 Nm |
| Clutch drum-to-primary driven gear bolts | 32 Nm |
| Clutch hose banjo bolt | 18 Nm |
| Clutch master cylinder mounting clamp bolts | 9 Nm |
| Clutch slave cylinder mounting bolts | 10 Nm |
| Connecting rod big-end bearing cap bolts | |
| Standard connecting rods | |
| Stage 1 | 20 Nm |
| Stage 2 | 35 Nm |
| Stage 3 | Angle-tighten 65° |
| Titanium connecting rods | see Section 32 |
| Crankcase breather valve | 40 Nm |
| Crankcase cover screws | 9 Nm |
| Crankcase screws | |
| M8 screws | |
| Standard screws | |
| Stage 1 | 19 Nm |
| Stage 2 | 25 Nm |
| Hollow M8 x 75 mm screw – see text | 15 Nm |
| M6 screws | 10 Nm |
| Cylinder head/barrel coolant outlet union/blanking cover screws | 9 Nm |
| Cylinder head nuts | |
| Stage 1 | 15 Nm |
| Stage 2 | 30 Nm |
| Stage 3 | 52 Nm |
| Cylinder head studs | 25 Nm |
| Cylinder head side cover bolts | 10 Nm |
| Cylinder head valve cover bolts | 10 Nm |
| Engine mounting bolt nuts | 44 Nm |

| | |
|---|---|
| Exhaust manifold nuts | 10 Nm |
| Gearchange lever clamp bolt | 10 Nm |
| Flywheel/alternator rotor – early models (pre 1999 model year) | |
| Flywheel/alternator rotor nut | 186 Nm |
| Starter clutch holder bolts | 10 Nm |
| Flywheel/alternator rotor – later models (1999-on model year) | |
| Flywheel/alternator rotor nut | 186 Nm |
| Alternator rotor-to-flywheel/starter clutch bolts | 13 Nm |
| Intake manifold nuts | 10 Nm |
| Oil cooler mounting bolt | 10 Nm |
| Oil drain plug | 42 Nm |
| Oil hose | |
| Banjo bolt | 12 Nm |
| Union nut | 18 Nm |
| Adapter | 24 Nm |
| Oil filter | 17 Nm |
| Oil filter adapter | 45 Nm |
| Oil pick-up gauze filter bolt | 42 Nm |
| Oil pump bolts | |
| M8 bolt | 25 Nm |
| M6 bolt | 10 Nm |
| Primary drive gear nut | 186 Nm |
| Rear brake master cylinder/pedal bracket | |
| Mounting bracket bolt | 43 Nm |
| Pedal pivot bolt | 29 Nm |
| Selector drum detent arm pivot bolt | 10 Nm |
| Selector drum detent bolt | 30 Nm |
| Sidestand bracket mounting bolts | 43 Nm |
| Spark plugs | 20 Nm |
| Starter idler gear pivot shaft bolt | 10 Nm |
| Swingarm pivot shaft bolt | 73 Nm |
| Timing belt driven gear nut | 45 Nm |
| Timing belt driveshaft pulley nut | |
| Driveshaft pulley nut | 62 Nm |
| Camshaft pulley nut | 71 Nm |
| Timing belt idler pulley bolt | 26 Nm |
| Timing belt tensioner pulley | |
| Retaining nut | 26 Nm |
| Mounting stud | 26 Nm |
| Transmission shaft bearing retaining/retaining plate screws | 10 Nm |
| General torque settings for unspecified fasteners | |
| M5 fixings | 6 Nm |
| M6 fixings | 10 Nm |
| M8 fixings | 24 Nm |
| M10 fixings | 36 Nm |

## 1 General information

The engine is a liquid-cooled 90° vee-twin cylinder unit mounted longitudinally in the frame. The four valves per cylinder are operated by Ducati's Desmodromic system whereby each valve has an opening and closing rocker arm operated by separate lobes on the camshaft. Each camshaft is driven by a toothed belt from a driveshaft housed in the crankcases. The driveshaft is driven off the left-hand side of the crankshaft by the timing gears.

The crankcases are divided vertically, with the crankshaft running in ball bearings. The alternator rotor, flywheel, starter clutch and timing gear are on the crankshaft left-hand end, and the primary drive gear is on its right-hand end. The pistons run in plated cylinder bores.

The clutch is a dry multi-plate unit which is driven off the primary drive gear. The unit is hydraulically operated by a lever and master cylinder on the left-hand handlebar. The clutch slave cylinder is mounted onto the left-hand crankcase cover and operates the clutch via a pushrod which passes through the centre of the transmission input shaft.

The transmission is of the six-speed constant mesh type. Final drive to the rear wheel is by chain and sprockets, the drive sprocket being mounted on the left-hand end of the output shaft.

The lubrication system is fed by the oil pump which is driven off the primary drive gear on the right-hand end of the crankshaft. The oil pump draws oil from the crankcases, via the pick-up gauze filter, and provides a pressurised supply to the engine via the oil filter. The crankshaft, pistons and transmission components are supplied via internal passages in the crankcases and the cylinder heads are supplied via an externally mounted pipe. On 748 SP and SPS models and all 916 and 996 models, an oil cooler is fitted to stabilise the oil temperature.

The water pump is fitted to the left-hand crankcase cover and is driven off the end of the timing belt driveshaft.

**Note:** *The identification marks on the cylinder heads, camshafts and pistons consist of the following four letters. These letters are abbreviations of the Italian words given in brackets and are as follows: O represents Horizontal (Orizzontale), V represents Vertical (Verticale), A represents Intake (Aspirazione) and S represents Exhaust (Scarico).*

## 2 Operations possible with the engine in the frame

The components and assemblies listed below can be removed without having to remove the engine from the frame. If however, a number of areas require attention at the same time, removal of the engine is recommended.

*Starter motor (see Chapter 9)*
*Alternator (see Chapter 9)*
*Water pump (see Chapter 3)*
*Timing belts and pulleys*
*Cylinder heads, barrels and pistons*
*Camshafts and rockers arms (see Section 11 and Chapter 1)*
*Crankcase covers*
*Flywheel, starter clutch and idler gear*
*Timing gears*
*Gearchange mechanism*
*Clutch*
*Oil pump*
*Primary drive gears*
*Oil pressure relief valve*

## 3 Operations requiring engine removal

It is necessary to remove the engine from the frame and separate the crankcase halves to gain access to the following components

*Timing belt driveshaft*
*Crankshaft and main bearings*
*Connecting rods and big-end bearings*
*Selector drum and forks*
*Transmission gear shafts*

## 4 Major engine repair – general note

**1** It is not always easy to determine when or if an engine should be completely overhauled, as a number of factors must be considered.

**2** High mileage is not necessarily an indication that an overhaul is needed, while low mileage, on the other hand, does not preclude the need for an overhaul. Frequency of servicing is probably the single most important consideration. An engine that has regular and frequent oil and filter changes, as well as other required maintenance, will most likely give many miles of reliable service. Conversely, a neglected engine, or one which has not been run in properly, may require an overhaul very early in its life.

**3** Exhaust smoke and excessive oil consumption are both indications that piston rings and/or valve guides are in need of attention, although make sure that the fault is not due to oil leakage.

**4** If the engine is making obvious knocking or rumbling noises, the connecting rod and/or main bearings are probably at fault.

**5** Loss of power, rough running, excessive valve train noise and high fuel consumption rates may also point to the need for an overhaul, especially if they are all present at the same time. If a complete tune-up does not remedy the situation, major mechanical work is the only solution.

**6** An engine overhaul generally involves restoring the internal parts to the specifications of a new engine. The piston rings and main and connecting rod bearings are usually renewed. Generally the valve seats are re-ground, since they are usually in less than perfect condition at this point. The end result should be a like new engine that will give as many trouble-free miles as the original.

**7** Before beginning the engine overhaul, read through the related procedures to familiarise yourself with the scope and requirements of the job. Overhauling an engine is not all that difficult, but it is time consuming. Plan on the motorcycle being tied up for a minimum of two weeks. Check on the availability of parts and make sure that any necessary special tools, equipment and supplies are obtained in advance.

**8** Most work can be done with typical workshop hand tools, although a number of precision measuring tools are required for inspecting parts to determine if they must be renewed. Often a dealer will handle the inspection of parts and offer advice concerning reconditioning and renewal. As a general rule, time is the primary cost of an overhaul so it does not pay to install worn or substandard parts.

**9** As a final note, to ensure maximum life and minimum trouble from a rebuilt engine, everything must be assembled with care in a spotlessly clean environment.

## 5 Engine – removal and installation

***Caution: The engine is very heavy. Engine removal and installation should be carried out with the aid of at least one assistant; personal injury or damage could occur if the engine falls or is dropped. A mechanical or hydraulic floor jack should be used to support and lower or raise the engine if possible.***

### Removal

**1** Support the bike securely upright using an auxiliary stand so it can't be knocked over during this procedure. Work can be made easier by raising the machine to a suitable working height on an hydraulic ramp or a suitable platform (see Section 1 of *Tools and Workshop Tips* in the *Reference* section).

***Caution: Ensure the bike is securely supported before proceeding.***

**2** Remove the fairing lower panels and seat cowling (see Chapter 8).

**3** If the engine is dirty, particularly around its mountings, wash it thoroughly before starting any major dismantling work. This will make work much easier and rule out the possibility of caked on lumps of dirt falling into some vital component.

**4** Remove the battery and its mounting tray (see Chapter 9).

**5** Drain the engine oil (see Chapter 1).

**6** Remove the oil cooler (where fitted) (see Section 27).

**7** Remove the fuel tank, airbox, throttle body assembly, vertical cylinder intake manifold and the complete exhaust system (see Chapter 4).

**8** Drain the cooling system (see Chapter 1) and remove the radiator and coolant overflow tank (see Chapter 3).

**9** Release the clips securing the top hose and thermostat hoses to their unions on the horizontal cylinder and water pump cover. Remove the top hose and the thermostat, complete with hoses, from the engine **(see illustration)**. Undo the three bolts securing the coolant outlet union to the left-hand side of the vertical cylinder head and position the union clear of the head **(see illustrations)**. Recover the sealing ring from the union and discard it; a new one must be used on installation.

**10** Slacken the retaining clip securing the crankcase breather tank hose to the breather valve on the top of the crankcase **(see**

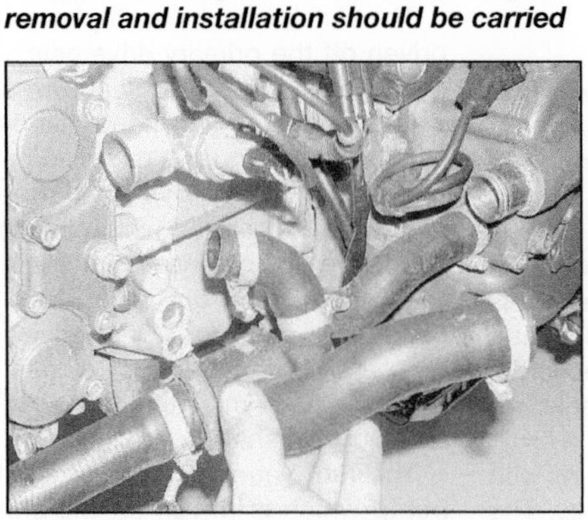

**5.9a Remove the thermostat complete with coolant hoses**

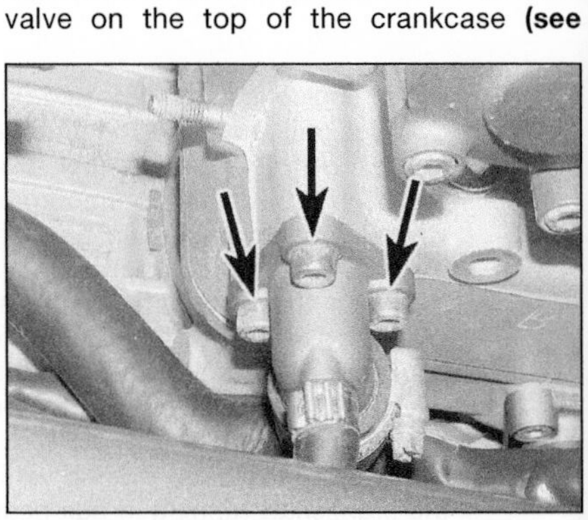

**5.9b Undo the three retaining bolts (arrowed) . . .**

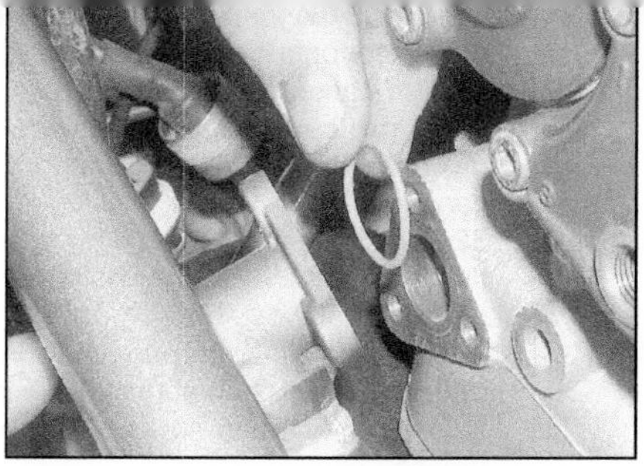

5.9c . . . then free the coolant outlet union from the vertical cylinder head and recover the sealing ring

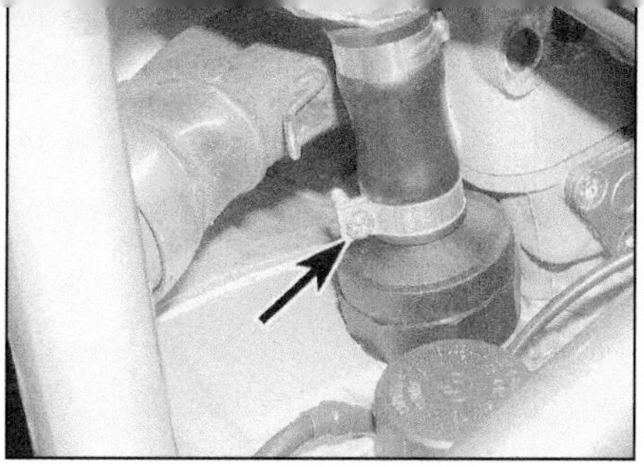

5.10a Slacken the retaining clip (arrowed) . . .

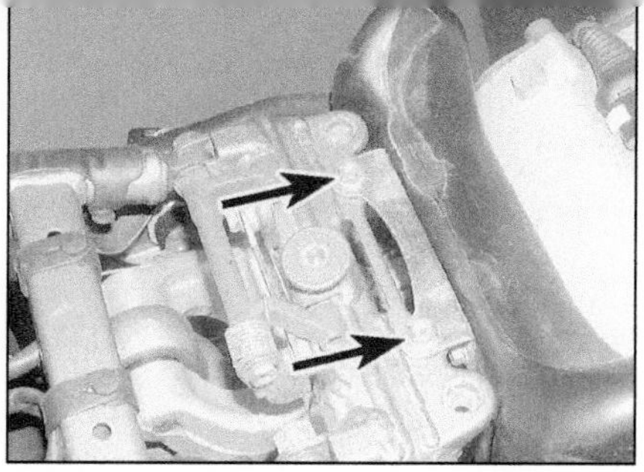

5.10b . . . then undo the retaining bolts (arrowed) . . .

**illustration)**. Undo the two bolts securing the tank mounting bracket to the frame and remove the breather tank assembly from the bike **(see illustrations)**.

**11** Remove the ignition HT coils (see Chapter 5).

**12** Disconnect the wiring connectors from the coolant temperature sensor, fan switch and temperature gauge sensor which are fitted to the coolant outlet on the left-hand side of the horizontal cylinder head **(see illustration)**.

**13** Disconnect the wiring connector from the timing sensor fitted to the left-hand side crankcase cover **(see illustration)**. On models with a P8 engine management system (see Chapter 4), also disconnect the RPM sensor wiring connector; label the wiring connectors to ensure they are connected correctly on installation (the RPM sensor wiring should be marked 'M').

**14** Peel back the rubber cover on the starter motor terminal then unscrew the nut and washer and detach the starter lead from the motor **(see illustration)**. Free the starter motor lead from any retaining clips and ties securing it to the engine, whilst noting its correct routing, and position it clear of the engine.

**15** Trace the wiring back from the neutral light switch (fitted to the rear of the crankcase) and disconnect its wiring connector from the main wiring harness.

**16** Disconnect the wiring connector from the oil pressure switch (fitted to the right-hand crankcase cover) **(see illustration)**.

**17** Undo the retaining bolt and free the earth (ground) lead from the top right-hand side of the crankcase **(see illustration)**.

**18** Undo the two bolts securing the sidestand mounting bracket to the left of the crankcase and remove the stand assembly from the bike. On later (2000 model year on) models, it will be necessary to remove the switch from the sidestand (see Chapter 9) before unbolting the bracket from the engine.

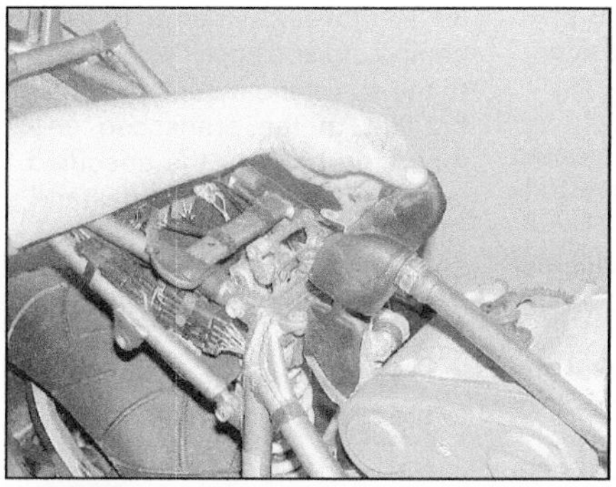

5.10c . . . and remove the crankcase breather tank assembly from the bike

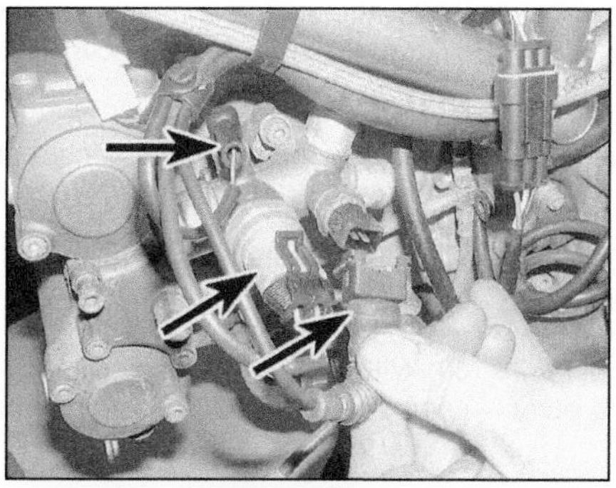

5.12 Disconnect the wiring connectors from the coolant temperature sensors and switch (arrowed)

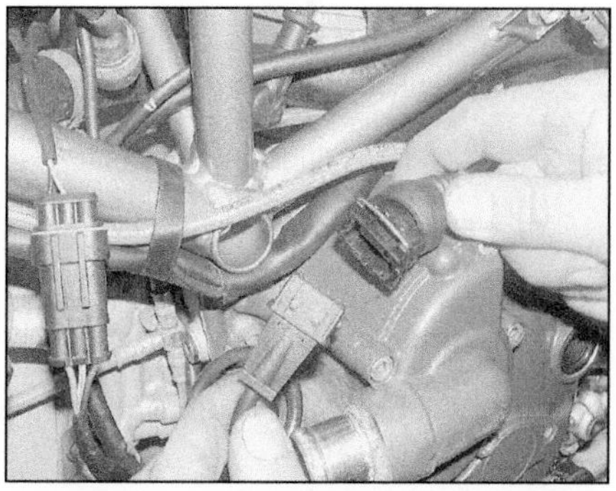

5.13 Disconnecting the timing sensor wiring connector

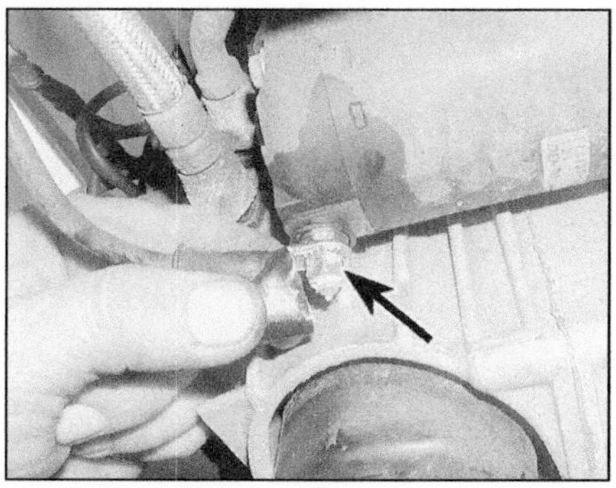

5.14 Peel back the rubber cover then undo the nut (arrowed) and free the lead from the starter motor

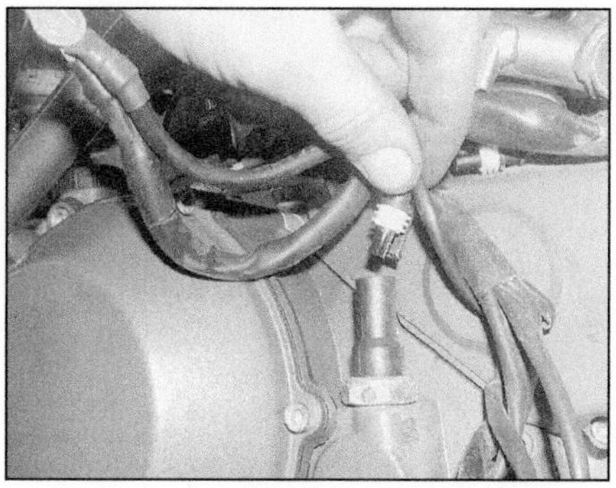

5.16 Disconnecting the oil pressure switch wiring connector

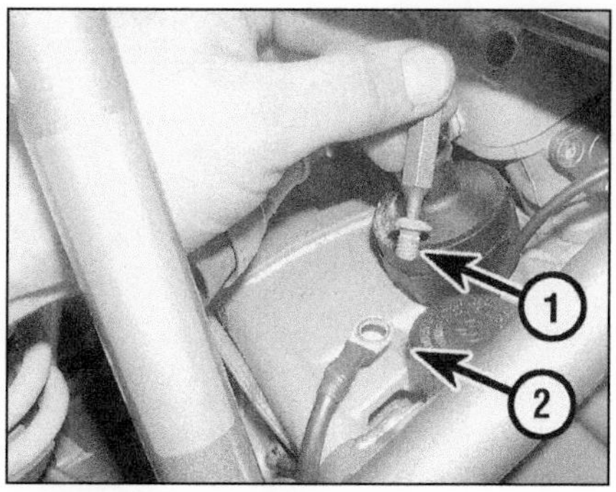


5.17 Undo the bolt (1) and free the earth lead (2) from the crankcase

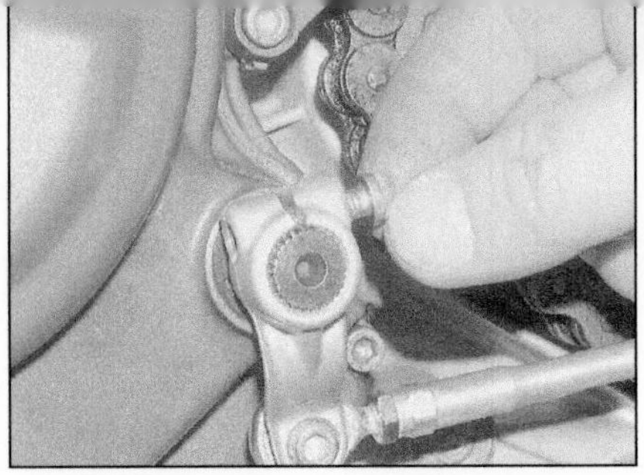
5.20 Unscrew the clamp bolt and free the gearchange lever from the engine

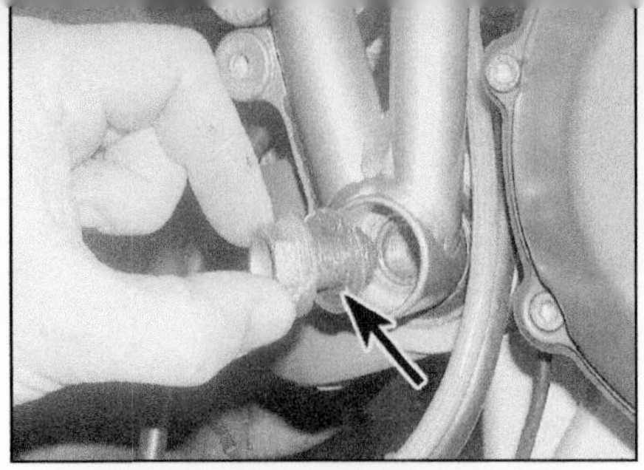
5.24a Unscrew the bolt and washer (arrowed) from the right-hand end of the swingarm pivot shaft . . .

19 Remove the front sprocket (see Chapter 6, Section 18).

20 Note the correct fitted location of the gearchange lever on its shaft (make alignment marks if necessary), then unscrew the clamp bolt and free the gearchange lever from the engine **(see illustration)**.

21 Slacken and remove the bolt securing the rear brake master cylinder/pedal bracket to the right-hand side of the crankcase. Unscrew the pedal pivot bolt from the crankcase without removing it from the pedal. Once the pivot bolt is free, position the master cylinder/pedal assembly clear of the engine. **Note:** *There is no need to disconnect any of the hydraulic hoses.*

22 At this point, position an hydraulic or mechanical jack under the engine with a block of wood between the jack head and crankcase. Make sure the jack is centrally positioned so the engine will not topple when the mounting bolts are removed. Take the weight of the engine on the jack.

23 Unscrew the nuts from the right-hand end of the engine mounting bolts.

24 Hold the left-hand end of the swingarm pivot shaft and slacken and remove the bolt and washer from its right-hand end **(see illustration)**. Withdraw the swingarm pivot shaft from the left-hand side of the frame **(see illustration)**.

25 Ensure the engine is securely supported then withdraw the engine mounting bolts from the left-hand side of the frame **(see illustration)**.

26 The engine is now free to be lowered out of position Check that all the wiring and hoses are disconnected and secured well clear, then carefully lower the engine out of position (see ***Caution*** at the start of this Section). The swingarm will remain attached to the frame by its inner sleeves

27 With the aid of an assistant lift the engine unit then remove the jack and lower the engine to the ground. The engine can then be manoeuvred out from underneath the frame. Whilst the engine is removed, refit the pivot shaft to the swingarm to secure it in position.

### Installation

28 Ensure the swingarm is correctly located in the frame and its inner sleeves are fully inserted.

29 Lubricate the engine mounting bolts and swingarm pivot shaft with a smear of molybdenum disulphide grease.

30 With the aid of an assistant, place the engine unit on top of the jack and block of position in the frame, making sure no wires or hoses become trapped between the engine and the frame.

31 Align the crankcase with the swingarm pivot then insert the pivot shaft from the left-hand side of the frame.

32 Align the engine mountings with the frame then insert the mounting bolts from the left-hand side of the frame.

33 Lubricate the threads and contact faces of the mounting bolt nuts and swingarm pivot shaft bolt with a smear of molybdenum grease.

34 Fit the nuts to the engine mounting bolts and tighten them to the specified torque.

35 Fit the bolt and washer to the swingarm pivot shaft and tighten it to the specified torque.

36 Clean the rear brake master cylinder/pedal mounting bracket and pivot bolts and apply a drop of locking compound to their threads. Align the bracket assembly with the crankcase and tighten the mounting bolt and pivot bolt to the specified torque settings.

37 Clean the gearchange lever clamp bolt and apply a drop of fresh locking compound to its threads. Engage the gearchange lever splines with those of the shaft so the gearchange lever is correctly positioned then refit the clamp bolt, tightening it to the specified torque.

38 Install the front sprocket (see Chapter 6, Section 18).

39 Remove all traces of original locking compound and apply fresh locking compound to the sidestand mounting bolts. Fit the stand bracket to the crankcase and tighten its mounting bolts to the specified torque. On later models, refit the sidestand switch (see Chapter 9).

40 Secure the earth (ground) lead to the crankcase, tightening its retaining bolt securely.

41 Securely reconnect the wiring connector to the oil pressure switch.

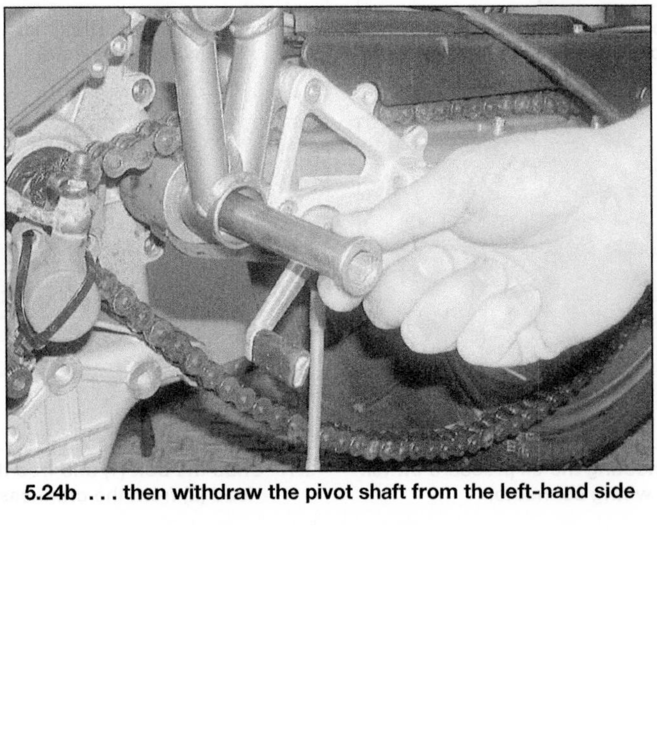
5.24b . . . then withdraw the pivot shaft from the left-hand side

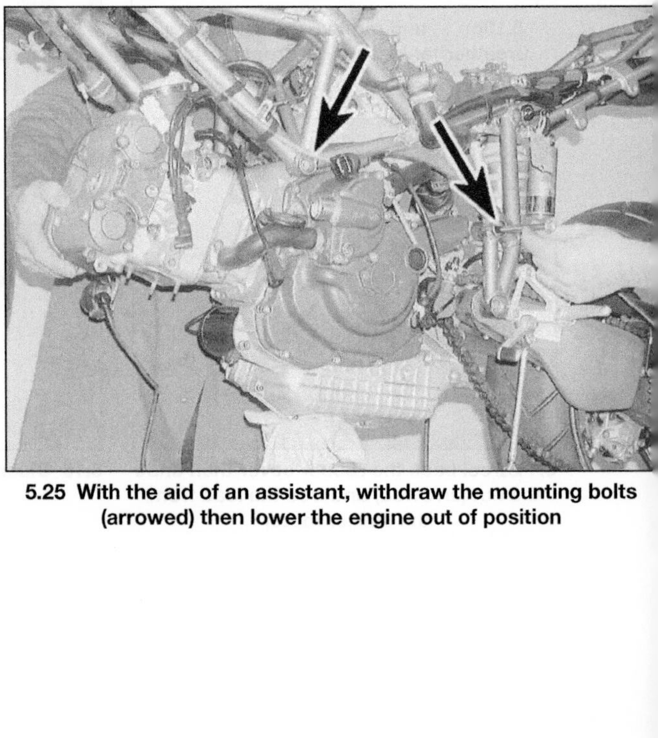
5.25 With the aid of an assistant, withdraw the mounting bolts (arrowed) then lower the engine out of position

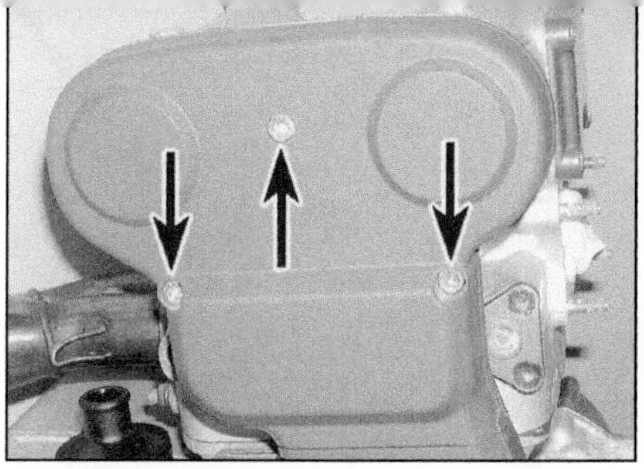

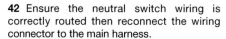

**6.4 Timing belt upper cover bolts (arrowed)**

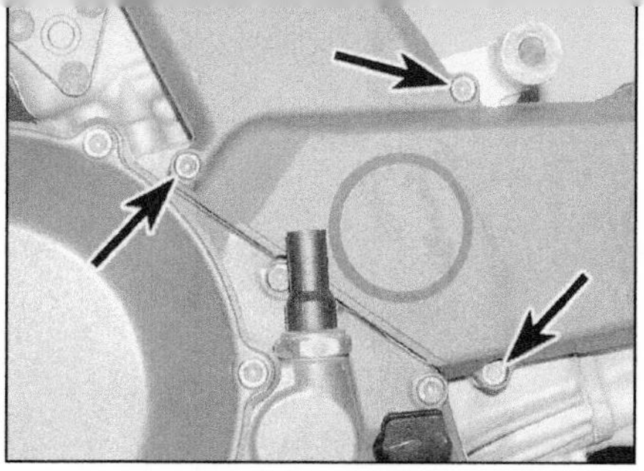

**6.5 Timing belt lower cover bolts (arrowed)**

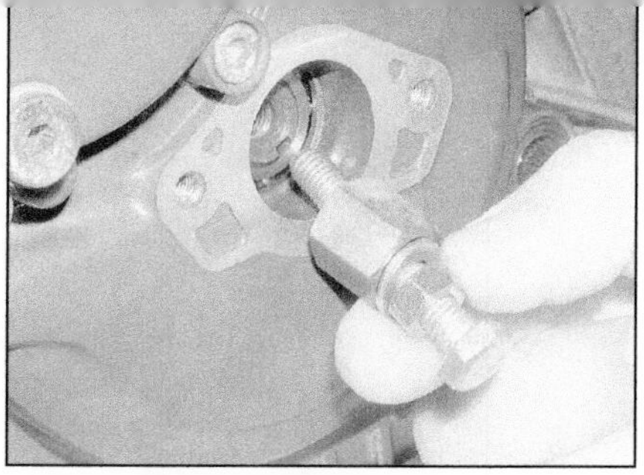

**6.7a Screw the M8 bolt, nut, washer and spacer arrangement into the end of the crankshaft . . .**

**42** Ensure the neutral switch wiring is correctly routed then reconnect the wiring connector to the main harness.

**43** Connect the starter lead to the motor terminal, ensuring it is correctly routed, and fit the washer and retaining nut, tightening it securely. Cover the terminal and nut with a smear of multi-purpose grease, to prevent corrosion, then seat the rubber cover correctly over the terminal. Also apply a smear of grease to the starter lead at the points where it contacts the engine/frame.

**44** Securely reconnect the wiring connector to the timing sensor. On models with a P8 engine management system also reconnect the RPM sensor connector ensuring the connectors are correctly remade (the RPM sensor wiring should be marked 'M').

**45** Reconnect the wiring connectors to the coolant temperature sensor, fan switch and temperature gauge sensor on the horizontal cylinder head outlet.

**46** Install the ignition coils (see Chapter 5).

**47** Clean the crankcase breather tank bolts and apply a drop of locking compound to their threads. Refit the tank to the frame and securely tighten its bolts. Reconnect the tank hose to the breather valve and securely tighten its retaining clip.

**48** Fit a new sealing ring to the coolant union groove then refit the union to the vertical cylinder head, tightening its retaining bolts securely. Refit the thermostat assembly and radiator top hose then install the radiator and overflow tank (see Chapter 3). Ensure all hoses are securely retained by their clips then refill the cooling system (see Chapter 1).

**49** Install the exhaust system, throttle body assembly and fuel tank (see Chapter 4).

**50** Install the oil cooler (where fitted) (see Section 27) and refill the engine with oil (see Chapter 1).

**51** Install the battery mounting tray and battery (see Chapter 9).

**52** Prior to installing the fairing panels, start the engine and check that there are no signs of fuel/coolant/oil leakage.

## 6 Engine – timing mark alignment and positioning at TDC (Top Dead Centre)

**Note:** *In order to accurately position the crankshaft for timing/adjusting the top end of the engine, it will be necessary to manually rotate the crankshaft. Ducati dealers use a service tool (88713-0123), which screws into the left-hand end of the crankshaft for this purpose. In the absence of the tool, an M8 bolt, nut, washer and spacer can be used (see Step 7).*

**1** Remove the fairing lower panels (see Chapter 8).

**2** Remove the battery and its mounting tray (see Chapter 9).

**3** Remove the fuel tank and airbox to gain access to the vertical cylinder head.

**4** Undo the three retaining screws and remove the timing belt upper covers from the right-hand side of both cylinder heads **(see illustration)**.

**5** Undo the retaining screws and remove the timing belt lower cover from the engine **(see illustration)**.

**6** Undo the retaining screws and remove the centre cap and sealing ring from the left-hand crankcase cover. Obtain a new sealing ring for use on refitting.

**7** In the absence of the Ducati service tool (88713-0123), obtain an M8 bolt, nut, washer and spacer **(see illustration)**. Screw the nut fully onto the bolt then slide on the washer and spacer. Screw the bolt fully into the end of the crankshaft and tighten the nut against the spacer to lock it in position; the bolt can then be used to rotate the crankshaft **(see illustration)**. **Note:** *It will be considerably easier to rotate the crankshaft if the spark plugs are removed (see Chapter 1).*

**8** Using a socket/spanner on the bolt, rotate the crankshaft until the timing mark on the timing belt driveshaft pulley is approaching the index mark on the right-hand crankcase cover. Continue rotating the crankshaft until the timing mark on the flywheel aligns with the pointer in the inspection window on the left-hand crankcase cover **(see illustrations)**. **Note:** *Always rotate the crankshaft in its normal direction of rotation (anti-clockwise when viewed from the left-hand side of the engine).*

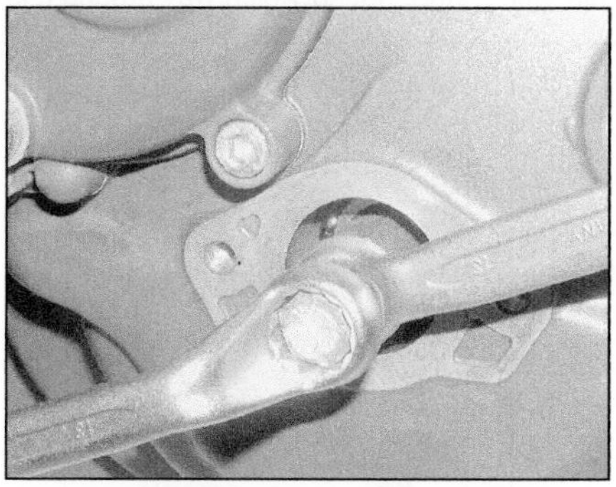

**6.7b . . . and securely tighten the nut against the spacer to lock the arrangement in position**

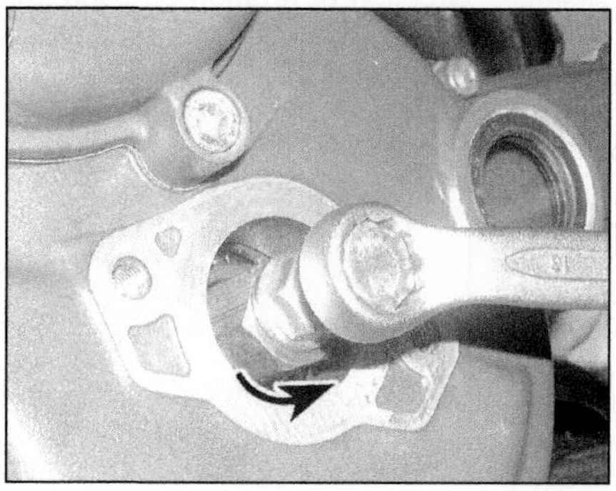

**6.8a Use the bolt to rotate the crankshaft anti-clockwise . . .**

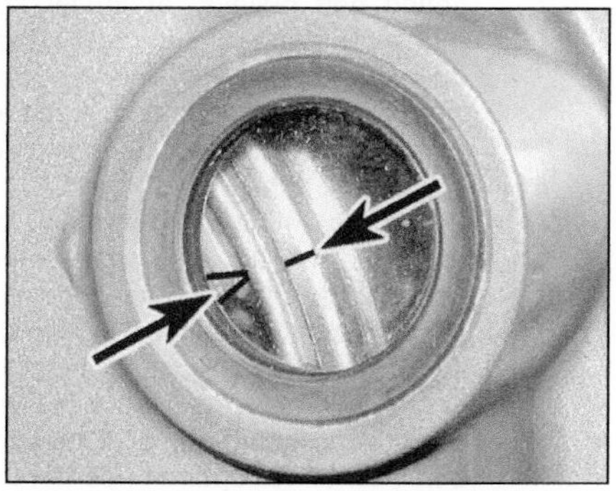

**6.8b . . . and align the flywheel timing mark with the pointer (arrowed) in the left-hand crankcase cover window**

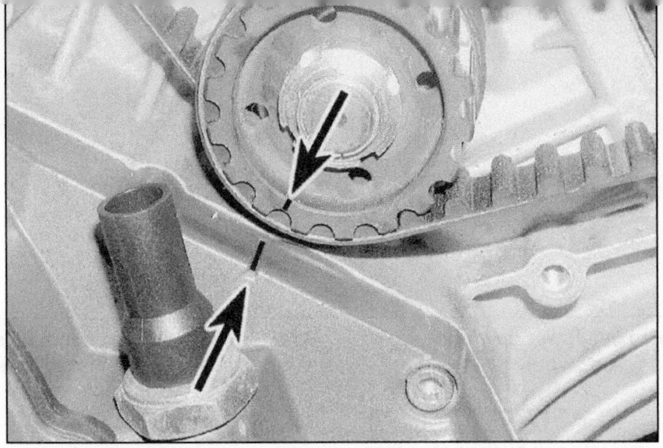

**6.9a Ensure the timing mark on the driveshaft pulley is aligned with the mark on the crankcase cover (arrowed) . . .**

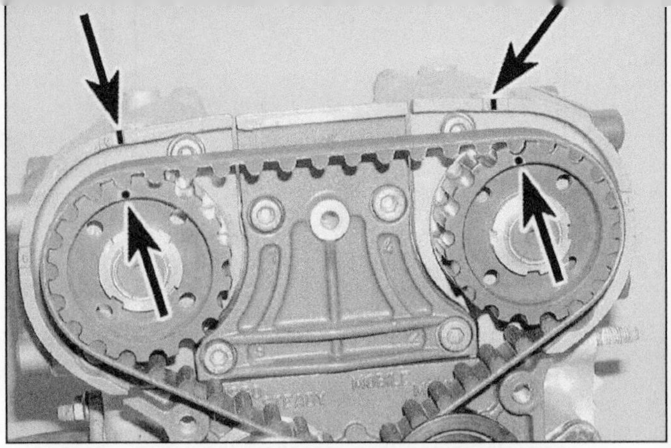

**6.9b . . . and the timing marks on the camshaft pulleys are correctly aligned with the V marks (arrowed) on the vertical cylinder head . . .**

**9** With the flywheel timing mark correctly positioned, check that the timing mark on the timing belt driveshaft pulley is correctly aligned with the index mark on the crankcase cover and the mark on each camshaft timing belt pulley is correctly aligned with the V marks on the vertical cylinder head and O marks on the horizontal cylinder head (see Note in Section 1) **(see illustrations)**.

**10** With the timing marks aligned as described, the horizontal cylinder piston is at TDC on its compression stroke. From this position, to bring the vertical cylinder piston to TDC on its compression stroke rotate the crankshaft a further 3/4 of a turn (270°) anti-clockwise and align the other flywheel timing mark with the pointer in the inspection window.

## 7 Valve timing – general information

**1** To compensate for manufacturing tolerances, the valve timing can be adjusted by the fitting of offset Woodruff keys to the timing belt pulleys. An offset key slightly repositions the timing belt pulley on the driveshaft/camshaft and so retards or advances the valve timing. A range of offset Woodruff keys is available to enable accurate adjustment to be made.

**2** The valve timing is set during production and, as far as the home mechanic is concerned, should never require checking again. The only time checking the valve timing might be necessary would be after a major engine overhaul, to ensure the engine was correctly assembled, or if the engine was being tuned for optimum performance, such as on SP and SPS engines.

**3** Checking of the valve timing is a complex procedure, requiring the use of several precision measuring tools to ensure accuracy. We advise that the motorcycle be taken to a Ducati dealer if a valve timing check is thought necessary.

## 8 Timing belts – removal, installation and tensioning

**Note:** *The timing belts can be removed with the engine in the frame. If the engine has already been removed, ignore the steps which do not apply. Access to the Ducati measuring gauge (88765.0999 or 051.2.001.1A), or a suitable aftermarket equivalent gauge, will be needed to accurately set the timing belt tension* **(see illustration)**. *If a gauge is not available it is recommend that timing belt removal and installation is entrusted to a Ducati dealer.*

### *Removal*

**1** Align the engine timing marks (see Section 6).

**2** If the timing belts are to be re-used, use chalk or similar to mark the belts H for horizontal and V for vertical. Also mark the direction of rotation on each belt. This will ensure they are refitted in their original locations.

**3** Working on the horizontal cylinder, slacken and remove the timing belt tensioner pulley hub retaining nut and washer **(see illustration)**. Slide the pulley assembly off is stud, noting which way around it is fitted, and

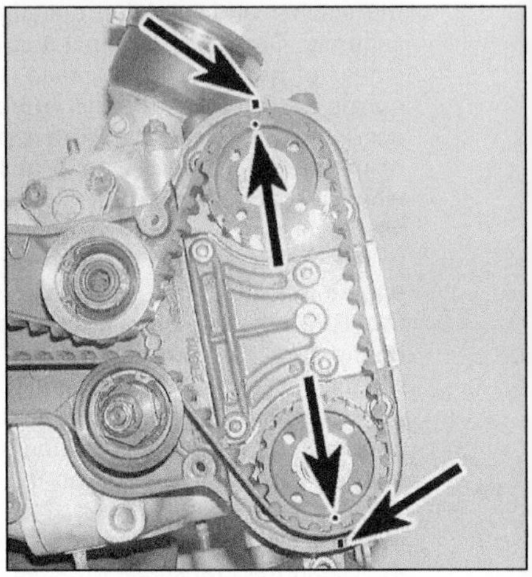

**6.9c . . . and the O marks (arrowed) on the horizontal cylinder head**

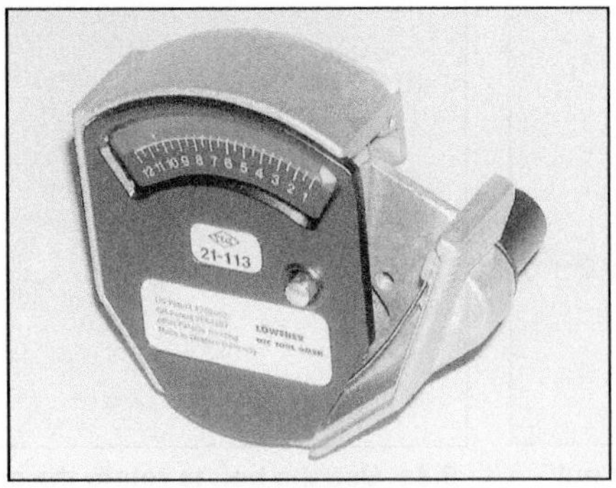

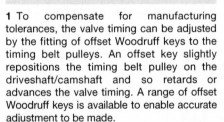

**8.0 Ducati gauge for measuring timing belt tension**

**8.3a Slacken and remove the retaining nut and washer . . .**

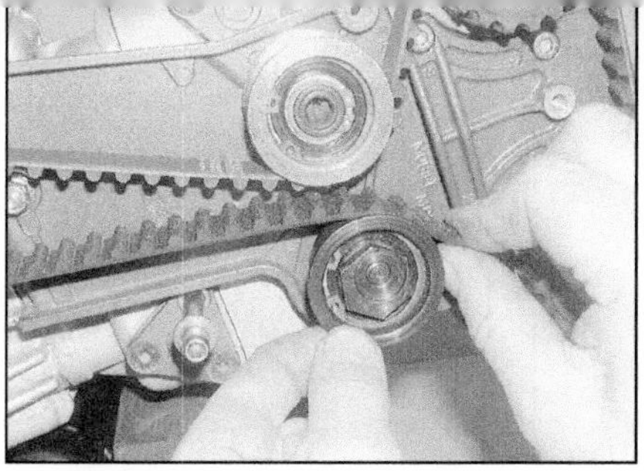

8.3b . . . then slide the tensioner pulley off its stud and remove the timing belt

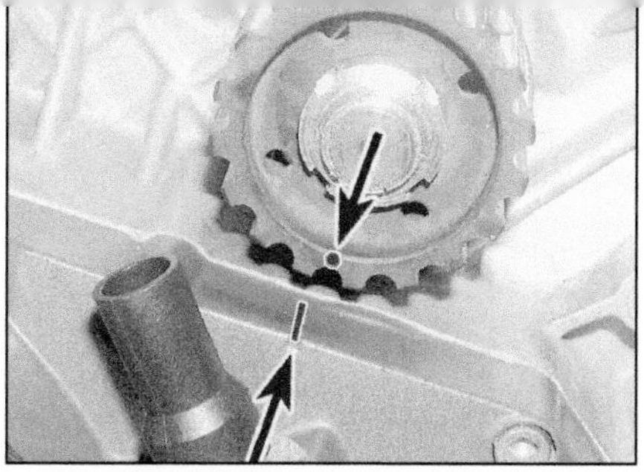

8.9a Ensure the timing marks on the driveshaft pulley and cover (arrowed) . . .

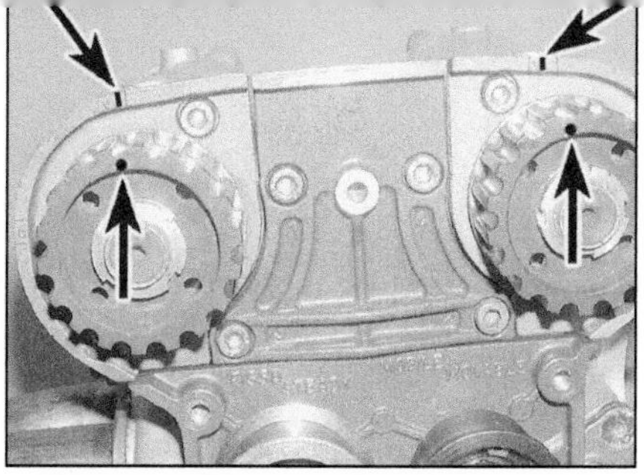

8.9b . . . camshaft pulleys and vertical cylinder head (arrowed) . . .

slip the timing belt off its pulleys and remove it from the engine **(see illustration)**.

***Caution: Do not rotate the camshafts or crankshaft whilst the timing belt is removed. If the crankshaft or either camshaft are rotated, the valves could contact the pistons, causing serious engine damage.***

**4** Once the horizontal cylinder belt has been removed, remove the vertical cylinder timing belt as described in Step 3.

## Inspection

**Note:** *It is strongly recommended that the timing belts are renewed whenever they are disturbed, regardless of their age and condition. Should a belt break in use, the valves will contact the pistons resulting in extensive engine damage and likely loss of control of the motorcycle.*

**5** Inspect each belt along its backing (flat side) and edges and check that it is not worn or damaged in any way. Check the working face of the belt for damaged teeth, cracking between the teeth and wear of the belt material – a shiny surface indicates extreme wear.

**6** Check for wear of the belt teeth by fitting the belt over one of the pulleys and feeling for play between the teeth and pulley slots.

**7** If either belt shows signs of wear or damage, renew both belts as a pair.

**8** Check the surfaces of all pulleys for damage. Also check that the tensioner and idler pulleys rotate easily without any sign of freeplay or roughness in their bearings. Renew worn or damaged pulleys and bearings (see Section 9).

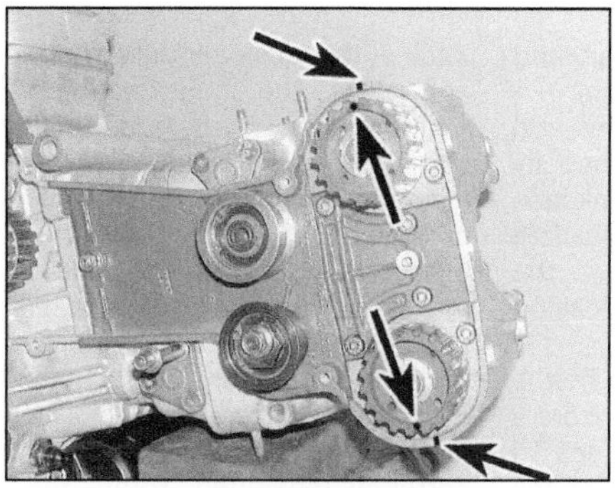

8.9c . . . and the pulleys and horizontal cylinder head are correctly aligned before installing the timing belts

## Installation

**9** Ensure the timing belt driveshaft pulley and all camshaft pulley timing marks are still correctly aligned with the marks on the crankcase cover and cylinder heads (see Section 6) **(see illustrations)**.

**10** Ensure that all the pulleys are clean and dry then manoeuvre the vertical cylinder timing belt into position. If the original belt is being reused, use the marks made on removal to ensure the correct belt is being installed and it is the right way around.

8.11a Fit the vertical cylinder timing belt over the driveshaft pulley . . .

**11** Taking care not to twist the timing belt sharply, fit the belt over the inner pulley on the driveshaft and around the fixed idler pulley **(see illustration)**. Engage the belt with the camshaft pulleys, making sure that the idler pulley and top run of the belt are taut, then seat the tensioner pulley against the belt ensuring its flange and hub hex are facing outwards and slip it onto its mounting stud **(see illustrations)**. Ensure that all slack is on the tensioner pulley side of the belt and that the belt teeth are seated centrally in the pulleys.

**12** Fit the washer to the tensioner pulley and thread the retaining nut on by hand **(see illustration)**. Pivot the pulley hub anti-clockwise to remove all freeplay from the

8.11b . . . around the idler pulley and camshaft pulleys . . .

8.11c . . . then seat the tensioner pulley against the belt and slip it onto its mounting stud

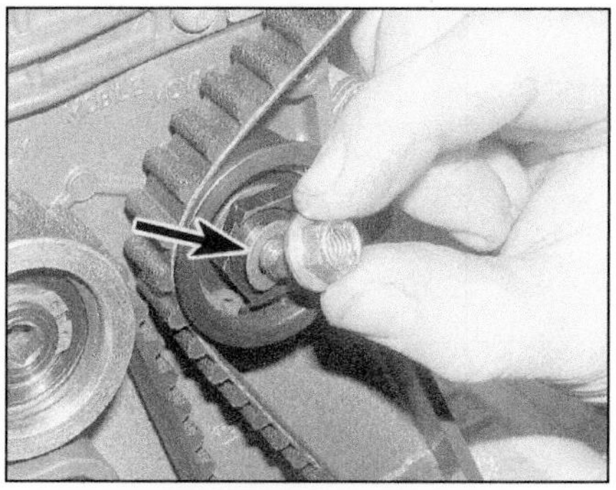

8.12a Fit the washer (arrowed) and nut to the tensioner pulley . . .

**8.12b . . . then rotate the pulley hub anti-clockwise to tension the belt before securely tightening the nut**

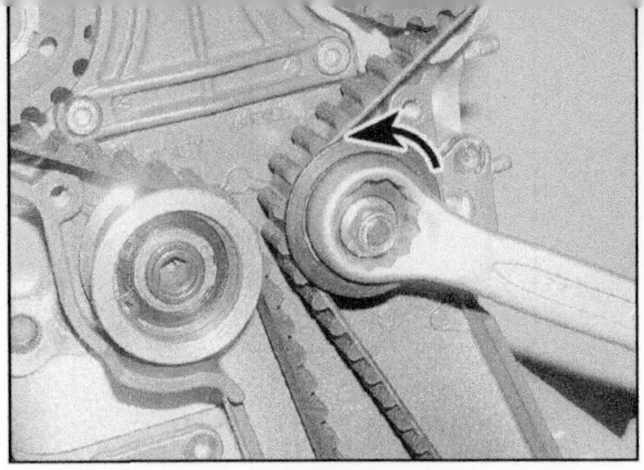

**8.18a Rotate the tensioner pulley hub anti-clockwise to tension the timing belt**

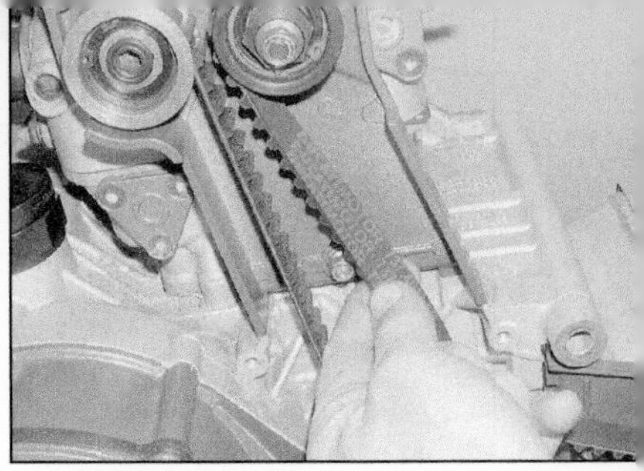

**8.18b If a measuring gauge is not available, tension the belt until it is just possible to twist the belt through 45° - see text**

timing belt then hold the hub stationary and securely tighten the nut **(see illustration)**.

**13** Check that the driveshaft pulley and camshaft pulley timing marks are all correctly aligned with their marks on the crankcase cover and cylinder head (see Section 6) before proceeding. If they are not, release the tensioner pulley and adjust the belt position on the pulleys.

**14** Once the vertical cylinder timing belt is correctly installed, install the horizontal cylinder timing belt as described in Steps 10 to 13, fitting the belt to the outer pulley on the driveshaft.

**15** Once both timing belts are correctly installed, adjust the timing belt tension as described under the relevant sub-heading.

## Tensioning without the Ducati measuring gauge

**Note:** *If this method is used, ensure that the belt tension is checked with a tensioning gauge at the earliest possible opportunity.*

**16** If the special measuring gauge is not available, an approximate setting may be achieved as follows. Timing belt tension is always adjusted with the cylinder at TDC on its compression stroke (see Section 6).

**17** Rotate the crankshaft through four complete rotations to settle the timing belts in position then realign the timing marks (see Section 6).

**18** Starting with the horizontal cylinder, slacken the tensioner pulley hub retaining nut and release the timing belt tension. Using a 22 mm spanner, rotate the pulley hub anti-clockwise until it is just possible to twist the timing belt through 45° by finger and thumb, midway between the driveshaft and tensioner pulleys **(see illustrations)**. The deflection of the belt at the mid-point between the pulleys should be approximately 5.0 mm. Hold the pulley hub stationary then tighten the retaining nut to the specified torque.

**19** Once the horizontal cylinder timing belt is correctly tensioned, rotate the crankshaft 270° anti-clockwise to bring the vertical cylinder to TDC on its compression stroke (see Section 6). Repeat the adjustment operation on the vertical cylinder timing belt.

**20** With both timing belts correctly tensioned, rotate the crankshaft through a further three and a quarter rotations to settle the timing belts in position.

**21** Realign the timing marks (see Section 6) then recheck the tension of the horizontal timing belt. If necessary, readjust the timing belt tension.

**22** Rotate the crankshaft 270° anti-clockwise to bring the vertical cylinder back to TDC on its compression stroke (see Section 6). Then recheck the tension of the vertical timing belt. If necessary, readjust the timing belt tension.

**23** Once both belts are correctly tensioned, install the belt lower cover and securely tighten its retaining bolts. Install both upper covers, tightening their retaining bolts securely.

**24** Slacken the nut and remove the bolt spacer, washer and nut used to rotate the crankshaft.

**25** Fit a new sealing ring then fit the centre cap to the left-hand crankcase cover **(see illustration)**. Apply a drop of locking compound to the retaining screws threads then fit the screws, tightening them securely.

**26** Install the airbox and fuel tank (see Chapter 4).

**27** Install the battery mounting tray and battery (see Chapter 9).

**28** Install the fairing lower panels (see Chapter 8).

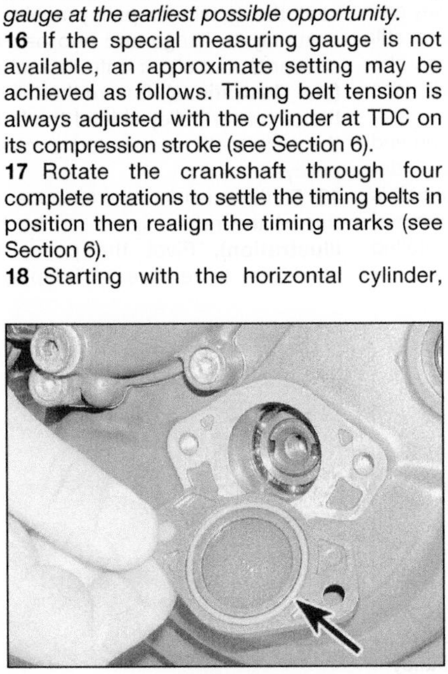

**8.25 Fit a new sealing ring (arrowed) to the crankcase cover centre cap**

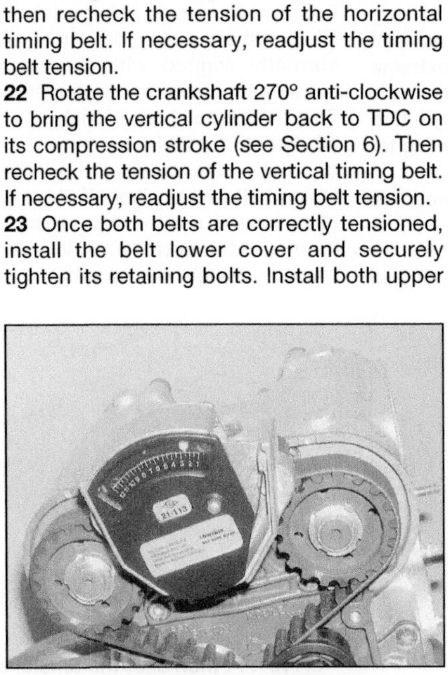

**8.30 Ducati timing belt tension gauge in position on engine**

## Tensioning using the Ducati measuring gauge

**Note:** *If an aftermarket gauge is being used follow the instructions supplied by the gauge manufacturer (the belt tension is measured in Lowener units).*

**29** Rotate the crankshaft through four complete rotations to settle the timing belts in position then realign the timing marks (see Section 6). Timing belt tension is always adjusted with the cylinder at TDC on its compression stroke (see Section 6).

**30** Starting on the horizontal cylinder, fit the measuring gauge to the 'top run' of the timing belt, midway between the camshaft pulleys **(see illustration)**.

**31** Slacken the tensioner pulley retaining nut and release the timing belt tension.

**32** Using a 22 mm spanner, rotate the pulley hub anti-clockwise to tension the timing belt whilst observing the measuring gauge pointer. Overtension the belt until the pointer reaches the end of its measuring scale then gradually release the tension until the needle returns to the 2.5 position on the scale **(see illustration)**. Hold the pulley hub stationary then tighten the retaining nut to the specified torque. Ensure the gauge reading is still 2.5 then remove the gauge from the timing belt.

**33** Once the horizontal cylinder timing belt is correctly tensioned, rotate the crankshaft 270° anti-clockwise to bring the vertical cylinder to TDC on its compression stroke

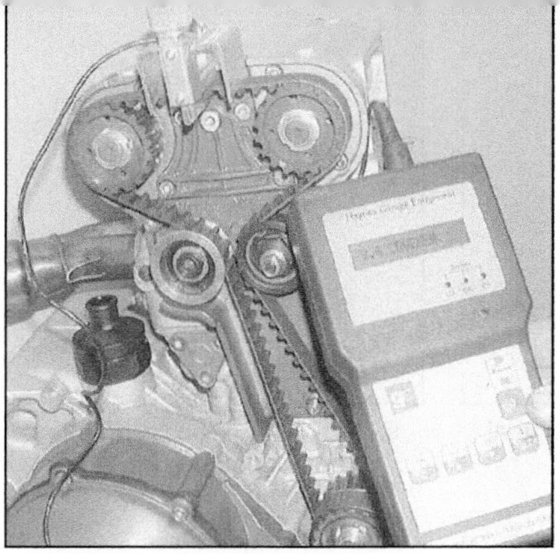

**8.32 Aftermarket timing belt tensioning gauge in position on engine**

(see Section 6). Tension the vertical cylinder timing belt as described in Steps 30 to 32.

**34** Once both timing belts are correctly tensioned, install all removed components as described in Steps 23 to 28.

## 9 Timing belt pulleys – removal and installation

**Note:** *The timing belt pulleys can be removed with the engine in the frame. If the engine has already been removed, ignore the steps which do not apply.*

### *Removal*

**Note:** *On some engines, offset Woodruff keys may be fitted to the driveshaft and camshaft pulleys (the keys are used to adjust the valve timing – see Section 7). Where an offset Woodruff key is used, make a careful note of which way around the key is fitted to ensure it is installed the correct way around on installation. If the key is incorrectly fitted the valve timing will be altered.*

**1** Remove the timing belt(s) (see Section 8). Proceed as described under the relevant sub-heading.

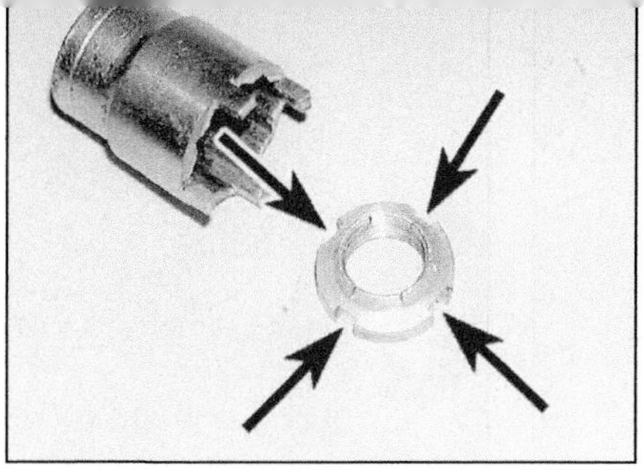

**9.2 Cut a socket as shown so its tabs are a snug-fit in the pulley nut cutouts (arrowed)**

***Caution: Do not rotate the camshafts or crankshaft whilst the timing belts are removed. If the crankshaft or either camshaft are rotated, the valves could contact the pistons, causing serious engine damage.***

### Driveshaft pulleys

**Note:** *A special socket and holding tool will be required to slacken/tighten the pulley nut. Alternatives to the Ducati socket and holding tool (88700.5644) are given in the text (see Steps 2 and 3).*

**2** In the absence of the Ducati tool, it will be necessary to fabricate a socket to enable the pulley retaining nut to be slackened/tightened. A suitable alternative can be made by cutting a spare socket (approximately 20 mm in size) as shown **(see illustration)**. Cut the socket so the tabs are a snug fit in the retaining nut cutouts.

**3** Another problem is preventing rotation whilst the nut is slackened/tightened. If the Ducati tool is not available, the options are as follows.

a) *Retain the pulley by gripping it with an old timing belt clamped firmly around it with a pair of self-locking grips* **(seeillustration)**. *If this method is used, note that it will be necessary to fit a new timing belt on installation – never reuse a timing belt which has been used to hold a pulley in this way.*

b) *Retain the pulley with the holding tool used to retain the clutch centre (see Section 20)* **(see illustration)**.

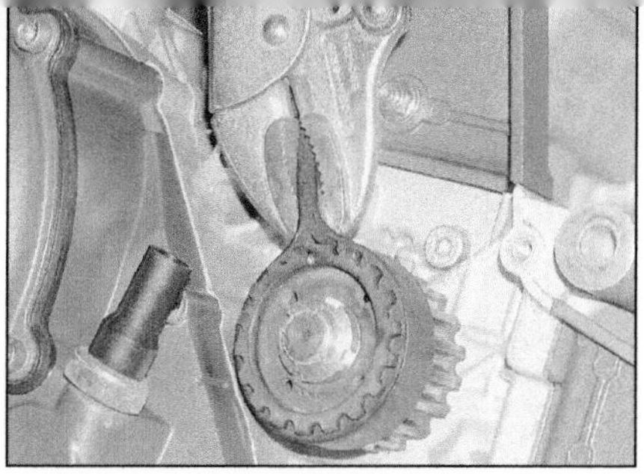

**9.3a Using an old timing belt and a pair of grips to retain the driveshaft pulley**

c) *If the engine is still in the frame, the driveshaft can be locked by placing the transmission in gear and having an assistant firmly apply the rear brake.*

**4** Slacken and remove the pulley retaining nut (see Steps 2 and 3) and washer from the driveshaft **(see illustration)**. Discard the retaining nut, a new one must be used on installation.

**5** Slide the outer (horizontal cylinder) pulley off the driveshaft **(see illustration)**. Mark the pulley for identification purposes to ensure it is correctly positioned on installation (both pulleys are the same. If the pulley Woodruff key is a loose-fit, remove it from the driveshaft and store it with the pulley for safe-keeping (see **Note** at the start of Section) **(see illustration)**.

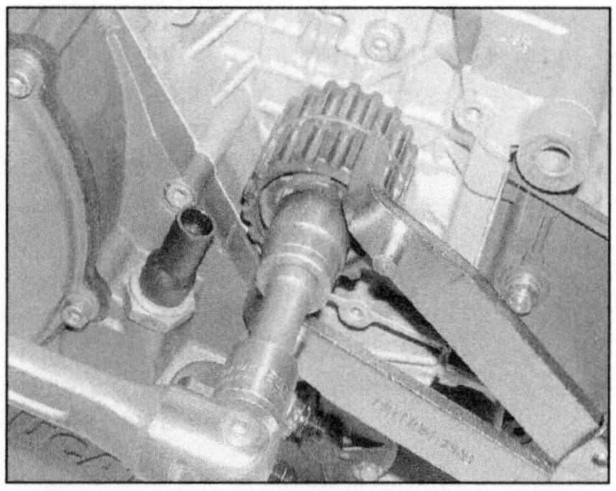

**9.3b Using a clutch holding tool to retain the driveshaft pulley whilst the nut is slackened**

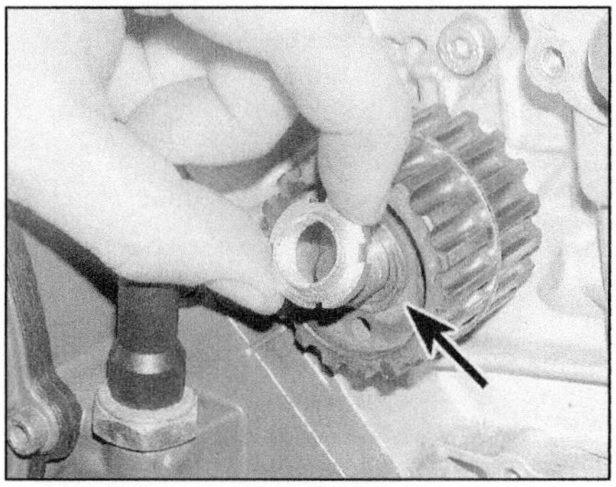

**9.4 Unscrew the nut and remove the washer (arrowed)**

**9.5a Remove the outer (horizontal cylinder) pulley, noting which way around it is fitted . . .**

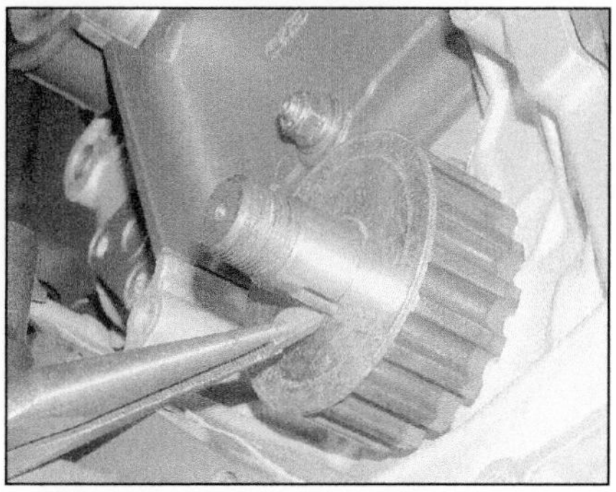

**9.5b . . . then remove the Woodruff key. If an offset key is fitted, make careful note which way around the key is installed**

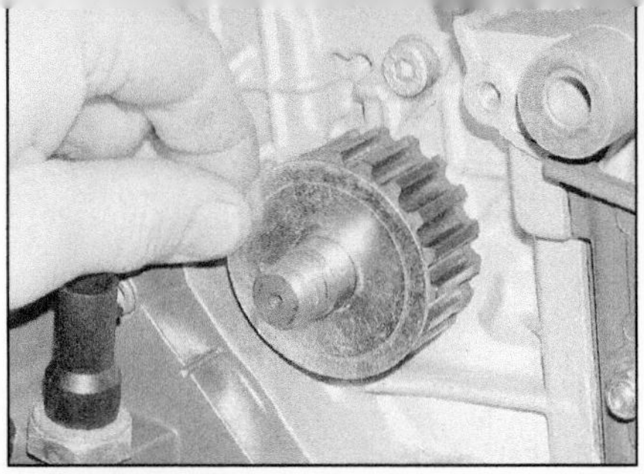
9.6 Slide off the large spacer . . .

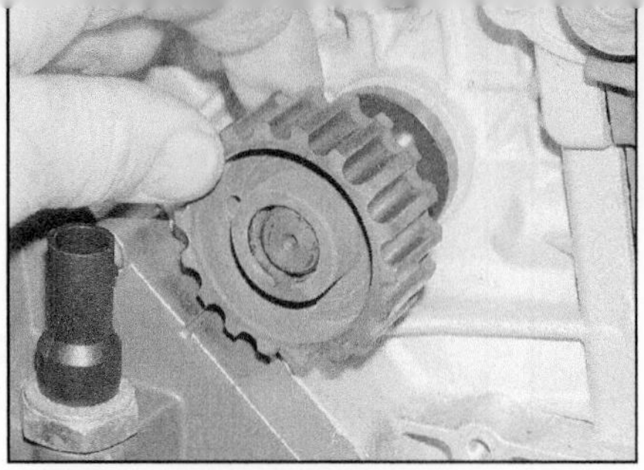
9.7a . . . then remove the inner (vertical cylinder) pulley . . .

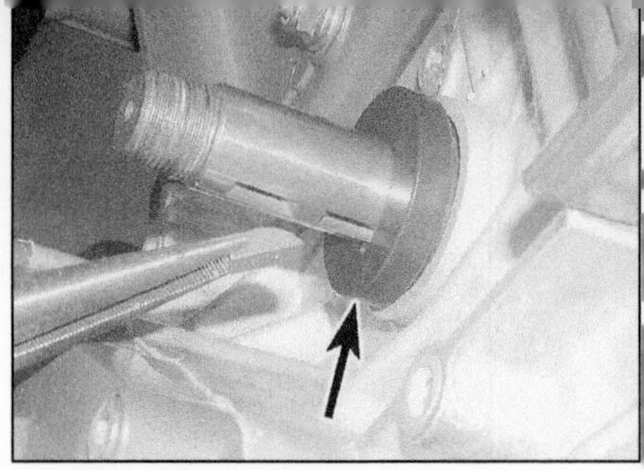
9.7b . . . and Woodruff key and slide off the smaller spacer (arrowed)

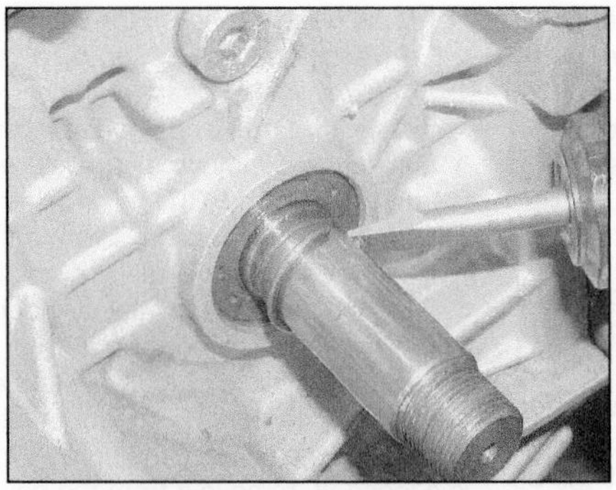
9.9 If necessary, remove the circlip from the timing belt driveshaft

9.11 Retain the camshaft pulley then slacken and remove the retaining nut

**6** Remove the large spacer from the driveshaft **(see illustration)**.

**7** Slide the inner (vertical cylinder) pulley off the driveshaft **(see illustration)**. If the pulley Woodruff key is a loose-fit, remove it from the driveshaft and store it with the pulley for safe-keeping (see **Note** at the start of Section) **(see illustration)**.

**8** Remove the smaller spacer from the driveshaft, noting which way around it is fitted.

**9** If necessary, remove the circlip from the driveshaft **(see illustration)**. Check the driveshaft oil seal for signs of leakage and, if necessary, rectify the problem before installing the pulleys.

## Camshaft pulleys

**Note:** *A special socket and holding tool will be required to slacken/tighten the pulley nut. Alternatives to the Ducati socket and holding tool (88700.5644) are given in the text (see Steps 2 and 3).*

**10** In the absence of the Ducati tool, it will be necessary to fabricate a socket to fit the pulley retaining nut (see Step 2). It will also be necessary to prevent camshaft rotation as the nut is slackened/tightened (see options a or b in Step 3).

**11** Slacken and remove the pulley retaining nut (see Steps 2 and 3) and washer from the camshaft **(see illustration)**. Discard the retaining nut, a new one must be used on installation.

**12** Slide the pulley off the camshaft, noting which way round it is fitted **(see illustration)**. If the pulley Woodruff key is a loose-fit, remove it from the driveshaft and store it with the pulley for safe-keeping (see **Note** at the start of Section).

**13** Remove the pulley spacer from the camshaft.

**14** If necessary, slide out the inner sleeve from the centre of the camshaft oil seal, noting which way around it is fitted **(see illustration)**. Check the camshaft oil seal for signs of leakage and, if necessary, rectify the problem before installing the pulley.

## Tensioner pulley

**15** The tensioner pulley is removed as part of the timing belt removal procedure.

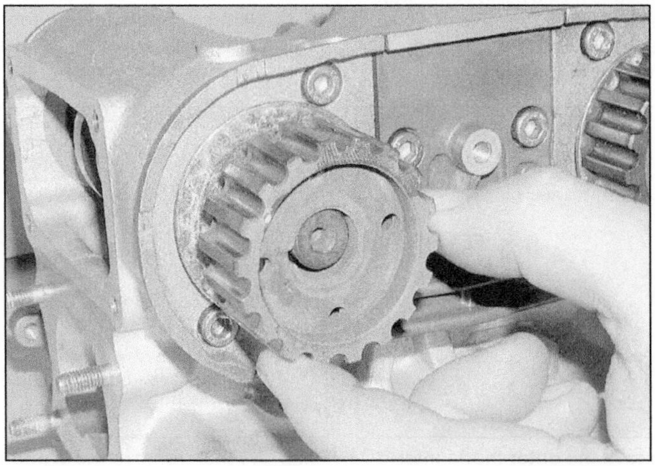
9.12 Remove the camshaft pulley noting which way around it is fitted

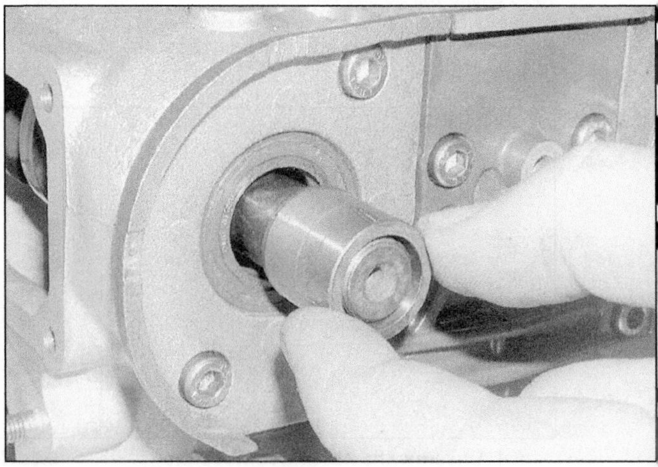
9.14 If necessary, slide the inner sleeve out from the centre of the camshaft oil seal

**9.16 Unscrew the tensioner pulley mounting stud from the side of the head**

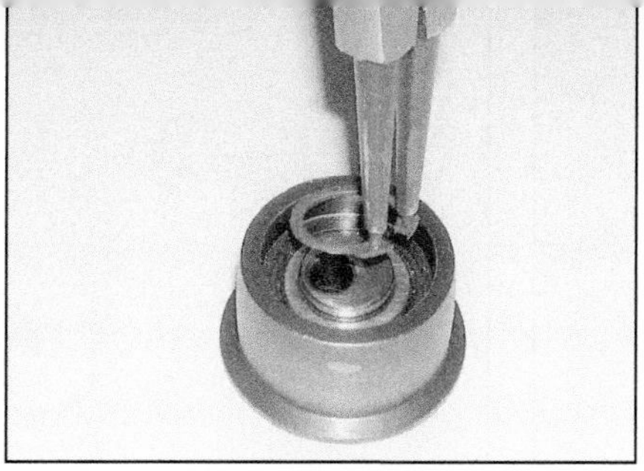

**9.17a To disassemble the pulley, remove the circlip . . .**

**9.17b . . . and slide out the pulley hub**

**16** If necessary, unscrew the mounting stud from the cylinder head **(see illustration)**.

**17** To disassemble the pulley, remove the circlip from the rear of the pulley hub then slide the hub out from the bearing **(see illustrations)**. Remove the circlip from the outside of the pulley then separate the pulley and bearing **(see illustration)**. Check that the pulley bearing inner race rotates freely and easily without any sign of freeplay or roughness; if not renew it.

### Idler pulley

**18** If the tensioner and idler pulleys are to be removed, note the correct fitted location of each one prior to removal. The idler pulley location should be indicated by the 'FISSO or STEADY' marking on the inner cover and the tensioner pulley by the 'MOBILE or MOVABLE' marking; if no marks are present make alignment marks to avoid confusion on installation **(see illustration)**. Using an Allen wrench, unscrew the mounting bolt and remove the pulley assembly from the cylinder head.

**19** To disassemble the pulley, remove the circlip from the end of the mounting bolt then slide the bolt out from the bearing **(see illustration)**. Remove the circlip from the outside of the pulley then separate the pulley and bearing **(see illustration)**. Check the pulley bearing inner race rotates freely and easily without any sign of freeplay or roughness; if not renew it.

## *Installation*

### Driveshaft pulleys

**20** Slide the circlip onto the driveshaft and locate it correctly in the driveshaft groove **(see illustration)**.

**21** Slide the smaller spacer onto the driveshaft, ensuring its inner recess engages correctly with the circlip **(see illustration)**.

**22** Fit the inner Woodruff key to the driveshaft. If an offset Woodruff key is fitted, ensure it is installed the same way around as

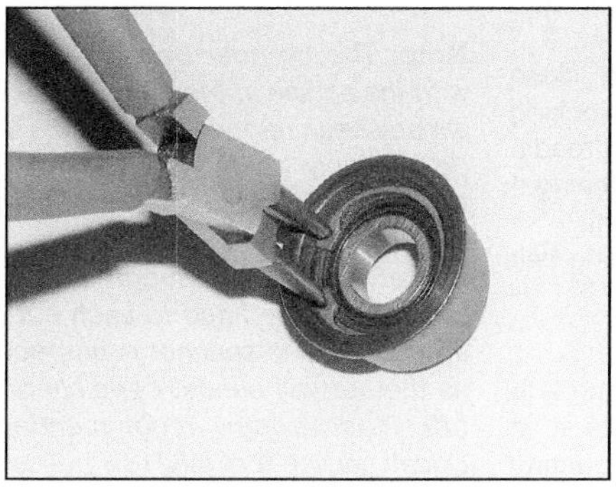

**9.17c The bearing can be separated from the pulley once the circlip has been removed**

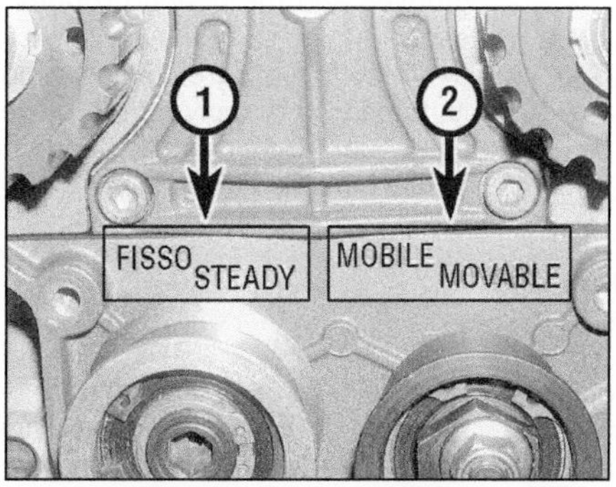


**9.18 The idler pulley location is marked FISSO or STEADY (1) and the tensioner pulley location MOBILE or MOVABLE (2)**

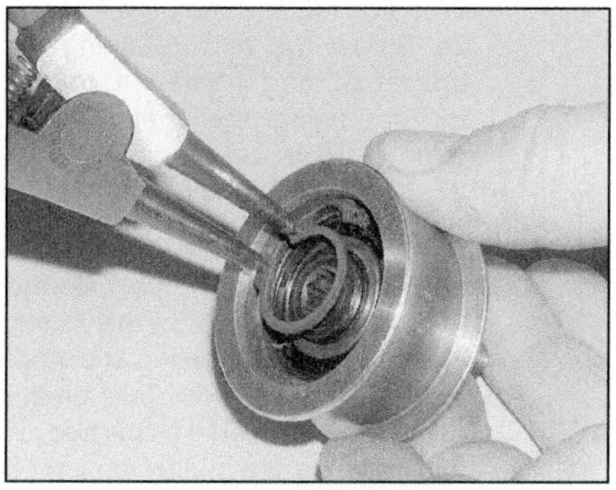

**9.19a Remove the circlip . . .**

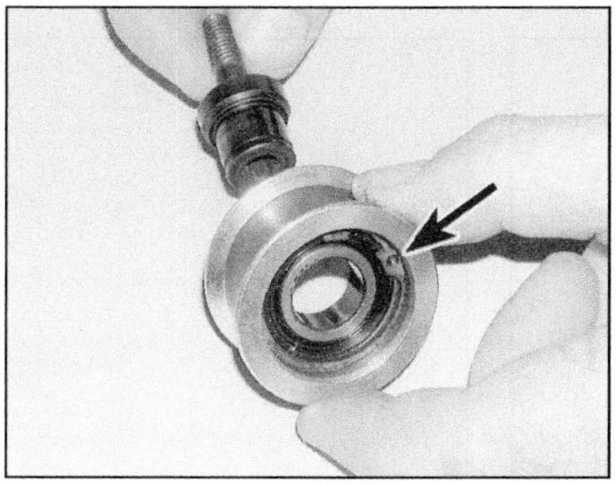

**9.19b . . . and slide out the idler pulley mounting bolt (bearing circlip arrowed)**

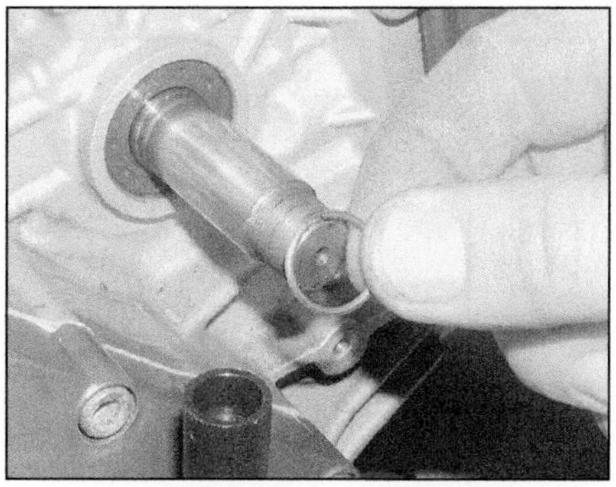

**9.20 Slide on the circlip and locate it in the driveshaft groove**

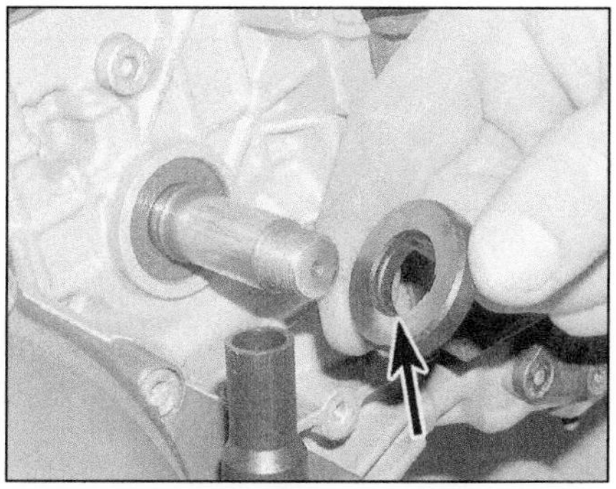

**9.21 Slide on the smaller spacer ensuring it is the correct way around so its inner recess (arrowed) engages with the circlip**

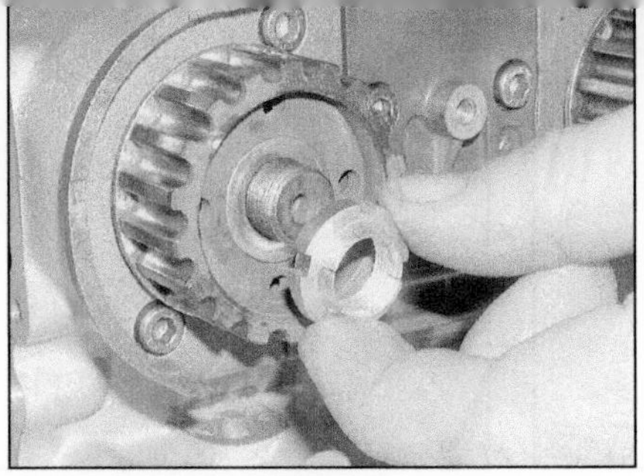

9.31a Fit the washer then thread on the new retaining nut . . .

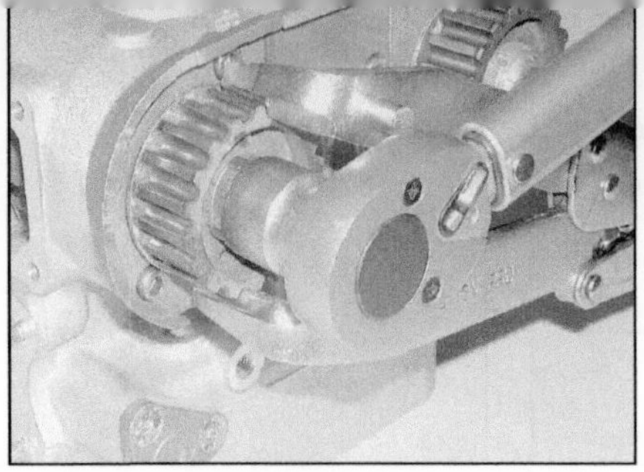

9.31b . . . and tighten it to the specified torque

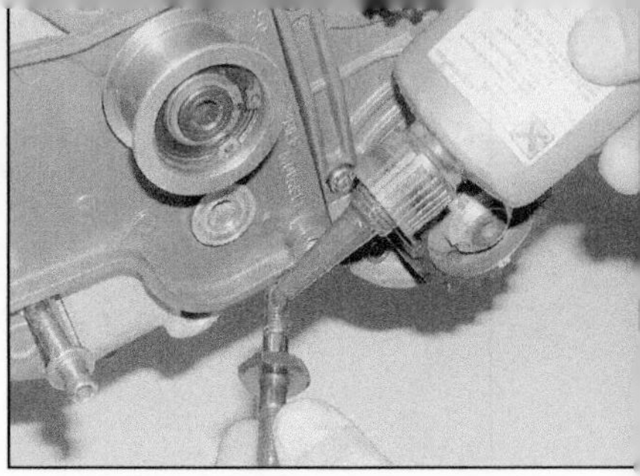

9.34 Apply locking compound to the threads of the tensioner pulley stud

was noted on removal (see **Note** at the start of Section).

**23** Slide on the inner (vertical cylinder) pulley, ensuring its timing mark is facing inwards (towards the crankcase), and engage it with the Woodruff key. If the original pulleys are being fitted, use the marks made to ensure they are correctly positioned.

**24** Slide on the large spacer then fit the outer Woodruff key to the driveshaft. If an offset Woodruff key is fitted, ensure it is installed the same way around as was noted on removal (see **Note** at the start of Section).

**25** Offer up the outer (horizontal cylinder) pulley to the driveshaft, ensuring its timing mark is facing outwards (away from the crankcase). Engage the pulley with the Woodruff key then refit the washer.

**26** Screw the new retaining nut onto the driveshaft and tighten it to the specified torque, using the method employed on removal to prevent rotation.

**27** Install the timing belt(s) (see Section 8).

### Camshaft pulley

**28** Where necessary, lubricate the oil seal lip with a smear of engine oil then carefully slide the inner sleeve into position ensuring its tapered end is facing inwards. Take great care not to damage the oil seal lip as the sleeve is fitted.

**29** Slide on the pulley spacer then fit the Woodruff key to the camshaft. If an offset Woodruff key is fitted, ensure it is installed the same way around as was noted on removal (see **Note** at the start of Section).

**30** Slide the pulley onto the camshaft, ensuring its timing mark is facing outwards, and engage it with the Woodruff key.

**31** Fit the washer to the camshaft then fit the new retaining nut **(see illustration)**. Tighten the nut to the specified torque, using the method employed on removal to prevent rotation **(see illustration)**.

**32** Install the timing belt(s) (see Section 8).

### Tensioner pulley

**33** Where necessary, insert the bearing into the centre of the pulley and secure it in position with the circlip. Insert the hub through from the front of the bearing and secure it in position with the circlip. Ensure both circlips are correctly located in their grooves and the bearing rotates freely and easily.

**34** If the mounting stud was removed, clean its threads and apply a drop of fresh locking compound to its cylinder head end threads. Screw the stud into position and tightening it to the specified torque **(see illustration)**.

**35** The pulley is installed with the timing belt (see Section 8).

### Idler pulley

**36** Where necessary, insert the bearing into the centre of the pulley and secure it in position with the circlip. Insert the mounting bolt through from the rear of the pulley bearing (the bearing circlip must face outwards) and secure it in position with the circlip. Ensure the circlip is correctly located in its groove and the bearing rotates freely and easily.

**37** Clean the threads of the mounting bolt and apply a drop of fresh locking compound to its threads **(see illustration)**. Screw the tensioner bolt into position (the idler pulley location is indicated by the 'FISSO or STEADY' marking on the inner cover) and tightening it to the specified torque **(see illustration)**.

**38** Install the timing belt(s) (see Section 8).

## 10 Cylinder heads – removal and installation

**Note:** *The cylinder heads can be removed with the engine in the frame. If the engine has already been removed, ignore the steps which do not apply.*

**Note:** *Access to the cylinder head nuts is very awkward and it is not possible to attach a socket to them. Although a very thin ring-spanner can be fitted to each nut (the use of an open-ended spanner is not recommended as the nut will almost certainly be rounded-off), it is strongly recommended that the Ducati service tool (88713.1139) is purchased* **(see illustration)**. *The service tool will enable the cylinder head nuts to be easily slackened and, more importantly, correctly tightened on installation.*

9.37a Apply locking compound to the threads of the idler pulley mounting bolt . . .

9.37b . . . then fit the pulley and tighten the bolt to the specified torque

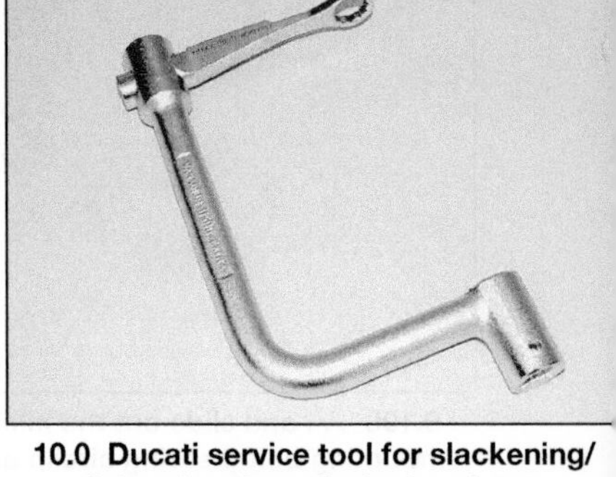

10.0 Ducati service tool for slackening/tightening the cylinder head nuts

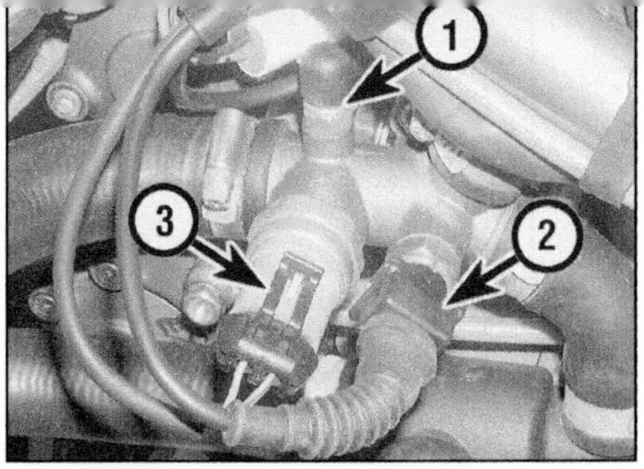


**10.5 Disconnect the wiring connectors from the coolant temperature sensors (1 and 2) and switch (3)**

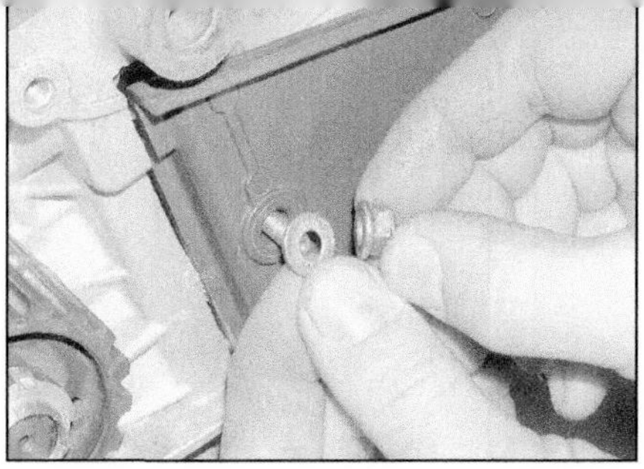

**10.9a Unscrew the retaining nut and washer . . .**

**10.9b . . . and remove the timing belt inner cover from the cylinder head**

***Caution: The engine must be completely cool before beginning this procedure or the cylinder head may become warped.***

> **HAYNES HiNT** ***The cylinder head nuts are likely to be corroded due to their exposed location, making them difficult to slacken. It is advisable to liberally spray each nut with penetrating fluid and allow it to soak in, preferably overnight, before attempting removal.***

## *Horizontal cylinder head*

### Removal

**1** Remove the fairing lower and inner panels (see Chapter 8).

**2** Remove the oil cooler (where fitted) (see Section 27).

**3** Remove the radiator and coolant overflow tank (see Chapter 3). Release the retaining clip and disconnect the top hose from the cylinder head.

**4** Remove the fuel tank, airbox and throttle body assembly (see Chapter 4). Also remove the exhaust system front downpipe (see Chapter 4).

**5** Disconnect the wiring connectors from the coolant temperature sensor, fan switch and temperature gauge sender which are fitted to the coolant outlet on the left-hand side of the cylinder head **(see illustration)**.

**6** Release the clip securing the thermostat hose and the vertical cylinder hose to the union on the left-hand side of the cylinder head.

**7** Remove the horizontal cylinder timing belt (see Section 8). **Note:** *There is no need to disturb the vertical cylinder timing belt.*

**8** Remove the timing belt tensioner and idler pulleys (see Section 9) noting the correct fitted location of each pulley.

**9** Unscrew the retaining nut and washer and remove the timing belt inner cover from the cylinder head **(see illustrations)**.

**10** Wipe clean the area around the oil hose union on the left-hand side of the cylinder head. Unscrew the banjo bolt and separate the hose from the head **(see illustration)**. Plug the hose end or wrap a plastic bag tightly around the hose to prevent dirt from entering the system. Discard the sealing washers, as new ones must be used on installation.

**11** Working in a criss-cross sequence, evenly and progressively slacken the four cylinder head nuts (see **Note** at the start of Section) **(see illustration)**. Once all nuts are loose, remove them along with their washers.

**12** Free the cylinder head from the barrel. If it is stuck, tap around the joint faces of the cylinder head with a soft-faced mallet to free the head. Don't attempt to free the head by inserting a screwdriver between the head and barrel – you'll damage the sealing surfaces. ***Caution: If the cylinder barrel is not being removed, great care must be taken not to disturb the cylinder base gasket as the head is freed from the barrel. If the base gasket joint is disturbed, the barrel must be removed and the gasket renewed before the cylinder head is installed. Otherwise there is a risk of oil leakage from the base gasket joint.***

**13** Lift the cylinder head off the engine.

**14** Remove the old head gasket and discard it. If they are loose, remove the cylinder head locating dowels and store them with the head for safe-keeping.

**15** Check the cylinder head gasket and the mating surfaces on the cylinder head and barrel for signs of leakage, which could indicate warpage. Check the flatness of the head as described in Section 11.

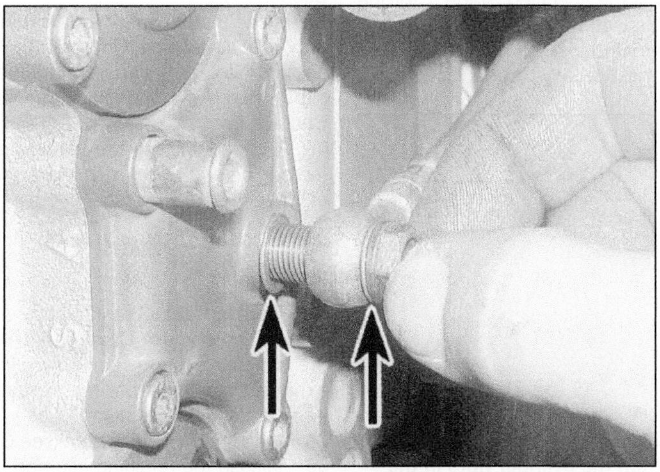

**10.10 Unscrew the oil hose banjo bolt and recover the sealing washers (arrowed)**

**10.11 Using the Ducati service tool to slacken the cylinder head nuts**

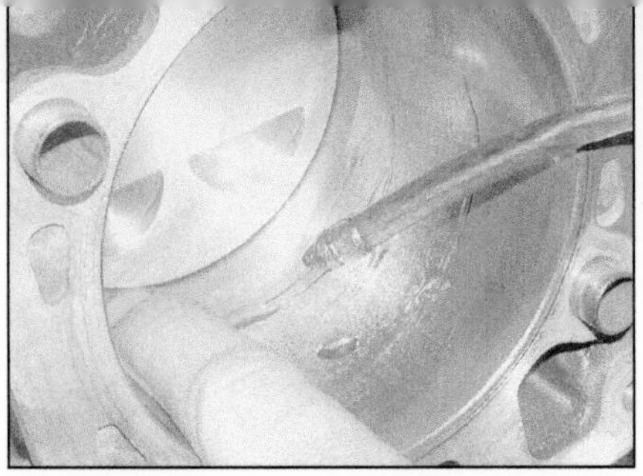

**10.19 Prior to installing the head, lubricate the cylinder bore with clean engine oil**

**10.20a Cylinder head gasket must be positioned so that the side with the most coolant holes (arrowed) is on the exhaust side**

**10.20b Ensure the gasket is fitted the correct way around and seat it on the locating dowels (arrowed)**

## *Installation*

**16** Prior to installation, ensure the cylinder head studs are in good condition. To renew a stud, screw two nuts onto the upper end of the stud and lock them securely together; the nuts can then be used to unscrew the stud **(see illustrations 13.13a to c)**. Remove the nuts and install them on the new stud. Alternatively, a stud removal tool can be used – see *Tools and Workshop Tips* in the Reference section at the end of this manual. When fitting a new stud, apply a drop of locking compound to the threads at the crankcase end then fit the stud to the crankcase and tighten it to the specified torque. Unlock the nuts and remove them from the stud.

**17** If the studs are in good condition, ensure they are all securely screwed into the crankcase. If any stud is loose, remove it and clean its threads. Apply a drop of locking compound to the crankcase end threads then refit the stud and tighten it to the specified torque, using two nuts locked together.

**18** Clean all traces of old gasket material from the cylinder head and barrel. If a scraper is used, take care not to scratch or gouge the soft aluminium. Also ensure that none of the gasket material is allowed to fall into the cylinder bores, oil passages or water jacket.

**19** Ensure the cylinder head and block mating surfaces are clean and fit the locating dowels to the cylinder barrel (if removed). Apply a smear of engine oil to the surface of the cylinder bore **(see illustration)**.

**20** Note that the cylinder head gasket is not symmetrical – there are more coolant flow holes on one side of the gasket than the other. Fit the gasket to the barrel ensuring its ALTO (TOP) marking (where present) is facing upwards and the side with the greater number of coolant flow holes is positioned on the exhaust side **(see illustrations)**.

***Caution: Failure to position the cylinder head gasket correctly could result in serious engine damage.***

**21** Lubricate the stud threads with a smear of molybdenum disulphide grease then manoeuvre the cylinder head into position and locate it correctly on the dowels.

**22** Fit the washers to the studs ensuring their flat edges are facing inwards **(see illustration)**.

**23** Lubricate the threads and contact faces of the cylinder head nuts with a smear of molybdenum disulphide grease. Screw the nuts onto the studs and tighten them by hand.

**24** Using the Ducati service tool (88713.1139), working in a criss-cross pattern tighten the cylinder head nuts evenly and progressively to the specified Stage 1 torque setting **(see illustration)**.

**25** Once the cylinder head nuts have been tightened to the Stage 1 torque, go around again in a criss-cross sequence and tighten them to the Stage 2 torque setting.

**26** Finally go around again, in a criss-cross pattern, and tighten the cylinder head nuts to the specified Stage 3 torque setting.

**27** Position a new sealing washer on each side of the oil hose union and screw in the banjo bolt. Ensure the end fitting is correctly positioned in relation to the cylinder head then tighten the banjo bolt to the specified torque.

**28** Fit the timing belt inner cover to the cylinder head and install its washer and retaining nut, tightening it securely.

**29** Fit the timing belt tensioner and idler pulleys (see Section 9).

**30** Install the timing belt (see Section 8).

**31** Reconnect the coolant hoses to the outlet on the left-hand side of the cylinder head, securing them in position with the retaining clips.

**32** Reconnect the wiring connectors to the coolant temperature sensor, fan switch and temperature gauge sender on the coolant outlet union.

**33** Install the exhaust system, throttle body assembly, airbox and fuel tank (see Chapter 4).

**34** Install the oil cooler (where fitted) (see Section 27).

**35** Install the coolant overflow tank, radiator and top hose (see Chapter 3). Ensure all coolant hoses are securely retained by their clips then refill the cooling system (see Chapter 1).

**36** Prior to installing the fairing panels, start the engine and check that there are no signs of fuel/coolant/oil leakage.

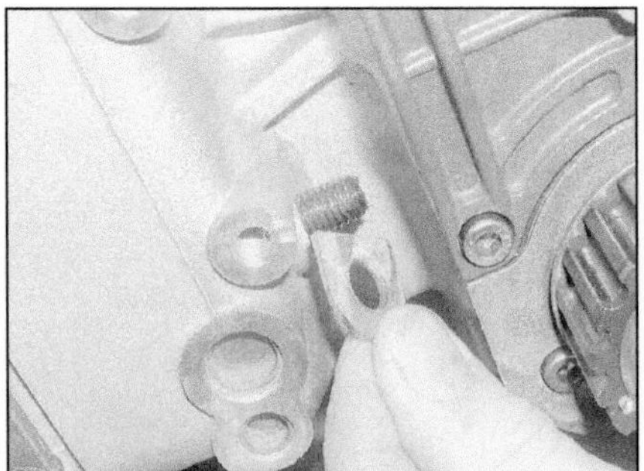

**10.22 Fit the washers to the studs ensuring their flat edges are facing inwards**

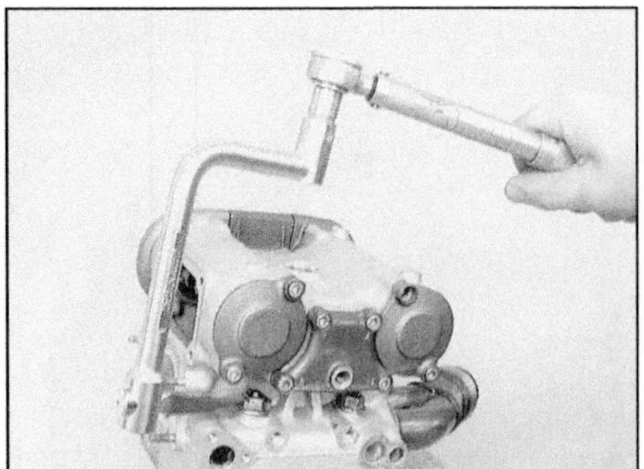

**10.24 Tighten the cylinder nuts in the sequence given in the text**

## *Vertical cylinder head*

### Removal

**37** Remove the fuel tank, airbox and throttle body assembly (see Chapter 4). Also remove the exhaust system rear downpipe and the exhaust manifold from the vertical cylinder (see Chapter 4).

**38** Drain the cooling system (see Chapter 1).

**39** Release the retaining clip and disconnect the coolant hose from the union on the left-hand side of the cylinder head.

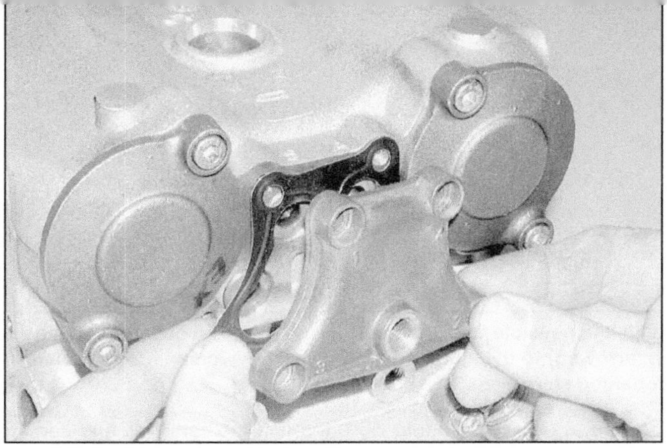

11.7 Remove the side covers and gaskets from the cylinder head

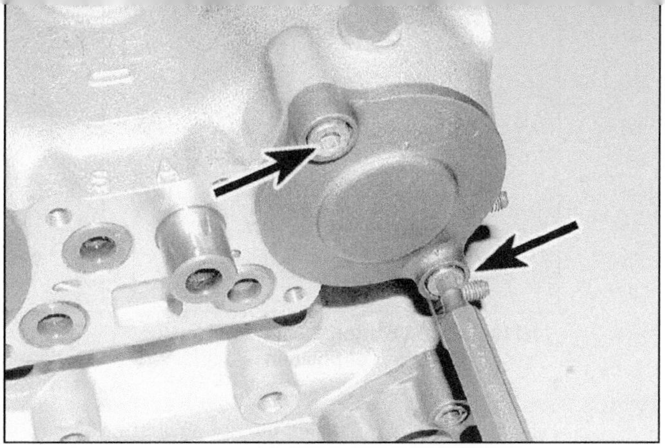

11.9 Unscrew the bolts (arrowed) and remove the left-hand end cap from the head

**40** Remove the timing belts (see Section 8).
**41** Remove the cylinder head as described in Steps 8 to 15.

### Installation

**42** Install the cylinder head as described in Steps 16 to 29.
**43** Install the timing belts (see Section 8).
**44** Reconnect the coolant hose to the head outlet and secure it in position with the retaining clip. Refill the cooling system (see Chapter 1).
**45** Install the exhaust system, throttle body assembly, airbox and fuel tank (see Chapter 4).

## 11 Cylinder heads, camshafts and valves – disassembly, inspection and reassembly

**Note:** *The following procedure is described with the cylinder head removed from the engine. However, the camshafts and rocker arms can be removed with the engine in the frame – this is necessary to enable the valve clearances to be adjusted. If the closing (lower) rocker arm is being removed, ensure precautions are taken to prevent the valve dropping into the cylinder. See 'Valve clearances – check and adjustment' in Chapter 1 for details.*

### *Disassembly*

**Note:** *Disassemble the cylinder heads separately to avoid interchanging components. Before proceeding, arrange to label and store the camshafts, rocker arms, shafts and valves along with their related components in such a way that they can be returned to their original locations without getting mixed up. Obtain a container which is divided into compartments and label each compartment with the identity of the valve which will be stored in it (i.e. intake or exhaust side, left- or right-hand side valve). Alternatively, labelled plastic bags will do just as well.*

**1** Remove the cylinder head from the engine (see Section 10).
**2** Undo the retaining nuts and remove the intake and exhaust manifolds from the cylinder head. Discard the gaskets; new ones will be needed on installation.
**3** If the vertical cylinder head is being overhauled, undo the retaining screws and remove the coolant outlet union from the left-hand side of the head and the blanking cover from the right-hand side of the head. Discard the sealing rings; new ones will be needed for installation.
**4** If the horizontal cylinder head is being overhauled, undo the retaining screw and remove the outer section of the coolant union from the left-hand side of the cylinder, then unbolt the inner section of the union from the cylinder head. Also unbolt the blanking cover from the right-hand side of the head. Discard all sealing rings; new ones will be needed for installation.
**5** Remove the camshaft pulleys and slide the inner sleeve out from the centre of each camshaft oil seal (see Section 9). **Note:** *If the camshaft and right-hand end cap are not being separated for bearing or oil seal renewal, there is no need to remove the camshaft pulley. The camshaft, timing belt pulley and right-hand end cap can then be removed/installed as an assembly.*
**6** Undo the retaining bolts and remove the intake and exhaust valve covers from the cylinder head. Discard the gaskets (where fitted – not all engines have them); new ones will be needed on installation.
**7** Undo the retaining bolts and remove the left- and right-hand side covers from the cylinder head to gain access to the rocker arm shafts. Discard the cover gaskets; new ones will be needed on installation **(see illustration)**. If the horizontal head is being overhauled, note the correct fitted location of the radiator locating peg when removing the covers.
**8** To minimise the risk of interchanging components, it is strongly recommended that the intake and exhaust camshaft, rocker arms and valves are treated as separate assemblies. Remove all the intake side components first and store them away safely before removing any of the exhaust side components (or vice-versa). Removal is as follows.
**9** Make identification markings between the camshaft left-hand end cap and the head to ensure it is installed in its original location (both intake and exhaust caps are the same). Undo the retaining bolts then ease the cap out of position and remove it from the cylinder head **(see illustration)**. Discard the cap sealing ring; a new one should be used on installation.
**10** Each rocker arm has its own rocker shaft and all rocker shafts are equipped with an M5 thread. The thread is provided to enable a service tool to be screwed into the shaft to draw the shaft out from the head. In the absence of Ducati service tool (88713.0862), obtain an M5 bolt, nut, washer and a socket to use a drawbolt. Screw the nut onto the bolt and fit the washer.
**11** Fit the socket to the M5 bolt then screw the bolt securely into the end of the opening (upper) rocker arm shaft **(see illustration)**. Draw the rocker arm shaft out from the

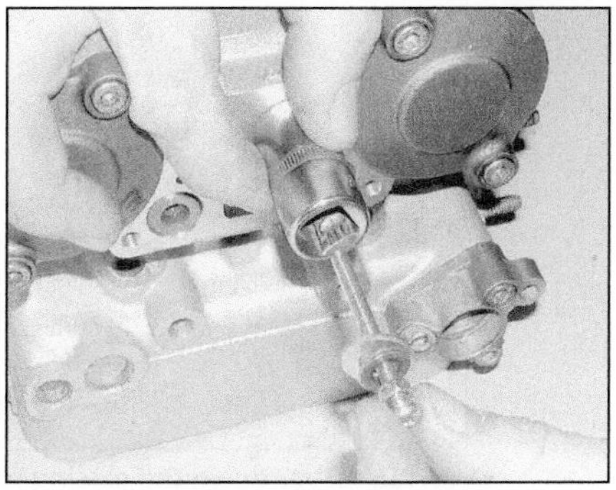

11.11a Fit the socket, bolt, nut and washer arrangement to the rocker shaft . . .

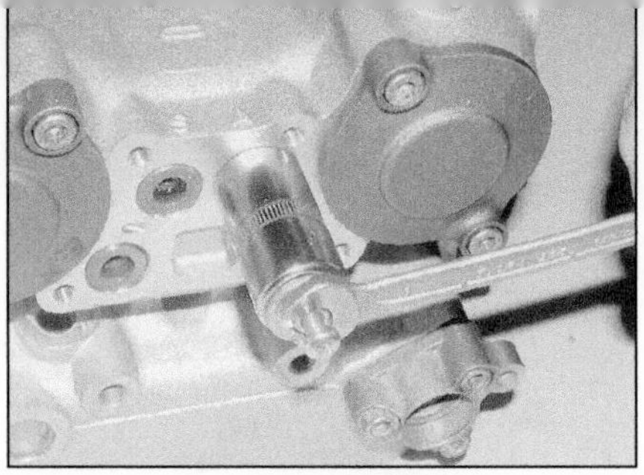

**11.11b . . . and tighten the nut to draw the shaft out of position . . .**

**11.11c . . . until it is possible to slide the rocker arm (arrowed) to the side and remove the opening shim from the valve**

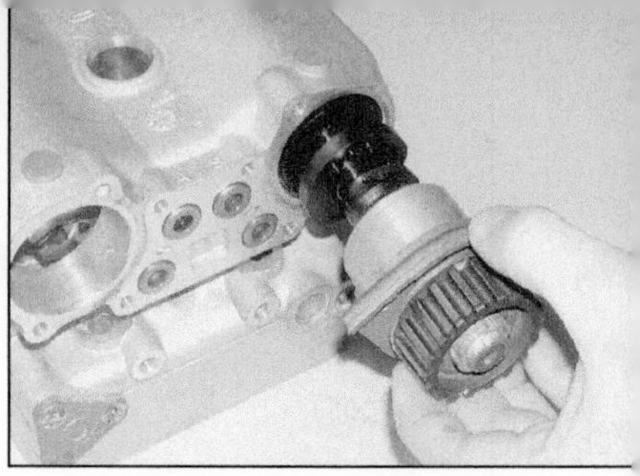

**11.13a The camshaft can be removed complete with pulley**

cylinder head, by tightening the nut against the washer and socket, until it is possible to move the opening rocker arm to the side of the valve **(see illustration)**. Position the rocker arm clear of the valve and remove the opening shim from the top of the valve **(see illustration)**.

**12** Repeat the operation on the other opening (upper) rocker arm and remove the other opening shim.

**13** With both opening shims removed, slacken and remove the bolts securing the camshaft right-hand end cap to the cylinder head. Ease the cap out of position and remove it from the cylinder head, complete with the camshaft **(see illustration)**. Discard the cap sealing ring; a new one should be used on installation. Note that all the camshafts are different and are not interchangeable. The camshaft identification marks are cast on the shafts; on the horizontal cylinder head the intake camshaft is marked OA and the exhaust camshaft OS and on the vertical cylinder head the intake camshaft is marked VA and the exhaust camshaft VS (see Note in Section 1) **(see illustration)**.

**14** With the camshaft removed, slide the rocker arm shafts out of position and remove both opening rocker arms **(see illustrations)**. Note that the right and left rocker arms are different and are not interchangeable.

**15** To remove the valve, insert a screwdriver through the camshaft end cap aperture anc carefully lever the closing (lower) rocker arn down to relieve the spring pressure from the valve closing shim. Slide the closing shin down the valve stem and remove the shin retaining half-rings **(see illustration)**. With both half-rings removed, slowly release the rocker arm and slide the closing shim from the end of the valve **(see illustration)**. The valve can then be withdrawn from its guide. Discarc the shim retaining half-rings; new ones mus be used on installation.

**16** To remove a closing (lower) rocker arm with the valve removed, first note the correc fitted location of the spring behind the cylinder head lug **(see illustration)**. Fit the

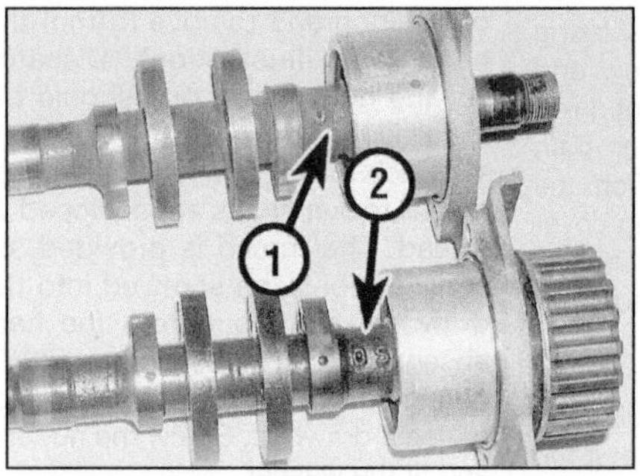


**11.13b Horizontal cylinder head camshaft identification markings. Intake camshaft is marked OA (1) and the exhaust camshaft OS (2)**

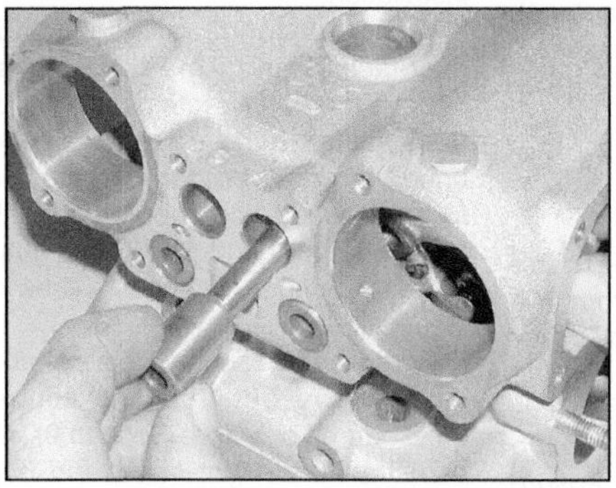

**11.14a Withdraw the rocker arm shaft . . .**

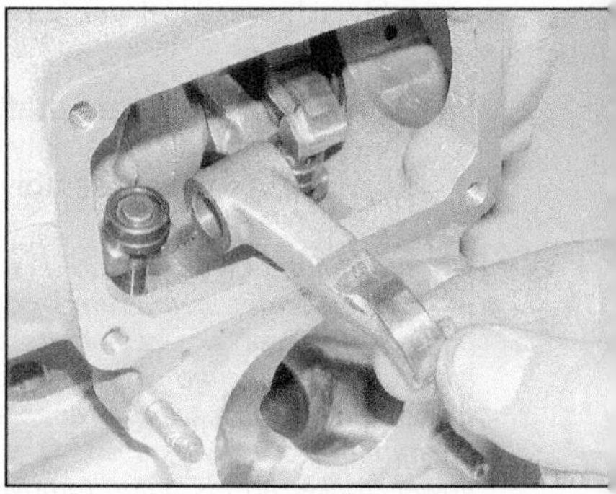

**11.14b . . . and remove the opening rocker arm**

**11.15a Lever down the closing rocker arm then remove the closing shim half-rings from the valve**

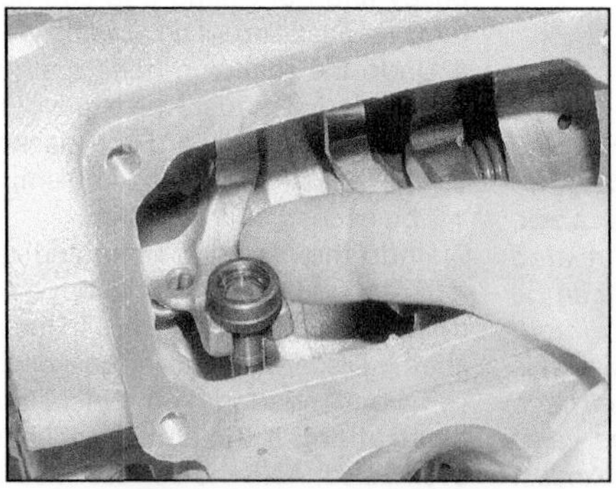

**11.15b With the half-rings removed, slowly release the rocker arm and slide off the closing shim from the valve**

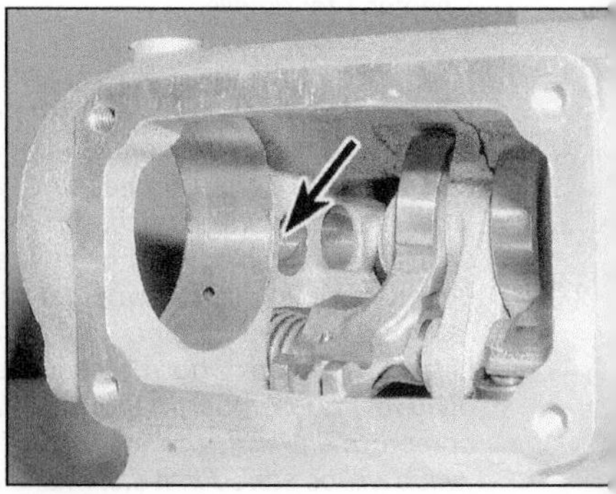

**11.16a The closing rocker arm spring end is located behind the cylinder head lug (arrowed)**

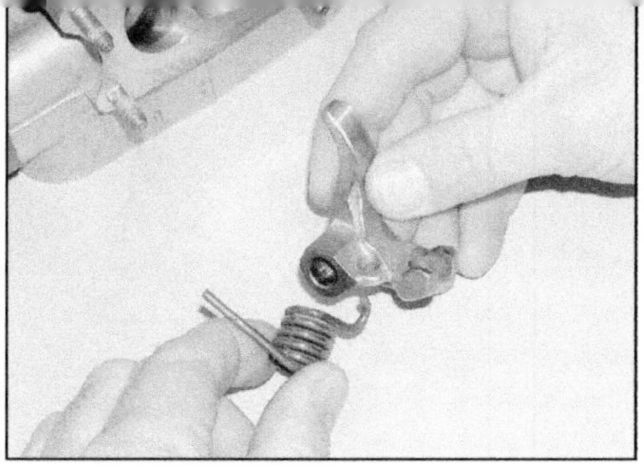

**11.16b Withdraw the rocker shaft then remove the closing rocker arm and spring assembly**

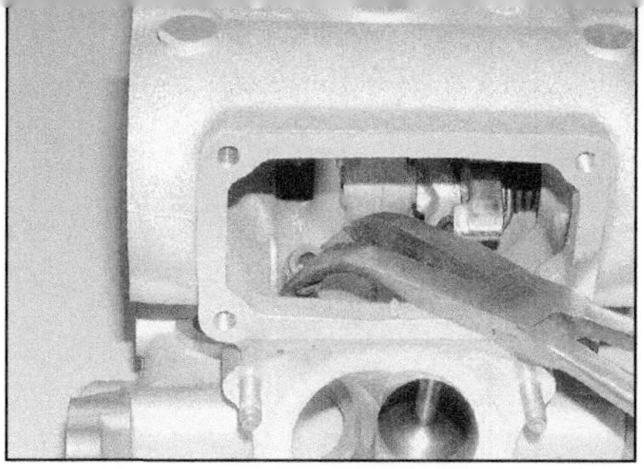

**11.17 Pull the valve stem seal off the valve guide**

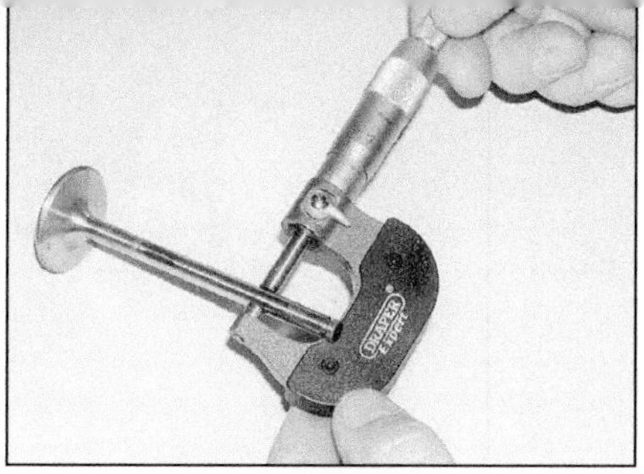

**11.23 Using a micrometer to measure valve stem diameter**

socket and bolt assembly to the rocker arm shaft and draw the shaft out from the cylinder head whilst retaining the rocker arm. Once the shaft is free, ease the closing rocker arm and spring out from the head, taking care to relieve the spring tension gently **(see illustration)**. Remove the drawbolt arrangement from the shaft and store the rocker arm, spring and shaft with its respective shim. Note that the right and left rocker arms are different and are not interchangeable.

**17** Pull the valve stem seal off the guide – a new one must be installed on reassembly **(see illustration)**.

## *Inspection*

### Cylinder head

**18** Thoroughly clean the cylinder head and remove any carbon deposits from the valve heads and combustion chamber area. Inspect the head very carefully for cracks and other damage. If cracks are found, a new head will be required.

**19** Using a precision straight-edge and a feeler gauge, check the head gasket mating surface for warpage. Refer to Section 3 of *Tools and Workshop Tips* in the *Reference* section for details of how to use the straight-edge. If there are signs of warpage or the surface is damaged, seek the advice of an engineering specialist. Ducati do not specify a limit for gasket face distortion but as a guide, anything above 0.03 mm is excessive.

**20** Examine the valve seats in the combustion chamber. If they are pitted, cracked or burned, the head will require work beyond the scope of the home mechanic. Measure the valve seat width and compare it to the figure given in the Specifications. Replacement valve seats are available for this engine but renewal should be entrusted to a Ducati dealer or suitably equipped engineering specialist.

### Valves and valve guides

**21** Carefully inspect each valve face for cracks, pits and burned spots. Check the valve stem and the closing shim half-ring groove area for cracks. Rotate the valve and check for any obvious indication that it is bent – if vee-blocks and a dial gauge are available, measure valve stem and head runout. Check the end of the stem for pitting and excessive wear. The presence of any of the above conditions indicates the need for valve servicing. The closing shim half-rings must be renewed, regardless of their apparent condition.

**22** Clean the valve guides to remove any carbon build-up, then measure the inside diameters of the guides (at both ends and the centre of the guide) with a small hole gauge and micrometer. These measurements, along with the valve stem diameter measurements, will enable you to compute the valve stem-to-guide clearance.

**23** Measure the valve stem diameter **(see illustration)**. By subtracting the stem diameter from the valve guide bore diameter, the valve stem-to-guide clearance is obtained. If the stem-to-guide clearance is greater than that listed in the specifications, the valves and guides must be renewed as a set by a Ducati dealer or suitably equipped engineering specialist.

### Rocker arms and shafts

**24** Taking care not to interchange components, inspect the rocker arms, rocker arm shafts and the closing rocker arm springs. If in any doubt about their condition replace them with new components. Measure the rocker arm inside diameter and the shaft outside diameter (at its point of contact with the rocker arm) **(see illustration)**. Subtract one from the other to obtain the rocker arm-to-shaft clearance. If in excess of the service limit the arm and shaft should be renewed.

### Camshaft

**25** Examine the camshaft lobe surfaces and the corresponding contact points on the rocker arms. All should be free from scratches, cracks or signs of excessive wear. Check the areas of the camshaft which locate in the ball bearings and needle roller bearings; there should be no sign of wear or scoring at these points. Make sure the oilways in the camshaft are clear. If vee-blocks and a dial gauge are available, measure the camshaft runout. Renew the camshaft if worn or damaged.

### Camshaft bearings

**26** Check the bearings in each camshaft end cap. The right-hand bearing inner races should rotate freely and easily without any sign of roughness. Renew any bearing which shows signs of wear or damage. It is recommended that the oil seals in the right-hand caps are renewed regardless of their apparent condition.

**27** To overhaul the right-hand end cap, first note the correct fitted location of the oil seal in the housing then carefully lever the seal out of position and discard it **(see illustration)**. Extract the circlip from the inside of the cap then press/tap the bearing out of position

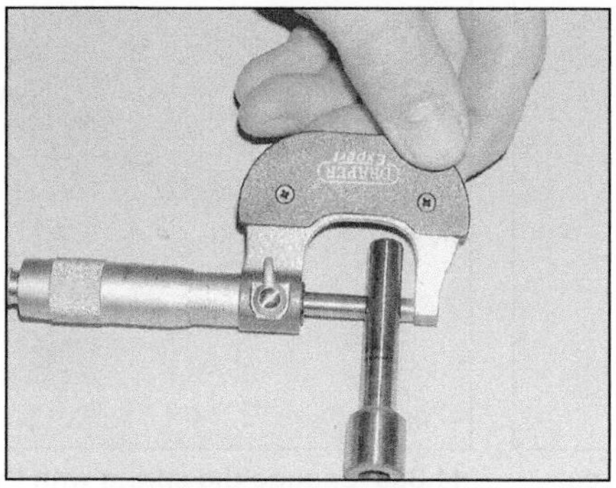

**11.24 Measuring rocker arm shaft diameter with a micrometer**

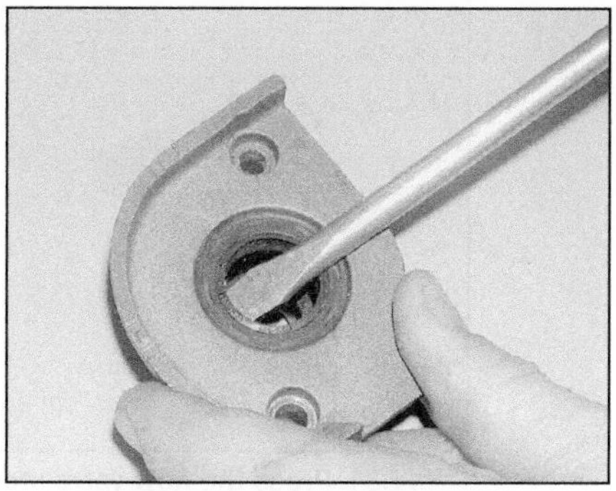

**11.27a Lever out the camshaft oil seal using a flat-bladed screwdriver**

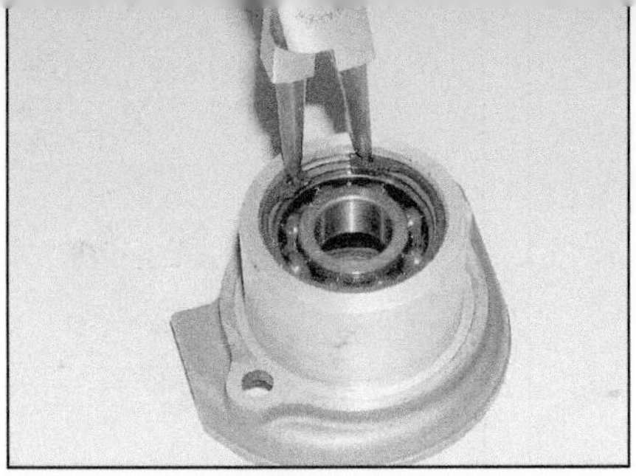

11.27b Remove the circlip to allow the bearing to removed from the right-hand end cap

11.27c Tap/press the new camshaft seal into the end cap . . .

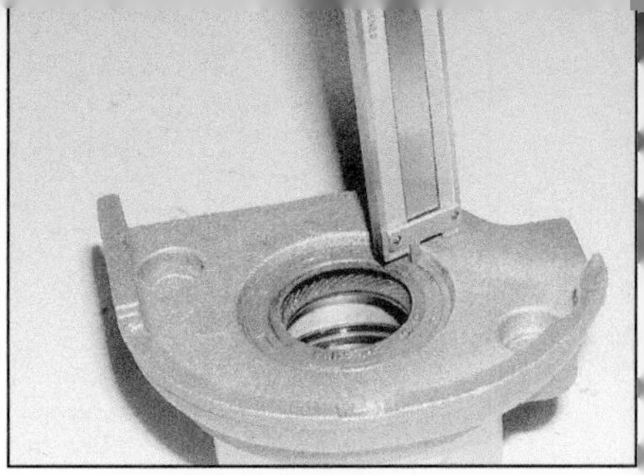

11.27d . . . and position it so the outer edge of the seal is 2 mm in from the end cap surface

**(see illustration)**. Clean the end cap bore and lubricate it with a smear of engine oil. Support the outer face of the cap and tap/press the new bearing squarely into position, using a socket which bears only on the bearing's outer race. Secure the bearing in position with the circlip, making sure it is correctly located in its groove. Turn the end cap over and fit the new oil seal, ensuring its sealing lip is facing inwards (towards the bearing). Press the seal squarely into position, using a socket which bears only on the hard outer edge of the seal, until its outer face is recessed 2 mm in from the end cap outer face **(see illustrations)**.

**28** To overhaul the left-hand end cap, remove the circlip from inside the cap then extract the bearing and oil seal **(see illustration)**. If the bearing is a tight-fit, a slide-hammer and bearing puller attachment will be required to removed it. Clean the end cap bore and lubricate it with a smear of engine oil. Fit the new oil seal, ensuring its sealing lip is facing away from the sealed end of the cap, and press it squarely into position using a socket which bears only on the hard outer edge of the seal. Tap/press the new bearing squarely into position, using a socket which bears only on the bearing's outer race, and secure the bearing in position with the circlip. Ensure the circlip is correctly located in its groove.

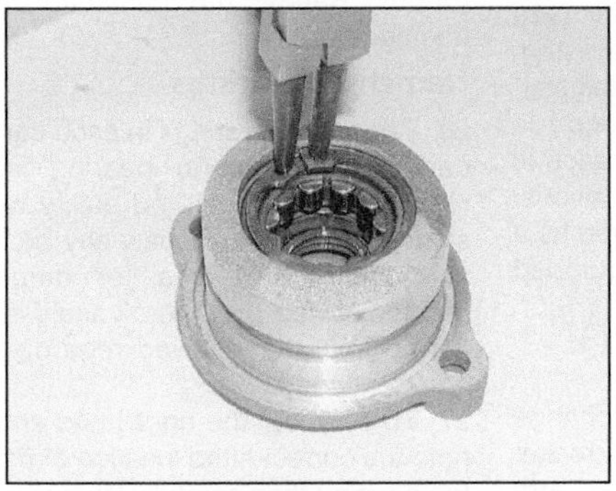

11.28 Left-hand end cap bearing is retained by a circlip

## *Reassembly*

**29** Before installing the valves in the head, they should be ground in (lapped) to ensure a positive seal between the valves and seats. This procedure requires coarse and fine valve grinding compound and a valve grinding tool. If a grinding tool is not available, a piece of rubber or plastic hose can be slipped over the valve stem (after the valve has been installed in the guide) and used to turn the valve.

**30** Apply a small amount of coarse grinding compound to the valve face, then slip the valve into the guide. **Note:** *Make sure each valve is installed in its correct guide and be careful not to get any grinding compound on the valve stem.*

**31** Attach the grinding tool (or hose) to the valve and rotate the tool between the palms of your hands. Use a back-and-forth motion (as though rubbing your hands together) rather than a circular motion (i.e. so that the valve rotates alternately clockwise and anti-clockwise rather than in one direction only). Lift the valve off the seat and turn it at regular intervals to distribute the grinding compound properly. Continue the grinding procedure until the valve face and seat contact area is of uniform width and unbroken around the entire circumference of the valve face and seat.

**32** Carefully remove the valve from the guide and wipe off all traces of grinding compound. Use solvent to clean the valve and wipe the seat area thoroughly with a solvent soaked cloth.

**33** Repeat the procedure with fine valve grinding compound, then repeat the entire procedure for the other valves.

**34** Lubricate the new valve stem oil seal with clean engine oil then press it squarely onto the top of the valve guide **(see illustration)**. Ensure the seal is correctly fitted before proceeding.

**35** Lubricate the closing (lower) rocker arm bore and shaft with clean engine oil. Engage the hooked end of the spring with the hole in the closing rocker arm then manoeuvre the assembly into position in the cylinder head **(see illustration)**. Ensure the spring end is correctly located behind the cylinder head lug, then align the rocker arm with the cylinder head bore and insert the rocker arm shaft, pressing it fully into position **(see illustration)**.

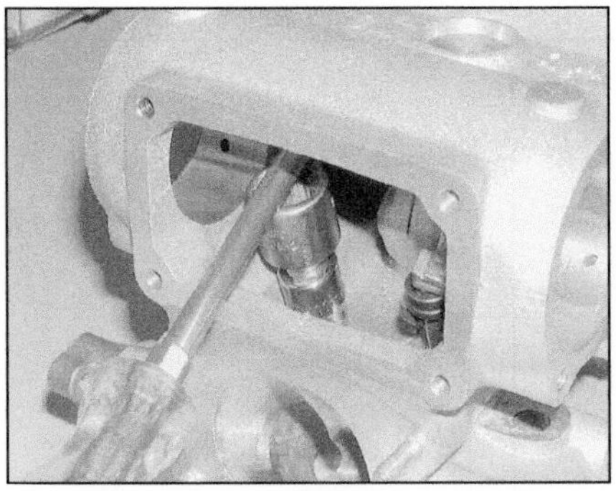

11.34 Press the new valve stem seal squarely onto the guide using a socket

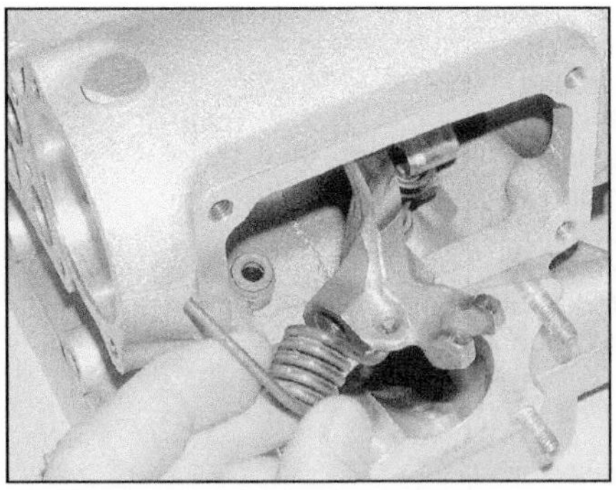

11.35a Engage the spring with the closing rocker arm then manoeuvre the assembly into position

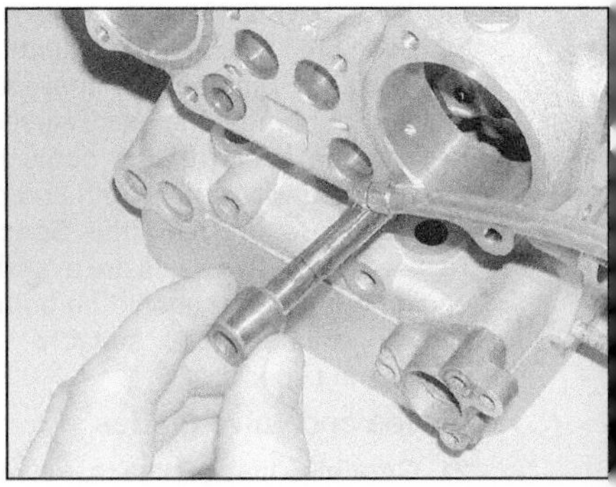

11.35b Lubricate the rocker arm shaft with clean engine oil then insert the shaft

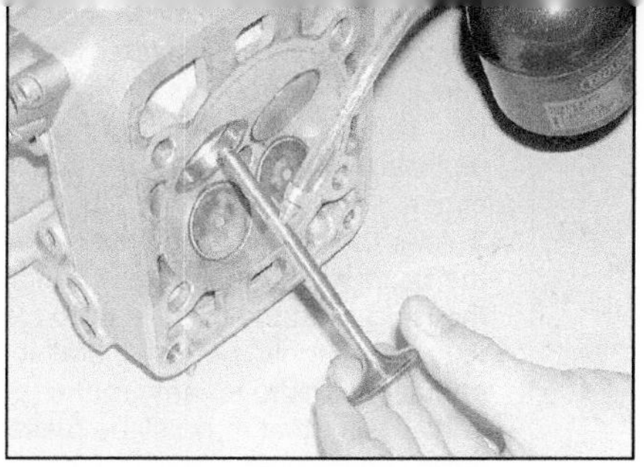


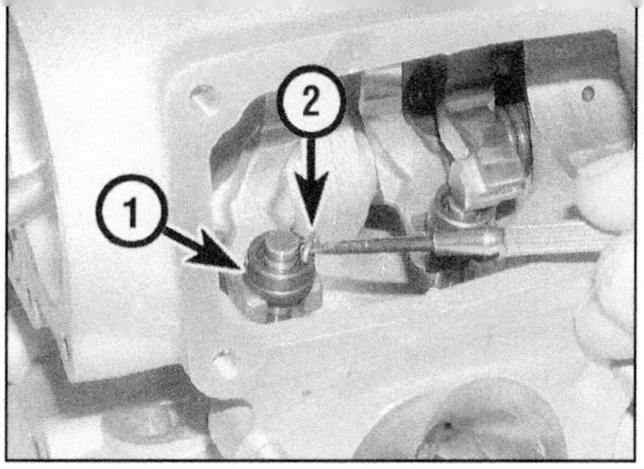

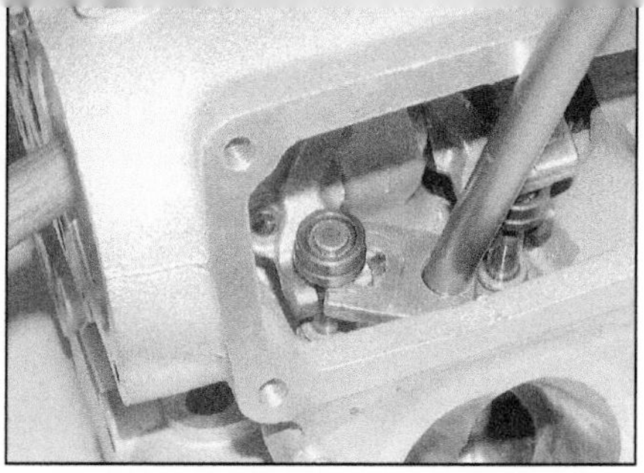

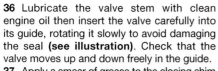

**11.36 Lubricate the valve stem with clean engine oil and insert the valve into its guide**

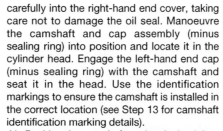

**11.38 Hold down the closing rocker arm then slide on the closing shim (1 – flange downwards) and fit the new half-rings (2)**

**11.39 Using a forked tool to pull up on the closing shim and seat the half-rings correctly in position**

**36** Lubricate the valve stem with clean engine oil then insert the valve carefully into its guide, rotating it slowly to avoid damaging the seal **(see illustration)**. Check that the valve moves up and down freely in the guide.

**37** Apply a smear of grease to the closing shim new half-rings to help hold them in position.

**38** Insert a screwdriver through the camshaft end cap aperture and lever the closing rocker arm down, ensuring its fork engages correctly with the valve stem. Hold the rocker arm down then slide the closing (lower) shim onto the valve stem, ensuring its flange is facing downwards **(see illustration)**. Locate the new half-rings correctly in the groove on the valve then slowly release the rocker arm.

**39** Ensure that the half-rings are correctly located in the valve groove and closing shim then forcibly raise the closing shim to seat them in the shim recess. Do this either by pushing on the rear of the rocker arm or by lifting the shim with a forked metal tool **(see illustration)**. Ensure the half-rings are in firm contact with the shoulder on the base of the shim before proceeding.

***Caution: It is essential that the half-rings are correctly seated in the closing shim recess. Failure to ensure the half-rings are in firm contact with the base of the shim will result in inaccurate valve clearances and serious engine damage.***

**40** With both closing rocker arms and valves correctly installed, insert the camshaft carefully into the right-hand end cover, taking care not to damage the oil seal. Manoeuvre the camshaft and cap assembly (minus sealing ring) into position and locate it in the cylinder head. Engage the left-hand end cap (minus sealing ring) with the camshaft and seat it in the head. Use the identification markings to ensure the camshaft is installed in the correct location (see Step 13 for camshaft identification marking details).

**41** Position the camshaft so the closing lobes are pointing away from the rocker arms and the valves are fully closed. Using feeler gauges, measure the clearance of each closing rocker arm (see Chapter 1).

**42** Remove the left-hand end cap again then withdraw the camshaft and right-hand end cap assembly from the cylinder head.

**43** If the closing rocker arm clearances were incorrect, remove the shims and adjust as necessary (see Chapter 1).

**44** Once the closing rocker arm clearances are both correctly adjusted, lubricate the opening (upper) rocker arm bores and shafts with clean engine oil. Manoeuvre the opening rocker arms into position and partially insert both rocker arm shafts. Locate the rocker arms on the end of the shafts and position them to the sides of the valves. Do not press the shafts fully in yet.

**45** Fit the new sealing rings to the grooves on the left- and right-hand end caps **(see illustration)**. Lubricate the sealing rings and camshaft bearing with clean engine oil.

**46** Lubricate the camshaft lobes and bearing surfaces with clean engine oil then carefully slide the right-hand end cap onto the camshaft end, taking care not to damage the oil seal **(see illustration)**.

**47** Manoeuvre the camshaft and end cap assembly into position, manoeuvring it past the rocker arms, and locate it correctly in the cylinder head **(see illustration)**. Fit the end cap retaining bolts and tighten them to the specified torque.

**48** Ensure the cap is positioned so that its oilway is facing towards the rocker arms then fit the left-hand end cap to the head, tightening its retaining bolts to the specified torque **(see illustration)**.

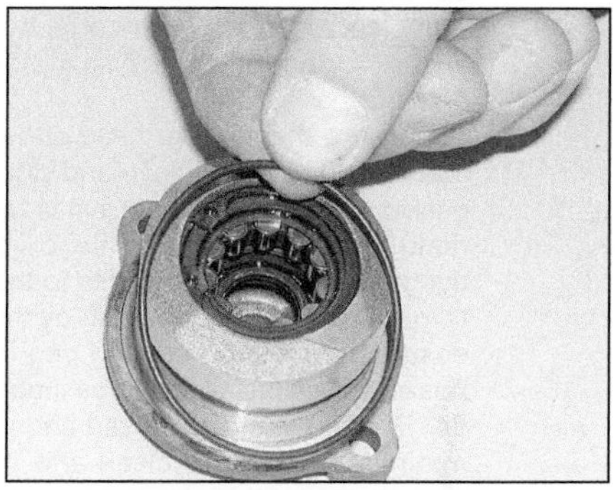

**11.45 Fit a new sealing ring to each camshaft end cap**

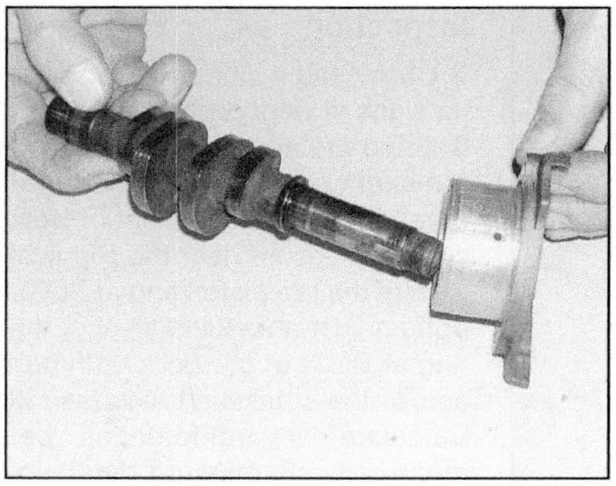

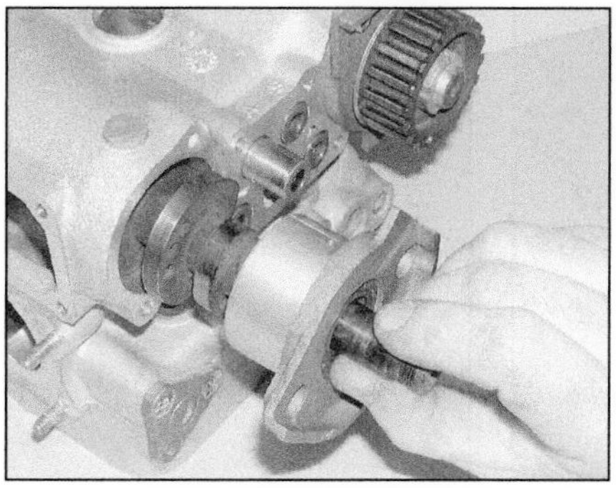

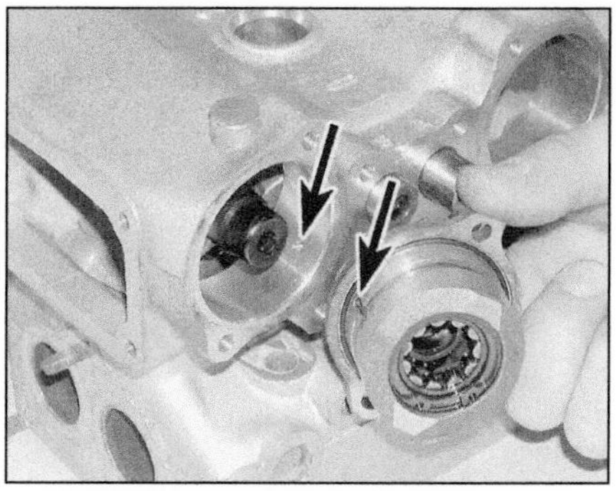

**11.46 Insert the camshaft into the end cap . . .**

**11.47 . . . then manoeuvre the assembly into the cylinder head**

**11.48 Fit the left-hand end cap ensuring its oilway is correctly aligned with the oilway in the head (arrowed)**

**11.49 Fit the opening shim (1) to the top of the valve then slide the opening rocker arm (2) back into position between the cam lobe and shim**

**49** Position the camshaft so the opening lobes are pointing away from the valves then fit the opening shim to the top of each valve. Slide the opening rocker arms into position between the shim and lobe then press the rocker arm shafts fully into position **(see illustration)**.

**50** Ensure the camshaft opening lobes are pointing away from the rockers arms then, using feeler gauges, measure the clearance of each opening rocker arm (see Chapter 1).

**51** If the opening rocker arm clearances are incorrect, partially withdraw the rocker arm shaft, slide the rocker arm to the side then remove the shim and adjust as necessary (see Chapter 1).

**52** Once both the closing and opening rocker arm clearances are both correctly adjusted, ensure all the rocker arm shafts are pushed fully into position.

**53** Ensure the cylinder head and side cover mating surfaces are clean and dry. Fit a new gasket to each cover then install the left- and right-hand side covers on the cylinder head, tightening their retaining bolts to the specified torque. On the horizontal cylinder head, ensure the radiator locating peg is correctly positioned on installation **(see illustration)**.

**54** Ensure the cylinder head and valve cover mating surfaces are clean and dry. Where gaskets were fitted, fit a new gasket to each cover then install the intake and exhaust valve covers on the cylinder head. Where no gaskets were fitted, apply a smear of sealant to the cover mating surfaces then fit the covers. Tighten the cover retaining bolts to the specified torque.

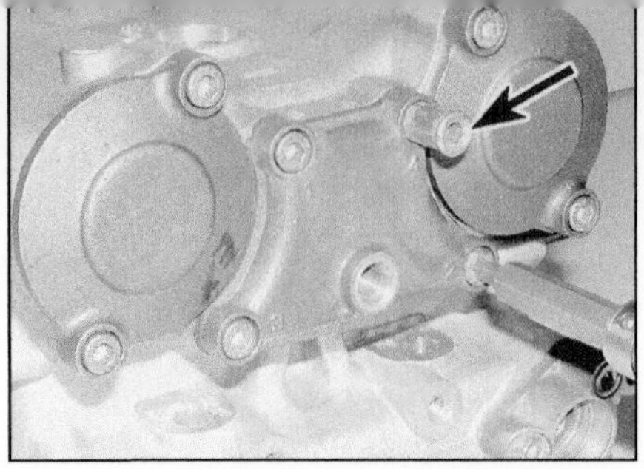

**11.53 On the horizontal cylinder head, ensuring the radiator peg (arrowed) is correctly positioned when fitting the left-hand side cover**

**55** Where necessary, install the inner sleeves and camshaft pulleys (see Section 9).

**56** On the horizontal cylinder head, fit new sealing rings and install the inner section of the coolant union and the blanking cover, tightening their screws to the specified torque. Fit the new sealing ring to the outer section of the coolant union and tighten its retaining screw to the specified torque.

**57** On the vertical cylinder head, fit new sealing rings and install the coolant union and the blanking cover, tightening their screws to the specified torque.

**58** Ensure the cylinder head and manifold mating surfaces are clean and dry. Fit a new gasket to each manifold then fit the intake and exhaust manifold to the cylinder head, tightening their retaining nuts to the specified torque.

**59** Install the cylinder head (see Section 10).

## 12 Valves and seats – servicing

**1** Because of the complex nature of this job and the special tools and equipment required, most owners leave servicing of the valves,

**2** The home mechanic can, however, remove the valves from the cylinder head, clean and check the components for wear and grind in the valves (see Section 11). Note that replacement valve seats are available for this engine.

**3** After the valve service has been performed, the head will be in like-new condition. When the head is returned, be sure to clean it again very thoroughly before installation on the engine to remove any metal particles or abrasive grit that may still be present from the valve service operations. Use compressed air, if available, to blow out all the holes and passages.

## 13 Cylinder barrels – removal, inspection and installation

**Note:** *The cylinder barrels can be removed with the engine in the frame. If the engine has already been removed, ignore the steps which do not apply.*

### *Horizontal cylinder barrel*

### Removal

**1** Remove the cylinder head (see Section 10).

**2** Release the retaining clips and remove the coolant hose connecting the barrel to the water pump.

**3** Remove all traces of dirt from around the base of the barrel and crankcase.

**4** Free the cylinder barrel from the crankcase. If it's stuck, tap around its perimeter with a soft-faced hammer. Don't attempt to pry between the barrel and the crankcase, as you'll ruin the sealing surfaces.

**5** Carefully lift the barrel off the crankcase. Prior to freeing the piston from the bore, stuff the crankcase mouth with clean, lint-free cloth to prevent any debris from falling into the crankcase **(see illustration)**. **Note:** *If both barrels are being removed, mark the barrel (H for horizontal cylinder, V for vertical cylinder) for identification purposes.*

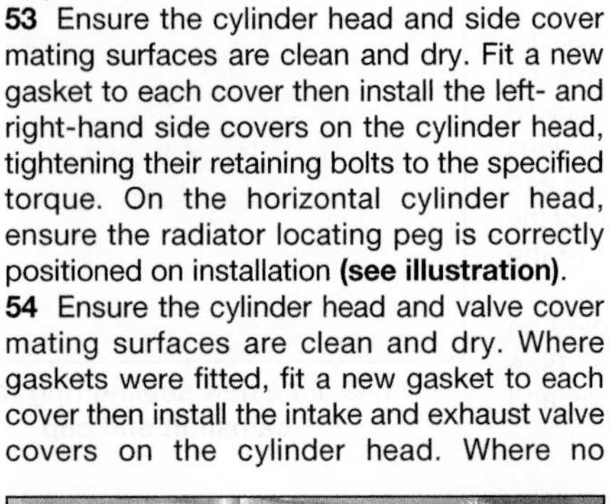

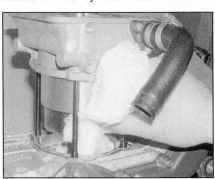

**13.5 Stuff the crankcase mouth with clean cloth to prevent debris falling into the crankcase**

**6** Remove the barrel base gasket and discard it. If the locating dowel is a loose-fit, remove it and store it with the barrel for safe-keeping.

### Inspection

**7** Check the cylinder bore carefully looking for signs of wear or damage.

**8** Using the appropriate precision measuring tools, check the dimensions of the cylinder bore to assess the amount of wear, taper and ovality. Measure near the top (just below the level of the top piston ring at TDC), centre and bottom (just above the level of the top piston ring at BDC) of the bore both parallel to and across the crankshaft axis **(see illustration)**. Calculate any differences between the measurements taken to determine any taper and ovality in the bore and compare the results to the specifications at the beginning of the Chapter. Calculate the piston-to-bore

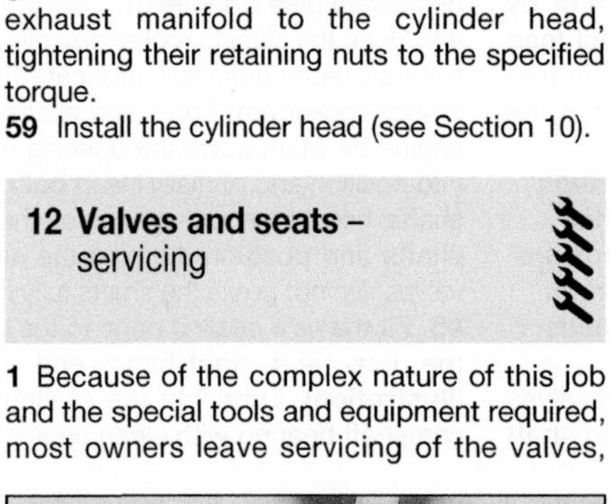

**13.8 Measuring cylinder bore diameter**

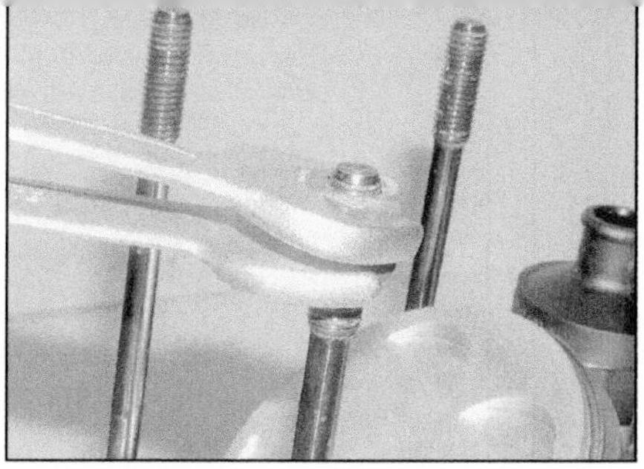
13.13a To remove a cylinder head stud, lock two nuts securely together . . .

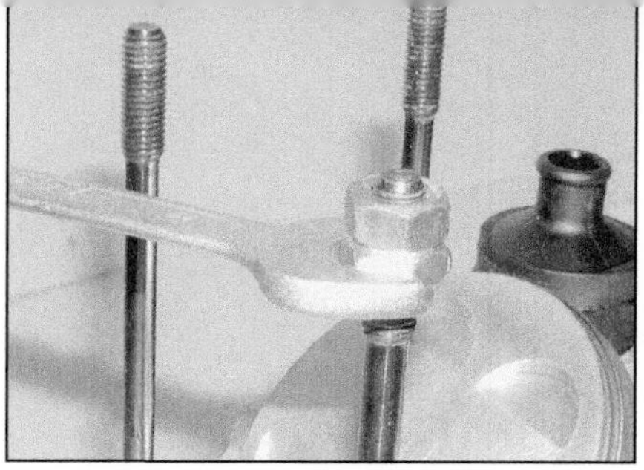
13.13b . . . then use the lower nut to unscrew the stud from the crankcase

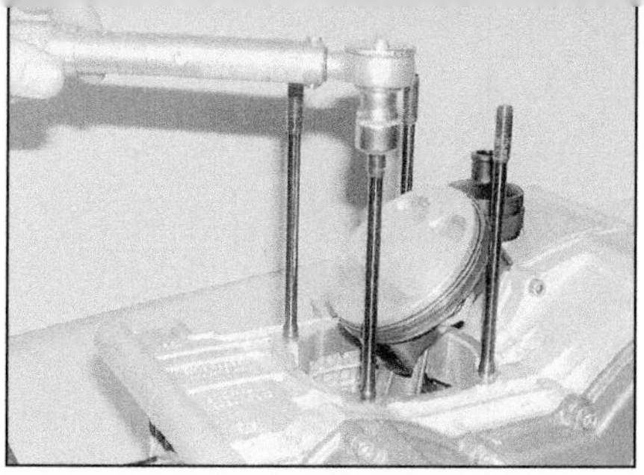
13.13c On installation, apply locking compound to the stud threads and tighten it to the specified torque

clearance as described in Section 14. If you do not have access to the precision measuring tools required, take the barrel and piston to a Ducati dealer for assessment and advice on their condition.

**9** If the cylinder bore is tapered, out-of-round, worn beyond the specified limits, or badly scuffed or scored, a new piston and cylinder barrel will have to be fitted – reboring is not possible. When purchasing a new barrel, ensure its size group matches that of the piston (see Section 14); the size group is indicated by the letter stamped on the tab on the side of the barrel. **Note:** *Before condemning the barrel, seek the advice of an engineering workshop as to whether it is possible to have the cylinder bore re-plated.*

**10** If the cylinder bore is in reasonably good condition and not worn to the outside of the limits, and if the piston-to-bore clearance can be maintained properly (see Section 14), then the cylinder barrel will not have to be renewed; hone the bore and fit new piston rings.

**11** To perform the honing operation you will need the proper size flexible hone with fine stones, or a 'bottle brush'-type hone, plenty of light oil or honing oil, some shop towels and an electric drill motor. Hold the cylinder barrel in a vice (cushioned with soft jaws or wood blocks) when performing the honing operation. Mount the hone in the drill motor, compress the stones and slip the hone into the bore. Lubricate the bore thoroughly, turn on the drill and move the hone up and down in the cylinder bore at a pace which will produce a fine crosshatch pattern on the cylinder wall with the crosshatch lines intersecting at approximately a 60° angle. Be sure to use plenty of lubricant and do not take off any more material than is absolutely necessary to produce the desired effect. Do not withdraw the hone from the cylinder while it is running. Instead, shut off the drill and continue moving the hone up and down in the cylinder until it comes to a complete stop, then compress the stones and withdraw the hone. Wipe the oil out of the cylinder and repeat the procedure on the remaining cylinder. Remember, do not remove too much material from the cylinder bore. If you do not have the tools, or do not desire to perform the honing operation, a dealer service department or motorcycle repair shop will generally do it for a reasonable fee.

**12** Next, the cylinder bore must be thoroughly washed with warm soapy water to remove all traces of the abrasive grit produced during the honing operation. Be sure to run a brush through the bolt holes and flush them with running water. After rinsing, dry the cylinder bore thoroughly and apply a coat of light, rust-preventative oil to all machined surfaces.

## Installation

**Note:** *It was found easier to insert the piston partially into the base of the barrel and install the barrel and piston as an assembly as opposed to trying to fit the barrel with the piston in position on the connecting rod. Details of both methods are given, decide on the procedure which suits you best.*

### Installing barrel with piston fitted to connecting rod

**13** Prior to installation, ensure the cylinder head studs are in good condition. To renew a stud, screw two nuts onto the upper end of the stud and lock them securely together; the nuts can then be used to unscrew the stud **(see illustrations)**. Remove the nuts and install them on the new stud. Alternatively, a stud removal tool can be used – see *Tools and Workshop Tips* in the Reference section at the end of this manual. Apply a drop of locking compound to the threads of the stud at the crankcase end then fit the stud to the crankcase and tighten it to the specified torque **(see illustration)**. Unlock the nuts and remove them from the stud.

**14** If the studs are in good condition, ensure they are all securely screwed into the crankcase. If any stud is loose, remove it and clean its threads. Apply a drop to the crankcase end threads then refit the stud and tighten it to the specified torque, using two nuts locked together.

**15** Clean all traces of old gasket material and sealant from the cylinder barrel and crankcase. If a scraper is used, take care not to scratch or gouge the soft aluminium. Also ensure that none of the gasket material is allowed to fall into the crankcase.

**16** Ensure the locating dowel is in position in the crankcase. If the dowel is a loose-fit, secure it in position with a drop of locking compound.

**17** Apply a thin coat of sealant to each side of the new base gasket **(see illustration)**. Ensure the gasket is correctly positioned so that its small hole is correctly aligned with the locating dowel then slide it down the studs and locate it on the crankcase **(see illustration)**. On most models the gasket will be marked 'TOP INLET' to aid installation; the gasket should be fitted with this marking

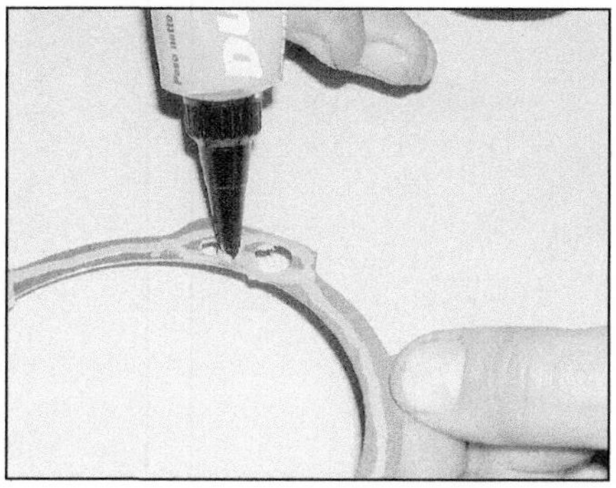
13.17a Apply a coat of sealant to each side of the new base gasket . . .

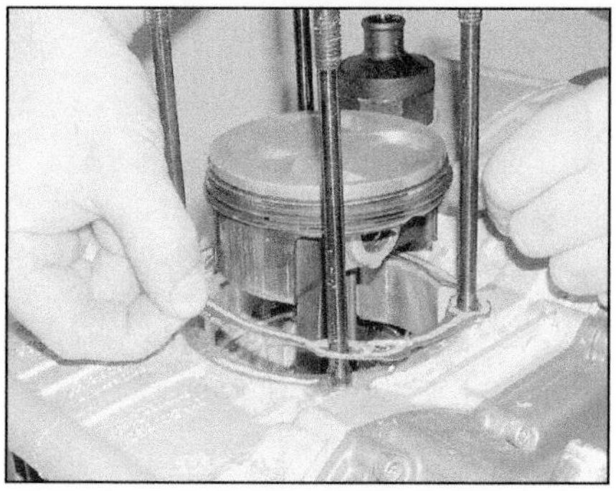
13.17b . . . then slide the gasket down the studs and onto its locating dowel . . .

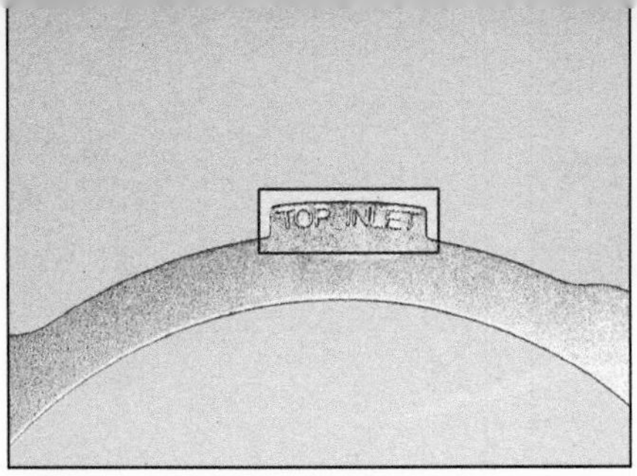


**13.17c . . . ensuring its TOP INLET marking is facing upwards and on the intake side of the barrel**

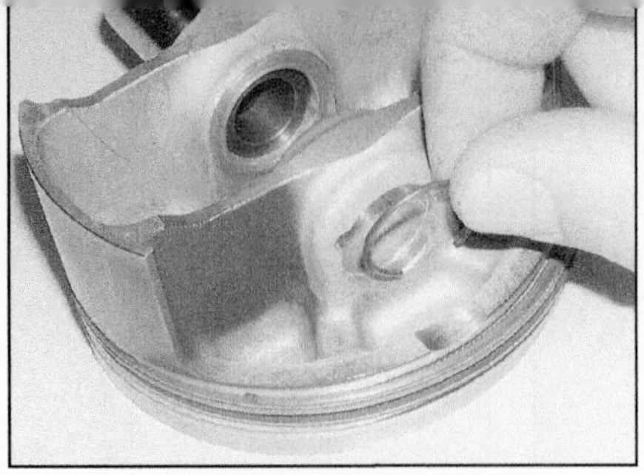

**13.24 Fit a new circlip to the piston ensuring it is correctly located in the piston groove**

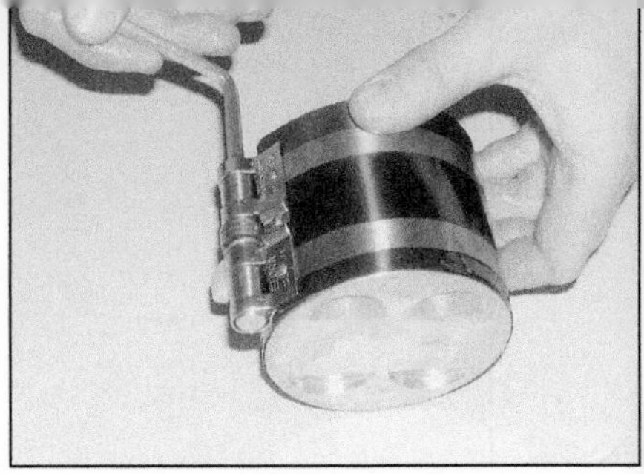

**13.25 Ensure the ring end gaps are correctly spaced then clamp them in position with a ring compressor**

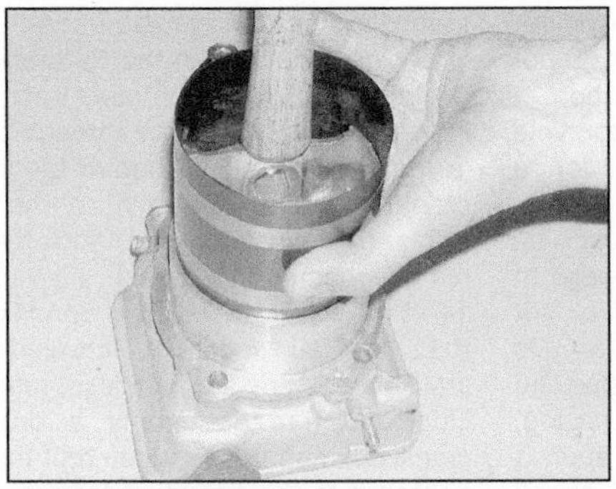

**13.27 Carefully fit the piston to the barrel, ensuring it is the correct way around. Once all the rings are inserted remove the ring compressor**

facing upwards on the intake side of the barrel **(see illustration)**.

**18** Position the piston ring end gaps so they are all evenly spaced 120° apart then lubricate the rings with clean engine oil. Also lubricate the cylinder bore with plenty of clean engine oil.

**19** Ensure the barrel is positioned the right way around then carefully lower it down over the studs and seat the piston crown in the base of the bore. Ensure the piston remains square then gently ease the barrel onto the piston whilst carefully easing the piston rings into the bottom of the cylinder bore.

***Caution: Ensure the piston rings do not snag and break as the piston enters the cylinder bore. The base of the bore is chamfered to ease installation but great care is still needed.***

**20** Once all the piston rings are correctly located in the bore, slide the barrel fully down the piston and seat it on the locating dowel.

**21** Install the hose connecting the barrel to the water pump and secure it in position with the retaining clips.

**22** Install the cylinder head (see Section 10).

### Installing barrel and piston as an assembly

**23** Carry out the operations described in Steps 13 to 17.

**24** Check that the piston has one new circlip fitted to it and that it is correctly seated in the piston groove with its end gap away from the removal notch in the piston **(see illustration)**. If the original piston is being installed, use the mark made on removal to ensure it is fitted in its original location.

**25** Position the piston ring end gaps so they are all evenly spaced 120° apart then lubricate the rings with clean engine oil. If a piston ring compressor is available, fit the compressor to the piston and clamp the rings in position **(see illustration)**.

**26** Lubricate the cylinder bore with plenty of clean engine oil.

**27** Fit the piston to the base of the cylinder barrel making sure that the smaller valve cutouts on the piston crown are positioned on the exhaust side. The piston crown may also have A and S markings, A is the intake side and S the exhaust side (see Note in Section 1). Ensure the piston remains square then gently ease it into the barrel until all the piston rings have entered the bore **(see illustration)**. Remove the piston ring compressor from the piston (where used).

***Caution: Ensure the piston rings do not snag and break as the piston enters the cylinder bore. The base of the bore is chamfered to ease installation but great care is still needed.***

**28** Ensure the piston is correctly positioned then lubricate the piston pin and connecting rod small-end bore with clean engine oil. Slide the piston pin partially into the piston **(see illustration)**.

**29** Position the connecting rod at TDC then stuff a clean, lint-free cloth into the crankcase mouth, around the connecting rod **(see illustration)**. This will prevent the circlip from

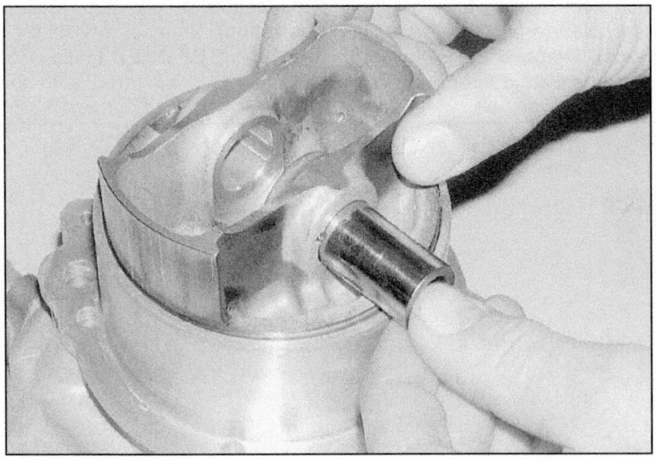

**13.28 Insert the piston pin partially into the piston**

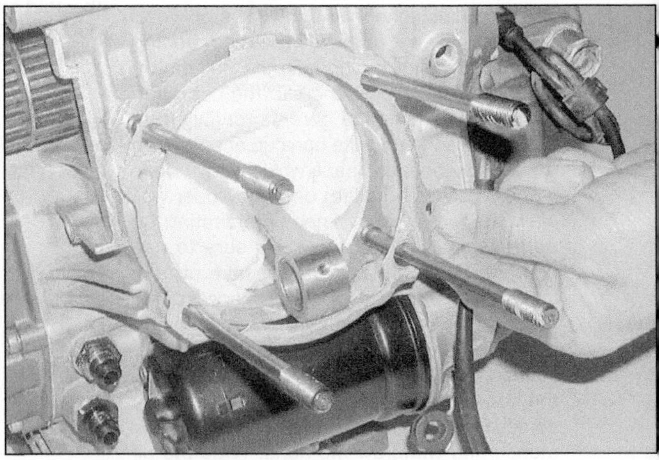

**13.29 Stuff the crankcase mouth with clean cloth . . .**

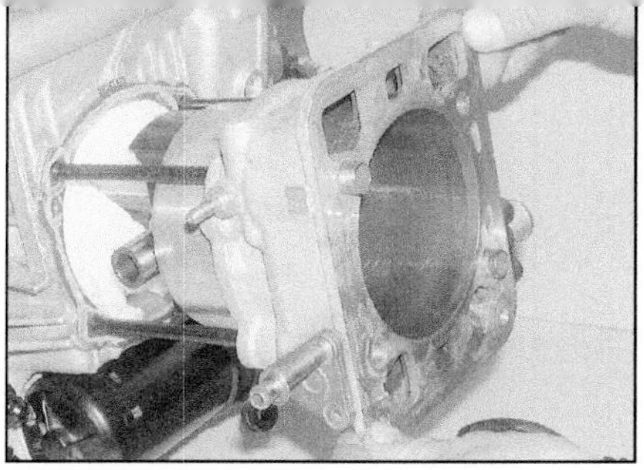

**13.30a . . . then slide the barrel and piston assembly down the studs**

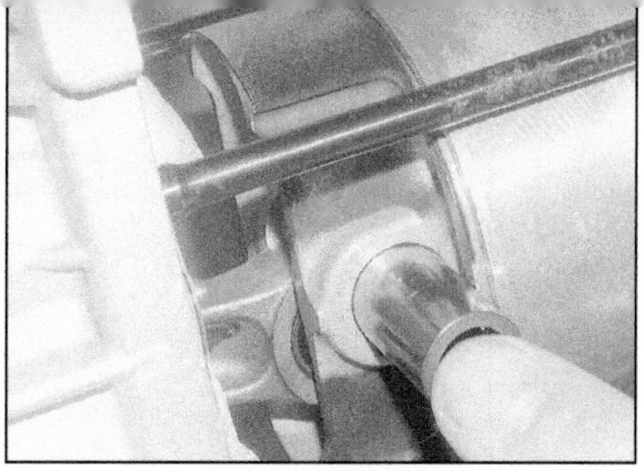

**13.30b Align the piston with the connecting rod then press the piston pin into position . . .**

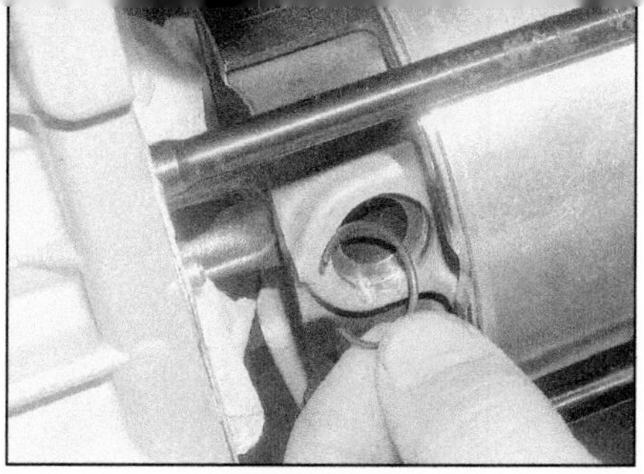

**13.30c . . . and secure it in position with the second new circlip**

falling into the crankcase if it is inadvertently dropped.

**30** Ensure both the barrel and piston are positioned the right way around then carefully lower the assembly down over the studs **(see illustration)**. Align the piston pin with the connecting rod bore then push the pin fully into position **(see illustration)**. If necessary the pin can be tapped carefully into position, using a hammer and suitable drift, whilst supporting the connecting rod and piston. Secure the piston pin in position with a second new circlip, making sure it is correctly seated in the piston groove with its end gap away from the removal notch in the piston **(see illustration)**.

**31** Ensure both circlips are correctly fitted then slide the barrel fully down the piston and seat it on the locating dowel.

**32** Install the hose connecting the barrel to the water pump and secure it in position with the retaining clips.

**33** Install the cylinder head (see Section 10).

### *Vertical cylinder barrel*

#### Removal

**34** Remove the cylinder head (see Section 10).

**35** Unscrew the retaining bolt and free the oil hose retaining clip from the left-hand side of the barrel.

**36** Remove the barrel as described in Steps 2 to 6. Recover the O-ring (where fitted – some engines don't have one) which is fitted

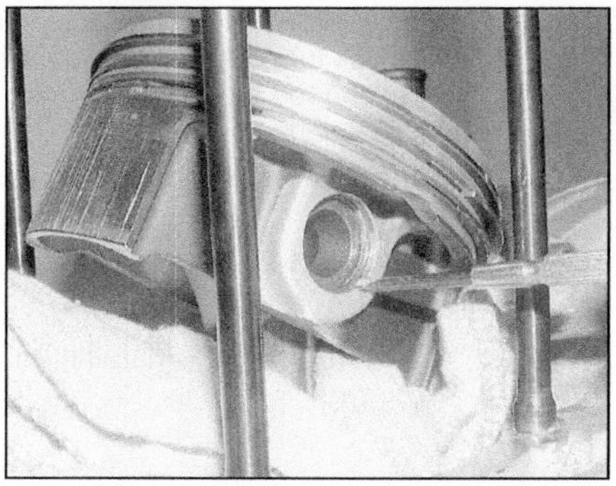

**14.4 Carefully prise out the circlip using a small, flat-bladed screwdriver**

to the oilway and discard it; a new one must be used on installation.

#### Inspection

**37** See Steps 7 to 12.

#### Installation

**38** Where an O-ring was fitted to the oilway, lubricate the new O-ring with a smear of multi-purpose grease and seat it the recess on the crankcase.

**39** Install the barrel as described in Steps 13 to 22 or Steps 23 to 33 (as applicable).

**40** Refit the oil hose retaining clip to the side of the barrel, tightening its retaining bolt securely.

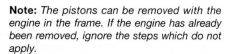

## 14 Pistons – removal, inspection and installation

**Note:** *The pistons can be removed with the engine in the frame. If the engine has already been removed, ignore the steps which do not apply.*

### *Removal*

**1** Remove the cylinder head and barrel (see Sections 10 and 13).

**2** Before removing the piston from the rod, stuff a clean, lint-free cloth into the crankcase mouth around the connecting rod. This will prevent the circlip from falling into the crankcase if it is inadvertently dropped.

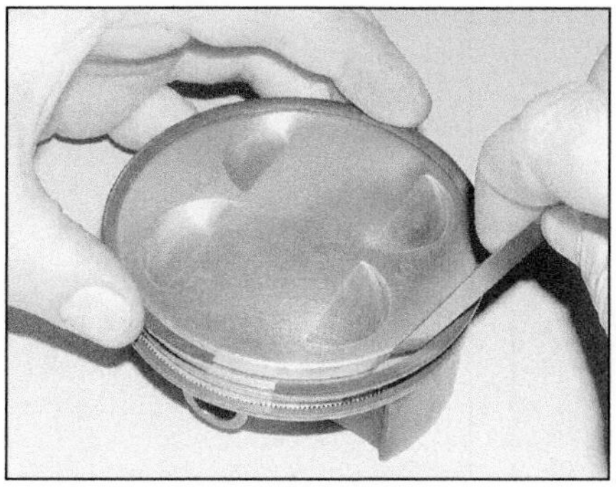

**14.7 Using a feeler gauge to remove a piston ring**

**3** If both pistons are being removed, mark the piston (H for horizontal cylinder, V for vertical cylinder) for identification purposes. Use a sharp scriber (or a marker pen if the piston is clean enough) to make the identification mark on the piston crown.

**4** Support the piston and prise one of the circlips out with a small, flat-bladed screwdriver **(see illustration)**. Discard the circlip; it must never be reused.

**5** Push the piston pin out from the opposite end to free the piston from the rod. You may have to deburr the area around the groove to enable the pin to slide out (use a triangular file for this procedure). If the pin won't come out, the pin can be tapped carefully out of position, using a hammer and suitable drift, whilst supporting the connecting rod and piston.

### *Inspection*

**6** Before the inspection process can be carried out, the piston must be cleaned and the old piston rings removed.

**7** Using a piston ring removal and installation tool or a feeler gauge, carefully remove the rings from the piston **(see illustration)**. Do not nick or gouge the pistons in the process.

**8** Scrape all traces of carbon from the top of the piston, taking care not to remove the identification marking. A hand-held wire brush or a piece of fine emery cloth can be used once most of the deposits have been scraped away. Do not, under any circumstances, use a wire brush mounted in a drill motor to remove deposits from the pistons; the piston material is soft and will be eroded away by the wire brush.

**9** Use a piston ring groove cleaning tool to remove any carbon deposits from the ring grooves. If a tool is not available, a piece broken off an old ring will do the job. Be very careful to remove only the carbon deposits. Do not remove any metal and do not nick or gouge the sides of the ring grooves.

**10** Once the deposits have been removed, clean the pistons with solvent and dry them thoroughly. Make sure the oil return holes below the oil ring grooves are clear.

**11** If the piston is not damaged or worn excessively and if the cylinder barrel is not

**14.15 Using a micrometer to measure piston diameter**

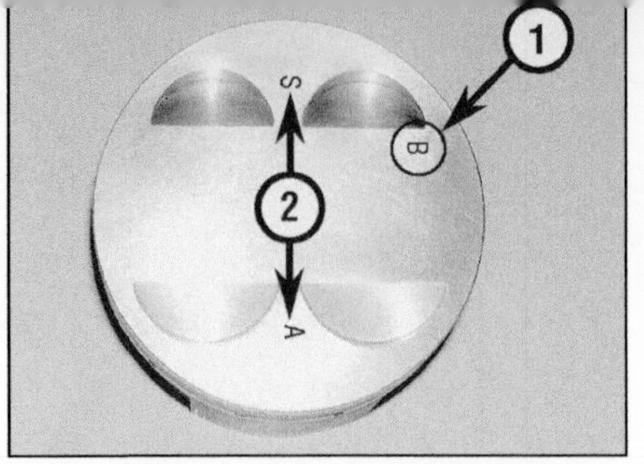


**14.16 Piston size group marking (1) and direction fitting marks (2)**

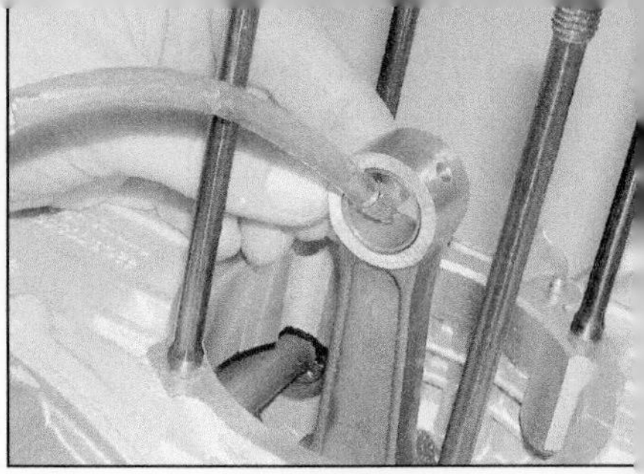

**14.19 Lubricate the small-end bush with clean engine oil**

being renewed, a new piston will not be necessary. Normal piston wear appears as even, vertical wear on the thrust surfaces of the piston and slight looseness of the top ring in its groove. Note that new piston rings should always be used when an engine is overhauled.

**12** Carefully inspect each piston for cracks around the skirt, at the pin bosses and at the ring lands.

**13** Look for scoring and scuffing on the thrust faces of the skirt, holes in the piston crown and burned areas at the edge of the crown. If the skirt is scored or scuffed, the engine may have been suffering from overheating and/or abnormal combustion, which caused excessively high operating temperatures. A hole in the piston crown, an extreme to be sure, is an indication that abnormal combustion (pre-ignition) was occurring. Burned areas at the edge of the piston crown are usually evidence of spark knock (detonation). If any of the above problems exist, the causes must be corrected or the damage will occur again.

**14** Measure the piston ring-to-groove clearance by fitting a new piston ring in the ring groove and slipping a feeler gauge in beside it. Check the clearance at three or four locations around the groove. Be sure to use the correct ring for each groove; they are different (see Section 15). If the clearance is greater than the service limit, new pistons will have to be used when the engine is reassembled.

**15** Calculate the piston-to-bore clearance by measuring the bore (see Section 13) and the piston diameter. Make sure that the piston and cylinder barrel are correctly matched. Measure the piston across the skirt on the thrust faces at a 90° angle to the piston pin, 6.8 mm up from the bottom of the skirt **(see illustration)**. Subtract the piston diameter from the bore diameter to obtain the clearance. If it is greater than specified in the Specifications at the beginning of this Chapter, a new piston and cylinder barrel will have to be fitted (the cylinder bores are plated and reboring is not possible – see Section 13).

**16** Apply clean engine oil to the pin, insert it into the piston and check for freeplay by rocking the pin back-and-forth. If the pin is loose, a new piston and pin must be installed. If the necessary measuring equipment is available measure the pin diameter and piston pin bore and subtract the pin diameter from the bore diameter to obtain the clearance. If it is greater than specified in the Specifications at the beginning of this Chapter, a new piston and pin will have to be fitted. When purchasing a new piston, ensure its size group matches that of the barrel (see Section 13); the size group is indicated by the letter stamped on the piston crown **(see illustration)**.

**17** Install the rings on the piston as described in Section 15.

### *Installation*

**Note:** *The piston can either be fitted to the connecting rod or inserted into the barrel and the piston and barrel fitted as an assembly (this was found to be the easier option, especially if a piston ring compressor is available). Continue as described under the relevant sub-heading.*

### Fitting piston to connecting rod

**18** Check that the piston has one new circlip fitted to it and that it is correctly seated in the piston groove with its end gap away from the removal notch in the piston. Insert the piston pin from the opposite side. If it is a tight fit, the piston should be warmed first. If the original piston is being installed, use the mark made on removal to ensure it is fitted in its original location.

**19** Lubricate the piston pin and connecting rod small-end bore with clean engine oil **(see illustration)**.

**20** Stuff a clean, lint-free cloth into each crankcase mouth, around the connecting rod. This will prevent the circlip from falling into the crankcase if it is inadvertently dropped.

**21** Fit the piston to its respective connecting rod making sure that the smaller valve cutouts on the piston crown are positioned on the exhaust side. The piston crown may also have A and S markings, A is the intake side and S the exhaust side (see Note in Section 1) **(see illustration 14.16)**.

**22** Push the piston pin through both piston bosses and the connecting rod bore **(see illustration)**. If necessary the pin can be tapped carefully into position, using a hammer and suitable drift, whilst supporting the connecting rod and piston. Secure the piston pin in position with a second new circlip making sure it is correctly seated in the piston groove with its end gap away from the removal notch in the piston **(see illustration)**.

**23** Check that the piston pivots freely on the connecting rod then fit the cylinder barrel and head (Sections 13 and 10).

### Fitting piston and barrel as an assembly

**24** See Steps 23 to 33 of Section 13.

## 15 Piston rings – installation

**1** Before installing new piston rings, their end gaps must be checked. **Note:** *Ensure the ring*

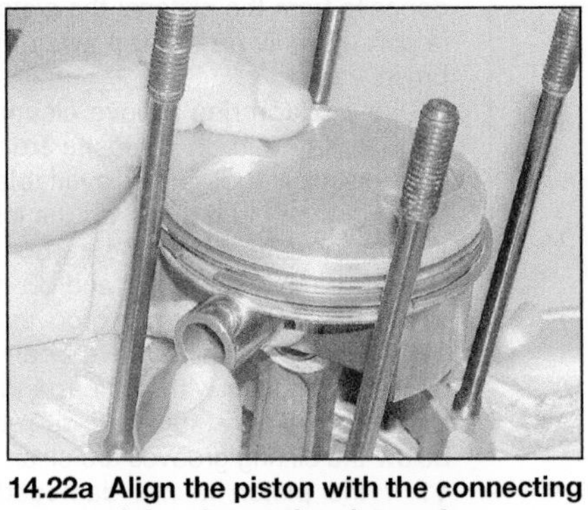

**14.22a Align the piston with the connecting rod then insert the piston pin . . .**

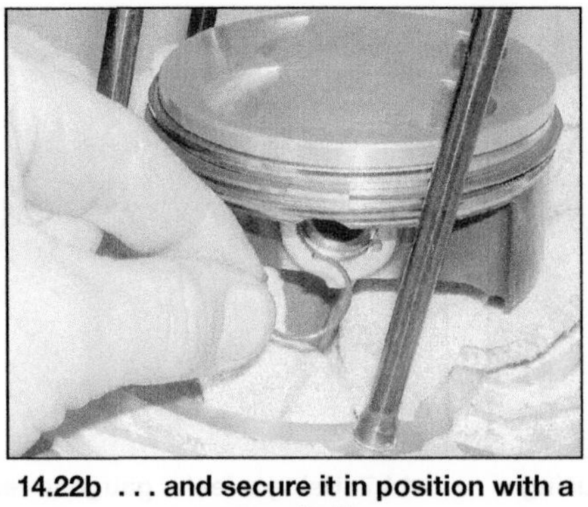

**14.22b . . . and secure it in position with a new circlip**

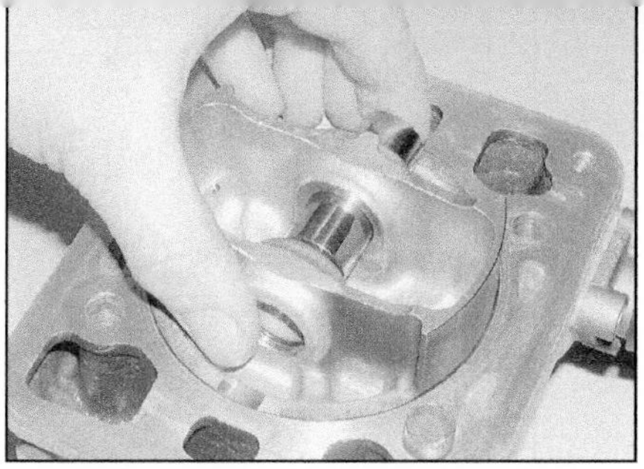

**15.2a Insert the piston ring into the cylinder bore and use the top of the piston crown to square it up**

*end gaps are checked in the cylinder bore in which they will be installed.*

**2** Insert the top compression ring into the bottom of the cylinder bore and square it up with the cylinder walls by pushing it in with the top of the piston **(see illustration)**. The ring should be about 25 mm down from the top of the bore. To measure the end gap, slip a feeler gauge between the ends of the ring and compare the measurement to that given in the Specifications at the beginning of this Chapter **(see illustration)**.

**3** If the gap is larger or smaller than specified, double check to make sure that you have the correct rings before proceeding.

**4** Repeat the procedure for the second compression ring and oil control ring that will be installed in the barrel. Remember to keep the rings, piston and barrel matched up.

**5** Once the ring end gaps have been checked/corrected, the rings can be installed on the piston. **Note:** *Do not expand the rings any more than is necessary to slide them into position. To avoid breaking the rings, the use of a piston ring installation tool is recommended.*

**6** The oil control ring (lowest on the piston) is installed first. It is composed of two separate components. Slip the expander into the lower groove on the piston then install the oil control ring, ensuring its 'TOP or SP' marking is facing upwards **(see illustrations)**.

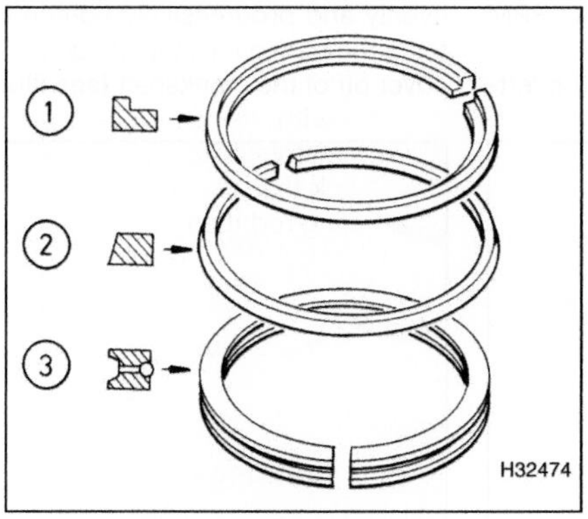


**15.7a Piston ring identification details**

1 *Top compression ring*
2 *Second compression ring*
3 *Oil control ring*

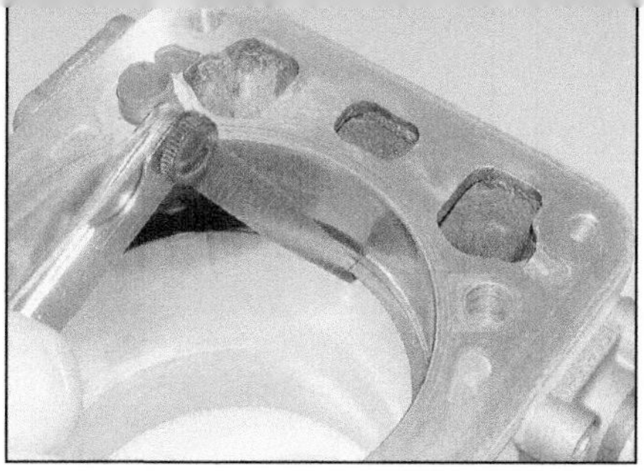

**15.2b Using a feeler gauge to measure piston ring end gap**

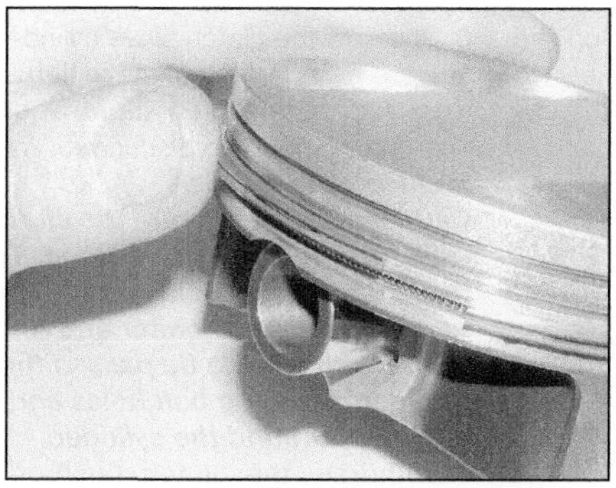

**15.6b . . . then install the oil control ring . . .**

**7** Next install the second compression ring. **Note:** *The second ring and top ring are different and cannot be interchanged. The second ring is easily identified by its tapered outer edge, the top ring is stepped* **(see illustration)**. Locate the ring in the middle groove on the piston, making sure it is fitted the correct way up with its widest point at the bottom and its 'TOP' marking facing upwards **(see illustrations)**.

**8** Finally, install the top ring in the piston upper groove, making sure it is fitted the correct way up with its stepped surface and 'TOP' marking facing upwards.

**9** With the piston rings correctly installed, check that each ring is free to rotate easily in its groove. Check the ring-to-groove clearance of each ring using feeler gauges and check that the clearance is within the specified range (this is very tricky on the top ring).

**10** Repeat the procedure for the remaining piston and rings.

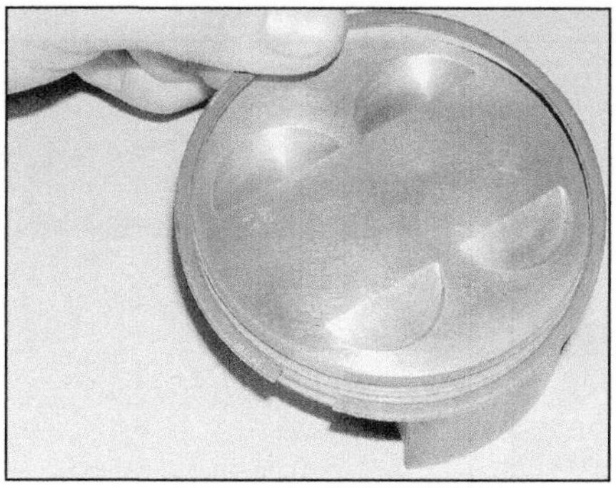

**15.7b Ensure the second and top compression rings are correctly positioned . . .**

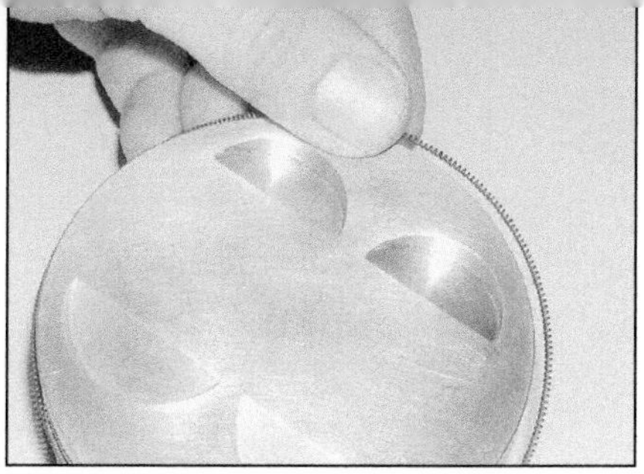

**15.6a Fit the expander to the lower groove on the piston . . .**

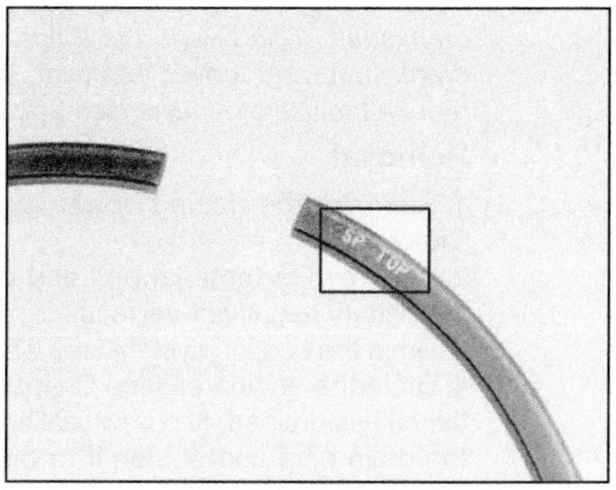

**15.6c . . . ensuring its identification marking is facing upwards**

## 16 Crankcase covers – removal, inspection and installation

**Note:** *The crankcase covers can be removed with the engine in the frame. If the engine has already been removed, ignore the steps which do not apply.*

### *Left-hand side crankcase cover*

**Note:** *The crankcase cover is fitted with a bearing which locates on the end of the*

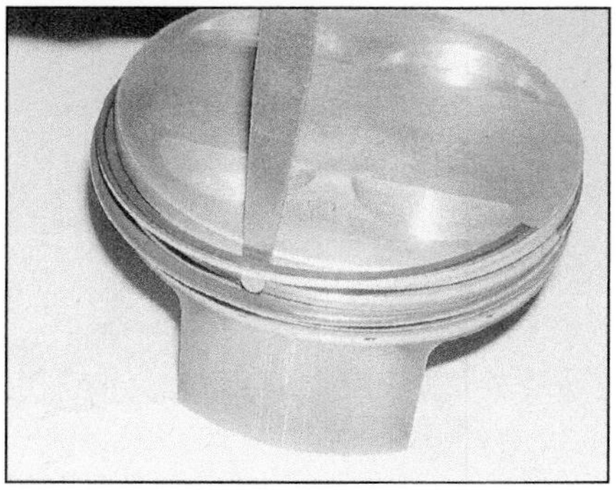

**15.7c . . . and fit them to the piston using a feeler gauge or ring installation tool**

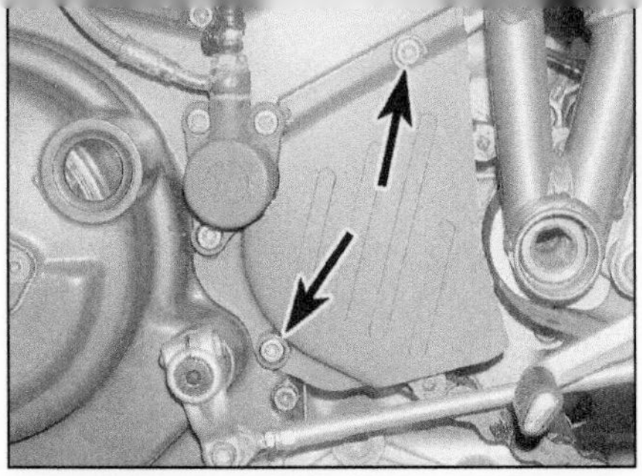

16.5 Undo the bolts (arrowed) and remove the sprocket cover from the engine

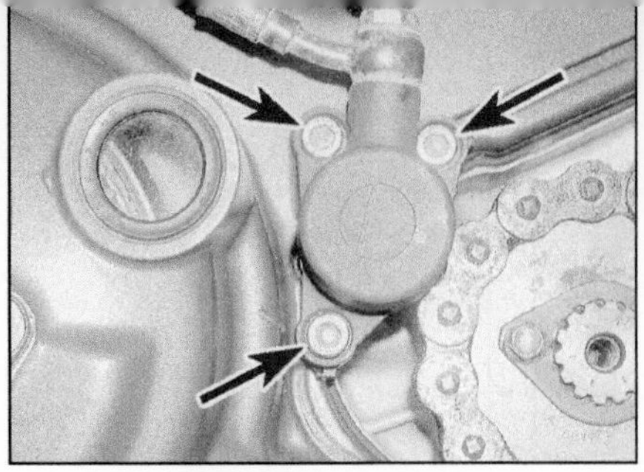

16.6a Undo the bolts (arrowed) . . .

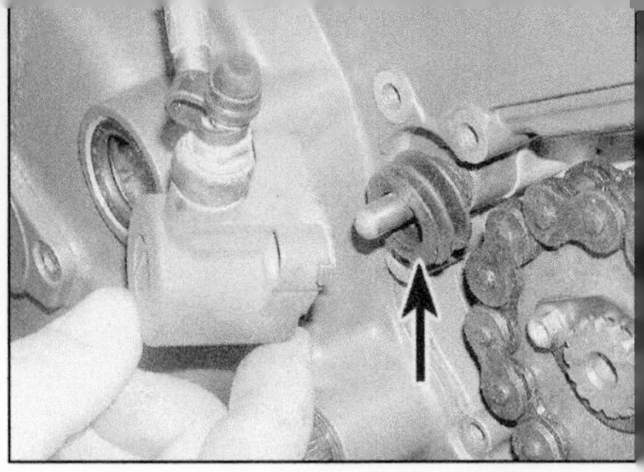

16.6b . . . then free the clutch slave cylinder from the engine and recover the rubber gaiter (arrowed)

*crankshaft. This bearing is a tight-fit on the crankshaft and cover removal is likely to require the use of a puller (see Step 14).*

### Removal

**1** Remove the fairing lower panels (see Chapter 8).

**2** Unscrew its terminal bolt and disconnect the battery negative (-ve) lead.

**3** Drain the cooling system (see Chapter 1).

**4** Drain the engine oil (see Chapter 1). Once the oil has drained, fit a new sealing washer to the drain plug and tighten it to the specified torque.

**5** Undo the two bolts and remove the sprocket cover from the engine **(see illustration)**.

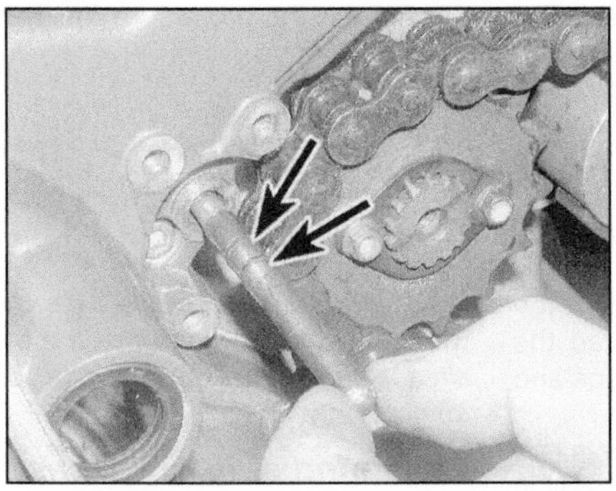

16.7 Withdraw the clutch pushrod noting which way around it is fitted (O-rings arrowed)

**6** Unscrew the clutch slave cylinder bolts and free the cylinder, complete with rubber gaiter, from the engine **(see illustrations)**. **Note:** *There is no need to disconnect the hydraulic hose from the cylinder.*

***Caution: Do not operate the clutch lever whilst the cylinder is detached. To prevent the piston being accidentally expelled, remove the rubber gaiter and retain the piston with a cable tie passed through the cylinder mounting bolt holes and securely tightened around the cylinder.***

**7** Withdraw the clutch pushrod from the engine, noting which way around it is fitted. If the pushrod O-rings show signs of damage or deterioration they must be renewed **(see illustration)**.

**8** Note the correct fitted location of the gearchange lever on its shaft (make alignment marks if necessary), then unscrew the clamp bolt and free the gearchange lever from the engine **(see illustration)**.

**9** Release the retaining clips and disconnect the coolant hoses from the water pump unions.

**10** Disconnect the wiring connector from the timing sensor fitted to the left-hand side crankcase cover. On models with a P8 engine management system (see Chapter 4), also disconnect the RPM sensor wiring connector; label the wiring connectors to ensure they are connected correctly on installation (the RPM sensor wiring should be marked 'M').

**11** Trace the alternator wiring from the left-hand crankcase cover and disconnect it at the regulator/rectifier unit connector(s). If necessary, to improve access to the connectors, unbolt the battery mounting tray from the frame (see Chapter 9).

**12** Undo the retaining screws and remove the centre cap and sealing ring from the crankcase cover. Obtain a new sealing ring for use on refitting.

**13** Working in a criss-cross pattern, evenly slacken and remove the crankcase cover retaining bolts, noting the correct fitted location of any relevant wiring clips and washers. Note each bolts' correct fitted location as it is removed; there are several different lengths of bolt used to secure the cover. **Note:** *There is no need to remove the water pump cover bolts; the pump cover can be left in position.*

**14** In the absence of the Ducati puller (88713.0144), obtain a length of stout metal bar, two M6 bolts, nuts and washers and an M8 bolt. Drill two 7 mm holes in the bar that align with the centre cap retaining screw holes in the crankcase cover. Screw the M8 bolt fully into the end of the crankshaft. Screw the nuts fully onto the M6 bolts and fit the washers then insert the bolts through the holes in the bar **(see illustration)**. Screw the M6 bolts fully into the centre cap retaining screw holes in the crankcase cover then evenly and progressively tighten the nuts to force the bar against the M8 bolt and draw the cover off of the crankshaft **(see illustrations)**.

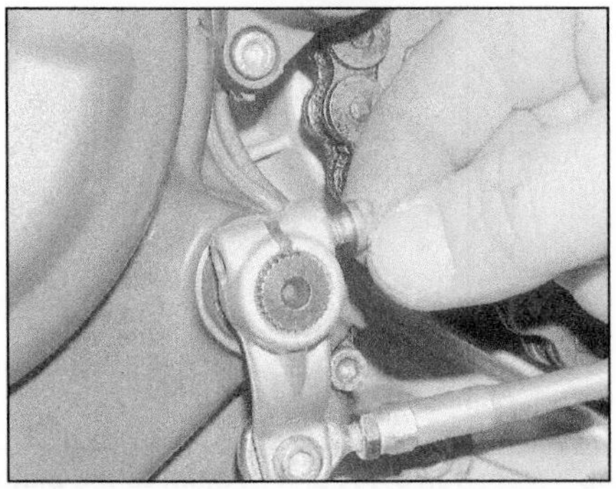

16.8 Unscrew the clamp bolt then detach the gearchange lever from the engine

16.14a Homemade tool for drawing left-hand crankcase cover off the crankshaft

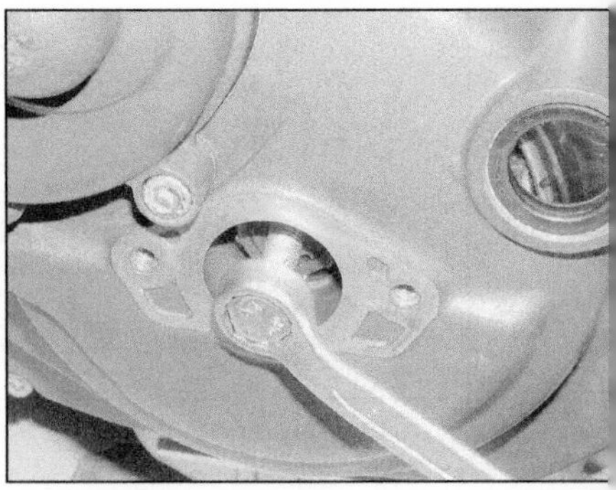

16.14b Securely fit the M8 bolt to the crankshaft end . . .

**16.14c . . . then screw the bolts, nuts and metal bar into the centre cap threads of the cover and use the nuts to draw the cover off**

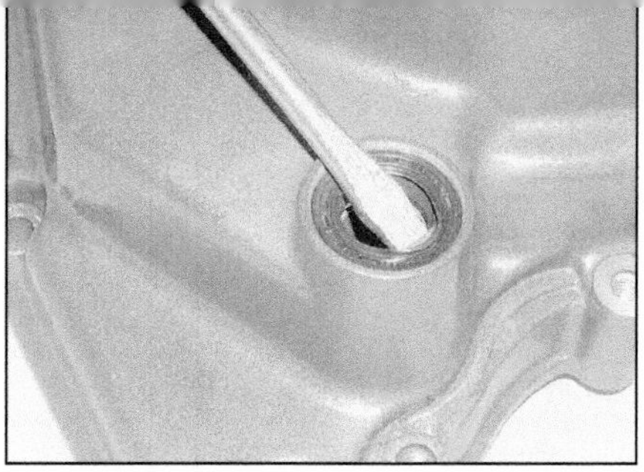

**16.20a Carefully lever out the gearchange shaft oil seal from the cover using a flat-bladed screwdriver**

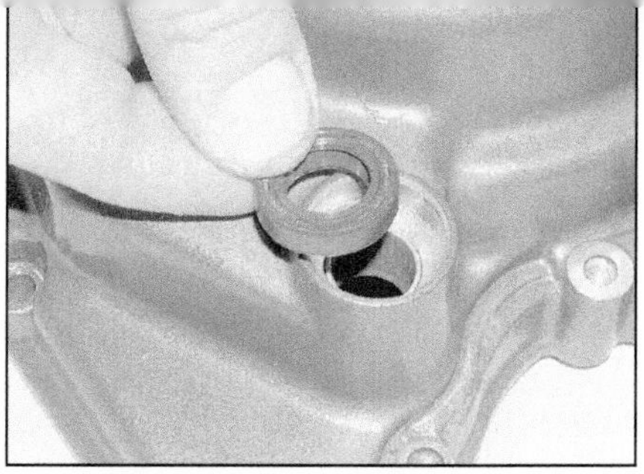

**16.20b Fit the new seal ensuring its sealing lip is facing inwards . . .**

**15** Remove the crankcase cover from the engine, being prepared to catch any residual oil which may be released as the cover is removed. Remove the puller from the cover. **Note:** *If the bearing remains on the end of the crankshaft (on early models the bearing was not secured in the cover with a circlip), use a bearing puller to remove it and fit the bearing to the crankcase cover (see Step 19) prior to installation.*

**16** Remove the gasket (where fitted – only early models have a gasket) and discard it. Note the two locating dowels fitted to the crankcase; remove these for safe-keeping if they are loose.

## Inspection

**17** Refer to Chapter 3 for information on water pump overhaul and Chapter 9 for information on alternator stator removal and installation.

**18** Inspect the crankshaft bearing for signs of wear or damage, the inner race must rotate freely without any sign of freeplay or roughness. Also check the gearchange shaft oil seal and bush for signs of wear or damage. Renew damaged components as necessary.

**19** To renew the crankshaft bearing, extract the circlip (where fitted) from inside the cover then support the cover and tap the bearing out of position. Clean the cover bore and lubricate it with clean engine oil then fit the new bearing. Tap the new bearing squarely into position, using a socket which bears only on the bearing's outer race. Where a circlip is fitted, secure the bearing in position with the circlip ensuring it is correctly located in the cover groove.

**20** To renew the gearchange shaft oil seal and bush, carefully lever the old seal out of position taking care not to damage the cover **(see illustration)**. If necessary, the bush can then be tapped/pressed out of position. Lubricate the new bush with clean engine oil then press it into position **(see illustrations)**. Press the new seal squarely into position ensuring its sealing lip is facing inwards.

## Installation

**21** Ensure the water pump and alternator stator are correctly installed (see Chapters 3 and 9).

**22** Ensure the mating surfaces of the crankcase and cover are clean and dry then fit both locating dowels to the crankcase **(see illustration)**.

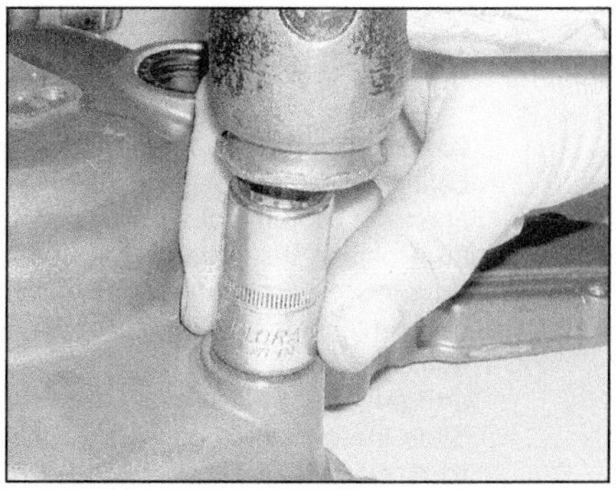

**16.20c . . . and press it squarely into position with a socket which bears only on the seal outer edge**

**23** On early models where a gasket is fitted, locate the new gasket on the dowels.

**24** On later models with no gasket, apply a thin coat of sealant (Ducati recommend the use of Three Bond sealant) to the mating surface of the crankcase cover and alternator wiring grommet **(see illustration)**.

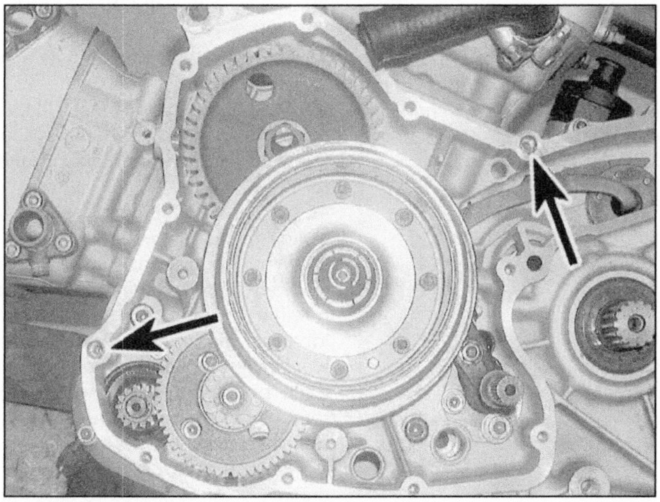

**16.22 Ensure the cover locating dowels (arrowed) are correctly fitted**

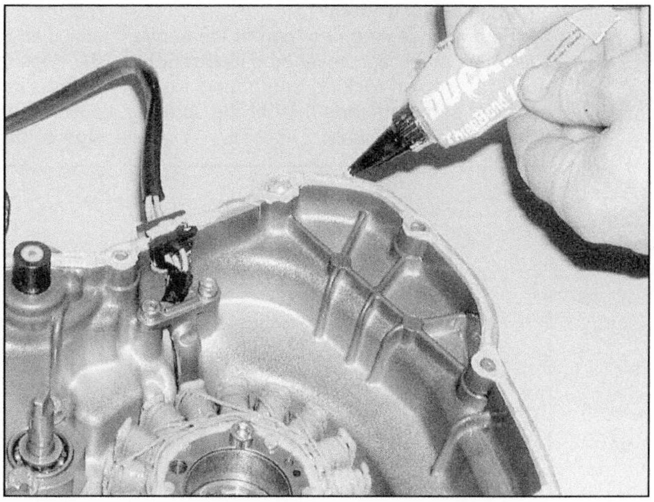

**16.24 On later models apply a coat of sealant to the mating surface of the cover**

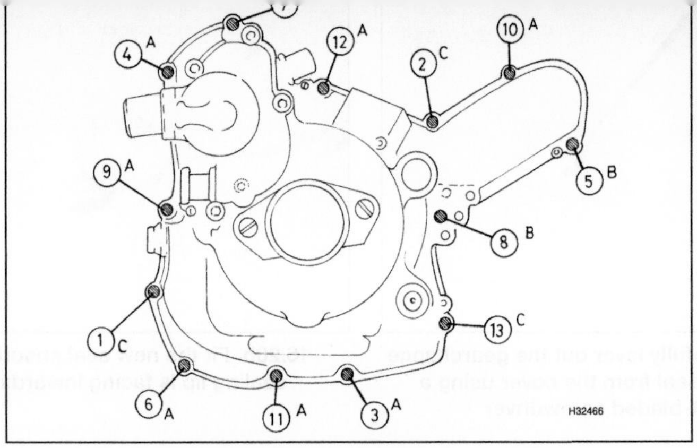


16.27 **Left-hand crankcase cover bolt locations. Tighten the bolts in the numerical sequence shown**

*A M6x25 bolt* *B M6x20 bolt* *C M6x30 bolt*

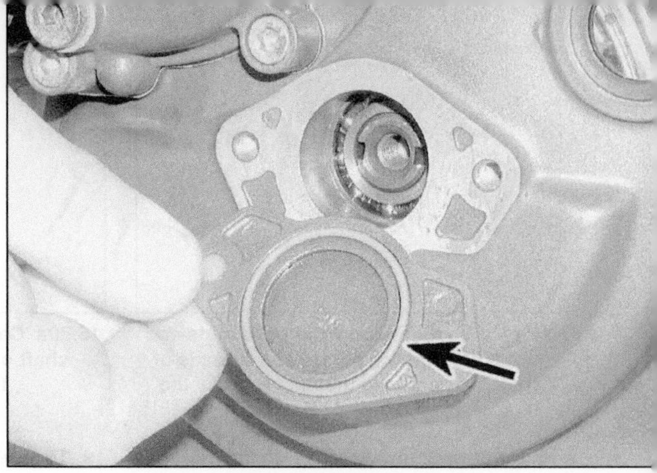

**16.28 Fit a new sealing ring (arrowed) to the centre cap**

**25** On all models, lubricate the crankshaft bearing with clean engine oil and apply a smear of engine oil to the gearchange shaft oil seal.

**26** Position the water pump shaft so that its drive dog will engage the slot on the timing belt driveshaft end as the cover is installed. Manoeuvre the crankcase cover into position and engage the bearing with the crankshaft. Slide the cover into position, taking care not to damage the oil seal on the gearchange lever splines, and locate it on the dowels. If necessary, tap the cover onto the crankshaft using a soft-faced mallet.

***Caution: Take care not to trap your fingers between the cover and the crankcase as the magnetic pull of the alternator draws the cover into position.***

**27** Ensure the cover is correctly seated on the crankcase then install the cover retaining bolts, complete with the wiring retaining clip and washers. Ensure all components are installed in their original locations then evenly and progressively tighten the bolts to the specified torque setting in the sequence shown **(see illustration)**.

**28** Fit a new sealing ring then fit the centre cap to the crankcase cover **(see illustration)**. Apply a drop of locking compound to the retaining screw threads then fit the screws, tightening them securely.

**29** Route the alternator wiring correctly back to the regulator/rectifier and securely reconnect the wiring connector(s). Where necessary, install the battery mounting tray (see Chapter 9).

**30** Securely reconnect the wiring connector to the timing sensor. On models with a P8 engine management system, also reconnect the RPM sensor connector ensuring the connectors are correctly remade (the RPM sensor wiring should be marked 'M'). **Note:** *Although not strictly necessary, it is highly recommended that the sensor air gap(s) is/are checked before proceeding (see Chapter 4, Section 9), especially if the engine has been overhauled.*

**31** Reconnect the coolant hoses to the water pump and secure them in position with the retaining clips.

**32** Clean the gearchange lever clamp bolt and apply a drop of fresh locking compound to its threads. Engage the gearchange lever splines with those of the shaft so the gearchange lever is correctly positioned then refit the clamp bolt, tightening it to the specified torque.

**33** Wipe the clutch pushrod clean. Ensure the O-rings are both correctly located in the pushrod groves (renew them if they show any sign of damage) then lubricate the pushrod with molybdenum disulphide grease **(see illustration)**. Insert the pushrod into the crankcase ensuring that the O-rings are positioned on the left-hand (slave cylinder end of the shaft.

**34** Ensure the clutch slave cylinder and engine surfaces are clean and dry then remove the cable tie (used for security). Refit the rubber gaiter to the slave cylinder then locate the cylinder on the cover, tightening its retaining bolts to the specified torque.

**35** Refit the sprocket cover to the engine and securely tighten its retaining bolts.

**36** Refill the engine with oil and refill the cooling system with coolant (see Chapter 1).

**37** Reconnect the battery negative (-ve) lead tightening its retaining bolt securely.

**38** Start the engine and check that there are no signs of oil and coolant leakage before installing the fairing panels.

## Right-hand side crankcase cover

### Removal

**39** Remove the clutch assembly (see Section 20).

**40** Remove the battery and its mounting tray (see Chapter 9).

**41** Drain the engine oil (see Chapter 1). Once the oil has drained, fit a new sealing washer to the drain plug and tighten it to the specified torque.

**42** Disconnect the oil pressure warning light switch wiring connector.

**43** Working in a criss-cross pattern, evenly slacken and remove the crankcase cover retaining bolts, noting the correct fitted location of wiring/hose clip, spacer and washer (some engines have two clips). Note each bolts' correct fitted location as it is removed; there are several different lengths of bolt used to secure the cover.

**44** Remove the crankcase cover from the engine, being prepared to catch any residual oil which may be released as the cover is removed **(see illustration)**.

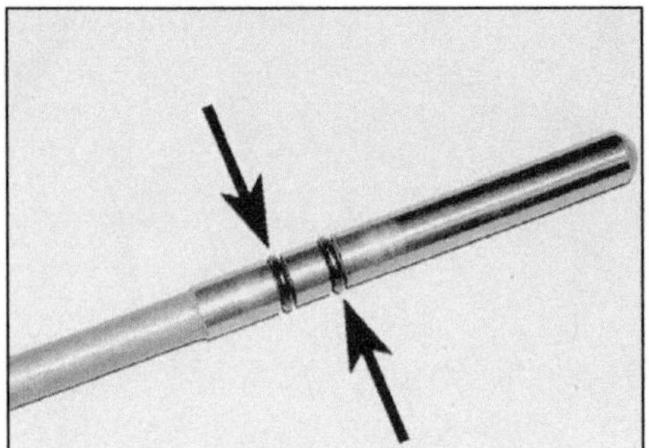

**16.33 Renew the pushrod O-rings (arrowed) if damaged**

**16.44 Removing the right-hand crankcase cover**

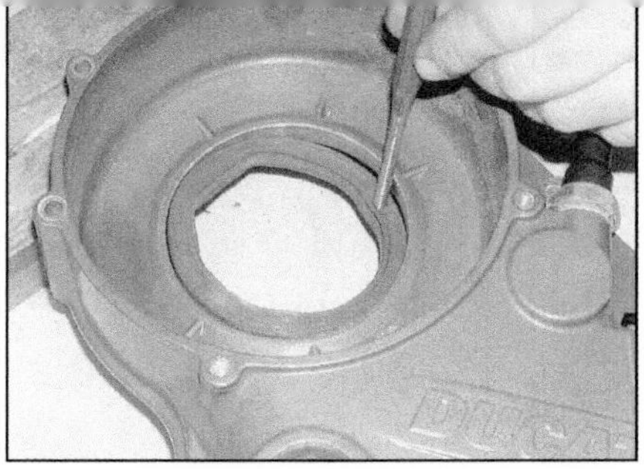

16.47 Tap the clutch assembly oil seal out of position and renew it if it shows signs of oil leakage

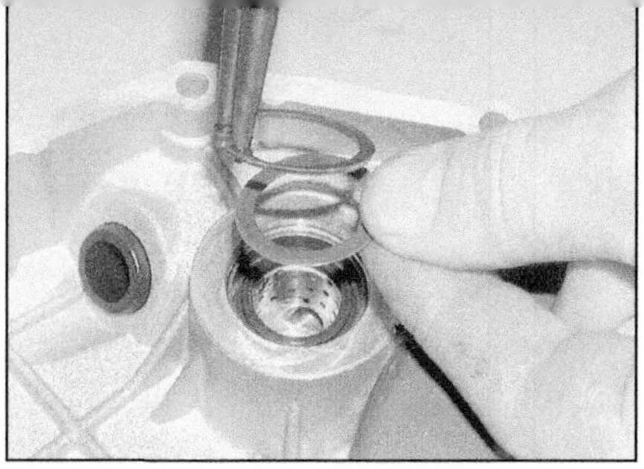

16.48 Remove the circlip and lift out the washer to gain access to the crankshaft oil seal

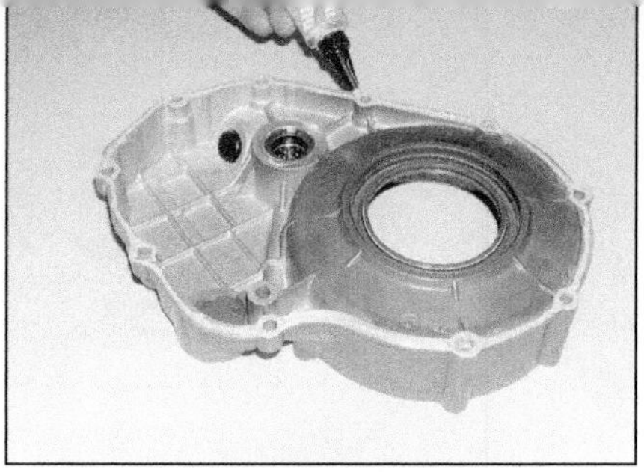

16.51 On later models apply a coat of sealant to the cover mating surface

45 Remove the cover gasket (where fitted – only early models have a gasket) and recover the O-ring from the oilway located to the rear of the oil pump. Discard the gasket (where fitted) and O-ring; new ones must be used on installation. Note the cover locating dowel fitted to the crankcase; remove it for safe-keeping if it is loose.

### Inspection

46 Inspect the clutch oil seal and crankshaft oil seal for signs of damage or deterioration.

47 To renew the clutch assembly oil seal, press/lever the original seal out of position taking care not to damage the cover **(see illustration)**. Support the cover then press/tap the new seal squarely into position ensuring its sealing lip is facing inwards.

48 To renew the crankshaft oil seal, remove the circlip from inside the cover and lift out the washer **(see illustration)**. Carefully lever the oil seal out of position, taking care not to damage the casing or bush. Clean the cover bore then fit the new oil seal, ensuring its sealing lip is facing away from the sealed end of the cover. Press the seal squarely into position, until it abuts the cover shoulder then refit the washer. Secure the washer in position with the circlip, ensuring it is correctly located in the cover groove.

### Installation

49 Ensure the mating surfaces of the crankcase and cover are clean and dry then fit the locating dowel to the crankcase.

50 On early models where a gasket is fitted, locate the new gasket on the dowels.

51 On later models with no gasket, apply a thin coat of sealant (Ducati recommend the use of Three Bond sealant) to the mating surface of the crankcase cover **(see illustration)**.

52 On all models, fit the new O-ring to the crankcase oilway, using a smear of multi-purpose grease to hold it in position **(see illustration)**.

53 Lubricate the lips of the clutch oil seal and crankshaft oil seal with a smear of engine oil then manoeuvre the crankcase cover into position and engage it with the crankshaft. Carefully ease the cover into position, taking care not to damage the lip of the clutch oil seal as it passes over the primary driven gear, and locate it on the dowel.

54 Install the cover retaining bolts in their original locations, ensuring the washer, hose/wiring clip and spacer is fitted to the correct bolt **(see illustration)**. Tighten all bolts by hand, then working in a criss-cross sequence, tighten them evenly and progressively to the specified torque.

55 Reconnect the wiring connector to the oil pressure warning light switch.

56 Install the clutch assembly (see Section 20).

57 Fit the battery and its mounting tray (see Chapter 9).

58 Refill the engine with oil (see Chapter 1).

59 Start the engine and check that there is no sign of oil leakage before installing the fairing panels.

## 17 Flywheel, starter motor clutch and idler gear – removal, inspection and installation

**Note:** *The flywheel, starter motor clutch and idler gear can be removed with the engine in the frame. It will be necessary to prevent engine rotation to enable the flywheel/alternator rotor nut to be slackened (see Step 2 or 26).*

**Note:** *There are two possible types of flywheel/starter clutch assembly. Early (pre 1999 model year) models are fitted with an assembly where the alternator rotor is mounted onto the crankshaft and rotates on the **inside** of the stator coil. Later (1999 models year on) models are fitted with an assembly where the alternator rotor is bolted onto the flywheel and rotates around the **outside** of the stator coil.*

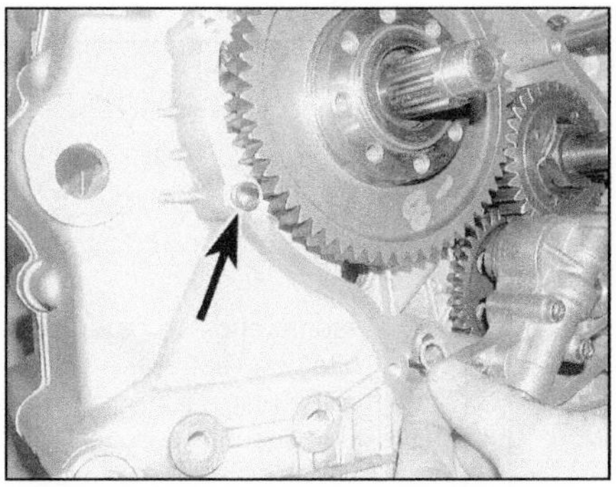

16.52 Fit a new O-ring to the crankcase oilway, using a smear of grease to hold it in position (locating dowel arrowed)

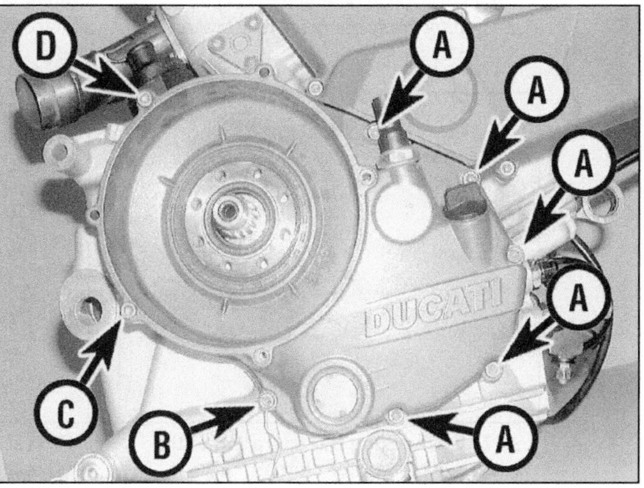

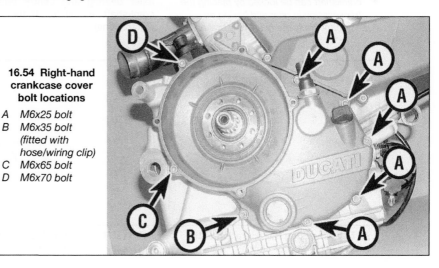

**16.54 Right-hand crankcase cover bolt locations**

A *M6x25 bolt*
B *M6x35 bolt (fitted with hose/wiring clip)*
C *M6x65 bolt*
D *M6x70 bolt*

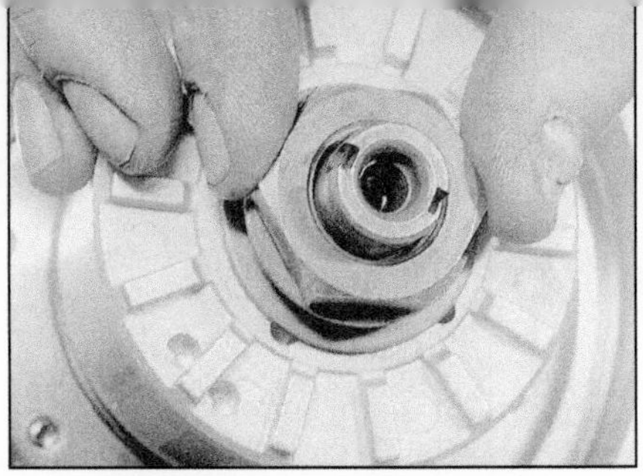

17.3a Slacken and remove the flywheel/alternator rotor nut . . .

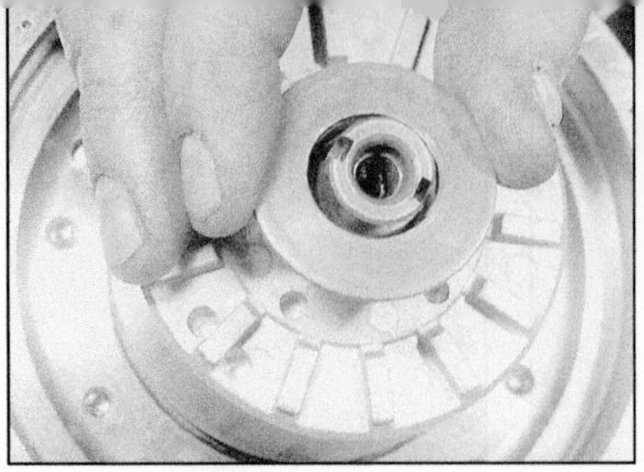

17.3b . . . and remove the dished washer

17.6a Slide off the needle roller bearing . . .

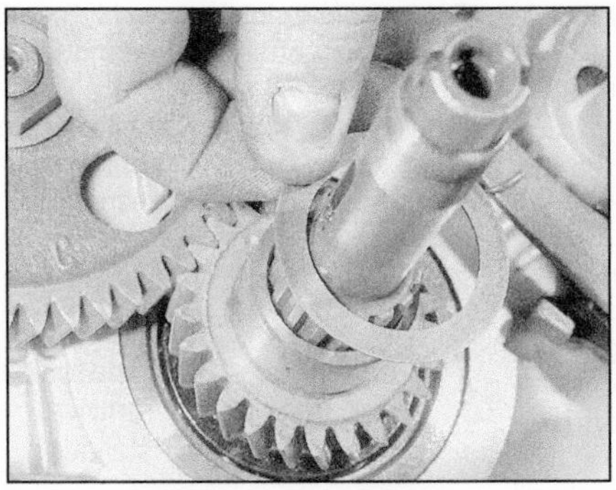

17.6b . . . and washer . . .

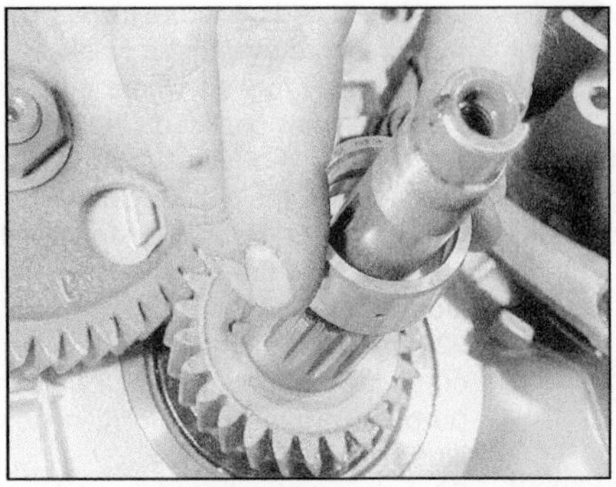

17.6c . . . then remove the centre bush

## *Early (pre 1999 model year) models*

### Removal

**1** Remove the left-hand crankcase cover (see Section 16).

**2** It is necessary to prevent crankshaft rotation to enable the flywheel/alternator rotor nut to be slackened. If the Ducati holding tool (88713.0710) is not available, the options are as follows.

- *a) Retain the flywheel or alternator rotor with a heavy-duty strap wrench.*
- *b) If the engine is still in the frame, the crankshaft can be locked by placing the transmission in gear and having an assistant firmly apply the rear brake.*

**3** Slacken the flywheel/alternator rotor retaining nut whilst preventing the crankshaft from rotating. Remove the nut from the end of the crankshaft and slide off the dished washer, noting which way around it is fitted **(see illustrations)**.

**4** Slide the alternator rotor off the end of the crankshaft. If the rotor Woodruff key is a loose-fit, remove it and store it with the rotor for safe-keeping.

**5** Remove the flywheel and starter clutch assembly from the end of the crankshaft.

**6** Remove the starter clutch needle roller bearing and centre bush from the crankshaft and slide off the washer **(see illustrations)**.

**7** Remove the circlip then slide the outer washer, starter idler gear and inner washer off the pivot shaft. If necessary, unscrew the retaining bolt and remove the pivot shaft from the crankcase.

### Inspection

**8** Inspect the starter clutch driven gear and idler gear teeth and renew them as a set if any teeth are chipped or missing. Check the idler gear shaft and gear bearing surfaces for signs of wear or damage, and renew if necessary. If the gear teeth are damaged, also check the condition of the starter motor pinion; the pinion is retained by a circlip and is easily renewed.

**9** Check the starter clutch driven gear, needle roller bearing and centre bush contact surfaces for wear or scoring. Renew worn components as necessary.

**10** Hold the flywheel in one hand and with the other, attempt to rotate the starter clutch driven gear **(see illustration)**. It should rotate freely in one direction and lock up in the other. If the driven gear turns freely in both directions, or is locked solid, dismantle the starter clutch assembly and inspect the components as follows.

**11** Remove the driven gear from the rear of the flywheel then remove the circlip from the centre of the starter clutch holder **(see illustrations)**. Make an identification mark on the one-way clutch assembly face then

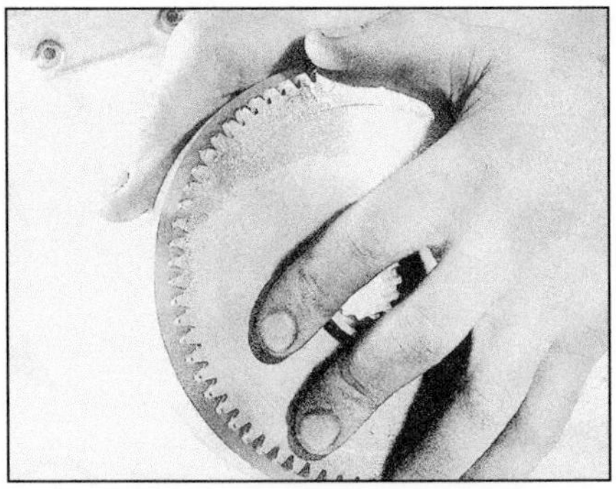

17.10 Checking the operation of the starter clutch

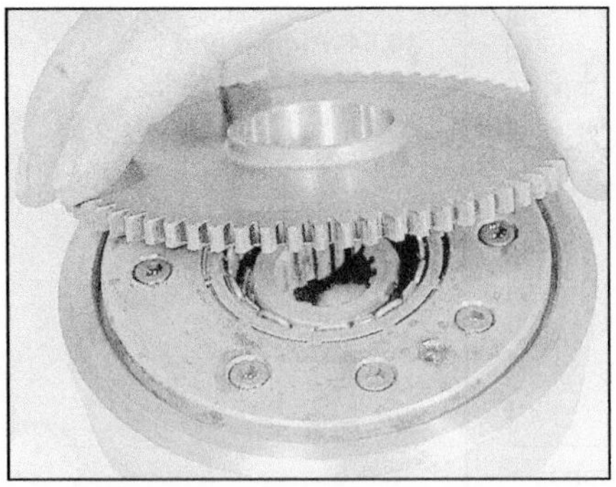

17.11a Remove the driven gear from the rear of the flywheel

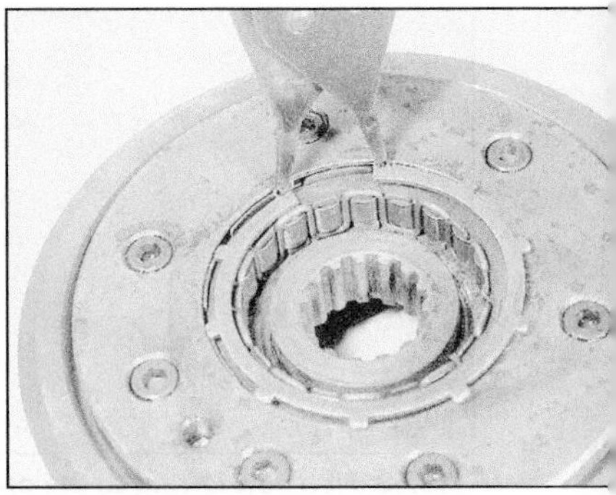

17.11b Remove the circlip . . .

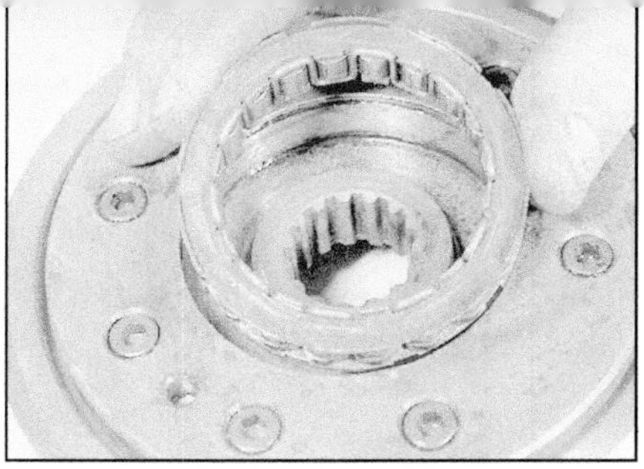

17.11c . . . and lift out the one-way clutch, noting which way around it is fitted

17.12 Examine the driven gear surface (arrowed) for signs of wear or damage

17.14 Ensure the circlip tabs are correctly located before installing the driven gear

remove the clutch from the centre of the holder **(see illustration)**.

**12** Inspect the one-way clutch rollers, driven gear and holder contact surfaces for signs of wear and scoring **(see illustration)**. The one-way clutch rollers and the gear and holder surfaces should be unmarked, with no signs of wear such as pitting or flat spots. Renew any component which shows signs of wear or damage.

**13** To renew the starter clutch holder, clamp the flywheel in a vice equipped with soft jaws then unscrew the retaining bolts. Separate the holder and flywheel and recover the locating pin and circlip arrangement. Clean the retaining bolts and apply a drop of fresh locking compound to the threads of each one. Ensure the locating pin and circlip arrangement are in position then assemble the holder and flywheel, aligning the pin with its holes. Clean the threads of the retaining bolts and apply a drop of thread locking compound to their threads, then tighten them evenly and progressively to the specified torque.

**14** On reassembly lubricate all components with clean engine oil. Using the mark made on disassembly to ensure it is the correct way around, fit the one-way clutch to the centre of the holder and secure it in position with the circlip. Ensure the circlip is correctly located in the holder groove then ease the driven gear into position **(see illustration)**. Check the operation of the starter clutch (see Step 10).

## Installation

**15** If the idler gear pivot shaft was removed, remove all traces of locking compound from its retaining bolt and apply a drop of fresh locking compound to its threads. Fit the pivot shaft to the crankcase and tighten its retaining bolt to the specified torque.

**16** Lubricate the idler gear shaft and gear with clean engine oil. Slide the inner washer onto the shaft then fit the gear, ensuring its smaller gear is facing outwards, and outer washer **(see illustrations)**. Secure all components in position with the circlip, locating it correctly in the shaft groove **(see illustration)**.

**17** Lubricate the starter clutch needle roller bearing and centre bush with clean engine oil. Slide the bush fully onto the crankshaft, then fit the washer and bearing onto the bush.

***Caution: Ensure the bush remains tight against the timing gear at all times. If not, the washer may slip off the rear of the bush and become trapped between the bush and gear. This would cause the flywheel not to seat properly on the crankshaft and will result in serious engine damage.***

**18** Ensure the driven gear is correctly installed and check the operation of the starter clutch (see Step 10).

**19** Slide the flywheel and starter clutch assembly onto the crankshaft. Align the punch mark on the flywheel hub with the alternator rotor Woodruff key slot then engage the flywheel on the crankshaft splines whilst aligning the driven gear teeth with those of the idler gear **(see illustration)**. Ensure the flywheel mark and key slot are correctly aligned before proceeding.

**20** Fit the Woodruff key to the crankshaft.

**21** Ensure the rotor is fitted so its 'DUCATI' marking is facing inwards (towards the flywheel) then align its slot with the Woodruff

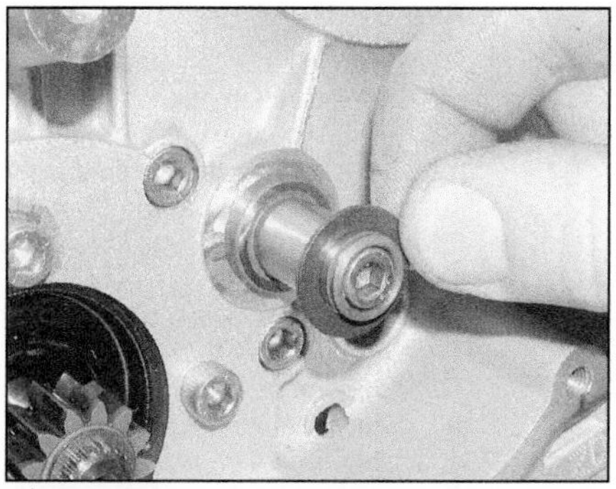

17.16a Fit the inner washer to the shaft . . .

17.16b . . . then install the idler gear and outer washer

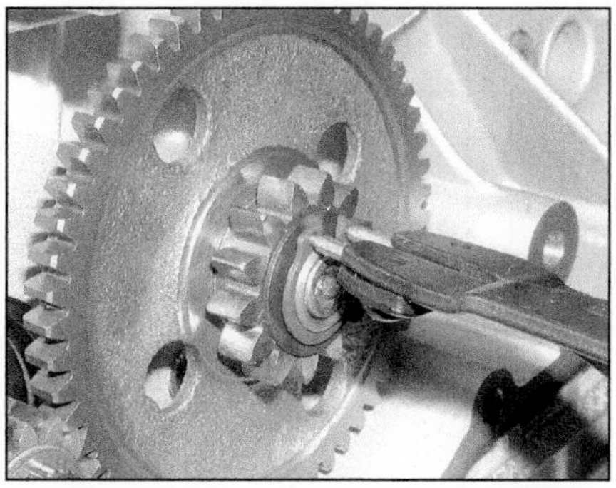

17.16c Secure the idler gear assembly in position with the circlip making sure it is correctly located in the shaft groove

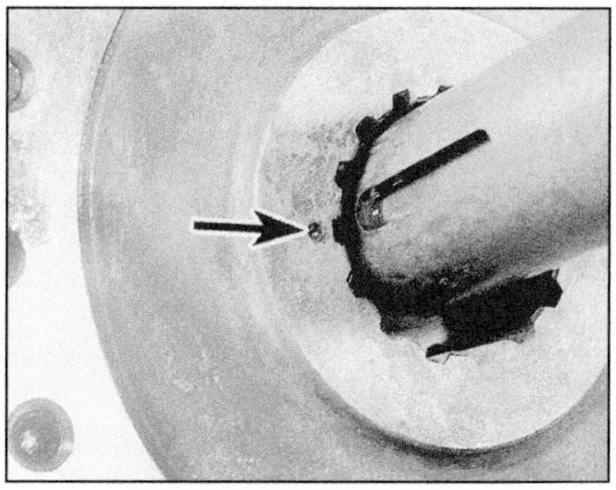

17.19 Slide the assembly onto the crankshaft aligning the punch mark (arrowed) with the Woodruff key slot

17.21 **Install the alternator rotor so its DUCATI marking faces inwards. Ensure the rotor engages correctly with the Woodruff key (arrowed)**

**17.27a Retain the rotor with a strap wrench then slacken the nut**

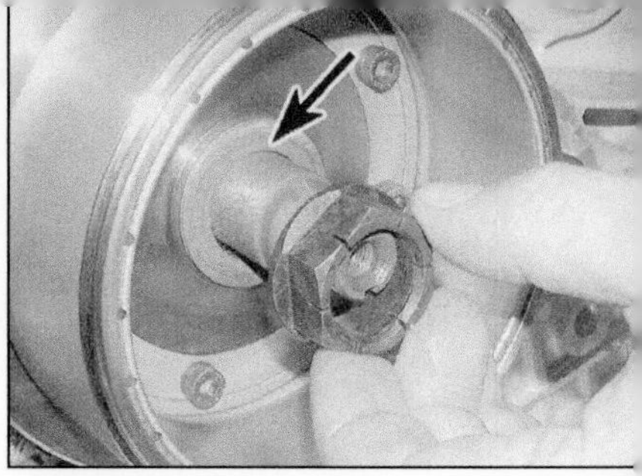

**17.27b Unscrew the flywheel/alternator rotor nut and remove the washer (arrowed)**

key and slide the rotor onto the crankshaft **(see illustration)**.

**22** Fit the dished washer to the crankshaft ensuring its convex side is facing outwards.

**23** Clean the threads of the crankshaft end and flywheel/alternator rotor nut and apply a drop of locking compound to the nut threads. Screw the nut onto the crankshaft and tighten it to the specified torque, preventing rotation using the method employed on removal.

**24** Remove any traces of excess locking compound from the crankshaft end then install the crankcase cover (see Section 16).

## Later (1999 model year on) models

### Removal

**25** Remove the left-hand side crankcase cover (see Section 16).

**26** It is necessary to prevent crankshaft rotation to enable the flywheel/alternator rotor nut to be slackened. If the Ducati holding tool (88713.1419) is not available, the options are as follows.

a) *Retain the flywheel or alternator rotor with a heavy-duty strap wrench.*

b) *If the engine is still in the frame, the crankshaft can be locked by placing the transmission in gear and having an assistant firmly apply the rear brake.*

**27** Slacken the flywheel/alternator rotor retaining nut whilst preventing the crankshaft from rotating **(see illustration)**. Remove the nut from the end of the crankshaft and slide off the dished washer, noting which way around it is fitted **(see illustration)**. Discard the nut; a new one must be used on installation.

**28** Remove the flywheel/alternator rotor and starter clutch assembly from the end of the crankshaft.

**29** Remove the starter clutch needle roller bearing and centre bush from the crankshaft and recover the washer.

**30** Remove the circlip then slide the outer washer, starter idler gear and inner washer off the pivot shaft. If necessary, unscrew the retaining bolt and remove the pivot shaft from the crankcase.

### Inspection

**31** Inspect the starter clutch driven gear and idler gear teeth and renew them as a set if any teeth are chipped or missing. Check the idler gear shaft and gear bearing surfaces for signs of wear or damage, and renew if necessary. If the gear teeth are damaged, also check the condition of the starter motor pinion; the pinion is retained by a circlip and is easily renewed.

**32** Check the starter clutch driven gear, needle roller bearing and centre bush contact surfaces for wear or scoring. Renew worn components as necessary.

**33** Hold the flywheel in one hand and with the other, attempt to rotate the starter clutch

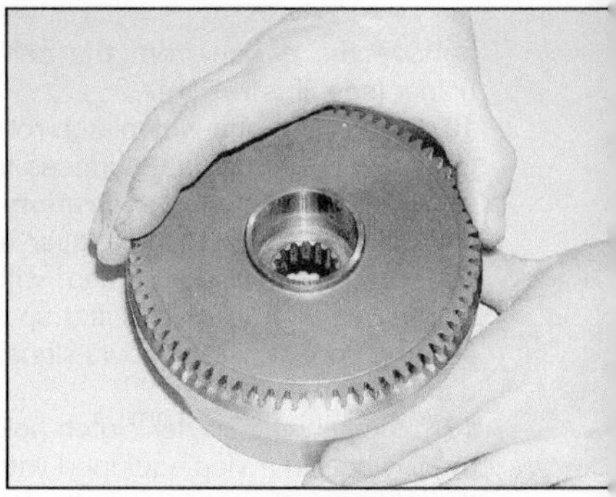

**17.33 Checking the starter clutch operation**

driven gear **(see illustration)**. It should rotate freely in one direction and lock up in the other. If the driven gear turns freely in both directions, or is locked solid, dismantle the starter clutch assembly and inspect the components as follows.

**34** Remove the driven gear from the rear of the flywheel **(see illustration)**. Retain the alternator rotor in a vice equipped with soft jaws then slacken and remove the bolts securing the alternator rotor to the flywheel and starter clutch holder. Separate the alternator rotor and flywheel and recover the locating pin and circlip arrangement **(see illustration)**. Remove the starter clutch holder from the rear of the flywheel, noting which way around it is fitted, then separate the one-way clutch and holder **(see illustration)**.

**17.34a Remove the driven gear from the rear of the flywheel**

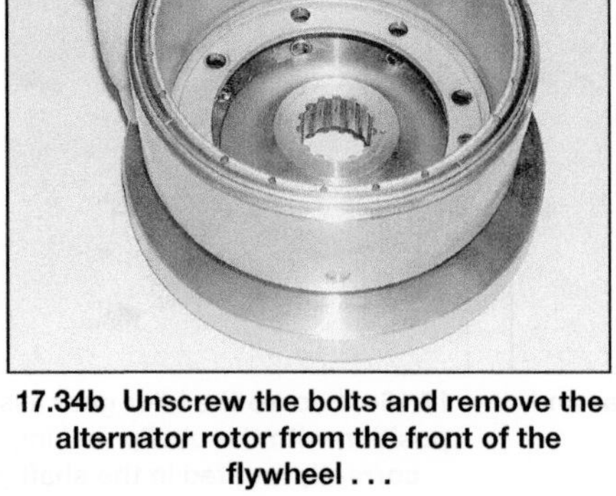

**17.34b Unscrew the bolts and remove the alternator rotor from the front of the flywheel . . .**

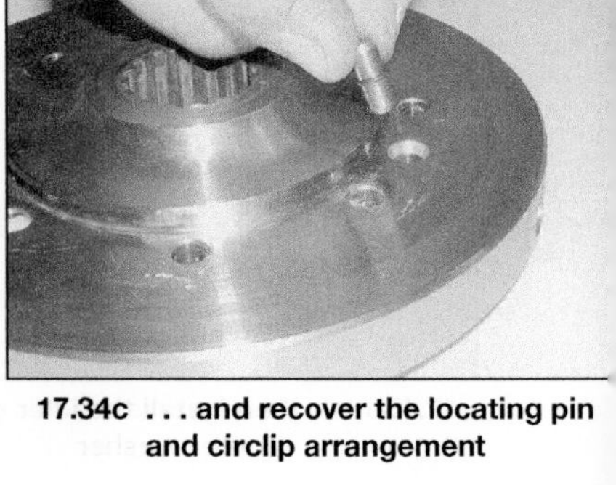

**17.34c . . . and recover the locating pin and circlip arrangement**

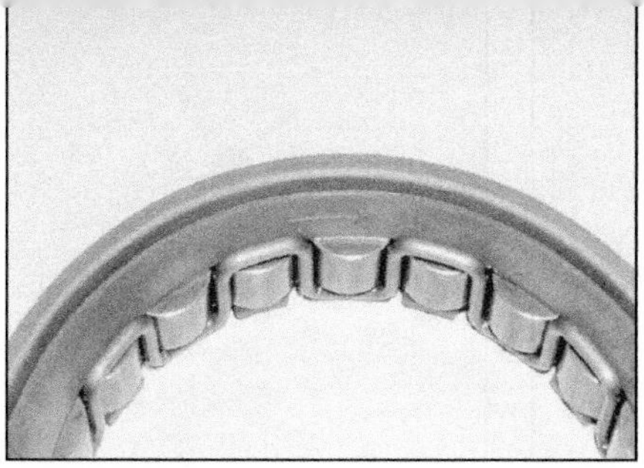

17.35 Check the one-way clutch rollers for signs of wear or damage

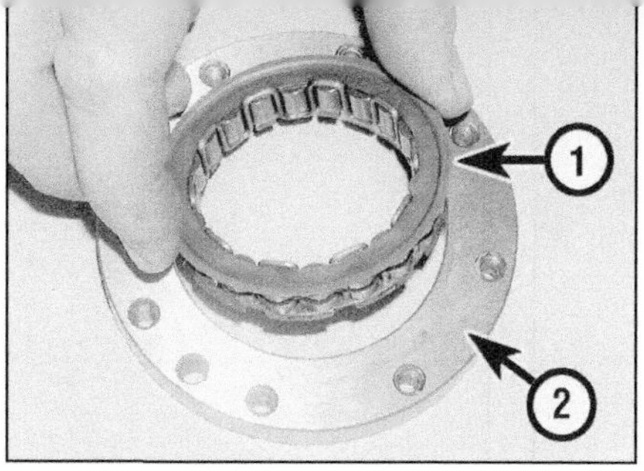


17.36a Fit the one-way clutch to the holder ensuring its flange (1) is against the side of the holder with the tapered outer edge (2)

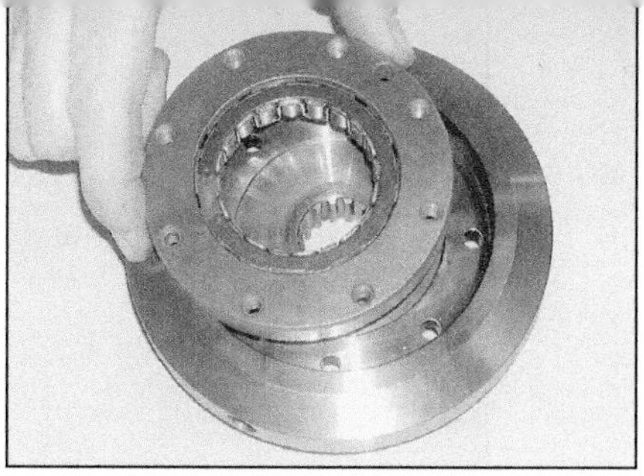

17.36b Fit the clutch and holder assembly to the flywheel ensuring the clutch flange and holder tapered edge are facing the flywheel . . .

**35** Inspect the one-way clutch rollers, driven gear and holder contact surfaces for signs of wear and scoring. The one-way clutch rollers and the gear and holder surfaces should be unmarked with no signs of wear such as pitting or flat spots **(see illustration)**. Renew worn components as necessary.

**36** On reassembly, remove all traces of locking compound from the threads of the retaining bolts and lubricate the clutch, holder and driven gear surfaces with clean engine oil. Fit the one-way clutch to the holder, ensuring its flange is correctly positioned against the side of the holder with the tapered outer edge **(see illustration)**. Fit the holder and clutch assembly to the rear of the flywheel, ensuring the holder's tapered outer edge and one-way clutch flange are facing the flywheel **(see illustration)**. Fit four of the retaining bolts and use the bolts to draw the starter clutch holder squarely into the flywheel **(see illustration)**. Once the holder is correctly seated remove the bolts. Fit the circlip and locating pin arrangement to the flywheel then fit the alternator rotor, engaging it with the pin. Apply a drop of locking compound to the threads of the alternator rotor bolts then install the bolts and tighten them evenly and progressively to the specified torque **(see illustration)**. Fit the driven gear and check the operation of the starter clutch (see Step 33).

## Installation

**37** Install the starter idler gear (see Steps 15 and 16).

**38** Lubricate the starter clutch needle roller bearing and centre bush with clean engine oil. Slide the bearing onto the bush then fit the washer **(see illustration)**. Slide the assembly fully onto the crankshaft, ensuring the washer is innermost and remains on the bush, until the bush is in firm contact with the timing gear **(see illustration)**.

***Caution: Ensure the bush remains tight against the timing gear at all times. If not, the washer may slip off the rear of the bush and become trapped between the bush and gear. This would cause the flywheel not to seat properly on the crankshaft and will result in serious engine damage.***

**39** Ensure the driven gear is correctly installed and check the operation of the starter clutch (see Step 33).

**40** Slide the flywheel and starter clutch assembly onto the crankshaft. Align the punch mark on the flywheel hub with the notch on the crankshaft and engage the flywheel with the crankshaft splines whilst aligning the driven gear teeth with those of the idler gear **(see illustration)**. Ensure the flywheel mark and crankshaft notch are correctly aligned before proceeding.

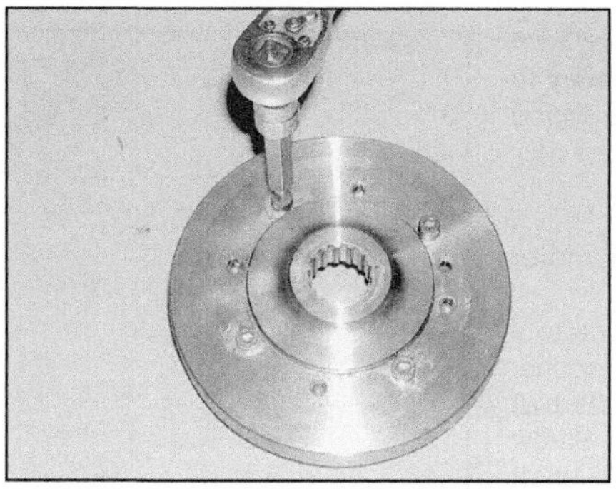

17.36c . . . and draw the assembly into position using the rotor bolts

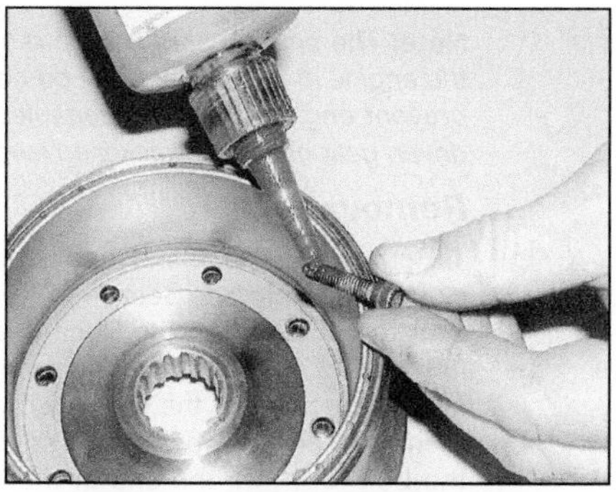

17.36d Apply locking compound to the retaining bolts and tighten them to the specified torque

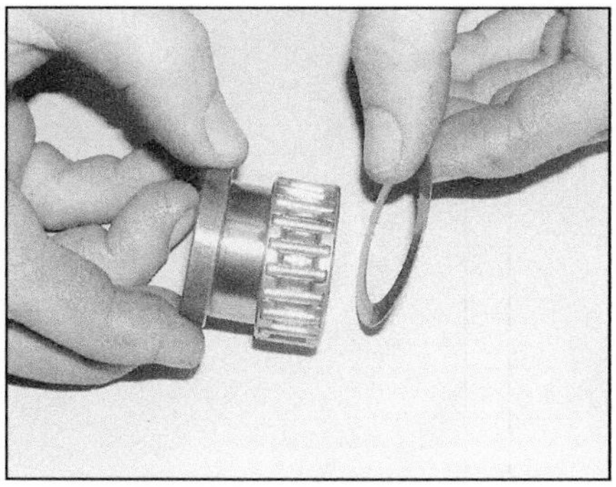

17.38a Slide the needle roller bearing and washer onto the centre bush . . .

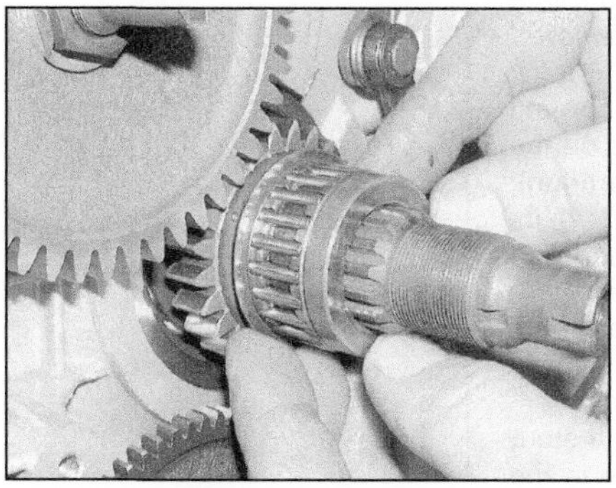

17.38b . . . then slide the assembly onto the crankshaft ensuring the washer is innermost

17.40 Engage the assembly with the crankshaft splines aligning the punch mark (1) with the crankshaft slot (2)

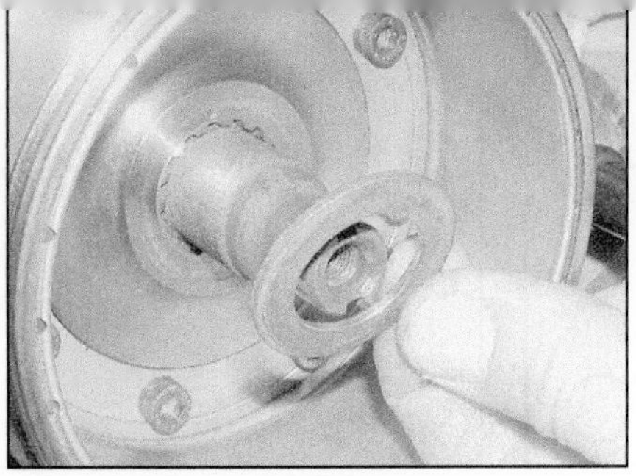

**17.41 Fit the dished washer with its convex surface facing outwards**

**41** Fit the dished washer to the crankshaft ensuring its convex side is facing outwards **(see illustration)**.

**42** Lubricate the threads and contact face of the new flywheel/alternator rotor nut with clean engine oil then screw the nut onto the crankshaft. Prevent rotation using the method employed on removal and tighten the nut to the specified torque **(see illustration)**.

**43** Install the crankcase cover (see Section 16).

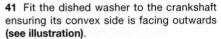

## 18 Timing gears – removal, inspection and installation

**Note:** *The timing gears can be removed with the engine in the frame. It will be necessary to prevent engine rotation to enable the timing driven gear nut to be slackened (see Step 5).*

### Removal

**1** Remove the flywheel and starter motor clutch assembly (see Section 17).

**2** In the absence of the Ducati service tool (88713-0123), obtain an M8 bolt, nut, washer and spacer. Screw the nut fully onto the bolt then slide on the washer and spacer. Screw the bolt fully into the end of the crankshaft and tighten the nut against the spacer to lock it in position; the bolt can then be used to rotate the crankshaft.

**Note:** *It will be considerably easier to rotate the crankshaft if the spark plugs are removed (see Chapter 1).*

**3** Using a socket/spanner on the bolt, rotate the crankshaft until the timing marks on the drive and driven gears align **(see illustration)**.

**Note:** *Always rotate the crankshaft in its normal direction of rotation (clockwise when viewed from the left-hand side of the engine).*

**4** Bend the lockwasher tab back clear of the driven gear nut, using a hammer and suitable chisel/punch **(see illustration)**.

**5** In order to prevent rotation, insert a stout metal rod or punch through the hole in the driven gear and locate it in the crankcase casing. Hold the rod/punch then unscrew the driven gear nut and remove the lockwasher

**17.42 Fit a new flywheel/alternator rotor nut and tighten it to the specified torque**

**(see illustration)**. Discard the lockwasher; a new one should be used on installation.

**6** Remove the driven gear from the timing belt driveshaft, noting which way around it is fitted **(see illustration)**. If the Woodruff key is a loose-fit in the driveshaft, remove it and store it with the gear. **Note:** *On some engines, an offset Woodruff key may be fitted to the driven gear (the key is used to adjust the valve timing – see Section 7). Where an offset Woodruff key is used, make a careful note of which way around the key is fitted to ensure it is installed correctly on installation. If the key is incorrectly fitted the valve timing will be altered.*

***Caution: If the cylinder heads are still installed, do not rotate the timing belt driveshaft or crankshaft whilst the timing gears are removed, otherwise the valves could contact the pistons, causing serious engine damage.***

**7** Slide the drive gear off the crankshaft noting which way around it is fitted **(see illustration)**. If the Woodruff key is a loose-fit remove it from the crankshaft and store it with the drive gear for safe-keeping.

### Inspection

**8** Inspect the gears for signs of damage, such as chipped or worn teeth. If either gear shows signs of wear of damage, renew both gears as a matched pair.

### Installation

**9** Fit the drive gear Woodruff key to the

**18.3 Align the timing marks (arrowed) on the timing gears prior to removal**

**18.4 Bend the lockwasher tab back clear of the driven gear nut . . .**

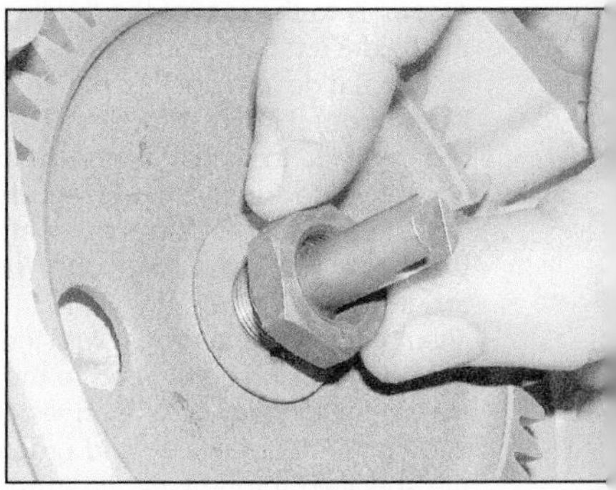

**18.5 . . . then slacken and remove the nut and lockwasher**

**18.6 Slide off the driven gear and recover the Woodruff key from the driveshaft**

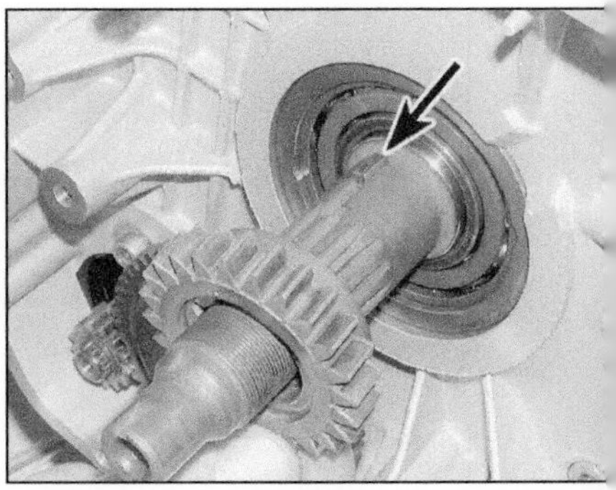

**18.7 Remove the drive gear from the crankshaft and recover the Woodruff key (arrowed)**

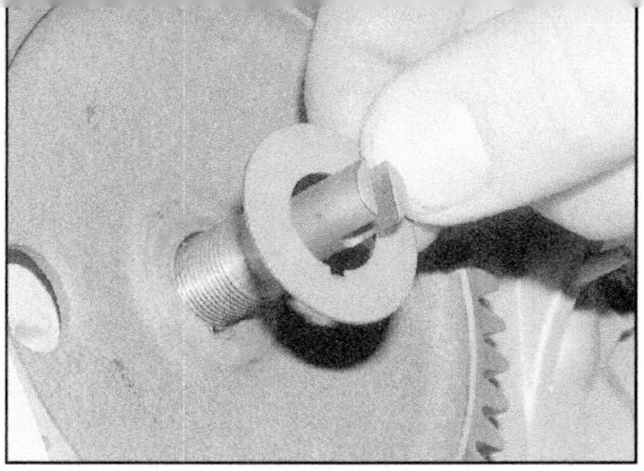

**18.12a Fit the new lockwasher to the drive gear . . .**

**18.12b . . . then tighten the nut to the specified torque whilst retaining the gear with a punch as shown**

**18.13 Secure the driven gear nut in position by bending the lockwasher up against one of the nut flats**

crankshaft. Ensure the drive gear timing mark is facing outwards then slide the gear onto the crankshaft, aligning its slot with the key. Ensure the crankshaft is positioned so the drive gear timing mark is facing towards the timing belt driveshaft.

**10** Fit the Woodruff key to the timing belt driveshaft. If an offset Woodruff key is fitted, ensure it is installed the same way around as was noted on removal (see **Note** in Step 6).

**11** Ensure the timing mark is facing outwards then locate the driven gear on the driveshaft. Align the driven gear timing mark with the mark on drive gear and engage the gear teeth whilst at the same time aligning the gear slot with its key. Slide the driven gear fully onto the driveshaft and ensure the timing marks are correctly aligned before proceeding **(see illustration 18.3)**.

**12** Fit the new lockwasher to the driveshaft and screw on the retaining nut. Prevent rotation using the rod/punch and tighten the nut to the specified torque **(see illustrations)**.

**13** Secure the driven gear nut in position by bending the lockwasher up against one of the nut flats **(see illustration)**.

**14** Install the flywheel and starter motor clutch assembly (see Section 17).

## 19 Gearchange mechanism – removal, inspection and installation

**Note:** *The external gearchange mechanism can be removed with the engine in the frame.*

### Removal

**1** Remove the flywheel and starter motor clutch assembly (see Section 17).

**2** Prior to removal, make alignment marks between the gearchange mechanism mounting bracket and the crankcase and also the selector claw and the crankcase **(see illustrations)**. These marks can then be used to realign the mechanism on installation (the retaining bolt holes are slotted for adjustment).

**3** Slacken and remove the two retaining bolts and washers and remove mechanism from the crankcase **(see illustrations)**.

### Inspection

**4** Examine the gearchange mechanism for signs of wear or damage, paying particular attention to the selector claw and the mechanism springs. Any worn component must be renewed; all components are available separately. Note that the selector drum pins can only be accessed once the drum is removed from the crankcase.

**5** To renew the selector claw, note the correct fitted location of the spring, then unhook it from the claw. Remove the retaining clip and washer then remove the claw and spring from the mechanism arm. On reassembly, fit the spring to the mechanism shoulder ensuring its shorter hook is correctly engaged with the arm. Fit the selector claw to the arm and secure it in position with the washer and retaining clip. Ensure the retaining clip is correctly located in its groove then hook the spring back over the claw **(see illustration)**.

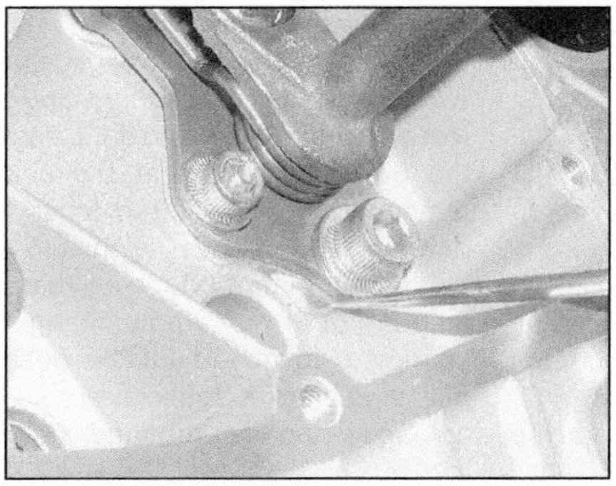

**19.2a Prior to removal, make alignment marks between the gearchange mechanism mounting bracket . . .**

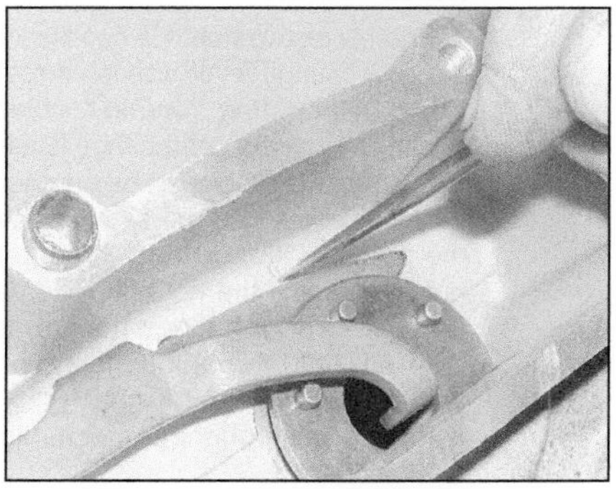

**19.2b . . . and the selector claw and crankcase to use on installation**

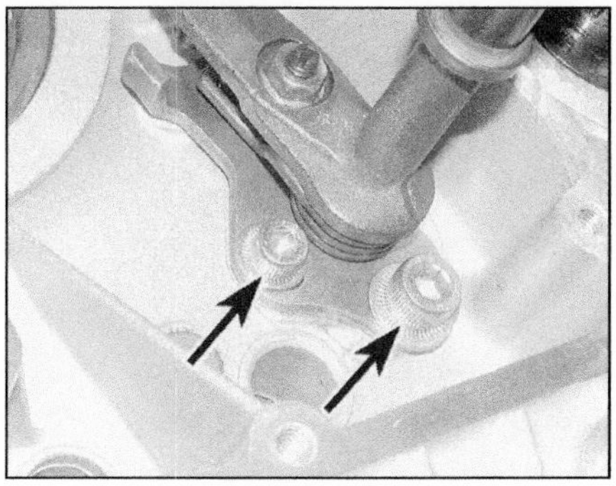

**19.3a Unscrew the retaining bolts (arrowed) . . .**

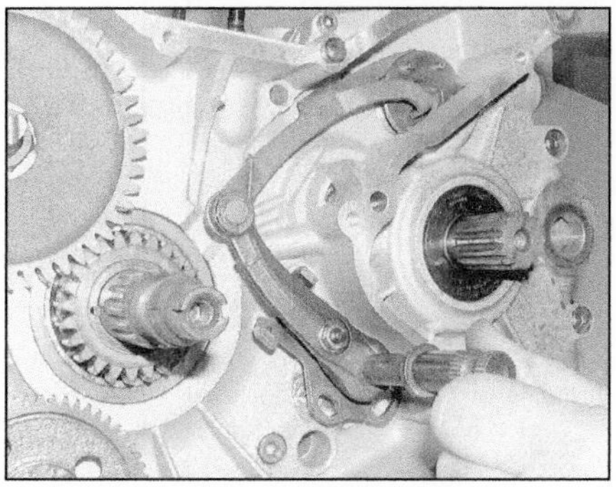

**19.3b . . . and remove the gearchange mechanism from the engine**

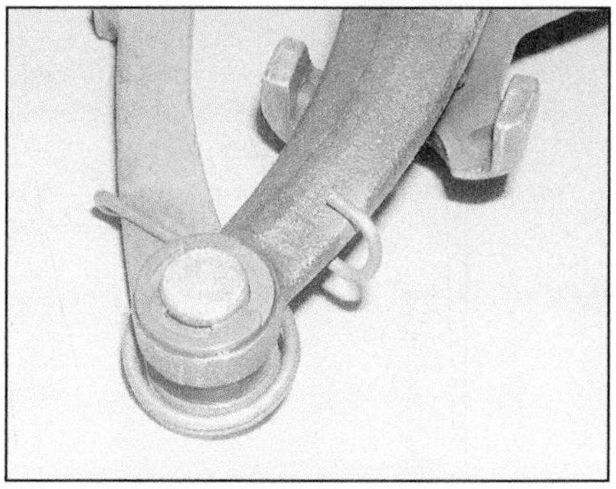

**19.5 Selector claw circlip and spring**

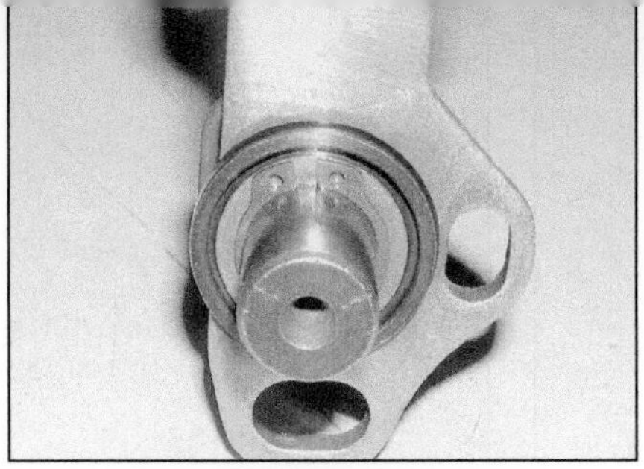

19.6 Gearchange lever circlip

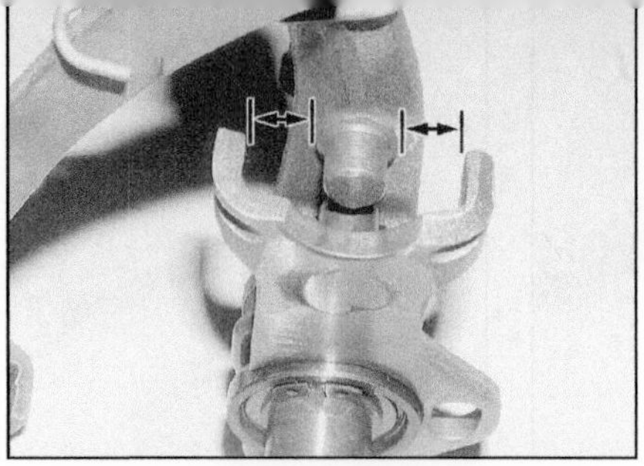

**19.7a Ensure the distance between the arm pin and mounting bracket tabs is equal on both sides**

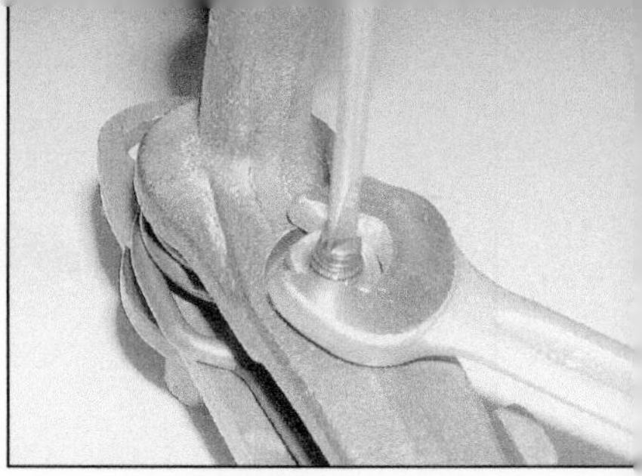

**19.7b If adjustment is necessary, slacken the locknut and rotate the eccentric adjustment pin**

**6** To renew the mechanism gearchange lever shaft, remove the circlip and washer then separate the shaft assembly from the mounting bracket **(see illustration)**. Remove the spacer and centring spring from the shaft then undo the nut and remove the adjustment pin. On reassembly, fit the adjustment pin to the lever arm and fit the nut. Fit the centring spring, engaging it with the adjustment pin, and slide on the spacer. Assemble the gearchange lever and mounting bracket ensuring the centring spring engages with the bracket pin. Fit the washer to the gearchange lever shaft and secure it in position with the circlip, ensuring it is correctly located in its groove. Adjust the mechanism as described in Step 7.

### Installation

**7** Prior to installation it is necessary to ensure the gearchange lever arm is correctly centred in the mounting bracket. Measure the distance from the gearchange lever arm pin to the mounting bracket tabs on each side; the distance should be the same on each side of the pin **(see illustration)**. If not, slacken the nut and rotate the eccentric adjustment pin **(see illustration)**. Once the arm is correctly centred, hold the adjustment pin stationary and securely tighten the nut.

**8** Fit the gearchange mechanism to the crankcase, engaging the selector claw with the drum, and fit the retaining bolts and washers. Align the marks made prior to removal and lightly tighten the retaining bolts.

**9** The mounting bracket must be positioned so the selector claw is centrally located in relation to the selector drum pins. The selector claw has a line scribed on it which is designed to be used with the Ducati alignment tool (88713.1091); fit the alignment tool to the end of the selector drum and align the claw mark with the edge of the tool. If the alignment tool is not available the centre position will have to be judged by eye.

**10** To check the mounting bracket is correctly positioned, temporarily fit the gearchange lever to the shaft and shift the transmission into second gear whilst observing the selector claw movement then return it to neutral (rotate the front sprocket to help engage the gear; this will mean using an auxiliary stand to raise the rear wheel off the ground if the engine is still in the frame). Check that the selector claw remains correctly centred around the drum, both when the transmission is in gear and in neutral, and that the claw has the same amount of travel when changing up and changing down. Adjust the position of the mounting bracket as necessary.

**11** Once the gearchange mechanism is correctly adjusted, taking great care not to move the bracket, remove one of the mounting bolts. Clean the bolt and apply a drop of fresh locking compound to its threads then refit it and tighten it securely. Remove the other bolt, apply locking compound to its threads, then refit it and tighten it securely.

**12** Ensure the mechanism is still correctly adjusted then refit the flywheel and starter motor clutch (see Section 17) and the crankcase cover (see Section 16).

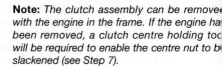

## 20 Clutch – removal, inspection and installation

**Note:** *The clutch assembly can be removed with the engine in the frame. If the engine has been removed, a clutch centre holding tool will be required to enable the centre nut to be slackened (see Step 7).*

### Removal

**1** Remove the fairing right-hand lower panel (see Chapter 8).

**2** Undo the retaining screws and remove the clutch cover from the right-hand crankcase cover **(see illustration)**. Remove the cover gasket (where fitted – not all models have one) **(see illustration)**.

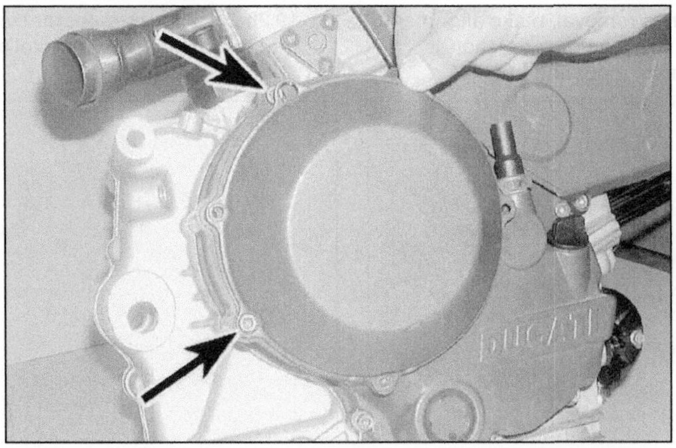

**20.2a Unscrew the retaining bolts (the two bolts arrowed do not need to be removed) and remove the clutch cover . . .**

**20.2b . . . and gasket (where fitted) from the engine**

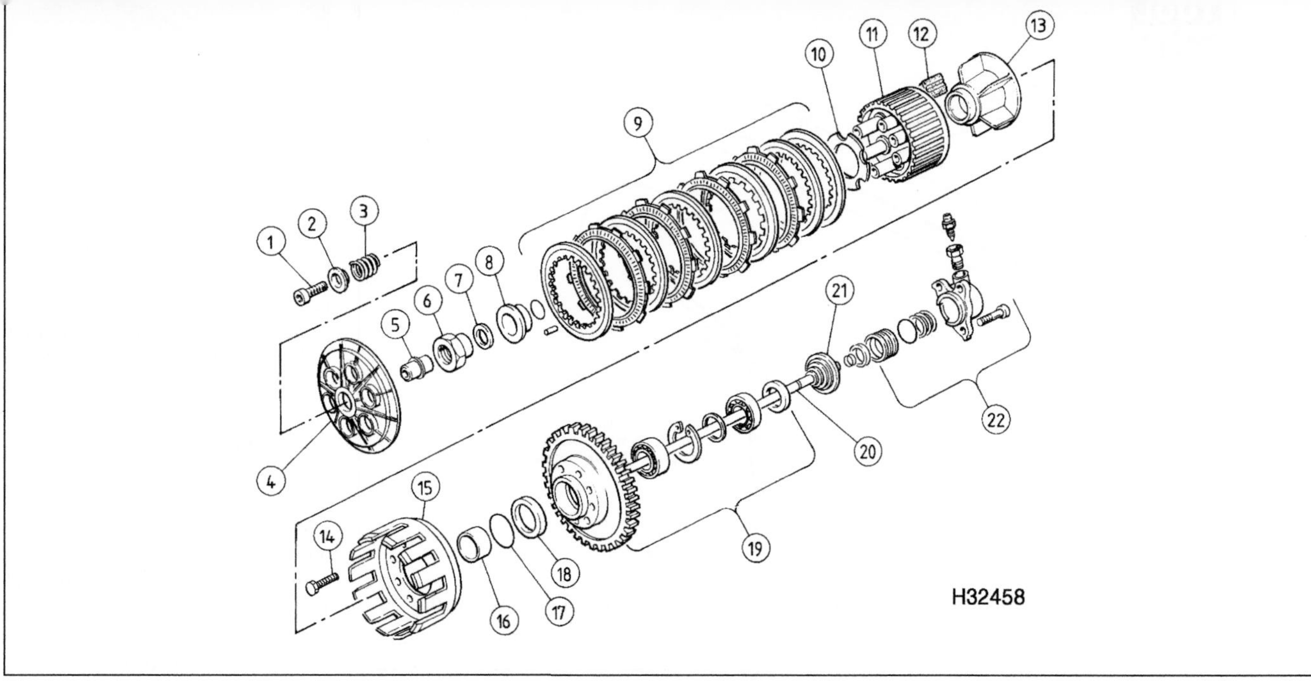


**20.3a Clutch components**

1 *Spring bolt*
2 *Collar*
3 *Spring*
4 *Pressure plate*
5 *Clutch lifter*
6 *Centre nut*
7 *Serrated washer*
8 *Locating collar*
9 *Friction and plain plates*
10 *Large thrust washer*
11 *Clutch centre*
12 *Cush drive rubber*
13 *Drive hub*
14 *Clutch drum bolt*
15 *Clutch drum*
16 *Inner sleeve*
17 *Sealing ring*
18 *Oil seal*
19 *Primary driven gear and associated components*
20 *Pushrod*
21 *Rubber gaiter*
22 *Clutch slave cylinder components*

**3** Working in a criss-cross pattern, gradually slacken the clutch spring retaining bolts until all spring pressure is released. Unscrew the bolts and remove them along with the collars and springs **(see illustrations)**.

**4** Remove the pressure plate, complete with release bearing and clutch lifter **(see illustration)**. Remove the lifter from the centre of the bearing. Remove the sealing ring (where fitted – not all models have one) from the clutch lifter and discard it; a new one should be used on installation.

**5** Slide the pushrod out of position, noting which way around it is fitted **(see illustration)**. If the pushrod sealing rings show signs of damage or deterioration they must be renewed.

**6** Withdraw the clutch friction plates and plain plates, keeping them in order **(see illustration)**. Note that not all the plain plates are identical (see Steps 28 and 29).

**7** To slacken the clutch centre nut the input shaft/clutch centre must be locked in one of the following ways.

a) *If the engine is in the frame, lock the clutch through the transmission, by selecting top gear and applying the rear brake hard whilst the nut is slackened.*
b) *Retain the clutch centre with Ducati service tool (88713.0148) or a universal clutch centre holding tool (available from most good motorcycle accessory*

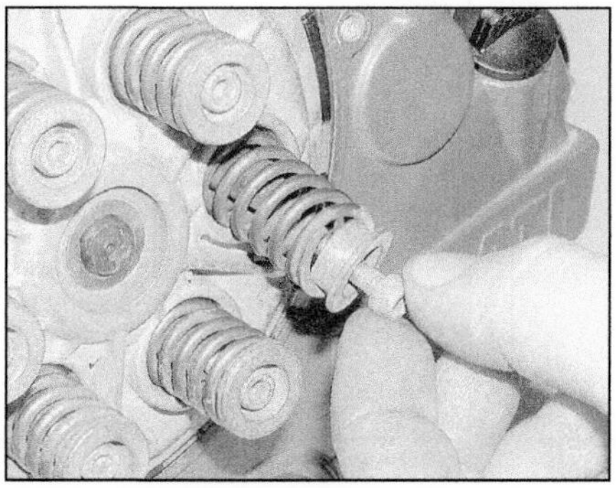

**20.3b Unscrew the clutch spring retaining bolts and remove them complete with the collars and springs . . .**

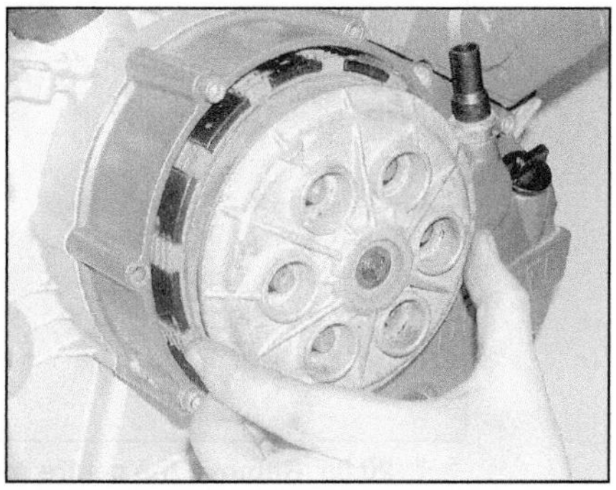

**20.4 . . . then remove the pressure plate . . .**

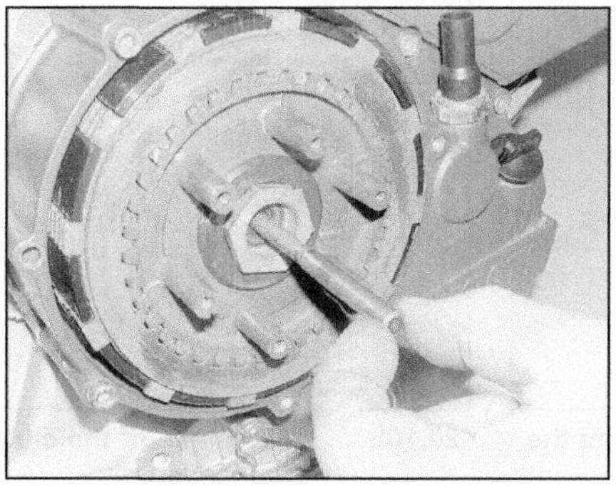

**20.5 . . . and slide out the pushrod**

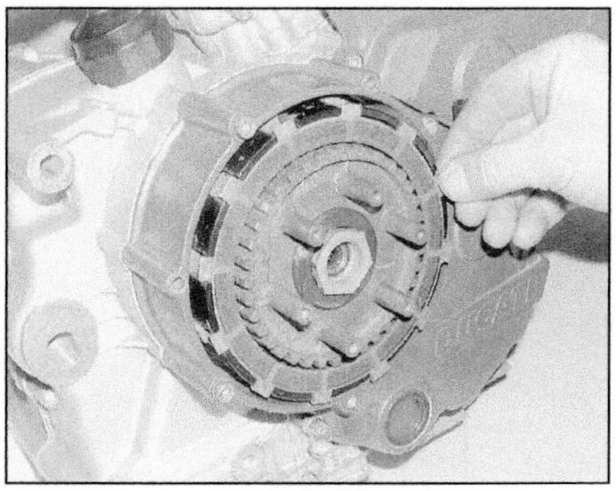

**20.6 Remove the clutch friction plates and plain plates, keeping them in their correct fitted order**

**TOOL TiP**

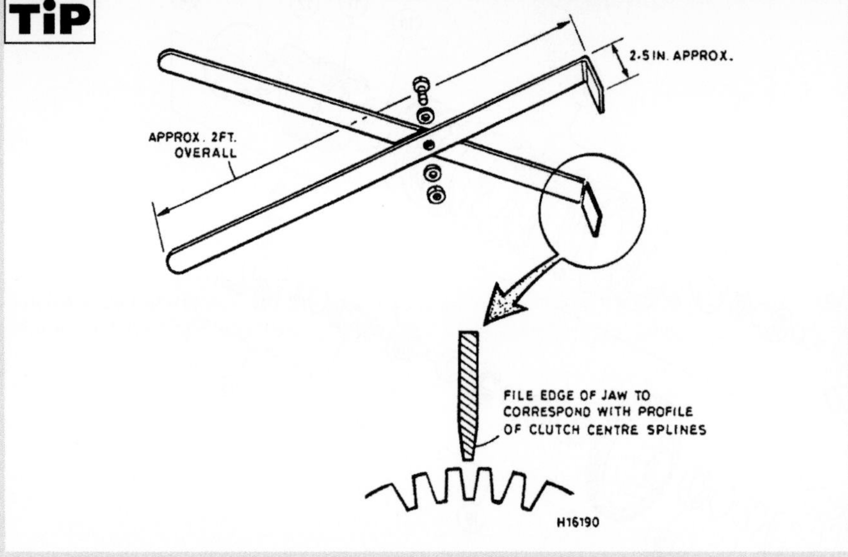


***A clutch centre holding tool can be made from two strips of steel, bent over at the ends and bolted together in the middle***

*dealers). Alternatively, a clutch centre holding tool can be fabricated from some steel strap, bent at the ends and bolted together in the middle **(see Tool Tip and illustration)**.*

**8** Slacken and remove the centre nut and serrated washer **(see illustrations)**.

**9** Remove the locating collar and large thrust washer from the clutch centre **(see illustration)**. If the collar locating pin is a loose-fit, remove it and store it with the collar.

**10** Remove the sealing ring from the end of

**20.7 Using a universal clutch centre holding tool to retain the clutch centre whilst the nut is slackened**

the input shaft then slide off the clutch centre assembly **(see illustrations)**. Discard the sealing ring, a new one must be used on installation.

**11** Withdraw the inner sleeve from the centre of the primary driven gear **(see illustration)**. Note the sealing ring which is fitted to the inside of the sleeve; discard the sealing ring if it must be renewed every time the clutch assembly is removed.

**12** Evenly and progressively slacken the bolts securing the clutch drum to the primary driven gear, preventing rotation using the same method/tool as for the clutch centre. Remove the bolts and manoeuvre the clutch

**20.8a Remove the centre nut . . .**

**20.8b . . . and serrated washer . . .**

**20.9 . . . then remove the large thrust washer**

**20.10a Remove the sealing ring from the end of the input shaft . . .**

**20.10b . . . then slide off the clutch centre assembly**

**20.11 Slide the inner sleeve out from the centre of the primary driven gear, noting which way around it is fitted**

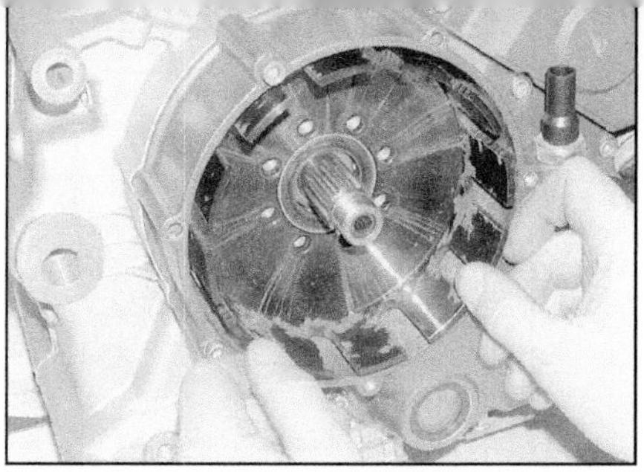

20.12 Unscrew the retaining bolts and remove the clutch drum from the driven gear

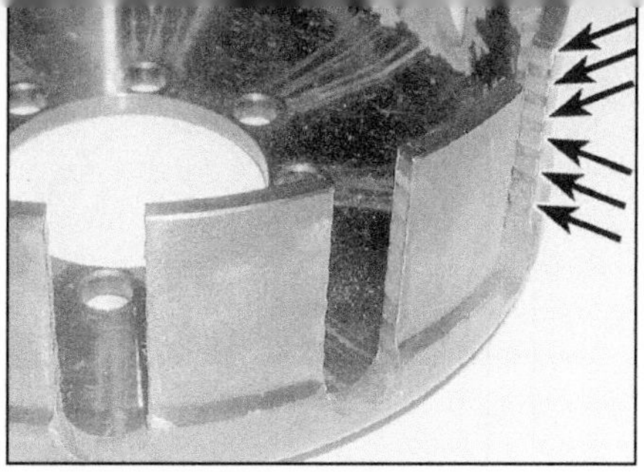

20.14 Check the clutch drum slots for signs of excessive wear

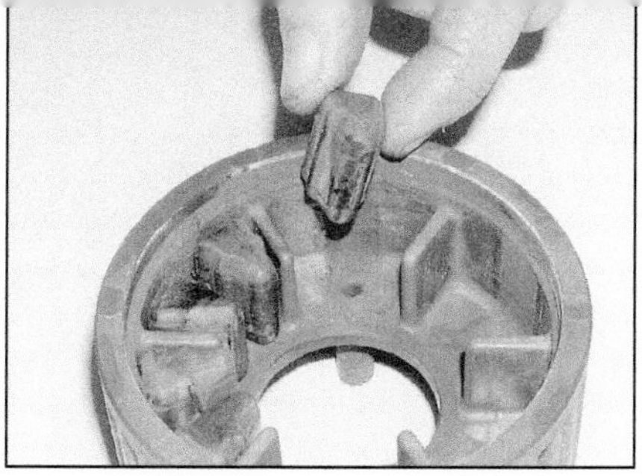

20.16a Ensure the cush drive rubbers are correctly seated in the clutch centre . . .

drum out from the crankcase cover **(see illustration)**. Discard the bolts; new ones should be used on installation.

**13** Whilst the clutch is removed, check the condition of the oil seal in the crankcase cover. If the seal shows signs of damage or leakage, the crankcase cover should be removed and the oil seal renewed (see Section 16). Also check the pushrod grease seal and bearing in the end of the input shaft for signs of damage and deterioration and, if necessary, renew them.

### *Inspection*

**14** Examine the slots in the clutch drum and the tangs of the friction plates for wear **(see illustration)**. A wear pattern will develop over a period of time, and if severe, will restrict clutch operation. If the slots and plate tangs are badly notched, the high spots can be filed off, but take care that this does not reduce the tang-to-slot clearance beyond the service limit.

**15** Inspect the splines of the clutch centre drive hub and the corresponding splines on the input shaft for wear.

**16** Check for signs of freeplay between the clutch centre and its drive hub. The clutch centre assembly incorporates a cush drive type shock absorber. If there is any sign of freeplay between the clutch centre and its drive hub, the cush drive rubbers are in need of renewal. To renew the rubbers, prise the drive hub out from the rear of the clutch centre taking care to damage either the hub or centre. Remove the cush drive rubbers from the inside of the clutch centre. Install the new cush drive rubbers, positioning one on each side of each clutch centre flange. Align the drive hub flanges with the gaps between the cush drive rubbers and push the hub fully into position **(see illustrations)**.

**17** If the lining material of the friction plates smells burnt or appears glazed, new plates are required. If the steel clutch plates are scored or discoloured, they must be renewed with new ones. Measure the thickness of each friction plate and compare the results to the service limit in this Chapter's Specifications **(see illustration)**. Renew the friction plates as a set if any are near the wear limit.

**18** Lay the plain plates, one at a time, on a perfectly flat surface (such as a piece of plate glass) and check for warpage by trying to slip a gauge between the flat surface and the plate **(see illustration)**. The feeler gauge should be the same thickness as the warpage limit listed in this Chapter's Specifications. Do this at several places around the plate's circumference. If the feeler gauge can be slipped under the plate, it is warped and should be renewed.

**19** Measure the free length of the clutch springs with a vernier caliper. If any spring has

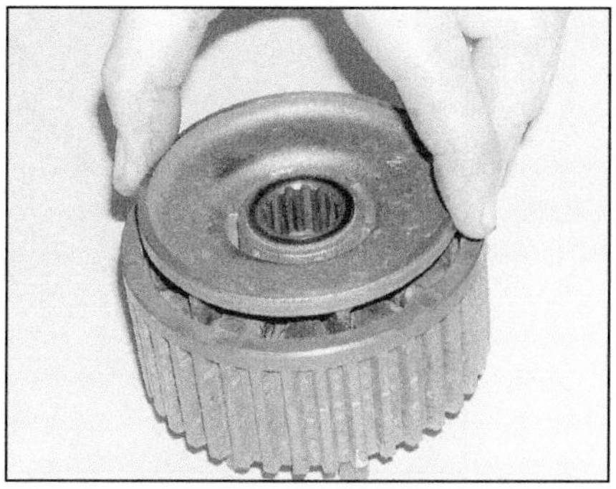

20.16b . . . then insert the hub aligning its flanges with the gaps between the rubbers

set to less than the service limit, all six springs must be renewed.

**20** Rotate the inner race of the pressure plate bearing **(see illustration)**. If it is noisy or notchy in operation renew it. The bearing can be tapped from the pressure plate using a drift. Use a socket or bearing driver which bears only on the bearing outer race to install it in the retainer plate.

### *Installation*

**21** Apply a smear of thread locking/sealing compound to the threads of each of the new clutch drum bolts. Align the drum with the primary driven gear and fit the new bolts **(see**

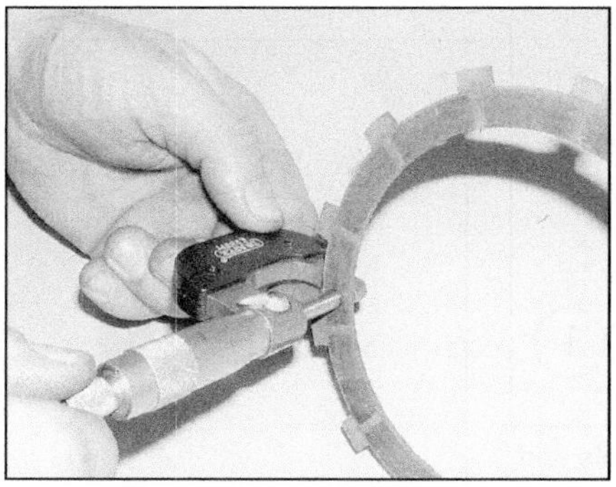

20.17 Measuring friction plate thickness with a micrometer

20.18 Checking a plain plate for warpage

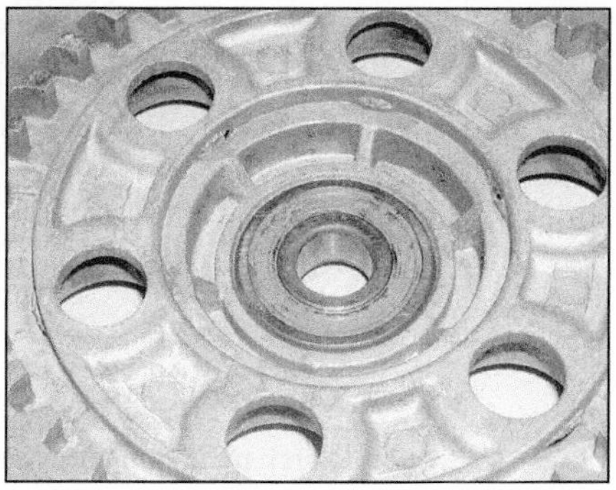

20.20 Check the pressure plate bearing for signs of roughness or freeplay and renew if worn

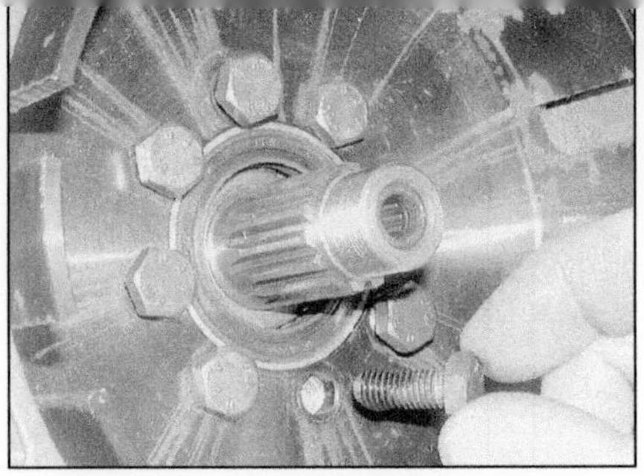

20.21a Apply thread locking/sealing compound to the clutch drum bolts . . .

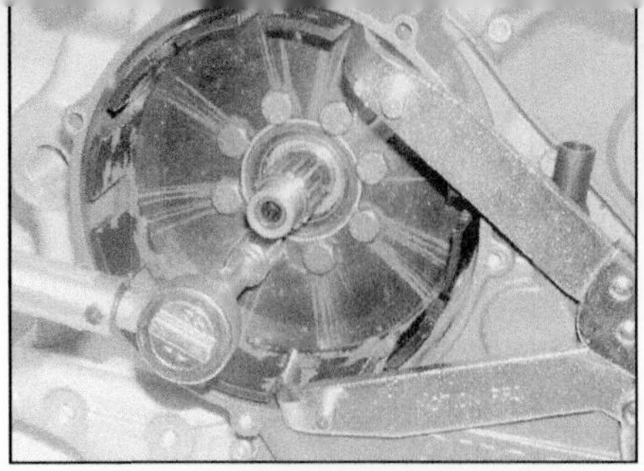

20.21b . . . then tighten them to the specified torque, using the holding tool to prevent rotation

20.22 Fit a new sealing ring to the inner recess of the primary driven gear inner sleeve

20.26 Fit the locating collar ensuring its hole (1) engages correctly with the locating pin (2)

20.27 Retain the clutch centre and tighten the nut to the specified torque

**illustration)**. Working in a criss-cross pattern, tighten the clutch drum bolts evenly and progressively to the specified torque, using the method/tool used on removal to prevent rotation **(see illustration)**.

**22** Fit the new sealing ring to the recess in the centre of the primary driven gear inner sleeve **(see illustration)**. Lubricate the sealing ring and seal lip of the primary driven gear with clean engine oil then carefully slide the inner sleeve into position, ensuring the sealin ring is positioned at the inner end of th sleeve.

**23** Ensure the clutch centre, drive hub an cush drive rubbers are correctly assemble (see Step 16) then slide the assembly onto th input shaft engaging the drive hub spline with those of the shaft.

**24** Ensure the collar locating pin is correct fitted to the clutch centre then fit the ne sealing ring to the end of the input shaft.

**25** Fit the large thrust washer to the clutc centre.

**26** Install the locating collar, ensuring its hol engages correctly with the locating pin, and f the serrated washer **(see illustration)**.

**27** Lubricate the threads and contact face c the clutch centre nut with a smear c molybdenum disulphide grease then fit the nu Tighten the nut to the specified torque settin whilst holding the clutch centre using th method employed on removal **(see illustration**

**28** On 916 SP and SPS models and 996 and SPS models there are three differer types of plain plate; there are six 2.0 mm thic plain plates, two 1.5 mm thick plain plates an two 1.5 mm thick dished plain plates. Ther are eight friction plates which are all identica The plates must be installed as follows **(se illustrations)**.

*a) First install a 2.0 mm plain plate.*

*b) Next fit a 1.5 mm dished plain plate ensuring its convex side is facing outwards (away from 2.0 mm plate).*

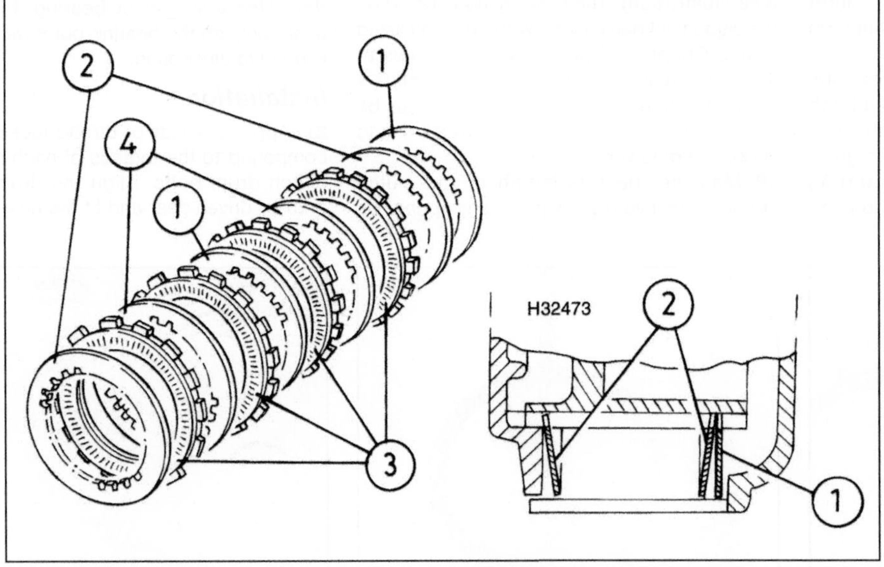


20.28a Clutch plate fitting locations (not all plates shown) – 916 SP and SPS models and 996 S and SPS models

*1 2.0 mm thick plain plate*
*2 1.5 mm thick dished plain plate*
*3 2.5 mm thick friction plate*
*4 1.5 mm thick plain plate*

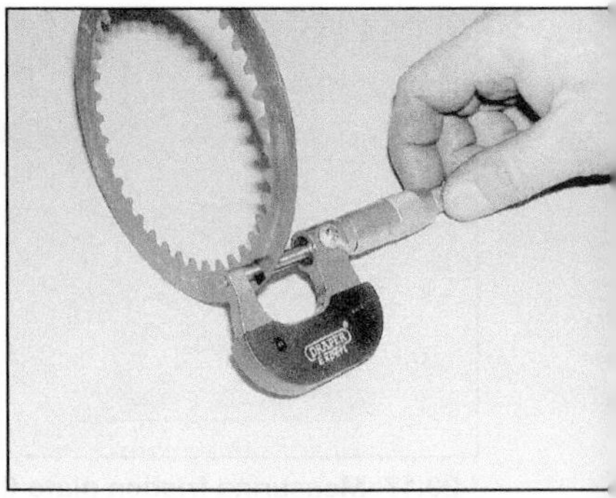

20.28b Use a micrometer to measure the plain plate thickness

*mm plain plate.*

d) *Alternately install the next six friction plates and five 2.0 mm plain plates.*

e) *Next fit the other 1.5 mm plain plate then install the final friction plate.*

f) *Fit the remaining 1.5 mm dished plain plate ensuring its convex side is facing inwards (towards the friction plate).*

**29** On all other models there are two different types of plain plate; there are eight 2.0 mm thick plain plates and a single 1.5 mm thick dished plain plate. There are seven friction plates which are all identical. The plates must be installed as follows **(see illustration)**.

a) *First install two 2.0 mm plain plates.*

b) *Next fit the first friction plate.*

c) *Next fit the 1.5 mm dished plain plate ensuring its convex side is facing outwards (away from installed friction plate).*

d) *Alternately install the remaining friction plates and 2.0 mm plain plates.*

**30** Wipe clean the clutch pushrod. Ensure the sealing rings are both correctly located in the pushrod groves (renew them if they show any sign of damage) then lubricate the pushrod and its grease seal in the end of the input shaft with molybdenum disulphide grease. Taking care not to damage the grease seal, carefully insert the pushrod into the input shaft ensuring that the sealing rings are positioned on left-hand end of the shaft **(see illustration)**. Wipe off any excess grease before proceeding.

**31** Lubricate the clutch lifter and pushrod contact surfaces with a smear of molybdenum disulphide grease. Where a sealing ring was fitted to the clutch lifter, fit the new sealing ring to the lifter recess. Press the clutch lifter into position in the centre of the release bearing and wipe off the excess grease **(see illustration)**.

**32** Fit the pressure plate, complete with the release bearing and clutch lifter. Position the pressure plate so that its clutch spring hole with the cutouts (indicated by the triangular mark on the plate) is correctly aligned with the spring bolt post on the clutch centre with the matching cutouts **(see illustration)**. Engage the pressure plate with the clutch centre ensuring its inner tangs are correctly engaged with the clutch centre slots.

**33** Fit the clutch springs and install the collars and retaining bolts. Gradually tighten the bolts evenly in a criss-cross pattern until they are all securely tightened.

**34** Check the operation of the clutch before proceeding.

**35** Ensure the mating surfaces are clean and dry then refit the clutch cover and gasket (where fitted) to the crankcase cover. Install the cover screws and tighten them evenly and progressively to the specified torque.

**36** Install the fairing panel (see Chapter 8).

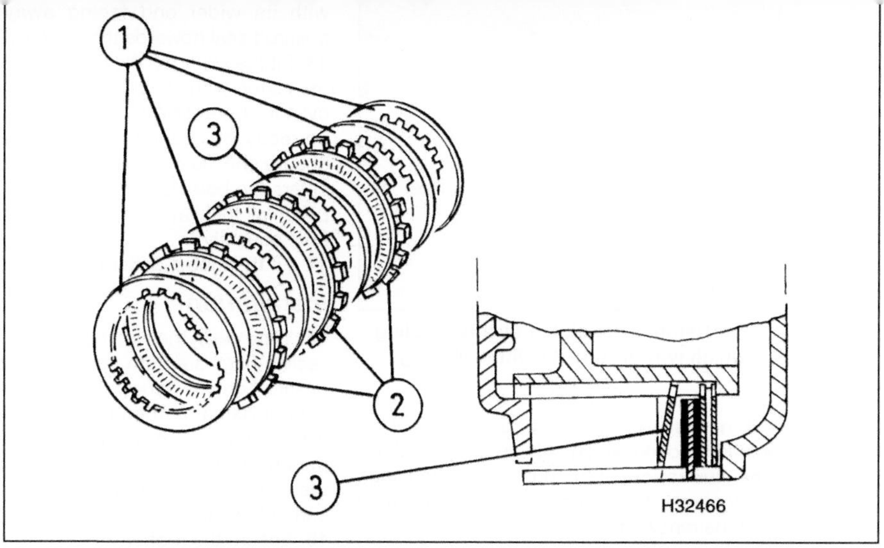


**20.29 Clutch plate fitting locations (not all plates shown) – all other models**

*1 2.0 mm thick plain plate 2 3 mm thick friction plate 3 1.5 mm thick dished plain plate*

## 21 Clutch slave cylinder – removal, overhaul and installation

***Caution: Disassembly, overhaul and reassembly of the slave cylinder must be done in a spotlessly clean work area to avoid contamination and possible failure of the hydraulic system components. Use care when working with hydraulic fluid as it can injure your eyes and it will damage painted surfaces and plastic parts.***

### Removal

**1** Remove the fairing left-hand lower panel as described in Chapter 8.

**2** Note the correct fitted location of the clutch hose end fitting (make alignment marks if necessary), then unscrew the banjo bolt and separate the hose from the slave cylinder. Plug the hose end, or wrap a plastic bag tightly around it, to minimise fluid loss and prevent dirt entering the system. Discard the sealing washers as new ones must be used on installation.

**3** Unscrew the clutch slave cylinder bolts and remove the cylinder from the engine, complete with its rubber gaiter.

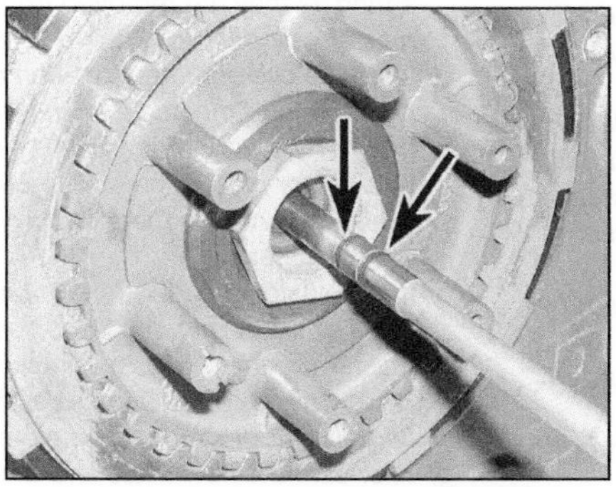

**20.30 Ensure the pushrod is fitted so the sealing rings (arrowed) are on the left-hand end**

**20.31 Insert the clutch lifter into the centre of the pressure plate bearing . . .**

**20.32 . . . then fit the pressure plate aligning its cutouts (1), indicated by the triangular mark (3) with those on the spring post (2)**

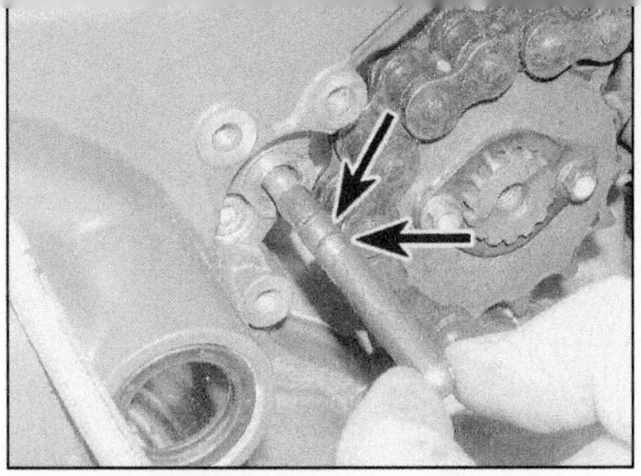

**21.4 Remove the clutch pushrod noting which way around it is fitted (O-rings arrowed)**

**4** If necessary, slide the pushrod out of position, noting which way around it is fitted **(see illustration)**. If the pushrod sealing rings show signs of damage or deterioration they must be renewed.

## Overhaul

**5** Clean the exterior of the cylinder with denatured alcohol or brake system cleaner.

**6** Remove the rubber gaiter then withdraw the piston from the cylinder.

> **HAYNES HiNT** ***If the piston cannot be withdrawn by hand, it can be pushed out by applying compressed air to the clutch hose union hole. Only low pressure should be required, such as is generated by a foot pump, and wrap the slave cylinder in a wad of rag to prevent the piston being forcibly expelled.***

**7** Recover the spring from the cylinder, noting which way round it is fitted.

**8** Carefully remove the fluid seal from the piston, noting which way round it is fitted. Also remove the pushrod seal from the end of the piston.

**9** Clean all parts with clean brake fluid or denatured alcohol. If compressed air is available, use it to dry the parts thoroughly (make sure it is filtered and unlubricated).

***Caution: Do not, under any circumstances, use a petroleum-based solvent to clean slave cylinder parts.***

**10** Inspect the cylinder bore and piston for signs of corrosion, nicks and burrs and loss of plating. If surface defects are present, the cylinder assembly must be renewed. If the cylinder is in bad shape, the master cylinder should also be checked. No specifications are given to check piston and bore wear.

**11** Pack the inside of the piston with molybdenum disulphide grease then press the new pushrod seal into position, ensuring its sealing lip is facing inwards. Wipe off any excess grease.

**12** Lubricate the new piston fluid seal with clean fluid. Fit the seal to the piston groove, with its wider end facing away from the pushrod seal (towards the slave cylinder).

**13** Fit the spring to the cylinder then lubricate the piston with clean fluid and install it in the cylinder bore. Make sure the spring remains correctly positioned and take great care to ensure the fluid seal is not damaged as it enters the bore. Using your thumbs, push the piston all the way in, making sure it enters the bore squarely.

**14** Fit the rubber gaiter to the slave cylinder.

## Installation

**15** Wipe clean the clutch pushrod. Ensure the sealing rings are both correctly located in the pushrod groves (renew them if they show any sign of damage) then lubricate the pushrod with molybdenum disulphide grease. Insert the pushrod into the crankcase ensuring that the sealing rings are positioned on left-hand end of the shaft.

**16** Ensure the rubber gaiter is correctly fitted to the slave cylinder then fit the clutch slave cylinder to the cover. Install the retaining bolts and tighten them to the specified torque setting.

**17** Position a new sealing washer on each side of the clutch hose end fitting, then connect the hose to the slave cylinder. Ensure the hose end fitting is correctly position so it is parallel to the engine, then tighten the banjo bolt to the specified torque.

***Caution: If the clutch hose end fitting is not correctly positioned, the hose may contact the surrounding bodywork, resulting in damage to the hose/paintwork.***

**18** Fill the master cylinder reservoir with the recommended clutch fluid (see *Daily (pre-ride) checks*) and bleed the hydraulic system as described in Section 23.

**19** Check that there are no leaks and thoroughly test the operation of the clutch before installing the fairing panel.

# 22 Clutch master cylinder – removal, overhaul and installation

> ***Warning: If the master cylinder requires overhaul (usually indicated by leaking fluid or failure to produce a firm lever feel, even after repeated bleeding), all old fluid should be flushed from the system. Do not, under any circumstances, use petroleum-based solvents to clean hydraulic parts. Use clean DOT 4 fluid, or denatured alcohol only.***

***Caution: To prevent damage to the paint from spilled fluid, always cover the surrounding components when working on the master cylinder.***

## Removal

**1** Remove all traces of dirt from around the master cylinder clutch hose union then note fitting in relation to the master cylinder. If necessary, make alignment marks to ensure the end fitting is correctly positioned on installation.

**2** Unscrew the banjo bolt and separate the hose from the master cylinder. Plug the hose end or wrap a plastic bag tightly around the hose to minimise fluid loss and prevent dirt from entering the system. Discard the sealing washers, as new ones must be used on installation.

**3** Unscrew the mounting clamp bolts and remove the master cylinder assembly from the handlebar.

**4** Unscrew the fluid reservoir cap and lift out the rubber diaphragm. Empty the reservoir contents into a suitable container.

**5** If necessary, unscrew the bolt securing the fluid reservoir bracket to the master cylinder then release the retaining clip and detach the reservoir hose. The master cylinder and fluid reservoir can then be separated.

## Overhaul

**6** Ducati specify that the master cylinder should not be overhauled and must be renewed if faulty. Therefore Ducati only supply replacement master cylinders and do not list any overhaul kits. The only components that are available separately are the fluid reservoir assembly and its connecting hose as well as the clutch lever.

**7** Before condemning the original master cylinder, check whether a pattern overhaul kit is available from a motorcycle accessory dealer. If a pattern overhaul kit is available carefully follow the instructions supplied with the kit noting the following points.

a) *Ensure absolute cleanliness at all times. Clean components only with denatured alcohol or brake system cleaner. Do not, under any circumstances, use a petroleum-based solvent to clean brake parts.*
b) *If compressed air is being used to dry the parts, make sure it's filtered and unlubricated.*
c) *Note the correct fitted location and orientation of the piston assembly and spring as they are removed from the master cylinder.*
d) *Note the correct fitted location and orientation of the seals on the piston before removing them. Use only a wooden or plastic tool to remove the seals. Never use a metal tool as this could cause damage.*
e) *If the master cylinder bore or piston show signs of wear, damage or corrosion, the master cylinder must be renewed.*
f) *Renew all the disturbed seals, the circlip and dust boot. Never re-use them.*
g) *Lubricate the new seals and the piston with clean brake fluid prior to installation. Ensure the seals are correctly fitted on the piston and make sure the piston and spring are correctly positioned (as noted*

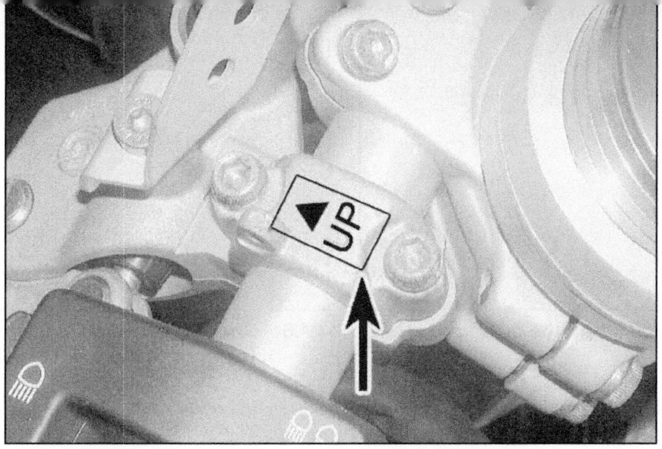


**22.9 Ensure the arrow marking on the master cylinder mounting clamp faces upwards or forwards (as applicable)**

**23.5 Bleeding the clutch hydraulic circuit**

*on removal). When installing the piston, take care not to turn the seal lips inside out as they slip into the bore.*

*h) Ensure the new circlip is correctly located in the cylinder body groove and the dust boot is correctly fitted.*

### Installation

**8** Where necessary, reconnect the fluid reservoir hose to the master cylinder and secure it in position with the retaining clip. Align the fluid reservoir bracket with the cylinder body and securely tighten its retaining bolt.

**9** Locate the master cylinder on the handlebar, aligning its lug with the handlebar hole. Fit the mounting clamp with its arrow mark facing upwards or forwards (as applicable) and install the mounting clamp bolts **(see illustration)**. Tighten the mounting clamp upper/front bolt to the specified torque first, followed by the lower/rear bolt, then recheck the upper/front bolt is correctly torqued.

**10** Position a new sealing washer on each side of the clutch hose union and screw in the banjo bolt. Ensure the end fitting is correctly positioned in relation to the master cylinder body then securely tighten the banjo bolt.

***Caution: If the clutch hose end fitting is not correctly positioned, the hose may contact the surrounding bodywork, resulting in damage to the hose/paintwork.***

**11** Fill the master cylinder reservoir with the recommended hydraulic fluid (see *Daily (pre-ride) checks*) and bleed the hydraulic system as described in Section 23.

**12** Ensure the fluid level is correct then fit the reservoir rubber diaphragm and cap.

**13** Check for leaks and thoroughly test the operation of the clutch before riding the motorcycle.

## 23 Clutch hydraulic system – bleeding

***Caution: To prevent damage to the paint from spilled hydraulic fluid, always cover the fuel tank and fairing panels when working on the master cylinder.***

**1** Bleeding the clutch is simply the process of removing all the air bubbles from the clutch master cylinder, the hose and the slave cylinder. Bleeding is necessary whenever an hydraulic connection is loosened, when a component or hose is renewed, or when the master cylinder or slave cylinder is overhauled. Leaks in the system may also allow air to enter, but leaking fluid will reveal their presence and warn you of the need for repair.

**2** To bleed the clutch, you will need some new DOT 4 hydraulic fluid, a length of clear vinyl or plastic tubing, a small container partially filled with clean hydraulic fluid, some rags and a spanner to fit the slave cylinder bleed valve.

**3** Remove the fairing left-hand lower panel (see Chapter 8) to gain access to the slave cylinder bleed valve.

**4** Remove the master cylinder reservoir cap and diaphragm (see *Daily (pre-ride) checks*). Slowly pump the clutch lever a few times until no air bubbles can be seen floating up from the holes in the bottom of the reservoir. This bleeds the air from the master cylinder end of the line. Loosely refit the reservoir cap.

**5** Pull the dust cap off the slave cylinder bleed valve. Attach one end of the clear vinyl or plastic tubing to the bleed valve and submerge the other end in the brake fluid in the container **(see illustration)**.

**6** Remove the reservoir cap and check the fluid level. Do not allow the fluid level to drop below the lower mark during the bleeding process.

**7** Carefully pump the clutch lever three or four times and hold it in while opening the bleed valve. When the valve is opened, fluid will flow out of the cylinder into the clear tubing.

**8** Retighten the bleed valve, then release the clutch lever gradually. Repeat the process until no air bubbles are visible in the fluid leaving the valve, and the clutch action feels smooth and progressive.

**9** Disconnect the bleeding equipment, then securely tighten the bleed valve and install the dust cap.

**10** Top the fluid level up to the upper level mark (see *Daily (pre-ride) checks*), then install the diaphragm and reservoir cap. Wipe up any spilled fluid and check the system for leaks before installing the fairing panel (see Chapter 8).

**Note:** *Failure to bleed satisfactorily after a reasonable repetition of the bleeding procedure may be due to worn master cylinder seals.*

## 24 Oil pump – removal, inspection and installation

**Note:** *The oil pump can be removed with the engine in the frame.*

### Removal

**1** Remove the right-hand crankcase cover (see Section 16).

**2** Slacken and remove the three retaining bolts and washers securing the oil pump to the crankcase **(see illustration)**.

**3** Free the pump from crankcase and primary

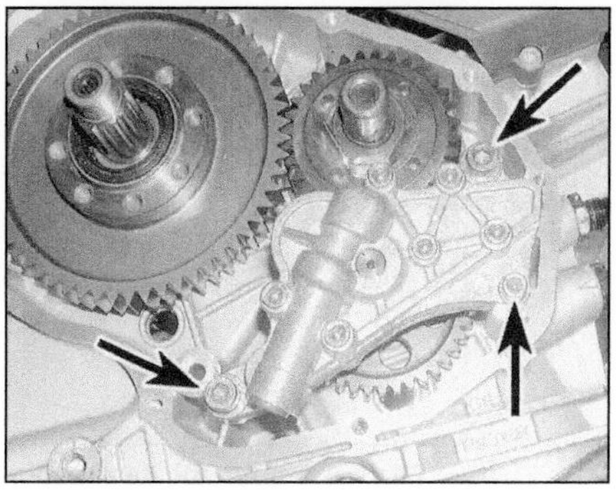

**24.2 Oil pump retaining bolts (arrowed)**

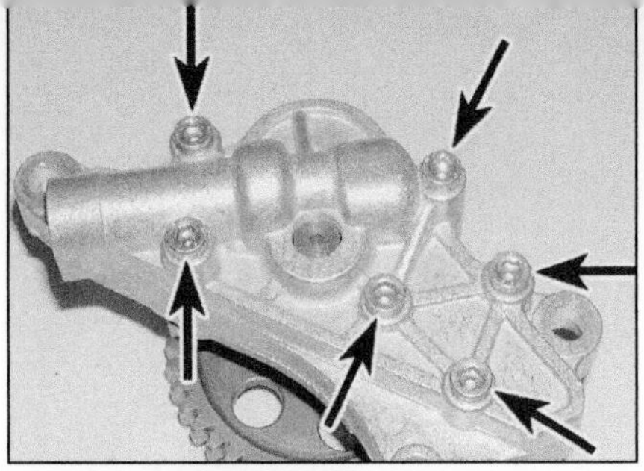

24.4a Unscrew the retaining screws (arrowed) . . .

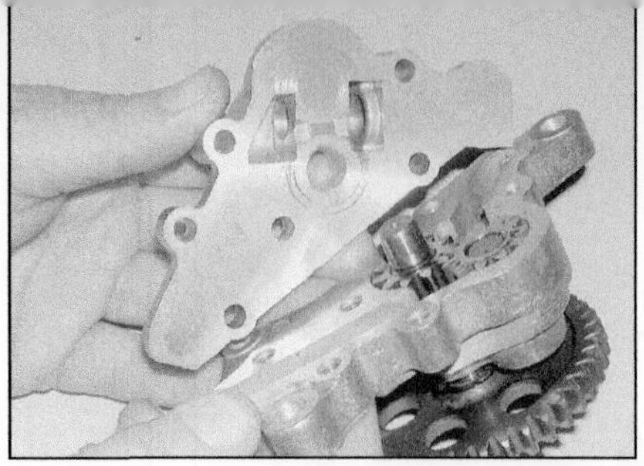

24.4b . . . and lift off the oil pump cover

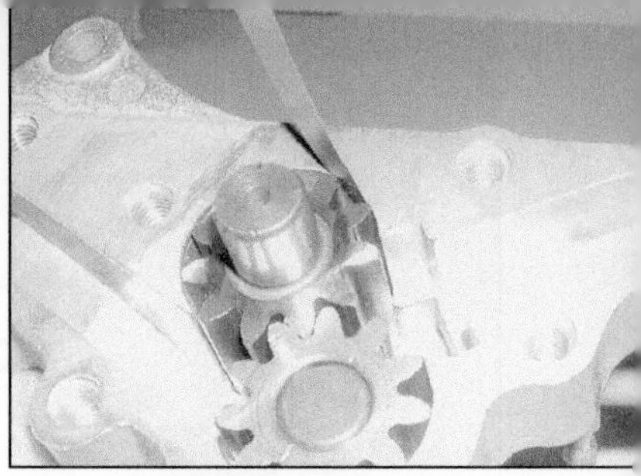

24.6a Checking oil pump gear-to-housing clearance using a feeler gauge

drive gears and manoeuvre it out of position. Recover the pump locating dowels and sealing rings from the crankcase. Discard the sealing rings; new ones must be used on installation.

### *Inspection*

**4** Slacken and remove the retaining screws and remove the pump cover **(see illustrations)**. Wash the oil pump in solvent, then dry it off.

**5** Inspect the cover inner surface and check that it is not badly scored. It can be checked for distortion with a straight-edge and feeler gauges. On 996 models (including the 916 SPS) and later 748 models also check the oil pressure relief valve which is fitted to the pump cover (see Section 26).

**6** Using a feeler blade (a very small set will be required), measure the clearance between the meshed gear teeth, then between the gear teeth and housing (on both gears) **(see illustration)**. Lay a straight-edge across the gear housing and measure the gap between the top surface of the gears and the straight-edge with feeler gauges **(see illustration)**. If any clearance exceeds the specified limits (see Specifications) renew the worn components. Providing the pump body and cover are unmarked the gears can be renewed as a matched pair. If the body or cover show signs of damage, the complete pump assembly should be renewed. To disassemble the pump, proceed a follows.

**7** Prior to disassembly, mark the outer face of the oil pump gear and driven gear fc identification purposes. With the cove removed lift the driven gear from the pum housing, noting which way around it is fitte **(see illustration)**. To remove the drive gea remove the outer circlip from the pump sha and slide off the spacer, noting which wa around it is fitted **(see illustration)**. Remov the centre circlip then slide off the oil pum gear, noting which way around it is fitted **(se illustration)**. Remove the Woodruff key fro the shaft then remove the inner circlip an slide the drive gear out from the housing **(se illustrations)**.

24.6b Using a feeler gauge and straight-edge to check gear endfloat

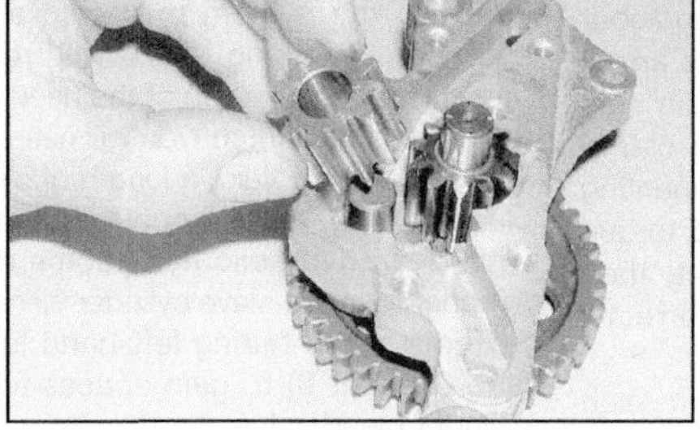

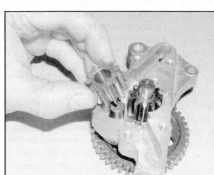

24.7a Remove the driven gear from the pump

24.7b Remove the outer circlip and slide off the spacer (arrowed)

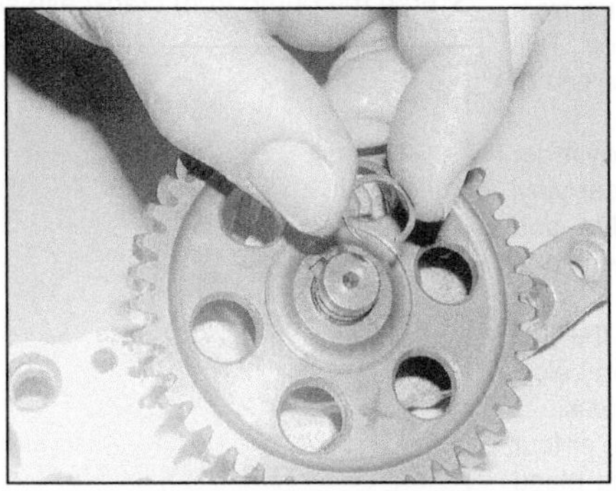

24.7c Remove the centre circlip then remove the drive gear and Woodruff key

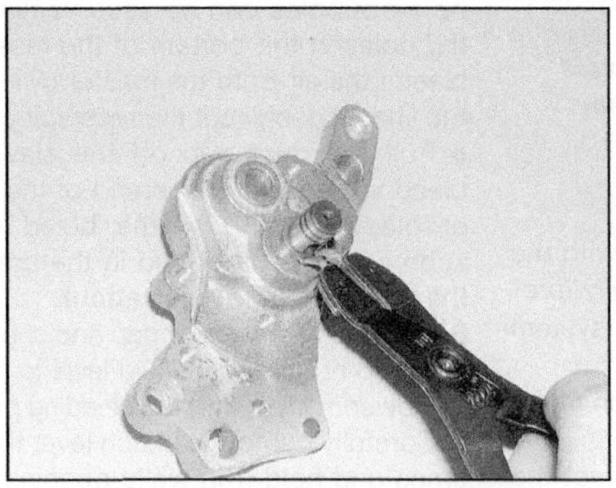

24.7d Remove the inner circlip . . .

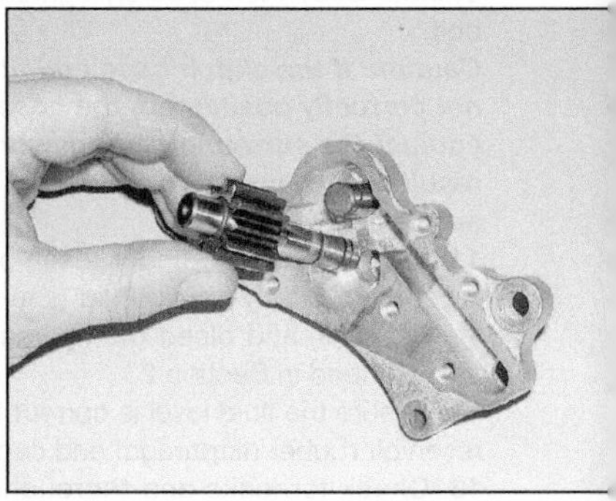

24.7e . . . then withdraw the drive gear from the pump housing

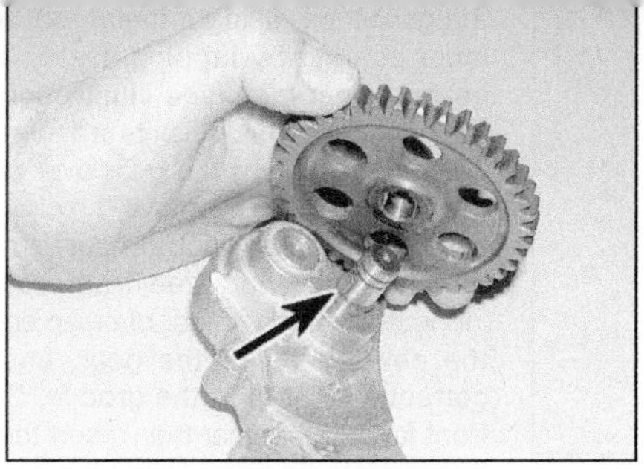

**24.8a Ensure the drive gear is fitted the correct way around and engages correctly with the Woodruff key**

**8** On reassembly lubricate all components with clean engine oil then slide the drive gear into position in the housing. Fit the inner circlip to the inner groove on the drive gear shaft and fit the Woodruff key. Slide on the oil pump gear, using the mark made prior to removal to ensure it is installed the correct way around, and engage it with the key **(see illustration)**. Fit the centre circlip to the next groove on the shaft then slide on the spacer ensuring it is fitted the correct way around so its inner recess engages correctly with the centre circlip **(see illustration)**. Secure the spacer in position with the outer circlip, making sure it is correctly located in the groove. Install the driven gear in the housing, using the mark made prior to removal to ensure it is fitted the same way around.

**9** Lubricate the pump gears with fresh engine oil then install the pump cover, tightening its retaining screws securely. Check the oil pump gears rotate freely before installing the pump.

### Installation

**Note:** *If the pump has been renewed or overhauled, change the engine oil and filter and clean the oil pick-up gauze filter (see Chapter 1).*

**10** Fit the pump locating dowels to the crankcase and install the new sealing rings in their recesses on the crankcase **(see illustration)**. If necessary, use a dab of grease to hold the sealing rings in position.

**24.8b Fit the spacer the correct way around so its inner recess (arrowed) engages with the centre circlip**

**11** Prime the oil pump with clean engine oil then manoeuvre the pump into position. Engage the oil pump gear with the primary drive gear then seat the pump on its locating dowels **(see illustration)**.

**12** Fit the pump retaining bolts and washers and tighten them evenly and progressively to the specified torque.

**13** Install the crankcase cover (see Section 16).

## 25 Primary drive gears – removal, inspection and installation

**Note:** *The primary drive gears can be removed with the engine in the frame. A holding tool will be required to enable the primary drive gear nut to be slackened (see Step 4) and a heavy-duty puller will be required to draw the drive gear off the crankshaft end (the drive gear is an extremely tight fit on the crankshaft taper).*

### Removal

**1** Remove the right-hand crankcase cover (see Section 16).

**2** If the primary drive gear is to be removed, remove the oil pump (see Section 24).

**3** Bend the lockwasher tab back clear of the primary drive gear nut, using a hammer and suitable chisel/punch **(see illustration)**.

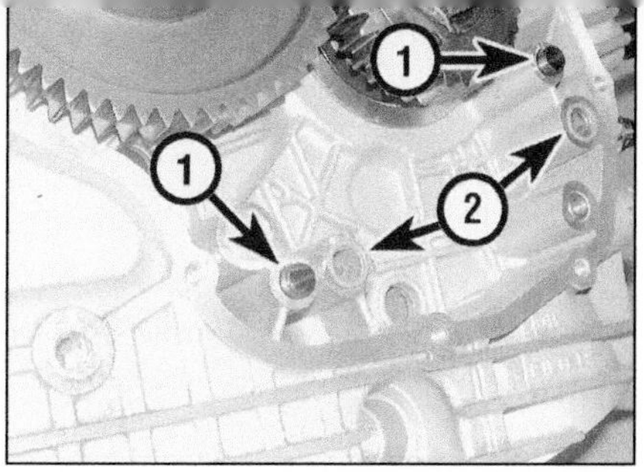


**24.10 Ensure the locating dowels (1) are in position and fit new sealing rings (2) to the crankcase recesses**

**4** In the absence of the Ducati holding tool (88713.0137 – a peg spanner which engages with the four holes in the drive gear **(see illustration)** a home-made holding tool can be fabricated to retain the driven gear whilst the drive gear nut is slackened. Obtain two lengths of steel strip (one long, the other short), and a nut and bolt and fabricate a forked tool, using the nut and bolt as the pivot. Drill a hole in the end of each 'fork' to align with the clutch drum holes in the driven gear then securely bolt the tool to the driven gear using two of the original clutch drum bolts.

**5** Slacken the drive gear nut and unscrew it a few turns **(see illustration)**. Once the nut is loose, unscrew the bolts and remove the holding tool from the driven gear.

**24.11 Prime the oil pump with clean engine oil before installing it**

**25.3 Bend the lockwasher tab back clear of the primary drive gear nut**

**25.4 Ducati service tool has four pegs which engage with the holes in the primary drive gear**

**25.5 Using the home-made tool to retain the driven gear whilst the drive gear nut is slackened**

25.6a Slide the driven gear assembly off the input shaft . . .

25.6b . . . and remove the spacer

**6** Slide the primary driven gear and its spacer off the input shaft and remove them from the engine **(see illustrations)**.

**7** Taking great care not to damage the gear teeth or crankcase, use a heavy-duty puller to free the primary drive gear from the crankshaft taper **(see illustration)**. Once the gear is free, remove the nut and lockwasher and remove the drive gear **(see illustration)**. Discard the lockwasher; a new one should be used on installation.

**8** If the drive gear Woodruff key is a loose-fit, remove it and store it with the drive gear for safe-keeping.

## Inspection

**9** Inspect the drive and driven gear teeth for signs of wear of damage. If damage is found, both gears should be renewed as a matched pair.

**10** Check the driven gear oil seal and bearings for signs of damage or deterioration. The bearing inner races should rotate smoothly and freely without any sign of roughness or freeplay. If either bearing is damage, both bearings should be renewed as a pair. It is recommended that the oil seal is renewed, regardless of its apparent condition.

**11** To renew the driven gear oil seal, carefully lever the original seal out of position using a flat-bladed screwdriver **(see illustration)**. Ensure the sealing lip of the new seal is facing inwards then press it squarely into position until it is flush with the surface of the gear hub **(see illustration)**.

**12** To renew the driven gear bearings first support the gear then, using a metal rod, remove the inner bearing by tapping evenly around the bearing inner race **(see illustration)**. Recover the spacer which is fitted between the bearings then turn the gear over and remove the outer bearing. Remove the circlip from the centre of the gear hub. Ensure the gear hub bore is clean and free from damage then lubricate it with a smear of clean engine oil. Fit the new circlip to the gear, ensuring it is correctly located in the groove. Support the front face of the gear then insert the new inner bearing into its bore. Using the old bearing, a bearing driver or a socket large enough to contact the outer race of the bearing, drive the bearing it in until it's completely seated against the circlip. Turn the gear over and support its rear face. Fit the spacer to the centre of the circlip then drive the outer bearing into place as described above. Ensure both bearings are in firm contact with the circlip then fit a new oil seal (see Step 11).

## Installation

**13** Ensure the crankshaft and primary drive gear mating surfaces are clean and dry then fit the Woodruff key to the crankshaft slot. Align the primary drive gear slot with the Woodruff key and slide the gear onto the crankshaft ensuring its smaller (oil pump) gear is innermost (facing towards the crankcase) **(see illustration)**.

**14** Fit the new lockwasher to the crankshaft

25.7a A heavy-duty puller will be needed to free the primary drive gear from the crankshaft

25.7b Once the drive gear is free, remove the retaining nut and lockwasher and slide off the gear

25.11a Lever out the driven gear oil seal using a large flat-bladed screwdriver . . .

25.11b . . . and tap/press the new seal into position using a socket which bears only on the seal outer edge

25.12 Support the rear of the gear and tap the inner bearing out of position using a drift passed through the outer bearing

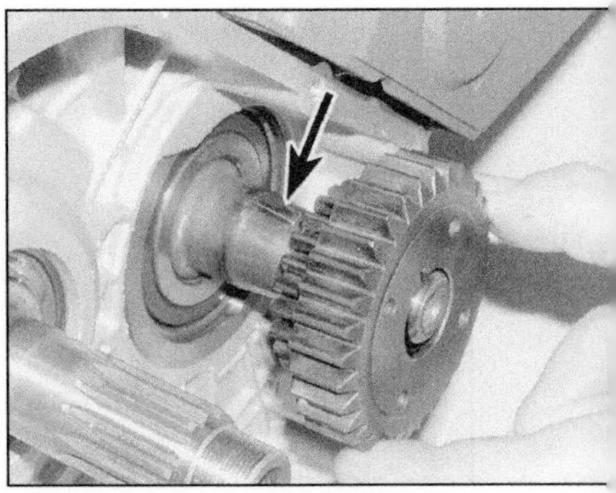
25.13 Ensure the Woodruff key (arrowed) is in position then slide on the primary drive gear and engage it with the key

**25.14 Fit the new lockwasher engaging its tab (arrowed) with the gear key slot**

**25.18 Tighten the nut to the specified torque and secure it in position by bending up the lockwasher against one of its flats**

engaging its tab with the gear slot **(see illustration)**.

**15** Lubricate the threads and contact face of the primary drive gear nut with a smear of molybdenum disulphide grease then thread the nut onto the crankshaft.

**16** Fit the driven gear spacer to the input shaft then slide on the driven gear, engaging its teeth correctly with the drive gear.

**17** Tighten the drive gear nut to the specified torque, whilst preventing rotation with the holding tool (see Step 4).

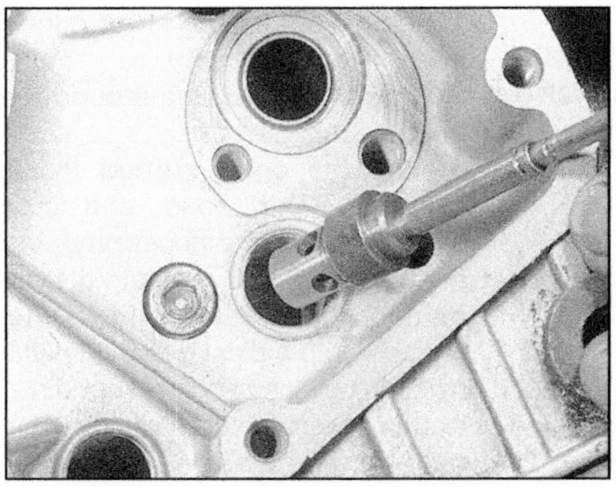

**26.4 On engines with a crankcase mounted valve, insert the piston . . .**

**18** Secure the drive gear nut in position by bending the lockwasher up against one of the nut flats **(see illustration)**.

**19** Install the oil pump (see Section 24).

**20** Install the crankcase cover (see Section 16).

## 26 Oil pressure relief valve and bypass valve – removal, inspection and installation

### *Oil pressure relief valve*

**Note:** *There are two types of oil pressure relief valve arrangement. All 916 (excluding SPS) models and early 748 models have a separate oil pressure relief valve which is fitted to the left-hand side of the crankcase, whereas on 996 models (including the 916 SPS) and later 748 models the oil pressure relief valve is fitted to the oil pump cover. The changeover occurred during the 1999 model year. Some 1999 models are fitted with the oil pump mounted valve, but also still have the crankcase-mounted valve; on these engines the oil pump valve is the only valve which actually functions because the crankcase valve is actually fitted with a modified plug which prevents the valve operating – see your Ducati dealer for further information.*

#### Crankcase mounted valve

**1** Remove the left-hand crankcase cover (see Section 16). The oil pressure relief valve is located behind the plug situated directly below the gearchange shaft.

**2** Unscrew the relief valve plug from the crankcase and remove the valve spring. Withdraw the valve piston from the crankcase, using a magnet if necessary, noting which way around it is fitted.

**3** Check the valve piston for signs of wear or damage and renew if necessary. Renew the valve spring is there is any doubt about its condition.

**4** Ensure the valve piston is clean then lubricate it with clean engine oil. Insert the piston into the crankcase passage ensuring it is positioned the right way around **(see illustration)**.

**5** Fit the spring to the piston making sure it is correctly located on the piston shoulder **(see illustration)**.

**6** Apply a drop of locking compound to the threads of the relief valve plug then fit the plug to the crankcase, tightening it securely **(see illustration)**.

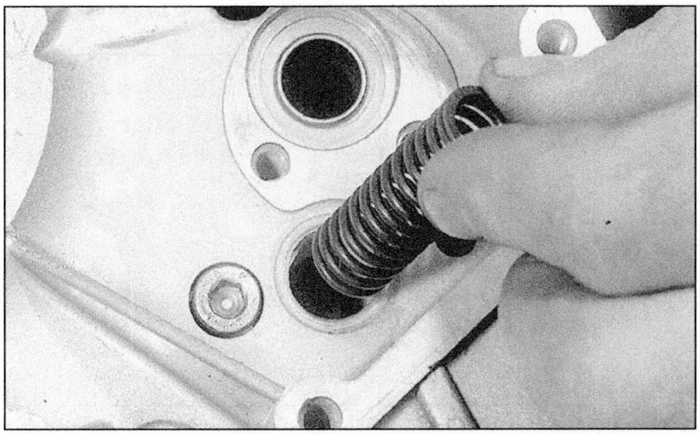

**26.5 . . . and spring . . .**

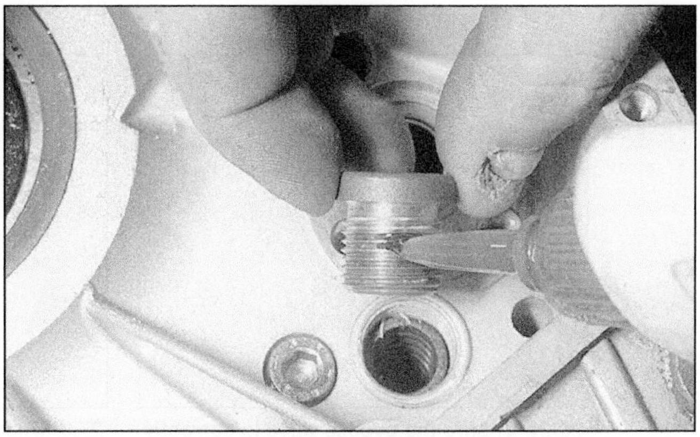

**26.6 . . . then apply thread locking compound to the valve plug and refit it to the crankcase**

**26.9a Unscrew the relief valve plug from the oil pump cover . . .**

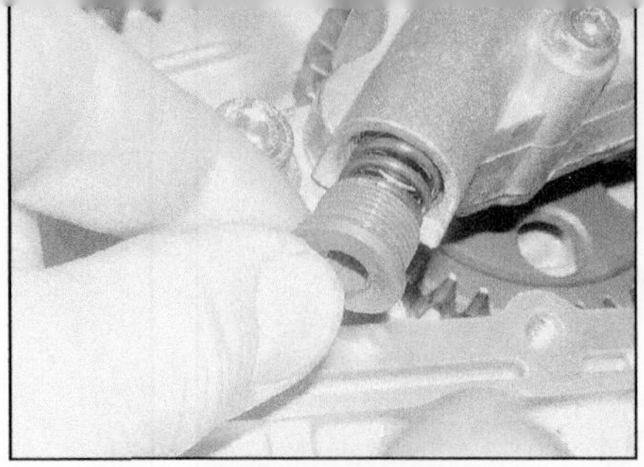

**26.9b . . . and remove the plug . . .**

**26.9c . . . valve spring and piston**

**7** Install the crankcase cover (see Section 16).

### Oil pump mounted valve

**8** Remove the right-hand crankcase cover (see Section 16). The oil pressure relief valve is fitted to the oil pump cover.

**9** Unscrew the relief valve plug from the pump cover and remove the valve spring. Withdraw the valve piston from the pump, using a magnet if necessary, noting which way around it is fitted **(see illustrations)**.

**10** Check the valve piston for signs of wear or damage and renew if necessary. Renew the valve spring is there is any doubt about its condition.

**11** Ensure the valve piston is clean then lubricate it with clean engine oil.

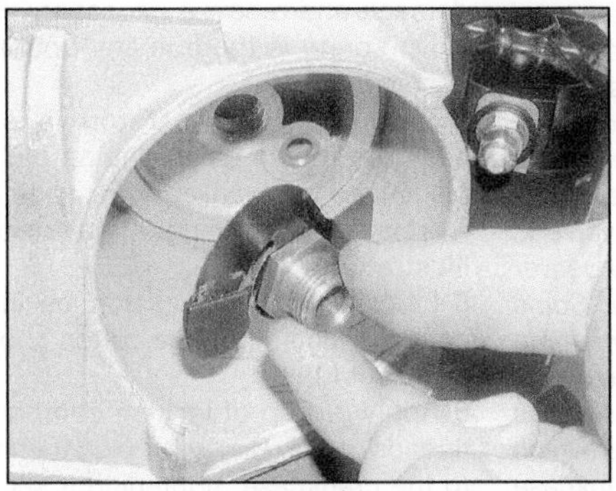

**26.17 Unscrew the oil filter adaptor from the crankcase and remove the bypass valve**

**12** Fit the piston to the end of the spring then insert the assembly into the oil pump.

**13** Apply a drop of locking compound to the threads of the relief valve plug then fit the plug to the pump, tightening it securely.

**14** Install the crankcase cover (see Section 16).

## *Oil bypass valve*

### Removal

**15** The oil bypass valve is fitted between the oil filter and crankcase.

**16** Drain the engine oil and remove the oil filter (see Chapter 1). Discard the oil filter (it is likely to be damaged on removal); on installation fit a new oil filter and fill the engine with fresh oil.

**17** Unscrew the oil filter adapter from the crankcase and remove the oil bypass valve, noting its correct fitted location **(see illustration)**.

### Inspection

**18** Inspect the bypass valve rubber pad for signs of damage or deterioration and renew it if damaged.

### Installation

**19** Ensure the crankcase mating surface and bypass valve are clean and undamaged.

**20** Clean the threads of the oil filter adapter and apply a drop of thread locking compound to its crankcase threads.

**21** Fit the bypass valve to the crankcase, ensuring it correctly located between th crankcase lugs, and screw in the oil filte adapter. Ensure the bypass valve is correct seated then tighten the adapter to th specified torque **(see illustration)**.

**22** Fit the new oil filter and fill the engine wi fresh oil (see Chapter 1).

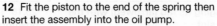

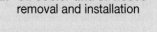

## 27 Oil cooler and oil hoses – removal and installation

## *Oil cooler*

### Removal

**1** Remove the fairing lower panels and inn panel (see Chapter 8).

**2** Wipe clean the area around the oil coole hose unions.

**3** Note the correct fitted location of th cylinder head hose end fitting (mak alignment marks if necessary), then unscre the banjo bolt and separate the hose from th oil cooler **(see illustration)**. Plug the hos end, or wrap a plastic bag tightly around it, minimise oil loss and prevent dirt entering th system. Discard the sealing washers as ne ones must be used on installation.

**4** Hold the oil cooler adapter with an oper ended spanner then loosen the union nu securing each crankcase hose to the coole **(see illustration)**. Disconnect both hoses an

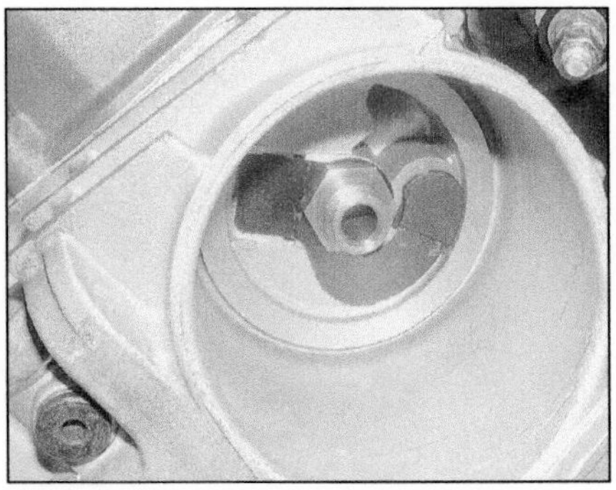

**26.21 Ensure the bypass valve is correctly seated on the crankcase before tightening the adaptor to the specified torque**

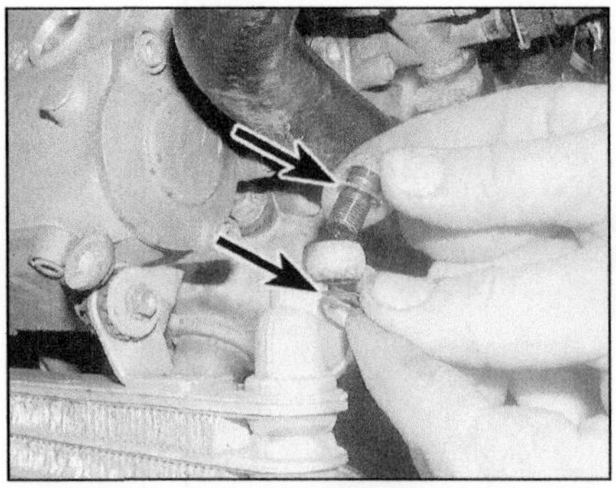

**27.3 Unscrew the oil hose banjo bolt from the cooler and recover the sealing washers (arrowed)**

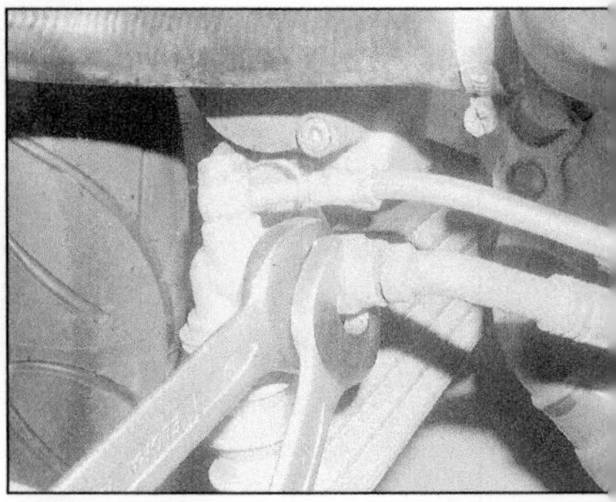

**27.4 Retain the oil cooler adaptor then slacken the union nut and detach the crankcase hose**

**27.5a Slacken and remove the mounting bolt . . .**

plug their ends or wrap a plastic bag tightly each hose, to minimise oil loss and prevent dirt entering the lubrication system.

**5** Slacken and remove the oil cooler mounting bolt from the left-hand side mounting then free the right-hand side mounting rubber from its mounting pin and remove the oil cooler from the bike **(see illustrations)**.

**6** Recover the collar from the left-hand side mounting rubber and inspect both mounting rubbers for signs of damage or deterioration, renewing them as a pair if necessary.

**7** If necessary, unscrew the hose adapters from the oil cooler, whilst counter-holding the oil cooler with an open-ended spanner. Discard the adapter sealing washers; new ones must be used on installation.

### Installation

**8** Where necessary, clean the threads of the crankcase hose adapter and apply a drop of locking compound to the oil cooler end threads of the adapter. Fit a new sealing washer then fit the adapter to the oil cooler. Retain the oil cooler with an open-ended spanner then tighten the adapter to the specified torque.

**9** Ensure the adapters and mounting rubbers are correctly fitted to the oil cooler and the mounting pin is securely fitted to the engine.

**10** Lubricate the right-hand side mounting rubber with a silicone-based spray lubricant then manoeuvre the oil cooler into position. Engage the right-hand side mounting rubber

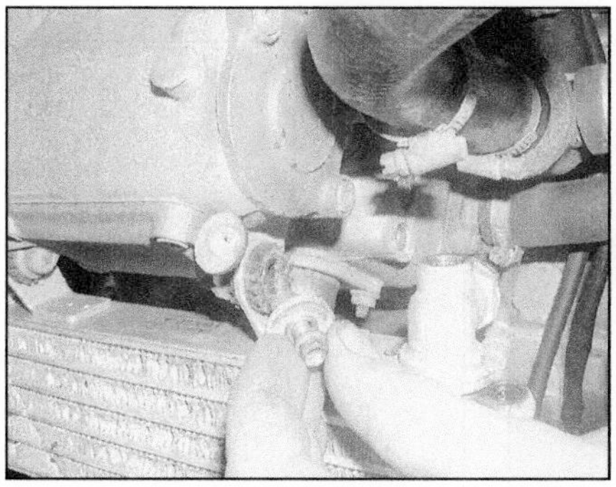

**27.10 Ensure the oil cooler is correctly located on the pin then refit the collar and mounting bolt**

**27.5b . . . then free the oil cooler from its mounting pin (arrowed) and remove it from the bike**

correctly on the mounting pin then insert the collar into the left-hand mounting rubber **(see illustration)**. Fit the oil cooler mounting bolt and tighten it to the specified torque.

**11** Connect the crankcase hoses to the oil cooler and tighten their union nuts to the specified torque. Counterhold the adapter whilst each union nut is tightened to prevent any excess strain being placed on the oil cooler.

**12** Position a new sealing washer on each side of the cylinder head hose union and screw in the banjo bolt. Ensure the end fitting is correctly positioned in relation to the oil cooler then tighten the banjo bolt to the specified torque.

**13** Check the engine oil level (see *Daily (pre-ride) checks*), then start the engine and check that there is no sign of oil leakage before installing the fairing panels (see Chapter 8).

## *Oil cooler crankcase hose*

### Removal

**14** Remove the fairing lower panels (see Chapter 8). To improve access to the crankcase end of the hose, unbolt the battery mounting tray from the frame (see Chapter 9). Each hose can be removed as follows.

**15** Wipe clean the area around the oil hose unions then slacken each union nut whilst retaining the adapter with an open-ended spanner. Unscrew both union nuts and remove the hose from the bike. Whilst the

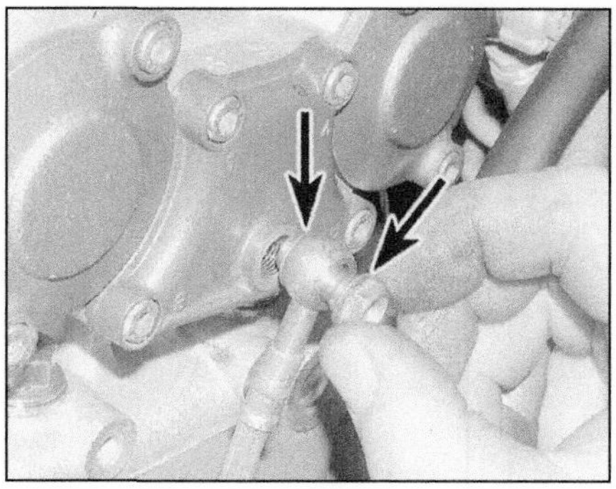

**27.22 Unscrew the oil hose banjo bolts and recover the sealing washers (arrowed)**

plastic bag tightly around each one, to minimise oil loss and prevent dirt entering the lubrication system.

**16** If necessary, unscrew the hose adapter from the oil cooler/crankcase and discard its sealing washer; a new one must be used on installation. When removing the oil cooler adapter, counter-holding the oil cooler with an open-ended spanner to prevent excess strain being placed on the cooler.

### Installation

**17** Where necessary, clean the threads of the hose adapter and apply a drop of locking compound to its oil cooler/crankcase (as applicable) end threads. Fit a new sealing washer then fit the adapter, tightening it to the specified torque. When installing the oil cooler adapter, counterhold the cooler with an open-ended spanner to prevent strain being placed on the cooler.

**18** Manoeuvre the hose into position, ensuring it is correctly routed. Ensure the hose is correctly positioned then tighten its union nuts to the specified torque, counterholding the adapter whilst each nut is tightened.

**19** Refit the battery mounting tray (where removed – see Chapter 9). Check the engine oil level (see *Daily (pre-ride) checks*), then start the engine and check for signs of oil leakage before installing the fairing panels (see Chapter 8).

## *Cylinder head hose – models with an oil cooler*

### Removal

**20** Remove the fairing left-hand lower panel (see Chapter 8).

**21** Wipe clean the area around the oil hose unions then slacken and remove the bolt securing the hose retaining clip to the side of the vertical cylinder barrel.

**22** Note the correct fitted location of the hose end fittings (make alignment marks if necessary), then unscrew the banjo bolts and remove the hose from the engine **(see illustration)**. Plug the cylinder head and oil cooler unions whilst the hose is removed to prevent dirt entering the lubrication system. Discard the sealing washers as new ones must be used on installation.

### Installation

**23** Manoeuvre the hose into position. Position a new sealing washer on each side of the hose unions and screw in the banjo bolts. Ensure all end fittings are correctly positioned in relation to the oil cooler/cylinders then tighten the banjo bolts to the specified torque.

**24** Fit the hose retaining clip to the vertical cylinder barrel and securely tighten its retaining bolt.

**25** Check the engine oil level (see *Daily (pre-ride) checks*), then start the engine and check that there is no sign of oil leakage before installing the fairing panels (see Chapter 8).

### without an oil cooler

#### Removal

26 Remove the fairing lower panels (see Chapter 8). To improve access to the crankcase end of the hose, unbolt the battery mounting tray from the frame (see Chapter 9).

27 Wipe clean the area around the oil hose unions, then slacken and remove the bolt securing the hose retaining clip to the side of the vertical cylinder barrel.

28 Retain the crankcase adapter with an open-ended spanner then loosen the union nut securing the hose to the adapter. Disconnect the hose, being prepared for some oil spillage, and plug the adapter or wrap a plastic bag tightly around it, to minimise oil loss and prevent dirt entering the lubrication system.

29 Note the correct fitted location of the hose end fittings in relation to the cylinder heads (make alignment marks if necessary), then unscrew the banjo bolts and remove the hose from the engine. Discard the sealing washers as new ones must be used on installation. Plug the cylinder head unions whilst the hose is removed to prevent dirt entering the lubrication system.

30 If necessary, unscrew the hose adapters (a dual adapter arrangement is used) from the crankcase. Discard the adapter sealing washers; new ones must be used on installation.

#### Installation

31 Where necessary, clean the threads of the crankcase adapters. Apply a drop of locking compound to the larger adapter then fit a new sealing washer. Screw the adapter into the crankcase and tighten it to the specified torque. Clean the threads of the smaller adapter and apply a drop of locking compound to the threads which screw into the larger adapter. Fit the smaller adapter and tighten it to the specified torque.

32 Manoeuvre the hose into position. Position a new sealing washer on each side of the each cylinder head hose union and screw in the banjo bolts. Ensure both end fittings are correctly positioned in relation to the cylinder specified torque.

33 Fit the hose retaining clip to the vertical cylinder barrel and securely tighten its retaining bolt.

34 Screw the hose union nut onto the crankcase adapter and tighten it to the specified torque whilst counterholding the adapter with an open-ended spanner.

35 Refit the battery mounting tray (where removed – see Chapter 9).

36 Check the engine oil level (see *Daily (pre-ride) checks*), then start the engine and check that there is no sign of oil leakage before installing the fairing panels (see Chapter 8).

## 28 Crankcase – separation and reassembly

### Separation

1 To examine and repair or renew the crankshaft, connecting rods and bearings, transmission shafts, selector drum and timing belt driveshaft, the crankcase must be split into two parts.

2 To enable the crankcases to be split the engine must be removed from the frame (see Section 5) and the following components first removed with reference to the relevant Sections.

*a) Oil filter and pick-up gauze filter (see Chapter 1).*
*b) ... (Chapter 9).*
*c) Cylinder heads.*
*d) Cylinder barrels.*
*e) Pistons.*
*f) Timing belt driveshaft pulleys.*
*g) Clutch.*
*h) Flywheel and starter clutch.*
*i) Timing gears – check the driveshaft endfloat before removing the driven gear (see Section 30).*
*j) Gearchange mechanism.*
*k) Oil pump.*
*l) Primary drive gears.**
*m) Oil pressure relief valve (crankcase mounted valve only).*

**If work no work is to be carried out on the crankshaft, there is no need to remove the primary drive gear. The gear can be left on the crankshaft and the crankshaft can remain in the right-hand crankcase half whilst the transmission components and/or timing belt driveshaft are overhauled.*

3 With all the relevant components removed proceed as follows.

4 Unscrew the selector drum detent bolt from the rear of the crankcase and recover the bolt sealing washer, the spring and detent ball **(see illustrations)**. Discard the sealing washer; a new one must be used on reassembly.

5 Unscrew the selector drum detent arm pivot bolt and remove the arm, washer and spring, noting the correct fitted location each component **(see illustrations)**.

**28.4a Unscrew the detent bolt from the rear of the crankcase . . .**

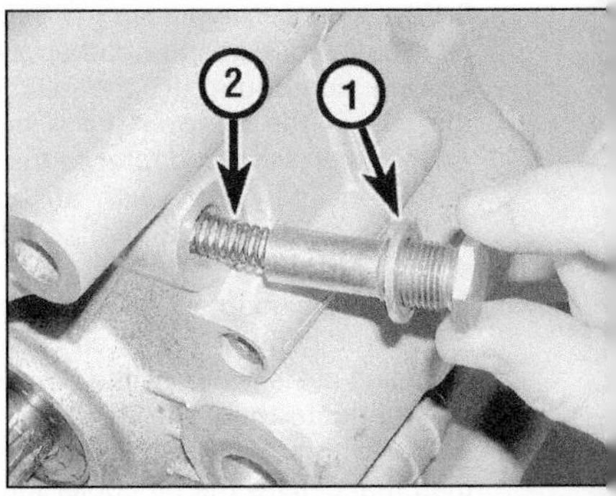


**28.4b . . . and remove the bolt, washer (1) and spring (2) . . .**

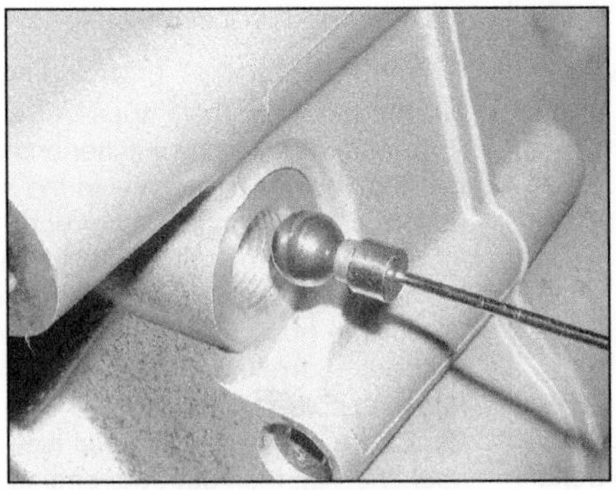

**28.4c . . . then recover the detent ball**

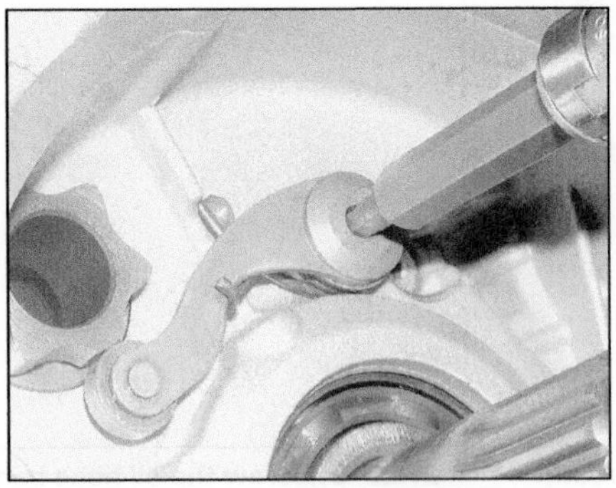

**28.5a Unscrew the pivot bolt . . .**

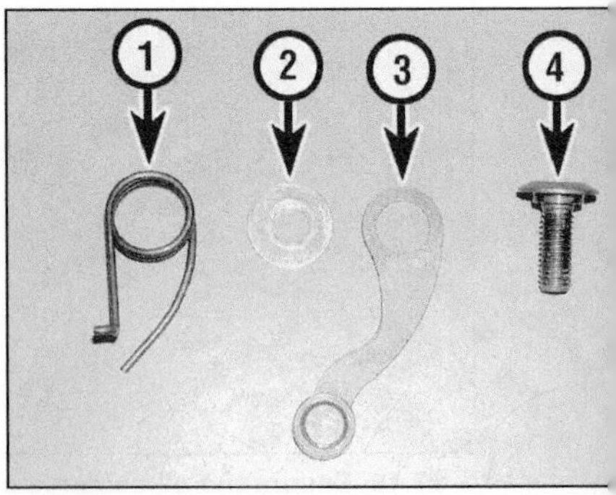


**28.5b . . . and remove the pivot bolt (4), detent arm (3), washer (2) and spring (1)**

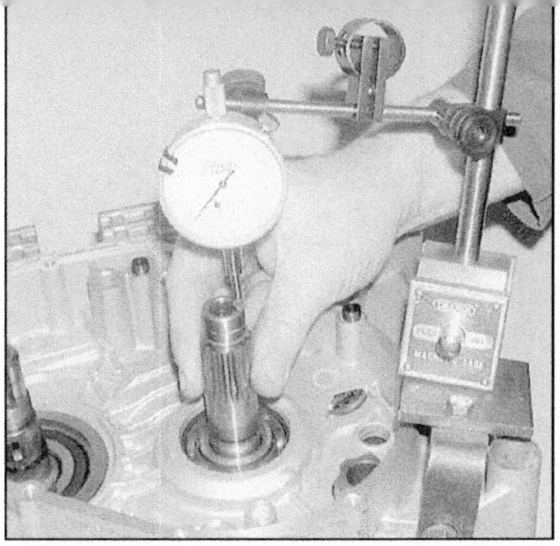

**28.7a Prior to separating the crankcase halves, use a dial gauge to check the endfloat of the crankshaft and transmission shafts . . .**

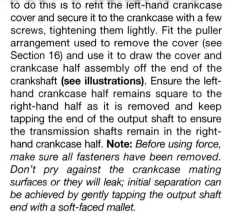

**28.7b . . . and the selector drum**

**6** Ensure the circlip has been removed from the right-hand end of the timing belt driveshaft.

**7** Before separating the crankcases feel for any endfloat in the crankshaft, both transmission shafts and the selector drum. If a dial gauge is available, mount it on the crankcase and record the exact amount of endfloat for each component **(see illustrations)**. Compare this figure to that specified. If endfloat is excessive, it will be necessary to adjust it prior to reassembling the crankcases (see Sections 31, 34 and 35).

**8** On 996 models (including the 916 SPS) and later 748 models, slacken and remove the two crankcase screws securing the right-hand crankcase half to the left-hand half **(see illustration)**.

**9** Position the engine on its side so that the left-hand crankcase half is uppermost. Support the right-hand half on wood blocks so that the crankshaft is not resting on the bench. Evenly and progressively slacken the crankcase screws in a diagonal sequence. Once all screws are loose, remove them noting their correct fitted location (there are several different lengths of screw). **Note:** *As each screw is removed, store it in its relative position in a cardboard template of the crankcase. This will ensure that each screw is returned to its original location on reassembly.* Make sure that all the crankcase screws have been removed before proceeding. **Note:** *All 916 and 996 SP and SPS models have a special hollow M8 x 75 mm screw fitted below, and just to the rear of the crankshaft axis (see Step 24 – the screw can be identified by its painted head). This hollow screw must be renewed every time it is disturbed. Discard the original screw and obtain a new one for reassembly. Some later Biposto models may also have this hollow screw fitted; if this is the case renew the screw.*

**10** It is now necessary to draw the left-hand crankcase half off the crankshaft. The best way to do this is to refit the left-hand crankcase cover and secure it to the crankcase with a few screws, tightening them lightly. Fit the puller arrangement used to remove the cover (see Section 16) and use it to draw the cover and crankcase half assembly off the end of the crankshaft **(see illustrations)**. Ensure the left-hand crankcase half remains square to the right-hand half as it is removed and keep tapping the end of the output shaft to ensure the transmission shafts remain in the right-hand crankcase half. **Note:** *Before using force, make sure all fasteners have been removed. Don't pry against the crankcase mating surfaces or they will leak; initial separation can be achieved by gently tapping the output shaft end with a soft-faced mallet.*

**11** Once the crankcase halves have separated, remove the tool and withdraw the crankcase cover from the left-hand crankcase half.

**12** Lift off the left-hand crankcase half ensuring all the endfloat shims remain on the crankshaft, transmission shafts and selector drum, if any have stuck to the casing, remove them and refit them on the relevant shaft **(see illustration)**. If the input shaft bearing inner race has remained on the end of the shaft, carefully lever it off, taking care not to damage the endfloat shim(s), and press it into the centre of the bearing in the left-hand crankcase half **(see illustration)**.

**13** Recover the O-ring (where fitted) from the

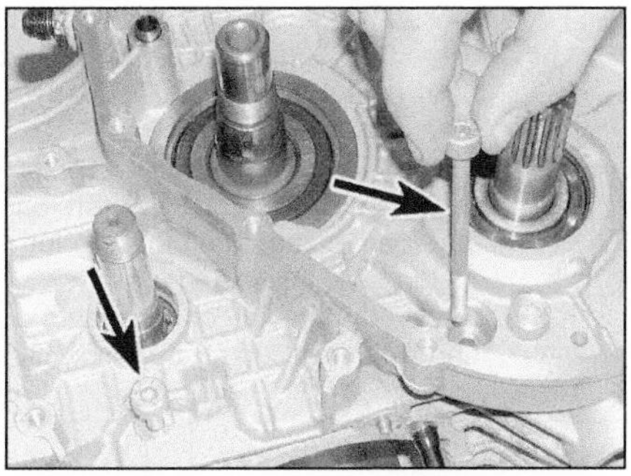

**28.8 Slacken and remove the two screws (arrowed) securing the right-hand crankcase half to the left**

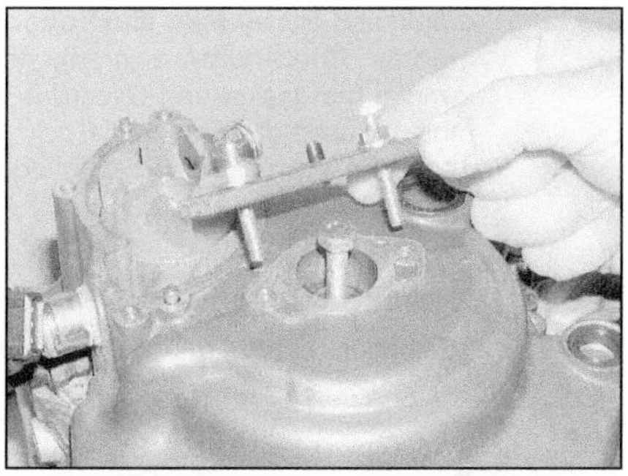

**28.10a Temporarily refit the left-hand crankcase cover then use the tool shown to draw the cover off the crankshaft . . .**

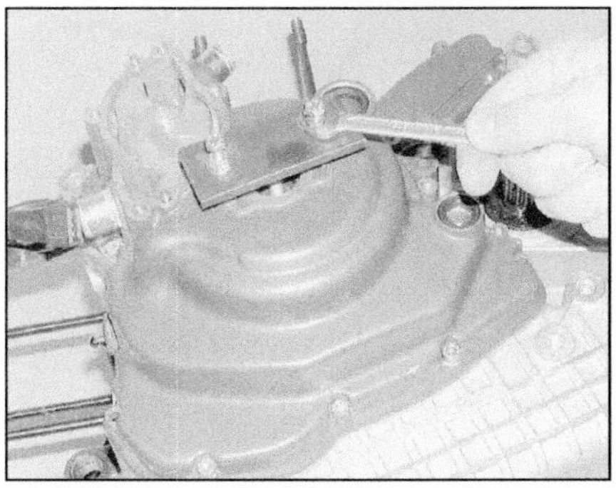

**28.10b . . . and separate the crankcase halves**

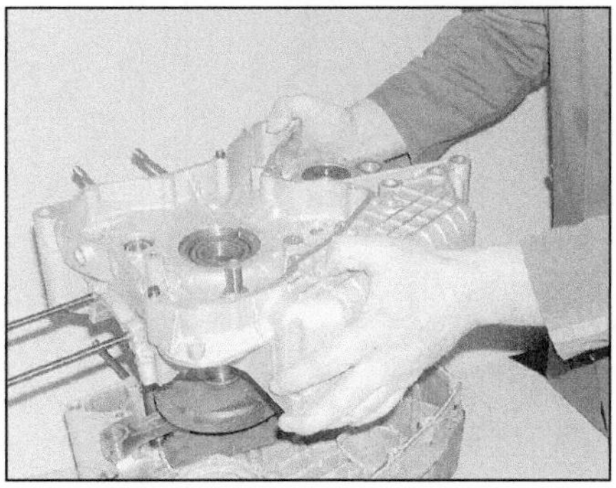

**28.12a Remove the crankcase cover and lift off the left-hand crankcase half**

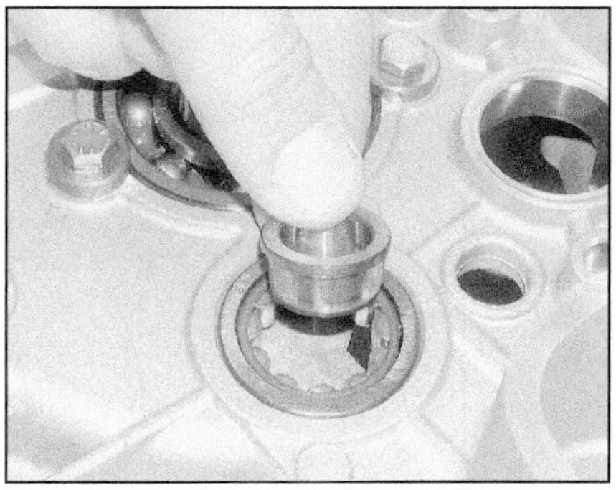

**28.12b If the inner race remains on the input shaft, remove it and press it into the bearing in the crankcase**

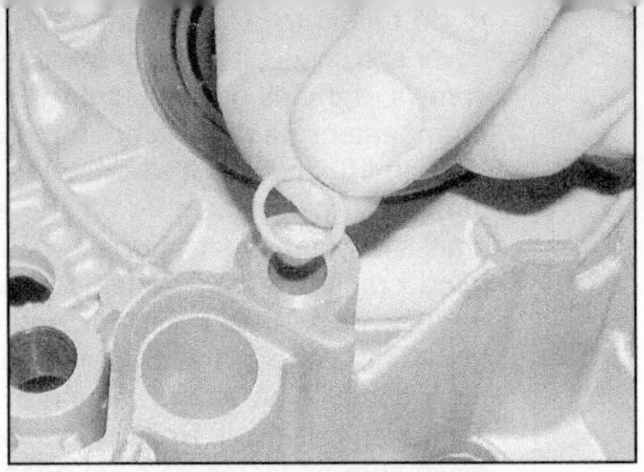

**28.13 Recover the O-ring (where fitted) from the crankcase recess**

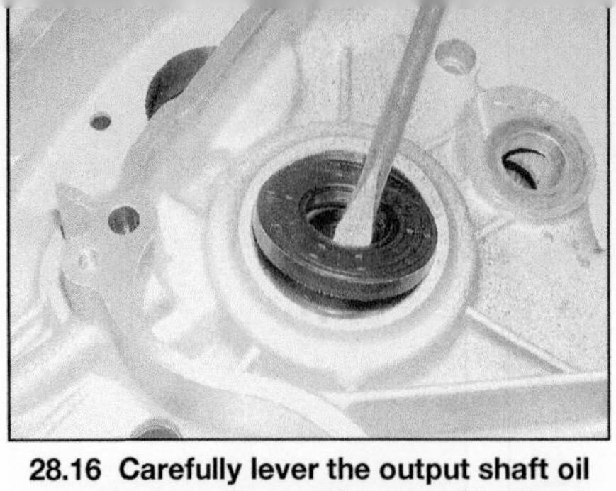

**28.16 Carefully lever the output shaft oil seal out from the crankcase half using a flat-bladed screwdriver**

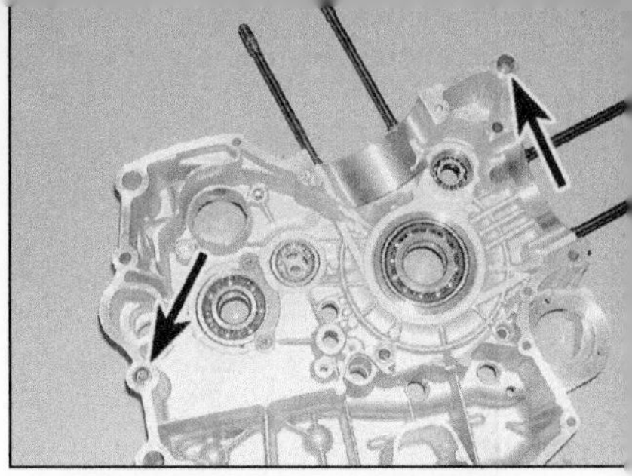

**28.19 Ensure the crankcase locating dowels are correctly fitted**

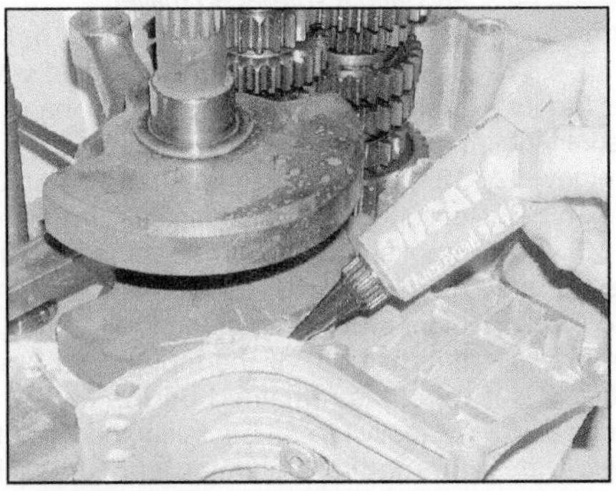

**28.21a On later models apply a coat of sealant to the areas of the crankcase mating surface . . .**

crankcase oilway **(see illustration)**. On early models fitted with a crankcase gasket, remove the gasket and discard it. A new one must be used on reassembly.

**14** If the crankcase locating dowels are a loose-fit, remove them and store them with the left-hand half for safe-keeping.

## *Reassembly*

**15** Check that the transmission shafts, timing belt driveshaft, crankshaft and selector drum are all correctly installed in the right-hand crankcase half and all endfloat adjustment shims are in position (see Sections 29 to 35). Ensure the input shaft bearing inner race is correctly installed in the bearing in the left-hand crankcase half and is not still on the end of the input shaft (see Step 12).

**16** Check the output shaft oil seal in the left-hand crankcase half for signs of damage and deterioration; it is recommended that the oil seal is renewed regardless of its apparent condition. To renew the oil seal, lever the original seal out of position using a flat-bladed screwdriver, taking care not to damage the casing **(see illustration)**. Ensure the sealing lip of the new seal is facing inwards then press it squarely into position until it is flush with the surface of the crankcase half. Lubricate the oil seal lip with a smear of grease.

**17** Remove all traces of sealant/gasket (as applicable) from the crankcase mating surfaces, being careful not to let any fall into the case as this is done.

**18** Check that all components are installed and that they can rotate smoothly and easily, then lubricate the transmission shafts ar crankshaft with clean engine oil. Use a ra soaked in high flash-point solvent to wip over the gasket surfaces of both halves t remove all traces of oil.

**19** Ensure the crankcase half matir surfaces are clean and dry then fit the locatir dowels **(see illustration)**.

**20** On early models where a crankcas gasket was fitted, fit the new gasket to th crankcase right-hand half, seating it on th locating dowels.

**21** On later models where no crankcas gasket was fitted, apply a thin smear suitable sealant (Ducati recommend the us of Three Bond liquid gasket sealant) to th areas of the right-hand crankcase half matir surface **(see illustrations)**.

***Caution: Do not use an excessive amount of sealant, as it will ooze out when the case halves are assembled and may obstruct oil passages and prevent the bearings from seating.***

**22** Fit a new O-ring (where fitted) to th recess in the crankcase left-hand half, using smear of multi-purpose grease to hold it position **(see illustration)**.

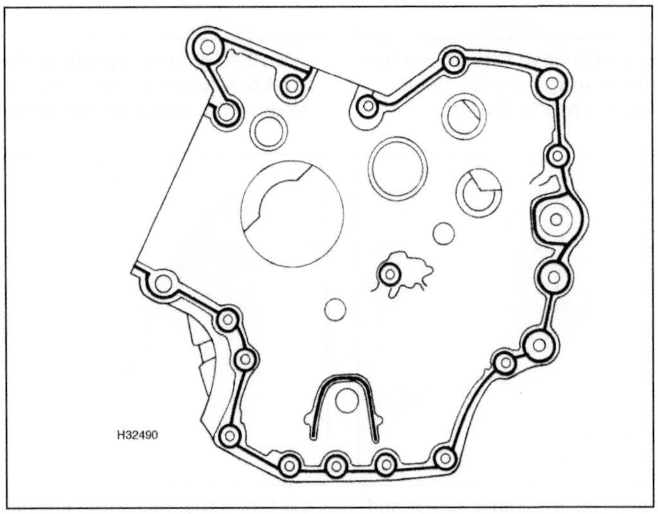


**28.21b . . . indicated by the black line**

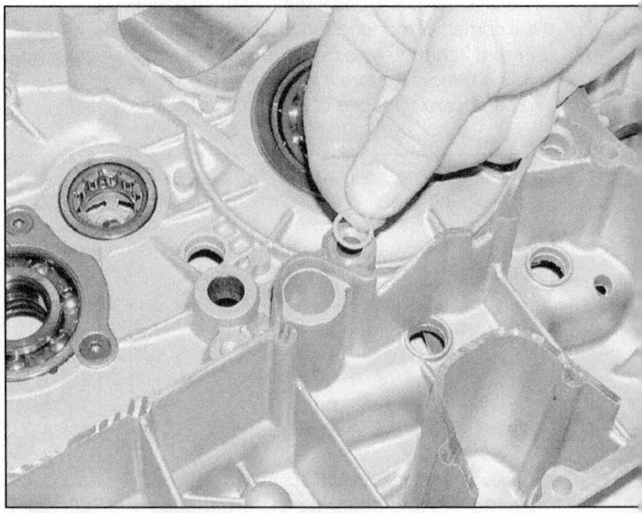

**28.22 Where necessary, fit a new O-ring to the recess in the left hand crankcase half, using a smear of grease to hold it in positio**

are correctly aligned with the crankcase mouths then carefully install the left-hand crankcase half. Align the bearings with the crankshaft and transmission components whilst gently tapping the left-hand casing gently onto the crankshaft with a soft-faced mallet. Ensure the left-hand casing remains square to the right-hand half as it is fitted and take care not to damage the oil seal lip on the output shaft. On models with an O-ring, check the O-ring is still correctly seated before the casings are joined.

***Caution: If the left-hand casing will not seat correctly, remove it and investigate the problem. Do not attempt to draw the crankcase halves together using the crankcase screws as the casing will crack and be ruined.***

**24** Ensure the crankcase halves are correctly joined then lubricate the threads of each crankcase screw with a smear of molybdenum disulphide grease. Install the screws in their original locations in the left-hand half and tighten them all by hand **(see illustrations)**. Ensure that the hollow M8 x 75 mm screw (where fitted – see Step 9) is installed in the correct location **(see illustrations)**.

**25** Evenly and progressively tighten the crankcase screws by hand then go around and evenly and progressively tighten them to the specified torque, working in a diagonal sequence.

**26** On 996 models (including 916 SPS) and later 748 models, fit the two crankcase screws securing the right-hand crankcase half to the left-hand half and tighten them to the specified torque.

**27** With all crankcase screws correctly tightened, check that the crankshaft, transmission shafts, selector drum and timing belt driveshaft all rotate freely. **Note:** *If new main bearings have been fitted, bear in mind that they are pre-loaded during the crankcase tightening sequence so resistance will be felt when turning the crankshaft.*

**28** Check the transmission shaft and selector drum endfloat (see Step 8). Check that all gears select by operating the selector drum cam, then return it to the neutral position.

**29** Temporarily fit the driven gear, washer and retaining nut to the timing belt driveshaft and securely tighten the nut. Check the driveshaft endfloat (see Section 30). Once the check is complete, remove the nut, washer and gear.

**30** If the endfloat of either the transmission shafts, the selector drum or the timing belt driveshaft is not within the specified limits, the crankcase must be separated again and the endfloat adjusted (see Sections 30, 34 and 35 – as applicable).

**31** Once the endfloat of all shafts is correctly set, fit the detent arm spring to its lug on the crankcase ensuring the inner end of the spring is correctly seated against the

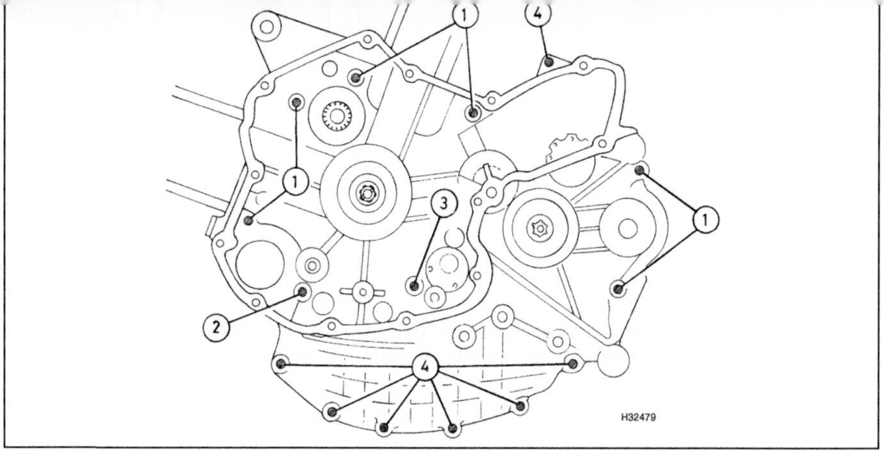


**28.24a Crankcase screw fitting locations - 916 models (excluding SPS) and early 748 models**

1 *M8 x 75 mm screw*
2 *M6 x 60 mm screw*
3 *M8 x 75 mm hollow screw (SP model) or normal M8 x 75 mm screw (as applicable)*
4 *M6 x 35 mm screw*

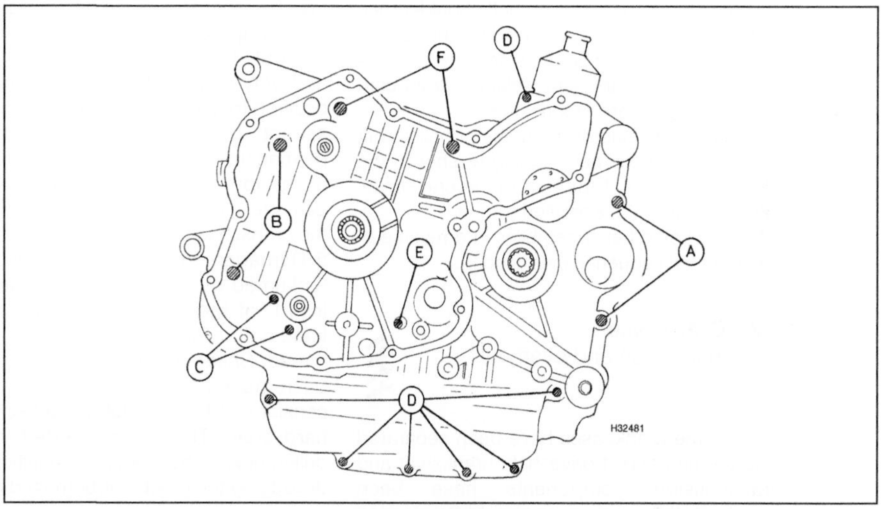


**28.24b Crankcase screw fitting locations - 996 models (including 916 SPS) and later 748 models**

A *M8 x 75 mm screw*
B *M8 x 90 mm screw*
C *M6 x 75 mm screw*
D *M6 x 35 mm screw*
E *M8 x 75 mm hollow screw (where fitted) or normal M8 x 75 mm screw (as applicable)*
F *M6 x 80 mm screw or M8 x 90 mm screw (depending on model)*

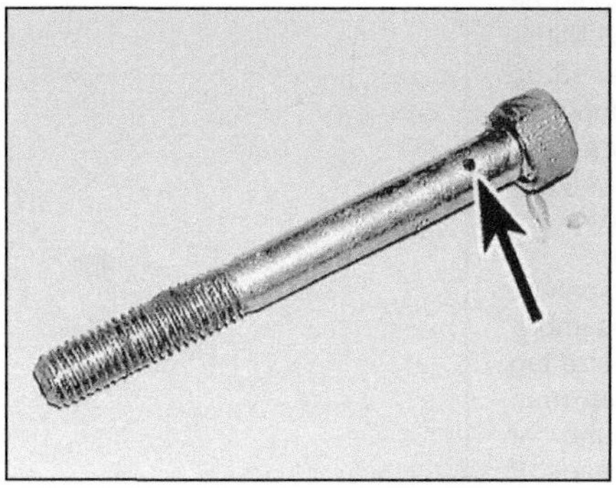

**28.24c On models with a hollow M8 x 75 mm screw (arrow shows oilway drilling) . . .**

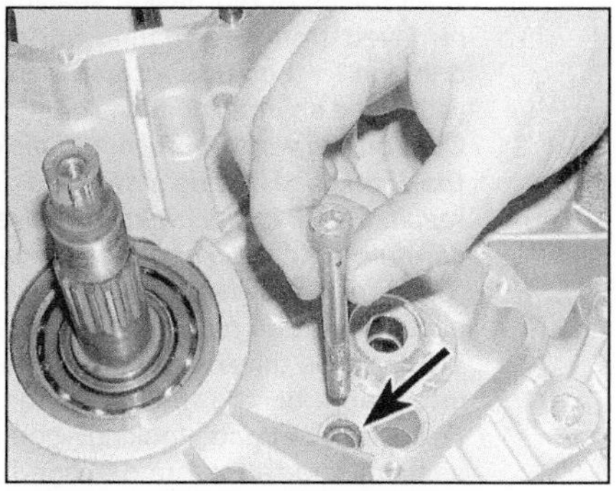

**28.24d . . . ensure the screw is fitted in the correct location (arrowed)**

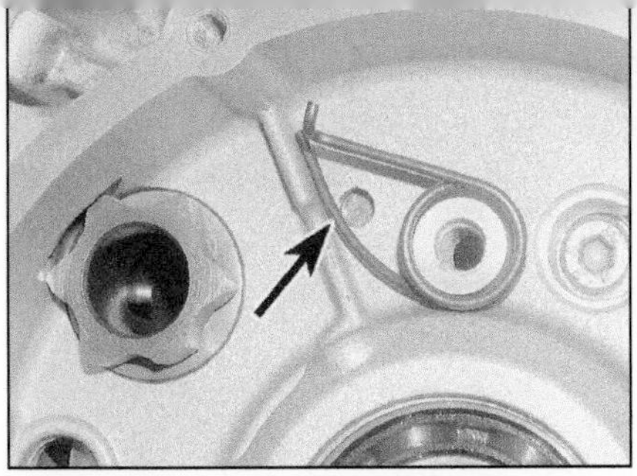

**28.31a Ensure the inner end of the detent arm spring is correctly located against the crankcase lug (arrowed) . . .**

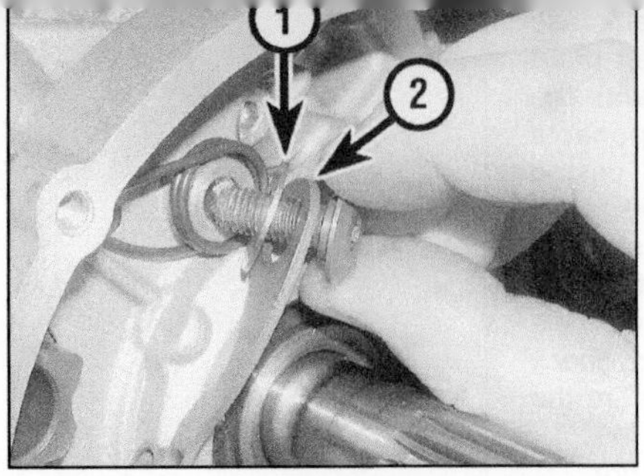


**28.31b . . . then install the pivot bolt complete with the washer (1) and detent arm (2)**

crankcase **(see illustration)**. Assemble the pivot bolt, detent arm and washer and apply a drop of locking compound to the bolt threads. Manoeuvre the assembly into position and screw in the pivot bolt a few turns **(see illustration)**. Engage the detent arm with its spring then screw the bolt into the crankcase. Ensure the detent arm is correctly seated on the selector drum and pivot bolt shoulder then tighten the bolt to the specified torque. Check the detent arm pivots smoothly and is securely held against the selector drum cam by its spring before proceeding.

**32** Insert the selector drum detent ball and fit the spring. Fit the new sealing washer to the detent bolt then fit the bolt to the crankcase, tightening it to the specified torque.

**33** Install all other assemblies in a reverse of the removal sequence (see Step 2).

## 29 Crankcase – inspection and overhaul

**1** After the crankcases have been separated and the timing belt driveshaft, crankshaft and transmission components have been removed, the crankcases should be cleaned thoroughly with new solvent and dried with compressed air.

***Warning: Wear eye protection when using compressed air!***

**2** All traces of old gasket sealant should be removed from the mating surfaces. Minor damage to the surfaces can be cleaned up with a fine sharpening stone or grindstone. ***Caution: Be very careful not to nick or gouge the crankcase mating surfaces or leaks will result. Check both crankcase halves very carefully for cracks and other damage.***

**3** All threaded holes must be clean, to ensure accurate torque readings during reassembly. To clean the threads, run the correct-size tap into each of the holes to remove rust, corrosion, thread locking compound or sealant, and to restore damaged threads. If possible, use compressed air to clear the holes of debris produced by this operation. A good alternative is to inject aerosol-applied water-dispersant lubricant into each hole, using the long spout usually supplied.

***Warning: Wear eye protection when cleaning out these holes in this way!***

**4** Small cracks or holes in aluminium castings may be repaired with an epoxy resin adhesive as a temporary measure. Permanent repairs can only be effected by argon-arc welding, and only a specialist in this process is in a position to advise on the economy or practical aspect of such a repair. Alternatively permanent repairs can be effected using one of the low temperature welding kits. If any damage is found that can't be repaired, renew the crankcase halves as a set.

**5** Damaged threads can be economically reclaimed by using a diamond section wire insert, of the Helicoil type, which is easily fitted after drilling and re-tapping the affected thread. Sheared studs or screws can usually be removed with screw extractors, which consist of a tapered, left thread screw of very hard steel. These are inserted into a pre-drilled hole in the stud, and usually succeed in dislodging the most stubborn stud or screw.

**HAYNES HiNT** ***Refer to Section 2 of Tools and Workshop Tips in the Reference section for details of thread repair methods and using screw extractors.***

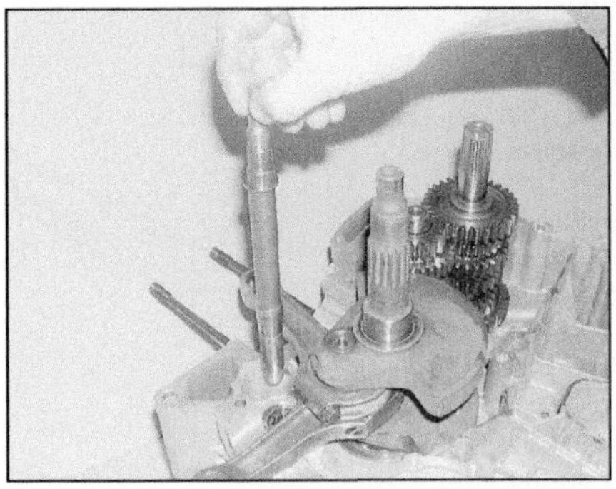

**30.2 Removing the timing belt driveshaft**

crankcase halves. Refer to Steps 13 and 14 of Section 13 for stud removal/installation details.

**7** The crankcase breather system is fully automatic in operation and will require no attention in normal use. If the separator unit in the top of the right-hand crankcase half is clogged with emulsified oil remove it from the crankcase and clean it thoroughly or renew it.

**8** Refer to the relevant following Section for information on crankcase bearing renewal.

## 30 Timing belt driveshaft and bearings – removal, inspection and installation

### Removal

**1** Separate the crankcase halves as described in Section 28. Prior to removing the driven gear from the timing belt driveshaft feel for any endfloat in the driveshaft. If a dial gauge is available, mount it on the crankcase and record the exact amount of endfloat. Compare this figure to that specified. If endfloat is excessive, it will be necessary to adjust it prior to reassembling the crankcases; driveshaft endfloat is adjusted by fitting a shim between the left-hand bearing and its circlip (see Step 5).

**2** Tap the driveshaft out of its bearing in the right-hand crankcase half using a soft-faced mallet **(see illustration)**.

### Inspection

**3** Examine the driveshaft for signs of wear or damage. If vee-blocks and a dial gauge are available, measure the driveshaft runout. Renew the driveshaft if worn or damaged.

**4** Check the driveshaft bearing in each crankcase half. Both bearing inner races should rotate freely and easily without any sign of roughness. Renew any bearing which shows signs of wear or damage. It is recommended that the oil seal in the right-hand crankcase half is renewed regardless of its apparent condition.

**5** To renew the left-hand bearing, remove the circlip from the inside of the crankcase half and remove the shim (where fitted). Support the inner face of the crankcase half then using a metal rod, remove the bearing by tapping evenly around its inner race. Ensure the crankcase bore is clean and free from damage then lubricate it with a smear of clean engine oil. Support the outer face of the crankcase half then insert the new bearing into its bore and tap it squarely into position using a tubular drift which bears only on the outer race of the bearing. Drive the bearing in until it's completely seated then fit the shim (this shim is used to adjust the shaft endfloat – Ducati recommend that one is fitted if the bearing is renewed) and secure it in position with the circlip, ensuring it is correctly located in the casing groove.

**6** To renew the right-hand bearing, first

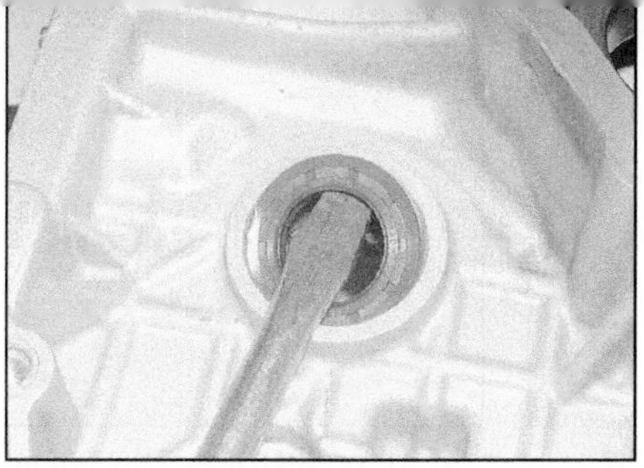

**30.6a Lever out the timing belt driveshaft oil seal with a flat-bladed screwdriver**

carefully lever out the oil seal **(see illustration)**. Remove the circlip from the inside of the crankcase half then support the inner face of the crankcase half **(see illustration)**. Using a metal rod, remove the bearing by tapping evenly around its inner race. Ensure the crankcase bore is clean and free from damage then lubricate it with a smear of clean engine oil. Support the outer face of the crankcase half then insert the new inner bearing into its bore. Tap the bearing squarely into position, using a tubular drift which contacts only the outer race of the bearing, until it's completely seated against the crankcase. Secure the bearing in position with the circlip, ensuring it is correctly located in the casing groove, then fit a new oil seal (see Step 7).

### *Installation*

**7** Check the driveshaft oil seal for signs of damage and deterioration; it is recommended that the oil seal is renewed regardless of its apparent condition. To renew the oil seal, lever the original seal out of position using a flat-bladed screwdriver, taking care not to damage the casing. Ensure the sealing lip of the new seal is facing inwards then press it squarely into position until it is flush with the surface of the crankcase half.

**8** Lubricate the oil seal lip with a smear of grease then fit the driveshaft to the right-hand crankcase half. Tap the driveshaft fully into position using a soft-faced mallet.

**9** Reassembly the crankcase halves as described in Section 28.

## 31 Crankshaft and main bearings – removal, inspection and installation

### *Removal*

**1** Separate the crankcase halves as described in Section 28.

**2** Remove the endfloat shim from the left-hand end of the crankshaft.

**3** Tap the crankshaft out from its bearing in the right-hand crankcase half, using a soft-faced mallet, and recover the endfloat shims, noting which way around the shims are fitted.

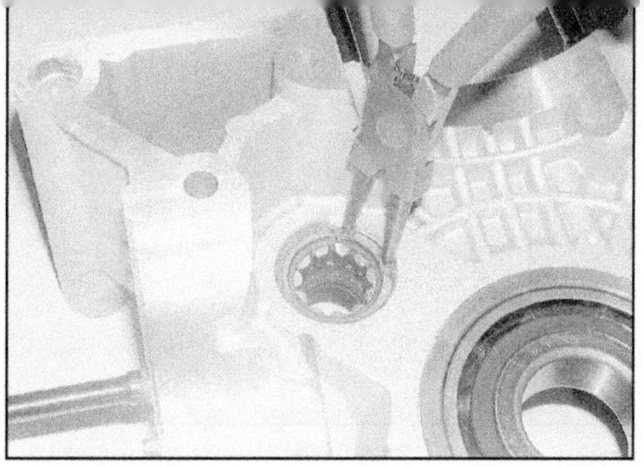

**30.6b Timing belt driveshaft right-hand bearing is retained by a circlip**

### *Inspection*

**4** Clean the crankshaft with solvent. Remove the oilway plugs from the edge and side of the crank webs, and from the left-hand end of the crankshaft, and blow through the oilways with compressed air to clear any obstructions. A rifle-cleaning brush may also be useful to clear any stubborn blockages. Clean the threads of the oilway plugs and apply a suitable thread-locking compound to them before tightening the plugs securely.

**5** The crankshaft journals should be given a close visual examination, paying particular attention where damaged bearings have been discovered. If the journals are scored or pitted in any way a new crankshaft will be required.

**6** Examine the main bearings; if their inner races show any sign of roughness or freeplay new bearings must be installed. Always renew the main bearings as a pair. Evidence of extreme heat, such as discoloration, indicates that lubrication failure has occurred. Be sure to thoroughly check the oil pump and pressure relief valve as well as all oilways and passages before reassembling the engine. **Note:** *Ducati recommended renewing the main bearings whenever the engine is overhauled.*

**7** To renew the main bearings, first remove the transmission shafts, selector drum and forks and the timing belt driveshaft (see Sections 30, 34 and 35). Each bearing can then be renewed as follows

**8** Ducati recommend heating the crankcase casting to 100°C to ease bearing removal and installation. This can be done either by heating the casing in an oven or by immersing it in boiling water for several minutes. Once the casing is hot, securely support the inner face of the crankcase half then tap the bearing evenly out of position, using a metal drift against the bearing inner race. With the bearing removed, check the bearing holder for signs of wear or damage; the holder should be renewed if damage is present or if it is no longer a tight-fit in the crankcase.

***Caution: Take great care not to burn your hands on the hot casing and bearing!***

**9** Support the outer face of the crankcase casting. Ensure the bearing holder is pressed fully into position and its bore is clean and undamaged. Locate the new bearing in outwards (towards the holder), and tap it squarely into position using a tubular drift which bears only on the bearing outer race. Ensure the bearing is in firm contact with the bearing holder shoulder and the holder is pressed firmly into the crankcase half then leave the assembly to cool. Once cool, check that the bearing rotates smoothly and ensure both the bearing and holder are a tight-fit in the casing.

### *Installation*

#### Endfloat check and adjustment

**Note:** *This procedure assumes new main bearings have been installed. If the engine is being reassembled with the original main bearings (not recommended), do not add the bearing preload (0.15 mm) when calculating the endfloat shims required. Only new bearings should be preloaded (to allow for manufacturing tolerances); preloading the original bearings will accelerate their rate of wear and could lead to bearing failure, resulting in serious engine damage.*

**10** Prior to installing the crankshaft, it is necessary to calculate the crankshaft endfloat to ensure the correct thickness shims are installed. Endfloat is calculated as follows by measuring the distance between the inner faces of the right-hand and left-hand main bearings and subtracting the length of the crankshaft **(see illustration)**.

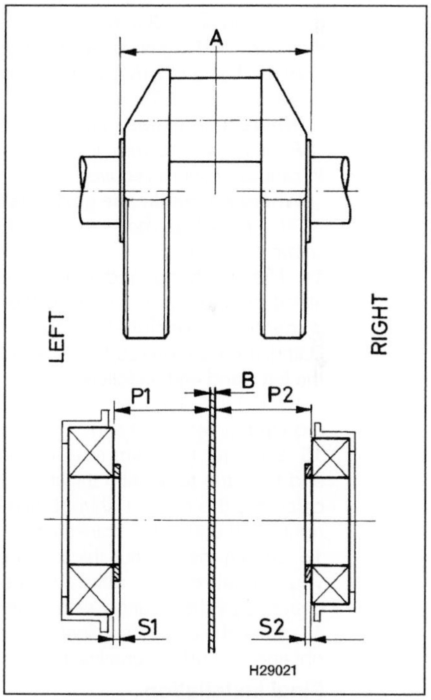


**31.10 Crankshaft endfloat shim calculation details**

*A* *Crankshaft width*
*B* *Crankcase gasket thickness (where fitted)*
*P1 and P2* *Crankcase surface-to-bearing inner race measurements*
*S1 and S2* *Endfloat shims*

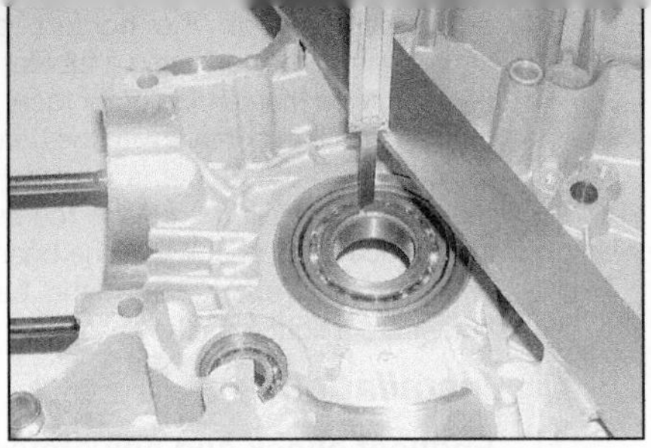

**31.11 Using a straight-edge and vernier caliper to measure the crankcase-to-bearing inner race measurement**

**11** Lay a straight-edge across the crankcase surface and using a depth gauge, measure the distance from the straight-edge to the surface of the main bearing inner race **(see illustration)**. Do the same on the other crankcase half. Record these measurements as P1 (left-hand crankcase) and P2 (right-hand crankcase).

**12** Using a vernier gauge, measure the width of the crankshaft from the bearing surface of its left-hand web to the bearing surface of the right-hand web. Record this measurement as A.

**13** To calculate crankshaft endfloat, add P1 and P2 together plus another 0.15 mm for bearing preload (new bearings only – see **Note**). On models which are fitted with a crankcase gasket also add 0.3 mm to compensate for the thickness of the gasket. Subtract dimension A from this figure to arrive at the correct thickness of shims required. Thus:

**Where a crankcase gasket is fitted:**

*P1 + P2 + 0.15 mm + 0.3 mm – A = total thickness of shims required*

**Where no crankcase gasket is fitted:**

*P1 + P2 + 0.15 mm – A = total thickness of shims required*

**14** The left-hand and right-hand endfloat shims should be arranged, so the crankshaft is centrally positioned in the crankcases. Calculate the required thickness of shims for the left-hand end as follows:

*P1 + 0.075 mm – (A ÷ 2) = shim thickness required for left-hand end*

**15** Subtract the shim size for the left-hand end from the total shim thickness required to calculate the correct shim thickness for the right-hand end of the crankshaft.

**16** Obtain the correct thickness shims from your Ducati dealer. Shim thickness can be checked by measuring it with a micrometer.

**17** Once the correct endfloat shims have been obtained, install the crankshaft as follows.

### Final installation

**18** Ensure the connecting rods are correctly installed (see Section 32) and obtain the correct thickness shims required to set the crankshaft endfloat correctly (see Steps 10 to 17).

**19** Lubricate the main bearing in the right-hand crankcase with clean engine oil.

**31.20 Fit the endfloat shim to the crankshaft right-hand end (flat surface facing away from crank web) . . .**

**20** Fit the correct thickness shim to the right-hand end of the crankshaft ensuring its chamfered inner edge is facing towards the crankshaft web (flat surface facing away from the crankshaft web) **(see illustration)**.

**21** Insert the crankshaft into the bearing **(see illustration)**. Ensure the connecting rods are correctly aligned with the crankcase mouths then tap on the end of the crankshaft with a soft-faced mallet to seat the crankshaft in its bearing.

**22** Ensure the crankshaft is correctly located then install the correct thickness shim on the left-hand end of the crankshaft again making sure its chamfered inner edge is facing the crankshaft web.

**23** Reassemble the crankcases (see Section 28). **Note:** *If new main bearings have been fitted, bear in mind that they are preloaded during the crankcase tightening sequence so resistance will be felt when turning the crankshaft.*

## 32 Connecting rods and big-end bearings – removal, inspection and installation

**Note:** *All SP and SPS models and the 996 S model are fitted with titanium connecting rods. All other models have standard connecting rods.*

### *Removal*

**Note:** *New big-end cap bolts must be used on installation.*

**1** Remove the crankshaft (see Section 28).

**2** Using paint or a felt marker pen, mark the relevant cylinder identity on each connecting rod and bearing cap and mark the cap in some way to indicate which way around it is fitted. Mark across the cap-to-connecting rod join to ensure that the cap is fitted the correct way around on reassembly.

**3** Unscrew the bearing cap bolts and remove the first connecting rod and bearing cap, complete with the bearing inserts and locating pins, from the crankshaft **(see illustration)**. Immediately install the bearing cap, locating pins and bolts on the connecting rod so that they are kept together as a matched set. Remove the remaining connecting rod in the same way.

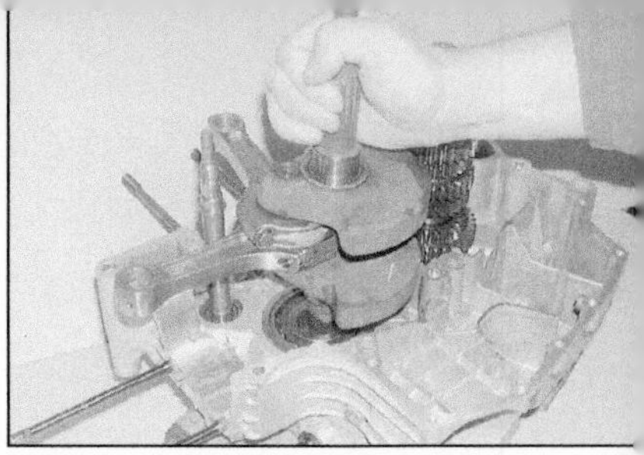

**31.21 . . . then insert the crankshaft into the crankcase**

### *Inspection*

#### General information

**4** Check the connecting rods for cracks ar other obvious damage. Lubricate the pistc pin for each rod, install it in its original rod ar check for play. Measure the pin OD and th small-end bush ID at their points of conta and calculate the difference between th measurements to obtain the piston pin-t small-end bush clearance. If the we exceeds the specified limit, renew th connecting rod small-end bush and/or th pin. Small-end bush renewal is a delicate ta which should be entrusted to a Ducati deal or a suitable-equipped engineering speciali **Note:** *On some models, small-end bus renewal is not possible. If the bush is worn th connecting rod will have to be renewed – ref to your Ducati dealer for details.*

**5** Refer to Section 33 and examine th connecting rod bearing inserts. If they a scored, badly scuffed or appear to hav seized, new bearings must be installe Always renew the bearings in the connectir rods as a set. If they are badly damage check the corresponding crankpin. Evidenc of extreme heat, such as discoloratio indicates that lubrication failure has occurre Be sure to thoroughly check the oil pump ar pressure relief valve as well as all oil holes ar passages before reassembling the engin **Note:** *It is recommended that new bearir inserts are fitted, regardless of the condition the original inserts.*

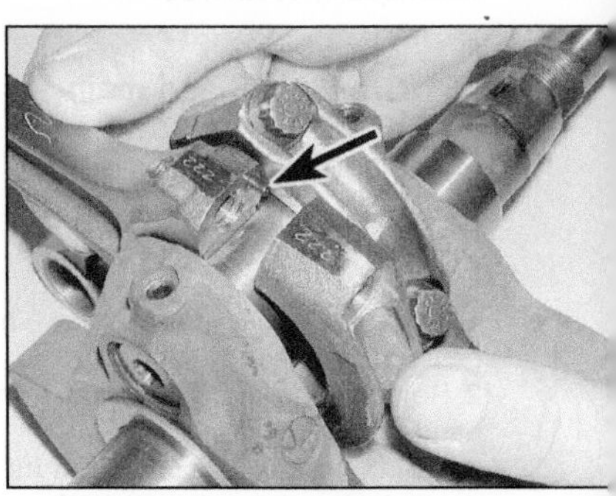

**32.3 Unscrew the bolts and remove the bearing cap and connecting rod from the crankshaft (locating pin arrowed)**

**32.9a Crankshaft crankpin journal diameter size group is marked on the crankshaft web (arrowed)**

**32.9b The crankpin size group can also be determined by measuring the crankpin with a micrometer**

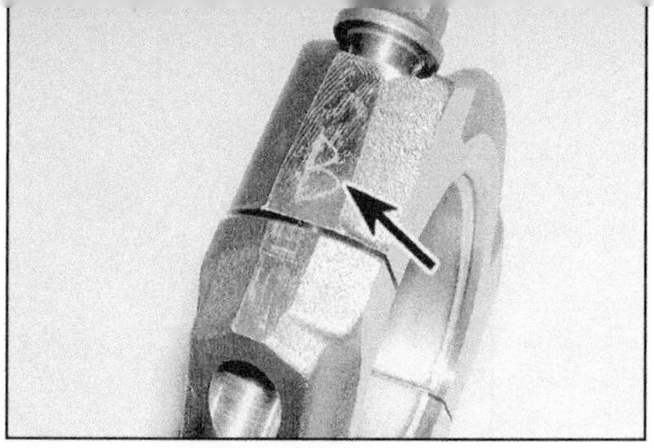

**32.10a Connecting rod big-end bore size group marking (arrowed)**

**6** Have the rods checked for twist and bending by a Ducati dealer or motorcycle engineering specialist.

**7** On all models with standard connecting rods, if a connecting rod is to renewed, be sure to state what size group it is when ordering. Ducati recommend that both connecting rods should be of the same size group as the crankshaft (see Step 10). **Note:** *On models with titanium connecting rods there is only one size group for the connecting rods.*

## Bearing selection

**8** The connecting rod bearing running clearance is controlled in production by selecting one of two grades of bearing insert. The grades are indicated by a colour-coding marked on the edge of each insert (this colour-code may no longer be visible on the original bearings). The Blue bearing inserts are the thickest and the Red inserts the thinnest. New bearing inserts are selected as follows using the crankpin and connecting rod size group markings.

**9** The standard crankpin journal diameter is divided into two size groups to allow for manufacturing tolerances. The size group of the crankpin can be determined from the letter (either A or B) marked on the outside of the left-hand crankshaft web **(see illustration)**. If the equipment is available, the size group can be checked by direct measurement **(see illustration)**.

**10** On all models fitted with standard connecting rods, the connecting rod big-end bore diameter is also divided into two size groups to allow for manufacturing tolerances. The size group of the connecting rod bore can be determined from the letter which is stamped on the connecting rod bearing cap **(see illustration)**. If the equipment is available, the size group can be checked by direct measurement **(see illustration)**. **Note:** *On models with titanium connecting rods there is only one size group for the connecting rods and the mark is on the connecting rod rather than the bearing cap.*

**11** Match the relevant connecting rod code with its crankshaft code and select the correct new bearing inserts using the relevant following table.

**Standard connecting rods**

| Connecting rod size code | Crankshaft crankpin size code | Bearing inserts required |
|---|---|---|
| A | A | 1 Red and 1 Blue |
| A | B | 2 Blue |
| B | A | 2 Red |
| B | B | 1 Red and 1 Blue |

**Titanium connecting rods**

| Connecting rod size code | Crankshaft crankpin size code | Bearing inserts required |
|---|---|---|
| A | A | 2 Red |
| A | B | 2 Blue |

## Oil clearance check

**12** Whether new bearing inserts are being fitted or the original ones are being re-used, the connecting rod bearing oil clearance should be checked prior to reassembly.

**13** Clean the backs of the bearing inserts and the bearing locations in both the connecting rod and bearing cap.

**14** Press the bearing inserts into their locations, ensuring that the tab on each insert engages the notch in the connecting rod/bearing cap **(see illustration)**. Make sure the bearings are fitted in the correct locations and take care not to touch any insert's bearing surface with your fingers.

**15** There are two possible ways of checking the oil clearance. The first method is by direct measurement (see Step 16) and the second by the use of a product known as Plastigauge (see Steps 17 to 20). **Note:** *Use the original connecting rod bearing cap bolts for the check, not the new ones.*

**16** If the first method is to be used, fit the bearing cap to the connecting rod, with the bearing inserts and locating pins in place. Make sure the cap is correctly fitted then tighten the cap retaining bolts (see Steps 22 to 27 for engines with titanium connecting rods and Steps 35 to 37 for engines with standard connecting rods) and measure the internal diameter of each assembled pair of bearing inserts **(see illustration)**. If the diameter of each corresponding crankpin journal is measured and then subtracted from the bearing internal diameter, the result will be the connecting rod bearing oil clearance.

**17** If the second method is to be used, each clearance can be checked as follows. Cut a

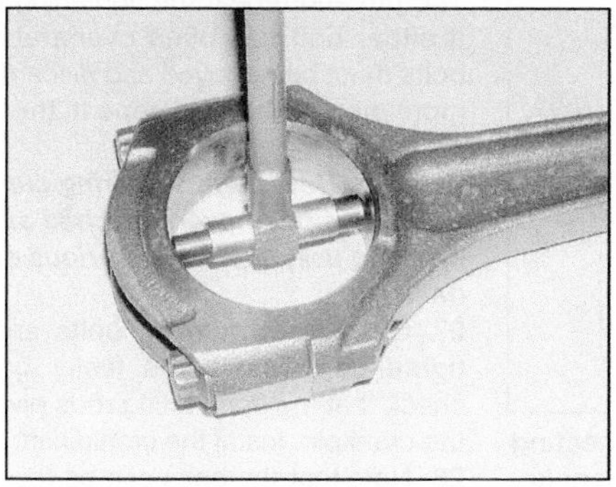

**32.10b Measuring connecting rod big-end bore diameter (bearing inserts removed)**

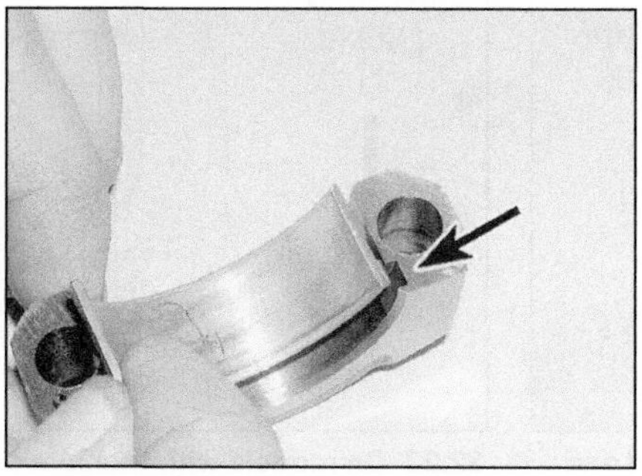

**32.14 Fit the big-end bearing inserts ensuring the tabs are correctly seated in the cutouts in the cap/connecting rod (arrowed)**

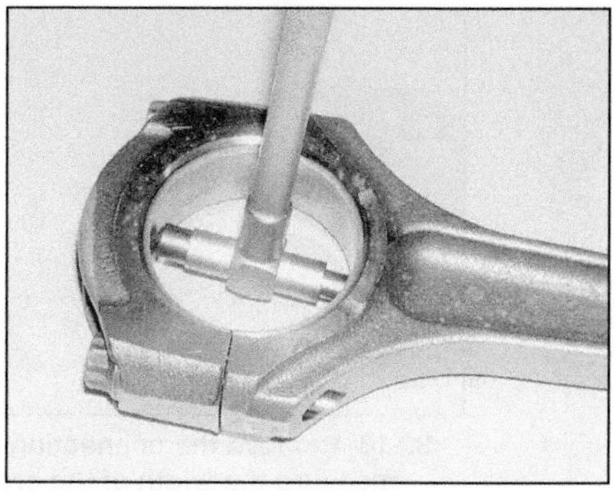

**32.16 Measuring the internal diameter of the connecting rod big-end bearing inserts**

**32.17a Place a strip of Plastigauge on the crankpin journal . . .**

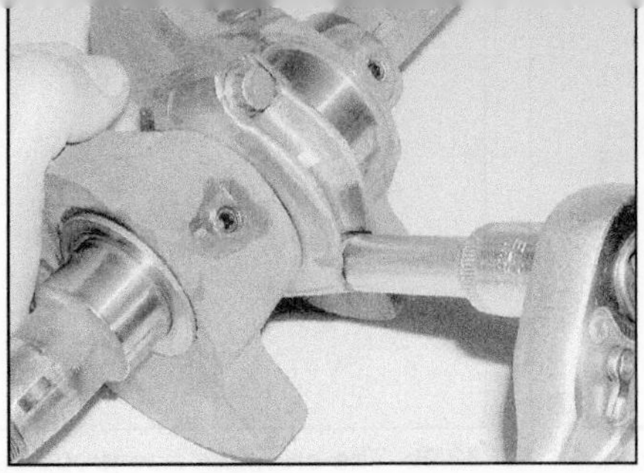

**32.17b . . . then assemble the connecting rod on the crankshaft**

length of the appropriate size Plastigauge (it should be slightly shorter than the width of the bearing insert) and place the strand on the relevant side of the (cleaned) crankpin journal **(see illustration)**. Fit the (clean) connecting rod assembly, complete with bearing insert and locating pins, and fit the bearing cap and insert. Make sure the cap is correctly fitted then fit the retaining bolts and tighten as specified (see Steps 22 to 27 for engines with titanium connecting rods and Steps 35 to 37 for all engines with standard connecting rods) whilst ensuring that the connecting rod does not rotate **(see illustration)**. Take care not to disturb the Plastigauge. Slacken the bearing cap bolts and remove the connecting rod assembly, again taking great care not to rotate the connecting rod.

**18** Compare the width of the crushed Plastigauge on the crankpin to the scale printed on the Plastigauge envelope to obtain the connecting rod bearing oil clearance **(see illustration)**. Repeat the check on the other connecting rod.

**19** If the clearance is not within the specified limits, the bearing inserts may be the wrong grade (or excessively worn if the original inserts are being re-used). Before deciding that different grade inserts are needed, make sure that no dirt or oil was trapped between the bearing inserts and the connecting rod or bearing cap when the clearance was measured. If the clearance is excessive, even with new inserts (of the correct size), the crankpin is worn and the crankshaft should be renewed. **Note:** *Before condemning the crankshaft, check whether it is possible to have the crankshaft reground and undersized bearing shells fitted. Refer to your Ducati dealer for further information.*

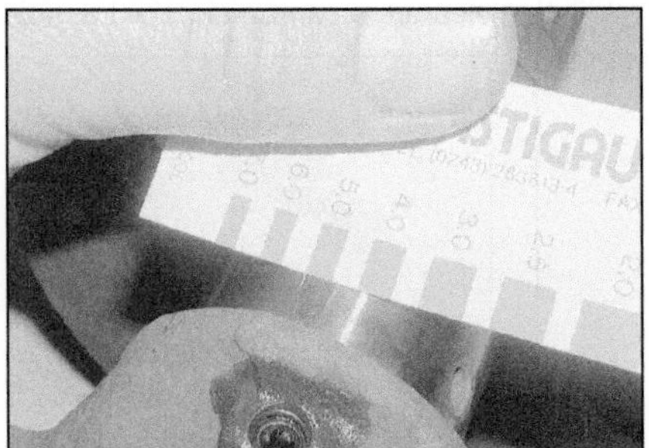

**32.18 Remove the connecting rod and measure the width of the crushed Plastigauge using the scale provided**

**20** On completion, carefully scrape away all traces of the Plastigauge material from the crankpin and bearing inserts using a fingernail or other object which is unlikely to score the inserts.

## *Installation*

### Titanium connecting rods

**Note:** *On these models, installation of the connecting rods is a very precise procedure requiring the use of a point micrometer with a 3 mm end. It is strongly recommended that connecting rod installation be entrusted to a Ducati dealer. Failure to correctly tighten the connecting rod bearing cap bolts could result in failure in use, causing serious engine damage.*

**21** Install the connecting rods as described in Steps 29 to 34 (Ducati recommend the use of Pankl PLB 05 to grease the bolts on titanium connecting rods). Tighten the new bearing cap bolts of each connecting rod as follows.

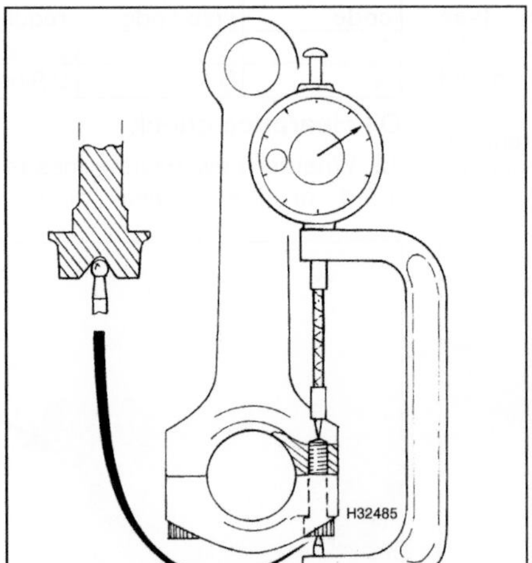


**32.22 On models with titanium connecting rods, specialist measuring equipment is required to ensure the big-end bearing cap bolts are correctly tightened**

bearing cap bolt with a point micrometer locating the point tips in the bolt indents **(see illustration)**. Note the exact length of each bolt.

**23** On 1994 to 1996 748 and 916 SP models tighten the connecting rod bolts as follows:

- Tighten both bolts to 15 Nm.
- Angle-tighten both bolts through 38° (this equates to a torque of 45 to 50 Nm).
- Angle-tighten both bolts through a further 38° (this equates to a torque of 75 to 80 Nm).
- With both bolts correctly tightened, measure the length of each bolt to check the total amount of stretch; this must be between 0.1 and 0.18 mm from their original lengths.

**24** On 1997 and 1998 748 and 916 SPS models tighten the connecting rod bolts as follows:

- Tighten both bolts to 30 Nm.
- Angle-tighten both bolts through 45°.
- With both bolts correctly tightened, measure the length of each bolt to check the total amount of stretch. This must be between 0.1 and 0.175 mm from their original lengths and corresponds to a torque of 65 to 90 Nm.

**25** On 996 S/SPS models tighten the connecting rod bolts as follows:

- Tighten the first bolt gradually in stages rechecking its length after each tightening. Continue tightening the bolt until it has stretched by 0.05 mm.
- Repeat the procedure on the other bolt tightening it until it has stretched by 0.05 mm.
- Working again on the first bolt, gradually tighten it in stages again, rechecking its length after each tightening. Continue tightening the bolt until it has stretched a **further** 0.105 mm.
- Repeat the procedure on the other bolt tightening it until it has stretched by a **further** 0.105 mm.
- With both bolts correctly tightened measure the length of each bolt to check the total amount of stretch; this must be 0.155 ± 0.005 mm from their original lengths. If the bolts are correctly stretched, check they are correctly tightened by apply a torque of 6 Nm to each one; if the tightening procedure has been correctly performed the bolts should not move.

**26** On all models, if either bolt is not tightened sufficiently, slacken both bolts by 1/4 turn and repeat the tightening procedure. If either bolt has been overstretched, both bolts must be removed and discarded. Fit two more new bolts and repeat the tightening procedure.

***Caution: Never use a bearing cap bolt which has been overstretched as it could break in use, leading to serious engine damage.***

**27** Once both pairs of bolts are correctly tightened, remove the feeler gauges and check that the connecting rods pivot freely on the crankpin. Instal the crankshaft.

**28** Note that the bolts can be reused up to a maximum of three times, after which they should be renewed.

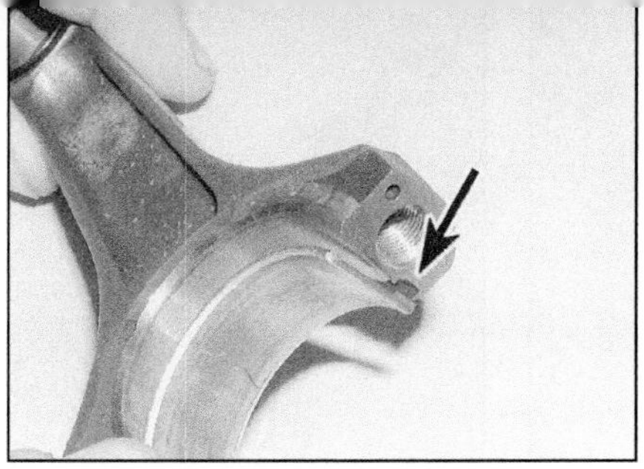

32.30 Fit the bearing inserts to the connecting rod and cap ensuring the tab is correctly located in the cutout (arrowed)

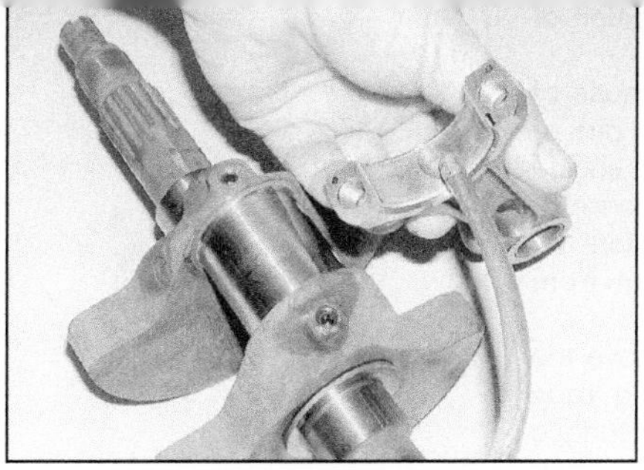

32.31 Lubricate the bearing inserts and crankpin with clean engine oil

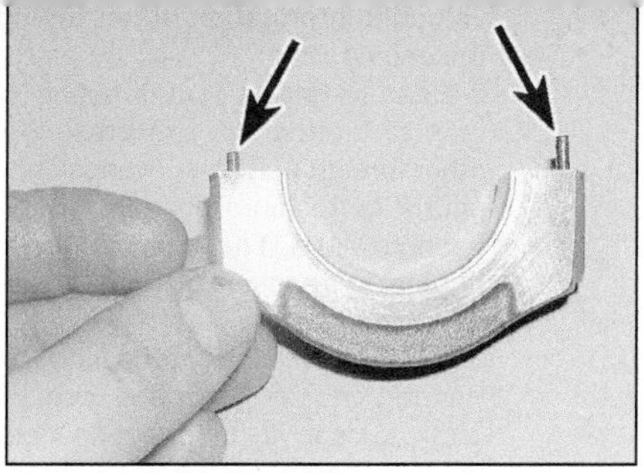

32.32a Ensure the locating pins (arrowed) are in position . . .

## Standard connecting rods

**29** Clean the backs of the bearing inserts and the bearing bores in the connecting rod and bearing cap. If new inserts are being fitted, ensure that all traces of the protective grease are cleaned off using paraffin (kerosene). Wipe dry the inserts and connecting rods with a lint-free cloth.

**30** Press the bearing inserts into their locations, making sure the tab on each insert engages the notch in the connecting rod or bearing cap **(see illustration)**. If the original bearing inserts are being reused, ensure they are installed in their original locations.

**31** Ensure the bearing inserts and crankpin are clean then liberally lubricate them with clean engine oil **(see illustration)**.

**32** Ensure the connecting rod and bearing cap mating surfaces are clean and dry and the locating pins are in position **(see illustration)**. Fit the connecting rod to the crankshaft and install the bearing cap, making sure the cap is fitted the correct way around **(see illustration)**. If the original connecting rod is being reused, use the identification marks made to ensure it is fitted to its original crankpin and is the same way around as was noted prior to removal.

**33** Lubricate the threads and contact faces of the heads of the new bearing cap bolts with a smear of grease (Ducati recommend the use of AGIP GR MU3 or Shell Retinax LX2). Fit both bolts to the connecting rod assembly and tighten them by hand **(see illustration)**.

**34** With both connecting rods correctly installed, remove all side clearance between them by inserting feeler gauges of the correct thickness **(see illustration)**. This will prevent the rods twisting as the bearing cap bolts are tightened. Tighten the bearing cap bolts of each connecting rod as follows.

**35** Evenly and progressively tighten the bolts to the specified Stage 1 torque setting **(see illustration)**.

**36** Once both bolts have been tightened to the specified stage 1 torque, tighten each bolt to the specified Stage 2 torque setting.

**37** Finally angle-tighten each bolt through the specified Stage 3 angle. To ensure accuracy, use an angle-measuring gauge **(see illustration)**.

**38** Once both pairs of bolts are correctly tightened, remove the feeler gauges and check the connecting rods pivot freely on the crankpin before installing the crankshaft.

## 33 Connecting rod big-end bearings – general information

**1** Even though the connecting rod bearings are generally renewed during the engine overhaul, the old bearings should be retained

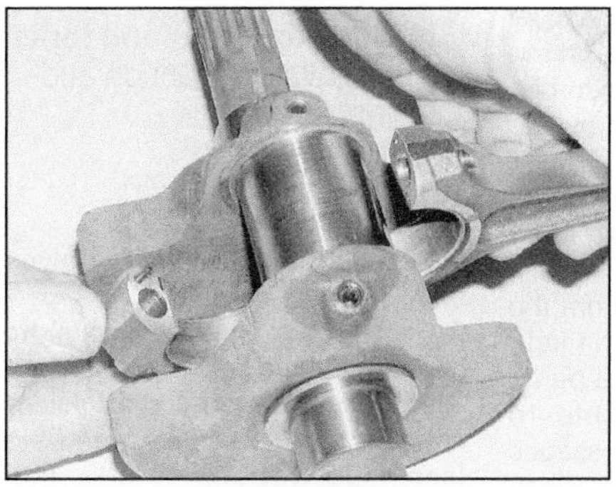

32.32b . . . then assemble the connecting rod and cap on the crankpin, ensuring it is the correct way around

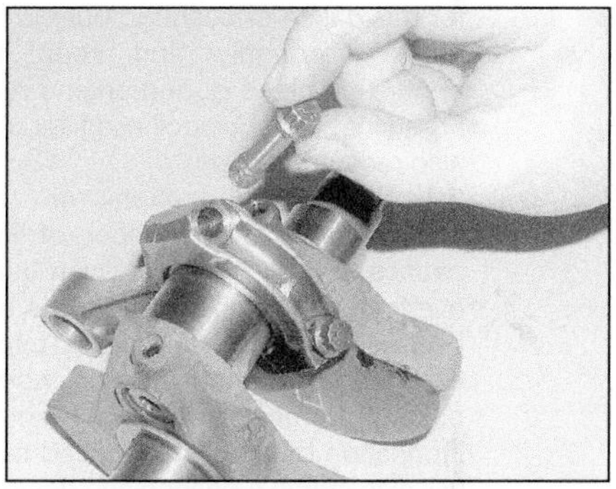

32.33 Lubricate the threads of the new bolts with grease and screw them into position

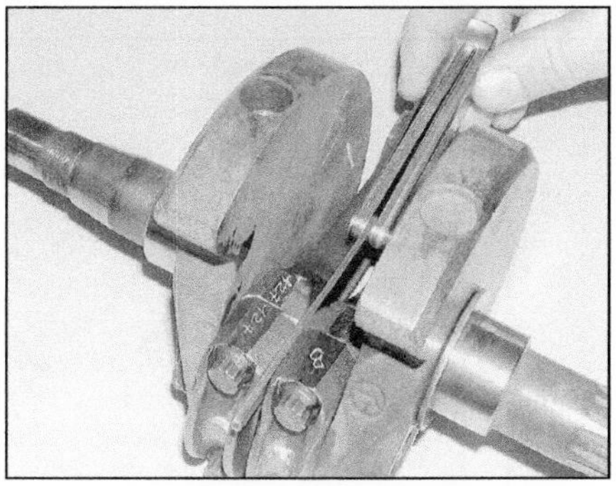

32.34 Remove all side clearance from between the connecting rods by insert feeler gauges of the required thickness

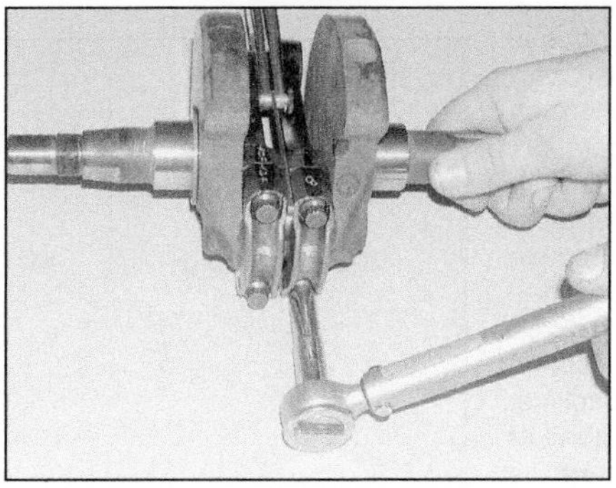

32.35 Tighten the bearing cap bolts to the specified Stage 1 and Stage 2 torque settings . . .

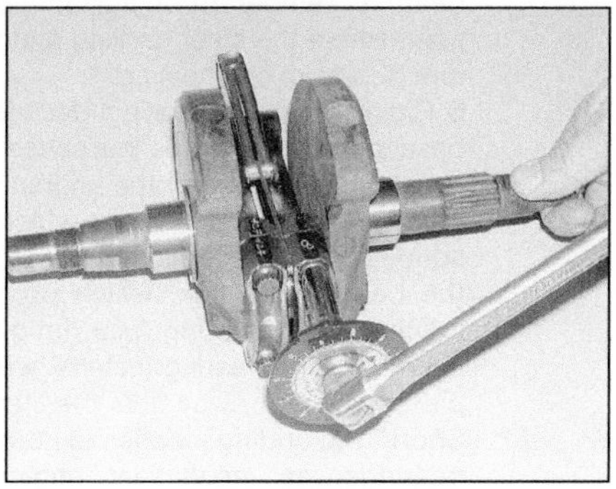

32.37 . . . and finally through the specified Stage 3 angle, using an angle-measuring gauge to ensure accuracy

valuable information about the condition of the engine.

2 Bearing failure occurs mainly because of lack of lubrication, the presence of dirt or other foreign particles, overloading the engine and/or corrosion. Regardless of the cause of bearing failure, it must be corrected before the engine is reassembled to prevent it from happening again.

3 When examining the bearings, remove the bearing inserts from the connecting rods and caps and lay them out on a clean surface in the same general position as their location on the crankshaft journals. This will enable you to match any noted bearing problems with the corresponding crankshaft journal.

4 Dirt and other foreign particles get into the engine in a variety of ways. It may be left in the engine during assembly or it may pass through filters or breathers. It may get into the oil and from there into the bearings. Metal chips from machining operations and normal engine wear are often present. Abrasives are sometimes left in engine components after reconditioning operations, especially when parts are not thoroughly cleaned using the proper cleaning methods. Whatever the source, these foreign objects often end up imbedded in the soft bearing material and are easily recognised. Large particles will not imbed in the bearing and will score or gouge the bearing and journal. The best prevention for this cause of bearing failure is to clean all parts thoroughly and keep everything spotlessly clean during engine reassembly. Frequent and regular oil and filter changes are also recommended.

5 Lack of lubrication or lubrication breakdown has a number of interrelated causes. Excessive heat (which thins the oil), overloading (which squeezes the oil from the bearing face) and oil leakage or throw off from excessive bearing clearances, worn oil pump or high engine speeds all contribute to lubrication breakdown. Blocked oil passages will also starve a bearing and destroy it. When lack of lubrication is the cause of bearing failure, the bearing material is wiped or extruded from the steel backing of the bearing. Temperatures may increase to the point where the steel backing and the journal turn blue from overheating.

6 Riding habits can have a definite effect on bearing life. Full throttle low speed operation, or labouring (lugging) the engine, puts very high loads on bearings, which tend to squeeze out the oil film. These loads cause the bearings to flex, which produces fine cracks in the bearing face (fatigue failure). Eventually the bearing material will loosen in pieces and tear away from the steel backing. Short trip riding leads to corrosion of bearings, as insufficient engine heat is produced to drive off the condensed water and corrosive gases produced. These products collect in the engine oil, forming acid and sludge. As the oil is carried to the engine bearings, the acid attacks and corrodes the bearing material.

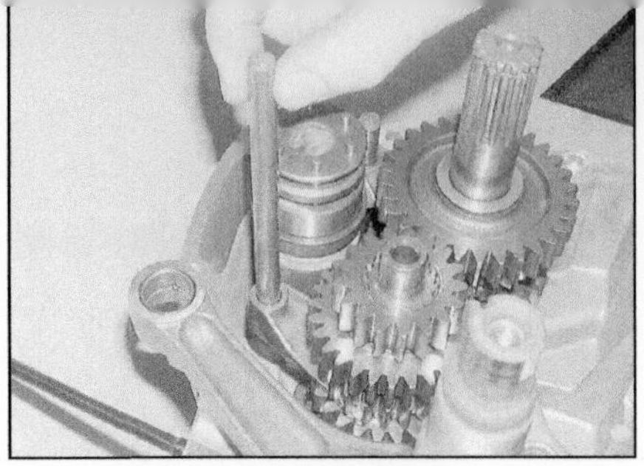

**34.3 Withdraw the selector fork rods from the input shaft . . .**

7 Incorrect bearing installation during engine assembly will lead to bearing failure as well. Tight fitting bearings which leave insufficient bearing oil clearances result in oil starvation. Dirt or foreign particles trapped behind a bearing insert result in high spots on the bearing which lead to failure.

8 To avoid bearing problems, clean all parts thoroughly before reassembly, double check all bearing clearance measurements and lubricate the new bearings with clean engine oil during installation.

## 34 Selector drum and forks – removal, inspection and installation

### *Removal*

1 Separate the crankcase halves (see Section 28).

2 Recover the endfloat shim(s) from the left-hand end of the selector drum.

3 Withdraw the input shaft selector fork rod and pivot the fork clear of the selector drum **(see illustration)**. Mark the rod for identification purposes to avoid interchanging it with the output shaft fork rod (both rods are the same).

4 Withdraw the output shaft selector fork rod from the crankcase and pivot bo forks clear of the selector drum **(s illustration)**.

**34.4 . . . and output shaft forks and pivo the forks clear of the selector drum**

5 Withdraw the selector drum from the righ hand crankcase half and recover its endflo shim(s) **(see illustration)**.

6 Free the selector fork from the input sh and remove it from the crankcase. Store th fork with its rod.

7 Free the selector forks from the outp shaft and remove them from the crankcas noting their correct fitted locations **(s illustration)**. To avoid confusion installation, using paint or a suitable mark pen, make identification marks on the for (left and right) to ensure they are installed their original locations (both forks a identical).

### *Inspection*

8 The selector forks and rods should closely inspected to ensure that they are n badly damaged or worn. Ensure the select drum neutral switch trigger is in go condition.

9 The selector fork rods can be checked f trueness by rolling them along a flat surface. bent rod will cause difficulty in selecting gea and make the gearchange action heavy. If th rod is bent it must be renewed.

10 Inspect the selector drum grooves a selector fork guide pins for signs of wear damage. If any component shows signs damage or has worn beyond the specifi

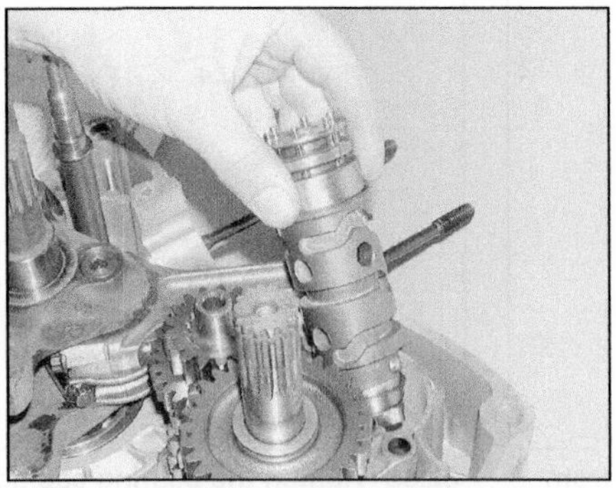

**34.5 Remove the selector drum from the crankcase and recover the endfloat shim**

**34.7 Remove the selector forks noting their location**

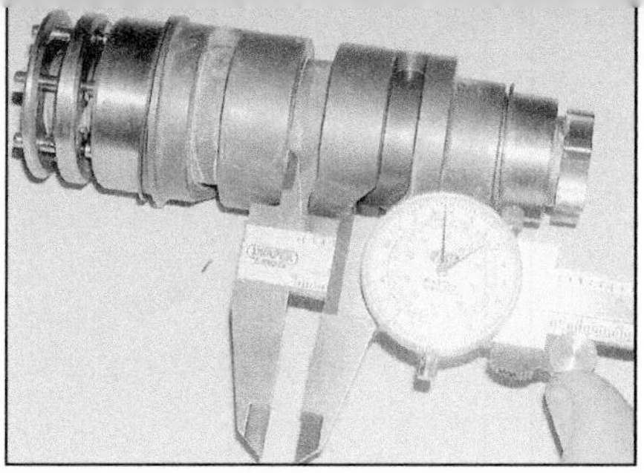

**34.10a Using a vernier caliper to measure a selector drum groove**

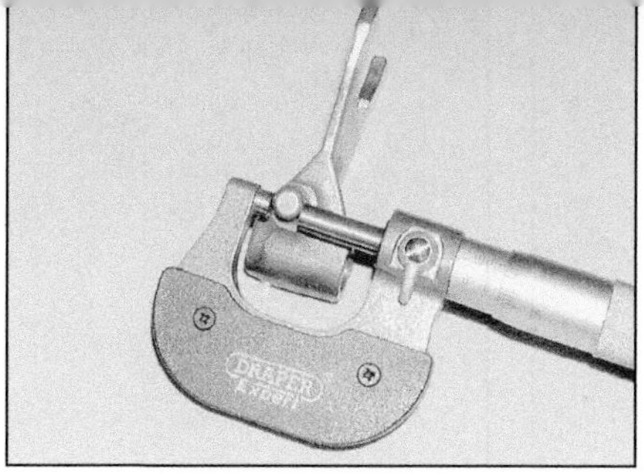


**34.10b Using a micrometer to measure a selector fork guide pin**

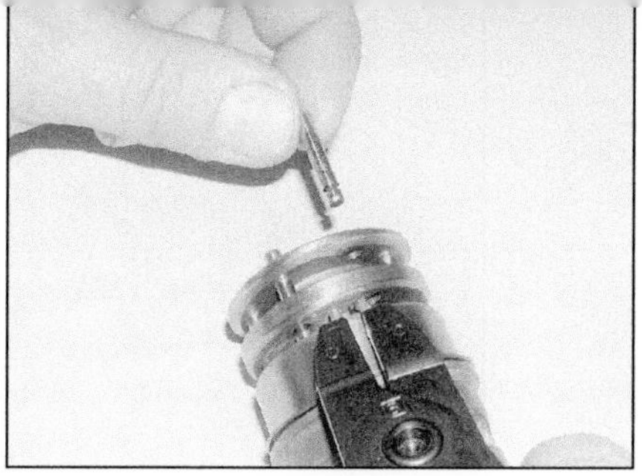

**34.11 Withdrawing a pin from the selector drum**

limits, the selector fork(s) and drum must be renewed **(see illustrations)**.

**11** Check the selector drum pins which engage with the gearchange mechanism selector claw. The pins must be undamaged, if there is any sign of wear, renew them as a set. To renew the pins, squeeze the ends of the pin retaining clip then slide each pin out of the drum **(see illustration)**. Slide each new pin into position, ensuring its groove is facing inwards. With all pins in position, seat the pin retaining clip correctly in the groove in every pin. Ensure all pins are securely held by the retaining clip before installing the selector drum.

**12** Check the bearing surfaces of the selector drum and crankcase. These surfaces shouldn't suffer from wear under normal conditions.

## *Installation*

### Endfloat check and adjustment

**13** Prior to installation, it is necessary to calculate the selector drum endfloat to ensure the correct thickness shims are installed. Endfloat is calculated as follows by measuring the distance between the inner faces of the right-hand and left-hand crankcase halves and subtracting the length of the selector drum and specified endfloat **(see illustration)**.

**14** Lay a straight-edge across the crankcase surface and using a depth gauge, measure the distance from the straight-edge to the crankcase selector drum bore shoulder. Do the same on the other crankcase half. Record these measurements as P1 (right-hand crankcase) and P2 (left-hand crankcase).

**15** Using a vernier gauge, measure the width of the selector drum from the bearing surface of its left-hand end to the bearing surface of its right-hand end **(see illustration)**. Record this measurement as A.

**16** To calculate selector drum endfloat, add P1 and P2 together. On models which are fitted with a crankcase gasket also add 0.3 mm to compensate for the thickness of the gasket. From this figure, subtract dimension A and 0.25 mm to allow for endfloat (0.25 mm is the mid-point of the specified endfloat range – see Specifications) to arrive at the correct thickness of shims required.

**Where a crankcase gasket is fitted:**

*P1 + P2 + 0.3 mm – A – 0.25 mm = total thickness of shims required*

**Where no crankcase gasket is fitted:**

*P1 + P2 – A – 0.25 mm = total thickness of shims required*

**17** The left-hand and right-hand endfloat shims should be arranged, so the selector drum is centrally positioned in the crankcases. Calculate the required thickness of shims for the left-hand end as follows:

*P1 – 0.125 mm – (A ÷ 2) = shim thickness for left-hand end of selector drum*

**18** Subtract the shim size for the left-hand end from the total shim thickness required to calculate the correct shim thickness for the right-hand end of the drum.

**19** Obtain the correct thickness shims from your Ducati dealer. Shim thickness can be checked by measuring with a micrometer.

**20** Once the correct endfloat shims have been obtained, install the selector drum and forks as follows.

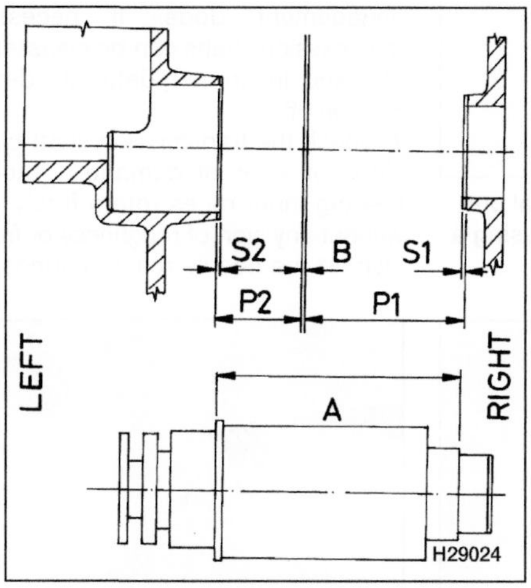


**34.13 Selector drum endfloat shim calculation details**

*A Selector drum width*
*B Crankcase gasket thickness (where fitted)*
*P1 and P2 Crankcase surface-to-selector drum bore shoulder measurements*
*S1 and S2 Endfloat shims*

### Final installation

**21** Obtain the correct thickness shims required to set the selector drum endfloat correctly (see Steps 13 to 20).

**22** Lubricate the transmission shaft gears and selector forks with clean engine oil. Also lubricate the selector fork rods and the fork bores.

**23** Engage the left and right selector forks (both forks are the same) with the output shaft gears, ensuring the fork pins are facing towards the selector drum. If the original forks are being fitted, use the marks made on removal to ensure they are installed in their original locations.

**24** Engage the remaining selector fork with the input shaft gear ensuring its pin is facing towards the selector drum location.

**25** Lubricate the selector drum bearing surface in the right-hand crankcase with clean engine oil.

**26** Fit the correct thickness shim(s) to the right-hand end of the selector drum then insert the drum into the right-hand crankcase half.

**27** Engage the output shaft left and right selector fork pins with their selector drum grooves then insert the selector fork rod. Align the rod with its crankcase bore and push it fully into position.

**28** Locate the input shaft selector fork pin in the selector drum groove then insert the selector fork rod. Align the rod with its crankcase bore and push it fully into position.

**29** Check the operation of the selector drum

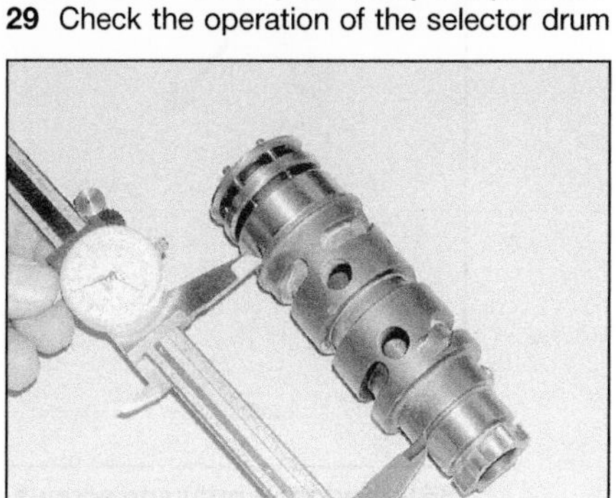

**34.15 Measure the width of the selector drum between the bearing surfaces**

**35.4 Remove the input and output shafts as an assembly**

**35.5a If the bearing inner race remains on the output shaft, carefully ease it off with a pair of screwdrivers . . .**

**35.5b . . . and press it into the centre of the bearing in the right-hand crankcase half**

then install the correct thickness endfloat shim(s) on its left-hand end.

**30** Reassemble the crankcases (see Section 28).

## 35 Transmission shafts – removal, inspection and installation

### *Removal*

**1** Separate the crankcase halves (see Section 28).

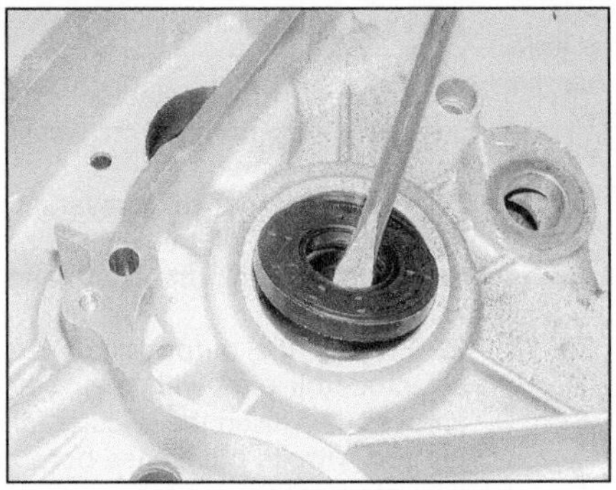

**35.8 Lever the output shaft oil seal out from the left-hand crankcase half using a flat-bladed screwdriver**

**2** Remove the selector drum and forks (see Section 34).

**3** Recover the endfloat shims from the left-hand end of the input and output shafts.

**4** Remove both shafts as an assembly, tapping the input shaft out from the casing using a soft-faced mallet **(see illustration)**. Recover the endfloat shims from the right-hand end of each shaft. **Note:** *On most models there will be a spacer and an endfloat shim on the right-hand end of the output shaft (the spacer is 2.0 to 2.3 mm thick, the endfloat shim is thinner).*

**5** If the bearing inner race has remained on the right-hand end of the output shaft, carefully lever it off, taking care not to damage the endfloat shim(s), and press it into the centre of the shaft bearing in the right-hand crankcase half **(see illustrations)**.

### *Inspection*

**6** Inspect the transmission gears looking for signs of damaged or chipped gear teeth and engagement dogs. If necessary, the transmission shafts can be disassembled and checked in greater detail as described in Section 36.

**7** Check the transmission shaft bearings for signs of wear of damage. Check the ball bearing inner races rotate freely and easily without any sign of roughness or freeplay and inspect the needle roller bearings and inner races for signs of wear or damage. Renew damaged bearings as follows.

### Output shaft left-hand bearing renewal

**8** Lever out the oil seal, taking care not to damage the casing **(see illustration)**. Discard the seal, a new one must be used.

**9** Undo the retaining screws and remove the bearing retaining plate from the inside the crankcase **(see illustration)**.

**10** Support the inner face of the crankcase half then tap the bearing evenly out of position, using a metal drift against the bearing inner race **(see illustration)**.

**11** Ensure the crankcase bore is clean and undamaged then lubricate it with clean engine oil to ease installation.

**12** Locate the new bearing in position ensuring its marked face is facing outwards (towards the casing), and tap it squarely into position using a tubular drift which bears only on the bearing's outer race **(see illustration)**. Ensure the bearing is in firm contact with the crankcase shoulder.

**13** Clean the threads of the retaining plate screws and apply a drop of fresh locking compound to the threads of each one. Fit the retaining plate to the crankcase and tighten the retaining screws to the specified torque.

**14** Fit the new oil seal prior to reassembling the crankcases (see Section 28).

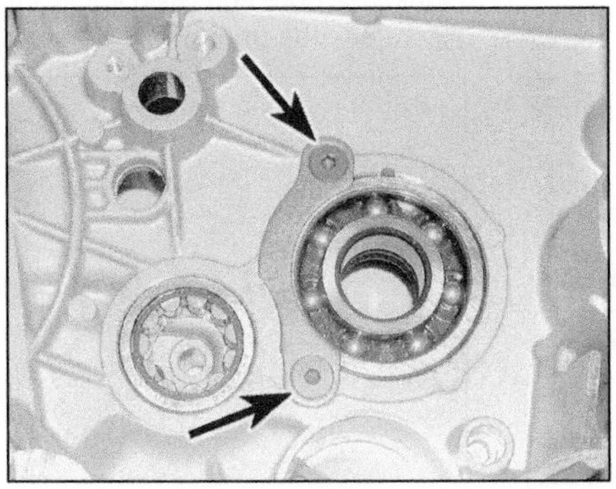

**35.9 Undo the retaining screws (arrowed) and remove the output shaft bearing retaining plate . . .**

**35.10 . . . then support the inner face of the crankcase and tap the bearing out of position**

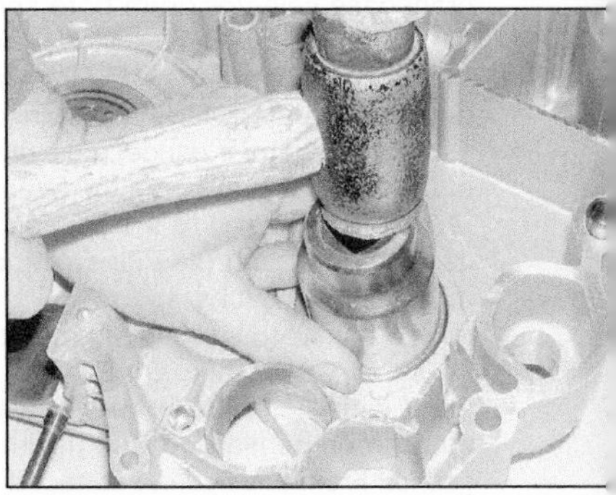

**35.12 Support the casing outer face and tap the new bearing into position using a socket which bears only on the bearing outer race**

## renewal

**15** Slacken and remove the bearing retaining screws from the inside of the crankcase **(see illustration)**.

**16** Renew the bearing as described in Steps 10 to 12.

**17** Clean the threads of the bearing retaining screws and apply a drop of fresh locking compound to the threads of each one. Fit the retaining screws and washers to the crankcase and tighten them to the specified torque.

## Output shaft right-hand bearing renewal

**Note:** *The needle roller bearing is fitted in a blind hole in the crankcase half and removal will require the use of a slide-hammer with bearing puller attachment.*

**18** Remove the bearing inner race then extract the needle roller bearing from the crankcase half using a slide-hammer and bearing puller attachment.

**19** Ensure the crankcase bore is clean and undamaged then lubricate it with clean engine oil to ease installation.

**20** Locate the new bearing in position, ensuring its marked face is facing outwards (towards the casing), and tap it squarely into position using a tubular drift which bears only on the bearing's outer race. Ensure the bearing is in firm contact with the crankcase shoulder.

## Input shaft left-hand bearing renewal

**Note:** *The needle roller bearing is fitted in a blind hole in the crankcase half and removal will require the use of a slide-hammer with bearing puller attachment.*

**21** Remove the bearing inner race then extract the needle roller bearing from the crankcase half using a slide-hammer and bearing puller attachment. Recover the washer fitted between the bearing and crankcase.

**22** Ensure the crankcase bore is clean and undamaged then lubricate it with clean engine oil to ease installation.

**23** Insert the washer into the bearing bore then locate the new bearing in position, ensuring its marked face is facing outwards (towards the casing). Tap the new bearing squarely into position using a tubular drift which bears only on the bearing's outer race. Ensure the bearing is in firm contact with the washer.

**35.15 Input shaft right-hand bearing retaining screws (arrowed)**

**35.26 Using a straight-edge and vernier caliper to measure the bearing inner race-to-crankcase depth**

## *Installation*

### Endfloat check and adjustment

**24** Prior to installation, it is necessary to calculate the input and output shaft endfloat to ensure the correct thickness shims are installed. Endfloat is calculated by measuring the distance between the inner races of bearings in the right-hand and left-hand crankcase and subtracting the length of each transmission shaft assembly and the specified endfloat **(see illustration)**.

**25** Before proceeding ensure the inner races of the input shaft left-hand bearing and the output shaft right-hand bearing are correctly fitted to the bearings and are not still in position on the shaft ends (see Step 5).

**26** Lay a straight-edge across the crankcase surface and using a depth gauge, measure the distance from the straight-edge to the inner race of each transmission shaft bearing **(see illustration)**. Do the same on the other crankcase half. Record these measurements as PA1 (right-hand crankcase) and PA2 (left-hand crankcase) for the input shaft and as PB1 (right-hand crankcase) and PB2 (left-hand crankcase) for the output shaft.

**27** Using a vernier gauge, measure the width of each complete transmission shaft assembly. On the input shaft, measure from the bearing surface of the integral 1st gear to the bearing surface of the 2nd gear and record this measurement as A. On the output shaft, measure from the bearing surface of the shoulder on its left-hand end to the bearing surface of the spacer (where fitted) or 1st gear (as applicable) on its right-hand end and record this measurement as B.

**28** To calculate shaft endfloat, add PA1 and PA2 (for input shaft) and PB1 and PB2 (for output shaft) together. On models which are fitted with a crankcase gasket also add 0.3 mm to compensate for the thickness of the gasket. From this figure, subtract dimension A (input shaft) or B (output shaft) and another 0.1 mm to allow for endfloat (0.1 mm is the mid-point of the specified endfloat range – see Specifications) to arrive at the correct thickness of shims required. Thus:

**Where a crankcase gasket is fitted:**

*PA1 + PA2 + 0.3 mm – A – 0.1 mm = total thickness of shims for input shaft*

*PB1 + PB2 + 0.3 mm – B – 0.1 mm = total thickness of shims for output shaft*

**Where no crankcase gasket is fitted:**

*PA1 + PA2 – A – 0.1 mm = total thickness of shims for input shaft*

*PB1 + PB2 – B – 0.1 mm = total thickness of shims for output shaft*

**29** The left-hand and right-hand endfloat shims should be arranged, so the transmission shafts are centrally positioned in the crankcases. Calculate the required thickness of shims for the left-hand end as follows:

*PA1 – 0.05 mm – (A ÷ 2) = shim thickness for left-hand end of input shaft*

*PB1 – 0.05 mm – (B ÷ 2) = shim thickness for left-hand end of output shaft*

**30** Subtract the shim size for the left-hand end of each shaft from the total shim

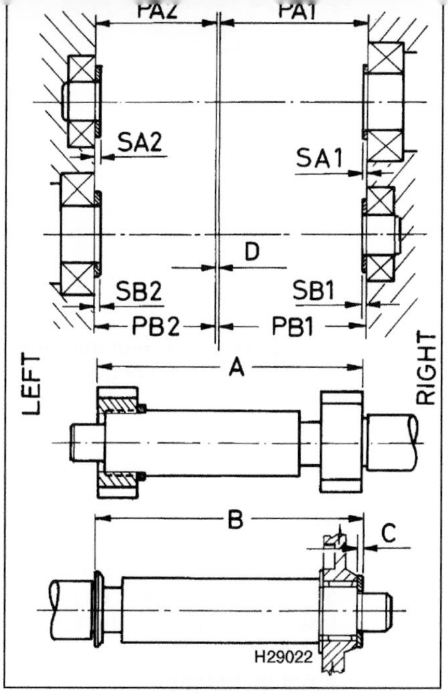


**35.24 Transmission shaft endfloat shim calculation details**

*A Input shaft width*
*B Output shaft width*
*C Output shaft spacer (where fitted)*
*D Crankcase gasket thickness (where fitted)*
*PA1 and PA2 Crankcase surface-to-input shaft bearing inner race measurements*
*PB1 and PB2 Crankcase surface-to-output shaft bearing inner race measurements*
*SA1 and SA2 Input shaft endfloat shims*
*SB1 and SB2 Output shaft endfloat shims*

**35.33 Fit the correct thickness endfloat shim to each end of the input and output shafts**

thickness required to calculate the correct shim thickness for the right-hand end of each shaft.

**31** Obtain the correct thickness shims from your Ducati dealer. Shim thickness can be checked by measuring with a micrometer.

**32** Once the correct endfloat shims have been obtained, install the transmission shafts as follows.

### Final installation

**33** Obtain the correct thickness shims required to set the transmission shaft endfloat correctly (see Steps 24 to 32) **(see illustration)**.

**34** Ensure the output shaft bearing inner race is correctly installed in the bearing in the right-hand crankcase half and is not still on the end of the input shaft (see Step 5).

**35** Lubricate the input and output shaft bearings in the right-hand crankcase with clean engine oil.

**36** Ensure both transmission shafts are correctly assembled and ensure the spacer (where fitted) is in position on the right-hand end of the output shaft. Fit the correct thickness endfloat shims to the right-hand end of both the input and output shafts.

**37** Mesh the input and output shafts gears together then fit the assembly to the right-hand crankcase half. Align both shafts with their bearings and tap them gently into position with a soft-faced mallet. Position the gears in the neutral position then check the shafts rotate freely.

**36.2 Slide the 2nd gear off the input shaft, noting which way around it is fitted**

**38** Install the correct thickness endfloat shims on the input and output shaft left-hand ends.

**39** Install the selector drum and forks then reassemble the crankcases (see Sections 34 and 28).

## 36 Transmission shafts – disassembly, checking and reassembly

**HAYNES HiNT** ***When disassembling the transmission shafts, place the parts on a long rod, or thread a wire through them to keep them in order and facing the proper direction.***

**1** Remove the transmission shafts as described in Section 35.

### *Input shaft*

**Note:** *Discard all circlips; new ones must be used on reassembly. On early models, the gears have two-piece needle roller bearings whereas on later models the gear bearings are one-piece items. When removing a one-piece bearing, do not expand the bearing any more than is necessary to remove/install it on the shaft.*

### Disassembly

**2** Slide off the 2nd gear, noting which way

**36.3a Remove the circlip . . .**

**36.3b . . . then slide off the splined thrus washer followed by the 6th gear (arrowe**

around it is fitted **(see illustration)**. To avo confusion on reassembly, use paint suitable marker pen to mark the outer face the gear; this mark can then be used c reassembly to ensure the gear is fitted tl same way around.

**3** Using circlip pliers, remove the first circl from the input shaft and slide off the spline thrust washer **(see illustrations)**.

**4** Remove the 6th gear followed by the 6 gear needle roller bearing and the next spline thrust washer **(see illustration)**.

**5** Remove the next circlip and slide off tl 3rd/4th gear, noting which way around it fitted **(see illustration)**.

**6** Remove the next circlip using a suitab pair of circlip pliers **(see illustration)**.

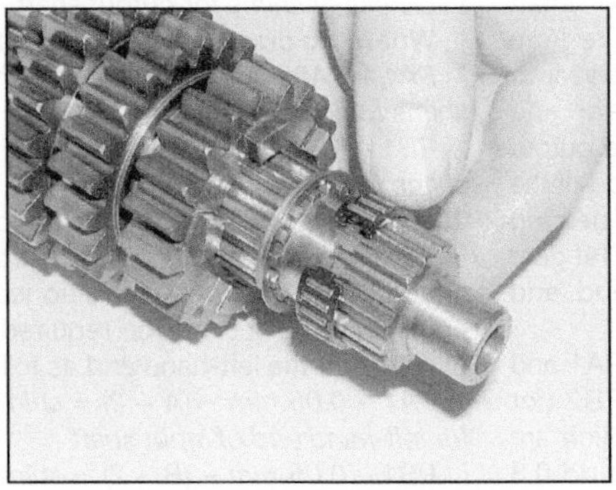

**36.4 Remove the 6th gear needle roller bearing (one-piece bearing shown) and slide off the next splined washer**

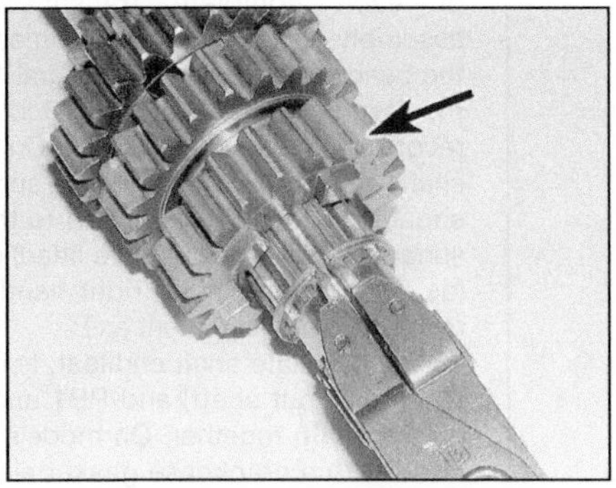

**36.5 Remove the next circlip then slide off the 3rd/4th gear (arrowed)**

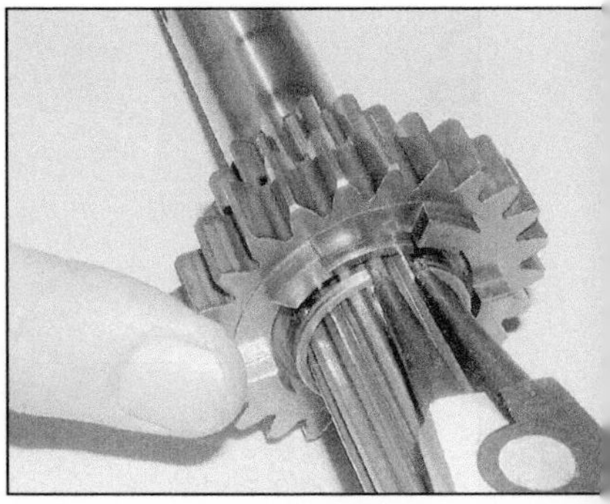

**36.6 Remove the next circlip then slide o the splined washer and 5th gear**

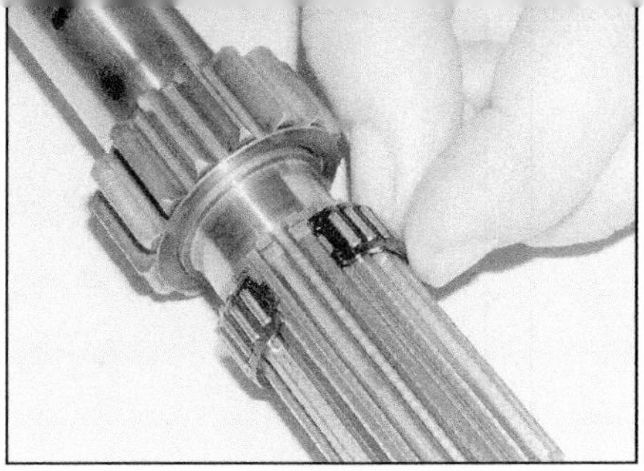

36.7 Remove the 5th gear needle roller bearing and final thrust washer

7 Slide off the splined thrust washer followed by the 5th gear, 5th gear needle roller bearing and thrust washer **(see illustration)**.

## Inspection

8 Wash all of the components in clean solvent and dry them off.

9 Check the gear teeth for cracking and other obvious damage. Check the gear bearings and the surface in the inner diameter of each gear for scoring or heat discoloration. If the gear or bearing is damaged, renew it. It is recommended that the bearings are renewed, regardless of their apparent condition.

10 Inspect the dogs and the dog holes in the gears for excessive wear. Renew the paired gears as a set if necessary.

11 The shaft is unlikely to sustain damage unless the engine has seized, placing an unusually high loading on the transmission, or the machine has covered a very high mileage. where a pinion turns on it, and renew the shaft if it has scored or picked up. Inspect the threads of the shafts and check them for trueness by setting them up in V-blocks and measuring any runout with a dial gauge. Damage of any kind can only be cured by renewal.

## Reassembly

12 During reassembly, lubricate all components with engine oil before assembling them **(see illustration)**. **Note:** *Always use new circlips on reassembly. If the circlips are examined closely it will be seen that they are chamfered on one side. During reassembly it is essential that each circlip is fitted so its chamfered side is facing away from the direction of thrust load (refer to Section 2 'Circlips' in Tools and Workshop Tips in the Reference section of this manual).*

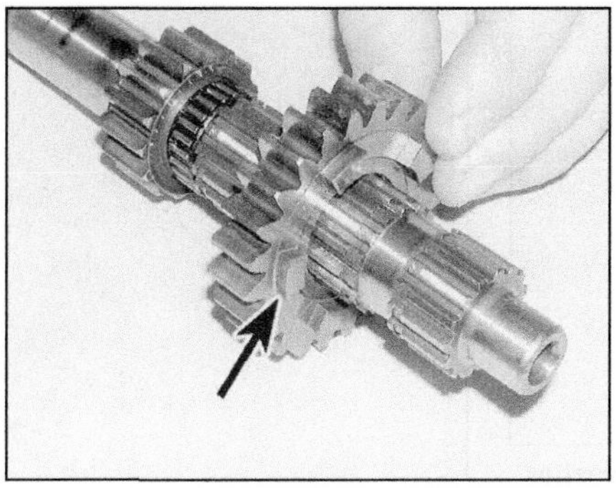

36.14 Ensure the 5th gear is installed with its dogs (arrowed) facing away from the 1st gear

gear needle roller bearing. On early models with two-piece bearings ensure the bearing halves are correctly assembled on the shaft.

14 Fit the 5th gear with its dogs facing away from the 1st gear and locate it correctly on its bearing **(see illustration)**. Slide on the splined thrust washer then secure the 5th gear components in position with a new circlip. Ensure the circlip is fitted the correct way around and is correctly located in the input shaft groove.

15 Install the 3rd/4th gear with its larger 4th gear facing the 5th gear **(see illustration)**.

16 Fit another new circlip to the shaft, making sure it the right way around and is correctly located in its groove.

17 Slide on the splined thrust washer and fit the 6th gear needle roller bearing. Fit the 6th gear so that its dogs are facing the 3rd/4th

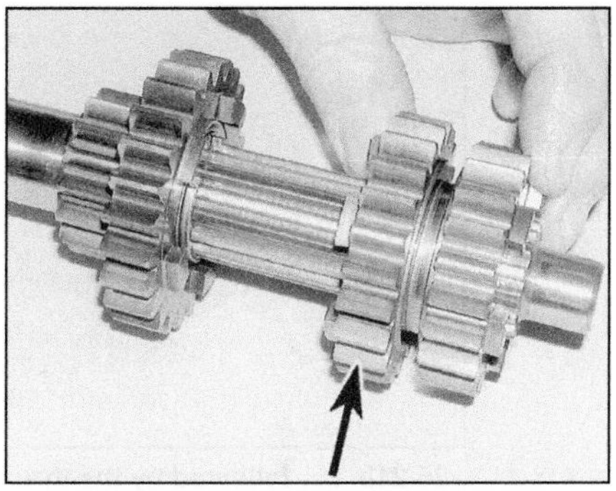

36.15 Install the 3rd/4th gear with its larger 4th gear (arrowed) facing the 5th gear

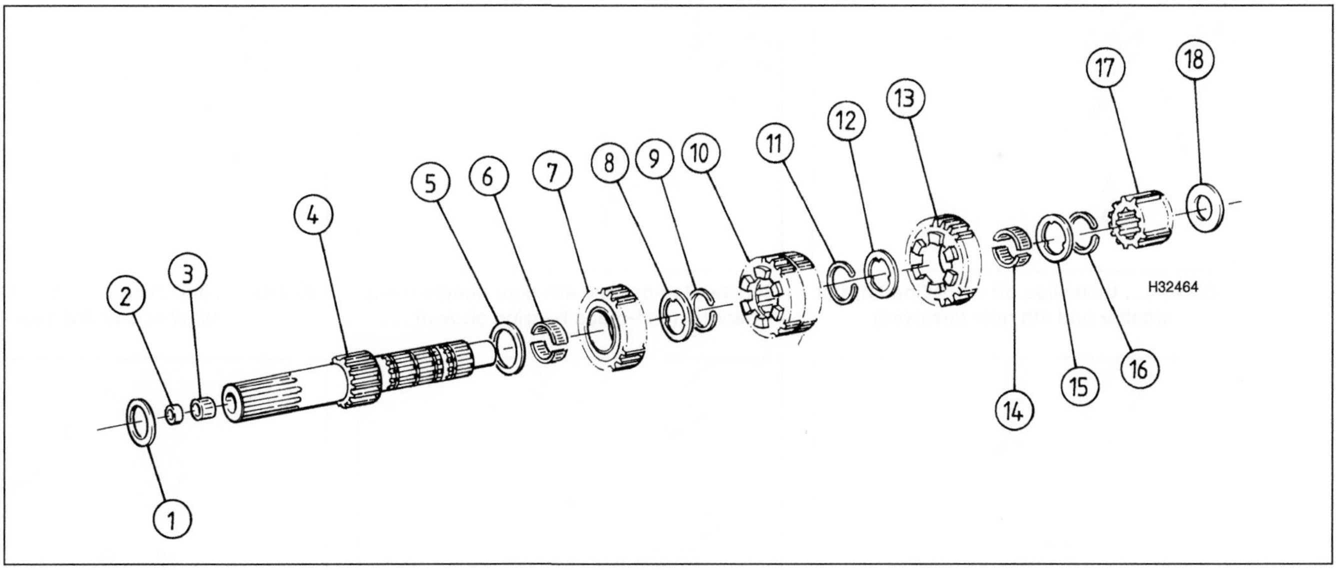


36.12 Input shaft components

*1 Endfloat shim*
*2 Pushrod oil seal*
*3 Pushrod needle roller bearing*
*4 Input shaft*
*5 Thrust washer*
*6 Needle roller bearing (two-piece bearing shown)*
*7 5th gear*
*8 Splined thrust washer*
*9 Circlip*
*10 3rd/4th gear*
*11 Circlip*
*12 Splined thrust washer*
*13 6th gear*
*14 Needle roller bearing (two-piece bearing shown)*
*15 Splined thrust washer*
*16 Circlip*
*17 2nd gear*
*18 Endfloat shim*

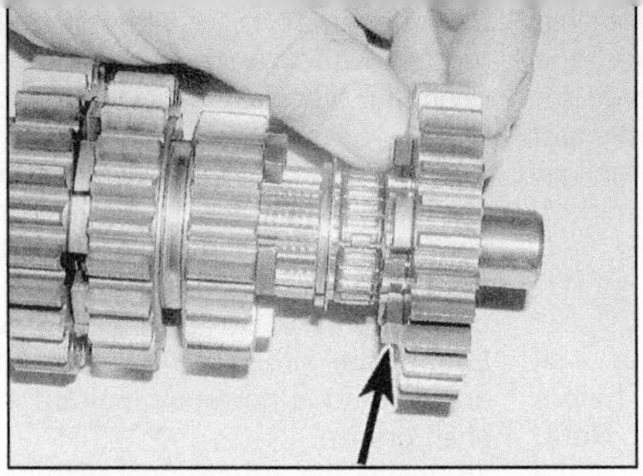

36.17 Fit the 6th gear with its dogs (arrowed) facing the 3rd/4th gear

36.20 Remove the spacer (where fitted) and slide off the 1st gear . . .

36.21a . . . and needle roller bearing . . .

gear and locate it on the bearing **(see illustration)**.

**18** Slide on the splined thrust washer then secure the 6th gear components in position with a new circlip. Ensure the circlip is fitted the correct way around and is correctly located in the input shaft groove.

**19** Fit the 2nd gear to the input shaft end. If the original gear is being installed, use th mark made prior to removal to ensure th gear is fitted the right way around.

## *Output shaft*

**Note:** *Discard all circlips; new ones must b used on reassembly. On early models, th gears have two-piece needle roller bearing whereas on later models the gear bearings ar one-piece items.*

### Disassembly

**20** Remove the spacer (where fitted) from th right-hand end of the output shaft **(se illustration)**.

**21** Remove the 1st gear, noting which wa around it is fitted, followed by the 1st gea needle roller bearing and thrust washer **(se illustrations)**.

36.21b . . . followed by the thrust washer and 5th gear

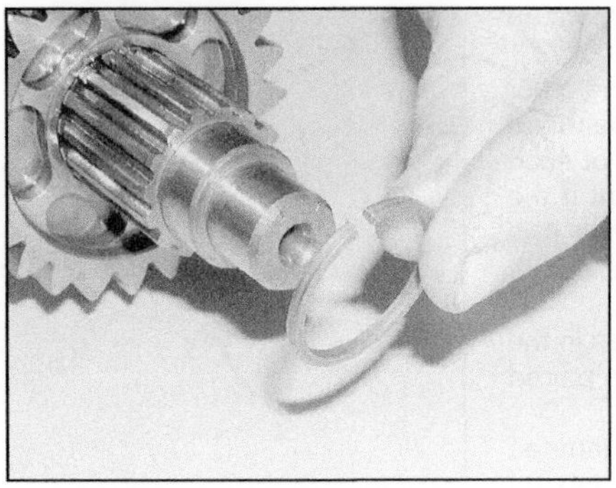

36.23a Remove the circlip . . .

36.23b . . . then slide off the splined thrust washer and 4th gear (arrowed)

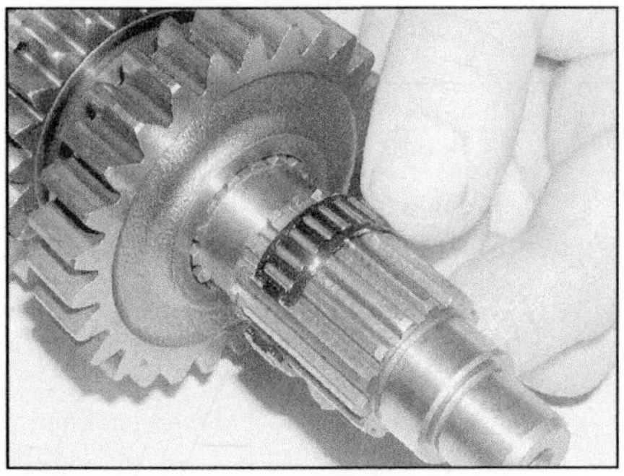

36.24a Remove the 4th gear needle roller bearing (one-piece bearing shown) . . .

36.24b . . . and slide off the splined thrust washer and 3rd gear

36.25a Remove the 3rd gear needle roller bearing . . .

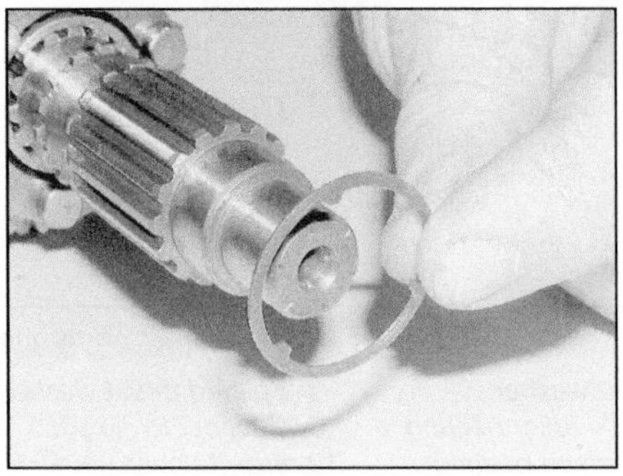

36.25b . . . and splined thrust washer

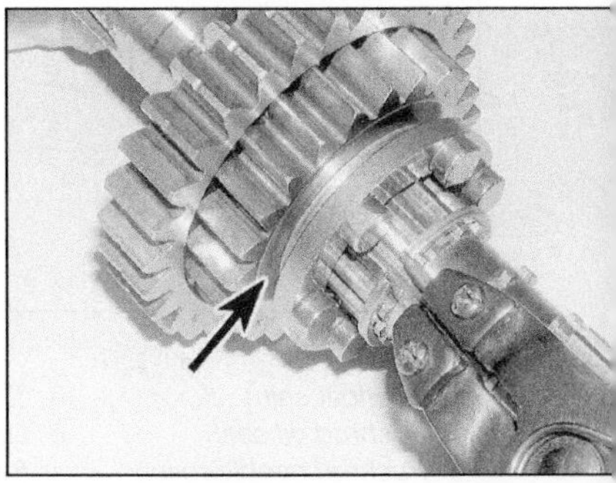

36.26 Remove the next circlip then slide off the 6th gear (arrowed)

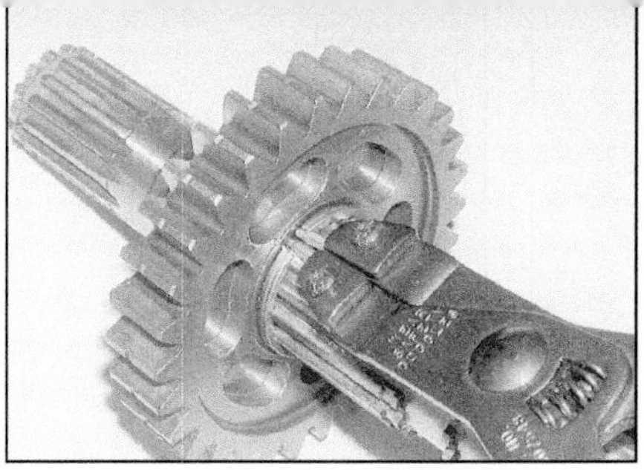

**36.27a Remove the next circlip . . .**

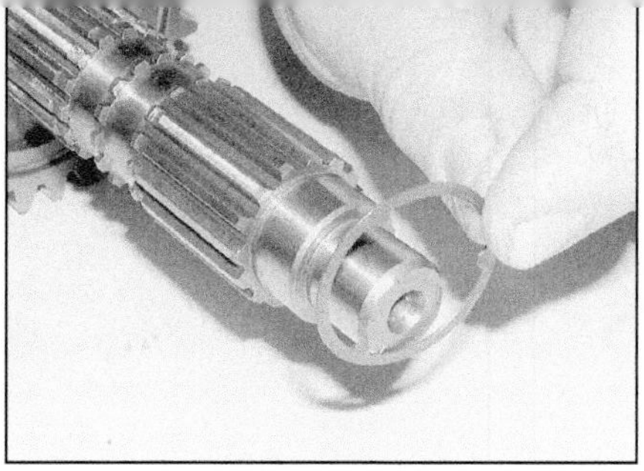

**36.27b . . . followed by the splined thrust washer and 2nd gear . . .**

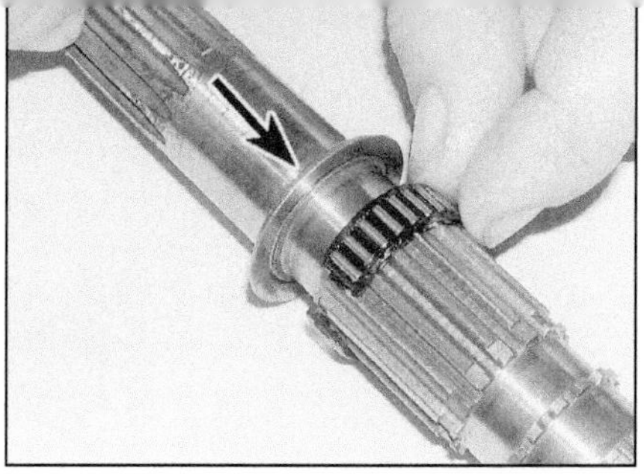

**36.28 . . . then remove the needle roller bearing and final thrust washer**

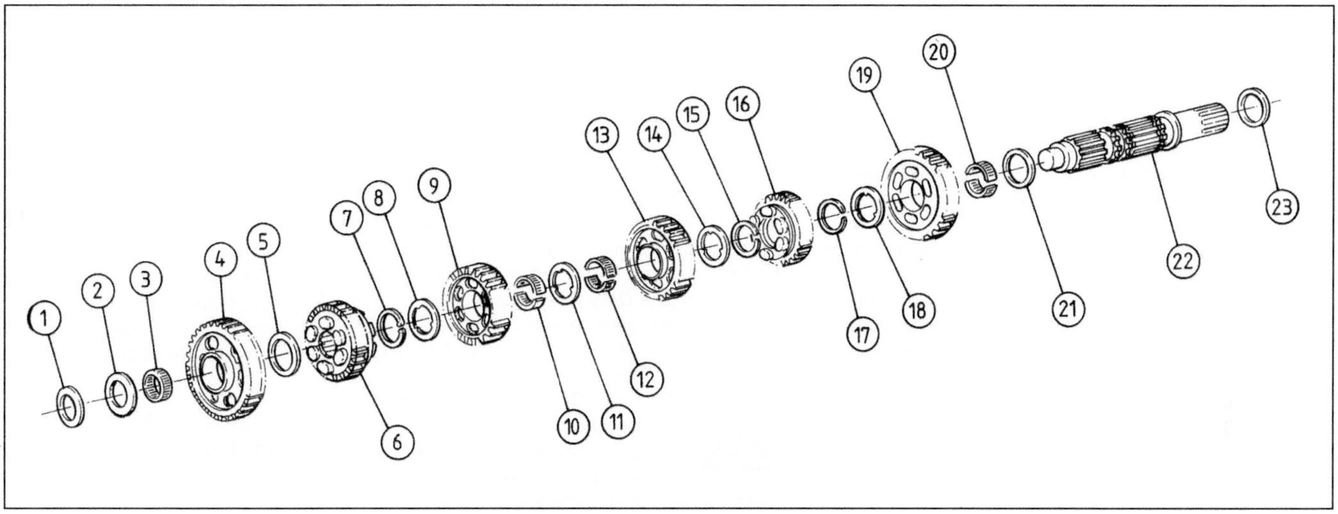


**36.30 Output shaft components**

1 *Endfloat shim*
2 *Spacer (where fitted)*
3 *Needle roller bearing*
4 *1st gear*
5 *Thrust washer*
6 *5th gear*
7 *Circlip*
8 *Splined thrust washer*
9 *4th gear*
10 *Needle roller bearing (two-piece bearing shown)*
11 *Splined thrust washer*
12 *Needle roller bearing (two-piece bearing shown)*
13 *3rd gear*
14 *Splined thrust washer*
15 *Circlip*
16 *6th gear*
17 *Circlip*
18 *Splined thrust washer*
19 *2nd gear*
20 *Needle roller bearing (two-piece bearing shown)*
21 *Thrust washer*
22 *Output shaft*
23 *Endfloat shim*

**22** Slide off the 5th gear, noting which way around it is fitted.

**23** Remove the circlip with a suitable pair of circlip pliers and slide off the splined thrust washer **(see illustrations)**.

**24** Slide off the 4th gear, noting which way around it is fitted, then remove the 4th gear needle roller bearing and thrust washer **(see illustrations)**.

**25** Slide off the 3rd gear, noting which way around it is fitted, followed by the 3rd gear needle roller bearing and splined thrust washer **(see illustrations)**.

**26** Remove the next circlip then slide off the 6th gear, noting which way around it is fitted **(see illustration)**.

**27** Remove the next circlip and slide off splined thrust washer **(see illustrations)**.

**28** Remove the 2nd gear, noting which way around it is fitted, then remove the 2nd gear needle roller bearing and the thrust washer **(see illustration)**. To avoid confusion on reassembly, use paint or suitable marker pen to mark the outer face of the gear.

## Inspection

**29** Refer to Steps 8 to 11.

## Reassembly

**30** During reassembly, lubricate all components with engine oil before assembling them **(see illustration)**. **Note:** *Always use new circlips on reassembly. If the circlips are examined closely it will be seen that they are chamfered on one side. During reassembly it is essential that each circlip is fitted so its chamfered side is facing away from the direction of thrust load (refer to Section 2 'Circlips' in Tools and Workshop Tips in the Reference section of this manual).*

**31** Slide on the thrust washer and fit the 2nd gear needle roller bearing. On early models with two-piece bearings ensure the bearing halves are correctly assembled on the shaft.

**32** Fit the 2nd gear, ensuring its engagement dog holes are facing to the right, and locate it on its bearing **(see illustration)**.

**36.32 Fit the 2nd gear with its engagement dog holes facing to the right**

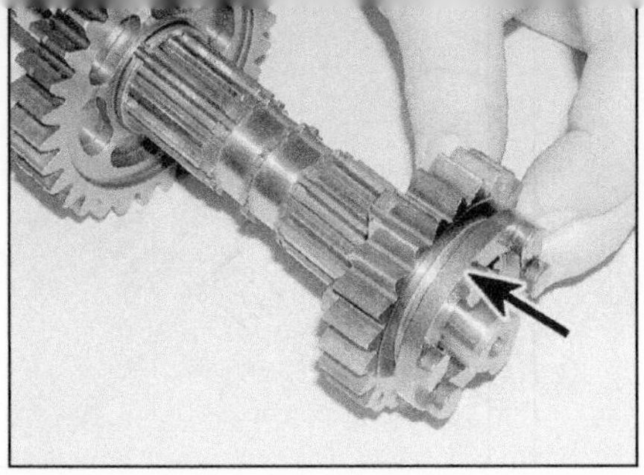

**36.34 Fit the 6th gear with its selector fork groove (arrowed) facing away from the 2nd gear**

**36.36 Fit the 3rd gear with its dog holes facing towards the 6th gear**

**36.37 Install the 4th gear with its dog holes facing away from the 3rd gear**

**33** Fit the splined thrust washer and secure the 2nd gear components with a new circlip. Ensure the circlip is fitted the right way around and is correctly located in the output shaft groove.
**34** Fit the 6th gear to the shaft so that its selector fork groove is facing away from the 2nd gear **(see illustration)**.
**35** Fit another new circlip ensuring it is the right way around and correctly located in the shaft groove.
**36** Slide on the splined thrust washer then fit the 3rd gear needle roller bearing. Fit the 3rd gear ensuring its dog holes are facing the 6th gear and locate it on its bearing **(see illustration)**.
**37** Slide on the splined thrust washer then fit the 4th gear needle roller bearing. Fit the 4th gear ensuring its dog holes are facing away from the 3rd gear and locate it on its bearing **(see illustration)**.
**38** Fit the splined thrust washer and secure the 4th gear components with a new circlip. Ensure the circlip is fitted the right way around and is correctly located in the output shaft groove.
**39** Fit the 5th gear ensuring its selector fork groove is facing the 4th gear **(see illustration)**.
**40** Fit the thrust washer and 1st gear needle roller bearing then fit the 1st gear ensuring its dog holes are facing towards the 5th gear **(see illustration)**.

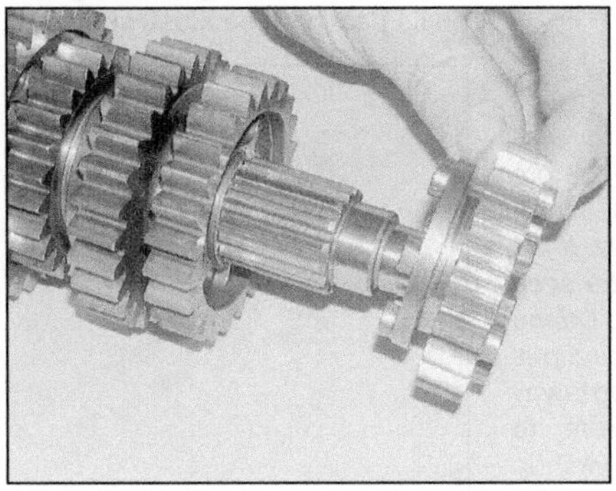

**36.39 Fit the 5th gear with its selector fork groove facing towards the 4th gear**

**41** Fit the spacer (where fitted) to the end of the output shaft.

## 37 Initial start-up after overhaul

**Note:** *Do not install the inner and lower fairing panels until after the engine has been run.*
**1** Make sure the engine oil and coolant levels are correct (see *Daily (pre-ride) checks*).
**2** Turn on the ignition switch and crank the engine over with the starter to prime the lubrication system of the engine.

***Warning: Operate the starter in 5 second bursts with at least a 15 second wait in between operations. This will prevent the starter motor and battery overheating and becoming damaged.***

**3** Make sure there is fuel in the tank then start the engine and allow it idle slowly.

***Warning: If the oil pressure warning light doesn't go off immediately or soon after the engine starts (a delay of a few seconds is usual), or it comes on while the engine is running, stop the engine immediately and investigate the cause.***

**4** Once the oil pressure warning light goes out, bleed the air from the cooling system (see Chapter 1) and top-up the expansion ta coolant level.

**36.40 Install the 1st gear so that its dog holes face the 5th gear**

**5** Warm the engine up to normal operati temperature whilst checking carefully for and coolant leaks. Check the operation of t clutch and transmission then switch off t engine.
**6** Make sure the transmission and contro especially the brakes, function properly befo road testing the machine. Refer to Section for the recommended break-in procedure.
**7** Upon completion of the road test, and aft the engine has cooled down complete check the engine oil and the coolant level.

## 38 Recommended running-in procedure

**1** Any rebuilt engine needs time to break-i even if parts have been installed in th original locations. For this reason, treat t machine gently for the first few miles to ma sure oil has circulated throughout the engi and any new parts installed have started seat.
**2** Even greater care is necessary if the engi has been fitted with new cylinder barrels a pistons or a new crankshaft. In the case new cylinder barrels and pistons, the engi will have to be run in as if the machine we new. This means greater use of t transmission and a restraining hand on t throttle until at least 500 miles (800 km) ha been covered. There's no point in keeping any set speed limit – the main idea is to ke from labouring (lugging) the engine and gradually increase performance until the 5 mile (800 km) mark is reached. The recommendations can be lessened to extent when only a new crankshaft installed. Experience is the best guide, sin it's easy to tell when an engine is runni freely.
**3** If a lubrication failure is suspected, stop t engine immediately and try to find the caus If an engine is run without oil, even for a sh period of time, irreparable damage will occu

# Chapter 3
## Cooling system

## Contents



## Degrees of difficulty

| | | | | |
|---|---|---|---|---|
| **Easy,** suitable for novice with little experience | **Fairly easy,** suitable for beginner with some experience | **Fairly difficult,** suitable for competent DIY mechanic | **Difficult,** suitable for experienced DIY mechanic | **Very difficult,** suitable for expert DIY or professional |

## Specifications

### Coolant

| | |
|---|---|
| Mixture type and capacity | see Chapter 1 |

### Cooling fan switch

| | |
|---|---|
| Switches on (fan cut-in temperature) | 92°C |
| Switches off (cooling fan cut-out temperature) | 87°C |

### Thermostat

| | |
|---|---|
| Opening temperature | 75°C |

### Torque wrench settings

| | |
|---|---|
| Cooling fan thermostatic switch | 42 Nm |
| Coolant temperature gauge sender | 10 Nm |
| Radiator mounting bolts | 10 Nm |
| Water pump | |
| Cover screws | 10 Nm |
| Bearing retaining bolts | 10 Nm |

## 1 General information

The cooling system uses a water/antifreeze coolant to carry away excess energy in the form of heat **(see illustration)**. The cylinders are surrounded by a water jacket, from which the heated coolant is circulated by thermo-siphonic action in conjunction with a water pump which is driven off the left-hand end of the timing belt driveshaft. The hot coolant flows down through the radiator core, where it is cooled by the passing air, then through the thermostat and water pump and back to the engine, where the cycle is repeated.

A thermostat is fitted in the system to prevent the coolant flowing through the radiator when the engine is cold, therefore accelerating the speed at which the engine reaches normal operating temperature.

The complete cooling system is partially sealed and pressurised, the pressure being controlled by a valve contained in the expansion tank pressure cap. By pressurising the coolant, the boiling point is raised – preventing premature boiling in adverse conditions. The overflow pipe from the expansion tank is connected to an overflow under pressure. The discharged coolant automatically returns to the expansion tank when the engine cools.

An electrically-operated cooling fan is fitted to aid cooling in extreme conditions. The fan is fitted to the rear of the radiator and is controlled by a thermostatic switch, which is screwed into the coolant outlet on the left-hand side of the horizontal cylinder, and a relay. The coolant temperature gauge is controlled by the temperature sender, which is also screwed into the coolant outlet.

***Warning: Do not remove the expansion tank cap when the engine is hot. Scalding hot coolant and steam may be blown out under pressure, which could cause serious injury. When the engine has cooled, place a thick rag such as a towel over the pressure cap then slowly unscrew the cap to allow any residual pressure to escape.***

***Warning: Do not allow antifreeze to come into contact with your skin or with the painted surfaces of the motorcycle. Rinse off any spills immediately with plenty of water. Antifreeze is highly toxic if ingested. Never leave antifreeze lying around in an open container or in puddles on the floor; children and pets are it. Check with the local authorities about disposing of used antifreeze. Many communities will have collection centres which will see that antifreeze is disposed of safely.***

***Caution: At all times use the specified type of antifreeze, and always mix it with distilled water in the correct proportion. The antifreeze contains corrosion inhibitors which are essential to avoid damage to the cooling system. A lack of these inhibitors could lead to a build-up of corrosion which would block the coolant passages, resulting in overheating and severe engine damage. Distilled water must be used as opposed to tap water to avoid a build-up of scale which would also block the coolant passages.***

## 2 Expansion tank pressure cap – check

**1** If problems such as overheating or loss of coolant occur, check the entire system as described in Chapter 1. The pressure cap opening pressure should be checked by a Ducati dealer with the special tester required to do the job. If the cap is defective renew it.

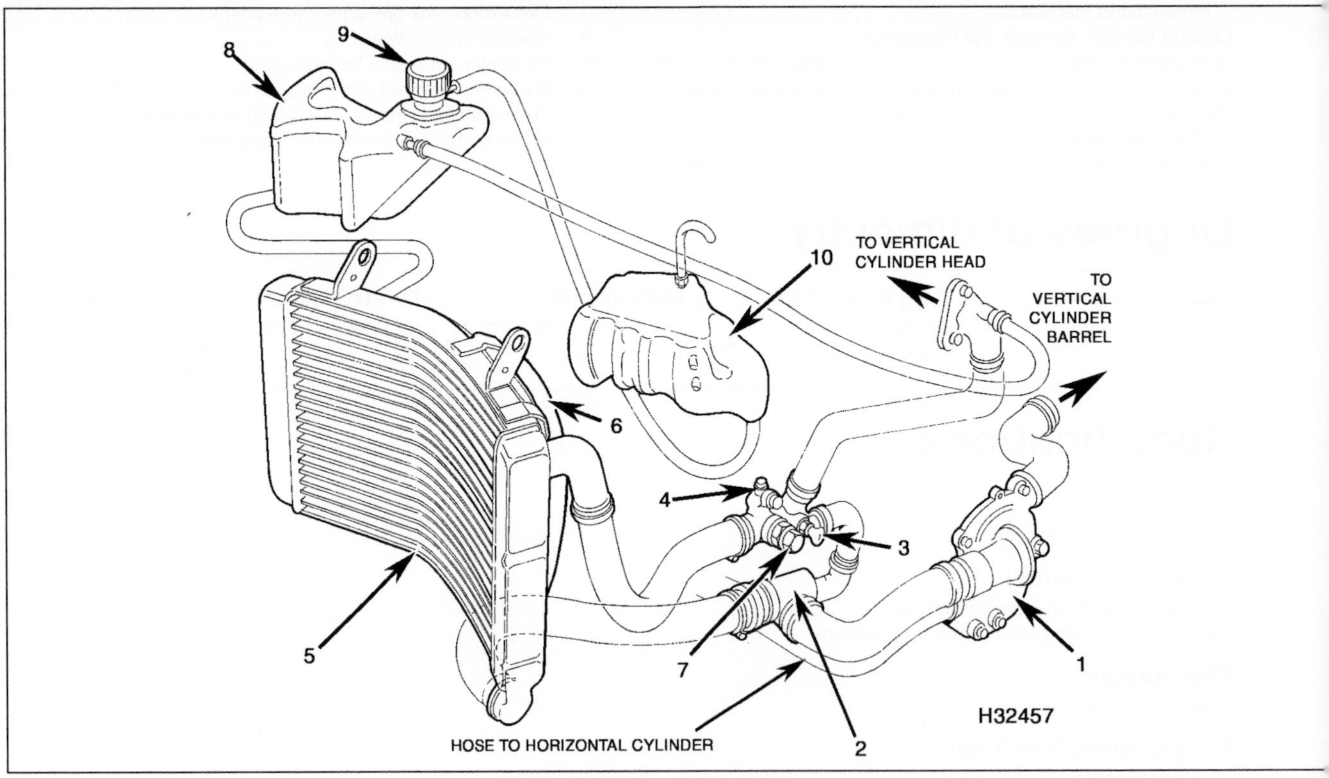


**1.1 Cooling system layout**

*1 Water pump*
*2 Thermostat*
*3 Engine management system coolant temperature sensor*
*4 Coolant temperature gauge sensor*
*5 Radiator*
*6 Cooling fan*
*7 Cooling fan temperature switch*
*8 Expansion tank*
*9 Pressure cap*
*10 Overflow tank*

3.3 Unscrew the bolts and free the ignition (main) switch from the frame

3.4 Remove the mounting rubber from the top of the expansion tank

3.5 Ease the atmospheric pressure sensor off its pegs and position it clear of the expansion tank

## 3 Coolant expansion tank and overflow tank – removal and installation

***Caution: Ensure the cooling system is cold before carrying out this procedure.***

### *Expansion tank*

#### Removal

**1** Remove the fairing right-hand lower panel (see Chapter 8).

**2** Remove the fuel tank and airbox (see Chapter 4).

**3** Unscrew the bolts securing the ignition (main) switch in position. Free the switch from the frame and position it clear of the expansion tank **(see illustration)**.

**4** Remove the mounting rubber from the top of the expansion tank **(see illustration)**.

**5** Carefully ease the atmospheric pressure sensor off its mounting pegs on the expansion tank and position it clear **(see illustration)**.

**6** Slacken the retaining clip then detach the expansion tank hose from the top of the radiator and drain the tank contents into a clean container **(see illustration)**.

**7** Slacken the retaining clips and disconnect the overflow hose from the filler neck and the cylinder head coolant hose from the top of the expansion tank **(see illustration)**.

**8** Manoeuvre the expansion tank out of position, noting its mounting rubber which is clipped to the frame tube **(see illustration)**.

#### Installation

**9** Ensure the mounting rubber is correctly fitted to the frame tube, then manoeuvre the tank into position.

**10** Connect the overflow hose to the tank filler neck, the cylinder head hose to the union on the top of the tank and the lower hose to the radiator union. Secure all hoses in position with their retaining clips.

**11** Lubricate the atmospheric pressure sensor mounting rubbers with a silicone-based spray lubricant then fit the sensor to its locating pegs on the tank.

**12** Fit the mounting rubber to the top of the expansion tank.

**13** Remove all traces of locking compound from the threads of the lock bolts and apply a few drops of fresh locking compound to each bolt. Fit the lock to the frame and tighten its retaining bolts to the specified torque (see Chapter 9).

**14** Refill the expansion tank with coolant (see *Daily pre-ride checks*).

**15** Install the airbox and fuel tank and fit the fairing panels (see Chapters 4 and 8).

### *Overflow tank*

#### Removal

**16** Remove the throttle body assembly (see Chapter 4).

**17** Drain the cooling system (see Chapter 1).

**18** Slacken the retaining clip and disconnect the overflow tank hose from the expansion tank **(see illustration)**.

**19** Slacken the retaining clip and disconnect the vertical cylinder head coolant hose

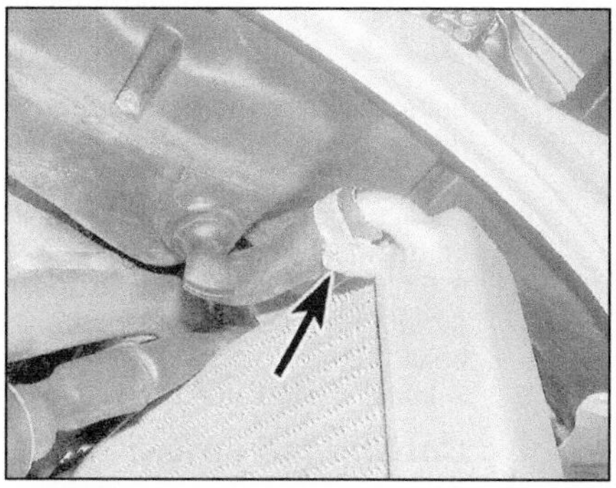

3.6 Slacken the clip (arrowed) then disconnect the expansion tank hose from the radiator and drain the tank contents

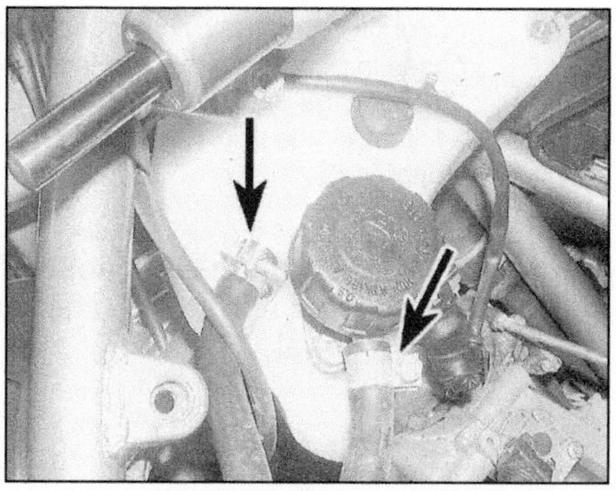

3.7 Slacken the retaining clips and disconnect the hoses (arrowed) from the top of the expansion tank

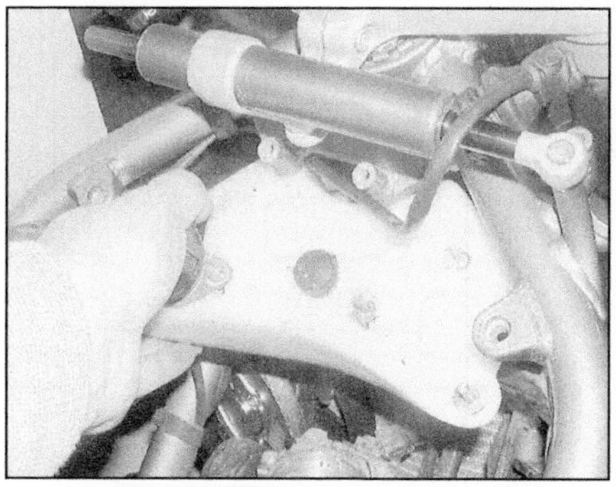

3.8 Removing the expansion tank

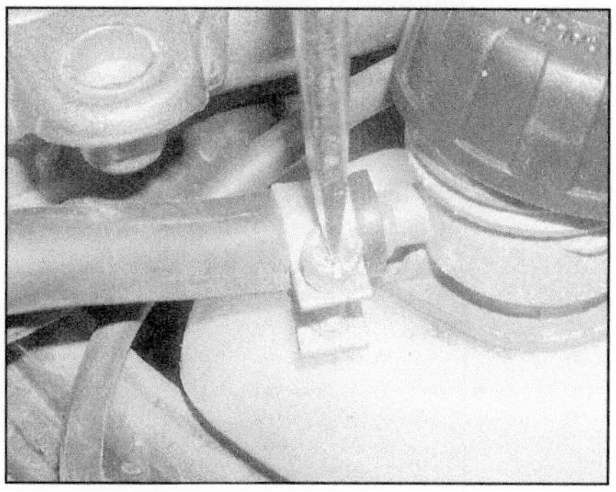

3.18 Slacken the retaining clip and disconnect the overflow tank hose from the expansion tank

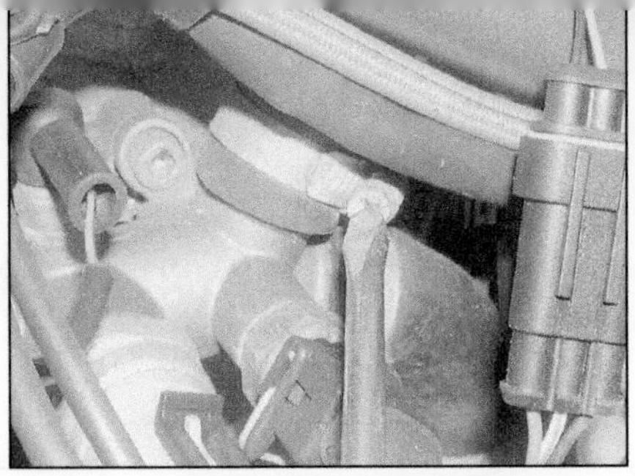

3.19 Slacken the retaining clip and disconnect the vertical cylinder head hose from the coolant union on the horizontal cylinder head

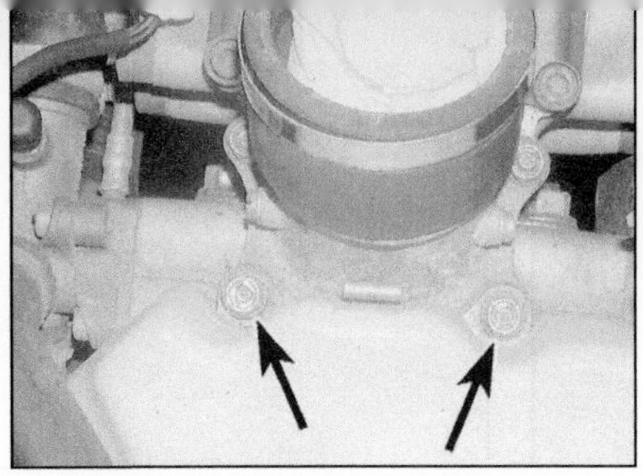

3.20a Unscrew the manifold nuts (arrowed) . . .

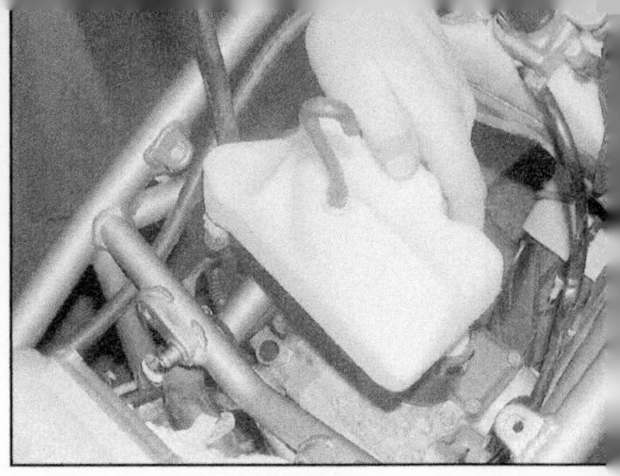

3.20b . . . and remove the coolant overflo tank

from the top of the union on the left-hand side of the horizontal cylinder head **(see illustration)**.

**20** Unscrew the retaining nuts and free the overflow tank mounting bracket from the manifold studs of the horizontal cylinder head **(see illustration)**. Remove the tank, complete with its hoses **(see illustration)**.

### Installation

**21** Seat the tank mounting bracket back on the manifold studs then refit the retaining nuts and tighten them to the specified torque (see Chapter 4).

**22** Reconnect the overflow tank hose to the expansion tank then connect the hose to the outlet union on the cylinder head. Secure both hoses in position with the retaining clips.

**23** Refill the cooling system (see Chapter 1).

**24** Install the throttle body assembly (see Chapter 4).

## 4 Cooling fan and cooling fan switch and relay – check and renewal

### *Cooling fan*

#### Check

**1** If the engine is overheating and the cooling fan is not coming on, first check the cooling fan circuit fuse (see Chapter 9) and then the fan switch (see Steps 8 to 14) and relay (see Step 21).

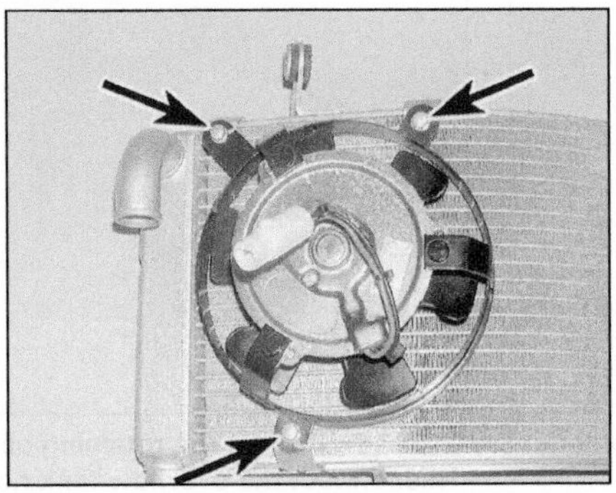

4.5 Cooling fan retaining bolts (arrowed)

**2** If the fuse, fan switch and relay are good and the fan still does not come on, the fault lies either in the cooling fan motor or in the relevant wiring. Test all the wiring and connections as described in Chapter 9.

**3** To test the cooling fan motor, disconnect the fan wiring connector and, using a 12 volt battery and two jumper wires, connect the battery across the terminals of the motor connector. Once connected the fan should operate. If it does not, and the wiring is good, then the fan motor is faulty.

#### Renewal

***Warning: Ensure the cooling system is cold before carrying out this procedure.***

**4** Remove the radiator (see Section 7).

**5** Unscrew the mounting bolts and remove the fan assembly from the rear of the radiator **(see illustration)**. There is little point in dismantling the fan assembly because no spare parts are available – it must be treated as a sealed unit.

**6** Fit the fan assembly to the rear of the radiator and securely tighten its retaining bolts.

**7** Install the radiator (see Section 7).

### *Cooling fan switch*

#### Check

**8** If the engine is overheating and the cooling fan is not coming on, first check the cooling

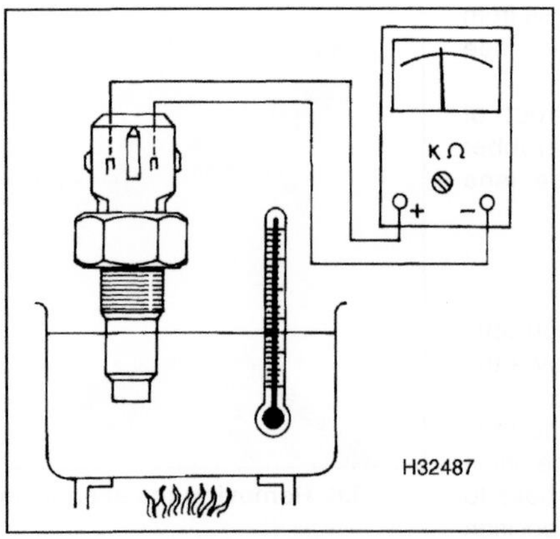


4.13 Cooling fan switch test set-up

fan circuit fuse (see Chapter 9). If the fuse blown, check the fan circuit for a short earth (see the wiring diagrams at the end this book).

**9** If the fuse is good, remove the fairing le hand lower panel (see Chapter 8) to ga access to the fan switch. The fan switch is th forwardmost of the two sensors screwed in the side of the coolant outlet on the horizon cylinder (the rear sensor is the engi management coolant temperature sens **(see illustration 4.16)**.

**10** Disconnect the wiring connector, th switch on the ignition and check that batte voltage is present at the fan switch purp wire terminal; if not, check the relay described in Step 21. If battery voltage present, using a jumper wire if necessa connect the fan switch connector termina together. The fan should come on. If it doe the fan switch is proven defective and mu be renewed. If it does not come on, the f motor should be tested (see Step 3).

**11** If the fan is on all the time, disconnect t switch wiring connector. The fan should sto If it does, the switch is proven defective a must be renewed. If it does not stop, che the wiring between the switch and the fan f a short (see Chapter 9).

**12** If the fan works but is suspected cutting in at the wrong temperature, a mo comprehensive test of the switch can made as follows.

**13** Remove the switch (see Steps 15 to 1 Fill a small, heatproof, container with wat and place it on a stove. Connect an ohmme across the terminals of the switch and, usi some wire or other support, suspend t switch in the water so that just the sensi portion and the threads are submerged **(s illustration)**. Also place a thermomet capable of reading temperatures up to 100 in the water so that its bulb is close to t switch. **Note:** *None of the components shou be allowed to directly touch the container.*

**14** Initially, the ohmmeter reading shou show an open circuit (infinite resistanc indicating that the switch is open. Heat t water, stirring it gently. When the wat reaches the specified temperature, the swit contacts should close and the meter shou

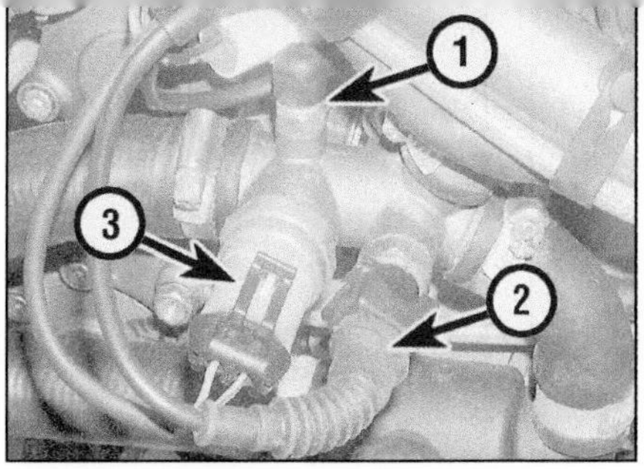


**4.16 Coolant temperature sensor and switch locations**

1 *Coolant temperature gauge sender*
2 *Engine management system coolant temperature sensor*
3 *Cooling fan temperature switch*

show continuity (zero resistance). Now turn the heat off. As the water temperature falls, the switch contacts should open at the specified temperature and the meter reading should show an open circuit (infinite resistance). If the meter readings obtained are different, or they are obtained at significantly different temperatures, then the fan switch is faulty and must be renewed.

***Warning: This must be done very carefully to avoid the risk of personal injury.***

### Renewal

***Warning: Ensure the cooling system is cold before carrying out this procedure.***

**15** Drain the cooling system (see Chapter 1).

**16** Disconnect the wiring connector from the fan switch. The fan switch is the forwardmost of the two sensors screwed into the side of the coolant outlet on the horizontal cylinder (the rear sensor is the engine management coolant temperature sensor) **(see illustration)**.

**17** Unscrew the switch and remove it from the coolant union. Discard the sealing washer, a new one should be used for installation.

**18** Fit the new sealing washer then fit the switch to the coolant union, tightening it to the specified torque.

**19** Reconnect the switch wiring connector then refill the cooling system (see Chapter 1).

## *Cooling fan relay*

### Check

**20** If there is no voltage at the fan switch purple wire terminal, and the fuse is in good condition, check the relay as follows.

**21** Remove the relay from its holder located on the rear of the battery mounting tray. Connect an ohmmeter across terminals 30 and 87 of the relay **(see illustration)**. Using a 12V battery and auxiliary wires, connect the

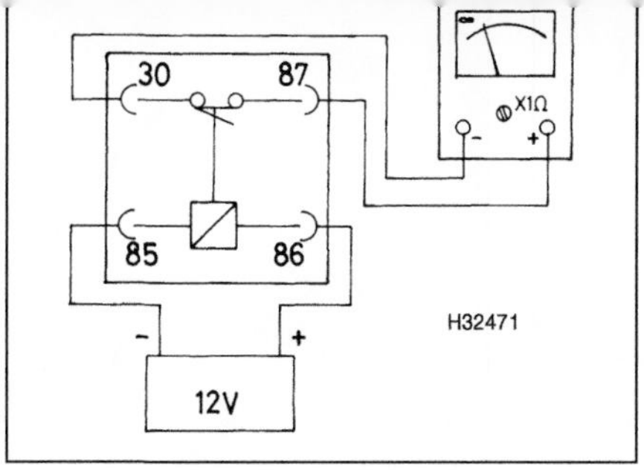


**4.21 Cooling fan relay test details**

battery positive (+ve) terminal to terminal 86 of the relay and the negative (–ve) terminal to terminal 85 of the relay and note the meter reading obtained. If the relay is operating correctly there should be continuity (zero resistance) whilst the battery is connected and no continuity (infinite resistance) whilst the battery is disconnected; the relay will be heard to 'click' as the battery is connected/disconnected. If this is not the case, renew the relay.

### Renewal

**22** Remove the fairing right-hand lower panel to gain access to the cooling fan relay which is mounted on the rear of the battery mounting tray **(see illustration)**.

**23** Ensure the ignition is switched OFF then free the relay from its mounting and disconnect it from its connector.

**24** On installation ensure the relay is securely fitted to the wiring connector and mounting tray, then install the fairing panel (see Chapter 8).

## 5 Coolant temperature gauge and sender – check and renewal

## *Check*

**1** The coolant temperature gauge is located in the instrument cluster and is operated by the coolant temperature sender on the coolant outlet on the left-hand side of the horizontal cylinder. If the gauge malfunctions, check first that the battery is fully charged and that the fuses are all good (see Chapter 9).

**2** If the gauge is not working, remove the fairing left-hand lower panel (see Chapter 8) to gain access to the sender. The temperature gauge sender is screwed into the top of the coolant outlet (those on the side of the outlet are the cooling fan switch and engine management system coolant temperature sensor) **(see illustration 4.16)**.

**3** Ensure the ignition is switched off, then disconnect the wiring connector from the sender. Turn the ignition switch on; the gauge needle should be at the left (cold) end of the

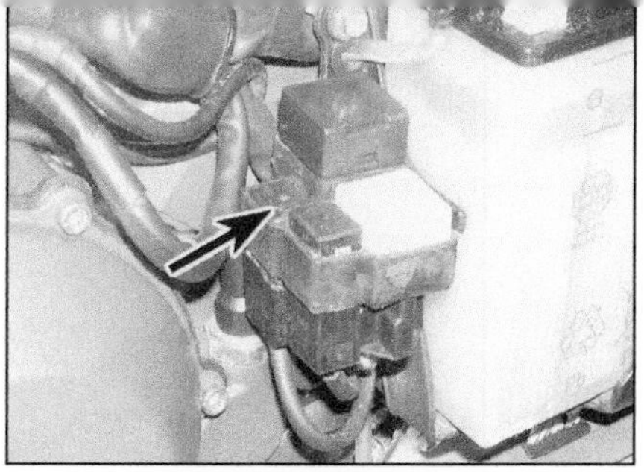

**4.22 Cooling fan relay (arrowed) is mounted on the rear of the battery tray**

scale. Turn the ignition switch off again, then earth the sensor wiring connector on the engine. Turn the ignition switch on again; the gauge needle should swing towards the right (hot) end of the scale. If the gauge performs as described, the coolant temperature sender is proven defective and should be renewed. **Note:** *Ducati do not specify any resistance readings for the temperature gauge sender so a comprehensive test of the sender is not possible.*

***Caution: Do not leave the ignition switched on for any longer than is necessary, or the gauge may be damaged.***

**4** If the temperature gauge does not perform as expected, the fault lies in the wiring or the gauge itself. Check all the relevant wiring and wiring connectors (see Chapter 9). If all appears to be well, the gauge is defective and must be renewed.

## *Renewal*

### Coolant temperature gauge

**5** Refer to Chapter 9.

### Temperature gauge sender

***Warning: Ensure the cooling system is cold before carrying out this procedure.***

**6** Drain the cooling system (see Chapter 1). Remove the fairing left-hand lower panel (see Chapter 8) to gain access to the sender.

**7** Disconnect the wiring connector from the coolant temperature gauge sender. The sender is screwed into the top of the coolant outlet on the left-hand side of the horizontal cylinder (those on the side of the union are the cooling fan switch and the engine management coolant temperature sensor) **(see illustration 4.16)**.

**8** Unscrew the sender and remove it from the coolant union.

**9** Clean the sender and apply a smear of sealant to its threads.

**10** Fit the sender to the coolant union, tightening it to the specified torque, and reconnect the wiring connector.

**11** Refill the cooling system (see Chapter 1). Refit the fairing panel (see Chapter 8).

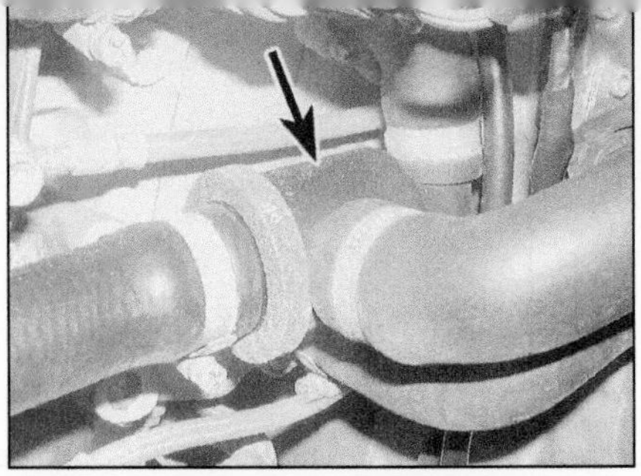

**6.3 The thermostat is located on the left-hand side of the engine**

## 6 Thermostat – removal, check and installation

> ***Warning: Ensure the cooling system is cold before carrying out this procedure.***

### Removal

**1** The thermostat is automatic in operation and should give many years of service without requiring attention. In the event of a failure, the valve will probably jam open, in which case the engine will take much longer than normal to warm up. Conversely, if the valve jams shut, the coolant will be unable to circulate and the engine will overheat. Neither condition is acceptable, and the fault must be investigated promptly.

**2** Drain the cooling system (see Chapter 1).

**3** Slacken the retaining clips securing the water pump, radiator and horizontal cylinder coolant hoses to the thermostat **(see illustration)**. Free the thermostat from the hoses and remove it from the bike.

### Check

**4** Examine the thermostat visually before carrying out the test. If it remains in the open position at room temperature, it should be renewed.

**5** Suspend the thermostat by a piece of wire in a container of cold water. Place a thermometer in the water so that the bulb is

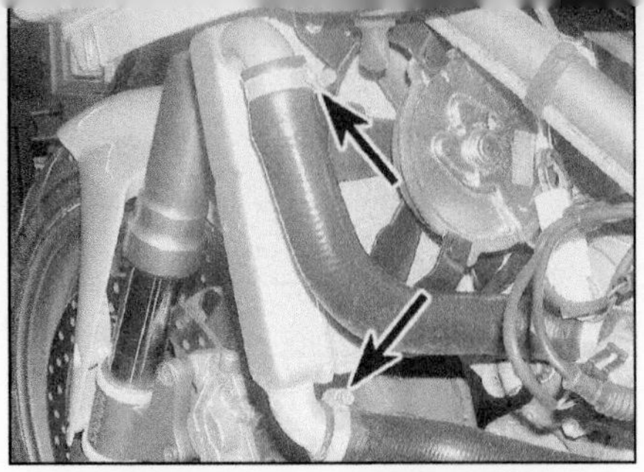

**7.4 Slacken the retaining clips and disconnect the top and bottom hoses (arrowed) from the left-hand side of the radiator . . .**

close to the thermostat. Heat the water, noting the temperature when the thermostat opens, and compare the result with the specifications given at the beginning of the Chapter. If the opening temperature differs significantly from that given, the thermostat is faulty and must be renewed.

> ***Warning: This must be done very carefully to avoid the risk of personal injury.***

### Installation

**6** Connect the coolant hoses to the thermostat, securing them in position with the retaining clips.

**7** Refill the cooling system (see Chapter 1).

## 7 Radiator – removal and installation

> ***Warning: Ensure the cooling system is cold before carrying out this procedure.***

### Removal

**1** Remove the complete fairing (see Chapter 8).

**2** Remove the fuel tank then unclip the right- and left-hand air filter housings and remove them from the airbox (see Chapter 4).

**3** Drain the cooling system (see Chapter 1).

**4** Slacken the retaining clips and disconnect

**7.5 . . . and the expansion tank hose from the right-hand side of the radiator**

the top and bottom coolant hoses from th left-hand side of the radiator **(see illustration**

**5** Slacken the retaining clip and disconnec the expansion tank hose from the right-han side of the radiator **(see illustration)**.

**6** Disconnect the cooling fan wiring connectc from the main wiring harness **(see illustration**

**7** Ease the mounting bracket out from th radiator lower mounting rubber and free from the mounting pin on the cylinder hea **(see illustration)**.

**8** Unscrew the mounting bolt from the radiatc left-hand upper mounting and recover the coll from the mounting rubber **(see illustration)**.

**9** Slacken and remove the mounting bolt an collar from the right-hand upper mounting c free the right-hand mounting rubber from it locating peg on the frame (as applicable) **(se illustration)**. The radiator can then b removed from the bike.

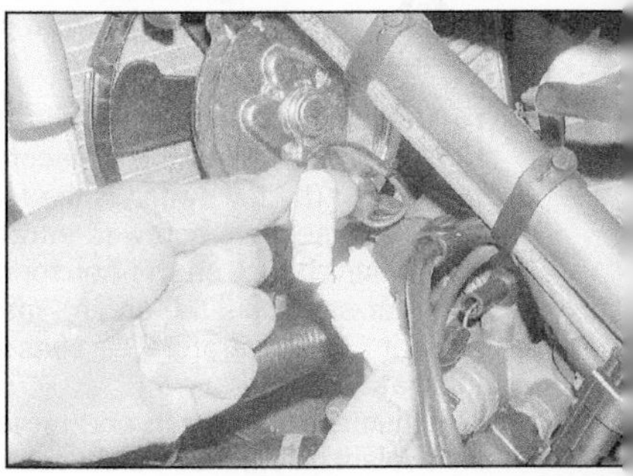

**7.6 Disconnecting the cooling fan wiring connector**

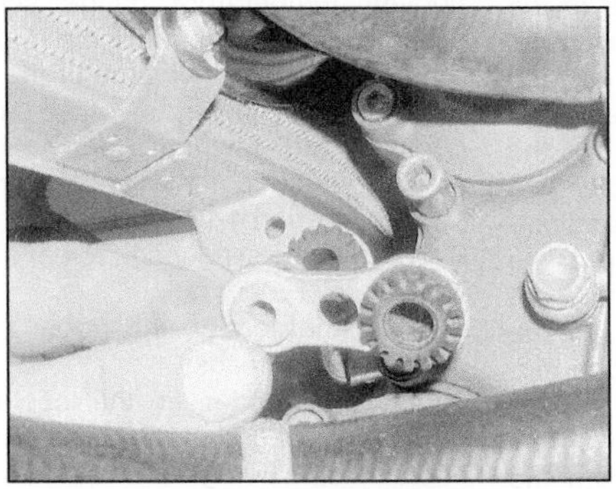

**7.7 Ease the mounting bracket out of position and remove it**

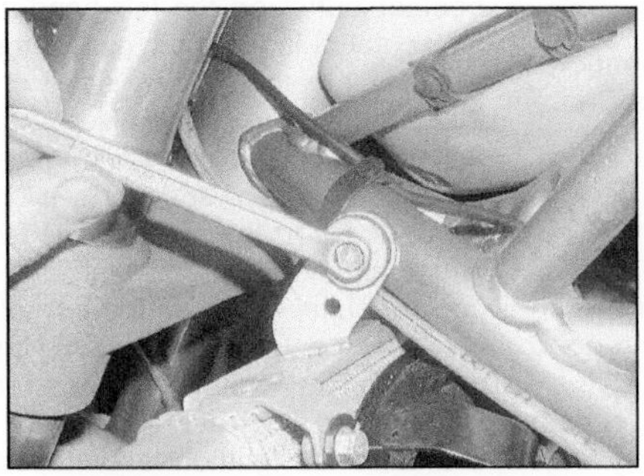

**7.8 Unscrew the mounting bolt and recover the collar from the mounting rubber**

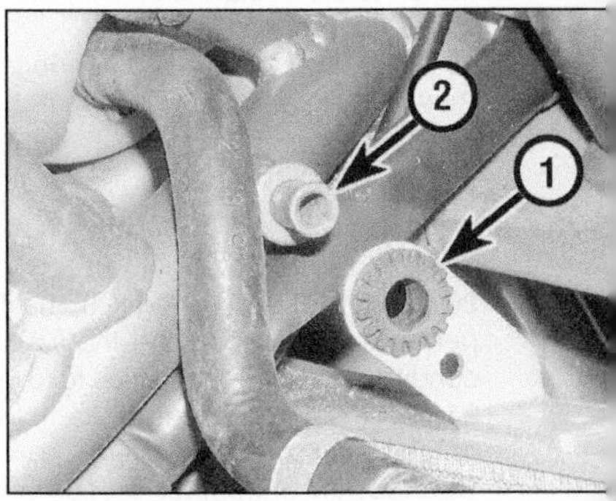


**7.9 Free the radiator mounting rubber (1) from its upper locating peg (2)**

of damage or deterioration, renewing them as a set if necessary.

### Installation

**11** Ensure the mounting rubbers are correctly fitted to the radiator upper and lower mounting lugs.

**12** Manoeuvre the radiator assembly into position. Locate the right-hand upper mounting rubber on its locating peg or align the mounting rubber with the frame and insert the collar and mounting bolt (as applicable). Insert the collar into the left-hand upper mounting rubber then fit the mounting bolt.

**13** Ensure the mounting pin is securely screwed into the cylinder head and the mounting rubber is correctly fitted to the lower mounting bracket. Lubricate the lower mounting rubbers with a silicone-based spray lubricant then ease the lower mounting bracket into position, taking care not to displace the mounting rubbers.

**14** Ensure the mounting rubbers are all correctly located then tighten the radiator mounting bolt(s) to the specified torque.

**15** Ensure the cooling fan motor wiring is correctly routed and reconnect it to the main wiring harness.

**16** Reconnect all the coolant hoses to the radiator, securing them in position with the retaining clips.

**17** Refill the cooling system (see Chapter 1).

**18** Install the air filter housings and the fuel tank then refit the fairing panels (see Chapters 4 and 8).

## 8 Water pump – removal, overhaul and installation

**Note:** *The water pump is located inside the left-hand crankcase cover. To prevent leakage of water from the cooling system to the lubrication system and vice versa, a mechanical seal is fitted on the impeller shaft. If this seal fails, the coolant will leak into the oil resulting in the oil turning a milky white colour. If it is noted that the engine oil is turning white, suspect a faulty water pump seal.*

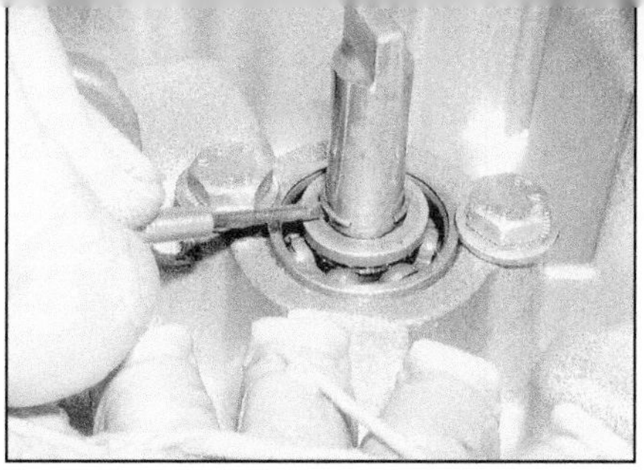

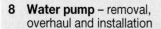

**8.3a Remove the circlip and spacer (where fitted) . . .**

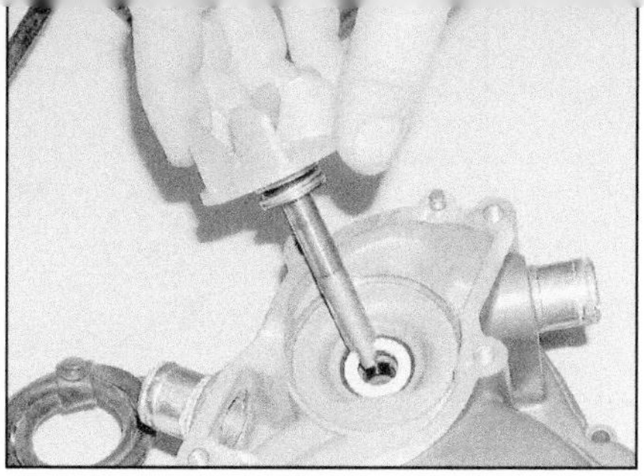

**8.3b . . . and slide out the water pump impeller**

### Removal

**1** Remove the left-hand crankcase cover from the engine (see Chapter 2). Prior to removing the cover, slacken the water pump cover retaining screws.

**2** With the crankcase cover removed, undo the retaining screws and remove the water pump cover, taking care not to lose the cover dowel pins. Discard the cover gasket.

**3** Remove circlip and the spacer (where fitted) from the pump impeller shaft **(see illustration)**. Withdraw the impeller from the cover; the mechanical seal will remain on the impeller shaft **(see illustration)**.

### Overhaul

**4** Check the impeller shaft, mechanical seal and the seal seat in the cover for signs of wear or damage, paying particular attention to the contact faces of the seal and seat **(see illustration)**. Also check the pump bearings for signs of wear; both bearing inner races should rotate freely and easily without any sign of freeplay or roughness. Renew worn or damaged components as follows.

#### Mechanical seal

**5** Pull the original seal off the impeller shaft, noting which way around it is fitted.

**6** Ensure the shaft and rear face of the impeller are clean and free from corrosion. If there is any sign of damage, the impeller must be renewed.

**7** Lubricate the impeller shaft with clean engine oil then slide on the new seal, ensuring its spring is facing the impeller. Press the seal squarely onto the shaft until its inner sealing lip is firmly in contact with the impeller shaft shoulder.

#### Seal seat

**8** Carefully lever the seal seat out from the cover using a flat-bladed screwdriver, noting which way around it is fitted **(see illustration)**.

**9** Ensure the cover bore is clean and free from damage then lubricate it with a smear of clean engine oil.

**10** Locate the seal seat in the cover (rubber surface towards the cover) and press it squarely into position, taking great care not to damage the seat face **(see illustration)**. **Note:** *On some early models the seal and seat are supplied separately. If this is the case, ensure the seal is fitted with its flat surface towards the cover/bearing washer and the seat with its rounded edge facing outwards (towards the impeller).*

#### Bearings

**Note:** *Make careful note of the correct fitted locations of the bearings and spacer/washer (as applicable) on removal and ensure all components are correctly fitted on installation. The bearing and washer/spacer arrangement has been modified several times during the model run.*

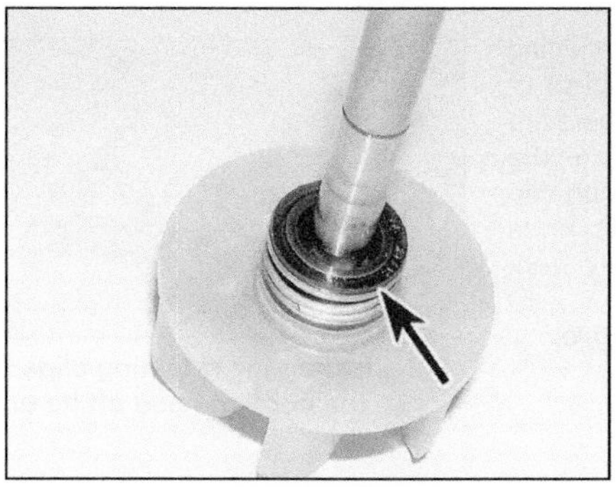

**8.4 Check the mechanical seal surface for signs of damage**

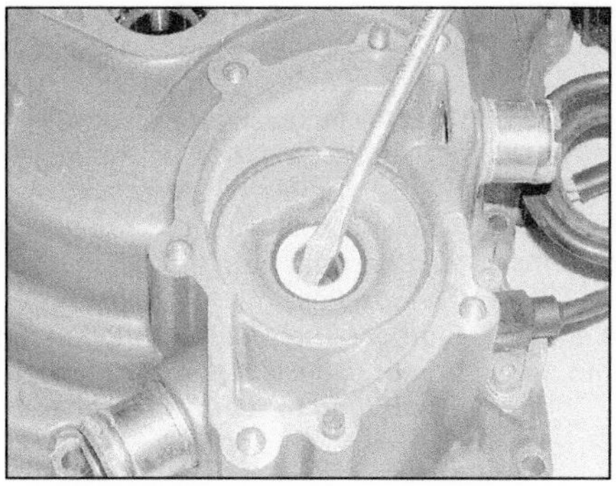

**8.8 Lever the seal seat out of the cover using a flat-bladed screwdriver**

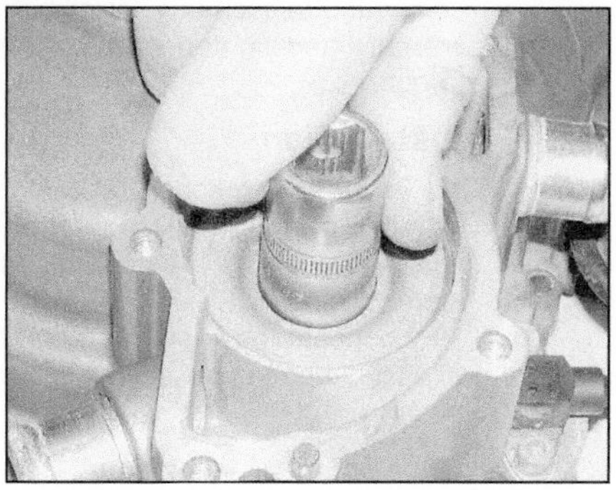

**8.10 Fit the new seal seat, ensuring its rubber surface is facing towards the cover, and press it squarely into position**

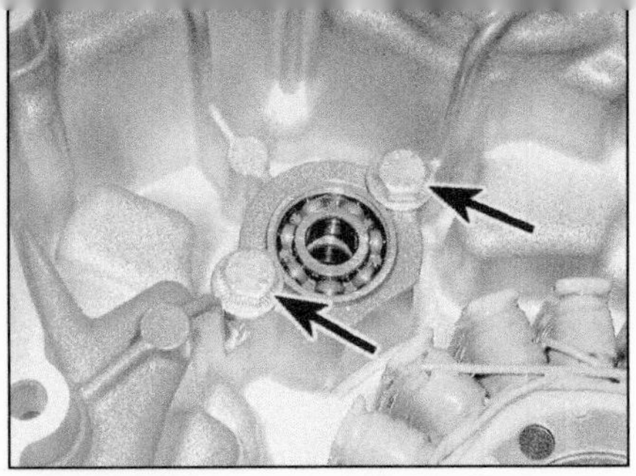

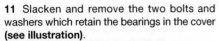

**8.11 Water pump bearing retaining bolts (arrowed)**

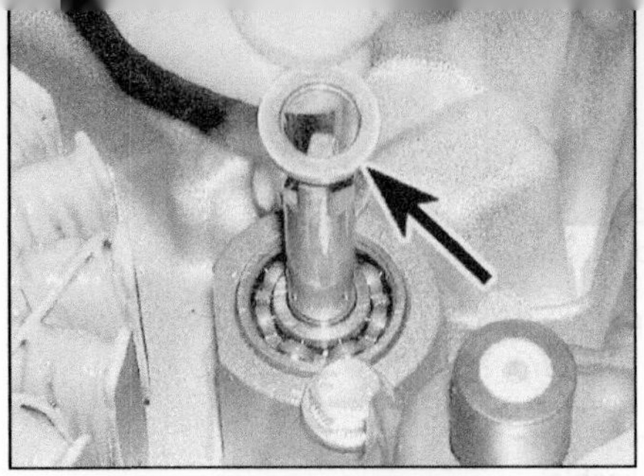

**8.20 Ensure the spacer is fitted with its recessed inner face (arrowed) facing away from the bearings**

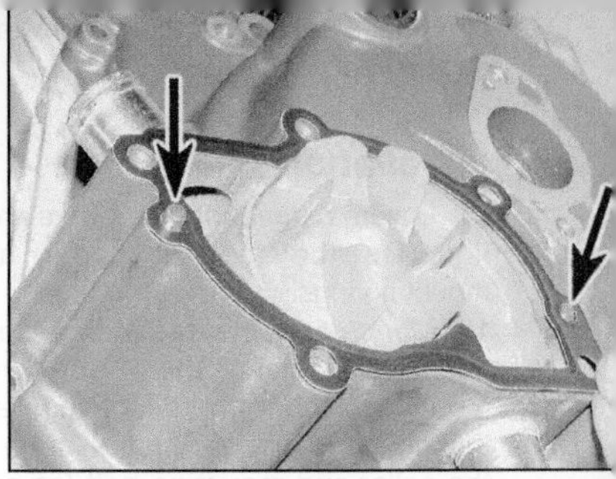

**8.23 Ensure the dowel pins (arrowed) ar in position then fit a new gasket to the cover**

**11** Slacken and remove the two bolts and washers which retain the bearings in the cover **(see illustration)**.

**12** Support the inner face of the crankcase cover then pass a drift through the centre of the seal seat. Tap evenly around the outer bearing inner race to remove both bearings and the spacer (where fitted) from the cover. **Note:** *The inner and outer bearings are different, the outer bearing has one sealed face whereas the inner bearing is unsealed.* Recover the washer located between the outer bearing and cover (where fitted).

**13** Ensure the cover bore is clean and free from damage then lubricate it with a smear of clean engine oil.

**14** Support the outer face of the cover then insert the washer (where fitted) ensuring its rounded edge is facing outwards (towards the pump impeller).

**15** Insert the outer bearing into its bore, ensuring its sealed face is facing outwards (towards the pump impeller). Using a tubular spacer, such as a socket, which contacts only the outer race of the bearing, drive the bearing in until it contacts the cover shoulder/washer (as applicable).

**16** Once the outer bearing is correctly seated, insert the spacer (where fitted) then fit the inner bearing (the bearing can be fitted either way around) in the same way.

**17** Clean the threads of the bearing retaining bolts and apply a drop of fresh locking compound to each one. Install both bolts and washers and tighten them to the specified torque.

### Installation

**18** Ensure the mechanical seal is correctly installed on the impeller shaft and the seal seat and bearings are correctly fitted to the crankcase cover.

**19** Lubricate the impeller shaft with a smear of clean engine oil then insert it into the bearings.

**20** On models where the impeller is retained by a spacer and circlip arrangement, slide the spacer onto the shaft making sure its recessed inner face is facing away from the bearings **(see illustration)**. Fit the impeller circlip, ensuring it is correctly seated in both the impeller shaft groove and the spacer recess.

**21** On models where the impeller is retained by a circlip, slide the circlip onto the impeller shaft and locate it correctly in the shaft groove.

**22** On all models, check that the impeller rotates freely and easily before proceeding.

**23** Ensure the cover mating surfaces are clean and dry and the dowel pins are in position. Fit a new gasket and locate the pump cover on the crankcase cover **(see illustration)**.

**24** Apply a smear of sealant to the threads of the pump cover lower retaining screw then install the screws and tighten them evenly and progressively to the specified torque.

**25** Fit the crankcase cover to the engine (see Chapter 2).

## 9 Coolant hoses – removal and installation

### Removal

**1** Before removing the hoses, drain the coolant (see Chapter 1).

**2** To disconnect a hose, release the retaining clips and move them along the hose, clear of the relevant union **(see illustration)**. There are two possible types of retaining clip – the standard screw-type clip, and the spring clip which is released by squeezing its ends together with a pair of pliers. Carefully work the hose free.

***Caution: The radiator unions are fragile. Do not use excessive force when attempting to remove the hoses.***

**3** If a hose proves stubborn, release it rotating it on its union before working it off all else fails, cut the hose with a sharp kni then slit it at each union so that it can peeled off in two pieces. Whilst this mea renewing the hose, it is preferable to buying new radiator.

### Installation

**4** Slide the clips onto the hose, and then wo it on to its respective union.

> **HAYNES HiNT** *If the hose is difficult to push on to its union, it can be softened by soaking it in very hot water, or alternatively a little soapy water can be used as a lubricant.*

**5** Rotate the hose on its unions to settle it position before sliding the clips into place a tightening them securely. Some hoses a equipped with alignment marks to ensure th are correctly positioned; align the paint ma on the hose with the raised mark on the uni before tightening the clip.

**6** On completion, refill the cooling syste (see Chapter 1).

**9.2 Slacken the retaining clips then eas the coolant hose off its union**

# Chapter 4
# Fuel and exhaust system

## Contents



## Degrees of difficulty

| | | | | |
|---|---|---|---|---|
| **Easy,** suitable for novice with little experience | **Fairly easy,** suitable for beginner with some experience | **Fairly difficult,** suitable for competent DIY mechanic | **Difficult,** suitable for experienced DIY mechanic | **Very difficult,** suitable for expert DIY or professional |

## Specifications

### Fuel

| | |
|---|---|
| Grade | Unleaded or leaded, minimum 95 RON (Research Octane Number) |
| Fuel tank capacity | 17 litres |

| | |
|---|---|
| System type | |
| 916 Strada models | Marelli IAW P8 engine management system with one injector per cylinder |
| 916 SP, SPS and 996 SPS models | Marelli IAW P8 engine management system with two injectors per cylinder |
| All other models | |
| 748 and 916 models | Marelli IAW 1.6M engine management system with one injector per cylinder |
| 996 models | Marelli IAW 1.6M engine management system with two injectors per cylinder |
| Fuel pump flow rate | 120 litres per hour |
| Fuel system operating pressure | 3 bar |
| Idle speed | see Chapter 1 |
| Component test data – see text for test details | |
| Air temperature sensor resistance | |
| At -20°C | 27.6 to 30.5 K-ohms |
| At -10°C | 15.7 to 17.4 K-ohms |
| At 0°C | 9.2 to 10.2 K-ohms |
| At 20°C | 2.8 to 3.1 K-ohms |
| At 60°C | 710 to 780 ohms |
| At 80°C | 350 to 390 ohms |
| Atmospheric pressure sensor output voltage | |
| 17 mm Hg | 0.25 volts |
| 787 mm Hg | 4.75 volts |
| Coolant temperature sensor resistance | |
| At -20°C | 26.6 to 33.3 K-ohms |
| At -10°C | 14.6 to 18.8 K-ohms |
| At 0°C | 8.7 to 11.0 K-ohms |
| At 20°C | 3.4 to 4.1 K-ohms |
| At 60°C | 670 to 830 ohms |
| At 80°C | 340 to 420 ohms |
| Fuel injector resistance | 14 ohms at 20°C |
| Throttle position sensor output voltage | |
| Throttle valve fully closed | 0.05 to 0.25 volts |
| Throttle valve 25° open | 2.64 to 2.97 volts |
| Throttle valve 35° open | 3.31 to 3.63 volts |
| Throttle valve 85° open | 4.77 to 5.00 volts |
| Timing sensor resistance | 680 ohms at 20°C |
| RPM sensor resistance | 680 ohms at 20°C |

## Torque settings

| | |
|---|---|
| Airbox mounting bolts | 19 Nm |
| Coolant temperature sensor | 15 Nm |
| Exhaust system | |
| Centre pipe | |
| Mounting bolt | 10 Nm |
| Mounting bracket bolts | |
| Bracket to pipe bolt | 10 Nm |
| Bracket to engine bolt | 24 Nm |
| Manifold | |
| Retaining nuts | 10 Nm |
| Studs | 10 Nm |
| Silencer | |
| Mounting bracket bolts | 10 Nm |
| Rear joining bolt | 5 Nm |
| Fuel tank | |
| Drain bolt | 15 Nm |
| Filler cap screws | 5 Nm |
| Front mounting bracket bolts | 10 Nm |
| Fuel pump mounting plate bolts | 10 Nm |
| Intake manifold | |
| Retaining nuts | 10 Nm |
| Studs | 10 Nm |
| RPM sensor bolt/nuts | 5 Nm |
| Throttle twistgrip housing bolts | 9 Nm |
| Timing sensor bolt/nuts | 5 Nm |
| Sensor air gap inspection cap | 15 Nm |

## 1 General information and precautions

### General information

The fuel system consists of the fuel tank, the fuel pump, pressure regulator and filter (which are all contained in the tank), the fuel feed and return hoses and the throttle body assembly. The fuel pump supplies fuel to the injectors in the throttle body assembly, which inject the fuel into the intake tracts. The injectors are operated by the electronic control unit (ECU) using the information obtained from the various sensors it monitors (refer to Section 7 for information on the fuel injection system operation). On 916 SP and SPS and all 996 models, each throttle body has two injectors per cylinder whereas all other models have only a single injector per cylinder.

Air is drawn into the throttle bodies via a dual air filter arrangement. The air filters are located in housings on each side of the frame. The housings are linked to the airbox situated beneath the fuel tank (the underside of the fuel tank actually forms the top of the airbox) from which the throttle body intakes are fed. The filter housing intakes are located in the upper fairing and use the forward motion of the motorcycle to create a ram-air effect in the airbox.

### Precautions

***Warning: Petrol (gasoline) is extremely flammable, so take extra precautions when you work on any part of the fuel system. Don't smoke or allow open flames or bare light bulbs near the work area, and don't work in a garage where a natural gas-type appliance is present. If you spill any fuel on your skin, rinse it off immediately with soap and water. When you perform any kind of work on the fuel system, wear safety glasses and have a fire (flammable liquids) on hand.***

Residual pressure will remain in the fuel feed hoses long after the motorcycle was last used. Bear this in mind before disconnecting any fuel line.

It is vital that dirt or debris is not allowed to enter the fuel tank, the fuel hoses or the injectors whilst the hoses are disconnected. Any foreign matter in the fuel system components could result in injector damage/malfunction.

Ensure the ignition is switched off before disconnecting/reconnecting any fuel injection system wiring connector. If a connector is disconnected/reconnected with the ignition switched on, the electronic control unit (ECU) may be damaged.

Always perform service procedures in a well-ventilated area to prevent a build-up of fumes.

Never work in a building containing a gas appliance with a pilot light, or any other form of naked flame. Ensure that there are no naked light bulbs or any sources of flame or sparks nearby.

Do not smoke (or allow anyone else to smoke) while in the vicinity of petrol (gasoline) or of components containing it. Remember the possible presence of vapour from these sources and move well clear before smoking.

Check all electrical equipment belonging to the house, garage or workshop where work is being undertaken (see the Safety first! section of this manual). Remember that certain electrical appliances such as drills, cutters etc. create sparks in the normal course of operation and must not be used near petrol (gasoline) or any component containing it. Again, remember the possible presence of fumes before using electrical equipment.

Always mop up any spilt fuel and safely dispose of the rag used.

Any stored fuel that is drained off during servicing work must be kept in sealed containers that are suitable for holding petrol (gasoline), and clearly marked as such; the containers themselves should be kept in a safe place. Note that this last point applies equally to the fuel tank if it is removed from the machine; also remember to keep its filler cap closed at all times.

Read the Safety first! section of this manual carefully before starting work.

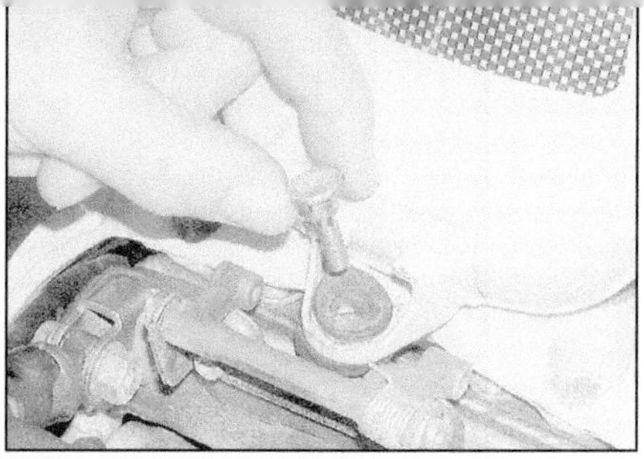

**2.2 Unscrew the mounting bolt from the rear of the fuel tank . . .**

## 2 Fuel tank – removal and installation

***Warning: Refer to the precautions given in Section 1 before starting work.***

### Removal

**1** Ensure the ignition is switched off then remove the seat cowling (see Chapter 8).

**2** Slacken and remove the mounting bolt securing the rear of the fuel tank to the frame **(see illustration)**.

**3** Lift the rear of the fuel tank and move the tank rearwards to free its front mounting bracket peg from the frame **(see illustration)**. Recover the collar from the tank rear mounting rubber.

**4** Taking care not to damage the paintwork, raise the tank to gain access to the fuel tank hoses and wiring.

**5** Disconnect the fuel tank wiring connector **(see illustration)**.

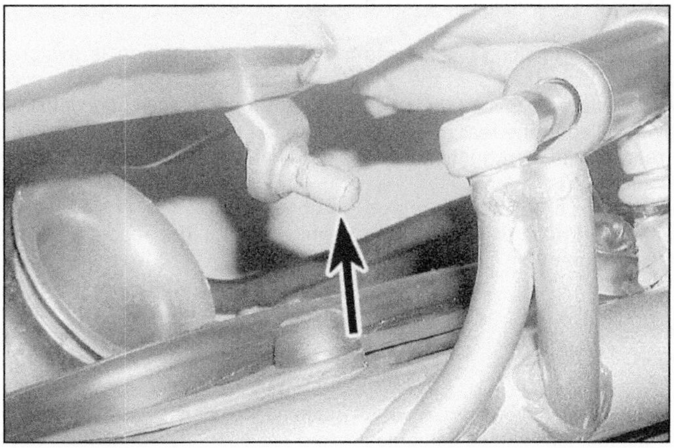

**2.3 . . . then move the tank to the rear to free its front mounting peg (arrowed) from the frame**

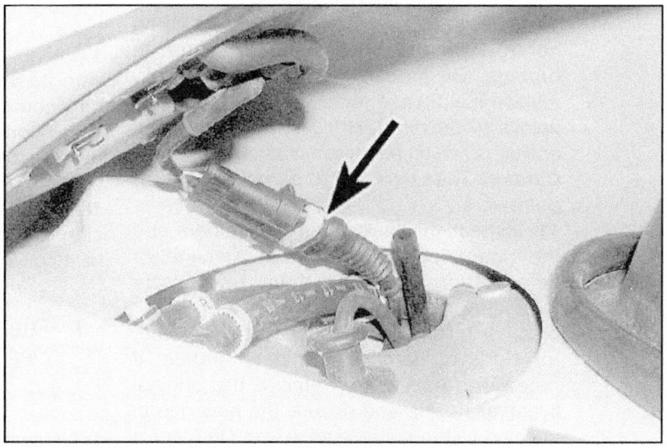

**2.5 Raise the fuel tank and disconnect the fuel tank wiring connector**

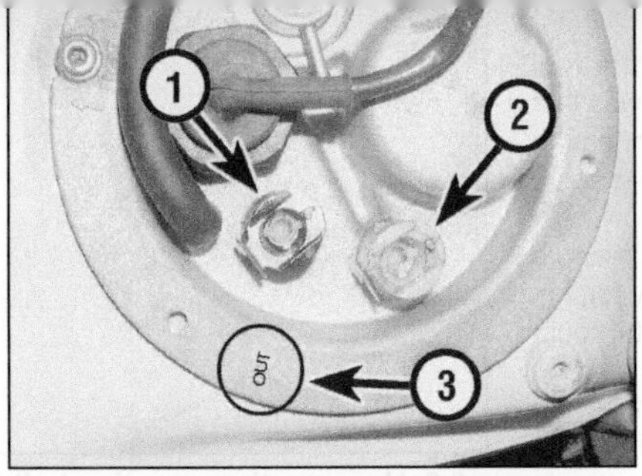


**2.8 The fuel tank outlet (1) and return (2) hose unions are colour-coded for identification (quick-release type fittings shown) and the mounting plate is marked OUT (3)**

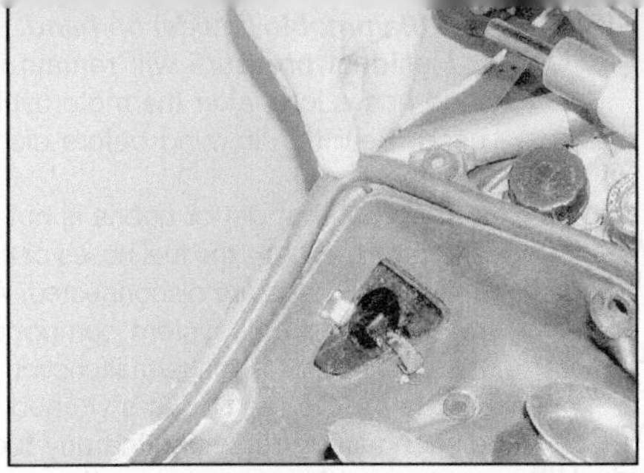

**2.11a Check the airbox seal for signs of wear or damage and renew if necessary**

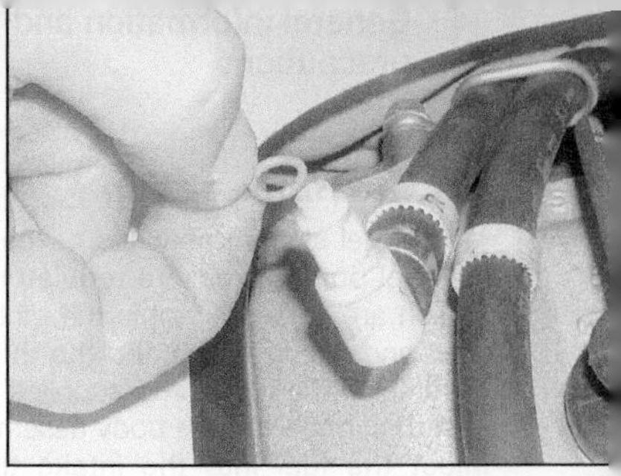

**2.11b On models with quick-release fue hose fittings, ensure the sealing rings ar in good condition**

**6** Disconnect the fuel tank breather/drain hose from the T-piece.

**7** On California models disconnect the evaporative emission system hose from the tank.

***Caution: Plug the evaporative emission system hose to prevent the vapour canister being contaminated.***

**8** Note the correct fitted positions of the fuel feed and return hoses. The fuel pump mounting plate outlet union is marked 'OUT' and the hoses are fitted with colour-coded end-fittings; the feed hose has a black end-fitting (and is fitted with an identification collar marked M) and the return hose has a white end-fitting (and is fitted with an identification collar marked R) **(see illustration)**. If the marking/end-fittings/collars are not present, make identification markings to avoid confusion on installation.

**9** Position a wad of rag around the fuel hose unions, to catch any residual fuel (pressure will still be present in the fuel hoses). On models with quick-release fuel hose end fittings, depress the retaining clips and detach the fuel hoses from the tank. On models without quick-release fittings, release the retaining clips and carefully disconnect the hoses from the fuel tank unions, whilst being prepared for fuel spillage.

**10** Remove the fuel tank from the bike taking not to lose the front and rear mounting rubbers. On models not fitted with quick-release fuel fittings, either plug the fuel tank unions to prevent fuel loss or store the tank upside-down on some soft cloth.

***Caution: Take care not to damage the paintwork.***

**11** Inspect the tank mounting rubbers and the airbox seal for signs of damage or deterioration and renew them if necessary **(see illustration)**. Also check the rubber breather nozzle, located under the filler cap, for signs of damage and deterioration; if renewal is necessary, remove the original breather nozzle and secure the new one in position with a suitable adhesive. On models with quick-release fuel hoses, inspect the end fitting sealing rings for signs of damage or deterioration and renew them if necessary **(see illustration)**.

### Installation

**12** Prior to installation, check that the tank front mounting bracket is securely fitted. If the bolts are loose, remove them apply a drop of locking compound to their threads then refit them and tighten to the specified torque.

**13** Ensure the tank front mounting rubber is correctly installed in the frame and the rear mounting rubber is securely fitted to the tank. Slide the collar into the underside of the rear mounting rubber.

**14** Ensure the rubber seal is correctly fitted to the top of the airbox and wipe clean the underside of the fuel tank.

**15** Manoeuvre the tank into position and securely reconnect the fuel hoses, using the identification collars to ensure they are correctly reconnected. On models with quick-release end fittings, ensure each end fitting sealing ring is in good condition and secure the hoses in position by pushing them fully in until they 'click' into position. On models without quick-release fittings, push the hoses onto their unions then secure them in position with the retaining clips.

**16** Securely reconnect the fuel tank wiring connector then reconnect the breather/drain hose to the T-piece. On California models also reconnect the evaporative emission system hose.

**17** Align the tank front mounting bracket peg with its mounting rubber then seat the fuel tank correctly on the airbox. Ensure the collar is still correctly installed in the rear mounting rubber then refit the tank mounting bolt, tightening it securely.

**18** Start the engine and check that there is no sign of fuel leakage. If all is well, install the seat cowling (see Chapter 8).

## 3 Fuel tank – cleaning and repair

**1** All repairs to the fuel tank should be carried out by a professional who has experience in this critical and potentially dangerous work. Even after cleaning and flushing of the fu system, explosive fumes can remain a ignite during repair of the tank.

**2** If the fuel tank is removed from the bike, should not be placed in an area where spar or open flames could ignite the fumes comi out of the tank. Be especially careful insi garages where a natural gas-type appliance located, because the pilot light could cau an explosion.

## 4 Fuel pump – check, removal and installation

***Warning: Refer to the precautions given in Section 1 before starting work.***

### Fuel pump circuit check

**1** The fuel pump is located inside the fu tank. The fuel pump runs for a few secon when the ignition is switched ON, pressurise the fuel system, and then cuts o until the engine is started. If the pump thought to be faulty, first check the fuses (s Chapter 9). If they are in good conditi proceed as follows.

**2** Free the fuel tank from the frame (see Ste 1 to 3 of Section 2) and support it so acce can be gained to the fuel tank wiri connector.

**3** Ensure the ignition is switched off th disconnect the fuel tank wiring connector **(s illustration 2.5)** and connect the positive (+v lead of a voltmeter to the brown/whi terminal of the connector and the negati (-ve) lead to the black terminal of t connector. Switch on the ignition swit whilst noting the reading obtained on t meter.

**4** If battery voltage is present for a fe seconds, the fuel pump circuit is operati correctly and the fuel pump is probably faul

**5** If no reading is obtained, check the fu pump circuit wiring for continuity and ma sure all the connectors are free from corrosi and are securely connected. Repair/repla the wiring as necessary and clean t connectors using electrical contact cleaner.

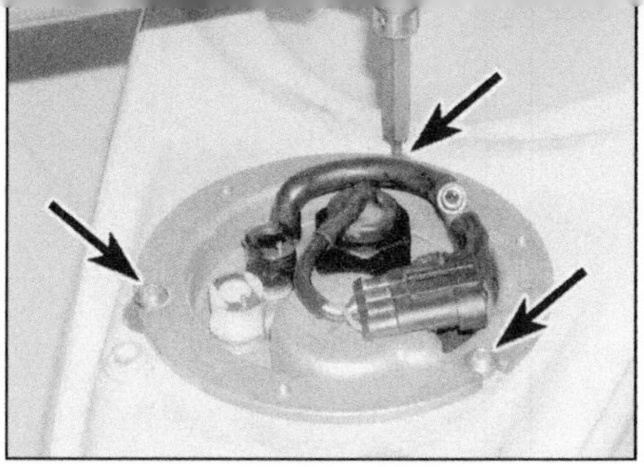

**4.11 Unscrew the fuel pump mounting plate bolts (arrowed)**

this fails to reveal the fault, check the following components.

*a) Engine stop switch (see Chapter 9).*
*b) Engine management system relays (see Section 9).*
*c) Electronic control unit (ECU) (see Section 9).*

### Fuel pump check

**Note:** *A suitable automotive-type fuel pressure gauge will be required to check the fuel pump cut-off pressure.*

**6** Remove the fuel pump assembly from the tank (see below). Check the pump wiring for loose or damaged terminals and check the wiring between the fuel tank connector and pump for continuity.

**7** If the wiring is fine, connect a fully charged 12 volt battery to the pump wiring terminals of the connector using two auxiliary wires; connect the positive (+ve) terminal of the battery to the brown/white connector terminal and the battery negative (-ve) terminal to the black connector terminal. The pump should operate. If not, it is faulty and must be renewed.

**8** If the pump operates but is thought to be delivering an insufficient amount of fuel, first check the fuel filter is not blocked and the pipes linking the pump, filter and separator chamber are not kinked, damaged or blocked.

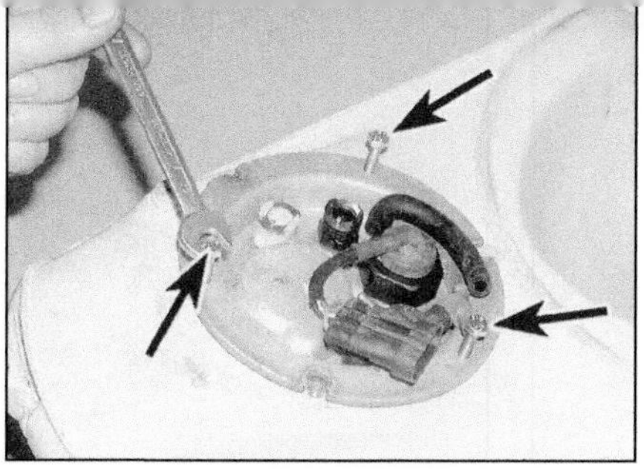

**4.12 If the mounting plate is tight, use three M6 bolts fitted to the threaded holes provided to draw it out of position**

If the equipment is available, the flow rate and operating pressure of the pump can be checked (see Specifications). Use paraffin, not petrol (gasoline) when testing the pump.

***Warning: Do NOT use petrol (gasoline) for this test! It is unnecessary and dangerous.***

### Removal

**9** Remove the fuel tank (see Section 2).

**10** Unscrew the drain bolt and sealing washer from the rear of the fuel tank base and drain its contents into a suitable container. Once the tank has finished draining, clean the threads of the drain bolt and fit a new sealing washer. Apply a smear of sealant to the drain bolt threads then refit the bolt to the tank, tightening it to the specified torque.

**11** With the fuel tank supported upside-down, unscrew the fuel pump mounting plate retaining bolts **(see illustration)**.

***Caution: Take care not to damage the paintwork.***

**12** Note the correct fitted location of the plate in relation to the tank then ease the plate out of position. If the plate is a tight-fit, screw three M6 bolts into the threaded holes provided and use the bolts to draw the plate squarely out of position **(see illustration)**.

**13** Once the mounting plate is free from the tank, slacken the retaining clips and disconnect the drain and breather hoses from their unions on each side of the plate **(see illustrations)**. The fuel pump assembly can then be removed from the tank. Remove the sealing ring from the mounting plate and discard it; a new one must be used on installation.

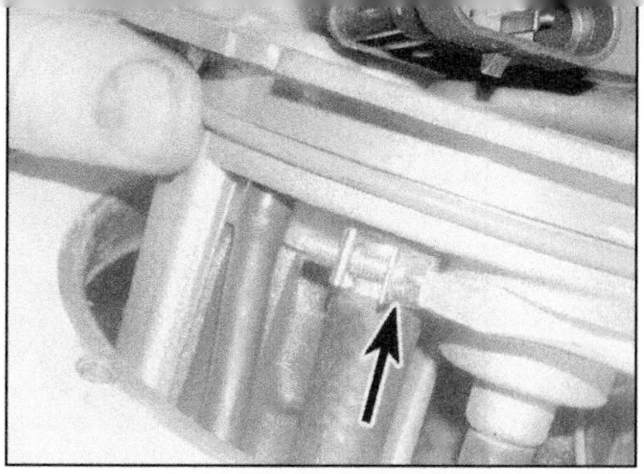

**4.13a Slacken the retaining clips . . .**

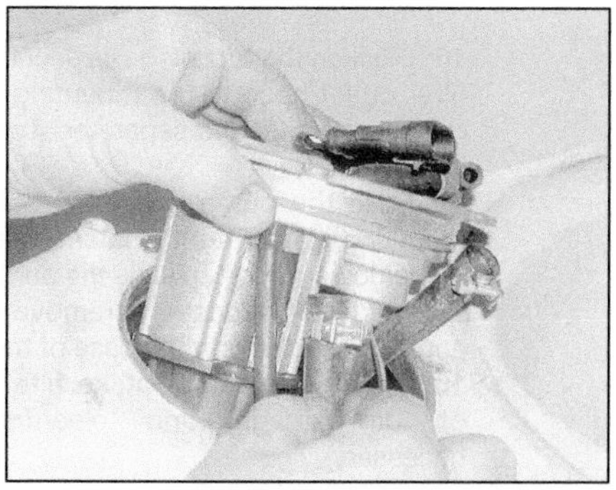

**4.13b . . . and disconnect the drain and breather hoses then manoeuvre the pump assembly out from the tank**

**14** To remove the pump, note the correct fitted locations of the wiring connector(s) then disconnect the pump wiring **(see illustration)**.

**15** Slacken the retaining clip and disconnect the fuel outlet hose from the pump and the separator hose from the pump intake filter **(see illustration)**.

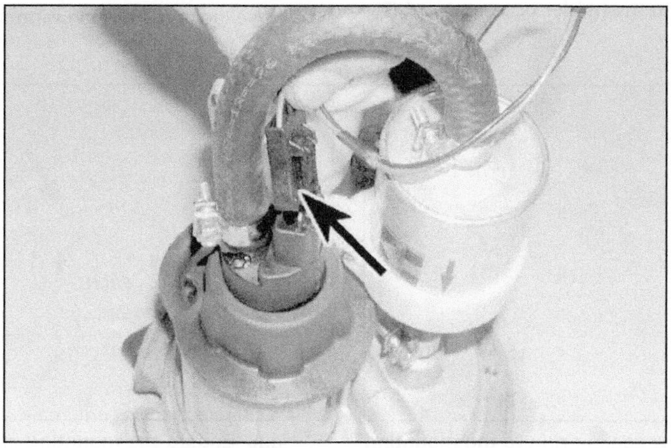

**4.14 Disconnect the fuel pump wiring**

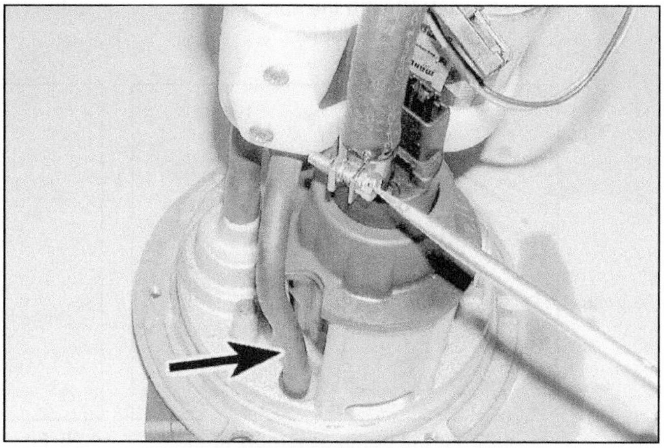

**4.15 Disconnect the fuel outlet hose and the separator hose (arrowed) from the pump**

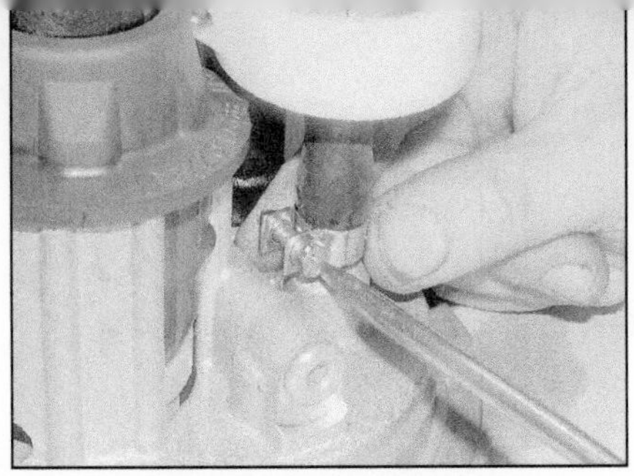

4.16a Disconnect the filter outlet hose from the mounting plate . . .

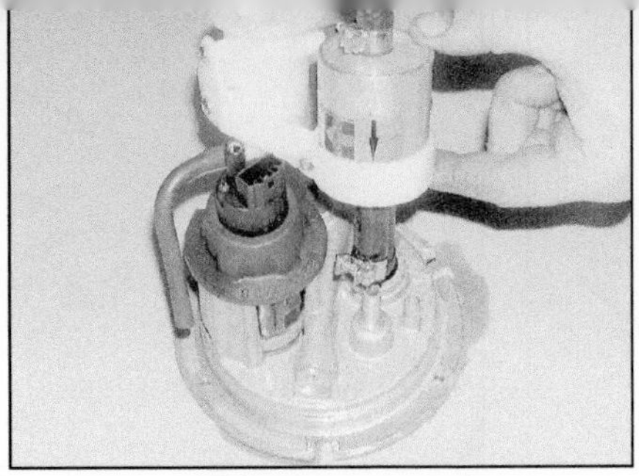

4.16b . . . then remove the filter and separator assembly

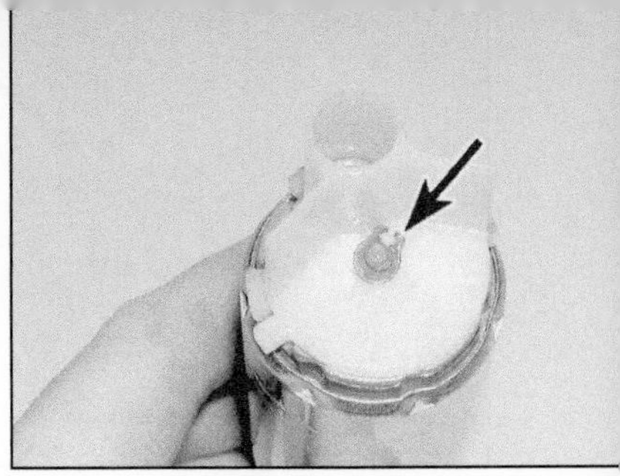

4.20a Fit the baffle plate to the pump an secure it in position with the retaining cli (arrowed)

16 Slacken the retaining clip securing the fuel filter outlet hose to the mounting plate then remove the filter and separator assembly **(see illustrations)**.

17 Ease the pump assembly out from the mounting plate. Free the intake filter from the holder lower end then slide the pump out from the holder. If necessary, remove the circlip and baffle plate from the base of the pump.

18 Check the pump intake filter for signs of dirt/damage and clean/renew (as necessary).

### Installation

19 If the pump has been dismantled carry out the operations in Steps 20 to 23. If not proceed to Step 24.

20 Where necessary, reassemble the pump and baffle plate and secure it in position with the circlip **(see illustration)**. Slide the pump into position in the holder, aligning the baffle plate tab with the holder lower cut-out **(see illustration)**.

21 Fit the intake filter to the holder, aligning its hose union with the holder outer cut-out **(see illustration)**.

22 Lubricate the holder with a silicone-based spray lubricant then fit the pump assembly to the mounting plate, aligning the filter union with the plate recess **(see illustration)**. Ensure the holder is correct seated in the mounting plate befor proceeding.

23 Fit the filter and separator assembly to th mounting plate and reconnect the fuel hose to the pump and intake filter. Secure the outl hoses in position with the retaining clip Securely reconnect the pump wirin connector(s).

24 Prior to refitting, check all the rubb hoses are undamaged and are secure connected.

25 Ensure the mounting plate and tar surfaces are clean and dry, then fit the ne sealing ring **(see illustration)**. Ensure th sealing ring is correctly located against th plate shoulder then lubricate it with silicon based spray lubricant to aid installation.

26 Install the mounting plate assembly in the fuel tank, ensuring its 'FRONT' marking cut-out (as applicable) is facing towards th front of the tank **(see illustration)**. Reconne the breather and drain hoses to the mountin plate and secure them in position with th retaining clips.

27 Align the mounting plate with its retainin bolt holes then press the plate squarely int position. If the plate is tight, fit nuts to the M bolts used to draw the plate out of positio then screw the bolts into the retaining bo holes. Use the nuts to squarely press the pla

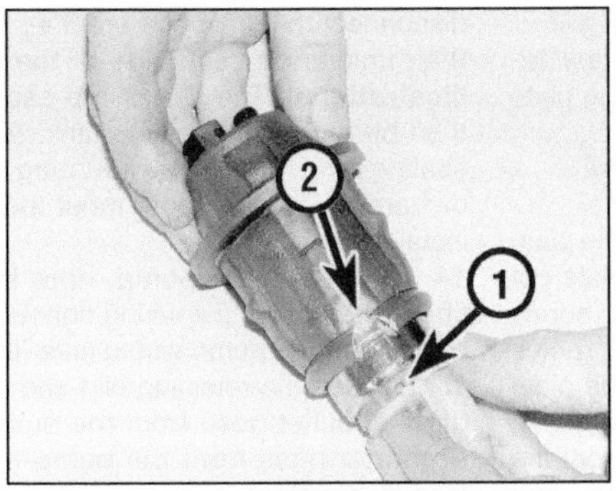


4.20b Insert the pump, aligning the baffle plate tab (1) with the holder lower cut-out (2)

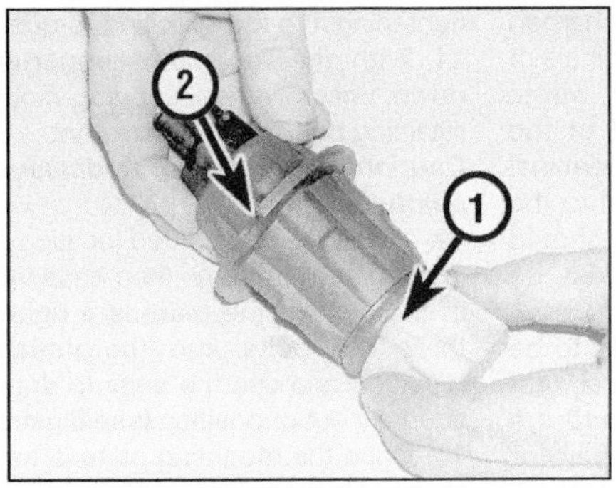


4.21 Fit the intake filter aligning its hose union (1) with the holder outer cut-out (2)

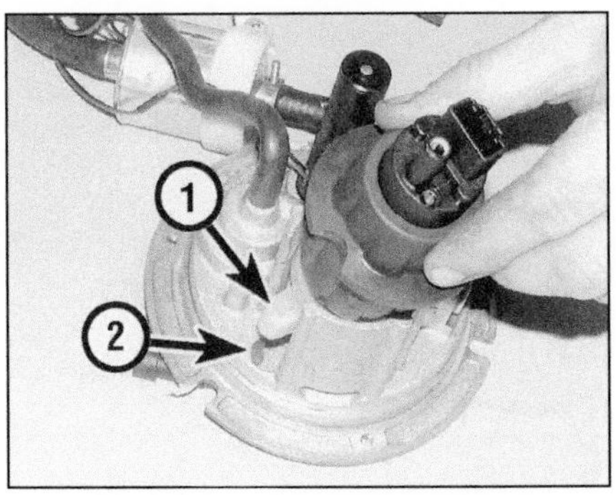


4.22 Fit the pump assembly to the mounting plate aligning the filter union (1) with the plate recess (2)

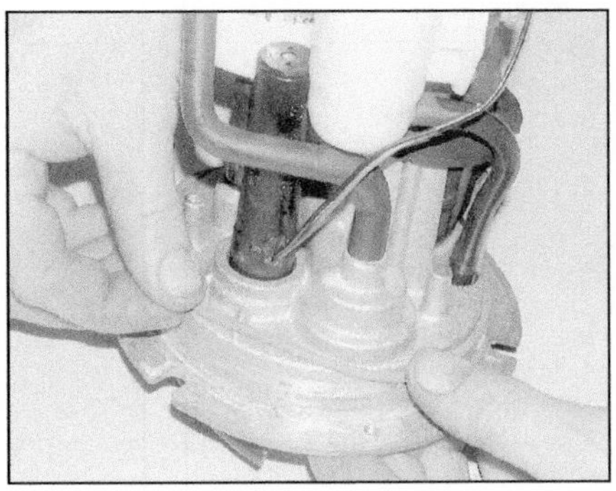

4.25 Fit a new sealing ring to the mounting plate

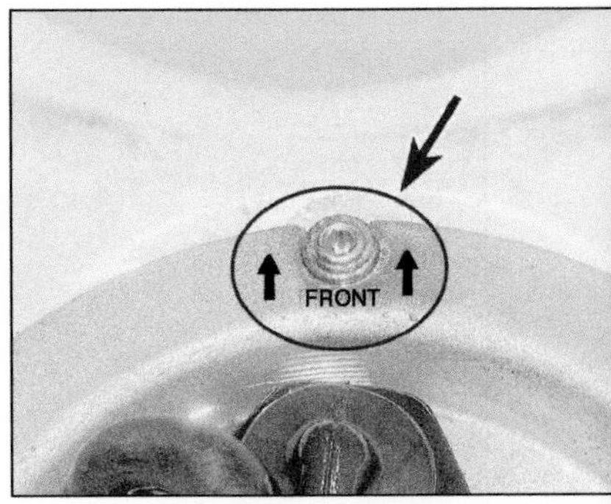


4.26 Ensure the mounting plate is correctly positioned so its FRONT markin is facing forwards

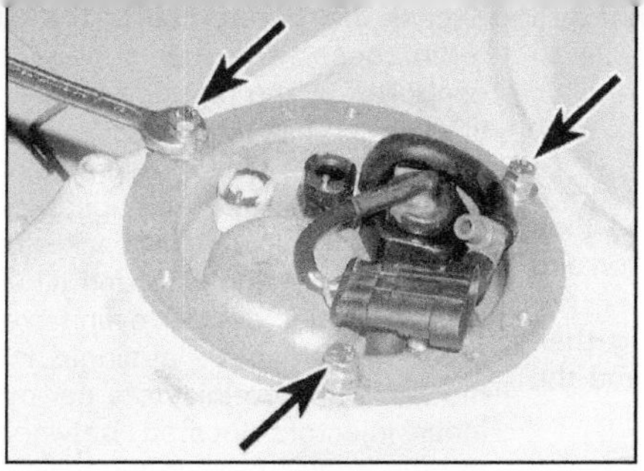

**4.27 If necessary, draw the mounting plate into position using M6 bolts and nuts fitted to the mounting bolt holes**

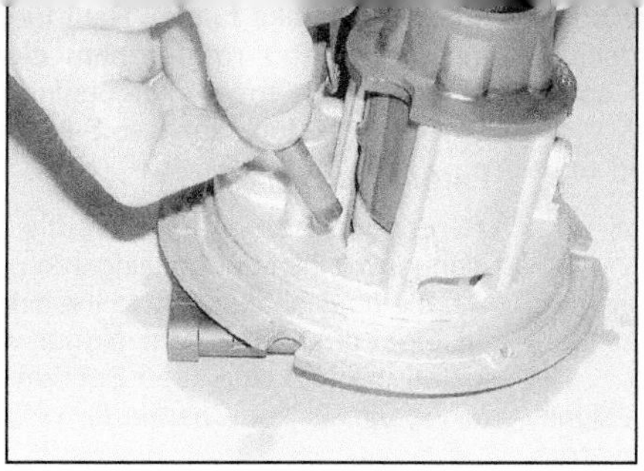

**5.4 Disconnect the separator hose from the pump intake filter**

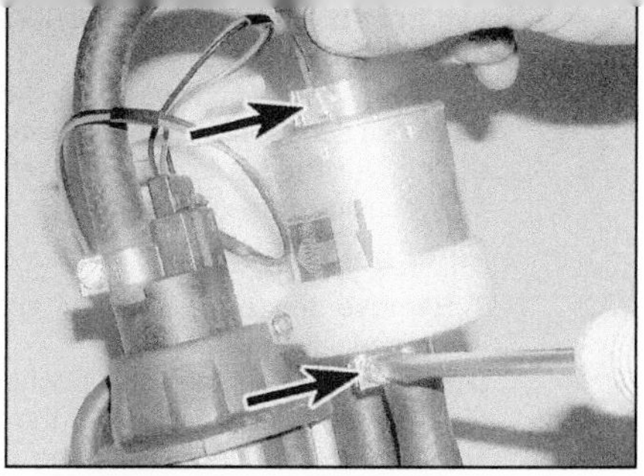

**5.5 Slacken the retaining clips (arrowed) and disconnect the fuel hoses then remove the filter and separator assembly**

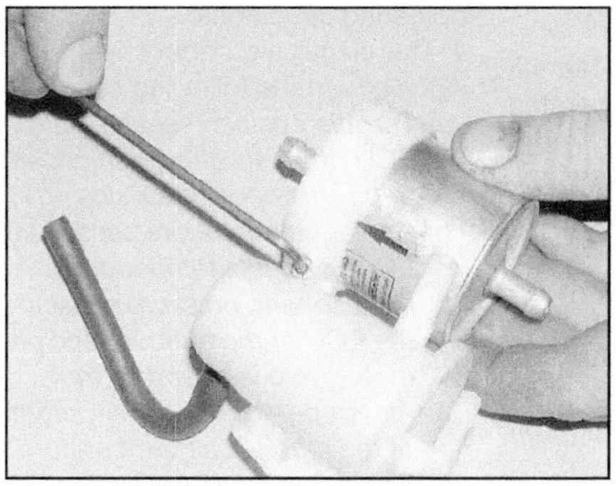

**5.6 Slacken the retaining screw and slide the filter out from its clamp**

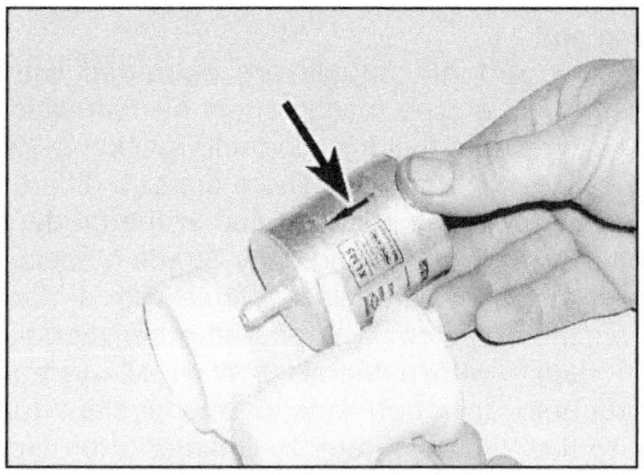

**5.7a Fit the filter to its clamp ensuring the arrow is pointing in the direction of fuel flow . . .**

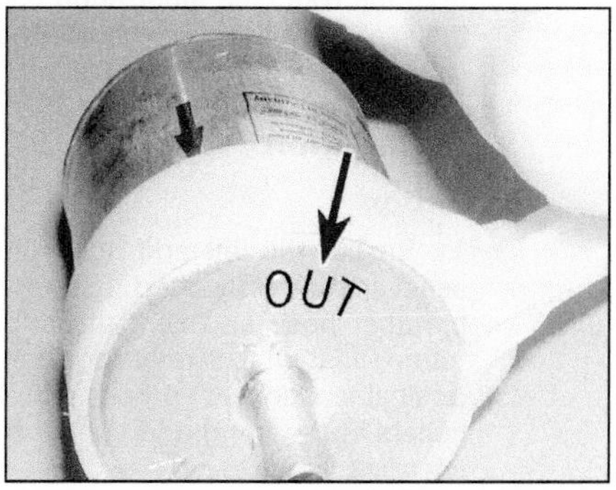


**5.7b . . . and the OUT marking (arrowed) is on the outlet side**

into position **(see illustration)**. Remove the M6 bolts (where fitted) then install the mounting plate retaining bolts and tighten them to the specified torque.
**28** Install the fuel tank (see Section 2).

## 5 Fuel filter – removal and installation

***Warning: Refer to the precautions given in Section 1 before starting work.***

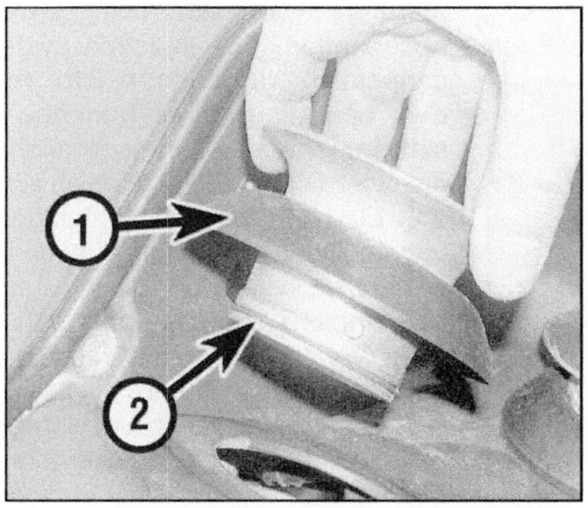

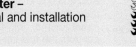

**6.3 Rotate the intake funnel anti-clockwise to release it and remove it complete with the rubber collar (1) and sealing ring (2)**

### *Removal*

**1** The filter is part of the fuel pump assembly which is housed inside the fuel tank.
**2** Remove the fuel tank (Section 2).
**3** Remove the fuel pump assembly from the tank as described in Steps 10 to 13 of Section 4.
**4** Disconnect the separator hose from the pump intake filter **(see illustration)**.
**5** Slacken the retaining clips then free the filter from the fuel hoses and remove the filter and separator assembly **(see illustration)**.
**6** Note which way around the filter is fitted, then slacken the clamp screw and slide the filter out of its clamp **(see illustration)**.

### *Installation*

**7** Slide the new filter into the retaining clamp, ensuring it is the correct way around, and securely tighten the clamp screw. The filter must be fitted with its arrow pointing in the direction of fuel flow (towards the mounting plate) and/or its OUT marking on the outlet (lower) side **(see illustrations)**.
**8** Connect the filter to the fuel hoses, tighten the hose clips securely, and reconnect the separator hose to the pump intake filter.
**9** Install the pump assembly in the tank as described in Steps 24 to 27 of Section 4.
**10** Fit the fuel tank to the bike (see Section 2).

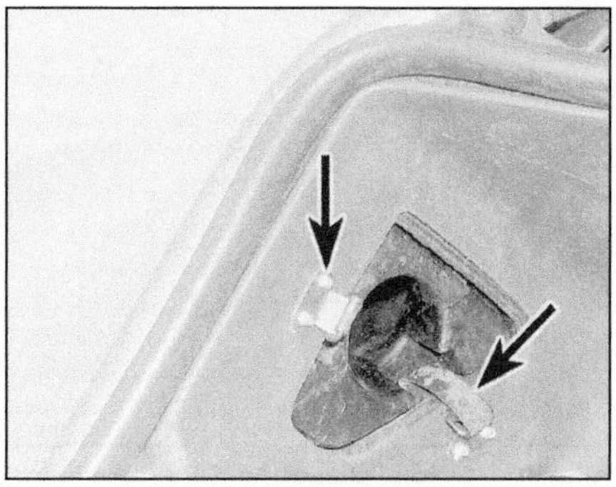

**6.4 Release the retaining clips securing the filter housings to the airbox**

## 6 Airbox and filter housings – removal and installation

### *Removal*

**1** The air filter assembly consists of three separate sections, the airbox and the left and right filter housings. Each section can be removed individually as follows.

#### Airbox

**2** Remove the fuel tank (see Section 2).
**3** Rotate the intake funnels anti-clockwise to release them from the throttle bodies then remove them from the airbox, complete with their rubber collars and sealing rings **(see illustration)**.
**4** Release the clips securing the left and right side filter housings to the airbox **(see illustration)**.

two front bolts are different to the rear bolts) and lift the airbox out of position, disconnecting the breather hose as it becomes accessible **(see illustrations)**.

**6** Recover the seals from the left and right filter housings **(see illustration)**.

### Filter housing

**7** Remove the upper fairing and relevant lower panel (see Chapter 8).

**8** Remove the fuel tank (see Section 2).

**9** Trace the wiring back from the turn signal light and disconnect its wiring connectors **(see illustration)**.

**10** Release the clips securing the filter housing to the airbox and remove the housing from the bike **(see illustration 6.4)**. Recover the seal fitted between the filter housing and airbox **(see illustration 6.6)**.

## *Installation*

### Airbox

**11** Ensure the left and right filter housing seals are correctly fitted then reconnect the breather hose and seat the airbox on the frame. Install the retaining bolts in their original locations (two bolts with the rubber collars at the front) and tighten them to the specified torque.

**12** Ensure the seals are still correctly positioned then clip the left and right filter housings securely to the airbox.

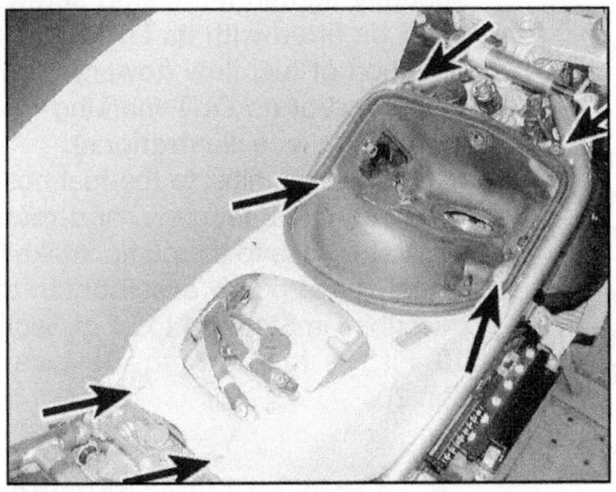

**6.5a Unscrew the retaining bolts (arrowed) . . .**

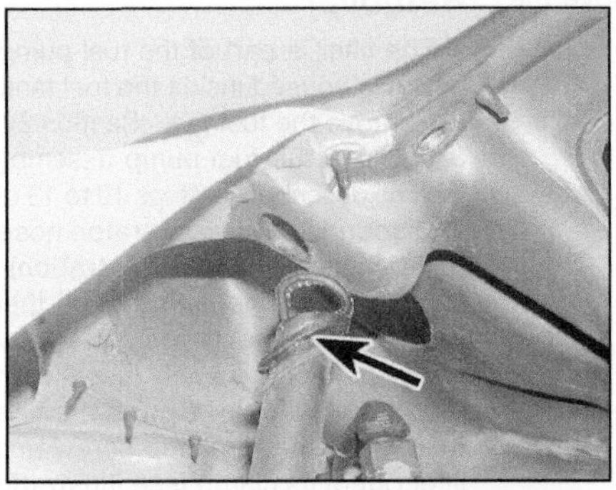

**6.5b . . . then remove the airbox from the bike, disconnecting the breather hose (arrowed) as it becomes accessible**

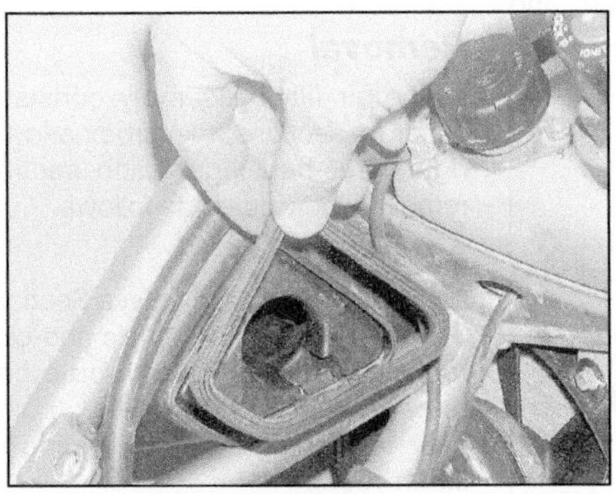

**6.6 Recover the seals from the air filter housings**

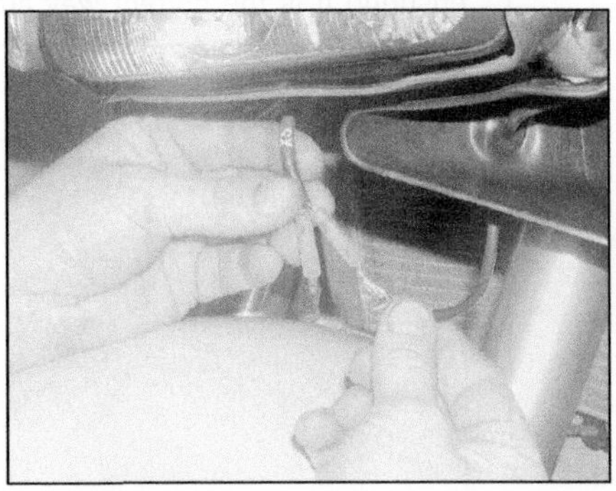

**6.9 Disconnect the turn signal wiring connectors so the light is free to be removed with the air filter housing**

onto each intake funnel. Refit the funnels to the airbox and rotate them clockwise to secure them to the throttle bodies.

**14** Install the fuel tank (see Section 2).

### Filter housing

**15** Ensure the seal is correctly fitted then manoeuvre the filter housing into position and clip the housing securely to the airbox.

**16** Reconnect the turn signal wiring then install the fuel tank (see Section 2) and the fairing panels (see Chapter 8).

## 7 Fuel injection system – general information

**1** All models are equipped with a Marelli engine management system which operates the fuel injection and ignition systems on the motorcycle. There are two different versions of the system used in the model range; 916 SP, SPS and early Strada models and all 996 SPS models are fitted with a Marelli IAW P8 system whereas all other models are fitted with a Marelli IAW 1.6M system. The fuel injection side of the system functions as follows; refer to Chapter 5 for information on the ignition system.

**2** The fuel pump, filter and pressure regulator are contained in the fuel tank. The pump supplies fuel to the injectors in the throttle

Excess fuel is returned to the tank via th return hose. The fuel supply pressure controlled by the pressure regulator which fitted to the fuel return passage on the pum mounting plate. The pressure regulator kee the pressure in the fuel hoses constant governing the flow of fuel back into the tank

**3** The 916 SP and SPS and all 996 mode have two injectors per cylinder whereas other models have a single injector. O models with two injectors per cylinder, th inner injectors located between the tw throttle bodies provide the main fuel supp and operate whenever the engine is runnir The outer injector for each cylinder is use only to supply additional fuel under certa operating conditions.

**4** The electronic control unit (ECU) monito signals from the following sensors.

*a) Throttle position sensor – informs the ECU of the throttle position, and the rate of throttle opening or closing.*

*b) Coolant temperature sensor – informs th ECU of engine temperature.*

*c) Atmospheric pressure sensor – informs the ECU of the atmospheric pressure th motorcycle is operating in.*

*d) Air temperature sensor – informs the EC of the ambient air temperature.*

*e) Timing sensor (1.6M system – fitted opposite timing gear) – informs the ECU of engine speed and crankshaft/camsha position.*

*f) Timing sensor (P8 system – fitted opposite timing gear) – informs the ECU of crankshaft/camshaft position.*

*g) RPM sensor (P8 system – fitted opposite flywheel) – informs the ECU of engine speed.*

**5** All the above information is analysed by th ECU and based on these signals it determin the appropriate ignition and fuelli requirements for the engine. The EC controls the fuel injector by varying its pul width – the length of time the injector is he open – to provide a richer or weaker mixtu The mixture is constantly varied by the EC to provide the best setting for crankin starting, warm-up, idle, cruising, a acceleration. The injection system is fu sequential, with each injector receiving own operating signal from the ECU. Th settings (or maps) for injection/ignition timi are stored on an EPROM which is fitted insi the ECU. If the fuelling/ignition settin require altering, to suit an aftermarket exhau system for instance, the original EPROM c be removed and replaced with a anoth EPROM with more suitable settings.

**6** If there is an abnormality in any of th readings obtained from any sensor, the EC enters its back-up mode. In this event, th ECU ignores the abnormal sensor signal, a assumes a pre-programmed value which w allow the engine to continue running (albeit reduced efficiency). If an engine manageme system fault is suspected, the bike should

opportunity. A complete test of the engine management system can then be carried out, using the Mathesis diagnostic tester which is simply plugged into the system's diagnostic connector (located underneath the seat cowling).

## 8 Fuel injection system – testing and adjustment

### Testing

**1** If a fault appears in the system, first ensure that all the system wiring connectors are securely connected and free of corrosion. Then ensure that the fault is not due to poor maintenance – i.e. check that the air filter elements are clean, that the spark plugs are in good condition and correctly gapped, that the valve clearances are correctly adjusted and the cylinder compression pressures are correct (refer to Chapter 1).

**2** If these checks fail to reveal the cause of the problem, the motorcycle should be taken to a suitably-equipped Ducati dealer for checking. They will have access to the Mathesis diagnostic tester which can be plugged into the system. The diagnostic tester will locate the fault quickly and simply, alleviating the need to check all the system components individually, which is a time-consuming operation (checking information for individual components is given in Section 9).

### Adjustment

**3** The ECU is equipped with an adjuster to alter the idle mixture (exhaust gas CO level) setting. See Chapter 1 for the throttle body synchronisation, engine idle speed and idle mixture setting adjustment procedure.

**4** The only other means of adjustment is to change the ECU's EPROM to alter the fuelling/ignition characteristics of the system. See Section 9 for removal and installation details.

## 9 Fuel injection system components – removal, check and installation

***Caution: Ensure the ignition is switched OFF before disconnecting and reconnecting any fuel injection system wiring connector. If a connector is disturbed with the ignition switched ON the electronic control unit (ECU) maybe damaged.***

**Note:** *To avoid unnecessary expense, if a check identifies a component as being faulty, have your findings confirmed by a Ducati dealer before condemning the component concerned. Bear in mind that most electrical parts cannot be exchanged once purchased.*

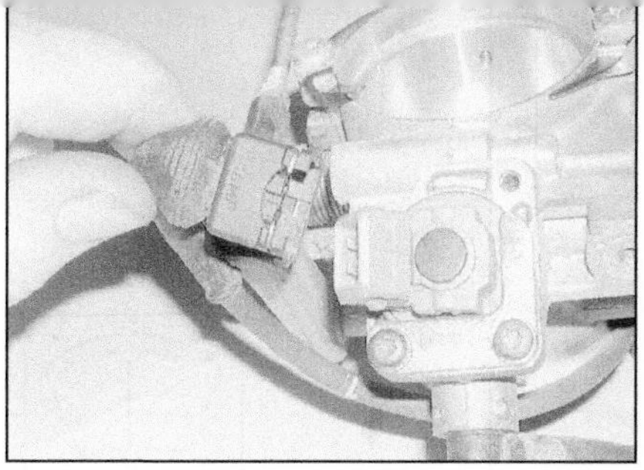

**9.4 Disconnect the wiring connector from the injector . . .**

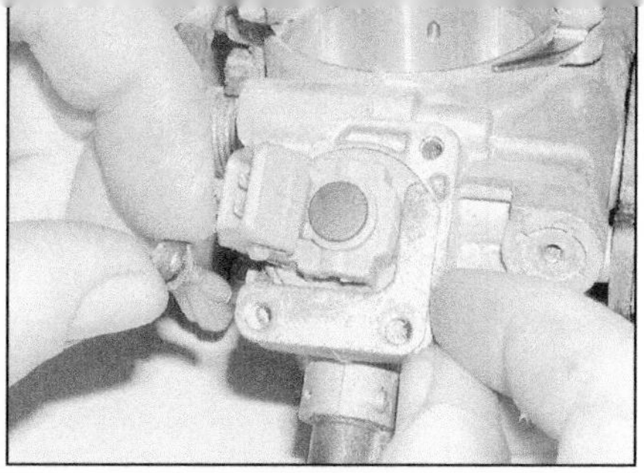

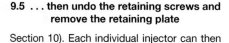

**9.5 . . . then undo the retaining screws and remove the retaining plate**

### Fuel injectors

***Warning: Refer to the precautions given in Section 1 before starting work.***

**Note:** *If the bike has been stored for a long period of time, Ducati recommend that a fuel additive (Tunap 231 – available from your Ducati dealer) is added to the fuel. The additive will break down any varnish or gum deposits on the injectors which may have built-up during the storage period.*

#### Check

**1** If the engine runs, start it and allow it to idle. Check the operation of each injector using a stethoscope or sounding rod; an injector will emit a 'clicking' noise when functioning. If any injector is silent, either the injector or its wiring harness is faulty. **Note:** *On models with two injectors per cylinder, only the inner injectors will be operating; the outer injectors are only used to provide extra fuel under certain operating conditions.*

**2** If the engine does not run, disconnect the wiring connector from the injectors (see Step 4). Connect an ohmmeter across the terminals of each injector and measure its resistance. Compare the readings obtained for each injector to that given in the Specifications. If the resistance of any injector is significantly different from that specified, the injector is faulty and should be renewed.

#### Removal

**3** Remove the throttle body assembly (see Section 10). Each individual injector can then be removed as follows.

**4** Disconnect the injector wiring connector **(see illustration)**. If more than one injector is being removed, note the correct fitted location of each wiring connector before disconnect them. If necessary, to avoid confusion on installation, label the connectors for identification; it is essential each one is connected to its original injector.

**5** Undo the retaining screws and remove the injector retaining plate from the throttle body **(see illustration)**.

**6** Remove the injector from the throttle body, complete with its seals **(see illustration)**. The seals must both be renewed.

#### Installation

**Note:** *On models with two injectors per cylinder (see Section 7), Ducati recommend swapping the inner and outer injector of each throttle body over occasionally to ensure optimum operation (all injectors are identical).*

**7** Remove the original seals from the injector and install the new ones. Ensure both seals are correctly located and lubricate them with a smear of engine oil to aid installation **(see illustration)**.

**8** Ease the injector into position in the throttle body, taking care not to damage the seals.

**9** Ensure the injector wiring connector is correctly positioned then refit the retaining plate.

**10** Remove all original locking compound and apply a drop of fresh locking compound

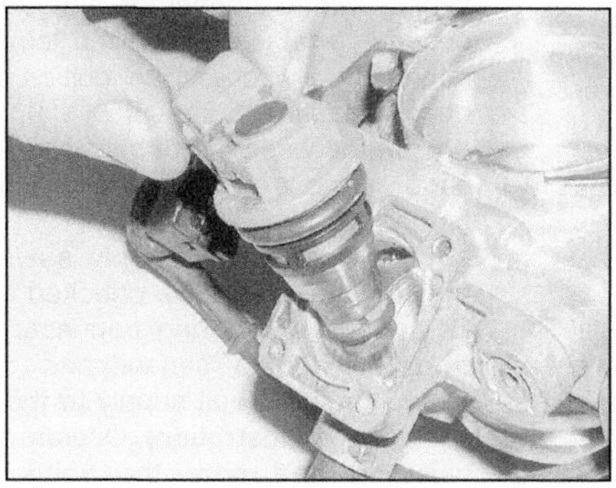

**9.6 Ease the injector out of position and remove it from the throttle body**

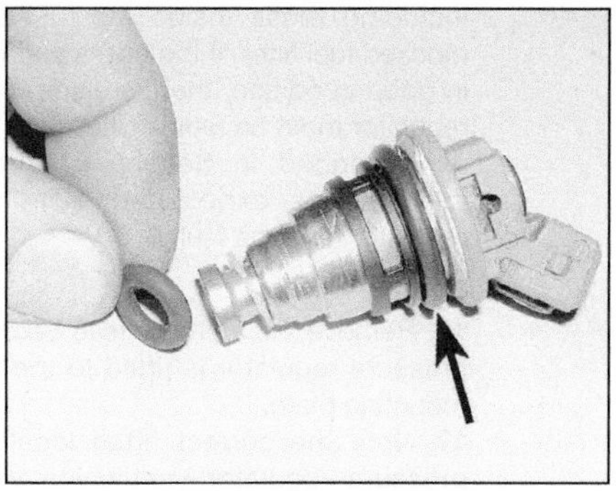

**9.7 Renew the injector upper (arrowed) and lower sealing rings every time the injector is removed**

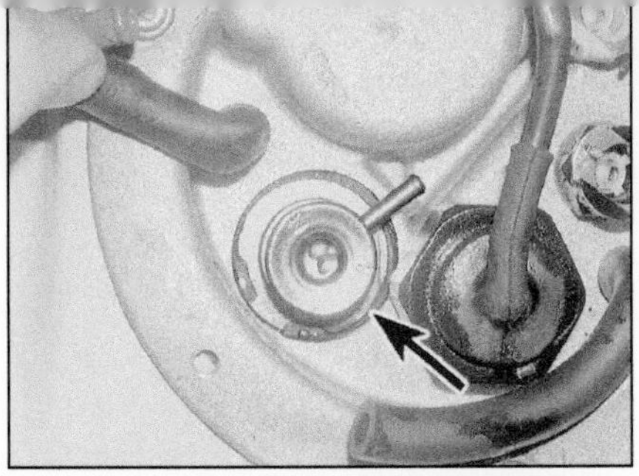

**9.17 Fuel pressure regulator circlip (arrowed)**

to each retaining plate screw. Refit the screws and tighten them securely.

**11** Securely reconnect the wiring connector to the injector. If more than one injector was removed, use the marks made on removal to ensure the connectors are reconnected to the correct injector.

***Caution: If the injector wiring connectors are incorrectly connected, the engine will not run.***

**12** Install the throttle body assembly (see Section 10).

## Fuel pressure regulator

***Warning: Refer to the precautions given in Section 1 before starting work.***

### Check

**13** If a fuel pressure gauge is available, the operation of the pressure regulator can be checked. Using a length of fuel hose and adapter, connect the gauge into the fuel hose between the tank and the throttle body then start the engine and allow it to idle. Note the pressure present in the fuel system then turn the engine off. Compare the reading obtained to that given in the Specifications.

**14** If the fuel pressure is higher than specified, check for blocked or restricted fuel hoses and passages. If all the hoses and passages are clear, the fuel pressure regulator must be faulty (check the regulator vent union is clear and unblocked before condemning it).

**15** If the fuel pressure is lower than specified, first check for signs of damaged fuel hoses, including those inside the fuel tank, or a blocked fuel filter. If the hoses and filter are all in good condition, the fuel pump or pressure regulator must be faulty. Check the fuel pump as described in Section 4. If the pump performs as expected the fuel pressure regulator must be faulty.

### Removal

**16** Remove the fuel tank (see Section 2). The pressure regulator is fitted to the fuel pump mounting plate.

**17** Note the correct fitted location of the pressure regulator vent union then, using circlip pliers, extract the regulator circlip from the mounting plate **(see illustration)**.

**18** Ease the pressure regulator out from the mounting plate along with its seals. The seals must both be renewed. **Note:** *Depending on the fuel level in the tank, fuel might leak out when the pressure regulator is removed. To prevent this drain the fuel tank (see Step 10 of Section 4).*

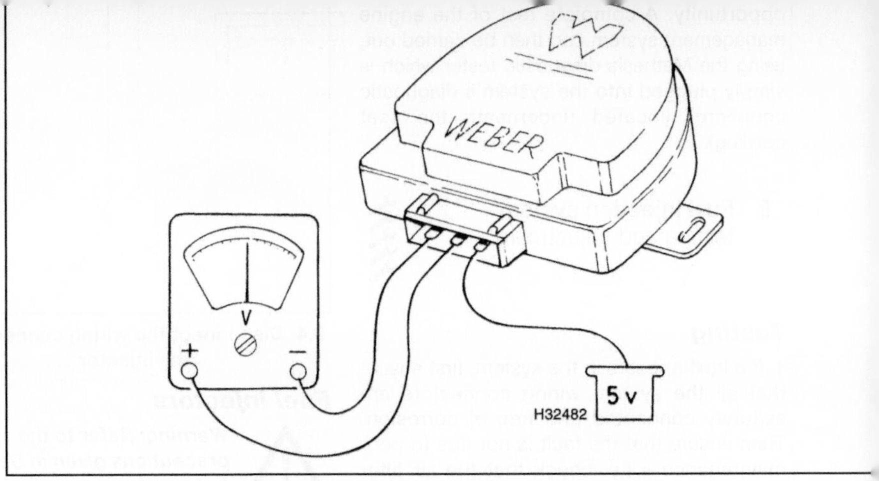


**9.23 Throttle position sensor test details**

### Installation

**19** Remove the original seals from the pressure regulator and install the new ones. Ensure both seals are correctly located and lubricate them with a smear of engine oil to aid installation.

**20** Ease the pressure regulator into position in the throttle body, taking care not to damage the seals. Ensure the vent union is correctly positioned then secure the regulator in position with the circlip.

**21** Install the fuel tank (see Section 2).

## Throttle position sensor

### Check

**22** The throttle position sensor is fed with a 5 volt supply from the electronic control unit (ECU). To check the power supply, disconnect the wiring connector from the sensor and connect the positive (+ve) lead of a voltmeter to the white/red terminal of the sensor wiring connector and connect the negative (–ve) lead to the red terminal of the connector. Switch on the ignition switch and check that a voltage of 5 ± 0.25 volts is present between the terminals. If the voltage supply is incorrect, there is a fault in the wiring harness or the ECU.

**23** If a 5 volt power supply is available, the throttle sensor can be checked as follows. Disconnect the wiring connector from the throttle position sensor and connect a voltmeter and 5 volt supply to the sensor as shown **(see illustration)**. Operate the throttle twistgrip and note the voltage reading obtained at the various throttle openings. Compare the readings obtained to those given in the Specifications. If the results differ greatly from that specified, the thrott position sensor is faulty and should b renewed.

### Removal

**Note:** *Accurate adjustment of the thrott position sensor requires the use of the Duca (Mathesis) diagnostic tester. If the tester is nc available, it is recommended that the thrott position sensor should not be disturbed.*

**24** Remove the airbox (see Section 6).

**25** Disconnect the wiring connector from th throttle position sensor which is located c the left-hand side of the horizontal cylind throttle body.

**26** Make alignment marks between th sensor and throttle body, then undo th retaining screws and remove the sensor.

### Installation

**27** Engage the sensor with the throttle valv spindle and refit its retaining screws. Align th marks made prior to removal then secure tighten the sensor screws and reconnect th wiring connector.

**28** Check the throttle body synchronisatio idle speed and mixture settings as describe in Chapter 1.

**29** On completion, refit the airbox (se Section 6).

## Coolant temperature sensor

### Check

**30** The coolant temperature sensor is fe with a 5 volt supply from the electronic contr unit (ECU). To check the power suppl disconnect the wiring connector from th sensor and connect the positive (+ve) lead c a voltmeter to the white/red terminal of th sensor wiring connector and connect th negative (–ve) lead to the green terminal of th connector. Switch on the ignition switch an check that a voltage of 5 ± 0.25 volts present between the terminals. If the voltag supply is incorrect, there is a fault in the wirin harness or the ECU.

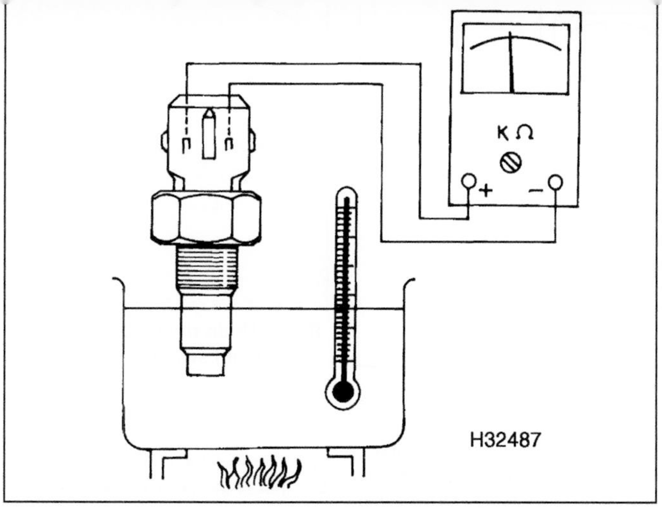


**9.31 Coolant temperature sensor test set-up**

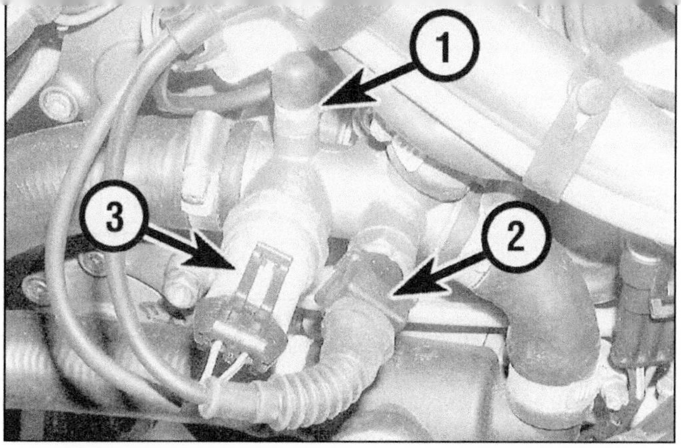


**9.32 Coolant temperature sensor and switch locations**

1 *Coolant temperature gauge sender*
2 *Engine management system coolant temperature sensor*
3 *Cooling fan temperature switch*

**31** The sensor can be checked as follows. Remove the sensor (see below) and fill a small, heatproof, container with water and place it on a stove. Connect an ohmmeter across the terminals of the sensor and, using some wire or other support, suspend the sensor in the water so that just the sensing portion and the threads are submerged **(see illustration)**. Also place a thermometer capable of reading temperatures up to 80°C in the water so that its bulb is close to the sensor. **Note:** *None of the components should be allowed to directly touch the container.* Heat the water and note the resistance reading of the sensor at the temperatures given in the Specifications; allow the temperature of the water and sensor to stabilise before taking each reading. If the meter readings obtained are significantly different then the coolant temperature sensor is faulty and must be renewed.

***Warning: This must be done very carefully to avoid the risk of personal injury.***

### Removal

**32** Remove the fairing left-hand lower panel (see Chapter 8). The coolant temperature sensor is the rearmost of the two sensors screwed into the side of the coolant outlet on the side of the horizontal cylinder (the front sensor is the cooling fan switch **(see illustration)**.

**33** Drain the cooling system (see Chapter 1).

**34** Disconnect the wiring connector then unscrew the coolant temperature sensor.

### Installation

**35** Clean the threads of the sensor and apply a smear of sealant to its threads. Screw the sensor into the coolant union, tightening it to the specified torque, then reconnect the wiring connector.

**36** Refill the cooling system and install the fairing panel (see Chapters 1 and 8).

## *Air temperature sensor*

### Check

**37** The air temperature sensor is fed with a 5 volt supply from the electronic control unit (ECU). To check the power supply, disconnect the wiring connector from the sensor and connect the positive (+ve) lead of a voltmeter to the white/red terminal of the sensor wiring connector and connect the negative (–ve) lead to the green/blue terminal of the connector. Switch on the ignition switch and check that a voltage of 5 ± 0.25 volts is present between the terminals. If the voltage supply is incorrect, there is a fault in the wiring harness or the ECU.

**38** The sensor can be checked as follows. Remove the sensor (see below) and connect an ohmmeter across its terminals. Heat the sensor gently with a hairdryer/hot air gun (hold the sensor with an insulated tool) and note the resistance readings of the sensor at the temperature given (accurate measurement of the temperature will be difficult but this check will give a general idea if the sensor is functioning). If the meter readings obtained are significantly different from those specified, the air temperature sensor is faulty and must be renewed.

### Removal

**39** Remove the upper fairing (see Chapter 8). The air temperature sensor is mounted on the base of the headlight mounting shell bracket on the front of the headstock.

**40** Undo the retaining screws and free the sensor from the mounting bracket **(see illustration)**.

**41** Disconnect the sensor from its wiring connector and remove it from the bike.

### Installation

**42** Reconnect the sensor to the wiring connector then fit it to the mounting bracket, tightening its retaining screws securely.

**43** Install the upper fairing (see Chapter 8).

## *Atmospheric pressure sensor*

### Check

**44** The atmospheric pressure sensor is fed with a 5 volt supply from the electronic control unit (ECU). To check the power supply, disconnect the wiring connector from the sensor and connect the positive (+ve) lead of a voltmeter to the white/red terminal of the sensor wiring connector and connect the negative (–ve) lead to the red terminal of the connector. Switch on the ignition switch and check that a voltage of 5 ± 0.25 volts is present between the terminals **(see illustration)**. If the voltage supply is incorrect,

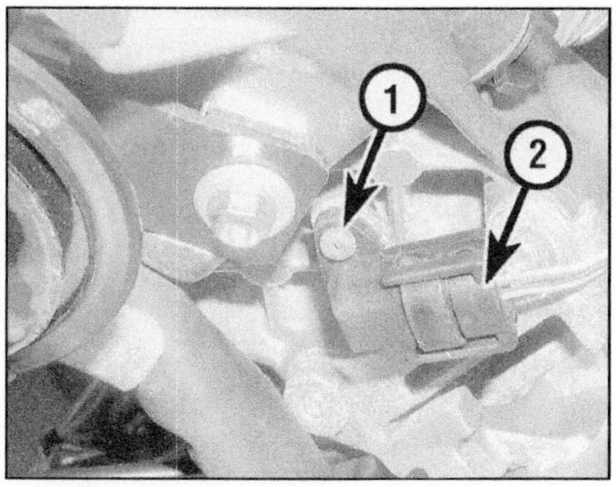


**9.40 Air temperature sensor retaining screw (1) and wiring connector (2)**

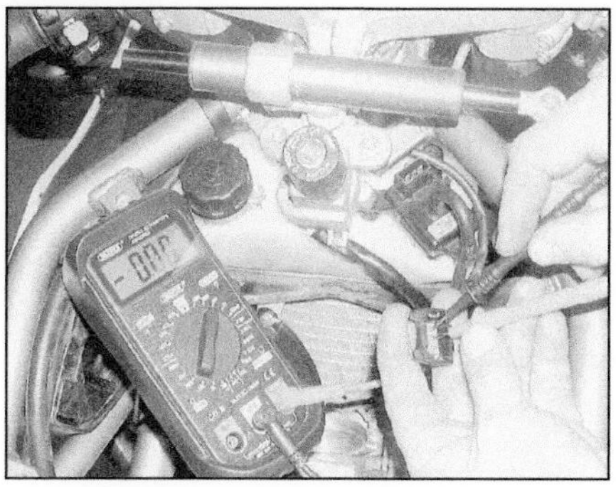

**9.44 Checking the atmospheric pressure sensor supply voltage – see text**

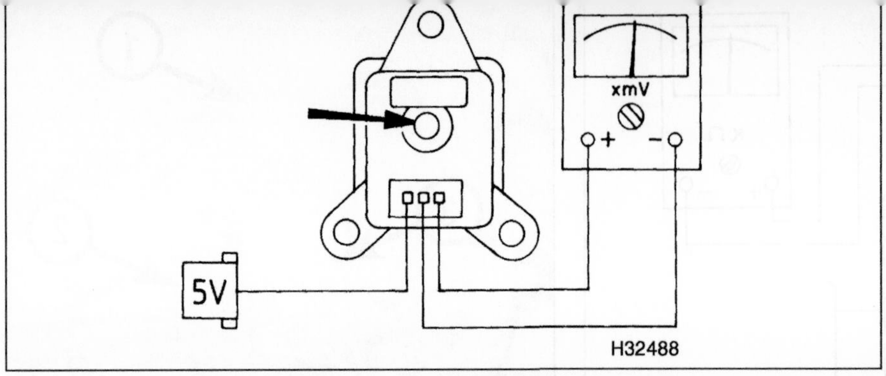


9.45 Atmospheric pressure sensor test details – apply vacuum to sensor port (arrowed)

there is a fault in the wiring harness or the ECU.

**45** If a 5 volt power supply and hand-operated vacuum pump and gauge are available, the pressure sensor can be checked as follows. Remove the fuel tank (see Section 2) to gain access to the sensor. Disconnect the wiring connector from the sensor and connect a voltmeter and 5 volt supply to the sensor as shown **(see illustration)**. Attach the vacuum pump to the sensor port and note the voltage reading obtained at the various vacuums. Compare the upper and lower readings obtained to those given in the Specifications and check that the voltage reading increases/decrease smoothly as the vacuum is applied/released.

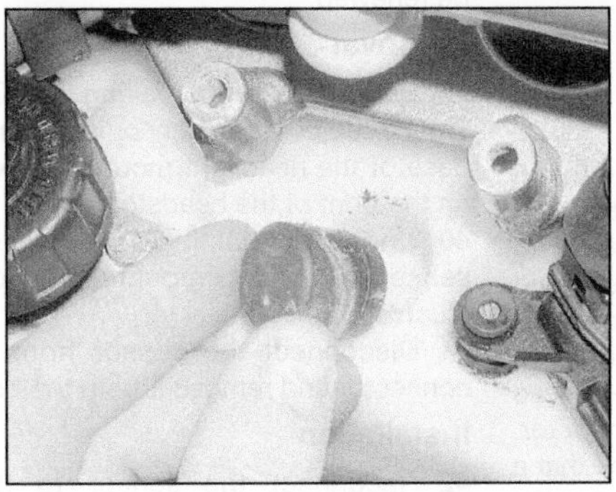

**9.47b . . . and remove the mounting rubber from the expansion tank**

If the results differ greatly from that specified, the atmospheric pressure sensor is probably faulty and should be renewed. **Note:** *If a vacuum pump is not available a rough idea of the sensor performance can be gained by sucking on the sensor port.*

***Caution: Never test the atmospheric pressure sensor outside its specified operating range (see Specifications) as this could damage the sensor diaphragm.***

### Removal

**46** The sensor is mounted to the top of the coolant expansion tank. Remove the airbox (see Section 6) to gain access.

**47** Undo the retaining bolts and free the ignition (main) switch from the frame, taking care not to displace the mounting rubber from the expansion tank **(see illustrations)**.

**48** Free the sensor from its mounting pins on the expansion tank then disconnect the wiring connector and remove it from the bike **(see illustrations)**.

### Installation

**49** Ensure the mounting rubbers are in good condition then lubricate them with a silicone-based spray to aid installation. Locate the sensor on its pins and securely reconnect the wiring connector.

**50** Ensure the mounting rubber is correctly fitted to the expansion tank. Remove all traces of locking compound from the threads of the lock bolts and apply a few drops of fresh

**9.47a Undo the bolts and free the ignitio (main) switch from the frame . . .**

locking compound to each bolt. Fit the lock the frame and tighten its retaining bolts to t specified torque (see Chapter 9).

**51** Install the airbox (see Section 6).

## *Timing sensor*

### Check

**52** Remove the fairing left-hand lower par (see Chapter 8) and disconnect the sens wiring connector. Connect an ohmme across the sensor connector terminals a measure its resistance, then check continuity between each of the connect terminals and earth (ground). Compare t reading obtained to that given in t Specifications noting that the specified val is only valid at 20°C (68°F). If the resistan reading differs greatly from that specified, there is continuity between either of t connector terminals and earth (ground) th the sensor is faulty.

**53** If the sensor resistance reading is specified, check the sensor air gap (see Ste 64 to 74).

**54** If the sensor resistance reading and gap are correctly set then the fault must be the wiring harness or the ECU.

### Removal

**55** Remove the fairing left-hand lower par (see Chapter 8). The timing sensor is fitted the left-hand crankcase cover where it located just in front of the water pump **(s illustration)**.

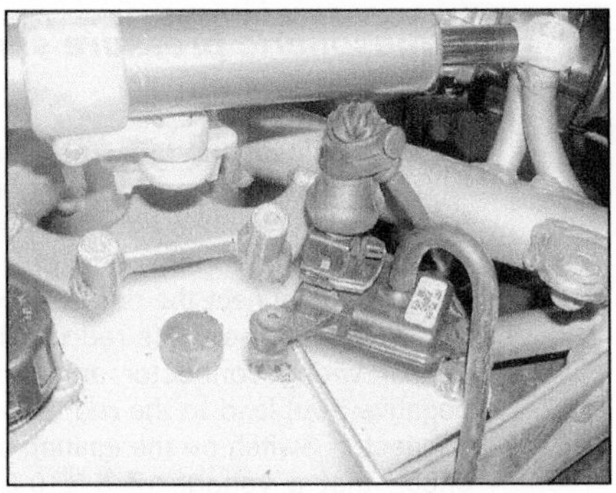

**9.48a Ease the atmospheric pressure sensor off its locating pegs . . .**

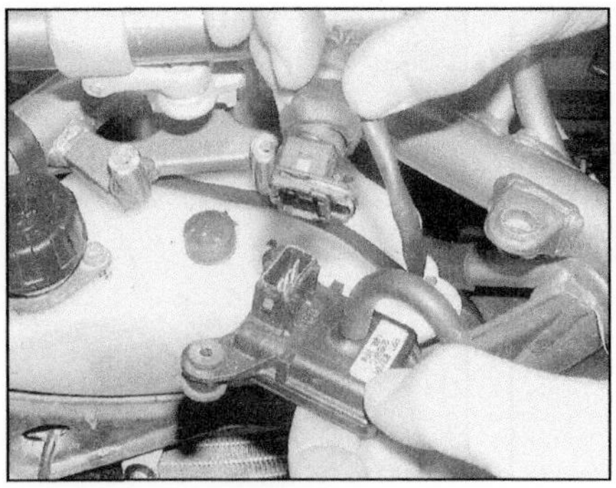

**9.48b . . . then disconnect its wiring connector**

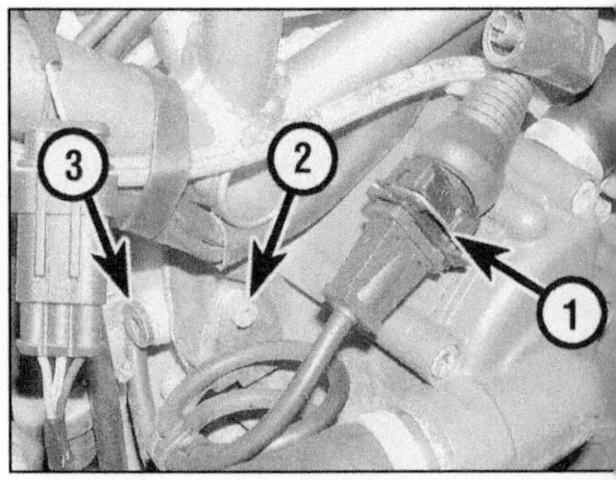


**9.55 Timing sensor wiring connector (1) retaining bolt (2) and air gap inspection plug (3)**

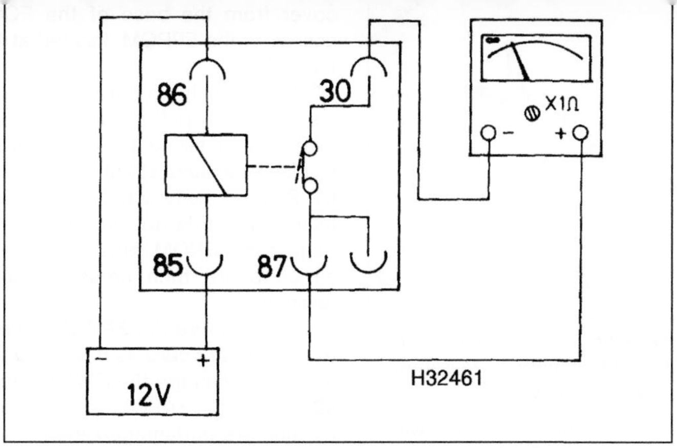


**9.76 Engine management system relay test details – later type relay (without fuse) shown**

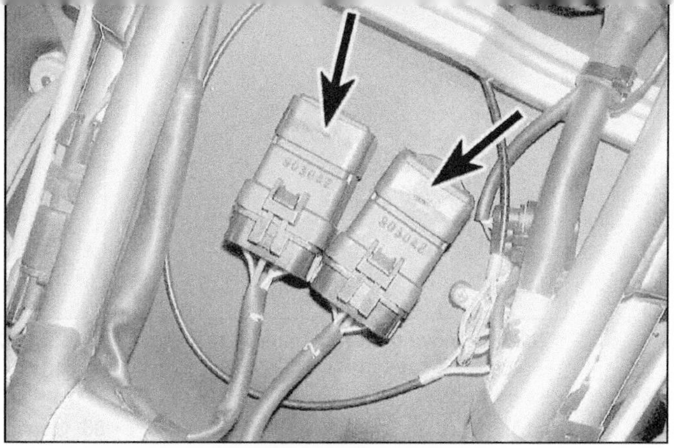

**9.77 Engine management relays (arrowed) are located underneath the seat cowling**

**56** Trace the wiring back from the sensor, freeing it from all its retaining clips and ties whilst noting its correct routing, and disconnect its connector from the main wiring harness.

**57** On 748 SPS models, unscrew the two nuts and remove the sensor retaining plate. Remove the sensor, complete with its holder, from the crankcase cover and slide off the sealing ring and shim(s) (as applicable). Discard the sealing ring; a new one must be used on installation.

**58** On all other models, undo the retaining bolt(s) and remove the sensor from the crankcase cover, complete with its sealing ring and shim(s) (as applicable). Discard the sealing ring; a new one must be used on installation.

### Installation

**59** Ensure the sensor and cover mating surfaces are clean and dry. On models with a sensor holder, ensure the holder is securely fitted to the cover or sensor (as applicable).

**60** Fit the shim(s) to the sensor and slide on the new sealing ring then ease the sensor into position.

**61** Clean the sensor bolt(s)/nuts and apply a drop of fresh locking compound to their threads. Fit the retaining bolt(s)/retaining plate and nuts (as applicable) and tighten to the specified torque.

**62** Check and, if necessary, adjust the sensor air gap (see Steps 64 to 74).

**63** Ensure the sensor wiring is correctly routed and retained by all the relevant clips and ties then reconnect its connector to the main wiring harness. Install the fairing panel (see Chapter 8).

### Air gap check and adjustment

**64** Remove the fairing left-hand lower panel (see Chapter 8).

**65** Undo the retaining screws and remove the centre cap and sealing ring from the left-hand crankcase cover. Obtain a new sealing ring for use on refitting.

**66** Unscrew the inspection plug and sealing washer from the front of the crankcase to gain access to the sensor tip. Obtain a new sealing washer for use on refitting.

**67** In the absence of the Ducati service tool (88713-0123), obtain an M8 bolt, nut, washer and spacer. Screw the nut fully onto the bolt then slide on the washer and spacer. Screw the bolt fully into the end of the crankshaft and tighten the nut against the spacer to lock it in position; the bolt can then be used to rotate the crankshaft.

**Note:** *It will be considerably easier to rotate the crankshaft if the spark plugs are removed (see Chapter 1).*

**68** Rotate the crankshaft until the timing driven gear is correctly positioned so its raised section is aligned with the sensor tip. On models with a P8 engine management system there is only a small raised section on the gear whereas on models with a 1.6M system the whole of the gear is raised except for one small section which is recessed.

**69** With the timing driven gear correctly positioned, using feeler gauges, measure the gap between the sensor tip and the outer face of the gear. This should be 0.6 to 0.8 mm.

**70** If the air gap is not as specified, note the measured gap then remove the sensor from the cover (see Step 57 or 58). Measure the thickness of the shim(s) fitted to the sensor then use this to calculate the required thickness of shim(s) required to correctly set the air gap. Shims are available in various thicknesses – refer to your Ducati dealer for details. Fit the correct thickness shim(s) and a new sealing ring then install the sensor (see Steps 59 to 61).

**71** Once the sensor air gap is correctly set, clean the inspection plug and fit the new sealing washer. Apply a drop of locking compound to the plugs threads then fit it to the crankcase, tightening it to the specified torque.

**72** Remove the bolt arrangement from the crankshaft.

**73** Fit a new sealing ring then fit the centre cap to the crankcase cover. Apply a drop of locking compound to the retaining screws threads then fit the screws, tightening them securely.

**74** Install the fairing panel (see Chapter 8).

## *RPM sensor – P8 engine management system*

**75** The RPM sensor is fitted to the left-hand crankcase cover where it is located to the rear of the water pump. The checking, removal, installation and air gap adjustment procedures are similar to those for the timing sensor. The inspection plug for checking the sensor air gap is on the crankcase cover and one of the raised tabs on the flywheel (there are four in total) should be aligned with the sensor tip when checking the gap.

## *Engine management system relays*

### Check

**Note:** *On early 916 models, the relays have integral fuses. Ensure the fuses are in good condition before testing the relay (see Chapter 9).*

**76** Remove the relay (see below). Connect an ohmmeter across terminals 30 and 87 of the relay **(see illustration)**. Using a battery and auxiliary wires, connect the battery positive (+ve) terminal to terminal 85 of the relay and the negative (–ve) terminal to terminal 86 of the relay and note the meter reading obtained. If the relay is operating correctly there should be continuity (zero resistance) when the battery is connected and no continuity (infinite resistance) when the battery is disconnected; the relay will be heard to 'click' as the battery is connected/disconnected. If this is not the case, renew the relay.

### Removal

**77** Unlock the seat cowling and pivot it forwards onto the fuel tank. The relays are located in front of the electronic control unit (ECU) **(see illustration)**.

**78** Free the relevant relay from its holder then disconnect it from its wiring connector.

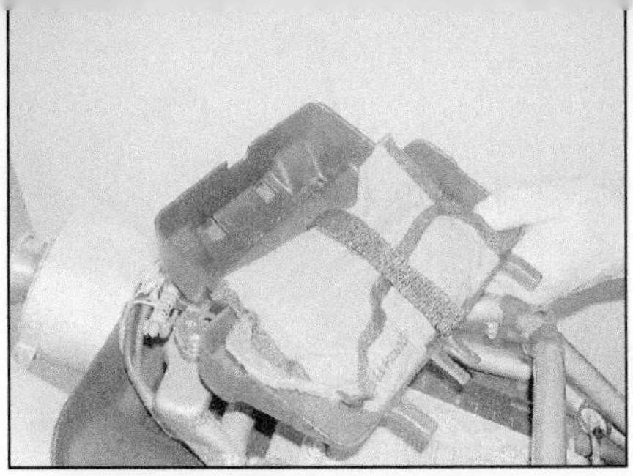

9.83 Remove the toolkit holder to gain access to the ECU

### Installation

**79** Securely connect the relay to the wiring connector then slide it into its holder.

**80** Lower the seat cowling and lock it in position.

## *Electronic control unit (ECU)*

### Check

**81** The electronic control unit (ECU) can only be checked using the Ducati (Mathesis) diagnostic tester (see Section 8).

### Removal

**82** Unlock the seat cowling and pivot it forwards onto the fuel tank. The electronic control unit (ECU) is mounted onto the rear of the subframe.

**83** Free the toolkit holder from its mounting rubbers and remove it from the bike **(see illustration)**.

**84** On models with a P8 engine management system, unscrew the bolts and free both ignition power modules from the ECU.

**85** On all models, unscrew the retaining nuts and free the ECU from its rubber mountings, noting the correct fitted location of the earth (ground) lead (where present) **(see illustration)**.

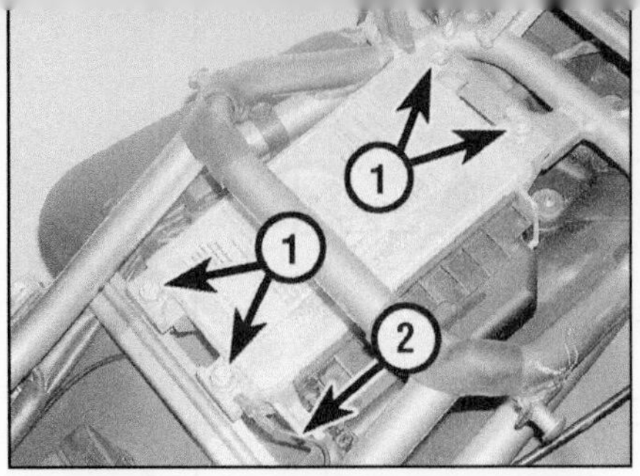


**9.85 ECU mounting nuts (1) and earth lead (2) – 996 models with 1.6M engine management system**

**86** Unclip and disconnect the wiring connector then remove the ECU.

### Installation

**87** Installation is the reverse of removal. If a new ECU has been installed, check the idle mixture setting (see Chapter 1).

## *Electronic control unit (ECU) EPROM*

***Caution: The ECU and EPROM are delicate components which are easily damaged. Ducati dealers have special tools for removing and installing the EPROM (88713.1097 and 88713.1140). Attempting to remove or install an EPROM without the special tools is highly likely to result in damage to the ECU or EPROM. It is therefore that recommended that this procedure is entrusted to a Ducati dealer.***

### Models with a P8 engine management system

**88** Remove the ECU from the bike (see above).

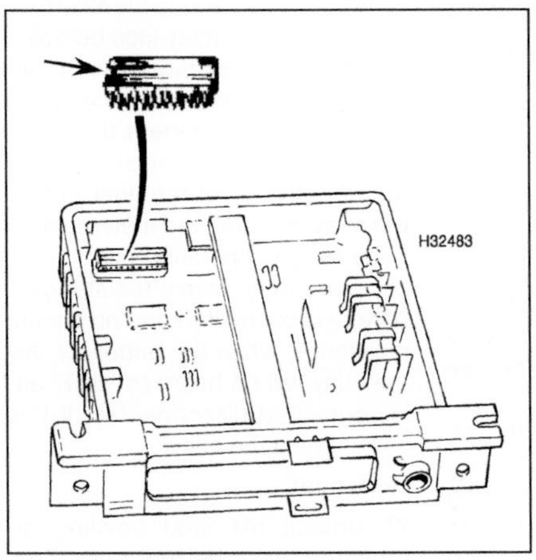


**9.90 ECU EPROM location – P8 engine management system**

*Ensure the EPROM is fitted with its cut-out (arrowed) facing towards the casing*

**89** ... cover from the base of the ECU to gai access to the EPROM, located at the rear c the unit.

**90** Note which way around the EPROM i installed then pull it squarely out from th circuit board, taking great care not to damag its pins **(see illustration)**.

**91** Position the new EPROM so its cut-out i facing outwards (towards the ECU casing Align the EPROM pins correctly with th circuit board then press it squarely int position.

***Caution: Ensure the EPROM is kept squar to the circuit board as it is fitted. Failure t do so will damage the EPROM pins.***

**92** Ensure the EPROM is securely fitted ar its pins are undamaged then refit the EC cover. Apply a drop of locking compound t each cover screw then refit the screw tightening them securely.

**93** Install the ECU.

### Models with a 1.6M engine management system

**94** Unlock and raise the seat cowling. Fre the toolkit holder from its mounting rubbe and remove it from the bike.

**95** Ensure the ignition is turned off the disconnect the wiring connector from th ECU.

**96** Peel the sticker off the top of the EC then remove the rubber plug to gain access t the EPROM. Discard the sticker and obtain new one **(see illustration)**.

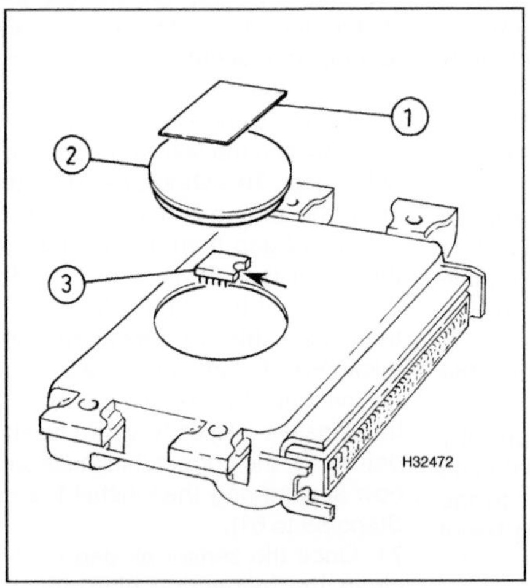


**9.96 ECU EPROM fitting details – 1.6M engine management system**

1 *Sticker*
2 *Rubber plug*
3 *EPROM (must be fitted with its cut-out (arrowed) facing towards the ECU wiring connector)*

**97** Note which way around the EPROM i installed then pull it squarely out from th circuit board, taking great care not to damag its pins.

**98** Position the new EPROM so its cut-out i facing the ECU wiring connector. Align th EPROM pins correctly with the circuit boar then press it squarely into position.

***Caution: Ensure the EPROM is kept squar to the circuit board as it is fitted. Failure t do so will damage the EPROM pins.***

**99** Ensure the EPROM is securely fitted ar its pins are undamaged then securely fit th rubber plug to the ECU casing. Secure th rubber plug in position with the new sticker.

**100** Reconnect the ECU wiring connector ar refit the toolkit holder then lower the se cowling and lock it in position.

## 10 Throttle body assembly – removal and installation

***Warning: Refer to the precautions given i Section 1 before starting work.***

## *Removal*

**1** Remove the fairing lower panels (se Chapter 8).

**2** Remove the fuel tank (see Section 2).

**3** Remove the airbox (see Section 6).

**4** Unscrew the retaining ring and disconne

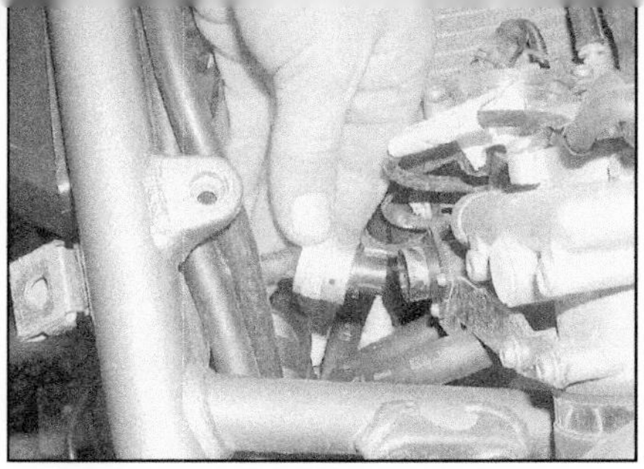

10.4 Unscrew the retaining ring and disconnect the throttle body wiring connector

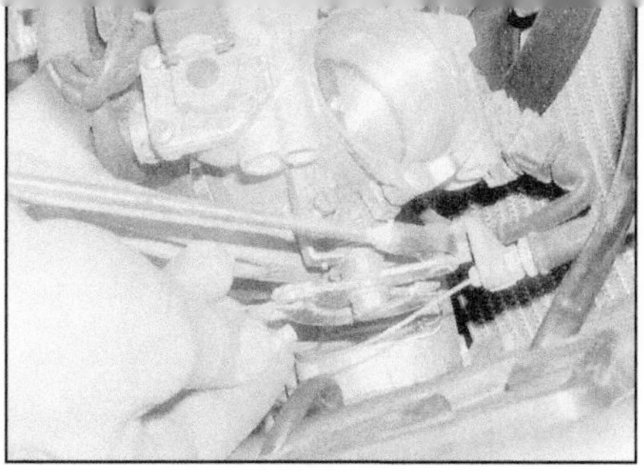

10.5a Free the throttle inner cable from the linkage . . .

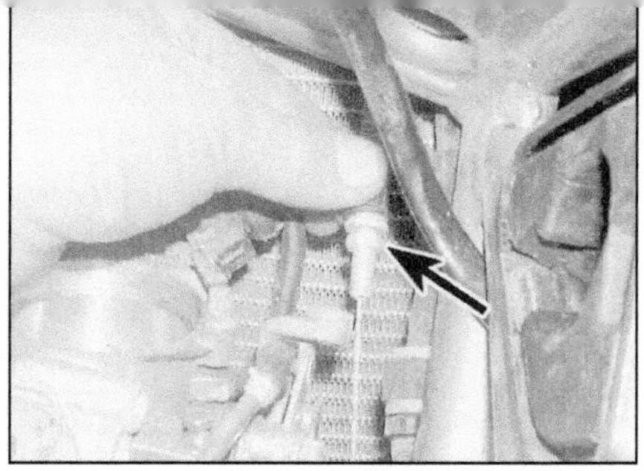

10.5b . . . then slacken the locknut (arrowed) and unscrew the cable adjuster from the mounting bracket

the wiring connector from the throttle body wiring harness connector on the left-hand side of the throttle body assembly **(see illustration)**.

**5** Unhook the throttle inner cable from the linkage **(see illustration)**. Slacken the locknut then unscrew the adjuster from its mounting bracket and position the cable clear of the throttle body **(see illustration)**.

**6** Unscrew the mounting bolt and washer securing the fuel hose guide to the side of the vertical cylinder head and recover the spacer fitted between the guide and head **(see illustration)**. Free one of the fuel hoses from the guide to enable the throttle body assembly to removed complete with hoses **(see illustration)**.

**7** Slacken the retaining clips securing the intake rubbers to the throttle body assembly **(see illustration)**. Ease the throttle body assembly out of position, noting the correct routing of the fuel hoses, and remove it from the bike **(see illustration)**.

**8** Check each intake rubber for signs of damage or deterioration and, if necessary, renew it. The rubber is an integral part of the intake manifold; undo the retaining nuts and remove the manifold and gasket from the cylinder head. Discard the gasket; a new one will be needed on installation.

***Caution: Whilst the throttle body assembly is removed, tape over/plug the intake ports to prevent dirt/debris from entering the cylinder head.***

## *Installation*

**9** Remove the tape/plugs from the intake ports.

**10** Where necessary, ensure the cylinder head and manifold mating surfaces are clean and dry and the manifold studs are securely fitted. If any stud is loose, remove it apply locking compound to its threads then refit it to the cylinder head and tighten it to the specified torque. Fit a new gasket then install the manifold, tightening its retaining nuts to the specified torque **(see illustrations)**.

**11** Lubricate the rubbers with a silicone-based spray to ease installation then ease the throttle body assembly in position. Ensure both throttle bodies are correctly seated in the

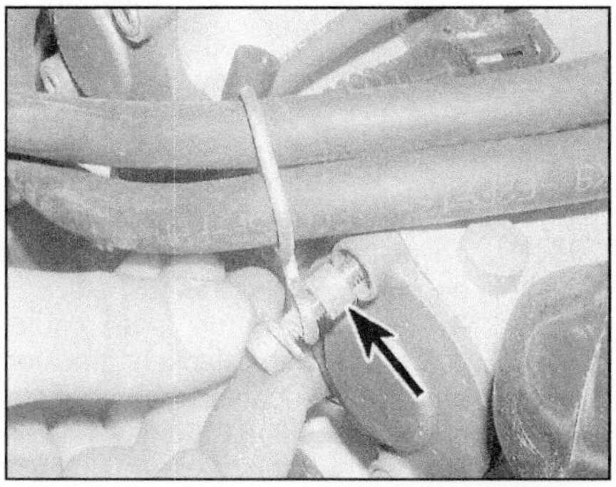

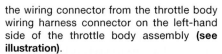

10.6a Unscrew the mounting bolt and washer and recover the spacer (arrowed) fitted between fuel hose guide and cylinder head

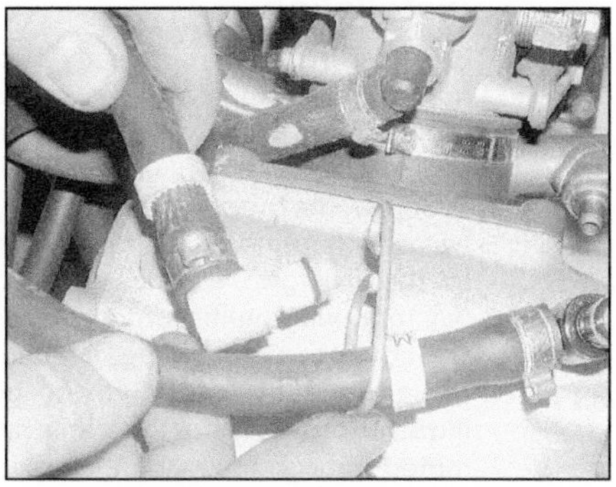

10.6b Free one of the hoses from the guide to enable the throttle body to be removed

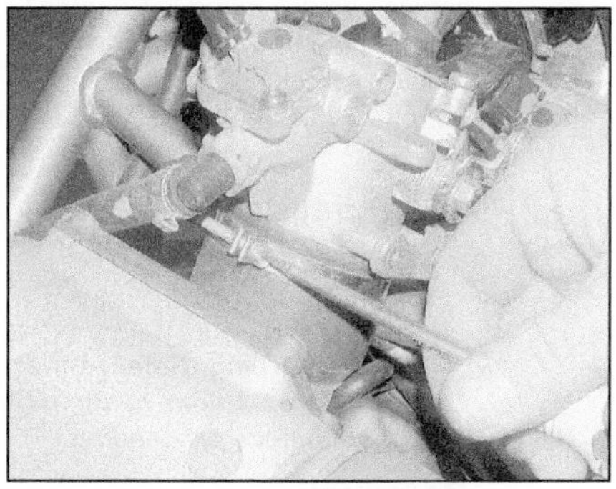

10.7a Slacken the intake rubber retaining clips . . .

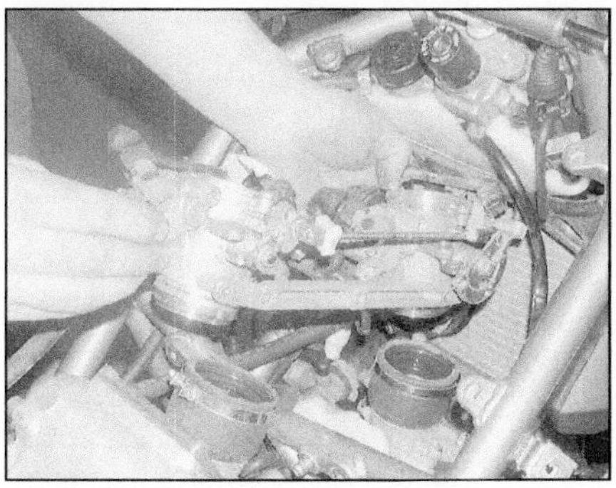

10.7b . . . then ease the throttle body assembly out of position

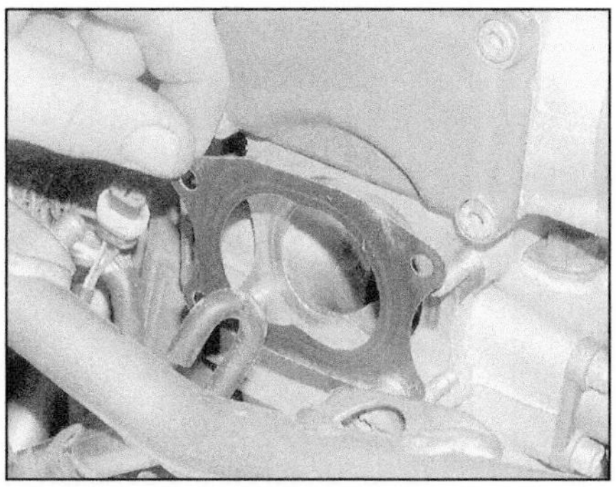

10.10a Fit a new gasket to the cylinder head . . .

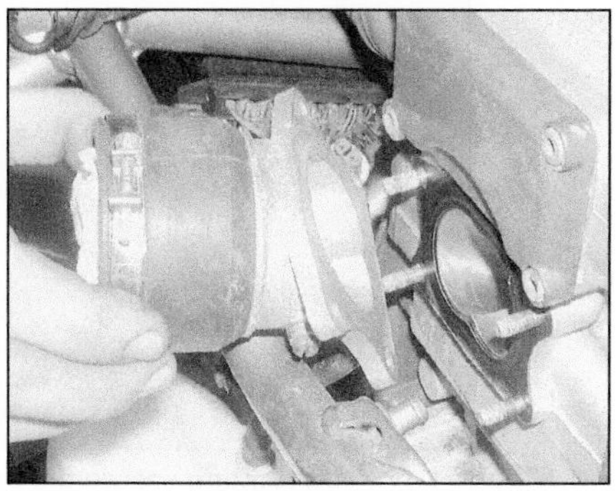

10.10b . . . then fit the intake manifold

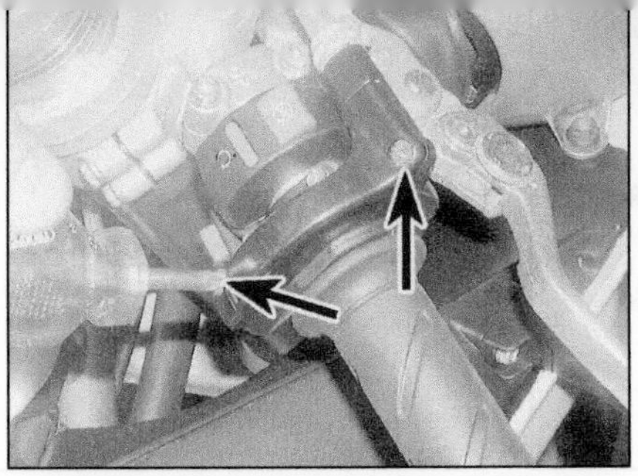

11.3 Undo the retaining screws (arrowed) and remove the cover from the twistgrip housing

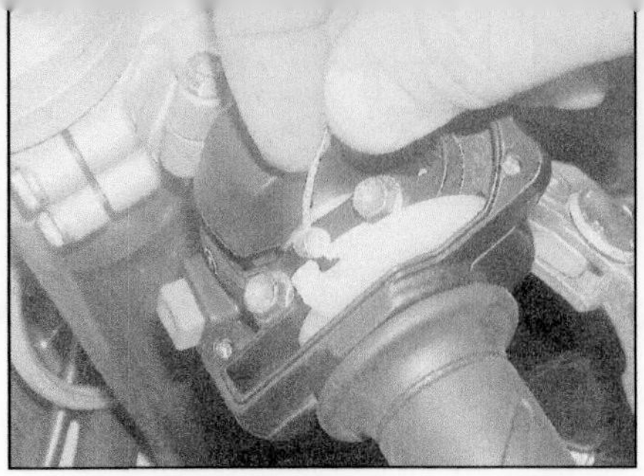

11.4a Free the inner cable from the twistgrip . . .

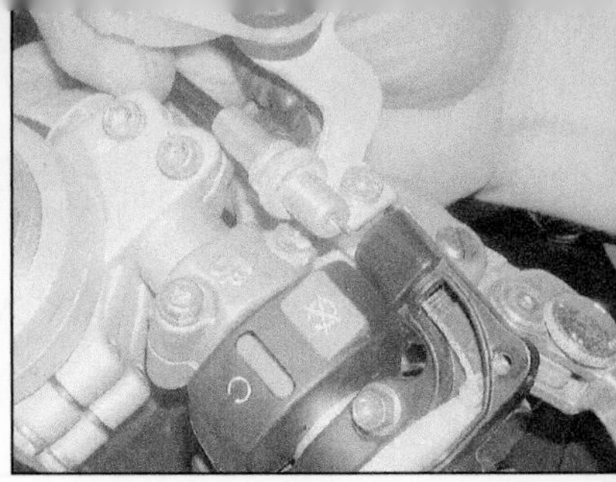

11.4b . . . then slacken the locknut and unscrew the cable adjuster from the housing

manifold rubbers then securely tighten the retaining clips.

12 Route the fuel hoses correctly around the frame then route both hoses through the guide. Position the spacer between the guide and vertical cylinder head then install the retaining bolt and washer, tightening it securely.

13 Screw the throttle cable adjuster fully into its bracket and connect the inner cable to the throttle linkage. Adjust the cable as described in Chapter 1.

14 Securely reconnect the wiring connector to the throttle body harness connector.

15 If a new throttle body assembly has been installed, check the throttle body synchronisation, idle speed and mixture settings as described in Chapter 1.

16 Install the airbox and the fuel tank (Sections 6 and 2).

17 Fit the fairing panels (see Chapter 8).

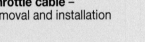

## 11 Throttle cable – removal and installation

**Warning: Refer to the precautions given in Section 1 before proceeding.**

### Removal

1 Remove the fairing right-hand lower panel (see Chapter 8) to gain access to the throttle body end of the cable.

2 Unhook the inner cable from the throttle body linkage then slacken the locknut and unscrew the lower adjuster from its mounting bracket **(see illustrations 10.5a and 10.5b)**.

3 Undo the retaining screws and remove the cover from the top of the throttle twistgrip housing **(see illustration)**.

4 Free the inner cable from the twistgrip then slacken the locknut and unscrew the cable upper adjuster from the twistgrip housing **(see illustrations)**.

5 Work along the cable, freeing it from the retaining clips and ties whilst noting its correct routing, and remove it from the bike.

### Installation

6 Route the cable correctly between the right-hand fork leg and the headstock and secure it in position with all the relevant clips and ties.

7 Screw the upper adjuster fully into the twistgrip housing then attach the inner cable to the twistgrip. Lubricate the cable and twistgrip with multi-purpose grease then fit the cover to the housing, seating the inner cable correctly in the cover guide **(see illustration)**. Ensure the cable is correctly routed through the guide then refit the cover retaining screws, tightening them securely.

8 Screw the lower adjuster fully into the bracket on the throttle body and connect the inner cable to the throttle linkage.

9 Adjust the cable as described in Chapter 1. Turn the handlebars back and forth to make sure the cable doesn't cause the steering to bind.

10 Start the engine and turn the handlebars back and forth to make sure the idle speed doesn't rise as the bars are turned. If it does, the cable is incorrectly routed and the problem must be sorted before the motorcycle is ridden.

11 On completion install the fairing panel (see Chapter 8).

## 12 Throttle twistgrip assembly – removal and installation

### Removal

1 Remove the end weight from the handlebar.

2 Undo the retaining screws and remove the cover from the top of the throttle twistgrip housing **(see illustration 11.3)**.

3 Free the throttle inner cable from the twistgrip then slacken the locknut and unscrew the cable upper adjuster from the housing **(see illustrations 11.4a and 11.4b)**.

4 Unscrew the two retaining bolts and remove the upper and lower halves of the twistgrip housing **(see illustrations)**. T

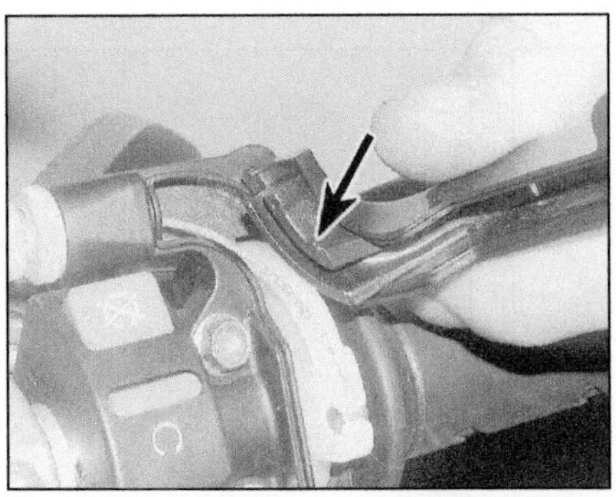

11.7 On refitting ensure the cable is correctly routed through the guide (arrowed) on the cover

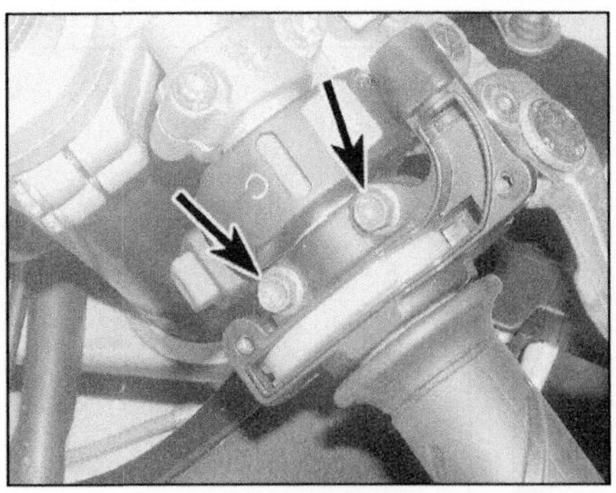

12.4a Unscrew the bolts (arrowed) . . .

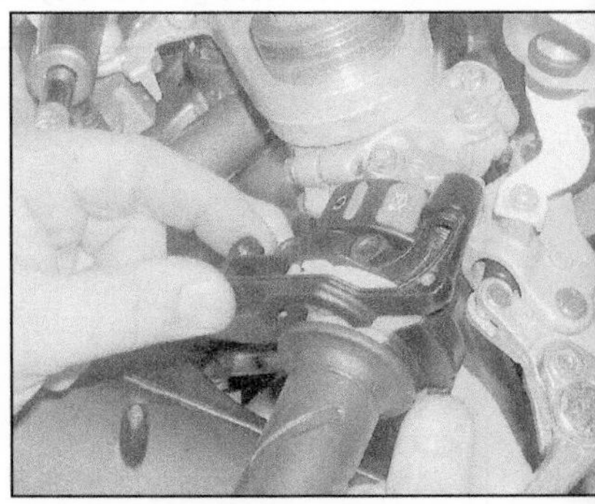

12.4b . . . and remove the upper and lower halves of the twistgrip housing . . .

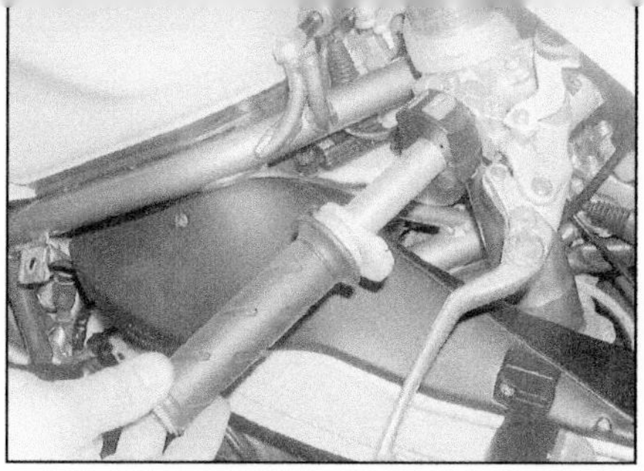

12.4c ... and slide the twistgrip off the handlebar

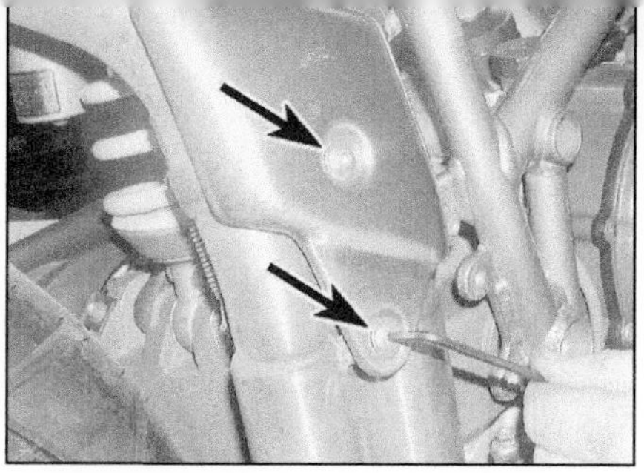

13.3 Undo the screws (arrowed) and remove the heatshield from the centre pipe

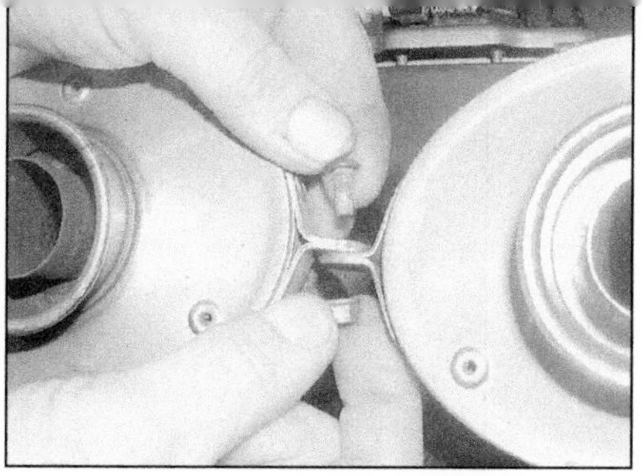

13.4 Unscrew the nut and bolt securing the rear of the silencers together

twistgrip can then be slid off the handlebar **(see illustration)**.

### Installation

**5** Lubricate the handlebar and twistgrip contact surfaces with multi-purpose grease then slide the twistgrip assembly onto the handlebar.

**6** Assemble the twistgrip housing halves around the twistgrip ensuring the locating peg in the lower half locates correctly in the handlebar hole. Ensure the twistgrip housing is correctly assembled then fit the retaining bolts, tightening them to the specified torque.

**7** Screw the cable upper adjuster fully into the twistgrip housing then attach the inner cable to the twistgrip. Lubricate the cable and twistgrip with multi-purpose grease then fit the cover to the housing, seating the inner cable correctly in the cover guide. Ensure the cable is correctly routed through the guide then refit the cover retaining screws, tightening them securely **(see illustration 11.7)**.

**8** Check the operation of the twistgrip then fit the end weight to the handlebar.

**9** Adjust the throttle cable as described in Chapter 1.

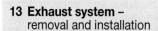

## 13 Exhaust system – removal and installation

***Warning: If the engine has been running the exhaust system will be very hot. Allow the system to cool before carrying out any work.***

### Silencers

#### Removal

**1** Unlock the seat cowling and pivot it forwards onto the fuel tank.

**2** Remove the rider's right-hand footrest bracket and (where fitted) both passenger footrest brackets (see Chapter 6).

**3** Slacken and remove the retaining screws, collars and washers securing the heatshield to the exhaust centre pipe assembly **(see illustration)**. Remove the heatshield and recover the insulating washers fitted between the shield and centre pipe.

**4** Slacken and remove the nut and bolt securing the brackets at the rear of the silencers together **(see illustration)**.

**5** Carefully unhook and remove the springs securing the silencers to the centre pipe assembly **(see illustration)**.

**6** Remove the bolt securing the silencer mounting brackets to the subframe. Recover the collar from each side of the brackets **(see illustration)**.

**7** Free the right-hand silencer from the centre pipe and remove it from the bike then remove the left-hand silencer **(see illustration)**.

**8** If necessary, unscrew the bolt and remove the mounting bracket and collars from the silencer mounting clamp **(see illustration)**. The mounting clamp and rubber can then be removed from the silencer. Inspect the mounting bracket and clamp rubbers for signs of damage or deterioration and, if necessary, renew them.

#### Installation

**9** Lubricate all the exhaust mounting bolts with a smear of molybdenum disulphide grease.

**10** Where necessary, fit the mounting rubber and clamp to the silencer. Fit the collars to the mounting bracket rubber then fit the bracket to the clamp and install the bolt.

**11** Ensure the silencer and centre pipe joints are clean and apply a thin smear of exhaust jointing paste to each joint.

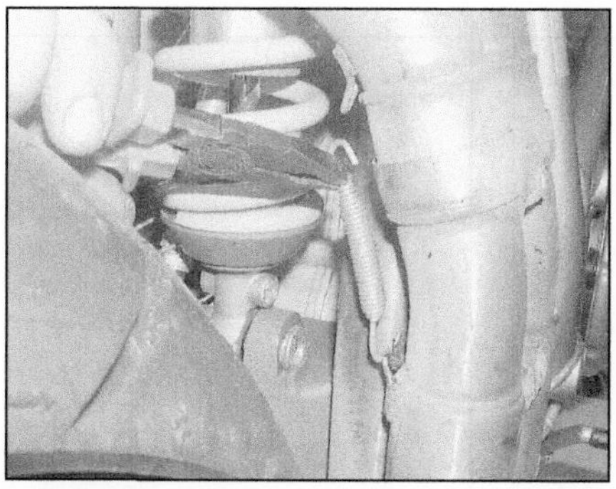

13.5 Unhook the springs securing each silencer to the centre pipe

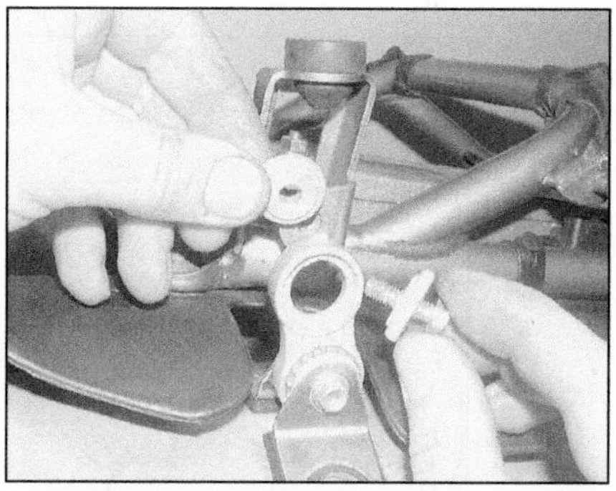

13.6 Unscrew the silencer mounting bolt and recover the collars from each side of the bracket

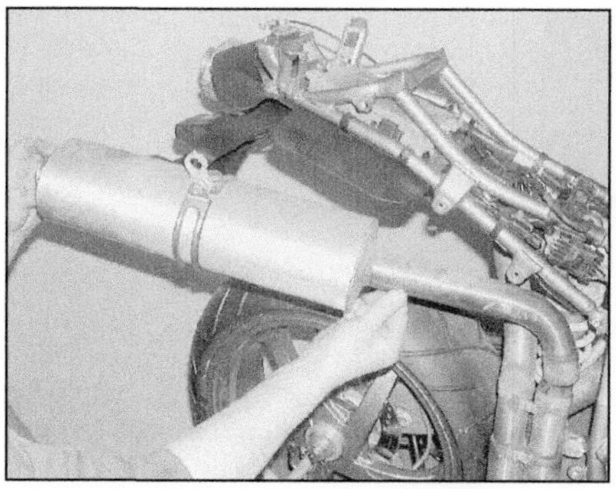

13.7 Free the silencer from the centre pipe and remove it from the bike

13.8 If necessary, undo the bolt and separate the silencer and mounting clamp components

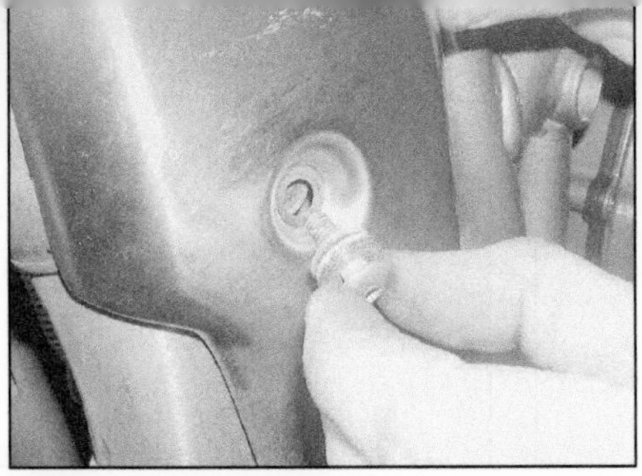

**13.17a Fit the collars and washers to the screws then fit the screws to heatshield . . .**

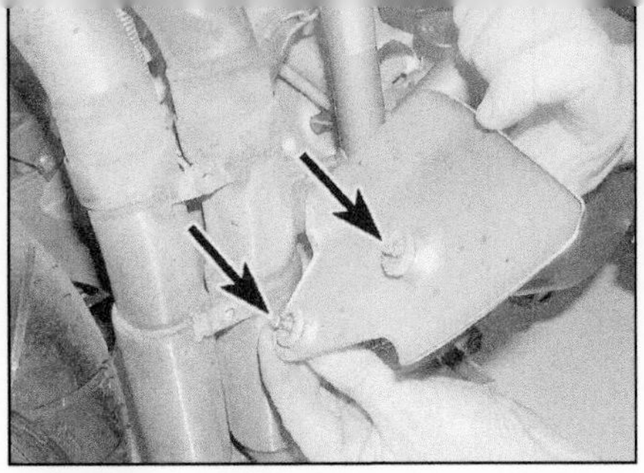

**13.17b . . . and position the insulating washers between the heatshield and centre pipe**

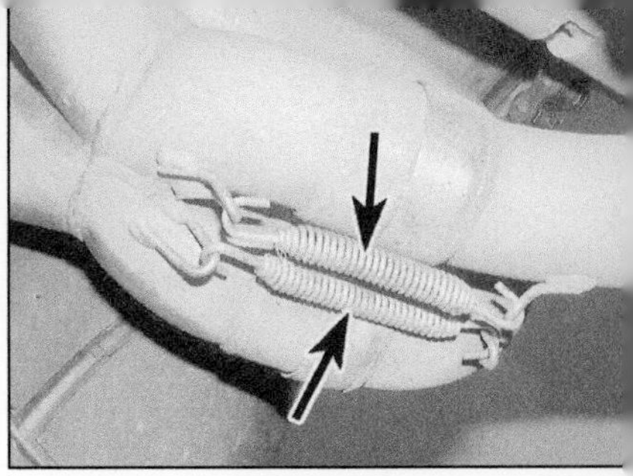

**13.20 Unhook the springs (arrowed) securing the centre pipe to the downpipe**

**12** Engage the left-hand silencer with the centre pipe and align its mounting bracket with the subframe. Position the collars on each side of the mounting bracket then screw in the bolt securing the bracket to the subframe.

**13** Fit the right-hand silencer in the same way.

**14** Secure both silencers to the centre pipe assembly with the springs.

**15** Align the brackets at the rear of the silencers and refit the retaining bolt and nut, tightening it to the specified torque.

**16** Adjust the position of the mounting clamps and rubbers on the silencers to relieve all strain from the mounting brackets, then tighten the mounting bracket bolts to the specified torque.

**17** Fit the collar and washers to each heatshield screw then fit the screws to the heatshield **(see illustration)**. Position the insulating washers between the heatshield and centre pipe then refit the heatshield, tightening the screws securely **(see illustration)**.

**18** Install the footrest bracket(s) (see Chapter 6) then lower the seat cowling and lock it in position.

## *Centre pipe assembly*

### Removal

**19** Remove the silencers (see Steps 1 to 8).

**20** Carefully unhook the springs securing th downpipes to the centre pipe **(se illustration)**.

**21** Unscrew the mounting nut and bo securing the centre pipe to the frame and i mounting bracket **(see illustrations)**.

**22** Slacken the bolt securing the pip mounting bracket to the engine then pivot th bracket clear of the pipe **(see illustration)**.

**23** Free the centre pipe from the downpipe and remove it from the bike **(see illustration** Recover the collars from the mountin bracket and frame lug mounting rubbers **(se illustration)**. Inspect the mounting rubbers f signs of damage or deterioration and, necessary, renew them.

### Installation

**24** Lubricate all the exhaust mounting bol with a smear of molybdenum disulphid grease.

**25** Ensure the mounting rubbers are correct fitted to the frame lug and bracket and pres in the collars.

**26** Ensure the centre pipe joints are clea and apply a thin smear of exhaust jointin paste to each joint.

**27** Engage the centre pipe with th downpipes and locate it correctly on th frame lug.

**28** Secure both downpipes to the centre pip assembly with the springs.

**29** Fit the bolts and nuts securing the cent

**13.21a Unscrew the nuts and bolts securing the centre pipe to the frame . . .**

**13.21b . . . and mounting bracket**

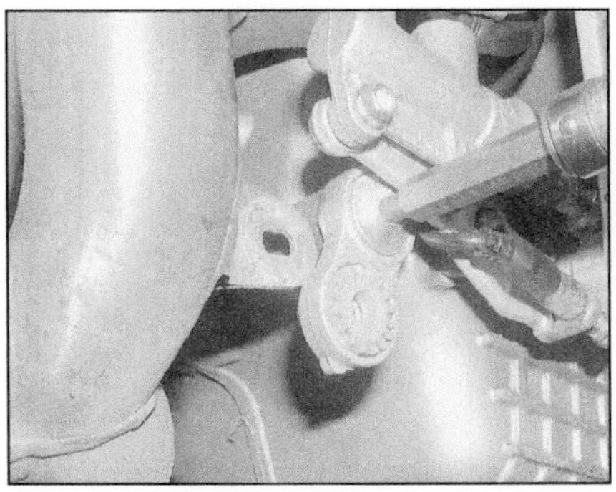

**13.22 Slacken the mounting bracket bolt and pivot the bracket clear of the centre pipe**

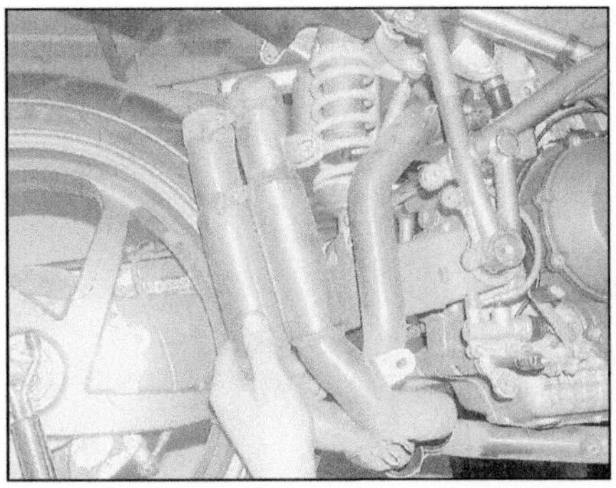

**13.23a Remove the centre pipe assembly from the bike . . .**

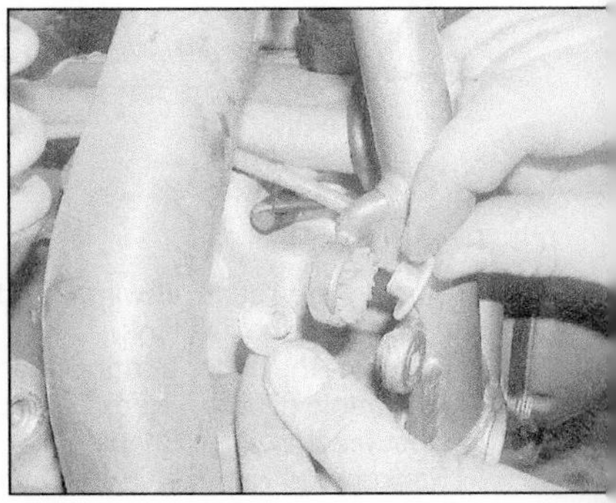

**13.23b . . . and recover the collars from the frame mounting**

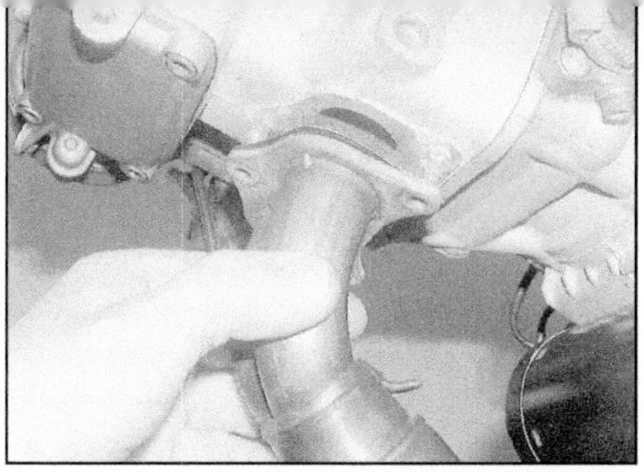

**13.38a Unscrew the retaining nuts and remove the exhaust manifold . . .**

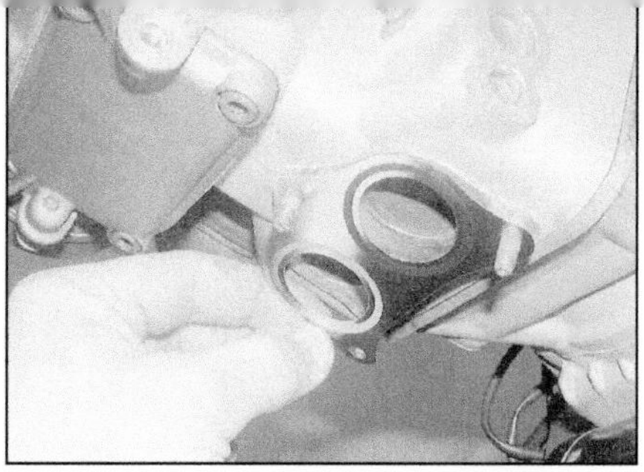

**13.38b . . . and gasket from the cylinder head**

pipe to the frame and mounting bracket. Ensure the centre pipe is correctly positioned then tightening its mounting bolts to the specified torque.

**30** Install the silencers (see Steps 9 to 18).

## *Downpipes*

### Removal

**31** Remove the silencers and centre pipe assembly as described above.

**32** To remove the rear downpipe, unhook the retaining spring then free the pipe from its manifold and manoeuvre it out of position.

**33** To remove the front downpipe, first remove the fairing lower panels (see Chapter 8). Unhook the retaining spring then free the pipe from its manifold and remove it from the bike.

### Installation

**34** Ensure the downpipe joints are clean and apply a thin smear of exhaust jointing paste to each joint.

**35** Manoeuvre the pipes into position and engage them with the exhaust manifolds.

**36** Install the centre pipe assembly and silencers (see above) then secure the downpipes to the manifolds with their springs. Refit the fairing panels.

## *Exhaust manifolds*

### Removal

**37** Remove the relevant downpipe (see above).

**38** Unscrew the retaining nuts and remove the exhaust manifold and gasket from the cylinder head **(see illustrations)**. Discard the gasket; a new one will be needed on installation. Renew any damaged studs.

### Installation

**39** Ensure the cylinder head and manifold mating surfaces are clean and dry and the manifold studs are securely fitted. If any stud its threads then refit it to the cylinder head and tighten to the specified torque.

**40** Fit a new gasket then install the manifold and tighten its retaining nuts to the specified torque.

**41** Install the downpipe, centre pipe assembly and silencers (see above).

## 14 Evaporative emission control (EVAP) system – California models

**1** On all California models, an evaporative emission control system is fitted to prevent the escape of fuel vapours into the atmosphere. The fuel tank is sealed and the tank filler cap has a one-way valve which allows air into the tank as the volume of fuel decreases, but prevents any fuel vapour from escaping.

**2** When the engine is stopped, fuel vapour from the tank is allowed to flow into a charcoal canister where it is absorbed and stored whilst the motorcycle is standing. Depending on the model, the canister is either located between the throttle bodies or mounted to the battery tray on the right-hand side of the frame.

**3** When the engine is started, intake manifold depression draws the stored vapours into the inlet tracts to be burned during the normal combustion process. The flow of the fuel vapours into the intake manifolds is controlled by restrictor(s) in the hose(s).

**4** The system is not adjustable and can be tested only by a Ducati dealer.

# Chapter 5
# Ignition system

## Contents



## Degrees of difficulty

| | | | | |
|---|---|---|---|---|
| **Easy,** suitable for novice with little experience | **Fairly easy,** suitable for beginner with some experience | **Fairly difficult,** suitable for competent DIY mechanic | **Difficult,** suitable for experienced DIY mechanic | **Very difficult,** suitable for expert DIY or professional |

## Specifications

### General information

| | |
|---|---|
| Cylinder identification | Horizontal (front), vertical (rear) |
| Spark plug type and electrode gap | see Chapter 1 |
| Ignition HT coils | |
| Primary winding resistance | 495 to 606 ohms at 20°C |
| Secondary winding resistance | 6.66 to 8.14 K-ohms at 20°C |
| Ignition timing | Controlled by engine management ECU – see Chapter 4 |

### Torque settings

| | |
|---|---|
| Ignition HT coil bracket mounting bolts | 10 Nm |

## 1 General information

The ignition system is integrated with the fuel injection system to form a combined engine management system which is operated by the electronic control unit (ECU) (see Chapter 4 for further information). The ECU uses its inputs from the various sensors to calculate the required ignition advance setting and ignition HT coil charging time. Note that there is no provision for checking or adjusting the ignition timing on these models.

On 916 SP, SPS and early Strada models and all 996 SPS models (fitted with a P8 engine management system), the only components which solely operate the ignition side of the system are the two ignition coils and their power modules (one for each cylinder).

On all other models (fitted with a 1.6M engine management system), the only components which solely operate the ignition side of the system are the two separate ignition HT coils, one for each cylinder. The power modules for the ignition coils are integrated into the engine management system ECU.

On later (2000 model year on) models, a safety interlock circuit will cut the ignition if the sidestand is put down whilst the engine is running. It also prevents the engine from being started when the sidestand is down.

## 2 Ignition system – check

***Warning: The energy levels in electronic systems can be very high. On no account should the ignition be switched on whilst the plugs or plug caps are being held. Shocks from the HT circuit can be most unpleasant. Secondly, it is vital that the engine is not turned over or run with any of the plug caps removed, and that the plugs are soundly earthed (grounded) when the system is checked for sparking. The ignition system components can be seriously damaged if the HT circuit becomes isolated.***

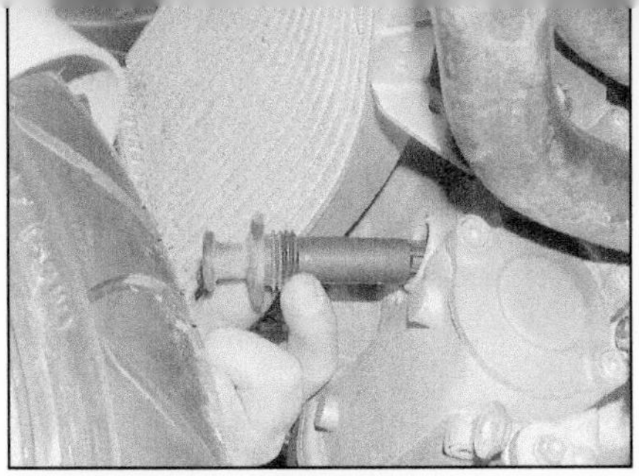

**2.2 Disconnecting the horizontal cylinder plug cap**

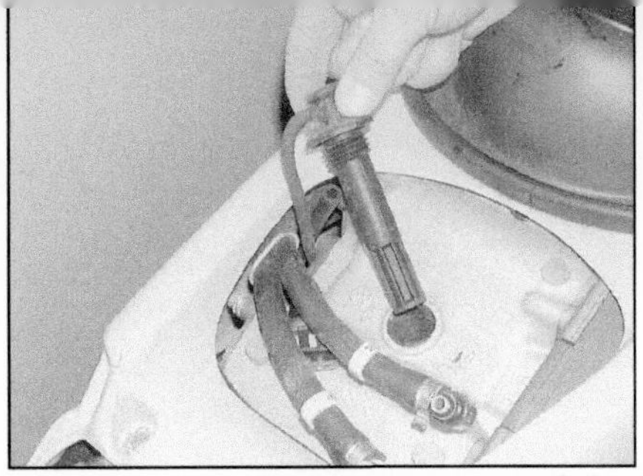

**2.3 Disconnecting the vertical cylinder plug cap**

**1** As no means of adjustment is available, any failure of the system can be traced to failure of a system component or a simple wiring fault. Of the two possibilities, the latter is by far the most likely. In the event of failure, check the system in a logical fashion, as described below.

**2** To gain access to the horizontal cylinder spark plug, remove the fairing lower and inner panels (see Chapter 8) **(see illustration)**.

**3** To gain access to the vertical cylinder spark plug, remove the fuel tank (see Chapter 4) **(see illustration)**.

**4** Disconnect the plug caps from the spark plugs. Connect each cap to a spare spark plug and lay each plug on the engine with its threads contacting the engine. If necessary, hold each spark plug with an insulated tool.

> ***Warning: Do not remove any of the spark plugs from the engine to perform this check – atomised fuel being pumped out of the open spark plug hole could ignite, causing severe injury!***

**5** Having observed the above precautions, check that the kill switch is in the RUN position and the transmission is in neutral. On later (2000 models year on) models it will also be necessary to support the bike on an auxiliary stand so the sidestand can be raised.

**6** Turn the ignition switch ON and turn the engine over on the starter motor. If the system is in good condition a regular, fat blue spark should be evident at each plug electrode. If the spark appears thin or yellowish, or is non-existent, further investigation will be necessary. Before proceeding further, turn the ignition OFF and remove the key as a safety measure.

**7** The ignition system must be able to produce a spark which is capable of jumping a particular size gap. Ducati do not provide a specification, but a healthy system should produce a spark capable of jumping at least 6 mm. A simple testing tool can be made to test the minimum gap across which the spark will jump (see **Tool Tip**) or alternatively it is possible to buy an ignition spark gap tester tool and some of these tools are adjustable to alter the spark gap.

**8** Connect the plug cap of the vertical cylinder coil to the protruding electrode on the test tool, and clip the tool to a good earth (ground) on the engine or frame. Turn the ignition switch ON and turn the engine over on the starter motor. If the system is in good condition a regular, fat blue spark should be seen to jump the gap between the nail ends. Repeat the test for the horizontal cylinder coil. If the test results are good the entire ignition system can be considered good. If the spark appears thin or yellowish, or is non-existent, further investigation is required.

**9** Ignition faults can be divided into two categories, namely those where the ignition system has failed completely, and those which are due to a partial failure. The likely faults are listed below, starting with the most probable source of failure. Work through the list systematically, referring to the subsequent sections for full details of the necessary checks and tests. **Note:** *Before checking the following items ensure that the battery is fully charged and that all fuses are in good condition.*

*a) Loose, corroded or damaged wiring connections, broken or shorted wiring between any of the component parts of the ignition system (see Chapter 9).*
*b) Faulty HT lead or spark plug cap, faulty spark plug, dirty, worn or corroded plug electrodes.*
*c) Faulty ignition (main) switch or engine kil switch (see Chapter 9).*
*d) Faulty sidestand switch – later (2000 model year on) models (see Chapter 9).*
*e) Faulty ignition HT coil(s).*
*f) Faulty ignition power module (P8 engine management system).*
*g) Faulty engine management system ECU or sensor (see Chapter 4).*

**TOOL TiP**

***A simple spark gap testing tool can be made from a block of wood, a large alligator clip and two nails, one of which is fashioned so that a spark plug cap or bare HT lead end can be connected to its end. Make sure the gap between the two nail ends is the same as specified.***

**10** If the above checks don't reveal the cau of the problem, have the ignition syste tested by a Ducati dealer.

**11** On completion, securely reconnect t plug caps to the plugs then install the fu tank and fairing panels (see Chapters and 8).

## 3 Ignition HT coils – check, removal and installation

### Check

**1** In order to determine conclusively that t ignition coils are defective they should b tested by a Ducati dealer. However, the co can be checked visually (for cracks and oth damage) and the primary and secondary c resistances can be measured with a ohmmeter. If the coils are undamaged, and the resistances are as specified, they a probably capable of proper operation.

**2** To gain access to the coils, HT leads a plug caps remove the fuel tank and airb (see Chapter 4).

**3** Unplug the primary circuit wiring connect and the spark plug HT lead from the coil a check the coil as follows. If necessar remove the coil to improve access.

**4** To check the primary winding resistanc set the ohmmeter to the ohms x 1 scale a connect one ohmmeter lead to one of t primary terminals and the other lead to t other primary terminal **(see illustratio** Compare the measured resistance to t value listed in this Chapter's Specifications.

**5** To check the secondary windi resistance, set the ohmmeter to t

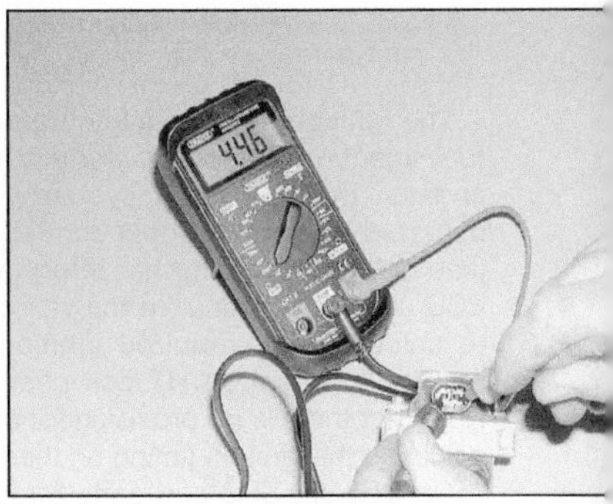

**3.4 Checking ignition HT coil primary winding resistance**

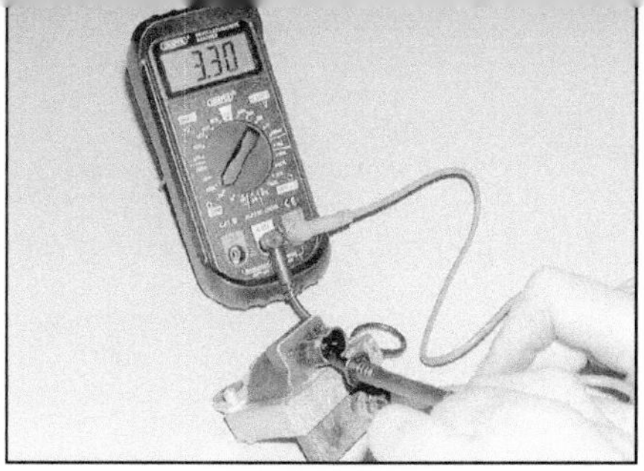

3.5 Checking ignition HT coil secondary winding resistance

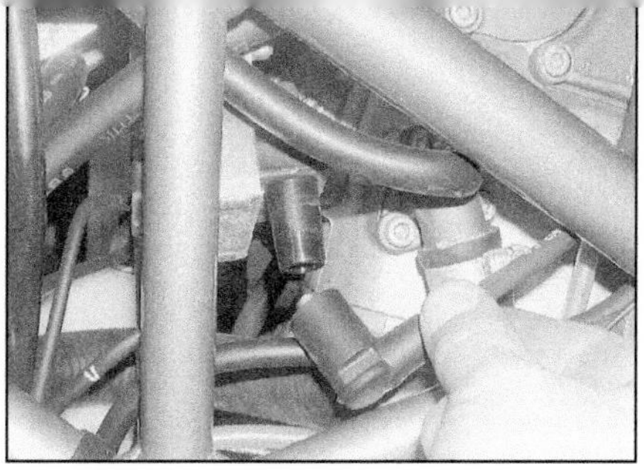

3.8a Disconnect the HT lead . . .

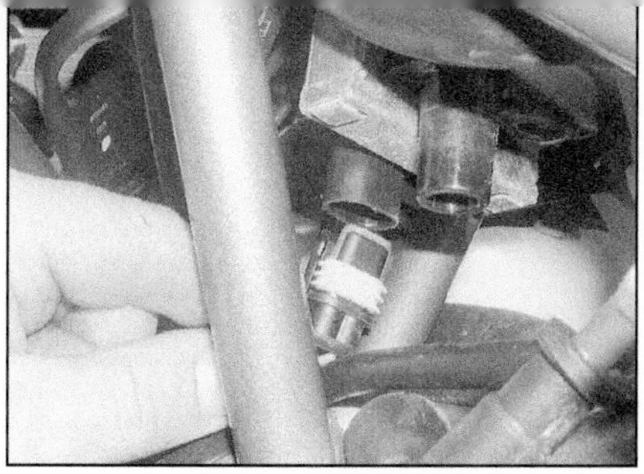

3.8b . . . and wiring connector . . .

K ohms scale. Connect one ohmmeter lead to one of the primary terminals and the other lead to the HT lead terminal of the coil **(see illustration)**. Compare the measured resistance to the value listed in this Chapter's Specifications.

**6** If the resistances are not as specified, the coil is probably defective. Have your findings confirmed by a Ducati dealer before condemning the coil.

### Removal

**Note:** *The spark plug cap/HT lead assembly is available separately and can be renewed without removing the coil. The HT lead is a push-fit in the coil terminal. Do not try and separate the plug cap from the HT lead.*

**7** To gain access to the coils, remove the fuel tank and airbox (see Chapter 4).

**8** Disconnect the primary circuit wiring connector and the spark plug HT lead from the coil **(see illustrations)**.

**9** Undo the bolt and washer then free the coil mounting bracket from its locating peg and remove it from the frame, taking care not to lose the collar from the mounting rubber **(see illustrations)**. If necessary, undo the screws and separate the coil and bracket. Inspect the bracket mounting rubbers for signs of damage and deterioration and, if necessary, renew them.

### Installation

**10** Assemble the coil and bracket, tightening the screws securely.

**11** Ensure the mounting rubbers are correctly fitted then insert the collar into the rear of the mounting bolt rubber **(see illustration)**. Lubricate the peg mounting rubber with a silicone-based spray lubricant, to ease installation, then install the coil seating it correctly on the locating peg. Refit the coil mounting bolt and washer and tighten to the specified torque.

**12** Securely reconnect the spark plug HT lead and primary wiring connector to the coil.

**13** Install the airbox and fuel tank (see Chapter 4).

## 4 Ignition power modules (P8 system) – check, removal and installation

### Check

**1** The ignition power modules (one for each coil) are delicate and expensive components requiring the use of specialist equipment for testing. If a power module is suspected of being faulty, the best way to determine this is to substitute it with another module which is known to be functioning correctly. Both modules are identical so if only one is faulty, they can easily be checked by swapping them over. If this transfers the problem to the other cylinder then the module is confirmed faulty.

### Removal

**2** Unlock the seat cowling, raise it and rest it on the fuel tank. The ignition power modules are mounted on each side of the engine management ECU.

**3** Ensure the ignition is switched off, then remove the bolt securing the relevant power module bracket to the side of the engine management ECU. Disconnect its wiring connector and remove the power module. If necessary, undo the retaining screws and washers and separate the module and bracket.

### Installation

**4** Ensure the power module and bracket mating surfaces are clean and dry. Assemble the module and bracket and securely refit the retaining screws and washers. Do not overtighten the screws.

**5** Ensure the ignition is switched off, then reconnect the wiring connector to the power module.

**6** Locate the module bracket on the side of the ECU and tighten its mounting bolt securely.

**7** Lower the seat cowling back down and lock it in position.

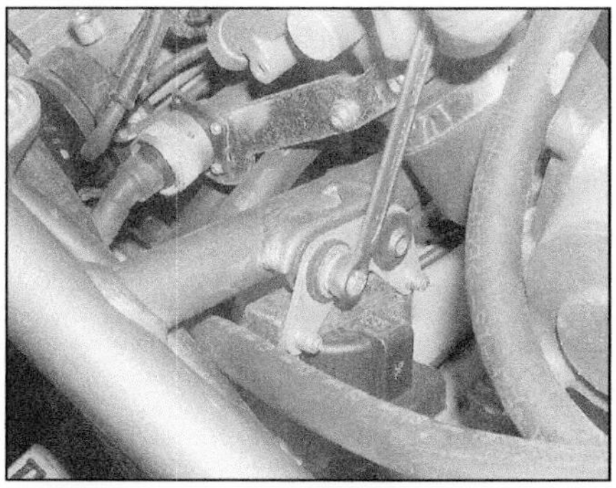

3.9a . . . then slacken and remove the retaining bolt and washer . . .

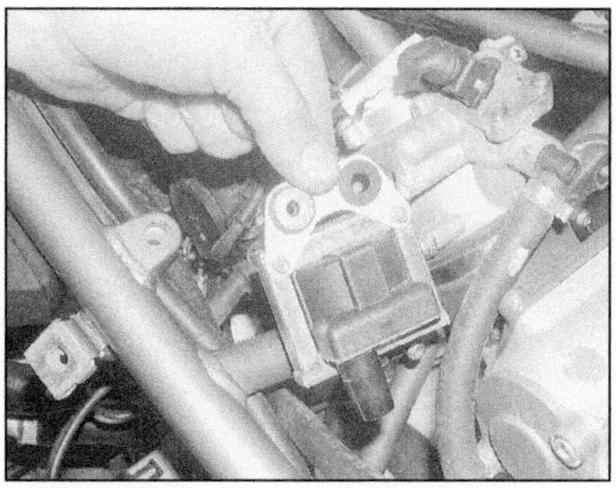

3.9b . . . and remove the ignition HT coil complete with mounting bracket

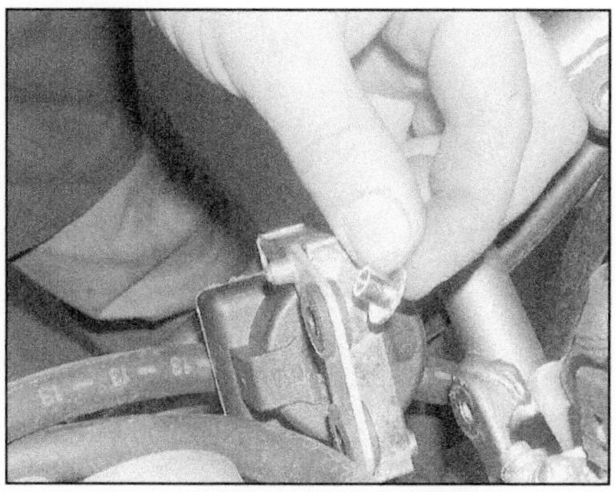

3.11 Ensure the collar is fitted to the rear of the mounting rubber

# Chapter 6
# Frame, suspension and final drive

## Contents



## Degrees of difficulty

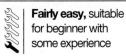

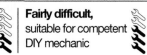

| | | | | |
|---|---|---|---|---|
| **Easy,** suitable for novice with little experience | **Fairly easy,** suitable for beginner with some experience | **Fairly difficult,** suitable for competent DIY mechanic | **Difficult,** suitable for experienced DIY mechanic | **Very difficult,** suitable for expert DIY or professional |

## Specifications

### Front forks (Showa)

***Note:*** *This information is only applicable to Showa front forks. For information on the Ohlins front forks, refer to your Ducati dealer or an Ohlins suspension specialist.*

| | |
|---|---|
| Fork inner tube diameter | 43 mm |
| Fork travel | 127 mm |
| Fork oil type | Shell advance fork 7.5 or Showa SS8 |
| Fork oil capacity | |
| 748 models | |
| SPS models | 492 ± 2.5 cc |
| All other models | |
| Early (pre 2000 model year) models | 480 cc |
| Later (2000-on model year) models | 492 ± 2.5 cc |
| 916 models | |
| SPS models | 492 ± 2.5 cc |
| All other models | 480 cc |
| 996 models | 492 ± 2.5 cc |

| | |
|---|---|
| Fork oil level* | |
| 748 models | |
| SPS models | 132 mm |
| All other models | |
| Early (pre 2000 model year) models | 135 mm |
| Later (2000-on model year) models | 132 mm |
| 916 models | |
| SPS models | 132 mm |
| All other models | 135 mm |
| 996 models | 132 mm |
| Fork spring minimum free length | 270 mm |
| Fork inner tube runout limit | 0.1 mm |

*Oil level is measured from the top of the outer tube with the fork spring and spacers removed, the leg fully compressed and the damper rod fully inserted.*

### Rear suspension

| | |
|---|---|
| Shock absorber stroke | 71 mm |
| Rear wheel travel | 130 mm |

### Chassis geometry

| | |
|---|---|
| Steering head angle (see Section 14) | |
| Models with an adjustable steering head | |
| 'Road' position | 24° 30' |
| 'Race' position | 23° 30' |
| Models with a fixed steering head | 24° 30' |
| Trail | |
| Models with an adjustable steering head | |
| 'Road' position | 97 mm |
| 'Race' position | 91 mm |
| Models with a fixed steering head | 97 mm |

### Final drive

| | |
|---|---|
| Chain type | |
| 748 models | 520 VL4 (94 links) |
| 916 and 996 models | 525 HV (94 links) |
| Final drive ratio (sprocket sizes) | |
| 748 models | |
| SP and SPS models | 2.64:1 (14 tooth front, 37 tooth rear) |
| All other models | 2.71:1 (14 tooth front, 38 tooth rear) |
| 916 models | |
| SP models | 2.57:1 (14 tooth front, 36 tooth rear) |
| All other models | 2.40:1 (15 tooth front, 36 tooth rear) |
| 996 models | 2.40:1 (15 tooth front, 36 tooth rear) |

### Torque settings

| | |
|---|---|
| Bottom yoke fork clamp bolt | 14 Nm |
| Chainguard | |
| Mounting screws | 8 Nm |
| Brake hose guide screws | 5 Nm |
| Footrest bracket bolts | |
| Mounting bolts | 31 Nm |
| Heel plate bolts | |
| Rider's footrest bracket | 10 Nm |
| Passenger's footrest bracket | 8 Nm |
| Fork damper assembly bolt | 35 Nm |
| Fork top cap | |
| Top cap to damper rod | 35 Nm |
| Top cap to fork tube | 35 Nm |
| Front sprocket retaining plate bolts | 6 Nm |
| Gearchange lever | |
| Clamp bolt | 10 Nm |
| Pivot bolt | 23 Nm |
| Handlebar clamp bolts | 10 Nm |
| Master cylinder mounting clamp bolts | 9 Nm |
| Rear suspension shock absorber, rocker arm and tie rod pivot bolts | 42 Nm |
| Rear sprocket coupling nut | 156 Nm |
| Rear sprocket cush drive bush nut | 48 Nm |

| | |
|---|---|
| Sidestand | |
| Pivot bolt nut | 26 Nm |
| Bracket mounting bolts | 43 Nm |
| Steering damper | |
| Clamp bolt | 8 Nm |
| Damper-to-frame bolt | |
| Standard damper | 12 Nm |
| Ohlins damper | 8 Nm |
| Mounting clamp bolt | 10 Nm |
| Steering head adjuster tube | |
| Detent screw | 19 Nm |
| Clamp bolts | 22 Nm |
| Steering stem nut | |
| Stage 1 | Tighten to 20 Nm |
| Stage 2 | Slacken by 30° |
| Steering stem nut clamp bolt | 20 to 24 Nm |
| Swingarm | |
| Pivot shaft bolt | 73 Nm |
| Drive chain slider screws | 10 Nm |
| Caliper bracket pin | 33 Nm |
| Throttle twistgrip housing bolts | 9 Nm |
| Top yoke clamp bolt | 23 Nm |

## 1 General information

All models use a trellis-type frame, manufactured from steel tubing, which uses the engine as a stressed member. On most models, with the exception of some later 748 models, the steering head angle can be adjusted to alter the steering and handling characteristics of the motorcycle (see Section 14).

Front suspension is by a pair of upside-down oil-damped telescopic forks which have a conventional damper system and are adjustable for spring pre-load and compression and rebound damping.

At the rear, a single-sided alloy swingarm acts on a single shock absorber which is linked to the frame by an adjustable rear suspension linkage. The swingarm pivot bolt passes through the frame and the rear of the engine crankcase. The shock absorber is adjustable for spring pre-load and compression and rebound damping. The suspension linkage is adjustable to compensate for changes in ride height, should the final drive ratio be changed (see Section 14).

The drive to the rear wheel is by chain.

## 2 Frame – inspection and repair

**1** The frame should not require attention unless accident damage has occurred. In most cases, frame renewal is the only satisfactory remedy for such damage. A few frame specialists have the jigs and other equipment necessary for straightening the frame to the required standard of accuracy, but even then there is no simple way of assessing to what extent the frame may have been over-stressed.

**2** After the machine has accumulated a lot of miles, the frame should be examined closely for signs of cracking or splitting at the welded joints. Loose engine mounting bolts can cause ovaling or fracturing of the mounting tabs. Minor damage can often be repaired by specialist welding, depending on the extent and nature of the damage.

**3** Remember that a frame which is out of alignment will cause handling problems. If misalignment is suspected as the result of an accident, it will be necessary to strip the machine completely so the frame can be thoroughly checked.

## 3 Footrests and brackets – removal and installation

### *Rider's footrest*

**1** Remove the retaining clip from the footrest pivot pin, then withdraw the pivot pin and remove the footrest, noting the correct fitting of the return spring.

**2** Installation is the reverse of removal, ensuring the return spring is correctly fitted.

### *Passenger's footrests*

**3** Remove the retaining clip from the footrest pivot pin.

**4** Withdraw the pivot pin and carefully remove the footrest from the bracket, complete with the detent plates and balls (on each side of the footrest) and the detent spring.

**5** Installation is the reverse of removal ensuring the detent plates, balls and spring are all correctly positioned. Check the detent mechanism functions correctly then secure the pivot pin in position with the retaining clip.

### *Rider's right-hand footrest bracket assembly*

**6** Unscrew the two bolts and remove the footrest bracket assembly from the frame **(see illustration)**. If necessary, undo the bolts and remove the heel plate from the bracket noting the spacers fitted between the two.

**7** Remove all traces of original locking compound and apply a drop of fresh locking compound to all removed bolts.

**8** Fit the bracket to the frame and tighten its bolts to the specified torque. Where necessary, offer up the heel plate to the bracket, position the spacers between the two, and tighten the retaining bolts to the specified torque.

### *Rider's left-hand footrest bracket assembly*

**9** Note the correct fitted location of the

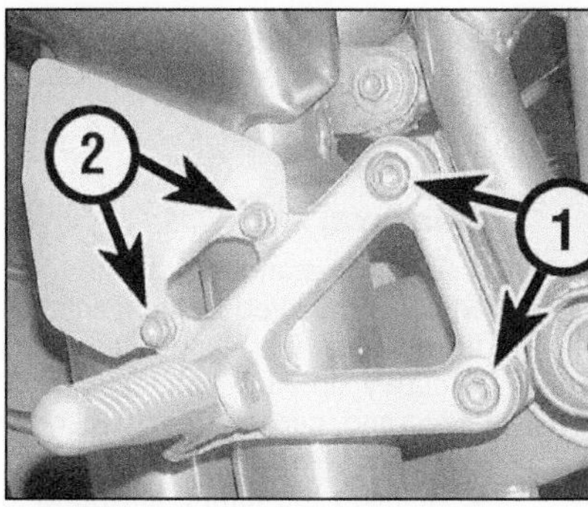


**3.6 Rider's footrest bracket bolts (1) and heel plate bolts (2)**

marks if necessary), then unscrew the clamp bolt and free the gearchange lever from the engine **(see illustration)**.

**10** Unscrew the two bolts securing the footrest bracket to the frame and remove the assembly from the bike. If necessary, undo the bolts and remove the heel plate from the bracket.

**11** If necessary, unscrew the pivot bolt and remove the gearchange lever assembly from the bracket. Recover the spacer fitted between the lever and bracket and the sealing rings (where fitted) from the lever bush. Renew the lever bush if it shows signs of wear or damage.

**12** Remove all traces of original locking compound and apply a drop of fresh locking compound to all removed bolts.

**13** Fit the bracket to the frame and tighten its bolts to the specified torque. Where necessary, fit the heel plate and tighten its bolts to the specified torque.

**14** If the gearchange lever was removed, position the sealing rings (where fitted) on each side of the lever bush then offer up the lever to the bracket. Ensure the spacer is fitted between the lever and bracket then fit the pivot bolt, tightening it to the specified torque.

**15** Engage the gearchange lever splines with those of the shaft so the gearchange lever is correctly positioned then refit the clamp bolt, tightening it to the specified torque.

### Passenger footrest bracket assembly

**16** Raise the seat cowling assembly (see Chapter 8).

**17** Unscrew the two mounting bolts and remove the footrest bracket from the rear subframe **(see illustration)**.

**18** Remove all traces of original locking compound and apply a drop of fresh locking compound to the bracket bolts.

**19** Fit the bracket to the subframe and tighten its bolts to the specified torque.

**20** Lower the seat cowling back down and lock it in position.

## 4 Sidestand – removal and installation

### Removal

**1** The sidestand is attached to a bracket which is mounted to the crankcase. A spring anchored to the stand ensures that it is held securely in the retracted position. The sidestand can be removed on its own or complete with its mounting bracket.

**2** Remove the fairing left-hand lower panel (see Chapter 8).

**3** Support the bike on an auxiliary stand.

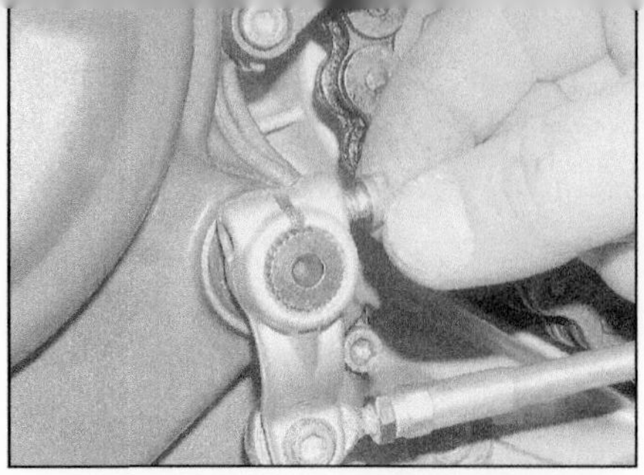

**3.9 Slacken and remove the clamp bolt and free the gearchange lever from the engine**

**4** On later models, undo the screw and free the sidestand switch from the stand pivot **(see illustration)**.

**5** To remove the stand on its own, carefully unhook the stand spring and remove it complete with its connecting plate (note which way around the plate is fitted) and cover. Unscrew the nut from the sidestand pivot bolt, then remove the pivot bolt and stand from the mounting bracket.

**6** To remove the stand and bracket, unscrew the two bolts securing the stand bracket to the crankcase, then remove the assembly as a unit.

### Installation

**7** To refit the stand and bracket assembly, remove all traces of original locking compound and apply fresh locking compound to the stand mounting bolts. Fit the stand bracket to the crankcase and tighten its mounting bolts to the specified torque.

**8** To refit the stand, apply multi-purpose grease to the pivot bolt shank then fit the sidestand to its bracket. Fit the pivot bolt then fit the nut to the bolt and tighten it to the specified torque. Ensure the spring (complete with cover) and connecting plate are correctly assembled, then locate the connecting plate on the bracket pin and carefully hook the spring over the pin on the stand.

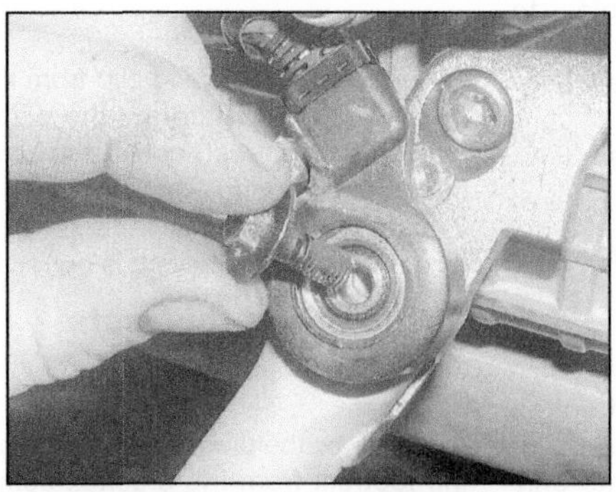

**4.4 On later models unscrew the screw and free the switch from the sidestand pivot**

**3.17 Passenger footrest bracket bolts (arrowed)**

**9** On later models remove the original locki compound from the threads of the sidesta switch screw and apply fresh locki compound to the screw. Locate the switch the sidestand, aligning its pin with the hole the stand and its cutout with the lug on stand bracket **(see illustration)**. Install t switch retaining screw and tighten it secure Check the operation of the sidestand swi (see Chapter 1).

**10** On all models, check that the spring ho the stand securely up when not in us then install the fairing panel (see Cha ter 8) – an accident is almost certain to oc if the stand extends while the machine is motion.

## 5 Handlebars – removal and installation

### Right-hand handlebar

#### Removal

**1** Remove the end weight from the handleb

**2** Trace the wiring back from the brake li switch, fitted to the base of the mas cylinder, and disconnect it at the wiri connector(s).

**3** Slacken and remove the throttle twistg housing bolts (not the cover screws) a

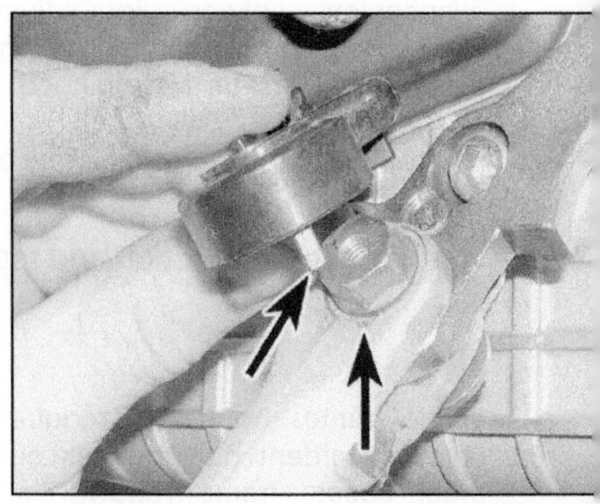

**4.9 Ensure the switch pin engages the sidestand hole (arrowed) on installatio**

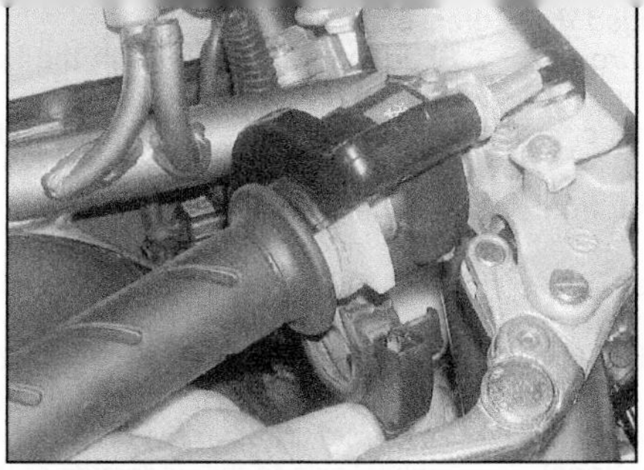
5.3 Unscrew the bolts and remove the lower half of the twistgrip housing

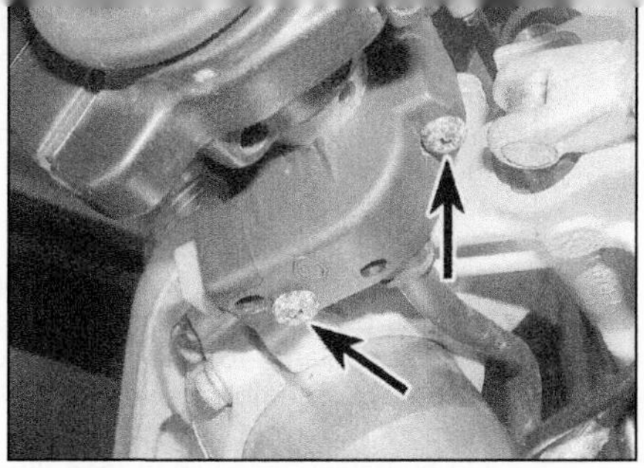
5.4a Remove the retaining screws (arrowed) . . .

5.4b . . . and free the switch assembly from the handlebar

remove the lower half of the housing **(see illustration)**.

**4** Unscrew the two handlebar switch screws then free the switch from the handlebar **(see illustrations)**.

**5** Unscrew the two master cylinder assembly clamp bolts and position the assembly clear of the handlebar, making sure no strain is placed on the hydraulic hose. Keep the fluid reservoir upright to prevent possible fluid leakage.

**6** Slacken and remove the clamp bolt(s) and free the handlebar mounting clamp from the fork tube. Slide off the throttle twistgrip and remove the handlebar assembly from the bike.

**7** If necessary, slacken the clamp bolts and separate the handlebar and mounting clamp.

### Installation

**8** If the handlebar was separated from the mounting clamp, remove the clamp bolts, clean them, lubricate them with molybdenum disulphide grease then refit them to the mounting clamp. Insert the handlebar, aligning it correctly with the clamp, and tighten its clamp bolts evenly and progressively to the specified torque.

**9** Clean the mounting clamp bolt(s) and lubricate it/them with molybdenum disulphide grease.

**10** Lubricate the contact surfaces of the throttle twistgrip and handlebar with a smear of multi-purpose grease then slide the twistgrip onto the handlebar.

**11** Assemble the handlebar clamp around the fork leg and install the clamp bolt(s). Slide the handlebar clamp up the fork leg and seat its locating pin correctly in the hole in the base of the top yoke. Hold the handlebar clamp firmly against the top yoke then tighten its clamp bolt(s) to the specified torque.

**12** Fit the lower half of the twistgrip housing, seating its locating peg correctly in the handlebar hole, then refit the housing bolts, tightening them to the specified torque.

**13** Assemble the switch on the handlebar, aligning its lug with the handlebar hole. Refit the retaining screws and tighten them securely, tightening the front screw first.

**14** Locate the master cylinder on the handlebar, aligning its lug with the handlebar hole. Fit the mounting clamp with its arrow mark facing upwards or forwards (as applicable) and install the mounting clamp bolts. Tighten the mounting clamp upper/front bolt to the specified torque first, followed by the lower/rear bolt then recheck the upper/front bolt is correctly torqued.

**15** Install the handlebar end weight.

**16** Reconnect the wiring connectors to the front brake light switch. Check the operation of the switch and throttle twistgrip before using the bike.

## *Left-hand handlebar*

### Removal

**17** Unscrew the two clutch master cylinder assembly clamp bolts and position the assembly clear of the handlebar, making sure no strain is placed on the hydraulic hose. Keep the fluid reservoir upright to prevent possible fluid leakage.

**18** Unscrew the two handlebar switch screws and position the switch clear of the handlebar.

**19** Slacken and remove the clamp bolt(s) then free the handlebar mounting clamp from the fork tube and remove the handlebar assembly from the bike.

**20** If necessary, slacken the clamp bolts and separate the handlebar and mounting clamp. The handlebar grip is glued to the bar (cut it off if necessary).

### Installation

**21** If the handlebar was separated from the mounting clamp, remove the clamp bolts, clean them, lubricate them with molybdenum disulphide grease then refit them to the mounting clamp. Insert the handlebar, aligning it correctly with the clamp, and tighten its clamp bolts evenly and progressively to the specified torque. Clean the handlebar surface then apply a suitable adhesive to the inside of the new handlebar grip. Slide the grip into position, making sure it is correctly positioned before the adhesive sets.

**22** Clean the mounting clamp bolt(s) and lubricate it/them with molybdenum disulphide grease.

**23** Assemble the handlebar clamp around the fork leg and install the clamp bolt(s) **(see illustration)**. Slide the handlebar clamp up the fork leg and seat its locating pin correctly in the hole in the base of the top yoke **(see illustration)**. Hold the handlebar clamp firmly against the top yoke then tighten its clamp bolt(s) to the specified torque.

**24** Assemble the switch on the handlebar, aligning its lug with the handlebar hole. Refit the retaining screws and tighten securely, tightening the front screw first.

**25** Locate the clutch master cylinder on the handlebar, aligning its lug with the handlebar hole. Fit the mounting clamp with its arrow mark facing upwards or forwards (as

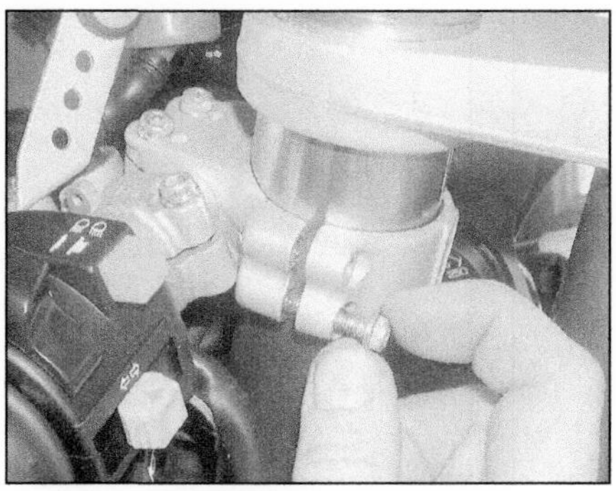
5.23a Assemble the handlebar clamp and fit the clamp bolts . . .

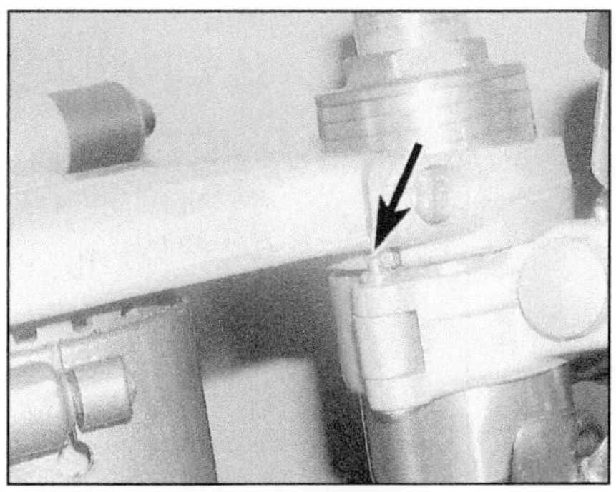
5.23b . . . then slide the clamp up against the top yoke and locate the pin (arrowed) in the yoke hole

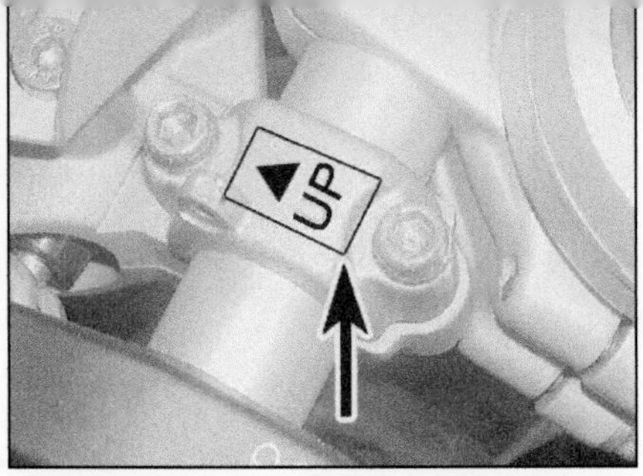


**5.25 Ensure the master cylinder mounting clamp is fitted with its arrow facing upwards/forwards (as applicable)**

applicable) and install the mounting clamp bolts. Tighten the mounting clamp upper/front bolt to the specified torque first, followed by the lower/rear bolt then recheck the upper/front bolt is correctly torqued.

**26** Check the operation of the switch and clutch before using the bike.

## 6 Forks – removal and installation

### *Removal*

**Note:** *The standard position of the fork leg is given in the installation procedure (see Step machine if a previous owner has changed the ride height (see Section 14). To ensure the forks are installed in the same positions make alignment marks or take measurements prior to removal.*

**1** Remove the complete fairing and front mudguard (see Chapter 8).

**2** Remove the front wheel (see Chapter 7).

**3** Unscrew the clamp bolt(s) securing the handlebar clamp to the fork leg. Position the handlebar assembly clear of the fork leg and support it to avoid any strain being placed on the hydraulic hose/wiring **(see illustrations)**. Ensure the master cylinder fluid reservoir is kept upright to prevent possible fluid leakage.

**4** If the fork is to be dismantled, unscrew the top cap from the fork tube by a few turns.

**5** Slacken and remove the top and bottom yoke clamp bolts and remove the fork by twisting it and pulling it downwards **(see illustrations)**.

HAYNES HiNT ***If the fork legs are seized in the yokes, spray the area with penetrating oil and allow time for it to soak in before trying again.***

### *Installation*

**6** Remove all traces of corrosion from the fork tube and the yokes. Clean the yoke and handlebar clamp bolts and lubricate them grease.

**7** Slide the fork up through the bottom ar top yokes and refit the clamp bolts to the to and bottom yokes. Position the fork correct in the yokes, as was noted prior to remov (align the marks, if made), then tighten th bottom yoke clamp bolts to the specifie torque. The standard fitting position for th fork legs is as follows:

*a) On 916 models and early (pre 2000 mod year) 748 models, position the fork leg s the distance from the centre of the front wheel axle to the underside of the botto yoke clamp is 408.5 mm* **(see illustration)**.

*b) On 996 models and later (2000 model year on) 748 models, position the fork le so the distance from the upper surface o the bottom yoke clamp to the upper surface of the top cap is 244 mm* **(see illustration)**.

***Caution: Ensure both fork legs are positioned at the same height. If the forks are not at the same height the handling o the motorcycle will be adversely affected Refer to Section 14 for information on steering geometry and ride height adjustment.***

**8** Ensure the fork top cap is tightened to th specified torque then tighten the top yo clamp bolt to the specified torque setting.

**9** Assemble the handlebar clamp around th fork leg and install the clamp bolt(s). Slide th

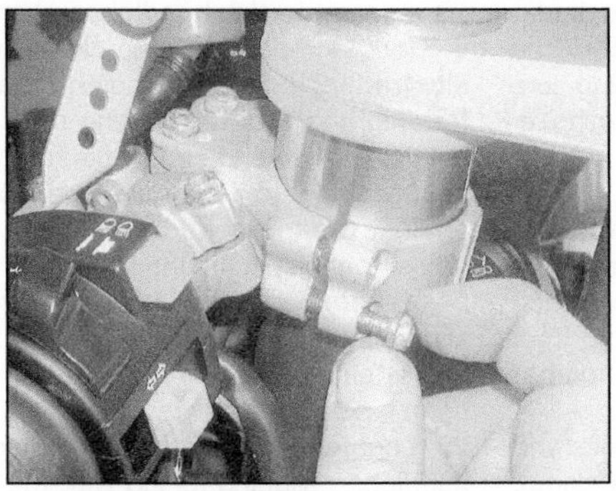

**6.3a Slacken and remove the clamp bolt(s) . . .**

**6.3b . . . and free the handlebar clamp from the fork**

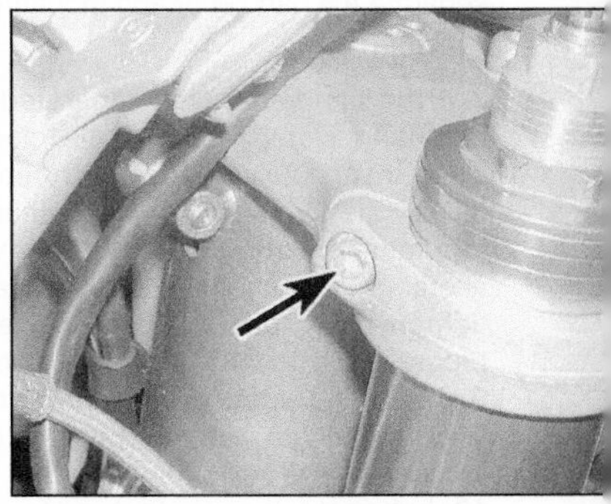

**6.5a Slacken the top yoke clamp bolt (arrowed) . . .**

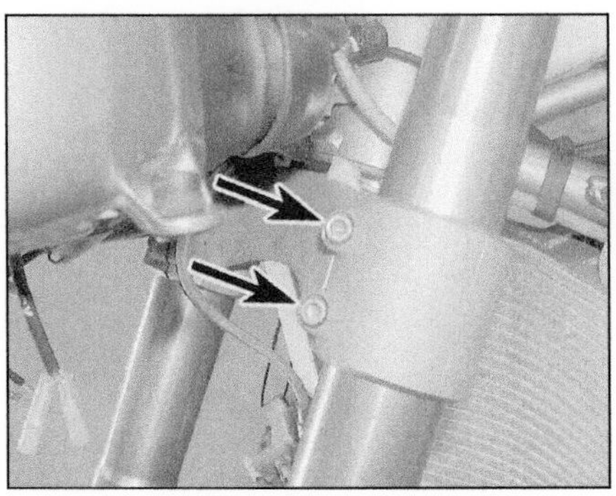

**6.5b . . . and bottom yoke clamp bolts (arrowed) then slide the fork out of position**

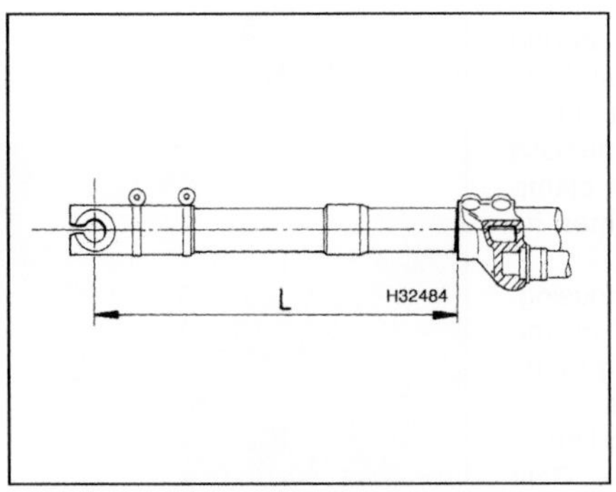


**6.7a Fork leg position measurement (L) – 916 models and early (pre 2000 model year) 748 models**

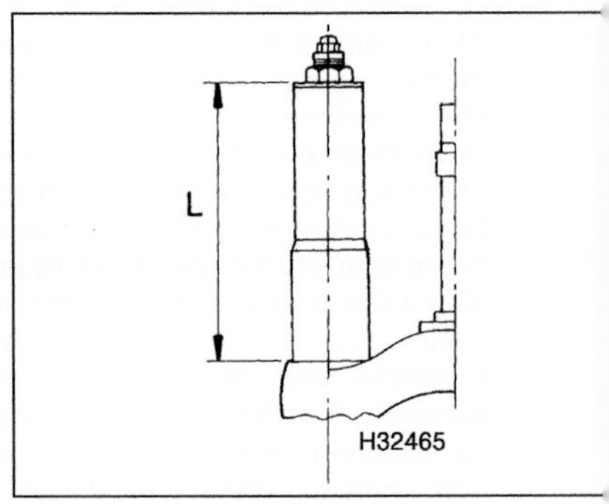


**6.7b Fork leg position measurement (L) 996 models and later (2000 model year o 748 models**

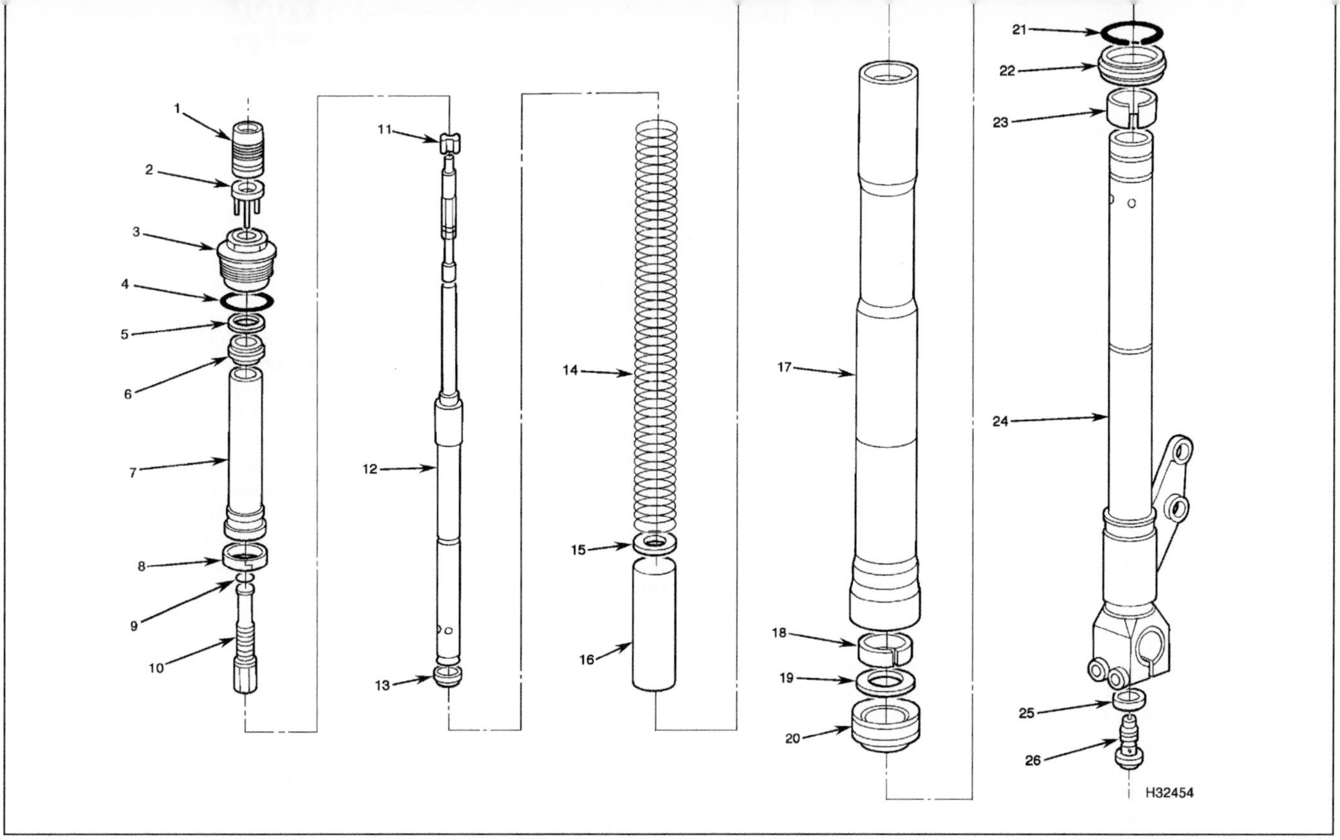


**7.1 Front fork assembly components**

*1 Spring preload adjuster*
*2 Adjuster seat*
*3 Top cap*
*4 Sealing ring*
*5 Upper washer*
*6 Collar*
*7 Upper spacer*
*8 Upper spacer piston ring*
*9 Sealing ring*
*10 Rebound damping adjuster (DO NOT REMOVE)*
*11 Rebound damping adjuster locknut (DO NOT REMOVE)*
*12 Damper assembly*
*13 Damper seat*
*14 Spring*
*15 Lower washer*
*16 Lower spacer*
*17 Outer tube*
*18 Bottom bush*
*19 Washer*
*20 Oil seal*
*21 Retaining clip*
*22 Dust seal*
*23 Top bush*
*24 Inner tube*
*25 Sealing washer*
*26 Damper bolt (contains compression damping adjuster)*

handlebar clamp up the fork leg and seat its locating pin correctly in the hole in the base of the top yoke. Hold the handlebar clamp firmly against the top yoke then tighten its clamp bolt(s) to the specified torque.

**10** Install the front wheel (see Chapter 7) and the front mudguard and fairing (see Chapter 8). Check the operation of the front forks and brakes before taking the machine out on the road.

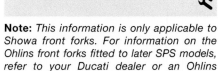

## 7 Forks – disassembly, inspection and reassembly

**Note:** *This information is only applicable to Showa front forks. For information on the Ohlins front forks fitted to later SPS models, refer to your Ducati dealer or an Ohlins suspension specialist (Ducati list no spare parts for the Ohlins front forks and supply them only as a complete assembly).*

### *Disassembly*

**Note:** *A holding tool and thick 10 mm washer will be required to compress and hold the fork spring in position (see Steps 6 and 7).*

**1** Always dismantle the fork legs separately to avoid interchanging any of the parts and thus causing an accelerated rate of wear **(see illustration)**. Store all components in separate, clearly marked containers.

**2** If the damper assembly is to be removed from the inner tube, it is advisable to slacken the damper bolt (which incorporates the compression damping adjuster) before dismantling begins. Remove the front wheel axle clamp bolts from the base of the inner tube to allow access to the damper bolt. If necessary, to prevent the damper rotating, compress the fork so that the spring exerts maximum pressure on the damper, then have an assistant slacken the bolt. **Note:** *The fork seals and bushes can be renewed without removing the damper assembly from the inner tube.*

**3** Support the fork in an upright position then back off the rebound damping adjuster.

**4** Carefully prise off the circlip from the top of the rebound damping adjuster then unscrew and remove the spring preload adjuster, complete with sealing ring **(see illustrations)**.

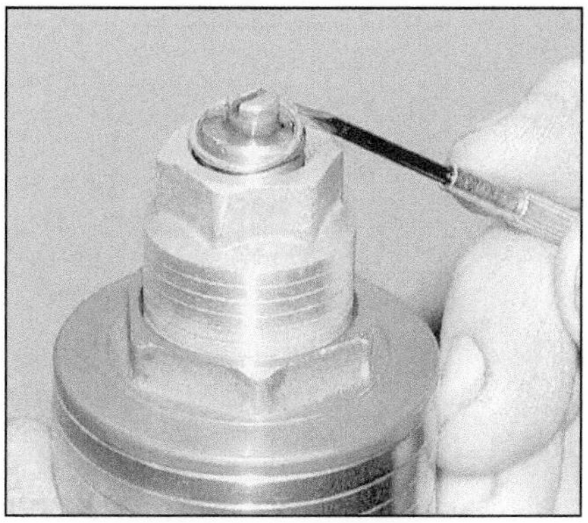

**7.4a Prise off the circlip . . .**

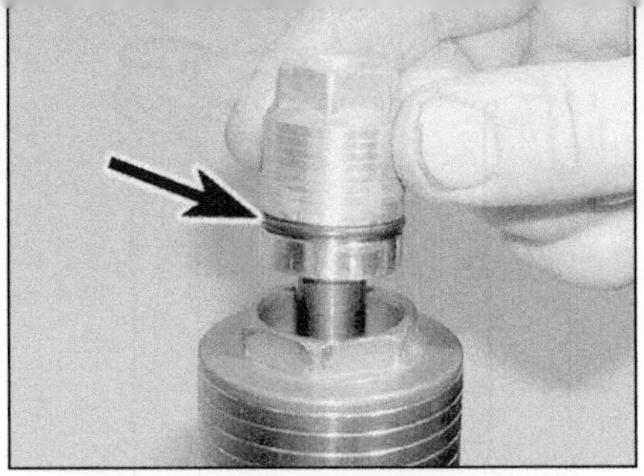

7.4b . . . then unscrew the preload adjuster (sealing ring arrowed) . . .

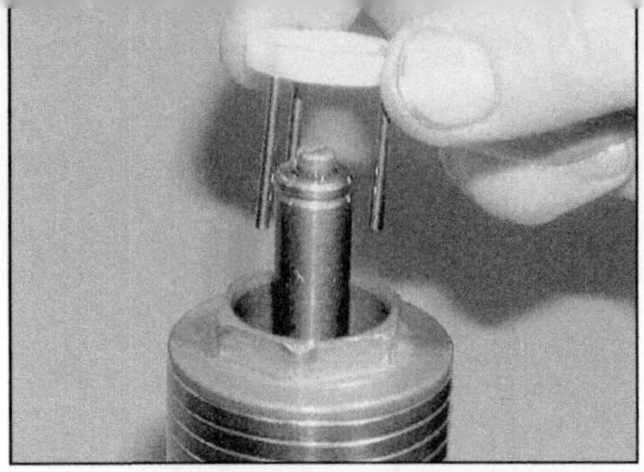

7.4c . . . and remove the adjuster seat

Remove the adjuster seat from the centre of the top bolt **(see illustration)**.

**5** Fully unscrew the top cap from the outer tube.

**6** In order to remove the top cap, it is necessary to compress the fork spring slightly and hold it in position by sliding a plate between the rebound damping adjuster locknut and the washer. In the absence of the Ducati special tool (88713.0957), obtain a thick washer with a 10 mm inside diameter and cut a slot in it to allow it to pass around the piston rod. In order to compress the fork spring sufficiently to allow the washer to be inserted, a holding tool will which engages the holes in the upper spacer will be needed **(see Tool Tip)**.

**7** With the aid of an assistant, compress the fork spring until it is possible to slide the slotted washer between the upper washer and the rebound damper adjuster locknut **(see illustrations)**. Once the washer is in position gently release the fork spring; the end of the rebound damping adjuster should now be clearly visible.

***Caution: Ensure the fork spring is securely held by the washer before proceeding.***

**8** Retain the rebound damping adjuster, then slacken and remove the top cap, complete with sealing ring **(see illustration)**.

**9** Compress the fork spring again until it is possible to remove the slotted washer, then carefully release the fork spring.

**10** Lift off the upper washer, collar and upper spacer then withdraw the fork spring, noting which way up it is fitted **(see illustrations)**.

**TOOL TiP**

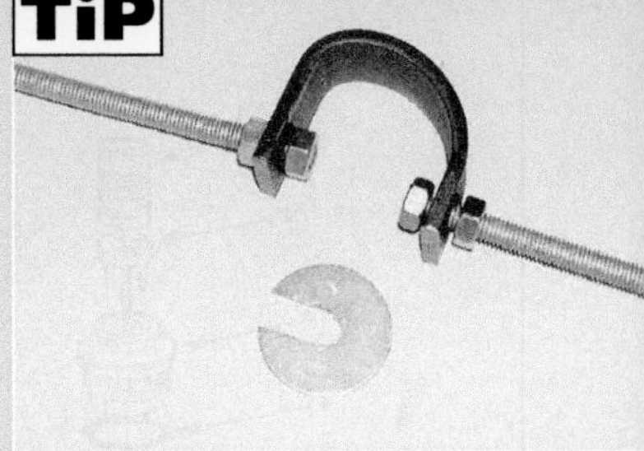

***A holding tool can be fabricated by drilling two holes in a strip of metal an bending it into a horseshoe shape. Fit a length of threaded rod into each hole with a nut positioned on each side of the metal strip. Engage the tool with the spacer holes and use the nuts to position the rods so they are securely located in the holes yet do not contact the damper rod or preload adjuster.***

**Note:** *Do not attempt to remove the rebou damper adjuster from the damper piston.*

**11** Invert the fork over a suitable contai and tip out the lower washer and spac Pump the fork outer tube and damper rod expel as much fork oil as possible.

**12** Carefully prise out the dust seal from t base of the outer tube to gain access to the seal retaining clip **(see illustration)**.

**13** Slide the inner tube out of the outer tu

7.7a Fit the tool to the upper spacer . . .

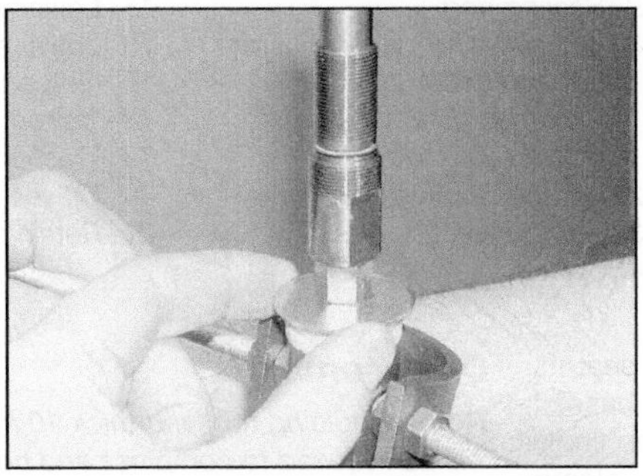

7.7b . . . and compress the fork spring until it is possible to insert the slotted washer between upper washer and locknut

7.8 Retain the rebound damping adjust and unscrew the top cap

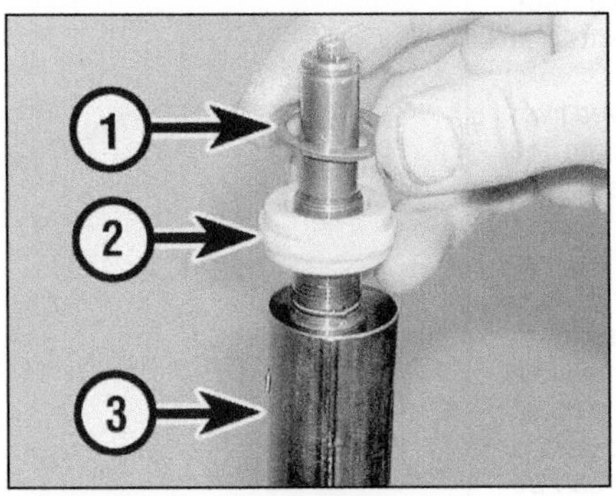


7.10a Remove the upper washer (1), collar (2) and upper spacer (3) . . .

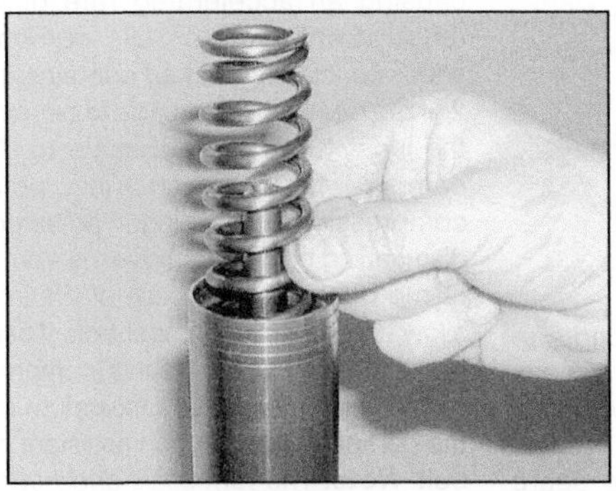

7.10b . . . then lift out the fork spring

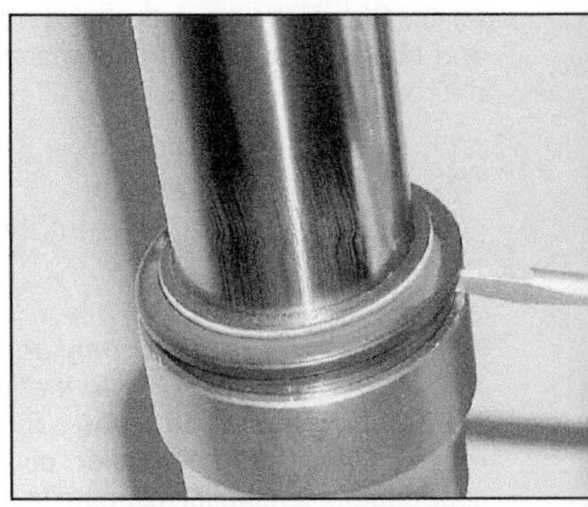

7.12 Carefully prise out the dust seal fr the outer tube . . .

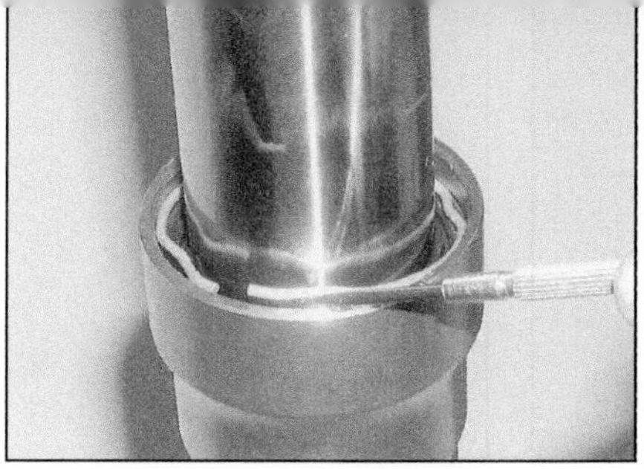

7.13 . . . and ease out the retaining clip

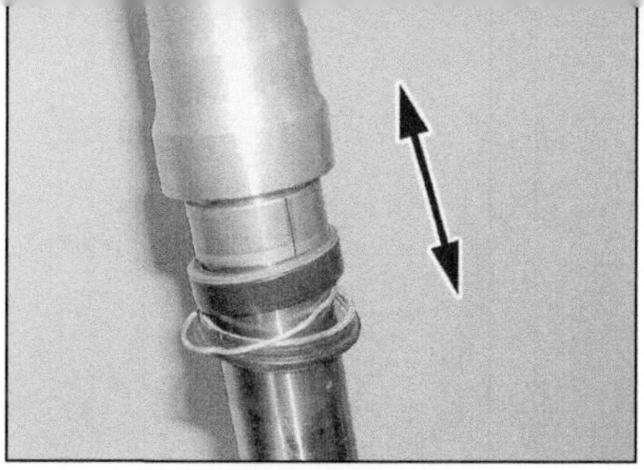

7.14 Repeatedly tap the top bush against the bottom bush to separate the inner and outer tubes

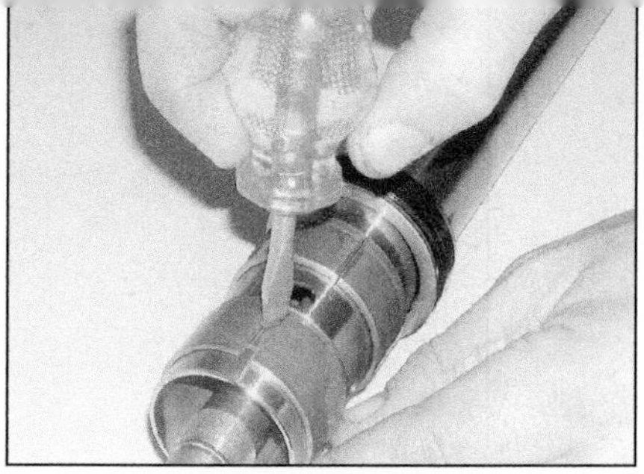

7.15 Open up the top bush and slide it off the inner tube

then ease the retaining clip out of position, taking care not to scratch the surface of the tube **(see illustration)**.

**14** To separate the outer tube from the inner tube it is necessary to displace the bottom bush and oil seal. The top bush should not pass through the bottom bush. Push the inner tube gently inwards then pull it sharply outwards until the top bush strikes the bottom bush **(see illustration)**. Repeat this operation until the bottom bush and seal are tapped out of the outer tube.

**15** With the outer tube removed, carefully open up the top bush by prising it apart at the slit using a flat-bladed screwdriver **(see illustration)**. Do not open up the bush any more than is necessary to slide it off the inner tube.

**16** Slide the bottom bush, washer, oil seal, retaining clip and dust seal off the inner tube, noting which way up they fit. Discard the dust seal and oil seal as new ones must be used. It is also highly recommended that the top and bottom bushes are renewed as well, regardless of their apparent condition.

**17** If necessary, remove the previously slackened damper bolt and its sealing washer from the bottom of the inner tube then invert the tube and tip out the damper assembly and its seat. Discard the sealing washer, as a new one must be used on reassembly.

### Inspection

**18** Clean all parts in solvent and blow them dry with compressed air, if available. Check the fork inner tube for score marks, scratches, flaking of the chrome finish and excessive or abnormal wear. Look for dents in the tube and renew the tube in both forks if any are found. Check the fork seal area of the tube for nicks, gouges and scratches. If damage is evident, leaks will occur. Also check the oil seal washer for damage or distortion and renew it if necessary. Renew all seals, regardless of their condition.

**19** Check the fork inner tube for runout using V-blocks and a dial gauge, or have it done by a dealer. If any discernible amount of runout is measured (Ducati specify a limit of 0.1 mm), the inner tube should be renewed.

***Warning: If the inner tube is bent, it should not be straightened; renew it.***

**20** Check the spring for cracks and other damage. Measure the spring free length and compare the measurement to the specifications at the beginning of the Chapter. If it is defective or sagged below the service limit, renew the springs in both forks. Never renew only one spring.

**21** Inspect the piston ring on the fork spring upper spacer for signs of wear or damage and, if necessary, renew it.

**22** Examine the working surfaces of the two bushes and the washer fitted between the bottom bush and oil seal; if worn or scuffed they must be renewed (it is recommend that both bushes are renewed every time the fork is stripped, regardless of their apparent condition).

**23** Check the damper assembly for damage and wear, and renew the assembly if necessary. **Note:** *Do not attempt to dismantle the damper assembly.*

### Reassembly

**24** Fit the seat to the base of the damper assembly (where removed) and insert the assembly into the inner tube. Fit a new copper sealing washer to the damper bolt then install the bolt into the bottom of the slider and tighten it to the specified torque setting. **Note:** *If the damper assembly rotates inside the tube, temporarily install the fork spring, spacers, collar and washer in the inner tube and fit the top cap to the outer tube. Fit the outer tube to the inner tube and compress the fork to hold the damper.*

**25** Oil the fork inner tube with the specified fork oil.

**HAYNES HiNT** ***Place a small plastic bag over the upper end of the inner tube and lubricate the bag with fork oil – this will help prevent damage to the seal lips as they pass over the tube end and top bush cutout.***

**26** Lubricate the lips of the new dust seal then slide it down the inner tube, ensuring it is the right way around.

**27** Fit the oil seal retaining clip to the inner tube **(see illustration)**.

**28** Lubricate the new oil seal with fork oil then carefully slide the seal onto the inner tube, making sure its marked surface is facing downwards (main sealing lip upwards) **(see illustration)**.

**29** Remove the plastic bag then fit the washer and slide the bottom bush onto the

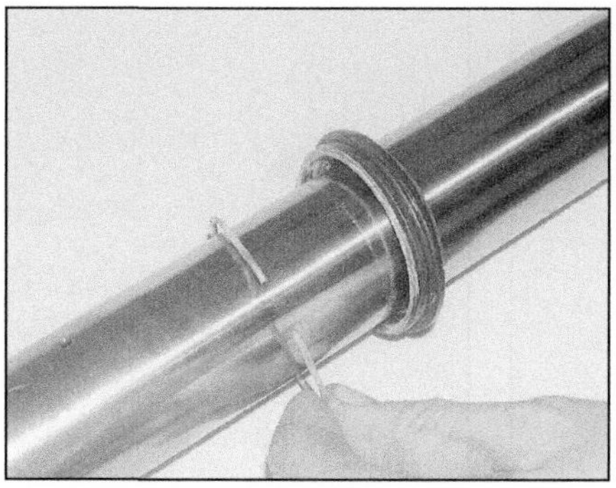

7.27 Slide the dust seal and retaining clip onto the inner tube . . .

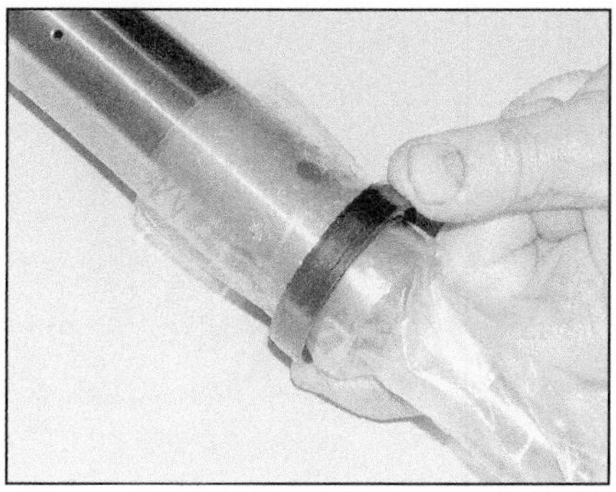

7.28 . . . then slide on the oil seal (note the use of the plastic bag to protect the seal lips)

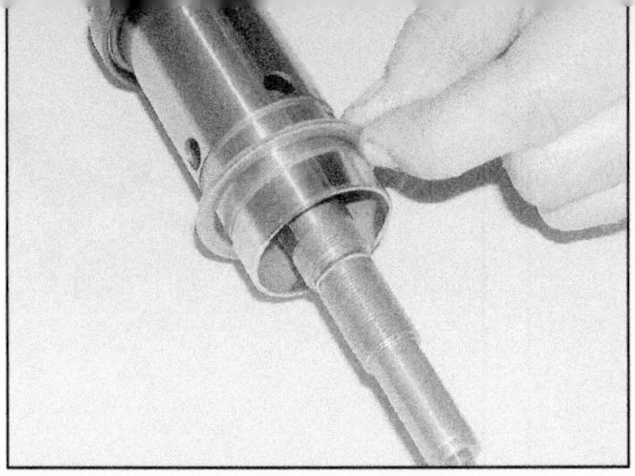

7.29a Fit the washer to the inner tube . . .

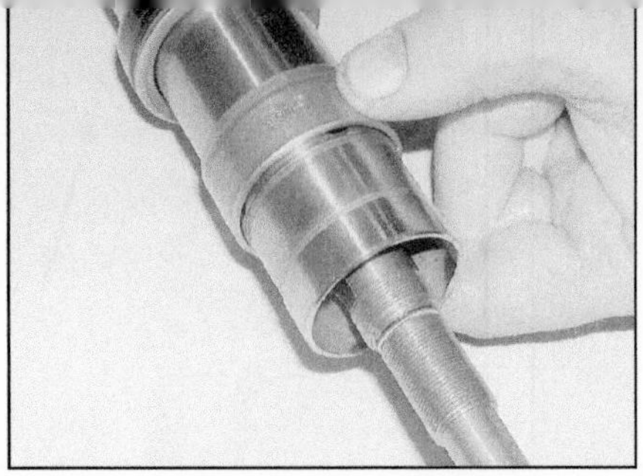

7.29b . . . then slide on the bottom bush

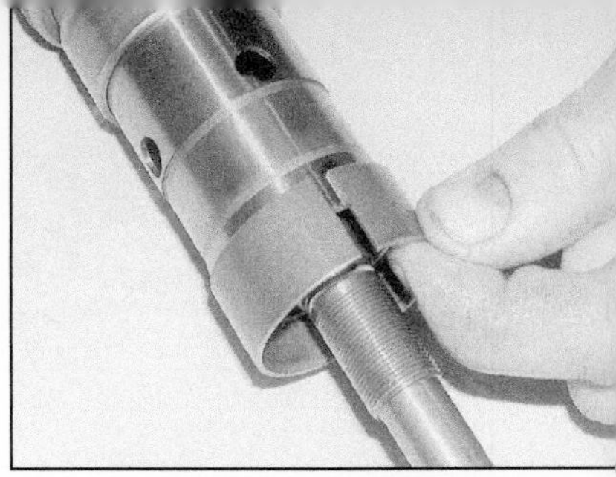

7.30 Fit the top bush and locate it correctly in the inner tube cutout

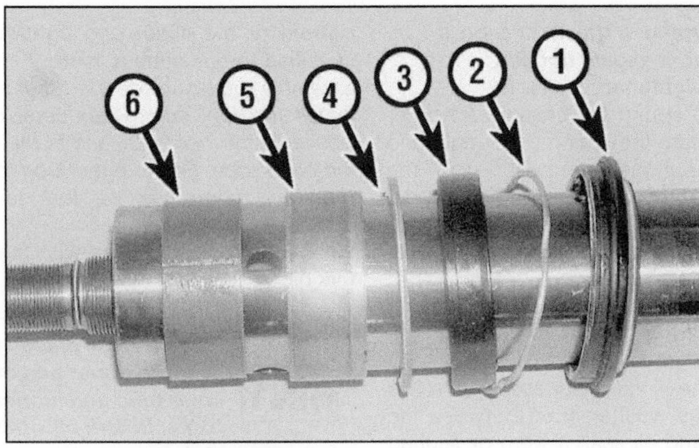


**7.31 Correct fitted order of fork components**

1 *Dust seal*
2 *Retaining clip*
3 *Oil seal*
4 *Washer*
5 *Bottom bush*
6 *Top bush*

inner tube having lubricated it with fork o
**(see illustrations)**.

**30** Lubricate the top bush with fork oil ar ease it onto the inner tube. Do not expand th bush anymore than is necessary and ensure is correctly located in the cutout on the tube

**31** Ensure all components are correct installed then insert the inner tube into th outer tube **(see illustration)**.

**32** Press the bottom bush squarely into i recess in the outer tube as far as possibl Seat the washer on the top of the bush the tap the bush squarely into position using hammer and punch, taking great care not scratch the fork tube. Ensure the bush correctly seated before continuing.

**HAYNES HiNT** ***Ensure the inner tube remains fully extended from the outer tube whilst the bush is being tapped into position. Any accidental damage will then be confined to the area of the inner tube which remains above the oil seal and bottom bush during normal use.***

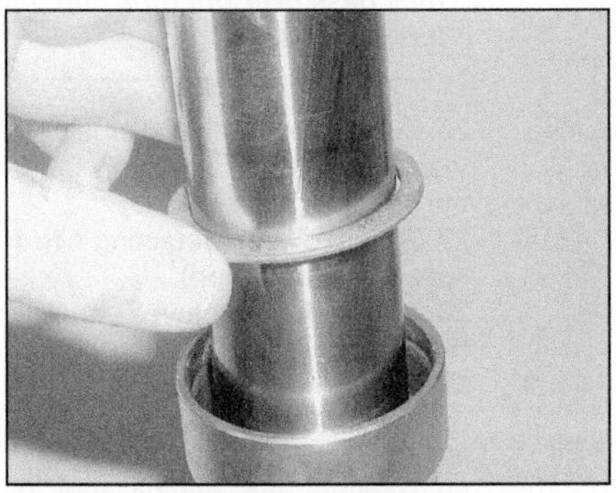

7.33a Ensure the bottom bush is correctly fitted then slide the washer into position . . .

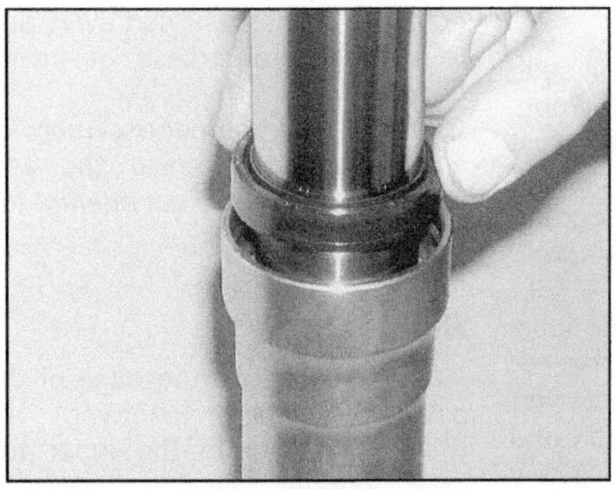

7.33b . . . and press the oil seal into the outer tube

**33** Slide the washer up against the botto bush then press the oil seal into the outer tub **(see illustrations)**. Carefully tap the seal in place as described in Step 32 until th retaining clip groove is visible.

**34** Once the seal is correctly seated, secu it in position with the retaining clip ensuring is correctly located in its groove **(se illustration)**.

**35** Slide the dust seal along the inner tub and press it fully into the outer tube.

**36** Support the fork in an upright positio then fully insert the rod into the damp assembly and slide the outer tube fully dov the inner tube.

**37** Measure out the correct amount of th specified fork oil (see Specifications at th beginning of the Chapter for fork oil typ capacity and level). Slowly pour in the whilst pushing the damper assembly rod u and down **(see illustration)**. Fill the fork w the oil, then slowly pump the outer tube and down a few times to purge the air fro

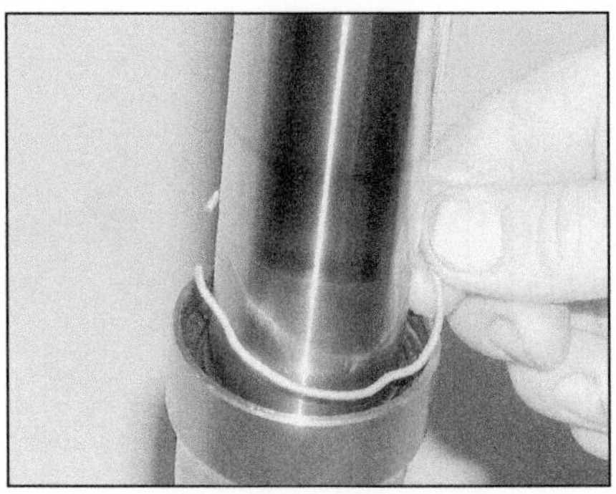

7.34 Secure the oil seal in position with the retaining clip

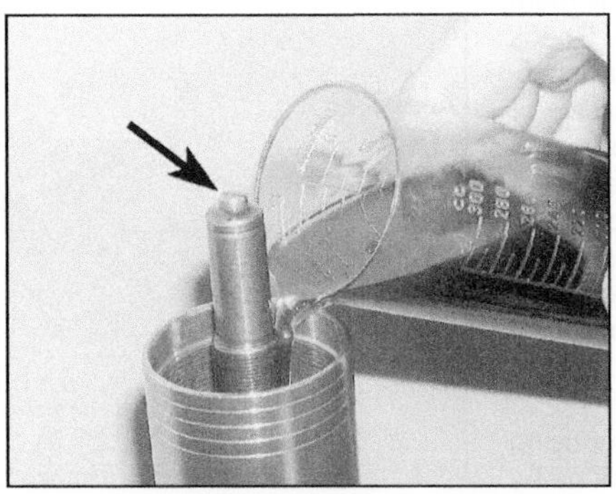

7.37a Fill the fork with the specified type and amount of oil whilst pumping the damper rod (arrowed)

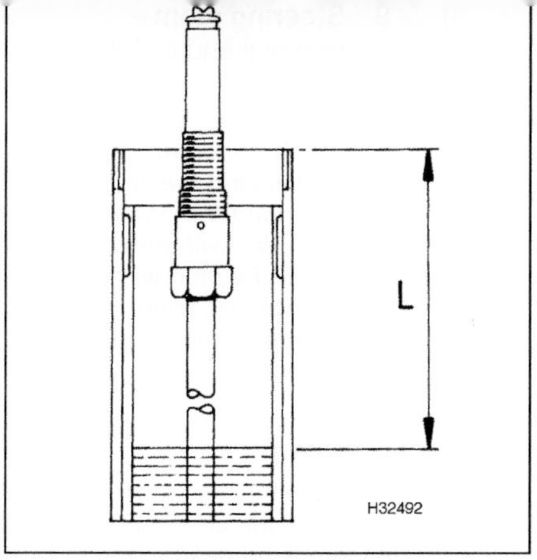


**7.37b Check the fork oil level is the specified distance (L) below the top of the outer tube**

between the inner and outer tubes. Add the remaining fork oil whilst pumping the damper rod. Once all the oil has been added, fully insert the rod into the damper and slide the outer tube fully down the inner tube. Leave the fork to stand for a few minutes to allow any trapped air to surface. Check the fork oil level from the top of the tube **(see illustration)**. Add or subtract fork oil until it is at the specified level.

**38** Fully extend the damper rod then install the fork spring lower spacer and washer **(see illustrations)**.

**39** Insert the fork spring ensuring that its smaller diameter (tapered) end is at the top (some fork springs are symmetrical and can be fitted either way up).

**40** Lubricate the piston ring with a smear of fork oil then insert the upper spacer into the fork tube, ensuring its piston ring is at the bottom **(see illustration)**.

**41** Fit the collar to the upper end of the spacer then fit the washer.

**42** With the aid of an assistant, hold the damper rod in the fully extended position then compress the fork spring until it is possible to slide the slotted washer between the base of the rebound damping adjuster locknut and the upper washer. Ensure the washer is correctly positioned then gently release the fork spring. ***Caution: Ensure the fork spring is securely held by the washer before proceeding.***

**43** Lubricate the top cap sealing ring with a smear of fork oil then screw the cap fully onto the rebound damping adjuster. Retain the adjuster and tighten the top cap to the specified torque.

**44** Compress the fork spring again until it is possible to remove the slotted washer, then carefully release the fork spring, making sure the upper washer and collar pass over the locknut and seat correctly against the top cap.

**45** Check that all components are correctly seated, then carefully screw the top cap into

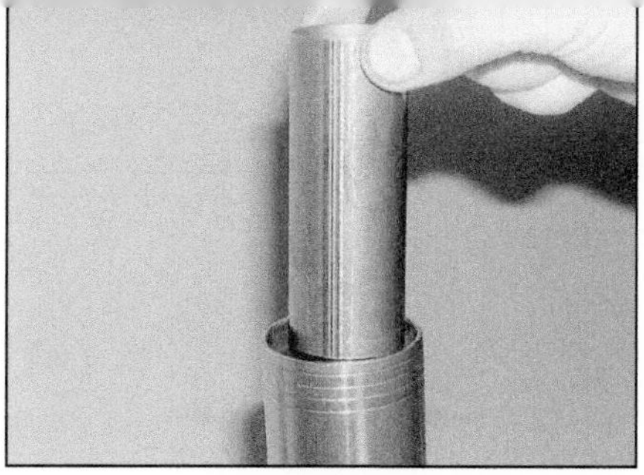

**7.38a Once the oil level is correct, fit the lower spacer . . .**

**7.38b . . . and insert the washer**

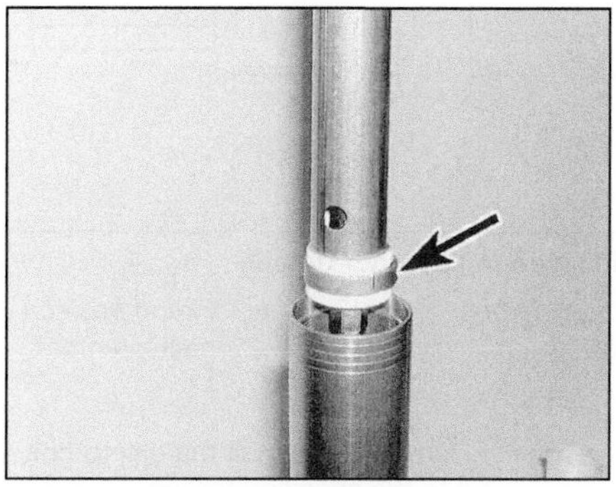

**7.40 Ensure the upper spacer is fitted with its piston ring (arrowed) at the bottom**

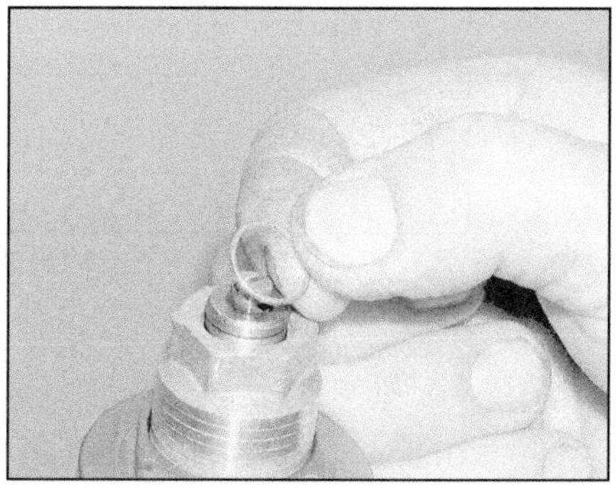

**7.46 Fit the circlip ensuring it is correctly located in the adjuster groove**

the outer tube, making sure it is not cross-threaded. **Note:** *The top cap can be tightened to its specified torque setting at this stage if the tube can be held firmly enough, but do not risk distorting the outer tube by overtightening it. A better method is to tighten the top cap when the fork has been reinstalled and is securely held in the bottom yoke.*

**46** Lubricate the spring preload adjuster sealing ring with a smear of fork oil. Slide the adjuster seat into position then screw on the adjuster. Secure the adjuster in position with the circlip, ensuring it is correctly located in its groove **(see illustration)**.

**47** Install the forks and set the fork adjustments as required (see Sections 6 and 13).

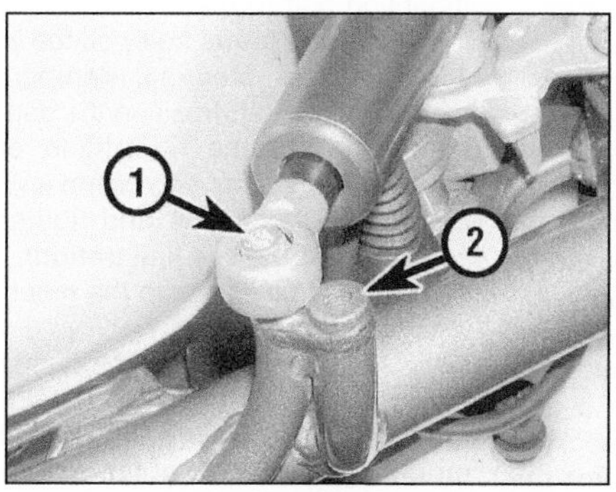


**8.1 Steering damper frame bolt (1). The front threaded hole (2) is for use only when the steering head angle is set to the race position**

## 8 Steering damper – removal, inspection and installation

### *Removal*

#### Standard damper

**1** Slacken and remove the bolt securing the steering damper to the frame and recover the washer (where fitted) positioned between the damper and frame **(see illustration)**.

**2** Slacken and remove the clamp bolt then slide the damper out from its mounting clamp **(see illustration)**.

**3** If necessary, unscrew the bolt and remove the mounting clamp, sealing ring and shouldered collar from the top yoke.

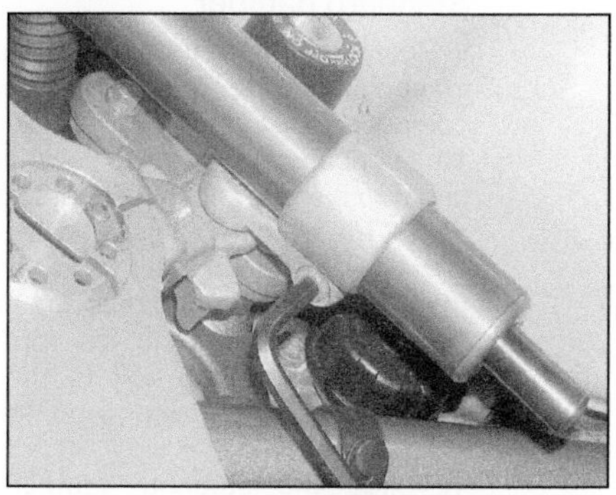

**8.2 Slacken the clamp bolt and slide out the steering damper**

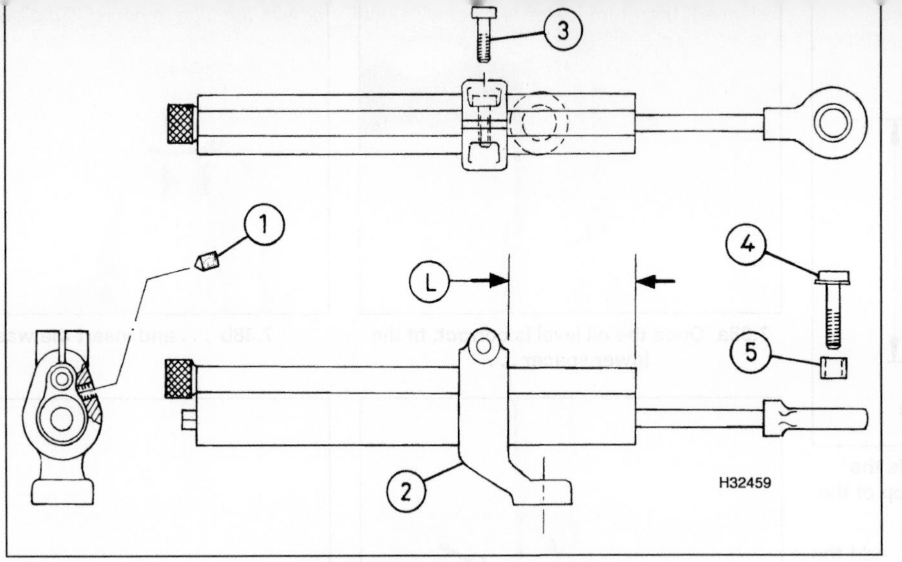


**8.16 Ohlins steering damper details**

1 *Grub screw*
2 *Mounting clamp*
3 *Clamp bolt*
4 *Mounting bolt*
5 *Collar*
L *Fitting position measurement*

### Ohlins damper (SPS models)

**4** Slacken and remove the bolt securing the steering damper to the frame and recover the collar from the damper rod end fitting.
**5** Slacken and remove the clamp bolt and grub screw from the damper mounting clamp, then slide out the damper and remove it from the bike.
**6** If necessary, unscrew the bolt and remove the mounting clamp, sealing ring and washer from the top yoke.

## *Inspection*

**7** Inspect the damper for signs of fluid leakage or damage to the damper rod. Check that the damper rod moves smoothly and the resistance remains constant throughout its entire travel. If any sign of wear or damage is found the damper must be renewed.
**8** Renew the mounting bracket if damage is evident.

## *Installation*

### Standard damper

**9** Remove all traces of the original locking compound and apply a drop of fresh locking compound to the threads of each bolt.
**10** Lubricate the top yoke, collar and sealing ring with a smear of multi-purpose grease.
**11** Fit the shouldered collar to the top yoke, ensuring its flat surface is facing downwards, then fit the sealing ring onto the collar. Refit the mounting clamp to the top yoke and tighten its mounting bolt to the specified torque. Check the clamp pivots freely on the yoke.
**12** Slide the steering damper into the mounting bracket. Align the raised section of the damper correctly with the mounting clamp, then install the clamp bolt and tighten it to the specified torque.
**13** Align the steering damper rod with the **rear** mounting point on the frame. Ensure the washer (where fitted) is correctly positioned between the damper and frame then refit the mounting bolt and tighten to the specified torque. **Note:** *On models with an adjustable steering head, if the steering angle has been altered from the standard 'road' setting, the steering damper should be fixed to the front mounting point on the frame (see Section 14).*

### Ohlins damper – SPS models

**14** Remove all traces of the original locking compound and apply a drop of fresh locking compound to the threads of each bolt and the grub screw.
**15** Lubricate the pivot pin on the top yoke with a smear of multi-purpose grease, then fit the washer and sealing ring onto the pin. Refit the mounting clamp to the top yoke and tighten its mounting bolt to the specified torque. Check that the clamp pivots freely on the yoke.
**16** Slide the steering damper into the mounting bracket. Position the damper so the distance from the right-hand end of the damper to the mounting clamp is 62 mm then install the clamp bolt and tighten it to the specified torque **(see illustration)**.
**17** Fit the grub screw to the mounting clamp and tighten it securely.
**18** Insert the collar into the damper rod end fitting then align the rod with the **rear** mounting point on the frame. Refit the damper mounting bolt and tighten to the specified torque. **Note:** *If the steering angle has been altered from the standard 'road' setting, the steering damper should be fixed to the front mounting point on the frame (see Section 14).*

## 9 Steering stem – removal and installation

***Caution: Although not strictly necessary, before removing the steering stem it is recommended that the fuel tank is removed. This will prevent accidental damage to the paintwork.***
**Note:** *A special socket will be needed slacken/tighten the steering stem nut (s Steps 4 and 5.*

## *Removal*

**1** Remove the front forks (see Section 6).
**2** Remove the steering damper (see Sect 8); there is no need to remove the mounti clamp.
**3** Slacken and remove the clamp b securing the top yoke to the steering stem then lift off the yoke.
**4** In order to slacken/tighten the steer stem nut, the Ducati service tool (88713.10 is required. If this tool is not available suitable alternative can be made using a s of metal, two M4 nuts and bolts and an nut and bolt (**see Tool Tip**).
**5** Support the bottom yoke then, using eit the Ducati service tool or a suita alternative, slacken and remove the steer stem nut.
**6** Lower the bottom yoke and steering st out of the frame. Remove the lower bear from the steering stem.
**7** Remove the dust seal and the up bearing and its inner race from the top of steering head.
**8** Remove all traces of old grease from bearings and races and check them for w or damage as described in Section 10. **No** *Do not attempt to remove the races from*

**TOOL TIP**

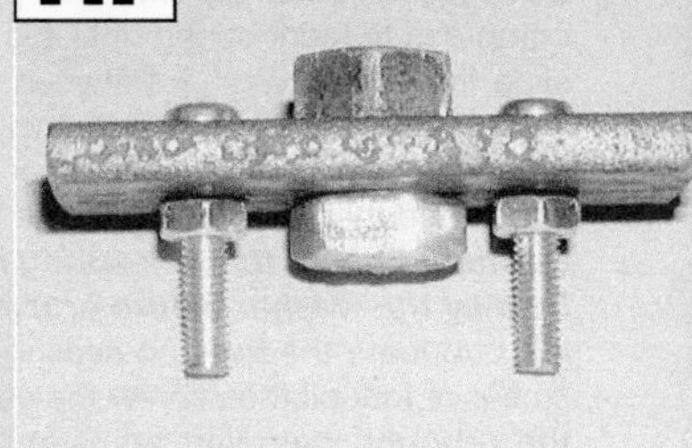

***Drill two 4 mm holes in the metal strip to align with holes around the top of the steering stem nut and drill an 8 mm hole at the mid-point between the two 4 mm holes. Fit the M8 nut and bolt to the centre hole and the M4 bolts and nuts to the outer holes. Align the M4 bolts with the nut holes and use a socket on the M8 nut to slacken/tighten the nut.***

*unless the bearings are to be renewed.*

**9** On models with an adjustable steering head, to remove the adjuster tube unscrew the tube detent screw from the right-hand side of the headstock. Make alignment marks between the tube and headstock then remove the circlip and washer from each adjuster tube clamp bolt. Unscrew both bolts and slide the adjuster tube assembly out of the bottom of the headstock.

### Installation

**10** If the steering head adjuster tube (where fitted) was removed, clean the outside of the tube and the inside of the headstock. Lubricate the headstock and tube contact surfaces with a thin film of multi-purpose grease then slide the adjuster tube into position. Align the marks made on removal so the adjuster tube hole is correctly aligned with the detent screw hole on the headstock then insert the detent screw and tighten it to the specified torque. Lubricate the threads of the clamp bolts with molybdenum disulphide grease then refit the bolts and tighten them to the specified torque. Fit each clamp bolt washer to the frame and secure them in position with the circlips, ensuring they are correctly located in their grooves.

**11** On all models, smear a liberal quantity of multi-purpose grease on the bearing races in the frame/adjuster tube and steering stem. Work the grease well into both the upper and lower bearings and oil the threads of the steering stem nut.

**12** Ensure the lower bearing is correctly seated on its inner race then carefully lift the steering stem/bottom yoke up through the frame. Install the upper bearing and its inner race in the top of the steering head/adjuster tube then install the dust seal and screw the nut firmly onto the steering stem.

**13** Fit the top yoke onto the steering stem nut. Lubricate the stem nut clamp bolt with a smear of molybdenum disulphide grease and install the bolt, tightening it lightly only at this stage.

**14** Slide one of the front forks into position to align the top and bottom yokes and lightly tighten the bottom yoke clamp bolt(s) to hold it in position.

**15** With the fork in position, ensure all the top yoke clamp bolts are loose then tighten the steering stem nut to the specified torque to preload the bearings. Turn the steering stem from lock-to-lock approximately 5 times to settle the bearings and races in position then slacken the steering stem nut by the specified angle. **Note:** *It is important to check the feel of the steering afterwards as described below; if it is too tight readjust the bearings as described below.*

**16** If it is not possible to tighten the nut to the specified torque, tighten the nut hard to preload the bearings then turn the steering stem from lock-to-lock approximately 5 times to settle the bearings in position. Slacken the released, then turn it slowly clockwise until resistance is just evident. The object is to set the nut so that the bearings are under a very light loading, just enough to remove any freeplay.

***Caution: Take great care not to apply excessive pressure because this will cause premature failure of the bearings.***

**17** With the bearings correctly adjusted, press down on the top yoke to ensure it is firm contact with the steering stem nut shoulder, then tighten the nut clamp bolt to the specified torque.

**18** Install the forks as described in Section 6 of this Chapter.

**19** Install the steering damper (see Section 8).

**20** On completion check the steering stem bearing adjustment as described in Chapter 1.

## 10 Steering head bearings – inspection and renewal

### Inspection

**1** Remove the steering stem (see Section 9).

**2** Remove all traces of old grease from the bearings and races and check them for wear or damage.

**3** The outer races should be polished and free from indentations. Inspect the bearing rollers for signs of wear, damage or discoloration, and examine the bearing ball retainer cage for signs of cracks or splits. Spin the bearings by hand. They should spin freely and smoothly. If there are any signs of wear on any of the above components both upper and lower bearing assemblies must be renewed as a set. Only remove the outer races and the lower bearing inner race if they need to be renewed – do not re-use them once they have been removed.

### Renewal

**Note:** *Obtain new bearings and new dust seals before proceeding.*

**Note:** *On models with an adjustable steering head, the outer races can be removed either or with the tube removed. If the bearing races are being removed with the adjuster tube still installed in the frame, do not use excessive force otherwise the adjuster tube/detent screw may be damaged.*

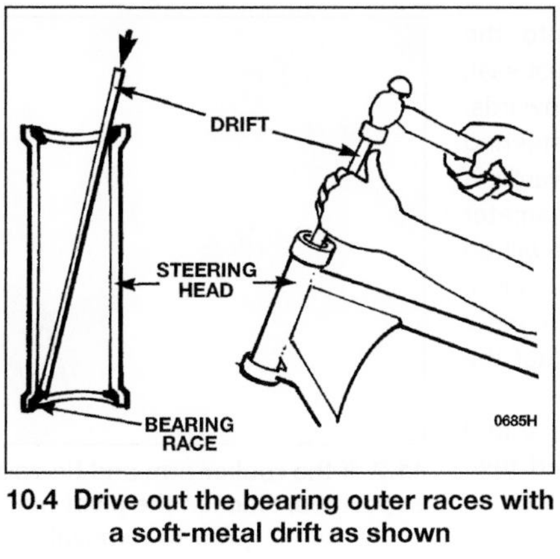


**10.4 Drive out the bearing outer races with a soft-metal drift as shown**

**4** The outer races are retained by circlips and are an interference fit in the frame headstock/adjuster tube. Remove the circlip. Each race can be tapped from position with a suitable drift **(see illustration)**. Tap firmly and evenly around each race to ensure that it is driven out squarely. It may prove advantageous to curve the end of the drift slightly to improve access. Alternatively, the races can be removed using a slide-hammer type bearing extractor; these can often be hired from tool shops.

**5** The new outer races can be pressed into position using a drawbolt arrangement, or by using a large diameter tubular drift **(see illustration)**. Ensure that the drawbolt washer or drift (as applicable) bears only on the outer edge of the race and does not contact the race bearing surface. Once both bearing races are correctly seated, secure them in position with the circlips.

> **HAYNES HiNT** ***Installation of new bearing outer races is made much easier if the races are left overnight in the freezer. This causes them to contract slightly making them a looser fit.***

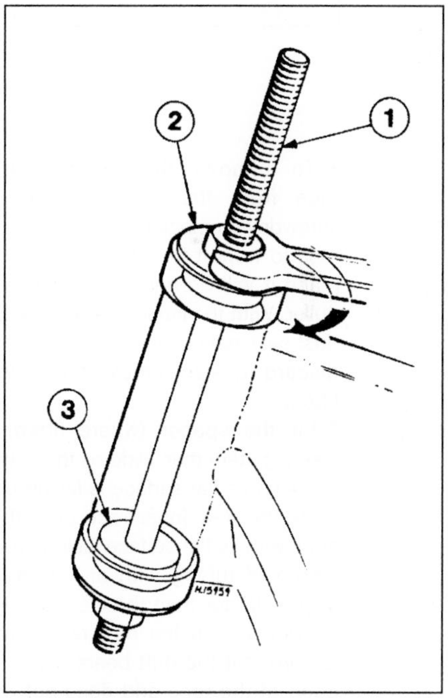


**10.5 Drawbolt arrangement for fitting steering stem bearing outer races**

1. *Long bolt or threaded rod*
2. *Thick washer*
3. *Guide for outer race*

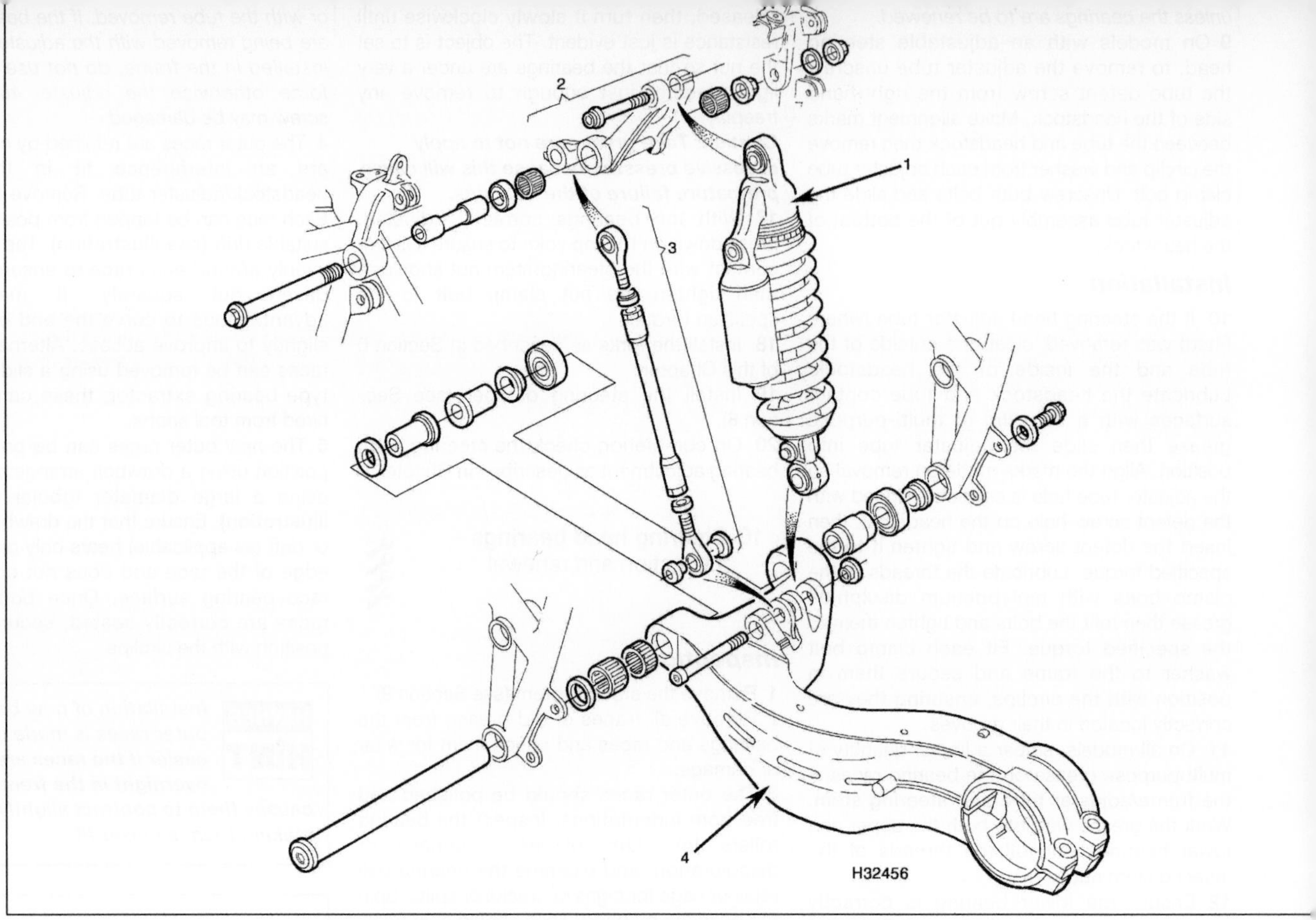


**11.1 Rear suspension and swingarm components**

*1 Shock absorber 2 Rocker arm 3 Tie-rod 4 Swingarm*

**6** To remove the lower bearing inner race from the steering stem, use two screwdrivers placed on opposite sides of the race to work it free. If the bearing is firmly in place it will be necessary to use a bearing puller. With the inner race removed, lift off the dust seal, noting which way up it is fitted, and discard it. Also remove the spacer (where fitted).

**7** Fit the spacer (where fitted) onto the steering stem then slide on the new dust seal, ensuring its flat surface is facing downwards. Slide the new inner race onto the steering stem with its flat surface facing downwards. A length of tubing with an internal diameter slightly larger than the steering stem will be needed to tap the new race into position. Ensure that the drift bears only on the inner edge of the race and does not contact the bearing surface.

**8** Ensure the lower bearing inner race and both outer races are correctly seated then install the steering stem as described in Section 9.

## 11 Rear suspension linkage – removal, inspection and installation

### *Removal*

**1** Remove the rear shock absorber (Section 12) **(see illustration)**.

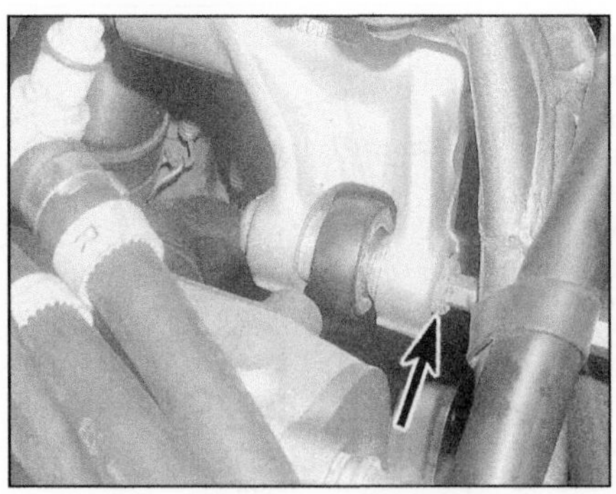

**11.2 If the rocker arm and tie-rod are to be separated, slacken the pivot bolt (arrowed) prior to removal**

**2** If the rocker arm and tie-rod are to b separated, slack the tie-rod pivot bolt **(se illustration)**.

**3** Unscrew the nut and washer from th suspension linkage rocker arm piv bolt.

**4** Withdraw the pivot bolt and manoeuvre th rocker arm and tie-rod assembly from the bi **(see illustrations)**.

**5** If necessary, note which way around th tie-rod is fitted then remove the bolt ar

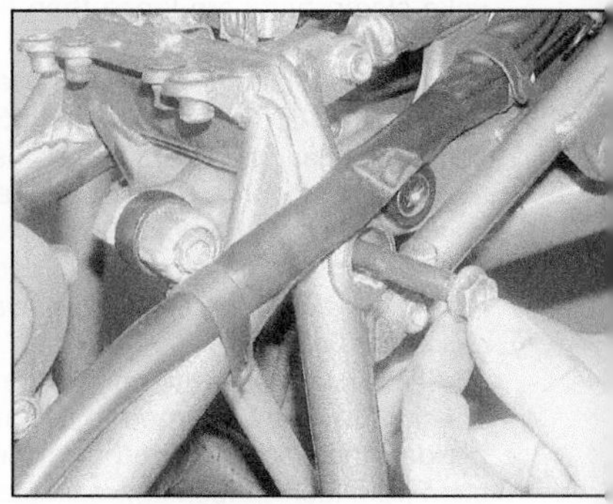

**11.4a Withdraw the pivot bolt . . .**

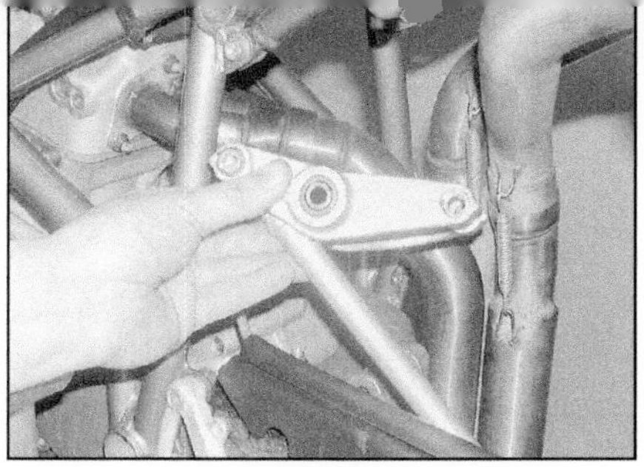

11.4b . . . and remove the rocker arm and tie-rod assembly

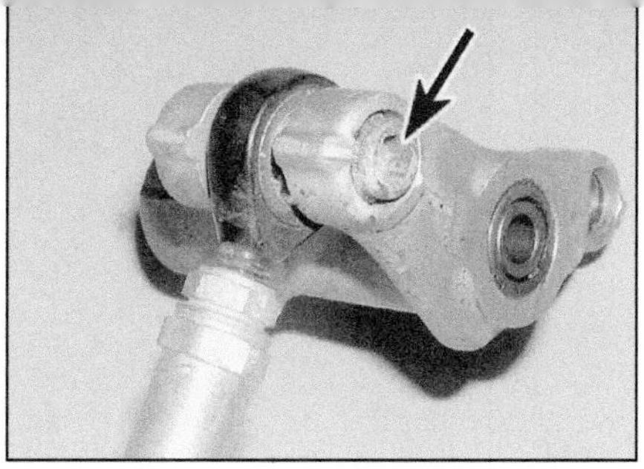

11.5a Unscrew the pivot bolt (arrowed) . . .

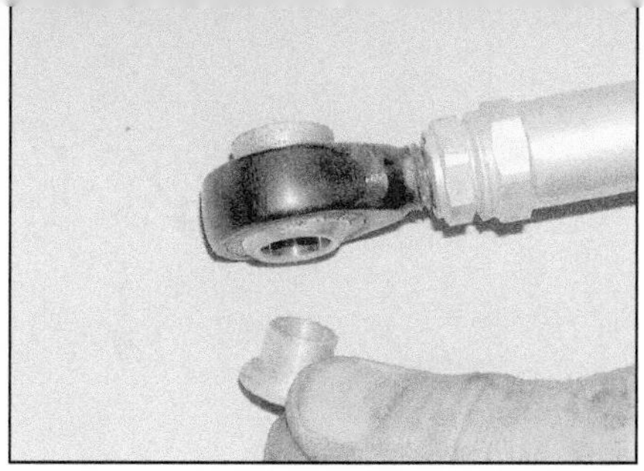

11.5b . . . then separate the tie-rod and rocker arm and recover the collars

separate the tie-rod and rocker arm **(see illustration)**. Recover the collars which are fitted on each side of the tie-rod end fitting **(see illustration)**.

## *Inspection*

### Rocker arm

**6** Withdraw the inner sleeve from the rocker arm and thoroughly clean all components, removing all traces of dirt, corrosion and grease **(see illustration)**.

**7** Inspect all components closely, looking for obvious signs of wear such as heavy scoring, or for damage such as cracks or distortion. Renew as necessary.

**8** If the dust seals are damaged, the old seals can be levered out of position using a flat-bladed screwdriver. Ensure the sealing lip of the new seal is facing inwards then press the seal squarely into position until it is flush with the link.

**9** If the bearings are damaged, it will be necessary to renew the bearings, inner sleeve and dust seals. Remove the dust seals and note the correct fitted location of each bearing before pressing/driving them out of position. The new bearings should be pressed or drawn into their bores rather than driven into position to prevent possible damage. In the absence of a press, a suitable drawbolt arrangement can be made up as described in *Tools and Workshop Tips* in the Reference section. Ensure both bearings are correctly positioned in the arm then press the new dust seals into position, ensuring their sealing lips are facing inwards.

**10** Lubricate the needle roller bearings, the inner sleeves and the dust seal lips with molybdenum disulphide grease then slide the inner sleeve carefully into position.

### Tie-rod

**11** Inspect the tie-rod closely, looking for obvious signs of wear such as heavy scoring, or for damage such as cracks or distortion. Check that the balljoint of each end fitting is free to move smoothly without excessive freeplay; if necessary the end fittings can be renewed individually as follows.

**12** Measure the length of the tie-rod between the pivot bolt centres then slacken the lock nut and unscrew the end fitting. **Note:** *The lower end fitting and locknut have a left-hand thread.* Transfer the lock nut onto the new end fitting then screw the end fitting into the tie-rod. Position the end fitting so the tie-rod length is as noted prior to removal, then securely tighten the locknut. **Note:** *The recommended setting for the tie-rod length is 261 mm (measured between the centres of the pivot bolt holes). The tie-rod length affects the rear ride height of the bike which in turn alters the handling characteristics of the machine (see Section 14). Ducati state that the tie-rod length should never be set to more than 261 mm.*

## *Installation*

**13** Where necessary, lubricate the tie-rod upper end fitting and pivot bolt with molybdenum disulphide grease. Fit the mounting collars to the end fitting (shoulders facing inwards) then assemble the tie-rod and rocker arm and insert the pivot bolt. **Note:** *Ensure the tie rod is fitted the right way up with its left-hand threaded end at the bottom. The left-hand thread end can be identified by the lines scored on both the tie-rod hexagonal section and the end fitting locknut* **(see illustration)**.

**14** If not already done, lubricate the rocker arm seals, needle roller bearings, inner sleeve and the pivot bolt with molybdenum disulphide grease.

**15** Manoeuvre the assembly into position then align the rocker arm with the frame and insert the pivot bolt from the left-hand side. Lubricate the threads and contact face of the pivot bolt nut with molybdenum disulphide grease then fit the washer and nut to the bolt and tighten to the specified torque.

**16** If the rocker arm and tie-rod were separated, tighten the tie-rod pivot bolt to the specified torque **(see illustration)**.

**17** Check that the rocker arm pivots smoothly then install the rear shock absorber (see Section 12). Check the operation of the rear suspension before taking the machine on the road.

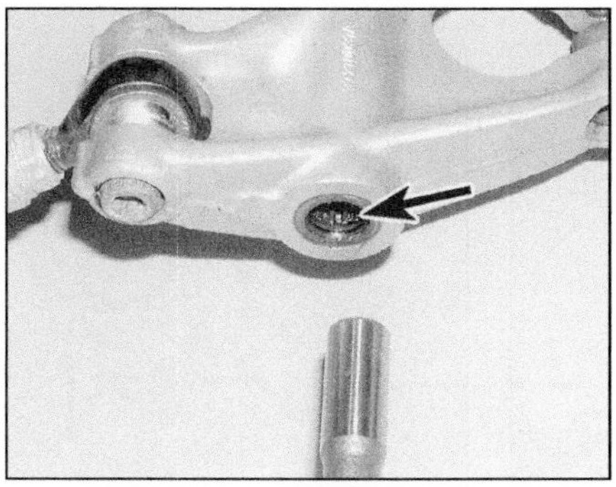

11.6 Withdraw the inner sleeve and check the rocker arm bearings (arrowed)

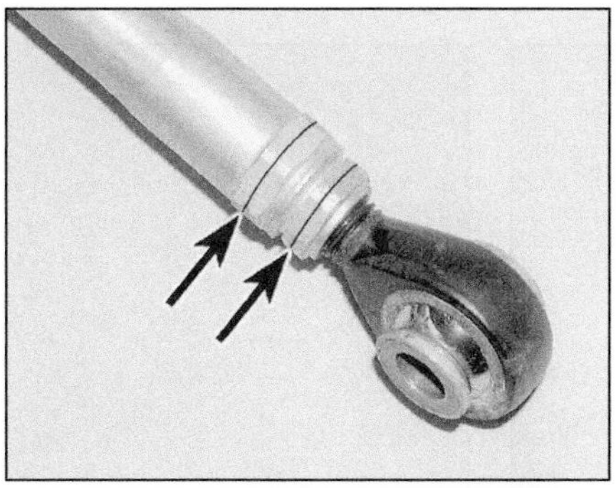

11.13 Ensure the tie-rod is fitted with its left-hand thread end (indicated by the lines on the nut and rod – arrowed) at the bottom

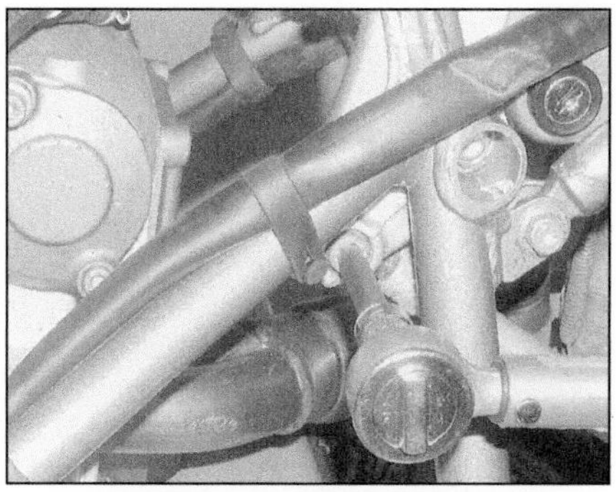

11.16 If the tie-rod pivot bolt was removed, tighten it to the specified torque before installing the shock absorber

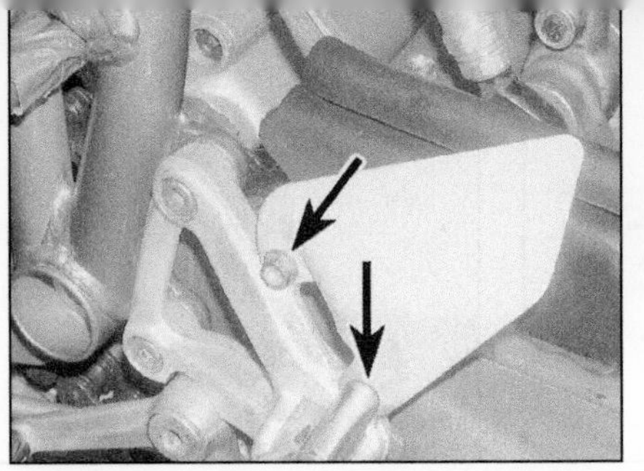

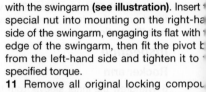

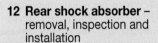

**12.3 Unscrew the bolts (arrowed) and remove the heel plate from the left-hand footrest bracket**

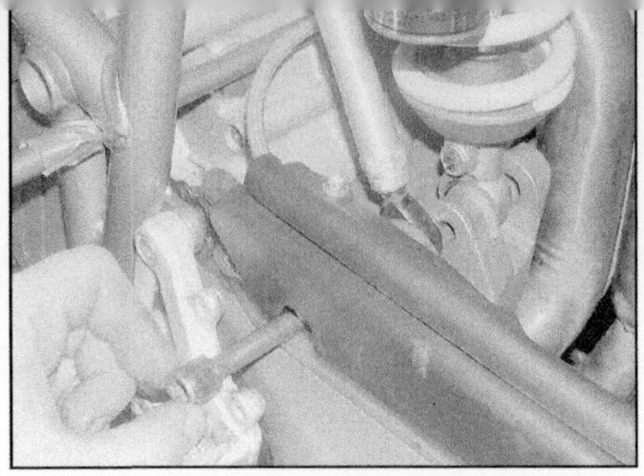

**12.4a Slacken and remove the pivot bolt securing the tie-rod and shock absorber to the swingarm . . .**

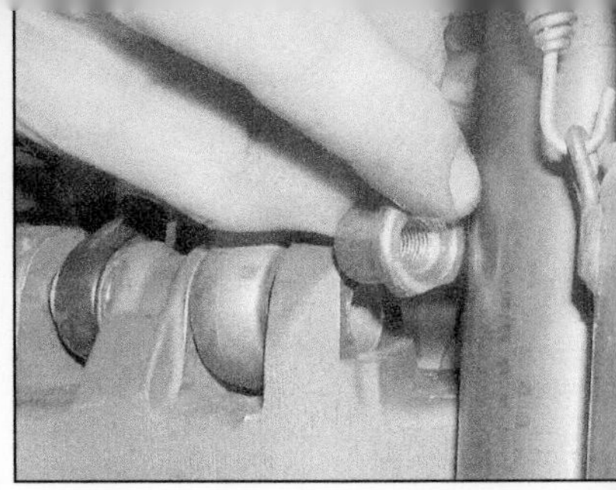

**12.4b . . . and recover the special nut**

## 12 Rear shock absorber – removal, inspection and installation

### Removal

**1** Support the motorcycle on an auxiliary stand so the rear wheel is raised clear of the ground with no weight on the rear suspension linkage. This can be done either by using an auxiliary stand which engages the swingarm pivot or by removing the lower fairing panels (see Chapter 8) and supporting the bike on an auxiliary stand(s) positioned underneath the engine. Once the bike is securely supported, position a block of wood between the tyre and the ground; this will prevent the swingarm dropping as the shock absorber bolts are withdrawn.

***Caution: Ensure the bike is securely supported before proceeding.***

**2** Remove the rear wheel (see Chapter 7).

**3** To gain access to the lower pivot bolt, unscrew the bolts which retain the heel plate to the rider's left-hand footrest bracket and remove the plate **(see illustration)**.

**4** Slacken and remove the pivot bolt and special nut securing the shock absorber and tie-rod to the swingarm **(see illustrations)**. Withdraw the bolt and recover the collars which are fitted on each side of the tie-rod end fitting.

**5** Unlock and raise the seat cowling to gain access to the shock absorber upper mounting bolt. Slacken and remove the upper mounting bolt, then manoeuvre the shock absorber out of position **(see illustrations)**.

### Inspection

**6** Inspect the shock absorber for obvious physical damage and oil leakage, and the coil spring for looseness, cracks or signs of fatigue.

**7** If damage is found, it will be necessary to renew the shock absorber assembly. Before condemning the original, it is worth checking whether overhaul of the unit is possible. Seek the advice of your Ducati dealer or a suspension specialist for the best course of action (Ducati do not list spare parts for the unit and supply the shock absorber only as a complete assembly).

### Installation

**8** Lubricate the bolts and the tie-rod end fitting and collars with molybdenum disulphide grease.

**9** Manoeuvre the shock absorber into position, ensuring the reservoir is on the left-hand side. Align the shock absorber with the rocker arm and fit the upper mounting bolt, tightening it to the specified torque.

**10** Fit the mounting collars to the tie-rod end fitting (shoulders facing inwards) then align the tie-rod and shock absorber lower mounting with the swingarm **(see illustration)**. Insert the special nut into mounting on the right-ha side of the swingarm, engaging its flat with the edge of the swingarm, then fit the pivot b from the left-hand side and tighten it to the specified torque.

**11** Remove all original locking compou and apply a drop of fresh locking compou to each heel plate bolt. Refit the heel plate the footrest bracket and tighten the bolts the specified torque.

**12** Install the rear wheel (see Chapter 7).

**13** Check the adjustment settings a operation of the rear suspension before tak the machine on the road.

## 13 Suspension – adjustments

**Note:** *The standard settings given here are those recommended at the time of writing. If the settings recommended in your Duc owners manual differ from those specif here, use the settings recommended in the manual which are specific to your machine.*

### Front forks

***Caution: Always make sure both left and right fork leg adjustments are equally se to ensure the motorcycle handles predictably.***

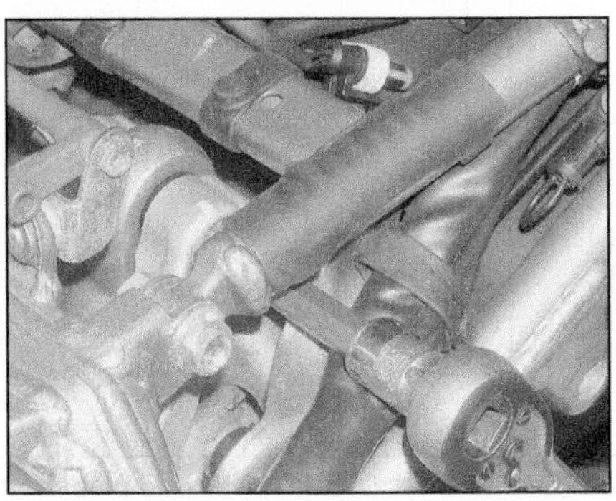

**12.5a Slacken and remove the upper mounting bolt . . .**

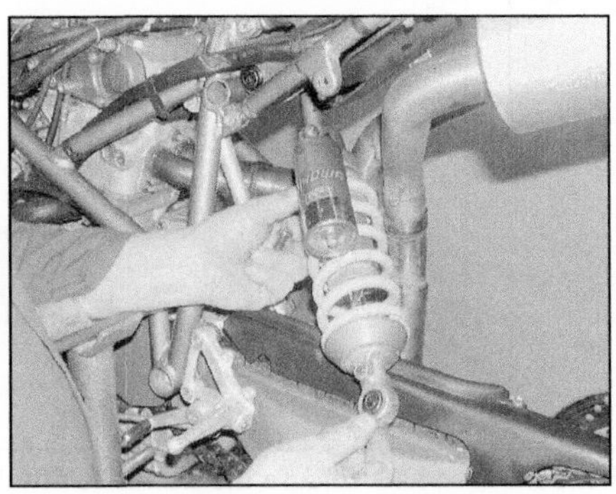

**12.5b . . . then manoeuvre the shock absorber out of position**

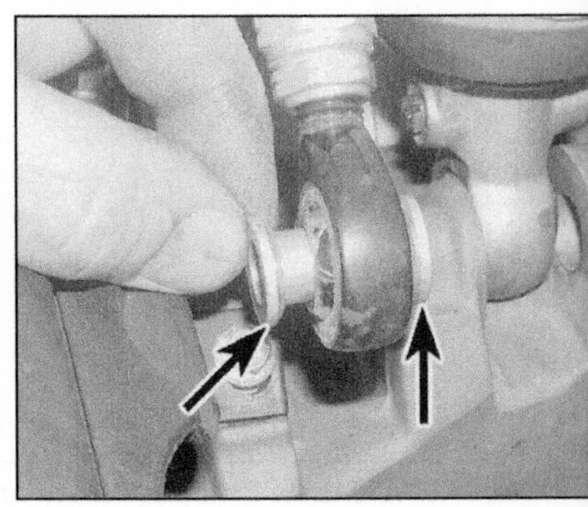

**12.10 Ensure the mounting collars are correctly fitted to the tie-rod lower mounting**

**13.1a Check the fork spring preload adjuster setting by measuring its height above the top cap surface**

**13.1b Adjust the fork spring preload adjuster with a ring spanner or socket**

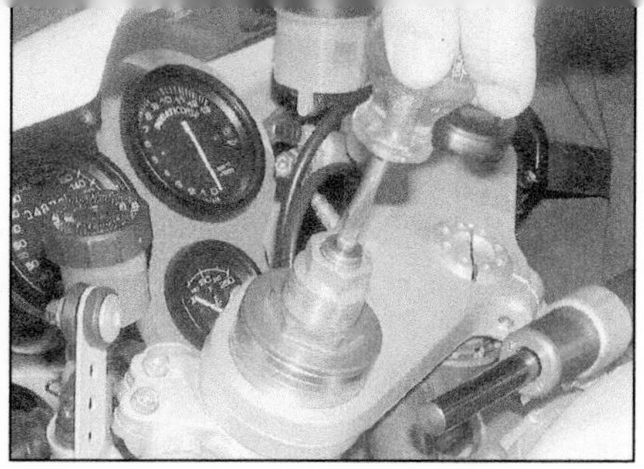

**13.2 Adjusting the fork rebound damping setting**

### Spring pre-load adjustment

**1** The spring pre-load is set using the adjuster fitted to the centre of each fork top cap. The preload adjustment is set by measuring the distance from the top of the adjuster to the upper surface of the top cap hexagonal section **(see illustration)**. The adjuster has a range of between 10 and 25 mm and the standard setting is 20 mm. Turn the adjuster clockwise to increase the pre-load and anti-clockwise to decrease it **(see illustration)**.

### Rebound damping adjustment

**2** The fork rebound damping is set using the adjuster located in the centre of the pre-load adjuster **(see illustration)**. The adjuster has a usable range of 14 clicks. To establish the standard setting, rotate the adjuster fully clockwise until it stops; do not force it. From this point, rotate the adjuster anti-clockwise whilst counting the number of clicks it emits; the standard setting is 10 or 11 clicks back from the fully clockwise position. To soften the damping, rotate the adjuster further anti-clockwise and to stiffen the damping rotate the adjuster further clockwise.

### Compression damping adjustment

**3** The fork compression damping is set using the adjuster on the bottom of the fork. The adjuster is not visible but is accessed through the base of the fork tube via the hole in the front wheel axle **(see illustrations)**. The adjuster has a usable range of between 14 and 17 clicks (depending on model). To establish the standard setting, rotate the adjuster fully clockwise until it stops; do not force it. From this point, rotate the adjuster anti-clockwise whilst counting the number of clicks it emits; the standard setting is 12 clicks back from the fully clockwise position. To soften the damping, rotate the adjuster further anti-clockwise and to stiffen the damping rotate the adjuster further clockwise.

## *Rear shock absorber*

### Spring pre-load adjustment

**4** Spring pre-load adjustment is made by repositioning the large locknut and adjuster nut, which form the spring upper seat, on the shock absorber body **(see illustration)**. Using a large C-spanner, slacken the locknut, then turn the adjuster nut clockwise to increase pre-load and anti-clockwise to decrease it. Once the adjustment is complete, secure the adjuster nut in position with the locknut.

**13.3a Adjusting the fork compression damping setting**

**5** On 916 models and early (pre 2000 models year) 748 models, no standard spring preload setting is specified by Ducati. Seek the advice of your Ducati dealer or a suspension specialist for the recommended setting.

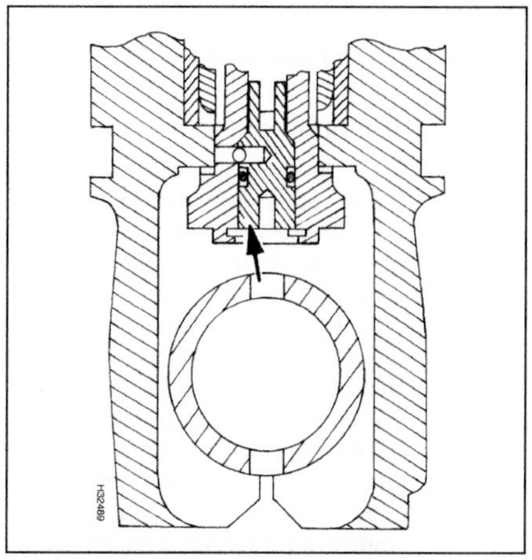


**13.3b Fork compression damping adjuster (arrowed) is fitted to the damper bolt**

**6** On 996 models and later (2000 model year on) 748 models, the standard pre-load setting can be established by measuring the length of the shock absorber spring, either with the shock absorber removed from the bike (see Section 12) or with the bike supported so there is no load on the rear suspension. The

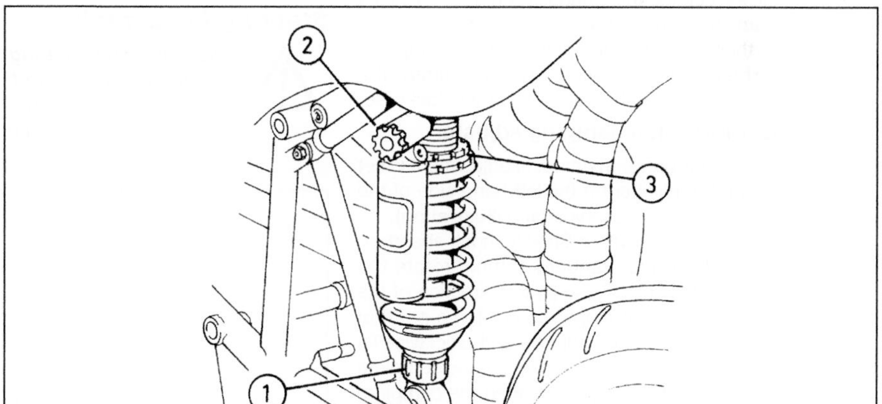


**13.4 Ohlins rear shock absorber adjustment details**

1 *Rebound damping adjuster*
2 *Compression damping adjuster*
3 *Spring preload locknut and adjuster nut*

**13.7 Adjusting the rebound damping setting – Showa rear shock absorber**

**13.9 Adjusting the compression damping setting – Showa rear shock absorber**

standard setting for the spring length is 160 mm on the Showa shock absorber, and 151 mm on the Ohlins shock absorber.

### Rebound damping adjustment

**7** On models with a Showa shock absorber, the rebound damping adjustment is set using the adjuster on the left-hand side of the shock absorber lower end **(see illustration)**. To establish the standard setting, rotate the adjuster fully clockwise (in the direction of the 'H' arrow) until it stops; do not force it. From this point, rotate the adjuster anti-clockwise (in the direction of the 'S' arrow) by one complete rotation (360°). To further soften the damping, rotate the adjuster further anti-clockwise (in the direction of the 'S' arrow) and to stiffen the damping rotate the adjuster further clockwise (in the direction of the 'H' arrow).

**8** On models with an Ohlins shock absorber, the rebound damping adjustment is set using the collar on the base of the shock absorber **(see illustration 13.4)**. To establish the standard setting, rotate the adjuster collar fully clockwise (when viewed from underneath the shock absorber) until it stops; do not force it. From this point, rotate the adjuster collar anti-clockwise whilst counting the number of clicks it emits; the standard setting is 14 clicks back from the fully clockwise position. To further soften the damping, rotate the adjuster further anti-clockwise and to stiffen the damping rotate the adjuster further clockwise.

### Compression damping adjuster

**9** The compression damping adjustment is set using the adjuster on the left-hand side of the shock absorber reservoir **(see illustration)**.

**10** On models with a Showa shock absorber, to establish the standard setting, rotate the adjuster fully clockwise (in the direction of the 'H' arrow) until it stops; do not force it. From this point, rotate the adjuster anti-clockwise (in the direction of the 'S' arrow) by one complete rotation (360°). To further soften the damping, rotate the adjuster further anti-clockwise (in the direction of the 'S' arrow) and to stiffen the damping rotate the adjuster further clockwise (in the direction of the 'H' arrow).

**11** On models with an Ohlins shock absorber, to establish the standard setting, rotate the adjuster fully clockwise until it stops; do not force it **(see illustration 13.4)**. From this point, rotate the adjuster anti-clockwise whilst counting the number of clicks it emits; the standard setting is 14 clicks back from the fully clockwise position. To further soften the damping, rotate the adjuster further anti-clockwise and to stiffen the damping rotate the adjuster further clockwise.

## 14 Chassis geometry – general information and adjustment

***Warning: Adjustments to chassis geometry will have a marked effect on the handling characteristics of the machine and should only be carried out by those with a good understanding of the principles of chassis/suspension geometry. The standard settings have been tried and tested by Ducati to give the best handling characteristics for normal road use. Any deviation from these settings could result in the handling of the machine becoming unpredictable, and even dangerous, on uneven road surfaces.***

### *Steering head angle*

***Warning: The steering head angle must be set to the 'road' position whenever the bike is used on the road (all machines set in this position). If the steering angle is set to the 'race' position, the steering lock becomes inoperable and the handling of the machine could become unpredictable on uneven road surfaces.***

### General information

**1** On most models (with the exception some later 748 models), the steering hea angle is adjustable. The adjuster is in the fo of a tube which is fitted inside the headsto of the frame and held in position by a dete screw and two clamp bolts. The holes in t centre of the adjuster tube in which t steering stem pivots are offset to facilita adjustment.

**2** The adjuster has two positions a 'roa position (steering angle 24°30') designed ensure safe and predictable handli characteristics on all kinds of road surfac and a 'race' position (steering angle 23°3 for use only on race tracks. The change steering angle alters the trail of the motorcyc which has a marked effect on the handli and stability of the bike.

**3** To allow for the movement of the t yoke, the steering damper has tv mounting points on the frame; the re mounting point is for use when the steeri angle is set to the 'road' position and the fro mounting point for use when the steeri angle is set to the 'race' position **(s illustration 8.1)**.

### Adjustment

**Note:** *Position the steering head just to t left of the central position whilst adjusting t steering head angle.*

**4** Slacken and remove the bolt securing t steering damper to the frame. Recover t washer (where fitted) positioned between t damper and frame or the collar from t damper end fitting (as applicable – s Section 8).

**5** Remove the circlip and washer from ea adjuster tube clamp bolt then slacken a remove both clamp bolts from the frame **(s illustrations)**.

**6** Unscrew the adjuster tube detent scre

**14.5a Remove the circlip . . .**

**14.5b . . . and washer from each clamp bolt . . .**

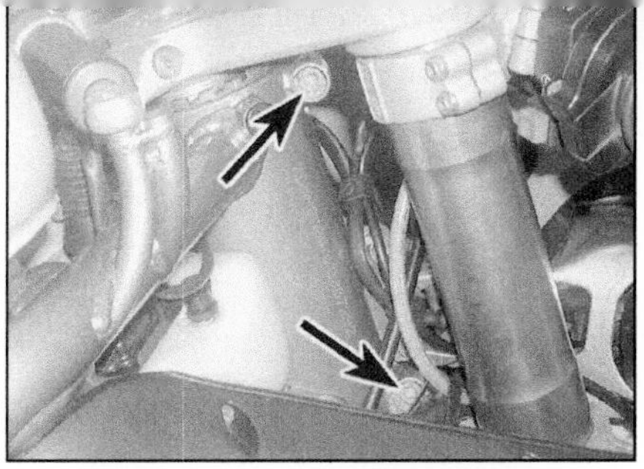

**14.5c . . . then unscrew both bolts (arrowed) from the headstock**

from the right-hand side of the headstock **(see illustration)**.

**7** Note the alignment marks on the top of the adjuster tube there are two marks positioned 180° (half-a-turn) apart **(see illustration)**. Using a C-spanner, rotate the adjuster tube 180° (half-a-turn) until the opposite mark is correctly aligned with the detent hole in the frame. Check the adjuster tube hole is correctly aligned with the frame then refit the detent screw, tightening it to the specified torque. Lubricate the clamp bolts with molybdenum disulphide grease then refit both bolts, tightening them to the specified torque. Fit the washer to each clamp bolt and secure them in position with the circlips, ensuring they are correctly located in their grooves.

**8** Remove all original locking compound from the steering damper bolt and apply a drop of fresh locking compound to its threads. Align the damper rod end fitting with the correct mounting point on the frame (rear mounting point if head angle is set to 'road' position, front mounting point for 'race' position), ensuring the washer/collar is in position (see Section 8). Refit the damper mounting bolt and tighten to the specified torque.

## Rear ride height

***Warning: Adjustments of the rear ride height are only recommended if the final drive ratio is changed. Any change will effect the handling of the machine and could result in unpredictable handling on uneven road surfaces.***

**14.7 Adjuster tube alignment mark (arrowed)**

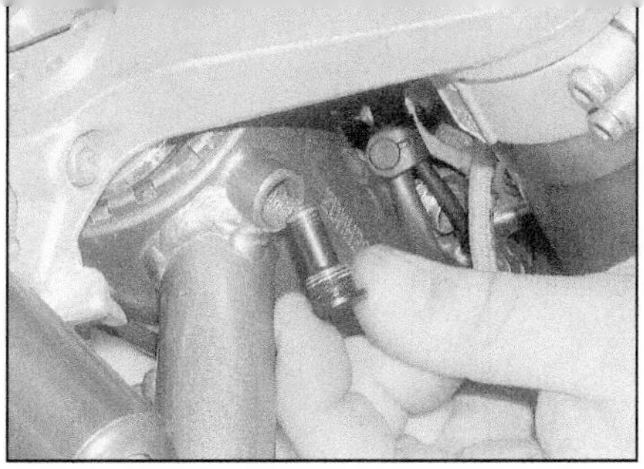

**14.6 Slacken and remove the detent screw from the adjuster tube**

### General information

**9** The tie-rod of the rear suspension linkage is adjustable to facilitate changes in the rear ride height of the bike. This adjustment should only be necessary to compensate for changes in the height of the rear axle (due to the eccentric adjustment mechanism of the final drive chain) if the final drive ratio of the sprockets is being changed.

### Adjustment

**Note:** *If the final drive ratio is to be changed from standard, before changing the sprockets measure the distance between the centre of the rear axle and a reference point on the frame (bike supported with no weight on the rear suspension). Once the sprockets have been installed and the final drive chain is correctly adjusted, adjust the ride height so the axle is at the same distance from the reference point on the frame (bike supported with no weight on the suspension). Ducati have a service tool which mounts on the engine rear mounting points on the frame to ensure the measurements are accurately taken* **(see illustration)**.

**10** To adjust the rear ride height, support the motorcycle on an auxiliary stand so the rear weight on the rear suspension linkage. This can be done either by using an auxiliary stand which engages with the swingarm pivot or by removing the lower fairing panels (see Chapter 8) and supporting the bike on an auxiliary stand(s) positioned underneath the engine.

**11** Once the bike is securely supported, slacken the tie-rod end fitting locknuts noting that the lower lock nut has a left-handed thread (identified by the lines scored on both the tie-rod hexagonal section and the locknut). With both locknuts loosened, rotate the tie-rod body to shorten/lengthen the tie-rod and alter the ride height. **Note:** *The standard setting for the tie-rod length is 261 mm (measured between the centres of the pivot bolt holes). Ducati state that the tie-rod length should never be set to more than 261 mm.*

**12** Once the tie-rod length is correctly set, securely tighten both locknuts, then lower the bike to the ground and (where necessary) install the fairing panels (see Chapter 8).

## Front forks

***Warning: Changes to the position of the front forks in the yokes will alter the steering characteristics of the bike. Whenever the bike is used on the road, it is recommended that the forks are positioned at the standard height (see Section 6). If the forks are repositioned in the yokes the handling of the machine could become unpredictable on uneven road surfaces.***

**13** The position of the front forks in the yokes also effects the chassis geometry and has a major effect on the steering characteristics of the bike. The standard fitting positions of the forks are given in Section 6.

**14** To adjust the position of the forks,

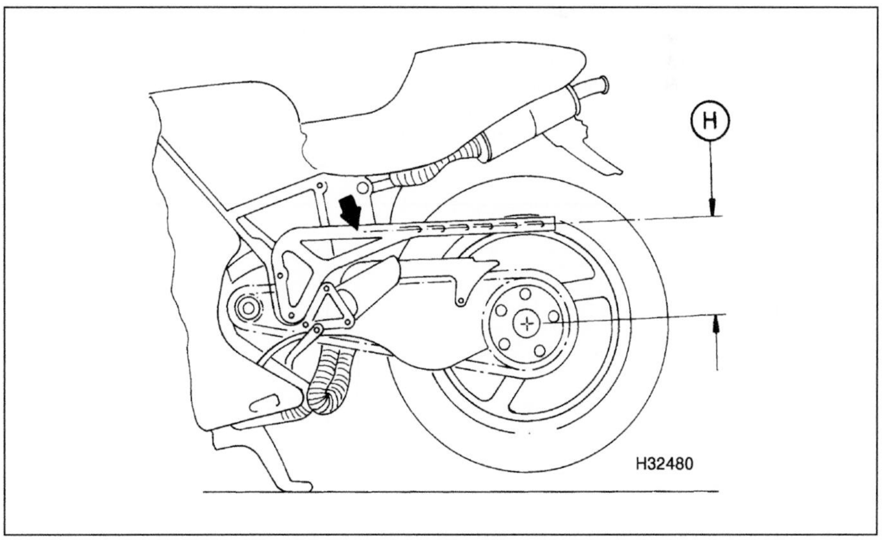


**14.9 Ducati service tool (arrowed) for adjusting the rear ride height (H)**

so the front wheel is raised clear of the ground. Slacken the top and bottom yoke clamp bolts and the handlebar clamp bolts, then reposition the forks in the yokes as necessary. Ensure both forks are exactly the same height, then tighten the clamp bolts to the specified torque, noting that the handlebar clamp locating pin must engage the hole in the top yoke.

## 15 Swingarm – removal and installation

**Note:** *Due to the design of the machine, the engine must be removed first to allow the swingarm to be removed (see Chapter 2).*

### Removal

1 Remove the rear wheel (see Chapter 7).

2 Remove the retaining screws and collars and free the chainguard from the swingarm. Recover the support plate fitted to the chainguard rear mounting point **(see illustration)**.

3 If the swingarm is to be renewed, remove the rear wheel bearing holder assembly (see Chapter 7). If the swingarm is to be installed again, remove the bolts securing the rear brake caliper to its mounting bracket then slide the caliper off the disc and tie it to the subframe to avoid any strain being placed on the hydraulic hoses. Release the drive chain tension and unhook the chain from the rear sprocket.

***Caution: Do not operate the rear brake whilst the caliper is removed.***

4 Remove the engine as described in Chapter 2.

5 With the engine removed, support the frame in such a way so that it will not topple over when the swingarm is removed. The easiest way to do this is to support the frame on axle stands with a plank of wood on the axle stand heads (shape the ends of the wood so they sit in the stands) positioned beneath the frame. Have an assistant lift the rear of the bike whilst you position the stands and wood correctly under the frame, then lower the frame onto the wood.

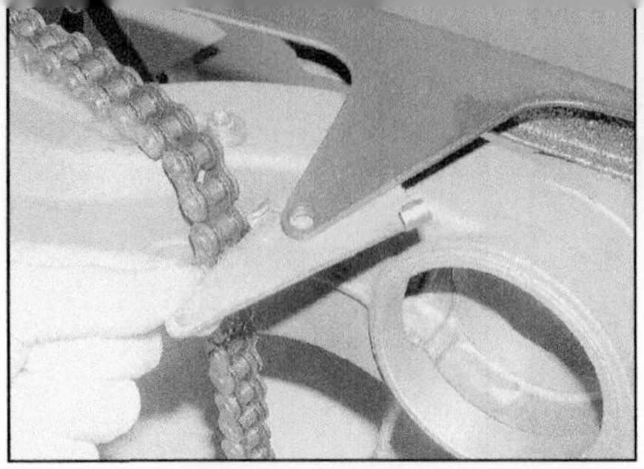

**15.2 Remove the support plate from the chainguard rear mounting**

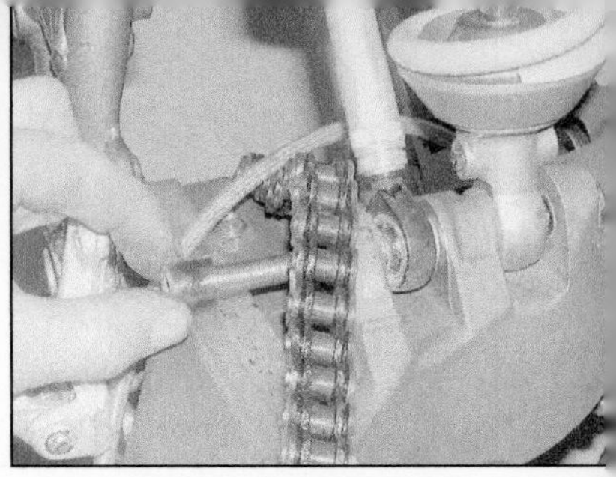

**15.7a Slacken and remove the pivot bo securing the tie-rod and shock absorber the swingarm . . .**

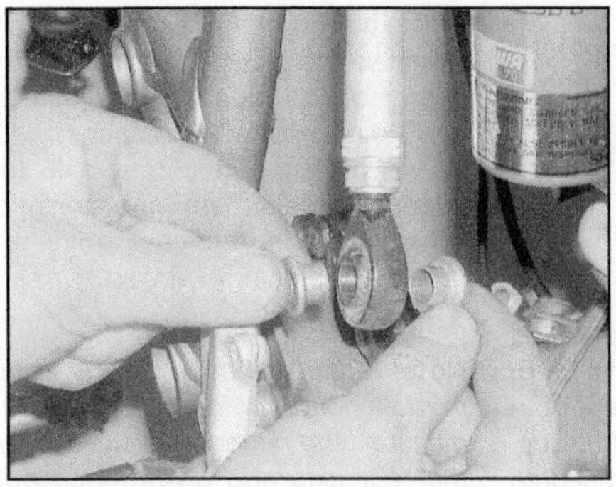

**15.7b . . . and recover the collars from the tie-rod lower end fitting**

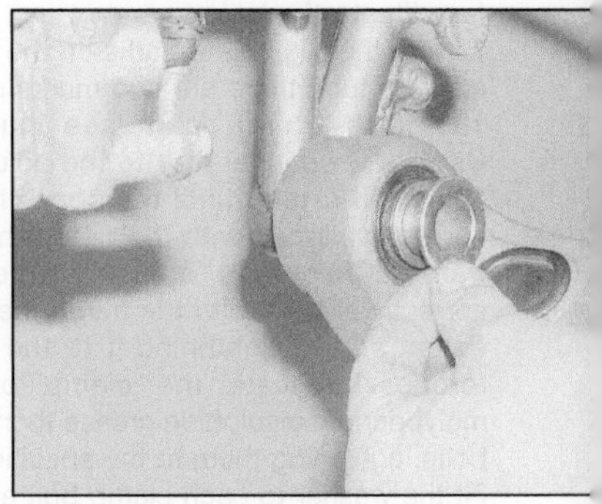

**15.8a Withdraw the inner sleeves from t left- and right-hand pivots . . .**

6 Unscrew the bolts and remove the heel plate from the rider's left-hand footrest bracket.

7 Support the swingarm then slacken and remove the pivot bolt and special nut securing the shock absorber and tie-rod to the swingarm. Withdraw the bolt and recover the collars fitted on each side of the tie-rod end fitting **(see illustrations)**.

8 Ensure the frame is securely supported then withdraw the inner sleeves from the swingarm left- and right-hand pivots **(see illustration)**. Remove the swingarm and drive chain from the frame and recover the inner and outer collars from the right-hand pivot **(see illustration)**. Inspect the assembly as described in Section 16.

### Installation

9 Lubricate the swingarm seals, bearin collars and inner sleeves with bearing grea Lubricate the pivot bolts and the tie-rod e fitting collars with molybdenum disulph grease.

10 Fit the inner and outer collars (should facing inwards) to the swingarm right-ha pivot, then partially insert both inner slee **(see illustrations)**.

11 Manoeuvre the swingarm and drive ch assembly into position. Align the swinga pivots with the frame and fully insert the in sleeves into the left- and right-hand pivots.

12 Lubricate the threads of the pivot bolt v molybdenum disulphide grease, then fit

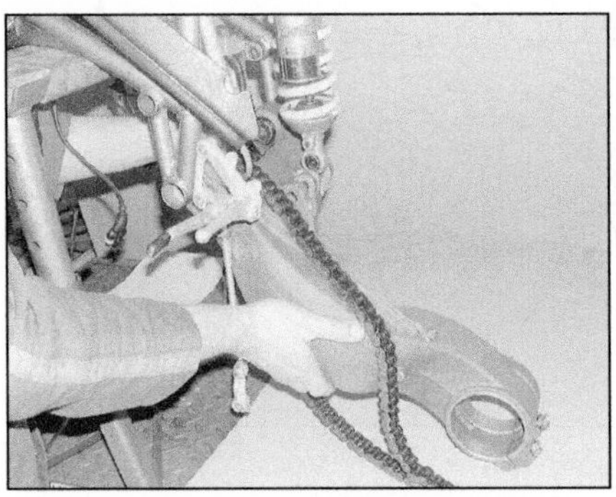

**15.8b . . . and remove the swingarm and drive chain**

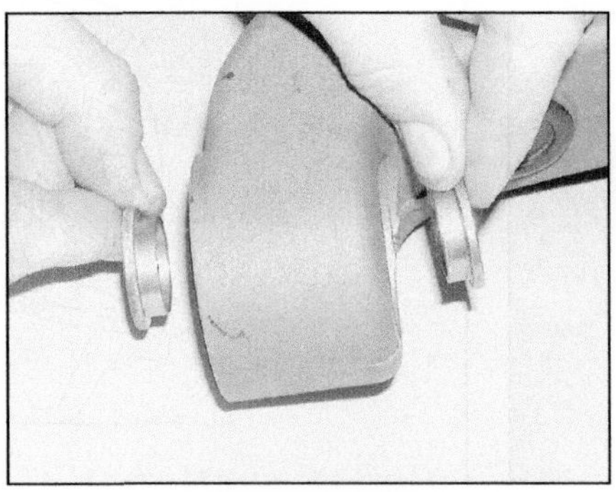

**15.10a Fit the inner and outer collars to the right-hand pivot . . .**

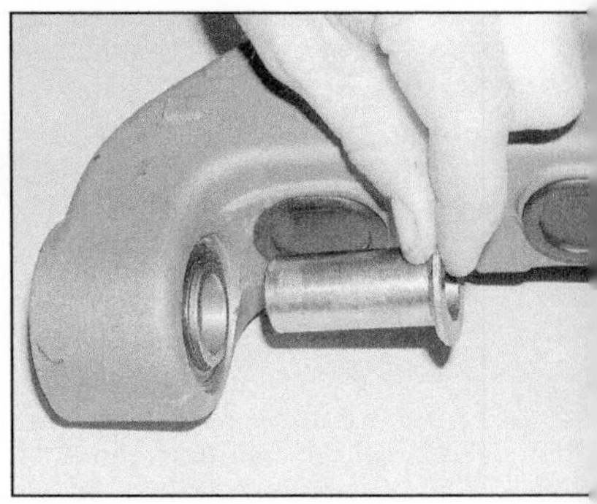

**15.10b . . . and insert the right-hand inn sleeve . . .**

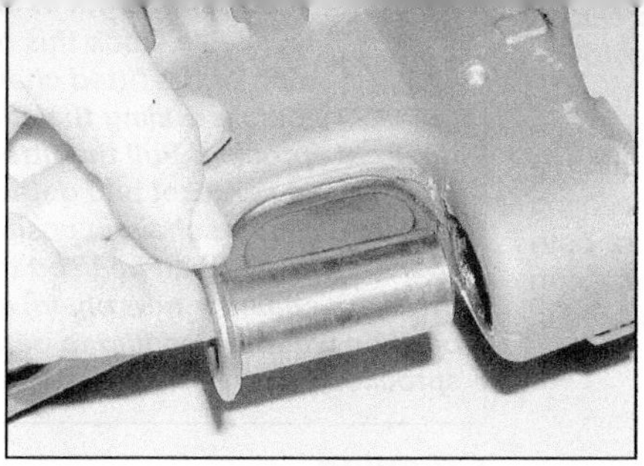

**15.10c . . . and left-hand inner sleeve into the swingarm**

special nut in its mounting on the right-hand side of the swingarm.

**13** Fit the mounting collars to the tie-rod end fitting (shoulders facing inwards) then align the tie-rod and shock absorber lower mounting with the swingarm. Insert the pivot bolt from the left-hand side of the swingarm and thread it into the special nut; tighten the bolt to the specified torque.

**14** Remove all original locking compound and apply a drop of fresh locking compound to each heel plate bolt. Refit the heel plate to the footrest bracket and tighten the bolts to the specified torque.

**15** Install the engine as described in Chapter 2.

**16** Where necessary, fit the rear wheel bearing holder and associated components (see Chapter 7).

**17** Hook the drive chain onto the rear sprocket then slide the brake caliper into position, ensuring the pads pass each side of the disc. Lubricate the caliper mounting bolts with molybdenum disulphide grease then refit the bolts, tightening them to the specified torque (see Chapter 7).

**18** Remove all original locking compound and apply a drop of fresh locking compound to each chainguard screw. Ensure the support plate is correctly fitted to the rear mounting, then locate the chainguard on the swingarm and refit the retaining screws and collars, tightening them to the specified torque.

**19** Fit the rear wheel (see Chapter 7) then adjust the drive chain slack as described in Chapter 1.

**20** Check the operation of the rear brake and suspension before taking the machine on the road.

## 16 Swingarm – inspection and bearing renewal

### Inspection

**1** Remove the swingarm and withdraw inner and outer collars from the swingarm right-hand pivot (see Section 15).

**2** Inspect all components closely, looking for obvious signs of wear such as heavy scoring, or for damage such as cracks or distortion **(see illustration)**. The right-hand pivot ball bearing inner races should rotate freely and easily without any sign of freeplay or roughness **(see illustration)**. Renew worn components as necessary.

**3** Inspect the swingarm drive chain upper and lower sliders along their entire length and renew them if they show signs of wear or damage. To renew the slider, slacken and remove the retaining screws and collars and remove the slider from the swingarm **(see illustration)**. Remove all original locking compound and apply a drop of fresh locking compound to each retaining screw. Fit the new slider to the swingarm and refit the collars and retaining screws, tightening them to the specified torque **(see illustration)**.

**4** Ensure the caliper mounting plate locating pin is securely fitted **(see illustration)**. If the

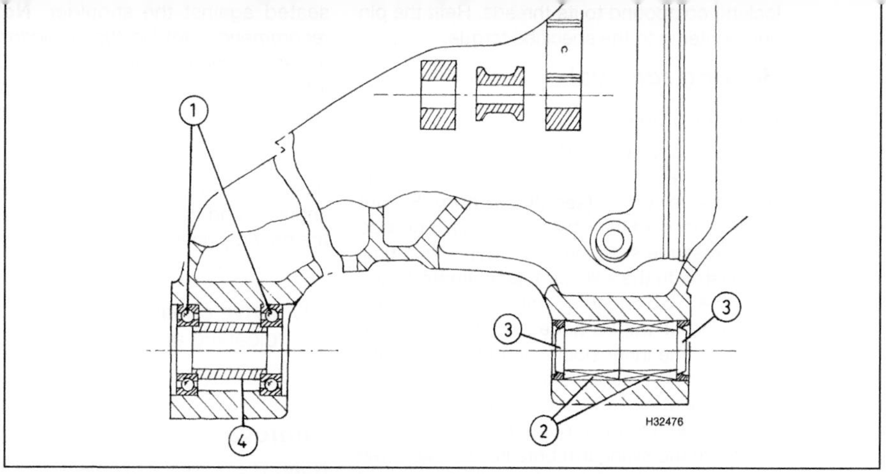


**16.2a Swingarm bearing arrangement**

*1 Right-hand bearings*
*2 Left-hand needle roller bearings*
*3 Dust seals*
*4 Spacer*

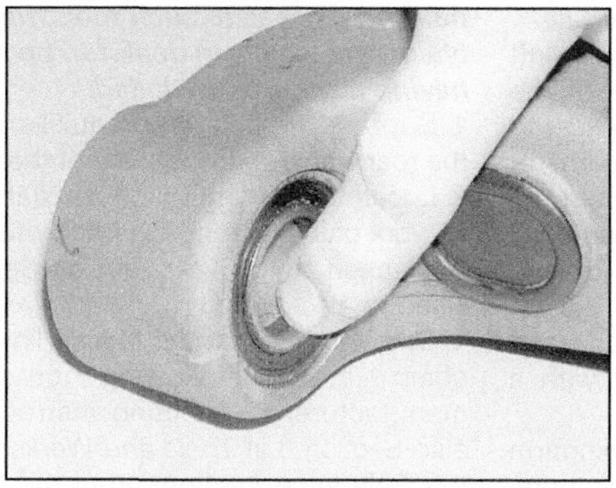

**16.2b Checking the swingarm right-hand pivot bearings for wear**

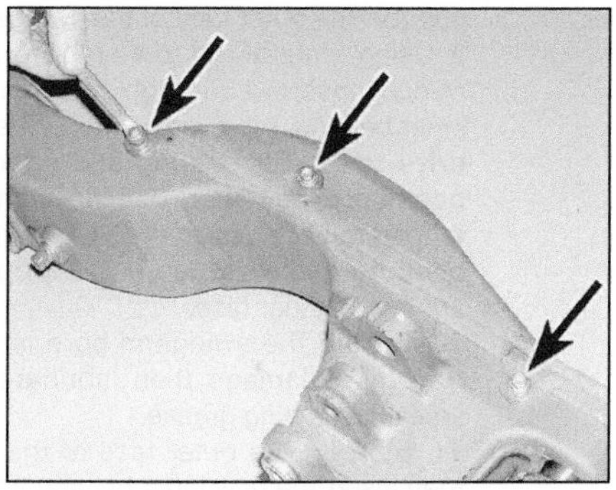

**16.3a Unscrew the retaining screws and collars and remove the drive chain upper slider**

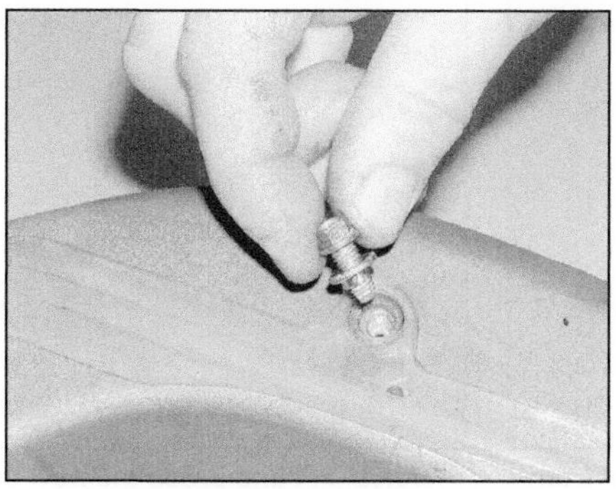

**16.3b Ensure the collars are correctly fitted to the slider bolts**

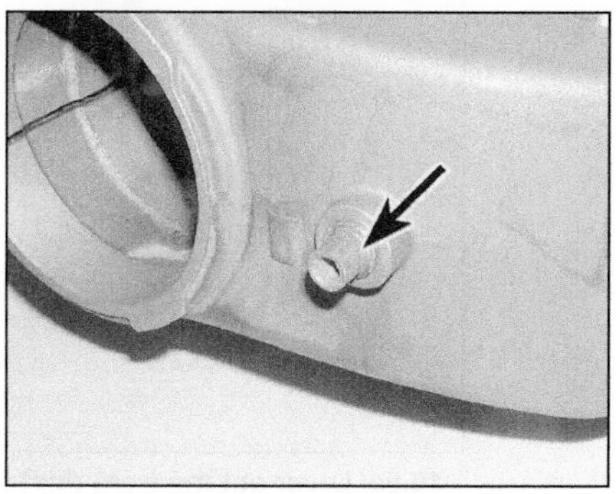

**16.4 Ensure the swingarm caliper plate pin (arrowed) is securely fitted**

locking compound to its threads. Refit the pin and tighten it to the specified torque.

## *Bearing renewal*

### Left-hand pivot

**5** If the dust seals are damaged, the old seals can be levered out of position using a flat-bladed screwdriver **(see illustration)**. Ensure the sealing lip of the new seal is facing inwards then press the seal squarely into position until it is flush with the swingarm **(see illustration)**.

**6** If the two needle roller bearings are damaged, it will be necessary to renew the bearings, the inner sleeve and the dust seals. Remove the dust seals and note the correct fitted location of the bearings before pressing/drifting them out of position.

**7** Ensure the swingarm bore is clean and free from damage then lubricate it with a smear of bearing grease. The new bearings should be pressed or drawn into the bore, rather than driven into position, to prevent possible damage. In the absence of a press, a suitable drawbolt arrangement can be made up as described in *Tools and Workshop Tips* in the Reference section. Ensure the bearing is correctly positioned in its bore then press the new dust seals into position, ensuring their sealing lips are facing inwards. **Note:** *Ducati recommend warming the swingarm to 150°C to ease bearing installation.*

### Right-hand pivot

**8** Remove the inner and outer collars then support the outer face of the swingarm.

**9** Using a metal rod (preferably a brass drift punch) inserted through the centre of the inner bearing, tap evenly around the spacer to drive the outer bearing and spacer out of position. The inner bearing can then be tapped out of position once the swingarm has been turned over and a support placed against its inner face.

**10** Ensure the swingarm bore is clean and free from damage then lubricate it with a smear of bearing grease.

**11** Support the outer face of the swingarm then insert the new inner bearing into its bore. Using the old bearing, a bearing driver or a socket large enough to contact the outer race seated against the shoulder. **Note:** *Ducati recommend warming the swingarm to 150°C to ease bearing installation.*

**12** Turn the swingarm over and support its inner face. Press the bearing spacer into the inner bearing race then drive the outer bearing into place as described above. Ensure both bearings are in firm contact with the swingarm shoulder and the spacer is correctly seated in the bearing inner races.

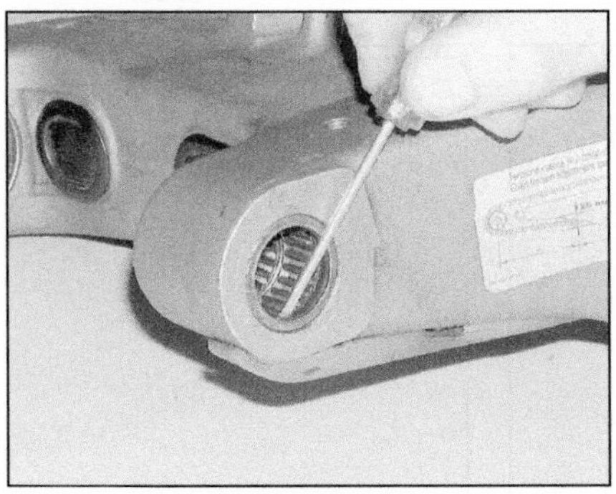

**16.5a Lever out the worn dust seal from the left pivot . . .**

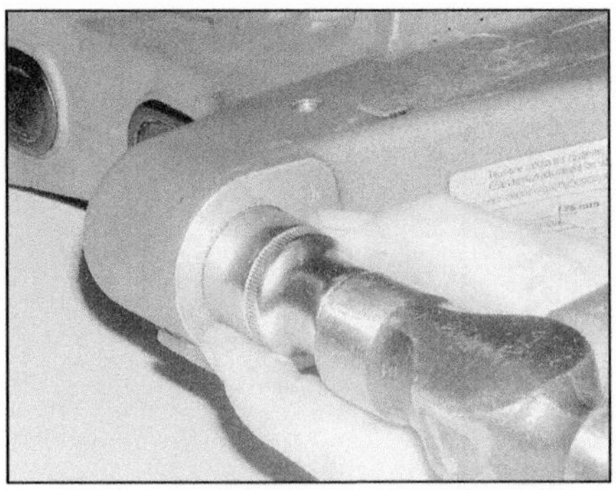

**16.5b . . . and press the new seal into position using a socket which bears only on the seal's outer edge**

## 17 Drive chain – removal, cleaning and installation

## *Removal*

**Note:** *The original equipment drive chain fitted to these models has a rivet-type joining link which can be disassembled using one of several commercially-available drive chain breaking/riveting tools. The joining link can be recognised by the identification marks on its side plate (and usually its different colour), as well as by the staked ends of the two pins which look as if they have been deeply centre-punched, instead of peened over as with all the other pins.*

***Warning: NEVER install a drive chain which uses a clip-type master (split) link. Use ONLY the correct service tools to secure the staked-type of master link – if you do not have access to such tools, have the chain renewed by a dealer to be sure of having it securely installed.***

**1** Support the bike on an auxiliary stand so the rear wheel is raised clear of the ground.

**2** Locate the joining link in a suitable position to work on by rotating the back wheel.

**3** Slacken the drive chain as described in Chapter 1.

**4** Split the chain at the joining link using the chain cutter, following carefully the manufacturer's operating instructions (see also Section 8 in *Tools and Workshop Tips* in the Reference Section). Free the chain from the rear sprocket then, with the transmission in neutral, pull it off the front sprocket.

**HAYNES HiNT** ***If a spare length of chain is available, hook this onto one end of the fitted chain before pulling the chain off the front sprocket. Pull the fitted chain off the front sprocket and detach it, leaving the spare chain in position. The spare chain can then be used to draw the fitted chain (or new chain) into position without needing to detach the sprocket cover.***

## *Cleaning*

**5** Soak the chain in paraffin (kerosene) f approximately five or six minutes.

***Caution: Don't use petrol (gasoline), solvent or other cleaning fluids which might damage its internal sealing properties. Don't use high-pressure wate Remove the chain, wipe it off, then blow dry it with compressed air immediately. The entire process shouldn't take longer than ten minutes – if it does, the O-rings the chain rollers could be damaged.***

## *Installation*

***Warning: If you do not have access to a chain riveting tool, have the chain fitted by a deal***

**6** If necessary, remove the front sprock cover from the engine as described in Se tion 18.

**7** Install the drive chain around the sprocke and leave the two ends in a convenie position to work on.

**8** Refer to Section 8 in *Tools and Worksh Tips* in the Reference Section. Fit an O-ring each of the new joining link pins, then ins the joining link from the inside of the chain. the second O-ring to each link pin then inst the new side plate with its identification mar facing out. Press the side plate securely or the link and secure it in position by spreadi the link pin ends using the chain riveting to following carefully the instructions of both t chain manufacturer and the tool manufactur **DO NOT** re-use old joining link components

**9** After staking, check the joining link a staking for any signs of cracking. If there any evidence of cracking, the joining lir O-rings and side plate must be renewed.

**10** Install the sprocket cover (where remov – see Section 18), then adjust and lubrica the chain following the procedures describ in Chapter 1.

## 18 Sprockets – check and renewal

## *Check*

**1** To gain access to the front sprock remove the fairing lower panel (see Chapter and unbolt the sprocket cover from t engine.

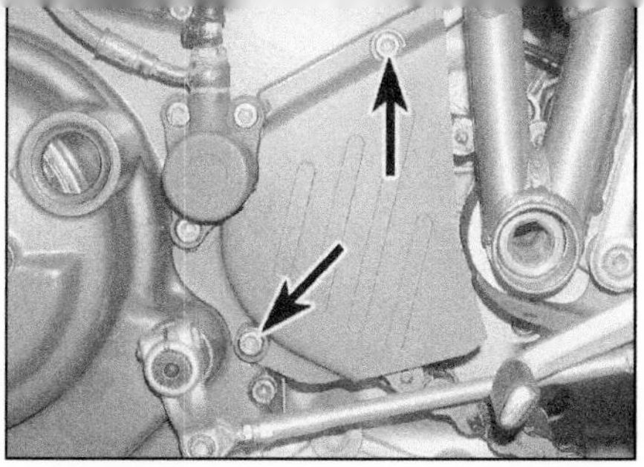

**18.6 Undo the bolts (arrowed) and remove the sprocket cover from the engine**

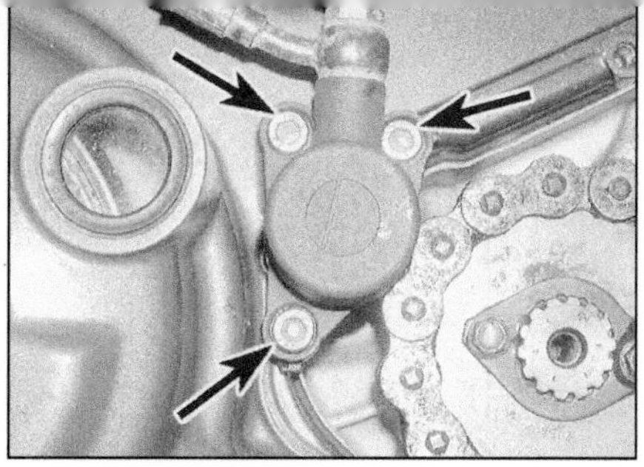

**18.7a Unscrew the bolts (arrowed) . . .**

**18.7b . . . then free the clutch slave cylinder from the engine and remove the rubber gaiter (arrowed)**

**2** Check the wear pattern on both sprockets (see Chapter 1, Section 33). If the sprocket teeth are worn excessively, renew the chain and both sprockets as a set. Whenever the sprockets are inspected, the drive chain and cush drive rubbers should also be inspected. If you are renewing the chain, renew the sprockets as well.

**3** Also check the drive chain upper and lower sliders on the swingarm for signs of wear or damage and renew if necessary (see Section 16).

**4** Install the sprocket cover, tightening its retaining bolts securely, and fairing panel (see Chapter 8) then adjust and lubricate the chain following the procedures described in Chapter 1, Section 4.

## *Renewal*

### Front sprocket

**5** Remove the fairing left-hand lower panel (see Chapter 8).

**6** Undo the two bolts and remove the sprocket cover from the engine **(see illustration)**.

**7** Unscrew the clutch slave cylinder bolts and free the cylinder, complete with rubber gaiter, from the engine **(see illustrations)**. **Note:** *There is no need to disconnect the hydraulic hose from the cylinder.*

***Caution: Do not operate the clutch lever whilst the cylinder is detached. To prevent the piston being accidentally expelled, remove the rubber gaiter and retain the piston with a cable tie passed through the cylinder mounting bolts holes and securely tightened around the cylinder.***

**8** Withdraw the clutch pushrod from the engine, noting which way around it is fitted **(see illustration)**. If the pushrod O-rings show signs of damage or deterioration they must be renewed.

**9** Place the transmission in gear then slacken the sprocket retaining plate bolts. Unscrew both bolts then rotate the retaining plate and slide it off the end of the output shaft **(see illustration)**. The retaining plate must be renewed if it shows signs of damage or wear.

**10** Slacken the bearing holder clamp bolts then adjust the drive chain until it is fully slack (see Chapter 1) and unhook it from the rear sprocket.

**11** Disengage the sprocket from the chain and slide it off the output shaft, noting which way around it is fitted **(see illustration)**.

**12** Slide the new sprocket onto the output shaft, ensuring it flange is facing towards the engine. Engage the drive chain with the sprocket and take up any slack in the chain.

**13** Slide the retaining plate onto the output shaft splines then align it with the shaft groove and rotate it to line it up with the sprocket holes. Remove all original locking compound and apply a drop of fresh locking compound to each retaining plate bolt then refit the bolts, tightening them to the specified torque **(see illustration)**. Ensure the sprocket is securely retained by the plate before proceeding.

**14** Wipe the clutch pushrod clean. Ensure the O-rings are both correctly located in the pushrod groves (renew them if they show any sign of damage) then lubricate the pushrod

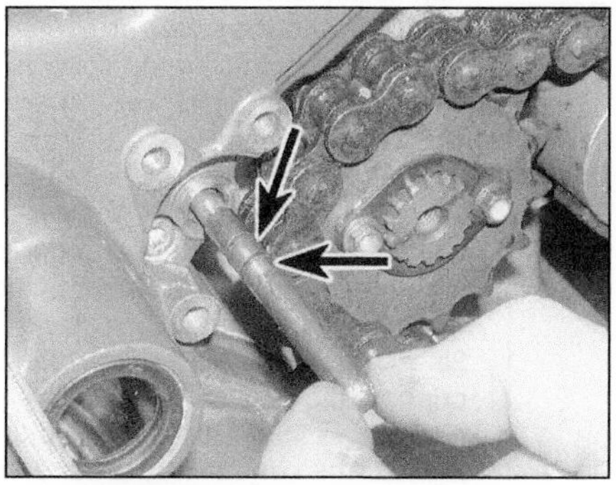

**18.8 Withdraw the clutch pushrod noting which way around it is fitted (O-rings arrowed)**

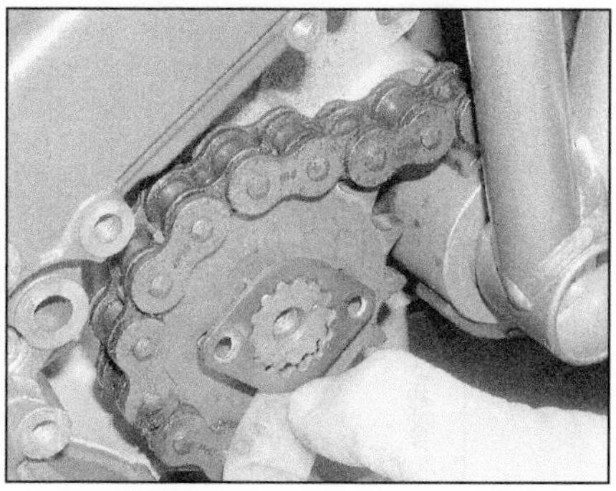

**18.9 Unscrew the bolts and remove the retaining plate from the output shaft**

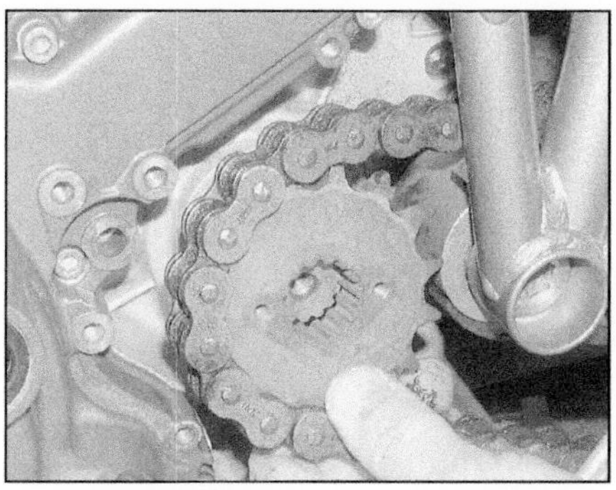

**18.11 Disengage the sprocket from the chain and remove it from the bike**

**18.13 Apply locking compound to the threads of the sprocket retaining plate bolts**

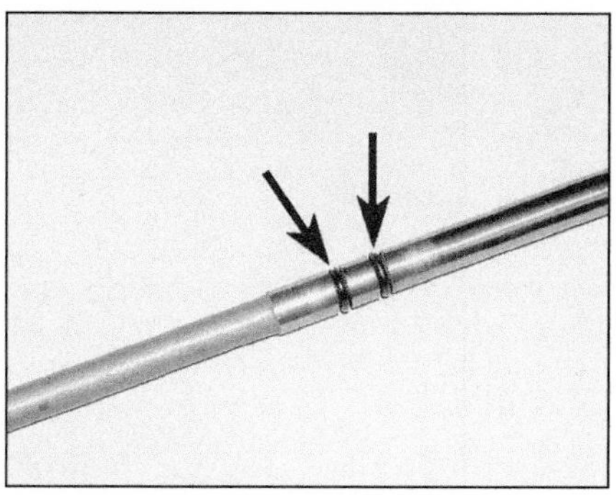

**18.14 Ensure the clutch pushrod O-rings (arrowed) are in good condition**

18.19a Remove the rear sprocket retaining circlip . . .

18.19b . . . and washer from the coupling

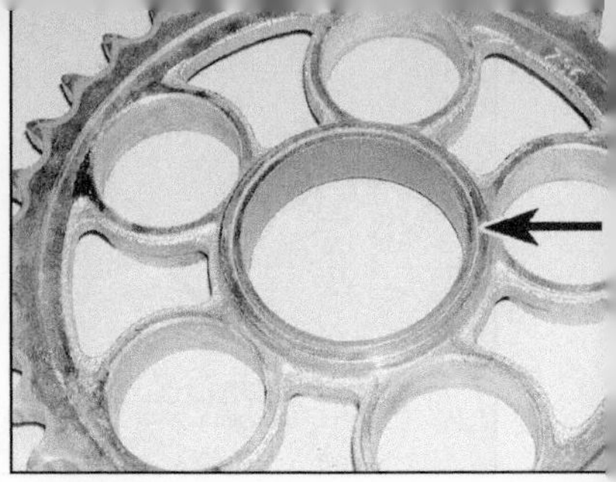

18.22 Ensure the collar (arrowed) is positioned flush with the rear sprocke

with molybdenum disulphide grease **(see illustration)**. Insert the pushrod into the crankcase ensuring that the O-rings are positioned on left-hand end of the shaft.

**15** Ensure the clutch slave cylinder and engine surfaces are clean and dry then remove the cable tie (used for security). Refit the rubber gaiter to the slave cylinder then locate the cylinder on the engine, tightening its retaining bolts to the specified torque (see Chapter 2).

**16** Refit the sprocket cover to the engine and securely tighten its retaining bolts.

**17** Install the fairing panel (see Chapter 8) then adjust and lubricate the chain following the procedures described in Chapter 1.

## Rear sprocket

**18** Remove the rear sprocket coupling as described in Section 19.

**19** Using a pair of circlip pliers, extract the large circlip securing the sprocket to the coupling flange, then remove the inner washer **(see illustrations)**.

**20** Note which way around the sprocket is fitted then, using a rubber mallet, tap the rear sprocket off the coupling assembly. The centre bush and outer washer should remain on the flange and the collar in the sprocket.

**21** Check the cush drive bushes and sprocket centre bush and collar for signs of wear or damage and, if necessary, renew them (see Section 19).

**22** Remove all traces of dirt from the sprocket and coupling flange and ensure all the cush drive bushes are securely installed. If the new sprocket is not supplied complete with collar, remove the collar from the original sprocket and press/tap it squarely into the new sprocket. Ensure the collar is positioned flush with the sprocket outer face **(see illustration)**.

**23** Ensure the outer washer and centre bush are correctly fitted to the flange.

**24** Lubricate the sprocket, bush and flange contact surfaces with a smear of molybdenum disulphide grease to aid installation.

**25** Align the sprocket with the cush drive bushes and press/tap it squarely onto the flange **(see illustration)**. Ensure the sprocket is fitted the correct way around with its size marking facing outwards.

**26** Once the sprocket is correctly seated, refit the inner washer and secure it in posit with the circlip, ensuring it is correctly loca in the coupling flange groove.

**27** Install the sprocket coupling as describ in Section 19.

18.25 Ensure the rear sprocket is fitted the correct way around

## 19 Rear sprocket coupling – removal, overhaul and installation

### *Removal*

**1** Remove the circlip from the sproc coupling nut, noting which way around i fitted (the inner end of the circlip is curv **(see illustration)**.

**2** Place the transmission in gear then have assistant support the bike and apply the brake hard whilst you slacken the coup nut.

**3** Position the motorcycle on an auxili stand so that the rear wheel is clear of ground.

**4** Slacken the bearing holder clamp bolts adjust the drive chain until it is fully slack ( Chapter 1).

**5** Remove the coupling nut and washer t unhook the drive chain from the rear sproc and hang it over the swingarm (s **illustration)**.

**6** Slide the sprocket coupling assembly the stub axle and recover the washer fit between the coupling and bearing holder (s **illustrations)**.

19.1 Remove the circlip then slacken the sprocket coupling nut

19.5 Remove the nut and washer . . .

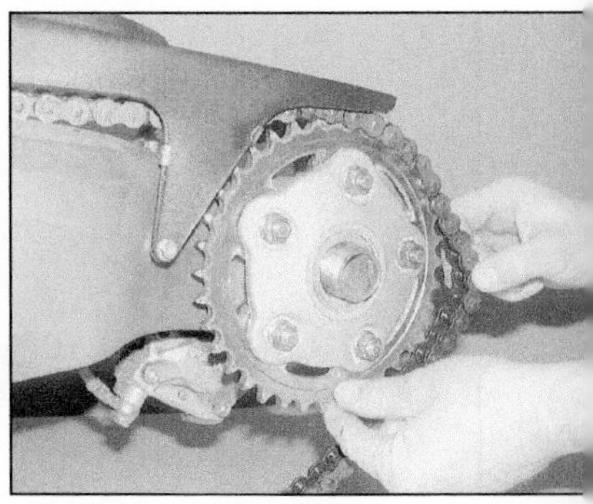

19.6a . . . then slide off the coupling assembly . . .

19.6b . . . and remove the washer

19.9a Retain the cush drive bush then unscrew the retaining nut . . .

19.9b . . . and remove the bush from the sprocket

### Overhaul

**7** Inspect the coupling assembly components closely, looking for obvious signs of wear such as heavy scoring, or for damage such as cracks or distortion.

**8** Check the cush drive bushes and the sprocket centre bush and collar for signs of wear or damage and renew if damaged. If wear or damage is found, renew the cush drive bushes as a set and renew the centre bush and collar as a matched pair.

**9** To renew a cush drive bush, retain the bush with an Allen key, then slacken and remove the retaining nut and remove the bush from the flange/sprocket **(see illustrations)**. Lubricate the threads and contact face of the retaining nut with molybdenum disulphide grease then fit the new bush to the flange/sprocket and tighten the retaining nut to the specified torque. Repeat as necessary until all bushes have been renewed.

**10** To renew the centre bush, first remove the rear sprocket (see Section 18). Lever the original bush off the sprocket flange using two screwdrivers **(see illustration)**. Clean the flange and lubricate it with a smear of molybdenum disulphide grease then tap the new bush squarely onto the flange. Reassemble the sprocket and flange (see Section 18).

**11** To renew the centre bush collar, remove the rear sprocket (see Section 18). Support the sprocket on blocks of wood then tap the collar out of position. Clean the sprocket bore then tap the new collar into position using a suitable tubular drift. Ensure the collar is positioned so that it is flush with the sprocket outer face. Reassemble the sprocket and flange (see Section 18).

### Installation

**12** Ensure the splines of the stub axle and sprocket coupling are clean then slide the washer onto the axle.

**13** Lubricate the axle splines with a smear of grease then install the sprocket coupling assembly.

**14** Lubricate the threads and contact face of the coupling nut with a smear of molybdenum disulphide grease then refit the washer and nut to the stub axle, tightening the nut firmly by hand.

**15** Hook the drive chain onto the sprocket and remove all slack from the chain. Remove the bike from its stand then adjust the drive chain as described in Chapter 1.

**16** Once the drive chain is correctly adjusted, tighten the coupling nut to the specified torque (prevent rotation in the same way as on removal). Check that the nut is correctly aligned with one of the stub axle holes to enable the circlip to be installed; if not tighten it slightly until alignment is correct.

**17** Insert the inner end of the circlip into the stub axle hole and seat the circlip correctly on the coupling nut shoulder. Note that the circlip must be fitted so the bend of its inner end curves towards the coupling **(see illustration)**.

**18** Operate the brake pedal several times to ensure the pads are in firm contact with the disc before using the bike on the road.

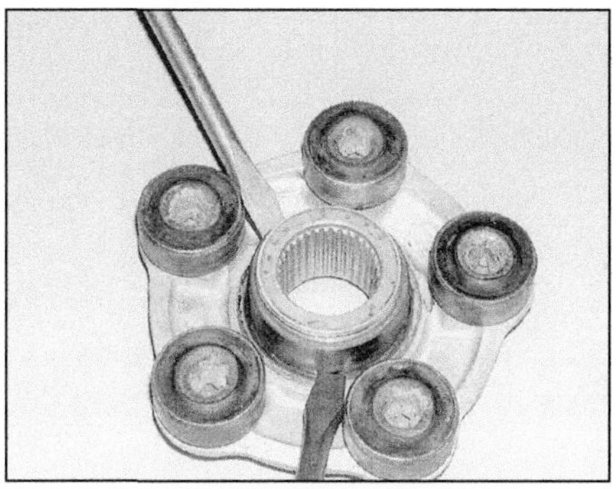

19.10 Lever the bush off the sprocket flange using two screwdrivers

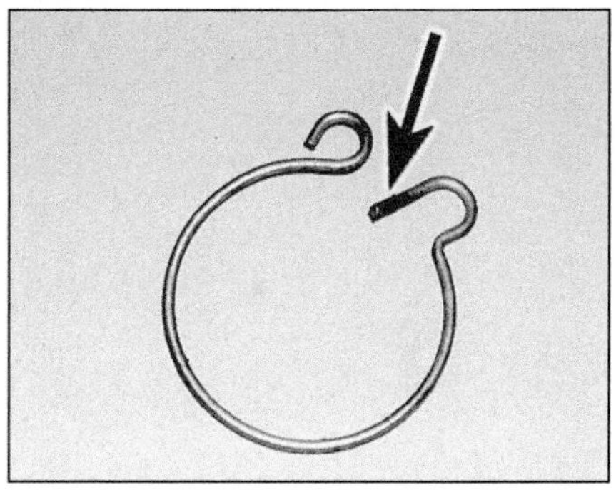

19.17 Ensure the circlip is installed with its bend (arrowed) curving in towards the sprocket coupling

# Chapter 7
# Brakes, wheels and tyres

## Contents



## Degrees of difficulty

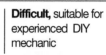

| | | | | |
|---|---|---|---|---|
| **Easy,** suitable for novice with little experience | **Fairly easy,** suitable for beginner with some experience | **Fairly difficult,** suitable for competent DIY mechanic | **Difficult,** suitable for experienced DIY mechanic | **Very difficult,** suitable for expert DIY or professional |

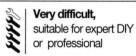

## Specifications

### Brakes

| | |
|---|---|
| Brake fluid type | DOT 4 |
| Brake pad friction material minimum thickness | 1 mm |
| Front discs | |
| Diameter | 320 mm |
| Thickness | |
| Steel disc | |
| Standard | 5.0 ± 0.1 mm |
| Service limit | 4.6 mm |
| Cast iron disc | |
| Standard | 4.5 ± 0.1 mm |
| Service limit | 3.5 mm |
| Front disc maximum runout | 0.3 mm |
| Rear disc | |
| Diameter | 220 mm |
| Thickness | |
| Standard | 6.0 ± 0.1 mm |
| Service limit | 5.4 mm |
| Rear disc maximum runout | 0.3 mm |

### Wheels

| | |
|---|---|
| Maximum wheel runout (front and rear) | |
| Axial (side-to-side) | 0.5 mm |
| Radial (out-of-round) | 0.8 mm |
| Maximum axle runout (front and rear) | 0.2 mm |

| | |
|---|---|
| Tyre pressures | see *Daily (pre-ride)* checks |
| Tyre sizes | |
| 748 models | |
| Front | 120/60 ZR17 |
| Rear | 180/55 ZR17 |
| 916 models | |
| Front | 120/70 ZR17 |
| Rear | 180/55 ZR 17 or 190/50 ZR17 |
| 996 models | |
| Front | 120/70 ZR17 |
| Rear | 190/50 ZR17 |

## Torque wrench settings

| | |
|---|---|
| Bleed valve | 12 Nm |
| Front brake caliper mounting bolts | 43 Nm |
| Front brake disc bolts | 25 Nm |
| Front brake master cylinder mounting clamp bolts | 9 Nm |
| Front wheel | |
| Axle nut | 63 Nm |
| Axle clamp bolts | 19 Nm |
| Rear brake caliper mounting bolts | 25 Nm |
| Rear brake disc bolts | |
| M6 bolts | 10 Nm |
| M8 bolts | 25 Nm |
| Rear brake master cylinder | |
| Mounting bolts | 10 Nm |
| Mounting bracket bolt | 43 Nm |
| Pedal pivot bolt | 29 Nm |
| Rear wheel nut | 176 Nm |
| Rear wheel driving pin bolts | 11 Nm |

## 1 General information

All models covered in this manual are fitted with cast alloy wheels designed for tubeless tyres only. Both front and rear brakes are hydraulically operated disc brakes of Brembo manufacture.

***Caution: Disc brake components rarely require disassembly. Do not disassemble components unless absolutely necessary. If a hydraulic brake line is loosened, the entire system must be drained then properly filled and bled upon reassembly. Do not use solvents on internal brake components. Solvents will cause the seals to swell and distort. Use only clean brake fluid or denatured alcohol for cleaning. Use care when working with brake fluid as it can injure your eyes and it will damage painted surfaces and plastic parts.***

## 2 Front brake pads – renewal

***Warning: Renew both sets of front brake pads at the same time – never renew the pads on only one disc, as uneven braking may result. Note that the dust created by wear of the pads may contain asbestos, which is a health hazard. Never blow it out with compressed air, and don't inhale any of it. An approved filtering mask should be worn when working on the brakes. DO NOT use petrol or petroleum-based solvents to clean brake parts; use brake cleaner or denatured alcohol only.***

**Note:** *There are two possible types of br[...] caliper fitted to the models covered in [...] manual; on early (pre 1999 model year) [...] models and all 916 models (excluding SPS) the brake pads are retained by a sin[...] retaining pin, and on all other models the pa[...] are retained by two pins.*

**1** Note the correct fitted locations of the [...] pin(s) and anti-rattle spring, then using pli[...] remove the R-clip(s) from the pad retain[...] pin(s) **(see illustration)**. **Note:** *If necessary [...] improve access for pad renewal, slacken [...] remove the caliper mounting bolts and s[...] the caliper off the brake disc.*

**2** Slide the pad retaining pin(s) out from [...] caliper and remove the anti-rattle spring, no[...] which way around it is fitted **(see illustratio[...]**

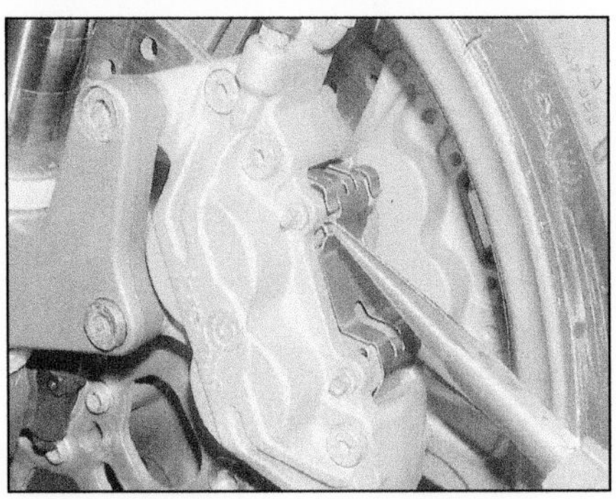

**2.1 Remove the R-clips . . .**

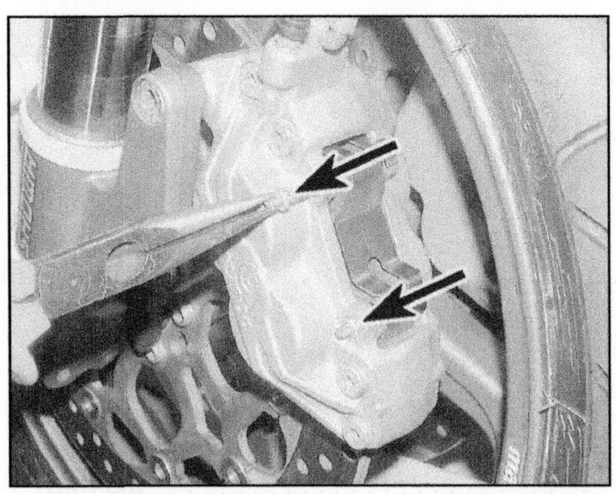

**2.2a . . . then slide out the pad retaining pins . . .**

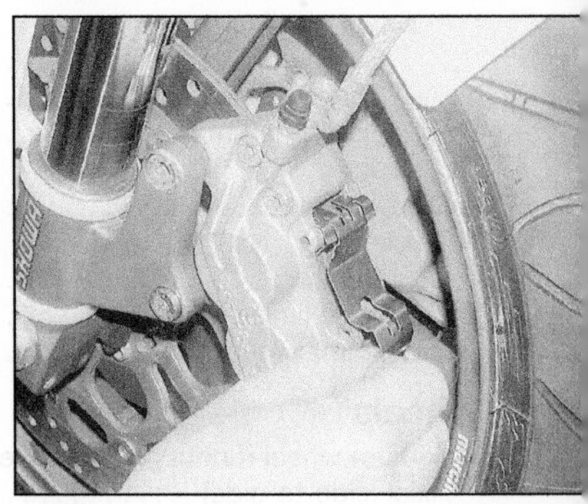

**2.2b . . . and lift out the anti-rattle spri[...]**

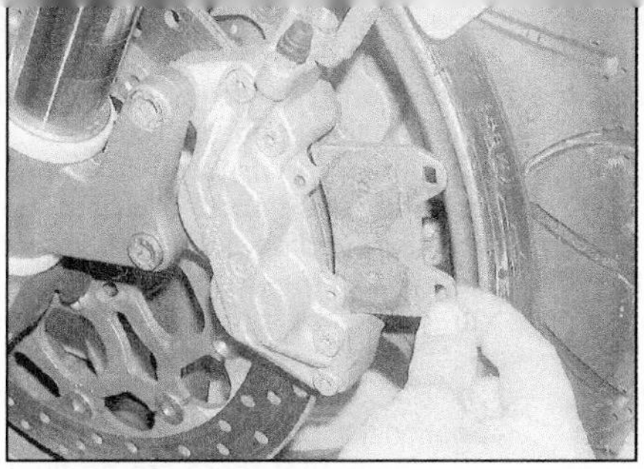

2.3 Remove both brake pads from the caliper

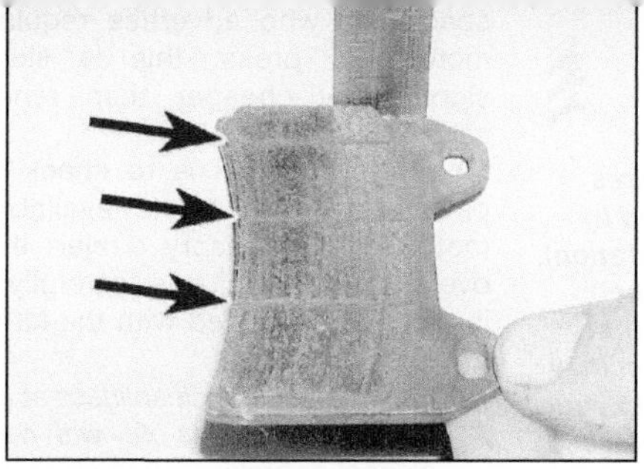

2.4 Measuring brake pad friction material thickness (wear limit grooves arrowed)

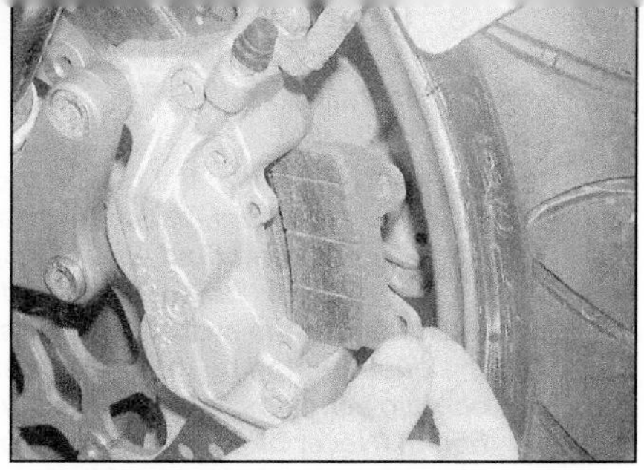

2.10 Insert both pads into the caliper ensuring their friction material is facing the disc

The spring has an arrow on it which should point in the direction of disc rotation.

**3** Withdraw both pads from the caliper **(see illustration)**.

**4** Inspect the surface of each pad for contamination and check that the friction material has not worn down to or beyond the wear limit grooves. Some after-market pads may not have wear limit grooves, in this case check that the friction material has not worn to less then the specified minimum **(see illustration)**. If the friction material on either pad has worn down to, or beyond, the wear limit/specified minimum thickness, is fouled with oil or grease, or heavily scored or damaged by dirt and debris, all pads must be renewed as a set. Note that it is not possible to degrease the friction material; if the pads are contaminated in any way they must be renewed. Also check that the pads have worn evenly at each end, and that each has the same amount of wear as the other. If uneven wear is noticed, one or more of the pistons are probably sticking in the caliper, in which case the calipers must be overhauled (see Section 3).

**5** If the pads are in good condition, clean them carefully to remove all traces of road dirt and corrosion, using a fine wire brush which is completely free of oil and grease. Using a pointed instrument, clean out the grooves in the friction material and dig out any embedded particles of foreign matter.

**6** Check the condition of the brake disc (see Section 4).

**7** Remove all traces of corrosion from the pad retaining pin(s). Inspect the pin(s) for signs of damage and renew them if necessary.

**8** If new pads are being installed, push the pistons as far back into the caliper as possible by hand or by using a piece of wood as a lever. Due to the increased friction material thickness of new pads, it may be necessary to remove the master cylinder reservoir cover and diaphragm and extract some fluid.

**9** Smear the backs of the pads and the shank of the pad retaining pin(s) with copper-based grease, making sure that none gets on the front or sides of the pads.

**10** Insert each pad into the caliper, making sure its friction material is facing the brake disc **(see illustration)**.

**11** On calipers with a single pad retaining pin, fit the anti-rattle spring to the caliper, ensuring it is correctly fitted with its arrow pointing in the direction of normal disc rotation. Slide in the pad retaining pin ensuring it passes through the hole in each brake pad and over the top of the anti-rattle spring, then secure it in position with the R-clip.

**12** On calipers with two pad retaining pins, fit the anti-rattle spring to the caliper, ensuring it is the correct way up with its arrow pointing in the direction of normal disc rotation **(see illustration)**. Slide both retaining pins into position ensuring they pass through the holes in both brake pads and the anti-rattle spring **(see illustration)**. Secure each pin in position with an R-clip, ensuring the clip is positioned between the outer pad and the caliper body **(see illustration)**.

**13** Where the caliper was removed for access, slide it back into position making sure the pads pass on each side of the disc. Lubricate the caliper mounting bolts with a smear of molybdenum disulphide grease then refit the bolts, tightening them to the specified torque.

**14** Operate the brake lever several times to bring the pads into contact with the disc.

**15** Repeat the above procedure and renew the pads on the opposite caliper.

**16** With both sets of pads renewed, operate the brake lever several times to ensure the pads are in firm contact with the discs, then check the master cylinder reservoir fluid level (see *Daily (pre-ride) checks*). Once the fluid level is correct, check the operation of the brake before riding the motorcycle.

***Warning: New pads will not give full braking efficiency until they have bedded in. Be prepared for this, and avoid hard braking as far as possible for the first few miles or so after pad renewal.***

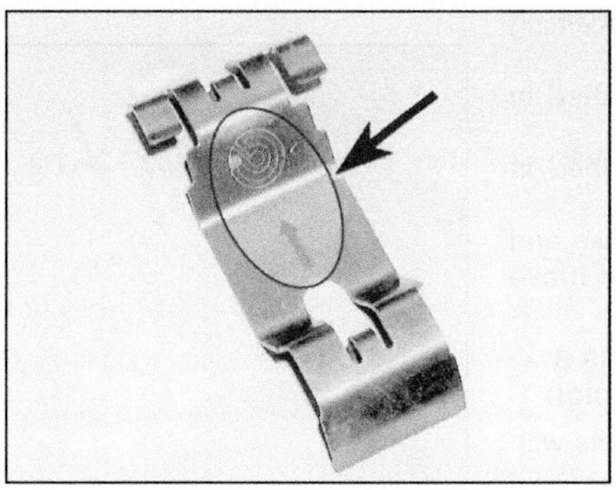

2.12a Pad anti-rattle spring must be fitted with its arrow pointing in the direction of normal disc rotation

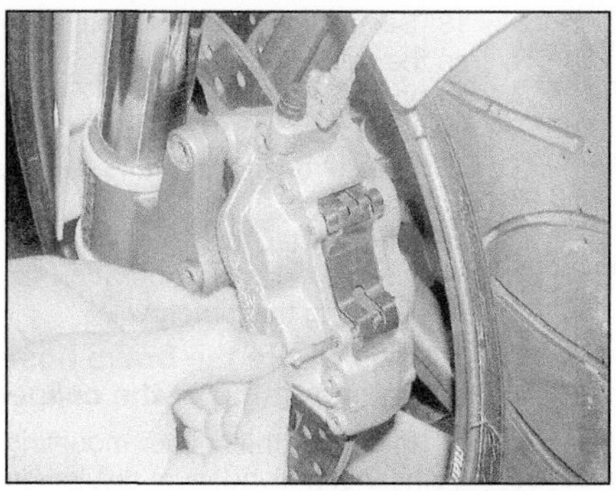

2.12b Ensure the anti-rattle spring is correctly fitted then insert the pad retaining pins . . .

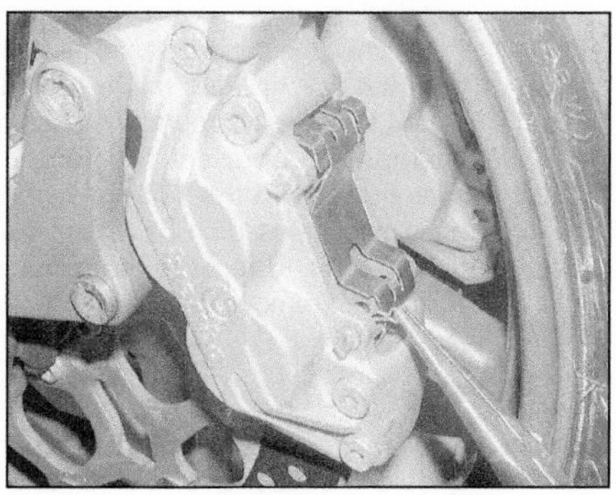

2.12c . . . and secure them in position with the R-clips

## 3 Front brake calipers – removal, overhaul and installation

***Warning: If a caliper requires overhaul (usually indicated by leaking fluid or sticky operation), all old brake fluid should be flushed from the system. Note also that the dust created by the brake system may contain asbestos, which is harmful to your health. Never blow it out with compressed air and don't inhale any of it. An approved filtering mask should be worn when working on the brakes. Do not, under any circumstances, use petroleum-based solvents to clean brake parts. Use clean brake fluid, brake cleaner or denatured alcohol only.***

***Caution: To prevent damage to the paint from spilled brake fluid, always cover the surrounding components when working on the brake calipers.***

### *Removal*

**1** Remove the brake pads from the caliper (see Section 2).

**2** Remove all traces of dirt from around the brake hose union then continue as described under the relevant sub-heading.

#### Models where the brake hose has a threaded end fitting at the caliper union

**3** Loosen the brake hose union end fitting from the caliper.

**4** Slacken and remove the caliper mounting bolts and free the assembly from the fork leg.

**5** Unscrew the caliper from the end of the brake hose and remove it from the bike. Plug the hose end or wrap a plastic bag tightly around the hose to minimise fluid loss and prevent dirt from entering the hydraulic system.

#### Models where the brake hose has a banjo end fitting at the caliper union

**6** Note the correct fitted position of the brake hose end fitting in relation to the caliper. If necessary, make alignment marks to ensure the end fitting is correctly positioned on installation.

**7** Unscrew the banjo bolt and separate the hose from the caliper. Plug the hose end or wrap a plastic bag tightly around the hose to minimise fluid loss and prevent dirt from entering the system. Discard the sealing washers, as new ones must be used on installation.

**8** Slacken and remove the caliper mounting bolts, then remove the assembly from the fork leg.

### *Overhaul*

**9** Ducati specify that the brake calipers should not be overhauled and must be renewed if faulty, thus replacement parts are not available. Before condemning the original caliper, it maybe worthwhile checking whether specialists who advertise regularly in the motorcycle press; this is likely to be significantly cheaper than renewing the caliper.

**10** Another option is to check whether a pattern overhaul kit is available from a motorcycle accessory dealer. If a pattern overhaul kit is available, carefully follow the instructions supplied with the kit noting the following points.

*a) Ensure absolute cleanliness at all times. Clean components only with denatured alcohol or brake system cleaner. Do not, under any circumstances, use a petroleum-based solvent to clean brake parts.*

*b) If compressed air is being used to dry the parts, make sure it's filtered and unlubricated.*

*c) Keep each piston matched to its caliper bore (make alignment marks to ensure they are refitted in their original locations). If the pistons are swapped, the rate of wear will be accelerated.*

*d) Use only a wooden or plastic tool to remove the seals from the caliper bores. Never use a metal tool as this could cause damage.*

*e) If the caliper bores or pistons show signs of wear, damage or corrosion, the caliper must be renewed.*

*f) Renew all the disturbed seals and sealing rings. Never re-use them.*

*g) Lubricate the new seals and the pistons with clean brake fluid prior to installation. Ensure the pistons are fitted closed-end first and enter their bores squarely.*

*h) Apply thread locking compound to the caliper body bolts.*

### *Installation*

#### Models where the brake hose has a threaded end fitting at the caliper union

**11** Lubricate the caliper mounting bolts with a smear of molybdenum disulphide grease.

**12** Screw the caliper fully onto the brake hose then locate the caliper on the fork leg. Refit the caliper mounting bolts, tightening them to the specified torque.

**13** Securely tighten the brake hose end fitting on the caliper.

**14** Install the brake pads as described in Section 2.

**15** Bleed the front brake as described in Section 11.

**16** Check that there are no fluid leaks and thoroughly test the operation of the brake before riding the motorcycle.

#### Models where the brake hose has a banjo end fitting at the caliper union

**17** Lubricate the caliper mounting bolts with a smear of molybdenum disulphide grease.

**18** Locate the caliper assembly on the fork leg and fit the mounting bolts, tightening them to the specified torque.

side of the brake hose union and screw in t banjo bolt. Ensure the end fitting is correc positioned in relation to the caliper body, th securely tighten the banjo bolt.

***Caution: If the brake hose end fitting is n correctly positioned, the hose may conta the surrounding bodywork, resulting in damage to the hose/paintwork.***

**20** Install the brake pads as described Section 2.

**21** Bleed the front brake as described Section 11.

**22** Check that there are no fluid leaks a thoroughly test the operation of the bra before riding the motorcycle.

## 4 Front brake discs – inspection, removal and installation

### *Inspection*

**1** Visually inspect the surface of the disc score marks and other damage. Lig scratches are normal after use and won't affe brake operation, but deep grooves and hea score marks will reduce braking efficiency a accelerate pad wear. If a disc is badly groov it must be machined or renewed.

**2** To check disc runout, position the bike an auxiliary stand so that the wheel is rais off the ground. Mount a dial gauge on a fo leg, with the plunger on the gauge touchi the surface of the disc about 10 mm from t outer edge. Rotate the wheel and watch t gauge needle, comparing the reading with t limit listed in the Specifications at t beginning of the Chapter. If the runout greater than the service limit, check the whe bearings for play (see Chapter 1). If t bearings are worn, renew them (s Section 15) and repeat this check. If t runout is still excessive, the disc will have be renewed, although machining by engineer may be possible.

**3** The disc must not be machined or allow to wear down to a thickness less than t service limit listed in this Chapte Specifications and as marked on the di itself **(see illustration)**. The thickness of t

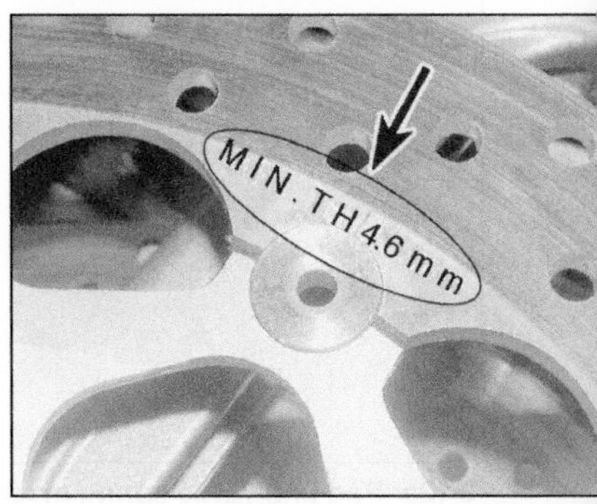


**4.3a Minimum thickness is stamped or the disc (arrowed)**

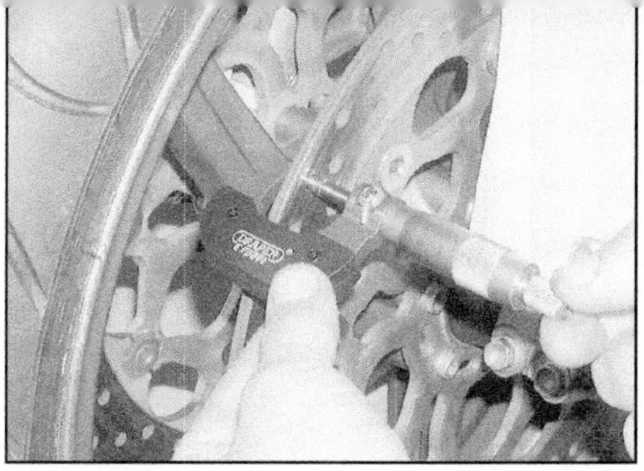

**4.3b Using a micrometer to measure front disc thickness**

disc can be checked with a micrometer **(see illustration)**. If the thickness of the disc is less than the service limit, it must be renewed. **Note:** *If either disc requires renewal, BOTH discs should be renewed at the same time to ensure even and consistent braking. New brake pads must also be fitted at the same time.*

### Removal

**4** Remove the front wheel (see Section 14). ***Caution: Do not lay the wheel down and allow it to rest on either disc – this could warp the disc. Set the wheel on wood blocks so that the disc doesn't support the weight of the wheel.***

**5** Mark the relationship of the disc to the wheel, so it can be installed in the same position. Unscrew the disc retaining bolts, loosening them a little at a time in a criss-cross pattern to avoid distorting the disc, then remove the disc from the wheel **(see illustration)**.

**6** If both discs are to be removed, make identification marks on removal to avoid confusion on installation.

### Installation

**7** Remove all traces of original locking compound from the threads of the disc retaining bolts.

**8** Install the disc on the wheel, making sure the marks made are on the outside. If the original disc is being installed, use the marks made prior to removal to ensure it is fitted on the correct side.

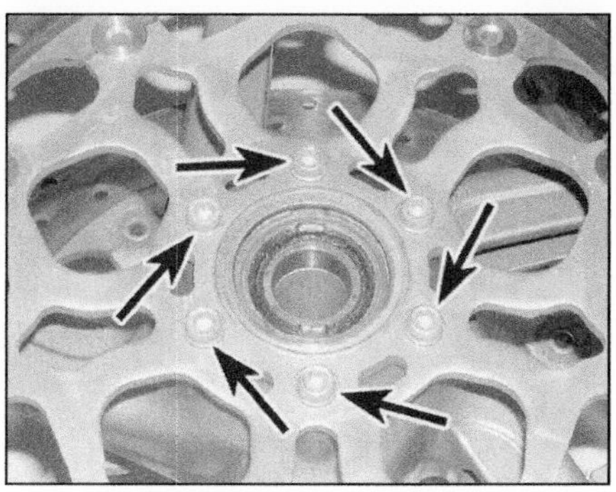

**4.5 Front disc retaining bolts (arrowed)**

**9** Apply a suitable non-permanent thread locking compound to the threads of each retaining bolt then fit the bolts. Tighten all bolts by hand then tighten them in a criss-cross pattern evenly and progressively to the specified torque.

**10** Clean all grease off the brake discs using brake system cleaner. If a new brake disc has been installed, remove any protective coating from its working surfaces.

**11** Install the wheel (see Section 14).

**12** Operate the brake lever several times to bring the pads into contact with the disc. Check the operation of the brake carefully before riding the bike.

## 5 Front brake master cylinder – removal, overhaul and installation

***Warning: If the master cylinder requires overhaul (usually indicated by leaking fluid or failure to produce a firm lever feel, even after repeated bleeding), all old brake fluid should be flushed from the system. Do not, under any circumstances, use petroleum-based solvents to clean brake parts. Use clean brake fluid, brake cleaner or denatured alcohol only.***

***Caution: To prevent damage to the paint from spilled brake fluid, always cover the surrounding components when working on the master cylinder.***

### Removal

**1** Trace the wiring back from the brake light switch, fitted to the base of the master cylinder, and disconnect it at the wiring connector(s).

**2** Remove all traces of dirt from around the master cylinder brake hose union then note the correct fitted position of the hose end fitting in relation to the master cylinder. If necessary, make alignment marks to ensure the end fitting is correctly positioned on installation.

**3** Unscrew the banjo bolt and separate the hose from the master cylinder. Plug the hose end or wrap a plastic bag tightly around the hose to minimise fluid loss and prevent dirt from entering the system. Discard the sealing

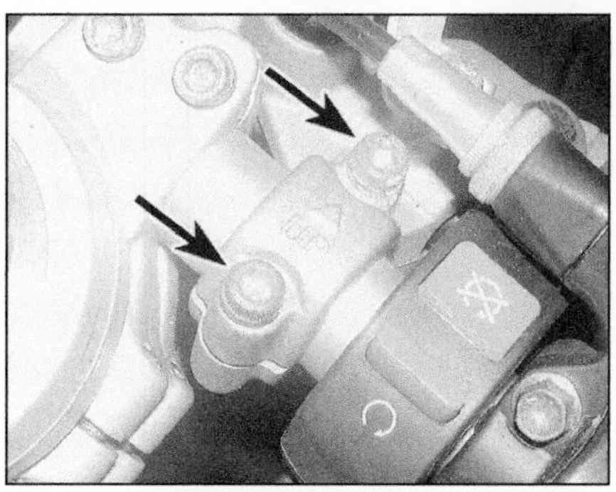

**5.4 Front brake master cylinder mounting clamp bolts (arrowed)**

installation.

**4** Unscrew the mounting clamp bolts and remove the master cylinder assembly from the handlebar **(see illustration)**.

**5** Remove the fluid reservoir cover retaining screws and nuts and lift off the cover. Remove the rubber diaphragm and empty the reservoir contents into a suitable container.

**6** If necessary, unscrew the bolt securing the fluid reservoir bracket to the master cylinder, then release the retaining clip and detach the reservoir hose. The master cylinder and fluid reservoir can then be separated.

### Overhaul

**7** Ducati specify that the master cylinder should not be overhauled and must be renewed if faulty. The only components that are available separately are the fluid reservoir assembly and its connecting hose, as well as the obvious components such as the brake lever and brake light switch.

**8** Before condemning the original master cylinder, check whether a pattern overhaul kit is available from a motorcycle accessory dealer. If a pattern overhaul kit is available, carefully follow the instructions supplied with the kit noting the following points.

a) *Ensure absolute cleanliness at all times. Clean components only with denatured alcohol or brake system cleaner. Do not, under any circumstances, use a petroleum-based solvent to clean brake parts.*
b) *If compressed air is being used to dry the parts, make sure it's filtered and unlubricated.*
c) *Note the correct fitted location and orientation of the piston assembly and spring as they are removed from the master cylinder.*
d) *Note the correct fitted location and orientation of the seals on the piston before removing them. Use only a wooden or plastic tool to remove the seals. Never use a metal tool as this could cause damage.*
e) *If the master cylinder bore or piston show signs of wear, damage or corrosion, the master cylinder must be renewed.*
f) *Renew all the disturbed seals, the circlip and dust boot. Never re-use them.*
g) *Lubricate the new seals and the piston with clean brake fluid prior to installation. Ensure the seals are correctly fitted on the piston and make sure the piston and spring are correctly positioned (as noted on removal). When installing the piston, take care not to turn the seal lips inside out as they slip into the bore.*
h) *Ensure the new circlip is correctly located in the cylinder body groove and the dust boot is correctly fitted.*

### Installation

**9** Where necessary, reconnect the fluid reservoir hose to the master cylinder and

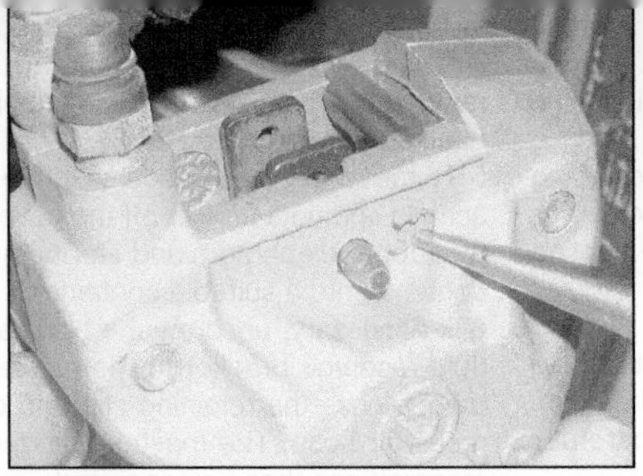

6.2 Remove the retaining clip . . .

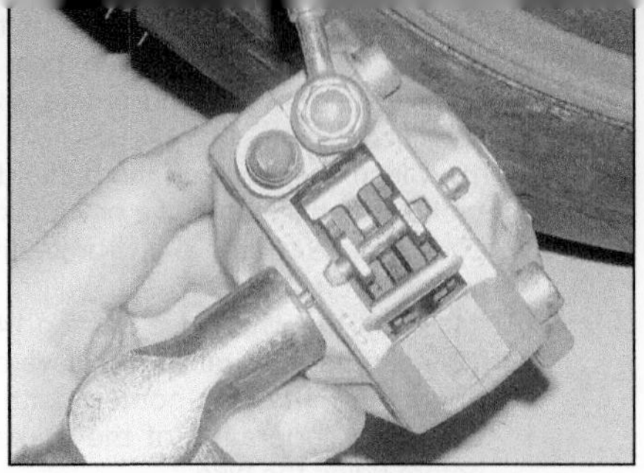

6.3 . . . then tap the pad pin out of position and remove the anti-rattle spring

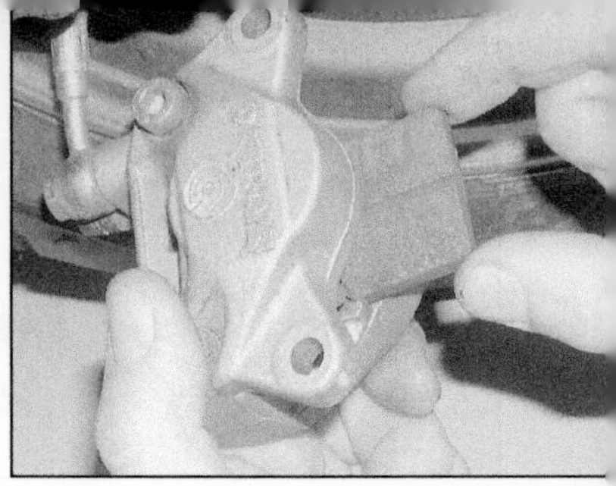

6.4 Slide the pads out of the caliper

secure it in position with the retaining clip. Align the fluid reservoir bracket with the cylinder body and securely tighten its retaining bolt.

**10** Locate the master cylinder on the handlebar, aligning its lug with the handlebar hole. Fit the mounting clamp with its arrow mark facing upwards or forwards (as applicable) and install the mounting clamp bolts. Tighten the mounting clamp upper/front bolt to the specified torque first, followed by the lower/rear bolt, then recheck that the upper/front bolt is correctly torqued.

**11** Position a new sealing washer on each side of the brake hose union and screw in the banjo bolt. Ensure the end fitting is correctly positioned in relation to the master cylinder body then securely tighten the banjo bolt.

***Caution: If the brake hose end fitting is not correctly positioned, the hose may contact the surrounding bodywork, resulting in damage to the hose/paintwork.***

**12** Reconnect the brake light switch wiring connectors.

**13** Fill the fluid reservoir with specified fluid (see *Daily (pre-ride) checks*), then bleed the air from the front brake as described in Section 11.

**14** Ensure the fluid level is correct then fit the reservoir rubber diaphragm and cover. Secure the cover in position with the retaining screws and nuts; do not overtighten the screws.

**15** Thoroughly check the operation of the front brake before riding the motorcycle.

## 6 Rear brake pads – renewal

***Warning: The dust created by the brake system may contain asbestos, which is harmful to your health. Never blow it out with compressed air and don't inhale any of it. An approved filtering mask should be worn when working on the brakes.***

**1** Note the correct fitted locations of the pad pin and anti-rattle spring. **Note:** *If necessary, to improve access for pad renewal, slacken and remove the caliper mounting bolts and slide the caliper off the brake disc.*

**2** Remove the retaining clip from the pad retaining pin **(see illustration)**.

**3** Slide the pin out from the caliper and remove the anti-rattle spring, noting which way around it is fitted; the arrow on the spring should point in the direction of disc rotation **(see illustration)**. If necessary, the pin can be tapped out of position using a hammer a punch.

**4** Withdraw both pads from the caliper (s illustration).

**5** Inspect the surface of each pad contamination and check that the frict material has not worn down to or beyond wear limit grooves **(see illustration)**. Sc after-market pads may not have wear li grooves, in this case check that the frict material has not worn to less then specified minimum **(see illustration)**. If friction material of either pad has worn do to, or beyond, the wear limit/specif minimum thickness, is fouled with oil grease, or heavily scored or damaged by and debris, both pads must be renewed a set. Note that it is not possible to degre the friction material; if the pads contaminated in any way they must renewed. Also check that both pads h worn evenly at their ends, and that one has the same amount of wear as the othe uneven wear is noticed, one or more of pistons are probably sticking in the calipe which case the calipers must be overhau (see Section 7).

**6** If the pads are in good condition, cl them carefully to remove all traces of road

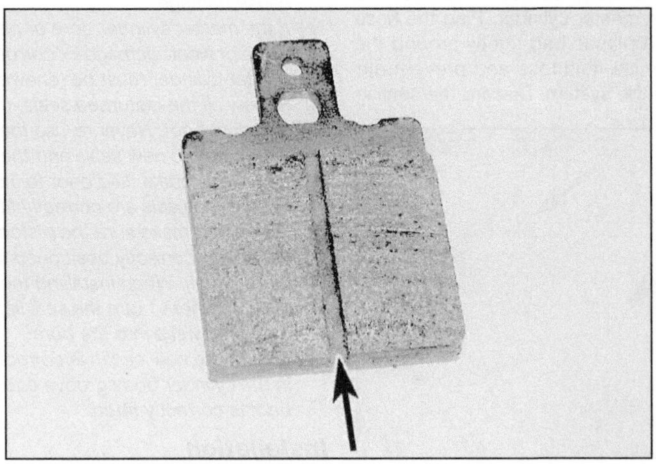

6.5a Caliper friction material wear limit groove (arrowed)

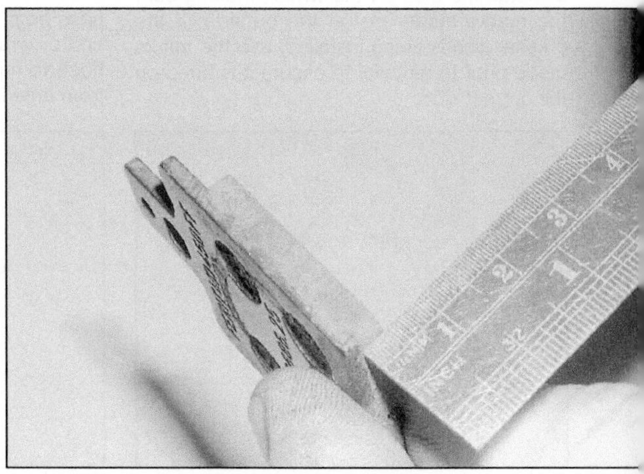

6.5b If no wear limit groove is present, measure the friction material thickness

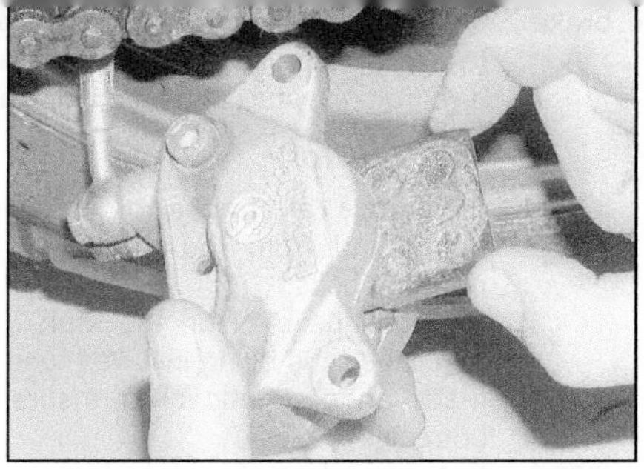

**6.11 Insert each pad into the caliper ensuring the friction material is facing the brake disc**

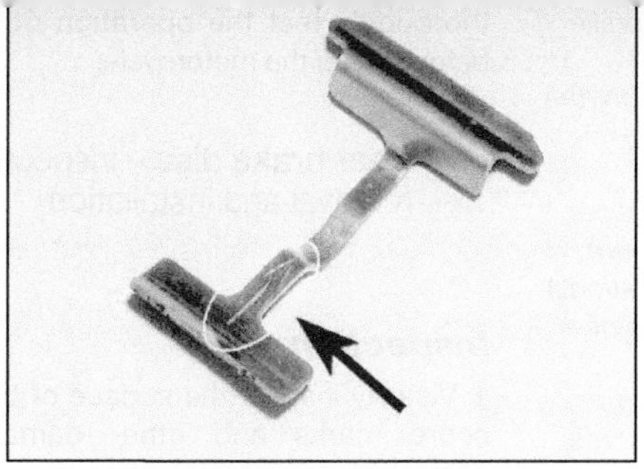

**6.12a Ensure the arrow on the anti-rattle spring points in the direction of normal disc rotation**

**6.12b Ensure the anti-rattle spring is correctly positioned then insert the pad retaining pin . . .**

and corrosion, using a fine wire brush which is completely free of oil and grease Using a pointed instrument, clean out the grooves in the friction material and dig out any embedded particles of foreign matter.

**7** Check the condition of the brake disc (see Section 8).

**8** Remove all traces of corrosion from the pad retaining pin. Inspect the pin for signs of damage and renew it if necessary.

**9** If new pads are being installed, push the pistons as far back into the caliper as possible by hand or by using a piece of wood as a lever. Due to the increased friction material thickness of new pads, it may be necessary to remove the master cylinder reservoir cover and diaphragm and extract some fluid.

**10** Smear the backs of the pads and the shank of the pad retaining pin with copper-based grease, making sure that none gets on the front or sides of the pads.

**11** Insert each pad into the caliper, making sure its friction material is facing the brake disc **(see illustration)**.

**12** Fit the anti-rattle spring to the caliper, ensuring it is correctly fitted with the arrow pointing in the direction of normal disc rotation **(see illustration)**. Slide in the pad retaining pin ensuring it passes through the hole in each brake pad and over the top of the anti-rattle spring **(see illustration)**. Ensure the pad pin is pushed fully into the caliper then secure it in position with the retaining clip **(see illustration)**.

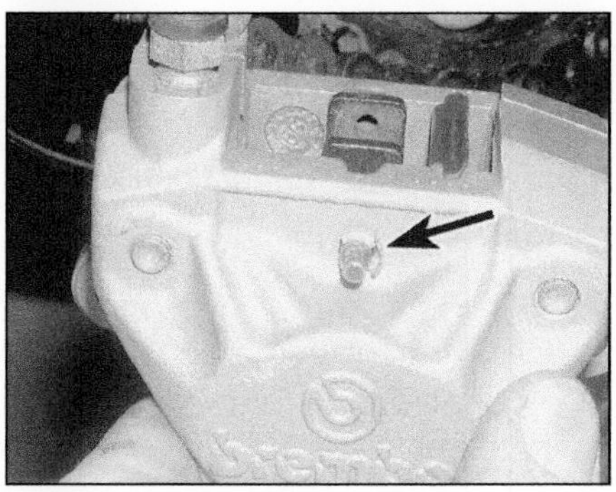

**6.12c . . . and secure it in position with the retaining clip**

**13** If the caliper was removed, slide it back into position making sure the pads pass on each side of the disc **(see illustration)**. Lubricate the caliper mounting bolts with a smear of molybdenum disulphide grease then refit the bolts, tightening them to the specified torque.

**14** Operate the brake pedal several times to bring the pads into firm contact with the disc.

**15** Check the master cylinder reservoir fluid level (see *Daily (pre-ride) checks*) and check the operation of the brake before riding the motorcycle.

***Warning: New pads will not give full braking efficiency until they have bedded in. Be prepared for this, and avoid hard braking as far as possible for the first few miles or so after pad renewal.***

## 7 Rear brake caliper – removal, overhaul and installation

***Warning: If a caliper requires overhaul (usually indicated by leaking fluid or sticky operation), all old brake fluid should be flushed from the system. Note also that the dust created by the brake system may contain asbestos, which is harmful to your health. Never blow it out with compressed air and don't inhale any of it. An approved filtering mask should be worn when working on the brakes. Do not, under any circumstances, use petroleum-based solvents to clean brake parts. Use clean brake fluid, brake cleaner or denatured alcohol only.***

***Caution: To prevent damage to the paint from spilled brake fluid, always cover the surrounding components when working on the brake caliper.***

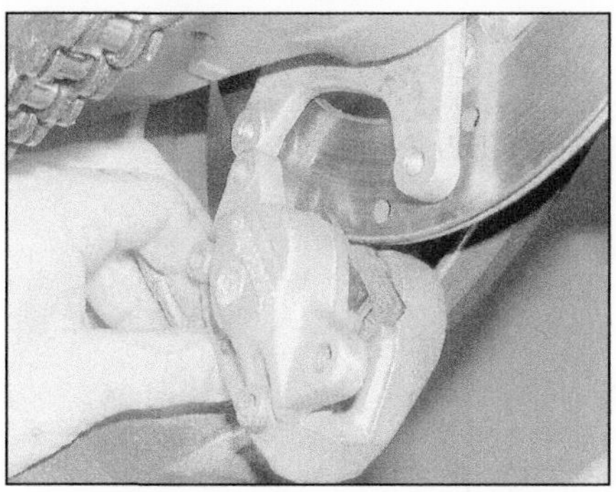

**6.13 Slide the caliper back into position ensuring the pads pass on each side of the disc**

### Removal

**1** Remove the brake pads from the caliper (see Section 6).

**2** Remove all traces of dirt from around the caliper brake hose union. Note the correct fitted position of the hose end fitting in relation to the caliper and if necessary, make alignment marks to ensure the end fitting is correctly positioned on installation.

**3** Unscrew the banjo bolt and separate the hose from the caliper. Plug the hose end or wrap a plastic bag tightly around the hose to minimise fluid loss and prevent dirt from entering the system. Discard the sealing washers, as new ones must be used on installation.

**4** Slacken and remove the caliper mounting bolts, then remove the assembly from its mounting bracket.

### Overhaul

**5** Ducati specify that the brake calipers should not be overhauled and must be renewed if faulty, thus replacement parts are not available. Before condemning the original caliper, it maybe worthwhile checking whether it can be overhauled by one of the many brake specialists who advertise regularly in the motorcycle press; this is likely to be significantly cheaper than renewing the caliper.

**6** Another option is to check whether a pattern overhaul kit is available from a motorcycle accessory dealer. If a pattern overhaul kit is available, carefully follow the instructions supplied with the kit noting the following points.

a) *Ensure absolute cleanliness at all times. Clean components only with denatured alcohol or brake system cleaner. Do not,*

*petroleum-based solvent to clean brake parts.*

*b) If compressed air is being used to dry the parts, make sure it's filtered and unlubricated.*

*c) Keep each piston matched to its caliper bore (make alignment marks to ensure they are refitted in their original locations). If the pistons are swapped, the rate of wear will be accelerated.*

*d) Use only a wooden or plastic tool to remove the seals from the caliper bores. Never use a metal tool as this could cause damage.*

*e) If the caliper bores or pistons show signs of wear, damage or corrosion, the caliper must be renewed.*

*f) Renew all the disturbed seals and sealing rings. Never re-use them.*

*g) Lubricate the new seals and the pistons with clean brake fluid prior to installation. Ensure the pistons are fitted closed-end first and enter their bores squarely.*

*h) Apply thread locking compound to the caliper body bolts.*

### Installation

**7** Install the brake pads as described in Section 6.

**8** Locate the caliper assembly on its mounting bracket and fit the mounting bolts. Do not fully tighten the bolts yet, it will be necessary to remove the caliper to bleed it.

**9** Position a new sealing washer on each side of the brake hose union and screw in the banjo bolt. Ensure the end fitting is correctly positioned in relation to the caliper body then securely tighten the banjo bolt.

***Caution: If the brake hose end fitting is not correctly positioned, the hose may contact the surrounding components.***

**10** Bleed the rear brake as described in Section 11.

**11** Once the brake has been correctly bled, install the caliper correctly making sure the brake pads pass on each side of the disc. Lubricate the caliper mounting bolts with a smear of molybdenum disulphide grease then refit them, tightening them to the specified torque.

thoroughly test the operation of the brake before riding the motorcycle.

## 8 Rear brake disc – inspection, removal and installation

### Inspection

**1** Visually inspect the surface of the disc for score marks and other damage. Light scratches are normal after use and won't affect brake operation, but deep grooves and heavy score marks will reduce braking efficiency and accelerate pad wear. If the disc is badly grooved it must be machined or renewed.

**2** To check disc runout, position the bike on an auxiliary stand so that the rear wheel is raised off the ground. Mount a dial gauge on the swingarm, with the plunger on the gauge touching the surface of the disc about 10 mm from the outer edge. Rotate the wheel and watch the gauge needle, comparing the reading with the limit listed in the Specifications at the beginning of the Chapter. If the runout is greater than the service limit, check the wheel bearings for play (see Chapter 1). If the bearings are worn, renew them (see Section 17) and repeat this check. If the runout is still excessive, the disc will have to be renewed, although machining by an engineer may be possible.

**3** The disc must not be machined or allowed to wear down to a thickness less than the service limit listed in this Chapter's Specifications and as marked on the disc itself **(see illustration)**. The thickness of the disc can be checked with a micrometer **(see illustration)**. If the thickness of the disc is less than the service limit, it must be renewed; new brake pads must also be fitted at the same time.

### Removal

**4** Remove the rear wheel stub axle (see Section 17).

**5** Mark the relationship of the disc to the axle, so it can be installed in the same position. Unscrew the disc retaining bolts, loosening them a little at a time in a criss-cross patte to avoid distorting the disc, then remove th disc from the stub axle **(see illustration)**.

### Installation

**6** Remove all traces of original lockin compound from the threads of the di retaining bolts.

**7** Install the disc on the stub axle. If th original disc is being installed, use the mar made prior to removal to ensure it is fitt correctly.

**8** Apply a drop of fresh locking compound each retaining bolt then fit the bolts. Tight all bolts by hand then tighten them in a cris cross pattern evenly and progressively to th specified torque.

**9** Clean all grease off the brake disc usi brake system cleaner. If a new brake disc h been installed, remove any protective coati from its working surfaces.

**10** Install the stub axle (see Section 17).

**11** Operate the brake pedal several times bring the pads into contact with the dis Check the operation of the brake carefu before riding the bike.

## 9 Rear brake master cylinder – removal, overhaul and installation

***Warning: If the master cylinder requires overhaul (usually indicated by leaking flu or failure to produce a firm pedal feel, ev after repeated bleeding), all old brake flu should be flushed from the system. Do n under any circumstances, use petroleum based solvents to clean brake parts. Use clean brake fluid, brake cleaner or denatured alcohol only.***

***Caution: To prevent damage to the paint from spilled brake fluid, always cover the surrounding components when working the master cylinder.***

### Removal

**1** Remove the fairing right-hand lower par (see Chapter 8).

**2** Remove all traces of dirt from the mast

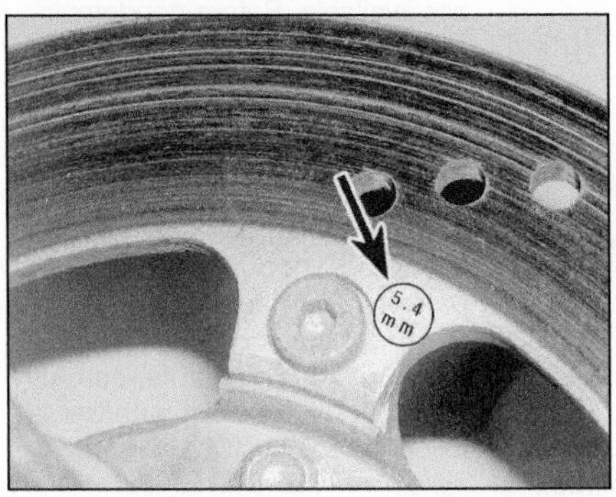


**8.3a Minimum thickness is stamped on the disc (arrowed)**

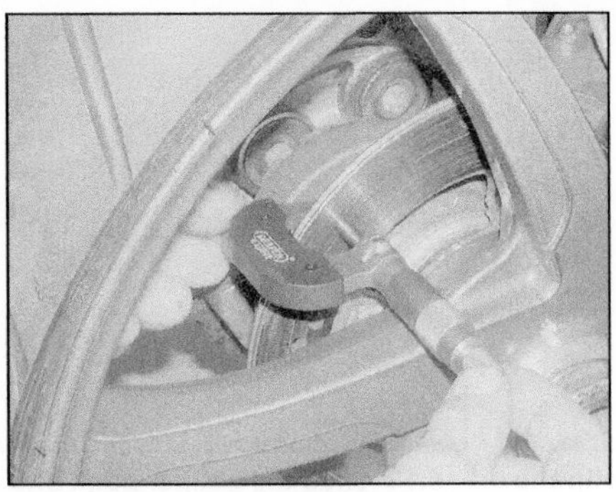

**8.3b Using a micrometer to measure rear disc thickness**

**8.5 Rear disc retaining bolts (arrowed)**

the hose end fitting in relation to the master cylinder. If necessary, make alignment marks to ensure the end fitting is correctly positioned on installation.

**3** Unscrew the banjo bolt and separate the hose from the master cylinder **(see illustration)**. Plug the hose end or wrap a plastic bag tightly around the hose to minimise fluid loss and prevent dirt from entering the system. Discard the sealing washers, as new ones must be used on installation.

**4** Release the retaining clip and disconnect the brake fluid reservoir hose from its union on the master cylinder body. Allow the fluid reservoir contents to drain into a container.

**5** Unscrew the master cylinder retaining bolts, then free the cylinder from the end of the pushrod and remove it from the bike.

### Overhaul

***Caution: Overhaul of the brake master cylinder must be done in a spotlessly clean work area to avoid contamination and possible failure of the brake hydraulic system components.***

**6** Ducati specify that the master cylinder should not be overhauled and must be renewed if faulty. However, overhaul kits are available for some master cylinders – check with your Ducati dealer for availability. If an original overhaul kit is not available, check whether a pattern overhaul kit is available from a motorcycle accessory dealer. If you cannot purchase an overhaul kit, renewal is the only option. Overhaul is as follows.

**7** Remove the dust boot from the master cylinder.

**8** Depress the piston and, using circlip pliers, remove the circlip. Withdraw the piston assembly and spring from the master cylinder. If they are difficult to remove, apply low pressure compressed air to the fluid outlet. Lay the parts out in the correct fitted order to prevent confusion during reassembly.

**9** Clean all parts with clean brake fluid or denatured alcohol.

***Caution: Do not, under any circumstances, use a petroleum-based solvent to clean brake parts. If compressed air is available, use it to dry the parts thoroughly (make sure it's filtered and unlubricated).***

**10** Check the master cylinder bore for corrosion, scratches, nicks and score marks. If damage or wear is evident, the master cylinder must be renewed. If the master cylinder is in poor condition, then the brake caliper should be checked as well. Check that the fluid inlet and outlet ports in the master cylinder are clear. Inspect the fluid reservoir, rubber diaphragm cover and its joining hose for cracks or splits and renew it if necessary.

**11** Insert the new spring into the master cylinder, ensuring it is the right way around.

**12** Lubricate the new piston and seal assembly with clean brake fluid. Ensure the assembly is the correct way round, then carefully ease it into the master cylinder, making sure the seal lips do not turn inside out as they slip into the bore.

**13** Depress the piston and secure it in position with the circlip. Ensure the circlip is correctly located in the master cylinder groove then fit the new dust boot to the master cylinder.

### Installation

**14** Lubricate the end of the pushrod with a smear of multi-purpose grease then manoeuvre the master cylinder assembly into position. Ensure the master cylinder is correctly engaged with its pushrod then refit its retaining bolts, tightening them to the specified torque.

**15** Reconnect the fluid reservoir hose to the master cylinder union and secure it in position with the retaining clip.

**16** Position a new sealing washer on each side of the brake hose union and screw in the banjo bolt. Ensure the end fitting is correctly positioned in relation to the master cylinder body then securely tighten the banjo bolt.

***Caution: If the brake hose end fitting is not correctly positioned, the hose may contact the surrounding bodywork, resulting in damage to the hose/paintwork.***

**17** Fill the fluid reservoir with specified fluid (see *Daily (pre-ride) checks*), then bleed the air from the rear brake as described in Section 11.

**18** Ensure the fluid level is correct then install the rubber diaphragm and securely refit the reservoir cap.

**19** Check the height of the rear brake pedal. Ducati recommend that the distance between the top of the brake pedal and the centre of the swingarm pivot bolt should be 46.6 mm **(see illustration)**. However, the pedal height can be altered to suit individual tastes. To alter the pedal height, slacken the locknut and alter the position of the pedal stop bolt. Once the desired pedal height is obtained, hold the stop bolt and securely tighten the locknut. After carry out pedal height adjustment ensure that there is approximately 1.5 to 2.0 mm of pedal freeplay before the pushrod contacts master cylinder piston. If adjustment is necessary, slacken the pushrod locknut and screw the pushrod into/out of (as applicable) its clevis. Once the pushrod length is correct, securely tighten the locknut.

**20** Install the fairing panel (see Chapter 8).

**21** Thoroughly check the operation of the rear brake before riding the motorcycle.

## 10 Brake hoses and unions – inspection and renewal

### Inspection

**1** The brake hoses and their associated fittings should be checked regularly (see Chapter 1).

**2** Twist and flex the rubber hoses while

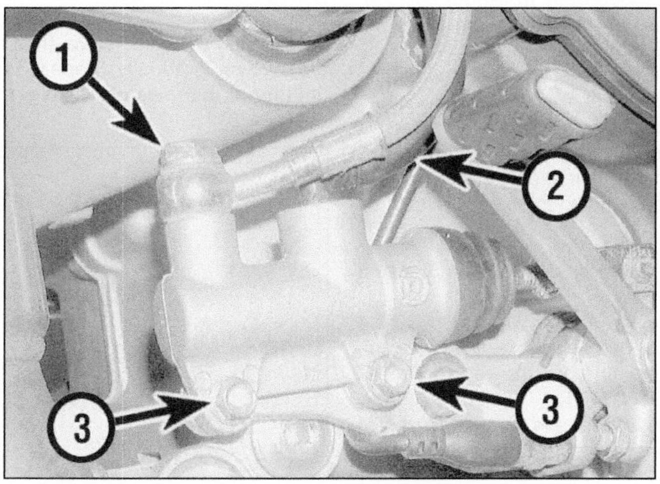

**9.3 Rear brake master cylinder banjo bolt (1), fluid reservoir hose (2) and mounting bolts (3)**

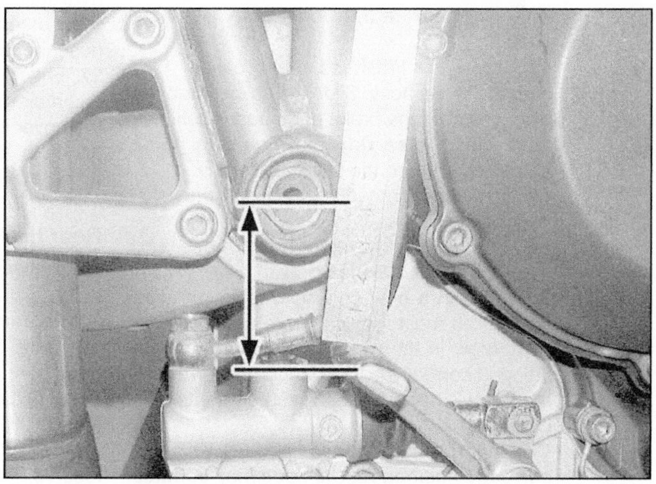
**9.19 Checking rear brake pedal height**

Check extra carefully around the areas where the hoses connect with the end fittings, as these are common areas for hose failure.

**3** Inspect the banjo fittings connected to the brake hoses. If the fittings are rusted, scratched or cracked, renew them.

## Renewal

***Caution: To prevent damage to the paint from spilled brake fluid, always cover the surrounding components when working on the brake hose.***

### Front brake hose – hose with threaded end fittings at caliper unions

**4** Remove all traces of dirt from around each of the brake hose end fittings.

**5** Note the correct fitted position of the hose end fitting in relation to the master cylinder. If necessary, make alignment marks to ensure the end fitting is correctly positioned on installation.

**6** Unscrew the banjo bolt and separate the hose from the master cylinder. Discard the sealing washers, as new ones must be used on installation. Plug the master cylinder outlet to minimise fluid loss and prevent the entry of dirt.

**7** Loosen the brake hose union end fitting from each caliper.

**8** Slacken and remove the left-hand brake caliper mounting bolts. Slide the caliper off the brake disc, then unscrew it from the end of the brake hose. Plug the caliper inlet to minimise fluid loss and prevent dirt from entering the hydraulic system.

**9** Repeat the procedure and remove the right-hand brake caliper.

**10** Note the correct routing of the hose, then free it from its retaining clips and guides and remove it from the bike.

**11** Fit the new hose, making sure it is correctly routed and isn't twisted or otherwise strained, and secure it in position with the necessary clips and guides.

**12** Lubricate the brake caliper mounting bolts with a smear of molybdenum disulphide grease.

**13** Screw the left-hand brake caliper fully onto the brake hose. Slide the caliper onto the disc, ensuring the brake pads pass each side of the disc, then refit the mounting bolts, tightening them to the specified torque.

**14** Repeat the procedure and install the right-hand brake caliper.

**15** Securely tighten the brake hose end fittings on both brake calipers.

**16** Position a new sealing washer on each side of the master cylinder brake hose union and screw in the banjo bolt. Ensure the end fitting is correctly positioned in relation to the master cylinder body then securely tighten the banjo bolt.

***Caution: If the brake hose end fitting is not correctly positioned, the hose may contact the surrounding bodywork, resulting in damage to the hose/paintwork.***

**17** Fill the fluid reservoir with fresh DOT 4 hydraulic fluid (see *Daily (pre-ride) checks*), then bleed the air from the front brake as described in Section 11.

**18** Ensure the fluid level is correct then fit the reservoir rubber diaphragm and cover. Secure the cover in position with the retaining screws and nuts; do not overtighten the screws.

**19** Thoroughly check the operation of the front brake before riding the motorcycle.

### Front brake hose – hose with banjo end fittings at caliper unions

**20** Remove all traces of dirt from around each of the brake hose end fittings.

**21** Note the correct fitted position of each hose end fitting in relation to the master cylinder and caliper. If necessary, make alignment marks to ensure the end fittings are correctly positioned on installation.

**22** Unscrew the banjo bolts and separate the hose from the master cylinder and brake calipers. Discard the sealing washers, as new ones must be used on installation. Plug the master cylinder/brake caliper unions to minimise fluid loss and prevent the entry of dirt.

**23** Note the correct routing of the hose, then free it from its retaining clips and guides and remove it from the bike.

**24** Fit the new hose, making sure it is correctly routed and isn't twisted or otherwise strained, and secure it in position with the necessary clips and guides.

**25** Position a new sealing washer on each side of the brake hose unions and screw in the banjo bolts. Ensure each end fitting is correctly positioned in relation to the master cylinder body/brake caliper then securely tighten the banjo bolts.

***Caution: If the brake hose end fittings are not correctly positioned, the hose may contact the surrounding bodywork, resulting in damage to the hose/paintwork.***

**26** Fill the fluid reservoir with fresh DOT 4 hydraulic fluid (see *Daily (pre-ride) checks*), then bleed the air from the front brake as described in Section 11.

**27** Ensure the fluid level is correct then fit the reservoir rubber diaphragm and cover. Secure the cover in position with the retaining screws and nuts; do not overtighten the screws.

**28** Thoroughly check the operation of the front brake before riding the motorcycle.

### Rear brake hose

**29** Renew the hose as described in Steps 20 to 25.

**30** Fill the fluid reservoir with fresh DOT 4 hydraulic fluid (see *Daily (pre-ride) checks*), then bleed the air from the rear brake as described in Section 11.

**31** Ensure the fluid level is correct then install the rubber diaphragm and securely refit the reservoir cap.

**32** Thoroughly check the operation of the rear brake before riding the motorcycle.

## 11 Brake system – bleeding

**1** Bleeding the brakes is simply the proc of removing all the air bubbles from the br fluid reservoirs, the hoses and the br calipers. Bleeding is necessary wheneve brake system hydraulic connection loosened, when a component or hose renewed, or when a master cylinder or cali is overhauled. Leaks in the system may a allow air to enter, but leaking brake fluid reveal their presence and warn you of need for repair.

**2** To bleed the brakes, you will need so new DOT 4 brake fluid, a length of clear v or plastic tubing, a small container parti filled with clean brake fluid, some rags an spanner to fit the brake caliper bleed valve

## Front brake

**3** Cover the fuel tank and other pain components to prevent damage in the ev that brake fluid is spilled.

**4** Remove the master cylinder fluid reser cover (see *Daily (pre-ride) checks*) and lift the rubber diaphragm and plate. Slowly pu the brake lever a few times, until no bubbles can be seen floating up from holes in the bottom of the reservoir; bleeds the air from the master cylinder en the line. Loosely refit the reservoir cover.

**5** Pull the dust cap off the bleed valve. Att one end of the clear vinyl or plastic tubing the bleed valve on one of the front calip and submerge the other end in the brake in the container **(see illustration)**.

**6** Check the fluid level. Do not allow this drop below the lower 'MIN' mark during bleeding process.

**7** Carefully pump the brake lever three or times and hold it in while opening the cal bleed valve. When the valve is opened, b fluid will flow out of the caliper into the c tubing and the lever will move towards handlebar.

**8** Retighten the bleed valve, then release brake lever gradually. Repeat the proc until no air bubbles are visible in the br

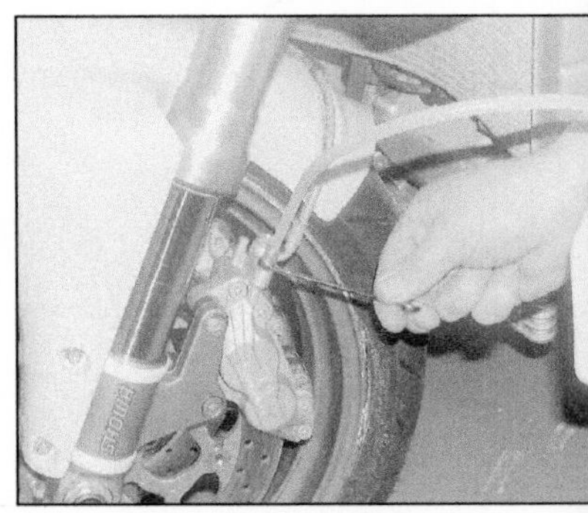

**11.5 Bleeding a front brake caliper usin one-way valve kit**

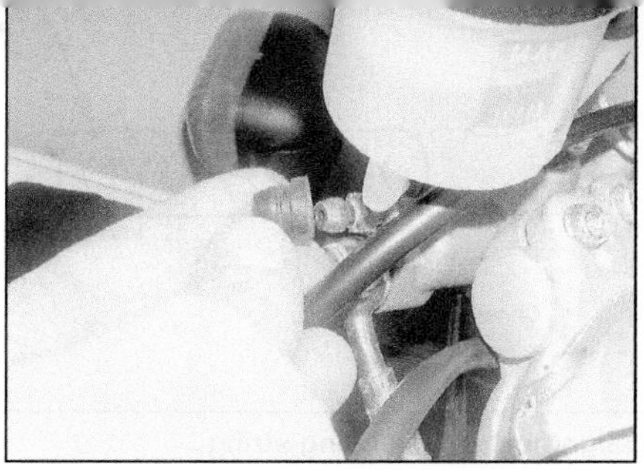

11.10 Later models also have a bleed valve on the front brake master cylinder

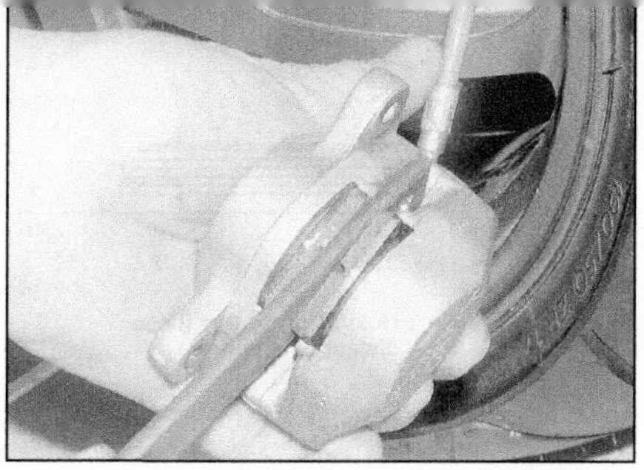

11.14 Insert a wedge between the brake pads to prevent the piston from being expelled during rear brake bleeding

11.15 Hold the caliper so the bleed valve is uppermost when bleeding the rear brake caliper

fluid leaving the valve, and the lever is firm when applied. Disconnect the bleeding equipment, then tighten the bleed valve to the specified torque and install the dust cap.

**9** Attach the tubing to the bleed valve on the opposite caliper (see Step 5) and repeat the procedure described in Steps 6 to 8, until all air is removed from the system and the brake lever feels firm again.

**10** On later models there is also be a bleed valve on the master cylinder. Where a master cylinder bleed valve is present, pull the dust cap and attach the tubing to the bleed valve **(see illustration)**. Submerge the other end of the tubing in the brake fluid in the container and repeat the procedure described in Steps 6 to 8, until all air is removed from the master cylinder and the brake lever feels firm again.

**11** Once the bleeding procedure is complete, top the fluid level up to the upper 'MAX' level mark (see *Daily (pre-ride) checks*) then install the rubber diaphragm and plate. Refit the reservoir cover and secure it in position with the retaining screws and nuts; do not overtighten the screws. Wipe up any spilled brake fluid and check the entire system for leaks. Thoroughly test the operation of the brake before riding the motorcycle.

### Rear brake

**Note:** *This procedure will be easier with the aid of an assistant.*

**12** Cover the area around the rear brake fluid reservoir to prevent damage in the event that brake fluid is spilled.

**13** Remove the master cylinder reservoir cap (see *Daily (pre-ride) checks)* and lift out the rubber diaphragm and plate. Slowly pump the brake pedal a few times, until no air bubbles can be seen floating up from the holes in the bottom of the reservoir. This bleeds the air from the master cylinder end of the line. Loosely refit the reservoir cover.

**14** Remove the rear brake caliper mounting bolts and slide the caliper off the disc. Insert a wooden wedge between the brake pads to prevent the pistons being expelled from the caliper during the bleeding procedure **(see illustration)**.

**15** Pull the dust cap off the bleed valve. Hold the caliper so the bleed valve is uppermost then attach one end of the clear vinyl or plastic tubing to the bleed valve on the rear caliper and submerge the other end in the brake fluid in the container **(see illustration)**.

**16** Check the fluid level. Do not allow this to drop below the lower 'MIN' mark during the bleeding process and ensure the caliper is held with its bleed valve uppermost at all times.

**17** Carefully pump the brake pedal three or four times and hold it down while opening the caliper bleed valve. When the valve is opened, brake fluid will flow out of the caliper into the clear tubing and the pedal will move further downwards.

**18** Retighten the bleed valve, then release the brake lever gradually. Repeat the process until no air bubbles are visible in the brake fluid leaving the valve, and the lever is firm when applied. Disconnect the bleeding equipment, then tighten the bleed valve to the specified torque and install the dust cap.

**19** Remove the wooden wedge from between the brake pads then slide the brake caliper back onto the disc, ensuring the brake pads pass each side of the disc **(see illustration)**. Lubricate the caliper mounting bolts with a smear of molybdenum disulphide grease then refit the bolts, tightening them to the specified torque **(see illustration)**.

**20** Repeatedly apply the brake pedal to force the pads back into firm contact with the disc. Top the fluid level up to the upper 'MAX' level mark (see *Daily (pre-ride) checks*) then install the rubber diaphragm and plate and securely refit the reservoir cap. Wipe up any spilled brake fluid and check the entire system for leaks. Thoroughly test the operation of the brake before riding the motorcycle.

> **HAYNES HiNT** ***If it's not possible to produce a firm feel to the lever or pedal, the fluid my be aerated. Let the brake fluid in the system stabilise for a few hours and, when the tiny bubbles in the system have settled out, repeat the procedure. Failure to bleed satisfactorily, after a reasonable repetition of the procedure, may be due to worn master cylinder seals.***

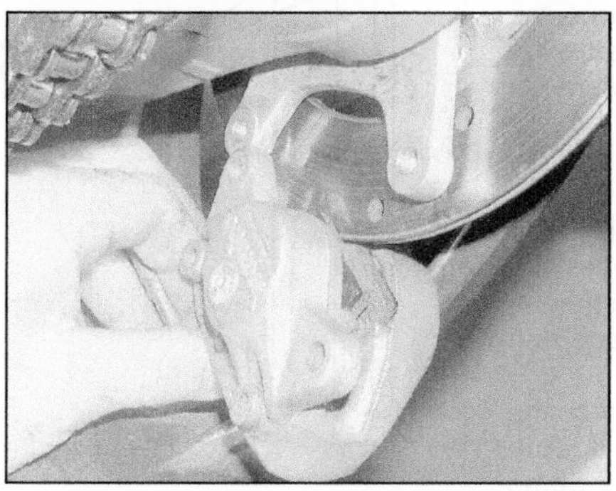

11.19a Slide on the caliper, ensuring the pads pass each side of the disc . . .

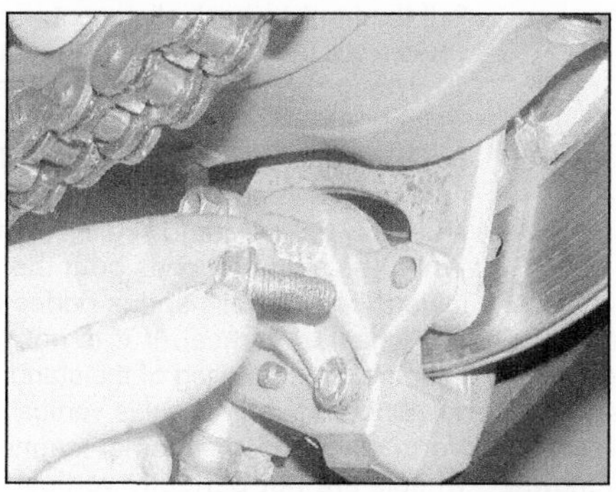

11.19b . . . and lubricate the bolts with molybdenum grease prior to installation

## 12 Wheels – inspection and repair

**1** In order to carry out a proper inspection of the wheels, place the bike on an auxiliary stand and support it so that the wheel being inspected is raised off the ground. Clean the wheels thoroughly to remove mud and dirt that may interfere with the inspection procedure or mask defects. Make a general check of the wheels (see Chapter 1) and tyres (see *Daily (pre-ride) checks*).

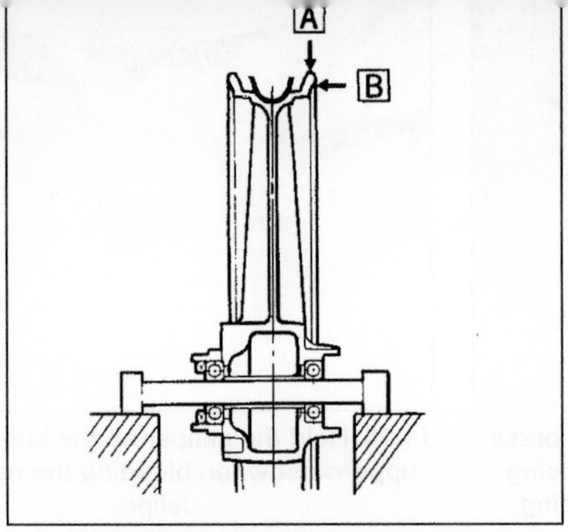


**12.2 Check the wheel for radial (out-of-round) runout (A) and axial (side-to-side) runout (B)**

2 Attach a dial gauge to the fork leg or the swingarm and position its stem against the side of the rim. Spin the wheel slowly and check the axial (side-to-side) runout of the rim. In order to check radial (out of round) runout accurately with the dial gauge, the wheel would have to be removed from the machine, and the tyre from the wheel. With the axle clamped in a vice and the dial gauge positioned on the top of the rim, the wheel can be rotated to check the runout **(see illustration)**.

3 An easier, though slightly less accurate, method is to attach a stiff wire pointer to the fork leg or the swingarm and position its end a fraction of an inch from the wheel (where the wheel and tyre join). If the wheel is true, the distance from the pointer to the rim will be constant as the wheel is rotated. **Note:** *If wheel runout is excessive, check the wheel bearings very carefully before renewing the wheel.*

4 The wheels should also be visually inspected for cracks, flat spots on the rim and other damage. Look very closely for dents in the area where the tyre bead contacts the rim. Dents in this area may prevent complete sealing of the tyre against the rim, which leads to deflation of the tyre over a period of time. If damage is evident, or if runout in either direction is excessive, the wheel will have to be renewed. Never attempt to repair a damaged cast alloy wheel.

## 13 Wheels – alignment check

1 Misalignment of the wheels, which may be due to a bent frame, fork yokes, swingarm or rear stub axle, can cause strange and possibly serious handling problems. If the frame, yokes, swingarm or stub axle are at fault, repair by a frame specialist or renewal are the only options.

2 To check the alignment you will need an assistant and a length of string or a perfectly straight piece of wood, and a ruler. A plumb bob or other suitable weight will also be required.

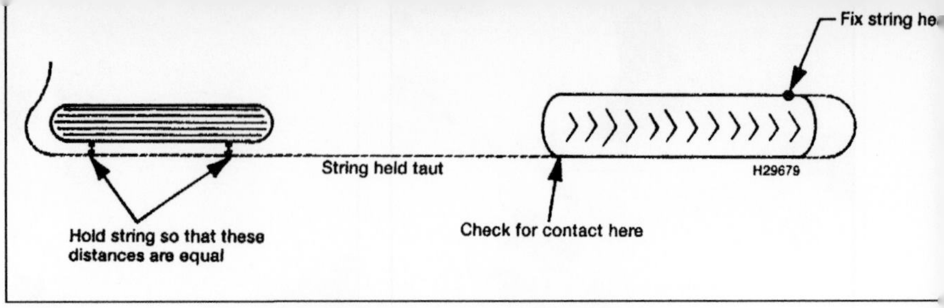


**13.5 Wheel alignment check using string**

3 In order to make a proper check of the wheels it is necessary to support the bike in an upright position, using an auxiliary stand. Measure the width of both tyres at their widest points. Subtract the smaller measurement from the larger measurement, then divide the difference by two. The result is the amount of offset that should exist between the front and rear tyres on both sides.

4 If a string is used, have your assistant hold one end of it about halfway between the floor and the rear axle, touching the rear sidewall of the tyre.

5 Run the other end of the string forward and pull it tight so that it is roughly parallel to the floor. Slowly bring the string into contact with the front sidewall of the rear tyre, then turn the front wheel until it is parallel with the string **(see illustration)**. Measure the distance from the front tyre sidewall to the string.

6 Repeat the procedure on the other side of the motorcycle. The distance from the front tyre sidewall to the string should be equal on both sides.

7 As was previously pointed out, a perfectly straight length of wood or metal bar may be substituted for the string **(see illustration)**. The procedure is the same.

8 If the distance between the string and the tyre is greater on one side, or if the rear wheel appears to be cocked, the frame, swingarm or rear stub axle must be damaged.

9 If the front-to-back alignment is correct, the wheels still may be out of alignment vertically.

10 Using the plumb bob, or other suitable weight, and a length of string, check the rear wheel to make sure it is vertical. To do this, hold the string against the tyre upper sidewall and allow the weight to settle just off the floor. When the string touches both the upper and lower tyre sidewalls and is perfectly straight, the wheel is vertical. If it is not, place thin spacers under one leg of the stand.

11 Once the rear wheel is vertical, check the front wheel in the same manner. If both wheels are not perfectly vertical, the frame and/or major suspension components are bent.

## 14 Front wheel – removal and installation

### *Removal*

1 Slacken and remove the mounting bo securing the brake calipers to the fork le

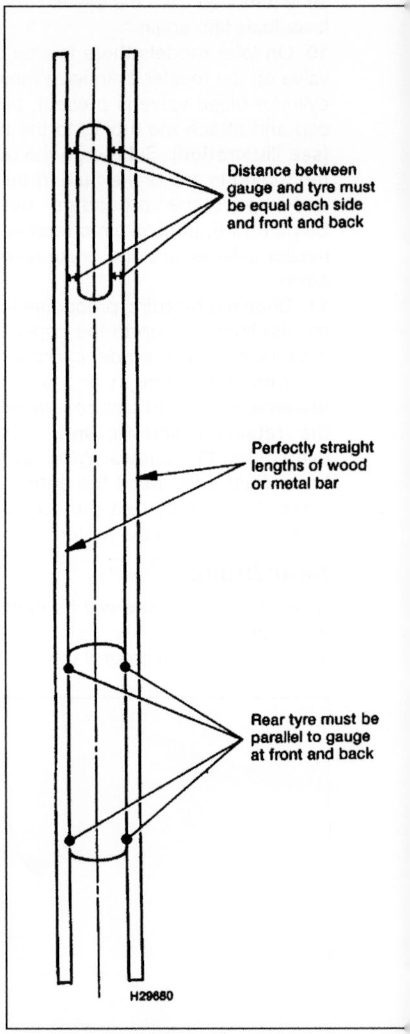


**13.7 Wheel alignment check using a straight edge**

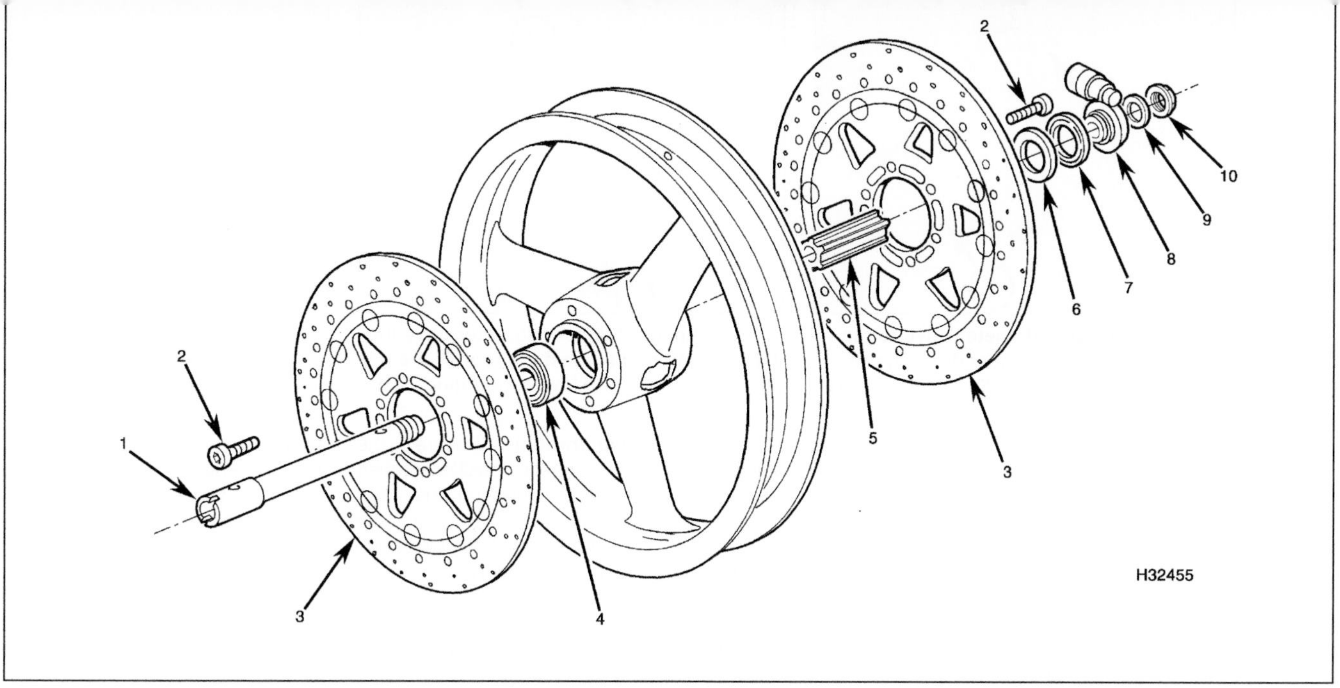


**14.1a Front wheel components**

1 *Axle*
2 *Disc retaining bolt*
3 *Brake disc*
4 *Wheel bearing - 2 off*
5 *Spacer*
6 *Speedometer driveplate*
7 *Dust seal*
8 *Speedometer drive*
9 *Washer*
10 *Axle nut*

**(see illustrations)**. Slide both caliper assemblies off the discs and position them clear of the wheel. Support each caliper with a piece of wire or a bungee cord so that no strain is placed on their hydraulic hoses. **Note:** *There is no need to disconnect the hoses from the calipers.*

***Caution: Do not operate the brake lever with the calipers removed.***

**2** Unscrew the knurled retaining ring and disconnect the speedometer cable from its drive on the left-hand side of the front wheel.

**3** Slacken the axle left-hand clamp bolts then slacken and remove the axle nut and washer **(see illustration)**.

**4** Slacken the axle right-hand clamp bolts, then position the motorcycle on an auxiliary stand and tie down the rear of the motorcycle to raise the front wheel off the ground. Alternatively, remove the fairing lower panels (see Chapter 8) and support the bike under the engine to raise the front wheel.

**5** Support the wheel, then withdraw the axle from the right-hand side and carefully lower the wheel to the ground **(see illustration)**. Manoeuvre the wheel out of position and recover the speedometer drive from its left-hand side. **Note:** *If the front of the bike has not been raised sufficiently to allow the wheel to be removed, remove the front mudguard (see Chapter 8).*

***Caution: Don't lay the wheel down and allow it to rest on a disc – the disc could become warped. Set the wheel on wood blocks so the disc doesn't support the weight of the wheel.***

**6** Check the axle for straightness by rolling it on a flat surface such as a piece of plate glass (first wipe off all old grease and remove any corrosion using fine emery cloth). If the equipment is available, place the axle in V-blocks and measure the runout using a dial gauge. If the axle is bent or the runout exceeds the limit specified, renew it.

**7** Refer to Section 15 if wheel bearing renewal is required.

## Installation

**8** Prior to installation remove the axle clamp bolts from the base of the fork legs. Clean each bolt then apply a smear of molybdenum

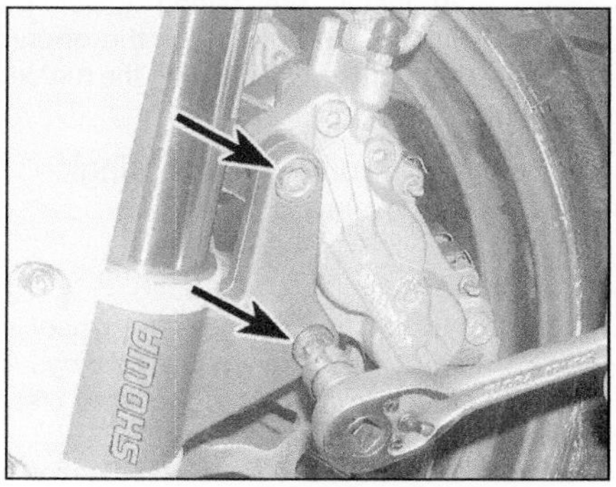

**14.1b Slacken and remove the mounting bolts (arrowed) and slide both brake calipers off the discs**

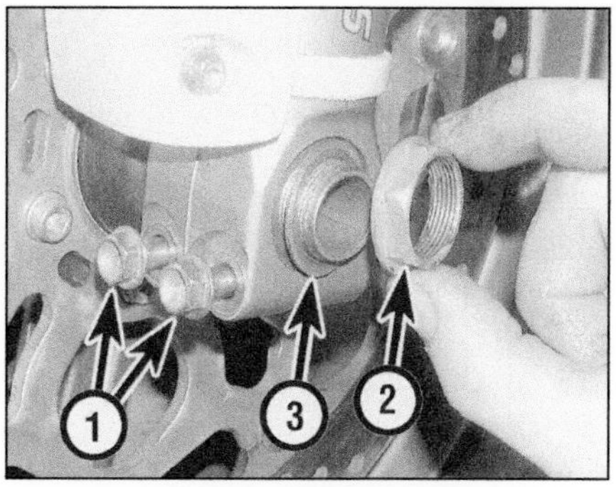


**14.3 Slacken the left-hand clamp bolts (1) then remove the axle nut (2) and washer (3)**

**14.5 Slide out the axle and manoeuvre the wheel out of position**

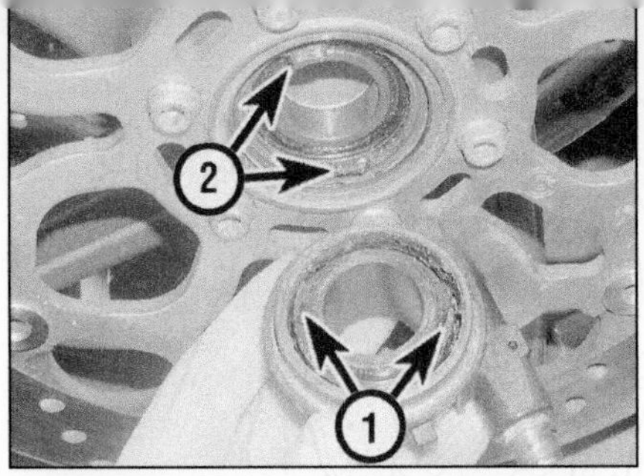


**14.9 Fit the speedometer drive to the wheel ensuring its gear dogs (1) are positioned between the driveplate tabs (2)**

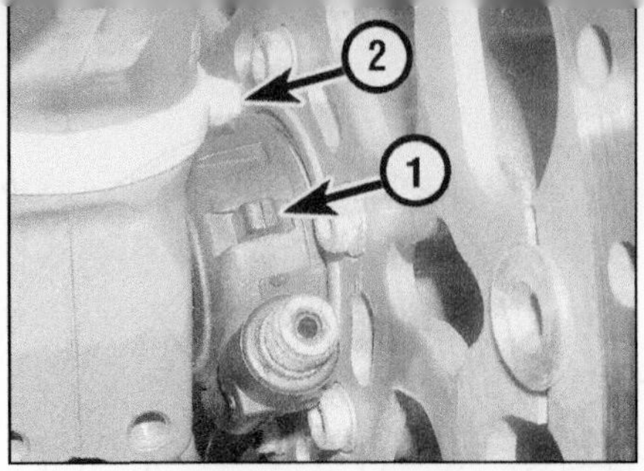


**14.11a Ensure the speedometer drive lug (1) is positioned against the rear of the lug (2) on the mudguard lower mounting clamp**

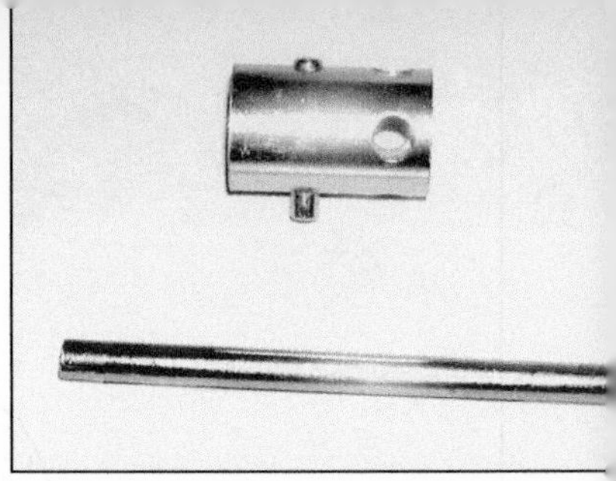

**14.11b Ducati tools provided in the too for aligning the front wheel axle**

disulphide grease to the bolts before refitting them to the fork legs. Also apply a smear of grease to the speedometer drive components and the axle.

**9** Fit the speedometer drive to the left-hand side of the wheel, ensuring its gear dogs are correctly positioned between the driveplate tabs **(see illustration)**.

**10** Manoeuvre the wheel into position, making sure the speedometer drive is on the left-hand side.

**11** Lift the wheel into position and position the lug on the speedometer drive housing against the rear of the lug on the mudguard mounting clamp **(see illustration)**. Ensure the speedometer drive is correctly positioned, then slide in the axle from the right-hand side. Align the slot in the right-hand end of the axle correctly with the slot on the fork leg then push the axle fully into position. **Note:** *A tool for aligning the axle slot with the fork leg is included in the toolkit originally supplied with the bike* **(see illustrations)**. *If the slot is not correctly aligned, it will not be possible to access to the fork compression damping adjusters (see Chapter 6).*

**12** Lubricate the threads and contact face of the axle nut with a smear of grease then refit the washer and nut to the axle.

**13** Ensure the special tool is correctly loca in the axle/fork leg slot then tighten the nut to the specified torque **(see illustrati** Remove the special tool from the axle check that the compression damp adjusters on both fork legs are accessi before proceeding **(see illustration)**. **Not** *the special tool is not available, pass a roc screwdriver, up through the compress damper adjuster access hole in the right-h fork leg and through the axle hole; this prevent the axle rotating as the nu tightened.*

**14** Slide the brake calipers into posit making sure the pads pass on each sid the discs. Lubricate the caliper mounting b with a smear of molybdenum disulph grease then refit the bolts, tightening then the specified torque **(see illustration)**.

**15** Reconnect the speedometer cable to drive and securely tighten its retaining ring

**16** Apply the front brake a few times to b the pads back into contact with the discs t check that the wheel rotates freely.

**17** Remove the bike from its stand.

**18** Apply the front brake and rock the b backwards and forwards a few times. This compress the fork legs and allow them settle in their natural position on the axle.

**19** Once the forks are correctly locat tighten both the left- and right-hand clamp bolts evenly and progressively to specified torque.

**20** Install the fairing lower panels ( Chapter 8) and check the operation of front brake before riding the motorcycle.

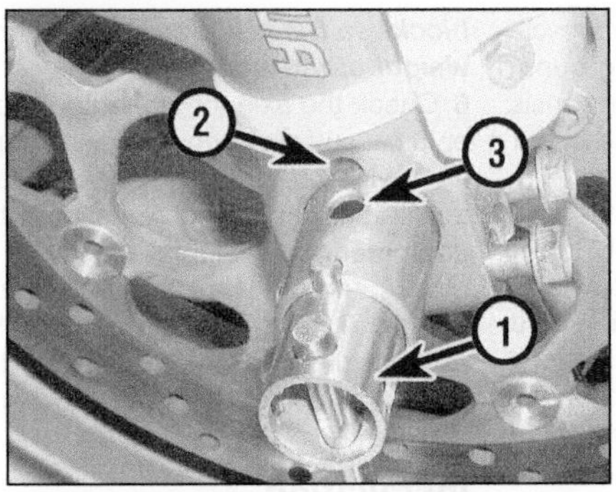


**14.11c Fit the tool (1) to the axle and align it with the fork leg cutout (2) to ensure the compression damping adjuster hole (3) is correctly positioned**

**14.13a Tighten the axle nut to the specified torque . . .**

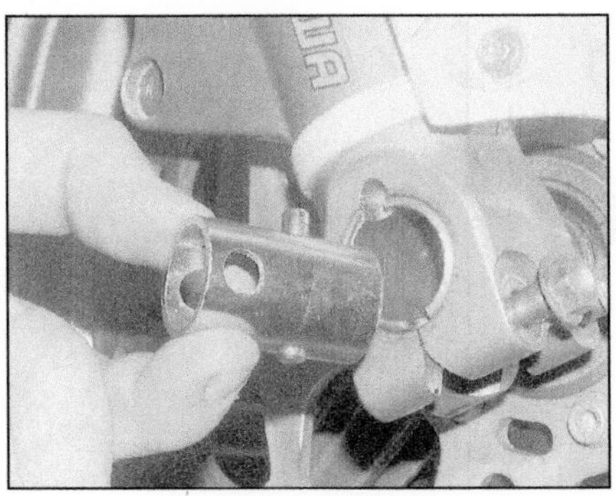

**14.13b . . . then remove the alignment tool**

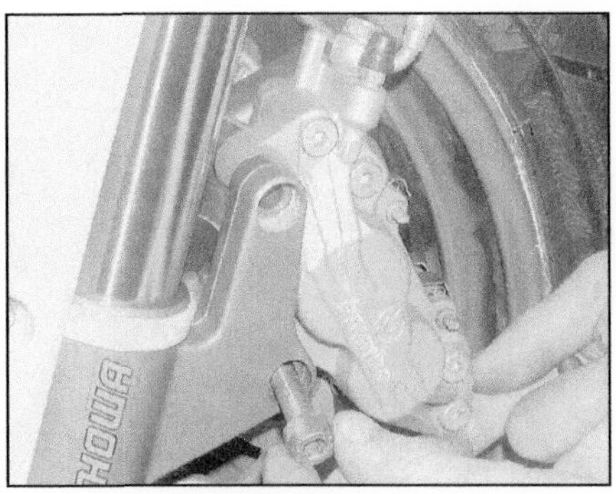

**14.14 Slide the brake calipers onto the discs ensuring the pads pass on each side of the disc**

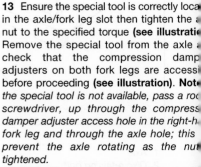

## 15 Front wheel bearings – renewal

**Note:** *Always renew the wheel bearing pairs. Never renew the bearings individu Avoid using a high pressure cleaner on wheel bearing area.*

**1** Remove the wheel (see Section 14).

**2** Set the wheel on blocks so as not to a the weight of the wheel to rest on either of brake discs.

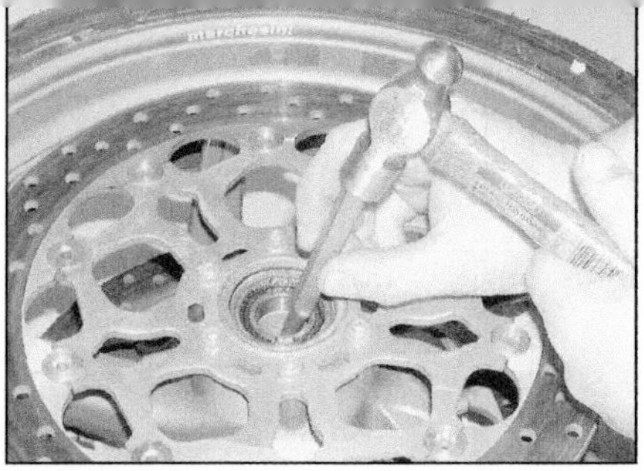

**15.4 Tap the front wheel bearing out of position using a drift passed through the opposite bearing inner race**

**3** Prise out the dust seal from the left-hand side of the wheel using a flat-bladed screwdriver, taking care not to damage the rim of the hub, and lift out the speedometer driveplate. Discard the seal, a new one should be used.

**4** Using a metal rod (preferably a brass drift punch) inserted through the centre of the left-hand bearing, tap evenly around the inner race of the right-hand bearing to drive it from the hub **(see illustration)**. The bearing spacer will also come out.

**5** Lay the wheel on its other side so that the left-hand bearing faces down. Drive the bearing out of the wheel using the same technique as above.

**6** If the bearings are only sealed on one side, clean them with a high flash-point solvent (one which won't leave any residue) and blow them dry with compressed air (don't let the bearings spin as you dry them). Apply a few drops of oil to the bearing. **Note:** *If the bearing is sealed on both sides don't attempt to clean it.*

**7** Hold the outer race of the bearing and rotate the inner race – if the bearing doesn't turn smoothly, has rough spots or is noisy, renew it.

HAYNES HiNT *Refer to Tools and Workshop Tips (Section 5) for more information about bearings.*

**15.9 Tap bearings into position using a socket which bears only on the bearing's outer race**

**8** If the bearing is good and can be re-used and isn't sealed on both sides, wash it in solvent once again and dry it, then pack the bearing with grease.

**9** Thoroughly clean the hub area of the wheel. First install the left-hand bearing into its recess in the hub, with the marked or sealed side facing outwards. Using the old bearing, a bearing driver or a socket large enough to contact the outer race of the bearing, drive it in until it's completely seated **(see illustration)**.

**10** Turn the wheel over and install the bearing spacer. Drive the right-hand bearing into place as described above.

**11** Once both bearings are correctly installed, fit the speedometer driveplate to the left-hand side of the hub. Ensure the hub cutouts then fit the new dust seal. Ensure the seal is fitted with its sealing lip facing inwards then press it squarely into position using a seal or bearing driver which contacts only the outer edge of the seal.

**12** Clean off all grease from the brake discs using brake system cleaner, then install the wheel (see Section 14).

## 16 Rear wheel – removal and installation

### *Removal*

**1** Remove the circlip from the rear wheel nut, noting which way around it is fitted (the inner end of the circlip is curved) **(see illustration)**.

**2** Place the transmission in gear then have an assistant support the bike and apply the rear brake hard whilst you slacken the wheel nut.

**3** Position the motorcycle on an auxiliary stand so that the rear wheel is clear of the ground.

**4** Remove the wheel nut and washer then slide off the tapered collar from the stub axle **(see illustrations)**. The rear wheel can then be removed.

### *Installation*

**5** Clean the mating surfaces of the wheel and stub axle and lubricate the axle driving pins with a smear of grease to prevent corrosion **(see illustration)**.

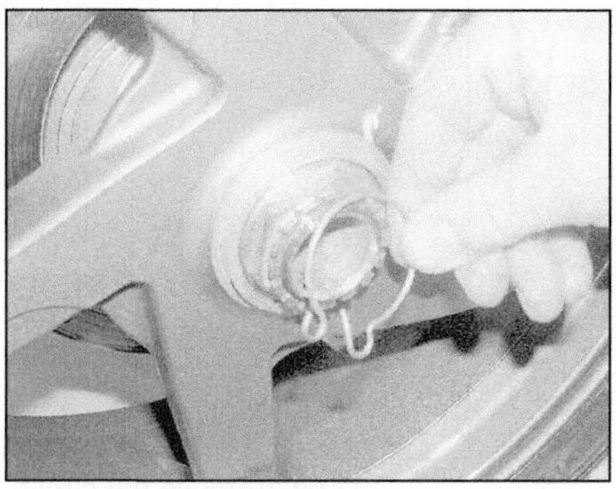

**16.1 Remove the circlip then slacken the rear wheel nut**

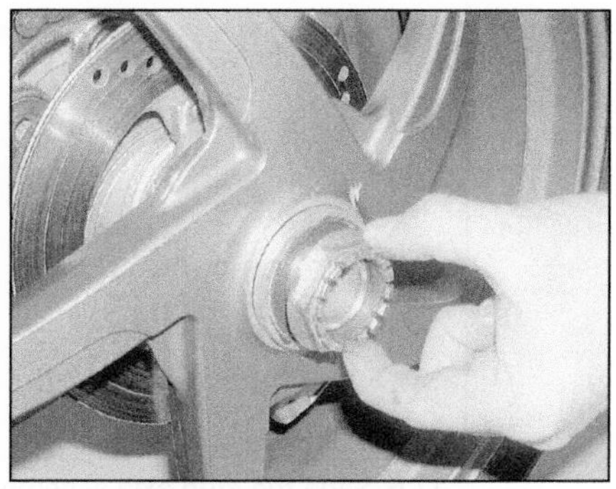

**16.4a Remove the wheel nut . . .**

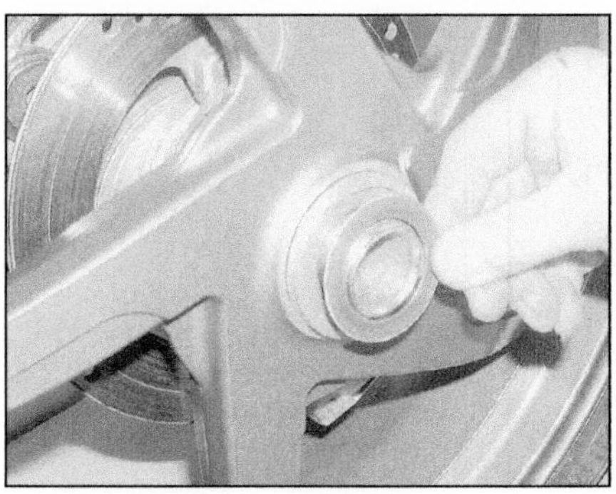

**16.4b . . . and washer . . .**

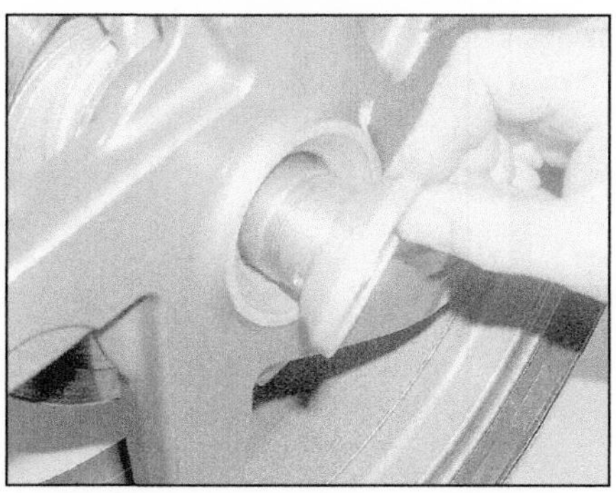

**16.4c . . . and slide off the tapered collar**

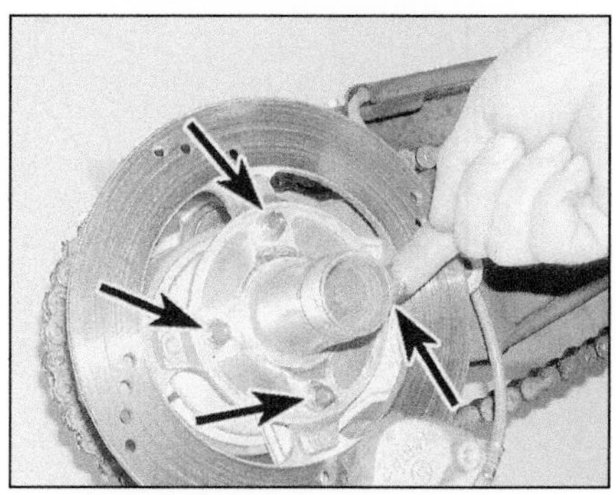

**16.5 Lubricate the driving pins with a smear of grease . . .**

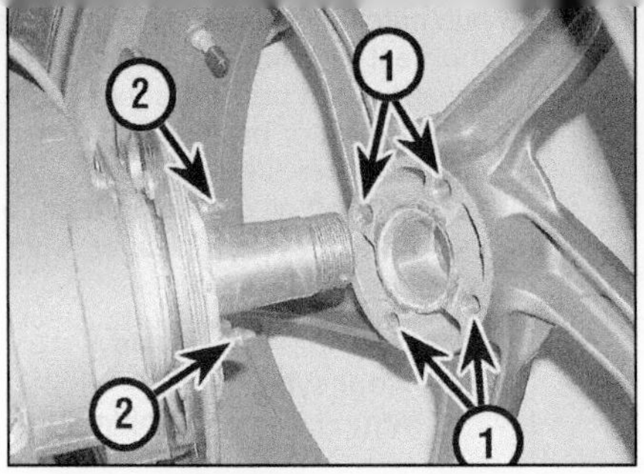


16.6 . . . then fit the wheel ensuring its holes (1) locate correctly on the pins (2)

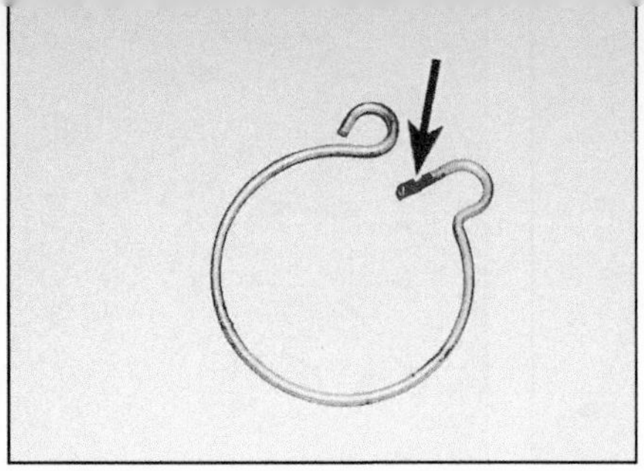

16.10 Ensure the circlip is fitted with its bend (arrowed) curving in towards the wheel

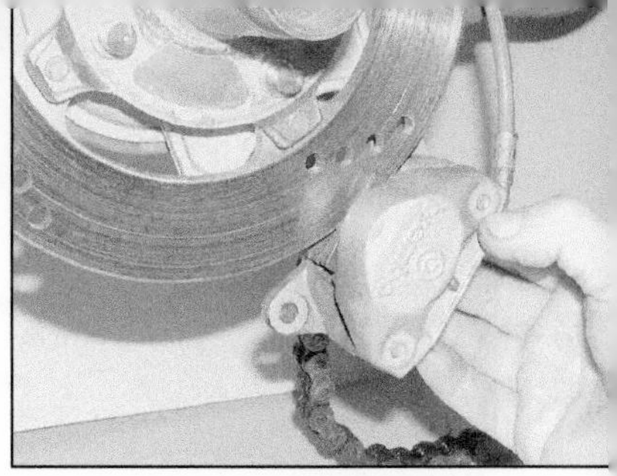

17.4 Unscrew the mounting bolts and sli the caliper off the disc

**6** Refit the rear wheel, engaging it with the stub axle driving pins **(see illustration)**.
**7** Slide the tapered collar onto the stub axle, ensuring its tapered end is facing the wheel, and locate it in the centre of the wheel.
**8** Fit the washer onto the stub axle.
**9** Lubricate the threads and contact face of the rear wheel nut with a smear of molybdenum disulphide grease. Refit the nut to the stub axle and tighten it to the specified torque (prevent rotation in the same way as on removal). Check that the nut is correctly aligned with one of the stub axle holes to enable the circlip to be installed; if not tighten the nut slightly until alignment is correct.
**10** Insert the inner end of the circlip into the stub axle hole and seat the circlip correctly on the wheel nut shoulder. Note that the circlip must be fitted so the bend of the inner end curves towards the wheel **(see illustration)**.
**11** Operate the brake pedal several times to ensure the pads are in firm contact with the disc, then remove the bike from its stand.

## 17 Rear wheel bearing holder – removal, overhaul and installation

### *Removal*

**1** Remove the circlip and slacken the rear wheel nut (see Steps 1 and 2 of Section 16)
**2** Remove the rear sprocket coupling described in Chapter 6.
**3** Remove the rear wheel (see Section 16).
**4** Slacken and remove the rear brake calip mounting bolts then slide the caliper off disc and tie it to the subframe/swingarm avoid any strain being placed on its hydrau hose **(see illustration)**.
**5** Withdraw the stub axle and brake d assembly from the bearing holder **(s illustration)**.
**6** Using a pair of circlip pliers, extract large circlip securing the caliper mounti plate to the bearing holder **(see illustratio** Remove the outer washer and sealing ri then remove the caliper mounting plate fr the bearing holder, noting which way aroun is fitted **(see illustrations)**. With the mounti plate removed, remove the inner sealing r and washer from the bearing holder. Disca the sealing rings; new ones should be used installation.
**7** Fully slacken the clamp bolts and withdr the bearing holder assembly from swingarm **(see illustration)**.

### *Overhaul*

**8** Inspect all components closely, looking obvious signs of wear such as heavy scori or for damage such as cracks or distorti

17.5 Slide the stub axle assembly out of position

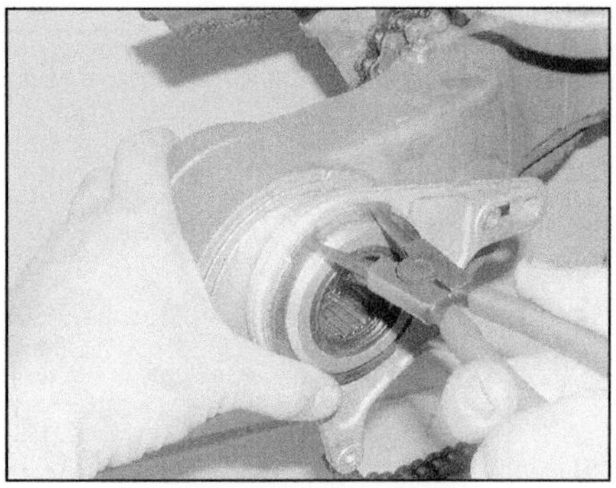

17.6a Remove the circlip . . .

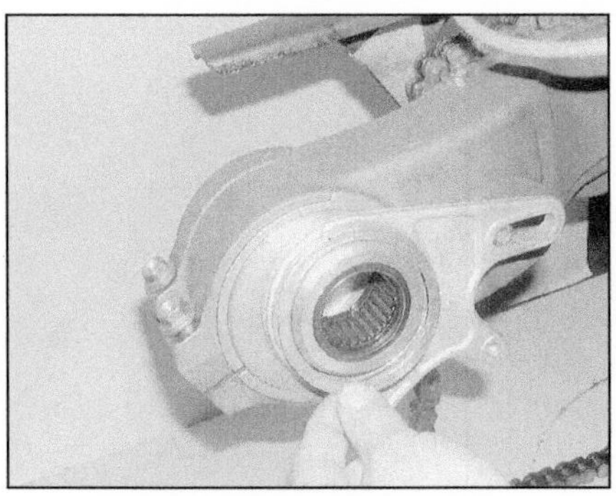

17.6b . . . and outer washer . . .

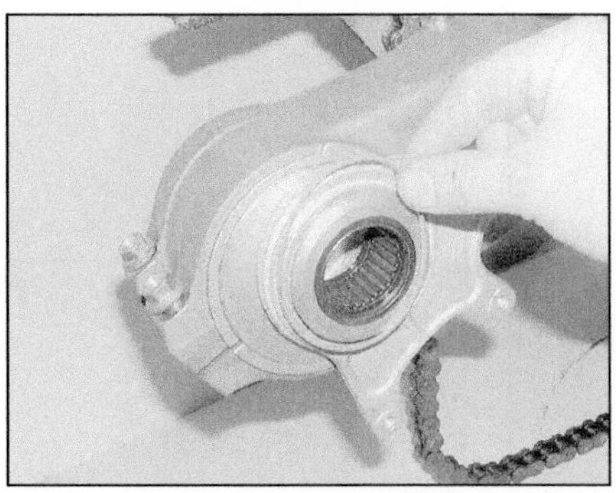

17.6c . . . then remove the sealing ring and caliper mounting plate

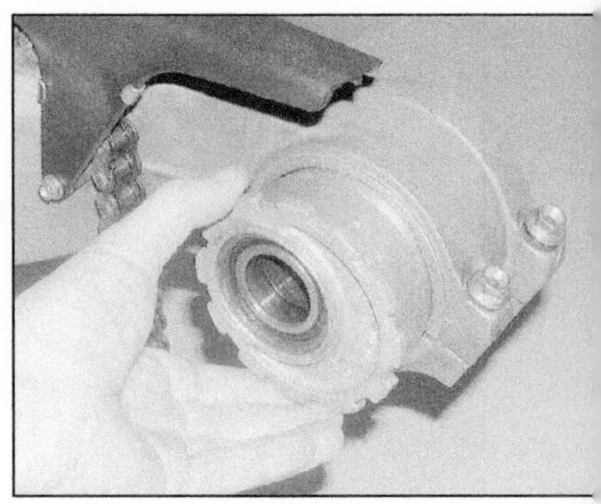

17.7 Removing the bearing holder assembly

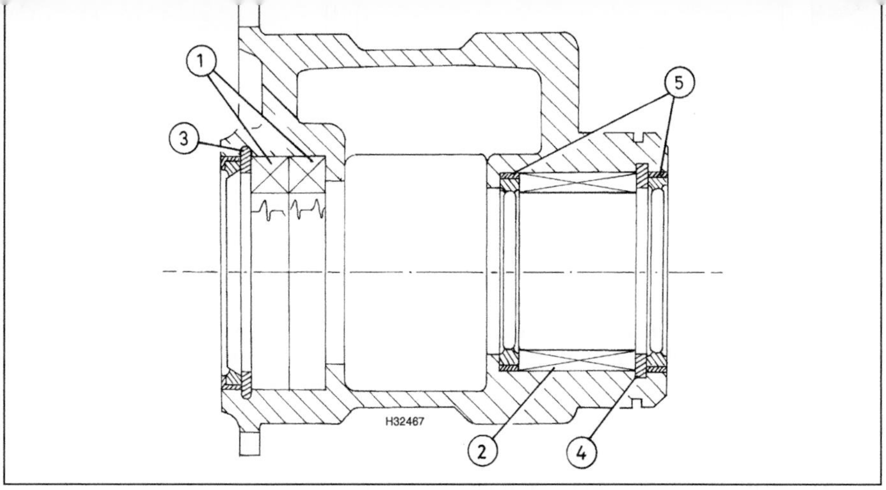


**17.8a Rear wheel bearing holder assembly components**

*1 Left-hand bearings*
*2 Right-hand needle roller bearing*
*3 Circlip*
*4 Circlip*
*5 Oil seal*

**(see illustration)**. The left-hand (sprocket) side bearing inner races should rotate freely and easily without any sign of freeplay or roughness **(see illustrations)**. If the stub axle shows visible signs of damage, it must be renewed.

**9** Ducati specify that the rear wheel bearing holder should not be overhauled and must be renewed as an assembly if the bearings are worn. However, Ducati do list the bearing holder components and stub axle as individual components for some models which means overhaul is possible – check with your Ducati dealer for spares availability. If you cannot purchase the components individually, renewal of the complete assembly is the only option. Should the components be available, overhaul is as follows.

## Left-hand (sprocket) side ball bearings

**10** Extract the bearing circlip from inside the holder **(see illustration)**.

**11** Support the left-hand side of the bearing holder and drive the bearings squarely out of position, using a hammer and suitable drift inserted through the holder from the right-hand side.

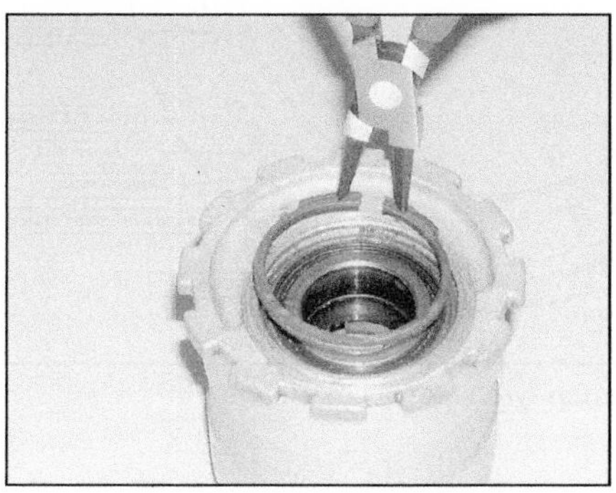

**17.10 Remove the circlip from the left-hand side of the bearing holder**

**12** Ensure the bearing holder bore is clean and undamaged then securely support the right-hand side of the bearing holder.

**13** Locate the first new bearing in its bore and tap it squarely into position using a tubular spacer (such as a socket) which bears only on the bearing's outer race. Ensure the bearing is firmly against its stop then install the second bearing in the same way.

**14** Once both bearings are correctly seated, then secure them in position with the circlip, ensuring it is correctly located in bearing holder groove.

## Right-hand (wheel) side needle roller bearing

**15** Carefully lever the outer dust seal out of position using a flat-bladed screwdriver, noting which way around it is fitted. Discard the seal; a new one must be used.

**16** Remove the bearing circlip from the holder.

**17** Support the right-hand side of the bearing holder then press/drive the bearing and inner seal out of position, noting which way around the seal is fitted.

**18** Ensure the bearing holder bore is clean and undamaged then securely support the left-hand side of the bearing holder.

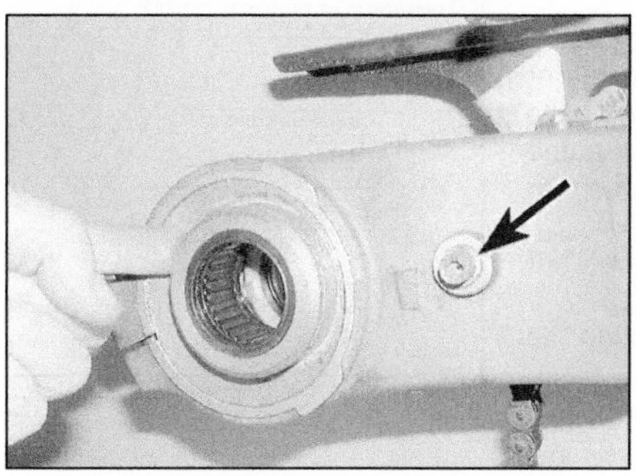

**17.25 Apply a smear of grease to the caliper plate surface of the holder and the locating pin (arrowed)**

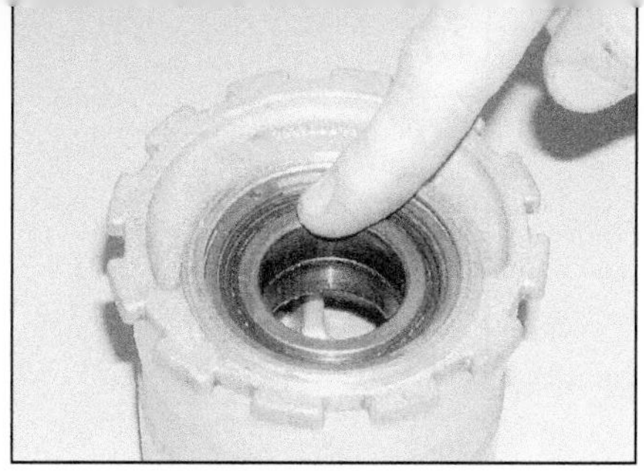

**17.8b Check the left-hand bearings for signs of wear . . .**

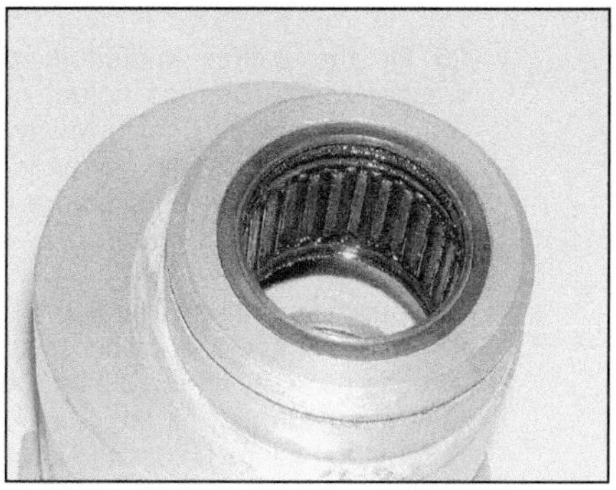

**17.8c . . . and the right-hand needle roller bearing for signs of damage**

**19** Locate the new inner seal in its bore, ensuring its sealing lip is facing outwards (towards the bearing). Press the seal squarely into position so it is firmly against its stop.

**20** The new bearing should be pressed or drawn into its bore rather than driven into position to prevent possible damage. In the absence of a press, a suitable drawbolt arrangement can be made up as described in *Tools and Workshop Tips* in the Reference section.

**21** Ensure the bearing is pressed fully home, then secure it in position with the circlip, ensuring it is correctly located in the holder groove.

**22** Fit the new outer seal, ensuring its sealing lip is facing inwards (towards the bearing), and press it squarely into position until it is flush with the holder.

## *Installation*

**23** Remove all traces of corrosion from the outside of the bearing holder assembly and the inside of the swingarm bore and lubricate the bearing holder surface with a smear of multi-purpose grease.

**24** Insert the bearing holder into the swingarm from the right-hand side and check that it is free to rotate smoothly before proceeding. Wipe off all excess grease.

**25** Lubricate the caliper mounting plate bearing surface of the holder and the locating pin on the swingarm with a smear of multi-purpose grease **(see illustration)**.

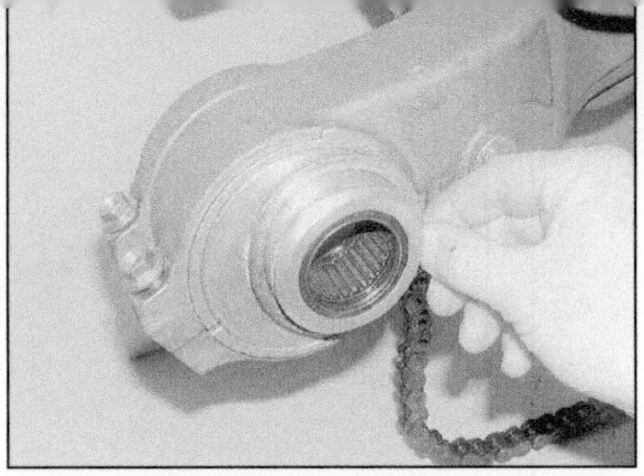
**17.26 Fit the inner washer to the bearing holder with its rounded edge facing away from the swingarm**

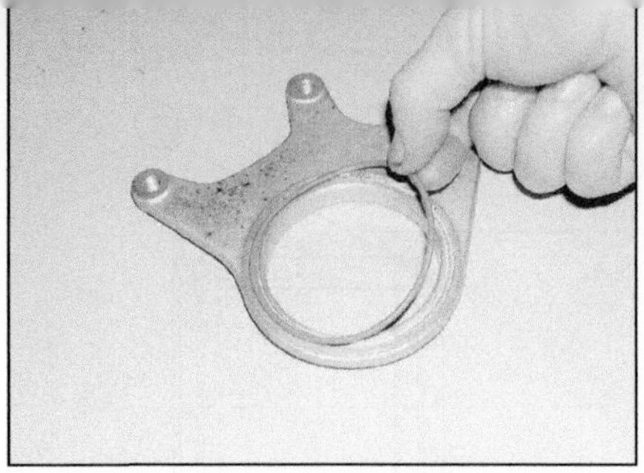
**17.27a Fit the sealing washer to the caliper mounting plate . . .**

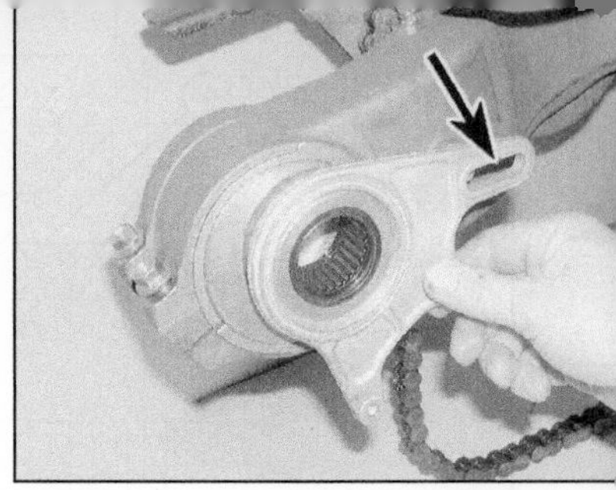
**17.27b . . . then fit the mounting plat ensuring its slot (arrowed) locates correctly over the pin**

**26** Fit the caliper mounting plate inner washer to the bearing holder ensuring its rounded edge is facing away from the swingarm; if the washer is studied closely it will be seen its has a square-edge on one side and a rounded edge on the other **(see illustration)**.

**27** Fit a new inner sealing ring to the bearing holder then install the caliper mounting plate, aligning its slot with the pin on the swingarm **(see illustrations)**. Fit the new outer sealing ring to the bearing holder and install the outer washer with its rounded edge facing away from the caliper mounting plate. Secure all components in position with the large circlip, ensuring it is correctly located in the holder groove.

**28** If a new stub axle is being installed, transfer the brake disc to the axle (see Section 8). Unscrew the bolts and remove the rear wheel driving pins from the original axle. Remove all traces of original locking compound and apply a drop of fresh locking compound to the threads of each bolt then fit the pins to the new stub axle, tightening their bolts to the specified torque.

**29** Apply a thin film of molybdenum disulphide grease to the bearing holder needle roller bearing and dust seal lips and also to the bearing surface of the stub axle. Carefully slide the stub axle (complete with brake disc and wheel locating pins) into the bearing holder, take care not to damage the dust seals. Clean off all excess grease using brake system cleaner.

**30** Slide the rear brake caliper into position, making sure the pads pass on each side of the disc. Lubricate the caliper mounting bolts with a smear of molybdenum disulphide grease then refit the bolts, tightening them to the specified torque.

**31** Fit the rear wheel, tightening the wheel nut lightly only (see Section 16).

**32** Install the rear sprocket coupling as described in Chapter 6.

**33** With the sprocket coupling correctly installed and the final drive chain adjusted, tighten the wheel nut to the specified torque and secure it in position with the circlip (see Section 16).

## 18 Tyres – general information and fitting

### *General information*

**1** The wheels fitted to all models are designed to take tubeless tyres only. Tyre sizes are given in the Specifications at the beginning of this Chapter.

**2** Refer to *Daily (pre-ride) checks* at the beginning of this manual for tyre maintenance, pressures and tread wear depth.

### *Fitting new tyres*

**3** When selecting new tyres, ensure they the correct size and speed rating and front and rear tyre types are compatibl necessary seek advice from a tyre fit specialist **(see illustration)**.

**4** It is recommended that tyre fitting is car out by a motorcycle tyre specialist rather t attempted in the home workshop. Thi particularly relevant in the case of tube tyres because the force required to break seal between the wheel rim and tyre bea substantial, and is usually beyond capabilities of an individual working normal tyre levers. Additionally, the speci will be able to balance the wheels after fitting.

**5** Note that punctured tubeless tyres ca some cases be repaired, but such rep must be carried out by a tyre fitting specia

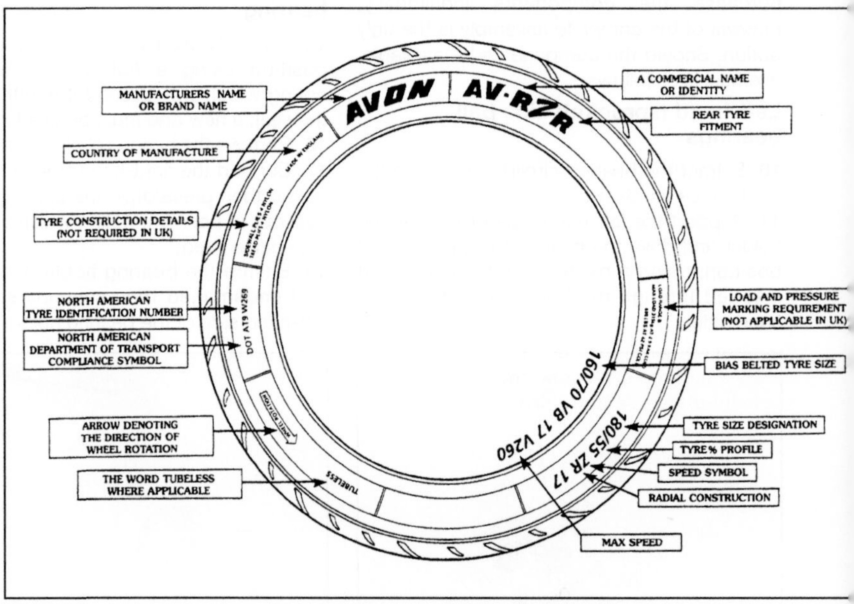

**18.3 Common tyre sidewall markings**

# Chapter 8
# Bodywork

## Contents



## Degrees of difficulty

| | | | | |
|---|---|---|---|---|
| **Easy,** suitable for novice with little experience | **Fairly easy,** suitable for beginner with some experience | **Fairly difficult,** suitable for competent DIY mechanic | **Difficult,** suitable for experienced DIY mechanic | **Very difficult,** suitable for expert DIY or professional |

## 1 General information

This Chapter covers the procedures necessary to remove and install the bodywork. Since many service and repair operations on these motorcycles require the removal of the bodywork, the procedures are grouped here and referred to from other Chapters.

In the case of damage to the bodywork, it is usually necessary to remove the broken component and renew it. The material the bodywork panels are composed of does not lend itself to conventional repair techniques. Note that there are, however, some companies that specialise in 'plastic welding', and there are a number of bodywork repair kits now available for motorcycles. On some models, certain panels are made from carbon fibre.

When attempting to remove any body panel, first study it closely, noting any fasteners and associated fittings, to be sure of returning everything to its correct place on installation. In some cases, the aid of an assistant will be required when removing panels, to help avoid the risk of damage to paintwork. If, after its fasteners have been removed, a panel will not release, DO NOT FORCE IT. Check that all fasteners have been removed and try again. Where a panel engages another by means of tabs, be careful not to break the tab or its mating slot, or to damage the paintwork. Remember that a few moments of patience at this stage will save you a lot of money in replacing broken fairing panels!

Before attempting to install a body panel, study its fasteners and associated fittings. Check that these are in good condition, including all trim nuts or clips and damping/rubber mounts; renew any faulty ones. Check also that all mounting brackets are straight and repair or renew them, if necessary. Where assistance was required to remove a panel, make sure your assistant is on hand to install it.

Tighten the fasteners securely but be careful not to overtighten any of them or the panel may break (not always immediately), due to the uneven stress. Where quick-release fasteners are fitted, turn them 180° anti-clockwise to release them, and 180° clockwise to secure them.

## 2 Seat cowling – removal and installation

### *Removal*

**1** Insert the ignition key into the seat lock. Apply slight downward pressure on the rear of the seat cowling, then turn the key clockwise to unlock the seat cowling. Raise the rear of the cowling slightly then move it backwards and pivot the seat cowling on its front hinge until it is resting on the fuel tank.

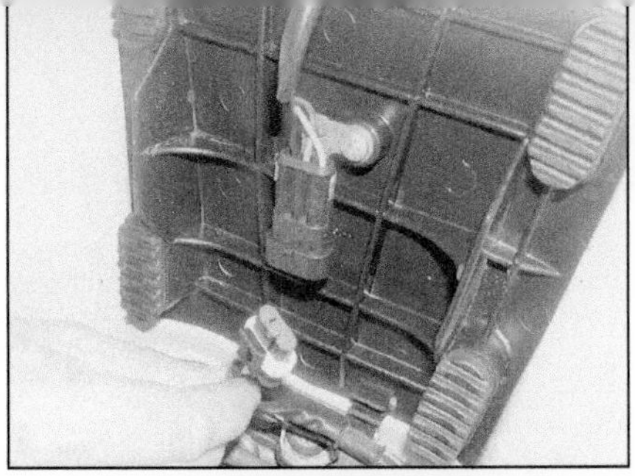

**2.2 Disconnect the tail light wiring connector**

**2.3 Remove the rubber retainer . . .**

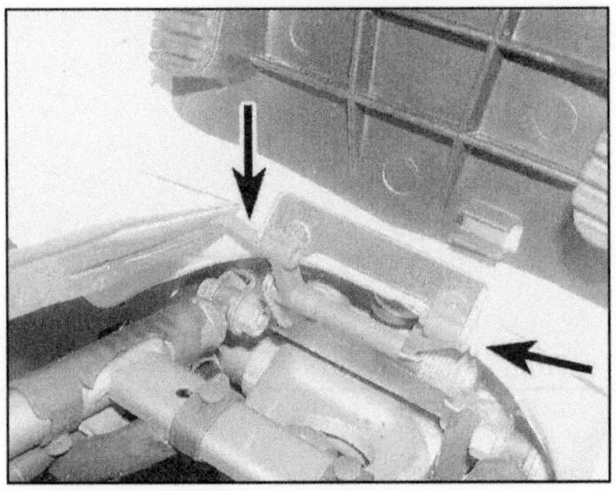

**2.4 . . . then slide out the pivot pins (arrowed) and remove the seat cowling assembly**

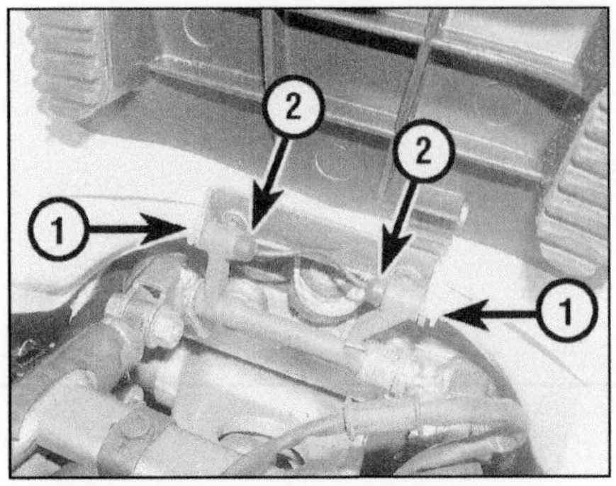


**2.7 Ensure the pivot pins (1) are fully inserted and secure them in position by fitting the rubber retainer caps (2) to their inner ends**

**2** Disconnect the tail light unit wiring connector **(see illustration)**.
**3** Remove the rubber retainer which links the seat cowling pivot pins **(see illustration)**.
**4** Slide out the pivot pins and remove the seat cowling assembly from the bike **(see illustration)**.
**5** If necessary, undo the two bolts and remove the seat cowling hinge assembly from the frame. Recover the spacers fitted between the hinge and frame.

### *Installation*

**6** If the hinge assembly was removed, remove all traces of the original locking compound then apply a drop of fresh locking compound to the threads of each retaining bolt. Offer up the hinge, positioning the spacers between the hinge and frame, then refit the retaining bolts and tighten them securely.
**7** Align the seat cowling assembly with the hinge then insert both pivot pins. Secure the pivot pins in position with the rubber retainer **(see illustration)**.
**8** Securely reconnect the tail light wiring connector.
**9** Ensure the tail light wiring is clipped securely in position and all the mounting of the cowling. Pivot the seat cowling ba down onto the subframe and lock it position.

## 3 Rear view mirrors – removal and installation

### *Removal*

**1** Unscrew the retaining bolt and remove mirror from the bike, complete with its rubb spacer.

### *Installation*

**2** Prior to installation, remove all traces of original locking compound and apply a dr of fresh locking compound to the threads the retaining bolt.
**3** Fit the rubber spacer and install the mirr Ensure the locating pegs are correctly locat in the mounting bracket then refit the retain bolt, tightening it securely.

## 4 Fairing panels – removal and installation

### *Lower panel*

#### Removal

**1** Remove the two quick-release fasten (twist them 180° anti-clockwise to relea them) or screws (as applicable) securing base of the left- and right-hand lower pan together. Recover the nylon washer fitted each fastener/screw.
**2** Each lower panel can then be removed removing the four quick-relea fasteners/screws securing the top of the pa to the upper fairing and frame (s **illustration)**. Recover the nylon washer fitt to each fastener/screw and remove the pa from the bike **(see illustration)**.
**3** If necessary, slacken and remove

**4.2a Four fasteners/screws retain the panel to the frame and upper fairing**

**4.2b Removing the lower panel from the bike**

**4.7 Remove the two fasteners/screws which retain the lower panels to the upper fairing**

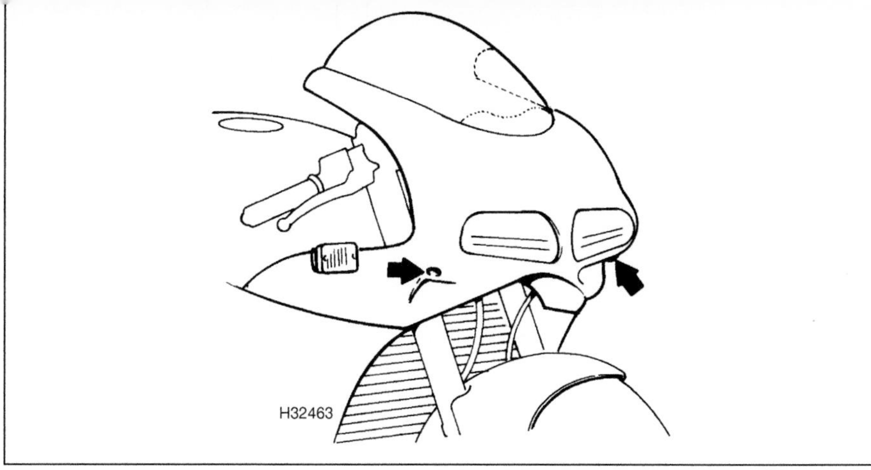


**4.8 Remove the two screws (arrowed) which retain the upper fairing to the headlight shell**

screws and nylon washers and separate the upper and lower sections of each lower panel.

### Installation

**4** Where necessary, ensure all the rubber nuts are in position then reassemble the upper and lower sections of the lower panel. Refit the screws and nylon washers.

**5** Manoeuvre the panel into position and secure it to the frame and fairing panels with the nylon washers and quick-release fasteners/screws (as applicable).

## *Upper fairing*

### Removal

**6** Remove both rear view mirrors (see Section 3).

**7** Remove the two fasteners/screws which retain the lower panel to the upper fairing on each side of the bike **(see illustration)**.

**8** Slacken and remove the two screws and nylon washers securing the upper fairing to the base of the headlight mounting shell **(see illustration)**.

**9** Free the upper fairing from the lower panels and air filter housings and manoeuvre it away from the bike. Whilst the upper fairing is removed, secure the air filter housings to the headlight mounting shell with the mounting bolts to prevent any strain being placed on the housings.

### Installation

**10** Prior to installation, check that the upper fairing rubber nuts on the headlight mounting shell and the mounting rubbers on the mounting brackets are in good condition. If not, renew them.

**11** Manoeuvre the upper fairing into position, engaging it with the lower fairing panels, and locate it on the headlight mounting shell.

**12** Ensure the air filter housings are correctly located, then refit the screws and nylon washers securing the upper fairing to the headlight mounting shell. Securely tighten the screws then retain the upper fairing to the lower panels with the nylon washers and quick-release fasteners/screws (as applicable).

**13** Refit the rear view mirrors (see Section 3).

## *Lower inner panel*

### Removal

**14** Remove both lower panels (see Steps 1 and 2).

**15** Slacken and remove the mounting screws and nylon washers and remove the inner panel from the bike **(see illustrations)**.

### Installation

**16** Engage the panel locating peg in its mounting rubber then refit the mounting screws and nylon washers and tighten them securely (do not overtighten the screws).

**17** Refit the lower panels (see Steps 4 and 5).

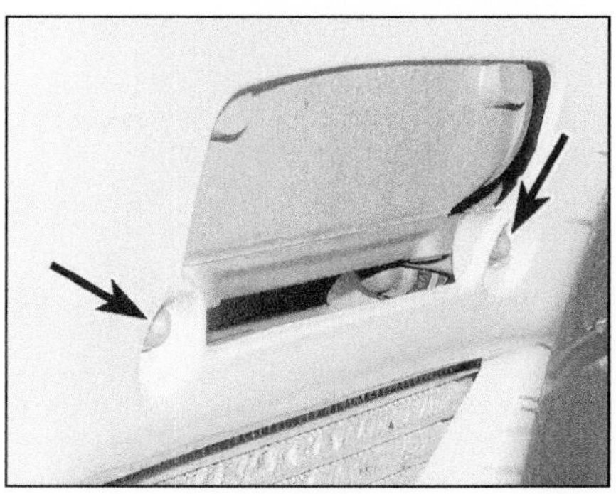

**4.15a Unscrew the mounting screws (arrowed) . . .**

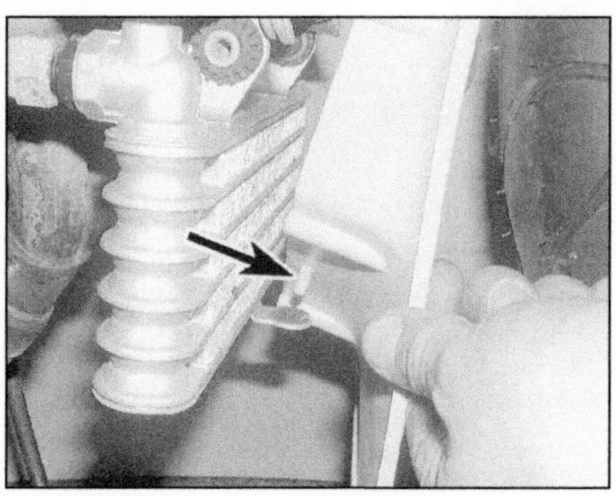

**4.15b . . . and remove the inner panel, freeing its locating peg (arrowed)**

## 5 Front mudguard – removal and installation

### *Removal*

**1** Unscrew the four screws and nylon washers securing the mudguard to the left- and right-hand fork legs, then manoeuvre the mudguard out of position.

**2** Check the mudguard mounting clamps for signs of damage and renew if necessary. Note that the lower clamp on the left-hand fork has the speedometer drive locating lug.

### *Installation*

**3** Installation is the reverse of removal. Do not overtighten the screws.

## 6 Windshield – removal and installation

### *Removal*

**1** Remove the upper fairing (see Section 4)

**2** Remove the screws, nylon washers and rubber nuts securing the windshield to the fairing, and remove the windshield, noting how it fits.

### *Installation*

**3** Prior to installation, check that the windshield rubber nuts are in good condition. If not, renew them.

**4** Align the windshield with the upper fairing and secure it in position with the retaining screws and nylon washers. Do not overtighten the screws.

# Chapter 9
# Electrical system

## Contents



## Degrees of difficulty

| | | | | |
|---|---|---|---|---|
| **Easy,** suitable for novice with little experience | **Fairly easy,** suitable for beginner with some experience | **Fairly difficult,** suitable for competent DIY mechanic | **Difficult,** suitable for experienced DIY mechanic | **Very difficult,** suitable for expert DIY or professional |

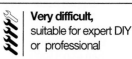

## Specifications

### Battery

| | |
|---|---|
| Capacity | 12V, 16Ah |
| Voltage | |
| Fully charged | 13.0 to 13.2V |
| Discharged | below 12.3V |
| Charging rate (normal) | 1.5A for 5 to 10 hrs |

### Charging system

| | |
|---|---|
| Alternator | |
| Pre 1999 model year | 350W |
| 1999-on model year | 520W three-phase |
| Current leakage (approximate) | 1.0mA (maximum) |
| Regulated voltage output (approximate) | 13.5 to 15.5V |
| Unregulated voltage output | |
| Pre 1999 model year | |
| At 1500 rpm | At least 35 volts |
| At 3000 rpm | At least 70 volts |
| At 6000 rpm | At least 140 volts |
| 1999-on model year | |
| At 2000 rpm | 38 ± 10 volts |
| At 6000 rpm | 110 ± 10 volts |
| Alternator stator coil resistance (approximate) | |
| Pre 1999 model year | 0.2 to 0.4 ohms |
| 1999-on model year | 0.1 to 1.0 ohms |

| | |
|---|---|
| Charging system fuse | |
| Pre 1997 model year | 30A |
| 1997-on model year | 40A |
| Fusebox fuses (location in brackets) | |
| Pre 1999 model year | |
| Ignition (main) switch (A1) | 30A |
| Cooling fan (B2) | 7.5A |
| Headlight main/dipped beam (C3) | 7.5A |
| Turn signal, tail light, and instrument cluster lights (D4) | 7.5A |
| Brake light and horn (E5) | 7.5A |
| Right handlebar switch (F6) | 3A |
| Spare (G7) | 30A |
| Spare (H8) | 7.5A |
| 1999-on model year | |
| Ignition (main) switch (A1) | 30A |
| Cooling fan (B2) | 7.5A |
| Left handlebar switch (C3) | 3A |
| Headlight high beam (D4) | 15A |
| Headlight dipped beam (E5) | 15A |
| Turn signal, tail light, and instrument cluster lights (F6) | 7.5A |
| Brake light and horn (G7) | 7.5A |
| Right handlebar switch (H8) | 3A |
| Engine management system fuse(s) | |
| Early 916 models (fuses integral with relays) | 2 x 15A |
| All other models | |
| Single fuse | 15A |
| Dual fuse arrangement | |
| 1.6M engine management system* | 5A and 20A |
| P8 engine management system* | 15A and 20A |

**See Chapter 4 for engine management system information – ensure the correct rating fuse is fitted to the relevant holder*

## Bulbs

| | |
|---|---|
| Headlight | |
| Dipped beam | 55W |
| Main beam | 55W |
| Sidelight | 5W |
| Brake/tail lights | 21/5W |
| Turn signal lights | 10W |
| Number plate light | 5W |
| Instrument cluster | |
| Illumination bulb | 2W |
| Warning light bulb | 1.2W |

## Torque settings

| | |
|---|---|
| Alternator | |
| Pre 1999 model year | |
| Stator bolts | 10 Nm |
| 1999-on model year | |
| Stator and wiring plate bolts | 10 Nm |
| Rotor bolts | 13 Nm |
| Battery mounting tray bolt(s) | 10 Nm |
| Horn bolt | 10 Nm |
| Ignition (main) switch bolt | 9 Nm |
| Neutral switch | 6 Nm |
| Oil pressure switch | 19 Nm |
| Starter motor mounting bolts | 10 Nm |
| Throttle twistgrip housing bolts | 9 Nm |

## 1 General information

All models have a 12-volt electrical system which is powered by an alternator with a separate regulator/rectifier unit. The regulator maintains the charging system output within the specified range to prevent overcharging, and the rectifier converts the ac (alternating current) output of the alternator to dc (direct current) to power the lights and other components and to charge the battery. The alternator rotor is mounted on the left-hand end of the crankshaft.

The starter motor is on the front of the crankcase. The starting system includes the motor, the battery, the relay and the various wires and switches. If the engine kill switch in the RUN position and the ignition (main) switch is ON, the starter relay allows the starter motor to operate. On later (2000-on) models, the sidestand must also be retracted before the starter motor can be operated.

**Note:** *Keep in mind that electrical parts, once purchased, cannot be returned. To avoid unnecessary expense, make very sure the faulty component has been positively identified before buying a new part.*

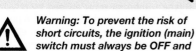

## 2 Electrical system – fault finding

***Warning: To prevent the risk of short circuits, the ignition (main) switch must always be OFF and the battery negative (–) terminal should be disconnected before any of the bike's other electrical components are disturbed. Don't forget to reconnect the terminal securely once work is finished or if battery power is needed for circuit testing.***

**1** A typical electrical circuit consists of an electrical component, the switches, relays, etc. related to that component and the wiring and connectors that hook the component to both the battery and the frame. To aid in locating a problem in any electrical circuit, refer to the wiring diagrams at the end of this Chapter.

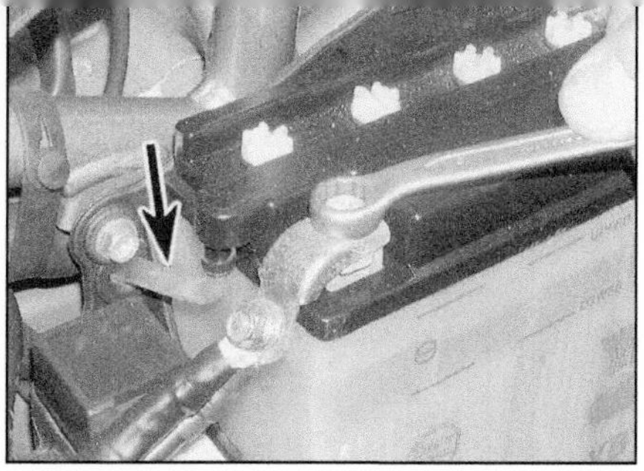

**3.2 Unscrew the bolt and disconnect the lead from the battery negative (-ve) terminal first (breather hose arrowed) . . .**

**2** Before tackling any troublesome electrical circuit, first study the wiring diagram (see end of Chapter) thoroughly to get a complete picture of what makes up that individual circuit. Trouble spots, for instance, can often be narrowed down by noting if other components related to that circuit are operating properly or not. If several components or circuits fail at one time, chances are the fault lies in the fuse or earth (ground) connection, as several circuits often are routed through the same fuse and earth (ground) connections.

**3** Electrical problems often stem from simple causes, such as loose or corroded connections or a blown fuse. Prior to any electrical fault finding, always visually check the condition of the fuse, wires and connections in the problem circuit. Intermittent failures can be especially frustrating, since you can't always duplicate the failure when it's convenient to test. In such situations, a good practice is to clean all connections in the affected circuit, whether or not they appear to be good. All of the connections and wires should also be wiggled to check for looseness which can cause intermittent failure.

**4** If testing instruments are going to be utilised, use the wiring diagram to plan where you will make the necessary connections in order to accurately pinpoint the trouble spot.

**5** The basic tools needed for electrical fault finding include a battery and bulb test circuit, a continuity tester, a test light, and a jumper wire. A multimeter capable of reading volts, ohms and amps is also very useful as an alternative to the above, and is necessary for performing more extensive tests and checks.

**3.3 . . . then unscrew the bolt and disconnect the positive (+ve) terminal lead**

> HAYNES HiNT *Refer to Fault Finding Equipment in the Reference section for details of how to use electrical test equipment.*

## 3 Battery and mounting tray – removal and installation

***Caution: Be extremely careful when handling or working around the battery. The electrolyte is very caustic and an explosive gas (hydrogen) is given off when the battery is charging.***

### Removal

**1** Remove the fairing right-hand lower panel (see Chapter 8).

**2** Unscrew the negative (–ve) terminal bolt first and disconnect the lead from the battery **(see illustration)**.

**3** Unscrew the positive (+ve) terminal bolt and disconnect the lead **(see illustration)**.

**4** Unscrew the bolt and remove the battery retaining clamp **(see illustrations)**.

**5** Disconnect the breather hose (unsealed battery only) from the battery and remove the battery from its mounting tray **(see illustration)**.

**3.4a Unscrew the retaining bolt . . .**

**3.4b . . . and remove the battery retaining clamp . . .**

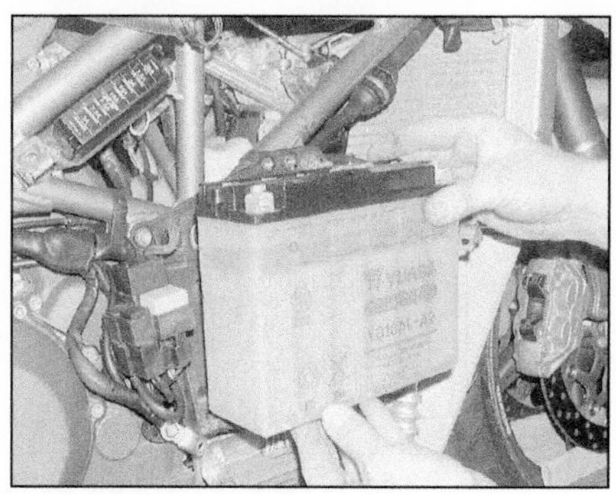

**3.5 . . . then lift out the battery**

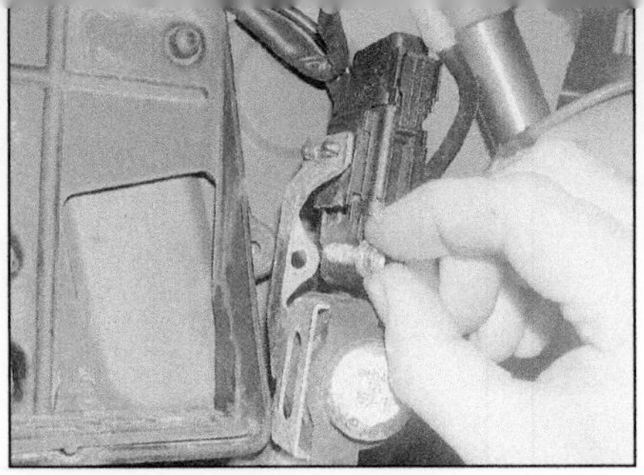

**3.6a Unscrew the bolt and free the starter relay and charging circuit fuse bracket from the front of the battery tray . . .**

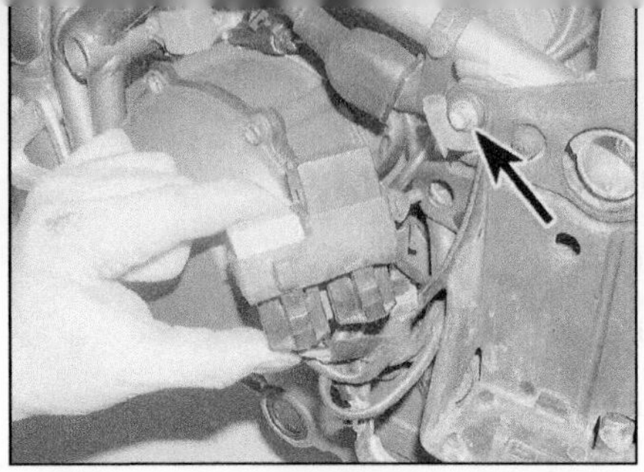

**3.6b . . . and unclip the relay mounting rubber, then unscrew the mounting bolt (arrowed)**

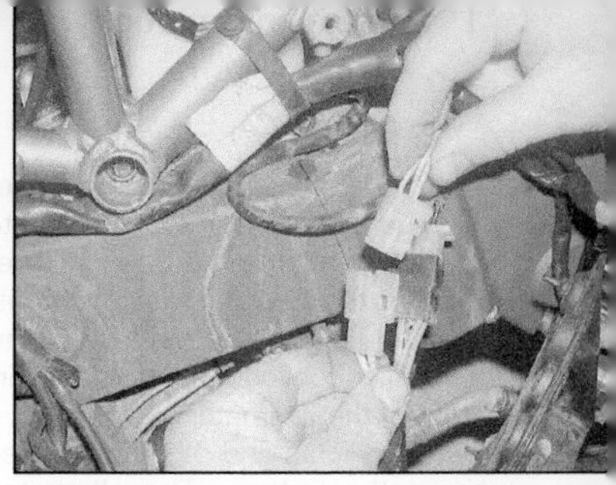

**3.6c Disconnect the regulator/rectifie wiring connectors . . .**

**6** To remove the mounting tray, undo the bolt and free the starter relay and charging circuit fuse holder from the front of the mounting tray, then unclip the relay mounting from the rear of the tray (there is no need to disconnect the relay and fuse wiring) **(see illustrations)**. Unscrew the retaining bolt(s) and free the mounting tray from the frame. Disconnect the regulator/rectifier wiring connectors and remove the mounting tray, complete with the regulator/rectifier unit; on some models it will also be necessary to unbolt the earth (ground) lead from the regulator/rectifier **(see illustrations)**.

### *Installation*

**7** If the mounting tray was removed, ensure the regulator/rectifier unit is securely fitted and the mounting rubber is in position. Securely reconnect the regulator/rectifier wiring connectors then locate the tray on the frame, tightening its retaining bolt(s) to the specified torque. Ensuring the wiring is correctly routed, clip the relay mounting back onto the rear of the tray then secure the starter relay and charging circuit fuse bracket in position with the retaining bolt. Where necessary, also reconnect the earth (ground) lead to the regulator/rectifier and securely tighten its bolt.

**8** Clean the battery terminals and lead ends with a wire brush or knife and emery paper.

**9** Locate the battery in the tray and securely reconnect the breather hose (unsealed battery). Refit the battery clamp and securely tighten its bolt.

**10** Reconnect the positive (+ve) lead to the battery first, then reconnect the negative (–ve) lead.

> **HAYNES HiNT** ***Battery corrosion can be kept to a minimum by applying a layer of petroleum jelly to the terminals after the cables have been connected.***

**11** Ensure both terminal bolts are securely tightened then install the fairing panel (see Chapter 8) **(see illustration)**.

## 4 Battery – charging

***Caution: Be extremely careful when handling or working around the battery. The electrolyte is very caustic and an explosive gas (hydrogen) is given off when the battery is charging.***

**1** Remove the battery (see Section 3). Connect the charger to the battery, making sure that the positive (+ve) lead on the charger is connected to the positive (+ve) terminal on the battery, and the negative (–ve) lea connected to the negative (–ve) terminal.

**2** Ducati recommend that the battery charged at a maximum rate of 1.5 amps f to 10 hours. Exceeding this figure can ca the battery to overheat, buckling the pla and rendering it useless. Few owners will h access to an expensive current contro charger, so if a normal domestic charge used check that after a possible initial pe the charge rate falls to a safe level ( **illustration)**. If the battery becomes during charging **stop**. Further charging cause damage.

**3** If the recharged battery discharges rap when left disconnected it is likely that internal short caused by physical damag sulphation has occurred. A new battery wi required. A sound item will tend to lose charge at about 1% per day.

**4** Install the battery (see Section 3).

**5** If the motorcycle sits unused for l periods of time, charge the battery once e month to six weeks and leave it disconnec

## 5 Fuses – check and renewal

**1** The electrical system is protected by fu of different ratings. Most fuses, except charging circuit fuse and the

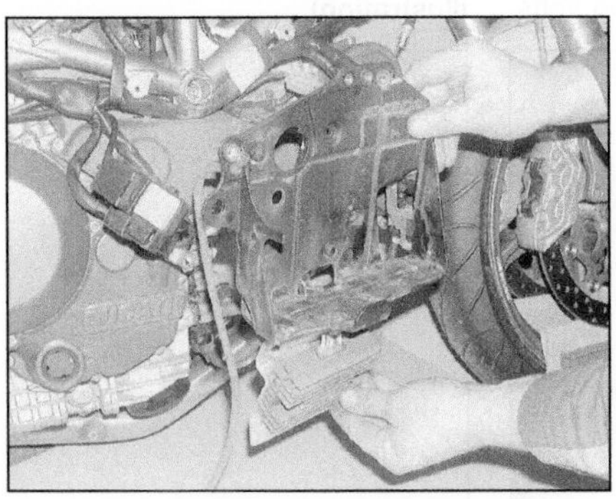

**3.6d . . . and remove the battery tray assembly from the bike**

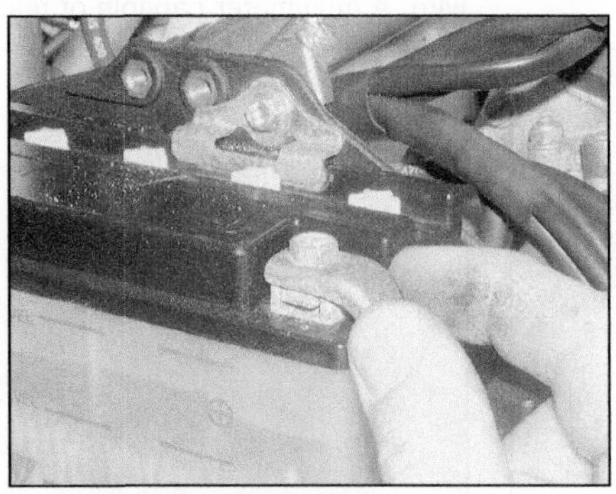

**3.11 Ensure the battery terminals are securely tightened before installing the fairing**

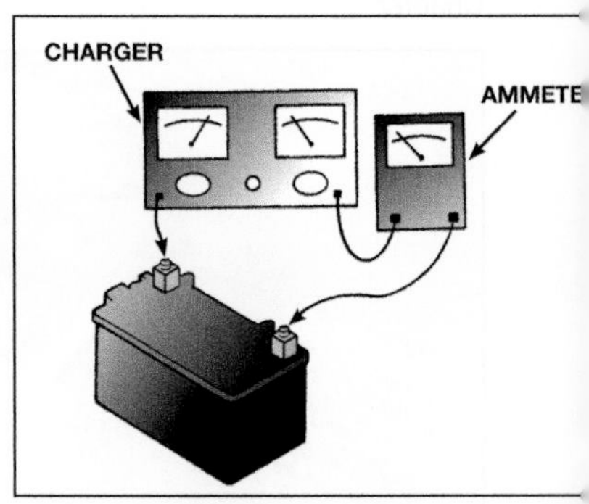


**4.2 If the charger doesn't have a built- ammeter, connector an ammeter in se as shown**

**5.1 The fusebox is mounted on the right-hand side of the frame**

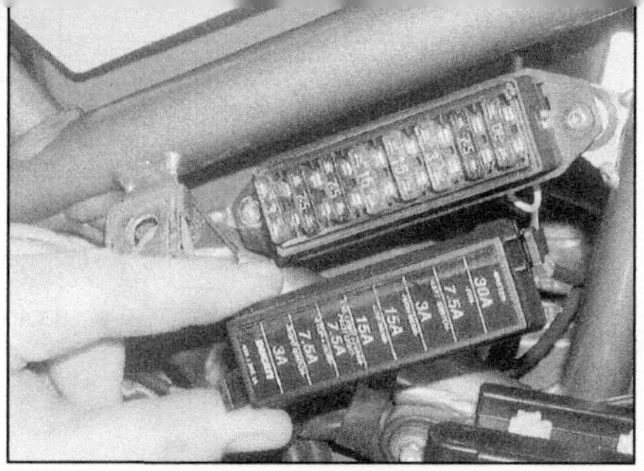

**5.2a Unclip the fusebox cover to gain access to the fuses. Fuse circuits are labelled on the cover**

**5.2b Charging circuit fuse is underneath the cover on the front of the battery tray**

injection/ignition system fuse(s), are located in the fusebox which is mounted on the right-hand side of the frame **(see illustration)**. The charging circuit fuse is located in a separate holder clipped to the front of the battery mounting tray and the engine management (fuel injection/ignition) system fuse(s) is/are located under the seat cowling.

**2** To access the fusebox and charging circuit fuseholder, remove the fairing right-hand lower panel (see Chapter 8), then unclip the relevant cover **(see illustrations)**.

**3** To gain access to the engine management (fuel injection/ignition system) fuse(s), unlock and raise the seat cowling (see Chapter 8). On early 916 models the fuses are fitted to the system relays (see Chapter 4). On all other models the fuse(s) is/are located in separate holder(s), located either in front of or on the right-hand side of the electronic control unit (ECU) – some models have a single fuse but most use a twin fuse arrangement **(see illustration)**. **Note:** *On early 916 models where the fuses are fitted to the engine management system relays, a special shim is fitted between the fuse and relay to secure it in position; do not omit this shim when installing the new fuse.*

**4** To remove a fuse, first switch off the ignition, then pull the fuse out of its terminals **(see illustration)**. If you can't pull the fuse out with your fingertips, use a pair of suitable pliers. A blown fuse is easily identified by a break in the element **(see illustration)**. Each fuse is clearly marked with its rating and must only be replaced by a fuse of the correct rating; the fuses are also colour-coded for easy recognition. It is recommended that spare fuses of all ratings should be carried on the bike at all times. On early models two spare fuses (7.5A and 30A) are fitted in the fusebox. If a spare fuse is used, always renew it so that a spare of each rating is available at all times.

***Warning: Never put in a fuse of a higher rating or bridge the terminals with any other substitute, however temporary it may be. Serious damage may be done to the circuit, or a fire may start.***

**5** If a new fuse blows immediately, find the cause before renewing it again; a short to earth (ground) as a result of faulty insulation is most likely. Look for bare wires and chafed, melted or burned insulation.

**6** Occasionally a fuse will blow or cause an open-circuit for no obvious reason. Corrosion of the fuse ends and fusebox terminals may occur and cause poor fuse contact. If this happens, remove the corrosion with a wire brush or emery paper, then spray the fuse end and terminals with electrical contact cleaner.

## 6 Lighting system - check

**1** The battery provides power for operation of the headlight, tail light, turn signals, brake light and instrument cluster lights. If none of the lights operate, always check battery voltage before proceeding. Low battery voltage indicates either a faulty battery or a defective charging system. Refer to Section 3 for battery checks and Sections 28 and 29 for charging system tests. Also, check the condition of the fuses.

### *Headlight*

#### Early (pre 1999) models

**2** If either headlight (main or dipped beam) fails to work, first check the fuse with the key ON (see Section 5), and then the bulbs (see Section 7). If they are both good, the problem lies in the wiring or one of the switches in the circuit. Check the wiring and switches (Sections 2 and 20) using the wiring diagrams at the end of this Chapter.

#### Later (1999-on) models

**3** If either headlight (main or dipped beam) fails to work, first check the fuse with the key ON (see Section 5), and then the bulb (see

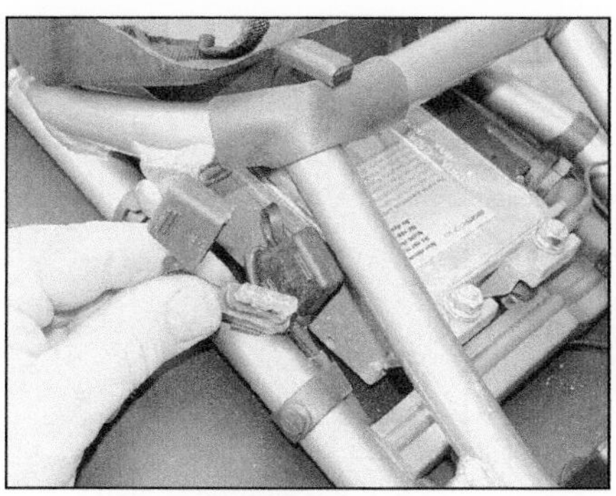

**5.3 Engine management system fuses – 996 model shown**

**5.4a Ensure the ignition is switched off then pull the fuse out of position**

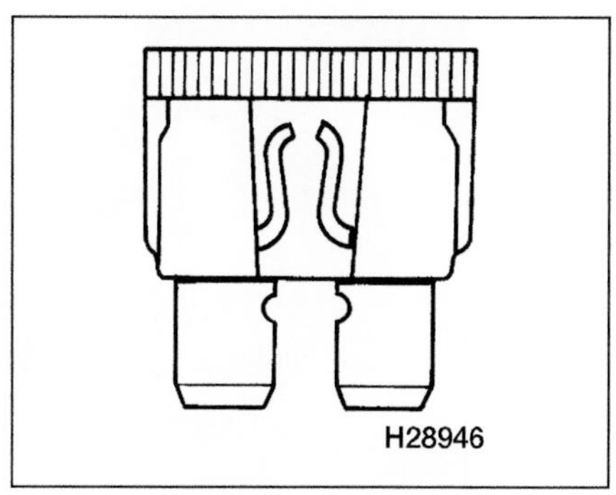


**5.4b A blown fuse is easily identified by a break in its element**

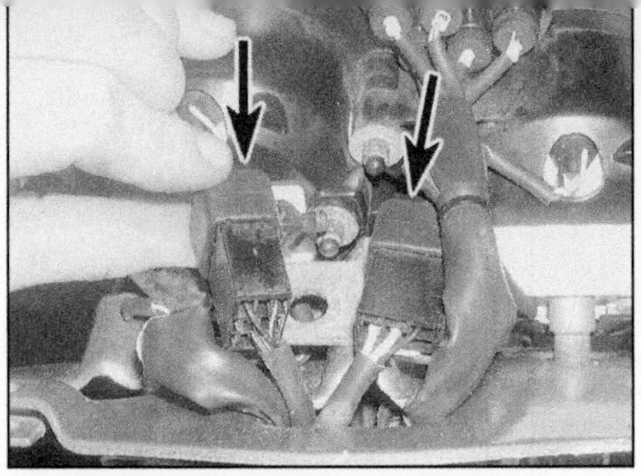

6.4 On later (1999-on) models, the headlight relays (arrowed) are mounted on the top of the headlight shell

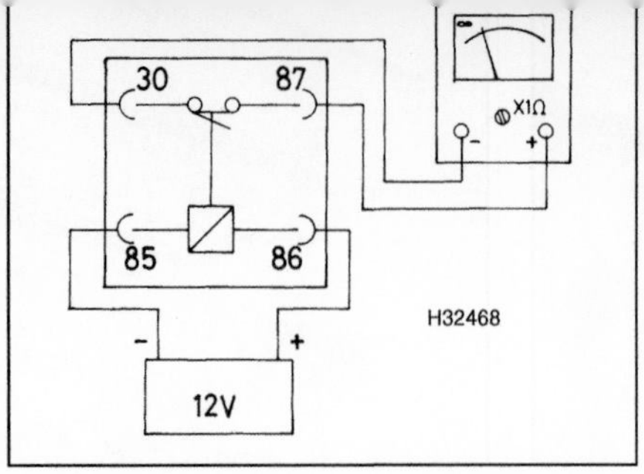


6.5 Relay test circuit – see text for details

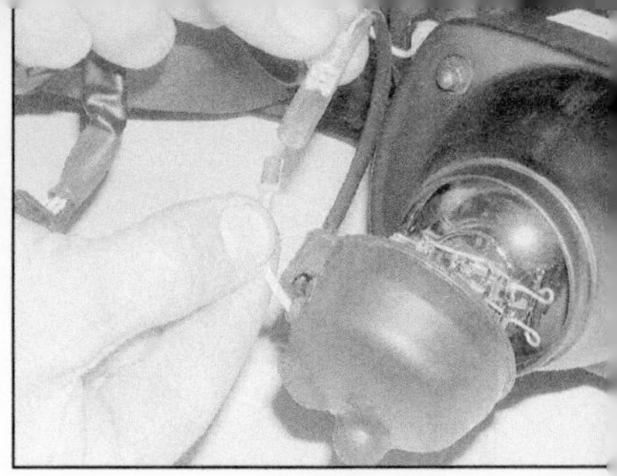

7.2a Disconnecting the main beam bul wiring connector (bulb comes complet with wire)

Section 7). If they are both good, the problem lies in the wiring, the relays (there are separate relays for the main and dipped beam), or one of the switches in the circuit.

**4** If either relay is suspected of being faulty, the best way to test it is to substitute it with another relay. Remove the upper fairing to access the relays (see Chapter 8) – they are mounted on the top of the headlight mounting shell **(see illustration)**. Both relays are identical so if only one is faulty the relays can be easily checked by swapping them over; if this transfers the problem to the other circuit then the relay is confirmed faulty. If both relays are faulty, check them as follows.

**5** Remove the relay and connect an ohmmeter across terminals 30 and 87 of the relay **(see illustration)**. Using a 12V battery and auxiliary wires, connect the battery positive (+ve) terminal to terminal 86 of the relay and the negative (–ve) terminal to the terminal 85 of the relay and note the meter reading obtained. If the relay is operating correctly there should be continuity (zero resistance) whilst the battery is connected and no continuity (infinite resistance) whilst the battery is disconnected; the relay will be heard to 'click' as the battery is connected/disconnected. If this is not the case, renew the relay.

**6** If the relays are proved good, check the wiring and switches (Sections 2 and 20) using the wiring diagrams at the end of this Chapter.

### Tail light

**7** If the tail light fails to work, check the bulbs and the bulb terminals first, then the fuse, then check for battery voltage at the yellow terminal on the supply side of the tail light wiring harness connector. If voltage is present, check the earth (ground) circuit for an open or poor connection.

**8** If no voltage is indicated, check the wiring between the tail light and the lighting switch.

### Brake light

**9** If the brake light fails to work, check the bulbs and the bulb terminals first, then the fuse. Check for battery voltage at the grey/red terminal on the supply side of the tail light wiring connector, with the brake lever pulled in or the pedal depressed; if voltage is present, check the earth (ground) circuit for an open or poor connection.

**10** If no voltage is indicated, check the brake light switches, then the wiring between the tail light and the switches.

**11** See Section 14 for brake switch checks and Section 9 for tail/brake light bulb renewal.

### Instrument and warning lights

**12** See Section 17 for instrument and warning light bulb renewal.

### Turn signal lights

**13** See Section 11 for the turn signal circ check.

## 7 Headlight and sidelight bulbs – renewal

### Headlight

**Note:** *The headlight bulbs are of the qua halogen type. Do not touch the bulb glass skin acids will shorten the bulb's service life the bulb is accidentally touched, it should wiped carefully when cold with a rag soake methylated spirit and dried before fitting.*

***Warning: Allow the bulbs time to cool before removing them if the headlight ha just been on.***

**1** Ensure the ignition (main) switch is off.

**2** Free the rubber dust cover from the rear the light unit, noting how it fits, th disconnect the bulb wiring connector (ther no need to disconnect the earth le connector from the holder) **(see illustration**

**3** Unhook the bulb retaining clip then rem the bulb **(see illustrations)**.

**4** Fit the new bulb, bearing in mind t information in the **Note** above. Make sure tabs on the bulb fit correctly in the slots in

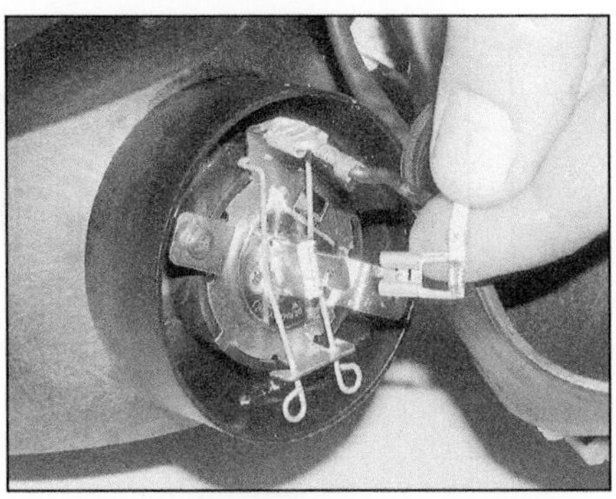

7.2b Disconnecting the dipped beam wiring connector

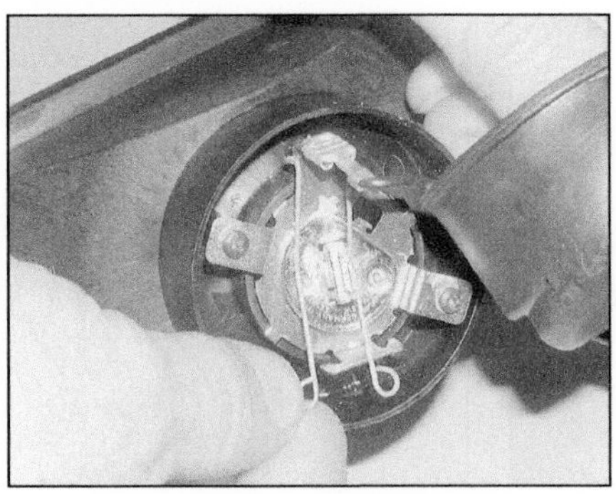

7.3a Unhook the retaining clip . . .

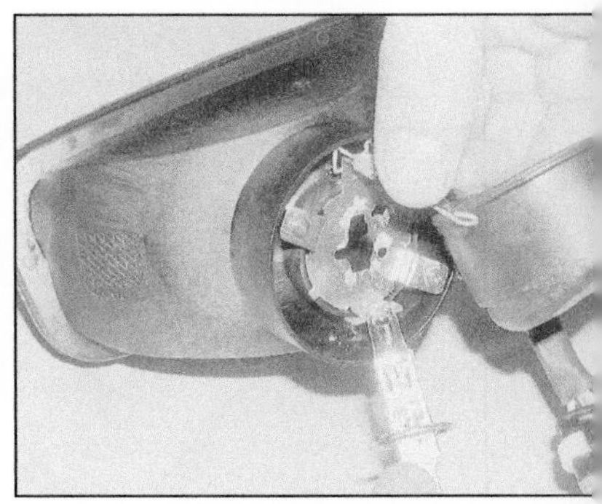

7.3b . . . and remove the bulb from the headlight (dipped beam bulb shown)

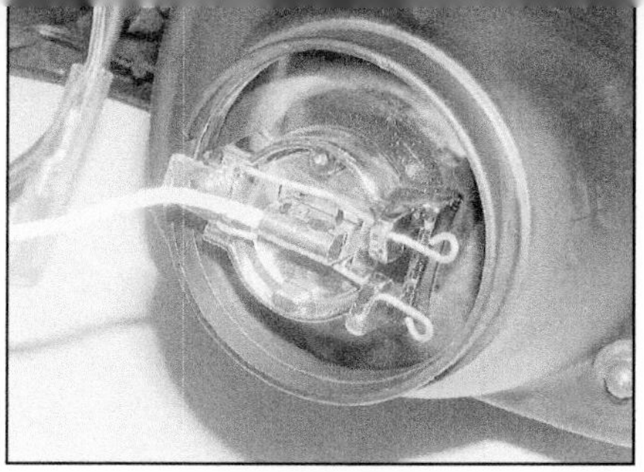

**7.4 Ensure the bulb is correctly located and the retaining clip is securely fitted (main beam bulb shown)**

bulb housing, and secure it in position with the retaining clip **(see illustration)**.

**5** Securely reconnect the bulb wiring connector then install the dust cover, making sure it is correctly seated on the light unit.

**6** Check the operation of the headlight.

> **HAYNES HiNT** ***Always use a paper towel or dry cloth when handling new bulbs to prevent injury if the bulb should break and to increase bulb life.***

### *Sidelight*

**Note:** *Either a single or double sidelight bulb arrangement may be fitted, depending on the model.*

**7** Remove the upper fairing (see Chapter 8).

**8** Undo the retaining bolt and collar and free the horn from the base of the headlight mounting shell.

**9** Pull the relevant bulbholder out of its socket in the base of the headlight, then carefully pull the bulb out of the holder. Check the socket terminals for corrosion and clean them if necessary. **Note:** *If necessary, remove the headlight to improve access to the sidelight bulbholders.*

**10** Fit the new bulb securely in the bulbholder, then install the bulbholder by pressing it in.

**11** Make sure the bulbholder is correctly seated then check the operation of the sidelight.

**12** Apply a drop of locking compound to the horn retaining bolt threads. Align the horn with its mounting and fit the retaining bolt and collar, tightening it to the specified torque.

**13** Install the upper fairing (see Chapter 8).

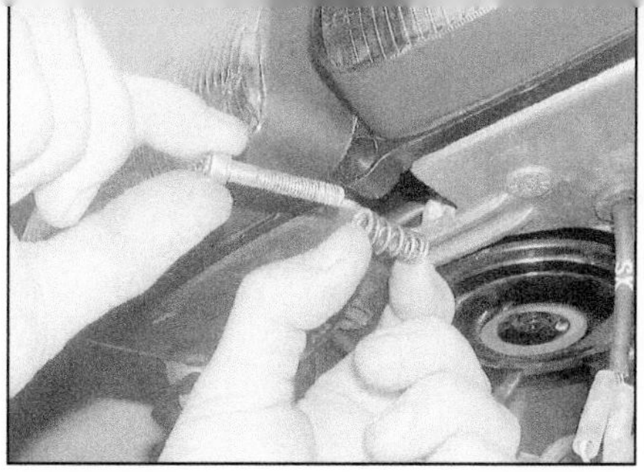

**8.3 Unscrew the adjuster bolt and recover the spring fitted between the headlight and mounting shell**

## 8 Headlight unit – removal and installation

### *Removal*

**1** Remove the upper fairing (see Chapter 8).

**2** Prior to removal, measure the distance between the headlight mounting shell and the base of the light unit. This measurement can then be used to set the headlight to the correct position on installation.

**3** Unscrew the adjuster bolt securing the headlight unit to the mounting shell and recover the spring fitted between the headlight and shell **(see illustration)**.

**4** Free the headlight unit upper mounting rubbers from the mounting shell tabs **(see illustration)**.

**5** Disconnect the headlight wiring connector and remove the headlight assembly from the bike **(see illustration)**.

**6** Check the headlight mounting rubbers for signs of damage and deterioration and renew them if necessary **(see illustration)**. If necessary, undo the retaining nuts and washers then remove the cover and seal from the rear of the headlight main beam unit **(see illustrations)**.

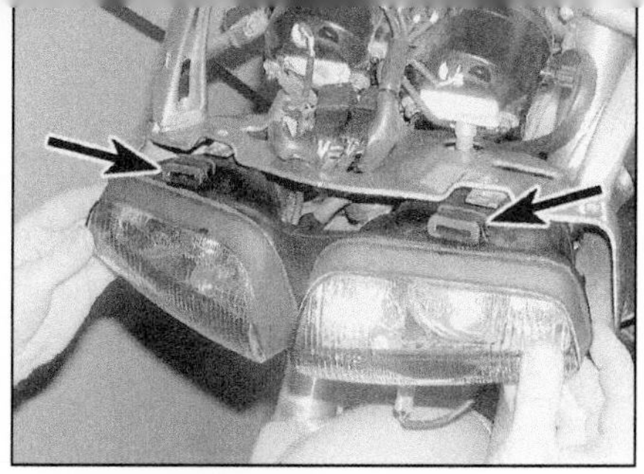

**8.4 Free the headlight upper mounting rubbers (arrowed) then withdraw the unit from the shell . . .**

### *Installation*

**7** Where necessary, ensure the seal is correctly located then install the cover to the rear of the main beam unit. Fit the washers and retaining nuts, tightening them securely.

**8** Ensure the upper mounting rubbers are correctly fitted to the headlight lugs and check the headlight wiring harness is correctly connected to the bulbs and the rubber dust covers are correctly seated. Lubricate the

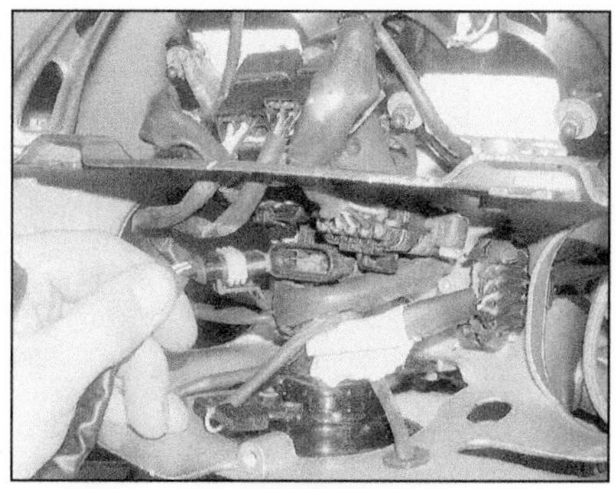

**8.5 . . . and disconnect its wiring connector**

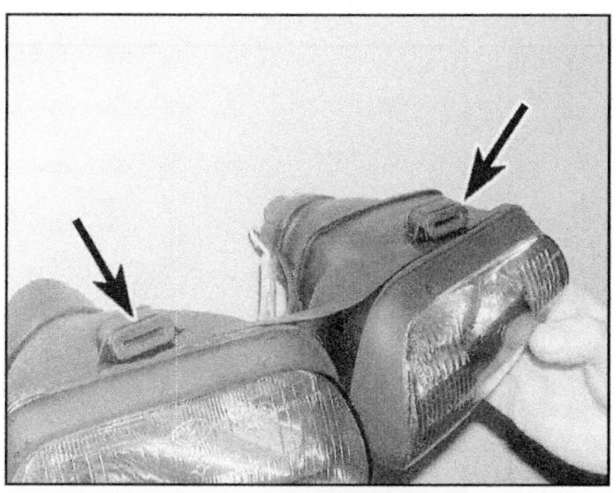

**8.6a Check the headlight mounting rubbers (arrowed) for signs of damage or deterioration**

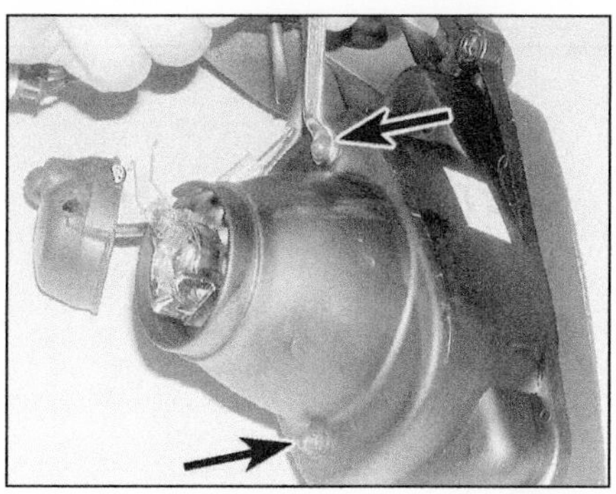

**8.6b If necessary, undo the retaining nuts (arrowed) . . .**

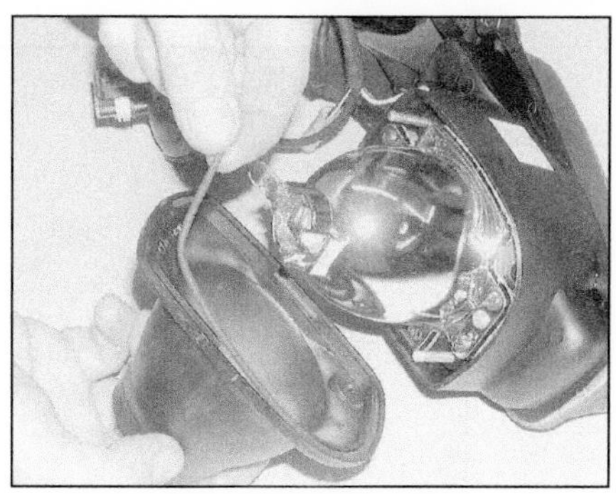

**8.6c . . . and remove the cover and seal from the rear of the main beam unit**

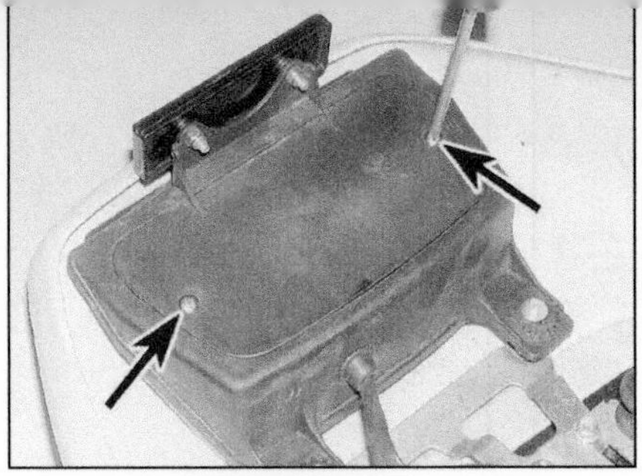

9.2a Undo the retaining screws (arrowed) . . .

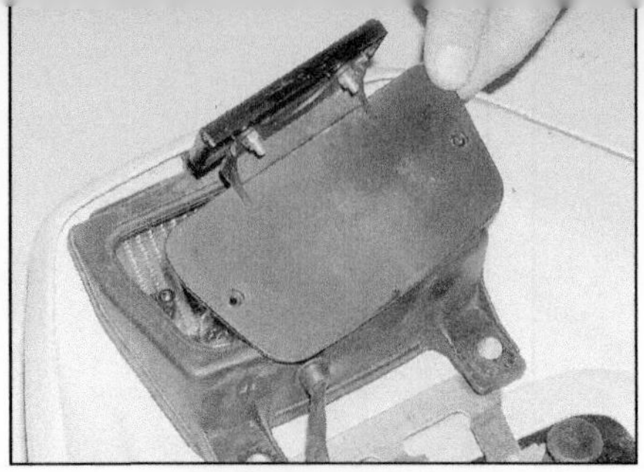

9.2b . . . and remove the access cover from the tail light unit

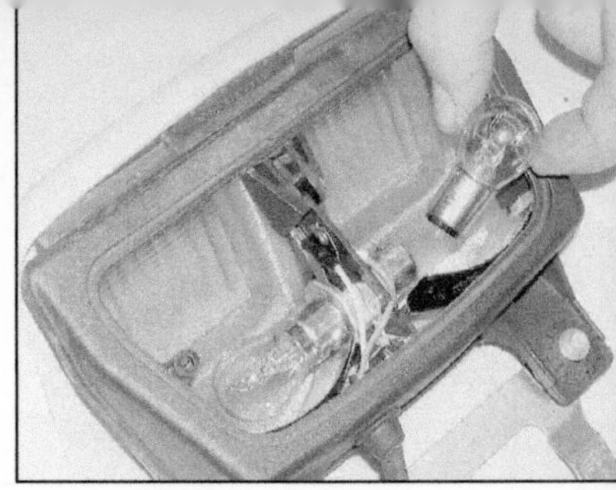

9.3 Push the relevant bulb into its hold and rotate it anti-clockwise to release

mounting rubbers with a silicone-based spray lubricant to ease installation.

9 Reconnect the headlight wiring harness connector then align the headlight mounting rubbers with the shell tabs. Position the spring between the base of the headlight unit and mounting shell then ease the headlight unit into position.

10 Ensure the headlight mounting rubbers are correctly located then fit the adjuster bolt, ensuring it passes through the spring. Screw the bolt into the shell until the distance between the headlight unit and base of the mounting shell is as noted prior to removal.

11 Check the operation of the headlight then fit the upper fairing (see Section 8).

12 On completion, adjust the headlight aim (see Chapter 1).

## 9 Tail light unit – bulb renewal, removal and installation

### Bulb renewal

1 Unlock and raise the seat cowling (see Chapter 8).

2 Undo the two retaining screws and remove the access cover from the base of the tail light unit **(see illustrations)**.

3 Push the relevant bulb into the light unit and rotate it anti-clockwise to remove it **(see illustration)**. Check the socket terminals for corrosion and clean them if necessary.

4 Line up the pins of the new bulb with the slots in the socket, then push the bulb in and turn it clockwise until it locks into place **(** **illustration)**. **Note:** *The pins on the bulb offset so it can only be installed one way. a good idea to use a paper towel or dry c when handling the new bulb to prevent in if the bulb should break, and to prolong l life.*

5 Fit the access cover to the tail light secure it in position with the retaining scre Do not overtighten the screws; the len easily broken.

### Removal

6 Unlock and raise the seat cowling ( Chapter 8).

7 Trace the wiring back from the light unit disconnect its wiring connector from the n wiring harness. Slacken and remove wiring connector retaining plate screw unclip the wiring from the underside of seat cowling so that it is free to be remo with the light **(see illustration)**.

8 Undo the two retaining bolts and rem the seat cowling lock catch bracket ( **illustration)**.

9 Remove the tail light unit and its moun bracket as an assembly then separate the **(see illustrations)**. Check the light mounting rubbers for signs of damage deterioration and, if necessary, renew then

### Installation

10 Ensure the mounting rubbers are corre fitted then assemble the tail light mounting bracket.

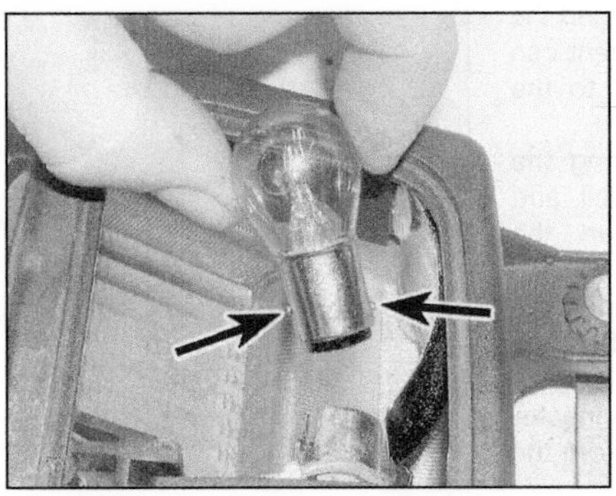

9.4 The brake/tail light bulbs have offset pins (arrowed) to ensure they are correctly fitted

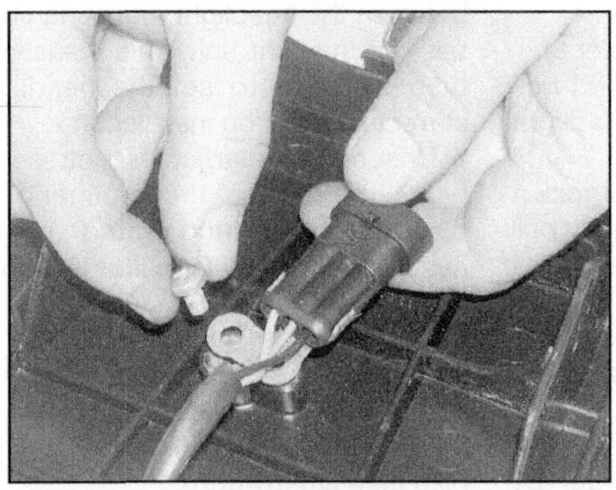

9.7 Undo the retaining screw and free the tail light wiring connector from the seat cowling

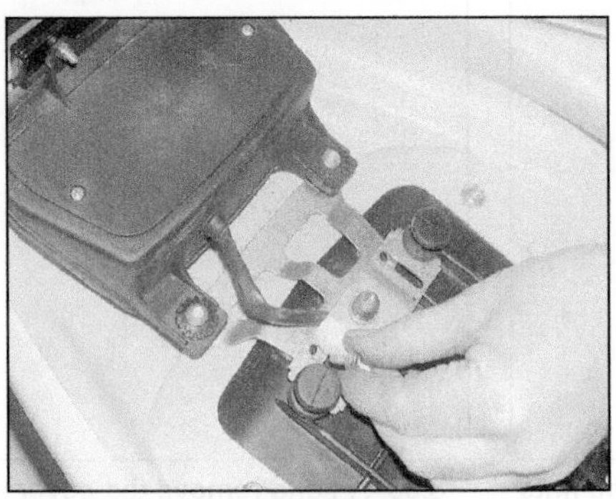

9.8 Undo the bolts and remove the seat cowling lock catch . . .

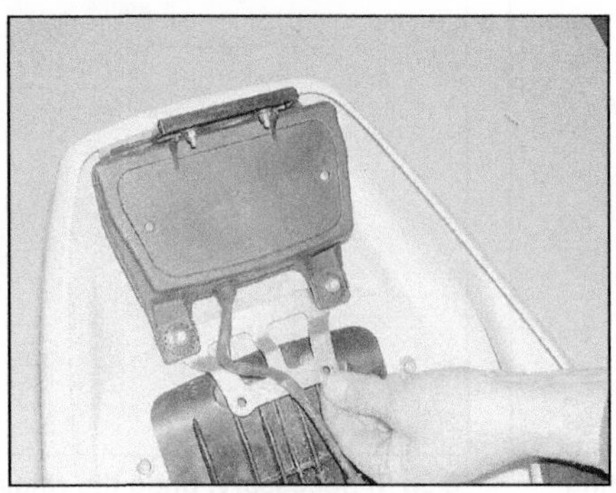

9.9a . . . then remove the tail light unit and mounting bracket as an assembly . . .

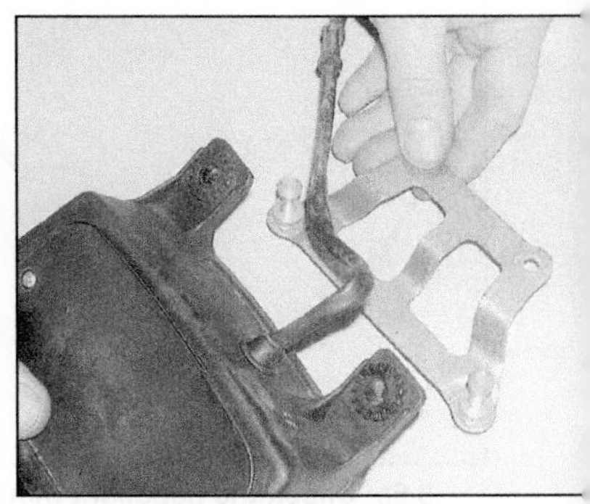

9.9b . . . and separate the two

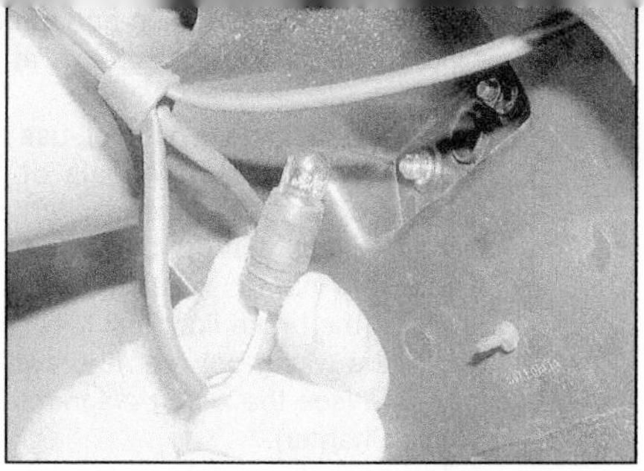

**10.1 Free the bulbholder from the rear of the number plate light unit then pull the bulb out of its holder**

**11** Fit the tail light unit and mounting bracket assembly to the seat cowling and install the lock catch bracket. Ensure the tail light unit wiring is correctly routed through the lock catch bracket then fit the bracket bolts and tighten them securely.
**12** Clip the wiring harness locating grommets correctly into the clips on the seat cowling and secure the wiring connector retaining plate to the seat cowling, tightening its retaining screw securely.
**13** Reconnect the tail light wiring connector and check the operation of the light unit before lowering the seat cowling and locking it in position.

## 10 Number plate light – bulb renewal, removal and installation

### *Bulb renewal*

**1** Free the bulbholder from the rear of the light unit and pull the bulb out of the holder to remove it **(see illustration)**. Check the socket terminals for corrosion and clean them if necessary.
**2** Fit the new bulb to the holder then fit the bulbholder securely back into the light unit.

### *Removal*

**3** Free the bulbholder from the rear of the light unit.

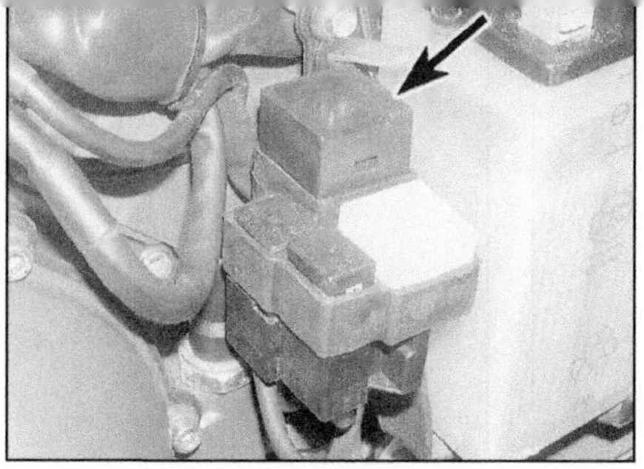

**11.3 Turn signal relay (arrowed) is mounted on the rear of the battery tray**

**4** Slacken and remove the retaining nuts and washers then free the light unit from the mudguard and remove it from the bike.

### *Installation*

**5** Fit the light unit to the mudguard and refit the washers and retaining nuts, tightening them securely.
**6** Refit the bulbholder to the light unit and check the operation of the light.

## 11 Turn signal circuit – check

**1** The battery provides power for operation of the turn signal lights, so if they do not operate, always check the battery voltage first. Low battery voltage indicates either a faulty battery or a defective charging system. Refer to Section 3 for battery checks and Sections 28 and 29 for charging system tests. Also, check the fuse (see Section 5) and the switch (see Section 20).
**2** Most turn signal problems are the result of a burned out bulb or corroded socket. This is especially true when the turn signals function properly in one direction, but fail to flash in the other direction. Check the bulbs and the sockets (see Section 12).
**3** If the bulbs and sockets are good, remove the fairing right-hand lower panel (see Chapter 8) for access to the relay, which is **illustration)**. Disconnect the wiring connector and check for power at the turn signal relay light blue wire with the ignition ON. Turn the ignition OFF when the check is complete.
**4** If no power was present at the relay, check the wiring from the relay to the ignition (main) switch for continuity.
**5** If power was present at the relay, using the appropriate wiring diagram at the end of this Chapter, check the wiring between the relay, turn signal switch and turn signal lights for continuity. If the wiring and switch are sound, renew the relay.

## 12 Turn signal bulbs – renewal

**1** Undo the retaining screw and remove the lens from the turn signal light unit **(see illustrations)**.
**2** Push the bulb into the light unit and rotate it anti-clockwise to remove it **(see illustration)**. Check the socket terminals for corrosion and clean them if necessary.
**3** Line up the pins of the new bulb with the slots in the socket, then push the bulb in and turn it clockwise until it locks into place. **Note:** *It is a good idea to use a paper towel or dry cloth when handling the new bulb to prevent injury if the bulb should break, and to prolong bulb life.*
**4** Fit the lens to the turn signal light and secure it in position with the retaining screw. Do not overtighten the screw; the lens is easily broken.

## 13 Turn signal assemblies – removal and installation

### *Front turn signals*

#### Removal

**1** Trace the wiring back from the turn signal and disconnect its wiring connectors from the main wiring harness. Tie a piece of string to

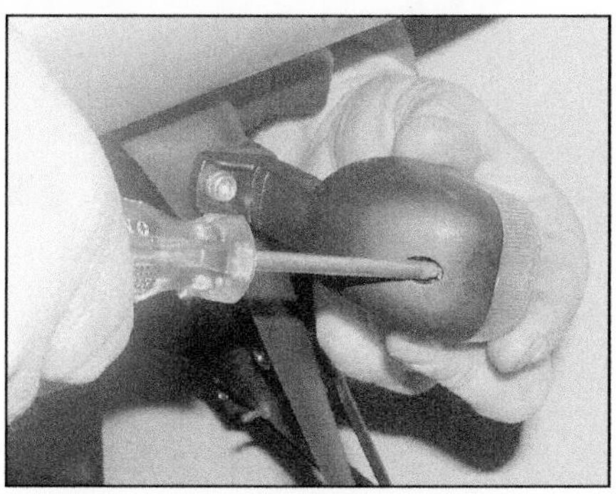

**12.1a Undo the retaining screw . . .**

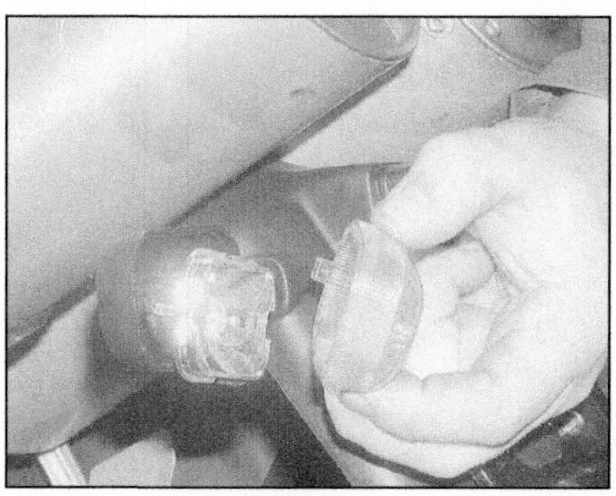

**12.1b . . . and remove the lens from the turn signal light**

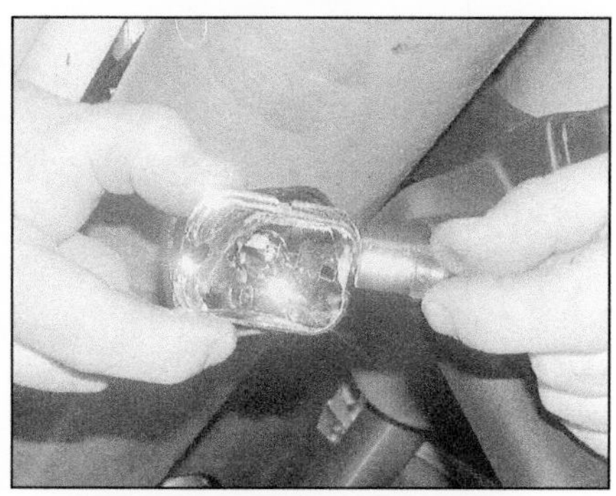

**12.2 Push the bulb into the holder and rotate it anti-clockwise to release it**

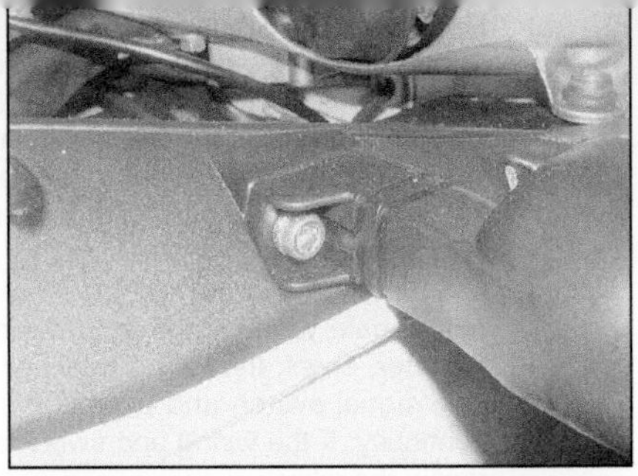

13.2 Front turn signal light unit retaining screw

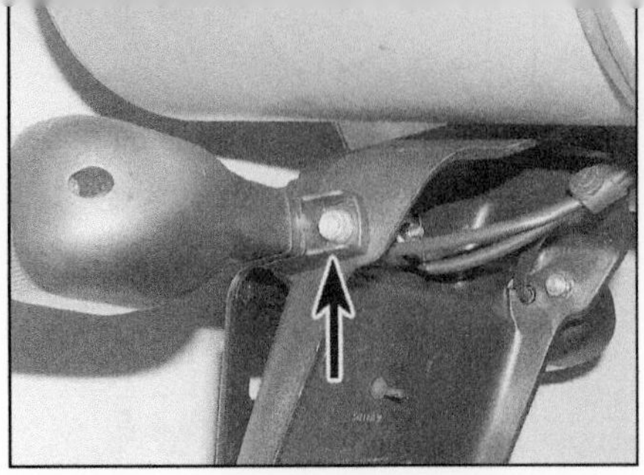

13.8 Rear turn signal light unit retaining screw (arrowed)

the end of the wiring; the string can then be used to draw the wiring back into position on installation.

**2** Undo the retaining screw then free the turn signal from the air filter housing and remove it from the bike **(see illustration)**. When the end of the string appears, untie it and leave it in position on the bike.

### Installation

**3** Tie the string to the turn signal wiring and use the string to draw the wiring through the air filter housing to the headlight unit shell.

**4** Fit the turn signal to the air filter housing and securely tighten its retaining screw.

**5** Untie and remove the string then reconnect the turn signal wiring connectors. Check the operation of the turn signal.

## *Rear turn signals*

### Removal

**6** Unlock and raise the seat cowling (see Chapter 8).

**7** Trace the wiring back from the turn signal and disconnect its wiring connectors from the main wiring harness.

**8** Slacken and remove the retaining nut and screw, then free the turn signal from the mudguard and remove it from the bike **(see illustration)**.

### Installation

**9** Fit the turn signal to the mudguard and tighten its retaining screw and nut.

**10** Route the wiring correctly, securing it in position with the necessary clips, and reconnect it to the main wiring harness connector.

**11** Check the operation of the turn signal unit then lower the seat cowling and lock it in position.

# 14 Brake light switches – check and renewal

## *Circuit check*

**1** Before checking any electrical circuit, check the bulb (see Section 9) and fuse (see Section 5). The following check is carried out at the switch wiring connector(s); remove the fairing right-hand lower panel (see Chapter 8) to gain access to the rear brake light switch wiring connector (the connector is located on the top of the crankcase).

**2** Disconnect the wiring connector and using a multimeter or test light connected to a good earth (ground), with the ignition ON check for battery voltage at the purple/black terminal of the brake light switch wiring connector(s). If between the switch, fuse and ignition (ma switch (see the *wiring diagrams* at the end this Chapter).

**3** If battery voltage is present, use an auxili wire to bridge the terminals of the wiri harness connector(s) then switch the igniti ON and check that the brake light comes If the light comes on the switch is prov faulty. If the brake light still fails to come check the wiring between the switch and light unit (see the *wiring diagrams* at the e of this Chapter).

**4** To check the switch, connect an ohmme across the terminals of the switch wiri connector(s) then pull the brake lever in depress the brake pedal (as applicable). Th should be continuity (zero resistan between the terminals when the brake applied and no continuity (infinite resistan with the brake released. If not, the switch faulty and must be renewed.

## *Switch renewal*

### Front brake lever switch

**5** The switch is mounted on the underside the brake master cylinder **(see illustratio** Disconnect the wiring connectors from switch.

**6** Remove the retaining screw/unclip applicable) the switch and remove it from master cylinder.

**7** Installation is the reverse of removal. T switch is not adjustable.

### Rear brake pedal switch

**8** The switch is screwed into the mas cylinder/brake pedal bracket **(s illustration)**. Remove the fairing right-ha lower panel for access (see Chapter 8).

**9** Trace the wiring back from the switch a disconnect it at the connector. Note correct routing of the wiring then free it fr the engine/frame.

**10** Unscrew the switch and remove it fr the mounting bracket.

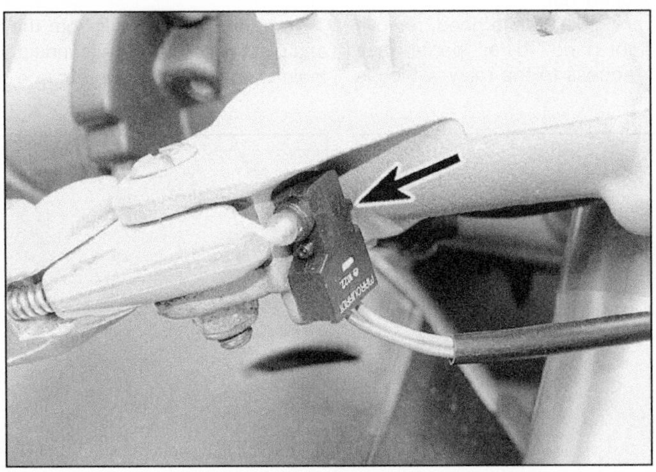

14.5 Front brake light switch (arrowed) – later-type master cylinder shown

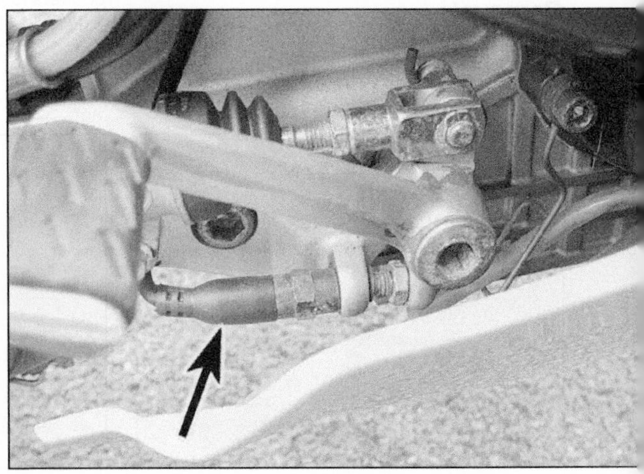

14.8 Rear brake light switch (arrowed) is screwed into the mas cylinder/brake pedal bracket

15.4 Disconnect the instrument cluster wiring connectors

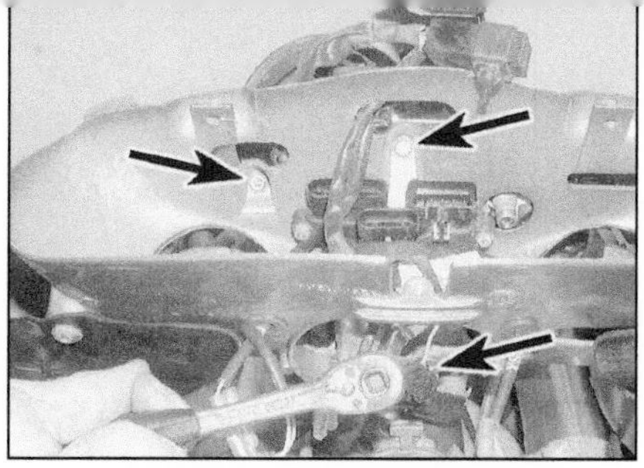

15.7a Unscrew the retaining nuts (arrowed) and remove the instrument cluster from the headlight shell

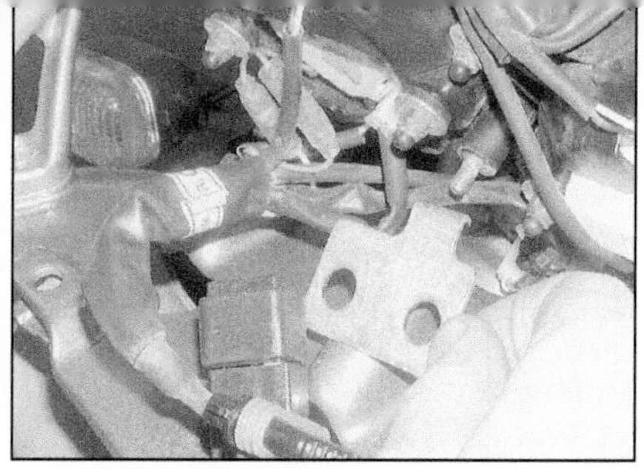

15.7b On later (1999-on) models recover the headlight relay mounting bracket fitted to the upper mounting stud

**11** Screw the new switch into the bracket and tighten it securely. Route the switch wiring correctly around the engine and frame and securely reconnect the connector to the main wiring harness.

**12** Check the operation of the switch then install the fairing panel (see Chapter 8).

## 15 Instrument cluster – removal and installation

**Note:** *Ensure the instrument cluster is kept the right way up when removed. If it is left face down for any length of time its gauges could become damaged.*

### *Removal*

**1** Remove the upper fairing (see Chapter 8).

**2** Remove the headlight unit (see Section 8).

**3** On later (1999-on) models, free the headlight relays from their mounting bracket.

**4** On all models, disconnect the instrument wiring harness connectors from their connectors located in the headlight shell **(see illustration)**.

**5** Unscrew the knurled retaining ring and detach the speedometer cable from the speedometer.

**6** Undo the retaining bolt and collar and free the horn from the base of the headlight mounting shell.

**7** Unscrew the nuts securing the instrument mounting studs to the headlight shell then remove the cluster assembly from the bike **(see illustration)**. On later (1999-on) models, recover the headlight relay bracket fitted to the upper mounting stud **(see illustration)**.

**8** Inspect the instrument cluster mounting studs and renew them if they are damaged.

### *Installation*

**9** Ensure the mounting studs are screwed securely into the instrument cluster.

**10** Manoeuvre the instrument cluster into position, ensuring its wiring is correctly routed, and locate it on the headlight mounting shell. On later models ensure the relay mounting bracket is correctly fitted to the upper stud.

**11** Fit the retaining nuts to the instrument panel mounting studs and tighten them securely.

**12** Reconnect the speedometer cable, tightening its retaining ring securely.

**13** Reconnect the instrument wiring harness connectors.

**14** Apply a drop of locking compound to the horn retaining bolt threads. Align the horn with its mounting and fit the retaining bolt and collar, tightening it to the specified torque.

**15** On later models refit the headlight relays to their mounting bracket.

**16** On all models install the headlight unit (see Section 8).

## 16 Instruments and cable/sensors – check and renewal

### *Speedometer*

#### Check

**1** Remove the cable as described in Steps 9 to 12 and check its condition.

**2** If the cable is in good condition, support the bike using an auxiliary stand so that the front wheel is off the ground. With the cable disconnected from the drive unit, spin the wheel and check that the drive unit gear spins. If not, remove the front wheel and check the drive unit and driveplate (see Chapter 7).

**3** If both the cable and drive unit are in good condition then the speedometer itself must be faulty.

#### Renewal

**4** Remove the instrument cluster as described in Section 15.

**5** Free the illumination bulbholders from the base of the speedometer **(see illustration)**.

**6** Undo the retaining screw and remove the trip meter reset knob from the speedometer **(see illustrations)**.

**7** Unscrew the speedometer retaining nuts and washers and remove the rubber collars

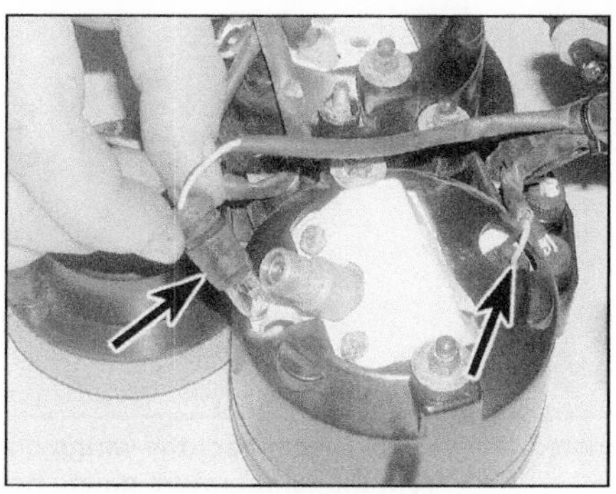

16.5 Free the bulbholders (arrowed) from the speedometer base

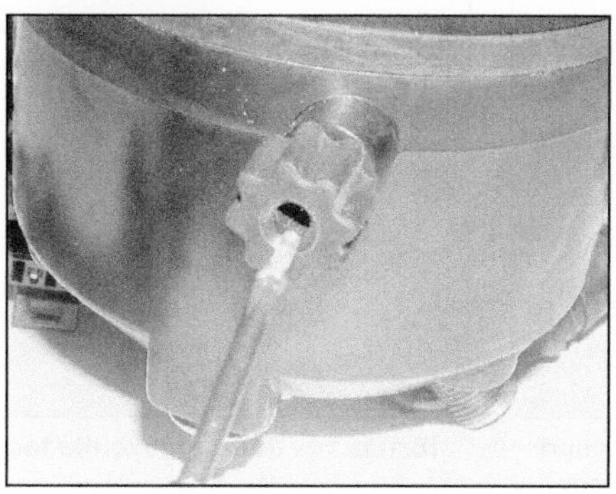

16.6a Undo the retaining screw . . .

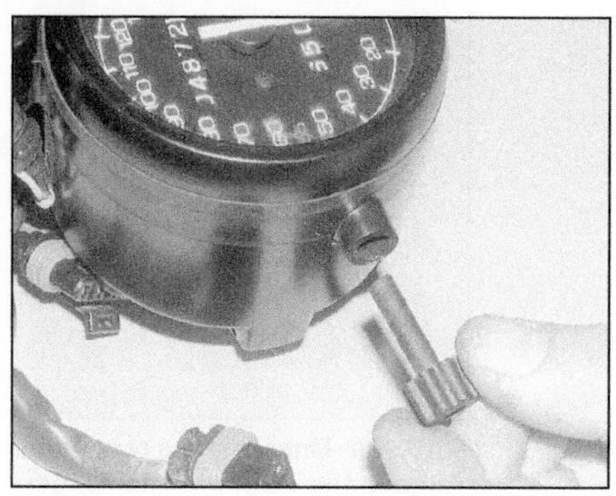

16.6b . . . and remove the trip meter reset knob

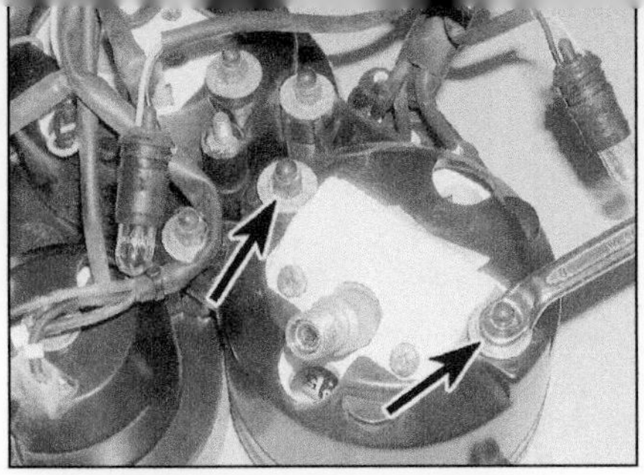

16.7a Unscrew the retaining nuts (arrowed) . . .

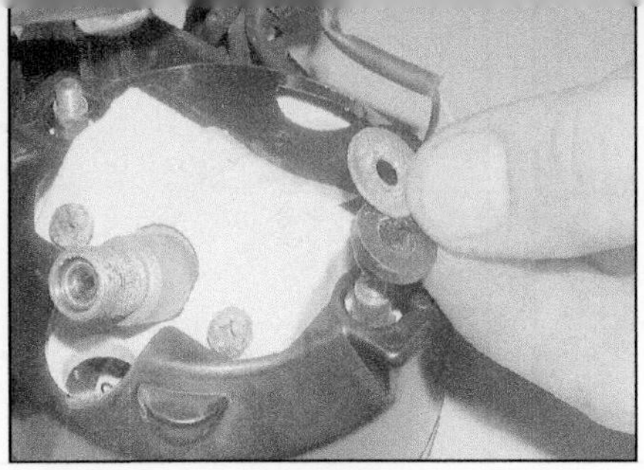

16.7b . . . and remove the washers and rubber collars . . .

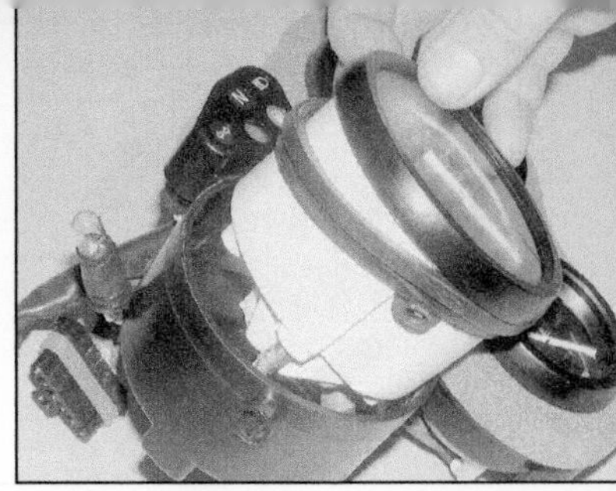

16.7c . . . then remove the speedomet complete with its rubber seat

from the studs **(see illustrations)**. Remove the speedometer from its housing, complete with its rubber seat **(see illustration)**.

**8** Installation is the reverse of removal, ensuring the rubber seat is correctly installed in the housing and the rubber collars are fitted to the speedometer mounting studs.

### Speedometer cable renewal

**9** Remove the upper fairing (see Chapter 8).

**10** Unscrew the knurled retaining ring and detach the speedometer cable from the speedometer.

**11** Unscrew the retaining ring securing the lower end of the cable to the drive unit on the wheel and detach the cable.

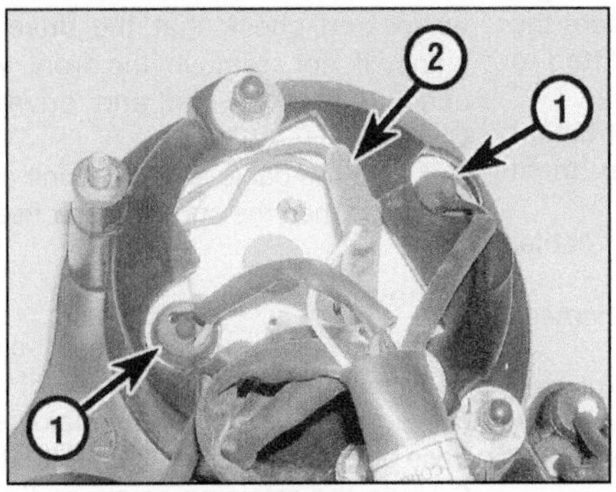


16.17 Free the bulbholders (1) from the tachometer and disconnect the wiring connectors (2)

**12** Free the cable from its retaining guides and clips and remove it from the bike, noting its correct routing.

**13** Route the cable correctly and pass it through its relevant guides and clips. Align the inner cable lower end with the drive gear and connect the cable to the drive unit, tightening its retaining ring securely.

**14** Connect the cable upper end to the instrument cluster and tighten the retaining ring. Check that the cable doesn't restrict steering movement or interfere with any other components, then install the upper fairing (see Chapter 8).

## *Tachometer*

### Check

**15** If the system malfunctions, first check that the battery is fully charged and that its terminals are clean, and that the wiring and fuses are in good condition. Remove the upper fairing (see Chapter 8) and the headlight unit (see Section 8) to gain access to the tachometer wiring terminals (the signal for the tachometer comes from the engine management system ECU via the green/grey wire). If the wiring and fuses are in good condition, then the fault either lies in the ECU (unlikely if the engine is running correctly) or the tachometer itself.

### Renewal

**16** Remove the instrument cluster described in Section 15.

**17** Disconnect the wiring connectors and the illumination bulbholders from tachometer **(see illustration)**.

**18** Unscrew the tachometer retaining r and washers and remove the rubber col from the studs **(see illustration)**. Remove tachometer from its housing ( **illustration)**.

**19** Installation is the reverse of remo ensuring the rubber collars are fitted to mounting studs and the wiring connectors securely connected.

## *Temperature gauge*

### Check

**20** The temperature gauge check described in Chapter 3.

### Renewal

**21** Remove the instrument cluster described in Section 15.

**22** Free the illumination bulbholder from base of the temperature gauge.

**23** Note the correct fitted location of three wiring connectors then disconnect th from the gauge terminals **(see illustrati** Each wire should have an identification c which matches the markings on the rear of gauge.

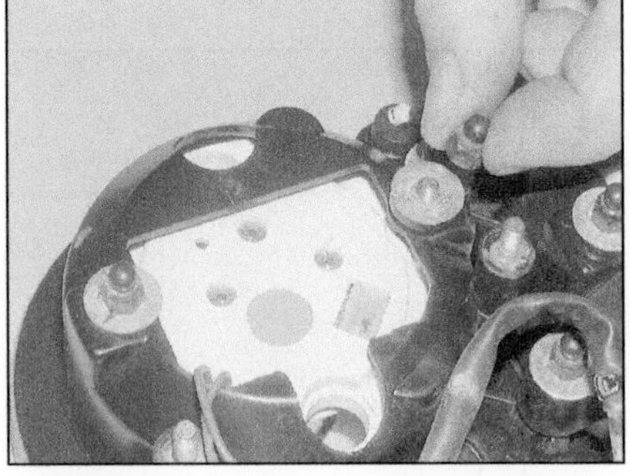

16.18a Unscrew the retaining nuts and remove the washers and rubber collars . . .

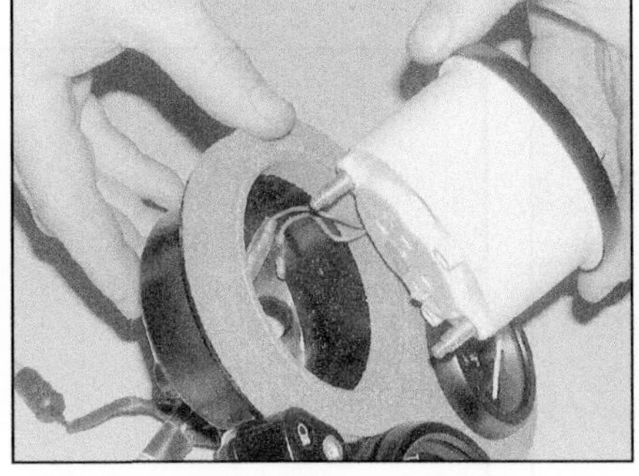

16.18b . . . then remove the tachometer

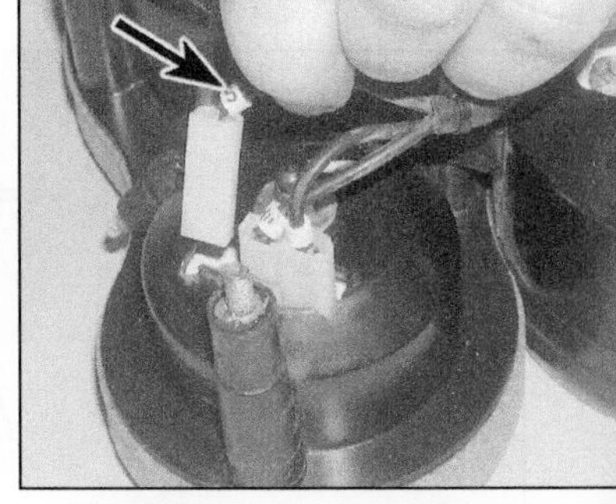

16.23 Disconnect the wiring connecto from the temperature gauge noting th correct fitted locations (identificatio collar arrowed)

**16.24a Unscrew the retaining nut and remove the washer and rubber collar . . .**

**16.24b . . . then remove the coolant temperature gauge**

**24** Unscrew the retaining nut and washer and remove the rubber collar from the stud **(see illustration)**. Remove the gauge from its housing **(see illustration)**.

**25** Installation is the reverse of removal, ensuring the rubber collar is fitted to the mounting stud and the wiring connectors are correctly reconnected.

## *Fuel level warning light*

### Check

**26** Before checking the electrical circuit, check the bulb (see Section 17) and fuses (see Section 5). The following check is carried out at the fuel tank wiring connector, free the fuel tank from the frame (see Section 2 of Chapter 4 – there is no need to disconnect the fuel hoses) and support it so access can be gained to the connector.

**27** Disconnect the wiring connector and using a multimeter or test light connected to a good earth (ground), with the ignition ON check for battery voltage at the light blue terminal of the connector. If there's no voltage present, check the wiring between the connector, fuse and ignition (main) switch (see the *wiring diagrams* at the end of this Chapter).

**28** If battery voltage is present, use an auxiliary wire to bridge the blue/black and

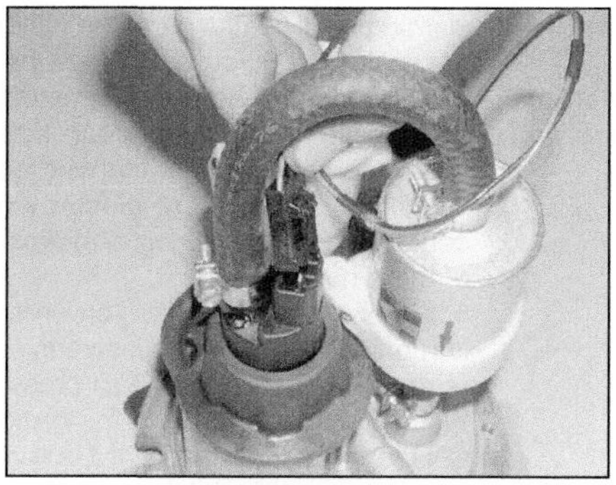

**16.30 Disconnect the fuel pump wiring connector . . .**

light blue terminals of the wiring harness connector then switch the ignition ON and check that the warning light comes on. If the light does come on the fuel level sensor is proven faulty. If the warning light still fails to come on, check the wiring between the tank and instrument cluster (see the *wiring diagrams* at the end of this Chapter).

### Fuel level sensor renewal

**29** Referring to Chapter 4, remove the fuel tank. Slacken the fuel level sensor then remove the fuel pump mounting plate assembly from the tank.

**30** Note the correct fitted locations of the fuel

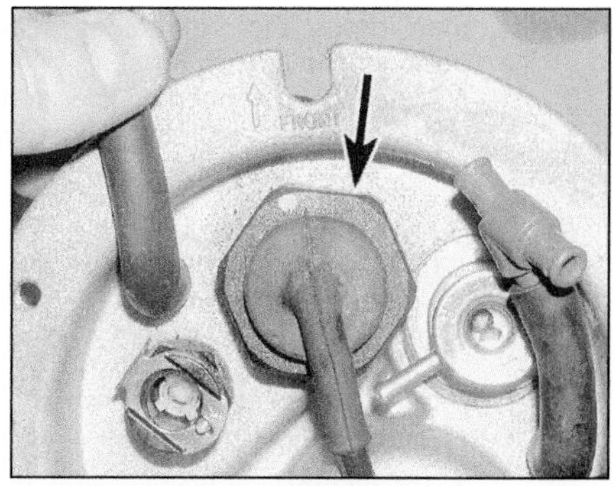

**16.31 . . . then unscrew the fuel level sensor (arrowed) from the mounting plate**

pump wiring connector(s) then disconnect them from the pump **(see illustration)**.

**31** Unscrew the fuel level sensor and remove it from the mounting plate **(see illustration)**. Recover the sensor sealing washer and discard it; a new should be used on installation.

**32** Fit the new sealing washer to the sensor then fit the sensor to the mounting plate, tightening it securely.

**33** Reconnect the fuel pump wiring connector(s) then refit the fuel pump mounting plate to the tank and install the fuel tank (see Chapter 4).

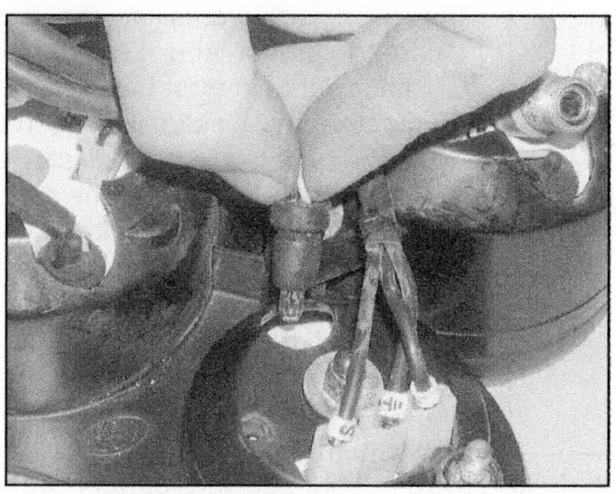

**17.2a Free the bulbholder from the instrument cluster . . .**

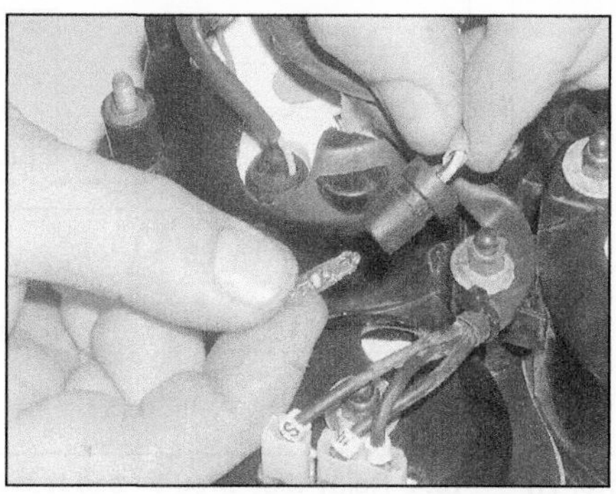

**17.2b . . . and pull out the bulb (coolant temperature gauge bulb shown)**

## 17 Instrument and warning light bulbs – renewal

**1** Access to the majority of bulbs can be gained by removing the upper fairing (see Chapter 8). To gain access to the coolant temperature gauge bulb, it will also be necessary to remove the headlight unit and free the instrument cluster from the headlight shell (see Sections 8 and 15).

**2** Ease the relevant bulbholder out of position then pull the bulb from its holder **(see illustrations)**.

**3** If the socket contacts are dirty or corroded,

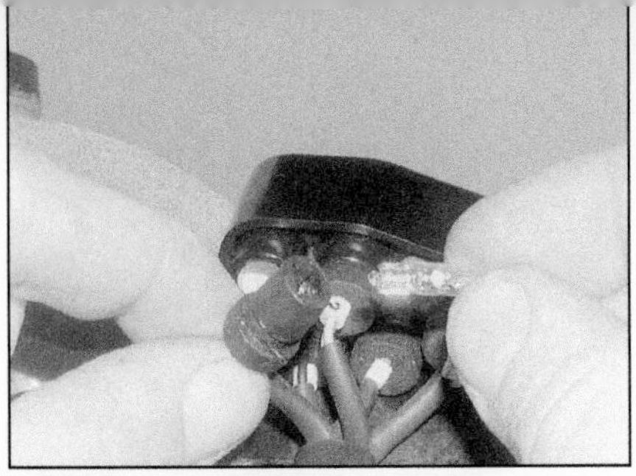

17.4a Push the new bulb firmly into its holder . . .

scrape them clean and spray them with electrical contact cleaner before a new bulb is installed.

**4** Push the new bulb carefully into the holder, then press the bulbholder securely into position **(see illustrations)**.

**5** Install the instrument cluster and headlight unit (where removed) and fit the upper fairing (see Chapter 8).

## 18 Oil pressure switch – check and renewal

### Check

**1** The oil pressure warning light should come on when the ignition (main) switch is turned ON and extinguish soon after the engine is started. If it comes on whilst the engine is running, stop the engine immediately and carry out an oil level check (see *Daily (pre-ride) checks*). If the level is correct, carry out an oil pressure check (see Chapter 1).

**2** If the oil pressure warning light does not come on when the ignition is turned on, check the bulb (see Section 17) and fuse (see Section 5).

**3** The oil pressure switch is screwed into the crankcase right-hand cover. To gain access to the switch, removing the fairing right-hand lower panel (see Chapter 8) then unclip the relay mounting rubber from the rear of the battery tray **(see illustration)**. Disconnect the wiring connector from the switch then, with the ignition switched ON, earth (ground) the wire on the crankcase and check that the warning light comes on. If the light comes on, the switch is defective and must be renewed.

**4** If the light still does not come on, check for voltage at the wire terminal. If there is no voltage present, check the wire between the switch, the instrument cluster and fuse for continuity (see the *wiring diagrams* at the end of this Chapter).

**5** If the warning light comes on whilst the engine is running, yet the oil pressure is satisfactory, remove the wire from the oil pressure switch. With the wire detached and the ignition switched ON the light should be out. If it is illuminated, the wire between the switch and instrument cluster must be earthed (grounded) at some point. If the wiring is good, the switch must be assumed faulty and renewed.

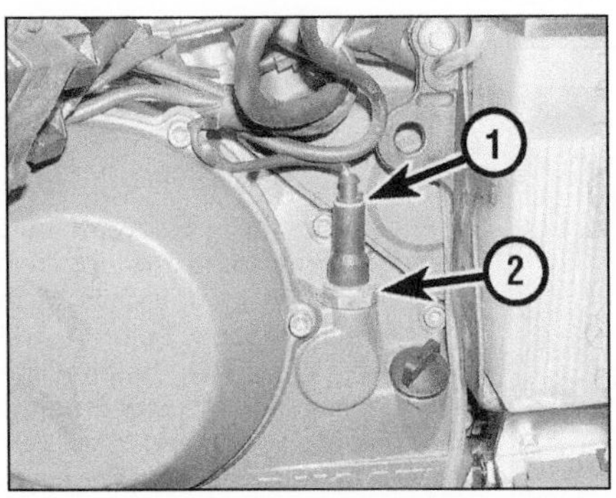

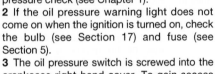

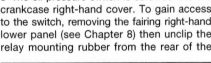

18.8 Disconnect the wiring connector (1) then unscrew the oil pressure switch (2) from the cover

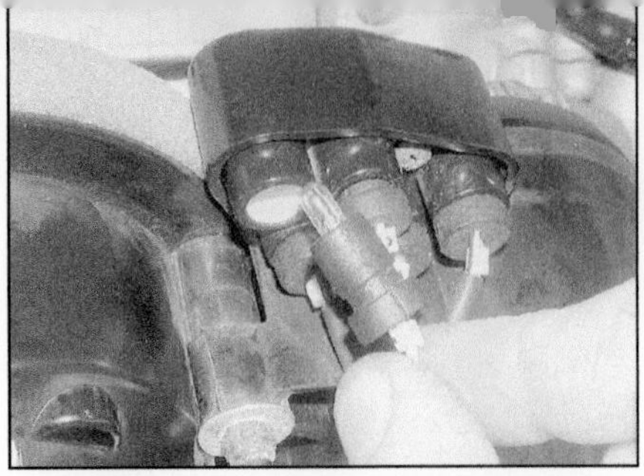

17.4b . . . then ease the holder into position (warning light bulb shown)

### Renewal

**6** Remove the fairing right-hand lower panel (see Chapter 8).

**7** Unclip the relay mounting rubber from the rear of the battery tray and position the relays clear of the switch.

**8** Disconnect the wiring connector from the oil pressure switch **(see illustration)**.

**9** Wipe clean the area around the switch then unscrew the switch from the crankcase cover. Discard the sealing washer and obtain a new one.

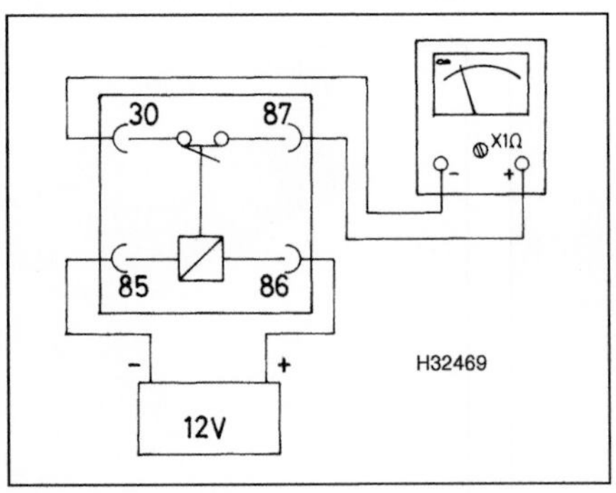


19.4 Relay test circuit – see text for details

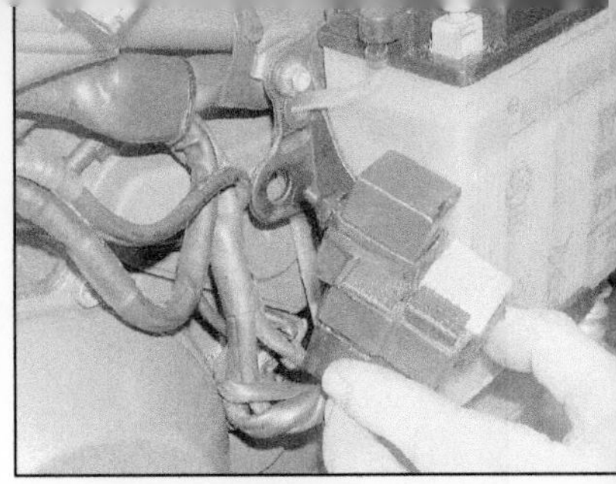

18.3 Free the relay mounting rubber fro the battery tray to gain access to the o pressure switch

***Caution: Do not allow any dirt or debris t enter the crankcase cover aperture whil the switch is removed.***

**10** Fit a new sealing washer to the swi then fit the switch to the crankcase cov tightening it to the specified torque.

**11** Reconnect the wiring connector then r the relay mounting rubber to the battery tra

**12** Run the engine and check that the swi operates correctly before installing the fai panel.

## 19 Ignition (main) switch and relay – check and renewal

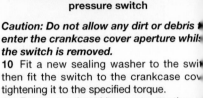

***Warning: To prevent the risk of short circuits, remove the fairing right-hand lower panel (see Chapter 8) and disconnect the battery negative (–ve) lea before making any ignition (main) switch checks.***

### Check

**1** If the ignition switch malfunctions, f check the fuses (see Section 5) and battery voltage before checking the swi operation. Remove the fairing right-ha lower panel (see Chapter 8) to gain access the ignition switch wiring connector and re

**2** Free the switch wiring from the frame a disconnect the wiring connector. Using ohmmeter or a continuity tester, check continuity of the connector terminal pairs ( the *wiring diagrams* at the end of t Chapter). Insert the key in the swit Continuity should exist between the termin connected by a solid line on the diagr when the switch is in the indicated position

**3** If the switch fails any of the tests, renew If the switch is good, check the ignition re as follows.

**4** Remove the relay from its holder located the rear of the battery mounting tray (s **illustration 19.11)**. Connect an ohmme across terminals 30 and 87 of the relay ( **illustration)**. Using a 12V battery and auxil wires, connect the battery positive (+ terminal to terminal 86 of the relay and negative (–ve) terminal to terminal 85 of

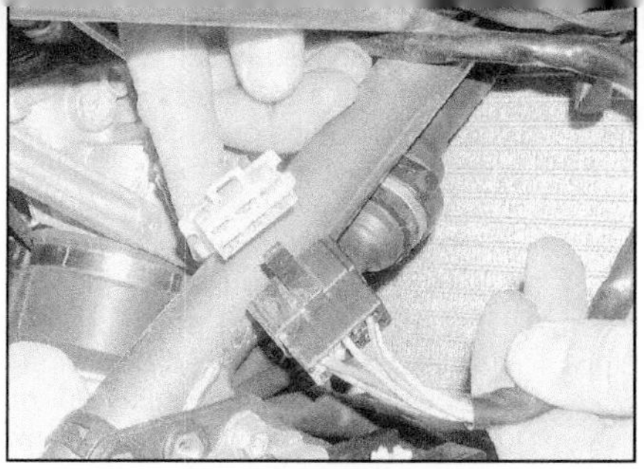

**19.7 Disconnecting the ignition switch wiring connector**

**19.8 Undo the retaining bolts and remove the ignition switch from the frame**

**19.9 Ensure the mounting rubber is correctly fitted to the expansion tank before installing the ignition switch**

relay and note the meter reading obtained. If the relay is operating correctly there should be continuity (zero resistance) whilst the battery is connected and no continuity (infinite resistance) whilst the battery is disconnected; the relay will be heard to 'click' as the battery is connected/disconnected. If this is not the case, renew the relay.

**5** If the switch and relay are proved good, check the circuit wiring and other switches (Sections 2 and 20) using the wiring diagrams at the end of this Chapter.

## *Renewal*

### Ignition switch

**6** Remove the airbox (see Chapter 4) and the fairing right-hand lower panel (see Chapter 8).

**7** Trace the ignition (main) switch wiring back from the base of the switch, freeing it from any retaining clips and ties whilst noting its correct routing. Disconnect the switch wiring connector located on the right-hand side of the frame **(see illustration)**.

**8** Unscrew the retaining bolts and remove the switch from the frame, taking care not to displace the mounting rubber from the top of the coolant expansion tank **(see illustration)**.

**9** On installation, remove all traces of locking compound from the threads of the lock bolts and apply a few drops of fresh locking compound to each bolt. Ensure the mounting rubber is in position, then fit the lock to the frame and tighten its retaining bolts to the specified torque **(see illustration)**.

**10** Ensure the lock wiring is correctly routed and retained by the necessary clips and ties then securely reconnect the wiring connector. Check the operation of the switch then refit the airbox and fairing panel (see Chapters 4 and 8).

### Ignition relay

**11** Remove the fairing right-hand lower panel (see Chapter 8). The ignition relay is mounted on the rear of the battery mounting tray **(see illustration)**.

**12** Ensure the ignition is switched OFF, then disconnect the wiring connector and free the relay from its mounting rubber **(see illustration)**.

**13** On installation ensure the relay is securely fitted to the connector and mounting. Check the relay operation before installing the fairing panel (see Chapter 8).

## 20 Handlebar switches – check

**1** Generally speaking, the switches are reliable and trouble-free. Most troubles, when they do occur, are caused by dirty or corroded contacts, but wear and breakage of internal parts is a possibility that should not be overlooked. If breakage does occur, the entire switch and related wiring harness will have to be renewed as individual parts are not available.

**2** The switches can be checked for continuity using an ohmmeter or a continuity test light. Always disconnect the battery negative (–ve) lead, which will prevent the possibility of a short circuit, before making the checks.

**3** Trace the wiring harness of the switch in question back to its connector, located on the rear of the headlight mounting shell, and disconnect it **(see illustration)**.

**4** Check for continuity between the terminals of the switch harness with the switch in the various positions (i.e. switch off – no continuity, switch on – continuity) – see the *wiring diagrams* at the end of this Chapter.

**5** If the continuity check indicates a problem exists, refer to Section 21, remove the switch and spray the switch contacts with electrical contact cleaner. If they are accessible, the contacts can be scraped clean with a knife or polished lightly with fine abrasive paper. If switch components are damaged or broken, it will be obvious when the switch is disassembled.

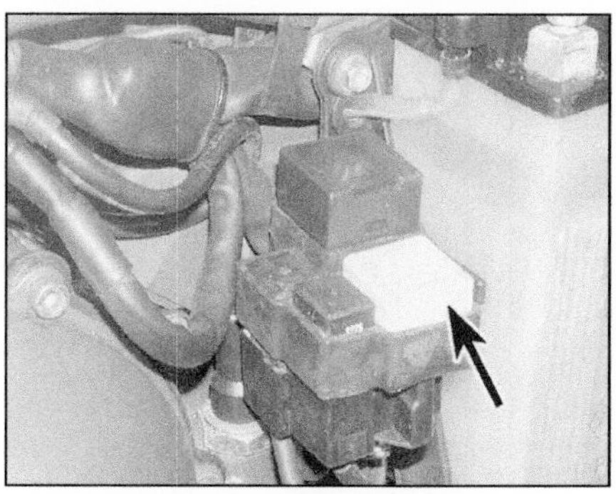

**19.11 The ignition relay (arrowed) is fitted to the rear of the battery tray**

**19.12 Disconnect the wiring connector then free the ignition relay from its mounting rubber**

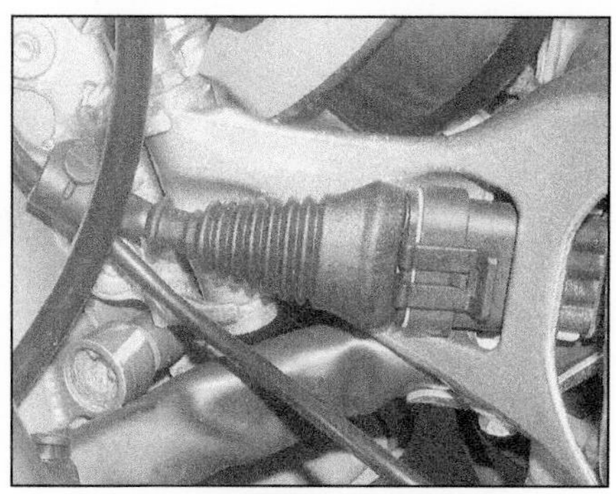

**20.3 The handlebar switch wiring connectors are located on the rear of the headlight shell**

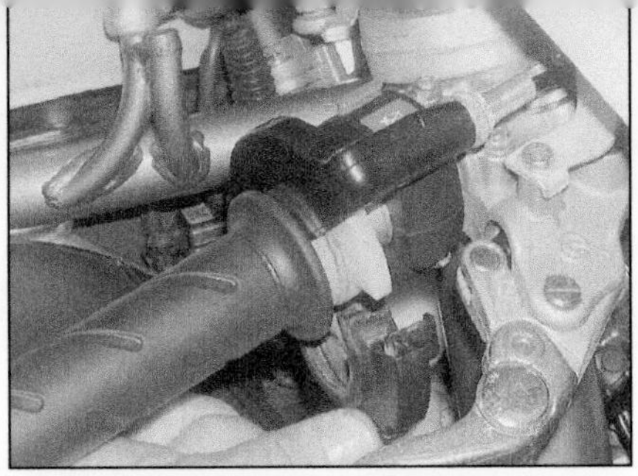

**21.1 Unscrew the throttle twistgrip housing bolts and remove the lower half of the housing to allow the housing to be positioned clear of the switch**

## 21 Handlebar switches – removal and installation

### *Right-hand handlebar switch*

#### Removal

**1** Unscrew the throttle twistgrip housing bolts (not the cover screws) and remove the lower half of the housing **(see illustration)**. Slide the housing clear of the switch.

**2** Trace the wiring harness of the switch back to its connector located on the rear of the headlight mounting shell, and disconnect it. Work back along the harness, freeing it from all the relevant clips and ties, noting its correct routing.

**3** Unscrew the two handlebar switch screws then free the switch from the handlebar and remove it from the bike **(see illustrations)**.

#### Installation

**4** Assemble the switch on the handlebar, aligning its lug with the handlebar hole. Refit the retaining screws and tighten them securely, tightening the front screw first.

**5** Ensure the switch wiring is correctly routed and retained by all the necessary clips and ties then securely reconnect the wiring connector.

**6** Fit the lower half of the twistgrip housing, handlebar hole, then refit the housing bolts, tightening them to the specified torque.

### *Left-hand handlebar switch*

#### Removal

**7** Remove the switch as described in Steps 2 and 3.

#### Installation

**8** Install the switch as described in Steps 4 and 5.

## 22 Neutral switch – check and renewal

### *Check*

**1** Before checking the electrical circuit, check the bulb (see Section 17) and fuse (see Section 5). The following check is carried out at the switch wiring connector. Remove the fairing right-hand lower panel (see Chapter 8) to gain access to the wiring connector (the connector is located on the right-hand side of the engine and the switch is screwed into the rear of the crankcase – see illustration 22.9).

**2** Make sure the transmission is in neutral then disconnect the wiring connector from the switch.

**3** With the connector disconnected and the ignition switched ON, the neutral light should be out. If not, the wire between the connector and instrument cluster must be earthed (grounded) at some point.

**4** With the ignition off, check for continuity between the switch wiring connectors (switch with two wires) or the switch wire and crankcase (switch with one wire). With the transmission in neutral, there should be continuity. With the transmission in gear, there should be no continuity. If the tests prove otherwise, then the switch is faulty or incorrectly adjusted. The successful operation of the neutral switch depends on its plunger being the correct distance from the trigger on the selector drum. Since crankcase thickness may vary from model to model, the sealing switch is set to the correct height. If proble are experienced with the neutral light stay on when the transmission is in gear, or light not coming on when in neutral, check neutral switch adjustment as follows.

**5** With the transmission in neutral, conne continuity tester across the two wires of switch connector (switch with two wires between the switch wiring connector and crankcase (switch with one wire). The te should indicate continuity (0 ohms). N unscrew the switch from the crankcase w noting the position where the tester indic no continuity (infinite resistance); this sh occur between a half turn and a whole tur the switch. If no continuity (switch open) oc before a half turn, the sealing washer shoul replaced with a thinner one. If no contin occurs after a whole turn of the switch sealing washer should be replaced wi thicker one. Sealing washers are availab 0.5 mm, 1 mm, 1.5 mm and 2 mm thicknes

**6** If the continuity tests prove the switc good, check for voltage (ignition on) at wire terminal (at the light blue wire termina the switch with two wires) using a test ligh there's no voltage present, check the wi between the switch, instrument cluster fusebox (see the *wiring diagrams* at the en this Chapter).

### *Renewal*

**7** The switch is screwed into the rear of crankcase and its wiring connector is loc on the top of the crankcase. Remove fairing right-hand lower panel to gain acc to the switch connector (see Chapter 8).

**8** Trace the wiring back from the switch t connector, noting its correct rout Disconnect the wiring connector then free wiring from the engine/frame.

**9** Remove all traces of dirt from around switch then unscrew it and remove it from crankcase; access to the switch is lim **(see illustration)**. Discard the switch sea washer and obtain a new one of the s thickness (washers are available in different thickness to facilitate sw adjustment – see Step 5).

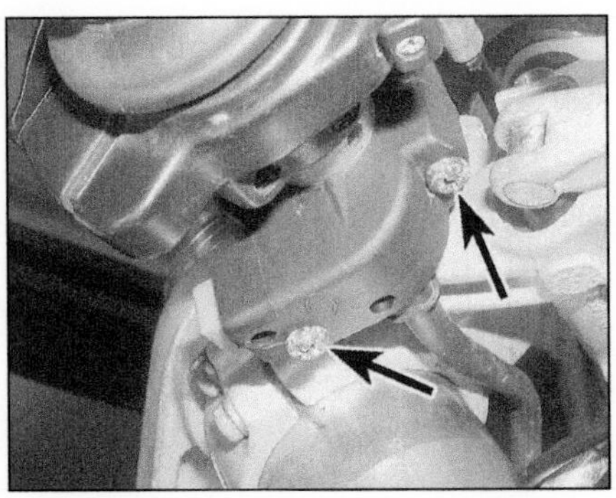

**21.3a Undo the retaining screws (arrowed) . . .**

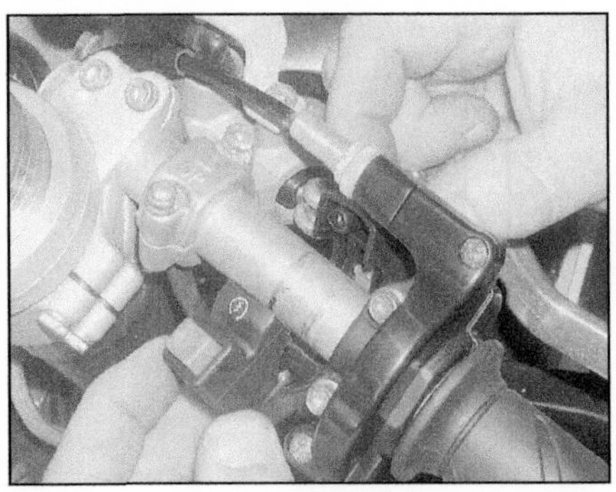

**21.3b . . . then free the right-hand switch from the handlebar and remove it from the bike**

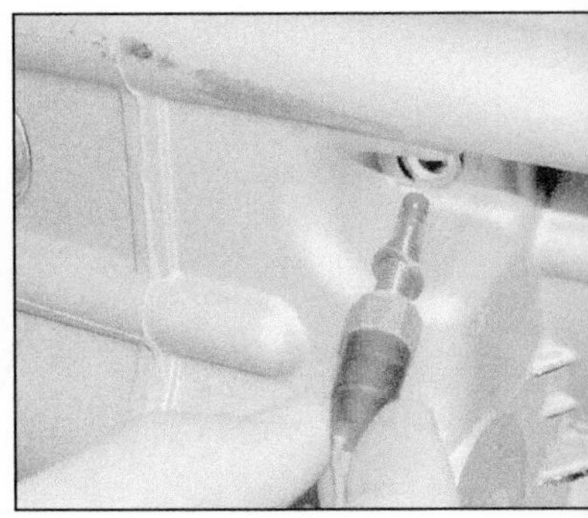

**22.9 Removing the neutral switch from crankcase**

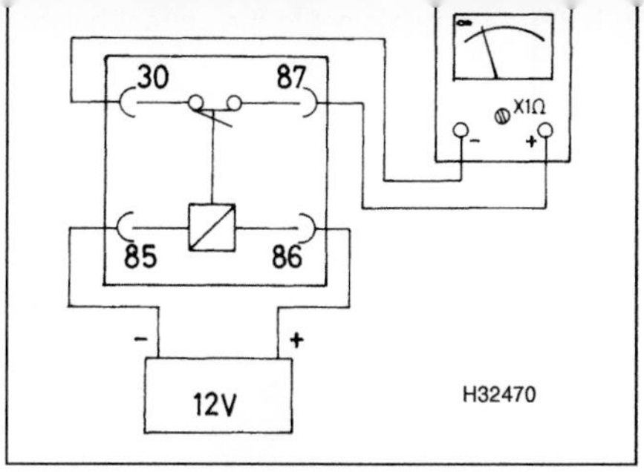


23.5 Relay test circuit – see text for details

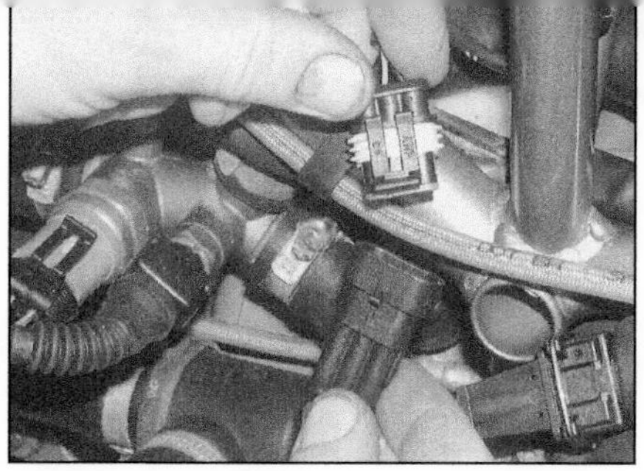

23.8 Disconnect the wiring connector . . .

23.9 . . . then undo the retaining screw and remove the switch from the sidestand pivot

***Caution: Do not allow any dirt or debris to enter the crankcase aperture whilst the switch is removed.***

**10** Fit the new sealing washer to the switch then fit the switch to the crankcase, tightening it to the specified torque.

**11** Check the operation of the switch to ensure it is correctly adjusted (see Step 5) then route the switch wiring correctly around the engine and frame and securely reconnect the connector to the main wiring harness.

**12** Check the operation of the neutral light then install the fairing panel (see Chapter 8).

## 23 Sidestand switch and relay (later models) – check and renewal

### *Check*

**1** The sidestand switch is mounted on the sidestand pivot and the relay is mounted on the rear of the battery mounting tray. The switch and relay control the safety circuit which prevents or stops the engine starting/running if the sidestand is down. Before checking the electrical circuit, check the fuses (see Section 5).

**2** Support the bike on an auxiliary stand. Remove the fairing left-hand lower panel to gain access to the switch and the right-hand lower panel to gain access to the relay (see Chapter 8).

**3** Trace the wiring back from the switch to its connector and disconnect the switch. Connect an ohmmeter across the switch terminals and check the operation of the switch. With the sidestand up there should be continuity (zero resistance) between the terminals, and with the sidestand down there should be no continuity (infinite resistance).

**4** If the switch does not perform as expected, it is defective and must be renewed. If the switch is good, check the relay as follows.

**5** Remove the relay from its holder located on the rear of the battery mounting tray. Connect an ohmmeter across the terminals 30 and 87 of the relay **(see illustration)**. Using a 12V battery and auxiliary wires, connect the battery positive (+ve) terminal to terminal 86 of the relay and the negative (–ve) terminal to terminal 85 of the relay and note the meter reading obtained. If the relay is operating correctly there should be continuity (zero resistance) whilst the battery is connected and no continuity (infinite resistance) whilst the battery is disconnected; the relay will be heard to 'click' as the battery is connected/disconnected. If this is not the case, renew the relay.

**6** If the switch and relay are proved good, check the circuit wiring (Section 2) using the wiring diagrams at the end of this Chapter.

### *Renewal*

#### Sidestand switch

**7** Remove the fairing left-hand lower panel (see Chapter 8).

**8** Trace the wiring back from the sidestand switch, freeing it from any retaining clips and ties, and disconnect its connector from the main wiring harness **(see illustration)**.

**9** Unscrew the retaining screw and remove the switch from the stand, noting how it fits **(see illustration)**.

**10** Prior to installation, remove the original locking compound from the switch screw and apply fresh locking compound to the screw threads. Locate the switch on the sidestand, aligning its pin with the hole in the stand and its cutout with the lug on the stand bracket. Install the switch retaining screw and tighten it securely **(see illustration)**.

**11** Make sure the wiring is correctly routed up to the connector and retained by all the necessary clips and ties then reconnect the connector. Check the operation of the switch before installing the fairing panel (see Chapter 8).

#### Sidestand relay

**12** Remove the fairing right-hand lower panel (see Chapter 8). The relay is mounted on the rear of the battery mounting tray **(see illustration)**.

**13** Ensure the ignition is switched OFF then free the relay from its mounting and disconnect it from its connector **(see illustration)**.

**14** On installation ensure the relay is securely fitted to the connector and mounting. Check the relay operation before installing the fairing panel (see Chapter 8).

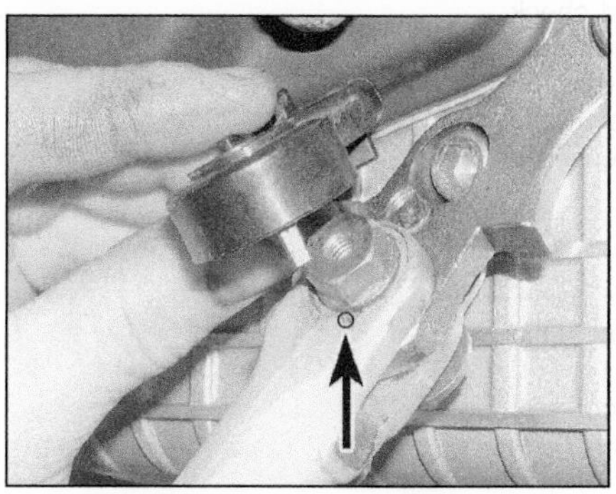

23.10 Install the switch ensuring its pin is correctly located in the stand hole (arrowed)

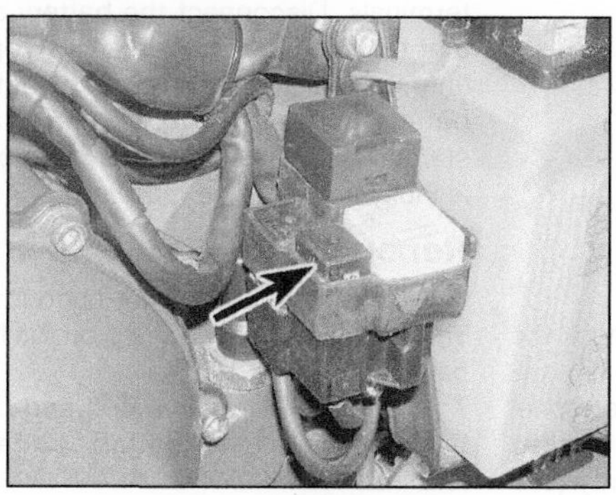

23.12 Sidestand relay (arrowed) is fitted to the rear of the battery tray

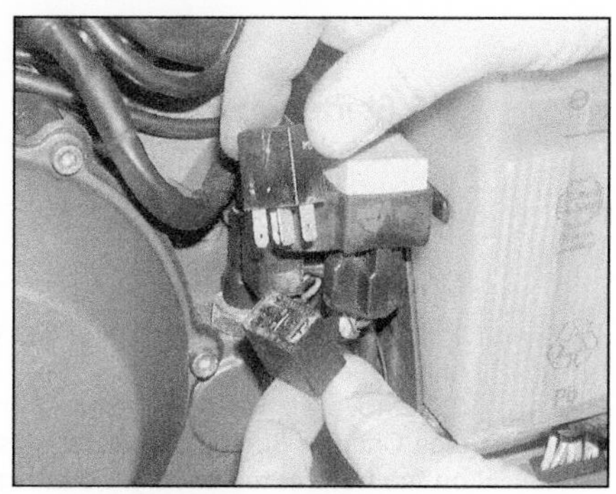

23.13 Free the sidestand relay from its mounting rubber and disconnect it from the wiring connector

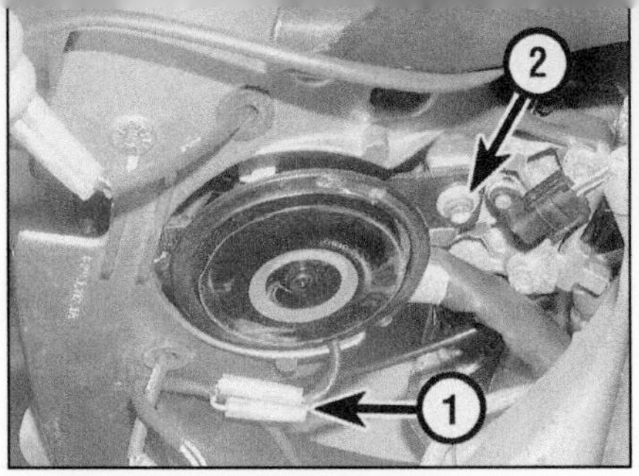


**24.5 Horn wiring connectors (1) and mounting bolt (2)**

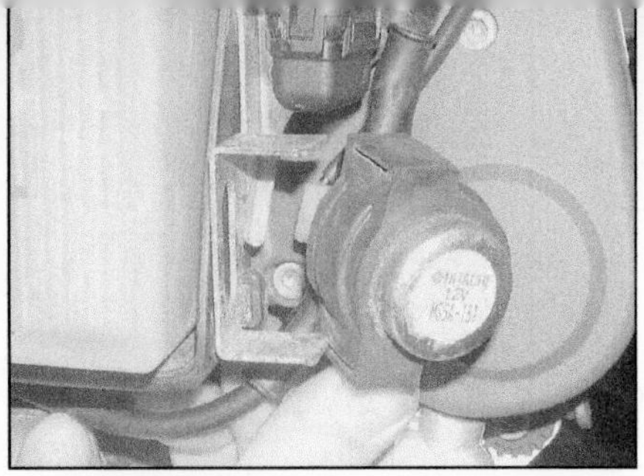

**25.8a Free the starter relay mounting rubber from the battery tray . . .**

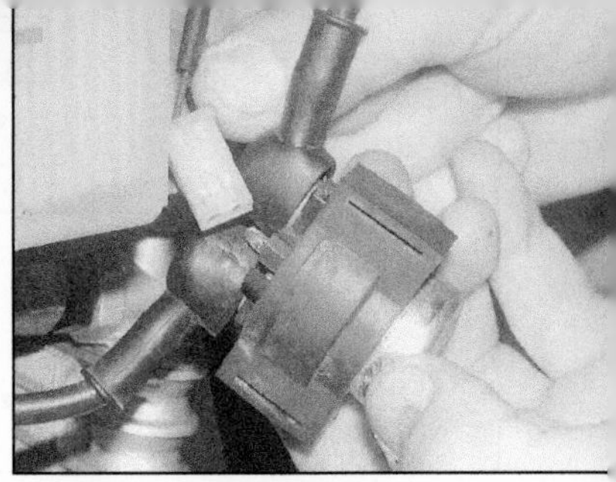

**25.8b . . . then disconnect the wiring connector**

## 24 Horn – check and renewal

### *Check*

**1** The horn is mounted on the underside of the headlight mounting shell. Remove the upper fairing for access (see Chapter 8).

**2** Disconnect the wiring connectors from the horn. Using two jumper wires, apply battery voltage directly to the horn terminals. If the horn sounds, check the fuse (see Section 5), switch (see Section 20) and the wiring between the switch and the horn (see the *wiring diagrams* at the end of this Chapter).

**3** If the horn doesn't sound, renew it.

### *Renewal*

**4** Remove the upper fairing (see Chapter 8).

**5** Disconnect the wiring connectors from the horn, then unscrew the bolt and collar securing the horn to the base of the headlight mounting shell and remove it from the bike **(see illustration)**.

**6** Apply a drop of locking compound to the threads of the horn bolt. Align the horn with the headlight shell and install the collar and mounting bolt. Tighten the bolt to the specified torque then reconnect the wiring connectors to the horn.

**7** Check the horn operation then install the upper fairing (see Chapter 8).

## 25 Starter relay – check and renewal

### *Check*

**1** If the starter circuit is faulty, first check the fuses (see Section 5).

**2** Remove the fairing right-hand lower panel (see Chapter 8). The starter relay is mounted on the front of the battery mounting tray **(see illustration 25.8a)**.

**3** With the ignition switch ON and the engine kill switch in the RUN position, press the starter switch. The relay should be heard to click. On later (2000-on) models, it will be necessary to retract the sidestand for the check.

**4** If the relay doesn't click, switch off the ignition and disconnect the wiring connector from the starter relay **(see illustration 25.8b)**. Connect the positive (+ve) lead of a voltmeter to the wiring connector red/blue terminal and connect the negative (–ve) lead to a good earth (ground) point. Switch on the ignition and press the starter button whilst noting the reading obtained on the meter; battery voltage should be present only when the starter button is depressed. If not check, the handlebar switch (Section 20) and the wiring between the relay, switch and fusebox (see *wiring diagrams* at the end of this Chapter). On later models also check the sidestand switch and relay (Section 23). If voltage is present, remove the relay as described below; test it as follows.

**5** Set a multimeter to the ohms x 1 scale and connect it across the relay's starter motor and battery lead terminals. Using a fully-charged 12 volt battery and two insulated jumper wires, connect the positive (+ve) terminal of the battery to the red/blue wire terminal of the relay, and the negative (–ve) terminal to the black wire terminal of the relay. If the relay is functioning correctly, it should be heard to click as the battery is connected and continuity (zero resistance) should be present between the battery and starter motor lead terminals. Disconnect the battery and check that the relay clicks again and an open circuit (infinite resistance) is present between the battery and starter motor terminals. If the starter relay does not perform as expected, it is faulty and must be renewed.

### *Renewal*

**6** Remove the fairing right-hand lower panel. The starter relay is mounted on the front of the battery mounting tray.

**7** Unscrew the terminal bolt and disconnect the lead from the battery negative (–ve) terminal.

**8** Free the starter relay mounting rubber from the battery tray, then disconnect the wiring connector from the relay **(see illustrations)**.

**9** Peel back their rubber covers then unsc the two nuts and washers securing the sta motor and battery leads to the relay (s **illustration)**. Detach the leads and remove relay from the bike. If necessary, separate relay and mounting rubber.

**10** On installation, connect the battery a starter motor leads to the relay terminals fit the washers and nuts. Securely tigh both nuts then seat the rubber insula covers correctly over the terminals.

**11** Locate the relay correctly in its moun rubber then reconnect the wiring connec Seat the relay mounting rubber on the bat tray then reconnect the battery negative (– lead. Check the operation of the relay bef installing the fairing panel.

## 26 Starter motor – removal and installation

### *Removal*

**1** Remove the fairing lower panels (s Chapter 8).

**2** Unscrew the terminal bolt and disconn the lead from the battery negative (– terminal.

**3** The starter motor is mounted on the fron the engine, below the horizontal cylinder. P back the rubber cover on the starter mo terminal then unscrew the nut and washer

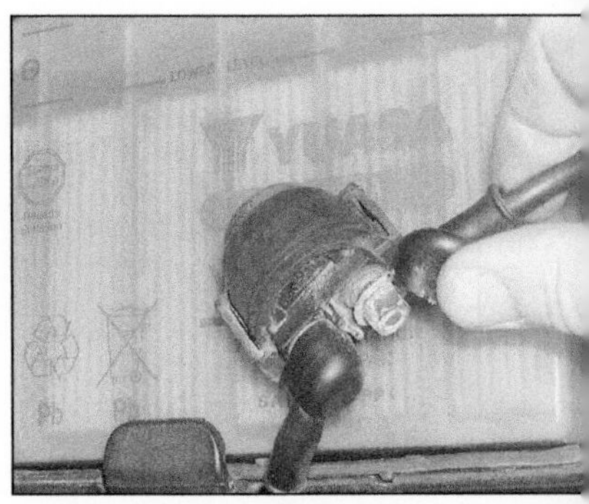

**25.9 Peel back the rubber covers the unscrew the retaining nuts securing th battery and starter motor leads to the re**

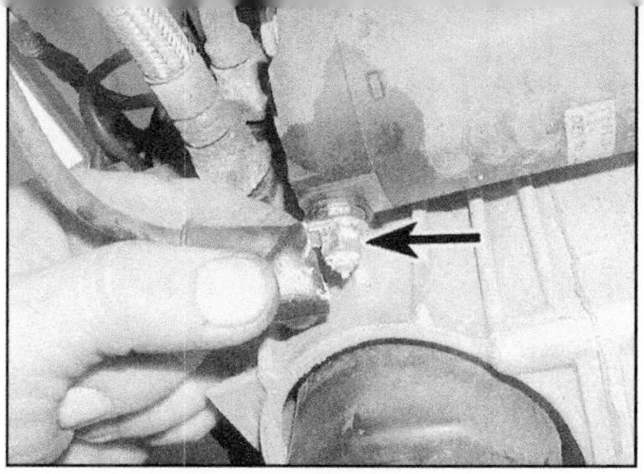

**26.3 Peel back the rubber cover then unscrew the nut and washer (arrowed) and detach the starter motor lead**

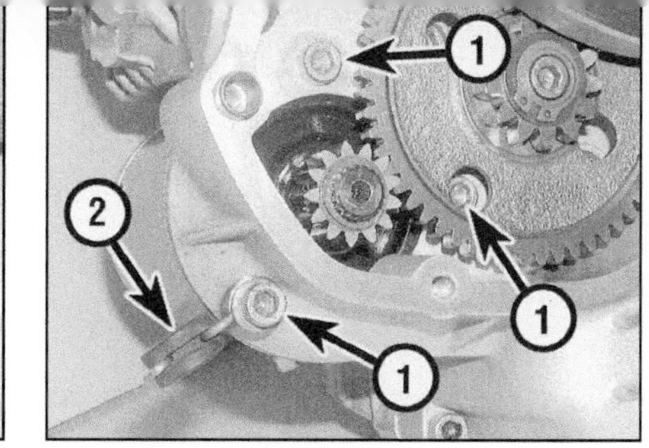


**26.5 Unscrew the starter motor mounting bolts (1) noting the location of the hose guide (2)**

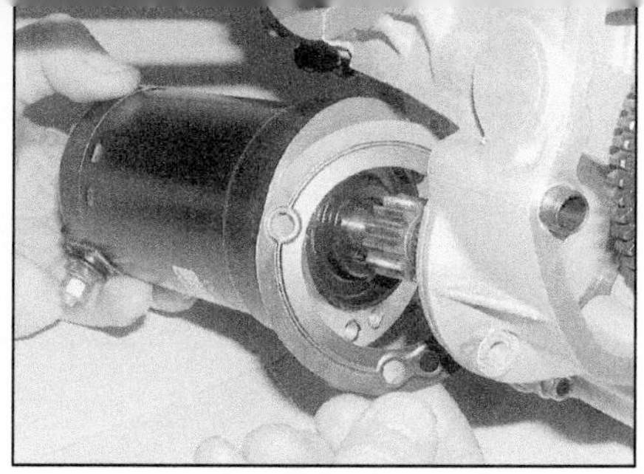

**26.7 Fit a new gasket and manoeuvre the starter motor into position**

detach the starter lead from the motor **(see illustration)**.

**4** Remove the crankcase left-hand cover from the engine (see Chapter 2, Section 16) to gain access to the starter motor bolts.

**5** Unscrew the three mounting bolts (the rear bolt can be accessed through the holes in the idler gear), noting the location of the hose guide, and remove the starter motor from the engine **(see illustration)**. Recover the gasket and discard it; a new one must be used on installation.

### *Installation*

**6** Ensure the mating surfaces of the motor and crankcase are clean and dry. Remove all traces of locking compound from the mounting bolt threads and apply a drop of fresh locking compound to each bolt.

**7** Fit the new gasket to the motor, aligning its holes with the motor bolt holes **(see illustration)**.

**8** Manoeuvre the motor into position and slide it into the crankcase, ensuring the starter motor pinion teeth mesh correctly with those of the starter idle gear. Fit the starter motor mounting bolts, ensuring the hose guide is correctly positioned, and tighten them to the specified torque.

**9** Install the crankcase cover (see Chapter 2, Section 16).

**10** Connect the starter lead to the motor terminal and fit the washer and retaining nut, tightening it securely. Cover the terminal and nut with a smear of multi-purpose grease, to prevent corrosion, then seat the rubber cover correctly over the terminal.

**11** Securely reconnect the lead to the battery negative (–ve) terminal and check the operation of the starter motor before installing the fairing panels (see Chapter 8).

## 27 **Starter motor** – disassembly, inspection and reassembly

### *Disassembly*

**1** Remove the starter motor (see Section 26).

**2** If no alignment marks are visible between the main housing and the end covers, make your own.

**3** Remove the circlip from the front end of the shaft and slide off the drive pinion, noting which way around it is fitted **(see illustrations)**.

**4** Unscrew the two long bolts and withdraw them from the starter motor, complete with their O-rings **(see illustration)**.

**5** Wrap some insulating tape around the teeth on the end of the starter motor shaft – this will protect the oil seal from damage as the front cover is removed **(see illustration)**. Remove the front cover from the motor and recover its sealing ring.

**6** Remove the rear cover and brushplate assembly from the main housing, complete with its sealing ring. Remove the shim(s) from the rear end of the armature shaft or from inside the rear cover, noting their location.

**7** Withdraw the armature from the main housing.

**8** Free the terminal bolt brush from its holder and separate the rear cover and brushplate.

**9** If necessary, noting the correct fitted location of each component, unscrew the terminal nut and remove it along with its insulating washer. Withdraw the terminal bolt and brushplate assembly from the rear cover and recover the O-ring and inner insulating cover from the bolt.

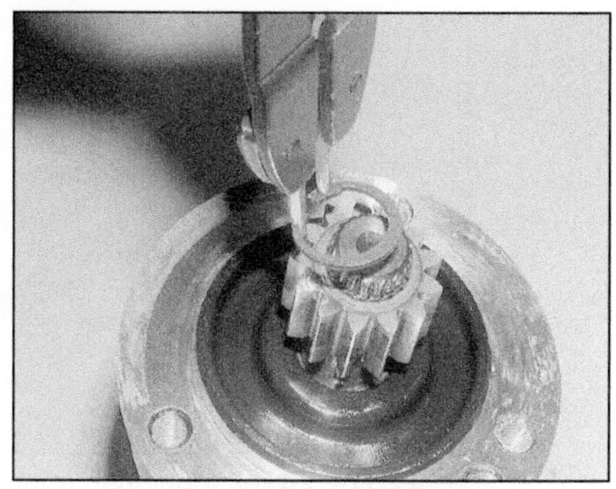

**27.3a Remove the circlip . . .**

**27.3b . . . and slide off the drive pinion from the starter motor**

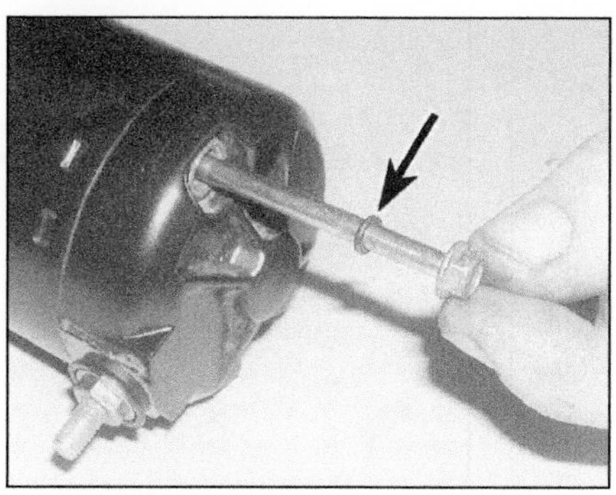

**27.4 Slacken and remove the long bolts complete with their O-rings (arrowed) . . .**

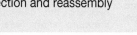

**27.5 . . . then remove the front cover from the motor**

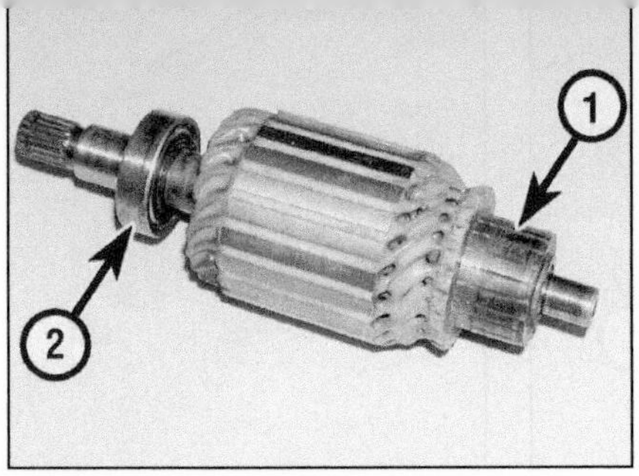


27.11 **Check the armature commutator bars (1) and bearing (2) for wear or damage as described in text**

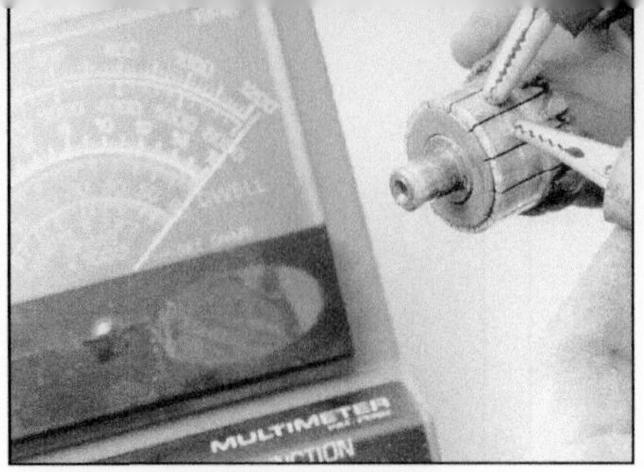

**27.12a Continuity should exist between the commutator bars**

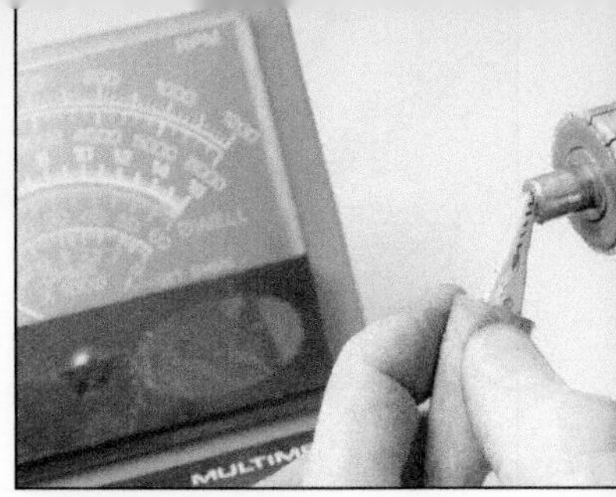

**27.12b There should be no continuit between the commutator bars and th armature shaft**

## *Inspection*

**Note:** *The only individual components Ducati list for the starter motor are the drive pinion and circlip and (on some models) replacement brushes. Check spares availability with your Ducati dealer. If the following checks reveal a worn or faulty internal component other than those listed, seek the advice of an auto electrical specialist before condemning the starter motor.*

**10** The parts of the starter motor that are most likely to require attention are the brushes. Check the brushes for signs of wear or damage, such as cracking or chipping (Ducati do not specify a service limit for brush length). If either brush is excessively worn or shows signs of damage, the brushes should be renewed as a set.

**11** Inspect the commutator bars on the armature for scoring, scratches and discoloration **(see illustration)**. The commutator can be cleaned and polished with crocus cloth, but do not use sandpaper or emery paper. After cleaning, wipe away any residue with a cloth soaked in electrical system cleaner or denatured alcohol.

**12** Using an ohmmeter or a continuity test light, check for continuity between the commutator bars **(see illustration)**. Continuity should exist between each bar and all of the others. Also, check for continuity between the commutator bars and the armature shaft **(see illustration)**. There should be no continuity (infinite resistance) between the commutator and the shaft. If the checks indicate otherwise, the armatur defective.

**13** Check for continuity between the br and the terminal bolt. There should continuity (zero resistance). Check continuity between the terminal bolt and housing (when assembled). There shoulc no continuity (infinite resistance).

**14** Check the starter motor drive pinior signs of wear or damage and, if necess renew it. If the pinion teeth are damaged, check the teeth of the idler gear and sta clutch driven gear.

**15** Inspect the end covers for signs of cra or wear. Inspect the magnets in the m housing and the housing itself for cracks.

**16** Inspect the shims and front cover oil sea signs of damage and renew them if necess Also check the armature front bearing.

## *Reassembly*

**17** Where necessary, fit the inner insula cover to the terminal bolt then insert the through the rear cover **(see illustration)** the O-ring and the insulating washer to terminal bolt then fit the nut, tightenir securely **(see illustrations)**.

**18** Slide the terminal bolt brush back intc holder and locate the brushplate assembl the rear cover, aligning its cutout with cover cutout **(see illustration)**. Ensure b springs are correctly seated on the brushe

**19** Slide the shim(s) onto the rear end of armature shaft, then lubricate the shaft wi drop of oil **(see illustration)**. Insert

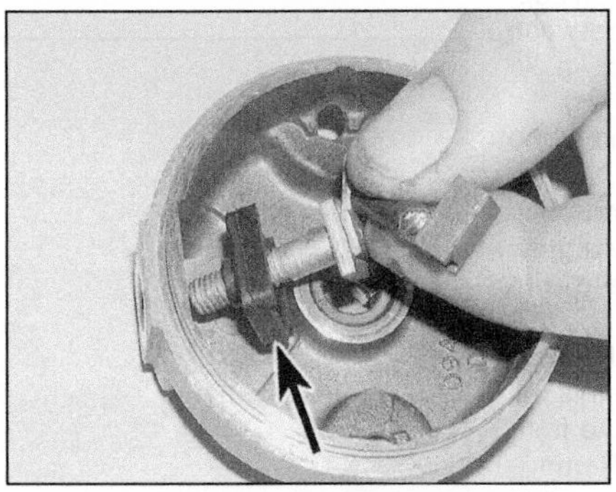

**27.17a Fit the inner insulating cover (arrowed) and locate the terminal bolt in the rear cover**

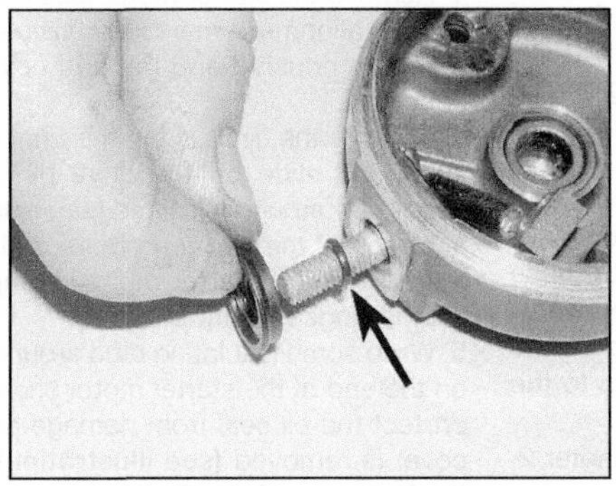

**27.17b Fit the O-ring (arrowed) and insulating washer to the bolt . . .**

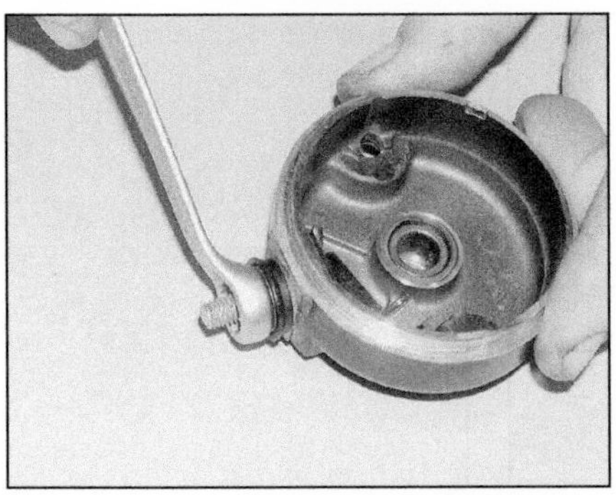

**27.17c . . . then fit the nut and tighten it securely**

**27.18 Align the brushplate cutout with the cutout (arrowed) in the rear cover**

**27.19a Fit the shim(s) to the rear of th armature shaft . . .**

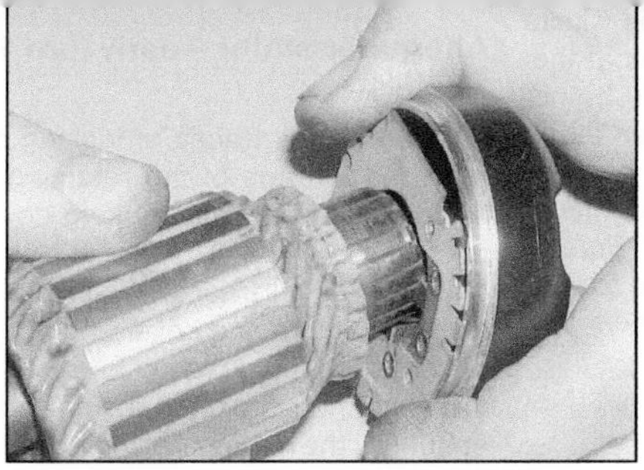

**27.19b . . . then locate the brushes correctly on the commutator and seat the armature in the rear cover**

armature into the rear cover, locating the brushes on the commutator bars as you do so, taking care not to damage them **(see illustration)**. Check that each brush is securely pressed against the commutator by its spring and is free to move easily in its holder.

**20** Fit the sealing ring to the rear cover then fit the housing over the armature and onto the rear cover, aligning the marks made on removal **(see illustration)**. Ensure the rear cover and brushplate cutouts are both correctly engaged with the housing before proceeding.

**21** Apply a smear of grease to the lips of the front cover oil seal and fit the sealing ring to the cover. Ensure the bearing is correctly fitted then install the cover, aligning the marks made on removal. Remove the protective tape from the shaft end.

**22** Check that the marks made on removal are correctly aligned, then install the long bolts, complete with their O-rings, and tighten them securely.

**23** Slide the drive pinion carefully onto the armature shaft, ensuring it is fitted the correct way around, and secure it in position with the circlip. Ensure the circlip is correctly located in the armature groove.

**24** Install the starter motor (see Section 26).

## 28 Charging system testing – general information and precautions

**1** If the performance of the charging system is suspect, the system as a whole should be checked first, followed by testing of the individual components. **Note:** *Before beginning the checks, make sure the battery is fully charged and that all system connections are clean and secure.*

**2** Checking the output of the charging system and the performance of the various components within the charging system requires the use of a multimeter (with voltage, current and resistance checking facilities).

**3** When making the checks, follow the procedures carefully to prevent incorrect

**27.20 Slide the main housing over the armature and seat it correctly in the rear cover, aligning the marks made/noted on removal**

connections or short circuits, as irreparable damage to electrical system components may result if short circuits occur.

**4** If a multimeter is not available, the job of checking the charging system should be left to a Ducati dealer or automotive electrician.

## 29 Charging system – leakage and output tests

**1** If the charging system of the machine is thought to be faulty, remove the fairing right-hand lower panel (see Chapter 8) and perform the following checks.

### Leakage test

***Caution: Always connect an ammeter in series, never in parallel with the battery, otherwise it will be damaged. Do not turn the ignition ON or operate the starter motor when the ammeter is connected – a sudden surge in current will blow the meter's fuse.***

**2** Turn the ignition switch OFF and disconnect the lead from the battery negative (–ve) terminal.

**3** Set the multimeter to the Amps function and connect its negative (–ve) probe to the battery negative (–ve) terminal, and positive (+ve) probe to the disconnected negative (–ve) lead **(see illustration)**. Always set the meter to a high amps range initially and then bring it down to the mA (milli Amps) range; if there is a high current flow in the circuit it may blow the meter's fuse.

**4** Ducati do not specify a limit for current leakage but if the current leakage indicated exceeds 1 mA, there is likely to be a short circuit in the wiring. Disconnect the meter and reconnect the negative (–ve) lead to the battery, tightening it securely. **Note:** *If the bike is fitted with an anti-theft alarm or immobiliser system, remember to take the current draw of the alarm/immobiliser system into account when taking the measurement (see manufacturers specifications for specified current draw of the system).*

**5** If leakage is indicated, use the wiring

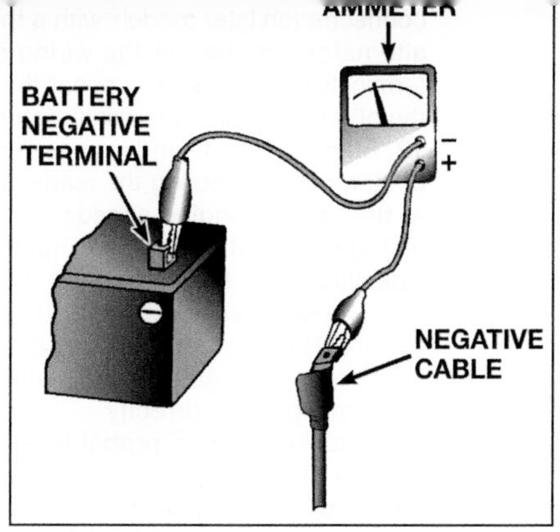


**29.3 Checking the charging system leakage rate. Connect the meter as shown**

diagrams at the end of this book to systematically disconnect individual electrical components and repeat the test until the source is identified.

### Regulated output test

**6** Start the engine and warm it up to normal operating temperature, then stop the engine.

**7** Start the engine and allow it to idle. Connect a multimeter set to the 0 to 20 volts DC scale across the terminals of the battery (positive (+ve) lead to battery positive (+ve) terminal, negative (–ve) lead to battery negative (–ve) terminal). Slowly increase the engine speed to 3000 rpm and note the reading obtained, then stop the engine and turn the ignition OFF; do not allow the engine to overheat. The regulated voltage should be approximately 13.5 to 15.5 volts (Ducati do not specify exact limits). If the voltage is outside these limits, check the unregulated output (see below).

HAYNES HiNT ***Clues to a faulty regulator are constantly blowing bulbs, with brightness varying considerably with engine speed, and battery overheating.***

### Unregulated output test

***Caution: Never disconnect/connect the alternator wiring with the engine running as this will damage the regulator/rectifier.***

**8** Start the engine and warm it up to normal operating temperature. Stop the engine.

**9** Remove the fairing left-hand lower panel (see Chapter 8).

**10** Trace the alternator wiring from the crankcase cover and disconnect it at the regulator/rectifier connector(s). On early models, if necessary, to improve access to the connectors unbolt the battery mounting tray from the frame (see Section 3).

**11** Using a multimeter set to 0 to 250 volts AC range, connect the meter probes to the connector (on later models with a three-phase alternator, any two of the wiring connector terminals can be used – repeat the check on the other two pairs of terminals later).

**12** Start the engine and increase its speed to 6000 rpm whilst noting the readings obtained at the various engine speeds. Compare the voltage output to those given in the Specifications. If the readings differ greatly from those specified, check the alternator stator coil resistance (see Section 30). If the readings are good, the alternator is functioning correctly and the regulator/rectifier is probably at fault (see Section 31).

**13** Stop the engine then reconnect the alternator wiring. Install the fairing panels (see Chapter 8).

## 30 Alternator – check, removal and installation

**Note:** *There are two possible types of alternator. On early (pre 1999) models the alternator rotor is mounted on the crankshaft end and rotates on the **inside** of the stator coil. Later (1999-on) models are fitted with a three-phase alternator where the alternator rotor is bolted onto the flywheel and rotates around the **outside** of the stator coil.*

### Check

**1** Remove the fairing lower panels (see Chapter 8).

**2** Trace the alternator wiring from the crankcase left-hand cover and disconnect it at the regulator/rectifier connector(s). If necessary, to improve access to the connectors unbolt the battery mounting tray from the frame (see Section 3).

**3** Using a multimeter set to the ohms x 1 (ohmmeter) scale measure the resistance between the yellow wires on the alternator side of the connector, then check for continuity between each terminal and ground (earth). On later models with a three-phase alternator, take measurements between each pair of yellow wires (a total of three readings).

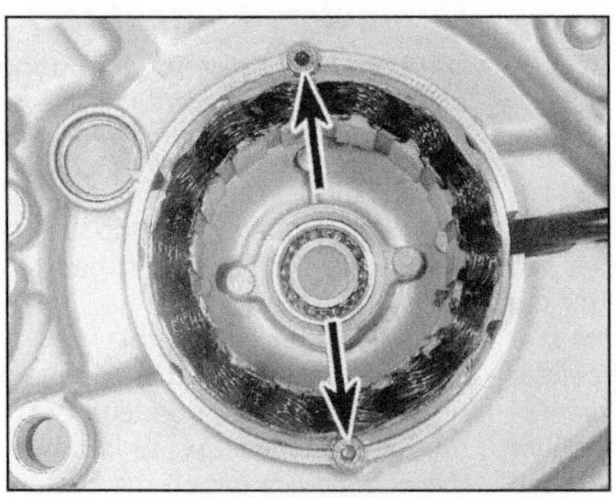

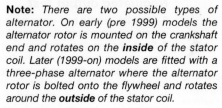

**30.6 On early models the stator coil assembly is retained by two bolts (arrowed)**

condition the three readings should be within the range shown in the Specifications at the start of this Chapter and there should be no continuity (infinite resistance) between all of the terminals and earth. If they differ greatly, the alternator stator coil assembly is at fault and should be renewed. **Note:** *Before condemning the stator coils, check the fault is not due to damaged wiring between the connector and coils.*

### Removal

**5** Remove the crankcase left-hand cover from the engine (see Chapter 2, Section 16). Proceed as described under the relevant sub-heading.

#### Alternator stator – early (pre 1999) models

**6** Undo the two stator retaining bolts and free the stator wiring grommet from the crankcase cover **(see illustration)**. The stator can then be removed, noting which way around it is fitted.

#### Alternator stator – later (1999-on) models

**7** Undo the retaining bolts and remove the stator wiring harness retaining plate from the inside of the cover **(see illustration)**.

**8** Undo the three stator retaining bolts then remove the stator from the cover, noting which way around it is fitted.

#### Alternator rotor – early (pre 1999) models

**9** Refer to Chapter 2, Section 17.

#### Alternator rotor – later (1999-on) models

**10** Slacken the bolts securing the rotor to the flywheel. If necessary, prevent rotation by placing the transmission in gear and having an assistant firmly apply the rear brake.

**11** Remove all the retaining bolts and free the rotor from the flywheel. Recover the locating pin and circlip arrangement fitted between the rotor and flywheel. Whilst the rotor is removed screw a couple of the bolts back into the flywheel to ensure the starter clutch holder remains correctly positioned.

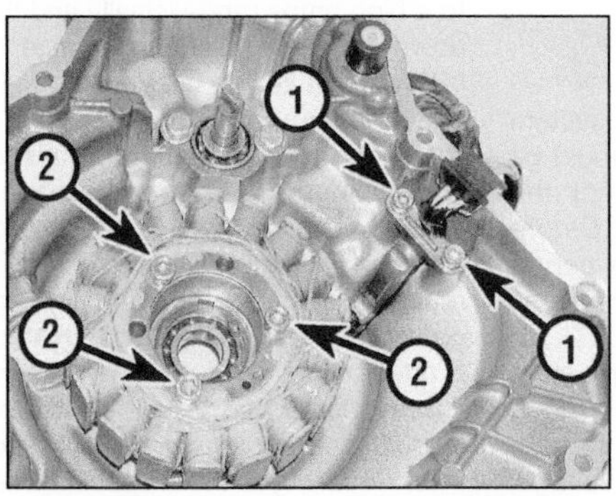


**30.7 Wiring harness plate bolts (1) and stator coil retaining bolts (2) – later models**

#### Alternator stator – early (pre 1999) models

**12** Remove all traces of locking compou from the threads of the retaining bolts a apply a drop of fresh locking compound each bolt.

**13** Remove all traces of oil from the sta wiring grommet and cover and apply a sm of sealant to the grommet.

**14** Align the stator with the crankcase co ensuring the wiring is facing towards cover. Route the wiring through the co aperture and seat the grommet correctly position. Align the stator cutouts with retaining bolt holes then fit the bo tightening them to the specified torque.

**15** Install the crankcase cover (see Ch ter 2, Section 16).

#### Alternator stator – later (1999-on) models

**16** Remove all traces of locking compou from the threads of the stator and wiring p retaining bolts and apply a drop of fr locking compound to each bolt.

**17** Align the stator with the crankcase co ensuring the wiring is facing towards cover. Route the wiring through cover guide and align the stator with retaining bolt holes. Fit the sta retaining bolts, tightening them to specified torque.

**18** Remove all traces of oil from the sta wiring grommet and cover and apply a sm of sealant to the grommet. Locate the sta wiring correctly in the cover cutout and s the grommet in its cutout. Secure the wirin position with the retaining plate, tightening bolts to the specified torque.

**19** Install the crankcase cover (see Ch ter 2, Section 16).

#### Alternator rotor – early (pre 1999) models

**20** Refer to Chapter 2, Section 17.

#### Alternator rotor – later (1999-on) models

**21** Remove all traces of locking compou from the threads of the rotor retaining bo and apply a drop of fresh locking compou to each bolt.

**22** Ensure the rotor and flywheel mat surfaces are clean and dry then fit the locat pin and circlip arrangement to the flywh Align the rotor with the pin and fit the retain bolts, tightening them evenly a progressively to the specified torque necessary, prevent rotation by placing transmission in gear and having an assist firmly apply the rear brake.

**23** Install the crankcase cover (see Ch ter 2, Section 16).

## 31 Regulator/rectifier – check and renewal

### Check

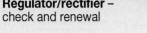

1 If the regulated voltage check shows up a charging system problem but the unregulated voltage check and stator coil checks show the alternator to be functioning correctly, then it is likely that the regulator/rectifier unit is faulty. Testing of the regulator/rectifier requires specialist equipment and if carried out carelessly, could actually damage the unit. If a fault is suspected, the unit should be taken to a Ducati dealer or an auto-electrical specialist for further testing. The best means of testing is to substitute the regulator/rectifier with a order.

### Renewal

2 Remove the battery mounting tray (see Section 3).

3 On early models, undo the mounting bolts and remove the regulator/rectifier and heatsink from the base of the battery tray.

4 On later models, undo the mounting bolts and remove the regulator/rectifier from its mounting bracket **(see illustration)**. If necessary, the mounting bracket can also be unbolted from the battery mounting tray.

5 Installation is the reverse of removal, tightening the mounting bolts securely. Install the battery mounting tray (Section 3).

***Caution: On early models never fit the regulator/rectifier unit without the heatsink otherwise the unit will overheat and be damaged.***

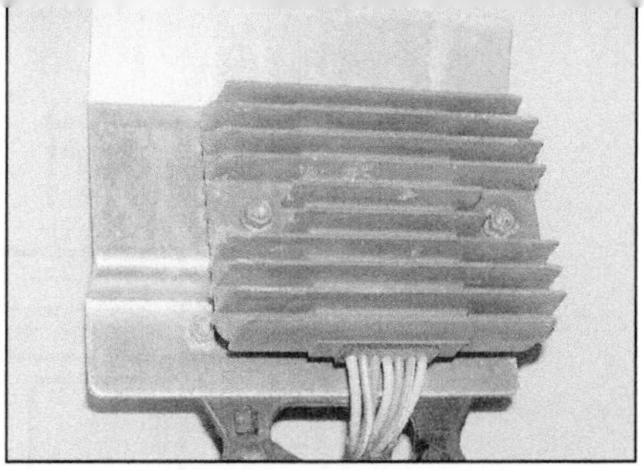

**31.4 Regulator/rectifier mounting bolts (later models)**

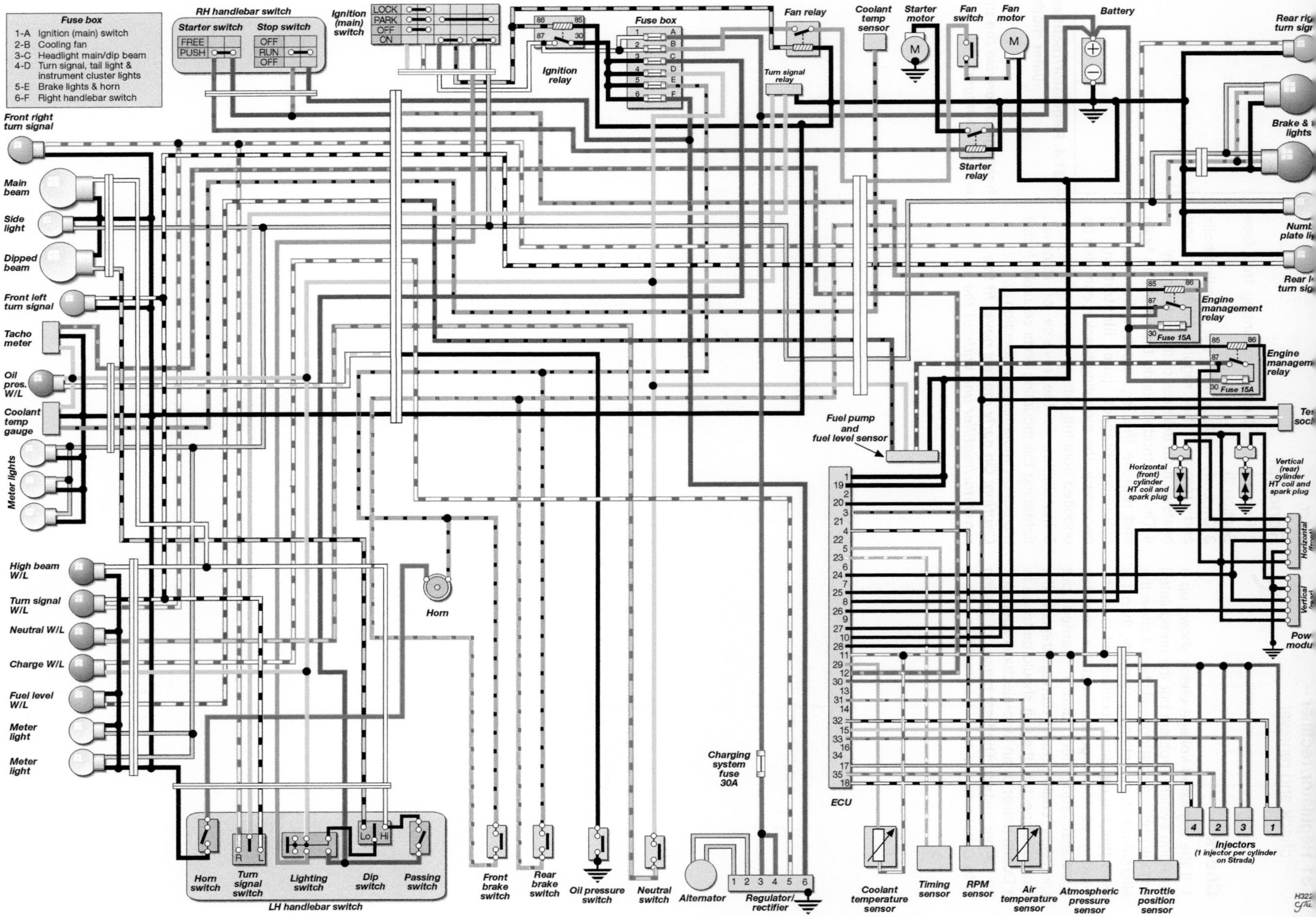
Fuse box
1-A Ignition (main) switch
2-B Cooling fan
3-C Headlight main/dip beam
4-D Turn signal, tail light & instrument cluster lights
5-E Brake lights & horn
6-F Right handlebar switch
RH handlebar switch
Starter switch
Stop switch
FREE
PUSH
OFF
RUN
OFF
Ignition (main) switch
LOCK
PARK
OFF
ON
Ignition relay
Fuse box
Fan relay
Turn signal relay
Coolant temp sensor
Starter motor
Fan switch
Fan motor
Starter relay
Battery
Front right turn signal
Main beam
Side light
Dipped beam
Front left turn signal
Tacho meter
Oil pres. W/L
Coolant temp gauge
Meter lights
High beam W/L
Turn signal W/L
Neutral W/L
Charge W/L
Fuel level W/L
Meter light
Meter light
Horn
Horn switch
Turn signal switch
Lighting switch
Dip switch
Passing switch
LH handlebar switch
Front brake switch
Rear brake switch
Oil pressure switch
Neutral switch
Alternator
Regulator/rectifier
Charging system fuse 30A
Fuel pump and fuel level sensor
ECU
Engine management relay
Fuse 15A
Horizontal (front) cylinder HT coil and spark plug
Vertical (rear) cylinder HT coil and spark plug
Coolant temperature sensor
Timing sensor
RPM sensor
Air temperature sensor
Atmospheric pressure sensor
Throttle position sensor
Injectors
(1 injector per cylinder on Strada)

**Ducati 1994 916 Strada model and 1994-95 916 SP model**

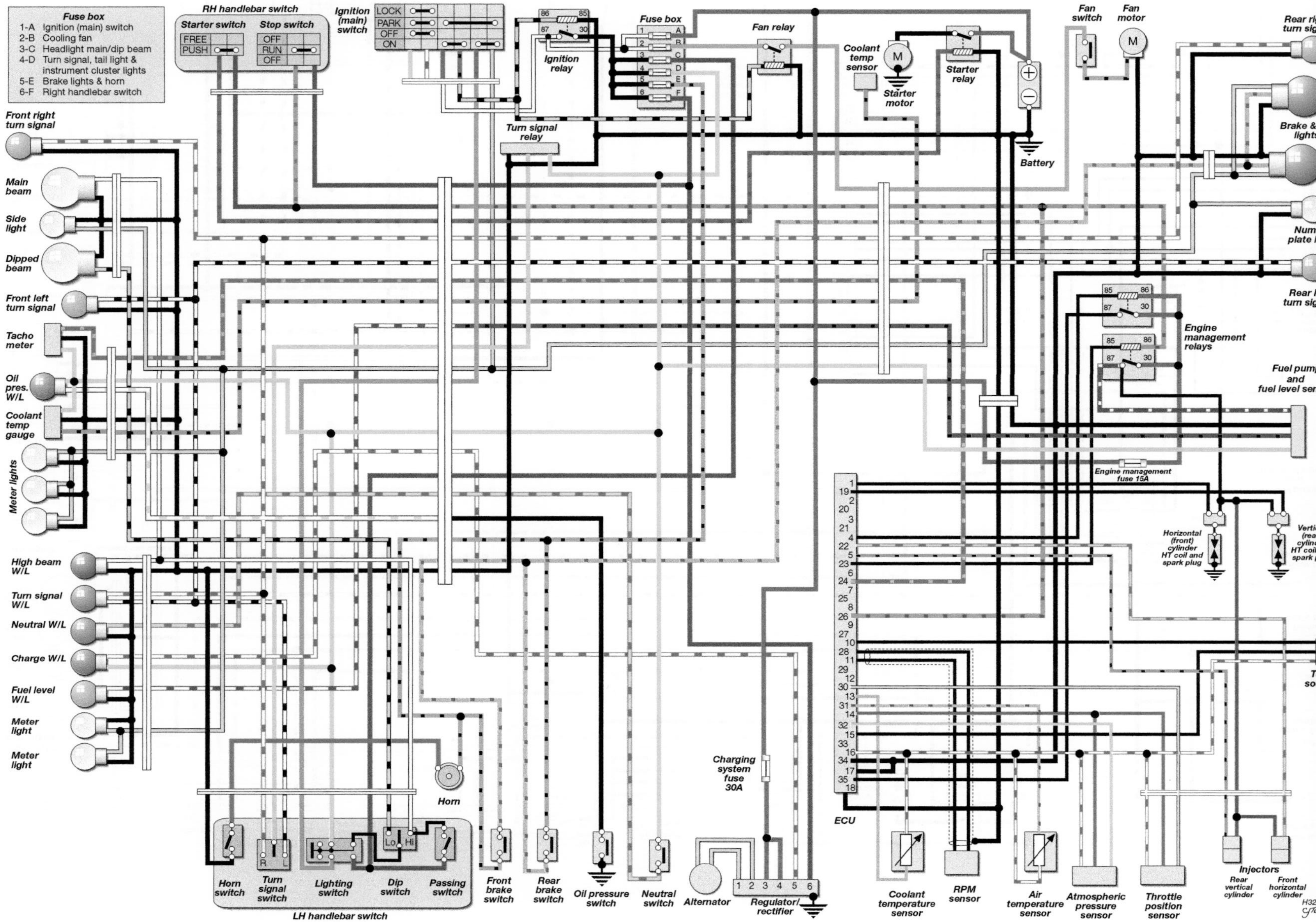


1995-97 748 Biposto and SP models, 1994-97 916 Biposto model

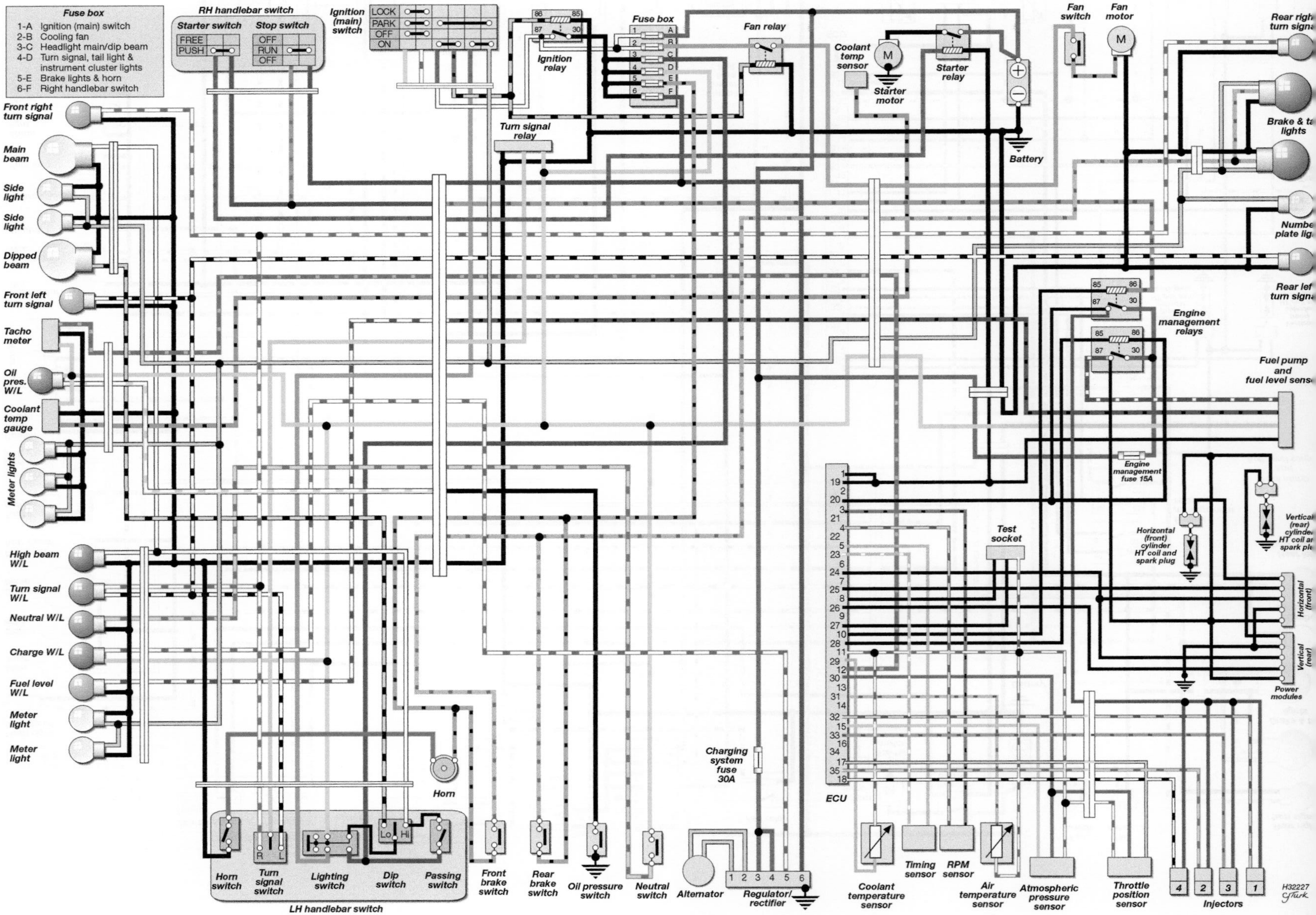


1996 916 SP and 1997 916 SPS models

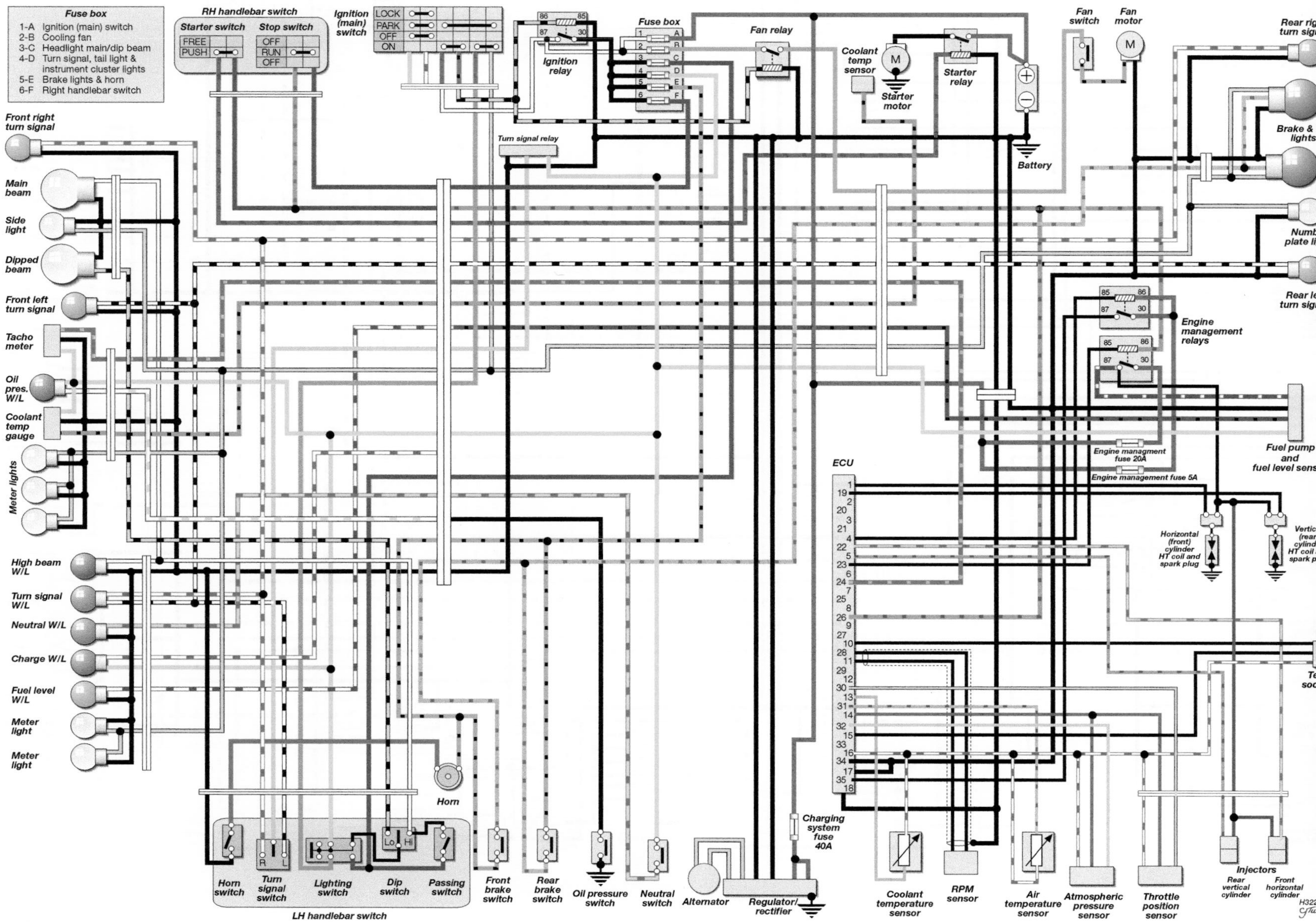


1998 748 Biposto and SPS models, 1998 916 Biposto model

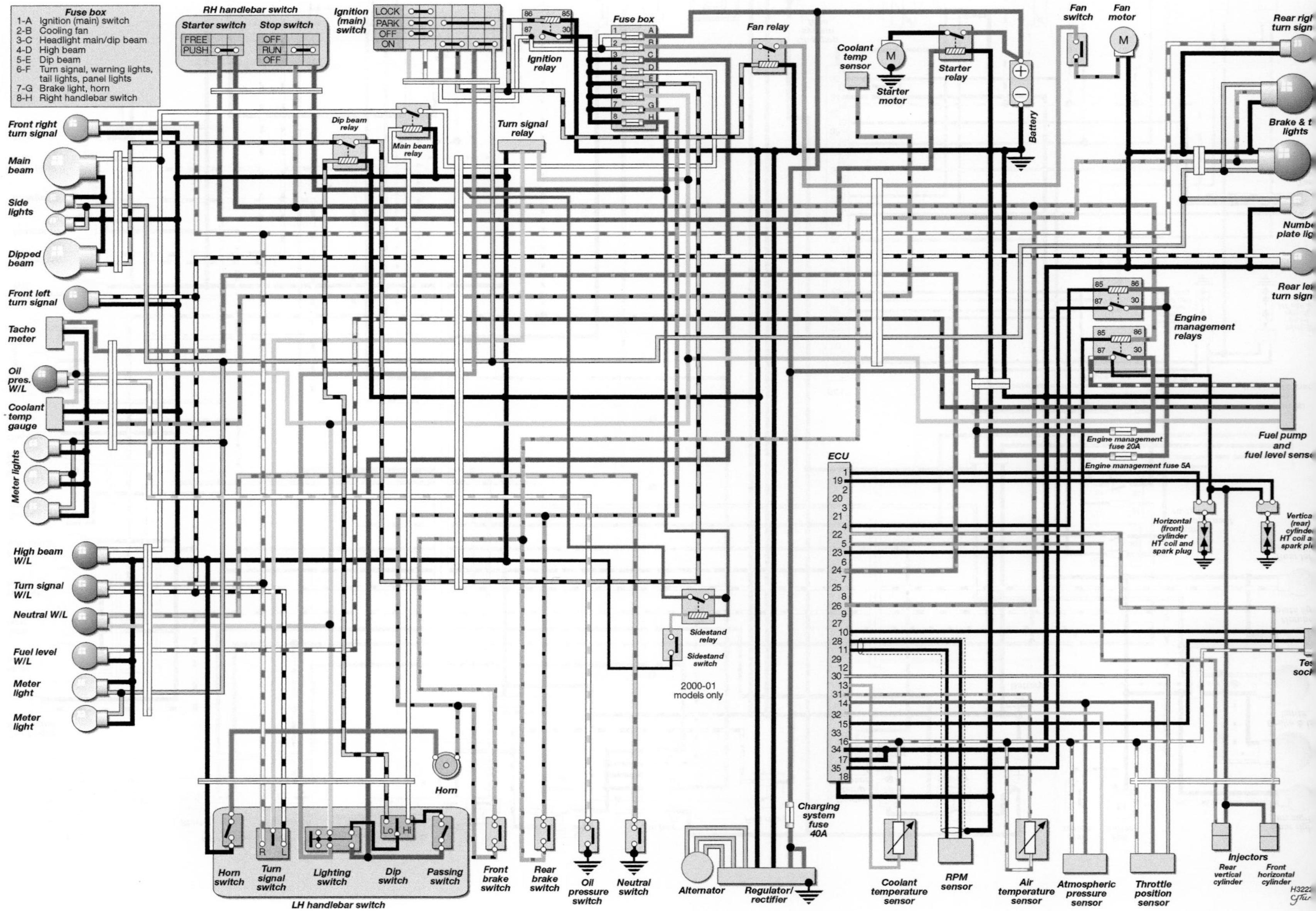


1999 748 Biposto and 748 SPS models, 2000-01 748 and 748 S models

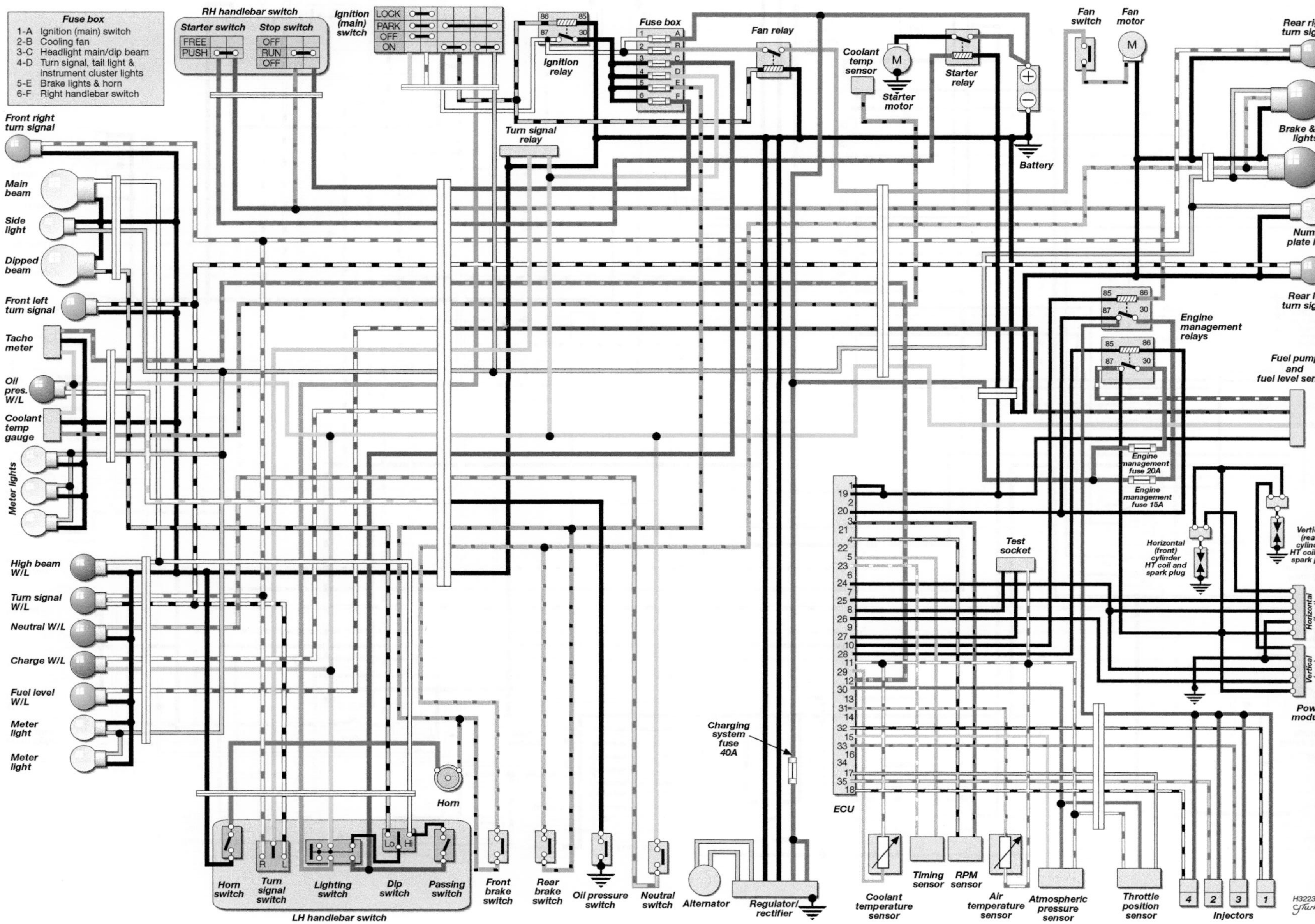


1998 916 SPS model

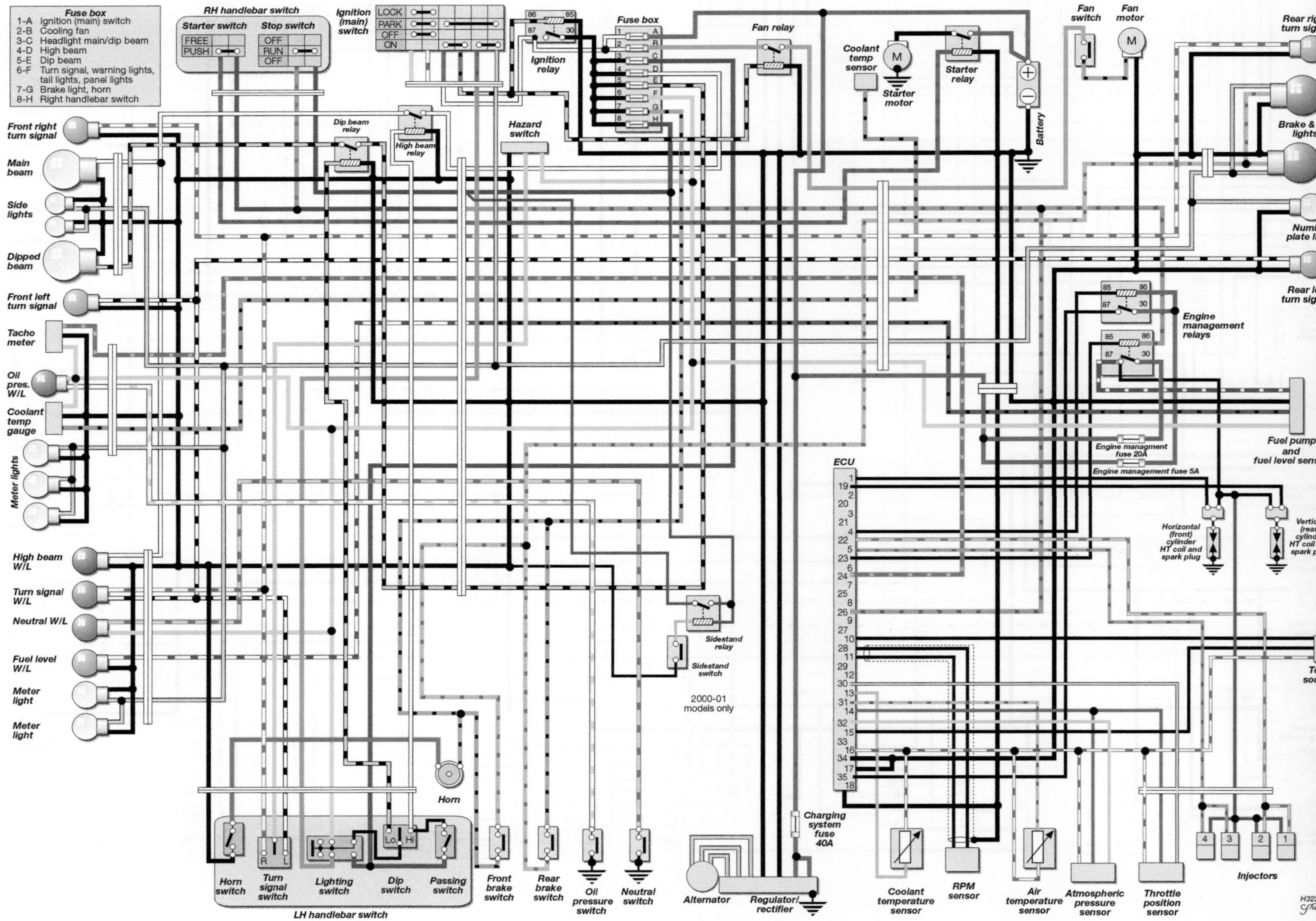


1999-01 996 Biposto and 996 S models

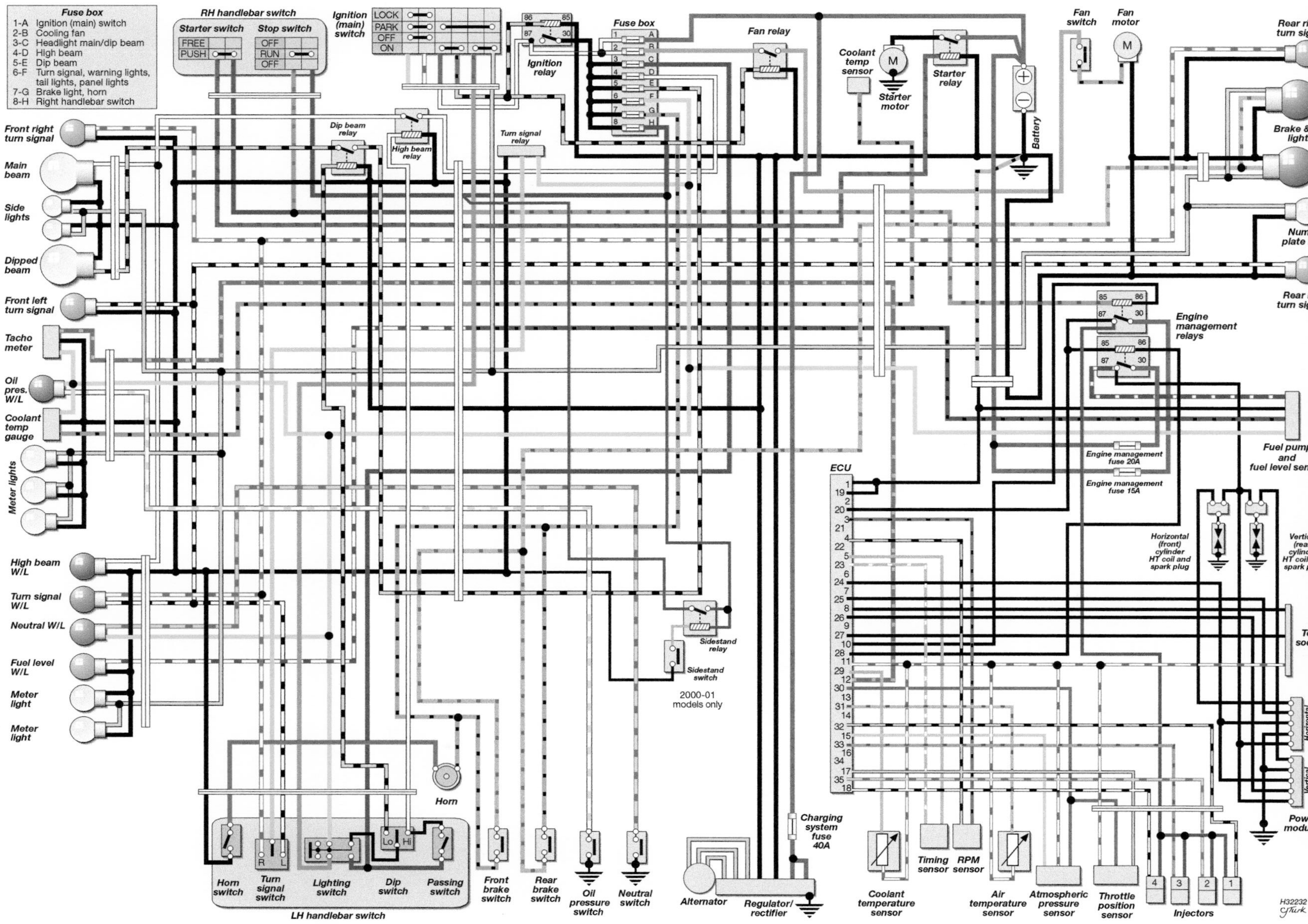


1999-00 996 SPS models

# Reference

## Tools and Workshop Tips — REF•2

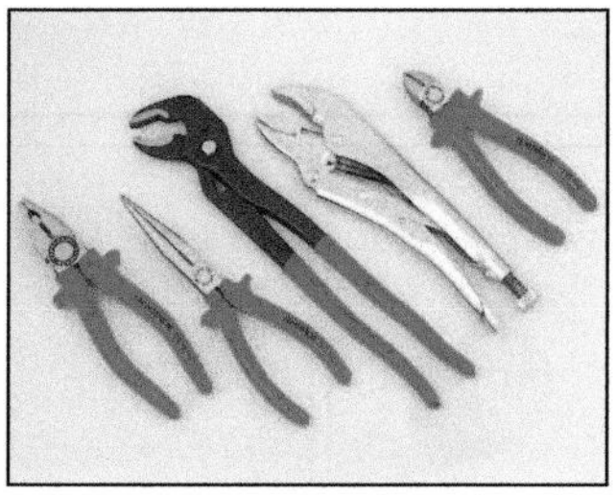

- Building up a tool kit and equipping your workshop ● Using tools
- Understanding bearing, seal, fastener and chain sizes and markings
- Repair techniques

## Security — REF•20

- Locks and chains
- U-locks ● Disc locks
- Alarms and immobilisers
- Security marking systems ● Tips on how to prevent bike theft

## Lubricants and fluids — REF•23

- Engine oils
- Transmission (gear) oils
- Coolant/anti-freeze
- Fork oils and suspension fluids ● Brake/clutch fluids
- Spray lubes, degreasers and solvents

## Conversion Factors — REF•26

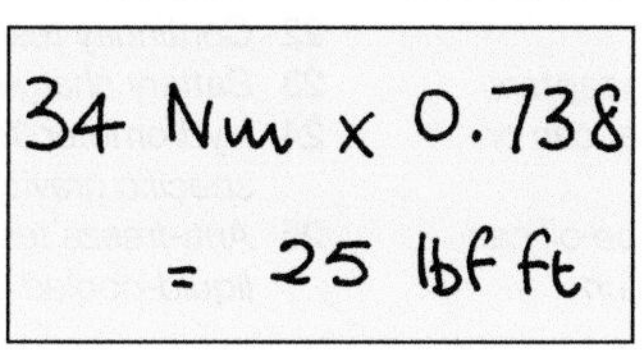


- Formulae for conversion of the metric (SI) units used throughout the manual into Imperial measures

## MOT Test Checks — REF•27

- A guide to the UK MOT test ● Which items are tested ● How to prepare your motorcycle for the test and perform a pre-test check

## Storage — REF•32

- How to prepare your motorcycle for going into storage and protect essential systems ● How to get the motorcycle back on the road

## Fault Finding — REF•35

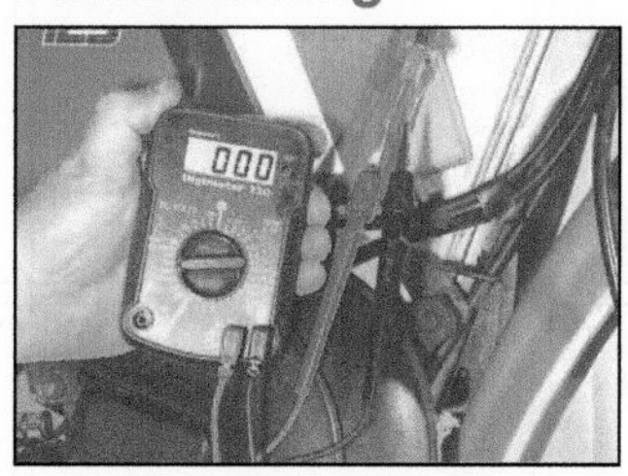

- Common faults and their likely causes ● How to check engine cylinder compression ● How to make electrical tests and use test meters

## Technical Terms Explained — REF•49

- Component names, technical terms and common abbreviations explained

## Index — REF•53

## Buying tools

A toolkit is a fundamental requirement for servicing and repairing a motorcycle. Although there will be an initial expense in building up enough tools for servicing, this will soon be offset by the savings made by doing the job yourself. As experience and confidence grow, additional tools can be added to enable the repair and overhaul of the motorcycle. Many of the specialist tools are expensive and not often used so it may be preferable to hire them, or for a group of friends or motorcycle club to join in the purchase.

As a rule, it is better to buy more expensive, good quality tools. Cheaper tools are likely to wear out faster and need to be renewed more often, nullifying the original saving.

***Warning: To avoid the risk of a poor quality tool breaking in use, causing injury or damage to the component being worked on, always aim to purchase tools which meet the relevant national safety standards.***

The following lists of tools do not represent the manufacturer's service tools, but serve as a guide to help the owner decide which tools are needed for this level of work. In addition, items such as an electric drill, hacksaw, files, soldering iron and a workbench equipped with a vice, may be needed. Although not classed as tools, a selection of bolts, screws, nuts, washers and pieces of tubing always come in useful.

the Haynes *Motorcycle Workshop Pract* *TechBook* (Bk. No. 3470).

## Manufacturer's service too

Inevitably certain tasks require the use c service tool. Where possible an alternat tool or method of approach is recommend but sometimes there is no option if perso injury or damage to the component is to avoided. Where required, service tools referred to in the relevant procedure.

Service tools can usually only be purcha from a motorcycle dealer and are identified a part number. Some of the commonly-us tools, such as rotor pullers, are available aftermarket form from mail-order motorcy tool and accessory suppliers.

# Maintenance and minor repair tools

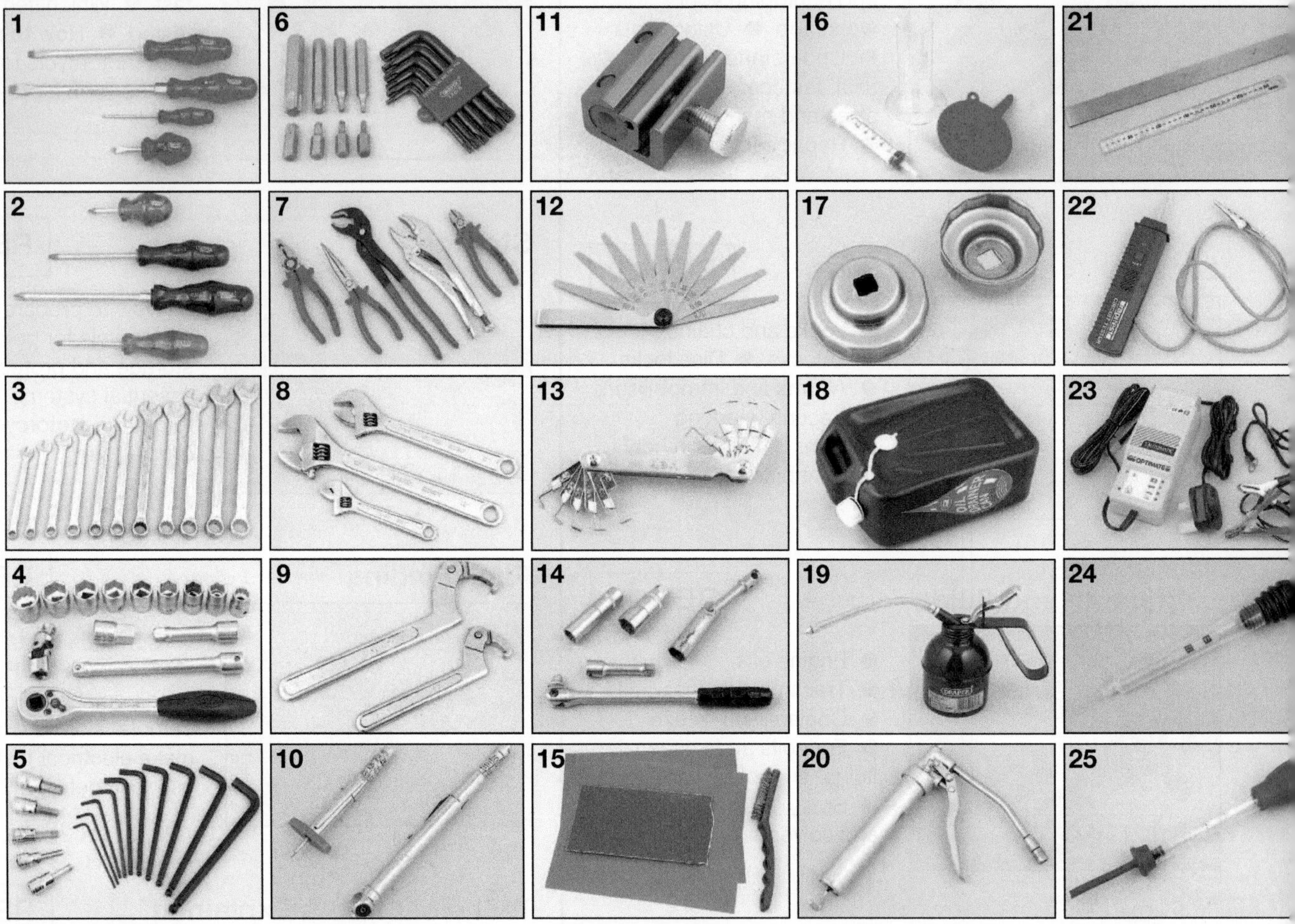

1 *Set of flat-bladed screwdrivers*
2 *Set of Phillips head screwdrivers*
3 *Combination open-end and ring spanners*
4 *Socket set (3/8 inch or 1/2 inch drive)*
5 *Set of Allen keys or bits*
6 *Set of Torx keys or bits*
7 *Pliers, cutters and self-locking grips (Mole grips)*
8 *Adjustable spanners*
9 *C-spanners*
10 *Tread depth gauge and tyre pressure gauge*
11 *Cable oiler clamp*
12 *Feeler gauges*
13 *Spark plug gap measuring tool*
14 *Spark plug spanner or deep plug sockets*
15 *Wire brush and emery paper*
16 *Calibrated syringe, measuring vessel and funnel*
17 *Oil filter adapters*
18 *Oil drainer can or tray*
19 *Pump type oil can*
20 *Grease gun*
21 *Straight-edge and steel rule*
22 *Continuity tester*
23 *Battery charger*
24 *Hydrometer (for batte specific gravity check*
25 *Anti-freeze tester (for liquid-cooled engines*

## Repair and overhaul tools

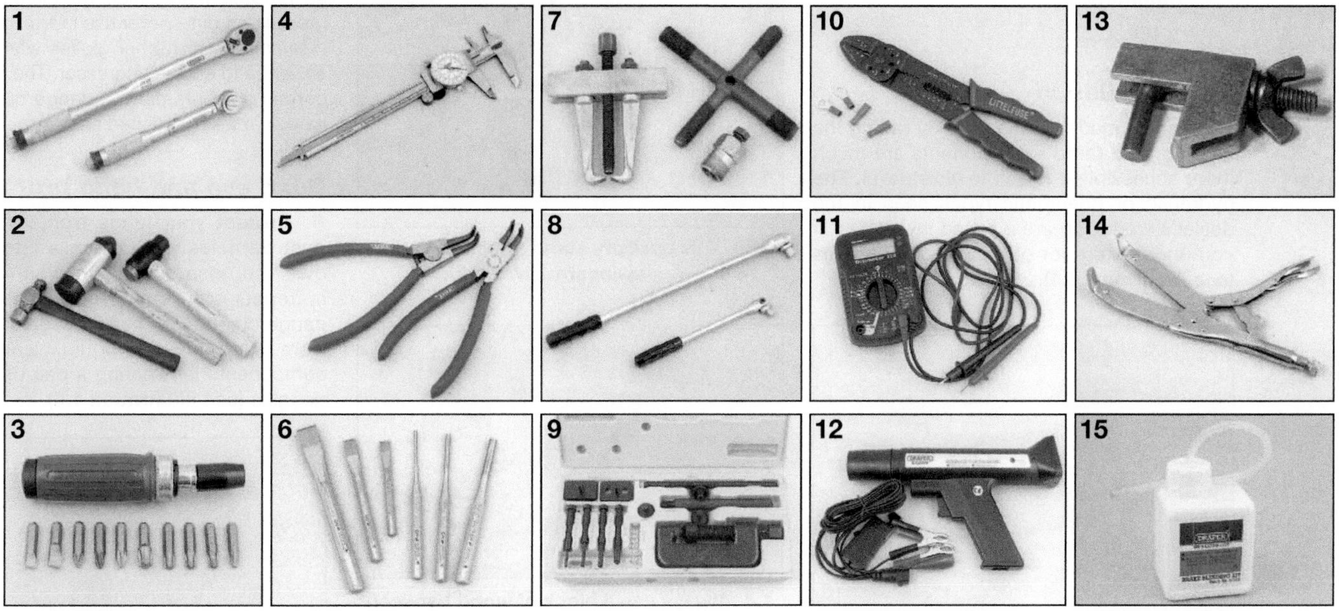

1 *Torque wrench (small and mid-ranges)*
2 *Conventional, plastic or soft-faced hammers*
3 *Impact driver set*
4 *Vernier gauge*
5 *Circlip pliers (internal and external, or combination)*
6 *Set of cold chisels and punches*
7 *Selection of pullers*
8 *Breaker bars*
9 *Chain breaking/riveting tool set*
10 *Wire stripper and crimper tool*
11 *Multimeter (measures amps, volts and ohms)*
12 *Stroboscope (for dynamic timing checks)*
13 *Hose clamp (wingnut type shown)*
14 *Clutch holding tool*
15 *One-man brake/clutch bleeder kit*

## Specialist tools

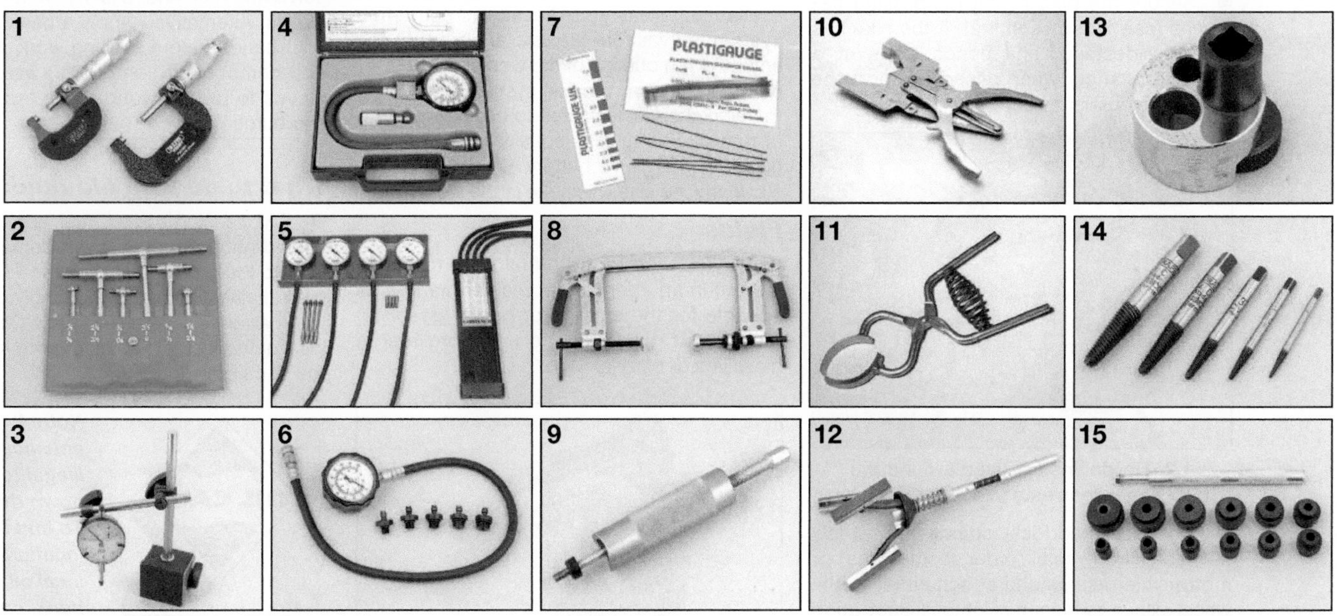


1 *Micrometers (external type)*
2 *Telescoping gauges*
3 *Dial gauge*
4 *Cylinder compression gauge*
5 *Vacuum gauges (left) or manometer (right)*
6 *Oil pressure gauge*
7 *Plastigauge kit*
8 *Valve spring compressor (4-stroke engines)*
9 *Piston pin drawbolt tool*
10 *Piston ring removal and installation tool*
11 *Piston ring clamp*
12 *Cylinder bore hone (stone type shown)*
13 *Stud extractor*
14 *Screw extractor set*
15 *Bearing driver set*

## 1 Workshop equipment and facilities

### The workbench

● Work is made much easier by raising the bike up on a ramp - components are much more accessible if raised to waist level. The hydraulic or pneumatic types seen in the dealer's workshop are a sound investment if you undertake a lot of repairs or overhauls **(see illustration 1.1)**.

**1.1 Hydraulic motorcycle ramp**

● If raised off ground level, the bike must be supported on the ramp to avoid it falling. Most ramps incorporate a front wheel locating clamp which can be adjusted to suit different diameter wheels. When tightening the clamp, take care not to mark the wheel rim or damage the tyre - use wood blocks on each side to prevent this.

● Secure the bike to the ramp using tie-downs **(see illustration 1.2)**. If the bike has only a sidestand, and hence leans at a dangerous angle when raised, support the bike on an auxiliary stand.

**1.2 Tie-downs are used around the passenger footrests to secure the bike**

● Auxiliary (paddock) stands are widely available from mail order companies or motorcycle dealers and attach either to the wheel axle or swingarm pivot **(see illustration 1.3)**. If the motorcycle has a centrestand, you can support it under the crankcase to prevent it toppling whilst either wheel is removed **(see illustration 1.4)**.

**1.3 This auxiliary stand attaches to the swingarm pivot**

**1.4 Always use a block of wood between the engine and jack head when supporting the engine in this way**

### Fumes and fire

● Refer to the Safety first! page at the beginning of the manual for full details. Make sure your workshop is equipped with a fire extinguisher suitable for fuel-related fires (Class B fire - flammable liquids) - it is not sufficient to have a water-filled extinguisher.

● Always ensure adequate ventilation is available. Unless an exhaust gas extraction system is available for use, ensure that the engine is run outside of the workshop.

● If working on the fuel system, make sure the workshop is ventilated to avoid a build-up of fumes. This applies equally to fume build-up when charging a battery. Do not smoke or allow anyone else to smoke in the workshop.

### Fluids

● If you need to drain fuel from the tank, store it in an approved container marked as suitable for the storage of petrol (gasoline) **(see illustration 1.5)**. Do not store fuel in glass jars or bottles.

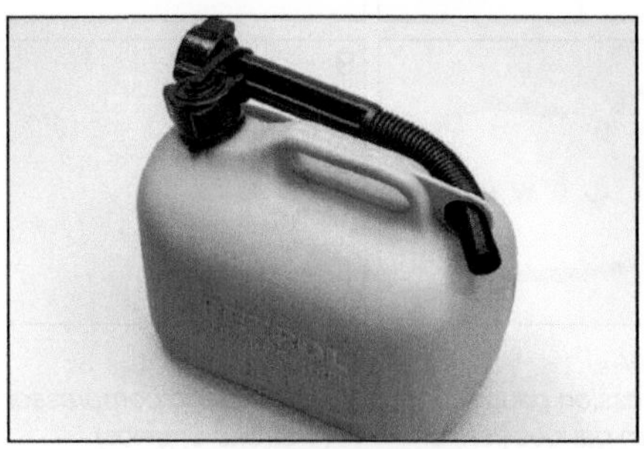

**1.5 Use an approved can only for storing petrol (gasoline)**

solvents which have a high flash-point, s as paraffin (kerosene), for cleaning off grease and dirt - never use petrol (gasoline cleaning. Wear rubber gloves when hanc solvent and engine degreaser. The fumes certain solvents can be dangerous - alw work in a well-ventilated area.

### Dust, eye and hand protection

● Protect your lungs from inhalatio dust particles by wearing a filtering m over the nose and mouth. Many fricti materials still contain asbestos whic dangerous to your health. Protect your from spouts of liquid and spr components by wearing a pair of protec goggles **(see illustration 1.6)**.

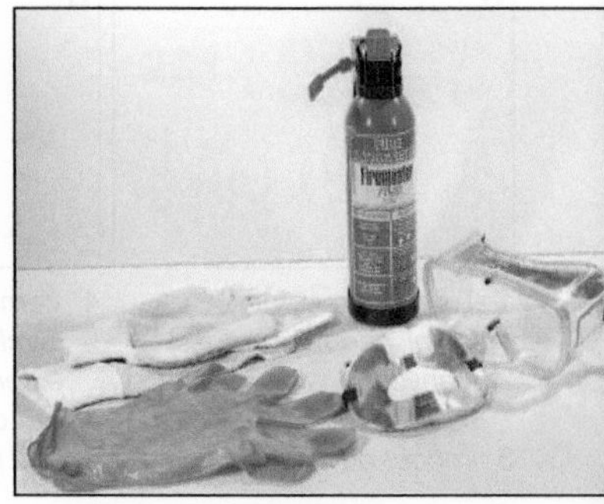

**1.6 A fire extinguisher, goggles, mas and protective gloves should be at ha in the workshop**

● Protect your hands from contact solvents, fuel and oils by wearing rul gloves. Alternatively apply a barrier crea your hands before starting work. If hanc hot components or fluids, wear suit gloves to protect your hands from scal and burns.

### What to do with old fluids

● Old cleaning solvent, fuel, coolant anc should not be poured down domestic dı or onto the ground. Package the fluid up ir oil containers, label it accordingly, and ta to a garage or disposal facility. Contact local authority for location of such sites or the oil care hotline.

OIL CARE
FOLLOW THE CODE
OIL BANK LINE
0800 66 33 66
www.oilbankline.org.uk

***Note: It is antisocial and illegal to dump down the drair To find the location of you local oil recycl bank, call this number free.***

***In the USA, note that any oil suppli must accept used oil for recycling.***

## 2 Fasteners - screws, bolts and nuts

### Fastener types and applications

#### Bolts and screws

● Fastener head types are either of hexagonal, Torx or splined design, with internal and external versions of each type **(see illustrations 2.1 and 2.2);** splined head fasteners are not in common use on motorcycles. The conventional slotted or Phillips head design is used for certain screws. Bolt or screw length is always measured from the underside of the head to the end of the item **(see illustration 2.11)**.

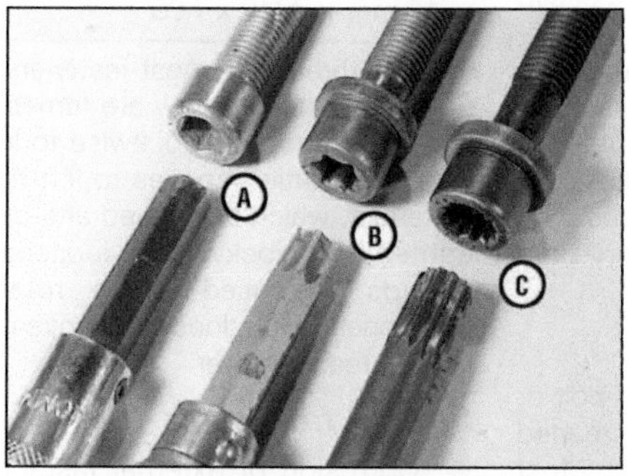


**2.1 Internal hexagon/Allen (A), Torx (B) and splined (C) fasteners, with corresponding bits**

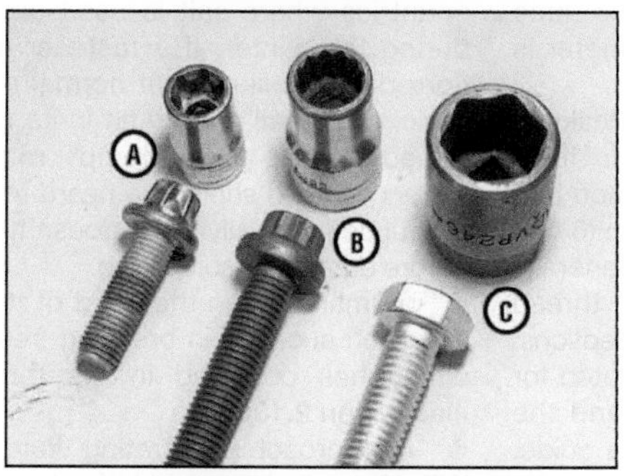


**2.2 External Torx (A), splined (B) and hexagon (C) fasteners, with corresponding sockets**

● Certain fasteners on the motorcycle have a tensile marking on their heads, the higher the marking the stronger the fastener. High tensile fasteners generally carry a 10 or higher marking. Never replace a high tensile fastener with one of a lower tensile strength.

#### Washers (see illustration 2.3)

● Plain washers are used between a fastener head and a component to prevent damage to the component or to spread the load when torque is applied. Plain washers can also be used as spacers or shims in certain assemblies. Copper or aluminium plain washers are often used as sealing washers on drain plugs.

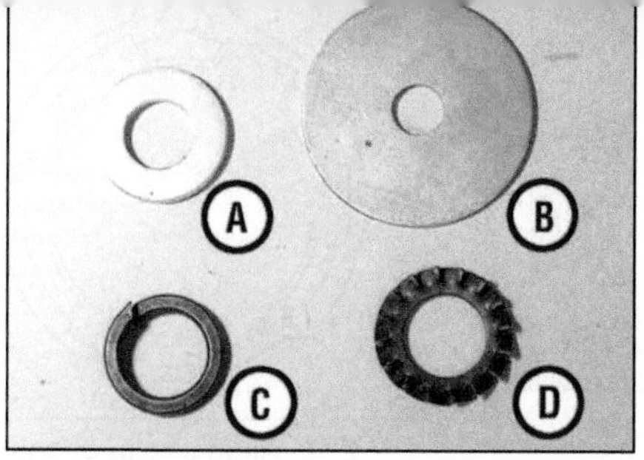


**2.3 Plain washer (A), penny washer (B), spring washer (C) and serrated washer (D)**

● The split-ring spring washer works by applying axial tension between the fastener head and component. If flattened, it is fatigued and must be renewed. If a plain (flat) washer is used on the fastener, position the spring washer between the fastener and the plain washer.

● Serrated star type washers dig into the fastener and component faces, preventing loosening. They are often used on electrical earth (ground) connections to the frame.

● Cone type washers (sometimes called Belleville) are conical and when tightened apply axial tension between the fastener head and component. They must be installed with the dished side against the component and often carry an OUTSIDE marking on their outer face. If flattened, they are fatigued and must be renewed.

● Tab washers are used to lock plain nuts or bolts on a shaft. A portion of the tab washer is bent up hard against one flat of the nut or bolt to prevent it loosening. Due to the tab washer being deformed in use, a new tab washer should be used every time it is disturbed.

● Wave washers are used to take up endfloat on a shaft. They provide light springing and prevent excessive side-to-side play of a component. Can be found on rocker arm shafts.

#### Nuts and split pins

● Conventional plain nuts are usually six-sided **(see illustration 2.4)**. They are sized by thread diameter and pitch. High tensile nuts carry a number on one end to denote their tensile strength.

**2.4 Plain nut (A), shouldered locknut (B), nylon insert nut (C) and castellated nut (D)**

insert, or two spring metal tabs, or a shoulder which is staked into a groove in the shaft - their advantage over conventional plain nuts is a resistance to loosening due to vibration. The nylon insert type can be used a number of times, but must be renewed when the friction of the nylon insert is reduced, ie when the nut spins freely on the shaft. The spring tab type can be reused unless the tabs are damaged. The shouldered type must be renewed every time it is disturbed.

● Split pins (cotter pins) are used to lock a castellated nut to a shaft or to prevent slackening of a plain nut. Common applications are wheel axles and brake torque arms. Because the split pin arms are deformed to lock around the nut a new split pin must always be used on installation - always fit the correct size split pin which will fit snugly in the shaft hole. Make sure the split pin arms are correctly located around the nut **(see illustrations 2.5 and 2.6)**.

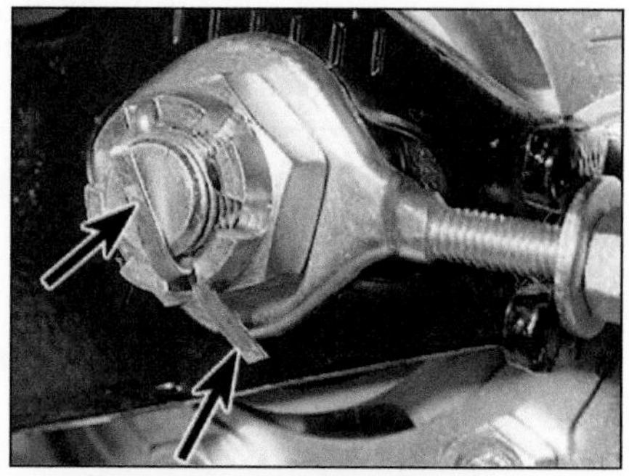

**2.5 Bend split pin (cotter pin) arms as shown (arrows) to secure a castellated nut**

**2.6 Bend split pin (cotter pin) arms as shown to secure a plain nut**

***Caution: If the castellated nut slots do not align with the shaft hole after tightening to the torque setting, tighten the nut until the next slot aligns with the hole - never slacken the nut to align its slot.***

● R-pins (shaped like the letter R), or slip pins as they are sometimes called, are sprung and can be reused if they are otherwise in good condition. Always install R-pins with their closed end facing forwards **(see illustration 2.7)**.

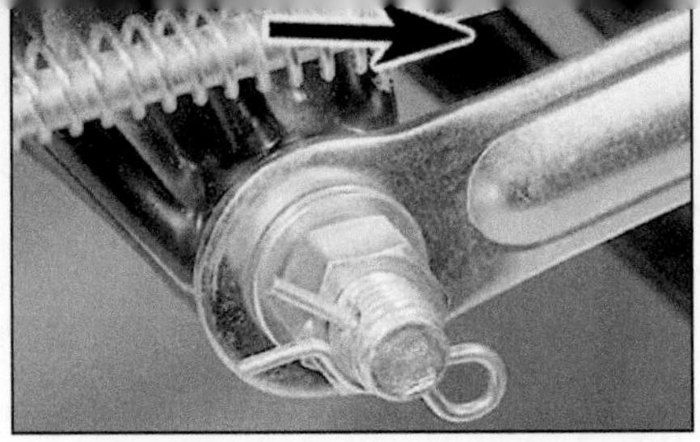

2.7 Correct fitting of R-pin. Arrow indicates forward direction

## Circlips (see illustration 2.8)

● Circlips (sometimes called snap-rings) are used to retain components on a shaft or in a housing and have corresponding external or internal ears to permit removal. Parallel-sided (machined) circlips can be installed either way round in their groove, whereas stamped circlips (which have a chamfered edge on one face) must be installed with the chamfer facing away from the direction of thrust load **(see illustration 2.9)**.

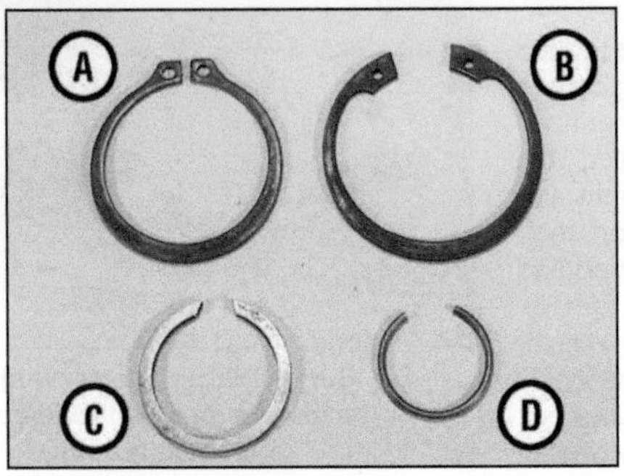


**2.8 External stamped circlip (A), internal stamped circlip (B), machined circlip (C) and wire circlip (D)**

● Always use circlip pliers to remove and install circlips; expand or compress them just enough to remove them. After installation, rotate the circlip in its groove to ensure it is securely seated. If installing a circlip on a splined shaft, always align its opening with a shaft channel to ensure the circlip ends are well supported and unlikely to catch **(see illustration 2.10)**.

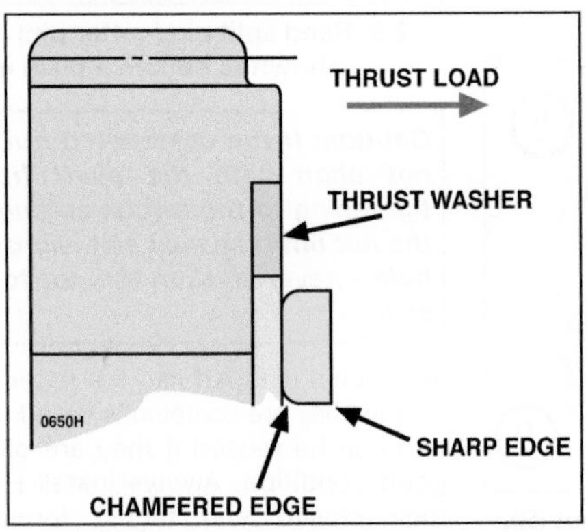


**2.9 Correct fitting of a stamped circlip**

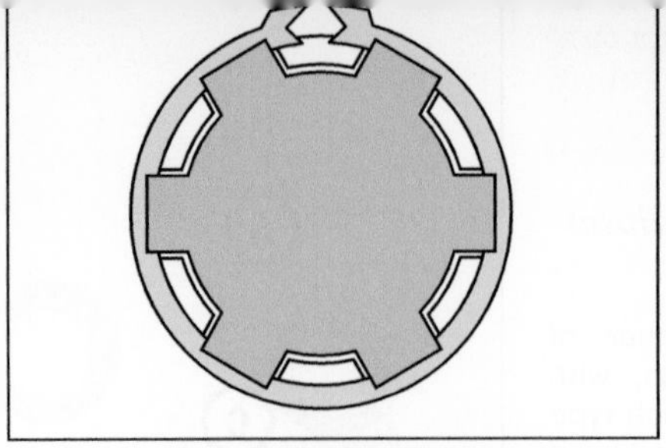

**2.10 Align circlip opening with shaft channel**

● Circlips can wear due to the thrust of components and become loose in their grooves, with the subsequent danger of becoming dislodged in operation. For this reason, renewal is advised every time a circlip is disturbed.

● Wire circlips are commonly used as piston pin retaining clips. If a removal tang is provided, long-nosed pliers can be used to dislodge them, otherwise careful use of a small flat-bladed screwdriver is necessary. Wire circlips should be renewed every time they are disturbed.

## *Thread diameter and pitch*

● Diameter of a male thread (screw, bolt or stud) is the outside diameter of the threaded portion **(see illustration 2.11)**. Most motorcycle manufacturers use the ISO (International Standards Organisation) metric system expressed in millimetres, eg M6 refers to a 6 mm diameter thread. Sizing is the same for nuts, except that the thread diameter is measured across the valleys of the nut.

● Pitch is the distance between the peaks of the thread **(see illustration 2.11)**. It is expressed in millimetres, thus a common bolt size may be expressed as 6.0 x 1.0 mm (6 mm thread diameter and 1 mm pitch). Generally pitch increases in proportion to thread diameter, although there are always exceptions.

● Thread diameter and pitch are related for conventional fastener applications and the accompanying table can be used as a guide. Additionally, the AF (Across Flats), spanner or socket size dimension of the bolt or nut **(see illustration 2.11)** is linked to thread and pitch specification. Thread pitch can be measured with a thread gauge **(see illustration 2.12)**.

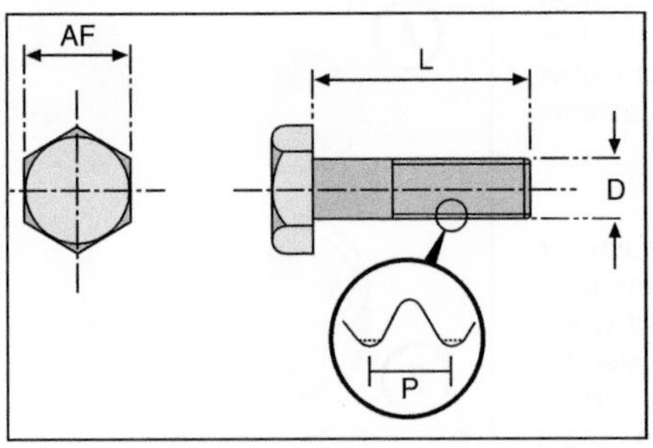


**2.11 Fastener length (L), thread diameter (D), thread pitch (P) and head size (AF)**

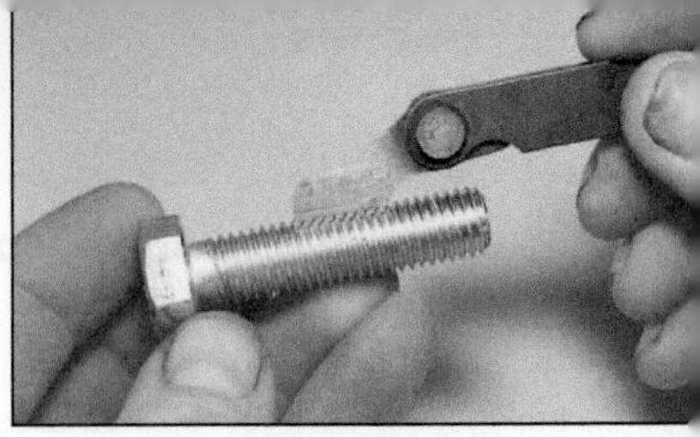

**2.12 Using a thread gauge to measure pitch**

| AF size | Thread diameter x pitch (mm |
|---|---|
| 8 mm | M5 x 0.8 |
| 8 mm | M6 x 1.0 |
| 10 mm | M6 x 1.0 |
| 12 mm | M8 x 1.25 |
| 14 mm | M10 x 1.25 |
| 17 mm | M12 x 1.25 |

● The threads of most fasteners are of right-hand type, ie they are turned clockw to tighten and anti-clockwise to loosen. reverse situation applies to left-hand thr fasteners, which are turned anti-clockwise tighten and clockwise to loosen. Left-h threads are used where rotation of component might loosen a conventional ri hand thread fastener.

## *Seized fasteners*

● Corrosion of external fasteners due water or reaction between two dissim metals can occur over a period of time. It build up sooner in wet conditions or countries where salt is used on the ro during the winter. If a fastener is seve corroded it is likely that normal methods removal will fail and result in its head be ruined. When you attempt removal, fastener thread should be heard to crack and unscrew easily - if it doesn't, stop th before damaging something.

● A smart tap on the head of the faste will often succeed in breaking free corros which has occurred in the threads ( **illustration 2.13)**.

● An aerosol penetrating fluid (such WD-40) applied the night beforehand may w its way down into the thread and ease remo Depending on the location, you may be abl make up a Plasticine well around the faste head and fill it with penetrating fluid.

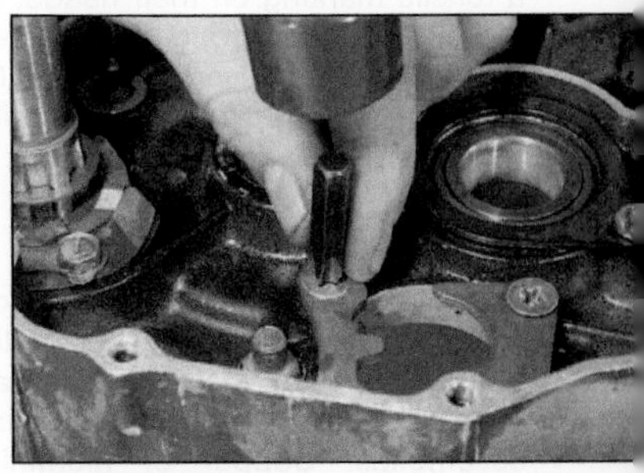

**2.13 A sharp tap on the head of a faste will often break free a corroded threa**

component, corrosion will most likely not be a problem due to the well lubricated environment. However, components can be very tight and an impact driver is a useful tool in freeing them **(see illustration 2.14)**.

**2.14 Using an impact driver to free a fastener**

- Where corrosion has occurred between dissimilar metals (eg steel and aluminium alloy), the application of heat to the fastener head will create a disproportionate expansion rate between the two metals and break the seizure caused by the corrosion. Whether heat can be applied depends on the location of the fastener - any surrounding components likely to be damaged must first be removed **(see illustration 2.15)**. Heat can be applied using a paint stripper heat gun or clothes iron, or by immersing the component in boiling water - wear protective gloves to prevent scalding or burns to the hands.

**2.15 Using heat to free a seized fastener**

- As a last resort, it is possible to use a hammer and cold chisel to work the fastener head unscrewed **(see illustration 2.16)**. This will damage the fastener, but more importantly extreme care must be taken not to damage the surrounding component.

> ***Caution: Remember that the component being secured is generally of more value than the bolt, nut or screw - when the fastener is freed, do not unscrew it with force, instead work the fastener back and forth when resistance is felt to prevent thread damage.***

**2.16 Using a hammer and chisel to free a seized fastener**

## *Broken fasteners and damaged heads*

- If the shank of a broken bolt or screw is accessible you can grip it with self-locking grips. The knurled wheel type stud extractor tool or self-gripping stud puller tool is particularly useful for removing the long studs which screw into the cylinder mouth surface of the crankcase or bolts and screws from which the head has broken off **(see illustration 2.17)**. Studs can also be removed by locking two nuts together on the threaded end of the stud and using a spanner on the lower nut **(see illustration 2.18)**.

**2.17 Using a stud extractor tool to remove a broken crankcase stud**

**2.18 Two nuts can be locked together to unscrew a stud from a component**

- A bolt or screw which has broken off below or level with the casing must be extracted using a screw extractor set. Centre punch the fastener to centralise the drill bit, then drill a hole in the fastener **(see illustration 2.19)**. Select a drill bit which is approximately half to three-quarters the

**2.19 When using a screw extractor, first drill a hole in the fastener . . .**

diameter of the fastener and drill to a depth which will accommodate the extractor. Use the largest size extractor possible, but avoid leaving too small a wall thickness otherwise the extractor will merely force the fastener walls outwards wedging it in the casing thread.

- If a spiral type extractor is used, thread it anti-clockwise into the fastener. As it is screwed in, it will grip the fastener and unscrew it from the casing **(see illustration 2.20)**.

**2.20 . . . then thread the extractor anti-clockwise into the fastener**

- If a taper type extractor is used, tap it into the fastener so that it is firmly wedged in place. Unscrew the extractor (anti-clockwise) to draw the fastener out.

> ***Warning: Stud extractors are very hard and may break off in the fastener if care is not taken - ask an engineer about spark erosion if this happens.***

- Alternatively, the broken bolt/screw can be drilled out and the hole retapped for an oversize bolt/screw or a diamond-section thread insert. It is essential that the drilling is carried out squarely and to the correct depth, otherwise the casing may be ruined - if in doubt, entrust the work to an engineer.
- Bolts and nuts with rounded corners cause the correct size spanner or socket to slip when force is applied. Of the types of spanner/socket available always use a six-point type rather than an eight or twelve-point type - better grip

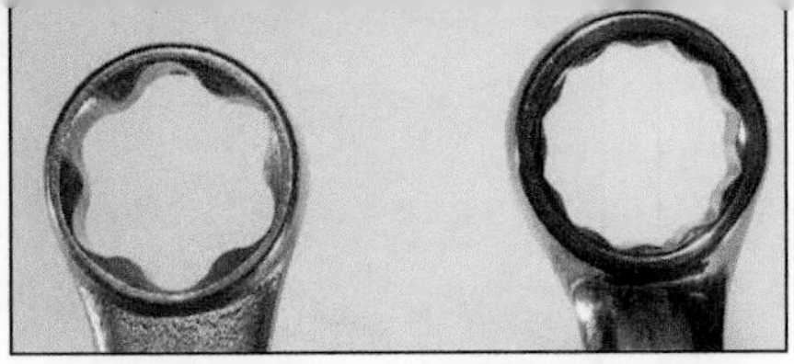

**2.21 Comparison of surface drive ring spanner (left) with 12-point type (right)**

is obtained. Surface drive spanners grip the middle of the hex flats, rather than the corners, and are thus good in cases of damaged heads **(see illustration 2.21)**.

● Slotted-head or Phillips-head screws are often damaged by the use of the wrong size screwdriver. Allen-head and Torx-head screws are much less likely to sustain damage. If enough of the screw head is exposed you can use a hacksaw to cut a slot in its head and then use a conventional flat-bladed screwdriver to remove it. Alternatively use a hammer and cold chisel to tap the head of the fastener around to slacken it. Always replace damaged fasteners with new ones, preferably Torx or Allen-head type.

***A dab of valve grinding compound between the screw head and screw-driver tip will often give a good grip.***

## *Thread repair*

● Threads (particularly those in aluminium alloy components) can be damaged by overtightening, being assembled with dirt in the threads, or from a component working loose and vibrating. Eventually the thread will fail completely, and it will be impossible to tighten the fastener.

● If a thread is damaged or clogged with old locking compound it can be renovated with a thread repair tool (thread chaser) **(see illustrations 2.22 and 2.23)**; special thread

**2.22 A thread repair tool being used to correct an internal thread**

**2.23 A thread repair tool being used to correct an external thread**

chasers are available for spark plug hole threads. The tool will not cut a new thread, but clean and true the original thread. Make sure that you use the correct diameter and pitch tool. Similarly, external threads can be cleaned up with a die or a thread restorer file **(see illustration 2.24)**.

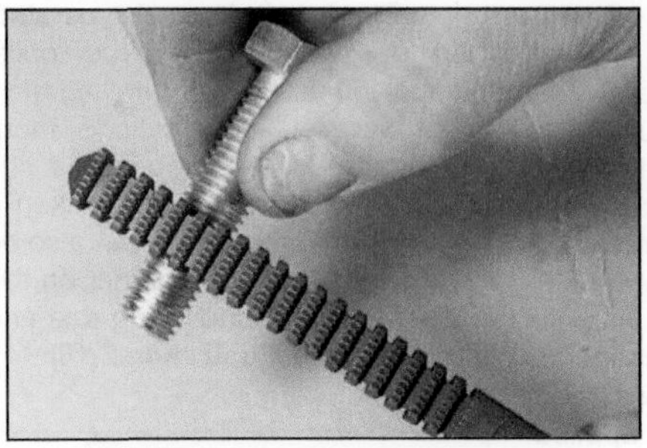

**2.24 Using a thread restorer file**

● It is possible to drill out the old thread and retap the component to the next thread size. This will work where there is enough surrounding material and a new bolt or screw can be obtained. Sometimes, however, this is not possible - such as where the bolt/screw passes through another component which must also be suitably modified, also in cases where a spark plug or oil drain plug cannot be obtained in a larger diameter thread size.

● The diamond-section thread insert (often known by its popular trade name of Heli-Coil) is a simple and effective method of renewing the thread and retaining the original size. A kit can be purchased which contains the tap, insert and installing tool **(see illustration 2.25)**. Drill out the damaged thread with the size drill specified **(see illustration 2.26)**. Carefully retap the thread **(see illustration 2.27)**. Install the

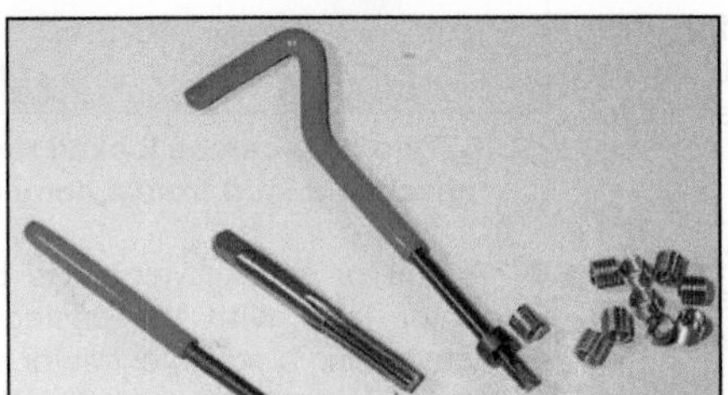

**2.25 Obtain a thread insert kit to suit the thread diameter and pitch required**

**2.26 To install a thread insert, first drill the original thread . . .**

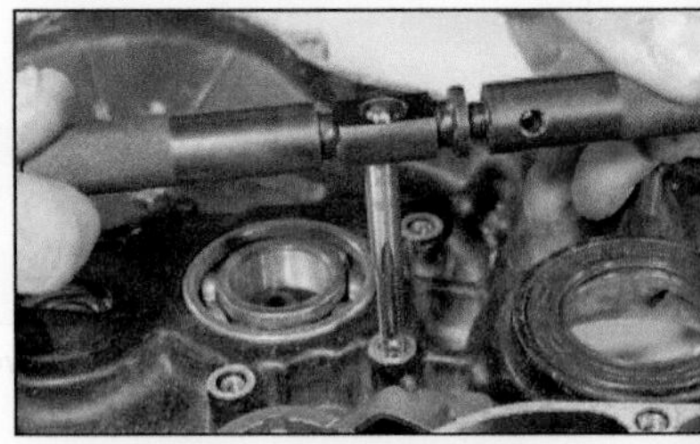

**2.27 . . . tap a new thread . . .**

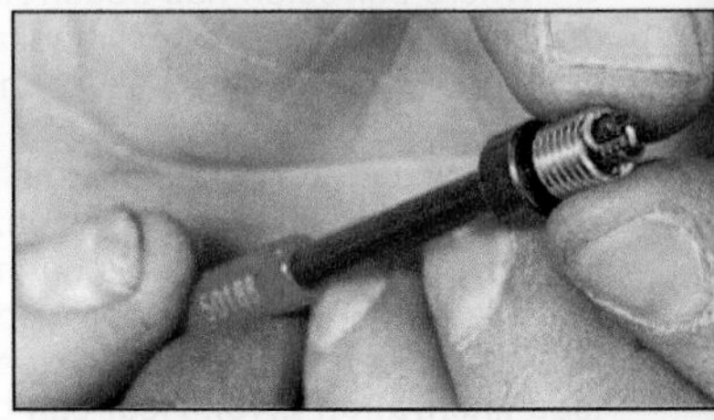

**2.28 . . . fit insert on the installing tool**

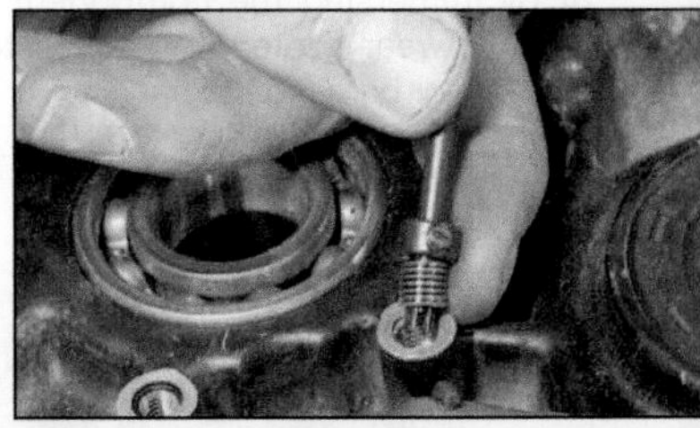

**2.29 . . . and thread into the componen**

**2.30 . . . break off the tang when comp**

insert on the installing tool and thread it sl into place using a light downward pres **(see illustrations 2.28 and 2.29)**. W positioned between a 1/4 and 1/2 turn b the surface withdraw the installing tool and the break-off tool to press down on the t breaking it off **(see illustration 2.30)**.

● There are epoxy thread repair kits o market which can rebuild stripped inte threads, although this repair should nc used on high load-bearing components.

## and sealing compounds

- Locking compounds are used in locations where the fastener is prone to loosening due to vibration or on important safety-related items which might cause loss of control of the motorcycle if they fail. It is also used where important fasteners cannot be secured by other means such as lockwashers or split pins.
- Before applying locking compound, make sure that the threads (internal and external) are clean and dry with all old compound removed. Select a compound to suit the component being secured - a non-permanent general locking and sealing type is suitable for most applications, but a high strength type is needed for permanent fixing of studs in castings. Apply a drop or two of the compound to the first few threads of the fastener, then thread it into place and tighten to the specified torque. Do not apply excessive thread locking compound otherwise the thread may be damaged on subsequent removal.
- Certain fasteners are impregnated with a dry film type coating of locking compound on their threads. Always renew this type of fastener if disturbed.
- Anti-seize compounds, such as copper-based greases, can be applied to protect threads from seizure due to extreme heat and corrosion. A common instance is spark plug threads and exhaust system fasteners.

# 3 Measuring tools and gauges

## Feeler gauges

- Feeler gauges (or blades) are used for measuring small gaps and clearances **(see illustration 3.1)**. They can also be used to measure endfloat (sideplay) of a component on a shaft where access is not possible with a dial gauge.
- Feeler gauge sets should be treated with care and not bent or damaged. They are etched with their size on one face. Keep them clean and very lightly oiled to prevent corrosion build-up.

**3.1 Feeler gauges are used for measuring small gaps and clearances - thickness is marked on one face of gauge**

gauge which is a light sliding fit between the two components. You may need to use two gauges together to measure the clearance accurately.

## Micrometers

- A micrometer is a precision tool capable of measuring to 0.01 or 0.001 of a millimetre. It should always be stored in its case and not in the general toolbox. It must be kept clean and never dropped, otherwise its frame or measuring anvils could be distorted resulting in inaccurate readings.
- External micrometers are used for measuring outside diameters of components and have many more applications than internal micrometers. Micrometers are available in different size ranges, eg 0 to 25 mm, 25 to 50 mm, and upwards in 25 mm steps; some large micrometers have interchangeable anvils to allow a range of measurements to be taken. Generally the largest precision measurement you are likely to take on a motorcycle is the piston diameter.
- Internal micrometers (or bore micrometers) are used for measuring inside diameters, such as valve guides and cylinder bores. Telescoping gauges and small hole gauges are used in conjunction with an external micro-meter, whereas the more expensive internal micrometers have their own measuring device.

### External micrometer

**Note:** *The conventional analogue type instrument is described. Although much easier to read, digital micrometers are considerably more expensive.*

- Always check the calibration of the micrometer before use. With the anvils closed (0 to 25 mm type) or set over a test gauge (for

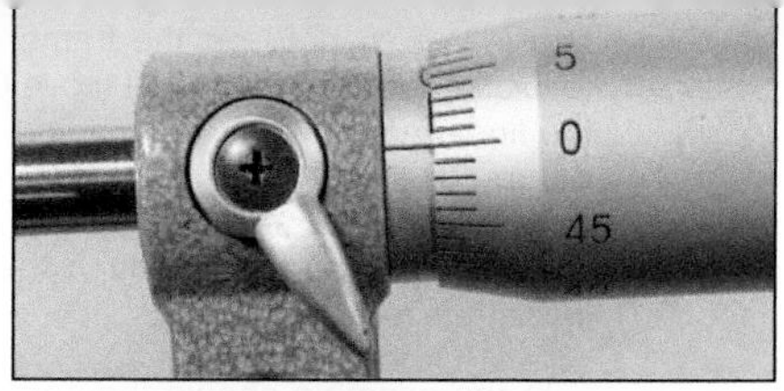


**3.2 Check micrometer calibration before use**

the larger types) the scale should read zero **(see illustration 3.2)**; make sure that the anvils (and test piece) are clean first. Any discrepancy can be adjusted by referring to the instructions supplied with the tool. Remember that the micrometer is a precision measuring tool - don't force the anvils closed, use the ratchet (4) on the end of the micrometer to close it. In this way, a measured force is always applied.
- To use, first make sure that the item being measured is clean. Place the anvil of the micrometer (1) against the item and use the thimble (2) to bring the spindle (3) lightly into contact with the other side of the item **(see illustration 3.3)**. Don't tighten the thimble down because this will damage the micrometer - instead use the ratchet (4) on the end of the micrometer. The ratchet mechanism applies a measured force preventing damage to the instrument.
- The micrometer is read by referring to the linear scale on the sleeve and the annular scale on the thimble. Read off the sleeve first to obtain the base measurement, then add the fine measurement from the thimble to obtain the overall reading. The linear scale on the sleeve represents the measuring range of the micrometer (eg 0 to 25 mm). The annular scale

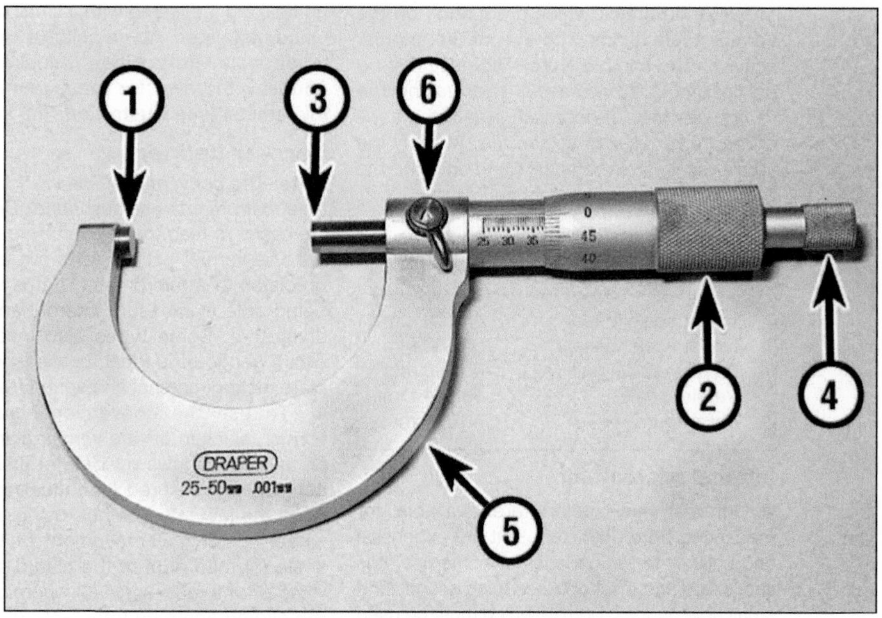


**3.3 Micrometer component parts**

*1 Anvil*
*2 Thimble*
*3 Spindle*
*4 Ratchet*
*5 Frame*
*6 Locking lever*

on the thimble will be in graduations of 0.01 mm (or as marked on the frame) - one full revolution of the thimble will move 0.5 mm on the linear scale. Take the reading where the datum line on the sleeve intersects the thimble's scale. Always position the eye directly above the scale otherwise an inaccurate reading will result.

In the example shown the item measures 2.95 mm **(see illustration 3.4)**:

| | |
|---|---|
| Linear scale | 2.00 mm |
| Linear scale | 0.50 mm |
| Annular scale | 0.45 mm |
| Total figure | **2.95 mm** |

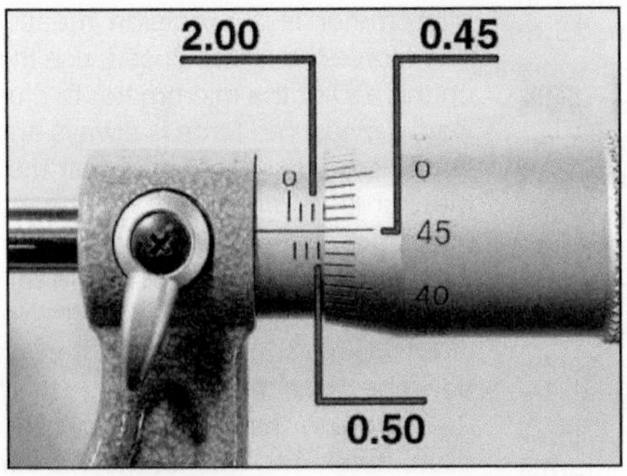


**3.4 Micrometer reading of 2.95 mm**

Most micrometers have a locking lever (6) on the frame to hold the setting in place, allowing the item to be removed from the micrometer.

- Some micrometers have a vernier scale on their sleeve, providing an even finer measurement to be taken, in 0.001 increments of a millimetre. Take the sleeve and thimble measurement as described above, then check which graduation on the vernier scale aligns with that of the annular scale on the thimble **Note:** *The eye must be perpendicular to the scale when taking the vernier reading - if necessary rotate the body of the micrometer to ensure this.* Multiply the vernier scale figure by 0.001 and add it to the base and fine measurement figures.

In the example shown the item measures 46.994 mm **(see illustrations 3.5 and 3.6)**:

| | |
|---|---|
| Linear scale (base) | 46.000 mm |
| Linear scale (base) | 00.500 mm |
| Annular scale (fine) | 00.490 mm |
| Vernier scale | 00.004 mm |
| Total figure | **46.994 mm** |

### Internal micrometer

- Internal micrometers are available for measuring bore diameters, but are expensive and unlikely to be available for home use. It is suggested that a set of telescoping gauges and small hole gauges, both of which must be used with an external micrometer, will suffice for taking internal measurements on a motorcycle.
- Telescoping gauges can be used to measure internal diameters of components. Select a gauge with the correct size range, make sure its ends are clean and insert it into the bore. Expand the gauge, then lock its position and withdraw it from the bore **(see illustration 3.7)**. Measure across the gauge ends with a micrometer **(see illustration 3.8)**.
- Very small diameter bores (such as valve guides) are measured with a small hole gauge. Once adjusted to a slip-fit inside the component, its position is locked and the gauge withdrawn for measurement with a micrometer **(see illustrations 3.9 and 3.10)**.

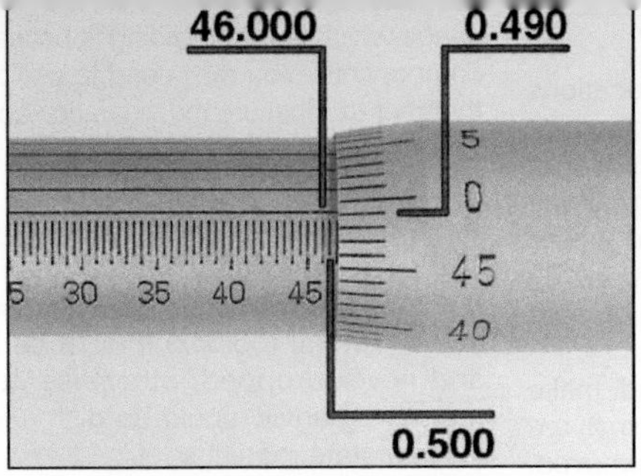


**3.5 Micrometer reading of 46.99 mm on linear and annular scales . . .**

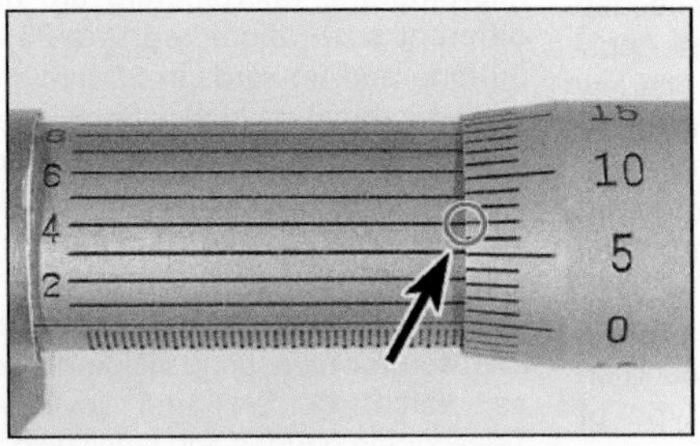

**3.6 . . . and 0.004 mm on vernier scale**

### Vernier caliper

**Note:** *The conventional linear and dial gauge type instruments are described. Digital types are easier to read, but are far more expensive.*

- The vernier caliper does not provide the precision of a micrometer, but is versatile in being able to measure internal and external diameters. Some types also incorporate a depth gauge. It is ideal for measuring clutch plate friction material and spring free lengths.
- To use the conventional linear scale vernier, slacken off the vernier clamp screws (1) and set its jaws over (2), or inside (3), the item to be measured **(see illustration 3.11)**. Slide the jaw into contact, using the thumb-wheel (4) for fine movement of the sliding scale (5) then tighten the clamp screws (1). Read off the main scale (6) where the zero on the sliding scale (5) intersects it, taking the whole number to the left of the zero; this provides the base measurement. View along the sliding scale and select the division which

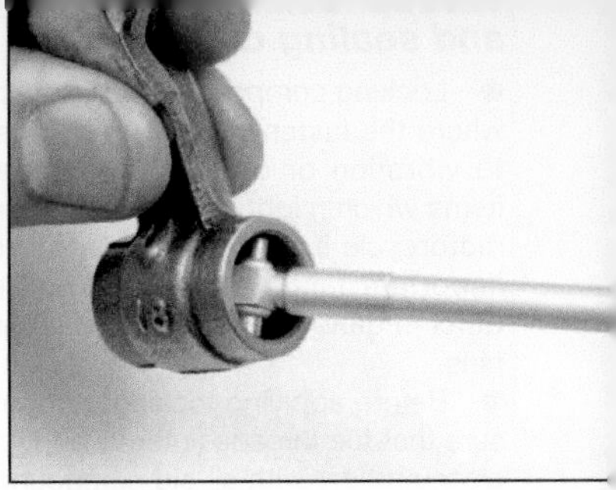

**3.7 Expand the telescoping gauge in the bore, lock its position . . .**

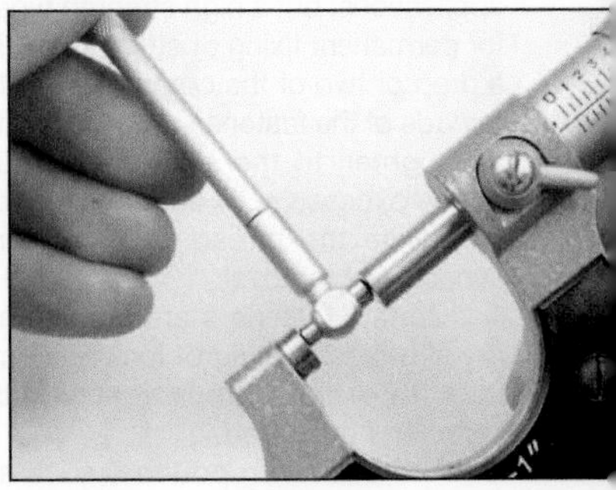

**3.8 . . . then measure the gauge with a micrometer**

**3.9 Expand the small hole gauge in the bore, lock its position . . .**

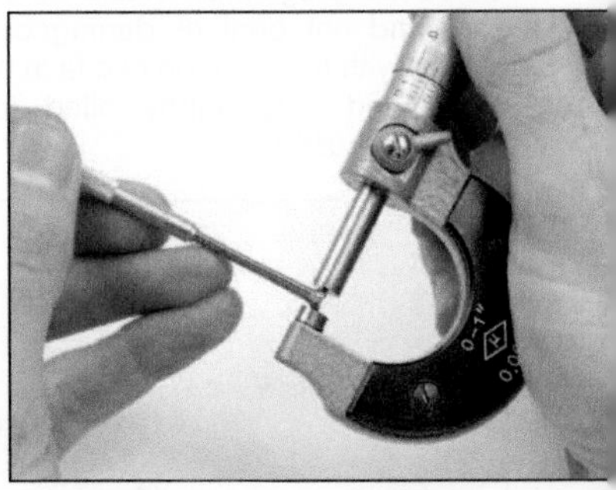

**3.10 . . . then measure the gauge with a micrometer**

lines up exactly with any of the divisions the main scale, noting that the divisi usually represents 0.02 of a millimetre. this fine measurement to the b measurement to obtain the total reading.

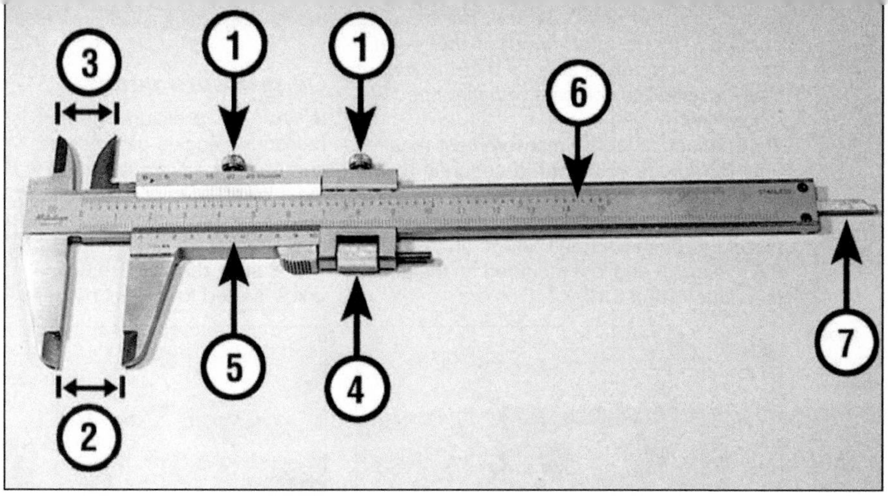


**3.11 Vernier component parts (linear gauge)**

*1 Clamp screws*
*2 External jaws*
*3 Internal jaws*
*4 Thumbwheel*
*5 Sliding scale*
*6 Main scale*
*7 Depth gauge*

In the example shown the item measures 55.92 mm **(see illustration 3.12)**:

| | |
|---|---|
| Base measurement | 55.00 mm |
| Fine measurement | 00.92 mm |
| Total figure | **55.92 mm** |

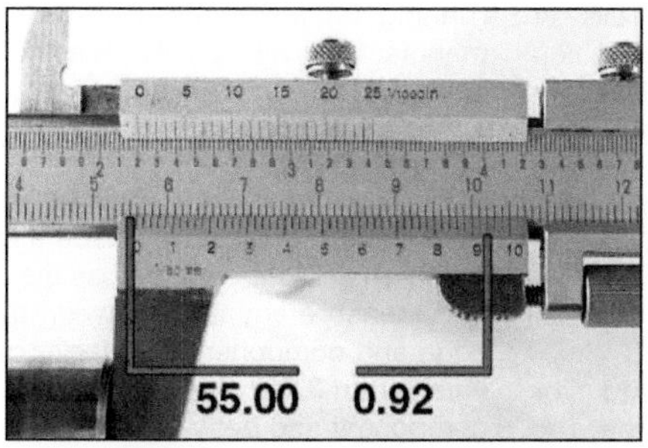


**3.12 Vernier gauge reading of 55.92 mm**

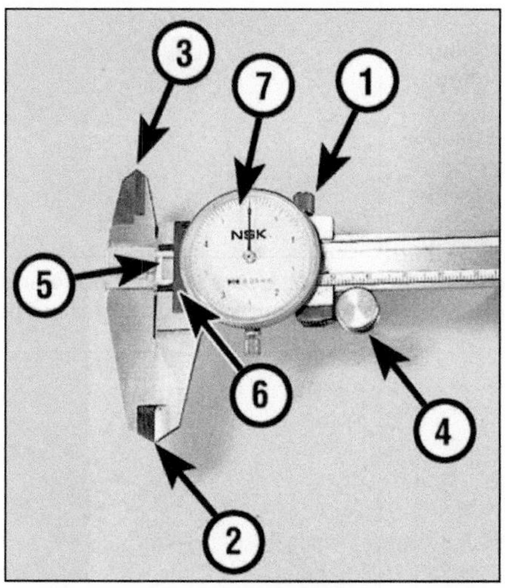


**3.13 Vernier component parts (dial gauge)**

*1 Clamp screw*
*2 External jaws*
*3 Internal jaws*
*4 Thumbwheel*
*5 Main scale*
*6 Sliding scale*
*7 Dial gauge*

- Some vernier calipers are equipped with a dial gauge for fine measurement. Before use, check that the jaws are clean, then close them fully and check that the dial gauge reads zero. If necessary adjust the gauge ring accordingly. Slacken the vernier clamp screw (1) and set its jaws over (2), or inside (3), the item to be measured **(see illustration 3.13)**. Slide the jaws into contact, using the thumbwheel (4) for fine movement. Read off the main scale (5) where the edge of the sliding scale (6) intersects it, taking the whole number to the left of the zero; this provides the base measurement. Read off the needle position on the dial gauge (7) scale to provide the fine measurement; each division represents 0.05 of a millimetre. Add this fine measurement to the base measurement to obtain the total reading.

In the example shown the item measures 55.95 mm **(see illustration 3.14)**:

| | |
|---|---|
| Base measurement | 55.00 mm |
| Fine measurement | 00.95 mm |
| Total figure | **55.95 mm** |

**3.14 Vernier gauge reading of 55.95 mm**

- Plastigauge is a plastic material which can be compressed between two surfaces to measure the oil clearance between them. The width of the compressed Plastigauge is measured against a calibrated scale to determine the clearance.
- Common uses of Plastigauge are for measuring the clearance between crankshaft journal and main bearing inserts, between crankshaft journal and big-end bearing inserts, and between camshaft and bearing surfaces. The following example describes big-end oil clearance measurement.
- Handle the Plastigauge material carefully to prevent distortion. Using a sharp knife, cut a length which corresponds with the width of the bearing being measured and place it carefully across the journal so that it is parallel with the shaft **(see illustration 3.15)**. Carefully install both bearing shells and the connecting rod. Without rotating the rod on the journal tighten its bolts or nuts (as applicable) to the specified torque. The connecting rod and bearings are then disassembled and the crushed Plastigauge examined.

**3.15 Plastigauge placed across shaft journal**

- Using the scale provided in the Plastigauge kit, measure the width of the material to determine the oil clearance **(see illustration 3.16)**. Always remove all traces of Plastigauge after use using your fingernails.

***Caution: Arriving at the correct clearance demands that the assembly is torqued correctly, according to the settings and sequence (where applicable) provided by the motorcycle manufacturer.***

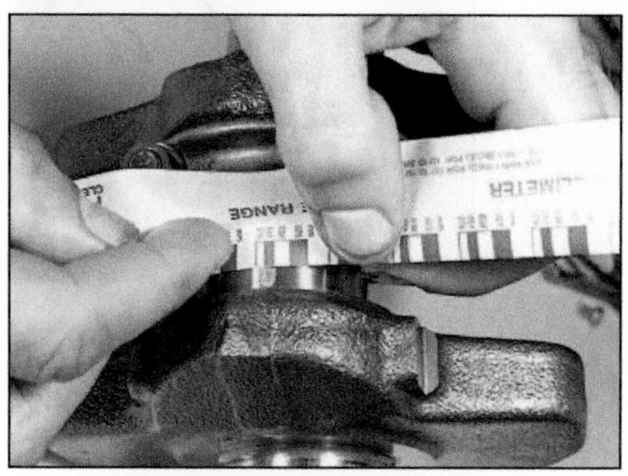

**3.16 Measuring the width of the crushed Plastigauge**

### *(Dial Test Indicator)*

- A dial gauge can be used to accurately measure small amounts of movement. Typical uses are measuring shaft runout or shaft endfloat (sideplay) and setting piston position for ignition timing on two-strokes. A dial gauge set usually comes with a range of different probes and adapters and mounting equipment.
- The gauge needle must point to zero when at rest. Rotate the ring around its periphery to zero the gauge.
- Check that the gauge is capable of reading the extent of movement in the work. Most gauges have a small dial set in the face which records whole millimetres of movement as well as the fine scale around the face periphery which is calibrated in 0.01 mm divisions. Read off the small dial first to obtain the base measurement, then add the measurement from the fine scale to obtain the total reading.

In the example shown the gauge reads 1.48 mm **(see illustration 3.17)**:

| | |
|---|---|
| Base measurement | 1.00 mm |
| Fine measurement | 0.48 mm |
| Total figure | **1.48 mm** |

**3.17 Dial gauge reading of 1.48 mm**

- If measuring shaft runout, the shaft must be supported in vee-blocks and the gauge mounted on a stand perpendicular to the shaft. Rest the tip of the gauge against the centre of the shaft and rotate the shaft slowly whilst watching the gauge reading **(see illustration 3.18)**. Take several measurements along the length of the shaft and record the

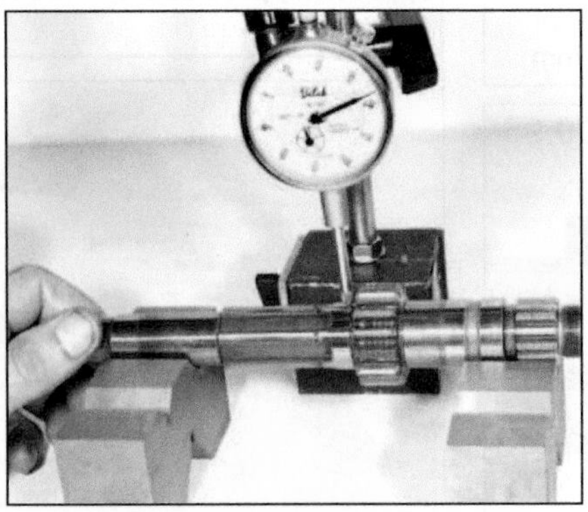

**3.18 Using a dial gauge to measure shaft runout**

runout in the shaft. **Note:** *The reading obtained will be total runout at that point - some manufacturers specify that the runout figure is halved to compare with their specified runout limit.*

- Endfloat (sideplay) measurement requires that the gauge is mounted securely to the surrounding component with its probe touching the end of the shaft. Using hand pressure, push and pull on the shaft noting the maximum endfloat recorded on the gauge **(see illustration 3.19)**.

**3.19 Using a dial gauge to measure shaft endfloat**

- A dial gauge with suitable adapters can be used to determine piston position BTDC on two-stroke engines for the purposes of ignition timing. The gauge, adapter and suitable length probe are installed in the place of the spark plug and the gauge zeroed at TDC. If the piston position is specified as 1.14 mm BTDC, rotate the engine back to 2.00 mm BTDC, then slowly forwards to 1.14 mm BTDC.

### *Cylinder compression gauges*

- A compression gauge is used for measuring cylinder compression. Either the rubber-cone type or the threaded adapter type can be used. The latter is preferred to ensure a perfect seal against the cylinder head. A 0 to 300 psi (0 to 20 Bar) type gauge (for petrol/gasoline engines) will be suitable for motorcycles.
- The spark plug is removed and the gauge either held hard against the cylinder head (cone type) or the gauge adapter screwed into the cylinder head (threaded type) **(see illustration 3.20)**. Cylinder compression is measured with the engine turning over, but not running - carry out the compression test as described in

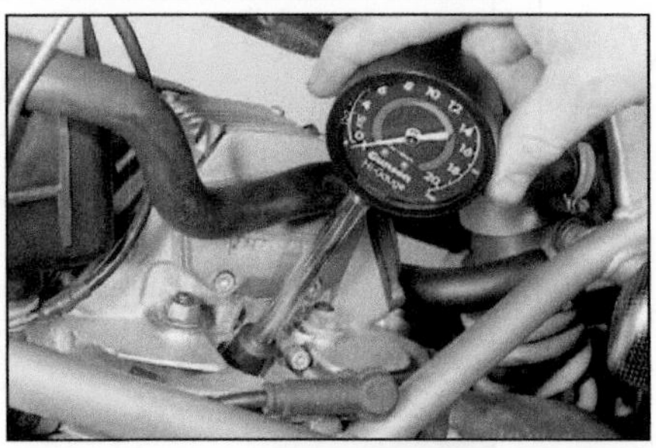

**3.20 Using a rubber-cone type cylinder compression gauge**

the reading until manually released.

### *Oil pressure gauge*

- An oil pressure gauge is used measuring engine oil pressure. Most ga come with a set of adapters to fit the thre the take-off point **(see illustration 3.21)**. take-off point specified by the motorc manufacturer is an external oil pipe u make sure that the specified replace union is used to prevent oil starvation.

**3.21 Oil pressure gauge and take-off p adapter (arrow)**

- Oil pressure is measured with the er running (at a specific rpm) and often manufacturer will specify pressure limits cold and hot engine.

### *Straight-edge and surface pla*

- If checking the gasket face c component for warpage, place a steel ru precision straight-edge across the gasket and measure any gap between the stra edge and component with feeler gauges **illustration 3.22)**. Check diagonally acros component and between mounting holes **illustration 3.23)**.

**3.22 Use a straight-edge and feele gauges to check for warpage**

**3.23 Check for warpage in these direct**

warpage, such as clutch plain (metal) plates, requires a perfectly flat plate or piece or plate glass and feeler gauges.

## 4 Torque and leverage

### What is torque?

- Torque describes the twisting force about a shaft. The amount of torque applied is determined by the distance from the centre of the shaft to the end of the lever and the amount of force being applied to the end of the lever; distance multiplied by force equals torque.
- The manufacturer applies a measured torque to a bolt or nut to ensure that it will not slacken in use and to hold two components securely together without movement in the joint. The actual torque setting depends on the thread size, bolt or nut material and the composition of the components being held.
- Too little torque may cause the fastener to loosen due to vibration, whereas too much torque will distort the joint faces of the component or cause the fastener to shear off. Always stick to the specified torque setting.

### Using a torque wrench

- Check the calibration of the torque wrench and make sure it has a suitable range for the job. Torque wrenches are available in Nm (Newton-metres), kgf m (kilograms-force metre), lbf ft (pounds-feet), lbf in (inch-pounds). Do not confuse lbf ft with lbf in.
- Adjust the tool to the desired torque on the scale **(see illustration 4.1)**. If your torque wrench is not calibrated in the units specified, carefully convert the figure (see *Conversion Factors*). A manufacturer sometimes gives a torque setting as a range (8 to 10 Nm) rather than a single figure - in this case set the tool midway between the two settings. The same torque may be expressed as 9 Nm ± 1 Nm. Some torque wrenches have a method of locking the setting so that it isn't inadvertently altered during use.

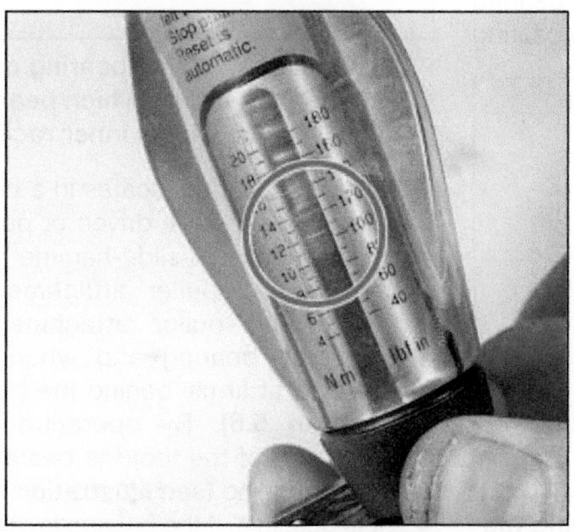


**4.1 Set the torque wrench index mark to the setting required, in this case 12 Nm**

- Install the bolts/nuts in their correct location and secure them lightly. Their threads must be clean and free of any old locking compound. Unless specified the threads and flange should be dry - oiled threads are necessary in certain circumstances and the manufacturer will take this into account in the specified torque figure. Similarly, the manufacturer may also specify the application of thread-locking compound.
- Tighten the fasteners in the specified sequence until the torque wrench clicks, indicating that the torque setting has been reached. Apply the torque again to double-check the setting. Where different thread diameter fasteners secure the component, as a rule tighten the larger diameter ones first.
- When the torque wrench has been finished with, release the lock (where applicable) and fully back off its setting to zero - do not leave the torque wrench tensioned. Also, do not use a torque wrench for slackening a fastener.

### Angle-tightening

- Manufacturers often specify a figure in degrees for final tightening of a fastener. This usually follows tightening to a specific torque setting.
- A degree disc can be set and attached to the socket **(see illustration 4.2)** or a protractor can be used to mark the angle of movement on the bolt/nut head and the surrounding casting **(see illustration 4.3)**.

**4.2 Angle tightening can be accomplished with a torque-angle gauge . . .**

**4.3 . . . or by marking the angle on the surrounding component**

- Where more than one bolt/nut secures a component, loosen each fastener evenly a little at a time. In this way, not all the stress of the joint is held by one fastener and the components are not likely to distort.
- If a tightening sequence is provided, work in the REVERSE of this, but if not, work from the outside in, in a criss-cross sequence **(see illustration 4.4)**.

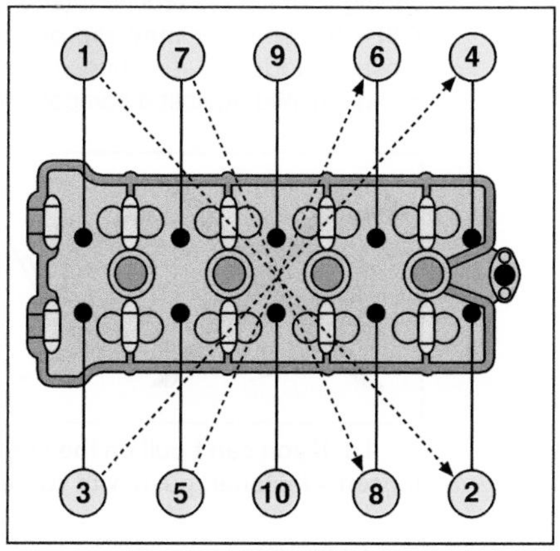


**4.4 When slackening, work from the outside inwards**

### Tightening sequences

- If a component is held by more than one fastener it is important that the retaining bolts/nuts are tightened evenly to prevent uneven stress build-up and distortion of sealing faces. This is especially important on high-compression joints such as the cylinder head.
- A sequence is usually provided by the manufacturer, either in a diagram or actually marked in the casting. If not, always start in the centre and work outwards in a criss-cross pattern **(see illustration 4.5)**. Start off by securing all bolts/nuts finger-tight, then set the torque wrench and tighten each fastener by a small amount in sequence until the final torque is reached. By following this practice,

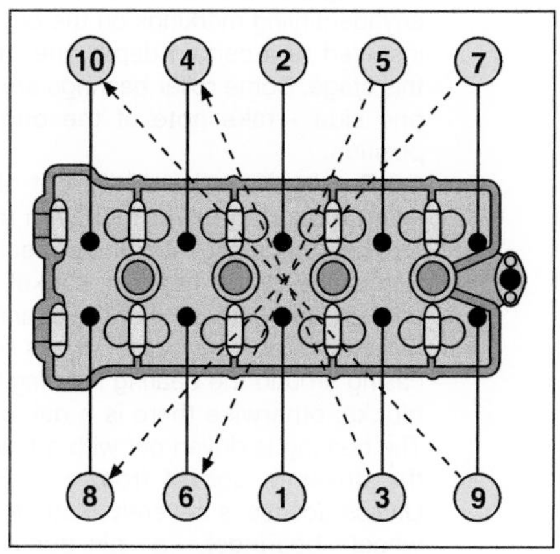


**4.5 When tightening, work from the inside outwards**

distorted. Important joints, such as the cylinder head and big-end fasteners often have two- or three-stage torque settings.

### Applying leverage

● Use tools at the correct angle. Position a socket wrench or spanner on the bolt/nut so that you pull it towards you when loosening. If this can't be done, push the spanner without curling your fingers around it **(see illustration 4.6)** - the spanner may slip or the fastener loosen suddenly, resulting in your fingers being crushed against a component.

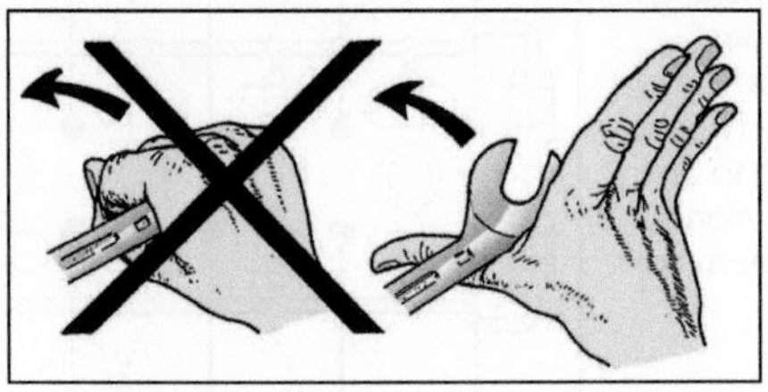

**4.6 If you can't pull on the spanner to loosen a fastener, push with your hand open**

● Additional leverage is gained by extending the length of the lever. The best way to do this is to use a breaker bar instead of the regular length tool, or to slip a length of tubing over the end of the spanner or socket wrench.

● If additional leverage will not work, the fastener head is either damaged or firmly corroded in place (see *Fasteners*).

## 5 Bearings

### Bearing removal and installation

#### Drivers and sockets

● Before removing a bearing, always inspect the casing to see which way it must be driven out - some casings will have retaining plates or a cast step. Also check for any identifying markings on the bearing and if installed to a certain depth, measure this at this stage. Some roller bearings are sealed on one side - take note of the original fitted position.

● Bearings can be driven out of a casing using a bearing driver tool (with the correct size head) or a socket of the correct diameter. Select the driver head or socket so that it contacts the outer race of the bearing, not the balls/rollers or inner race. Always support the casing around the bearing housing with wood blocks, otherwise there is a risk of fracture. The bearing is driven out with a few blows on the driver or socket from a heavy mallet. Unless access is severely restricted (as with wheel bearings), a pin-punch is not recommended unless it is moved around the bearing to keep it square in its housing.

install bearings. Make sure the bearing housing is supported on wood blocks and line up the bearing in its housing. Fit the bearing as noted on removal - generally they are installed with their marked side facing outwards. Tap the bearing squarely into its housing using a driver or socket which bears only on the bearing's outer race - contact with the bearing balls/rollers or inner race will destroy it **(see illustrations 5.1 and 5.2)**.

● Check that the bearing inner race and balls/rollers rotate freely.

**5.1 Using a bearing driver against the bearing's outer race**

**5.2 Using a large socket against the bearing's outer race**

#### Pullers and slide-hammers

● Where a bearing is pressed on a shaft a puller will be required to extract it **(see illustration 5.3).** Make sure that the puller clamp or legs fit securely behind the bearing and are unlikely to slip out. If pulling a bearing

**5.3 This bearing puller clamps behind the bearing and pressure is applied to the shaft end to draw the bearing off**

locate the puller behind a gear pinion if there no access to the race and draw the gear pi off the shaft as well **(see illustration 5.4).**

***Caution: Ensure that the puller's cent bolt locates securely against the end the shaft and will not slip when pressu is applied. Also ensure that puller do not damage the shaft end.***

**5.4 Where no access is available to the r of the bearing, it is sometimes possible draw off the adjacent component**

● Operate the puller so that its centre exerts pressure on the shaft end and dr the bearing off the shaft.

● When installing the bearing on the sh tap only on the bearing's inner race - con with the balls/rollers or outer race with des the bearing. Use a socket or length of tub as a drift which fits over the shaft end ( **illustration 5.5).**

**5.5 When installing a bearing on a sha use a piece of tubing which bears only the bearing's inner race**

● Where a bearing locates in a blind hol a casing, it cannot be driven or pulled ou described above. A slide-hammer with kr edged bearing puller attachment will required. The puller attachment pas through the bearing and when tighte expands to fit firmly behind the bearing ( **illustration 5.6)**. By operating the sl hammer part of the tool the bearing is ja out of its housing **(see illustration 5.7).**

● It is possible, if the bearing is of reasona weight, for it to drop out of its housing if casing is heated as described opposite. If

**5.6 Expand the bearing puller so that it locks behind the bearing . . .**

**5.7 . . . attach the slide hammer to the bearing puller**

method is attempted, first prepare a work surface which will enable the casing to be tapped face down to help dislodge the bearing - a wood surface is ideal since it will not damage the casing's gasket surface. Wearing protective gloves, tap the heated casing several times against the work surface to dislodge the bearing under its own weight **(see illustration 5.8)**.

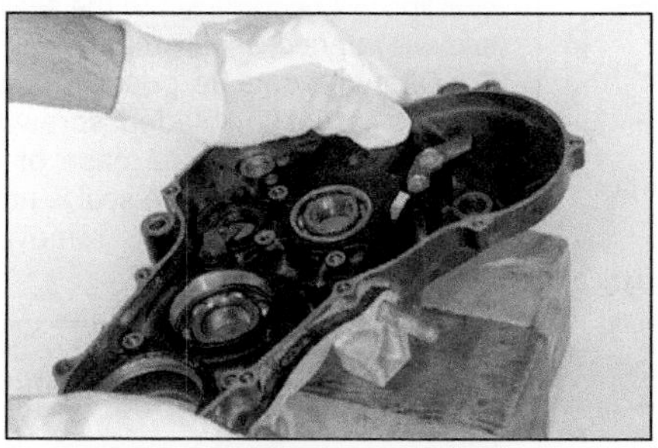

**5.8 Tapping a casing face down on wood blocks can often dislodge a bearing**

● Bearings can be installed in blind holes using the driver or socket method described above.

## Drawbolts

● Where a bearing or bush is set in the eye of a component, such as a suspension linkage arm or connecting rod small-end, removal by drift may damage the component. Furthermore, a rubber bushing in a shock absorber eye cannot successfully be driven out of position. If access is available to a engineering press, the task is straightforward. If not, a drawbolt can be fabricated to extract the bearing or bush.

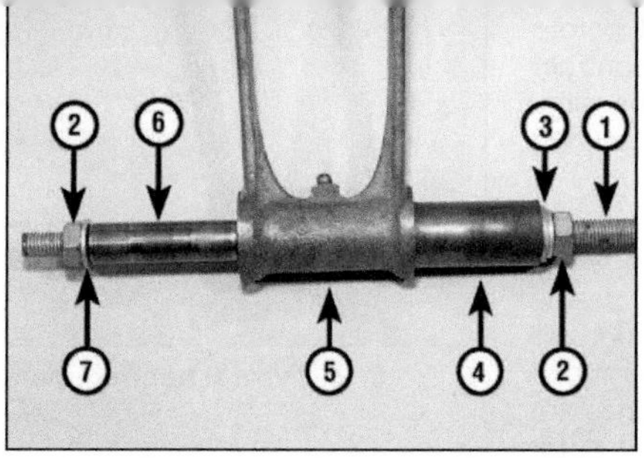


**5.9 Drawbolt component parts assembled on a suspension arm**

1 *Bolt or length of threaded bar*
2 *Nuts*
3 *Washer (external diameter greater than tubing internal diameter)*
4 *Tubing (internal diameter sufficient to accommodate bearing)*
5 *Suspension arm with bearing*
6 *Tubing (external diameter slightly smaller than bearing)*
7 *Washer (external diameter slightly smaller than bearing)*

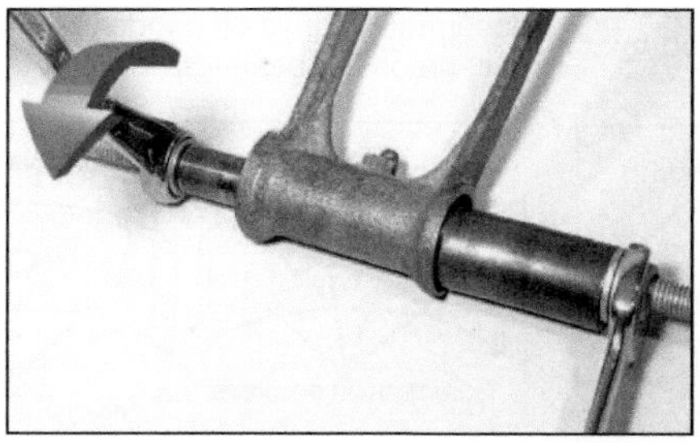

**5.10 Drawing the bearing out of the suspension arm**

● To extract the bearing/bush you will need a long bolt with nut (or piece of threaded bar with two nuts), a piece of tubing which has an internal diameter larger than the bearing/bush, another piece of tubing which has an external diameter slightly smaller than the bearing/bush, and a selection of washers **(see illustrations 5.9 and 5.10)**. Note that the pieces of tubing must be of the same length, or longer, than the bearing/bush.

● The same kit (without the pieces of tubing) can be used to draw the new bearing/bush back into place **(see illustration 5.11)**.

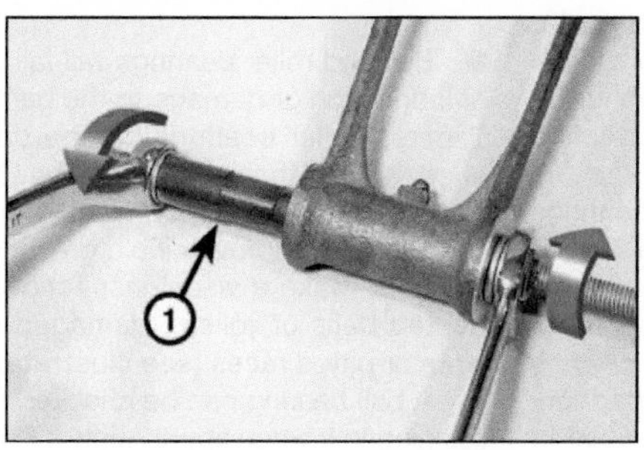


**5.11 Installing a new bearing (1) in the suspension arm**

● If the bearing's outer race is a tight fit in the casing, the aluminium casing can be heated to release its grip on the bearing. Aluminium will expand at a greater rate than the steel bearing outer race. There are several ways to do this, but avoid any localised extreme heat (such as a blow torch) - aluminium alloy has a low melting point.

● Approved methods of heating a casing are using a domestic oven (heated to 100°C) or immersing the casing in boiling water **(see illustration 5.12)**. Low temperature range localised heat sources such as a paint stripper heat gun or clothes iron can also be used **(see illustration 5.13)**. Alternatively, soak a rag in boiling water, wring it out and wrap it around the bearing housing.

***Warning: All of these methods require care in use to prevent scalding and burns to the hands. Wear protective gloves when handling hot components.***

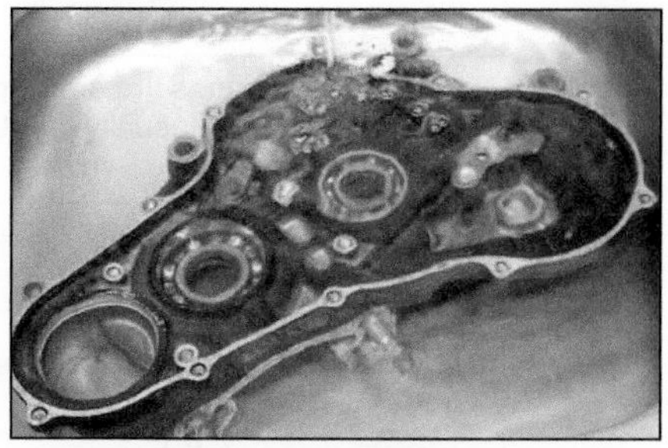

**5.12 A casing can be immersed in a sink of boiling water to aid bearing removal**

**5.13 Using a localised heat source to aid bearing removal**

● If heating the whole casing note that plastic components, such as the neutral switch, may suffer - remove them beforehand.

● After heating, remove the bearing as described above. You may find that the expansion is sufficient for the bearing to fall out of the casing under its own weight or with a light tap on the driver or socket.

● If necessary, the casing can be heated to aid bearing installation, and this is sometimes the recommended procedure if the motorcycle manufacturer has designed the housing and bearing fit with this intention.

placing them in a freezer the night before installation. The steel bearing will contract slightly, allowing easy insertion in its housing. This is often useful when installing steering head outer races in the frame.

## Bearing types and markings

● Plain shell bearings, ball bearings, needle roller bearings and tapered roller bearings will all be found on motorcycles **(see illustrations 5.14 and 5.15)**. The ball and roller types are usually caged between an inner and outer race, but uncaged variations may be found.

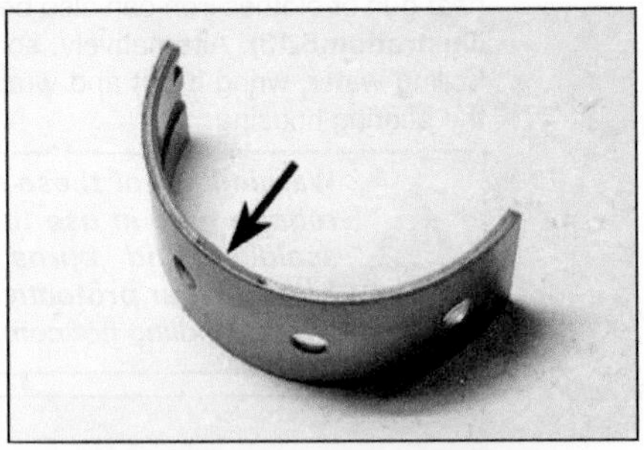

**5.14 Shell bearings are either plain or grooved. They are usually identified by colour code (arrow)**

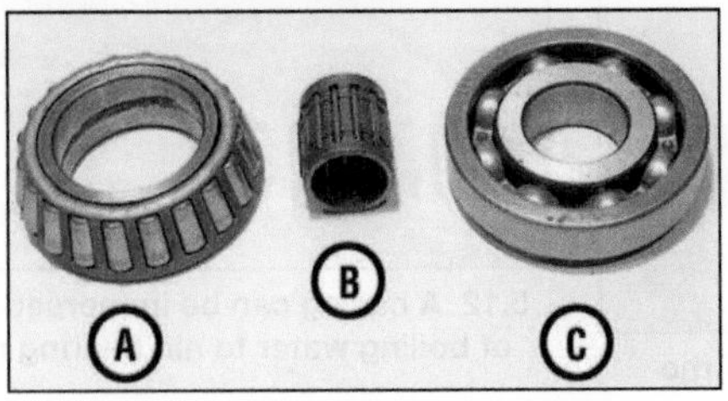


**5.15 Tapered roller bearing (A), needle roller bearing (B) and ball journal bearing (C)**

● Shell bearings (often called inserts) are usually found at the crankshaft main and connecting rod big-end where they are good at coping with high loads. They are made of a phosphor-bronze material and are impregnated with self-lubricating properties.

● Ball bearings and needle roller bearings consist of a steel inner and outer race with the balls or rollers between the races. They require constant lubrication by oil or grease and are good at coping with axial loads. Taper roller bearings consist of rollers set in a tapered cage set on the inner race; the outer race is separate. They are good at coping with axial loads and prevent movement along the shaft - a typical application is in the steering head.

● Bearing manufacturers produce bearings to ISO size standards and stamp one face of the bearing to indicate its internal and external diameter, load capacity and type **(see illustration 5.16)**.

● Metal bushes are usually of phosphor-bronze material. Rubber bushes are used in suspension mounting eyes. Fibre bushes have also been used in suspension pivots.

**5.16 Typical bearing marking**

## Bearing fault finding

● If a bearing outer race has spun in its housing, the housing material will be damaged. You can use a bearing locking compound to bond the outer race in place if damage is not too severe.

● Shell bearings will fail due to damage of their working surface, as a result of lack of lubrication, corrosion or abrasive particles in the oil **(see illustration 5.17)**. Small particles of dirt in the oil may embed in the bearing material whereas larger particles will score the bearing and shaft journal. If a number of short journeys are made, insufficient heat will be generated to drive off condensation which has built up on the bearings.

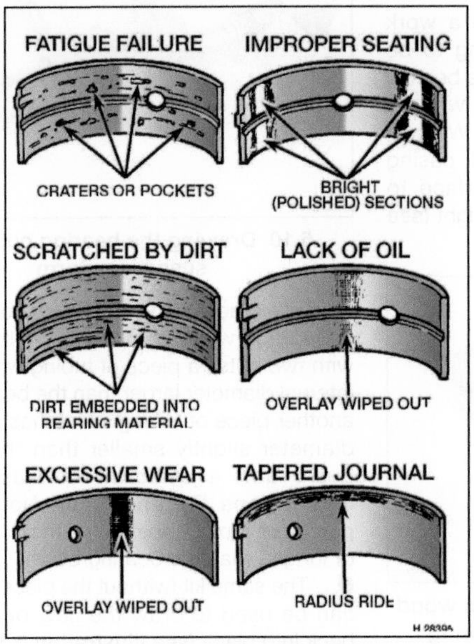


**5.17 Typical bearing failures**

● Ball and roller bearings will fail due to lack of lubrication or damage to the balls or rollers. Tapered-roller bearings can be damaged by overloading them. Unless the bearing is sealed on both sides, wash it in paraffin (kerosene) to remove all old grease then allow it to dry. Make a visual inspection looking to dented balls or rollers, damaged cages and worn or pitted races **(see illustration 5.18)**.

● A ball bearing can be checked for wear by listening to it when spun. Apply a film of light oil to the bearing and hold it close to the ear - hold the outer race with one hand and spin the inner race with the other hand **(see illustration 5**. The bearing should be almost silent w spun; if it grates or rattles it is worn.

**5.18 Example of ball journal bearing w damaged balls and cages**

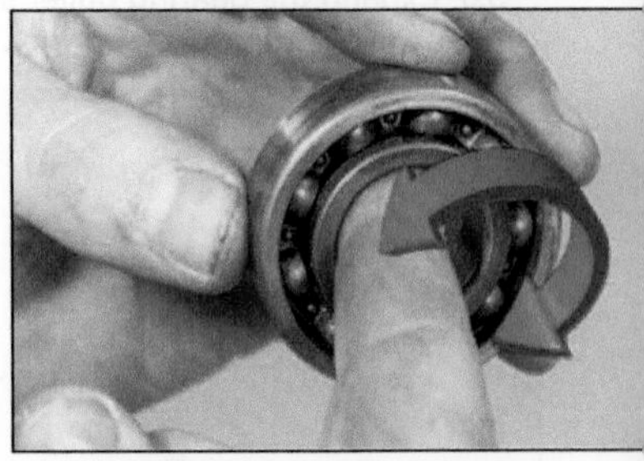

**5.19 Hold outer race and listen to inn race when spun**

## 6 Oil seals

## Oil seal removal and installati

● Oil seals should be renewed every ti component is dismantled. This is because seal lips will become set to the sealing sur and will not necessarily reseal.

● Oil seals can be prised out of pos using a large flat-bladed screwdriver **illustration 6.1)**. In the case of crank seals, check first that the seal is not lippe the inside, preventing its removal with crankcases joined.

**6.1 Prise out oil seals with a large flat-bladed screwdriver**

● New seals are usually installed with marked face (containing the seal refer code) outwards and the spring side tow the fluid being retained. In certain cases, as a two-stroke engine crankshaft se double lipped seal may be used due to t being fluid or gas on each side of the join bears only on the outer hard edge of the seal to install it in the casing - tapping on the inner edge will damage the sealing lip.

### Oil seal types and markings

- Oil seals are usually of the single-lipped type. Double-lipped seals are found where a liquid or gas is on both sides of the joint.
- Oil seals can harden and lose their sealing ability if the motorcycle has been in storage for a long period - renewal is the only solution.
- Oil seal manufacturers also conform to the ISO markings for seal size - these are moulded into the outer face of the seal **(see illustration 6.2)**.

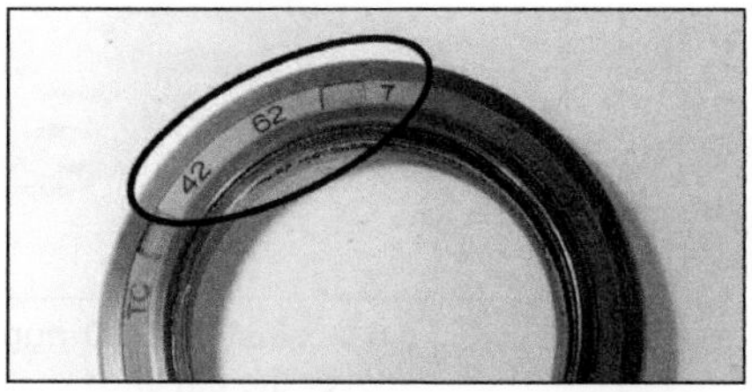


**6.2 These oil seal markings indicate inside diameter, outside diameter and seal thickness**

## 7 Gaskets and sealants

### Types of gasket and sealant

- Gaskets are used to seal the mating surfaces between components and keep lubricants, fluids, vacuum or pressure contained within the assembly. Aluminium gaskets are sometimes found at the cylinder joints, but most gaskets are paper-based. If the mating surfaces of the components being joined are undamaged the gasket can be installed dry, although a dab of sealant or grease will be useful to hold it in place during assembly.
- RTV (Room Temperature Vulcanising) silicone rubber sealants cure when exposed to moisture in the atmosphere. These sealants are good at filling pits or irregular gasket faces, but will tend to be forced out of the joint under very high torque. They can be used to replace a paper gasket, but first make sure that the width of the paper gasket is not essential to the shimming of internal components. RTV sealants should not be used on components containing petrol (gasoline).
- Non-hardening, semi-hardening and hard setting liquid gasket compounds can be used with a gasket or between a metal-to-metal joint. Select the sealant to suit the application: universal non-hardening sealant can be used on virtually all joints; semi-hardening on joint faces which are rough or damaged; hard setting sealant on joints which require a permanent bond and are subjected to high temperature and pressure. **Note:** *Check first if the paper gasket has a bead of sealant* [illegible] *additional sealant.*
- When choosing a sealant, make sure it is suitable for the application, particularly if being applied in a high-temperature area or in the vicinity of fuel. Certain manufacturers produce sealants in either clear, silver or black colours to match the finish of the engine. This has a particular application on motorcycles where much of the engine is exposed.
- Do not over-apply sealant. That which is squeezed out on the outside of the joint can be wiped off, whereas an excess of sealant on the inside can break off and clog oilways.

### Breaking a sealed joint

- Age, heat, pressure and the use of hard setting sealant can cause two components to stick together so tightly that they are difficult to separate using finger pressure alone. Do not resort to using levers unless there is a pry point provided for this purpose **(see illustration 7.1)** or else the gasket surfaces will be damaged.
- Use a soft-faced hammer **(see illustration 7.2)** or a wood block and conventional hammer to strike the component near the mating surface. Avoid hammering against cast extremities since they may break off. If this method fails, try using a wood wedge between the two components.

***Caution: If the joint will not separate, double-check that you have removed all the fasteners.***

**7.1 If a pry point is provided, apply gently pressure with a flat-bladed screwdriver**

**7.2 Tap around the joint with a soft-faced mallet if necessary - don't strike cooling fins**

### Removal of old gasket and sealant

- Paper gaskets will most likely come away complete, leaving only a few traces stuck on the sealing faces of the components. It is imperative that all traces are removed to ensure correct sealing of the new gasket.
- Very carefully scrape all traces of gasket away making sure that the sealing surfaces are not gouged or scored by the scraper **(see illustrations 7.3, 7.4 and 7.5)**. Stubborn deposits can be removed by spraying with an aerosol gasket remover. Final preparation of

**HAYNES HiNT**

***Most components have one or two hollow locating dowels between the two gasket faces. If a dowel cannot be removed, do not resort to gripping it with pliers - it will almost certainly be distorted. Install a close-fitting socket or Phillips screwdriver into the dowel and then grip the outer edge of the dowel to free it.***

**7.3 Paper gaskets can be scraped off with a gasket scraper tool . . .**

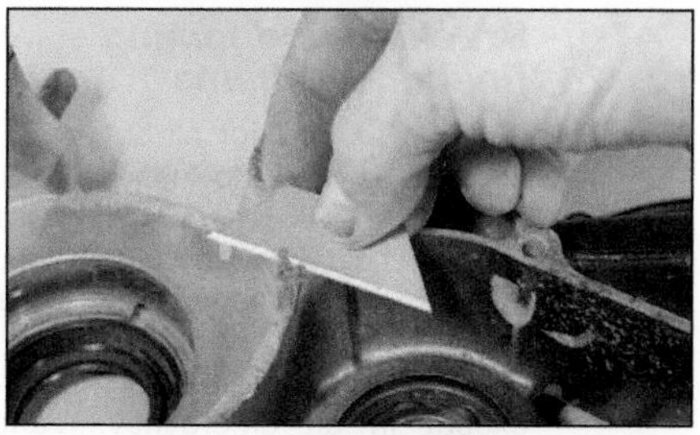

**7.4 . . . a knife blade . . .**

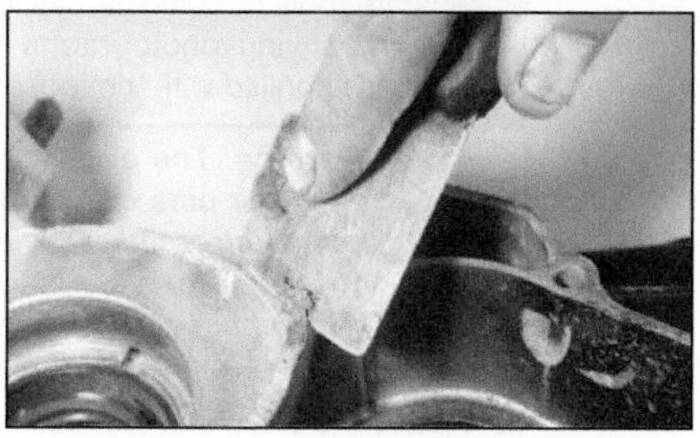

**7.5 . . . or a household scraper**

7.6 Fine abrasive paper is wrapped around a flat file to clean up the gasket face

7.7 A kitchen scourer can be used on stubborn deposits

the gasket surface can be made with very fine abrasive paper or a plastic kitchen scourer **(see illustrations 7.6 and 7.7)**.

● Old sealant can be scraped or peeled off components, depending on the type originally used. Note that gasket removal compounds are available to avoid scraping the components clean; make sure the gasket remover suits the type of sealant used.

## 8 Chains

### *Breaking and joining final drive chains*

● Drive chains for all but small bikes are continuous and do not have a clip-type connecting link. The chain must be broken using a chain breaker tool and the new chain securely riveted together using a new soft rivet-type link. Never use a clip-type connecting link instead of a rivet-type link, except in an emergency. Various chain breaking and riveting tools are available, either as separate tools or combined as illustrated in the accompanying photographs - read the instructions supplied with the tool carefully.

> ***Warning: The need to rivet the new link pins correctly cannot be overstressed - loss of control of the motorcycle is very likely to result if the chain breaks in use.***

● Rotate the chain and look for the soft link. The soft link pins look like they have been

8.1 Tighten the chain breaker to push the pin out of the link . . .

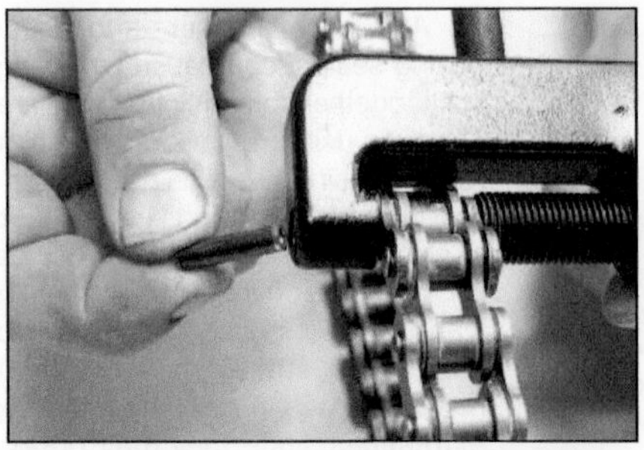

8.2 . . . withdraw the pin, remove the tool . . .

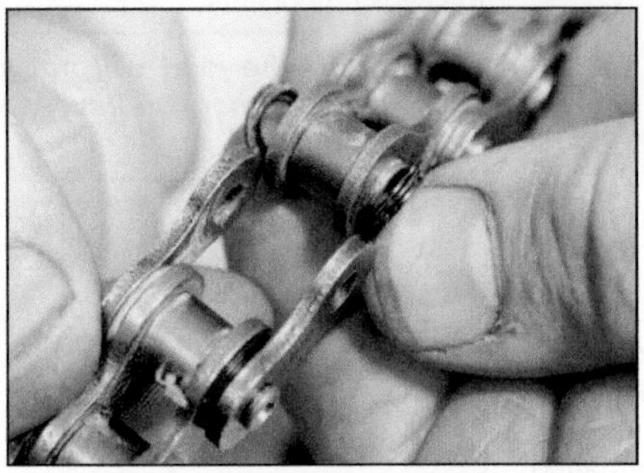

8.3 . . . and separate the chain link

deeply centre-punched instead of peened over like all the other pins **(see illustration 8.9)** and its sideplate may be a different colour. Position the soft link midway between the sprockets and assemble the chain breaker tool over one of the soft link pins **(see illustration 8.1)**. Operate the tool to push the pin out through the chain **(see illustration 8.2)**. On an O-ring chain, remove the O-rings **(see illustration 8.3)**. Carry out the same procedure on the other soft link pin.

> ***Caution: Certain soft link pins (particularly on the larger chains) may require their ends to be filed or ground off before they can be pressed out using the tool.***

● Check that you have the correct size and strength (standard or heavy duty) new soft link - do not reuse the old link. Look for the size marking on the chain sideplates **(see illustration 8.10)**.

● Position the chain ends so that they are engaged over the rear sprocket. On an O-ring

8.4 Insert the new soft link, with O-ring through the chain ends . . .

8.5 . . . install the O-rings over the pin ends . . .

8.6 . . . followed by the sideplate

chain, install a new O-ring over each pin of link and insert the link through the two ch ends **(see illustration 8.4)**. Install a new O- over the end of each pin, followed by sideplate (with the chain manufactur marking facing outwards) **(see illustrati 8.5 and 8.6)**. On an unsealed chain, insert link through the two chain ends, then ins the sideplate with the chain manufactur marking facing outwards.

● Note that it may not be possible to ins the sideplate using finger pressure alon using a joining tool, assemble it so that plates of the tool clamp the link and press sideplate over the pins **(see illustration 8** Otherwise, use two small sockets placed

8.7 Push the sideplate into position using a clamp

8.8 Assemble the chain riveting tool over one pin at a time and tighten it fully

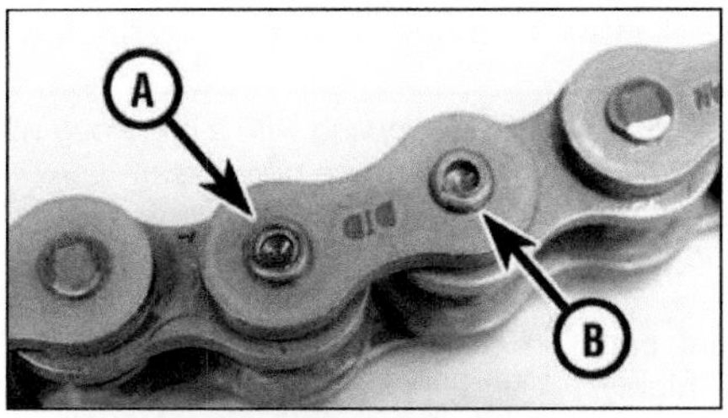


8.9 Pin end correctly riveted (A), pin end unriveted (B)

the rivet ends and two pieces of the wood between a G-clamp. Operate the clamp to press the sideplate over the pins.

- Assemble the joining tool over one pin (following the maker's instructions) and tighten the tool down to spread the pin end securely **(see illustrations 8.8 and 8.9)**. Do the same on the other pin.

> ***Warning: Check that the pin ends are secure and that there is no danger of the sideplate coming loose. If the pin ends are cracked the soft link must be renewed.***

### *Final drive chain sizing*

- Chains are sized using a three digit number, followed by a suffix to denote the chain type **(see illustration 8.10)**. Chain type is either standard or heavy duty (thicker sideplates), and also unsealed or O-ring/X-ring type.
- The first digit of the number relates to the pitch of the chain, ie the distance from the centre of one pin to the centre of the next pin **(see illustration 8.11)**. Pitch is expressed in eighths of an inch, as follows:

8.10 Typical chain size and type marking

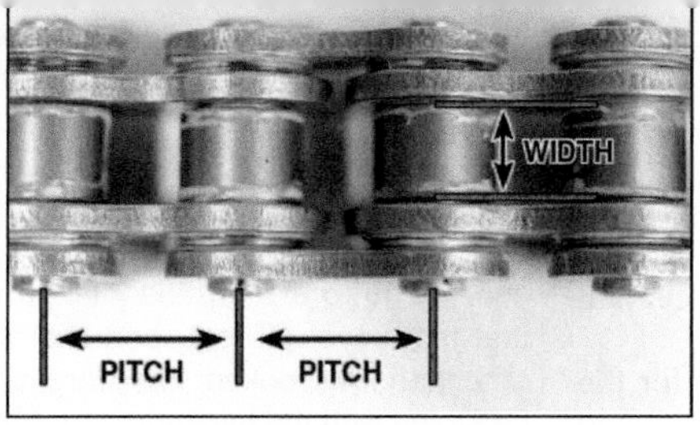


8.11 Chain dimensions

Sizes commencing with a 4 (eg 428) have a pitch of 1/2 inch (12.7 mm)

Sizes commencing with a 5 (eg 520) have a pitch of 5/8 inch (15.9 mm)

Sizes commencing with a 6 (eg 630) have a pitch of 3/4 inch (19.1 mm)

- The second and third digits of the chain size relate to the width of the rollers, again in imperial units, eg the 525 shown has 5/16 inch (7.94 mm) rollers **(see illustration 8.11)**.

## 9 Hoses

### *Clamping to prevent flow*

- Small-bore flexible hoses can be clamped to prevent fluid flow whilst a component is worked on. Whichever method is used, ensure that the hose material is not permanently distorted or damaged by the clamp.

*a) A brake hose clamp available from auto accessory shops **(see illustration 9.1)**.*

*b) A wingnut type hose clamp **(see illustration 9.2)**.*

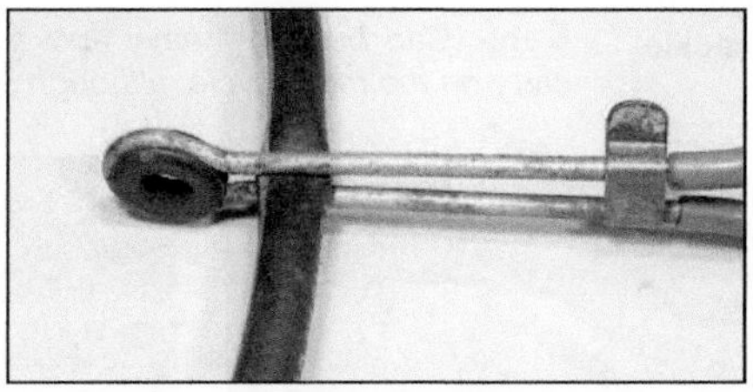

9.1 Hoses can be clamped with an automotive brake hose clamp . . .

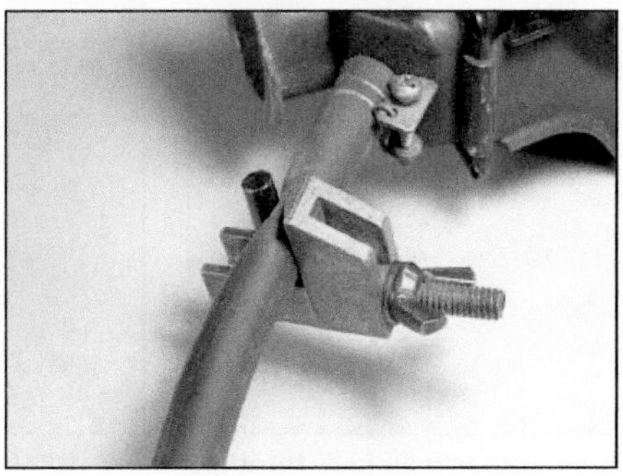

9.2 . . . a wingnut type hose clamp . . .

*and held with straight-jawed self-locking grips **(see illustration 9.3)**.*

*d) Thick card each side of the hose held between straight-jawed self-locking grips **(see illustration 9.4)**.*

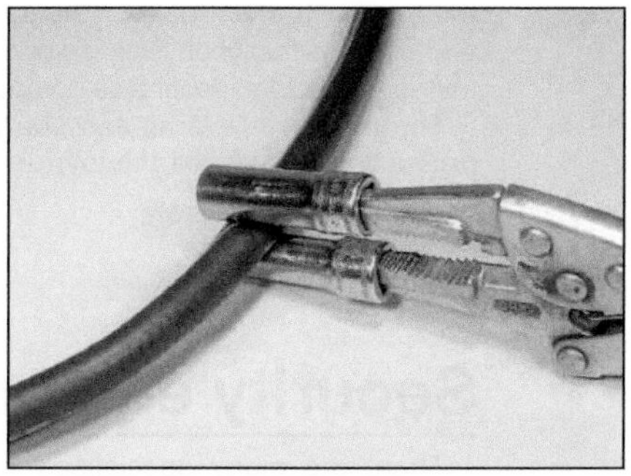

9.3 . . . two sockets and a pair of self-locking grips . . .

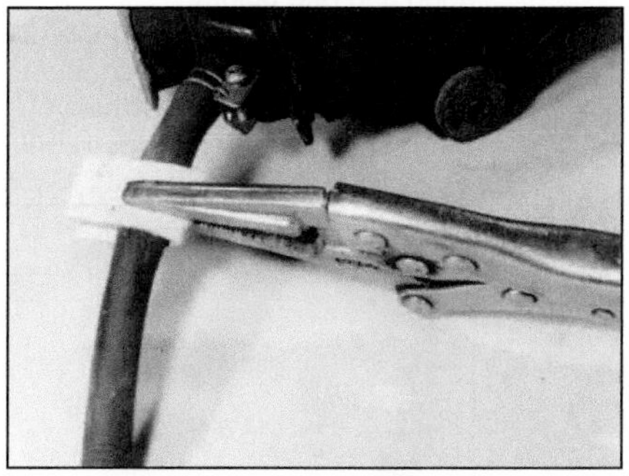

9.4 . . . or thick card and self-locking grips

### *Freeing and fitting hoses*

- Always make sure the hose clamp is moved well clear of the hose end. Grip the hose with your hand and rotate it whilst pulling it off the union. If the hose has hardened due to age and will not move, slit it with a sharp knife and peel its ends off the union **(see illustration 9.5)**.
- Resist the temptation to use grease or soap on the unions to aid installation; although it helps the hose slip over the union it will equally aid the escape of fluid from the joint. It is preferable to soften the hose ends in hot water and wet the inside surface of the hose with water or a fluid which will evaporate.

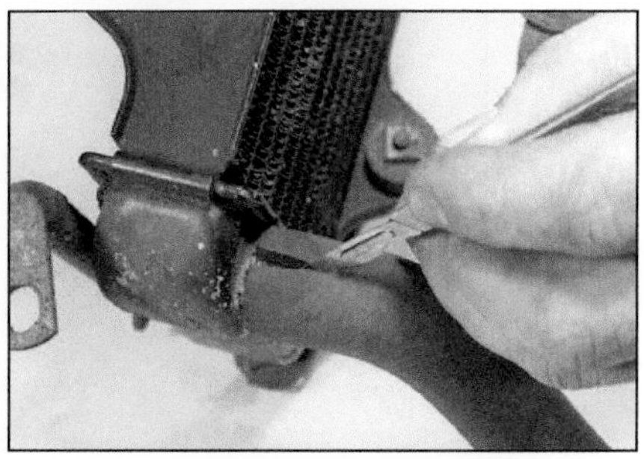

9.5 Cutting a coolant hose free with a sharp knife

## Introduction

In less time than it takes to read this introduction, a thief could steal your motorcycle. Returning only to find your bike has gone is one of the worst feelings in the world. Even if the motorcycle is insured against theft, once you've got over the initial shock, you will have the inconvenience of dealing with the police and your insurance company.

The motorcycle is an easy target for the professional thief and the joyrider alike and for depressing reading; on average a motorcycle is stolen every 16 minutes in the UK!

Motorcycle thefts fall into two categories, those stolen 'to order' and those taken by opportunists. The thief stealing to order will be on the look out for a specific make and model and will go to extraordinary lengths to obtain that motorcycle. The opportunist thief on the other hand will look for easy targets which can be stolen with the minimum of effort and risk.

make your machine 100% secure, estimated that around half of all st motorcycles are taken by opportunist thi Remember that the opportunist thief is al on the look out for the easy option: if ther two similar motorcycles parked side-by- they will target the one with the lowest le security. By taking a few precautions, you reduce the chances of your motorcycle b stolen.

# Security equipment

There are many specialised motorcycle security devices available and the following text summarises their applications and their good and bad points.

Once you have decided on the type of security equipment which best suits your needs, we recommended that you read one of the many equipment tests regularly carried out by the motorcycle press. These tests compare the products from all the major manufacturers and give impartial ratings on their effectiveness, value-for-money and ease of use.

Ensure the lock and chain you buy is of good quality and long enough to shackle your bike to a solid object

No one item of security equipment can provide complete protection. It is highly recommended that two or more of the items described below are combined to increase the security of your motorcycle (a lock and chain plus an alarm system is just about ideal). The more security measures fitted to the bike, the less likely it is to be stolen.

### Lock and chain

**Pros:** *Very flexible to use; can be used to secure the motorcycle to almost any immovable object. On some locks and chains, the lock can be used on its own as a disc lock (see below).*

**Cons:** *Can be very heavy and awkward to carry on the motorcycle, although some types will be supplied with a carry bag which c strapped to the pillion seat.*

- Heavy-duty chains and locks ar excellent security measure **(see illustratic** Whenever the motorcycle is parked, us lock and chain to secure the machine solid, immovable object such as a po railings. This will prevent the machine being ridden away or being lifted into the of a van.

- When fitting the chain, always ensur chain is routed around the motorcycle f or swingarm **(see illustrations 2 an** Never merely pass the chain around o the wheel rims; a thief may unbolt the w and lift the rest of the machine into a leaving you with just the wheel! Try to a having excess chain free, thus maki difficult to use cutting tools, and kee chain and lock off the ground to pre thieves attacking it with a cold chisel. Po the lock so that its lock barrel is fa downwards; this will make it harder fo thief to attack the lock mechanism.

Pass the chain through the bike's frame, rather than just through a wheel . . .

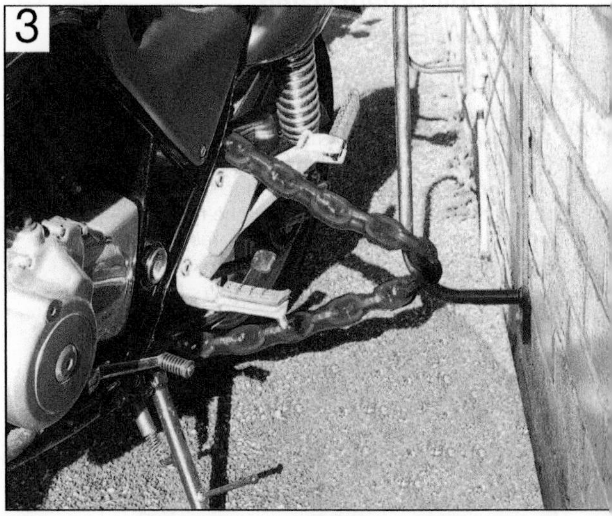

. . . and loop it around a solid object

## U-locks

**Pros:** *Highly effective deterrent which can be used to secure the bike to a post or railings. Most U-locks come with a carrier which allows the lock to be easily carried on the bike.*

**Cons:** *Not as flexible to use as a lock and chain.*

- These are solid locks which are similar in use to a lock and chain. U-locks are lighter than a lock and chain but not so flexible to use. The length and shape of the lock shackle limit the objects to which the bike can be secured **(see illustration 4)**.

4

**U-locks can be used to secure the bike to a solid object – ensure you purchase one which is long enough**

## Disc locks

**Pros:** *Small, light and very easy to carry; most can be stored underneath the seat.*

**Cons:** *Does not prevent the motorcycle being lifted into a van. Can be very embarrassing if you forget to remove the lock before attempting to ride off!*

5

**A typical disc lock attached through one of the holes in the disc**

- Disc locks are designed to be attached to the front brake disc. The lock passes through one of the holes in the disc and prevents the wheel rotating by jamming against the fork/brake caliper **(see illustration 5)**. Some are equipped with an alarm siren which sounds if the disc lock is moved; this not only acts as a theft deterrent but also as a handy reminder if you try to move the bike with the lock still fitted.

- Combining the disc lock with a length of cable which can be looped around a post or railings provides an additional measure of security **(see illustration 6)**.

## Alarms and immobilisers

**Pros:** *Once installed it is completely hassle-free to use. If the system is 'Thatcham' or 'Sold Secure-approved', insurance companies may give you a discount.*

**Cons:** *Can be expensive to buy and complex to install. No system will prevent the motorcycle from being lifted into a van and taken away.*

- Electronic alarms and immobilisers are available to suit a variety of budgets. There are three different types of system available: pure alarms, pure immobilisers, and the more expensive systems which are combined alarm/immobilisers **(see illustration 7)**.
- An alarm system is designed to emit an audible warning if the motorcycle is being tampered with.
- An immobiliser prevents the motorcycle being started and ridden away by disabling its electrical systems.
- When purchasing an alarm/immobiliser system, check the cost of installing the system unless you are able to do it yourself. If the motorcycle is not used regularly, another consideration is the current drain of the system. All alarm/immobiliser systems are powered by the motorcycle's battery; purchasing a system with a very low current drain could prevent the battery losing its charge whilst the motorcycle is not being used.

6

**A disc lock combined with a security cable provides additional protection**

7

**A typical alarm/immobiliser system**

8

**Indelible markings can be applied to most areas of the bike – always apply the manufacturer's sticker to warn off thieves**

### Security marking kits

**Pros:** *Very cheap and effective deterrent. Many insurance companies will give you a discount on your insurance premium if a recognised security marking kit is used on your motorcycle.*

**Cons:** *Does not prevent the motorcycle being stolen by joyriders.*

● There are many different types of security marking kits available. The idea is to mark as many parts of the motorcycle as possible with a unique security number **(see illustrations 8, 9 and 10)**. A form will be included with the kit to register your personal details and those of the motorcycle with the kit manufacturer. This register is made available to the police to help them trace the rightful owner of any motorcycle or components which they recover should all other forms of identification have been removed. Always apply the warning stickers provided with the kit to deter thieves.

9

**Chemically-etched code numbers can be applied to main body panels . . .**

### Ground anchors, wheel clamps and security posts

**Pros:** *An excellent form of security which will deter all but the most determined of thieves.*

**Cons:** *Awkward to install and can be expensive.*

10

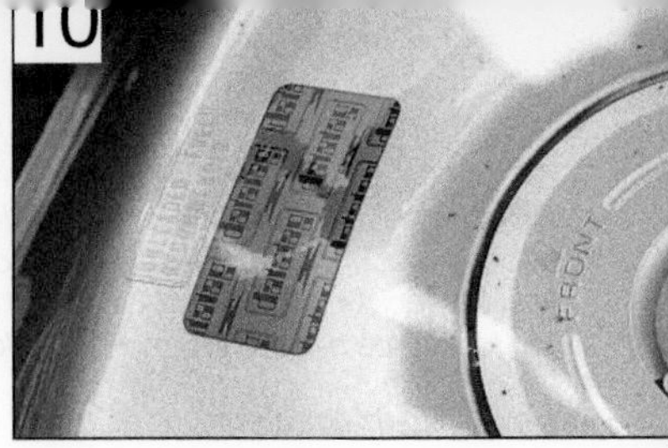

**. . . again, always ensure that the kit manufacturer's sticker is applied in a prominent position**

● Whilst the motorcycle is at home, it i good idea to attach it securely to the floor solid wall, even if it is kept in a securely loc garage. Various types of ground anch security posts and wheel clamps are availa for this purpose **(see illustration 11)**. Th security devices are either bolted to a s concrete or brick structure or can cemented into the ground.

11

**Permanent ground anchors provide an excellent level of security when the bike is at ho**

## Security at home

A high percentage of motorcycle thefts are from the owner's home. Here are some things to consider whenever your motorcycle is at home:

✔ Where possible, always keep the motorcycle in a securely locked garage. Never rely solely on the standard lock on the garage door, these are usual hopelessly inadequate. Fit an additional locking mechanism to the door and consider having the garage alarmed. A security light, activated by a movement sensor, is also a good investment.

✔ Always secure the motorcycle to the ground or a wall, even if it is inside a securely locked garage.

✔ Do not regularly leave the motorcycle outside your home, try to keep it out of sight wherever possible. If a garage is not available, fit a motorcycle cover over the bike to disguise its true identity.

✔ It is not uncommon for thieves to follow a motorcyclist home to find out where the bike is kept. They will then return at a later date. Be aware of this whenever you are returning home on your motorcycle. If you suspect are being followed, do not return ho instead ride to a garage or shop and stop precaution.

✔ When selling a motorcycle, do not pro your home address or the location where bike is normally kept. Arrange to meet buyer at a location away from your ho Thieves have been known to pose as poter buyers to find out where motorcycles are k and then return later to steal them.

## Security away from the home

As well as fitting security equipment to your motorcycle here are a few general rules to follow whenever you park your motorcycle.

✔ Park in a busy, public place.

✔ Use car parks which incorporate security features, such as CCTV.

✔ At night, park in a well-lit area, preferably directly underneath a street light.

✔ Engage the steering lock.

✔ Secure the motorcycle to a solid, immovable object such as a post or railings with an additional lock. If this is not possible, secure the bike to a friend's motorcy Some public parking places provide secu loops for motorcycles.

✔ Never leave your helmet or lugg attached to the motorcycle. Take them you at all times.

# Lubricants and fluids

A wide range of lubricants, fluids and cleaning agents is available for motor-cycles. This is a guide as to what is available, its applications and properties.

## Four-stroke engine oil

- Engine oil is without doubt the most important component of any four-stroke engine. Modern motorcycle engines place a lot of demands on their oil and choosing the right type is essential. Using an unsuitable oil will lead to an increased rate of engine wear and could result in serious engine damage. Before purchasing oil, always check the recommended oil specification given by the manufacturer. The manufacturer will state a recommended 'type or classification' and also a specific 'viscosity' range for engine oil.
- The oil 'type or classification' is identified by its API (American Petroleum Institute) rating. The API rating will be in the form of two letters, e.g. SG. The S identifies the oil as being suitable for use in a petrol (gasoline) engine (S stands for spark ignition) and the second letter, ranging from A to J, identifies the oil's performance rating. The later this letter, the higher the specification of the oil; for example API SG oil exceeds the requirements of API SF oil. **Note:** *On some oils there may also be a second rating consisting of another two letters, the first letter being C, e.g. API SF/CD. This rating indicates the oil is also suitable for use in a diesel engines (the C stands for compression ignition) and is thus of no relevance for motorcycle use.*
- The 'viscosity' of the oil is identified by its SAE (Society of Automotive Engineers) rating. All modern engines require multigrade oils and the SAE rating will consist of two numbers, the first followed by a W, e.g. 10W/40. The first number indicates the viscosity rating of the oil at low temperatures (W stands for winter – tested at –20°C) and the second number represents the viscosity of the oil at high temperatures (tested at 100°C). The lower the number, the thinner the oil. For example an oil with an SAE 10W/40 rating will give better cold starting and running than an SAE 15W/40 oil.
- As well as ensuring the 'type' and 'viscosity' of the oil match the recommendations, another consideration to make when buying engine oil is whether to purchase a standard mineral-based oil, a semi-synthetic oil (also known as a synthetic blend or synthetic-based oil) or a fully-synthetic oil. Although all oils will have a similar rating and viscosity, their cost will vary considerably; mineral-based oils are the cheapest, the fully-synthetic oils the most expensive with the semi-synthetic oils falling somewhere in-between. This decision is very much up to the owner, but it should be noted that modern synthetic oils have far better lubricating and cleaning qualities than traditional mineral-based oils and tend to retain these properties for far longer. Bearing in mind the operating conditions inside a modern, high-revving motorcycle engine it is highly recommended that a fully synthetic oil is used. The extra expense at each service could save you money in the long term by preventing premature engine wear.
- As a final note always ensure that the oil is specifically designed for use in motorcycle engines. Engine oils designed primarily for use in car engines sometimes contain additives or friction modifiers which could cause clutch slip on a motorcycle fitted with a wet-clutch.

## Two-stroke engine oil

- Modern two-stroke engines, with their high power outputs, place high demands on their oil. If engine seizure is to be avoided it is essential that a high-quality oil is used. Two-stroke oils differ hugely from four-stroke oils. The oil lubricates only the crankshaft and piston(s) (the transmission has its own lubricating oil) and is used on a total-loss basis where it is burnt completely during the combustion process.
- The Japanese have recently introduced a classification system for two-stroke oils, the JASO rating. This rating is in the form of two letters, either FA, FB or FC – FA is the lowest classification and FC the highest. Ensure the oil being used meets or exceeds the recommended rating specified by the manufacturer.
- As well as ensuring the oil rating matches the recommendation, another consideration to make when buying engine oil is whether to purchase a standard mineral-based oil, a semi-synthetic oil (also known as a synthetic blend or synthetic-based oil) or a fully-synthetic oil. The cost of each type of oil varies considerably; mineral-based oils are the cheapest, the fully-synthetic oils the most expensive with the semi-synthetic oils falling somewhere in-between. This decision is very much up to the owner, but it should be noted that modern synthetic oils have far better lubricating properties and burn cleaner than traditional mineral-based oils. It is therefore recommended that a fully synthetic oil is used. The extra expense could save you money in the long term by preventing premature engine wear, engine performance will be improved, carbon deposits and exhaust smoke will be reduced.

designed for use in an injector system. Many high quality two-stroke oils are designed for competition use and need to be pre-mixed with fuel. These oils are of a much higher viscosity and are not designed to flow through the injector pumps used on road-going two-stroke motorcycles.

## Transmission (gear) oil

- On a two-stroke engine, the transmission and clutch are lubricated by their own separate oil bath which must be changed in accordance with the Maintenance Schedule.
- Although the engine and transmission units of most four-strokes use a common lubrication supply, there are some exceptions where the engine and gearbox have separate oil reservoirs and a dry clutch is used.
- Motorcycle manufacturers will either recommend a monograde transmission oil or a four-stroke multigrade engine oil to lubricate the transmission.
- Transmission oils, or gear oils as they are often called, are designed specifically for use in transmission systems. The viscosity of these oils is represented by an SAE number, but the scale of measurement applied is different to that used to grade engine oils. As a rough guide a SAE90 gear oil will be of the same viscosity as an SAE50 engine oil.

## Shaft drive oil

- On models equipped with shaft final drive, the shaft drive gears are will have their own oil supply. The manufacturer will state a recommended 'type or classification' and also a specific 'viscosity' range in the same manner as for four-stroke engine oil.
- Gear oil classification is given by the number which follows the API GL (GL standing for gear lubricant) rating, the higher the number, the higher the specification of the oil, e.g. API GL5 oil is a higher specification than API GL4 oil. Ensure the oil meets or

the correct viscosity. The viscosity of gear oils is also represented by an SAE number but the scale of measurement used is different to that used to grade engine oils. As a rough guide an SAE90 gear oil will be of the same viscosity as an SAE50 engine oil.

- If the use of an EP (Extreme Pressure) gear oil is specified, ensure the oil purchased is suitable.

## Fork oil and suspension fluid

- Conventional telescopic front forks are hydraulic and require fork oil to work. To ensure the forks function correctly, the fork oil must be changed in accordance with the Maintenance Schedule.
- Fork oil is available in a variety of viscosities, identified by their SAE rating; fork oil ratings vary from light (SAE 5) to heavy (SAE 30). When purchasing fork oil, ensure the viscosity rating matches that specified by the manufacturer.
- Some lubricant manufacturers also produce a range of high-quality suspension fluids which are very similar to fork oil but are designed mainly for competition use. These fluids may have a different viscosity rating system which is not to be confused with the SAE rating of normal fork oil. Refer to the manufacturer's instructions if in any doubt.

## Brake and clutch fluid

- All disc brake systems and some clutch systems are hydraulically operated. To ensure correct operation, the hydraulic fluid must be changed in accordance with the Maintenance Schedule.
- Brake and clutch fluid is classified by its DOT rating with most motorcycle manufacturers specifying DOT 3 or 4 fluid. Both fluid types are glycol-based and can be mixed together without adverse effect; DOT 4 fluid exceeds the requirements of DOT 3

system designed for use with DOT 3 never use DOT 3 fluid in a system w specifies the use of DOT 4 as this will adve affect the system's performance. The required for the system will be marked o fluid reservoir cap.

- Some manufacturers also produce a D hydraulic fluid. DOT 5 hydraulic flui silicone-based and is not compatible wit glycol-based DOT 3 and 4 fluids. Never DOT 5 fluid with DOT 3 or 4 fluid as this seriously affect the performance of hydraulic system.

## Coolant/antifreeze

- When purchasing coolant/antifreeze, always ensure it is suitable for use in an aluminium engine and contains corrosion inhibitors to prevent possible blockages of the internal coolant passages of the system. As a general rule, most coolants are designed to be used neat and should not be diluted whereas antifreeze can be mixed with distilled water to provide a coolant solution of the requ strength. Refer to the manufactu instructions on the bottle.
- Ensure the coolant is change accordance with the Maintenance Sched

## Chain lube

- Chain lube is an aerosol-type spray lubricant specifically designed for use on motorcycle final drive chains. Chain lube has two functions, to minimise friction between the final drive chain and sprockets and to prevent corrosion of the chain. Regular use of a good-quality chain lube will extend the life of the drive chain and sprockets and thus maximise the power being transmitted from the transmission to the rear wheel.
- When using chain lube, always a some time for the solvents in the lub evaporate before riding the motorcycle. will minimise the amount of lube which

is used. If the motorcycle is equipped with an 'O-ring' chain, ensure the chain lube is labelled as being suitable for use on 'O-ring' chains.

## Degreasers and solvents

● There are many different types of solvents and degreasers available to remove the grime and grease which accumulate around the motorcycle during normal use. Degreasers and solvents are usually available as an aerosol-type spray or as a liquid which you apply with a brush. Always closely follow the manufacturer's instructions and wear eye protection during use. Be aware that many solvents are flammable and may give off noxious fumes; take adequate precautions when using them (*see Safety First!*).

● For general cleaning, use one of the many solvents or degreasers available from most motorcycle accessory shops. These solvents are usually applied then left for a certain time before being washed off with water.

**Brake cleaner** is a solvent specifically designed to remove all traces of oil, grease and dust from braking system components. Brake cleaner is designed to evaporate quickly and leaves behind no residue.

**Carburettor cleaner** is an aerosol-type solvent specifically designed to clear carburettor blockages and break down the hard deposits and gum often found inside carburettors during overhaul.

**Contact cleaner** is an aerosol-type solvent designed for cleaning electrical components. The cleaner will remove all traces of oil and dirt from components such as switch contacts or fouled spark plugs and then dry, leaving behind no residue.

**Gasket remover** is an aerosol-type solvent designed for removing stubborn gaskets from engine components during overhaul. Gasket remover will minimise the amount of scraping required to remove the gasket and therefore reduce the risk of damage to the mating surface.

## Spray lubricants

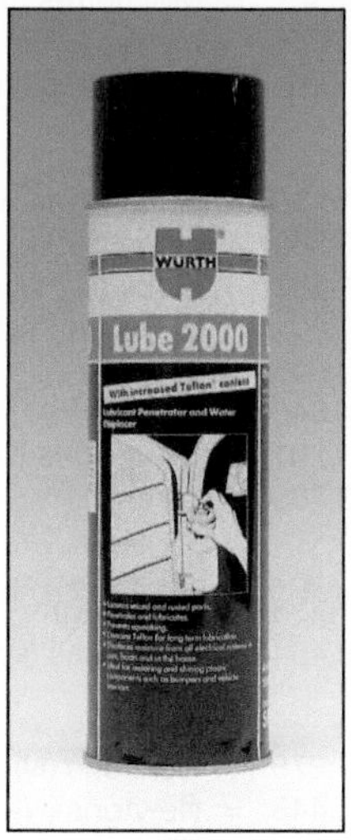


● Aerosol-based spray lubricants are widely available and are excellent for lubricating lever pivots and exposed cables and switches. Try to use a lubricant which is of the dry-film type as the fluid evaporates, leaving behind a dry-film of lubricant. Lubricants which leave behind an oily residue will attract dust and dirt which will increase the rate of wear of the cable/lever.

● Most lubricants also act as a moisture dispersant and a penetrating fluid. This means they can also be used to 'dry out' electrical components such as wiring connectors or switches as well as helping to free seized fasteners.

## Greases

● Grease is used to lubricate many of the pivot-points. A good-quality multi-purpose grease is suitable for most applications but some manufacturers will specify the use of specialist greases for use on components such as swingarm and suspension linkage bushes. These specialist greases can be purchased from most motorcycle (or car) accessory shops; commonly specified types include molybdenum disulphide grease, lithium-based grease, graphite-based grease, silicone-based grease and high-temperature copper-based grease.

## Gasket sealing compounds

● Gasket sealing compounds can be used in conjunction with gaskets, to improve their sealing capabilities, or on their own to seal metal-to-metal joints. Depending on their type, sealing compounds either set hard or stay relatively soft and pliable.

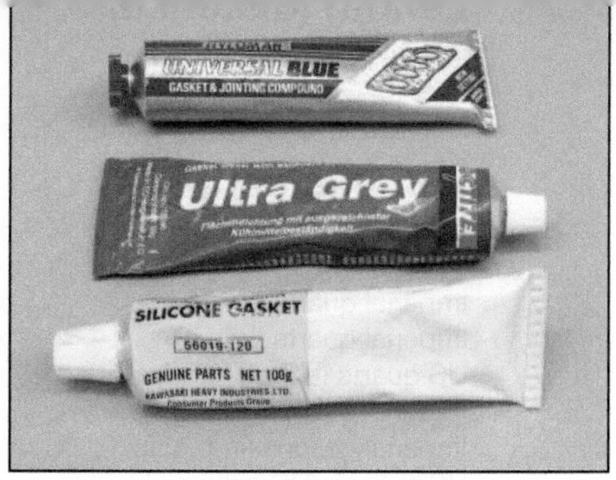


● When purchasing a gasket sealing compound, ensure that it is designed specifically for use on an internal combustion engine. General multi-purpose sealants available from DIY stores may appear visibly similar but they are not designed to withstand the extreme heat or contact with fuel and oil encountered when used on an engine (*see 'Tools and Workshop Tips' for further information*).

## Thread locking compound

● Thread locking compounds are used to secure certain threaded fasteners in position to prevent them from loosening due to vibration. Thread locking compounds can be purchased from most motorcycle (and car) accessory shops. Ensure the threads of the both components are completely clean and dry before sparingly applying the locking compound (*see 'Tools and Workshop Tips' for further information*).

## Fuel additives

● Fuel additives which protect and clean the fuel system components are widely available. These additives are designed to remove all traces of deposits that build up on the carburettors/injectors and prevent wear, helping the fuel system to operate more efficiently. If a fuel additive is being used, check that it is suitable for use with your motorcycle, especially if your motorcycle is equipped with a catalytic converter.

● Octane boosters are also available. These additives are designed to improve the performance of highly-tuned engines being run on normal pump-fuel and are of no real use on standard motorcycles.

## Length (distance)

| | | | | |
|---|---|---|---|---|
| Inches (in) | x 25.4 | = Millimetres (mm) | x 0.0394 | = Inches (in) |
| Feet (ft) | x 0.305 | = Metres (m) | x 3.281 | = Feet (ft) |
| Miles | x 1.609 | = Kilometres (km) | x 0.621 | = Miles |

## Volume (capacity)

| | | | | |
|---|---|---|---|---|
| Cubic inches (cu in; $in^3$) | x 16.387 | = Cubic centimetres (cc; $cm^3$) | x 0.061 | = Cubic inches (cu in; $in^3$) |
| Imperial pints (Imp pt) | x 0.568 | = Litres (l) | x 1.76 | = Imperial pints (Imp pt) |
| Imperial quarts (Imp qt) | x 1.137 | = Litres (l) | x 0.88 | = Imperial quarts (Imp qt) |
| Imperial quarts (Imp qt) | x 1.201 | = US quarts (US qt) | x 0.833 | = Imperial quarts (Imp qt) |
| US quarts (US qt) | x 0.946 | = Litres (l) | x 1.057 | = US quarts (US qt) |
| Imperial gallons (Imp gal) | x 4.546 | = Litres (l) | x 0.22 | = Imperial gallons (Imp gal) |
| Imperial gallons (Imp gal) | x 1.201 | = US gallons (US gal) | x 0.833 | = Imperial gallons (Imp gal) |
| US gallons (US gal) | x 3.785 | = Litres (l) | x 0.264 | = US gallons (US gal) |

## Mass (weight)

| | | | | |
|---|---|---|---|---|
| Ounces (oz) | x 28.35 | = Grams (g) | x 0.035 | = Ounces (oz) |
| Pounds (lb) | x 0.454 | = Kilograms (kg) | x 2.205 | = Pounds (lb) |

## Force

| | | | | |
|---|---|---|---|---|
| Ounces-force (ozf; oz) | x 0.278 | = Newtons (N) | x 3.6 | = Ounces-force (ozf; oz) |
| Pounds-force (lbf; lb) | x 4.448 | = Newtons (N) | x 0.225 | = Pounds-force (lbf; lb) |
| Newtons (N) | x 0.1 | = Kilograms-force (kgf; kg) | x 9.81 | = Newtons (N) |

## Pressure

| | | | | |
|---|---|---|---|---|
| Pounds-force per square inch (psi; $lbf/in^2$; $lb/in^2$) | x 0.070 | = Kilograms-force per square centimetre ($kgf/cm^2$; $kg/cm^2$) | x 14.223 | = Pounds-force per square inch (psi; $lbf/in^2$; $lb/in^2$) |
| Pounds-force per square inch (psi; $lbf/in^2$; $lb/in^2$) | x 0.068 | = Atmospheres (atm) | x 14.696 | = Pounds-force per square inch (psi; $lbf/in^2$; $lb/in^2$) |
| Pounds-force per square inch (psi; $lbf/in^2$; $lb/in^2$) | x 0.069 | = Bars | x 14.5 | = Pounds-force per square inch (psi; $lbf/in^2$; $lb/in^2$) |
| Pounds-force per square inch (psi; $lbf/in^2$; $lb/in^2$) | x 6.895 | = Kilopascals (kPa) | x 0.145 | = Pounds-force per square inch (psi; $lbf/in^2$; $lb/in^2$) |
| Kilopascals (kPa) | x 0.01 | = Kilograms-force per square centimetre ($kgf/cm^2$; $kg/cm^2$) | x 98.1 | = Kilopascals (kPa) |
| Millibar (mbar) | x 100 | = Pascals (Pa) | x 0.01 | = Millibar (mbar) |
| Millibar (mbar) | x 0.0145 | = Pounds-force per square inch (psi; $lbf/in^2$; $lb/in^2$) | x 68.947 | = Millibar (mbar) |
| Millibar (mbar) | x 0.75 | = Millimetres of mercury (mmHg) | x 1.333 | = Millibar (mbar) |
| Millibar (mbar) | x 0.401 | = Inches of water ($inH_2O$) | x 2.491 | = Millibar (mbar) |
| Millimetres of mercury (mmHg) | x 0.535 | = Inches of water ($inH_2O$) | x 1.868 | = Millimetres of mercury (mmHg) |
| Inches of water ($inH_2O$) | x 0.036 | = Pounds-force per square inch (psi; $lbf/in^2$; $lb/in^2$) | x 27.68 | = Inches of water ($inH_2O$) |

## Torque (moment of force)

| | | | | |
|---|---|---|---|---|
| Pounds-force inches (lbf in; lb in) | x 1.152 | = Kilograms-force centimetre (kgf cm; kg cm) | x 0.868 | = Pounds-force inches (lbf in; lb in) |
| Pounds-force inches (lbf in; lb in) | x 0.113 | = Newton metres (Nm) | x 8.85 | = Pounds-force inches (lbf in; lb in) |
| Pounds-force inches (lbf in; lb in) | x 0.083 | = Pounds-force feet (lbf ft; lb ft) | x 12 | = Pounds-force inches (lbf in; lb in) |
| Pounds-force feet (lbf ft; lb ft) | x 0.138 | = Kilograms-force metres (kgf m; kg m) | x 7.233 | = Pounds-force feet (lbf ft; lb ft) |
| Pounds-force feet (lbf ft; lb ft) | x 1.356 | = Newton metres (Nm) | x 0.738 | = Pounds-force feet (lbf ft; lb ft) |
| Newton metres (Nm) | x 0.102 | = Kilograms-force metres (kgf m; kg m) | x 9.804 | = Newton metres (Nm) |

## Power

| | | | | |
|---|---|---|---|---|
| Horsepower (hp) | x 745.7 | = Watts (W) | x 0.0013 | = Horsepower (hp) |

## Velocity (speed)

| | | | | |
|---|---|---|---|---|
| Miles per hour (miles/hr; mph) | x 1.609 | = Kilometres per hour (km/hr; kph) | x 0.621 | = Miles per hour (miles/hr; mph) |

## Fuel consumption*

| | | | | |
|---|---|---|---|---|
| Miles per gallon (mpg) | x 0.354 | = Kilometres per litre (km/l) | x 2.825 | = Miles per gallon (mpg) |

## Temperature

Degrees Fahrenheit = (°C x 1.8) + 32

Degrees Celsius (Degrees Centigrade; °C) = (°F - 32) x 0.56

** It is common practice to convert from miles per gallon (mpg) to litres/100 kilometres (l/100km), where mpg x l/100 km = 282*

## About the MOT Test

In the UK, all vehicles more than three years old are subject to an annual test to ensure that they meet minimum safety requirements. A current test certificate must be issued before a machine can be used on public roads, and is required before a road fund licence can be issued. Riding without a current test certificate will also invalidate your insurance.

For most owners, the MOT test is an annual cause for anxiety, and this is largely due to owners not being sure what needs to be checked prior to submitting the motorcycle for testing. The simple answer is that a fully roadworthy motorcycle will have no difficulty in passing the test.

This is a guide to getting your motorcycle through the MOT test. Obviously it will not be possible to examine the motorcycle to the same standard as the professional MOT tester, particularly in view of the equipment required for some of the checks. However, working through the following procedures will enable you to identify any problem areas before submitting the motorcycle for the test.

It has only been possible to summarise the test requirements here, based on the regulations in force at the time of printing. Test standards are becoming increasingly stringent, although there are some exemptions for older vehicles. More information about the MOT test can be obtained from the TSO publications, *How Safe is your Motorcycle* and *The MOT Inspection Manual for Motorcycle Testing*.

Many of the checks require that one of the wheels is raised off the ground. If the motorcycle doesn't have a centre stand, note that an auxiliary stand will be required. Additionally, the help of an assistant may prove useful.

Certain exceptions apply to machines under 50 cc, machines without a lighting system, and Classic bikes - if in doubt about any of the requirements listed below seek confirmation from an MOT tester prior to submitting the motorcycle for the test.

Check that the frame number is clearly visible.

**HAYNES HiNT** ***If a component is in borderline condition, the tester has discretion in deciding whether to pass or fail it. If the motorcycle presented is clean and evidently well cared for, the tester may be more inclined to pass a borderline component than if the motorcycle is scruffy and apparently neglected.***

# Electrical System

### Lights, turn signals, horn and reflector

✔ With the ignition on, check the operation of the following electrical components. **Note:** *The electrical components on certain small-capacity machines are powered by the generator, requiring that the engine is run for this check.*

- *a) Headlight and tail light. Check that both illuminate in the low and high beam switch positions.*
- *b) Position lights. Check that the front position (or sidelight) and tail light illuminate in this switch position.*
- *c) Turn signals. Check that all flash at the correct rate, and that the warning light(s) function correctly. Check that the turn signal switch works correctly.*
- *d) Hazard warning system (where fitted). Check that all four turn signals flash in this switch position.*
- *e) Brake stop light. Check that the light comes on when the front and rear brakes are independently applied. Models first used on or after 1st April 1986 must have a brake light switch on each brake.*
- *f) Horn. Check that the sound is continuous and of reasonable volume.*

✔ Check that there is a red reflector on the rear of the machine, either mounted separately or as part of the tail light lens.

✔ Check the condition of the headlight, tail light and turn signal lenses.

### Headlight beam height

✔ The MOT tester will perform a headlight beam height check using specialised beam setting equipment **(see illustration 1)**. This equipment will not be available to the home mechanic, but if you suspect that the headlight is incorrectly set or may have been maladjusted in the past, you can perform a rough test as follows.

✔ Position the bike in a straight line facing a brick wall. The bike must be off its stand, upright and with a rider seated. Measure the height from the ground to the centre of the headlight and mark a horizontal line on the wall at this height. Position the motorcycle 3.8 metres from the wall and draw a vertical line up the wall central to the centreline of the motorcycle. Switch to dipped beam and check that the beam pattern falls slightly lower than the horizontal line and to the left of the vertical line **(see illustration 2)**.

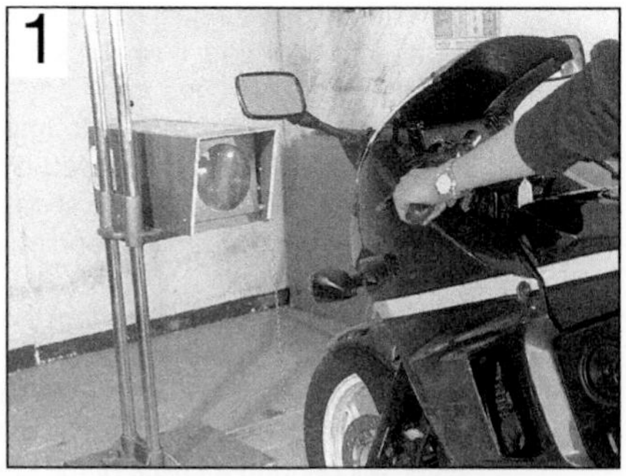


**Headlight beam height checking equipment**

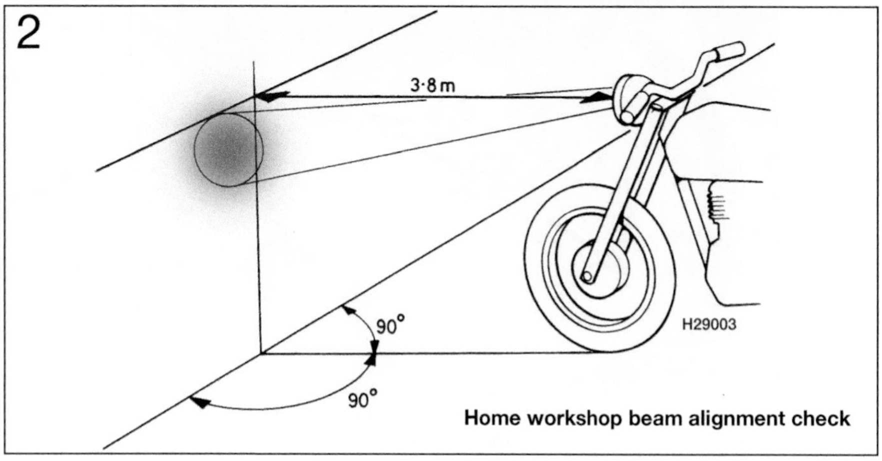


**Home workshop beam alignment check**

# Exhaust System and Final Drive

## Exhaust

✔ Check that the exhaust mountings are secure and that the system does not foul any of the rear suspension components.

✔ Start the motorcycle. When the revs are increased, check that the exhaust is neither holed nor leaking from any of its joints. On a linked system, check that the collector box is not leaking due to corrosion.

✔ Note that the exhaust decibel level ("loudness" of the exhaust) is assessed at the discretion of the tester. If the motorcycle was first used on or after 1st January 1985 the silencer must carry the BSAU 193 stamp, or a marking relating to its make and model, or be of OE (original equipment) manufacture. If the silencer is marked NOT FOR ROAD USE, RACING USE ONLY or similar, it will fail the MOT.

## Final drive

✔ On chain or belt drive machines, ch that the chain/belt is in good condition does not have excessive slack. Also ch that the sprocket is securely mounted or rear wheel hub. Check that the chain guard is in place.

✔ On shaft drive bikes, check for oil lea from the drive unit and fouling the rear tyr

# Steering and Suspension

## Steering

✔ With the front wheel raised off the ground, rotate the steering from lock to lock. The handlebar or switches must not contact the fuel tank or be close enough to trap the rider's hand. Problems can be caused by damaged lock stops on the lower yoke and frame, or by the fitting of non-standard handlebars.

✔ When performing the lock to lock check, also ensure that the steering moves freely without drag or notchiness. Steering movement can be impaired by poorly routed cables, or by overtight head bearings or worn bearings. The tester will perform a check of the steering head bearing lower race by mounting the front wheel on a surface plate, then performing a lock to lock check with the weight of the machine on the lower bearing **(see illustration 3)**.

✔ Grasp the fork sliders (lower legs) and attempt to push and pull on the forks **(see illustration 4)**. Any play in the steering h bearings will be felt. Note that in extr cases, wear of the front fork bushes ca misinterpreted for head bearing play.

✔ Check that the handlebars are secu mounted.

✔ Check that the handlebar grip rubbers secure. They should by bonded to the ba end and to the throttle cable pulley on right end.

3

**Front wheel mounted on a surface plate for steering head bearing lower race check**

## Front suspension

✔ With the motorcycle off the stand, the front brake on and pump the front fork and down **(see illustration 5)**. Check they are adequately damped.

4

**Checking the steering head bearings for freeplay**

5

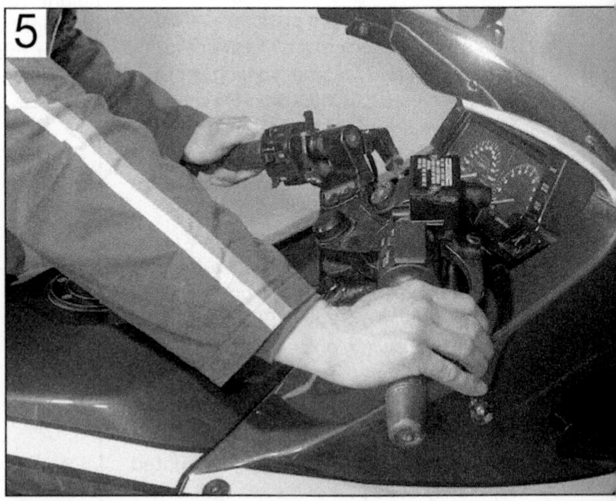

**Hold the front brake on and pump the front forks up and dow check operation**

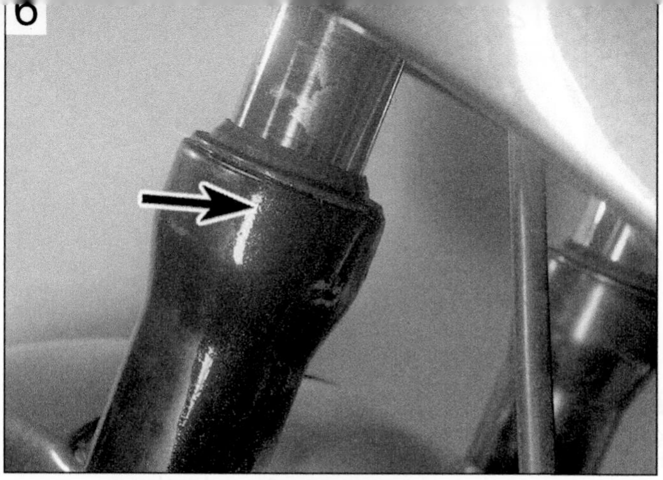


**Inspect the area around the fork dust seal for oil leakage (arrow)**

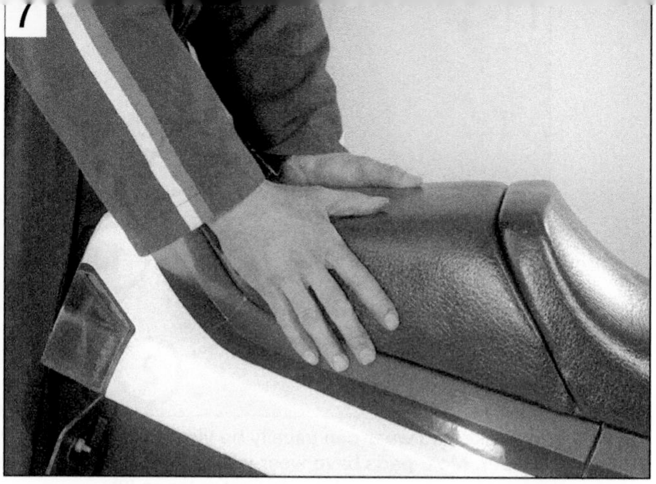


**Bounce the rear of the motorcycle to check rear suspension operation**

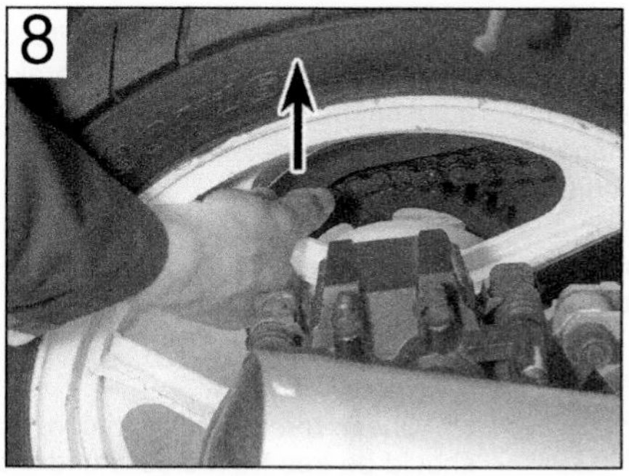


**Checking for rear suspension linkage play**

✔ Inspect the area above and around the front fork oil seals **(see illustration 6)**. There should be no sign of oil on the fork tube (stanchion) nor leaking down the slider (lower leg). On models so equipped, check that there is no oil leaking from the anti-dive units.

✔ On models with swingarm front suspension, check that there is no freeplay in the linkage when moved from side to side.

## Rear suspension

✔ With the motorcycle off the stand and an assistant supporting the motorcycle by its handlebars, bounce the rear suspension **(see illustration 7)**. Check that the suspension components do not foul on any of the cycle parts and check that the shock absorber(s) provide adequate damping.

✔ Visually inspect the shock absorber(s) and check that there is no sign of oil leakage from its damper. This is somewhat restricted on certain single shock models due to the location of the shock absorber.

✔ With the rear wheel raised off the ground, grasp the wheel at the highest point and attempt to pull it up **(see illustration 8)**. Any play in the swingarm pivot or suspension linkage bearings will be felt as movement. **Note:** *Do not confuse play with actual suspension movement.* Failure to lubricate suspension linkage bearings can lead to bearing failure **(see illustration 9)**.

✔ With the rear wheel raised off the ground, grasp the swingarm ends and attempt to move the swingarm from side to side and forwards and backwards - any play indicates wear of the swingarm pivot bearings **(see illustration 10)**.

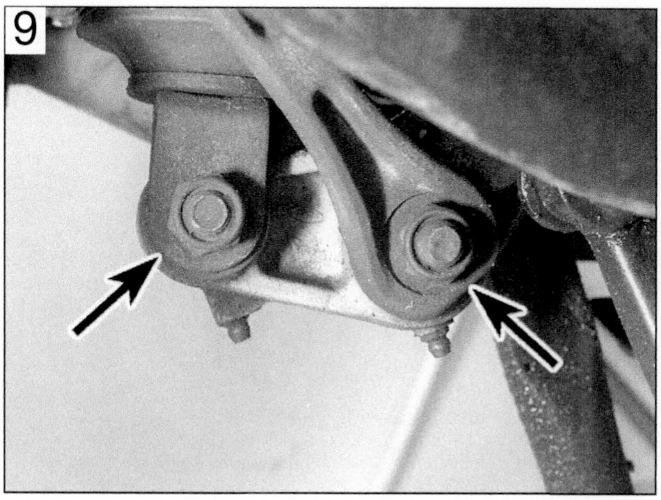


**Worn suspension linkage pivots (arrows) are usually the cause of play in the rear suspension**

**Grasp the swingarm at the ends to check for play in its pivot bearings**

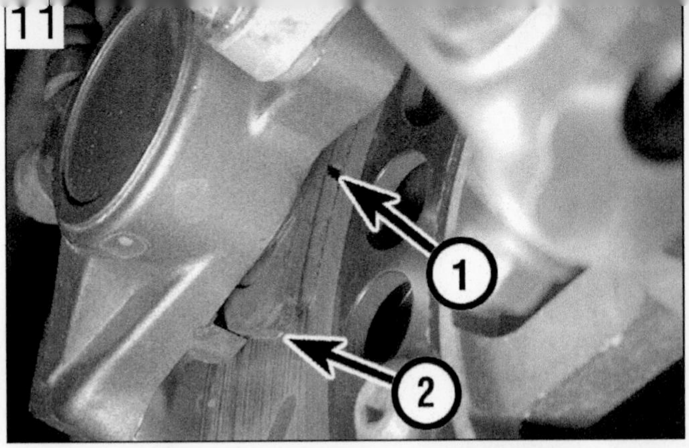

Brake pad wear can usually be viewed without removing the caliper. Most pads have wear indicator grooves (1) and some also have indicator tangs (2)

On drum brakes, check the angle of the operating lever with t brake fully applied. Most drum brakes have a wear indicato pointer and scale.

# Brakes, Wheels and Tyres

## Brakes

✔ With the wheel raised off the ground, apply the brake then free it off, and check that the wheel is about to revolve freely without brake drag.

✔ On disc brakes, examine the disc itself. Check that it is securely mounted and not cracked.

✔ On disc brakes, view the pad material through the caliper mouth and check that the pads are not worn down beyond the limit **(see illustration 11)**.

✔ On drum brakes, check that when the brake is applied the angle between the operating lever and cable or rod is not too great **(see illustration 12)**. Check also that the operating lever doesn't foul any other components.

✔ On disc brakes, examine the flexible hoses from top to bottom. Have an assistant hold the brake on so that the fluid in the hose is under pressure, and check that there is no sign of fluid leakage, bulges or cracking. If there are any metal brake pipes or unions, check that these are free from corrosion and damage. Where a brake-linked anti-dive system is fitted, check the hoses to the anti-dive in a similar manner.

✔ Check that the rear brake torque arm is secure and that its fasteners are secured by self-locking nuts or castellated nuts with split-pins or R-pins **(see illustration 13)**.

✔ On models with ABS, check that the self-check warning light in the instrument panel works.

✔ The MOT tester will perform a test of the motorcycle's braking efficiency based on a calculation of rider and motorcycle weight. Although this cannot be carried out at home, you can at least ensure that the braking systems are properly maintained. For hydraulic disc brakes, check the fluid level, lever/pedal feel (bleed of air if its spongy) pad material. For drum brakes, ch adjustment, cable or rod operation and s lining thickness.

## Wheels and tyres

✔ Check the wheel condition. Cast wh should be free from cracks and if of the b up design, all fasteners should be sec Spoked wheels should be checked broken, corroded, loose or bent spokes.

✔ With the wheel raised off the ground, the wheel and visually check that the tyre wheel run true. Check that the tyre does foul the suspension or mudguards.

✔ With the wheel raised off the grou grasp the wheel and attempt to move it a the axle (spindle) **(see illustration 14)**. play felt here indicates wheel bearing failu

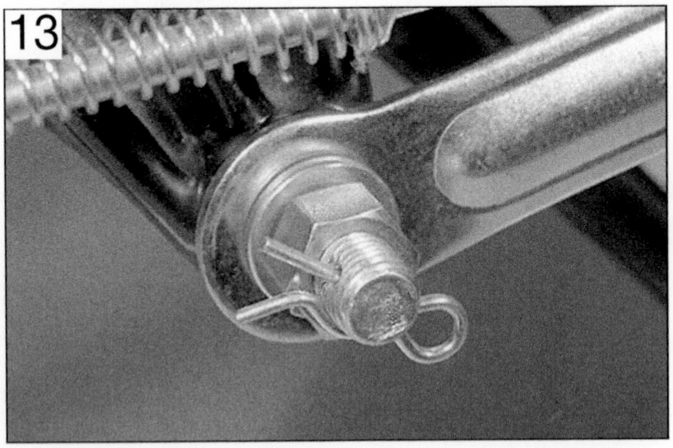

Brake torque arm must be properly secured at both ends

Check for wheel bearing play by trying to move the wheel ab the axle (spindle)

Checking the tyre tread depth

Tyre direction of rotation arrow can be found on tyre sidewall

**Castellated type wheel axle (spindle) nut must be secured by a split pin or R-pin**

✔ Check the tyre tread depth, tread condition and sidewall condition **(see illustration 15)**.

✔ Check the tyre type. Front and rear tyre types must be compatible and be suitable for road use. Tyres marked NOT FOR ROAD USE, COMPETITION USE ONLY or similar, will fail the MOT.

**Two straightedges are used to check wheel alignment**

✔ If the tyre sidewall carries a direction of rotation arrow, this must be pointing in the direction of normal wheel rotation **(see illustration 16)**.

✔ Check that the wheel axle (spindle) nuts (where applicable) are properly secured. A self-locking nut or castellated nut with a split-pin or R-pin can be used **(see illustration 17)**.

✔ Wheel alignment is checked with the motorcycle off the stand and a rider seated. With the front wheel pointing straight ahead, two perfectly straight lengths of metal or wood and placed against the sidewalls of both tyres **(see illustration 18)**. The gap each side of the front tyre must be equidistant on both sides. Incorrect wheel alignment may be due to a cocked rear wheel (often as the result of poor chain adjustment) or in extreme cases, a bent frame.

# General checks and condition

✔ Check the security of all major fasteners, bodypanels, seat, fairings (where fitted) and mudguards.

✔ Check that the rider and pillion footrests, handlebar levers and brake pedal are securely mounted.

✔ Check for corrosion on the frame or any load-bearing components. If severe, this may affect the structure, particularly under stress.

# Sidecars

A motorcycle fitted with a sidecar requires additional checks relating to the stability of the machine and security of attachment and swivel joints, plus specific wheel alignment (toe-in) requirements. Additionally, tyre and lighting requirements differ from conventional motorcycle use. Owners are advised to check MOT test requirements with an official test centre.

# Preparing for storage

## Before you start

If repairs or an overhaul is needed, see that this is carried out now rather than left until you want to ride the bike again.

Give the bike a good wash and scrub all dirt from its underside. Make sure the bike dries completely before preparing for storage.

## Engine

- Remove the spark plug(s) and lubricate the cylinder bores with approximately a teaspoon of motor oil using a spout-type oil can **(see illustration 1)**. Reinstall the spark plug(s). Crank the engine over a couple of times to coat the piston rings and bores with oil. If the bike has a kickstart, use this to turn the engine over. If not, flick the kill switch to the OFF position and crank the engine over on the starter **(see illustration 2)**. If the nature on the ignition system prevents the starter operating with the kill switch in the OFF position, remove the spark plugs and fit them back in their caps; ensure that the plugs are earthed (grounded) against the cylinder head when the starter is operated **(see illustration 3)**.

***Warning: It is important that the plugs are earthed (grounded) away from the spark plug holes otherwise there is a risk of atomised fuel from the cylinders igniting.***

**HAYNES HiNT** ***On a single cylinder four-stroke engine, you can seal the combustion chamber completely by positioning the piston at TDC on the compression stroke.***

- Drain the carburettor(s) otherwise there is a risk of jets becoming blocked by gum deposits from the fuel **(see illustration 4)**.

- If the bike is going into long-term stor consider adding a fuel stabiliser to the fu the tank. If the tank is drained comple corrosion of its internal surfaces may occ left unprotected for a long period. The can be treated with a rust prevent especially for this purpose. Alternati remove the tank and pour half a litre of m oil into it, install the filler cap and shake tank to coat its internals with oil be draining off the excess. The same effect also be achieved by spraying WD40 similar water-dispersant around the insic the tank via its flexible nozzle.

- Make sure the cooling system contains correct mix of antifreeze. Antifreeze contains important corrosion inhibitors.

- The air intakes and exhaust can be se off by covering or plugging the openi Ensure that you do not seal in condensation; run the engine until it is

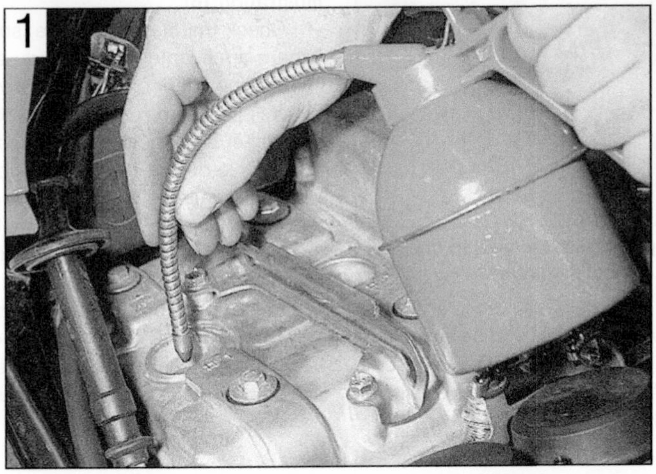

Squirt a drop of motor oil into each cylinder

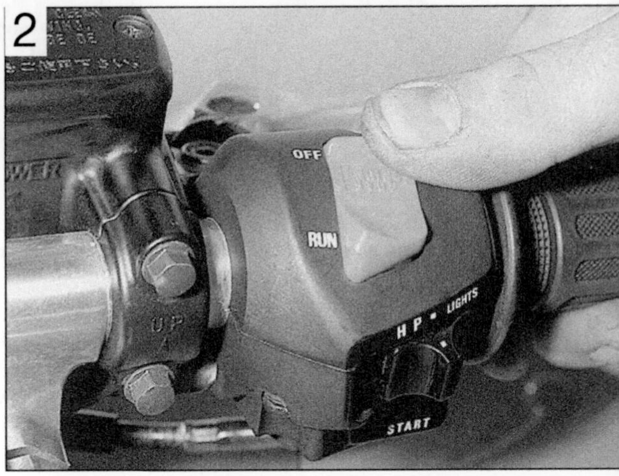


Flick the kill switch to OFF . . .

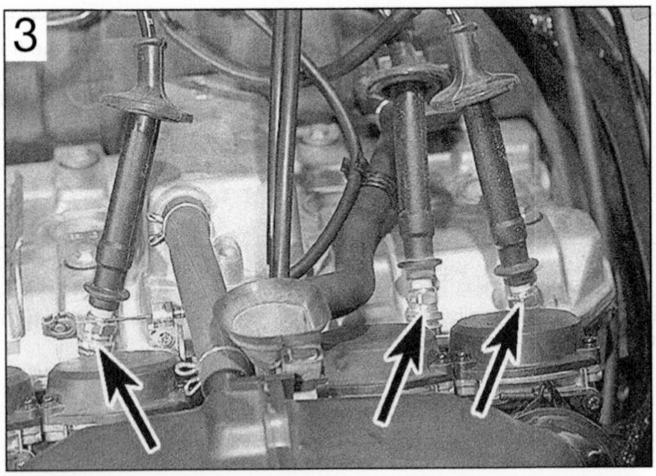

. . . and ensure that the metal bodies of the plugs (arrows) are earthed against the cylinder head

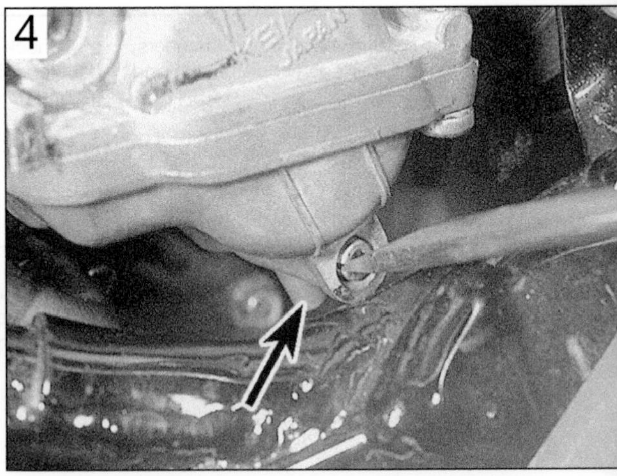

Connect a hose to the carburettor float chamber drain stu (arrow) and unscrew the drain screw

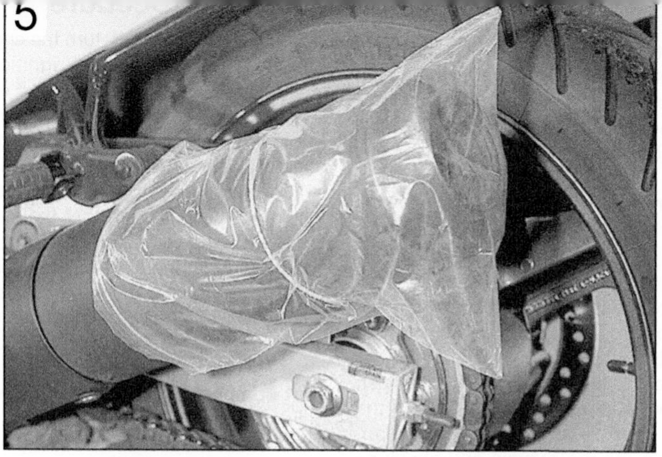

**Exhausts can be sealed off with a plastic bag**

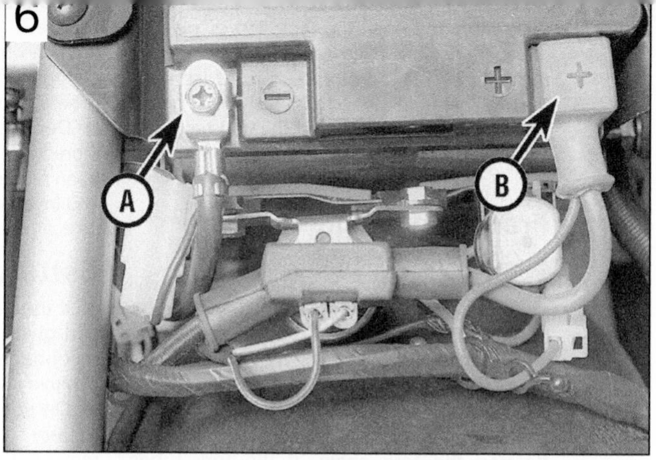


**Disconnect the negative lead (A) first, followed by the positive lead (B)**

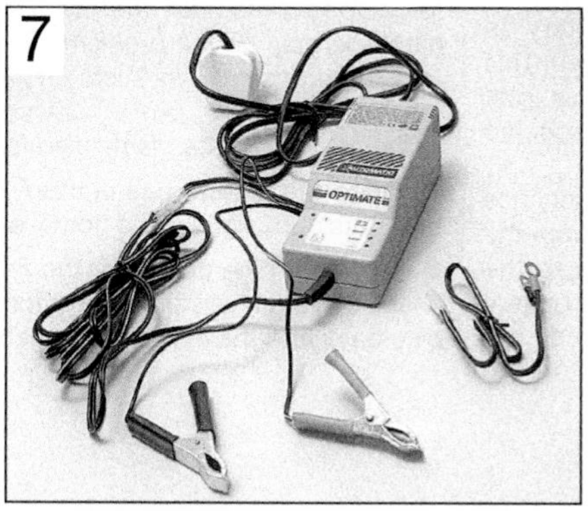

**Use a suitable battery charger - this kit also assess battery condition**

then switch off and allow to cool. Tape a piece of thick plastic over the silencer end(s) **(see illustration 5)**. Note that some advocate pouring a tablespoon of motor oil into the silencer(s) before sealing them off.

## Battery

● Remove it from the bike - in extreme cases of cold the battery may freeze and crack its case **(see illustration 6)**.

● Check the electrolyte level and top up if necessary (conventional refillable batteries). Clean the terminals.

● Store the battery off the motorcycle and away from any sources of fire. Position a wooden block under the battery if it is to sit on the ground.

● Give the battery a trickle charge for a few hours every month **(see illustration 7)**.

## Tyres

● Place the bike on its centrestand or an auxiliary stand which will support the motorcycle in an upright position. Position wood blocks under the tyres to keep them off the ground and to provide insulation from damp. If the bike is being put into long-term storage, ideally both tyres should be off the ground; not only will this protect the tyres, but will also ensure that no load is placed on the steering head or wheel bearings.

● Deflate each tyre by 5 to 10 psi, no more or the beads may unseat from the rim, making subsequent inflation difficult on tubeless tyres.

## Pivots and controls

● Lubricate all lever, pedal, stand and footrest pivot points. If grease nipples are fitted to the rear suspension components, apply lubricant to the pivots.

● Lubricate all control cables.

## Cycle components

● Apply a wax protectant to all painted and plastic components. Wipe off any excess, but don't polish to a shine. Where fitted, clean the screen with soap and water.

● Coat metal parts with Vaseline (petroleum jelly). When applying this to the fork tubes, do not compress the forks otherwise the seals will rot from contact with the Vaseline.

● Apply a vinyl cleaner to the seat.

## Storage conditions

● Aim to store the bike in a shed or garage which does not leak and is free from damp.

● Drape an old blanket or bedspread over the bike to protect it from dust and direct contact with sunlight (which will fade paint). This also hides the bike from prying eyes. Beware of tight-fitting plastic covers which may allow condensation to form and settle on the bike.

# Getting back on the road

## Engine and transmission

● Change the oil and replace the oil filter. If this was done prior to storage, check that the oil hasn't emulsified - a thick whitish substance which occurs through condensation.

● Remove the spark plugs. Using a spout-type oil can, squirt a few drops of oil into the cylinder(s). This will provide initial lubrication as the piston rings and bores comes back into contact. Service the spark plugs, or fit new ones, and install them in the engine.

● Check that the clutch isn't stuck on. The plates can stick together if left standing for some time, preventing clutch operation. Engage a gear and try rocking the bike back and forth with the clutch lever held against the handlebar. If this doesn't work on cable-operated clutches, hold the clutch lever back against the handlebar with a strong elastic band or cable tie for a couple of hours **(see illustration 8)**.

● If the air intakes or silencer end(s) were blocked off, remove the bung or cover used.

● If the fuel tank was coated with a rust

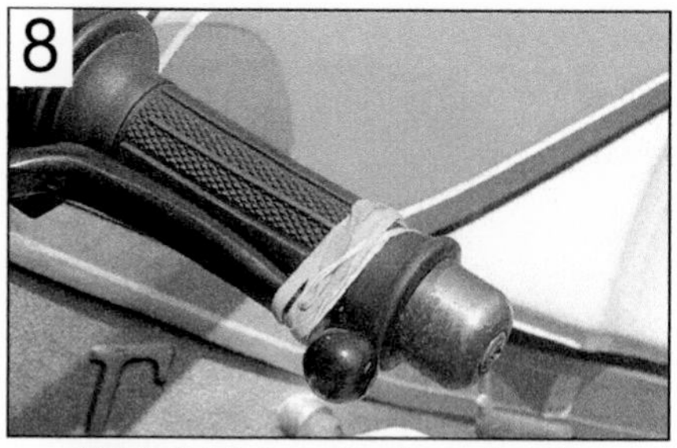

**Hold clutch lever back against the handlebar with elastic bands or a cable tie**

preventative, oil or a stabiliser added to the fuel, drain and flush the tank and dispose of the fuel sensibly. If no action was taken with the fuel tank prior to storage, it is advised that the old fuel is disposed of since it will go off over a period of time. Refill the fuel tank with fresh fuel.

## Frame and running gear

- Oil all pivot points and cables.
- Check the tyre pressures. They will definitely need inflating if pressures were reduced for storage.
- Lubricate the final drive chain (where applicable).
- Remove any protective coating applied to the fork tubes (stanchions) since this may well destroy the fork seals. If the fork tubes weren't protected and have picked up rust spots, remove them with very fine abrasive paper and refinish with metal polish.
- Check that both brakes operate correctly. Apply each brake hard and check that it's not possible to move the motorcycle forwards, then check that the brake frees off again once released. Brake caliper pistons can stick due to corrosion around the piston head, or on the sliding caliper types, due to corrosion of the slider pins. If the brake doesn't free after repeated operation, take the caliper off for examination. Similarly drum brakes can stick due to a seized operating cam, cable or rod linkage.
- If the motorcycle has been in long-term storage, renew the brake fluid and clutch fluid (where applicable).
- Depending on where the bike has been stored, the wiring, cables and hoses may have been nibbled by rodents. Make a visual check and investigate disturbed wiring loom tape.

## Battery

- If the battery has been previously removal and given top up charges it can simply be reconnected. Remember to connect the positive cable first and the negative cable last.
- On conventional refillable batteries, if the battery has not received any attention, remove it from the motorcycle and check its electrolyte level. Top up if necessary then charge the battery. If the battery fails to hold a charge and a visual checks show heavy white sulphation of the plates, the battery is probably defective and must be renewed. This is particularly likely if the battery is old. Confirm battery condition with a specific gravity check.
- On sealed (MF) batteries, if the battery has not received any attention, remove it from the motorcycle and charge it according to the information on the battery case - if the battery fails to hold a charge it must be renewed.

## St ting procedure

- If a kickstart is fitted, turn the engine ov couple of times with the ignition OFF distribute oil around the engine. If no kicks is fitted, flick the engine kill switch OFF the ignition ON and crank the engine ov couple of times to work oil around the u cylinder components. If the nature of ignition system is such that the starter w work with the kill switch OFF, remove spark plugs, fit them back into their caps earth (ground) their bodies on the cylir head. Reinstall the spark plugs afterwards
- Switch the kill switch to RUN, operate choke and start the engine. If the engine w start don't continue cranking the engine - only will this flatten the battery, but the st motor will overheat. Switch the ignition off try again later. If the engine refuses to s go through the fault finding procedures in manual. **Note:** *If the bike has been in stor for a long time, old fuel or a carbure blockage may be the problem. Gum depo in carburettors can block jets - if a carbure cleaner doesn't prove successful carburettors must be dismantled for clean*
- Once the engine has started, check the lights, turn signals and horn work prop
- Treat the bike gently for the first ride check all fluid levels on completion. Settle bike back into the maintenance schedule.

This Section provides an easy reference-guide to the more common faults that are likely to afflict your machine. Obviously, the opportunities are almost limitless for faults to occur as a result of obscure failures, and to try and cover all eventualities would require a book. Indeed, a number have been written on the subject.

Successful troubleshooting is not a mysterious 'black art' but the application of a bit of knowledge combined with a systematic and logical approach to the problem. Approach any troubleshooting by first accurately identifying the symptom and then checking through the list of possible causes, starting with the simplest or most obvious and progressing in stages to the most complex.

Take nothing for granted, but above all apply liberal quantities of common sense.

The main symptom of a fault is given in the text as a major heading below which are listed the various systems or areas which may contain the fault. Details of each possible cause for a fault and the remedial action to be taken are given, in brief, in the paragraphs below each heading. Further information should be sought in the relevant Chapter.

### Starter motor doesn't rotate

- ☐ Ignition switch OFF.
- ☐ Engine kill switch OFF.
- ☐ Fuse blown. Check main fuse and starter circuit fuse (Chapter 9).
- ☐ Battery voltage low. Check and recharge battery (Chapter 9).
- ☐ Starter motor defective. Make sure the wiring to the starter is secure. Make sure the starter relay clicks when the start button is pushed. If the relay clicks, then the fault is in the wiring or motor.
- ☐ Starter relay faulty. Check it according to the procedure in Chapter 9.
- ☐ Starter switch not contacting. The contacts could be wet, corroded or dirty (Chapter 9).
- ☐ Wiring open or shorted. Check all wiring connections and harnesses to make sure that they are dry, tight and not corroded. Also check for broken or frayed wires that can cause a short to ground (earth) (see wiring diagram, Chapter 9).
- ☐ Ignition (main) switch defective. Check the switch according to the procedure in Chapter 9. Renew the switch with a new one if it is defective.
- ☐ Engine kill switch defective. Check for wet, dirty or corroded contacts. Clean or renew the switch as necessary (Chapter 9).
- ☐ Faulty side stand switch – later models. Check the wiring to the switch and the switch itself according to the procedures in Chapter 9.

### Starter motor rotates but engine does not turn over

- ☐ Starter motor clutch defective. Inspect and repair or renew (Chapter 2).
- ☐ Damaged idler or starter gears. Inspect and renew the damaged parts (Chapter 2).

### Starter works but engine won't turn over (seized)

- ☐ Seized engine caused by one or more internally damaged components. Failure due to wear, abuse or lack of lubrication. Damage can include seized valves, followers/rocker arms, camshafts, pistons, crankshaft, connecting rod bearings, or transmission gears or bearings. Refer to Chapter 2 for engine disassembly.

### No fuel flow

- ☐ No fuel in tank.
- ☐ Fuel tank breather hose obstructed.
- ☐ Fuel pump faulty, filter is blocked or internal fuel tank hoses are split/disconnected (see Chapter 4).

### Engine flooded

- ☐ Starting technique incorrect. Under normal circumstances the machine should start with little or no throttle. When the engine is cold, the fast idle button should be operated and the engine started without opening the throttle. When the engine is at operating temperature, only a very slight amount of throttle should be necessary.

### No spark or weak spark

- ☐ Battery voltage low. Check and recharge the battery as necessary (Chapter 9).
- ☐ Spark plugs dirty, defective or worn out. Locate reason for fouled plugs using spark plug condition chart and follow the plug maintenance procedures (Chapter 1).
- ☐ Spark plug caps or secondary (HT) wiring faulty. Check conditi[on]. Renew either or both components if cracks or deterioration are evident (Chapter 5).
- ☐ Spark plug caps not making good contact. Make sure that the plug caps fit snugly over the plug ends.
- ☐ Ignition HT coils defective. Check the coils, referring to Chapte[r]
- ☐ Ignition power module defective (P8 engine management syste[m]). Refer to Chapter 5 for details.
- ☐ Engine management system ECU defective. Referring to Chap[ter] 4 for details.
- ☐ Ignition or kill switch shorted. This is usually caused by water, corrosion, damage or excessive wear. The switches can be cleaned with electrical contact cleaner. If cleaning does not he[lp,] renew the switches (Chapter 9).
- ☐ Wiring shorted or broken between:
  - *a) Ignition (main) switch and engine kill switch (or blown fus[e])*
  - *b) Engine management ECU and engine kill switch*
  - *c) Engine management ECU and ignition HT coils and ignit[ion] power modules (P8 engine management system only)*
  - *d) Ignition HT coils and spark plugs*
- ☐ Make sure that all wiring connections are clean, dry and tight. Look for chafed and broken wires (Chapters 5 and 9).

### Compression low

- ☐ Spark plugs loose. Remove the plugs and inspect their thread[s]. Reinstall and tighten to the specified torque (Chapter 1).
- ☐ Cylinder head not sufficiently tightened down. If the cylinder h[ead] is suspected of being loose, then there's a chance that the gas[ket] or head is damaged if the problem has persisted for any length [of] time. The head nuts should be tightened to the proper torque i[n] the correct sequence (Chapter 2).
- ☐ Improper valve clearance. This means that the valve is not clos[ing] completely and compression pressure is leaking past the valve. Check and adjust the valve clearances (Chapter 1).
- ☐ Cylinder and/or piston worn. Excessive wear will cause compression pressure to leak past the rings. This is usually accompanied by worn rings as well. A top-end overhaul is necessary (Chapter 2).
- ☐ Piston rings worn, weak, broken, or sticking. Broken or stickin[g] piston rings usually indicate a lubrication or fuelling problem th[at] causes excess carbon deposits or seizures to form on the pist[ons] and rings. Top-end overhaul is necessary (Chapter 2).
- ☐ Piston ring-to-groove clearance excessive. This is caused by excessive wear of the piston ring lands. Piston renewal is necessary (Chapter 2).
- ☐ Cylinder head gasket damaged. If a head is allowed to becom[e] loose, or if excessive carbon build-up on the piston crown and combustion chamber causes extremely high compression, the head gasket may leak. Retorquing the head is not always sufficient to restore the seal, so gasket renewal is necessary (Chapter 2).
- ☐ Cylinder head warped. This is caused by overheating or improperly tightened head nuts. Machine shop resurfacing or renewal is necessary (Chapter 2).
- ☐ Valve not seating properly. This is caused by a bent valve (fro[m] over-revving or improper valve adjustment), burned valve or se[at] (improper fuelling) or an accumulation of carbon deposits on t[he] seat (from fuelling or lubrication problems). The valves must b[e] cleaned and/or renewed and the seats serviced if possible (Chapter 2).

### Stalls after starting

- ☐ Improper fast idle button action. Make sure the button is clipping into position and holds the throttle twistgrip slightly open.
- ☐ Engine management (fuel injection/ignition) system malfunction. See Chapter 4.
- ☐ Fuel contaminated. The fuel can be contaminated with either dirt or water, or can change chemically if the machine is allowed to sit for several months or more. Drain the tank (Chapter 4).
- ☐ Intake air leak. Check for loose throttle body intake rubber retaining clips and damaged/disconnected vacuum hoses (Chapter 4).
- ☐ Engine idle speed incorrect. See adjustment procedure in Chapter 1.

### Rough idle

- ☐ Engine management (fuel injection/ignition) system malfunction. See Chapter 4.
- ☐ Throttle bodies not synchronised/idle speed incorrect. See adjustment procedure in Chapter 1.
- ☐ Fuel contaminated. The fuel can be contaminated with either dirt or water, or can change chemically if the machine is allowed to sit for several months or more. Drain the tank (Chapter 4).
- ☐ Intake air leak. Check for loose throttle body intake rubber retaining clips and damaged/disconnected vacuum hoses. Renew the intake manifolds if the rubbers are split or perished (Chapter 4).
- ☐ Air filters clogged. Renew the air filter elements (Chapter 1).

## 2 Poor running at low speeds

### Spark weak

- ☐ Battery voltage low. Check and recharge battery (Chapter 9).
- ☐ Spark plugs fouled, defective or worn out. Refer to Chapter 1 for spark plug maintenance.
- ☐ Spark plug cap or HT wiring defective. Refer to Chapters 1 and 5 for details on the ignition system.
- ☐ Spark plug caps not making contact.
- ☐ Incorrect spark plugs. Wrong type, heat range or cap configuration. Check and install correct plugs listed in Chapter 1.
- ☐ Ignition HT coils defective. See Chapter 5.
- ☐ Engine management (fuel injection/ignition) system malfunction. See Chapter 4.

### Fuel/air mixture incorrect

- ☐ Mixture adjustment screw incorrectly set (Chapter 1)
- ☐ Fuel injector(s) blocked/faulty. Use the recommended fuel additive to clean the injectors (see Chapter 4). If this fails to solve the problem the injector(s) will have to be renewed.
- ☐ Air filters clogged, poorly sealed or missing (Chapter 1).
- ☐ Air filter housings poorly sealed. Look for cracks, holes or loose clamps and renew or repair defective parts.
- ☐ Fuel tank breather hose obstructed.
- ☐ Intake air leak. Check for loose throttle body intake rubber retaining clips and damaged/disconnected vacuum hoses. Renew the intake manifolds if the rubbers are split or perished (Chapter 4).

### Compression low

- ☐ Spark plugs loose. Remove the plugs and inspect their threads. Reinstall and tighten to the specified torque (Chapter 1).
- ☐ Cylinder head not sufficiently tightened down. If the cylinder head is suspected of being loose, then there's a chance that the gasket and head are damaged if the problem has persisted for any length of time. The head nuts should be tightened to the proper torque in the correct sequence (Chapter 2).
- ☐ Improper valve clearance. This means that the valve is not closing completely and compression pressure is leaking past the valve. Check and adjust the valve clearances (Chapter 1).
- ☐ Cylinder and/or piston worn. Excessive wear will cause compression pressure to leak past the rings. This is usually accompanied by worn rings as well. A top-end overhaul is necessary (Chapter 2).
- ☐ Piston rings worn, weak, broken, or sticking. Broken or sticking piston rings usually indicate a lubrication or fuelling problem that causes excess carbon deposits or seizures to form on the pistons and rings. Top-end overhaul is necessary (Chapter 2).
- ☐ Piston ring-to-groove clearance excessive. This is caused by excessive wear of the piston ring lands. Piston renewal is necessary (Chapter 2).
- ☐ Cylinder head gasket damaged. If a head is allowed to become loose, or if excessive carbon build-up on the piston crown and combustion chamber causes extremely high compression, the head gasket may leak. Retorquing the head is not always sufficient to restore the seal, so gasket renewal is necessary (Chapter 2).
- ☐ Cylinder head warped. This is caused by overheating or improperly tightened head nuts. Machine shop resurfacing or head renewal is necessary (Chapter 2).
- ☐ Valve not seating properly. This is caused by a bent valve (from over-revving or improper valve adjustment), burned valve or seat (improper fuelling) or an accumulation of carbon deposits on the seat (from fuelling, lubrication problems). The valves must be cleaned and/or renewed and the seats serviced if possible (Chapter 2).

### Poor acceleration

- ☐ Engine management (fuel injection/ignition) system malfunction. See Chapter 4.
- ☐ Engine oil viscosity too high. Using a heavier oil than that recommended in Chapter 1 can damage the oil pump or lubrication system and cause drag on the engine.
- ☐ Brakes dragging. Usually caused by debris which has entered the brake piston seals, or from a warped disc or bent axle. Repair as necessary (Chapter 7).

## 3 Poor running or no power at high speed

### Firing incorrect

- ☐ Air filters restricted. Renew filters (Chapter 1).
- ☐ Spark plugs fouled, defective or worn out. See Chapter 1 for spark plug maintenance.
- ☐ Spark plug caps or HT wiring defective. See Chapters 1 and 5 for details of the ignition system.
- ☐ Spark plug caps not in good contact. See Chapter 5.
- ☐ Incorrect spark plugs. Wrong type, heat range or cap configuration. Check and install correct plugs listed in Chapter 1.
- ☐ Ignition coils defective. See Chapter 5.
- ☐ Engine management (fuel injection/ignition) system malfunction. See Chapter 4.

### Fuel/air mixture incorrect

- ☐ Fuel injector(s) blocked/faulty. Use the recommended fuel additive to clean the injectors (see Chapter 4). If this fails to solve the problem the injector(s) will have to be renewed.
- ☐ Air filters clogged, poorly sealed, or missing (Chapter 1).
- ☐ Air filter housings poorly sealed. Look for cracks, holes or loose clamps, and renew or repair defective parts.
- ☐ Fuel tank breather hose obstructed.
- ☐ Intake air leak. Check for loose throttle body intake rubber retaining clips and damaged/disconnected vacuum hoses. Renew the intake manifolds if the rubbers are split or perished (Chapter 4).

### Compression low

- ☐ Spark plugs loose. Remove the plugs and inspect their threads. Reinstall and tighten to the specified torque (Chapter 1).
- ☐ Cylinder head not sufficiently tightened down. If the cylinder head is suspected of being loose, then there's a chance that the gasket and head are damaged if the problem has persisted for any length of time. The head nuts should be tightened to the proper torque in the correct sequence (Chapter 2).
- ☐ Improper valve clearance. This means that the valve is not closing completely and compression pressure is leaking past the valve. Check and adjust the valve clearances (Chapter 1).
- ☐ Cylinder and/or piston worn. Excessive wear will cause compression pressure to leak past the rings. This is usually accompanied by worn rings as well. A top-end overhaul is necessary (Chapter 2).
- ☐ Piston rings worn, weak, broken, or sticking. Broken or sticking piston rings usually indicate a lubrication or fuelling problem that causes excess carbon deposits or seizures to form on the pistons and rings. Top-end overhaul is necessary (Chapter 2).
- ☐ Piston ring-to-groove clearance excessive. This is caused by excessive wear of the piston ring lands. Piston renewal is necessary (Chapter 2).
- ☐ Cylinder head gasket damaged. If a head is allowed to become loose, or if excessive carbon build-up on the piston crown and combustion chamber causes extremely high compression, the head gasket may leak. Retorquing the head is not always sufficient to restore the seal, so gasket renewal is necessary (Chapter 2).
- ☐ Cylinder head warped. This is caused by overheating or improperly tightened head nuts. Machine shop resurfacing or h renewal is necessary (Chapter 2).
- ☐ Valve not seating properly. This is caused by a bent valve (from o revving or improper valve adjustment), burned valve or seat (improper fuelling) or an accumulation of carbon deposits on the s (from fuelling or lubrication problems). The valves must be cleane and/or renewed and the seats serviced if possible (Chapter 2).

### Knocking or pinking

- ☐ Carbon build-up in combustion chamber. Use of a fuel additive that will dissolve the adhesive bonding the carbon particles to t crown and chamber is the easiest way to remove the build-up. Otherwise, the cylinder head will have to be removed and decarbonised (Chapter 2).
- ☐ Incorrect or poor quality fuel. Old or improper grades of fuel ca cause detonation. This causes the piston to rattle, thus the knocking or pinking sound. Drain old fuel and always use the recommended fuel grade.
- ☐ Spark plug heat range incorrect. Uncontrolled detonation indica the plug heat range is too hot. The plug in effect becomes a glo plug, raising cylinder temperatures. Install the proper heat rang plug (Chapter 1).
- ☐ Improper air/fuel mixture. This will cause the cylinders to run ho which leads to detonation. An intake air leak can cause this imbalance. See Chapter 4.

### Miscellaneous causes

- ☐ Throttle valve doesn't open fully. Adjust the throttle twistgrip freeplay (Chapter 1).
- ☐ Clutch slipping. May be caused by loose or worn clutch components. Refer to Chapter 2 for clutch overhaul procedure
- ☐ Engine oil viscosity too high. Using a heavier oil than the one recommended in Chapter 1 can damage the oil pump or lubrication system and cause drag on the engine.
- ☐ Brakes dragging. Usually caused by debris which has entered t brake piston seals, or from a warped disc or bent axle. Repair a necessary.

### Engine overheats

- ☐ Coolant level low. Check and add coolant (Daily (pre-ride) checks).
- ☐ Leak in cooling system. Check cooling system hoses and radiator for leaks and other damage. Repair or renew parts as necessary (Chapter 3).
- ☐ Thermostat sticking open or closed. Check and renew as described in Chapter 3.
- ☐ Faulty pressure cap. Remove the cap and have it pressure tested (Chapter 3).
- ☐ Coolant passages clogged. Have the entire system drained and flushed, then refill with fresh coolant (Chapter 1).
- ☐ Water pump defective. Remove the pump and check the components (Chapter 3).
- ☐ Clogged radiator fins. Clean them by blowing compressed air through the fins from the rear face of the radiator.
- ☐ Cooling fan or fan switch fault (Chapter 3).

### Firing incorrect

- ☐ Spark plugs fouled, defective or worn out. See Chapter 1 for spark plug maintenance.
- ☐ Incorrect spark plugs.
- ☐ Faulty ignition coils. See Chapter 5.
- ☐ Ignition power module defective (P8 engine management system). Refer to Chapter 5 for details.
- ☐ Engine management system ECU defective. Referring to Chapter 4 for details.

### Fuel/air mixture incorrect

- ☐ Fuel injector(s) blocked/faulty. Use the recommended fuel additive to clean the injectors (see Chapter 4). If this fails to solve the problem the injector(s) will have to be renewed.
- ☐ Air filters clogged, poorly sealed, or missing (Chapter 1).
- ☐ Air filter housings poorly sealed. Look for cracks, holes or loose clamps, and renew or repair defective parts.
- ☐ Fuel tank breather hose obstructed.
- ☐ Intake air leak. Check for loose throttle body intake rubber retaining clips and damaged/disconnected vacuum hoses. Renew the intake manifolds if the rubbers are split or perished (Chapter 4).

### Compression too high

- ☐ Carbon build-up in combustion chamber. Use of a fuel additive that will dissolve the adhesive bonding the carbon particles to the piston crown and chamber is the easiest way to remove the build-up. Otherwise, the cylinder head will have to be removed and decarbonised (Chapter 2).
- ☐ Improperly machined head surface or installation of incorrect gasket during engine assembly.

### Engine load excessive

- ☐ Clutch slipping. Can be caused by damaged, loose or worn clutch components. Refer to Chapter 2 for overhaul procedures.
- ☐ Engine oil level too high. The addition of too much oil will cause pressurisation of the crankcase and inefficient engine operation. Check Specifications and drain to proper level (Chapter 1).
- ☐ Engine oil viscosity too high. Using a heavier oil than the one recommended in Chapter 1 can damage the oil pump or lubrication system as well as cause drag on the engine.
- ☐ Brakes dragging. Usually caused by debris which has entered the brake piston seals, or from a warped disc or bent axle. Repair as necessary.

### Lubrication inadequate

- ☐ Engine oil level too low. Friction caused by intermittent lack of lubrication or from oil that is overworked can cause overheating. The oil provides a definite cooling function in the engine. Check the oil level (Chapter 1).
- ☐ Poor quality engine oil or incorrect viscosity or type. Oil is rated not only according to viscosity but also according to type. Some oils are not rated high enough for use in this engine. Check the Specifications section and change to the correct oil (Chapter 1).
- ☐ Blocked oil filter or pick-up gauze filter. Renew the engine oil and filter and clean the pick-up filter (Chapter 1).

### Miscellaneous causes

- ☐ Modification to exhaust system. Most aftermarket exhaust systems cause the engine to run leaner, which make them run hotter.

## 5 Clutch problems

### Clutch slipping

- ☐ Clutch fluid level too high. Check fluid level (see Daily (pre-ride) checks).
- ☐ Friction plates worn or warped. Overhaul the clutch assembly (Chapter 2).
- ☐ Plain plates warped (Chapter 2).
- ☐ Clutch springs broken or weak. Old or heat-damaged (from slipping clutch) springs should be renewed with new ones (Chapter 2).
- ☐ Clutch pushrod bent. Check and, if necessary, renew (Chapter 2).
- ☐ Clutch centre or drum unevenly worn. This causes improper engagement of the plates. Renew the damaged or worn parts (Chapter 2).

### Clutch not disengaging completely

- ☐ Clutch fluid level too low. Top-up and bleed the hydraulic system (Chapter 2).
- ☐ Clutch plates warped or damaged. This will cause clutch drag, which in turn will cause the machine to creep. Overhaul the clutch assembly (Chapter 2).
- ☐ Clutch spring tension uneven. Usually caused by a sagged or broken spring. Check and renew the springs as a set (Chapter 2).
- ☐ Clutch drum bearings seized (fitted to the primary driven gear). Lack of lubrication, severe wear or damage can cause the bearings to seize on the input shaft. Overhaul of the bearings, and perhaps transmission, may be necessary to repair the damage (Chapter 2).
- ☐ Clutch hydraulic release mechanism defective. Bleed the hydraulic system (Chapter 2). If this fails to cure the problem overhaul the clutch master and slave cylinders (Chapter 2).
- ☐ Loose clutch centre nut. Causes housing and centre misalignment putting a drag on the engine. Engagement adjustment continually varies. Overhaul the clutch assembly (Chapter 2).

# 6 Gearchanging problems

### Doesn't go into gear or lever doesn't return

- ☐ Clutch not disengaging. See above.
- ☐ Selector fork(s) bent or seized. Often caused by dropping the machine or from lack of lubrication. Overhaul the transmission (Chapter 2).
- ☐ Gear(s) stuck on shaft. Most often caused by a lack of lubrication or excessive wear in transmission bearings and bushings. Overhaul the transmission (Chapter 2).
- ☐ Selector drum binding. Caused by lubrication failure or incorrect endfloat adjustment. Separate the crankcase halves and investigate (Chapter 2).
- ☐ Gearchange mechanism worn or incorrectly adjusted (Chapter 2). Adjust or renew as necessary (Chapter 2).
- ☐ Selector drum detent arm or ball damaged or worn. Uncontrolled rotary movement of selector drum results, causing unpredictable gearchange operation. Renew the arm assembly and/or ball an spring (Chapter 2).

### Jumps out of gear

- ☐ Selector fork(s) worn. Overhaul the transmission (Chapter 2).
- ☐ Selector drum groove(s) worn. Overhaul the transmission (Chapter 2).
- ☐ Gear dogs or dog holes worn or damaged. The gears should b inspected and renewed. No attempt should be made to service the worn parts.

### Overselects

- ☐ Detent arm or ball spring weak or broken (Chapter 2).
- ☐ Gearchange mechanism springs broken or distorted or mechanism incorrectly adjusted (Chapter 2).

# 7 Abnormal engine noise

### Knocking or pinking

- ☐ Carbon build-up in combustion chamber. Use of a fuel additive that will dissolve the adhesive bonding the carbon particles to the piston crown and chamber is the easiest way to remove the build-up. Otherwise, the cylinder head will have to be removed and decarbonised (Chapter 2).
- ☐ Incorrect or poor quality fuel. Old or improper fuel can cause detonation. This causes the pistons to rattle, thus the knocking or pinking sound. Drain the old fuel and always use the recommended grade fuel (Chapter 4).
- ☐ Spark plug heat range incorrect. Uncontrolled detonation indicates that the plug heat range is too hot. The plug in effect becomes a glow plug, raising cylinder temperatures. Install the proper heat range plug (Chapter 1).
- ☐ Improper air/fuel mixture. This will cause the cylinders to run hot and lead to detonation. Blocked injectors or an air leak can cause this imbalance. See Chapter 4.

### Piston slap or rattling

- ☐ Cylinder-to-piston clearance excessive. Caused by improper assembly. Inspect and overhaul top-end parts (Chapter 2).
- ☐ Connecting rod bent. Caused by over-revving, trying to start a badly flooded engine or from ingesting a foreign object into the combustion chamber. Renew the damaged parts (Chapter 2).
- ☐ Piston pin or piston pin bore worn or seized from wear or lack of lubrication. Renew damaged parts (Chapter 2).
- ☐ Piston ring(s) worn, broken or sticking. Overhaul the top-end (Chapter 2).
- ☐ Piston seizure damage. Usually from lack of lubrication or overheating. Renew the pistons and renew the cylinders, as necessary (Chapter 2).
- ☐ Connecting rod big-end bearing clearance excessive. Caused excessive wear or lack of lubrication. Renew worn parts.

### Valve noise

- ☐ Incorrect valve clearances. Adjust the clearances by referring t Chapter 1.
- ☐ Camshafts worn or damaged. Lack of lubrication at high rpm i usually the cause of damage. Insufficient oil or failure to chang the oil at the recommended intervals are the chief causes (Chapter 2).

### Other noise

- ☐ Cylinder head gasket leaking.
- ☐ Exhaust pipe leaking at cylinder head connection. Caused by improper fit of pipe(s) or loose exhaust manifold nuts. All exha fasteners should be tightened evenly and carefully. Failure to c this will lead to a leak.
- ☐ Crankshaft runout excessive. Caused by a bent crankshaft (fr over-revving) or damage from an upper cylinder component failure. Can also be attributed to dropping the machine on eith the crankshaft ends.
- ☐ Engine mounting bolts loose. Tighten all engine mount bolts (Chapter 2).
- ☐ Crankshaft main bearings worn (Chapter 2).

## 8 Abnormal drive line noise

### Excessive clutch noise

- ☐ Clutch outer drum/friction plate clearance excessive (Chapter 2).
- ☐ Loose or damaged clutch pressure plate and/or bolts (Chapter 2).

### Transmission noise

- ☐ Bearings worn. Also includes the possibility that the shafts are worn. Overhaul the transmission (Chapter 2).
- ☐ Gears worn or chipped (Chapter 2).
- ☐ Metal chips jammed in gear teeth. Probably pieces from a broken gear or shift mechanism that were picked up by the gears. This will cause early bearing failure (Chapter 2).
- ☐ Engine oil level too low. Causes a howl from transmission. Also affects engine power and clutch operation (Chapter 1).

### Final drive noise

- ☐ Chain not adjusted properly (Chapter 1).
- ☐ Front or rear sprocket loose. Tighten fasteners (Chapter 6).
- ☐ Sprockets worn. Renew sprockets (Chapter 6).
- ☐ Rear sprocket warped. Renew sprockets (Chapter 6).

## 9 Abnormal frame and suspension noise

### Front end noise

- ☐ Low fluid level or improper viscosity oil in forks. This can sound like spurting and is usually accompanied by irregular fork action (Chapter 6).
- ☐ Spring weak or broken. Makes a clicking or scraping sound. Fork oil, when drained, will have a lot of metal particles in it (Chapter 6).
- ☐ Steering head bearings loose or damaged. Clicks when braking. Check and adjust or renew as necessary (Chapters 1 and 6).
- ☐ Fork yokes loose. Make sure all clamp bolts are tightened to the specified torque (Chapter 6).
- ☐ Fork tube bent. Good possibility if machine has been dropped. Renew tube with a new one (Chapter 6).
- ☐ Front axle bolt or axle clamp bolts loose. Tighten them to the specified torque (Chapter 7).
- ☐ Loose or worn wheel bearings. Check and renew as needed (Chapter 7).

### Shock absorber noise

- ☐ Fluid level incorrect. Indicates a leak caused by defective seal. Shock will be covered with oil. Renew shock or seek advice on repair from a Ducati dealer (Chapter 6).
- ☐ Defective shock absorber with internal damage. This is in the body of the shock and can't be remedied. The shock must be renewed with a new one (Chapter 6).
- ☐ Bent or damaged shock body. Renew the shock with a new one (Chapter 6).
- ☐ Loose or worn suspension linkage components. Check and renew as necessary (Chapter 6).

### Brake noise

- ☐ Squeal caused by dust on brake pads. Usually found in combination with glazed pads. Clean using brake cleaning solvent (Chapter 7).
- ☐ Contamination of brake pads. Oil, brake fluid or dirt causing brake to chatter or squeal. Clean or renew pads (Chapter 7).
- ☐ Pads glazed. Caused by excessive heat from prolonged use or from contamination. Do not use sandpaper/emery cloth or any other abrasive to roughen the pad surfaces as abrasives will stay in the pad material and damage the disc. A very fine flat file can be used, but pad renewal is suggested as a cure (Chapter 7).
- ☐ Disc warped. Can cause a chattering, clicking or intermittent squeal. Usually accompanied by a pulsating lever and uneven braking. Renew the disc (Chapter 7).
- ☐ Loose or worn wheel bearings. Check and renew as needed (Chapter 7).

## 10 Oil pressure warning light comes on

### Engine lubrication system

- ☐ Engine oil pump defective, blocked oil pick-up gauze filter or failed relief valve. Carry out oil pressure check (Chapter 1).
- ☐ Engine oil level low. Inspect for leak or other problem causing low oil level and add recommended oil (Chapter 1).
- ☐ Engine oil viscosity too low. Very old, thin oil or an improper weight of oil used in the engine. Change to correct oil (Chapter 1).
- ☐ Camshaft or journals worn. Excessive wear causing drop in oil pressure. Renew cam and/or/cylinder head. Abnormal wear could be caused by oil starvation at high rpm from low oil level or improper weight or type of oil (Chapter 1).
- ☐ Crankshaft and/or bearings worn. Same problems as above. Check and renew crankshaft and/or bearings (Chapter 2).

### Electrical system

- ☐ Oil pressure switch defective. Check the switch according to the procedure in Chapter 9. Renew it if it is defective.
- ☐ Oil pressure warning light circuit defective. Check for pinched, shorted, disconnected or damaged wiring (Chapter 9).

# 11 Excessive exhaust smoke

### White smoke

- ☐ Piston oil ring worn. The ring may be broken or damaged, causing oil from the crankcase to be pulled past the piston into the combustion chamber. Renew the rings with new ones (Chapter 2).
- ☐ Cylinders worn, cracked, or scored. Caused by overheating or oil starvation. Install a new cylinder barrel (Chapter 2).
- ☐ Valve oil seal damaged or worn. Renew oil seals with new ones (Chapter 2).
- ☐ Valve guide worn. Perform a complete valve job (Chapter 2).
- ☐ Engine oil level too high, which causes the oil to be forced past the rings. Drain oil to the proper level (Daily (pre-ride) checks).
- ☐ Head gasket broken between oil return and cylinder. Causes oil to be pulled into the combustion chamber. Renew the head gasket and check the head for warpage (Chapter 2).
- ☐ Abnormal crankcase pressurisation, which forces oil past the rings. Clogged breather is usually the cause.

### Black smoke

- ☐ Air filters clogged. Clean or renew the element (Chapter 1).
- ☐ Engine management system malfunction (Chapter 4).

# 12 Poor handling or stability

### Handlebar hard to turn

- ☐ Steering head bearing adjuster nut too tight. Check adjustment as described in Chapter 1.
- ☐ Bearings damaged. Roughness can be felt as the bars are turned from side-to-side. Renew bearings and races (Chapter 6).
- ☐ Races dented or worn. Denting results from wear in only one position (e.g., straight ahead), from a collision or hitting a pothole or from dropping the machine. Renew races and bearings (Chapter 6).
- ☐ Steering stem lubrication inadequate. Causes are grease getting hard from age or being washed out by high pressure car washes. Disassemble steering head and repack bearings (Chapter 6).
- ☐ Steering stem bent. Caused by a collision, hitting a pothole or by dropping the machine. Renew damaged part. Don't try to straighten the steering stem (Chapter 6).
- ☐ Front tyre air pressure too low (Chapter 1).

### Handlebar shakes or vibrates excessively

- ☐ Tyres worn or out of balance (Chapter 7).
- ☐ Swingarm bearings worn. Renew worn bearings (Chapter 6).
- ☐ Wheel rim(s) warped or damaged. Inspect wheels for runout (Chapter 7).
- ☐ Wheel bearings worn. Worn front or rear wheel bearings can cause poor tracking. Worn front bearings will cause wobble (Chapter 7).
- ☐ Handlebar clamp bolts loose (Chapter 6).
- ☐ Fork yoke bolts loose. Tighten them to the specified torque (Chapter 6).
- ☐ Engine mounting bolts loose. Will cause excessive vibration with increased engine rpm (Chapter 2).

### Handlebar pulls to one side

- ☐ Frame bent. Definitely suspect this if the machine has been dropped. May or may not be accompanied by cracking near the bend. Renew the frame (Chapter 6).
- ☐ Wheels out of alignment. Caused by bent steering stem, frame, swingarm or stub axle (Chapter 6).
- ☐ Swingarm bent or twisted. Caused by age (metal fatigue) or impact damage. Renew the arm (Chapter 6).
- ☐ Steering stem bent. Caused by impact damage or by dropping motorcycle. Renew the steering stem (Chapter 6).
- ☐ Stub axle bent or damaged. Renew the axle and bearings (Chapter 6).
- ☐ Fork tube bent. Disassemble the forks and renew the damaged parts (Chapter 6).
- ☐ Fork oil level uneven. Check and add or drain as necessary (Chapter 6).

### Poor shock absorbing qualities

- ☐ Too hard:
  - *a) Fork oil level excessive (Chapter 6).*
  - *b) Fork oil viscosity too high. Use a lighter oil (see the Specifications in Chapter 6).*
  - *c) Fork tube bent. Causes a harsh, sticking feeling (Chapter 6).*
  - *d) Shock shaft or body bent or damaged (Chapter 6).*
  - *e) Fork internal damage (Chapter 6).*
  - *f) Shock internal damage.*
  - *g) Tyre pressure too high (Chapter 1).*
- ☐ Too soft:
  - *a) Fork or shock oil insufficient and/or leaking (Chapter 6).*
  - *b) Fork oil level too low (Chapter 6).*
  - *c) Fork oil viscosity too light (Chapter 6).*
  - *d) Fork springs weak or broken (Chapter 6).*
  - *e) Shock internal damage or leakage (Chapter 6).*

## 13 Braking problems

### Brakes are spongy, don't hold

- ☐ Air in brake line. Caused by inattention to master cylinder fluid level or by leakage. Locate problem and bleed brakes (Chapter 7).
- ☐ Pad or disc worn (Chapters 1 and 7).
- ☐ Brake fluid leak. See paragraph 1.
- ☐ Contaminated pads. Caused by contamination with oil, grease, brake fluid, etc. Clean or renew pads. Clean disc thoroughly with brake cleaner (Chapter 7).
- ☐ Brake fluid deteriorated. Fluid is old or contaminated. Drain system, replenish with new fluid and bleed the system (Chapter 7).
- ☐ Master cylinder internal parts worn or damaged causing fluid to bypass (Chapter 7).
- ☐ Master cylinder bore scratched by foreign material or broken spring. Repair or renew master cylinder (Chapter 7).
- ☐ Disc warped. Renew disc (Chapter 7).

### Brake lever or pedal pulsates

- ☐ Disc warped. Renew disc (Chapter 7).
- ☐ Axle bent. Renew axle (Chapter 7).
- ☐ Brake caliper bolts loose (Chapter 7).
- ☐ Wheel warped or otherwise damaged (Chapter 7).
- ☐ Wheel bearings damaged or worn (Chapter 7).

### Brakes drag

- ☐ Master cylinder piston seized. Caused by wear or damage to piston or cylinder bore (Chapter 7).
- ☐ Lever binding. Check pivot and lubricate (Chapter 7).
- ☐ Brake caliper piston seized in bore. Caused by wear or ingestion of dirt past deteriorated seal (Chapter 7).
- ☐ Brake pad damaged. Pad material separated from backing plate. Usually caused by faulty manufacturing process or from contact with chemicals. Renew pads (Chapter 7).
- ☐ Pads improperly installed (Chapter 7).

## 14 Electrical problems

### Battery dead or weak

- ☐ Battery faulty. Caused by sulphated plates which are shorted through sedimentation. Also, broken battery terminal making only occasional contact (Chapter 9).
- ☐ Battery cables making poor contact (Chapter 9).
- ☐ Load excessive. Caused by addition of high wattage lights or other electrical accessories.
- ☐ Ignition (main) switch defective. Switch either grounds (earths) internally or fails to shut off system. Renew the switch (Chapter 9).
- ☐ Regulator/rectifier defective (Chapter 9).
- ☐ Alternator stator coil open or shorted (Chapter 9).
- ☐ Wiring faulty. Wiring grounded (earthed) or connections loose in ignition, charging or lighting circuits (Chapter 9).

### Battery overcharged

- ☐ Regulator/rectifier defective. Overcharging is noticed when battery gets excessively warm (Chapter 9).
- ☐ Battery defective. Renew battery with a new one (Chapter 9).
- ☐ Battery amperage too low, wrong type or size. Install manufacturer's specified amp-hour battery to handle charging load (Chapter 9).

## Checking engine compression

- Low compression will result in exhaust smoke, heavy oil consumption, poor starting and poor performance. A compression test will provide useful information about an engine's condition and if performed regularly, can give warning of trouble before any other symptoms become apparent.
- A compression gauge will be required, along with an adapter to suit the spark plug hole thread size. Note that the screw-in type gauge/adapter set up is preferable to the rubber cone type.
- Before carrying out the test, first check the valve clearances as described in Chapter 1.

**1** Run the engine until it reaches normal operating temperature, then stop it and remove the spark plug(s), taking care not to scald your hands on the hot components.

**2** Install the gauge adapter and compression gauge in No. 1 cylinder spark plug hole **(see illustration 1)**.

**Screw the compression gauge adapter into the spark plug hole, then screw the gauge into the adapter**

**3** On kickstart-equipped motorcycles, make sure the ignition switch is OFF, then open the throttle fully and kick the engine over a couple of times until the gauge reading stabilises.

**4** On motorcycles with electric start only, the procedure will differ depending on the nature of the ignition system. Flick the engine kill switch (engine stop switch) to OFF and turn the ignition switch ON; open the throttle fully and crank the engine over on the starter motor for a couple of revolutions until the gauge reading stabilises. If the starter will not operate with the kill switch OFF, turn the ignition switch OFF and refer to the next paragraph.

**5** Install the plugs back in their caps and arrange the plug electrodes so that their metal bodies are earthed (grounded) against the cylinder heads; this is essential to prevent damage to the engine management system **(see illustration 2)**. Position the plugs well away from the plug holes otherwise there is a

**All spark plugs must be earthed (grounded) against the cylinder head**

risk of atomised fuel escaping from the plug holes and igniting. As a safety precaution, cover the cylinder heads with rag and disconnect the fuel tank wiring connector (see illustration 2.5 in Chapter 4). Turn the ignition switch and kill switch ON, open the throttle fully and crank the engine over on the starter motor for a couple of revolutions until the gauge reading stabilises.

**6** After one or two revolutions the pressure should build up to a maximum figure and then stabilise. Take a note of this reading and on multi-cylinder engines repeat the test on the remaining cylinders.

**7** The correct pressures are given in Chapter 1. If the results fall within the specified range and on multi-cylinder engines all are relatively equal, the engine is in good condition. If there is a marked difference between the readings, or if the readings are lower than specified, inspection of the top-end components will be required.

**8** Low compression pressure may be due to worn cylinder bores, pistons or rings, failure of the cylinder head gasket, worn valve seals, or poor valve seating.

**9** To distinguish between cylinder/piston wear and valve leakage, pour a small quantity of oil into the bore to temporarily seal the piston rings, then repeat the compression tests **(see illustration 3)**. If the readings show

**Bores can be temporarily sealed with a squirt of motor oil**

a noticeable increase in pressure this confirms that the cylinder bore, piston, or rings are worn. If, however, no change is indicated, the cylinder head gasket or valves should be examined.

**10** High compression pressure indicates excessive carbon build-up in the combustion chamber and on the piston crown. If this is the case the cylinder head should be removed and the deposits removed. Note that excessive carbon build-up is less likely with the used on modern fuels.

## Checking battery open-circuit voltage

***Warning: The gases produced by the battery are explosive - never smoke or create any sparks in the vicinity of the battery. Never allow the electrolyte to contact your skin or clothing - if it does, wash it off and seek immediate medical attention.***

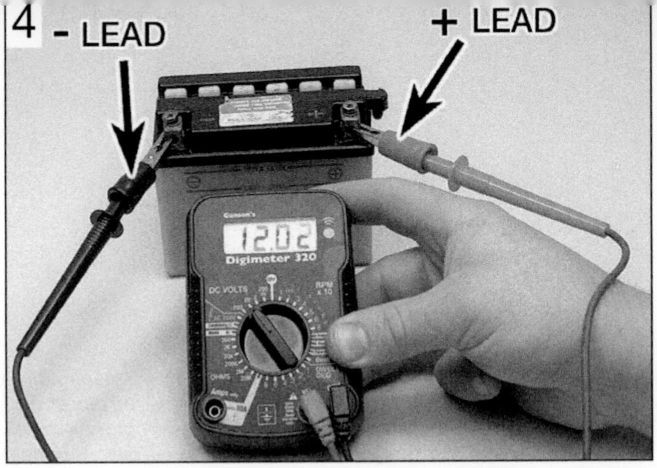


Measuring open-circuit battery voltage

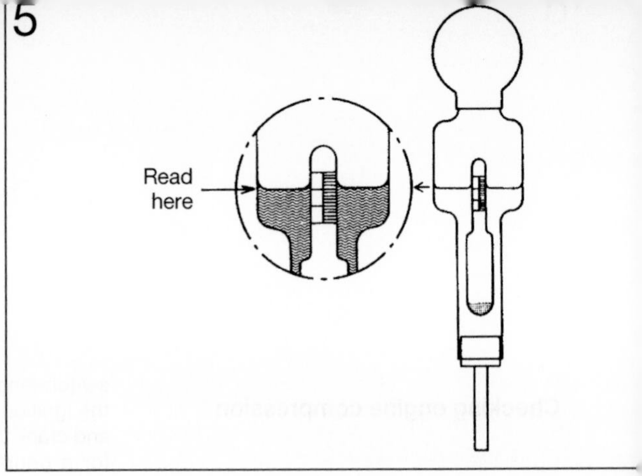


Float-type hydrometer for measuring battery specific gravit

● Before any electrical fault is investigated the battery should be checked.

● You'll need a dc voltmeter or multimeter to check battery voltage. Check that the leads are inserted in the correct terminals on the meter, red lead to positive (+ve), black lead to negative (-ve). Incorrect connections can damage the meter.

● A sound fully-charged 12 volt battery should produce between 12.3 and 12.6 volts across its terminals (12.8 volts for a maintenance-free battery). On machines with a 6 volt battery, voltage should be between 6.1 and 6.3 volts.

**1** Set a multimeter to the 0 to 20 volts dc range and connect its probes across the battery terminals. Connect the meter's positive (+ve) probe, usually red, to the battery positive (+ve) terminal, followed by the meter's negative (-ve) probe, usually black, to the battery negative terminal (-ve) **(see illustration 4)**.

**2** If battery voltage is low (below 10 volts on a 12 volt battery or below 4 volts on a six volt battery), charge the battery and test the voltage again. If the battery repeatedly goes flat, investigate the motorcycle's charging system.

## Checking battery specific gravity (SG)

***Warning: The gases produced by the battery are explosive - never smoke or create any sparks in the vicinity of the battery. Never allow the electrolyte to contact your skin or clothing - if it does, wash it off and seek immediate medical attention.***

● The specific gravity check gives an indication of a battery's state of charge.

● A hydrometer is used for measuring specific gravity. Make sure you purchase one which has a small enough hose to insert in the aperture of a motorcycle battery.

● Specific gravity is simply a measure of the electrolyte's density compared with that of water. Water has an SG of 1.000 and fully-charged battery electrolyte is about 26% heavier, at 1.260.

● Specific gravity checks are not possible on maintenance-free batteries. Testing the open-circuit voltage is the only means of determining their state of charge.

**1** To measure SG, remove the battery from the motorcycle and remove the first cell cap. Draw some electrolyte into the hydrometer and the reading **(see illustration 5)**. Return electrolyte to the cell and install the cap.

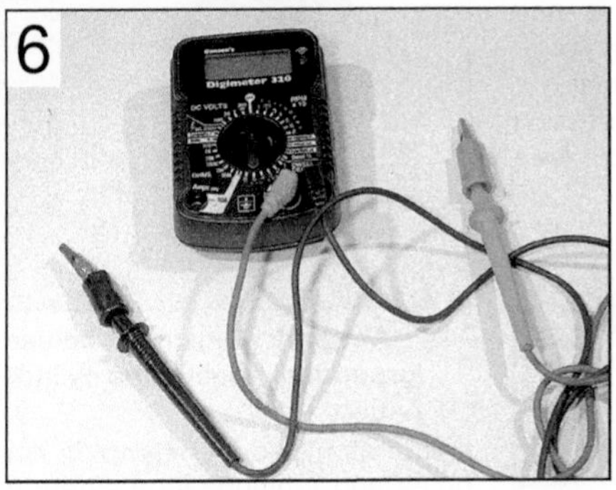


Digital multimeter can be used for all electrical tests

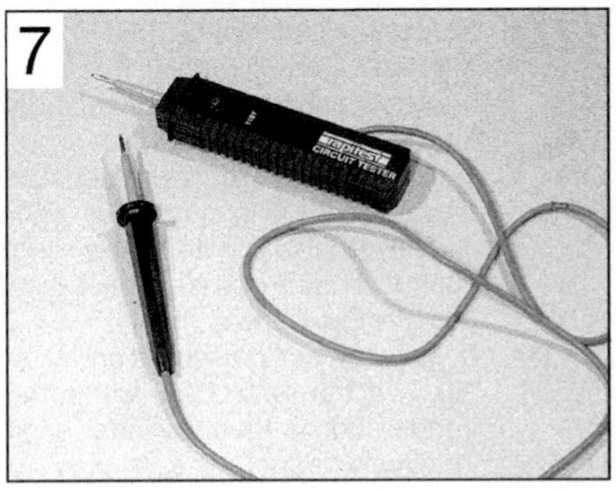


Battery-powered continuity tester

**2** The reading should be in the regio 1.260 to 1.280. If SG is below 1.200 battery needs charging. Note that SG will with temperature; it should be measure 20°C (68°F). Add 0.007 to the reading every 10°C above 20°C, and subtract 0. from the reading for every 10°C below 2 Add 0.004 to the reading for every 10°F ab 68°F, and subtract 0.004 from the readin every 10°F below 68°F.

**3** When the check is complete, rinse hydrometer thoroughly with clean water.

## Checking for continuity

● The term continuity describes uninterrupted flow of electricity throug electrical circuit. A continuity check determine whether an **open-circuit** situa exists.

● Continuity can be checked with ohmmeter, multimeter, continuity teste battery and bulb test circuit **(see illustrati 6, 7 and 8)**.

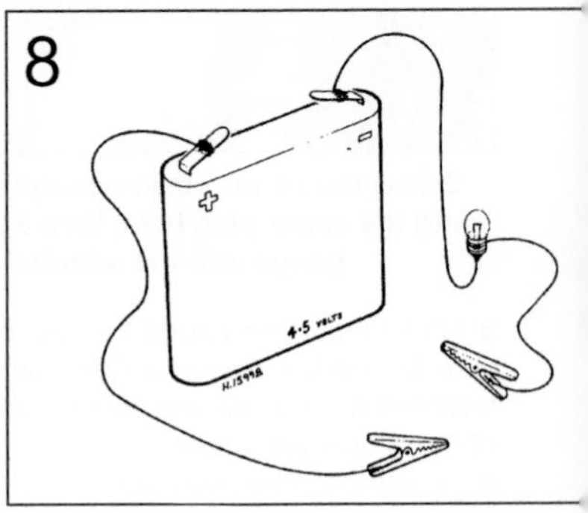


Battery and bulb test circuit

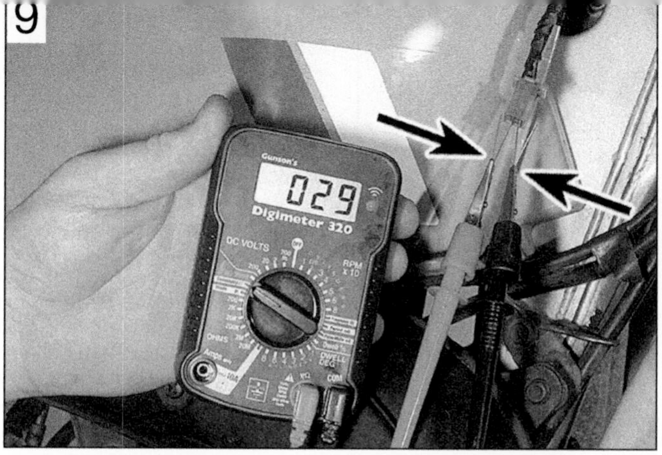


**Continuity check of front brake light switch using a meter - note split pins used to access connector terminals**

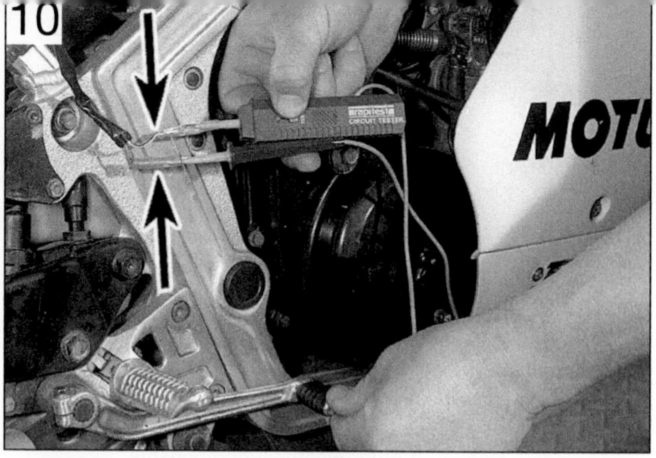


**Continuity check of rear brake light switch using a continuity tester**

- All of these instruments are self-powered by a battery, therefore the checks are made with the ignition OFF.
- As a safety precaution, always disconnect the battery negative (-ve) lead before making checks, particularly if ignition switch checks are being made.
- If using a meter, select the appropriate ohms scale and check that the meter reads infinity (∞). Touch the meter probes together and check that meter reads zero; where necessary adjust the meter so that it reads zero.
- After using a meter, always switch it OFF to conserve its battery.

### *Switch checks*

**1** If a switch is at fault, trace its wiring up to the wiring connectors. Separate the wire connectors and inspect them for security and condition. A build-up of dirt or corrosion here will most likely be the cause of the problem - clean up and apply a water dispersant such as WD40.

**2** If using a test meter, set the meter to the ohms x 10 scale and connect its probes across the wires from the switch **(see illustration 9)**. Simple ON/OFF type switches, such as brake light switches, only have two wires whereas combination switches, like the ignition switch, have many internal links. Study the wiring diagram to ensure that you are connecting across the correct pair of wires. Continuity (low or no measurable resistance - 0 ohms) should be indicated with the switch ON and no continuity (high resistance) with it OFF.

**3** Note that the polarity of the test probes doesn't matter for continuity checks, although care should be taken to follow specific test procedures if a diode or solid-state component is being checked.

**4** A continuity tester or battery and bulb circuit can be used in the same way. Connect its probes as described above **(see illustration 10)**. The light should come on to indicate continuity in the ON switch position, but should extinguish in the OFF position.

### *Wiring checks*

- Many electrical faults are caused by damaged wiring, often due to incorrect routing or chaffing on frame components.
- Loose, wet or corroded wire connectors can also be the cause of electrical problems, especially in exposed locations.

**1** A continuity check can be made on a single length of wire by disconnecting it at each end and connecting a meter or continuity tester across both ends of the wire **(see illustration 11)**.

**2** Continuity (low or no resistance - 0 ohms) should be indicated if the wire is good. If no continuity (high resistance) is shown, suspect a broken wire.

## Checking for voltage

- A voltage check can determine whether current is reaching a component.
- Voltage can be checked with a dc voltmeter, multimeter set on the dc volts scale, test light or buzzer **(see illustrations 12 and 13)**. A meter has the advantage of being able to measure actual voltage.
- When using a meter, check that its leads are inserted in the correct terminals on the meter, red to positive (+ve), black to negative (-ve). Incorrect connections can damage the meter.
- A voltmeter (or multimeter set to the dc volts scale) should always be connected in parallel (across the load). Connecting it in series will destroy the meter.
- Voltage checks are made with the ignition ON.

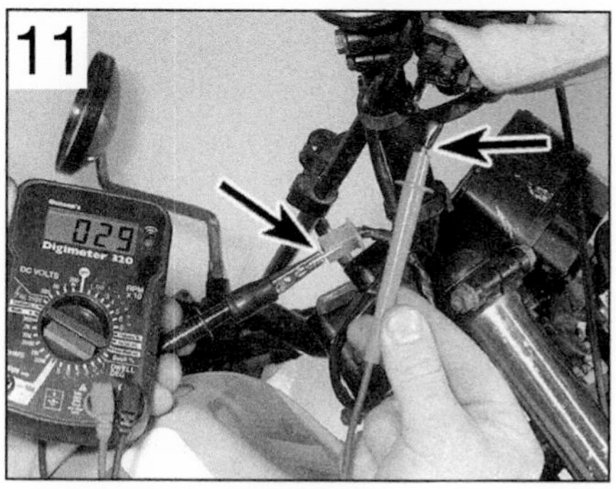


**Continuity check of front brake light switch sub-harness**

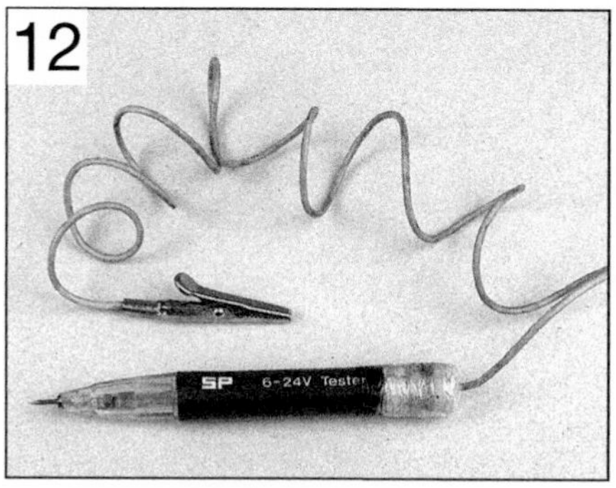


**A simple test light can be used for voltage checks**

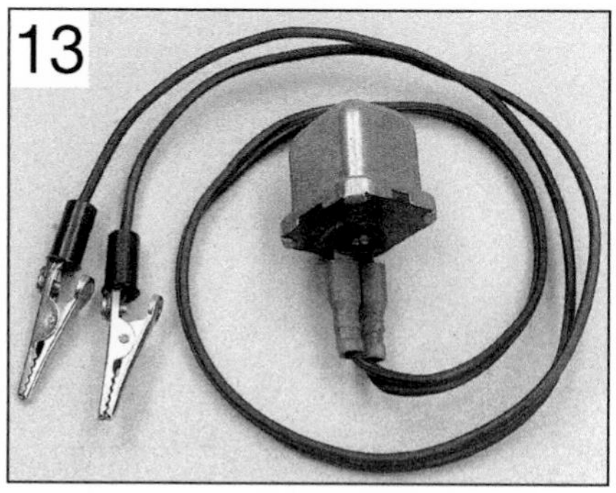


**A buzzer is useful for voltage checks**

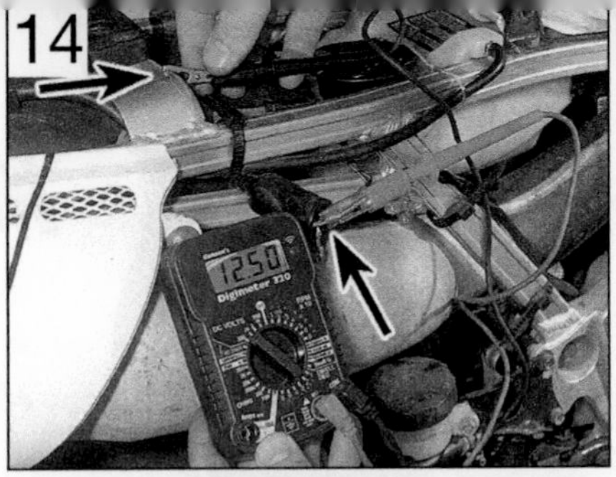


**Checking for voltage at the rear brake light power supply wire using a meter . . .**

**1** First identify the relevant wiring circuit by referring to the wiring diagram at the end of this manual. If other electrical components share the same power supply (ie are fed from the same fuse), take note whether they are working correctly - this is useful information in deciding where to start checking the circuit.

**2** If using a meter, check first that the meter leads are plugged into the correct terminals on the meter (see above). Set the meter to the dc volts function, at a range suitable for the battery voltage. Connect the meter red probe (+ve) to the power supply wire and the black probe to a good metal earth (ground) on the motorcycle's frame or directly to the battery negative (-ve) terminal **(see illustration 14)**. Battery voltage should be shown on the meter

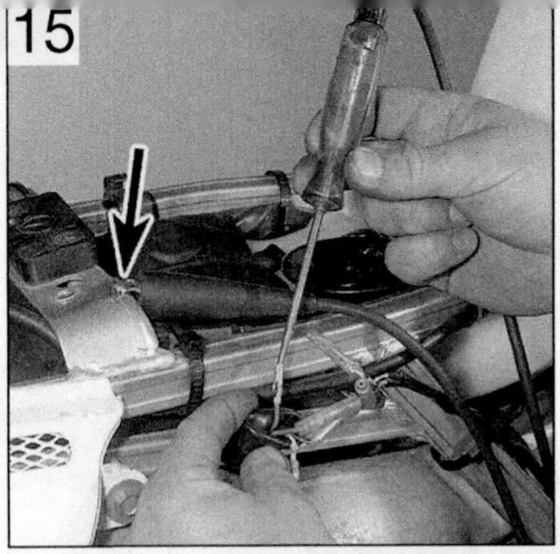


**. . . or a test light - note the earth connection to the frame (arrow)**

with the ignition switched ON.

**3** If using a test light or buzzer, connect its positive (+ve) probe to the power supply terminal and its negative (-ve) probe to a good earth (ground) on the motorcycle's frame or directly to the battery negative (-ve) terminal **(see illustration 15)**. With the ignition ON, the test light should illuminate or the buzzer sound.

**4** If no voltage is indicated, work back towards the fuse continuing to check for voltage. When you reach a point where there is voltage, you know the problem lies between that point and your last check point.

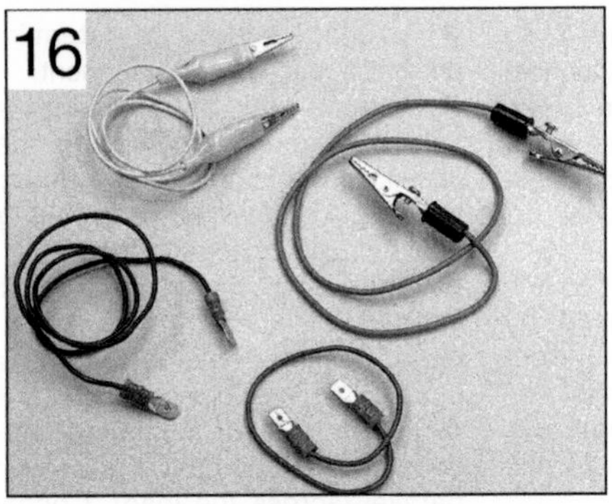


**A selection of jumper wires for making earth (ground) checks**

## Checking the earth (ground)

- Earth connections are made either directly to the engine or frame (such as sensors, neutral switch etc. which only have a positive feed) or by a separate wire into the earth circuit of the wiring harness. Alternatively a short earth wire is sometimes run directly from the component to the motorcycle's frame.
- Corrosion is often the cause of a poor earth connection.
- If total failure is experienced, check the security of the main earth lead from the

the main earth (ground) point on the w
harness. If corroded, dismantle the connec
and clean all surfaces back to bare metal.

**1** To check the earth on a component, us
insulated jumper wire to temporarily by
its earth connection **(see illustration**
Connect one end of the jumper wire betv
the earth terminal or metal body of
component and the other end to
motorcycle's frame.

**2** If the circuit works with the jumper
installed, the original earth circuit is fa
Check the wiring for open-circuits or
connections. Clean up direct e
connections, removing all traces of corro
and remake the joint. Apply petroleum je
the joint to prevent future corrosion.

## Tracing a short-circuit

- A short-circuit occurs where current s
to earth (ground) bypassing the ci
components. This usually results in a b
fuse.
- A short-circuit is most likely to occur w
the insulation has worn through due to w
chafing on a component, allowing a d
path to earth (ground) on the frame.

**1** Remove any bodypanels necessar
access the circuit wiring.

**2** Check that all electrical switches in
circuit are OFF, then remove the circuit
and connect a test light, buzzer or voltn
(set to the dc scale) across the fuse termi
No voltage should be shown.

**3** Move the wiring from side to side w
observing the test light or meter. Wher
test light comes on, buzzer sounds or n
shows voltage, you have found the caus
the short. It will usually shown up as dam
or burned insulation.

**4** Note that the same test can be perfor
on each component in the circuit, ever
switch.

**ABS (Anti-lock braking system)** A system, usually electronically controlled, that senses incipient wheel lockup during braking and relieves hydraulic pressure at wheel which is about to skid.
**Aftermarket** Components suitable for the motorcycle, but not produced by the motorcycle manufacturer.
**Allen key** A hexagonal wrench which fits into a recessed hexagonal hole.
**Alternating current (ac)** Current produced by an alternator. Requires converting to direct current by a rectifier for charging purposes.
**Alternator** Converts mechanical energy from the engine into electrical energy to charge the battery and power the electrical system.
**Ampere (amp)** A unit of measurement for the flow of electrical current. Current = Volts ÷ Ohms.
**Ampere-hour (Ah)** Measure of battery capacity.
**Angle-tightening** A torque expressed in degrees. Often follows a conventional tightening torque for cylinder head or main bearing fasteners **(see illustration)**.

**Angle-tightening cylinder head bolts**

**Antifreeze** A substance (usually ethylene glycol) mixed with water, and added to the cooling system, to prevent freezing of the coolant in winter. Antifreeze also contains chemicals to inhibit corrosion and the formation of rust and other deposits that would tend to clog the radiator and coolant passages and reduce cooling efficiency.
**Anti-dive** System attached to the fork lower leg (slider) to prevent fork dive when braking hard.
**Anti-seize compound** A coating that reduces the risk of seizing on fasteners that are subjected to high temperatures, such as exhaust clamp bolts and nuts.
**API** American Petroleum Institute. A quality standard for 4-stroke motor oils.
**Asbestos** A natural fibrous mineral with great heat resistance, commonly used in the composition of brake friction materials. Asbestos is a health hazard and the dust created by brake systems should never be inhaled or ingested.
**ATF** Automatic Transmission Fluid. Often used in front forks.
**ATU** Automatic Timing Unit. Mechanical device for advancing the ignition timing on early engines.
**ATV** All Terrain Vehicle. Often called a Quad.
**Axial play** Side-to-side movement.
**Axle** A shaft on which a wheel revolves. Also known as a spindle.

# B

**Backlash** The amount of movement between meshed components when one component is held still. Usually applies to gear teeth.
**Ball bearing** A bearing consisting of a hardened inner and outer race with hardened steel balls between the two races.
**Bearings** Used between two working surfaces to prevent wear of the components and a build-up of heat. Four types of bearing are commonly used on motorcycles: plain shell bearings, ball bearings, tapered roller bearings and needle roller bearings.
**Bevel gears** Used to turn the drive through 90°. Typical applications are shaft final drive and camshaft drive **(see illustration)**.

**Bevel gears are used to turn the drive through 90°**

**BHP** Brake Horsepower. The British measurement for engine power output. Power output is now usually expressed in kilowatts (kW).
**Bias-belted tyre** Similar construction to radial tyre, but with outer belt running at an angle to the wheel rim.
**Big-end bearing** The bearing in the end of the connecting rod that's attached to the crankshaft.
**Bleeding** The process of removing air from an hydraulic system via a bleed nipple or bleed screw.
**Bottom-end** A description of an engine's crankcase components and all components contained there-in.
**BTDC** Before Top Dead Centre in terms of piston position. Ignition timing is often expressed in terms of degrees or millimetres BTDC.
**Bush** A cylindrical metal or rubber component used between two moving parts.
**Burr** Rough edge left on a component after machining or as a result of excessive wear.

# C

**Cam chain** The chain which takes drive from the crankshaft to the camshaft(s).
**Canister** The main component in an evaporative emission control system (California market only); contains activated charcoal granules to trap vapours from the fuel system rather than allowing them to vent to the atmosphere.
**Castellated** Resembling the parapets along the top of a castle wall. For example, a castellated wheel axle or spindle nut.
**Catalytic converter** A device in the exhaust system of some machines which converts certain pollutants in the exhaust gases into less harmful substances.
**Charging system** Description of the components which charge the battery, ie the alternator, rectifer and regulator.
**Circlip** A ring-shaped clip used to prevent endwise movement of cylindrical parts and shafts. An internal circlip is installed in a groove in a housing; an external circlip fits into a groove on the outside of a cylindrical piece such as a shaft. Also known as a snap-ring.
**Clearance** The amount of space between two parts. For example, between a piston and a cylinder, between a bearing and a journal, etc.
**Coil spring** A spiral of elastic steel found in various sizes throughout a vehicle, for example as a springing medium in the suspension and in the valve train.
**Compression** Reduction in volume, and increase in pressure and temperature, of a gas, caused by squeezing it into a smaller space.
**Compression damping** Controls the speed the suspension compresses when hitting a bump.
**Compression ratio** The relationship between cylinder volume when the piston is at top dead centre and cylinder volume when the piston is at bottom dead centre.
**Continuity** The uninterrupted path in the flow of electricity. Little or no measurable resistance.
**Continuity tester** Self-powered bleeper or test light which indicates continuity.
**Cp** Candlepower. Bulb rating commonly found on US motorcycles.
**Crossply tyre** Tyre plies arranged in a criss-cross pattern. Usually four or six plies used, hence 4PR or 6PR in tyre size codes.
**Cush drive** Rubber damper segments fitted between the rear wheel and final drive sprocket to absorb transmission shocks **(see illustration)**.

**Cush drive rubbers dampen out transmission shocks**

# D

**Degree disc** Calibrated disc for measuring piston position. Expressed in degrees.
**Dial gauge** Clock-type gauge with adapters for measuring runout and piston position. Expressed in mm or inches.
**Diaphragm** The rubber membrane in a master cylinder or carburettor which seals the upper chamber.
**Diaphragm spring** A single sprung plate often used in clutches.
**Direct current (dc)** Current produced by a dc generator.

**Decarbonisation** The process of removing carbon deposits - typically from the combustion chamber, valves and exhaust port/system.
**Detonation** Destructive and damaging explosion of fuel/air mixture in combustion chamber instead of controlled burning.
**Diode** An electrical valve which only allows current to flow in one direction. Commonly used in rectifiers and starter interlock systems.
**Disc valve (or rotary valve)** A induction system used on some two-stroke engines.
**Double-overhead camshaft (DOHC)** An engine that uses two overhead camshafts, one for the intake valves and one for the exhaust valves.
**Drivebelt** A toothed belt used to transmit drive to the rear wheel on some motorcycles. A drivebelt has also been used to drive the camshafts. Drivebelts are usually made of Kevlar.
**Driveshaft** Any shaft used to transmit motion. Commonly used when referring to the final driveshaft on shaft drive motorcycles.

# E

**Earth return** The return path of an electrical circuit, utilising the motorcycle's frame.
**ECU (Electronic Control Unit)** A computer which controls (for instance) an ignition system, or an anti-lock braking system.
**EGO** Exhaust Gas Oxygen sensor. Sometimes called a Lambda sensor.
**Electrolyte** The fluid in a lead-acid battery.
**EMS (Engine Management System)** A computer controlled system which manages the fuel injection and the ignition systems in an integrated fashion.
**Endfloat** The amount of lengthways movement between two parts. As applied to a crankshaft, the distance that the crankshaft can move side-to-side in the crankcase.
**Endless chain** A chain having no joining link. Common use for cam chains and final drive chains.
**EP (Extreme Pressure)** Oil type used in locations where high loads are applied, such as between gear teeth.
**Evaporative emission control system** Describes a charcoal filled canister which stores fuel vapours from the tank rather than allowing them to vent to the atmosphere. Usually only fitted to California models and referred to as an EVAP system.
**Expansion chamber** Section of two-stroke engine exhaust system so designed to improve engine efficiency and boost power.

# F

**Feeler blade or gauge** A thin strip or blade of hardened steel, ground to an exact thickness, used to check or measure clearances between parts.
**Final drive** Description of the drive from the transmission to the rear wheel. Usually by chain or shaft, but sometimes by belt.
**Firing order** The order in which the engine cylinders fire, or deliver their power strokes, beginning with the number one cylinder.
**Flooding** Term used to describe a high fuel level in the carburettor float chambers, leading to fuel overflow. Also refers to excess fuel in the combustion chamber due to incorrect starting technique.
**Free length** The no-load state of a component when measured. Clutch, valve and fork spring lengths are measured at rest, without any preload.
**Freeplay** The amount of travel before any action takes place. The looseness in a linkage, or an assembly of parts, between the initial application of force and actual movement. For example, the distance the rear brake pedal moves before the rear brake is actuated.
**Fuel injection** The fuel/air mixture is metered electronically and directed into the engine intake ports (indirect injection) or into the cylinders (direct injection). Sensors supply information on engine speed and conditions.
**Fuel/air mixture** The charge of fuel and air going into the engine. See **Stoichiometric ratio**.
**Fuse** An electrical device which protects a circuit against accidental overload. The typical fuse contains a soft piece of metal which is calibrated to melt at a predetermined current flow (expressed as amps) and break the circuit.

# G

**Gap** The distance the spark must travel in jumping from the centre electrode to the side electrode in a spark plug. Also refers to the distance between the ignition rotor and the pickup coil in an electronic ignition system.
**Gasket** Any thin, soft material - usually cork, cardboard, asbestos or soft metal - installed between two metal surfaces to ensure a good seal. For instance, the cylinder head gasket seals the joint between the block and the cylinder head.
**Gauge** An instrument panel display used to monitor engine conditions. A gauge with a movable pointer on a dial or a fixed scale is an analogue gauge. A gauge with a numerical readout is called a digital gauge.
**Gear ratios** The drive ratio of a pair of gears in a gearbox, calculated on their number of teeth.
**Glaze-busting** see **Honing**
**Grinding** Process for renovating the valve face and valve seat contact area in the cylinder head.
**Gudgeon pin** The shaft which connects the connecting rod small-end with the piston. Often called a piston pin or wrist pin.

# H

**Helical gears** Gear teeth are slightly curved and produce less gear noise that straight-cut gears. Often used for primary drives.

**Installing a Helicoil thread insert in a cylinder head**

**Helicoil** A thread insert repair system. Commonly used as a repair for stripped sp plug threads **(see illustration)**.
**Honing** A process used to break down the g on a cylinder bore (also called glaze-busti Can also be carried out to roughen a rebo cylinder to aid ring bedding-in.
**HT (High Tension)** Description of the elect circuit from the secondary winding of the igni coil to the spark plug.
**Hydraulic** A liquid filled system used to tran pressure from one component to anot Common uses on motorcycles are brakes clutches.
**Hydrometer** An instrument for measuring specific gravity of a lead-acid battery.
**Hygroscopic** Water absorbing. In motorc applications, braking efficiency will be reduc DOT 3 or 4 hydraulic fluid absorbs water from air - care must be taken to keep new brake in tightly sealed containers.

# I

**lbf ft** Pounds-force feet. An imperial uni torque. Sometimes written as ft-lbs.
**lbf in** Pound-force inch. An imperial uni torque, applied to components where a very torque is required. Sometimes written as in-lb
**IC** Abbreviation for Integrated Circuit.
**Ignition advance** Means of increasing timing of the spark at higher engine spe Done by mechanical means (ATU) on e engines or electronically by the ignition co unit on later engines.
**Ignition timing** The moment at which the s plug fires, expressed in the number of cranks degrees before the piston reaches the top o stroke, or in the number of millimetres before piston reaches the top of its stroke.
**Infinity (∞)** Description of an open-ci electrical state, where no continuity exists.
**Inverted forks (upside down forks)** The sli or lower legs are held in the yokes and the tubes or stanchions are connected to the w axle (spindle). Less unsprung weight and s construction than conventional forks.

# J

**JASO** Quality standard for 2-stroke oils.
**Joule** The unit of electrical energy.
**Journal** The bearing surface of a shaft.

# K

**Kickstart** Mechanical means of turning engine over for starting purposes. Only us fitted to mopeds, small capacity motorcycles off-road motorcycles.
**Kill switch** Handebar-mounted switch emergency ignition cut-out. Cuts the ign circuit on all models, and additionally pre starter motor operation on others.
**km** Symbol for kilometre.
**kmh** Abbreviation for kilometres per hour.

# L

**Lambda (λ) sensor** A sensor fitted in exhaust system to measure the exhaust oxygen content (excess air factor).

**LCD** Abbreviation for Liquid Crystal Display.
**LED** Abbreviation for Light Emitting Diode.
**Liner** A steel cylinder liner inserted in a aluminium alloy cylinder block.
**Locknut** A nut used to lock an adjustment nut, or other threaded component, in place.
**Lockstops** The lugs on the lower triple clamp (yoke) which abut those on the frame, preventing handlebar-to-fuel tank contact.
**Lockwasher** A form of washer designed to prevent an attaching nut from working loose.
**LT Low Tension** Description of the electrical circuit from the power supply to the primary winding of the ignition coil.

# M

**Main bearings** The bearings between the crankshaft and crankcase.
**Maintenance-free (MF) battery** A sealed battery which cannot be topped up.
**Manometer** Mercury-filled calibrated tubes used to measure intake tract vacuum. Used to synchronise carburettors on multi-cylinder engines.
**Micrometer** A precision measuring instrument that measures component outside diameters **(see illustration)**.

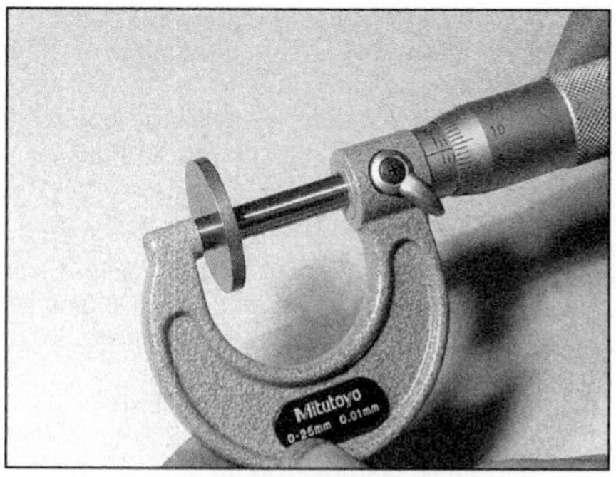


**Tappet shims are measured with a micrometer**

**MON (Motor Octane Number)** A measure of a fuel's resistance to knock.
**Monograde oil** An oil with a single viscosity, eg SAE80W.
**Monoshock** A single suspension unit linking the swingarm or suspension linkage to the frame.
**mph** Abbreviation for miles per hour.
**Multigrade oil** Having a wide viscosity range (eg 10W40). The W stands for Winter, thus the viscosity ranges from SAE10 when cold to SAE40 when hot.
**Multimeter** An electrical test instrument with the capability to measure voltage, current and resistance. Some meters also incorporate a continuity tester and buzzer.

# N

**Needle roller bearing** Inner race of caged needle rollers and hardened outer race. Examples of uncaged needle rollers can be found on some engines. Commonly used in rear suspension applications and in two-stroke engines.
**Nm** Newton metres.
**NOx** Oxides of Nitrogen. A common toxic pollutant emitted by petrol engines at higher temperatures.

# O

**Octane** The measure of a fuel's resistance to knock.
**OE (Original Equipment)** Relates to components fitted to a motorcycle as standard or replacement parts supplied by the motorcycle manufacturer.
**Ohm** The unit of electrical resistance. Ohms = Volts ÷ Current.
**Ohmmeter** An instrument for measuring electrical resistance.
**Oil cooler** System for diverting engine oil outside of the engine to a radiator for cooling purposes.
**Oil injection** A system of two-stroke engine lubrication where oil is pump-fed to the engine in accordance with throttle position.
**Open-circuit** An electrical condition where there is a break in the flow of electricity - no continuity (high resistance).
**O-ring** A type of sealing ring made of a special rubber-like material; in use, the O-ring is compressed into a groove to provide the sealing action.
**Oversize (OS)** Term used for piston and ring size options fitted to a rebored cylinder.
**Overhead cam (sohc) engine** An engine with single camshaft located on top of the cylinder head.
**Overhead valve (ohv) engine** An engine with the valves located in the cylinder head, but with the camshaft located in the engine block or crankcase.
**Oxygen sensor** A device installed in the exhaust system which senses the oxygen content in the exhaust and converts this information into an electric current. Also called a Lambda sensor.

# P

**Plastigauge** A thin strip of plastic thread, available in different sizes, used for measuring clearances. For example, a strip of Plastigauge is laid across a bearing journal. The parts are assembled and dismantled; the width of the crushed strip indicates the clearance between journal and bearing.
**Polarity** Either negative or positive earth (ground), determined by which battery lead is connected to the frame (earth return). Modern motorcycles are usually negative earth.
**Pre-ignition** A situation where the fuel/air mixture ignites before the spark plug fires. Often due to a hot spot in the combustion chamber caused by carbon build-up. Engine has a tendency to 'run-on'.
**Pre-load (suspension)** The amount a spring is compressed when in the unloaded state. Preload can be applied by gas, spacer or mechanical adjuster.
**Premix** The method of engine lubrication on older two-stroke engines. Engine oil is mixed with the petrol in the fuel tank in a specific ratio. The fuel/oil mix is sometimes referred to as "petroil".
**Primary drive** Description of the drive from the crankshaft to the clutch. Usually by gear or chain.
**PS** Pfedestärke - a German interpretation of BHP.
**PSI** Pounds-force per square inch. Imperial measurement of tyre pressure and cylinder pressure measurement.
**PTFE** Polytetrafluroethylene. A low friction substance.
**Pulse secondary air injection system** A process of promoting the burning of excess fuel present in the exhaust gases by routing fresh air into the exhaust ports.

# Q

**Quartz halogen bulb** Tungsten filament surrounded by a halogen gas. Typically used for the headlight **(see illustration)**.

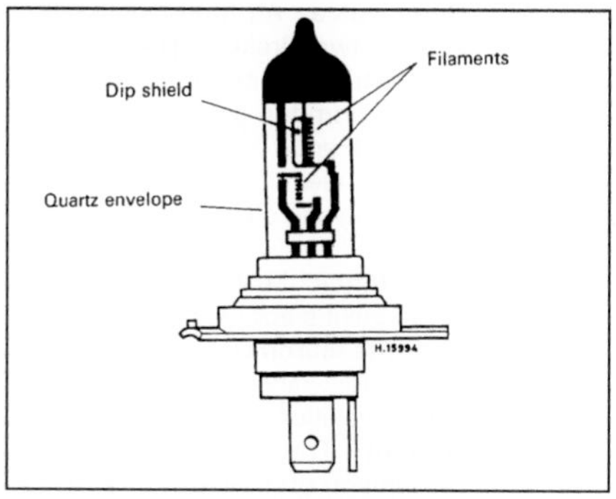


**Quartz halogen headlight bulb construction**

# R

**Rack-and-pinion** A pinion gear on the end of a shaft that mates with a rack (think of a geared wheel opened up and laid flat). Sometimes used in clutch operating systems.
**Radial play** Up and down movement about a shaft.
**Radial ply tyres** Tyre plies run across the tyre (from bead to bead) and around the circumference of the tyre. Less resistant to tread distortion than other tyre types.
**Radiator** A liquid-to-air heat transfer device designed to reduce the temperature of the coolant in a liquid cooled engine.
**Rake** A feature of steering geometry - the angle of the steering head in relation to the vertical **(see illustration).**

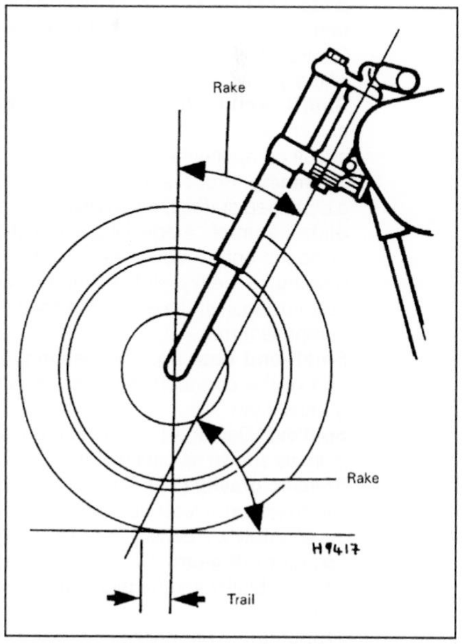


**Steering geometry**

**Rebore** Providing a new working surface to the cylinder bore by boring out the old surface. Necessitates the use of oversize piston and rings.
**Rebound damping** A means of controlling the oscillation of a suspension unit spring after it has been compressed. Resists the spring's natural tendency to bounce back after being compressed.
**Rectifier** Device for converting the ac output of an alternator into dc for battery charging.
**Reed valve** An induction system commonly used on two-stroke engines.
**Regulator** Device for maintaining the charging voltage from the generator or alternator within a specified range.
**Relay** A electrical device used to switch heavy current on and off by using a low current auxiliary circuit.
**Resistance** Measured in ohms. An electrical component's ability to pass electrical current.
**RON (Research Octane Number)** A measure of a fuel's resistance to knock.
**rpm** revolutions per minute.
**Runout** The amount of wobble (in-and-out movement) of a wheel or shaft as it's rotated. The amount a shaft rotates 'out-of-true'. The out-of-round condition of a rotating part.

# S

**SAE (Society of Automotive Engineers)** A standard for the viscosity of a fluid.
**Sealant** A liquid or paste used to prevent leakage at a joint. Sometimes used in conjunction with a gasket.
**Service limit** Term for the point where a component is no longer useable and must be renewed.
**Shaft drive** A method of transmitting drive from the transmission to the rear wheel.
**Shell bearings** Plain bearings consisting of two shell halves. Most often used as big-end and main bearings in a four-stroke engine. Often called bearing inserts.
**Shim** Thin spacer, commonly used to adjust the clearance or relative positions between two parts. For example, shims inserted into or under tappets or followers to control valve clearances. Clearance is adjusted by changing the thickness of the shim.
**Short-circuit** An electrical condition where current shorts to earth (ground) bypassing the circuit components.
**Skimming** Process to correct warpage or repair a damaged surface, eg on brake discs or drums.
**Slide-hammer** A special puller that screws into or hooks onto a component such as a shaft or bearing; a heavy sliding handle on the shaft bottoms against the end of the shaft to knock the component free.
**Small-end bearing** The bearing in the upper end of the connecting rod at its joint with the gudgeon pin.
**Spalling** Damage to camshaft lobes or bearing journals shown as pitting of the working surface.
**Specific gravity (SG)** The state of charge of the electrolyte in a lead-acid battery. A measure of the electrolyte's density compared with water.
**Straight-cut gears** Common type gear used on gearbox shafts and for oil pump and water pump drives.
**Stanchion** The inner sliding part of the front forks, held by the yokes. Often called a fork tube.
**Stoichiometric ratio** The optimum chemical air/fuel ratio for a petrol engine, said to be 14.7 parts of air to 1 part of fuel.
**Sulphuric acid** The liquid (electrolyte) used in a lead-acid battery. Poisonous and extremely corrosive.
**Surface grinding (lapping)** Process to correct a warped gasket face, commonly used on cylinder heads.

# T

**Tapered-roller bearing** Tapered inner race of caged needle rollers and separate tapered outer race. Examples of taper roller bearings can be found on steering heads.
**Tappet** A cylindrical component which transmits motion from the cam to the valve stem, either directly or via a pushrod and rocker arm. Also called a cam follower.
**TCS** Traction Control System. An electronically-controlled system which senses wheel spin and reduces engine speed accordingly.
**TDC** Top Dead Centre denotes that the piston is at its highest point in the cylinder.
**Thread-locking compound** Solution applied to fastener threads to prevent slackening. Select type to suit application.
**Thrust washer** A washer positioned between two moving components on a shaft. For example, between gear pinions on gearshaft.
**Timing chain** See **Cam Chain.**
**Timing light** Stroboscopic lamp for carrying out ignition timing checks with the engine running.
**Top-end** A description of an engine's cylinder block, head and valve gear components.
**Torque** Turning or twisting force about a shaft.
**Torque setting** A prescribed tightness specified by the motorcycle manufacturer to ensure that the bolt or nut is secured correctly. Undertightening can result in the bolt or nut coming loose or a surface not being sealed. Overtightening can result in stripped threads, distortion or damage to the component being retained.
**Torx key** A six-point wrench.
**Tracer** A stripe of a second colour applied to a wire insulator to distinguish that wire from another one with the same colour insulator. For example, Br/W is often used to denote a brown insulator with a white tracer.
**Trail** A feature of steering geometry. Distance from the steering head axis to the tyre's central contact point.
**Triple clamps** The cast components which extend from the steering head and support the fork stanchions or tubes. Often called fork yokes.
**Turbocharger** A centrifugal device, driven by exhaust gases, that pressurises the intake air. Normally used to increase the power output from a given engine displacement.
**TWI** Abbreviation for Tyre Wear Indicator. Indicates the location of the tread depth indicator bars on tyres.

# U

**Universal joint or U-joint (UJ)** A double-pivoted connection for transmitting power from a driving to a driven shaft through an angle. Typically found in shaft drive assemblies.
**Unsprung weight** Anything not supported by the bike's suspension (ie the wheel, tyres, brakes, final drive and bottom (moving) part of the suspension).

**Vacuum gauges** Clock-type gauges measuring intake tract vacuum. Used carburettor synchronisation on multi-cyli engines.
**Valve** A device through which the flow of li gas or vacuum may be stopped, starte regulated by a moveable part that opens, s or partially obstructs one or more port passageways. The intake and exhaust valv the cylinder head are of the poppet type.
**Valve clearance** The clearance betweer valve tip (the end of the valve stem) anc rocker arm or tappet/follower. The clearance is measured when the valve is clc The correct clearance is important - if too the valve won't close fully and will burn whereas if too large noisy operation will resu
**Valve lift** The amount a valve is lifted off its by the camshaft lobe.
**Valve timing** The exact setting for the op and closing of the valves in relation to p position.
**Vernier caliper** A precision meas instrument that measures inside and ou dimensions. Not quite as accurate a micrometer, but more convenient.
**VIN** Vehicle Identification Number. Term fc bike's engine and frame numbers.
**Viscosity** The thickness of a liquid c resistance to flow.
**Volt** A unit for expressing electrical "pressu a circuit. Volts = current x ohms.

# W

**Water pump** A mechanically-driven devic moving coolant around the engine.
**Watt** A unit for expressing electrical pc Watts = volts x current.
**Wear limit** see **Service limit**
**Wet liner** A liquid-cooled engine design w the pistons run in liners which are dir surrounded by coolant **(see illustration)**.

**Wet liner arrangement**

**Wheelbase** Distance from the centre of the wheel to the centre of the rear wheel.
**Wiring harness or loom** Describes the elec wires running the length of the motorcycl enclosed in tape or plastic sheathing. W coming off the main harness is usually refer as a sub harness.
**Woodruff key** A key of semi-circular or s section used to locate a gear to a shaft. used to locate the alternator rotor or crankshaft.
**Wrist pin** Another name for gudgeon or p pin.

**Note:** *References throughout this index are in the form - "Chapter number" • "Page number"*

# F



# G



# H

## L



## M



## N



## O



## R



## S

# T



# V



# W

# Preserving Our Motoring Heritage

<
*The Model J Duesenberg Derham Tourster. Only eight of these magnificent cars were ever built – this is the only example to be found outside the United States of America*

Almost every car you've ever loved, loathed or desired is gathered under one roof at the Haynes Motor Museum. Over 300 immaculately presented cars and motorbikes represent every aspect of our motoring heritage, from elegant reminders of bygone days, such as the superb Model J Duesenberg to curiosities like the bug-eyed BMW Isetta. There are also many old friends and flames. Perhaps you remember the 1959 Ford Popular that you did your courting in? The magnificent 'Red Collection' is a spectacle of classic sports cars including AC, Alfa Romeo, Austin Healey, Ferrari, Lamborghini, Maserati, MG, Riley, Porsche and Triumph.

## *A Perfect Day Out*

Each and every vehicle at the Haynes Motor Museum has played its part in the history and culture of Motoring. Today, they make a wonderful spectacle and a great day out for all the family. Bring the kids, bring Mum and Dad, but above all bring your camera to capture those golden memories for ever. You will also find an impressive array of motoring memorabilia, a comfortable 70 seat video cinema and one of the most extensive transport book shops in Britain. The Pit Stop Cafe serves everything from a cup of tea to wholesome, home-made meals or, if you prefer, you can enjoy the large picnic area nestled in the beautiful rural surroundings of Somerset.

\>
*John Haynes O.B.E., Founder and Chairman of the museum at the wheel of a Haynes Light 12.*

<
*The 1936 490cc sohc-engined International Norton – well known for its racing success*

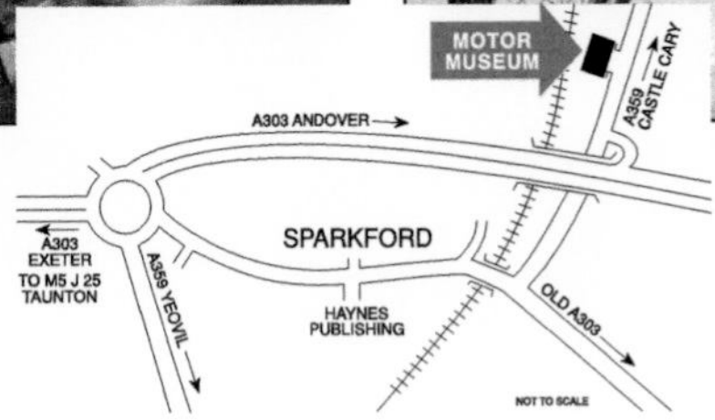


The Museum is situated on the A359 Yeovil to Frome road at Sparkford, just off the A303 in Somerset. It is about 40 miles south of Bristol, and 25 minutes drive from the M5 intersection at Taunton.

Open 9.30am - 5.30pm (10.00am - 4.00pm Winter) 7 days a week, *except Christmas Day, Boxing Day and New Years Day*

Special rates available for schools, coach parties and outings Charitable Trust No. 292048

Printed and bound by CPI Group (UK) Ltd, Croydon, CR0 4YY
18/01/2024
08224409-0001